Discovering Italy

What other country in Europe, or indeed the world, offers such a fascinating wealth of natural and artistic riches? From the drama of the Alps to the rolling hills of Tuscany and the fertile fields of Campania, each region has its own unique character. The artworks of Botticelli, Leonardo da Vinci and Michelangelo, the architecture of Rome, Florence and Venice, the poetry of Dante, the operas of Verdi and Puccini, the cinema of Federico Fellini and the couture of Versace and Armani represent just a fraction of the beauty of Italy and the talent of its people.

The famous "boot" is the ideal location for a holiday filled with activity. Enjoy walking, skiing or watersports. Marvel at some of the historical treasures on show at the many archaeological sites and in the museums. Sample the Carnivale and other lively festivals – religious, traditional or culinary. The passion of the Italians for La Dolce Vita is infectious and their welcome is enhanced by the warmth of the sunshine.

Whatever your plans for your Italian Journey, The Green Guide team have done everything to ensure that this 2002 edition of the guide will be an essential companion.
The guide has been entirely revised and updated and the addresses of hundreds of hotels, restaurants, shops and venues have been added. The preparation of this new edition was co-ordinated in the United Kingdom by Alison Westwood, in close collaboration with Erica Zane and Maura Marca, members of our editorial staff in Italy. As in each of the titles which make up The Green Guide collection, every map and town plan has been expertly drafted by our team of cartographers from first-hand observation.

All the information in the guide is checked regularly but we welcome comments from our readers on any discrepancies or changes which may have occurred since publication.

Thank you for choosing The Green Guide Italy. Buon viaggio!

H Deguine
International Director, The Green Guide

Contents

Genoa, St Andrea cloisters and Porta Soprana

Pasta

Selected Sights

The Islands

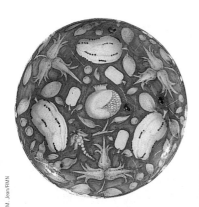

Faenza earthenware, 16C

Bologna

Maps and plans

Companion publications

Internet users can access personalised route plans, Michelin maps and town plans, and addresses of hotels and restaurants featured in The Red Guide Italia through the website at www.ViaMichelin.com

All Michelin publications are cross-referenced. For each sight covered in the Selected Sights section of the guide, a map reference is given under the heading "Location". From our range of products we recommend the following:

● **Michelin map 988 Italy,** a practical map on a scale of 1:1 000 000 which shows the whole Italian road network

● **Michelin Atlas Italy,** a practical, spiral-bound road atlas, on a scale of 1:300 000, with an alphabetical index of places and maps of 70 cities and conurbations.

● **Michelin map 428,** Italy North-West (Lombardy, Piedmont, Valle d'Aosta, Liguria), on a scale of 1:400 000 which gives detailed information on the area you wish to tour.

● **Michelin map 429,** Italy North-East (Veneto, Trentino-Alto Adige, Friuli-Venezia Giulia, Emilia-Romagna), on a scale of 1:400 000 which gives detailed information on the area you wish to tour.

● **Michelin map 430,** Italy Centre (Tuscany, Umbria, Lazio, Marches, Abruzzi, Repubblica di San Marino), on a scale of 1:400 000 which gives detailed information on the area you wish to tour.

● **Michelin map 431,** Italy South (Puglia, Molise, Campania, Calabria, Basilicata), on a scale of 1:400 000 which gives detailed information on the area you wish to tour.

● **Michelin map 432,** Sicily, on a scale of 1:400 000 which gives detailed information on the area you wish to tour.

● **Michelin map 433,** Sardinia, on a scale of 1:400 000 which gives detailed information on the area you wish to tour.

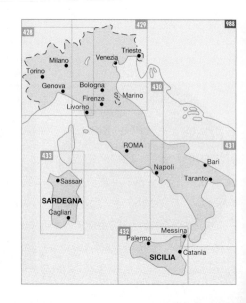

List of maps

Town plans

Maps of archaeological sites

Touring maps

Key

Selected monuments and sights

Tour - Departure point

Catholic church

Protestant church, other temple

Synagogue - Mosque

Building

Statue, small building

Calvary, wayside cross

Fountain

Rampart - Tower - Gate

Château, castle, historic house

Ruins

Dam

Factory, power plant

Fort

Cave

Troglodyte dwelling

Prehistoric site

Viewing table

Viewpoint

Other place of interest

Sports and recreation

Racecourse

Skating rink

Outdoor, indoor swimming pool

Multiplex Cinema

Marina, sailing centre

Trail refuge hut

Cable cars, gondolas

Funicular, rack railway

Tourist train

Recreation area, park

Theme, amusement park

Wildlife park, zoo

Gardens, park, arboretum

Bird sanctuary, aviary

Walking tour, footpath

Of special interest to children

Special symbols

Police station (Carabinieri)

Nuraghe

Palace, villa

Temple, Greek and Roman ruins

Abbreviations

H   Town hall (Municipio)

J   Law courts (Palazzo di Giustizia)

M   Museum (Museo)

P   Local authority offices (Prefettura)

POL.   Police station (Polizia) (in large towns: Questura)

T   Theatre (Teatro)

U   University (Università)

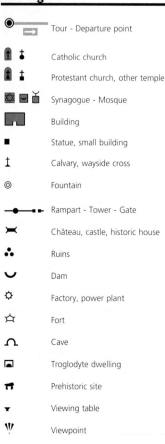

	Sight	Seaside resort	Winter sports resort	Spa
Highly recommended ★★★	☆☆☆	✲✲✲	ⳋⳋⳋ
Recommended ★★	☆☆	✲✲	ⳋⳋ
Interesting ★	☆	✲	ⳋ

Additional symbols

	Tourist information
	Motorway or other primary route
	Junction: complete, limited
	Pedestrian street
	Unsuitable for traffic, street subject to restrictions
	Steps - Footpath
	Train station - Auto-train station
	Coach (bus) station
	Tram
	Metro, underground
	Park-and-Ride
	Access for the disabled
	Post office
	Telephone
	Covered market
	Barracks
	Drawbridge
	Quarry
	Mine
	Car ferry (river or lake)
	Ferry service: cars and passengers
	Foot passengers only
③	Access route number common to Michelin maps and town plans
Bert (R.)...	Main shopping street
AZ B	Map co-ordinates
►►	Visit if time permits

Hotels and restaurants

20 rooms €118.79/ €180.76	Numbers of rooms: price for one person/two people, including breakfast
double rooms	Double occupancy only
5.16	Price of breakfast when it is not included in the price of the room
half-board or full board €78.45	Price per person, based on double occupancy (half or full board obligatory)
100 apart/ room week. €200/300	Number of apartments or rooms, minimum/maximum price per week ("agriturismo" or units rented on a weekly basis only, in summer)
100 beds €15.49	Number of beds (youth hostels, refuges, etc) and price per person
150 sites €19.63	Number of camp sites and cost for two people with a car
€10/26	Restaurant: minimum/maximum price for a full meal (not including drinks)
reserv	Reservation recommended
	No credit cards accepted
P	Reserved parking for hotel patrons
	Swimming Pool
	Air conditioning
	Hotel: non-smoking rooms Restaurant: non-smoking section
	Rooms accesible to persons of reduced mobility

Principal sights

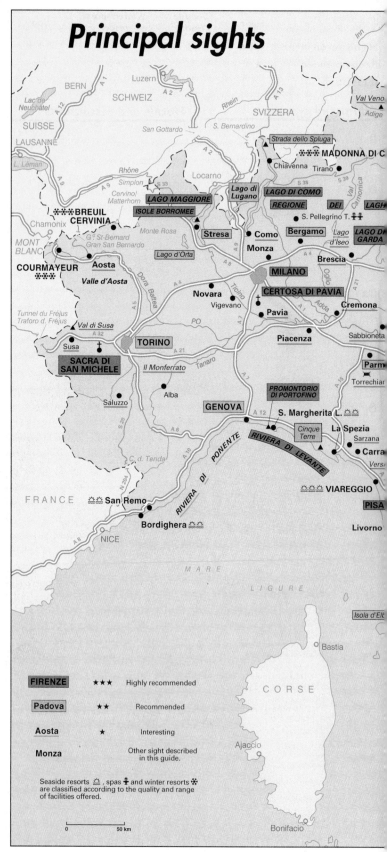

FIRENZE	★★★	Highly recommended
Padova	★★	Recommended
Aosta	★	Interesting
Monza		Other sight described in this guide.

Seaside resorts ♨, spas ✝ and winter resorts ✸ are classified according to the quality and range of facilities offered.

0   50 km

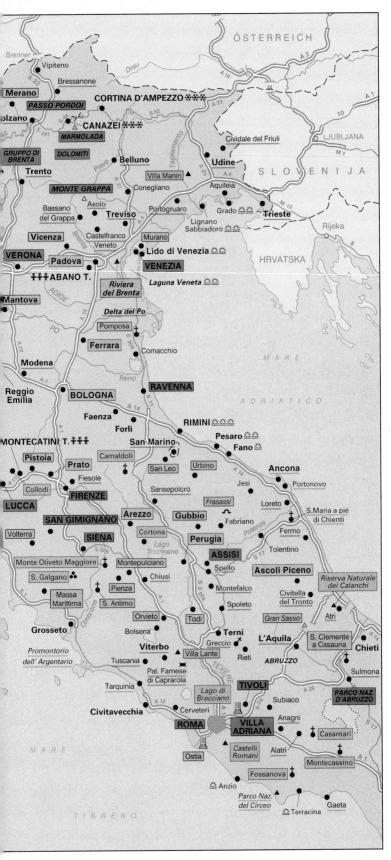

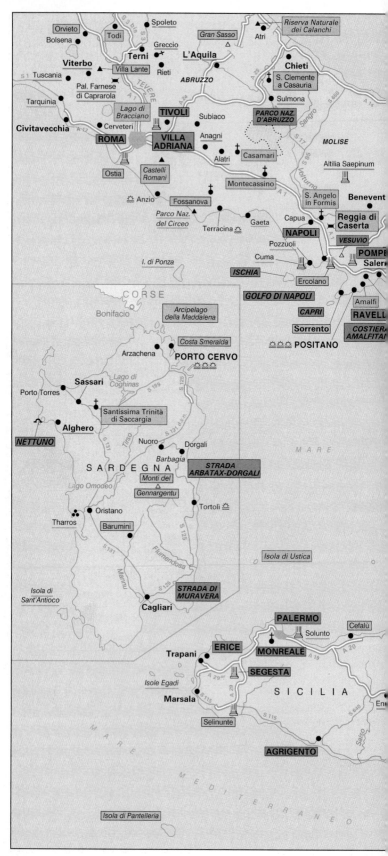

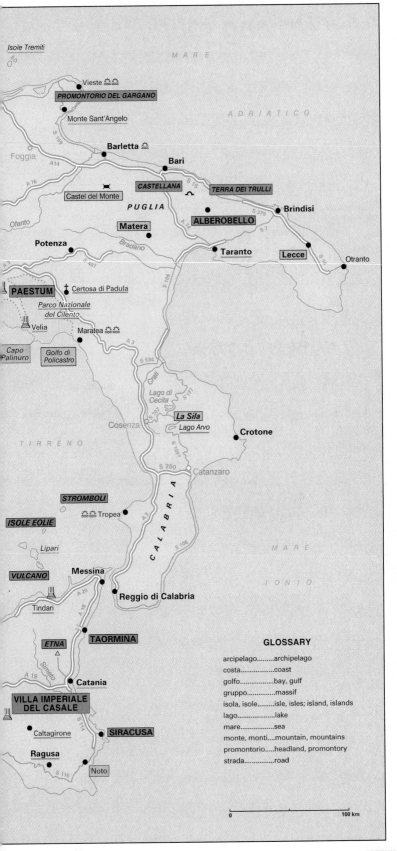

GLOSSARY

arcipelago.........archipelago
costa.................coast
golfo.................bay, gulf
gruppo...............massif
isola, isole.........isle, isles; island, islands
lago....................lake
mare..................sea
monte, monti....mountain, mountains
promontorio.....headland, promontory
strada...............road

Driving tours

For descriptions of these tours, turn to the Practical Points section following.

1. The Gulf of Genoa and the Italian Riviera : 700 km-435 miles (7 days)

2. From the Valle d'Aosta to the wine-growing Monferrato region : 600 km-375 miles (4 days including one day in Turin)

3. From the great lakes of Lombardy to the Po Valley : 850 km-530 miles (10 days)

4. From the Dolomites to Venice and Trieste : 800 km-500 miles (10 days including 2 in Venice)

5. From the rich cities of the plain to the lagoons of the Adriatic : 600 km-375 miles (10 days including 2 in Venice)

6. Art, nature and spirituality in Tuscany and Umbria : 750 km-465 miles (15 days including 2 in Florence)

7. From the heart of Umbria to the Adriatic : 850 km-530 miles (8 days)

8. From Rome and its region to the Abruzzi : 1 000 km-620 miles (8 days including 3 in Rome)

✳✳✳ CORTINA D'AMPEZZO

Bolzano

CANAZEI ✳✳✳

★ Udine

★ Belluno

Trento ★

DOLOMITI ★★★

4

★ Treviso

Vicenza ★★

VENEZIA ★★★

Aquileia

Portogruaro ★ Grado ♨♨

Trieste ★

ERONA ★★★

★★ Padova Riviera del Brenta ★★

5

Chioggia ★

Mantova ★★

★★ Ferrara

PO

Pomposa ★★

Modena ★

★Delta del Po

RAVENNA ★★★

BOLOGNA ★★

‡‡‡
MONTECATINI T.

Pistoia ★★

RIMINI ♨♨♨

★ San Marino

Pesaro ♨♨

Prato ★★

Fano ♨

Fiesole ★

Ancona ★

LUCCA ★★★

FIRENZE ★★★

★★ Urbino

6

7

★★★ SAN GIMIGNANO

Arezzo ★★

Volterra ★★

Cortona ★

Gubbio ★★

★★ SIENA

Montepulciano

Perugia ★★

ASSISI ★★★

Ascoli Piceno ★★

★★
Chiusi ★

★★ Monte Oliveto Maggiore

★★ Pienza

★★ Todi

Spoleto ★

Gran Sasso ★★

★★ Orvieto

Terni ★

★ L'Aquila

★★ S. Clemente a Casauria

★ Viterbo

Rieti

ABRUZZO

Sulmona ★

★ Tarquinia

8

★★★ TIVOLI

PARCO NAZIONALE D'ABRUZZO ★★★

Scanno ★

★★★ ROMA

★ Anagni

Casamari ★

★★ Ostia

★ Alatri

Montecassino ★★

★★ Castelli Romani

♨ Anzio

DOLOMITI ★★★   Region described in the guide accompanied by a detailed map.

★★★ = ✳✳✳ = ‡‡‡ = ♨♨♨
★★ = ✳✳ = ‡‡ = ♨♨
★ = ✳ = ‡ = ♨

0   50 km

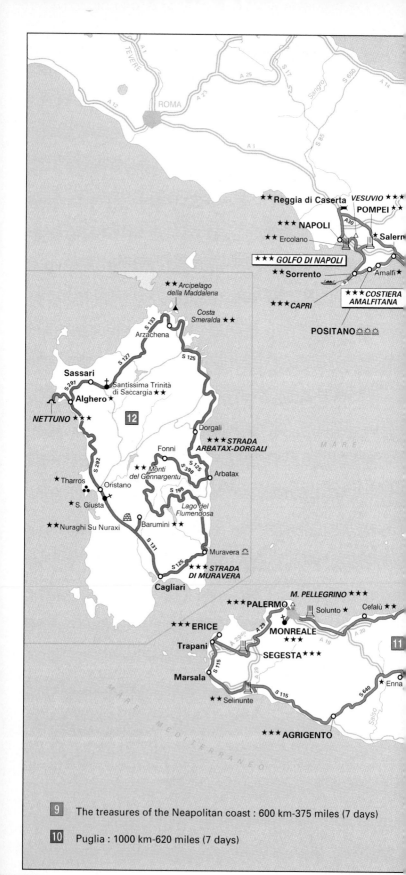

9 The treasures of the Neapolitan coast : 600 km-375 miles (7 days)

10 Puglia : 1000 km-620 miles (7 days)

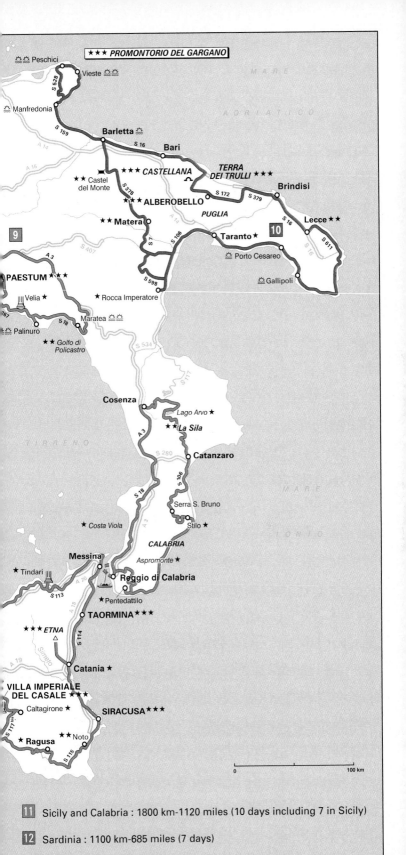

★★★ *PROMONTORIO DEL GARGANO*

⌂⌂ Peschici
Vieste ⌂⌂
⌂ Manfredonia
Barletta ⌂
Bari
★★ Castel del Monte
★★★ *CASTELLANA*
TERRA DEI TRULLI ★★★
Brindisi
★★★ **ALBEROBELLO**
PUGLIA
★★ **Matera**
Lecce ★★
10
★ **Taranto** ★
⌂ Porto Cesareo
9
⌂ Gallipoli
PAESTUM ★★★
Velia ★
★ Rocca Imperatore
⌂ Palinuro
Maratea ⌂⌂
★★ *Golfo di Policastro*

Cosenza
Lago Arvo ★
★★ *La Sila*
Catanzaro
TIRRENO
Serra S. Bruno
Stilo ★
★ *Costa Viola*
CALABRIA
Messina
Aspromonte ★
★ Tindari
Reggio di Calabria
★ Pentedattilo
MARE
IONIO
TAORMINA ★★★
★★★ *ETNA*
△
Catania ★
VILLA IMPERIALE DEL CASALE ★★★
Caltagirone ★
SIRACUSA ★★★
★ **Ragusa**
★★ Noto

MARE ADRIATICO

0   100 km

11 Sicily and Calabria : 1800 km-1120 miles (10 days including 7 in Sicily)

12 Sardinia : 1100 km-685 miles (7 days)

Practical Points

Planning your Trip

Useful Addresses

INTERNET

The Internet is a useful source of information, enabling visitors to contact tourist offices, consult programmes and brochures and make bookings on line.
www.initaly.com Travel tips, accommodation information and internet links
www.discoveritalia.com Tourist information
www.governo.it Website of the Italian government

A view of the Tuscan countryside in Val d'Orcia

B. Morandi/MICHELIN

TOURIST ORGANISATIONS

Italian State Tourist Office – ENIT (Ente Nazionale Italiano per il Turismo) – For information, brochures, maps and assistance in planning a trip to Italy, apply to the ENIT in your country or consult the ENIT website, www.enit.it
1 Princes Street, London W1B 2AY, ☎ (020) 7408 1254; 24-hour Brochure Request Line: ☎ 090 65 508 925 (calls charged at premium rate)
630 Fifth Avenue, Suite 1565, New York, NY 10111, ☎ 212 245 4822
12400 Wilshire Boulevard, Suite 550, Los Angeles, CA 90025, ☎ 310 820 1898
175 Bloor Street, Suite 907 – South Tower, Toronto M4W 3R8, ☎ 416 925 4882

ITALIAN EMBASSIES AND CONSULATES

EMBASSIES

14 Three Kings' Yard, London W1Y 2EH, ☎ (020) 7312 2200; Fax (020) 7499 2283; emblondon@embitaly.org.uk; www.embitaly.org.uk
3000 Whitehaven Street, NW Washington, DC 20008,

☎ (202) 612 4400; Fax (202) 518 2154; www.italyemb.org
275 Slater Street, 21st Floor, Ottawa, Ontario, K1P 5H9, ☎ (613) 232 2401; Fax (613) 233 1484; ambital@italyincanada.com; www.italyincanada.com

CONSULATES

38 Eaton Place, London SW1X 8AN; ☎ (020) 7235 9371, Fax (020) 7823 1609.
Rodwell Tower, 111 Piccadilly, Manchester M1 2HY, ☎ (0161) 236 9024; Fax (0161) 236 5574; passaporti@italconsulman.demon.co.uk
32 Melville Street, Edinburgh EH3 7HA, ☎ (0131) 226 3631; Fax (0131) 226 6260; consedimb@consedimb.demon.co.uk
690 Park Avenue, New York, NY 10021, ☎ (212) 737 9100; Fax (212) 249 4945; info@italconsulnyc.org; www.italconsulnyc.org
3489 Drummond Street, Montreal, Quebec, H3G 1X6, ☎ (514) 849 8351; Fax (514) 499 9471; cgi@italconsul.montreal.qc.ca; www.italconsul.montreal.qc.ca
136 Beverley Street, Toronto, Ontario, M5T 1Y5, ☎ (416) 977 1566; (416) 977 1119; CGToronto@toronto.italconsulate.org; www.toronto.italconsulate.org

Formalities

DOCUMENTS

Passport – Visitors entering Italy must be in possession of a valid national passport. Citizens of European Union countries need only a national identity card. In case of loss or theft, report to the embassy or consulate and the local police.

Visa – Entry visas are required by Australian, New Zealand, Canadian and US citizens (if their intended stay exceeds three months). Apply to the Italian Consulate (visa issued same day; delay if submitted by mail). US citizens should obtain the booklet *A Safe Trip Abroad* ($1), which provides useful information on visa requirements, customs regulations and medical care for international travellers. Published by the Government Printing Office, it can be ordered by phone (☎ (202) 512-1800) or consulted on-line at www.access.gpo.gov

Driving licence – Nationals of EU countries require a valid national driving licence. Nationals of non-EU countries require an **international driving licence**. This is available in the US from the American Automobile Association for US$10 (an application form can be found at www.aaa.com) and in Canada from the Canadian Automobile Association for $13 (see www.caa.com for details). If you are bringing your own car into the country, you will need the vehicle registration papers

Car insurance – If you are bringing your own car to Italy, an International Insurance Certificate (Green Card), although no longer a legal requirement, is the most effective proof of insurance cover and is internationally recognised by the police and other authorities. This is available from your insurer.

HEALTH
British citizens should apply to the Department of Health and Social Security for **Form E111**, which entitles the holder to urgent treatment for accident or unexpected illness in EU countries.

Nationals of non-EU countries should check that their insurance policy covers them specifically for overseas travel, including doctor's visits, medication and hospitalisation in Italy (in most cases you will probably have to take out supplementary medical insurance).

American Express offers its cardholders a service called *Global Assist* to help in financial, legal, medical or personal emergencies. For further information, consult their website: www.americanexpress.com

All prescription drugs should be clearly labelled, and it is recommended that you carry a copy of the prescription with you. A list of chemists open at night or on Sundays may be obtained from chemists' shops (*farmacia* – red cross sign). First Aid service (*pronto soccorso*) is available at airports, railway stations and in hospitals. Dial ☎ 113 for police, Red Cross and emergency first aid.

CUSTOMS REGULATIONS
As of 30 June 1999, those travelling between countries within the European Union can no longer purchase "duty-free" goods. For further information, there is a free leaflet, **Duty Paid**, available from HM Customs and Excise, Finchley Excise Advice Centre, Berkeley House, 304 Regents Park Road, London N3 2JY, ☎ 0845 010 9000; www.hmce.gov.uk The US Customs Service offers a free publication for US citizens entitled *Know Before You Go*. Consult www.customs.gov for details.

Seasons

THE BEST TIME
The best time of year to visit Italy is during the months of April, May, June, September and October, when the weather is generally pleasant throughout the country and the cities and beaches are not overrun with visitors. June and September are the best months for beach holidays, especially in the south for those who feel the cold. July and August should be avoided where possible, because of the high temperatures, crowds and increased prices. Flights, ferries, train tickets and hotels should be booked well in advance during these two months.

PUBLIC HOLIDAYS
Museums and other **monuments** are usually closed on Mondays and public holidays. **Churches** are often closed at lunchtime and cannot be visited during services. The following are days when museums and other monuments may be closed or vary their hours of admission:
1 January
6 January (Epiphany)
Easter Day and Easter Monday
25 April (anniversary of the 1945 liberation)
1 May
15 August ("Ferragosto")
1 November (All Saints)
8 December
25 and 26 December
Each town also celebrates the feast day of its patron saint (details of local festivals can be obtained from the local tourist offices).

TIME DIFFERENCE
In winter, standard time is Greenwich Mean Time + 1 hour. In summer the clocks go forward an hour to give Italian Summer Time (GMT + 2 hours) from the last weekend in March to the last weekend in September.

Budget

The cost of living in Italy is relatively cheap compared to other European countries and it is possible to get by on a limited budget, although this very much depends on the location and time of year. In the tourist centres it is not always easy to find value for money, especially when looking for accommodation, and during the summer months prices may well go up.

The hotels and restaurants in the Directory sections of the guide have been subdivided into three categories to suit all budgets. The **Budget** section includes campsites, youth hostels and modest but decent and well-located hotels and *pensioni* with single rooms for under €45. Restaurants in this category, without sacrificing quality, will charge less than €22 for a three-course meal (including drinks). Those on a larger budget will find hotels of greater comfort and charm and better quality restaurants in the **Moderate** category. Rooms in this category will cost from €45 to €85 for a single and expect to pay between €22 and €42 for a meal. For those in search of a truly memorable stay, the **Expensive** category includes luxurious hotels, B&Bs and guest farmhouses with a wide range of facilities, as well as enormous charm and atmosphere. Restaurants in this category will satisfy the most demanding taste buds with prices to match.

Basic meals are cheap and easy to find in Italy: for a meal in a pizzeria, expect to pay about €13 a head including drinks; a quick snack, especially at lunchtime, will cost around €5 for a sandwich and €10 for a simple dish, including drinks.

For suggestions on how to make your money go further, especially when buying airline or train tickets, see "Concessions" below.

Special needs

Many of the sights described in this guide are accessible to people with special needs. Sights marked with the symbols ♿ or (♿) offer full or partial access for wheelchairs. However, it is advisable to check beforehand by telephone.

For further information contact the **Associazione Italiana Disabili**, Via S. Barnaba 29, 20122 Milan, ☎ 02 55 01 75 64, and **CO.IN** (Consorzio Cooperative Integrate), Via Enrico Giglioli 54/A; ☎/Fax 06 71 29 011, 800 27 10 27 (freephone for the Vacanze Serene service). Offices are open Mon-Fri, 9am-5pm and 9am-1pm Sat and on the eve of public holidays. Visit the website at www.coinsociale.it

Transport

Getting there

BY AIR

Many international and other independent airlines operate services to Rome and to the major provincial airports (Milan, Turin, Verona, Genoa, Bologna, Pisa, Naples; Florence often requires a change in Milan, although there are direct trains from Pisa airport to the centre of Florence – transport time about 1 hour). There are several flights per day from London (Heathrow) to Rome and Milan; there are also daily flights from London (Heathrow) to Turin, Verona, Genoa, Bologna, Pisa and Naples, from London (Gatwick) to Rome, Naples and Genoa, and from Manchester or Birmingham to Milan; and a few flights per week from Dublin to Rome. There are package tour flights and Fly-Drive schemes available. Information, brochures and timetables are available from airlines and travel agents:

Alitalia
4 Portman Square, Marble Arch, London W1H 9PS; ☎ (020) 7486 8432; Fax (020) 7486 8431. Reservations can also be made on ☎ 08705 448 259; www.alitalia.co.uk
4-5 Dawson Street, Dublin 2; ☎ (01) 677 5171; Fax (01) 677 3373.

666 Fifth Avenue, New York, NY 10103; ☎ (212) 903 3300; Fax (212) 903 3350.
Viale Marchetti 111, 00148 Rome, ☎ 06 65 621.

British Airways
156 Regent Street, London W1; ☎ 0845 77 999 77 (enquiries); 0845 77 333 77 (reservations); Fax (020) 7434 4640 (reservations); www.britishairways.com
USA – ☎ (1-800) AIRWAYS.
Via Bissolati 54, 00187 Rome; ☎ 199 712 266 (from Italy only).

British Midland
Flights from London Heathrow to Milan. ☎ 0870 607 0555; www.flybmi.com

Go
Flights to Bologna, Milan, Naples, Rome and Venice from London Stanstead and various regional airports in the UK. ☎ 0870 60 76543; www.go-fly.com

Ryanair
Flights to Alghero (Sardinia), Ancona, Bologna, Genoa, Milan, Pescara, Pisa, Rome, Trieste, Turin, Venice and Verona from London Stanstead. ☎ 0870 156 9569; www.ryanair.com

Virgin Express
Flights from London Heathrow to Milan and Rome. ☎ (020) 7744 0004; www.virgin-express.com

For information on discounts on flights to Italy, see "Concessions".

BY SEA

Details of passenger ferry and car ferry services from the UK and Republic of Ireland to the Channel ports, linking up with the European rail and motorway network can be obtained from travel agents and from the main operators:

Hoverspeed – International Hoverport, Marine Parade, Dover CT17 9TG. ☎ 08705 240 241; www.hoverspeed.co.uk

P & O European Ferries – Channel House, Channel View Road, Dover CT17 9TJ. ☎ 0990 980 980; www.p-and-o.com

P & O Stena Line – Charter House, Park Street, Ashford, TN24 8EX ☎ 0990 70 70 70; www.posl.com

For details of crossing via the **Channel Tunnel** (35-minute high-speed undersea rail link between Folkestone and Calais), ☎ 08705 35 35 35; www.eurotunnel.com

BY TRAIN

From London and the Channel ports there are rail services to many Italian towns including many high-speed passenger trains and motorail services. For tourists residing outside Italy, there are rail passes offering unlimited travel, and group travel tickets offering savings for parties on the Italian Railways network.

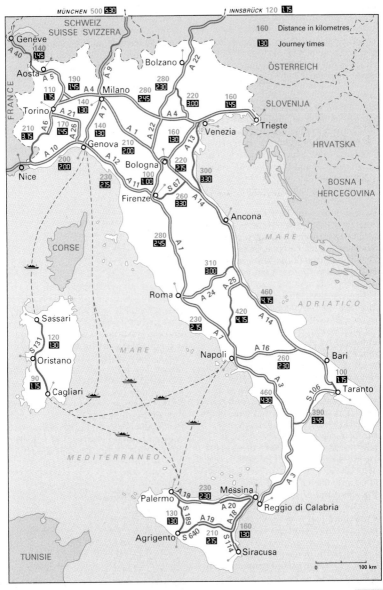

Italian State Railway –
www.fs-on-line.com
Rail Europe – www.raileurope.com
Eurostar – ☎ 0870 160 6600;
www.eurostar.co.uk
Tickets are also available from
principal British and American Rail
Travel Centres and travel agencies.
Travelling by rail is a particularly good
way of getting to Milan, Venice and
Florence, as the rail stations here are
within easy reach of the centre of town.

By coach

Regular coach services are operated
from London to Rome and to large
provincial Italian towns. Services
from Victoria Coach Station in London
to Italy are operated by Eurolines,
4 Cardiff Road, Luton, Bedfordshire
L41 1PP; ☎ 08705 143 219 (calls
charged at standard rate);
Fax 01582 400 694;
welcome@eurolinesuk.com;
www.eurolines.co.uk Alternatively,
contact National Express, 75 Davies
Street, London W1K 5HT, ☎ 0870 901
3190; 08705 80 80 80;
www.gobycoach.com

By car

*See "Formalities" above for details of the
documents necessary for driving in Italy.*
Roads from France into Italy, with the
exception of the Menton/Ventimiglia
(Riviera) coast road, are dependent on
Alpine passes and tunnels. The main
roads go through the Montgenèvre
pass near Briançon, the Fréjus tunnel
and Mont-Cenis pass near Saint-Jean-
de-Maurienne, the Petit-Saint-Bernard
pass near Bourg-Saint-Maurice and the
Mont-Blanc tunnel near Chamonix.
Via Switzerland, three main routes are
possible – through the tunnel or pass
at Grand-Saint-Bernard, through the
Simplon pass, and through the
St Gottard pass which goes via Ticino
and Lugano to the great lakes of
Lombardy. Those planning to drive
through Switzerland should remember
to budget for the Swiss road tax
(vignette), which is levied on all motor
vehicles and trailers with a maximum
weight of 3.5 tonnes, instead of
charging tolls on the motorways (the
vignette costs 40 Swiss francs and can
be bought at the border crossings, post
offices, petrol stations, garages and
cantonal motor registries, or in
advance from the Swiss Centre,
Swiss Court, London W1V 8EE,
☎ (020) 7734 1921).
For those driving down through
Germany and Austria, there is the
Brenner pass south of Innsbruck.
Remember that most of these tunnels
or passes levy a toll *(see "Motoring"
below)*
Use **Michelin maps 987, 989 and 988**
or the **Michelin Atlas Europe** to help
you plan your route.

Getting about

MOTORING

Italian roads are excellent, and there
is a wide network of motorways
(autostrade) (see map). The Italian
motorway website can be found at
www.autostrade.it

HIGHWAY CODE

The minimum driving age is 18.
Traffic drives on the right. It is
compulsory for the driver and front-
seat passengers to wear seat belts, and
seat belts must be worn in the back
where they are fitted. Children under
12 must travel in the back seats,
unless the front seat is fitted with a
child restraint system. Full or dipped
headlights must be switched on in
poor visibility and at night; use
sidelights only when a stationary
vehicle is not clearly visible.
In the event of a breakdown, a red
warning triangle must be displayed in
the road; these can be hired from the
ACI offices at the frontier (deposit
refunded).
Drivers should watch out for
unfamiliar road signs and take great
care on the road (it is not without
some justification that people say
Italian drivers prefer using their horn
to their brakes!). At crossroads drivers
coming from the right have priority.
Severe penalties are applicable for
drink-driving offences.

Speed limits: in built-up areas,
50kph/31mph; on country roads,
90kph/55mph; on motorways,
90kph/55mph for vehicles up to
1 000cc and 130kph/80mph for
vehicles over 1 100cc.

PARKING

There are many car parks with
attendants, particularly in the Naples
area. Obviously, you should check the
rates before parking, to avoid any
unpleasant surprises as you leave, but
it is advisable, particularly in the
south, to make use of these car parks
rather than leave vehicles unattended.
In many large towns, the historical
town centre is subject to traffic
restrictions (authorised vehicles only
may enter), indicated by large
rectangular signs saying **"Zona a
traffico limitato riservata ai veicoli
autorizzati"**. In this case, park your
vehicle outside the town before
proceeding on foot, as the streets are
often very narrow and have no
pavements or sidewalks.

ROAD SIGNS

Motorways *(autostrade* – subject to
tolls) and dual carriageways
(superstrade) are indicated by green
signs; ordinary roads by blue signs;
tourist sights by yellow signs.

ROAD TOLLS

Tolls are payable on most motorways. The toll is calculated according to the distance between the car axles and engine capacity. Bear in mind that motorway tolls can be paid in cash (look for lanes with signs representing toll collectors), with the Via Card (look for lanes with the Via Card sign and blue stripes on the road surface) and by credit card. Don't worry if you get into the Via Card lane by mistake: credit cards can be inserted into the appropriate slot as well as the Via Card.

PETROL

Gasolio = diesel. *Super* = super leaded (98 octane).
Senza piombo = premium unleaded petrol (95 octane).
Super Plus or *Euro Plus* = super unleaded petrol (98 octane).
Petrol stations are usually open from 7am to 7pm. Many close at lunchtime (between 12.30pm and 3pm), on Sundays and public holidays, and many refuse payment by credit card.

MAPS AND PLANS

Michelin map 988 at a scale of 1:1 000 000 covers the whole country. At 1:400 000, **Michelin map 428** covers the northwest, **429** the northeast, **430** the centre, **431** the south, **432** Sicily and **433** Sardinia; at 1:200 000, **218** covers Bolzano and **219** covers from Aosta to Milan; at 1:100 000, **115** covers the westernmost stretch of the Italian Riviera. The **Michelin Atlas Italy** (1:300 000) contains a complete index of towns, 80 plans of the largest cities and covers all of Italy; it is also available in mini format.
Maps **38** (1:10 000) and **46** (1:15 000) cover the cities of Rome and Milan; these are also available in spiral atlas format.
The **Touring Club Italiano (TCI)**, Corso d'Italia 10, 20139 Milan, ☎ 02 85 26 72, publishes a regional map series at 1:200 000.
Michelin Travel Publications has created a website to help motorists prepare for their journey. The service enables travellers to select their preferred route (fastest, shortest etc) and to calculate distances between towns and cities. Consult **www.ViaMichelin.com**

MOTORING ORGANISATIONS

Road Rescue Services – In case of breakdown, contact ACI (Automobile Club Italia), ☎ 116 (24hr). This breakdown service (tax levied) is operated by the ACI for foreign motorists. The ACI also offers a telephone information service in English (and other languages) for road and weather conditions as well as for tourist events: ☎ 06 4477.

CAR RENTAL

There are car rental agencies at airports, railway stations and in all large towns and resorts throughout Italy. The main agencies are Avis, Hertz, Eurodollar, Europcar and Maggiore Budget. Fly-drive schemes or train-and-car packages are available. European cars usually have manual transmission, but automatic cars are available on demand. An **international driving licence** is required for non-EU nationals.

BY AIR

Frequent domestic flights cover the whole country. There are transfer buses to town terminals and railway stations.
Useful telephone numbers for Italian airports *(the approximate time and method of transport for some cities is given in brackets)*:
For **Alitalia** information:
☎ 8488 65643 (freephone), 06 65 643, www.alitalia.it
Alghero: Fertilia, ☎ 079 93 50 33 (bus 15min)
Ancona: Falconara, ☎ 071 28 271 (bus 30min)
Bari: Palese, ☎ 080 58 35 230 (bus 30min)
Bergamo: Orio al Serio, ☎ 035 32 61 11 (bus 20min)
Bologna: Guglielmo Marconi, ☎ 051 64 79 615 (bus 20min)
Bolzano: ☎ 0471 25 40 70 (bus 15min)
Brindisi: Papola Casale, ☎ 0831 41 88 05
Cagliari: Elmas, ☎ 070 21 12 11 (bus 15min)
Catania: Fontanarossa, ☎ 095 34 05 05 (bus 30min)
Florence: Amerigo Vespucci, ☎ 055 30 615 (bus 20min)
Genoa: Cristoforo Colombo, ☎ 010 60 151 (bus 30min)
Gorizia: Ronchi dei Legionari, ☎ 0481 77 32 24 (bus 40min)
Lamezia Terme: S. Eufemia, ☎ 0968 51 766
Lampedusa: ☎ 0922 97 02 99
Milan: Forlanini and Malpensa, ☎ 02 74 85 22 00 (bus 1hr from Malpensa; Malpensa Express train from Stazione di Cadorna 35min)
Naples: Capodichino, ☎ 081 78 96 111 (bus 30min)
Olbia: Costa Smeralda, ☎ 0789 52 634
Palermo: Punta Raisi, ☎ 091 70 20 111 (bus 1hr)
Pantelleria: ☎ 0923 91 13 98
Perugia: S. Egidio, ☎ 075 59 21 41
Pisa: Galileo Galilei, ☎ 050 50 07 07
Reggio Calabria: Ravagnese, ☎ 0965 64 32 91
Rome: Fiumicino-Leonardo da Vinci, ☎ 06 65 951 (train 30min)
Turin: Caselle, ☎ 011 56 76 361 (bus 30min)

Venice: Marco Polo, ☎ 041 26 06 111
(bus 20min)
Verona: Villafranca Veronese,
☎ 045 80 95 666

By rail

The railway network also enables
visitors to travel the length and
breadth of Italy. Special train tickets
can be bought once in the country.
The *biglietto chilometrico* (kilometre
ticket) is valid for a distance of
3 000km/1 875mi (for a maximum
of 20 journeys) and allows travellers
to save approximately 15% off the full
price of a ticket. It is valid for two
months from the date of the first
journey and can be bought up to a
month prior to travelling. A *carnet*
allows the purchase of a minimum
of 4 tickets with a 10% (if the distance
is between 71km/44mi and
350km/218mi) or 20% (for longer
journeys) discount. Other special
railcards include the *Carta Verde*
(for those under 26) and the *Carta
d'Argento* (for those over 60) which
give 20% discounts on all journeys.
The **Pendolino** or high-speed train
runs between Milan-Rome (4hr),
Turin-Rome (5hr), Genoa-Rome (4hr),
Rome-Venice (4hr) and Rome-Bari
(4hr 30min).
Bicycles can be taken on those trains
with a guard van (usually all local
trains) for a supplement of about €3.

*For discounts on train fares see the
"Concessions" section.*

By boat

SICILY AND SARDINIA

These two islands are linked to the
mainland by ferries and hydrofoils
and are very popular, especially
during the summer months. Visitors
are therefore advised to book their
crossing well in advance, especially
if travelling with a car or if a cabin is
required. For those for whom comfort
is less of a priority, seats are available
on deck; although it is preferable to
book these ahead of time, they can

Capri

also be purchased a couple of hours
before departure from the ferry
terminal.

Crossings to Sicily are operated from
the following cities:
Cagliari: Tirrenia Navigazione,
Agenzia Agenave, Via Campidano 1,
☎ 070 66 60 65, Fax 070 66 38 53
(14hr 30min to Palermo, 11hr to
Trapani)
Genoa: Grandi Navi Veloci, Via
Fieschi 17, ☎ 010 58 93 31,
Fax 010 50 92 25 (20hr to Palermo)
Livorno: Grandi Navi Veloci,
Varco Galvani Darsena 1,
☎ 0586 40 98 04, Fax 0586 42 97 17
(17hr to Palermo)
Naples: Tirrenia Navigazione,
Stazione Marittima,
Molo Angioino, ☎ 081 31 72 999,
Fax 081 25 14 767 (11hr to Palermo),
☎ 199 123 199
Reggio di Calabria: Stazione Ferrovie
dello Stato, ☎ 0965 97 957 (25min to
Messina) and Aliscafi SNAV, Stazione
Marittima, ☎ 0965 29 568 (15min to
Messina)
Villa San Giovanni: Ferrovie dello
Stato, Piazza Stazione, and Società
Caronte, Via Marina 30,
☎ 0965 79 31 31, Fax 0965 79 31 28
(20min to Messina)

Crossings to **Sardinia** are operated
from the following cities:
Civitavecchia: Sardinia Ferries,
Calata Laurenti, ☎ 0766 50 07 14,
Fax 0766 50 07 18 (7hr to Golfo
Aranci), Tirrenia Navigazione,
Stazione Marittima, ☎ 0766 58 191,
Fax 0766 28 804 (to Cagliari, Olbia,
Arbatax)
Fiumicino: Tirrenia Navigazione,
Agenzia DA.NI.MARI Shipping,
Via Bignami 43, ☎ 06 65 80 351,
Fax 06 65 83 060 (to Arbatax and
Golfo Aranci)
Genoa: Tirrenia Navigazione, Nuovo
Terminal Traghetti, Via Milano 51,
☎ 010 26 981, Fax 010 26 98 255
(20hr to Cagliari, 15hr to Olbia, 19hr
to Arbatax, 10hr to Porto Torres);
Grimaldi, Grandi Navi Veloci,
Via Fieschi 17, ☎ 010 58 93 31,
Fax 010 50 92 25
La Spezia: Tirrenia Navigazione,
Agenzia Lardon, Viale S. Bartolomeo
109, ☎ 0187 55 11 11,
Fax 0187 55 13 01 (5hr 30min to Golfo
Aranci)
Livorno: Sardinia Ferries, Calata
Carrara, ☎ 0586 89 89 79,
Fax 0586 89 61 03 (9hr to Golfo
Aranci)
Palermo: Tirrenia Navigazione, Calata
Marinai d'Italia, ☎ 091 60 21 111,
Fax 091 60 21 211
Trapani: Tirrenia Navigazione,
Agenzia Salvo, Molo Sanità,
☎ 0923 54 54 33, Fax 0923 54 54 44
(11hr to Cagliari)

G. Targat/MICHELIN

Where to Stay and Where to Eat

Addresses listed in the Guide

To offer you a pleasant stay we have scoured all regions of the country in search of guesthouses, hotels, restaurants, campsites and even convents and monasteries that best typify Italy either for their striking location or traditional food, keeping all budgets in mind and not forgetting younger travellers.

CATEGORIES

Our selection is divided into three price brackets: **Budget** (€45 or under for a single room), **Moderate** (singles from €45 to €85) and **Expensive** (single rooms for over €85).

WHERE TO STAY

For regions and cities popular with tourists, it is advisable to book accommodation well in advance, especially if you plan to go from April to October. In general from November to March (with the exception of the art cities such as Florence, Venice and Rome), prices are considerably lower and many hotels offer discounts or special weekend deals.

For each establishment, the first figure refers to the price of a single room, the second figure to the price of a double room. Exceptions to this are highlighted (rural guesthouses, for example, which generally only have double rooms). Breakfast is usually included in the price although this may not be the case in smaller hotels. When not included in the price of the room, the cost of breakfast immediately follows the price of the room. Whatever type of accommodation you choose, it is advisable to check prices before booking, as rates can vary depending on the time of year and availability of rooms.

HOTELS AND PENSIONI

It is not always easy to distinguish between a hotel and a *pensione*. Generally, the word *pensione* is used to describe a small family-run hotel, which is sometimes situated within a residential building and which offers simple, basic rooms, often without a private bathroom.

RURAL ACCOMMODATION

Rural guesthouses were originally conceived as an opportunity to combine accommodation and the chance to taste the products made on

The culinary delights of Norcia

the farm (among them olive oil, wine, honey, vegetables and meat). In the last few years some regions of Italy have witnessed a huge growth in popularity of such guesthouses, some of which are as elegant as the best hotels, with prices to match. As a result, in some you will find a menu that makes use of the farm's own produce while in others you may be provided with a kitchenette in an apartment that will offer you complete independence; others still may only offer breakfast. The guesthouses included in the guide usually accept bookings for one night only but in high season the majority prefer weekly stays or offer half or full board as well as requiring a minimum stay. Prices for the latter are only given when this formula is compulsory. Bear in mind that the majority of these rural guesthouses only have double rooms and prices shown here are based on two people sharing a double room. People travelling alone should try asking for a discount. In any case because of the ever-increasing popularity of this type of accommodation it is advisable to book well in advance.

To get an idea of what is on offer in this category consult the following guides: *Vacanze e Natura* (published by Associazione Terranostra, ☎ 06 46 821), *Agriturismo e Vacanze Verdi* (published by Associazione Agriturist, ☎ 06 68 52 342), *Guida all'Agriturismo*, published by Demetra and *Vacanze Verdi* published by Edagricole, which offers a selection of over 400 addresses. Information is also available from *Turismo Verde*, Via Flaminia 56, Rome, ☎ 06 36 11 051, www.turismoverde.it

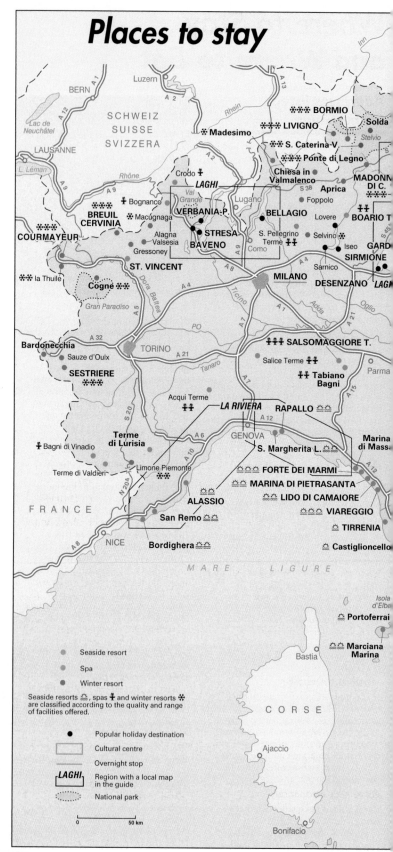

Places to stay

Seaside resort (grey dot)

Spa (orange dot)

Winter resort (black dot)

Seaside resorts ♨, spas ♱ and winter resorts ✳ are classified according to the quality and range of facilities offered.

● Popular holiday destination

▢ Cultural centre

— Overnight stop

LAGHI Region with a local map in the guide

⬭ National park

0   50 km

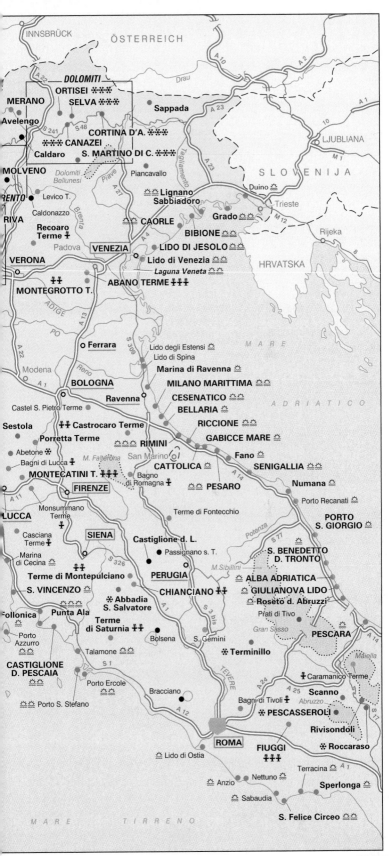

INNSBRÜCK — ÖSTERREICH

DOLOMITI
ORTISEI ✱✱✱
SELVA ✱✱✱
Sappada

MERANO
Avelengo

CORTINA D'A. ✱✱✱
✱✱✱ CANAZEI
Caldaro — S. MARTINO DI C. ✱✱✱

LJUBLIANA

MOLVENO
Dolomiti Bellunesi
Piancavallo

S L O V E N I J A

RENTO — Levico T.
Caldonazzo
RIVA
Recoaro Terme
Padova

Duino ♨
Trieste
Rijeka

♨♨ Lignano Sabbiadoro
♨♨ CAORLE
BIBIONE ♨♨
Grado ♨♨
LIDO DI JESOLO ♨♨

VERONA
♨♨ MONTEGROTTO T.
VENEZIA
Lido di Venezia ♨♨
Laguna Veneta ♨♨
ABANO TERME ♨♨♨

HRVATSKA

Ferrara
Modena
BOLOGNA
Ravenna
Castel S. Pietro Terme

Lido degli Estensi ♨
Lido di Spina
Marina di Ravenna ♨
MILANO MARITTIMA ♨♨
CESENATICO ♨♨
BELLARIA ♨
RICCIONE ♨♨
GABICCE MARE ♨

M A R E

A D R I A T I C O

Sestola
♨♨ Castrocaro Terme
Porretta Terme
Abetone ✱
Bagni di Lucca ♨
MONTECATINI T. ♨♨♨

M. Falterona
San Marino
Bagno di Romagna ♨
RIMINI
CATTOLICA ♨
♨♨ PESARO
Fano ♨
SENIGALLIA ♨♨
Numana ♨
Porto Recanati ♨

FIRENZE
LUCCA
Monsummano Terme ♨
Casciana Terme ♨
Marina di Cecina ♨
Terme di Montepulciano ♨♨
S. VINCENZO ♨

SIENA
Castiglione d. L.
Passignano s. T.
PERUGIA
CHIANCIANO ♨♨

Terme di Fontecchio
Potenza
M.Sibillini
PORTO S. GIORGIO ♨
S. BENEDETTO D. TRONTO ♨
ALBA ADRIATICA ♨
GIULIANOVA LIDO ♨
Roseto d. Abruzzi ♨

♨♨ Punta Ala
✱ Abbadia S. Salvatore
Terme di Saturnia ♨♨
Follonica
Porto Azzurro
CASTIGLIONE D. PESCAIA ♨♨
Talamone ♨♨
Porto Ercole ♨♨
♨♨ Porto S. Stefano

Bolsena
S. Gemini
Bracciano
Bagni di Tivoli ♨

Prati di Tivo
Gran Sasso
✱ Terminillo
PESCARA
Maiella
♨ Caramanico Terme
Scanno
Abruzzo
✱ PESCASSEROLI
Rivisondoli
✱ Roccaraso

ROMA
FIUGGI ♨♨♨
♨ Lido di Ostia
♨ Anzio
Nettuno ♨
♨ Sabaudia
Terracina ♨
Sperlonga ♨
S. Felice Circeo ♨♨

M A R E — T I R R E N O

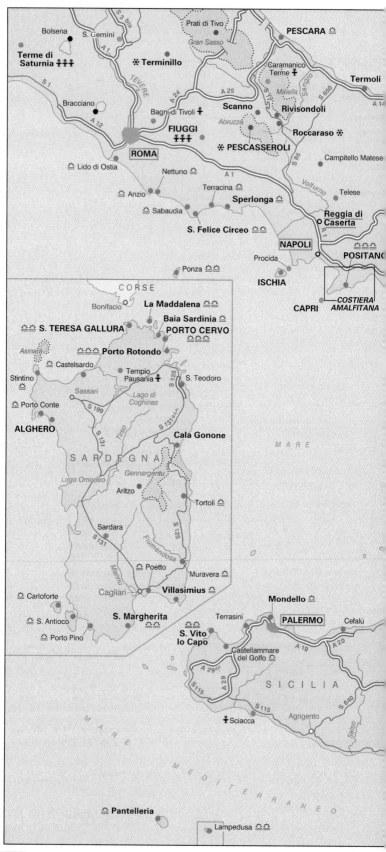

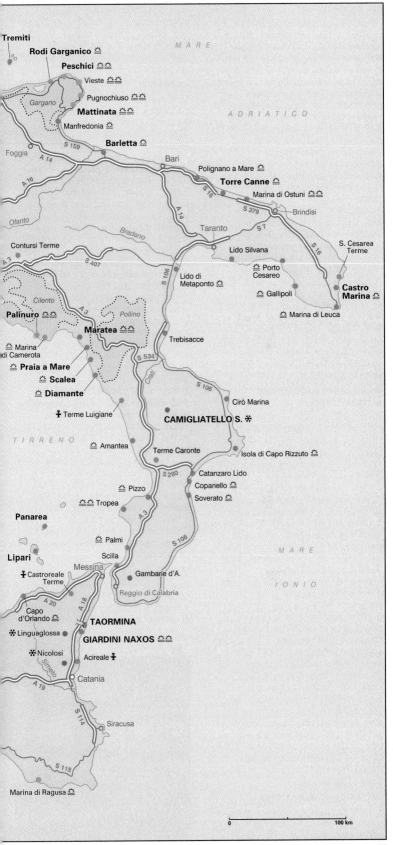

Tremiti

Rodi Garganico ⛺

Peschici ⛺⛺

Vieste ⛺⛺

Pugnochiuso ⛺⛺

Gargano

Mattinata ⛺⛺

Manfredonia ⛺

MARE

ADRIATICO

Barletta ⛺

Foggia

S 159

A 14

Bari

Polignano a Mare ⛺

A 16

Torre Canne ⛺

Marina di Ostuni ⛺⛺

S 16

Ofanto

Bradano

A 14

S 379

Brindisi

Taranto

S 7

Contursi Terme

S 407

S 106

Lido Silvana

Lido di Metaponto ⛺

S. Cesarea Terme

S 16

Porto Cesareo ⛺

Cilento

A 3

Pollino

Gallipoli ⛺

Castro Marina ⛺

Palinuro ⛺⛺

Maratea ⛺⛺

Marina di Leuca ⛺

⛺ Marina di Camerota

Trebisacce

⛺ Praia a Mare

S 534

⛺ Scalea

Crati

⛺ Diamante

S 106

✚ Terme Luigiane

Cirò Marina

CAMIGLIATELLO S. ✳

TIRRENO

⛺ Amantea

Terme Caronte

Isola di Capo Rizzuto ⛺

S 280

Catanzaro Lido

⛺ Pizzo

Copanello ⛺

⛺⛺ Tropea

Soverato ⛺

Panarea

A 3

⛺ Palmi

S 106

MARE

Scilla

Lipari

Messina

Gambarie d'A.

IONIO

✚ Castroreale Terme

Reggio di Calabria

A 20

A 18

Capo d'Orlando ⛺

TAORMINA

✳ Linguaglossa

GIARDINI NAXOS ⛺⛺

✳ Nicolosi

Acireale ✚

Simeto

Catania

A 19

S 114

Siracusa

S 115

Marina di Ragusa ⛺

0   100 km

BED AND BREAKFAST

A varied category, where often the difference between a hotel and a bed and breakfast is indistinguishable. The house or apartment is also often the home of the hosts, who let out a few of their rooms (usually between one and three). Guests are usually required to stay for a minimum period and credit cards are rarely accepted. Generally speaking a bed and breakfast offers a cosier atmosphere than a hotel at competitive prices.

Although in Italy the notion of "rooms to let" does not have an entirely positive image in the collective imagination, many regions offer delightful accommodation often, though not necessarily always, at very reasonable prices.

To get an idea of what is on offer contact **Bed & Breakfast Italia**, Palazzo Sforza Cesarini, Corso Vittorio Emanuele II 282, 00186 Rome, ☎ 06 68 78 618, Fax ☎ 06 68 78 619, www.bbitalia.it, or **Bed & Breakfast Bon Voyage**, Via Procaccini 7, 20154 Milan, ☎ 02 33 11 814, 02 33 11 820, Fax 02 33 13 009. Also visit the websites at: www.dolcecasa.it, www.caffelletto.it

YOUTH HOSTELS AND BUDGET ACCOMMODATION

Hostel accommodation is only available to members of the Youth Hostel Association. It is possible to join the organisation at any of the YHA hostels; membership then provides access to the many YHA hostels located around the world. There is no age limit for membership, which must be renewed annually. Apart from official youth hostels there are many establishments, mainly frequented by young people, with dormitories or rooms with several beds all of which have very reasonable prices. Visit the websites www.italiayhf.org and www.hostels-aig.org

In Italy youth hostels are run by the **Associazione Italiana Alberghi per la Gioventù** (AIG), situated at Via Cavour 44, 00184 Rome, ☎ 06 48 71 152. *Case per ferie* (holiday homes), generally to be found in the big cities, offer simple but decent accommodation at low prices, the only disadvantage being the curfew: visitors are expected to be back by 10.30pm. For more information contact the tourist offices and CITS, Centro Italiano Turismo Sociale, Associazione dell'ospitalità religiosa, ☎ 06 48 73 145.

CONVENTS AND MONASTERIES

A number of religious orders provide rooms for visitors in the major cities. Accommodation is simple, but clean and reasonably priced. The only disadvantage is the curfew; visitors are usually expected to be in by around 11pm. For information, contact tourist offices or the archdioceses.

CAMPSITES

Italy has over 16 000 officially graded campsites with varying ranges of facilities. There are very few possibilities for camping other than on an officially recognised site, and in the summer it is highly recommended that you **reserve a pitch in advance**, as campsites get extremely crowded in high season. They generally have a restaurant, bar and food shop and some have swimming pools. For less spartan travellers some sites have bungalows and caravans; for prices contact each site individually. Prices shown in the guide are daily rates for two people, one tent and one car. An International Camping Carnet for caravans is useful, but not compulsory; it can be obtained from the motoring organisations or the **Camping and Caravanning Club,** Greenfields House, Westwood Way, Coventry CV4 8JH, ☎ 02476 694 995; www.campingandcaravanningclub.co.uk

For more information contact the **Federazione Italiana del Campeggio e del Caravanning**, Via Vittorio Emanuele 11, 50041 Calenzano (FI), ☎ 055 88 23 91, Fax 055 88 25 918; www.federcampeggio.it The organisation publishes a map of campsites and a list of those which offer special rates to holders of the international camping card. It also publishes an annual guide *Campeggi e Villagi Turistici in Italia* in collaboration with the TCI. Local tourist boards also supply information on campsites.

WHERE TO EAT

Restaurant opening times vary from region to region (in the centre and south of Italy they tend to open and close later). Generally they are open

Tuscan tomatoes

for lunch from 12.30pm to 2.30pm and for dinner from 7.30pm to 11pm. Service is usually included but it is customary to leave a tip in proportion to customer satisfaction. Restaurants where service is not included, a rarity, are brought to the reader's attention; after the price of the meal an appropriate percentage for a tip is suggested. By law bread and the cover charge should be included in the price but in some *trattorie* and especially in *pizzerie* they are calculated separately.

For more information on Italian food see "A Riot of Flavours", p 54.

RESTAURANTS, TRATTORIE AND OSTERIE

Although the distinction between these different types of restaurants is not as obvious as it once was, in general, a ristorante offers elegant cuisine and service, while a **trattoria or osteria** is more likely to be a family-run establishment serving home-made dishes in a more relaxed, informal atmosphere. In typical trattorie, the waiter or owner will often tell you what dishes of the day are on offer – if ordering these, make sure that you know how much you are paying ahead of time to avoid any unpleasant shocks when the bill arrives! (A list is usually available; if in doubt ask to see it.) Be wary of choosing the tourist menu, which usually has very limited choice. Trattorie used to have almost exclusively house wine on offer (served by the carafe), but you can now expect to find a proper wine list which often has a good selection of local wines.

PIZZERIE

A pizza is the ideal solution for those in search of a tasty, quick and reasonable priced meal. We have made a selection of pizzerie that struck us as particularly good but since there are so many on offer, it is often readers themselves that alert us to an "authentic" address happened upon by chance.

The succulent lemons of the amalfi coast

WINE BARS

Wine bars *(enoteche)* are becoming increasingly popular in Italy. Like osterie they often have a kitchen and serve daily specials and light starters as well as a varied choice of wines served by the glass or bottle.

AND DON'T FORGET THE RED GUIDE

THE RED GUIDE ITALIA

For a more exhaustive list of hotels consult *The Red Guide Italia* which provides a whole host of details on Italy's hotels and restaurants.

Choosing Where to Stay

The map of Places to Stay on p 28 shows places of interest marked to denote suitability for different kinds of trips.
Those interested in **cultural centres** should look for place names framed in green. For visitors on brief trips who want to stay in one of the many cities of artistic interest, destinations suitable for an **overnight stop** are underlined in green.
Among the many other **places to stay** look for areas shaded in green (nature parks) and for the symbols ⨥ **(spas)**, ⌓ **(seaside resort)** and ❋ **(winter sports resort)**.

Services

Concessions

Visitors trying to keep costs down will find information on budget accommodation (*pensioni*, youth hostels, campsites, convents and monasteries) in the **Where to Stay** sections in the various chapters (*see also above*).

DISCOUNTS ...

BY TRAIN

The **Carta Prima** (€67.14, valid for a year) gives card-holders a 20% discount on first-class travel throughout Italy. This card is valid for the card-holder only and is non-transferrable.

The **Carta Amicotreno** (€51.13, valid for a year) gives a 50% discount on some local trains and a 20% discount on many medium- and long-distance trains, and is ideal for travellers spending an extended period in Italy, doing most of their travelling by rail. Certain restrictions apply to days of travel. Concessions also apply to a companion travelling with the card-holder.

BY AIR

Alitalia has various special offers for passengers buying their ticket one, two or three weeks before departure. The airline also offers special weekend rates for travellers departing on a Saturday and returning on a Sunday of the same weekend (*tipo corto*) and for the same type of ticket, but valid for a month (*tipo lungo*).

DISCOUNTS FOR YOUNG PEOPLE UNDER THE AGE OF 26

BY TRAIN

The **Carta Verde** (€25.82, valid for a year) gives young people a 20% discount in both first and second class, on all trains within Italy, including fast Eurocity trains and Eurostar. This card is valid for the card-holder only and is non-transferrable.

BY AIR

Discounted rates exist for young people aged between 12 and 26 (under 26 on the day of departure).

DISCOUNTS FOR SENIOR CITIZENS

BY TRAIN

For travellers over 60 years of age, the **Carta d'Argento** (€25.82, valid for a year) offers a 20% discount in first and second class on the Italian section of all routes, including fast Eurocity trains and Eurostar. This card is valid for the card-holder only and is non-transferrable.

BY AIR

Senior citizens aged 60 or over are also eligible for discounts on some airlines, and senior citizens who are at least 65 on the day of travel are entitled to a 10% discount on some tariffs.

DISCOUNTS FOR FAMILIES AND SMALL GROUPS

BY TRAIN

Families and groups of at least three people and no more than five are entitled to a 20% discount in both first and second class if they are travelling together. Children aged between 4 and 12 travel at half-price of the discounted fare and children under 4 travel free. This discount is available on all trains, including the Italian sections of Eurocity trains and on Eurostar, although it is not valid in July and August, or during the Easter and Christmas holiday periods.

BY AIR

Families qualify for discounted tickets on certain airlines if they fulfil the following conditions: the family must travel together and must comprise at least four people, with a maximum of two adults and a minimum of two children (between the ages of two and eleven). At least one of the adults must be a parent of the children, while the second adult does not necessarily need to be related to the family.

Practical Information

ELECTRICITY

The voltage is 220ac, 50 cycles per second; the sockets are for two-pin plugs. It is therefore advisable to take an adaptor for hairdryers, shavers, computers etc.

EMERGENCIES

☎ **113**: General emergency services (*soccorso pubblico di emergenza*); to be called only in cases of real danger. Calls are free.

☎ **112**: Police (*carabinieri*). Calls are free.

☎ **115**: Fire Brigade (*vigili del fuoco*). Calls are free.

☎ **118**: Emergency Health Services (*emergenza sanitaria*). Calls are free.

☎ **1515**: Forest Fire Service. Environmental emergencies. Calls are free.

☎ **803 116**: Automobile Club d'Italia Emergency Breakdown Service. Calls are free.

Foreign Embassies and Consulates in Italy

Australia – Via Alessandria 215, 00198 Rome; ☏ 06 85 27 21; www.australian-embassy.it

Canada – Via G.B. de Rossi 27, 00161 Rome; ☏ 06 44 59 81; rome@dfait-maeci.gc.ca

Ireland – Piazza di Campitelli 3, 00186 Rome; ☏ 06 69 79 121; Fax 06 67 92 354.

UK – Via XX Settembre 80a, Rome; ☏ 06 42 20 00 01; Fax 06 48 73 324.

USA – Via Veneto 119a, 00187 Rome; ☏ 06 46 741; Fax 06 48 82 672; www.usembassy.it

Money

The unit of currency is the **euro** which is issued in notes (€5, €10, €20, €50, €100, €200 and €500) and in coins (1 cent, 2 cents, 5 cents, 10 cents, 20 cents, 50 cents, €1 and €2).

BANKS

Banks are usually open Monday to Friday, 8.30am-1.30pm and 2.30pm-4pm. Some branches are open in city centres and shopping centres on Saturday mornings; almost all are closed on Saturdays, Sundays and public holidays. Most hotels will change travellers' cheques. Money can be changed in post offices (except travellers' cheques), money-changing bureaux and at railway stations and airports. Commission is always charged.

CREDIT CARDS

Payment by credit card is widespread in shops, hotels and restaurants and also some petrol stations. *The Red Guide Italia* and *The Red Guide Europe* indicate which credit cards are accepted at hotels and restaurants. Money may also be withdrawn from a bank but may incur interest pending repayment.

Newspapers

The main Roman newspapers (available throughout Italy) are *La Repubblica*, *Il Messaggero* and *Il Giorno*. The *Osservatore Romano* is the official newspaper of the Vatican City. Foreign newspapers are available in the cities and large towns.

Pharmacies

These are identified by a red and white cross. When closed each will advertise the names of the pharmacy on duty and a list of doctors on call.

Post

OPENING HOURS

Post offices are open 8am-2pm on weekdays, 8.30am-noon on Saturday. Stamps are also sold at tobacconists (*tabacchi*) which display a black *valori bollati* sign outside.

STAMPS

Stamps for letters or postcards cost €0.41.
Express service stamps (*posta prioritaria*) cost €0.62.

Shopping

(see also "What to buy locally" below)
Most shops open from 8.30/9am to 12.30/1pm and 3.30/4pm to 7.30/8pm, although in the centre of large towns and cities, shops usually remain open at lunchtime. Credit cards are accepted in most stores, with the exception of small food shops.
In northern Italy, shops often take a shorter midday break and close earlier. Late-night shopping is frequent in seaside resorts. Many tourist resorts have an open-air market once or twice a week.

Telecommunications

The telephone service is organised by TELECOM ITALIA (formerly SIP). Each office has public booths where the customer pays for units used (*scatti*) at the counter after the call. Reduced rates operate after 6.30pm and are even less between 10pm and 8am.

PHONECARDS

Phonecards (*schede telefoniche*) are sold in denominations of €1, €2.50, €5 and €8 and are supplied by CIT offices and post offices as well as tobacconists (sign bearing a white T on a black background).

PUBLIC PHONES

Telephone boxes may be operated by telephone cards (sold in post offices and tobacconists) and by telephone credit cards. To make a call: lift the receiver, insert payment, await dialling signal, punch in the required number and wait for a response.

TELEPHONING

When making a call within Italy, the area code (eg 06 for Rome, 055 for Florence) is always used, both from outside and within the city you are calling.
For international calls dial 00 plus the following country codes:
61 for Australia
1 for Canada
64 for New Zealand
44 for the UK
1 for the USA

If calling from outside the country, the international code for Italy is 39. Dial the full area code, even when making an international call; for example, when calling Rome from the UK, dial 00 39 06, followed by the correspondent's number.

USEFUL NUMBERS

(See also "Emergencies" above)
☏ 176: International Directory

Conversion Tables

Weights and measures

| 1 kilogram (kg) | 2.2 pounds (lb) | 2.2 pounds |
| 1 metric ton (tn) | 1.1 tons | 1.1 tons |

to convert kilograms to pounds, multiply by 2.2

| 1 litre (l) | 2.1 pints (pt) | 1.8 pints |
| 1 litre | 0.3 gallon (gal) | 0.2 gallon |

to convert litres to gallons, multiply by 0.26 (US) or 0.22 (UK)

| 1 hectare (ha) | 2.5 acres | 2.5 acres |
| 1 square kilometre (km²) | 0.4 square miles (sq mi) | 0.4 square miles |

to convert hectares to acres, multiply by 2.4

1 centimetre (cm)	0.4 inches (in)	0.4 inches
1 metre (m)	3.3 feet (ft) - 39.4 inches - 1.1 yards (yd)	
1 kilometre (km)	0.6 miles (mi)	0.6 miles

to convert metres to feet, multiply by 3.28, kilometres to miles, multiply by 0.6

Clothing

Women

	EU	US	UK	
	35	4	2½	
	36	5	3½	
	37	6	4½	
Shoes	38	7	5½	
	39	8	6½	
	40	9	7½	
	41	10	8½	
	36	6	8	
	38	8	10	
Dresses &	40	10	12	
suits	42	12	14	
	44	14	16	
	46	16	18	
	36	30	8	
	38	32	10	
Blouses &	40	34	12	
sweaters	42	36	14	
	44	38	16	
	46	40	18	

Men

	EU	US	UK	
	40	7½	7	
	41	8½	8	
	42	9½	9	
	43	10½	10	Shoes
	44	11½	11	
	45	12½	12	
	46	13½	13	
	46	36	36	
	48	38	38	
	50	40	40	Suits
	52	42	42	
	54	44	44	
	56	46	46	
	37	14½	14½	
	38	15	15	
	39	15½	15½	Shirts
	40	15¾	15¾	
	41	16	16	
	42	16½	16½	

Sizes often vary depending on the designer. These equivalents are given for guidance only.

Speed

kph	10	30	50	70	80	90	100	110	120	130
mph	6	19	31	43	50	56	62	68	75	81

Temperature

Celsius (°C)	0°	5°	10°	15°	20°	25°	30°	40°	60°	80°	100°
Fahrenheit (°F)	32°	41°	50°	59°	68°	77°	86°	104°	140°	176°	212°

To convert Celsius into Fahrenheit, multiply °C by 9, divide by 5, and add 32.
To convert Fahrenheit into Celsius, subtract 32 from °F, multiply by 5, and divide by 9.

Notes and Coins

The euro banknotes were designed by Robert Kalinan, an Austrian artist. His designs were inspired by the theme "Ages and styles of European Architecture". Windows and gateways feature on the front of the banknotes, bridges feature on the reverse, symbolising the European spirit of openness and co-operation.

The images are stylised representations of the typical architectural style of each period, rather than specific structures.

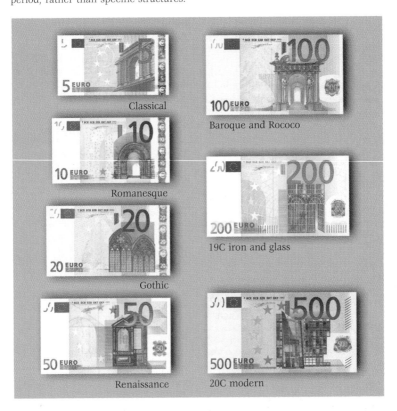

Classical

Baroque and Rococo

Romanesque

19C iron and glass

Gothic

200EURO

Renaissance

20C modern

Euro coins have one face common to all 12 countries in the European single currency area or "Eurozone" (currently Austria, Belgium, Finland, France, Germany, Greece, Ireland, Italy, Luxembourg, The Netherlands, Portugal and Spain) and a reverse side specific to each country, created by their own national artists.

Euro banknotes look the same throughout the Eurozone. All Euro banknotes and coins can be used anywhere in this area.

Enquiries. Provides phone numbers outside of Italy in English and Italian. Note that calls to this number are subject to a charge.

☎ 170: Operator Assisted International Calls. Note that calls to this number are subject to a charge.

TOBACCONISTS

Besides cigarettes and tobacco, *tabacchi* sell postcards and stamps, confectionery, phonecards, public transport tickets, lottery tickets and such like.

Sightseeing

Information on admission times and charges for museums and monuments is given in the "Selected Sights" section of the guide.

Admission times and charges are liable to alteration without prior notice. Due to fluctuations in the cost of living and the constant change in opening times as well as possible closures for restoration work, the information given in this guide should merely serve as a guideline. Visitors are advised to phone ahead to confirm opening times.

The admission prices indicated are for single adults benefiting from no special concession; reductions for children, students, the over 60s and parties should be requested on site and be endorsed with proof of ID. Special conditions often exist for groups but arrangements should be made in advance. For nationals of European Union member countries many institutions provide free admission to visitors under 18 and over 65 with proof of identification, and a 50% reduction for visitors under 25 years of age. Many museums require visitors to leave bags and backpacks in a luggage deposit area at the museum entrance. Taking photos with a flash is usually forbidden.

During **National Heritage Week** (Settimana dei Beni Culturali), which takes place at a different time each year, access to a large number of sights is free of charge. Contact the tourist offices for more detailed information.

Churches and chapels are usually open from 8am to noon and from 2pm to dusk. Notices outside a number of churches formally request visitors to dress in a manner deemed appropriate when entering a place of worship – this excludes sleeveless and low-cut tops, short miniskirts or skimpy shorts and bare feet. Visitors are not admitted during services and so tourists should avoid visiting at that time. Visitors are advised to visit churches in the morning, when the natural light provides better illumination of the works of art; also churches are occasionally forced to close in the afternoons due to lack of staff. Works of art are often illuminated by coin-operated lighting. When visits to museums, churches or other sites are accompanied by a custodian, it is customary to leave a donation.

SYMBOLS AND ABBREVIATIONS

Sights marked with the symbols &
or (&) offer full or partial access for wheelchairs.
Days of the week: Mon, Tue, Wed, Thu, Fri, Sat, Sun.
Months: Jan, Feb, Mar, Apr, May, Jun, Jul, Aug, Sep, Oct, Nov, Dec.
Hours and minutes: hr, min

Ideas for your Visit

Touring by Car

The map of **Driving Tours** (*see p 14*) shows recommended itineraries for those with their own transport. Visitors interested in Dante country should consult *The Green Guide Tuscany* which has recommended itineraries for those with a weekend, a few days or a whole week at their disposal.

THE GULF OF GENOA AND THE ITALIAN RIVIERA 1

This itinerary follows the Ligurian coast, from the **Cinque Terre** to the Cte d'Azure before moving inland, passing through the Colle di Tenda (not recommended for those prone to travel sickness!).

FROM THE VALLE D'AOSTA TO THE WINE-GROWING MONFERRATO REGION 2

An ideal route for mountain lovers, this itinerary reaches the French **Alps** and includes a cultural stop in **Turin**, the nearby **Sacra di S. Michele**, which evokes the sometimes sinister atmosphere of Umberto Eco's *The Name of the Rose*, and a stop in the wine-growing **Monferrato** region, a land of gentle, rolling hills.

FROM THE PO VALLEY TO THE GREAT LAKES OF LOMBARDY 3

This itinerary starts in the heart of Lombardy, the frenetic city of **Milan**.

Visitors with time and patience might be able to see past the glitter of yuppie executives and glamorous shops and discover a rich, if discreet, cultural heritage.

The route continues to the **Bassa Padana**, a land of mist and fog with a slightly melancholy charm, poetically described in the stories of Giovannino Guareschi. Finally, **Verona** is an ideal starting point to discover the **lake district**.

FROM THE DOLOMITES TO VENICE AND TRIESTE 4

Start from **Venice** *(see The Green Guide Venice)* before exploring this area with its blend of Italian and Central European culture. In **Trieste** we recommend a stop in the classic Caffè San Marco to savour the literary atmosphere of the city.

The route continues through the harsh and atmospheric Dolomites between **Cortina** and **Bolzano**, with the sounds of the German- and Ladin-accented local dialect, before descending to **Trent**, dominated by the Buonconsiglio castle with its ancient fresco cycle of the Months. The itinerary concludes in the Palladian town of **Vicenza**.

FROM THE RICH CITIES OF THE PLAIN TO THE LAGOONS OF THE ADRIATIC 5

This itinerary straddles the Veneto, Lombardy and Romagna. There is a decidedly Byzantine atmosphere in this area which embraces the **Po Delta**, **Bologna**, the mosaics of **Ravenna**, the noble city of **Ferrara**, the **Palladian villas of the Brenta** and the **Venetian lagoon**.

ART, NATURE AND SPIRITUALITY IN TUSCANY AND UMBRIA 6

This programme takes in the art cities of Tuscany, starting from **Florence** and progressing through the area around **Lucca** with its fine villas, **Pisa**, the Balze of **Volterra** and **San Gimignano** with its profusion of towers. The heart of Tuscany is embodied by the charm of **Siena**, a city that is at the same time gentle and aggressive. Here the itinerary takes on the character of some of the saints that populated the region: St Bernardino with his sermons that shook the walls *(see Fashion, p 108)*, St Catherine and, in **Umbria**, Saints Francis and Clare.

FROM THE HEART OF UMBRIA TO THE ADRIATIC 7

This itinerary offers contrasting landscapes, from the gentle Umbrian countryside with its treasures of art and spirituality (**Gubbio**, **Perugia**, **Assisi** and **Spoleto**), to the **Abruzzi** and the Adriatic, with a stopover in the beautiful piazza of **Ascoli Piceno**. From **Rimini** we move inland to **San Marino** and the majestic palace of the Duke of Montefeltro in **Urbino**.

FROM ROME AND ITS REGION TO THE ABRUZZI 8

Rome *caput mundi*: several days are essential to explore Italy's capital (consult *The Green Guide Rome*). Afterwards, explore the surrounding region with its lakes, castles and the Etruscan remains of **Tarquinia**. Finally, proceed to the **Parco Nazionale d'Abruzzo**, a blend of nature and culture, and the abbeys of **Casamari**, **Monte Cassino** and **San Clemente a Casauria**.

THE TREASURES OF THE NEAPOLITAN COAST 9

This is probably the most colourful itinerary, with the intense blue of the sea, the deep pink of the bougainvillea and the white houses overlooking the **Amalfi coast**.

Visit **Naples** and the surrounding bay, **Capri**, Mount Vesuvius and its illustrious victim **Pompeii**, and then onto **Paestum** before reaching **Calabria** and the **Gulf of Policastro**.

PUGLIA 10

This itinerary is one that combines the sea and varied and unusual architecture, from the **Gargano** to the **Terra dei Trulli**, from the Baroque town of **Lecce** to the Ionian sea and the **Sassi di Matera**.

SICILY AND CALABRIA 11

This programme includes **Scilla** and Cariddi, **Sila** and the **Aspromonte** as well as remains of ancient monasteries all the way down to **Sicily** *(see The Green Guide Sicily)*.

SARDINIA 12

Sardinia has a harsh landscape formed by a wind that is redolent of the scent of wild plants. Discover nature in its purest form as well as startling and primordial expressions of art before immersing yourself in a sea that is so crystalline as to be almost invisible.

Themed Tours

Historic Routes

Italy has a wide network of roads laid down by some its most illustrious inhabitants of days gone by. Listed here are a few of them, beginning with an ancient road of pilgrimage.

VIA FRANCIGENA

You may come across the logo of the Via Francigena which depicts a pilgrim who looks like a Roman statue, a little squat, with a cane in his hand and a bundle on his shoulder.

The Via Francigena ran from Canterbury to Rome, and was used by medieval pilgrims who managed to cover about 20km a day on foot.

The stopovers were: Canterbury, Calais, Bruay, Arras, Reims, Chalons sur Marne, Bar sur Aube, Besançon, Pontarlier, Lausanne, Gran San Bernardo, Aosta, Ivrea, Santhià, Vercelli, Pavia, Piacenza, Fiorenzuola, Fidenza, Parma, Fornovo, Pontremoli, Aulla, Luni, Lucca, S. Genesio, S. Gimignano, Siena, S. Quirico, Bolsena, Viterbo, Sutri and Rome. For more information see www.viafrancigena.com

VIA AURELIA

Of ancient Roman origin, the Via Aurelia (S 1) has linked Rome to Genoa since 109 BC! Construction began in 241 BC.

VIA APPIA

Construction of this road began in 312 BC. At its longest, it linked Rome to Brindisi. Nowadays it is limited to Rome and its surrounding area.

VIA CASSIA

Laid down in the 2C BC, this road runs through Etruria, linking Rome to Arezzo and then extending to Florence and Modena and, in another direction, to Luni. The current S 2, which still bears the same name, links Rome and Florence.

VIA EMILIA

This road links Rimini to Piacenza and gave its name to the region. It was built in 187 BC. During the period of the Roman Empire it extended to Aosta and Aquileia. Today the Via Emilia follows the same route.

VIA FLAMINIA

Built in 220 BC, the Via Flaminia linked Rome to Rimini. Nowadays it is one of the principal arteries of the capital.

Sport and Leisure

Italy has such a varied landscape that there is something for everyone. The Alps provide footpaths and mountains suitable for all levels of athletic expertise. The lake district, the mountain streams and rivers are ideal for fishing. Trentino-Alto Adige, the Riviera del Brenta, Tuscany and Umbria are among the more suitable regions for cycling. The Maremma offers a perfect landscape for horse riding. The entire coast of Italy is an Eden for those who enjoy swimming, windsurfing and the beach: the Adriatic coast with its shallow waters and long beaches is ideal for families with children, while the waters of the Gargano, the Gulf of Policastro, Sicily and Sardinia are renowned for their crystalline purity and splendid colours which on the Costa Smeralda really are emerald green. The Amalfi coast and the Faraglioni of Capri are perhaps the best known part of Italy's coasts; Versilia, with the Apuan Alps as a backdrop, is an essential venue for *habitués* of the beach, and the Ligurian Riviera offers striking views and beaches that nestle between the hills that lead down to the sea.

For information on sporting and leisure activities see the addresses of information offices for each region or sight in the introduction to each chapter in the guide.

A windsurfer sailboarding in the sea of Otranto

G. Bludzin/MICHELIN

Nature parks

National nature parks are the ideal destination for holidaymakers who prefer nature to regular tourist pursuits. An excellent website for further information is www.cts.it/parchionline (in Italian only). The principal Italian nature parks are:

Parco Nazionale del Gran Paradiso – Extends from the Valle d'Aosta to Piedmont. From Turin follow the SS 460. After Rivarolo Canavese, take the Ceresole Reale road or the A5 motorway and the S 47 to Cogne *(see VALLE D'AOSTA)*.

Parco Nazionale dello Stelvio – This includes the Ortles-Cevedale and Valfurva massifs and the Martello, Ultimo, Solda and Trafoi valleys. The park can be reached via Lombardy on the SS 38 to Bormio, or via Trentino by taking first the motorway, then the SS 43 to Rabbi. For further information, contact the tourist offices of Solda ☎ 0473 61 30 15 or Malè ☎ 0473 90 12 80, or Associazione Turistica Val Martello ☎ 0473 74 45 98.

Parco Nazionale delle Dolomiti Bellunesi – This park runs along the right bank of the Piave river, between Feltre and Belluno, and covers three main mountain ranges: the Vette Feltrine, the Monti del Sole and the Schiara massif. The park can be reached by taking the SS 50 from Grappa, or the SS 348 from Treviso as far as Feltre. The park authority office is in Feltre, Piazzale Zancanaro 1, ☎ 0439 33 28.

Parco Naturale della Maremma – The Monti dell'Uccellina are located in the heart of this park. Take the A 12 motorway to Grosseto. After Grosseto, follow signs to Alberese where the visitor centre is located.

Parco Nazionale dei Monti Sibillini – This park comprises a large limestone massif which stretches from the Marches to Umbria. It can be reached from Macerata on the S 78 to Sarnano and Amandola and from Spoleto the Forca di Cerro pass on the S 209, S 320 and S 396 to Norcia. For information on the park, contact the Marches regional tourist office: Servizio Turismo della Regione Marche, Via Gentile da Fabriano 9, 60125 Ancona, ☎ 071 80 61.

Parco Nazionale del Gran Sasso – *(See ABRUZZO).* For information on the park, contact the L'Aquila region tourist office, Piazza S. Maria Paganica 5, 67100 L'Aquila, ☎ 0862 41 08 08.

Parco Nazionale d'Abruzzo – *(See ABRUZZO).* For information on the park, contact Ufficio di Zona di Pescasseroli, Via Consultore 1, ☎ 0863 91955.

Parco Nazionale della Maiella – This can be reached via the A 5 motorway, exits Sulmona, Bussi, Torre de' Passeri and Scafa. For information, contact the park authorities (Ente Parco) at Presidenza della Regione Abruzzo, Viale Bovio 425, 65123 Pescara, ☎ 085 74 003.

Parco Nazionale del Circeo – *(See TERRACINA).*

Parco Nazionale del Cilento e Vallo di Diano – *(See Parco Nazionale del CILENTO).*

Parco Nazionale del Gargano – This park runs along the promontory of the same name and also includes the Tremiti islands. There arc visitor centres at San Marco in Lamis, Piazza Carlo Marx 1, ☎ 0882 83 32 82 and at Monte Sant'Angelo, loc. Foresta Umbra, ☎ 0884 56 09 44. Information is also available from the Azienda di Promozione Turistica di Foggia, Via E. Perrone 17, ☎ 0881 72 31 41.

Parco Nazionale del Pollino – This park covers the area around Monte Pollino (2 248m/7 380ft), which is part of the Calabrian Apennine chain. The park also contains several museums: the Museo del Lupo di Alessandria del Carretto, the Museo Naturalistico del Pollino di Rotonda, the Museo Albanese di Civita and the Museo della Cultura Arberesh di San Paolo Albanese. *For further information see CALABRIA.*

Parco Nazionale della Calabria – Situated in the heart of Calabria, this park covers the wooded massifs of Sila Grande, Sila Piccola and Aspromonte. For information, contact the Ufficio Parco Nazionale della Calabria, Viale della Repubblica 26, Cosenza, ☎ 0984 76 760.

Parco Nazionale del Golfo di Orosei, Gennargentu e Asinara – The best base for trips into the park is Nuoro. For information, contact the Ente Provinciale per il Turismo, Piazza Italia 19, Nuoro, ☎ 0784 32 307.

The following is a list of the main theme parks in Italy, which provide a range of imaginative and thrilling amusements and rides for both young and old:

Edenlandia – Viale Kennedy 76, Naples, ☎ 081 23 99 693, www.edenlandia.it

Fantasy World Minitalia – Via Vittorio Veneto 52, Capriate (MI), ☎ 02 90 90 169, www.minitaliaworld.com A 4, motorway, exit at Capriate.

Fiabilandia – Loc. Rivazzurra di Rimini, ☎ 0541 37 20 64, www.fiabilandia.it A 4 motorway, exit at Rimini Sud.

Gardaland – Castelnuovo del Garda, loc. Ronchi, ☎ 045 64 49 777, www.gardaland.it Take the A 4 motorway and exit at Peschiera del Garda or take A 22 and exit at Affi, then take the dual carriageway to Peschiera.

Italia in Miniatura –Via Popilia 239, Viserba (RN), ☎ 0541 73 20 04, www.italiainminiatura.com Take A 14 motorway, exit at Rimini Nord.

Mirabilandia – Statale Adriatica 16, km 162, Savio di Ravenna, ☎ 0544 56 11 11, www.mirabilandia.it Take A 14 motorway, exit at Ravenna (coming from the north) or Cesena Nord, then take E 45, exit at Mirabilandia; from Rome take A 1 to Orte, then E 45.

Sport

MOUNTAINEERING AND RAMBLING

For information contact the **Federazione Italiana Escursionismo**, Via La Spezia 58r, 16149 Genoa, ☎ 010 41 41 94; **CAI (Milan office)**, Via S. Pellico 6, 20122 Milan, ☎ 02 86 46 35 16, www.caimilano.it

HUNTING

For information contact Federazione Italiana della Caccia, Viale Tiziano 70, 00196 Rome, ☎ 06 32 33 779.

CANOEING

For information contact Federazione Italiana Canottaggio e Federazione Italiana Canoa e Kayak, Viale Tiziano 70, 00196 Rome, ☎ 06 32 33 801 and ☎ 06 36 85 85 25.

CYCLING

For information contact **Federazione Ciclistica Italiana**, Stadio Olimpico, Curva Nord, Cancello L, Porta 91, 00194 Foro Italico, Rome, ☎ 06 32 34 192.

RIDING AND PONY TREKKING

For information contact **Federazione Italiana di Turismo Equestre**, Piazza Antonio Mancini 4, 00196 Rome, ☎ 06 32 65 02 30, www.fiteec-ante.it

GOLF

For information contact **Federazione Italiana Golf**, Viale Tiziano 74, 00196 Rome, ☎ 06 32 31 825.

SAILING AND WINDSURFING

For information contact **Federazione Italiana Vela**, Piazza Borgo Pila 40, Corte Lambruschini, Torre A, Genoa ☎ 010 54 45 41.

FISHING

For information contact **Federazione Italiana Pesca Sportiva e Attività Subacquee**, via Vittorio Colonna 27, ☎ 06 32 31 709 (for Rome), **CONI**, Viale Tiziano, 70, ☎ 06 36 851.

SKIING

For information contact **Federazione Italiana Sport Invernali**, Via Piranesi, 44b, 20137 Milan, ☎ 02 75 731, www.fisi.org

WATER SKIING

For information contact **Federazione Italiana Sci nautico**, Via Piranesi, 44, 20137 Milan, ☎ 02 75 29 181, www.scinautico.com

SPELEOLOGY

For information contact **Società Speleologica Italiana**, Via Zamboni, 67, 40127 Bologna, ☎ 051 25 00 49, www.ssi.speleo.it

Spa Resorts

The map of Places to Stay on p 28 gives an overview of the location of Italian spas. For further information consult the ENIT website *(see "Useful Addresses" above).*

What to Buy Locally

Every region produces crafts of which it is justly proud.

Alabaster and stone – Alabaster is mostly crafted in Volterra in Tuscany. Objects in slate can be found in Liguria.

Paper and papier mâché – These can be found in Fabriano in the Marches, in Florence, Amalfi, Syracuse in Sicily, Lecce in Puglia, Bassano del Grappa and Verona in the Veneto region.

Ceramics – These are mainly produced in Romagna (Faenza), Umbria (Deruta, Gubbio, Orvieto, Città di Castello) and Sicily (Caltagirone).

Coral – Coral is mainly to be found in Naples, Torre del Greco and in Alghero, Sardinia.

Filigree – Can mainly be found in Genoa and Sardinia.

Wood – Trentino-Alto Adige (particularly in Val Gardena) and Valle d'Aosta are the most notable regions for woodcraft.

Lace – Lovers of lace should head for the Paese di Bengodi in Burano, the colourful island in the Venetian lagoon, but also for Tuscany and Umbria.

Porcelain – Can be found in Campania, Capodimonte, and Bassano del Grappa in the Veneto.

Glass – Watch the almost magical creation of glass objects on the island of Murano in the Venetian lagoon, known the world over for glass production. Glass objects can also be found in Liguria, at Altare, near Savona.

One should not of course forget the vast array of food products: pasta, Parmesan, Parma and San Daniele ham. *See A Riot of Flavours, p 54.*

Books

Italy has long been a favourite subject with writers of all nationalities. Some, which may be out of print, will be available only from libraries.

HISTORY AND ART

A Concise Encyclopaedia of the Italian Renaissance by JR Hale (*Thames and Hudson*)

A History of Italian Renaissance Art by F Hartt (*Thames and Hudson*)

Architecture of the Italian Renaissance by Peter Murray (*Thames and Hudson*)

Leonardo da Vinci by Martin Kemp, Jane Roberts and Philip Steadman (*Yale University Press*)

Michelangelo by Howard Hibbard (*Penguin*)

Rise and Fall of the House of Medici by Christopher Hibbert (*Penguin*)

Roman Italy by TW Potter (*British Museum Publications Ltd*)

Siena: A City and its History by Judith Hook (*Hamish Hamilton*)

The Art of the Renaissance by Linda and Peter Murray (*Thames and Hudson*)

The Grandeur that was Rome by JC Stobart (*Sidgwick and Jackson*)

The Italian World by JJ Norwich (*Thames and Hudson*)

Venetian Painting: A Concise History by John Steer (*Thames and Hudson*)

Villas of Tuscany by H Acton (*Thames and Hudson*)

A Traveller's History of Italy by Valerio Lintner (*The Windrush Press*)

Italy: The Unfinished Revolution by Matt Frei (*Mandarin*)

TRAVEL

DH Lawrence and Italy (*Penguin*)

Guide to Tuscany by Bently (*Penguin*)

Living in Italy by YM Menzies (*Hale*)

Mediterranean Island Hopping by Dana Facaros and Michael Pauls (*Gentry Books Ltd*)

The Path to Rome by Hilaire Belloc (*Penguin*)

Stones of Florence and Venice by Mary McCarthy (*Penguin*)

Venetian Evenings by James Lees-Milne (*Collins*)

Venice by John Kent (*Viking*)

Under the Tuscan Sun by Frances Mayes (*Bantam Books*)

FOOD AND WINE

Italy: The Beautiful Cookbook by Lorenza Medici (*Murdoch Books*)

Life beyond Lambrusco (Understanding Italian Fine Wine) by N Belfrage (*Sidgwick and Jackson*)

Traditional Italian Food by LB Birch (*Fontana*)

The Fratelli Camisa Cookery Book by Elizabeth Camisa (*Penguin*)

Italian Short Stories by R Trevelyan *(Penguin Parallel Text)*

A Room with a View by EM Forster *(Penguin)*

Where Angels Fear to Tread by EM Forster *(Penguin)*

Garden of the Finzi-Continis by Giorgio Bassani *(Penguin)*

Sicilian Carousel by Lawrence Durrell *(Faber)*

The Ant Colony by F King *(Flamingo)*

The Leopard by Giuseppe Tomasi di Lampedusa *(Flamingo)*

The Slow Train to Milan by Lisa St Aubin de Teran *(Penguin)*

The Name of the Rose by Umberto Eco *(Vintage)*

Films

See the chapter on CINEMA, p 106.

1935 **The Last Days of Pompeii** by Merian C Cooper

1945 **Roma, Città Aperta** (Rome Open City) by Roberto Rossellini

1948 **Ladri di biciclette** (Bicycle Thieves) by Vittorio de Sica

1950 **Domenica d'Agosto** (Sunday in August) by Luciano Emmer

1950 **Francesco, Giullare di Dio** (Francis, God's Jester) by Roberto Rossellini

1950 **September Affair** by William Dieterle (Capri)

1951 **Quo Vadis** by Mervyn Le Roy

1951 **The Little World of Don Camillo** by Julien Duvivier (in a village in the Po Plain). Followed by three sequels featuring Don Camillo and Peppone.

1953 **Roman Holiday** by William Wyler

1955 **Summertime** (Summer Madness) by David Lean

1957 **Le Notti di Cabiria** by Federico Fellini

1959 **Ben Hur** by William Wyler

1960 **Il Bell'Antonio** by Piero Piccioni (Sicily)

1960 **La Dolce Vita** by Federico Fellini

1960 **L'Avventura** by Michelangelo Antonioni (Lipari Islands and Sicily)

1960 **Spartacus** by Stanley Kubrick

1963 **Il Gattopardo** (The Leopard) by Luchino Visconti

1969 **Il Conformista** (The Conformist) by Bernardo Bertolucci

1971 **Death in Venice** by Luchino Visconti

1975 **Cadaveri eccellenti** (Illustrious Corpses) by Francesco Rosi

1976 **Novecento** (1900) by Bernardo Bertolucci (Italy 1900-45)

1977 **Un giornata particolare** by Ettore Scola

1978 **L'albero degli zoccoli** (The Tree of Wooden Clogs) by Ermanno Olmi (19C Lombardy)

1979 **Christ stopped at Eboli** by Francesco Rosi (Campania)

1985 **A Room with a View** by James Ivory (Florence and thereabouts)

1987 **Cronica di una Morta Annunciata** (Chronicle of a Death Foretold) by Francesco Rosi

1987 **Oci Ciornie** (Black Eyes) by Nikita Mikhalkov

1987 **The Belly of an Architect** by Peter Greenaway (Rome)

1989 **Cinema Paradiso** by Giuseppe Tornatore

1994 **Caro Diario** (Dear Diary) by Gianni Moretti

1994 **Il Postino** (The Postman) by Michael Radford

1997 **La vita è bella** (Life is Beautiful) by Roberto Benigni

Events and Festivals

More details can be obtained from local Tourist Information offices (APT).

30 and 31 January — Aosta
St Orso Fair: craft fair with sale of articles from the Valle d'Aosta.

First two weeks of February — Agrigento
Almonds in bloom festival.

Carnival — Venice / Ivrea / Viareggio / Verona
Parties and events in the *calli* and *campi* of Venice.
Folk festival, including the famous battle of the oranges.
Procession of allegorical floats.
"Venerdì gnocolar" procession.

1 April — San Marino
Investiture of the regents of the Republic.

Holy Week (Maundy Thursday and Good Friday) — Taranto
Holy Week rites: procession of Our Lady of Sorrows and the Mysteries.

Easter Day — Florence
Scoppio del Carro: At noon, in Piazza del Duomo, fireworks display from a decorated float – the fireworks are set off by a dove sliding along a wire from the high altar of the cathedral to the float. Parade in Renaissance costume.
Feast of the "Madonna che scappa in piazza". — Sulmona

1 May — Cagliari
Feast of Sant'Efisio.

First Sunday of May — Naples
Feast of the Miracle of St Januarius in the cathedral.

First Thursday after 1 May — Assisi
Calendimaggio.

First week of May — Bari
Feast of St Nicholas: 7 May: procession in period costume through the city; 8 May: Mass and procession along the shore; the statue is taken out to sea and worshipped.

15 May — Gubbio
Ceri ("candle") race.

Second or third Sunday in May — Venice
Vogalonga.

Last Sunday in May — Sassari
Cavalcata Sarda.

Last Sunday in May — Gubbio
Palio della Balestra in Piazza Grande.

Late May-early June — Taormina
Festival of Sicilian costumes and carts.

Early June — Castelrotto, Siusi and Fiè allo Scilia
Cavalcata Oswald von Wolkenstein: tournament and medieval fair inspired by the south Tyrolese poet.

June-November, even years — Venice
Biennale art festival.

16-17 June — Pisa
Feast of St Ranieri.

24 June and two other days of the month

Calcio Storico fiorentino: ball game in costume in Piazza S. Croce, accompanied by a procession in 16C costumes. Fireworks in Piazzale Michelangelo.

Florence

Penultimate Sunday in June

Giostra del Saracino – Saracen's Tournament.

Arezzo

Late June-mid July

Spoleto Festival: international theatre, music and dance festival.

Spoleto

July-August

Umbria Jazz Festival.

Perugia

Late June-late August

Opera season in the Roman amphitheatre.

Verona

2 July

Palio delle Contrade – historic horse race.

Siena

Second Saturday in July

Festa della Quintana at 8pm: procession of representatives of the various districts in 15C costumes; jousting.

Ascoli Piceno

Third Saturday in July

Feast of the Redeemer: fireworks display on Saturday night; religious services and regatta on Sunday.

Venice

Last week in August

Ferrara Buskers Festival: street music festival.

Ferrara

First Sunday in August

Festa della Quintana joust at 3.30pm.

Ascoli Piceno

14 August

Feast of the candles.

Sassari

16 August

Palio delle Contrade.

Siena

29 August and previous Sunday

Feast of the Redeemer.

Nuoro

Late August-early September

International Film Festival at the Lido.

Venice

First Sunday in September

Giostra del Saracino – Saracen's Joust.

Arezzo

Historical Regatta on the Grand Canal.

Venice

7 September

Feast of the Rificolona (coloured paper lanterns). Musical and folklore events in the various districts.

Florence

7 and 8 September

Feast of the Nativity of the Virgin.

Loreto

Second weekend in September in even years

Partita a scacchi – chess tournament with human chess pieces.

Marostica

Second Sunday in September

Palio della Balestra: crossbow competition in medieval costume.

Sansepolcro

Festival delle Sagre and "Douja d'or" wine festival

Asti

13 September

Luminara di S. Croce.

Lucca

Second Sunday in September

Quintana Games.

Foligno

19 September

Feast of the Miracle of St Januarius, in the cathedral.

Naples

UNESCO World Heritage List

In 1972, the United Nations Educational, Scientific and Cultural Organization (UNESCO) adopted a Convention for the preservation of cultural and natural sites. To date, more than 150 States Parties have signed this international agreement, which has listed over 500 sites "of outstanding universal value" on the World Heritage

List. Each year, a committee of representatives from 21 countries, assisted by technical organisations (ICOMOS – International Council on Monuments and Sites; IUCN – International Union for Conservation of Nature and Natural Resources; ICCROM – International Centre for the Study of the Preservation and Restoration of Cultural Property, the Rome Centre), evaluates the proposals for new sites to be included on the list, which grows longer as new nominations are accepted and more countries sign the Convention. To be considered, a site must be nominated by the country in which it is located.

The protected cultural heritage may be monuments (buildings, sculptures, archaeological structures etc) with unique historical, artistic or scientific features; groups of buildings (such as religious communities, ancient cities); or sites (human settlements, examples of exceptional landscapes, cultural landscapes) which are the combined works of man and nature of exceptional beauty. Natural sites may be a testimony to the stages of the earth's geological history or to the development of human cultures and creative genius or represent significant ongoing ecological processes, contain superlative natural phenomena or provide a habitat for threatened species.

Signatories of the Convention pledge to co-operate to preserve and protect these sites around the world as a common heritage to be shared by all humanity.

Some of the most well-known places which the World Heritage Committee has inscribed include: Australia's Great Barrier Reef (1981), the Canadian Rocky Mountain Parks (1984), The Great Wall of China (1987), the Statue of Liberty (1984), the Kremlin (1990), Mont-Saint-Michel and its Bay (France, 1979), Durham Castle and Cathedral (1986).

UNESCO World Heritage sites included in this guide are:

Valcamonica cave paintings

Historic centre of Rome, the Vatican City and San Paolo fuori le Mura

Santa Maria delle Grazie church and refectory, Milan

Historic centre of Florence

Venice and the Venetian lagoon

Piazza del Duomo, Pisa

Historic centre of San Gimignano

Rock dwellings, Matera

Vicenza and the Palladian villas

Historic centre of Siena

Historic centre of Naples

Crespi d'Adda

The Renaissance city of Ferrara

Castel del Monte

Trulli dwellings, Puglia

Palaeo-Christian monuments, Ravenna

Historic centre of Pienza La Reggia

palace and gardens, Vanvitelli aquaduct and San Leucio buildings, Caserta

Residence of the House of Savoy, Turin

Botanical gardens, Padua

Portovenere, the Cinque Terre and Palmaria, Tino and Tinetto islands

The Cathedral, Torre Civica and Piazza Grande, Modena

Pompeii, Herculaneum and Torre Annunziata

The Amalfi Coast

Agrigento archaeological site

Villa Romana del Casale

Su Nuraxi, Barumini

The Cilento region and Vallo di Diano, the archaeological sites of Paestum and Velia, and Padula Carthusian monastery

Historical centre of Urbino

Aquileia Basilica and archaeological site

A view of the Odle mountains from Val di Funes

Insights
and Images

La Dolce Vita

Land of saints, poets, heroes and navigators, Italy is a country whose traditions are deeply rooted in an ancient faith. Scars attest to years of domination and a long struggle for freedom and, proud as the nation is of its bountiful landscape, the people's eyes are fixed on what lies beyond the horizon ...

Pizza, spaghetti and mandolins

Sweeping generalisations are always risky, since the line separating description from judgement is so subtle that you could easily mistake a compliment for caricature. In a scene from one of the films in the *Fantozzi* series, the comic character played by Paolo Villaggio, sums up the Italians from a tourist's point of view in three words, "Pizza, spaghetti and mandolins".

And this is precisely what has happened with elements of the strongest Italian traditions – they have been held up to ridicule by the rest of the world's understanding of all that is Italian. These "caricatures" have been exacerbated by various well-known songs and ballads such as *That's Amore*, by Dean Martin, in which Italian phrases are distorted by the rather stilted and clumsy English of the Italian emigrant.

The hackneyed cliché of the downtrodden Neapolitan emigrant is again portrayed in the film *Ricomincio da tre* by **Massimo Troisi**. Having admitted that he is Neapolitan, the character Gaetano, as played by Troisi, is forever being asked if he is an emigrant. Tired of always having to explain that he is just a tourist, he eventually mutters a weary "yes" to the question.

As for the reputation of the macho Italian male and the Latin lover, this is best interpreted by **Alberto Sordi**, in *Un americano a Roma*, who apes the xenophile Italian who denounces his origins but cannot tear himself away from his plate of spaghetti.

It goes without saying that the way the Italians perceive themselves is inevitably very different from the way they are perceived by foreigners whose only experience of them is on holiday.

On the other hand you want to seek out the more informed opinion of illustrious travellers to Italy there is no shortage of writers to refer to. The list includes the literary legend Goethe and his *Italian Journey* as well as the more light-hearted Mark Twain with his book *The Innocents Abroad*.

Italy, the Bel Paese

Long before it became the name of a cheese, *Bel Paese* was an affectionate term for Italy and the title of a book by the abbot Antonio Stoppani (1824-91).

Issues about cheese apart, everybody agrees on how beautiful (*bel*) and surprisingly varied the country (*paese*) is. Jutting out into the sea as it does, the coastline offers beautiful beaches and pine woods, and inlets lapped by emerald green water; away from the coast, the misty, haunting plains rise up to form a high and rugged terrain where even the snow struggles to settle. And then there are the towns where the pace of life is astonishingly frenetic contrasting sharply with those sleepy hilltop villages where little has changed since the Middle

Churches

Santa Maria Maggiore

Piazza di Santa Maria Maggiore. Tel: 06 483195. Open: daily 0700–1900. £.

The largest of Rome's 80 churches dedicated to the Virgin, and arguably the most beautiful, Santa Maria Maggiore is especially famed for its blend of architectural styles – from 5th-century to baroque, via medieval and Renaissance – its shimmering mosaics and its sumptuous papal chapels, extravagant even by baroque standards.

Pope Liberius planned the **original basilica**, following a dream in which the Virgin instructed him to build a church on the spot where snow would fall the next morning, 5 August, AD 352. This miracle is commemorated annually at the feast of the *Madonna della Neve* **(Our Lady of the Snow)**, when thousands of white petals are released from the roof of the church. Santa Maria Maggiore is also the only church where Mass has been celebrated every day since the 5th century.

The most fabulous treasures of the church's interior are its gleaming mosaics: the 36 scenes from the Old Testament in the nave date from the 5th century. There are gold-tinged Byzantine-style scenes in the altar's triumphal arch, but most spectacular of all are the 13th-century mosaics in the apse – considered by many to be the height of Rome's mosaic tradition.

The basilica most prizes its relic of five pieces of wood bound with iron, said to be pieces of Christ's crib from Bethlehem, putting it on view only on the 25th of every month.

Bohemian Rome

Don't miss the atmospheric neighbourhood of Trastevere, long known as Rome's 'bohemian' district. By day, children kick footballs around church squares, locals sit gossiping in doorways and laundry hangs over the medieval flower-splashed façades of ochre-coloured houses. Its patchwork of tiny streets, its tumbledown houses and its sun-bleached piazzete, with their galleries and craft shops, might appear sleepy but, by night, this is where Rome's heart beats the loudest, as Romans come flocking to Trastevere's popular pizzerias and trendy bars.

187

Santa Maria in Trastevere

Piazza Santa Maria in Trastevere. Open: 0700–1300 and 1530–1900. £.

Of the many historic churches in the ancient – and now fashionable – district of Trastevere ('Across the Tiber'), Santa Maria is the greatest treasure. Its shimmering golden mosaics, adorning both the inside and the outside, count among Rome's finest.

This beautiful basilica was the first to be dedicated to the Virgin. It was founded in AD 222 on the site of a miraculous fountain of oil which, according to legend, sprang from nowhere the day Christ was born.

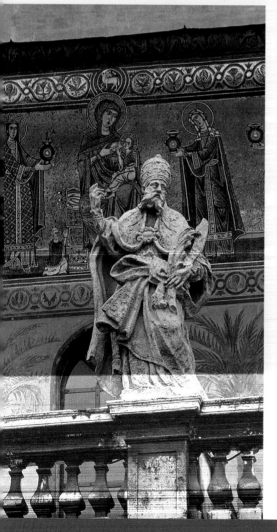

Its present appearance dates from the 12th century, the work of *Trasteverino* Pope Innocent II; the arched portico with its papal statues was added 500 years later. The choir contains six mosaics – bold, innovative works by Cavallini depicting episodes from the *Life of St Mary*. Cavallini's delicate 12th-century mosaic on the façade shows Mary feeding baby Jesus, flanked by ten maidens with lamps. This golden mosaic provides a stunning backdrop for **Piazza Santa Maria in Trastevere**, a popular meeting-place both day and night, and an ideal spot to while away the hours.

ROME

Ascoli Piceno: Piazza del Popolo

G. Bludzin/MICHELIN

Against this backdrop of landscapes are mapped out the different lives, characters and dialects of the inhabitants of this land. In Umbria, for example, the Milanese would be teased for their obsession with punctuality and efficiency. And a Tuscan visiting one of the many *bacari* (a typical bar in Venice) would find an enormous difference in rhythm, tone and sense of humour as he eavesdrops on the more lyrical chatter of the Venetians in the background.

A film, a fashion and a way of life

In 1960 Federico Fellini made *La Dolce Vita*, a film that was to exert a powerful influence on modern culture, linguistically as well as socially. This was the first time that the word "paparazzo" entered into general parlance and the fashion for polo-neck (*dolcevita*) jumpers, as worn by some of the main characters in the film, was born.

However, *la dolce vita*, or life of luxury and self-indulgence, as led by those strolling along the prestigious Via Veneto and epitomised by the now legendary frolicking of Anita Ekberg in the Fontana di Trevi, is more a reflection of Fellini's own way of life than that of the Italians generally.

Their pleasures are more modest and their lives are more humble. A good many Italians display an open and cheerful personality, a healthy interest in good food, a deep respect for traditions, especially those linked to nature (springtime feasts) and religion (Easter and Christmas celebrations), even if the character of the people, cooking and traditions change from region to region. And herein lies the danger of generalising about the Italians ...

For Italians, *la dolce vita* is the desire to live in harmony with mother nature, helped along by a little bit of passion and imagination, of which the Italians have plenty.

Pasta alla Norma

A Riot of Flavours

Whereas some of the world's best-known dishes and ingredients have their origins in the Italian kitchen, you would be wrong in thinking that the cuisine has a national flavour. Mediterranean it might be – but only in the south – whereas in the north, the hearty cooking reflects the proximity of the Alps beyond. It all depends on where your journey takes you.

Regional specialities: from north to south

Piedmont – Cooking here is done with butter. A popular dish is **fonduta**, a melted cheese dip of milk, eggs and white truffles *(tartufi bianchi)*. Typical of the region are *Cardi* (chards), prepared *alla bagna cauda*, ie with a hot sauce containing oil, anchovies, garlic and truffles. Other dishes include **agnolotti** (a kind of ravioli), braised beef in red Barolo wine, boiled meat, **fritto misto alla Piemontese** and **bonet** dessert (a type of chocolate pudding). Monferrato and the Langhe hills are also famous for their excellent cheeses, such as **robiola**, **castelmagno** and **bra**, and delicious wines: **Barolo** (used for braising), Barbaresco, **Barbera**, Grignolino, red Freisa wines, white Gavi and dessert wines such as **Asti**, still or sparkling *(spumante)* and Moscato.

Lombardy – Milan, where cooking is done with butter, gives its name to several dishes; *minestrone alla milanese*, a soup of green vegetables, rice and bacon; *risotto alla milanese*, rice cooked with saffron; **costoletta** *alla milanese*, a fillet of veal fried in egg and breadcrumbs with cheese; **osso buco**, a knuckle of veal with the marrow-bone. **Polenta**, maize semolina, is a staple food in traditional country cooking. Also worth trying are the **tortelli di zucca** (pumpkin fritters) from Mantua. The most popular cheeses are the creamy **Gorgonzola**, the hard **Grana Padana** and **Taleggio**. **Panettone** is a large fruit cake containing raisins and candied lemon peel and **torrone** (nougat) is a speciality of Cremona. Wines produced include Franciacorta (red, white and sparkling) and the red wines of the Valtellina and Pavia districts. The Valtellina is also renowned for its **pizzoccheri** (a type of large tagliatelle made from buckwheat) and its **bitto** cheese.

Veneto – As in the Po Delta, the people of the Veneto eat **polenta**, **bigoli** (a type of spaghetti), **risi e bisi** (rice and peas), **risotto** with chicory and **fegato alla veneziana** (calf's liver fried with onions). The excellent fish dishes include shellfish, eels, dried cod *(baccalà)* and **sardelle in saor** (sardines in brine). Black spaghetti made with squid ink is a popular Venetian dish. The most renowned cheese of the region is **asiago**. **Pandoro**, a star-shaped cake delicately flavoured with orange flower, is a speciality of Verona. The best wines come from the district of Verona: **Valpolicella** and **Bardolino**, rosé or red, perfumed and slightly sparkling, and **Soave**, which is white and strong.

Trentino-Alto Adige and Friuli-Venezia Giulia – In the Alto Adige, **canederli** is a type of gnocchi (dumplings) made with bread and flour served separately or in a broth. Other specialities include **gröstl** (potato and meat pie) and smoked pork served with sauerkraut. There are delicious pastries, in particular the **Strüdel** cake. Friuli is famous for **cialzons** (a type of ravioli), **jota** (meat soup), pork-butchers' specialities (ham – **prosciutto di San Daniele),** fish dishes (**scampi**, **grancevole** – spider crabs), **frico** (fried cheese) and montasio cheese. Trentino-Alto Adige is an important wine-producing region: white wines include Chardonnay, Pinot Bianco, Müller-Thurgau and Riesling, while Pinot and Cabernet are two of the best-known red wines. Friuli produces white Sauvignon, Pinot and Tocai and red Cabernet and Merlot wines.

Liguria – The chief speciality of Genoa is **pesto**, a sauce made with olive oil, basil, pine-kernels, garlic and ewes' cheese. It is served with **trenette** (long, thin noodles) and lasagne (flat pasta leaves). Other dishes include **cima** (stuffed meat parcels) and the excellent **pansotti** (a type of ravioli) served with a walnut sauce. The delicious seafood includes **buridda** (fish soup), **cappon magro** (fish and vegetable salad) and **zuppa di datteri**, a shellfish soup from **La Spezia**, with which the Ligurians drink Vermentino or Pigato, strong white wines. Sciacchetrà is an excellent dessert wine from the region.

Emilia-Romagna – The region has a fine gastronomic reputation; its pork-butchers' meat is the most famous in Italy: Bologna **salami** and **mortadella**, Modena **zamponi** (pigs' trotters), Parma **prosciutto** (ham). *Pasta* is varied and tasty when served *alla bolognese* – that is, with a meat and tomato sauce. **Parmesan cheese** *(parmigiano)*, hard and pale yellow, is strong yet delicate in flavour. Emilia produces **Lambrusco**, a fruity, sparkling red wine, and white Albano.

Tuscany – This is where Italian cooking was born, at the court of the Medici. The most typical first courses of the region are minestrones and soups, including the famous **ribollita**, and **pappardelle**, a type of lasagna. Florence also offers its *alla fiorentina* specialities: **baccalà**, dried cod**, bistecca**, grilled steak fillets, **fagioli all'ucelletto**, beans with quails, or fagioli "al fiasco" with oil, onions and herbs cooked in a round bottle *(fiasco)* on a coal fire. Livorno produces **triglie** (red mullet) and **cacciucco** (fish soup) and Siena offers **panforte**, a cake containing almonds, honey and candied melon, orange and lemon. Tuscan cheeses include **pecorino** and **caciotta**. **Chianti** (both red and white) is the most popular wine but there are other notable red **(Brunello di Montalcino, Nobile di Montepulciano)** and white **(Vernaccia di San Gimignano, Vin Santo)** wines.

Umbria and Marches – Norcia is the capital of Umbrian cuisine with the black truffles **(tartufo nero)** and pork dishes. The regional dish is the **porchetta**, a whole suckling pig roasted on the spit. Specialities from the Marches include *vincigrassi* (pasta cooked in the oven with a meat and cream sauce), **stringozzi** (a type of hollow spaghetti), stuffed olives, **brodetto** (a fish soup), and **stocco all'anconetana** (dried cod). The region produces both white wine (the famous **Orvieto** and Verdicchio) and red (Rosso Conero and Rosso Piceno).

Lazio – There are many Roman specialities: **fettucine** or flat strips of pasta, **spaghetti all'amatriciana** (with a spicy sauce) or **alla carbonara** (with a creamy sauce), **gnocchi** *alla Romana*, **saltimbocca** (a fillet of veal rolled in ham and flavoured with sage, fried in butter and served with a Marsala sauce), and **abbacchio al forno** (roast lamb) or lamb *alla cacciatora* (with an anchovy sauce). Vegetables include *carciofi alla Giudia*, artichokes cooked in oil with garlic and parsley, which take their name from their origins in the Jewish quarter of Rome. **Pecorino** (ewes' milk cheese), **caciotta**, **ricotta** and the famous white wines of Montefiascone and the **Castelli** (Frascati) will satisfy the most discerning gourmet.

Abruzzi and Molise – Among the pasta note **maccheroni alla chitarra**, made by hand and cut into strips. **Latticini** (fresh mountain cheeses) are popular.

Campania – Naples is the home of **spaghetti**, which is often prepared with shellfish *(alle vongole)*. *Trattorie* and *pizzerie* serve *costata alla pizzaiola*, a fillet steak with wild marjoram, **mozzarella** *in carrozza* (cheese savoury) and especially **pizza** and **calzone** (a folded pizza), topped with cheese *(mozzarella)*, tomato and anchovy and flavoured with capers and wild marjoram. The local **mozzarella di bufala** (buffalo mozzarella cheese) is especially delicious. Wines from volcanic soil have a delicate, slightly sulphurous taste: red and white Capri, white Ischia, **Lacryma Christi**, Fiano di Avellino and Greco di Tufo and red Gragnano and Taurasi.

Puglia, Basilicata and Calabria – **Orecchiette con cime di rapa** (pasta with turnip tops), rice with mussels *(cozze)*, the delicious oysters *(ostriche)* of Taranto and **capretto ripieno al forno** (roast kid stuffed with herbs) are among the typical dishes of the Apulia region. Wines include the white Locorotondo and San Severo and the rosé Castel del Monte. The specialities of Basilicata include **pasta alla potentina** and a range of lamb and mutton dishes, as well as a good selection of cheeses *(caciocavallo, scamorza* and ricotta), while Calabria is famous for its stuffed macaroni. Red Cirò is the most popular local wine.

Sicily – Specialities include **pasta con le sarde** (with sardines) and **alla Norma** (with aubergines, tomatoes and ricotta cheese), swordfish dishes and, in the Trapani region, **cuscusu** (couscous), a dish inherited from the Arabs and served with a type of fish soup. The real Sicilian **cassata** is a partly-frozen cream cake containing chocolate cream and candied fruits. Other traditional sweets and pastries include **cannoli** (filled with ricotta and candied fruit), almond cakes and marzipan. The best-known wine is **Marsala**, which is dark and strong, but **Malvasia** and the white wines of Etna and Lipari are also delicious.

Sardinia – The island of Sardinia is famous for **malloreddus** (pasta shells with sausage and tomato), delicious lobster soup and pork cooked on a spit. Meals are accompanied by **carasau**, the local soft-doughed bread (known as *carta da musica* in the rest of Italy). The many cheeses include goats' cheese, Sardinian **fiore** and Sardinian **pecorino**. **Sebadas** are round doughnuts which are fried and covered with honey. The best-known local wines are the red **Cannonau** and the white Vermentino.

The Regions of Italy

The boot of Italy which stretches 1 300km/808mi from north to south, juts out into the Mediterranean between Greece and Spain.

Geographical notes

Italy's rugged relief rises from great swathes of plain which cover approximately a quarter of its total area of 301 262km²/116 317sq mi. Its coastline (almost 7 500km/4 660mi long) is washed by the waters of four inner seas: the Ligurian, Tyrrhenian, Ionian and Adriatic.

The **Alps**, which were created as the earth's crust folded in the Tertiary Era, form a gigantic barrier with northern Europe and are a formidable source of hydroelectric power. Several passes and tunnels cross the Alps, which reach their highest peak at Mont Blanc (4 810m/15 780ft), to link Italy with France and northern Europe. On the southern side of the Alps between the fertile Po valley and the foothills there are several lakes of glacial origin.

The **Apennines**, a range of limestone hills formed by a more recent Tertiary geological movement, extend from Genoa down into Sicily, dividing the country into two zones. The peaks of this limestone chain are generally lower than those of the Alps. The Corno Grande at 2 914m/9 566ft is the highest mountain of the chain's tallest massif, the Gran Sasso. The section between Naples and Sicily is subject to tectonic plate movements resulting in earthquakes, restless volcanoes and marked changes in sea level. Such activity in turn has altered the relief of this southern part of the peninsula.

Exploring the regions

The 1948 constitution established 20 regions, although it was not enacted until 1970. Five of these (Sicily, Sardinia, Trentino-Alto Adige, Friuli-Venezia Giulia and Valle d'Aosta) have a special statute and enjoy greater administrative autonomy. The regions are subdivided into 95 provinces, which are themselves composed of districts, each headed by a *Sindaco*.

Aosta Valley (Valle d'Aosta)

This great deep furrow between the highest mountains in Europe is watered by the Dora Baltea River, whose tributaries run along picturesque lateral valleys: the Valtournenche, Val di Gressoney, Val d'Ayas, Val Grisenche. The **Parco Nazionale del Gran Paradiso** is found in the southwest of the region.

Aosta, well situated in the centre of the valley, is the capital of this region and has enjoyed a degree of administrative autonomy since 1947. In addition to the pastoral activities of the mountain people, the valley's economy depends primarily on tourism which has developed as a result of the Great St Bernard and Mont Blanc tunnels and the hydroelectric and iron and steel industries.

From Pont-St-Martin to Courmayeur the towns and villages have retained French names; many of the local inhabitants still speak French and other varied dialects.

Piedmont (Piemonte)

Piedmont, at the foot of the mountain range, consists mainly of the extensive Po Delta. Surrounded on three sides by the Alps and the Apennines this fertile area is made up of grassland alternating with fields planted with cereals and rice (three-

Some of the highest mountains in Europe

fifths of the Italian rice production is concentrated in the districts of Vercelli and Novara). The many rivers which cross the region (the Ticino, Sesia, Dora Baltea and Riparia, Tanaro, Bormida and Scrivia) are mainly found in the valley of the river **Po**, which has its source at Pian del Re on Monviso (approximately 100km/62mi southwest of Turin), and which flows for 652km/407mi before joining the Adriatic. Numerous hydroelectric power stations supply electricity to local industry: textile factories in Biella and the metal, engineering and chemical works in Turin.

Lombardy (Lombardia)

Lombardy's emphasis on commercial activity is mainly due to its favourable geographical location in the green Po Delta between the Ticino and the Mincio, which together with the Adda feed Lakes Maggiore, Como and Garda. To the north the great lake valleys give access to the Alpine passes. Lombardy, with the mulberry bushes of the **Brianza** district, takes first place in the production of silk. The permanent grazing and grasslands are used by modern dairy farming and processing industries. In the **Lomellina** district, large areas are given over to rice growing.

The many towns, scattered throughout the countryside, were important banking and trading centres in medieval and Renaissance times and spread the name of the Lombards all over Europe. Today Como is the centre of the silk industry, Brescia has steel, chemical and engineering industries, Bergamo textile and engineering works, Mantua petrochemicals and plastics, Cremona is the agricultural focus and Pavia the seat of an important university.

It is **Milan**, the economic capital of Italy, that has the highest density of population and businesses. This town with its modern architecture and numerous commercial enterprises and cultural institutions has an outer ring of industrial suburbs which are the home base of textile, oil, chemical, steel and food industries.

Venetia (Veneto)

This comprises mainly the vast alluvial Po Delta and its tributaries which are overlooked in the north by the Venetian Pre-Alps, and further north again in the **Cadore** district by the western massifs of the Dolomites. It is an agricultural region growing wheat, maize, mulberry bushes, olives, fruit trees and vines. The industrial sector includes oil refineries, smelting works and chemical plants which are concentrated in the vicinity of Venice at Mestre-Marghera, as well as a large production of hydroelectric energy in the valleys of the Pre-Alps. The latter supplies the textile industry.

The landscape is punctuated by two small volcanic groups, the **Berici Mountains** south of Vicenza and the **Euganean Hills** near Padua. The slopes of these blackish heights support vines and peach orchards, and there are several hot springs.

In the **Po Delta** and that of the Adige lie impoverished and desolate areas, subject to flooding. Following reclamation certain areas are farmed on an industrial scale for wheat and sugar beet. The coastline takes the form of lagoons *(lagune)* separated from the sea by spits of sand pierced by gaps *(porti)*. It is one of these lagoons that both provides and threatens the survival of Venice.

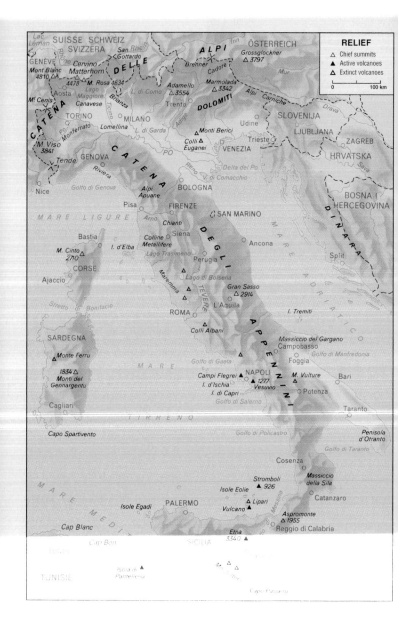

Trentino-Alto Adige

This is one of five Italian regions to enjoy a special autonomous statute and the people are partly of Germanic culture and German-speaking. The area includes the Adige and Isarco valleys and the surrounding mountains. The Adige Valley, at the southern exit from the Brenner Pass, has always been easy of access and much used by traffic. Though deep, it opens out towards the sunny south and is very fertile. Cereals are grown on the flatter areas of the valley bottom, with vines and fruit trees on the lower slopes and pastures above. Avelengo in the vicinity of Merano is well known for its breed of horses.

The highly-eroded limestone massif of the **Dolomites** extends across the Veneto and Trentino-Alto Adige.

Friuli-Venezia Giulia

This region prolongs the Veneto to the east and it forms the Italian boundary with Austria and Slovenia. The area enjoys a large degree of autonomy in administrative and cultural affairs. In the north is the schistose massif of the **Carnic Alps** with its forests of conifers and alpine pastures. Friuli-Venezia Giulia is an important silkworm breeding and spinning area. Traditional farming activites have been superseded by heavy industry which has grown up around Udine and Pordenone. **Trieste**, the region's capital, was once the busy port of Austria

Emilia-Romagna

The plain skirting the Apennines derives its name from the Via Emilia, a straight Roman road that crosses it from Piacenza to Rimini. South and east of Bologna the district is known as **Romagna.** Its soil, which is intensively cultivated, is among the best in Italy for wheat and beet. The rhythm of the landscape of extensive fields is punctuated at intervals by rows of mulberries and vines clinging to tall poles, and of maples or elms. Other vines grow on the slopes of the Apennines. The towns are strung out along the Via Emilia: the most important, **Bologna**, famous for its very old university, is today a communications and industrial (steel, engineering and food) centre and a market for wheat and pigs.

The region to the east of Ferrara through which the Po river runs is devoted to rice growing. To the south is an area of great lagoons, **Valli di Comacchio**, where fishermen catch eels.

Liguria

Liguria, furrowed by deep, narrow valleys at right angles to the coast, had a maritime civilisation before the Roman era. The steep slopes of the inner valleys are dotted with poor hilltop villages, watching over groves of chestnut or olive trees and cultivated terraces. The rocky, indented coastline has few fish to offer but has enjoyed heavy coastal traffic since the time of the Ligurians, facilitated by many small deep-water ports. The Roman Empire gave its present appearance to the country, with olive groves and vineyards, now complemented by vegetables, fruit (melons and peaches) and flowers grown on an industrial scale.

The **Riviera di Ponente** (Western Riviera) west of Genoa is sunnier and more sheltered than the **Riviera di Levante** (Eastern Riviera), but the latter has a more luxuriant vegetation. The chief towns are Imperia, Savona and **Genoa** (shipyards, steel production, oil terminal and thermal power station) and La Spezia (naval base, commercial port, thermal power station and arms manufacture).

Tuscany (Toscana)

The harmony of the beautiful Tuscan landscape of low-lying hills with graceful curves affording wide views and planted with olive groves, vineyards and cypress trees bathed in the soft, golden light, reflects the great artistic sense of the Tuscan people.

The region has a variety of soils. The Tuscan Archipelago, with the mountainous **Island of Elba** and its rich iron-bearing deposits, faces a shore which is sometimes rocky (south of Livorno), sometimes flat and sandy as in the area around Viareggio, known as **Versilia**. To the north of the Arno the **Apuan Alps** are quarried for marble (Carrara).

In the heart of Tuscany lies the fertile and beautiful **Arno Basin**, an ideal setting for **Florence**. Vines and silvery olives alternate with fields of wheat, tobacco and maize. Peppers, pumpkins and the famous Lucca beans grow among the mulberries. The old farms, with their distinctive grand architectural style, often stand alone on hilltops.

Southern Tuscany is a land of hills, soft and vine-clad in the **Chianti** district south of Florence, quiet and pastoral near Siena, dry and desolate round Monte Oliveto Maggiore, and massive and mysterious in the area of the **Colli Metalliferi** (metal-bearing hills) south of Volterra. Bordering Lazio, **Maremma**, with its melancholy beauty, was once a marshy district haunted by bandits and shepherds. Much of the area has now been reclaimed.

Umbria

The land of St Francis is a country of hills, valleys and river basins, where the poplars raise their rustling heads to limpid skies. This is the green Umbria of the Clitumnus Valley **(Valle del Clitunno)**, whose pastures were famous in ancient times. Umbria has two lakes, **Trasimeno** and Piediluco, and many rivers, including the Tiber. Medieval cities which succeeded Etruscan settlements over-look ravines and valleys: grim Gubbio, haughty **Perugia**, the capital of Umbria, Assisi, Spoleto and Spello. Others stand in the centre of a plain, such as Foligno and Terni, the metallurgical centre.

Marches (Marche)

So called because they were formerly frontier provinces of the Frankish Empire and papal domains, the Marches form a much subdivided area between San Marino and Ascoli Piceno, where the parallel spurs of the Apennines run down into the Adriatic, forming a series of deep, narrow valleys. There is, however, a flat and rectangular coastal belt dotted with beaches and canalports.

Apart from the capital, **Ancona**, a busy port, most of the old towns are built on commanding sites; Urbino (centre of the arts), Loreto (pilgrimage centre) and Macerata (manufacture of musical instruments).

Lazio

Lying between the Tyrrhenian Sea and the Apennines, from Tuscan Maremma to Gaeta, Latium, the cradle of Roman civilisation, borders a sandy coast whose ancient ports, such as Ostia at the mouth of the Tiber, have silted up. Civitavecchia today is the only modern port on the coastline. In the centre of Lazio, **Rome**, the Italian capital and seat of the Catholic Church, is mainly a residential city and the headquarters of both public and religious organisations.

To the east and north, volcanic hills, with lonely lakes in their craters, overlook the famous **Roman Campagna**, beloved by the writers and painters who have often described its great, desolate expanses, dotted with ancient ruins. Today this area, formerly a hotbed of malaria, has regained a degree of activity: the drainage of the Pontine Marches, near Latina, was a spectacular achievement.

The landscape around Pienza in Tuscany

B. Morandi/MICHELIN

To the south is the distinctive **Cio-ciaria**. This area takes its name from the shoes *(ciocie)*, which are part of the traditional costume. They have thick soles and thongs wound round the calf of the leg. The main centres are Frosinone and Casino.

Abruzzi (Abruzzo)

This is the part of the Apennines which most suggests a country of high mountains, grand and wild, with its **Gran Sasso** and **Maiella Massifs**. The **Parco Nazionale d'Abruzzo**, the doyen of the Italian national parks, was established in the Upper Sangro Valley in 1921. In basins sheltered from the wind are vineyards, and almond and olive groves, while industry is concentrated in the Chieti-Pescara zone and other areas such as Vasto (glass making), Sulmona (car factories), L'Aquila (steel works) and Avezzano (textile and food industries). The tourist industry is also important for the coastal regions and the winter resorts of the Gran Sasso massif.

Molise

Molise, with its capital, **Campobasso**, extends south of the Abruzzi, with which it has several common features: a mountainous relief, dark valleys and wild forests which are still haunted by wolves. The region is bordered to the west by the Maiella. The main industry can be found in the Termoli area, although agriculture still forms the basis of the local economy. The main crops are wheat, oats, maize, potatoes and vines.

Campania

Campania forms a fertile crescent around the Bay of Naples, where hemp, tobacco and cereals alternate with olive groves and vineyards. The charm and mystery of the **Bay of Naples**, which once stirred the imagination of the ancients, is dominated by the characteristic silhouette of **Vesuvius**. Although the coast has lost much of its charm owing to building developments, the **Sorrento Peninsula** and the **Island of Capri** are two notable beauty spots.

Puglia, Basilicata and Calabria

These three regions cover the foot of the Italian "boot". Puglia, on the east side, facing the Adriatic, has many assets. Cereals are grown in the plain between Foggia and Manfredonia and in the plains of Bari, Taranto, Lecce and Brindisi. Vines flourish almost everywhere, often alongside olive trees (the Apulian production of olive oil is very important to the world market) and almonds on the coast. The elevation of the **Gargano Promontory**, otherwise known as the "boot's spur", is distinctive.

Bari, the capital of Puglia, is a busy port, which still enjoys numerous trading links with the Middle East. Along with Taranto and Brindisi it is one of the three main industrial centres in the region. Basilicata or **Lucania**, and Calabria, comprise very different types of country; the rocky corniche from the Gulf of Policastro to Reggio; the grim, grand mountains of the **Sila Massif** with its extensive mountain pastures and wide horizons; and at the southern extremity of the peninsula between two inner seas, lies the **Aspromonte Massif** clad with pine, beech and chestnut forests.

Between Basilicata and Calabria is the **Parco Nazionale del Pollino** (inaugurated in 1990) which is covered in pine forests. Formed by the Pollino Massif it boasts an interesting array of fauna and flora. There are also several natural history museums in the area. *See also CALABRIA.*

Sardinia and Sicily

See SARDEGNA and SICILIA at the end of the guide.

Ancient Civilisations

Since 2000 BC and throughout antiquity, Italy has been a meeting-place of races, with Etruscan, Greek and Latin civilisations flourishing on her soil.

The Greeks

After the **Phoenicians** had settled at Carthage and set up trading posts, the Greeks founded a large number of colonies on the coasts of Sicily and southern Italy (8C BC), known as **Magna Graecia**. It included Ionian, Achaean and Dorian colonies, named after the Greek peoples who had colonised them. The social unit was the "city". The 6C and 5C BC marked the zenith of Greek civilisation in Italy, corresponding to the period of Pericles in Athens. Greek seaborne trade was so successful that Syracuse soon rivalled Athens. Syracuse and Taranto were the two main centres of this refined civilisation. Philosophers, scientists and writers settled in Sicily. Aeschylus lived at Gela. Theocritus defined the rules of bucolic poetry and Archimedes was murdered by a Roman soldier in Syracuse. But rivalry between these many and varied cities led to warfare, which, with Carthaginian raids, led to decline, culminating in the Roman conquest at the end of the 3C BC.

Art

Cities – Territory in the Greek settlements was roughly divided into three different areas from the 8C BC onwards, when the first colonists arrived in Italy: places of worship, public spaces and residential areas. Generally the city was laid out in an octagonal grid – designed by **Hippodamus of Miletus**, a Greek philosopher and town planner who lived in Asia Minor in the 5C BC – organised around two main axes, the **cardo** (*stenopos* in Greek), which ran from north to south, and the **decumanus** (*plateia* in Greek), running from east to west. The road network was completed with minor cardi and decumani, which

[Map of ancient Italy showing Etruria, Etruscan cities, Magna Graecia and Greek cities]

Legend:
- Etruria
- Etruscan city
- Magna Graecia
- Greek city
- **Veneti** Tribe

Celts, Raetians, Veneti, Ligurians, Felsina, Spina, Pisae, Faesulae, Volaterrae, Arretium, Populonia, Cortona, Umbrians, Vetulonia, Clusium, Volsinii (veteres), Perusia, Vulci, Tuder, MARE, Tarquinii, Volsinii Novi, Sabines, Veii, Caere, Roma, Samnites, ADRIATICUM, Veltrae, Latins, Campanians, Cumae, Capua, Pytheousa, Vesuvius, Neapolis, Oscans, Poseidonia, Tarentum, MARE, Metapontum, Messapii, MARE TYRRHENUM, Sybaris, Croton, Aeoliae I., Segesta, Himera, Tyndaris, Zancle, Locri, Sicani, Rhegion, MARE, Selinus, Etna, Naxos, Enna, IONIUM, Akragas, Siculi, Megara Hyblaea, Gela, Camarina, Syracusae

The Arezzo
Chimera

formed blocks. A number of public areas and buildings were situated within the town, such as the *agorà*, the main, central square where much of public life took place, the *ekklesiastérion*, a public building used for the meeting of the public assembly *(ekklesìa)*, and the *bouleutérion*, which housed meetings of the citizens' council (the *boulé*). The temples, sometimes built outside the city limits, were often surrounded by other sacred buildings, which in the most monumental structures could include porticoes, votive monuments, gymnasia and theatres. The city itself was usually protected by fortifications, outside of which lay the agricultural land, subdivided into family plots, and the area used for burials.

Temples – The focus of the building was the *naos*, also known as the cella, which housed the statue of the god; the temple faced east so that the statue was illuminated by the rising sun, considered to be the source of all life. In front of the *naos* was the *pronaos*, a kind of antechamber, while the back of the temple, the *opistodomos*, acted as a treasury room. The temple was surrounded by columns **(peristyle)** and supported by a base; the columns which supported the entablature rested on the last steps **(stylobate)** of the temple. The building was covered by a two-sided sloping roof.

The dominant style in Magna Graecia and in Sicily is the Doric style, with its imposing and plain columns, which are placed directly on the stylobate without a base. The capital has no sculpted carvings, but consists simply of a round buffer (echinus) placed on a square block (abacus). The Doric entablature comprises a smooth architrave, the upper section of which presents a frieze with alternating metopes (panels of sculpted low reliefs) and triglyphs (panels depicting two deep vertical grooves in the centre and two smaller grooves on each side).

The architectural style of the Doric temple has long been considered by many to be the prototype of ideal beauty as a result of its simple structure and perfect harmony of proportions. Architects, who took into account the tendency of the human eye to distort the lines of large buildings, were able to make a few optical corrections to the conventional structure. The entablatures, the upper section of which seemed to lean forward slightly, were raised in the centre, thus acquiring an imperceptible arched shape. To create an impression of perfect equilibrium, the columns situated to the sides of the temple façade were bent slightly towards the inside of the building, in order to avoid the effect of leaning outwards. Finally, in very large buildings (such as the Temple of Concord in Agrigento and the Basilica in Paestum) where the columns seemed to contract towards the top of the temple, this optical illusion was addressed by increasing the diameter of the shaft at about two-thirds of its height. The temples were often decorated with groups of sculptures and low reliefs and were usually painted in red, blue and white in order to provide the sculptures and columns with maximum relief.

The Doric harmony and elegance of Neptune's Temple at Paestum

When compared with the architecture of mainland Greece, the temples of Magna Graecia and Sicily are more monumental, pay more attention to spatial effect and show a particular taste for abundant decoration.

Sculpture – The scarcity of marble and the particular Italian taste for pictorial and chiaroscuro effects resulted in the predominant use of limestone and sandstone as raw materials. Clay was widely used in the pediments and acroteria of the temples, as well as for votive statues. The Ionic style was employed in the colonies from the end of the 6C BC and was characterised by a greater individualisation of features, an increasingly dramatic sense of pathos and the use of softer shapes. The main artistic centres of the period were Taranto, Naples, Paestum, Agrigento and Syracuse.

Painting and ceramics – Painting was considered by the Greeks to be the most noble and eloquent form of art; unfortunately the perishable nature of the pigments used means that little remains of this art. The only examples of Greek painting to have survived are to be found inside tombs or on the façades of hypogea (underground chambers).
Vases with black figures painted against a red or yellow background date from the Archaic and beginning of the Classical periods. The detail on the figures was obtained by simply engraving the black varnish with a steel tip. Mythological subjects or scenes depicting daily life were the most common designs used. Red figure vases appeared in southern Italy towards the end of the 5C BC. The black varnish, previously used only for figures, was now used for the background, with the figures 'reserved' in the natural brick red clay and painted with touches of black and white. This reversal, which gave artists a greater freedom of expression, constituted a revolutionary discovery and allowed artists to produce more subtle designs. The themes used remained much the same. From the 3C BC the art of the native Italian peoples and of Magna Grecia became more decorative in style.

The Etruscans

While the Greeks were disseminating their civilisation throughout the south of the peninsula and Sicily, the Etruscans were building up in central Italy, from the 8C BC onwards, a powerful empire whose growth was checked only by that of Rome (4C BC). They are a little-known people whose alphabet, along with certain tombstone inscriptions, has now been deciphered. Some authorities think they were natives of these parts, others, following the example of Herodotus, say they came from Lydia in Asia Minor. The Etruscans at first occupied the area between the Arno and the Tiber (see map) but later spread into Campania and the Po Plain. They reached their zenith in the 6C BC. **Etruria** then comprised a federation of 12 city-states known as *lucumonies*, which comprised the cities of Tarquinia, Vulci, Veiulonia, Cerveteri, Arezzo, Chiusi, Roselle, Volterra, Cortona, Perugia, Veii and Volsinii (present-day Bolsena). Having grown rich by working iron (the Island of Elba), copper and silver mines and by trading in the western Mediterranean, the Etruscans, who were excellent artisans and technicians, had a civilisation based on a mixture of barbarism and refinement.

Art

The Etruscan towns, built on elevated sites with walls of huge stones, show an advanced sense of town planning, often based on Greek models. Near the towns are vast burial grounds with underground chambers or hypogea filled with objects revealing the customs and art of the Etruscan people. Etruscan art is essentially primitive in character, though strongly influenced by the Orient and especially by Greece from the 6C BC onwards. It has a marked individuality sustained by realism and expressive movement. The discovery in the 19C of masterpieces like the Apollo and Hermes of Veii and the systematic study of artefacts in the 20C have given this very individual and powerful art the place it deserved.

Figurative arts – Sculpture makes up the main body of Etruscan art. The great period is the 6C BC, when large groups of statuary adorned the pediments of temples: the famous Apollo of Veii (in the Villa Giulia museum in Rome), of obvious Greek influence, belongs to this period. Some portrait busts are more original in their striking realism, intensity of expression and stylised features: their large prominent eyes and enigmatic smiles are characteristic of the Etruscan style. The same applies to the famous groups of semi-recumbent figures on the sarcophagi, many of which are portraits. The Etruscans also excelled in bronze sculpture, as demonstrated by the magnificent Arezzo Chimera (in the Archaeological Museum of Florence).

The only surviving **paintings** are in the burial chambers of the cemeteries (Cerveteri, Veii and especially Tarquinia), where they were supposed to remind the dead of the pleasures of life: banquets, games and plays, music and dancing, hunting etc. These colourful and delicate wall paintings show amazing powers of observation and form an excellent record of Etruscan habits and customs.

Pottery and goldsmiths' work – The Etruscans were artisans of genius. In pottery they used the little known **bucchero** technique, producing black earthenware with figures in relief. Initially decorated with motifs in *pointillé*, the vases developed more elaborate shapes with a more complicated ornamentation, although in general these were not of the same quality as the earlier work. In the 7C BC they modelled beautiful burial urns, *canopae*, in animal or human shape. Both men and women wore heavy often solid gold ornaments of remarkable workmanship, showing the skill of Etruscan goldsmiths particularly in the Filigree and granulation techniques.

Roman Architecture

For information on Roman history, see the section starting on p 68

A Roman town – Newly founded Roman towns often have a military origin or were planned as an extension to the *castrum*, the military camp. The new towns built in this way, which had been surrounded with walls during troubled periods, were generally divided into four quarters by two main streets, the *decumanus* and the *cardo*, intersecting at right angles and ending in gateways. Other streets parallel to these two gave the town a grid plan.

The **streets** were edged with footpaths, sometimes 50cm/18in high, and lined with porticoes to shelter pedestrians. The roadway, paved with large flagstones which fitted together perfectly, was crossed at intervals by stepping-stones laid at the same level as the pavements but with grooves between, where horses and cartwheels could pass.

A Roman house – Excavations at Herculaneum, Pompeii and especially Ostia have uncovered two main types of Roman house: the *insulae*, dwellings of several storeys divided into apartments, often with shops open to the street, and the *domus*, large, luxurious mansions for single families with an *atrium*, which had evolved from the earlier Greek model.

These last had a modest external appearance owing to their bare walls and few windows. But the interiors, adorned with mosaics, statues, paintings and marbles and sometimes including private baths and a fish pond, revealed the riches of their owners. A vestibule overlooked by the porter's lodge led to the *atrium*.

The *atrium* **(1)**, originally the heart of the *domus*, later came to refer to the internal courtyard built around the *impluvium*, a basin under the open section which caught rainwater. The bedrooms *(cubiculae)* opened off the atrium, which was the only part of the house to which strangers were usually admitted. At the far end was the *tablinum* **(2)**, or the living and dining room. The atrium and adjoining rooms constituted the oldest form of the Roman house, later inhabited only by less wealthy citizens.

The *peristyle* **(3)**, a court surrounded by a portico in the centre of the part of the house reserved for the family, was generally made into a garden with basins lined with mosaics, fountains and statues. The living quarters opened on to it. The *cubiculae* were simple sleeping chambers, containing a stone platform built against the wall or a movable bed. There were mattresses, cushions and blankets but no

Roman house

sheets. The dining room or *triclinium* **(4)**, takes its name from the three couches for the guests, who, adopting a custom that originated in Greece, adopted a reclining pose for eating, stretched out on cushions and leaning on one elbow. In the centre was a table at which the slaves busied themselves. Lastly, there was the great hall or *oecus* **(5)**, which was sometimes embellished with a colonnade. The outbuildings included the kitchen with a sink and drain, and built-in stove and oven; baths, which were like the public baths on a smaller scale, and the slaves' quarters, barns, cellars, stables etc. The latrines were usually in a corner of the kitchen in order to make use of the same drainage system.

The Forum – The forum was a large square, often surrounded by a portico during the Imperial period. Originally it was a market, usually at the crossing of the two main streets, as well as the centre of the public and commercial life of Roman towns. Government offices surrounded the forum. These included the *curia* or headquarters of local government; the voting hall for elections; the public tribune from which candidates for office harangued the crowd; the "basilica of finance" or exchange *(argentaria)*; the municipal treasury; the public granaries; the "basilica of justice" or law courts; the prison; temples and many commemorative monuments.

The tombs – Roman cemeteries were placed along the roads, at some distance from the towns. The tombs were marked by a simple stele, by an altar or, for the most important families, by a mausoleum. The remains of less affluent families were placed in a *columbarium*, a vault containing a series of niches in the wall for funerary urns. The most famous Roman cemetery is that on the Via Appia Antica, south of Rome. Directly after death the body of the deceased was exposed on a funeral couch surrounded with candlesticks and wreaths of flowers. Then it was buried or cremated by the family. The deceased was provided with objects for use in the after life: clothes, arms and tools for men, toys for children, and jewellery and toilet articles for women.

Trajan's Arch, Benevento

Architecture – The Romans borrowed certain elements from Greek architecture, yet Roman architecture differs from Greek in its basic "plastic" and organic conception, the strict relationship between the external shape and the internal space, and in the important technical innovations which allowed the use of softer, more flexible curved shapes, such as the arch, dome and vault. The column, which was the foundation of the Greek trilithic system (based on two columns and the architrave) was replaced by the wall and the pilaster. The use of **concrete**, thrown into moulds, allowed huge covered spaces to be built. Also noteworthy were the many public civil engineering projects carried out by the Romans, as testified by the huge constructions they have left behind, such as bridges, aqueducts, roads, tunnels, sewerage systems, baths, theatres and amphitheatres, stadia and circuses, basilicas and nymphaea, gymnasia and colonnades, triumphal arches and the many public and private monuments (the private often rivalling the public in terms of size and splendour).

Temples – The temples were dedicated to the worship of gods or emperors, raised to divine status from the time of Augustus. The Roman temple, inspired by the Greek model, consists of a closed chamber, the *cella*, containing the image of the god, and an open vestibule. The building is surrounded, partly or completely, by a colonnade and is built on a podium.

Triumphal arches – In Rome these commemorated the "triumphs" of generals or conquering emperors. The low reliefs on the arches recorded their feats of arms. In the provinces, such as Aosta, Benevento and Ancona, there are municipal arches commemorating important events or erected in honour of some member of the Imperial family.

The baths – The Roman baths, which were public and free, were not only baths but also physical fitness centres, casinos, clubs, recreation centres, libraries, lecture halls and meeting-places, which explains the amount of time people spent there. Decoration in these great buildings was lavish: mosaic ornaments, coloured marble facings, columns and statues. The bather followed a medically approved circuit. From the gymnasium *(palestra)* he entered a lukewarm room *(tepidarium)* to prepare for the high temperature of the hot baths *(caldarium)*; he then returned to a luke-warm room before taking a plunge in the cold baths *(frigidarium)* to tone up the skin. To heat air and water a number of underground furnaces *(hypocausts)* were used. The hot air was circulated to heat the rooms from below and from the sides.

The amphitheatre – This typically Roman structure, several storeys high, encir-cles the elliptical arena and was destined to seat the spectators. Posts were fixed to the upper part of the external wall to carry a huge adjustable awning, the *velarium*, which sheltered the spectators from the sun and rain. Inside, enclosing the arena, a wall protected the spectators in the front rows from the wild animals in the ring. A complex of circular galleries, staircases and corridors enabled all the spectators to reach their seats quickly without crowding through the *vomitaria* or passageways.

Always very popular, the performances included fighting of three kinds: between animals, between gladiators and animals, and between gladiators. In principle, a duel between gladiators always ended in the death of one of the opponents. The public could ask for a gladiator's life to be spared and the President of the Games would indicate a reprieve by turning up his thumb. The victorious gladiator received a sum of money if he was a professional, or he was freed if he was a slave or a prisoner.

In some amphitheatres the stage could be flooded for naval battles *(naumachia)*, in which special flat-bottomed boats were used.

The circus – The circus, which was usually connected to the Imperial palace and was used for horse and chariot races, was long and narrow, with a short curved side and a straight side, where the races started. Spectators were seated on the terraces, while the competitors raced around the track. In the later Roman Empire many different types of games took place here. The circus was very similar in shape to the smaller **stadium**, which was copied from the Greek model and which was originally used for athletic competitions.

The theatre – Theatres had rows of seats, usually ending in colonnades, a central area or **orchestra** occupied by distinguished spectators or used for acting, and a raised **stage**. The actors performed in front of a wall which was the finest part of the building and which imitated the façade of a palace in style: its decoration included several tiers of columns, niches containing statues, marble facings and mosaics. The perfect acoustics were generally due to a combination of sophisti-cated devices. The scenery was either fixed or mobile and there was an ingenious array of machinery either in the wings or below stage, as well as an impressive range of special effects (smoke, lightning, thunder, and the appearance of gods – the famous *deus ex machina* – or heroes).

The chief function of the theatre was the performance of comedies and tragedies; however, Roman theatres were also used for competitions, lottery draws and the distribution of bread or money.

Until the end of the 2C BC all actors wore wigs of different shapes and colours according to the nature of the character they represented. After that date they adopted pasteboard masks and again each character had a distinctive mask. Tragic actors, to make themselves more impressive, wore buskins or sandals with thick cork soles.

From the foundation of Rome to today

To travel around Italy is to stroll down ancient roads, following in the footsteps of the Italians and their history. We set off with the she-wolf of legend and then accompany Caesar and his subjects along the path they took. We are witness to the arrival of the barbarians, the rise and fall of empires, the war between the Guelfs and the Ghibellines and eventually arrive at our destination: a fascinating place where we can look back and gaze in wonder at human progress. Let us commence our journey ...

B. Morandi/MICHELIN

BC: from the Origins to the Empire (753-27 BC)

- **753** – Foundation of Rome by Romulus according to legend. (In fact it was born of the union of Latin and Sabine villages in the 8C.)
- **7C-6C** – Royal dynasty of the Tarquins. Power is divided between the king, the senate, representing the great patrician families, and the *comitia*, representing the rich families.
- **509** – Establishment of the Republic: the king's powers are conferred on two consuls, elected for one year.
- **451-449** – Law of the XII Tables, instituting equality between patricians and plebeians.
- **390** – The Gauls invade Italy and take Rome but are expelled by Camillus.
- **281-272** – War against Pyrrhus, King of Epirus; submission of the southern part of the peninsula to Rome.
- **264-241** – First Punic War: Carthage abandons Sicily to the Romans.
- **218-201** – Second Punic War.
Hannibal crosses the Alps and defeats the Romans at Lake Trasimeno. Hannibal routs the Romans at Cannae and halts at Capua (see *Capua, p 160*)
In 210 **Scipio** carries war into Spain, and in 204 he lands in Africa. Hannibal is recalled to Carthage.
Scipio defeats Hannibal at Zama in 202.
- **146** – Macedonia and Greece become Roman provinces. Capture and destruction of Carthage.
- **133** – Occupation of all Spain and end of the Mediterranean campaigns.
- **133-121** – Failure of the policy of the Gracchi, who promoted popular agrarian laws.
- **118** – The Romans in Gaul.
- **112-105** – War against Jugurtha, King of Numidia (now Algeria).
- **102-101** – Marius, vanquisher of Jugurtha, stops invasions of Cimbri and Teutoni.
- **88-79** – Sulla, the rival of Marius, triumphs over Mithridates (King of Pontus in Asia Minor) and establishes his dictatorship in Rome.

- **70** – Pompey and Crassus, appointed Consuls, become masters of Rome.
- **63** – Plot of Catiline against the Senate exposed by Cicero.
- **60** – The first Triumvirate: **Pompey**, **Crassus**, **Julius Caesar**. Rivalry of the three rulers.
- **59** – Julius Caesar as Consul.
- **58-51** – The Gallic War (52: Surrender of Vercingetorix at Alesia).
- **49** – Caesar crosses the Rubicon and drives Pompey out of Rome.
- **49-45** – Caesar defeats Pompey and his partisans in Spain, Greece and Egypt. He writes his history of the Gallic War.
- **Early 44** – Caesar is appointed Dictator for life.
- **15 March 44** – Caesar is assassinated by Brutus, his adopted son, among others.
- **43** – The second Triumvirate: **Octavian** (great-nephew and heir of Caesar), **Antony**, Lepidus.
- **41-30** – Struggle between Octavian and Antony. Defeat (at Actium) and suicide of Antony.

The Early Empire (27 BC – AD 284)

- **27** – Octavian, sole master of the Empire, receives the title of **Augustus Caesar** and plenary powers.

AD

- **14** – Death of Augustus.
- **14-37** – Reign of Tiberius.
- **54-68** – Reign of Nero, who causes the death of Britannicus, his mother Agrippina and his wives Octavia and Poppaea, and initiates violent persecution of the Christians.
- **68** – End of the **Julio-Claudian Dynasty** (Augustus, Tiberius, Caligula, Claudius, Nero).
- **69-96** – **Flavian Dynasty**: Vespasian, Titus, Domitian.
- **96-192** – The Century of the **Antonines**, marked by the successful reigns of Nerva, Trajan, Hadrian, Antoninus and Marcus Aurelius, who consolidated the Empire.
- **193-275** – **Severus Dynasty**: Septimius Severus, Caracalla, Heliogabalus, Alexander Severus, Decius, Valerian, Aurelian.
- **235-68** – Military anarchy; a troubled period. The legions make and break emperors.
- **270-75** – Aurelius re-establishes the unity of the Empire.

The Later Empire and the Decline (AD 284-476)

- **284-305** – Reign of **Diocletian**. Institution of **Tetrarchy** or 4-man government; persecution of the Christians (303) and reign of Diocletian known as "the age of martyrs".
- **306-37** – Reign of **Constantine**. By the **Edict of Milan** (313) Constantine decrees religious freedom. Constantinople becomes the new capital.
- **379-95** – Reign of Theodosius the Great, the Christian Emperor, who establishes Christianity as the state religion in 382. At his death the Empire is divided between his two sons, Arcadius (Eastern Empire) and Honorius (Western Empire) who settled at Ravenna.

- **5C** – The Roman Empire is repeatedly attacked by the barbarians: in 410, Alaric, King of the Visigoths, captures Rome. Capture and sack of Rome in 455 by the Vandals under Genseric.
- **476** – Deposition by **Odoacer** of the Emperor Romulus Augustus ends the Western Empire.

From the Roman Empire to the Germanic Holy Roman Empire

- **493** – Odoacer is driven out by the Ostrogoths under Theodoric.
- **535-53** – Reconquest of Italy by the Eastern Roman Emperor **Justinian** (527-65).
- **568** – **Lombard** invasion by King Alboin.
- **590-604** – Papacy of Gregory the Great, responsible for the evangelisation of the Germans and Anglo-Saxons.
- **752** – Threatened by the Lombards, the Pope appeals to Pepin the Short, King of the Franks.
- **756** – Donation of Querzy-sur-Oise. Pepin the Short returns the Byzantine territories conquered by the Lombards to Pope Stephen II, leading to the birth of the *Patrimonium Petri*, otherwise known as the Papal States, and the temporal power of the Pope.
- **774** – Pepin's son, **Charlemagne** (Charles the Great), becomes King of the Lombards.
- **800** – Charlemagne is proclaimed Emperor of the **Holy Roman Empire** by Pope Leo III.
- **9C** – The break-up of the Carolingian Empire causes complete anarchy and the formation of many rival States in Italy. This is an unsettled period for the Papacy, which is often weak and dissolute. Widespread corruption among the ecclesiastical hierarchy.
- **951** – Intervention in Italy of **Otto I**, King of Saxony, who becomes King of the Lombards.
- **962** – Otto I, now crowned Emperor, founds the Germanic Holy Roman Empire.

The Quarrel of the Church and the Empire

- **9C** – Progressive establishment of the **Normans** in Sicily and southern Italy.
- **1076** – The Gregorian Reform of Pope Gregory VII attempts to re-establish the influence of the Church. The dispute between the Pope and the Emperor Henry IV leads to the **Investiture Controversy**.
- 1077 – Humbling of the Emperor before the Pope at Canossa (see *REGGIO EMILIA*)
- 1155 – **Frederick Barbarossa** crowned Emperor. Resumption of the struggle between the Empire and the Papacy, with the **Ghibellines** supporting the Emperor and the **Guelphs** supporting the Pope.
- 1167 – Creation of the **Lombard League**. An association of Lombard cities with Guelph tendencies to counter the Emperor.
- 1176 – Reconciliation between Frederick Barbarossa and Pope Alexander III.
- 1216 – Triumph of the Papacy on the death of Pope Innocent III.
- 1227-50 – A new phase in the struggle between the Empire (Frederick II) and the Papacy (Gregory IX). New triumph of the Papacy.

French Influence and Decline of Imperial Power

Lorenzo the Magnificent

- **13C** – Peak of economic prosperity of the Communes.
- **1265** – Charles of Anjou, brother of St Louis, crowned King of Sicily.
- **1282** – Sicilian Vespers: massacre of French settlers in Sicily *(see SICILIA)*.
- **1300** – First Jubilee declared by Pope **Boniface VIII**.
- **1302** – The **Anjou Dynasty** establishes itself in Naples.
- **1303** – Attack of Anagni, instigated by King Philip of France, on Pope **Boniface VIII** *(see ANAGNI)*.
- **1309-77** – The popes established at Avignon, France. The Avignon popes included Clement V to Gregory XI who took the Papacy back to Rome at the instigation of St Catherine of Siena. This period is referred to as the **Avignon Captivity.**
- **1328** – Failure of the intervention in Italy by the Emperor Ludwig of Bavaria. This is the first sign of the slow erosion of the German Emperors' will to exercise political and economic power over the territories of the old Roman empire.
- **1378-1418** – The **Great Schism of the West** (anti-popes in Pisa and Avignon) is brought to an end by the Council of Constance (1414-18).
- **1402** – Last German intervention in Italy (Emperor defeated by Lombard militia).
- **1442** – Alfonso V, King of **Aragon**, becomes King of the Two Sicilies.
- **1453** – Constantinople, capital of the Christian Eastern territories, falls to the Turks.
- **1492** – Death of **Lorenzo de' Medici**, the Magnificent. **Christopher Columbus** discovers America.
- **1494** – Intervention of King Charles VIII of France for Ludovico II Moro.

Economic and Cultural Golden Age (15C, early 16C)

The centre and the north of the country were transformed by the commercial activity of craftsmen and merchants, while the south kept its feudal structures based on land ownership. The economic importance of Italy derived from the large-scale production of consumer goods (cloth, leather, glass, ceramics, arms etc) as well as from trade and wide-ranging banking activities.

Merchants and bankers who had settled in countries throughout Europe spread the influence of the Italian civilisation, which flourished at the courts of the Italian rulers. There was great rivalry regarding the patronage of artists and the commissioning of splendid palaces among enlightened patrons of the arts such as the Medici of Florence, the Sforza of Milan, the Montefeltro of Urbino, the Este of Ferrara, the Gonzaga of Mantua and the Popes in Rome (Julius II, Leo X).

Decline set in as trade shifted towards the Atlantic with grave consequences for the maritime republics which had prospered during the Middle Ages. **Genoa** soon faced ruin, **Pisa** was taken over by its age-old rival Florence, and **Amalfi** and **Venice** were in serious trouble as the Turks advanced westwards. In addition, the political fragmentation of the country made Italy an inevitable target for the more powerful nation-states now emerging within Europe.

Cosimo de' Medici, *by Cellini*

From the 16C to the Napoleonic era

- **16C** – France and Spain engage in a struggle for the supremacy of Europe.
- **1515-26** – François I, victor at Marignano but vanquished at Pavia, is forced to give up the Italian heritage.
- **1527** – Capture and **sack of Rome** by the troops of the Constable of Bourbon, in the service of Charles V.
- **1545-63** – The Church attempts to re-establish its authority and credibility, much damaged by the Protestant Reformation, with the Council of Trent.
- **1559** – Treaty of Cateau-Cambrèsis: Spanish domination over Naples and the district of Milan, Sicily and Sardinia until the early 18C.
- **17C** – Savoy becomes the most powerful State in northern Italy.
- **1713** – Victor-Amadeus II of Savoy acquires Sicily and the title of King. The Duke of Savoy is compelled to exchange Sicily for Sardinia in 1720.
- **1796** – **Napoleon's campaign** in Italy. Creation of the Cispadan Republic.
- **1797** – Battle of Rivoli. Treaty of Campo-Formio. Creation of the Cisalpine and Ligurian Republics.
- **1798** – Proclamation of the Roman Republic.
- **1799** – Proclamation of the Parthenopaean (Naples) Republic.
- **1801** – The Cisalpine Republic becomes the Italian Republic.
- **1805** – Napoleon transforms the Italian Republic into a Kingdom, assumes the iron crown of the Lombard kings and confers the viceroyalty on his stepson, Eugène de Beauharnais.
- **1808** – Rome is occupied by French troops. Murat becomes King of Naples.
- **1809** – The Papal States are attached to the French Empire.
- **1812** – Pius VII is taken to France as a prisoner.
- **1814** – Collapse of the Napoleonic regime. Pius VII returns to Rome.

Towards Italian Unity (1815-70)

Although Machiavelli had already dreamed of a united Italy in the 16C, it was not until after the French Revolution that the question of uniting the various regions under the same political regime was seriously contemplated. After the Congress of Vienna in 1815, a number of revolts by the "Carbonari" patriots who opposed the Austrian occupation were crushed and in 1831 the Young Italy movement was founded by **Giuseppe Mazzini**. This period, known as the **Risorgimento**, provided the initial impetus which resulted in the **First War of Independence** against Austria, led by Charles Albert of Savoy, King of Sardinia. Initial Italian successes were followed by a violent Austrian counter-attack, the abdication of Charles Albert in March 1849 and the accession of **Victor Emmanuel II** to the throne. The skilful campaigning of his minister **Camillo Cavour**, an ardent advocate of Italian liberty, and the participation of Piedmont in the Crimean War as France's ally brought the problem of Italian unity to the forefront of European affairs. The Plombières agreement signed by Cavour and Napoleon III in 1858 led to the outbreak of the **Second War of Independence** in the following year, with combined Franco-Piedmontese victories in Magenta and Solferino. Following popular uprisings in central and northern Italy, Lombardy, Emilia-Romagna and Tuscany were annexed to the Kingdom of Sardinia. In 1860, after **Garibaldi** liberated Sicily and southern Italy from the domination of the Bourbons, southern Italy, the Marches and Umbria were annexed to the emerging Italian State. On 17 March 1861 the inauguration of the Kingdom of

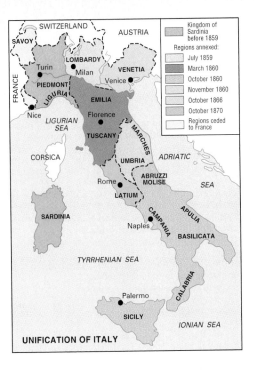

Italy was proclaimed with Turin as the capital and Victor Emmanuel as king. In 1866, for political reasons, the capital was moved to Florence. In the same year, the **Third War of Independence**, with the Prussians as Italy's allies against Austria, led to the annexation of Veneto. Four years later, on 20 September 1870, General Cadorna's troops entered Rome through Porta Pia. Rome was finally annexed to Italy and proclaimed the capital in 1871.

From 1870 to the Present Day

- **1882** – Italy, Germany and Austria sign the **Triple Alliance**.
- **1882-85** – The Italians gain a footing in Eritrea and on the Somali Coast.
- **1900** – Assassination of King Umberto I by an anarchist. Accession of Victor Emmanuel III.
- **1904-06** – Rapprochement of Italy with Britain and France.
- **1911-12** – War breaks out between Italy and the Turks. Occupation of Libya and the Dodecanese.
- **1914** – Outbreak of the **First World War**. Italy enters the First World War on 24 May 1915 on the side of France, Great Britain and Russia (the Triple Entente) in their struggle against Austria-Hungary, and then against Germany (28 August 1916).
- **1918** – The Battle of Vittorio Veneto marks the end of the First World War for Italy (4 November).
- **1919** – Treaty of St Germain-en-Laye: Istria and the Trentino are attached to Italy.
- **1920-21** – Social disturbances fomented by the Fascist Party led by **Benito Mussolini**.
- **1922-26** – The **March on Rome**. Mussolini becomes Prime Minister, then *Duce* (Leader).
- **1929** – **Lateran Treaty** concluded between the Italian Government and the Papacy. This defined the relationship between the Church and State and brought to an end the age-old "Roman Question".
- **1936** – Italian occupation of Ethiopia. Rapprochement with Germany. Rome-Berlin Axis formed.
- **1939** – Outbreak of the **Second World War**.
- **1940** – Italy enters the Second World War, allied with Germany against Britain and France.
- **1943** – 10 July: The Allies land in Sicily. 25 July: Overthrow and arrest of Mussolini. 8 September: Armistice.

THE "ROMAN QUESTION"

The Papacy became involved in the Risorgimento during the 19C, when it became clear that the Unification of Italy could not take place unless the Pope was willing to relinquish the temporal power that he exercised over part of the country. When the troops of Victor Emmanuel II entered Rome in 1870, Pope Pius IX retired to the Vatican, declaring himself a prisoner of the Italian State. The "Roman Question" was only finally resolved in 1929, under the papacy of Pius XI, with the Lateran Treaty drawn up between the Holy See and the Fascist government of Benito Mussolini. These pacts recognised the sovereignty of the Pope within the Vatican City, as well as over certain buildings and organisations in Rome, and granted the Church specific authority regarding education and marriage in Italy. The Lateran Pacts were then included in the new Constitution of the Italian Republic in 1947. They have continued to govern relations between the Italian State and the Church since the end of the Second World War, and were modernised in a new Concordat in 1984.

Much of the country is occupied by German troops. 12 September: Mussolini is freed by the Germans and sets up the **Italian Socialist Republic** in the north of the country with Salò as its capital.

- **1944-45** – The Allies slowly reconquer Italy. The country is liberated (25 April 1945) and the war ends. Mussolini is arrested while trying to flee into Switzerland, is tried and shot.
- **1946** – Abdication of Victor Emmanuel III and accession of Umberto II. Proclamation of the **Republic** after a referendum.
- **1947** – Treaty of Paris: Italy loses its colonies as well as Albania, Istria, Dalmatia and the Dodecanese. Frontier redefined to the benefit of France.
- **1948** – 1 January: The new Constitution comes into effect.
- **1954** – Trieste is attached to Italy.
- **1957** – Treaty of Rome instituting the European Economic Community (now the European Union): Italy is one of the six founding members.
- **1968** – Uprisings against the socio-economic system: *Autunno caldo* (literally, hot autumn).
- **1970-80** – Riots and terrorism as a result of political unrest.
- **1970** – Institution of the regional system.
- **1978** – Aldo Moro, former Presidente del Consiglio, assassinated.
- **1981** – Attack on Pope John Paul II in St Peter's Square by Turkish terrorist Mehmet Alì Agca.
- **1982** – Prefect of Palermo, Alberto Dalla Chiesa, his wife and one of his entourage killed on 3 September.
- **1991** – Italian Communist Party (PCI), led by Achille Occhetto, splits into two new parties, the Democratic Party of the Left (PDS) and the Communist Refoundation (RC).
The first wave of Albanian refugees arrives in Puglia in March.
- **1992** – Operation to fight economic and political corruption in Italy commences, and leads to the collapse of the ruling classes of the Republic. Two judges, Giovanni Falcone and Paolo Borsellino, are assassinated in Sicily.
- **1994** – The centre-right led by Silvio Berlusconi wins the first political elections to take place under the new majority electoral system. Beginning of the Second Republic.
- **29 January 1996** – Teatro La Fenice destroyed by fire in Venice.
- **21 April 1996** – Electoral victory of the Ulivo alliance. The left is in government for the first time in the history of the Republic.
- **27 March 1998** – Italy passes the final test and signs up to the single European currency.
- **13 May 1999** – Carlo Azeglio Ciampi, Governor of the Bank of Italy, becomes the 10th President of the Italian Republic.
- **13 May 2001** – Electoral victory for the central-right alliance and Berlusconi forms his second government.

Paul III Farnese and his nephews in a painting by Titian

"YOU ARE PETER AND ON THIS ROCK I WILL BUILD MY CHURCH" (MATTHEW 16, 18)

The title of "Pope", derived from the Greek pápas meaning father, was originally used for patriarchs and bishops from the Orient. From the 5C on, it became widely used in the west, where with the increasing importance of the Roman See, it was eventually reserved for the Bishop of Rome alone. The Bishop of Rome maintained that his See in the traditional capital of the Empire had been founded by the Apostles, Peter and Paul, and therefore claimed first place in the ecclesiastical hierarchy. The Pope was initially chosen by both the people and the clergy, until the Conclave of the Cardinals was established in 1059. Strict regulations regarding this method of election were set out by Gregory X in the 13C. Nowadays the cardinals meet in conclave in the Sistine Chapel and a vote is held twice a day; after each inconclusive vote the papers are burned so as to produce dark smoke. A majority of two thirds plus one is required for an election to be valid; then a plume of white smoke appears above the Vatican. The senior cardinal appears at the window in the façade of St Peter's from which papal blessings are given and announces the election in the Latin formula: Annuntio vobis gaudium magnum: habemus papam (I announce to you with great joy: we have a Pope …).

Over the centuries the Pope gradually assumed greater political power so that the history of the Papacy is inevitably linked with that of the relationship between the Church and the main political powers of the time. After the Unification of Italy, the Lateran Pacts of 1929 defined the present configuration of the Vatican City, which constitutes a separate State within the Italian State, of which the Pope is the sovereign ruler. The Holy Father is the undisputed leader of the Roman Catholic church and exercises absolute infallibility over all ecclesiastical dogma, as set out in the first Vatican Council in 1870. Through the figure of the Pope, the spiritual influence of the Roman Catholic church can be felt throughout the world.

Elements of Architecture

Ancient Art

Peripteral temple

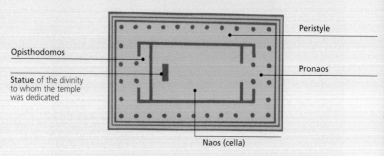

Peristyle

Opisthodomos

Pronaos

Statue of the divinity to whom the temple was dedicated

Naos (cella)

Elevation of a Corinthian order temple

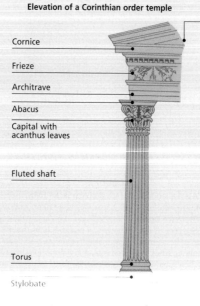

Pediment

Cornice

The section comprising the architrave, frieze and cornice is known as the **entablature**

Frieze

Architrave

Abacus

Capital with acanthus leaves

Fluted shaft

Torus

Stylobate

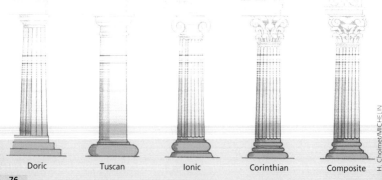

Doric

Tuscan

Ionic

Corinthian

Composite

H. Choimet/MICHELIN

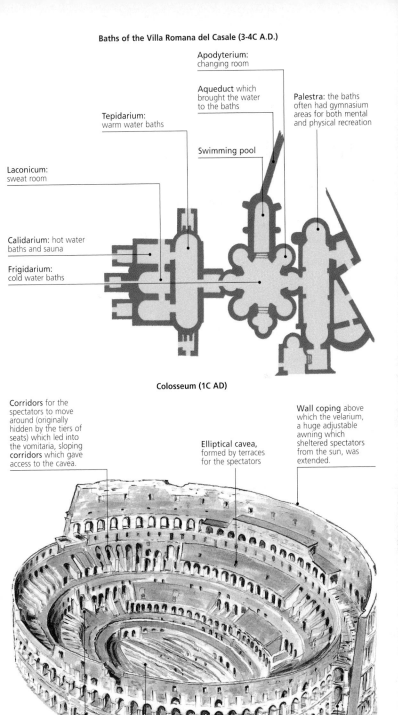

Baths of the Villa Romana del Casale (3-4C A.D.)

Apodyterium: changing room

Aqueduct which brought the water to the baths

Palestra: the baths often had gymnasium areas for both mental and physical recreation

Tepidarium: warm water baths

Swimming pool

Laconicum: sweat room

Calidarium: hot water baths and sauna

Frigidarium: cold water baths

Colosseum (1C AD)

Corridors for the spectators to move around (originally hidden by the tiers of seats) which led into the vomitaria, sloping **corridors** which gave access to the cavea.

Elliptical cavea, formed by terraces for the spectators

Wall coping above which the velarium, a huge adjustable awning which sheltered spectators from the sun, was extended.

Northern entrance to the amphitheatre, reserved for the Emperor and his suite. A further three main entrances corresponded to the two axes of the ellipsis.

Ambulacrum

Arena: originally covered by a wooden floor.

Entrance arches: numbered from I to LXXX (except the four main entrances) to correspond with the entrance number on the spectator's ticket; seating was arranged according to social status.

R. Corbel

Religious architecture

Plan of Parma cathedral (12-14C)

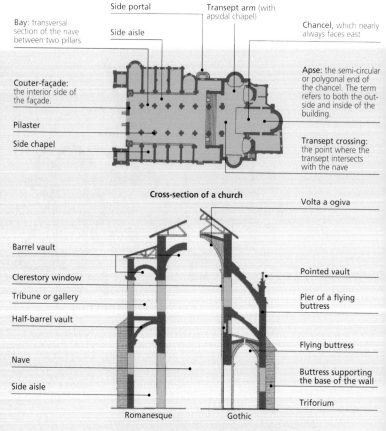

Side portal

Transept arm (with apsidal chapel)

Bay: transversal section of the nave between two pillars.

Side aisle

Chancel, which nearly always faces east

Couter-façade: the interior side of the façade.

Apse: the semi-circular or polygonal end of the chancel. The term refers to both the outside and inside of the building.

Pilaster

Side chapel

Transept crossing: the point where the transept intersects with the nave

Cross-section of a church

Volta a ogiva

Barrel vault

Clerestory window

Tribune or gallery

Half-barrel vault

Nave

Side aisle

Pointed vault

Pier of a flying buttress

Flying buttress

Buttress supporting the base of the wall

Triforium

Romanesque

Gothic

ROMANESQUE ARCHITECTURE
Milano – Basilica di Sant' Ambrogio (11-12C.)

A masterpiece of harmony and balance, Sant'Ambrogio is striking for the apparent simplicity of its composition and for the juxtaposition between the light and the building materials used..

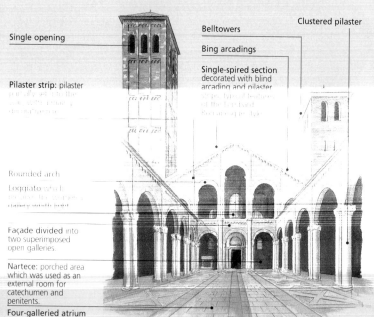

Single opening

Belltowers

Bing arcadings

Single-spired section decorated with blind arcading and pilaster

Clustered pilaster

Pilaster strip: pilaster partially set into the wall with purely decorative use.

Rounded arch

Loggiato which replaces the external gallery with light

Façade divided into two superimposed open galleries.

Nartece: porched area which was used as an external room for catechumen and penitents.

Four-galleried atrium

H. Chomer/MICHELIN

GOTHIC
Milano – Cathedral apse (14-15C)

Milano cathedral is a unique and extraordinary example of the late-Gothic style in Italy. It was started in 1386 and was not finished until the façade was completed in the 19C. The building, commissioned by Gian Galeazzo Visconti, clearly demonstrates a transalpine cultural influence far removed from contemporary Tuscan architecture.

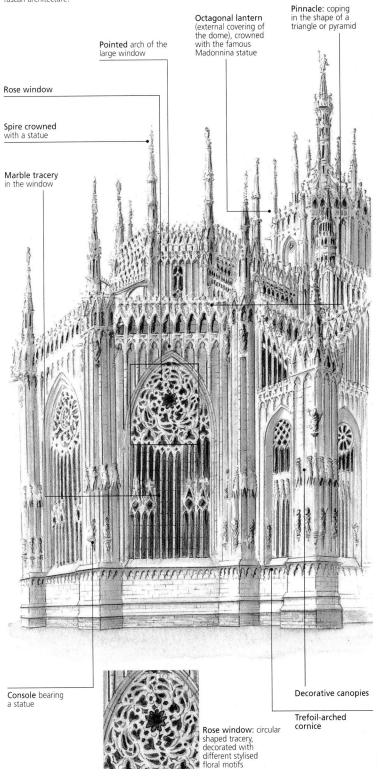

Octagonal lantern (external covering of the dome), crowned with the famous Madonnina statue

Pinnacle: coping in the shape of a triangle or pyramid

Pointed arch of the large window

Rose window

Spire crowned with a statue

Marble tracery in the window

Console bearing a statue

Rose window: circular shaped tracery, decorated with different stylised floral motifs

Decorative canopies

Trefoil-arched cornice

H. Choimet

THE RENAISSANCE
Rimini – Tempio Malatestiano (Leon Battista Alberti, 15C)

Built in honour of Sigismondo Malatesta, this church is a celebration of classical cultures and civilisations, from which many of its structural and decorative features are taken, re-interpreted and adapted to the religious role of the building.

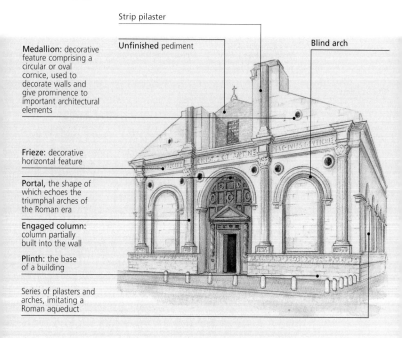

Strip pilaster

Unfinished pediment

Blind arch

Medallion: decorative feature comprising a circular or oval cornice, used to decorate walls and give prominence to important architectural elements

Frieze: decorative horizontal feature

Portal, the shape of which echoes the triumphal arches of the Roman era

Engaged column: column partially built into the wall

Plinth: the base of a building

Series of pilasters and arches, imitating a Roman aqueduct

Firenze – The interior of the Cappella dei Pazzi (Filippo Brunelleschi, 1430-1445)

The harmony of the proportions and the elegant play on colours between the grey of the *pietra serena* stone (which emphasises the architectural features) and the white of the plaster create an atmosphere of dignified and austere simplicity.

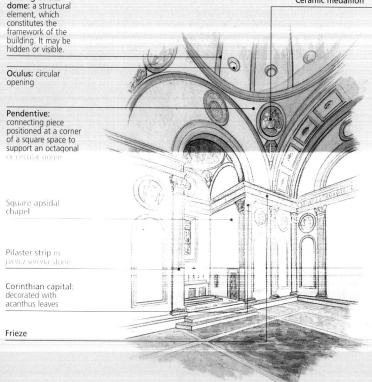

Ribbing of the dome: a structural element, which constitutes the framework of the building. It may be hidden or visible.

Ceramic medallion

Oculus: circular opening

Pendentive: connecting piece positioned at a corner of a square space to support an octagonal or circular dome.

Square apsidal chapel

Pilaster strip in *pietra serena* stone

Corinthian capital: decorated with acanthus leaves

Frieze

H. Choimet

BAROQUE
Lecce – Basilica di Santa Croce (15-17C)

The Baroque style of Lecce is influenced both by Roman and Spanish architecture. The exuberant, highly-worked decoration evokes the Spanish Plateresque style (15-16C), in which façades were decorated with the precise detail of a goldsmith (platero in Spanish).

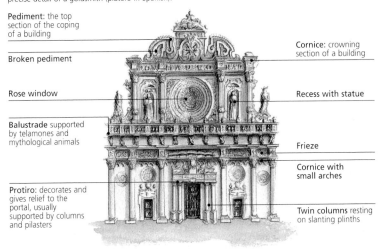

Pediment: the top section of the coping of a building

Broken pediment

Rose window

Balustrade supported by telamones and mythological animals

Protiro: decorates and gives relief to the portal, usually supported by columns and pilasters

Cornice: crowning section of a building

Recess with statue

Frieze

Cornice with small arches

Twin columns resting on slanting plinths

Roma – Interior of St John Lateran (4-17C)

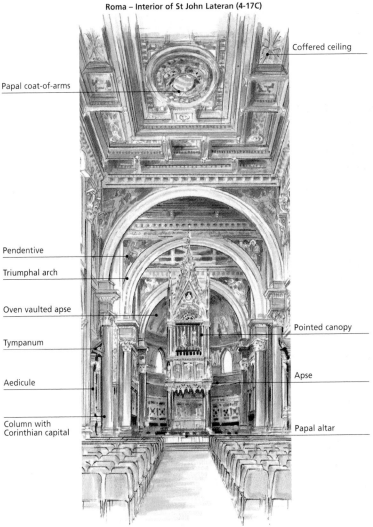

Coffered ceiling

Papal coat-of-arms

Pendentive

Triumphal arch

Oven vaulted apse

Tympanum

Aedicule

Column with Corinthian capital

Pointed canopy

Apse

Papal altar

H. Choimet

Civil architecture

Castel del Monte (13C)

Built by Frederick II, probably as a leisure residence, the castle is dominated by the number eight: the ground plan is octagonal, there are eight octagonal towers and eight rooms on each floor.

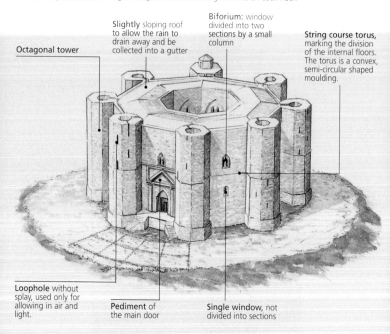

Slightly sloping roof to allow the rain to drain away and be collected into a gutter

Biforium: window divided into two sections by a small column

String course torus, marking the division of the internal floors. The torus is a convex, semi-circular shaped moulding.

Octagonal tower

Loophole without splay, used only for allowing in air and light.

Pediment of the main door

Single window, not divided into sections

Firenze – Palazzo Rucellai (Leon Battista Alberti, 1446-1451)

The palace is composed of three superimposed levels of the three classical orders (Doric, Ionic and Corinthian) and presents a pattern of vertical (the pilasters) and horizontal (the cornices) lines.

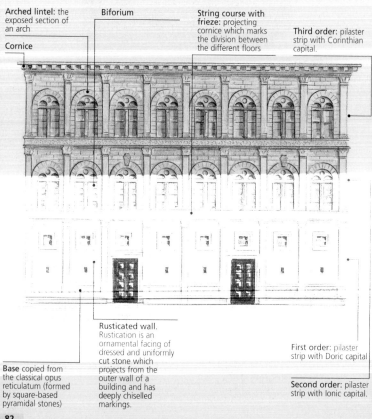

Arched lintel: the exposed section of an arch

Biforium

String course with frieze: projecting cornice which marks the division between the different floors

Third order: pilaster strip with Corinthian capital.

Cornice

Rusticated wall. Rustication is an ornamental facing of dressed and uniformly cut stone which projects from the outer wall of a building and has deeply chiselled markings.

First order: pilaster strip with Doric capital

Base copied from the classical opus reticulatum (formed by square-based pyramidal stones)

Second order: pilaster strip with Ionic capital.

H. Choimet

82

Torino – Palazzo Carignano (Guarino Guarini, 1679-1681)

The façade is striking for the juxtaposition of its straight and curved lines, while the use of brick is a reminder of the Emilian origins of the architect.

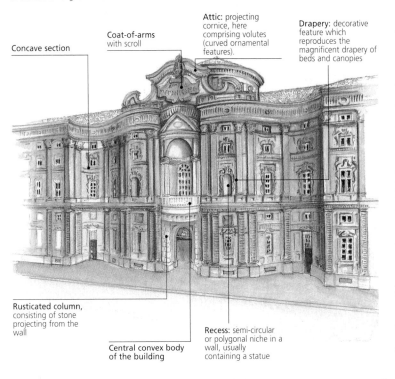

Concave section

Coat-of-arms with scroll

Attic: projecting cornice, here comprising volutes (curved ornamental features).

Drapery: decorative feature which reproduces the magnificent drapery of beds and canopies

Rusticated column, consisting of stone projecting from the wall

Central convex body of the building

Recess: semi-circular or polygonal niche in a wall, usually containing a statue

Milano – Teatro alla Scala (Giuseppe Piermarini, 1776-1778)

The sober and measured simplicity of the façade of this famous Milanese theatre contrasts with the rich decor of the interior. The theatre soon became a model for future neo-Classical theatres.

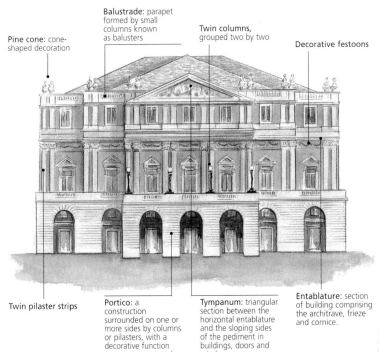

Pine cone: cone-shaped decoration

Balustrade: parapet formed by small columns known as balusters

Twin columns, grouped two by two

Decorative festoons

Twin pilaster strips

Portico: a construction surrounded on one or more sides by columns or pilasters, with a decorative function or as a monumental entrance.

Tympanum: triangular section between the horizontal entablature and the sloping sides of the pediment in buildings, doors and windows.

Entablature: section of building comprising the architrave, frieze and cornice.

H. Choimet

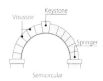

| Semicircular | Pointed | Horseshoe (Moorish) |

Glossary of Architecture

Some of the terms given below are further explained by the illustrations on the previous pages. Words in italics are Italian.

Altarpiece (or **ancona**): a large painting or sculpture adorning an altar.

Ambulatory: extension of the aisles around the chancel for processional purposes.

Apse: semicircular or polygonal end of a church behind the altar; the outer section is known as the chevet.

Architrave: the lowermost horizontal division of a Classical entablature sitting directly on the column capital and supporting the frieze.

Archivolt: arch moulding over an arcade or upper section of a doorway.

Atlantes (or **Telamones**): male figures used as supporting columns.

Atrium (or **four-sided portico**): a court enclosed by colonnades in front of the entrance to a early Christian or Romanesque church.

Bastion: in military architecture, a polygonal defensive structure projecting from the ramparts.

Buttress: external support of a wall, which counterbalances the thrust of the vaults and arches.

Caisson (or **lacunar**): decorative square panel sunk into a flat roof or vaulted stonework.

Cappella: chapel.

Cathedra: high-backed throne in Gothic style.

Ciborium: a canopy (baldaquin) over an altar.

Cortile: interior courtyard of a palace.

Counter-façade: internal wall of church façade.

Cross (church plan): churches are usually built either in the plan of a **Greek cross**, with four arms of equal length, or a **Latin cross**, with one arm longer than the other three.

Crypt: Underground chamber or vault usually beneath a church, often used as a mortuary, burial place or for displaying holy relics. Sometimes it was a small chapel or church in its own right.

Diptych: *see Polyptych*.

Duomo: cathedral.

Entablature: in certain buildings, the section at the top of a colonnade consisting of three parts: the architrave (flat section resting on the capitals of a colonnade), the frieze (decorated with carvings) and the cornice (projecting top section).

Exedra: section in the back of Roman basilicas containing seats; by extension, curved niche or semicircular recess outside.

Fresco: mural painting applied over a fresh undercoat of plaster.

Ghimberga: a triangular Gothic pediment adorning a portal.

Grotesque: a decorative style popular during the Renaissance in which parts of human, animal and plant forms are distorted and mixed. The term comes from the old Italian word *grotte*, the name given in the Renaissance period to the Roman ruins of the Domus Aurea.

High relief: sculpture or carved work projecting more than one half of its true proportions from the background (half-way between low relief and in-the-round figures).

Jamb or **pier**: pillar flanking a doorway or window and supporting the arch above.

Lantern: turret with windows on top of a dome.

Lesene (or **Lombard strips**): decorative band of pilasters joined at the top by an arched frieze.

Low relief: bas-relief, carved figures slightly projecting from their background.

Merlon: part of a crowning parapet between two crenellations.

Modillion: small console supporting a cornice.

Moulding: an ornamental shaped band which projects from the wall.

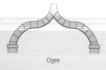

Ogee

Pointed horseshoe

Raised

Multifoil

Narthex: interior vestibule of a church.

Nave: the area between the entrance and chancel of a church, with or without aisles.

Oculus: round window.

Ogee arch: a pointed arch of double curvature: Cyma Recta where the lower curve is convex and the upper curve concave; Cyma Reversa where the lower curve is concave and the upper curve convex.

Order: system in Classical architecture ensuring a unity of style characterised by its columns (base, shaft, capital) and entablature. The orders are: Doric (capitals with mouldings), Ionic (capitals with volutes), Corinthian (capitals with acanthus leaves) and the Composite, derived from the Corinthian but more complex.

Pala: Italian term for altarpiece or reredos.

Palazzo: a town house usually belonging to the head of a noble family; the word derives from the Palatine Hill in Rome where the Caesars had their residences and came to mean the official residence of a person in authority.

Pediment: ornament in Classical architecture (usually triangular or semicircular) above a door or window.

Pendentive: connecting piece positioned at a corner of a square space to support an octagonal or circular dome.

Piano nobile: the principal floor of a *palazzo* raised one storey above ground level.

Pieve: Romanesque parish church.

Peristyle: the range of columns surrounding a Classical building or courtyard.

Pilaster strip: structural column partially set into a wall.

Pluteus: decorated balustrade made from various materials, separating the chancel from the rest of the church.

Polyptych: a painted or carved work consisting of more than three folding leaves or panels (diptych: 2 panels; triptych: 3 panels).

Portico: an open gallery facing the nave in early Christian churches; it later became a decorative feature of the external part of the church.

Predella: base of an altarpiece, divided into small panels.

Pronaos: the space in front of the *cella* or *naos* in Greek temples; later the columned portico in front of the entrance to a church or palace.

Pulpit: an elevated dais from which sermons were preached in the nave of a church.

Pyx: cylindrical box made of ivory or glazed copper for jewels or the Eucharistic host.

Retable: large and ornate altarpiece divided into several painted or carved panels, especially common in Spain after the 14C.

Rose-window: A circular window usually inserted into the front elevation of a church, often filled with stained glass, and decorated with tracery arranged symmetrically about its centre.

Splay: a surface of a wall that forms an oblique angle to the main surface of a doorway or window opening.

Tambour: a circular or polygonal structure supporting a dome.

Tempera: a painting technique in which pigments are ground down and bound usually by means of an egg-based preparation. The technique was replaced by oil.

Tondo: a circular picture, fashionable in Italy in the mid-15C.

Triforium: an open gallery above the arcade of the nave, comprised mainly of three-light windows.

Triptych: *see Polyptych.*

Trompe l'oeil: two-dimensional painted decoration giving the three-dimensional illusion of relief and perspective.

Tympanum: the section above a door (or window) between the lintel and archivolt.

Vault: arched structure forming a roof or ceiling; **barrel vault**: a continuous rounded arch; **cross vault**: the intersection of two barrel vaults; **oven vault**: semicircular in shape, usually over apsidal chapels, the termination of a barrel-vaulted nave.

Rampant

Volute: architectural ornament in the form of a spiral scroll.

Basket-handle

Italian Art

Associazione Turistica di Naturno

A tour of Italy's art treasures can be rather disorientating in the sheer breadth and scale of what the country's artists have achieved over the centuries. From saints and symbols to glistening mosaics, Italy boasts a wonderful array of dazzling images.

Introduction

8C fresco depicting S. Procolo

To appreciate Italian art in all its diversity and richness from the late Classical period to the end of the 18C, it is necessary to keep in mind the illustrious historical context. The rightful heir of the Greek, Etruscan and Roman civilisations, Italian art has adopted from each period some of the most essential principles and characteristics. Italy, with its vast geographical area from the Alps in the north down to Sicily, has always been open to diverse foreign influences. Following the fall of the Western Roman Empire, it was Byzantium that held sway and greatly influenced the northern Adriatic shores for several centuries, while a succession of invading peoples, namely the Ostrogoths, Lombards, Franks, Arabs and Normans, left their imprint on the conquered territory in southern Italy.

The extraordinarily malleable Italian character absorbed the various foreign influences and one after another the cities of Florence, Siena, Verona, Ferrara, Milan, Rome, Venice, Naples, Genoa and many other centres of minor or major importance, became the cradle of a flourishing artistic movement.

As early as the 12C, in spite of the regional diversities, Italian artists were already beginning to show certain common characteristics: a shared taste for harmony and solidity of form as well as an innate sense of space inherited from the Classical culture. Italian art is characterised by a sense of harmony and restraint, not present in other artistic traditions, which aims to depict the rational and intelligible order of things.

The Italians rejected the importance accorded to naturalistic art which was so popular with northern schools, and tempered the excessive emphasis placed on intellectual abstraction and decoration by Oriental artists. Slowly, the Italian artist evolved a representational technique which reflected his emotions. The Classical preoccupation with idealisation is evident in the emphasis given to human figures whether these be profane or religious in inspiration.

In spite of this scholarly and well-mastered image, Italian art has a strong social component. Parallel to the artist's intellectual attempt to impose order on reality, art gradually developed a feeling for naturalism, influenced by the memory of Classical models. A good example of this is the medieval square, the famous piazza, containing the main public buildings as in the Roman forum: the church, baptistery, town hall or princely seat. Law courts, a hospital or a fountain were sometimes added. This was the venue for local markets and meetings. Often designed like stage scenery and embellished with ornamentation, the piazza is also the place for business, political decision-making and other important events. It is usually the result of centuries of construction, depicting aesthetic influences and social moods; history can be interpreted by studying how certain elements were reused, ornamental motifs copied and styles mingled or superimposed. This is where the artist who also aspires to be architect, sculptor and painter can best exercise his talents where it may be admired by all.

These excellent town planners, however, retained harmony with nature and the Italian countryside. From Roman times on they embellished the countryside with sumptuous **villas**, splendid terraced gardens with basins, fountains and springs, all landscaped with skill to create shade and please the eye. Follies invited the passer-by to rest, meditate or simply enjoy the beauty of nature. Thus the Italian architects and landscape gardeners, often indifferent to the solemn grandeur of French classicism, have created a great many places where man has established a harmonious relationship with nature: they range from Hadrian's Villa near Rome to the flower-bedecked terraces of the Borromean Islands, including the Oriental charm of the Villa Rufolo in Ravello, the elegant buildings of the Florentine countryside, the fantastic Mannerist creations of Rome, Tivoli or Bomarzo adorned with grottoes and statues, the urban and regional projects designed by Juvarra in Piedmont, and finally the delightful mansions of the Brenta Riviera, all the work of Palladio.

Byzantine influence

The barbarian invasions were to have noticeable consequences for Italian art, bringing about the decline of the late Roman Imperial tradition and encouraging the popular and narrative early Christian art which later formed the basis of the Romanesque style. Ravenna was chosen by Honorius and his sister Galla Placidia as the capital of the Empire, and after the death of Theodoric and the Gothic invasions, the town came under direct Byzantine rule in the reign of Justinian (AD 527-65). The Byzantine Emperors ruled the region of Ravenna and Venezia Giulia only until the 8C, but they held sway in Sicily and part of southern Italy until the 11C. Byzantine art inherited a certain naturalism and Classical sense of space from the Greek and Latin artistic traditions, and a rich decorative style from its Oriental roots.

Architecture and sculpture

Byzantine architecture inherited the vault and dome from the late-Roman period and developed the potential of these structures with often extraordinary results, culminating in the basilica of San Vitale in Ravenna. More simple basilicas were also built, combining plain and sober exteriors with dazzling interior decoration in mosaic and marble. The bas-reliefs on the sides of sarcophagi, chancel parcloses, ambos and pulpits, assume an essentially decorative character which features symbolic and stylised figures and animals etc.

Mosaics

Byzantine artists excelled in this sumptuous art form. The precious materials used made this the perfect technique for portraying mystical characters from the Bible or striking courtly figures. Mosaics consisted of *tesserae*, fragments of hard stone or glass, glazed and irregularly cut to catch the light. They covered oven vaults, walls and cupolas, their gold highlights sparkling in the mysterious semidarkness. Enigmatic, grandiose figures stood out against midnight blue backgrounds and landscapes with trees,

SCALA

Peter and Andrew leave their fishing nets to follow Jesus – *Sant'Apollinare Nuovo, Ravenna*

Guidoriccio da Fogliano *by Simone Martini*

plants and animals. The most famous mosaics are those of Ravenna (5C-6C). However, the Byzantine style still prevailed in the 11C-12C at St Mark's in Venice and in Sicily (Cefalù, Palermo, Monreale), and in various forms up to the 13C in Rome

Romanesque and Gothic (11C-14C)

As elsewhere in Europe, cathedrals were built all over Italy, but here the Italian predilection for harmony and the Roman tradition of monumental ensembles meant that architecture did not reach the sublime heights of the great Gothic achievements of religious art in France and northern Europe.

Romanesque Period

The development of a new architectural style in the 11C was encouraged by a period of renaissance in the countryside, as well as in the towns and cities. New cathedrals and Benedictine monasteries drew on both the Classical heritage of Carolingian and Ottonian traditions and various regional influences. The main features of Romanesque architecture are alternating columns and pilasters, which provide buildings with rhythm, space and depth, and their continuation into the roof structure, where the square vaults are supported by archivolts and ribs. The structural function of individual architectural features is always visible.

Initially the most flourishing school was in northern Italy, where the master masons were known as the **Maestri Comacini**, who created exceptional buildings in stone in the mountains and in brick in the valleys, and the **Maestri Campionesi**, who came from the Lugano region and the Lombard lakes.

The regions of central Italy were influenced by other cultural models and produced quite different styles. The Classical legacy is strongly felt in Florence, where the highly original medieval Classical style is characterised by a delicate use of colours and a subtle intellectual character, while Rome draws on the early Christian tradition of the magnificent Constantinian basilicas. In Tuscany, especially in Pisa, Lucca and Pistoia, the Romanesque style shows strong Lombard and Classical Florentine influences, embellished by detailed decorative work which is perhaps borrowed from Oriental art. Typical features include tiers of arcades with a multitude of small columns on the façades, tall blind arcades on the side walls and east end, decorative lozenges and different coloured marble encrustations.

In Latium in the 12C-13C, the **Maestri Cosmati**, a Roman guild of mosaic and marble workers, held sway. They specialised in assembling fragments of multi-coloured marble (pavings, episcopal thrones, ambos or pulpits and candelabra) and the encrustation of columns and friezes in the cloisters with enamel mosaics.

Finally, in southern Italy and Sicily, Lombard, Saracen, Byzantine and Norman influences mingled. The result was the monumental and noble **Sicilian-Norman style** *(see SICILIA)*, which is Oriental in its highly decorative façades and Classical in the perfectly poised rhythm of its colonnades.

Sculpture was closely linked with architecture, with a marked use of low relief, occasionally presented as complex cycles of didactic or symbolic figures, both Biblical and secular. Various influences can be detected in this new, highly expressive artistic style.

Painting was developed alongside mosaics in the large cathedrals, where the vast walls and vaults were literally covered with colour. The bare and often austere walls that can be seen in churches today are almost always the result of the ravages of time or restoration work. Originally the bright and imaginative decoration would have alternated with large frescoes illustrating stories from the Bible, where new experimental artistic forms mingled with old Byzantine influences.

Gothic Period

From a structural viewpoint, Gothic architecture represents the evolution of some of the ideas introduced during the Romanesque period. The development of the use of the pointed arch, the potential of which had not been previously exploited to the full, allowed the height above the transept to be increased by concentrating the weight of the building on tall, spectacular pilasters formed by bands of columns and in so doing, released the walls from their weight-bearing role. As a result, it became possible to replace the opaque mass of the walls with huge glass openings which flooded the church with "divine" light. The buildings reached hitherto unimagined heights, supported externally by a mass of buttresses and flying buttresses, hidden from sight to those inside the church, thus accentuating the impression of space and vertical movement. The Cistercians introduced Gothic architecture into Italy, although the style remained close to earlier architectural traditions, with the emphasis purely on a heightened use of light as a structural element. The solid structure of the building and the omnipresent Classical heritage remained of primary importance. The widespread adoption of the Gothic style was due to the many new religious orders, especially the Franciscans and Dominicans, who often used the traditional model of the early Christian basilica, which was practical and economical, and adapted it to current trends.

There was more originality in civil architecture of the Gothic period. Numerous prosperous towns chose to show their civic pride by embellishing their city centres with municipal palaces and loggias. In Venice the ornate Gothic style relieved bare façades with window openings and loggias. Venetian Gothic was to persist until the late 15C.

The **Pisano** family from Pisa gave a decisive impetus to the art of **sculpture** by combining their continued use of ancient traditions seen through the classicism championed by Frederick II (**Nicola**, 1215?-c 80) and their vigorously expressive realism which was explicitly Gothic in tone (**Giovanni**, 1248-after 1314). These masters and the architect and sculptor **Arnolfo di Cambio** (c 1245-1302) introduced new iconography and ambitious projects for pulpits and funerary monuments, all of which exhibited the new humanism.

The painted Crucifixes in relief which appeared in the 12C were the first specimens of Italian painting. Gradually the hieratic tradition inherited from Byzantine art lost its extreme rigidity. In the 13C a Roman, **Pietro Cavallini**, (1273-1321) executed frescoes and mosaics with a greater breadth of style reminiscent of Antique art. His Florentine contemporary, **Cimabue** (1240-1302), adorned the Upper Basilica of Assisi with frescoes displaying a new sense of pathos which broke away from the Byzantine tradition. This new approach influenced **Giotto** (1266-1337), who revolutionised painting by introducing naturalism into his works:

movement, depth and atmosphere were indicated or suggested, and emotion came to light in the frescoes at Assisi, Padua and Florence. All successive painting was influenced in some way by this artist, including Masaccio and Michelangelo, who were directly inspired by his work.

In Siena at the same time **Duccio** di **Buoninsegna's** (c 1255-1318) work still showed a strong Byzantine influence. He founded the Siena school which continued to employ a graceful linear technique and showed a pronounced taste for the decorative use of colour. Some of the most delicate exponents of this school were **Simone Martini** (c 1284-1344) and the brothers **Pietro** (c 1280-1348?) and **Ambrogio Lorenzetti** (1285-1348?).

The masters of the Florentine Trecento period (14C) developed a mystical and realistic style far removed from the lively work of Giotto, a style characterised by harmonies of line and colour as well as a great refinement in the decorative elements. At the same time the **International Gothic** style developed in the courts of Europe, practised by artists from central and northern Italy and perfected in the frescoes painted by Simone Martini and Matteo Giovannetti (?-1367) in Avignon. Other exponents of this refined, stately and occasionally decadent artistic movement which lasted until the 15C include **Stefano da Zevio** (c 1379-after 1438) from Verona, **Pisanello** (c 1380-1455) a portraitist, animal painter and distinguished medallist and **Gentile da Fabriano** (c 1370-1427).

Quattrocento (15C)

The early Renaissance was characterised by an abiding passion for Antiquity, by the well-organised city-states governed by a noble or princely patron, a new vision of man's place at the centre of the universe, and a large number of artists, scholars and poets. The Medici city of Florence united all these conditions and it was an appropriate birthplace for this cultural movement, designated much later as the **Renaissance**.

Architecture

A new concept of art was introduced by the Florentine sculptor and architect **Filippo Brunelleschi** (1377-1446), who was an enthusiastic admirer of Antiquity. His strong personality transformed the practical approach of the medieval master builder into the creative role of the architect who designed new projects on the drawing board. Brunelleschi was both an artist and an intellectual, whose invention of geometrical perspective allowed him to plan harmonious and rationally designed buildings. His intuitive understanding of the reproduction of three-dimensional objects on two-dimensional canvas provided the foundation for all future painting. His intellectual abilities and the abstract character of his architectural creations were imitated and made commonplace by his followers, but were never fully understood. **Leon Battista Alberti** (1404-72) used his knowledge of ancient art to give life to a new expressive style, based on a dramatically emotional relationship between objects and space, which is thought to have influenced Bramante.

Sculpture

The magnificent doors of the Baptistery at Florence designed by **Lorenzo Ghiberti** (1378-1455) show the influence of Gothic tradition and ancient art. However, the most powerful sculptor of the period was undoubtedly **Donatello** (1386-1466), who was deeply interested in man and had little inclination for intellectual speculation. He was able to interpret Classical forms with a free and innovative spirit, breathing dynamism into his work and bringing it to the height of expressive power. After working in Padua, where he created works that set a standard for all of northern Italy, he returned to Florence and in the changing climate of the second half of the century he gave life to a humanity acquired through suffering, presaging the crisis of the end of the century. His contemporary, **Luca della Robbia** (1400-82), specialised in coloured and glazed terracotta works, while **Agostino di Duccio** (1418-c 81), **Desiderio da Settignano** (c 1430-c 64) and **Mino da Fiesole** (1429-84) continued in the Donatello tradition, at the same time moving away from Donatello's intense dramatical style.

Primavera by Botticelli (Galleria degli Uffizi, Florence)

Ph. Benet, R. Holbachova/MICHELIN

Painting

Masaccio (1401-28) was, with Brunelleschi and Donatello, the third major figure of the 15C. He applied Brunelleschi's laws of perspective and added a use of light which gave his figures volume so that for the first time for centuries they cast a shadow, creating an illusion of perspective and the notion of space. His substantial figures thus acquire a certain realism and their solidity lends them a moral dignity. **Paolo Uccello** (c 1397-1475) gave this new concept of space an alternative interpretation, using perspective based on two vanishing points and perhaps demonstrating that more than one method exists for reproducing reality, with the philosophical implications that this entails. At the same time, the Dominican friar **Fra Angelico** (1387-1455), who remained very attached to Gothic tradition, was attracted to the new theories of the Renaissance, while **Benozzo Gozzoli** (1420-97) adapts his style to the portrayal of brilliant festivities, always purely secular. **Andrea del Castagno** (1423-57) emphasised modelling and monumental qualities *(see FIRENZE)*. **Sandro Botticelli** (1444-1510) produced a miraculous purity of line which gives a graceful and almost unreal fragility to his figures and a deep sense of mystery to his allegorical scenes. At the turn of the century, with the crisis in humanist values, he created dazzling figures of sharp lines and muted colours. **Domenico Ghirlandaio** (1449-94) reveals his gift for narrative painting in monumental frescoes which depicted the ruling class of Florence in an atmosphere of stately serenity.

The work of **Piero della Francesca** (c 1415-92) from Sansepolcro is a supreme example of Tuscan Renaissance art displaying faultless harmony and sure draughtsmanship with his use of form, colour and light *(see AREZZO)*.

At the Gonzaga court in Mantua, **Andrea Mantegna** (1431-1506) painted scenes full of grandeur and rigour, using the ancient models to create paintings of strong and inscrutable heroes. In the esoteric, astrological and alchemical atmosphere of the court of Ferrara, **Cosmè (Cosimo) Tura** (1430-95) created troublingly strange yet original compositions in which men and objects are hurled together in a mix of colours that resemble sharp metals and semiprecious stones.

The second major centre of art at this time was Venice, where **Giovanni Bellini** (1432-1516) created a sense of optical and empirical space in his paintings, emphasising the use of colour and tones in contrast to the geometric, intellectual and anti-naturalist painting of Florence. Bellini was much influenced by the work in the 1470s of **Antonello da Messina** (1430-79), who had in turn drawn on the work of the Flemish masters and his knowledge of Piero della Francesca.

Cinquecento (16C)

The 16C saw the development of human sensibility which had already marked the previous century. Artists were attracted more and more by Antiquity, mythology and the discovery of humanity. The artistic centre of the Renaissance moved from Florence to Rome where the popes rivalled one another in embellishing palaces and churches. The artist became more independent and acquired a certain prestige. By the end of the century, the canons of Renaissance art were already being exported and put into practice elsewhere in Europe. However, this golden age of poets and humanists was destined to come to an end before reaching its zenith as a result of the political upheavals in Europe and the conflict brought about by the new Lutheran ideas of the time.

Architecture

The century begins with the return of **Donato Bramante** (1444-1514) from Milan to Rome, where he laid the foundations for the new basilica of St Peter's, later to be completed by Michelangelo. Despite appearances, Bramante's architectural style was not completely Classical in tone; he made use of *trompe l'oeil* effects (such as the false chancel created in San Satiro church in Milan) which feigned a depth that did not exist. As a result, architecture becomes more than just a rational representation of what actually exists, a development that would find perfect expression in the later Baroque style. **Michelangelo**, partly inspired by Bramante's ideas, thought of architecture as a form of sculpture and attempted to give moulded form to large architectural structures. **Giacomo da Vignola** (1507-73) also worked in Rome, while **Andrea Palladio** (1508-80) designed a number of buildings in Vicenza *(see VICENZA)*. In his important works on architecture he advocated the Classicism of ancient art and was himself responsible for many churches, palaces and luxury villas in Venetia.

Sculpture

Michelangelo (1475-1564) did most of his life's work in either Florence or Rome and was the most outstanding character of the century owing to his creative, idealistic and even troubled genius which found its expression in masterpieces of unsurpassed vitality. His art explored questions such as divine revelation, the human longing for something beyond its dissatisfying earthly existence, the soul struggling to release itself from the prison of the body, and the struggle between faith and the intellect. He draws inspiration from ancient art and the work of Donatello, which he reinterprets with impressive moral tension. In his later works this leads to a representation of the disintegration of matter, symbolising the human body, and the immateriality of light, symbolising the spirit, thus shattering the optimisim of Humanist Classicism. Michelangelo towered above his contemporaries, including the elegant and refined **Benvenuto Cellini** (1500-71), a skilled goldsmith and able sculptor known for his Perseus now in Florence, and the powerful sculptor **Giovanni Bologna** (or **Giambologna**, 1529-1608) of Flemish origin, and author of numerous group sculptures, who, together with other contemporaries, followed the dictates of a stately and courtly art.

Painting

The 16C is an important period for painting with numerous outstanding artists producing works in the new humanist vein, and with Rome and later Venice replacing Florence as artistic centres. The century began with exceptional but complementary masters. The fascinating **Leonardo da Vinci** (1452-1519) was the archetype of the enquiring mind of the new humanists. He is famous in painting for his *sfumato* (literally mist), a sort of impalpable, luminous veil which created an impression of distance between persons and things. His insatiable desire for knowledge and interest in the mechanics of how things actually worked, and his attempt to form his observations into a coherent system make him a precursor of modern scientists. His reflections on the workings of the soul and his interpretation of such reflections in paintings such as *The Last Supper* in Milan were to have a lasting effect on future painters. **Raphael** (1483-1520) was not only a prodigious portraitist and painter of gently drawn madonnas, but also a highly inventive decorator with an exceptional mastery of composition which was given free rein in the Stanze of the Vatican. His style is classical in the fullest sense of the term and he is able to communicate the most intellectual and sophisticated ideas in logical, fascinating and deceptively simple paintings.

Michelangelo (1475-1564), the last of the three great men, although he was really a sculptor, took on the formidable task of decorating the ceiling of the Sistine Chapel where his skill with relief and his power are triumphant. His paintings portray a magnificent and heroic humanity, which appears devastated by the message of God. The bright optimism of contemporary Classicism is thus shattered and future artists were forced to choose between the art of the divine Raphael or that of the terrifying Michelangelo.

The 16C Venetian school produced many great colourists. **Giorgione** (1478-1510) explores the relationship between man and nature by creating a wonderful sense of landscape and atmosphere. **Titian** (c 1490-1576), a disciple of Bellini, was as a

The Tempest by *Giorgione*
(Gallerie dell'Accademia, Venice)

Gallerie dell'Accademia, Venice/SCALA

youth influenced by Giorgione and imbued with his skill for both mythological and religious compositions. He was also a fine portraitist and was commissioned by numerous Italian princes and European sovereigns. His later work, characterised by bold compositions and densely coloured brushwork, is the impressive and personal document of one of the greatest artists of the century. **Tintoretto** (1518-94) added a tormented violence to the luminosity of his predecessors, and ably exploited this in his dramatic religious compositions. **Paolo Veronese** (1528-88) was first and foremost a decorator in love with luxury and sumptuous schemes who delighted in crowd scenes with grandiose architectural backgrounds. As for **Jacopo Bassano** (1518-92), he handled rustic and nocturnal scenes, imbued with a new sense of reality, with a freedom of touch and composition.

The unsettled years

The crisis at the end of the 15C, the invasion of Italy by foreign armies, with the resulting loss of liberty for many states, the increase in religious tensions, which led to the Lutheran Protestant movement, the sack of Rome and the Counter-Reformation all had a dramatic effect on the artists of the time. In northern Italy, **Lorenzo Lotto** (1480-1556) interpreted with sharp psychological insight the spiritual and moral anxieties of the provincial aristocracy and bourgeoisie. In Brescia, following the work of Foppa, artists paid particular attention to reality and morality. Various painters portrayed the distressing reality of their time: the work of **Romanino** (1484-1559) is characterised by a northern and anti-Classical expressive violence, **Giovanni Girolamo Savoldo** (c 1480-1548) demonstrates a deep, lyrical intensity, while the paintings of **Alessandro Moretto** (1498-1554) are humble in their touching spirit of faith. But the most obvious examples of the anti-Classical crisis were in Florence, where **Jacopo Pontormo** (1494-1556) was the typical incarnation of a genial but tormented and neurotic artist, a visionary given to bouts of insanity. His paintings were influenced by the works of Raphael and Michelangelo and disturbed the harmony of the Renaissance with their troubled tension, sharp colours and unreal sense of space.

Mannerism

The art of the Counter-Reformation, with its continued use of the Renaissance canon often in an exaggerated or mannered way, marked the transition between Renaissance and Baroque and attempted to give intellectual voice to the preoccupations of the previous generation. It could be described as a stately and refined art, which addressed the cultured public of the Italian and European courts and which pursued ideals of supreme and artificial beauty by copying the stylistic solutions of Raphael and Michelangelo, whose tragic sense would however be crystallised in mannered solutions which rendered the meaning ambiguous. A typical exponent of this style was **Giorgio Vasari** (1511-74), author of the *Lives of the Artists,* who has had a strong influence on historical and critical judgement up to the present day. While Mannerism was widely adopted throughout Europe, it was countered in Italy by the opposition of the Roman Catholic Church which, following the Council of Trent, proposed that religious art be subjected to greater doctrinal clarity.

Pinacoteca Ambrosiana, Milan/SCALA

Basket of Fruit *by Caravaggio*

17C – Naturalism, Classicism and Baroque

Painting

In reaction against Mannerism, a group of Bolognese artists founded the **Accademia degli Incamminati** (Academy of the Eclectic), under the leadership of the **Carracci** family (Annibale, the most original, Lodovico and Agostino). They proposed a less artificial style of art which was truer to nature and which paved the way for future artistic trends. Classicism evolved firstly in Bologna and Rome, and later throughout Italy, following the premises laid down by the Carracci. One of the basic concepts of this style is that certain classical artistic forms, used in ancient art and by Raphael, constitute models of perfection and should be used as a paradigm for any type of creation of high spiritual content. The vault of Palazzo Farnese in Rome, painted by Annibale Carracci, presages the Baroque style with its overwhelming dynamics and its use of *trompe l'oeil*. Baroque painting and architecture are characterised by a sense of movement, by broken perspectives, by scrolls and a taste for false reliefs. Painting is used in conjunction with architecture to give life to disturbing visions of impressive verisimilitude. A good example is the ceiling of the Gesù church in Rome, where **Baciccia** (1639-1709) created a credible illusion of the sky in the physical architectural space of the ceiling.

It was the work of **Michelangelo da Caravaggio** (1573-1610) which revolutionised several centuries of Italian idealism. His intense and often cruel realism, inspired by the artistic traditions of Lombardy and Brescia, drew its inspiration from everyday life in Rome. His unusual use of contrasting light and shadow gave a dramatic visual impact to his work and was often employed to highlight the moral reasons behind human actions and sentiments. He was widely imitated both in Italy and in France and the Netherlands and was without doubt the most influential artist in 17C Europe.

Architecture and sculpture

The main differences between Mannerist architecture, which is developed on a single level and is therefore intellectual and static in style, and Baroque, is the use of spatial dynamism, the continual intermingling between the exterior and interior, the use of curved and broken lines, the use of light as a vehicle of divine intervention, the combining of different artistic styles, and the use of scenic devices to amaze and confuse the spectator, convincing the latter of the existence of what he sees. The true Baroque style, which is structural and found mainly in Rome, is often the creation of artists who worked as architects, painters, sculptors and scenographers. The transformation of St Peter's basilica by **Gian Lorenzo Bernini** (1598-1680) offers typical examples: the famous colonnade solves the problem of the unharmonious extension of the church and of the monumental but static façade, making the façade the background to the dynamic piazza, which turns towards the city of Rome and open its arms to welcome the faithful. Inside the cathedral, the light flooding into the building and the immense bulk of the baldaquin compensate for the loss of centrality due to the extension of the nave, which is transformed into an extraordinary tunnel of perspective of increasing tension. However, the architecture of **Francesco Borromini** (1599-1667) shows the tensions, contrasts and resolutions of a troubled and tormented spirit, more inclined to find inspiration in the dilemmas and contradictions of modern spiritual suffering than in praising the representatives of the Almighty on earth. An interesting variation of Baroque architecture can be seen in Puglia (especially Lecce) and in Sicily, where buildings of ornate and imaginative decoration clearly show the influence of the Spanish Plateresque style.

Settecento (18C)

The deep cultural changes of the new century, with its emphasis on rational and enlightened thinking, were reflected in art where the Baroque style, exhausted of its most intimate religious content, became even more secular and decorative in tone. Art was beginning to free itself from symbolic significance and becoming more autonomous with its own aims and more inclined to entertain rather than to educate. This trend began in France, where the style was known as *rocaille*. Italy had by now relinquished its leading role in art, although the peninsula still produced some important artistic figures, especially in Piedmont. The most extraordinary project of the time was the urban and architectural revival of Turin, raising the city to the status of European capital. **Filippo Juvarra** (1678-1736) moved beyond the tension and drama of the 17C Baroque architecture of his predecessor **Guarino Guarini** (1624-83), designing an urban architecture and town plan (10km-long tree-lined avenues surrounding the buildings) of grandiose theatricality which provided the perfect backdrop for the fine costumes of the Court of Savoy. Art takes another important step away from a mere representation of physical objects with the work of the Venetian **Giovanni Battista (Giambattista) Tiepolo** (1696-1770), whose luminous painting produced *trompe l'oeil* perspectives created for pure visual pleasure with no real regard for verisimilitude or the content of the stories represented: art was now being valued for its artistic qualities alone.

Ottocento (19C)

In the late 18C and early 19C the vogue for all things Classical spread throughout Italy and all over Europe, following the excavations of Herculaneum and Pompeii. The sober, simple and harmonious lines of this style, which is modelled on the immortal examples of Antiquity, provide a stark contrast to the exuberant irregular lines of Baroque. The Italian neo-Classical style is exemplified by the sculptor **Antonio Canova** (1757-1822), whose works seem to follow perfectly the "noble simplicity and quiet grandeur" of Greek art as described by Winckelmann (and only really observed through Roman copies). In his most famous sculpture, The Three Graces (in the Victoria and Albert Museum, London), the extreme formal perfection is transformed into an ambiguous sensuality, which resonates with nostalgia for a perfect world which has been lost forever, a subtle allusion to the impalpable screen between life and death which characterises all of his work, as well as the Romantic poetry of the period.

The neo-Classical style can also be seen in the field of architecture, alongside the eclectic style, influenced by so many sources and which was to last throughout the century, with often very erratic results. An exception is **Alessandro Antonelli** (1798-1888), who enlivened the neo-Classical idiom with new engineering principles, binding the academic tradition to the boldest experiments in Europe.

In painting, the often explicitly academic tone of **Francesco Hayez** (1791-1882) demonstrates the Romantic style which existed alongside the neo-Classical tradition. This friend of Canova creates paintings of medieval history which he uses to refer to the contemporary events of the Risorgimento and which are highly sentimental in tone. The **Macchiaioli** group, founded in 1855, started a revolt against academicism, which was to last about 20 years. The group (who were also known as the "spotters") were in some ways the precursors of the Impressionist school; they often worked outdoors, using colour and simple lines and drawing inspiration from nature. The main exponents of this movement were **Giovanni Fattori** (1825-1908), **Silvestro Lega** (1826-95) and **Telemaco Signorini** (1835-1901). Some artists worked with the Impressionists in Paris: their influence had an indirect but powerful effect on Italian art. At the end of the 19C, in parallel with the growth of a flowing and sketch-like style of painting, **Giovanni Segantini** (1858-99), **Pellizza da Volpedo** (1868-1907) and **Gaetano Previati** (1852-1920) developed the Divisionist school. This art reflected the theories of the French Post-Impressionists, on the one hand developing a deeper analysis of reality, with strong connotations of a social character, while at the same time lending itself to allegorical and symbolist themes, in line with artistic developments in the rest of Europe. Their solutions were of fundamental importance for the avant-garde trends of the 20C.

Brawl in the Galleria
by Boccioni

Novecento (20C)

The 20C began in an explosive manner with the sensational and anti-aesthetic style of the **Futurists**, who under the leadership of the poet **Filippo Tommaso Marinetti** (1876-1944), the movement's theorist, proclaimed their belief in the age of speed, crowds and machinery. This was an explicit and anarchic reaction to bourgeois traditionalist values, which were attacked in the name of a vehement and sometimes superficial vitality; the movement soon adopted a nationalist tone, which in some cases developed into a sympathy for the Fascist movement. The Futurists attempted to render the dynamism of the modern world often by fragmented forms similar to the Cubist style. However, they differed from the Cubists in their marked sense of rebellion, which was influenced both by the writing of contemporary philosophers such as Bergson and by the violent and impassioned disharmony of the Expressionist movement.

The members of this avant-garde movement were **Umberto Boccioni** (1882-1916), **Giacomo Balla** (1871-1958), **Gino Severini** (1883-1966), **Carlo Carrà** (1881-1966) and the architect **Antonio Sant'Elia** (1888-1916). **Giorgio de Chirico** (1888-1978), together with Carrà, created **metaphysical painting**, a disturbing form of art where objects are placed in unlikely but credible positions in an ambiguous and enigmatic atmosphere. **Giorgio Morandi** was inspired by some of the same ideas, although his still-life paintings of everyday objects invite the observer to meditate more deeply on history and the meaning of the painting.

After the First World War, the return to normality brought about an increase in artistic activity both in Italy and abroad. This included the founding of the **Novecento** group which developed naturalistic premises through Magical Realism, interpreted through a re-reading of metaphysics and of Italian medieval and classical art, with often highly poetic and stylised results. Most of the painters, sculptors and architects in Italy either belonged to or were influenced by this group, especially when the political regime declared itself in favour of this stylistic trend in the 1920s, opposing any relationship with contemporary European art. A few isolated voices, often criticised by the authorities, were raised in explicit or tacit opposition to these artistic trends by those who were in favour of a less provincial approach. Some of the most important forces in Italian art during this period were involved in the **Corrente** group from Milan, the **Scuola romana**, and the **Sei di Torino**, which, although following individual paths, shared a common interest in expressionism, which often gave their art a highly dramatic realism, a social tension and a deeply humane content. A good example is the painter **Renato Guttoso** (1912-87), with his personal interpretation of post-Cubist art which he used in combination with explicitly anti-fascist material; even in the general post-war crisis he nearly always managed to avoid the risks of socialist realism, thanks to his openness to different cultural influences. One of the most important contemporary sculptors was **Giacomo Manzù** (1908-91), who succeeded in breathing new life into Christian art. Through the use of a clear and luminous sensitivity, which gives his works, especially the low reliefs, an almost Donatellian vitality, Manzù succeeds in making a sorrowful and humane statement against violence, which is shown to be the inexorable and universal human destructive tendency.

The post-war period

The tragedy of war always makes an indelible impression on art: in such circumstances artists query the significance of artistic creation in a world in which
all moral values have been brutally set aside. The phrase "the death of art" was
also used in the new consumer society of the 1950s and 1960s. The classical artistic
language is no longer understood as a system of signs able to give form to the aesthetic experience of reality. New artistic expression is therefore fundamentally
anti-aesthetic in style and develops in accordance with trends which were up to
this point unrelated to the world of art. To put it more simply, new trends often
shared a lack of interest in or even the destruction of the old physical support,
the canvas. This is partly true in the case of **Alberto Burri** (1915-95), who came
to painting later in life, avoiding the traditional academic circles. By pasting old
torn bags onto his canvas, Burri's intention was not to represent ideas or objects,
but to exhibit a fragment of reality, of matter, which only acquired significance
because it had been transformed by the artist and therefore became a part of his
personal experience. **Lucio Fontana** (1899-1968) also stretched the physical limits
inherent in the traditional method of creating art and cut his canvas in an attempt
to find new solutions to the old problem of space, which can be created but not
represented, emphasising the importance of the "gesture" and of the action which
puts the here and now in contact with the other world of the canvas, destroying
the classical pretence of space. Other artists belonged to the movement known as
arte povera, which was in explicit opposition to the "rich" world. For these artists
the break with the classical method of creating and understanding art is complete,
right up to the radical refusal of the artist to develop a role, which he believes to
be a hoax, dominated by the system against which he is struggling.

Literature

A story that began at the time of St Francis and continues today ...

Birth and Effulgence of Italian literature

The Italian language acquired a literary form in the 13C. At Assisi **St Francis** (1182-1226) wrote his moving *Canticle of the Creatures* in the vernacular instead of the traditional Latin, so that the people could read the word of God. The 13C also gave rise to the **Sicilian School** which, at the court of Frederick II, developed a language of love inspired by traditional ballads from Provence. The most famous of the 13C poetical trends was, however, that of the **dolce stil nuovo** ("sweet new style"): followers included Guinezzelli and Cavalcanti. The term was appropriated by **Dante Alighieri** (1265-1321), author of *Vita Nuova (New Life)*, *Convivio (The Banquet)* and *De vulgari eloquentia (Concerning Vernacular Eloquence)*, to indicate the lyrical quality of this poetry which would celebrate a spiritual and edifying love for an angel-like woman in verse. It was with this new tool that he wrote one of the most powerful masterpieces of Italian literature: the *Divine Comedy* is the account of a lively, enquiring and impassioned visitor to Inferno, Purgatory and Paradise *(Inferno, Purgatorio, Paradiso)*. It is also an epic account of the Christianised Western world and the height of spiritual knowledge of the period. During the 14C **Petrarch** (1304-74), the precursor of humanism and the greatest Italian lyrical poet *(see PADOVA)*, and his friend **Giovanni Boccaccio** (1313-75), the astonishing storyteller who seems almost modern at times *(see SAN GIMIGNANO: Certaldo)*, continued in the tradition of Dante. Each enriched the Italian language in his own way.

Humanism and Renaissance

Florentine humanism reinterpreted the ancient heritage and invented a scholarly poetry in which the tension of the words and images reflected the aspiration of the soul to attain an ideal. **Politian**, **Lorenzo de' Medici** (1449-92) and especially **Michelangelo** were exponents of the neo-Platonic notion of ideal poetry. However the Florentine Renaissance also favoured the development of other quite different lines of thought: scientific with Leonardo da Vinci, theorist with Leon Battista Alberti, philosophical with Marsile Ficin and encyclopaedic with the fascinating personality of Pico della Mirandola. Later Giorgio Vasari *(see FIRENZE)* became the first ever art historian.

In the 16C writers and poets perfected the Italian language to a height of refinement and elegance rarely attained, and all this in the service of princes whom they counselled or entertained. The most famous was **Niccolò Machiavelli** (1469-1527) *(see Index)*, the statesman and political theorist whose name now symbolises cunning and duplicity. In his work entitled *The Prince* he defined with clarity and intelligence the processes which control society, and the moral and political consequences of these relationships.

At the court in Ferrara, **Matteo Maria Boiardo** (1441-94) fused the epic poetry of the Carolingian cycles with the courtly poetry of the Breton cycles in the poem celebrating chivalry, *Orlando Innamorato (Roland in love)*. **Ludovico Ariosto** (1475-1533) and **Torquato Tasso** (1544-95) provided an element of intellectual brilliance. The former wrote *Orlando Furioso (Roland the Mad)*, an epic poem in episodes which enjoyed an extraordinary vogue, and Tasso, his successor at court in this genre, published his *Jerusalem Delivered (Gerusalemme Liberata)*.

*Dante explaining
the Divine Comedy
to the city of Florence*

S. Senini/MICHELIN

At Urbino, **Baldassare Castiglione** (1478-1529) was the author of one of the great works of the period *The Courtier (Il cortegiano)* which was read throughout Europe. In Venice, **Aretino** (1492-1556) sketched the unsentimental portrait of his contemporaries *(Letters)* while in Padua, **Ruzzante** (1502-42) favoured realism in the local dialect.

The Counter-Reformation and the Baroque period

After the discovery of America in 1492, an event which affected the Mediterranean economy adversely, and the spread of Lutheran Protestantism, the 17C to the early 18C marked a period of decadence for Italian literature. The exception was **Galileo** (1564-1642), a scientist, who, taking Archimedes as his point of reference rather than Aristotle, made a distinction between scientific methods and those applicable to theology and philosophy. He was implacably opposed by the Church in an attempt to reassert its influence under the onslaught of the Reformation. The fear of the Inquisition hampered original thought and favoured the development of Baroque poetical concepts in a quest for fantasy.

The Age of Enlightenment and Romanticism

The early 18C was marked by Arcadia, a literary academy which preached "good taste" inspired by the purity of Classical bucolic poetry, in opposition to the "bad taste" of the Baroque period.

The philosopher **Giambattista Vico** (1668-1744) elaborated the theory of the ebb and flow of history based on three stages (sense, imagination and reason). The dramatist **Pietro Metastasio** (1698-1783) was also a leading figure of the period whose biting yet well-thought out vision advanced scientific and philosophical thought.

In Venice, the 18C was dominated by the dramatist **Carlo Goldoni** (1707-93), known as the Italian Molière, who peopled his plays in an amusing, alert and subtle manner with the stock characters and situations of the *Commedia dell'Arte (see BERGAMO)*, an art form which was then highly popular in Venice.

From the end of the 18C writers began to express a new national spirit (consciousness which developed until the upheaval of the Risorgimento). **Giuseppe Parini** (1729-99), a didactic writer, and **Vittorio Alfieri** (1749-1803) who became known for his tragedies on the themes of liberty and opposition to tyranny, were the precursors of the violent and tormented **Ugo Foscolo** (1778-1827) whose patriotic pride is given full vent in *Of the Sepulchres*.

It was **Giacomo Leopardi** (1798-1837) who in some of the finest poems of his verse collection *Canzoni* expresses with a certain lucidity and lyrical purity the growing gulf between the old faith and a fear of the unknown future. He was the main exponent of Italian romanticism and of the theory of historical pessimism based on the contrast between a happy natural state and reason (or civilisation) which brings unhappiness. This was followed by cosmic pessimism which posits the condemnation of Nature and unhappiness as an intrinsic human condition. The Milanese author, **Alessandro Manzoni** (1785-1873), wrote one of the most important novels of 19C Italian literature, *The Betrothed (I promessi sposi)*, a grandiose epic of ordinary folk based on the notion of providence in human existence.

Realism and decadence

The Sicilian **Giovanni Verga** (1840-1922) assured the transition between the 19C and 20C with his novels. He was one of the most important members of the Italian Realist *(Verismo)* school of novelists which took its inspiration from the French naturalist movement. In his extravagant fiction series entitled *Vinti* he presents his pessimistic vision of the world and his compassion for the disinherited.

In the field of lyrical poetry in the second half of the 19C **Giosuè Carducci** (1835-1907), a Nobel prize winner in 1906, drew inspiration from Classical poetry. He was a melancholy figure who criticised the sentimentality of the romantic movement. **Gabriele d'Annunzio** (1863-1938) adopted a refined and precious style to express his sensual love of language. The complex and anxious voice of the poet **Giovanni Pascoli** (1855-1912) filled the early years of the century. His nostalgic poetry recalls the age of innocence and a sense of wonder.

Modern and contemporary authors

In the early 20C, magazines devoted to political, cultural, moral and literary themes were published. Giuseppe Prezzolini (1882-1982) and Giovanni Papini (1881-1956) were among the contributors.

Futurism, which influenced other forms of artistic expression, was the most important of the contemporary literary movements. In his *Manifesto* (1909) **Filippo Tommaso Marinetti** (1876-1944), the leader and theoretician of the movement, exalted the attractions of speed, machines, war and "feverish insomnia", ideas which were echoed by the disjointed syntax, punctuation and words employed in this literary style.

In line with the European sensibility expressed by Musil, Proust and Joyce, Italian letters favoured the theme of discovery which was influenced by studies on repression and the unconscious in the early years of psychoanalysis. In *Zeno's Conscience*, **Italo Svevo** (1861-1928) examines the alienation of the main protagonist as past and present unfold in a long internal monologue. The Sicilian dramatist **Luigi Pirandello** (1867-1936) also analyses man's tragic solitude and the way in which the identity of the individual is eclipsed by the perceptions of the different persons with whom he associates. The only escape is madness.

Traces of realism and the influence of D'Annunzio can be detected in the work of **Grazia Deledda** (1871-1936), who shrouds her portrayals of Sardinian society in mythology. Her tales are dominated by passionate emotions and a deep religious sense of life and death.

The **Hermetic Movement**, which developed after the First World War, celebrated the essential nature of words, liberated from the burden of a grandiloquent and commemorative tradition. The poetry of **Giuseppe Ungaretti** (1888-1970) is evocative and intense, while another leading figure of this movement, **Salvatore Quasimodo** (1901-68), produced successful translations of Greek and Latin Classical literature and of Shakespeare.

The poetry of **Eugenio Montale** (1896-1981) relates with sharp and incisive eloquence the anguish which afflicts human nature. **Umberto Saba** (1883-1957), whose native Trieste was strongly marked by Central European culture, uses both noble language and everyday vocabulary in his intensely lyrical and autobiographical work.

After the Second World War, **neo-Realism** – which was ideally suited to the cinema with its popular appeal – gave a graphic account of the life and misery of the working class, of peasants and street children.

The recurring themes in the works of **Cesare Pavese** (1908-50) are the loneliness and difficulty of existence, described with anguish in his diary which was published posthumously with the title *This Business of Living*.

During recent decades the Italian novel has shown a strong vitality with such diverse personalities as Pratolini *(A Tale of Poor Lovers)*, Guido Piovene *(Pietà contro pietà)*, Ignazio Silone *(Fontarama)*, Mario Soldati *(A cena col commendatore)*, Carlo Levi *(Christ stopped at Eboli)* and Elsa Morante *(Arthur's Island)*.

In the 20C, a handful of Italian authors have achieved international fame: **Alberto Moravia** (1907-90) is regarded as a significant narrator of modern Italy identifying the importance of such issues as sex and money. His book, *The Time of Indifference*, recounts the decline and forbearance of a bourgeois Roman family. Another well-known neo-Realist author was **Italo Calvino** (1923-85) who experimented with the mechanisms of language and who wrote short stories tinged with subtle irony. **Leonardo Sciascia** (1921-89) concentrated on revealing some of the ills of Italian society, such as the Mafia. He wrote essays, detective stories, historical memoirs and romantic surveys. **Carlo Emilio Gadda**, known as the "engineer", experiments with language in his works and succeeds in portraying the hypocrisy, follies and obscure ills of contemporary society. **Pier Paolo Pasolini** (1922-75) provoked and contested the received ideas of his time, contrasting Marxist ideology with Christian spirituality and peasant values. **Dino Buzzati** (1906-72), an original figure, was a poet, writer, illustrator and journalist. His penchant for fantasy and surrealism is tinged with scepticism and is reminiscent of Kafka and Poe.

The 1980s saw the huge success of *The Name of the Rose* (1980), a Gothic thriller written by the semiologist and essayist **Umberto Eco** (b 1932). The century came to a triumphant close with the awarding of the 1997 Nobel Prize for literature to the playwright and actor **Dario Fo** (b 1926), a kind of latter-day court jester who in his plays attacks the powerful and defends the oppressed.

Luigi Pirandello

HARLINGUE VIOLLET

Music

Italy has played a significant role in the evolution of music with the invention of the musical scale and the development of the violin. It is the birthplace of Vivaldi, who inspired Bach and who was surprisingly neglected until the beginning of the 20C, and of Verdi who created operatic works to celebrate the Risorgimento in the 19C.

La Scala c 1830

Early musical composition and religious music

As early as the end of the 10C, a Benedictine monk, **Guido** of Arezzo (997-c 1050), invented the scale, naming the notes with the initial syllables of the first six lines of John the Baptist's hymn *"Ut queant laxis / Resonare fibris / Mira gestorum / Famuli tuorum / Solve polluti / Labii reatum Sancte Johannes"*. The "Si" formed by the initials of *Sancte Johannes* was added to these and the *Ut* was changed to *Do* in the 17C. In the 16C, the golden age of vocal polyphony which was then very popular was marked by **Giovanni Pierluigi da Palestrina** (c 1525-94), a prolific composer of essentially religious music (105 masses). During that period, **Andrea Gabrieli** (c 1510-86) and his nephew **Giovanni** (c 1557-1612) who were the organists at St Mark's in Venice were masters of sacred and secular polyphonic music. The latter composed the first violin sonatas.

From the Baroque period to the 18C

It was only in the 17C and 18C that a proper musical school (for operatic as well as instrumental works) was born in Italy, characterised by charm and freshness of inspiration and melodic talent. The old and new musical forms evolved with the expressive and stylistic innovations of **Girolamo Frescobaldi** (1583-1643) for the organ and harpsichord, **Corelli** (1653-1713) for the violin and **Domenico Scarlatti** (1685-1757) for the harpsichord. The talented Venetian, **Antonio Vivaldi** (1675-1741), composed a wealth of lively music greatly admired by Bach, particularly his concertos divided into three parts, *allegro adagio allegro* and with descriptive interludes as in the *Four Seasons*. **Baldassare Galuppi** (1706-85), a native of Burano near Venice composed the music for the librettos of Goldoni as well as sonatas for harpsichord with a lively tempo. Although Venice was in its final period of glory, her musical reputation grew with the **Marcello** brothers, **Benedetto** (1686-1739) and **Alessandro** (1684-1750). The latter composed a famous concerto for oboe, stringed instruments and organ with a splendid adagio. The instrumental compositions of **Tomaso Albinoni** (1671-1750) are reminiscent of Vivaldi's masterpieces.

In the 18C important Italian composers worked outside Italy. In the field of chamber music, **Luigi Boccherini** (1743-1805), a native of Lucca working in Spain, was famous for his melodies and minuets. He also wrote a powerful symphony, *The House of the Devil*.

Antonio Salieri (1750-1825) from the Veneto was an active composer and a famous teacher who taught Beethoven, Schubert and Liszt. Towards the end of his life, he became mentally disturbed and blamed himself for Mozart's death. This episode

is the theme of the film *Amadeus* by Milos Forman (1984). The Piedmontese **Giovanni Battista Viotti** (1755-1824), Salieri's contemporary, enriched the violin repertory with 29 fine violin concertos. He lived in Paris and London and died after the failure of his wine business.

Although not a musician, **Lorenzo Da Ponte** deserves a mention for his poetic contribution to great musical works. His love of adventure took him not only to New York where he died, but also to Vienna, Europe's musical capital at that time. He collaborated with Mozart and wrote librettos for *The Marriage of Figaro, Don Giovanni* and *Così fan tutte* which won him great fame.

This great period ended with the Romantic movement which is wonderfully celebrated by the great violinist **Niccolò Paganini** (1782-1840) although by that time the piano had become more popular than the violin. His adventurous life, genius of interpretation and legendary virtuosity as well as his slim, tall build turned him into a demonic figure. His most famous works include 24 **Capricci** and six concertos; the finale of the second concerto is the well-known *Campanella*.

Opera

Modern opera originated with **Claudio Monteverdi** (1567-1643) from Cremona whose masterpiece was *Orfeo*. Monteverdi heralded this musical idiom combining words and music, which was immediately very successful and became a popular pursuit influencing the whole cultural scene in Italy.

At the end of the 17C, Neapolitan opera with **Alessandro Scarlatti** established the distinction between arias which highlight virtuoso singing and recitatives which are essential for the development of the action. In the 18C, **Giovan Battista Pergolese, Domenico Cimarosa** and **Giovanni Paisiello** were the leading composers of comic opera *(opera buffa)*, which is in a lighter vein and entirely sung.

In the 19C there were few great composers of instrumental music apart from

THE VIOLIN

The violin was created as a new and improved model of the viola da braccio. Nowadays its fame is so closely linked to that of the old stringed instrument workshops (second half of the 16C-beginning of the 18C), almost all of which were based in Cremona, that the manufacturer's name (Gasparo da Salò, Amati, Guarneri, Stradivari etc) is almost synonymous with that of the instrument and is often mentioned on concert programmes. The most important composers for the violin include **Arcangelo Corelli** (1653-1713), who wrote a number of sonatas for the violin and basso continuo (the bass part over which the solo instrument plays the melody), including the well-known La Follia; **Giuseppe Torelli** (1658-1709), the composer of many concerti grossi (compositions for an orchestra and a group of soloists); **Giuseppe Tartini** (1692-1770), who wrote the anguished sonatas *The Devil's Trill* (the devil appears to have been the inspiration for many musical pieces, especially those composed for the violin) and *Dido Abandoned*; **Pietro Locatelli** (1695-1764), who perfected violin techniques in his Capricci and Sonate; Giovanni Battista Viotti, and the incomparable Niccolò Paganini.

Vivaldi

Paganini, as lyrical art was made to reflect the intense passions of the Risorgimento. **Gioacchino Rossini** (1782-1868) marked the transition from the classical to the romantic period *(Othello, William Tell* and the comic operas *The Italian Girl in Algiers, The Thieving Magpie* and *The Barber of Seville)*. **Vincenzo Bellini** (1801-35) composed undistinguished orchestral music but admirable melodies and arias *(La Sonnambula, Norma)*. His rival **Gaetano Donizetti** (1797-1848) wrote several melodramas *(Lucia di Lammermoor)* where the action takes second place to the singing, as well as some charming comic operas: *L'Elisir d'Amore, Don Pasquale*. **Amilcare Ponchielli** (1834-86) is remembered mainly for his successful opera *La Gioconda*.

The greatest composer of the genre during the troubled period of the fight for independence from Austria was **Guiseppe Verdi** (1813-1901) with his dramatic yet romantic works: *Nabucco, Rigoletto, Il Trovatore, La Traviata, Aida* etc; he also wrote an admirable *Requiem*. The Realist movement *(Verismo)* then became popular, with Mascagni *(Cavalleria Rusticana)*, Leoncavallo *(I Pagliaci)*, and especially **Giacomo Puccini** (1858-1924) whose *Tosca, Madame Butterfly, La Bohème* and other works crowned this lyrical era.

Modern music

In reaction, the next generation concentrated on orchestral music; it included **Ottorino Respighi** (1879-1937) who composed symphonic poems *(The Fountains of Rome, The Pines of Rome, Roman festivals)*. 20C composers include Petrassi who explored all musical forms and **Dallapiccola** (1904-75), the leader of the dodecaphonic movement (the 12 notes of the scale are used) in Italy. The sensitive and passionate **Luigi Nono** (1924-90) used serial music to express his political and liberating message; he wrote instrumental, orchestral, vocal and choral works.

THE PIANO
The piano was invented by **Bartolomeo Cristofori** (1655-1732), who modified the harpsichord by replacing the plectra, which "plucked" the strings, with hammers which struck them. The first Italian to introduce this new instrument to the rest of Europe was **Muzio Clementi** (1752-1832), a rival of Mozart. He wrote a hundred studies for the piano, including Gradus ad Parnassum, and Six Sonatas, which were influenced by the work of both Mozart and Beethoven. The piano's wide range of tones and notes made it the ideal instrument for the Romantics, who composed a number of melancholic and passionate pieces for it. In more recent times some of Bach's compositions were adapted for the piano by **Ferruccio Busoni** (1866-1924).

Venues and artists

The only relatively recent unification of the country accounts for the numerous and famous opera houses and concert halls: the prestigious La Scala in Milan, for which Visconti created marvellous sets, the Rome Opera House, the San Carlo theatre in Naples, the Poncielli in Cremona, the Politeama in Palermo, the Fenice in Venice (destroyed by fire in January 1996), the Carlo Fenice in Genoa, and the Regio and the modern Lingotto in Turin. In spring Florence hosts a renowned music festival, and in summer splendid performances are held in the amphitheatre at Verona and in Caracalla's Baths in Rome.

Among the great orchestras and chamber music groups, the Orchestra of the Accademia di Santa Cecilia in Rome, the Filarmonica of La Scala in Milan, the Solisti Veniti and the Orchestra of Padua and the Veneto are noteworthy.

Among the great Italian conductors, Arturo Toscanini was renowned for the verve and originality of his interpretations. Other famous names include Victor De Sabata and nowadays, Claudio Abbado, Carlo Maria Giulini, Riccardo Muti, who perform all over the world. Artists of international reputation include the violinists Accardo and Ughi, the pianists Campanella, Ciccolini, Lucchesini and Maria Tipo, the cellists Brunello and Filippini and the ballet dancers Carla Fracci, Luciana Savignano and Alessandra Ferri.

The famous singers Cecilia Bartoli, Renato Bruson, Fiorenza Cossotto, Cecilia Gasdia, Katia Ricciarelli, Renata Scotto, Lucia Valentini Terrani as well as Ruggiero Raimondi and Luciano Pavarotti are worthy successors to La Malibran, Renata Tebaldi, Maria Callas, Caruso and Beniamino Gigli.

GIUSEPPE SINOPOLI
When he died in Berlin during a performance of Aida that he was conducting on 20 April 2001, this great Italian conductor was only 54 years old. Sinopoli was a man of many talents. Not only was he an accomplished musician and scholar of Wagner he was passionate about psychiatry and archaeology and achieved professional qualifications in both these fields.

Cinema

From Turin, which even has a museum dedicated to the town's film-making history, to Venice, Cannes and Hollywood ...

The early years and neo-Realism

The Italian cinema industry was born in Turin at the beginning of the 20C and grew rapidly (50 production companies in 1914) with great successes on the international scene. Film-makers specialised first in historical epics, then in the 1910s they turned to adventure films and in the 1930s to propaganda and escapist films subsidised by the State, which distracted spectators temporarily from the reality of the Fascist State. In 1935 the Cinecittà studios and the experimental cinematographic centre which numbered Rossellini and De Santis among its pupils were founded in Rome.
During the years of Fascist rule the cinema had become divorced from real life, and to bridge the gap film directors advocated a return to realism and close observation of daily life. The first major theme of **neo-Realism** was the war and its aftermath. **Roberto Rossellini** denounced Nazi and Fascist oppression in *Rome Open City* and *Germany Year Zero*. **Vittorio de Sica**'s *Sciuscia* (1946) and *Bicycle Thieves* (1948) depicted the unemployment and misery of the post-war years. In *Bitter Rice* (1949) and *Bloody Easter* (1950) **De Santis** portrays the working class divided between the prevailing ideology and revolutionary ambitions.
Neo-Realism ended in the early 1950s as it no longer satisfied the public who wanted to forget this bleak period, but its influence was still felt by future generations of film-makers.

1960s to the present day

In the 1960s Italian cinema flourished and a large number of films (over 200 a year), generally of very high quality, was made with the support of a strong industrial infrastructure. Three great directors dominated this period. **Federico Fellini** (1920-93) shot the hugely successful *La Strada (The Street)* in 1954 and *La Dolce Vita* in 1960. His fantasy world is reflected in the original camerawork. **Michelangelo Antonioni** (1912) made his debut in 1959 with *L'Avventura*, and his work (*The Red Desert*, 1960 and *Blow Up*, 1967) underlines the ultimate isolation of the individual. **Luchino Visconti** (1906-76) made *Rocco and his brothers* in 1960 and *The Leopard* in 1963. His films, which are characterised by opulence and beauty, examine closely the themes of impermanence, degradation and death.
During the same period a new generation of film-makers made a political and social statement: **Pier Paolo Pasolini**, **Ermanno Olmi**, Rosi, Bertolucci and the Taviani brothers.
Italian cinema won great international success with several masterpieces until the mid 1970s: *Death in Venice* (1970) and *Ludwig* (1972) by Visconti, *Casanova* (1976) by Fellini, *The Passenger* (1974) by Antonioni, *L'Affair Mattei* (1971) by **Francesco Rosi** and *The Last Tango in Paris* by **Bernardo Bertolucci**. Since the late 1970s the industry has been in a state of crisis, as it faces competition from television and the collapse of the market. However, some films made by famous directors have won acclaim: *The Night of San Lorenzo* (1982) by the **Taviani brothers**, *The Ball* (1983) by **Ettore Scola**, *The Last Emperor* (1987) by Bertolucci, *Cinema Paradiso* (1989) by **Giuseppe Tornatore**.
An introduction to Italian cinema would be incomplete without mentioning the famous "Italian comedies", which include masterpieces such as *Guardie e ladri* (1951), *I soliti ignoti* (1958), *La grande guerra* (1959), *L'Armata Brancaleone* (1966) and *Amici miei* (1975) by **Mario Monicelli** and *Divorzio all'Italiana* (1962) by **Pietro Germi**.

The younger generation of film-makers embraced realism and their protagonists are engaged in the social struggle. The most interesting films include *Bianca* (1984), *La messa è finita* (1985) and *Caro Diario* (1993) by **Nanni Moretti**, *Il portaborse* (1990) and *La Scuola* (1995) by **Daniele Luchetti**; *Regalo di Natale* (1986) by **Pupi Avati**; *Mery per sempre* (1989), *Ragazzi fuori* (1989) and *Il muro di gomma* (1991) by **Marco Risi** and *Notte italiana* (1987) and *Vesna va veloce* (1996) by **Carlo Mazzacurati**. In 2000, **Silvio Soldini** made a name for himself with a charming film, *Pane e tulipani*, in which the rather eccentric protagonists go about their daily life in Venice (and not a tourist in sight).

Different strands of comedy can also be seen in many Italian films made during the last 20 years. A number of talented actor-writers have succeeded in exporting some of these Italian films abroad. Examples include *Ricomincio da tre* (1981), *Non ci resta che piangere* (1984), *Le vie del Signore sono finite* and *The Postman* (1994) by **Massimo Troisi**; *Un sacco bello* (1980), *Compagni di scuola* (1988) and *Maledetto il giorno che ti ho incontrato* (1992) by **Carlo Verdone**; *Il ciclone* (1996) by **Leonardo Pieraccioni**, and *Il piccolo diavolo* (1988), *Johnny Stecchino* (1991) and *Il mostro* (1994) by **Roberto Benigni**, who also produced the 1999 Oscar-winning master-piece *Life is beautiful* (1997).

The success of Italian cinema is above all due to its famous stars, such as Vittorio Gasmann, Gina Lollobrigida, Sophia Loren, Anna Magnani, Giulietta Masina, Marcello Mastroianni, Alberto Sordi, Ugo Tognazzi, Totò and many others.

Awards and Oscars

Oscar Academy Awards

Life is beautiful by Roberto Benigni – 3 Oscars, including Best Foreign Film 1999
Mediterraneo by Gabriele Salvatores – Best Foreign Film 1992
Cinema Paradiso by Giuseppe Tornatore – Best Foreign Film 1990
The Last Emperor by Bernardo Bertolucci – 9 Oscars, including Best Film and Best Director 1988
Amarcord by Federico Fellini – Best Foreign Film 1975
Il Giardino dei Finzi-Contini by Vittorio De Sica – Best Foreign Film 1972
Indagine di un cittadino al di sopra di ogni sospetto by Elio Petri – Best Foreign Film 1971
Ieri, oggi, domani by Vittorio De Sica – Best Foreign Film 1965
8 1/2 by Federico Fellini – Best Foreign Film 1964
Le notti di Cabiria by Federico Fellini – Best Foreign Film 1958
La Strada by Federico Fellini – Best Foreign Film 1957

Cannes Film Festival

La stanza del figlio by Nanni Moretti, 2001
L'albero degli zoccoli (The Tree of Wooden Clogs) by Ermanno Olmi, 1978
Padre padrone by Paolo and Vittorio Taviani, 1977
Il Caso Mattei by Francesco Rosi and *La classe operaia va in Paradiso* by Elio Petri, 1972
Signore e signori by Pietro Germi, 1966
Il Gattopardo (The Leopard) by Luchino Visconti, 1963
La dolce vita by Federico Fellini, 1960
Due soldi di speranza by Renato Castellani, 1952
Miracolo a Milano by Vittorio De Sica, 1951

Venice Film Festival

Così ridevano by Gianni Amelio, 1998
La leggenda del santo bevitore by Ermanno Olmi, 1988
La Battaglia di Algeri by Gillo Pontecorvo, 1966
Vaghe stelle dell'orsa by Luchino Visconti, 1965
Deserto rosso by Michelangelo Antonioni, 1964
Le mani sulla città by Francesco Rosi, 1963
Il generale Della Rovere by Roberto Rossellini and *La grande guerra* by Mario Monicelli, 1959
Giulietta e Romeo by Renato Castellani, 1954

Fashion

Is it art?

What is the purpose of this rather fickle aspect of the lives of many, if indeed it has any purpose at all? The most obvious answer is that it is the **search for beauty**, for harmonisation with the physical and spiritual enlightenment that most people seek.

Then there is the **desire to be different**. At this point we should make the distinction between luxury and elegance. The former tends to be showy, with clothes and accessories purchased solely on the basis of price and not their aesthetic quality, which remains the main parameter of elegance. **St Bernardino** was of the opinion that luxury was "for the most part, synonymous with usury, and the blood, sweat and tears of the peasants" and that "elegance passed unnoticed and was not influenced by the transitory nature of fashion".

Colour, an essential element

The trend for **colour** was particularly in evidence during the Renaissance, but tastes in colour changed from century to century. Until the 13C the fashion was for the dark blue of the Byzantine mosaics at San Vitale (Ravenna) but during the 13C came the vogue for two-tone clothes. Pink was all the rage in the Quattrocento; in the 16C the fashion for gold, silver and black gave clothes a more solemn air (think of the portraits by Titian). Whereas pale colours were very popular in the 17C, the 18C saw a preference for white and pastel shades. The last word in fashion in the 19C was black and white with the vogue for dark colours also continuing into the early 20C.

Today, as in the past...

Whether they are artists, designers or just ordinary Italians, and whether they live in town or in the country, everybody seems to have inherently good taste. This is often most in evidence in their choice of clothes and accessories and applies as much to those who can afford to shop in Via Monte Napoleone (Milan) or Via dei Condotti (Rome) as the locals who go to the market. For the Italians, dressing casually is no excuse for shabby, slovenly attire.

The big names

The activities of the major Italian fashion houses extend to clothes, perfumes, jewellery and furnishings.

Giorgio Armani's creativity is best exemplified by the "deconstructed jacket", as well as evening wear, low-heeled shoes and concepts drawn from traditional Oriental dress.

The **Benetton** label is recognised by young people all over the world. The label is also famous for the controversial publicity photographs taken by Oliviero Toscani.

Laura Biagiotti has made a name for herself in cashmere.

COSTUME OR FASHION?
The term "costume" dates back to the 16C. Its meaning, "way of dressing", had traditional and lasting connotations. "Fashion" is a 17C term which refers to novelty in dress codes and implied something short-lived.

Lara Pessina/MICHELIN

In the 13C the austerity of centuries past gave way to the occasional concession to variety. There were also two new developments which influenced fashion: **buttons** and **glasses** (Cardinale Ugo di Provenza is depicted wearing spectacles in a 1352 fresco in Treviso's Capitolo di San Nicolò, a first in the history of art). **Hair** also got longer.

Pierre Cardin introduced geometric designs and experimented with the unisex style.

The **Enrico Coveri** brand goes for bold patterns.

Dolce and Gabbana are best known for their cheeky approach to fashion. Their free and easy style is typically exemplified by highly colourful clothing, lacy shirts, chunky belts and snakeskin fabrics.

Fendi is the name of four sisters who strive for "refinement, craftsmanship, originality and quality".

Gianfranco Ferré focuses on "quality, comfort, individuality and simplicity". Classic is the best way to describe **Gucci**, the designer label preferred by some of the world's most stylish women including Grace Kelly, Audrey Hepburn, Jacqueline Kennedy and Maria Callas.

Krizia and Mariuccia Mandelli are about "perfectionism, a high-quality finish and attention to detail".

Colour is what **Missoni** is all about. The family business is mostly known for its stripey knitwear.

Moschino takes its name from the avant-garde designer who died in 1994 and whose motto was *De gustibus non est disputandum*. Many of the company's designs have a larger-than-life quality to them.

Prada is one of the labels most strongly associated with sharp, classic lines.

Trussardi favours simple lines, focusing on high-quality tailoring and finishing.

Valentino recognised that women should cultivate their own style which enhanced their self-confidence. His designs tended to be both elegant and classical.

Versace is the surname of Gianni, Donatella and Santo. Before his death in 1997, Gianni's designs, which were both exotic and exciting, were very popular with rockstars: fans included Elton John and Jon Bon Jovi.

In the 16C Italy's influence on neighbouring countries was such that Erasmus of Rotterdam declared "let he who is learned be Italian". **Strange...but true:** heels could be as high as 60cm/2ft! In Venice, it was said that "such was the height of the heels they wore, the Venetian ladies passing through Piazza San Marco looked like dwarfs dressed up as giants". Women also began to wear earrings around this time, something that had previously been denounced as unbecoming because it was the sort of thing that Moors did.

In the 18C black veils, masks and three-cornered hats were the height of fashion in Venice. **Even more curious...:** fans and snuffboxes were all the rage, for men and women. In the 19C jackets and coats were worn long and straight with a high waistline and there was a certain romanticism in clothing. Very much in vogue were huge puffed sleeves and corsets designed to make the waist as small as possible (vitino di vespa or wasp waist). **And then...:** the crinoline arrived on the scene, worn over ornately decorated undergarments.

Rocca di Gradara

Selected Sights

Abruzzo

The splendours of the Abruzzi region lie in the grandeur and diversity of the wild and rugged terrain it occupies: stark karst formations give way to lush woodland, and barren plateaus to fertile pastures. Enclosed by three national parks – the long-established Parco Nazionale d'Abruzzo, the Parco Nazionale del Gran Sasso and Parco Nazionale della Maiella – the region also offers plenty of scope for both summer holidays and winter sports. Other attractions include a number of well-known seaside resorts including Alba Adriatica, Giulianova Lido, Roseto degli Abruzzi, Silvi Marina and Vasto.

Location

Michelin map 430 N-R 21-26. The Abruzzi is easily accessible from Rome, taking A 24, and from the Adriatic coast, taking A 25. ⬛ Via N. Fabrizi 171, 65122 Pescara, ☎ 085 42 90 01, Freephone (in Italy): 800 502 520; www.regione.abruzzo.it/turismo. By car the main access routes are Bisegna in the north, Barrea to the east and Forca d'Acero in the west. For information on park activities: ⬛ Centro Parchi Internazionale in Rome or local offices at Pescasseroli, Villetta Barrea, Civitella Alfedena, Villavallelonga and Campoli Appennino, open 9am-noon and 3-7pm. The Ufficio Operativo del Parco is in Pescasseroli, Viale S. Lucia, ☎ 0863 91 07 15; the main office is in Rome, Viale Tito Livio 12, ☎ 06 35 40 33 31.

See ASCOLI PICENO, L'AQUILA, SULMONA. Surrounding area: see MOLISE.

Directory

WHERE TO EAT

• Budget

Al Focolare di Bacco – *Via Solagna 18 – 64026 Roseto degli Abruzzi – 31km/19mi northeast of Pescara on S 16 –* ☎ 085 89 41 004 – *Closed Tue, Wed, at lunchtime (except public holidays), Nov –* ⬛ – €19/26. A popular spot, tucked away in the peace and tranquillity of the Abruzzi hills. Well-known for its cooking alla brace (flame grilled). A curious mix of rustic and elegant – with panoramic views out to sea and earthy aromas wafting from the kitchen. Attractive rooms. A unique base for a seaside vacation.

Peppe di Sora – *Via Benedetto Croce 1 – 67032 Pescasseroli –* ☎ 0863 91 908 – *Closed Mon (winter) – €21/31.* Riverside setting. A classic trattoria serving hearty local fare. Warmed by a roaring fire during the winter months. Also has rooms to let, simple but clean.

• Moderate

Don Ambrosio – *Contrada Piomba 49 – 64029 Silvi Marina – 14km/8.5mimi northeast of Pescara on S 16 –* ☎ 085 93 51 060 – *Closed Tue, 3-15 Nov, 15-28 Feb – €22.20/34.65.* A short trip into the hinterland brings you to this old farmhouse. Inside, the walls of exposed stonework bear witness to its agricultural heritage. Regional dishes and specialities, generous servings. Al fresco dining in summer.

WHERE TO STAY

• Budget

Hotel Il Vecchio Pescatore – *Via Benedetto Virgilio – 67030 Villetta Barrea – 15.5km/10mi east of Pescasseroli on S 83 –* ☎ 0864 89 274 – *Fax 0864 89 255 – 12 rm €28.41/49.06* ⬛ *– Restaurant €15/23.* A simple but comfortable hotel situated in the heart of the Parco Nazionale d'Abruzzo. Warm welcome. Rooms are small but light and airy. Pale-coloured modern furnishings. A stone's throw from the restaurant of the same name which is run by the same people.

• Moderate

Albergo Archi del Sole – *Via della Pretara 12 – 67033 Pescocostanzo –* ☎ 0864 64 00 07 – *Fax 0864 64 00 07 – archidelsole@virgilio.it – Closed Mon (winter) – 10 rm €67.14/82.63* ⬛. A charming hotel in this village frozen in time. All the rooms are named after a flower, with colour-coordinated decor and furnishings. Parquet floors and beamed ceilings add to the atmosphere.

• Expensive

Hotel Villino Mon Repos – *Via le Colli del-l'Oro – 67032 Pescasseroli –* ☎ 0863 91 28 58 – *Fax 0863 91 28 30 – 17 rm from €87.80* ⬛. A fine early-20C villa which used to be the summer residence of Benedetto Croce. Set in splendid parkland with some magnificent old trees. Comfortable rooms, tastefully furnished, with much attention to detail. A touch of class.

Background

Various Italic populations dominated the region until the 3C BC when Rome took over the territory definitively. After the fall of the Roman Empire the region became a Lombard territory before being taken over by the Franks. In the 12C it became part of the Kingdom of Naples and remained so until the Unification of Italy.

In the Middle Ages the diffusion of Benedictine rule from the neighbouring abbey at Monte Cassino (see *Abbazia di MONTECASSINO*) led to the construction of cathedrals, abbeys and churches whose beautifully ornate ciboria and pulpits constitute the definitive glory of Abruzzi art. In the 15C-16C the finest examples of Renaissance art were to be found in the work of the painter and architect **Cola dell'Amatrice**, the painter **Andrea de Litio**, the sculptor **Silvestro dell'Aquila** and in the refined work of the goldsmith **Nicola da Guardiagrele**.

Notable figures of the Abruzzi region include Publius Ovidius Naso (43 BC-AD 17), the poets Ovid and Gabriele D'Annunzio (1863-1938), philosopher and statesman Benedetto Croce (1866-1952) and novelist Ignazio Silone (1900-78).

Special Feature

Parco Nazionale d'Abruzzo★★★

Open 10am-1pm and 3-7pm. By car the main access routes are Bisegna in the north, Barrea to the east and Forca d'Acero in the west. For information on park activities contact Centro Parchi Internazionale in Rome or local offices at Pescasseroli, Villetta Barrea, Civitella Alfedena, Villavallelonga and Alvito. The main office is temporarily situated in Pescasseroli, Viale S. Lucia, ☎ 0863 91 07 15, the representative office is in Rome, Viale Tito Livio 12, ☎ 06 35 40 33 31; Fax 06 35 40 32 53; www.pna.it

A nature reserve was founded in 1923 in the very heart of the massif to protect the fauna, flora and outstanding landscapes of the region. The park extends over an area of approximately 40 000ha/100 000 acres, not including the 4 500ha/11 119 acres of the Mainarde territory (in the Molise region), and is surrounded by an external protected area of 60 000ha/150 000 acres. Two-thirds of the park is made up of forests (mainly beech, maple, oak and black pine) and it offers the last refuge for animals that once lived all over the Apennine range: brown bears, Apennine wolves, Abruzzi chamois, wild cats, otters, martens and royal eagles. **Pescasseroli***, situated in a small valley whose borders are covered with beech and pine forests, is the principal town in the Sangro valley and headquarters of the park.

Tours

GRAN SASSO★★ ①

From L'Aquila to Castelli

160km/99mi – allow 1/2 day, excluding tour of L'Aquila and surrounding area.

This is the highest massif in the Abruzzi and its main peak is **Corno Grande** (alt 2 912m/9 560ft). On the northern side, spines with many gullies slope away gently, while on the southern face Gran Sasso drops abruptly to the great glacial plateaux edged by deep valleys. The lush pastures and tree-covered slopes to the north contrast with the desolate and grandiose expanses to the south.

L'Aquila★ *See L'AQUILA*

Campo Imperatore★★

Access by cable car, 8.30am-5pm, Aug 8.30am-6pm. Sat and public holidays €11.50 return ticket (roundtrip), Mon-Fri €9.50 return ticket (round trip). ☎ 0862 60 61 43 or 0862 40 00 07. Access also by car from Fonte Cerreto taking S 17 (closed Dec-Apr).

The road passes through a splendid mountainous landscape grazed by large flocks of sheep and hordes of wild horses. It was from here that Mussolini escaped on 12 September 1943, in a daring raid by German airmen whose plane landed and took off near the hotel in which the Duce had been interned.

Return to Fonte Cerreto, follow directions for the Valico delle Capannelle road (closed Dec-Apr) and then take the S 80 in the direction of Montorio al Vomano.

The road then skirts the lower slopes of the Gran Sasso, as it follows the long green valley, **Valle del Vomano★★**, before entering the magnificent gorges which have striking stratified rock walls.

On leaving Montorio, take the S 491 to the right, the road to Isola del Gran Sasso. At Isola del Gran Sasso follow directions for Castelli.

Castelli★

This town, which stands on a wooded promontory at the foot of Monte Camicia, has been famous since the 13C for its ceramics of which the 17C **ceiling*** in the **church of San Donato** is a fine example. Just outside the town, the ex-Franciscan convent (17C) houses the **Museo delle Ceramiche**, which relates the history of Castelli ceramic production from the 15C to the 19C through the display of works of its leading exponents. (&) *Open daily, Jul-Sep 10am-1pm and 3-7pm, Oct-Mar 10am-1pm, Apr-Jun 9am-1pm, 20 Dec-11 Jan 10am-1pm and 3-6pm. €2.58.* ☎ 0861 97 93 98.

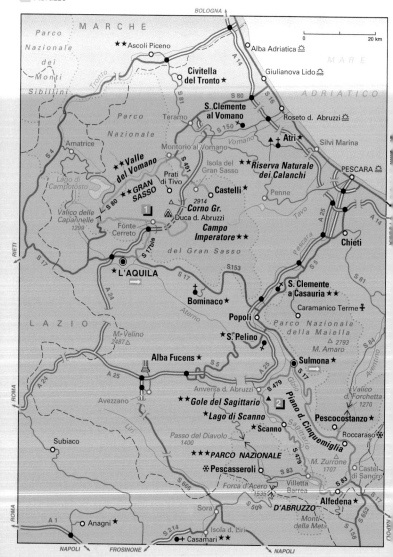

GREAT PLATEAUX ②

Round trip leaving from Sulmona

140km/87mi – allow at least 1 day excluding tour of Sulmona.

Sulmona★ *See SULMONA*

Piano delle Cinquemiglia

Beyond, the road sometimes runs along a corniche which affords good views of the Sulmona valley, and eventually reaches the **Piano delle Cinquemiglia**, largest of the Great Plateaux situated between Sulmona and Castel di Sangro. With an average altitude of more than 1 200m/3 900ft, the plateau, 5 Roman miles long (8km/5mi), was once the obligatory route for stage-coaches journeying to Naples and was much feared for its harsh winter climate and highway robbers.

Near the village of Rivisondoli, take S 84 to the left.

Pescocostanzo★

This attractive village with its paved streets and old houses is a flourishing craft centre specialising in wrought-iron work, copper, gold and woodwork as well as lace-making.

The **collegiate church of Santa Maria del Coll**, although built to a Renaissance plan, has several Romanesque features and Baroque additions (organ loft, ceiling and grille of the north aisle). *Open 8.30-11.45am and 5-6pm, Sun and public holidays 8.30-10am. Donations welcome. For information, contact Fr Angelo di Ianni* ☎ *0864 64 14 30.*

Alfedena★

The houses of this small town are grouped about the ruined castle. Paths lead northwards to the ancient city of Alfedena with its cyclopean walls and necropolis.

Scanno★

From its high mountain site, Scanno overlooks the lovely Lake Scanno (Lago di Scanno★) formed by a landslide which blocked the bed of the river Sagittario. The steep and narrow streets of this attractive holiday resort are lined with old houses and churches.

Continuing towards Anversa degli Abruzzi, the road hollowed out of the rock skirts the series of deep, wild gorges (Gole del Sagittario★★) which afford 10km/6mi of spectacularly wild and majestic nature.

Worth a visit

Alba Fucens

50km/30mi south of L'Aquila. Excavations: Open 9am-1hr before sunset. Donations welcome. For information, contact Sig. Di Mattia several days in advance of your visit. ☎ 0863 23 561.

These are the **excavations** of a Roman colony founded in 303 BC. Amid the foundations (of Italic origin) are the remains of a basilica, the forum, baths, the covered market complete with paved streets, wells, latrines and an **amphitheatre**. Above the ruins rises the **church of San Pietro★**, erected in the 12C on the remains of a temple of Apollo of the 3C BC. The **interior** houses two notable examples of Cosmati work, unusual in Romanesque Abruzzi buildings: the **ambo★★** and the stunning **iconostasis★★** of the 13C.

Atri

40km/24mi northwest of Chieti. The ancient settlement of *Hatria-Picena*, founded by an Italic people and later becoming a Roman colony, has a beautiful hillside setting and overlooks the Adriatic sea. The historic centre of the city has splendid medieval, Renaissance and Baroque buildings as well as scenic vistas.

Cathedral★ – *Open Jun-Sep 10am-noon and 4-8pm, the rest of the year 10am-noon and 3-5pm. Closed Wed (except public holidays). €2.58* ☎ *085 87 98 140.*

Built in the 13C-14C on the foundations of a Roman edifice, the cathedral is a good example of the transitional Romanesque-Gothic style, with a series of sculpted **doorways★** which became a model on which later work in the Abruzzi region was based. The lower part of the Romanesque campanile is square but becomes polygonal in its upper part which is of Lombard design. The **interior** has tall Gothic arches and, in the apse, **frescoes★★** by the Abruzzi artist, **Andrea de Litio** (1450-73). These depict scenes from the life of Joachim and Mary and fuse Gothic formal opulence with the solid geometry and realism of the Tuscans. Under the presbytery are remains of Roman baths and 3C AD mosaic floors.

The adjoining cloisters lead to the Roman cistern and the **Chapter Museum** with its fine collection of ceramics from the Abruzzi region.

In Piazza Duomo traces of the ancient Roman city are still visible.

Bominaco

30km/18mi southeast of L'Aquila. Churches: Guided tours only. Apply in advance to Sig. Cassiani. Donations welcome. ☎ *0862 93 604; www.webabruzzo.it/bominaco*

Two Romanesque churches stand about 500m/1 640ft above the hamlet of Bominaco, and are all that remain of a Benedictine monastery which was destroyed in the 15C. The **church of San Pellegrino★** is a 13C oratory decorated with contemporary **frescoes★**, portraying in a rather naive but detailed way the Life of Christ and St Pellegrino. Two elegant 10C plutei demarcate the chancel whose central wall is decorated with the delightful *Calendario bominacense,* depicting courtly scenes which are influenced by the French tradition. The **church of Santa Maria Assunta★** (11C and 12C), with its beautifully ornamented apses, is one of the most significant examples of Romanesque architecture in Abruzzi. The elegantly simple interior, with its distinctly Benedictine imprint, has a graceful Romanesque colonnade which makes skilful use of light and volume. Note the striking 12C **ambo★**.

Chieti

Chieti is built on the summit of a hill planted with olive trees and enclosed by imposing mountains. Due to its panoramic position it is known as "Abruzzi's balcony". **Corso Marrucino**, bordered by elegant arcades, is the town's principal street.

Museo Archeologico Nazionale d'Abruzzo★★ – ♿ *Open 8am-8pm. €4* ☎ *0871 33 16 68; www.muvi.org/musarc*

The archaeological museum is housed in the neo-Classical town hall (**Villa Comunale**) set in lovely **gardens★**, and possesses the most important collection of artefacts excavated in the Abruzzi region. The ground floor has displays from

Roman Abruzzi. Statues and portraits (note the *Seated Hercules* discovered at Alba Fucens) relate local history and customs. An interesting coin display, the collection formed by the Sulmonese **Giovanni Pansa** (ex-votos, domestic objects and bronze figures such as the *Venafro Hercules*) and the stunning bone **bier★** (1C BC-1C AD) complete the section. The first floor is dedicated to funerary cults of pre-Roman Abruzzi with displays of burial accoutrements from the most important necropoleis in Abruzzi (10C-6C BC). The famous *Warrior of Capestrano★★* (6C BC) has come to symbolise the Abruzzi region and is the most significant artefact of Picenum civilisation. Both disturbing and magical, it was used to protect royal tombs as can be seen in the inscription on the right pilaster: "Me, beautiful image, made by Aninis for King Nevio Pompuledonio".

Roman remains – Three 1C AD small **temples** *(tempietti)* were discovered in 1935 near Corso Marrucino. Nearby there are remains of a **theatre** (1C AD) which was able to house 5 000 spectators. The **baths** (1C AD) are in the eastern part of the town, outside the ancient city centre. Powered by a nine-chamber cistern dug out of the hill, the baths were heated by series of double-walls and interconnecting furnaces.

Civitella del Tronto★ See ASCOLI PICENO

Riserva Naturale dei Calanchi★★

2km/1.2mi northwest of Atri on SS 353. Calanchi, known locally as *scrimoini* (streaks) are the result of the natural phenomenon that occurred in the Tertiary Era when a plateau was eroded over the ages by water. Comparable to scenes from Dante's *Inferno* this landscape is characterised by precipices descending for hundreds of metres, sparse vegetation and white sediment which gives it an almost lunar appearance.

Abbazia di San Clemente a Casauria★★

30km/18mi southwest of Chieti on SS 5. Open from dawn to dusk. Guided tours available. Book several days in advance. ☎ 085 88 85 828; www.torredepasseri.com

This imposing abbey was founded in 871 for Emperor Ludovic II. After devastating Saracen attacks it was restored in the 12C by Cistercian monks who rebuilt the church in a style that was a crossover between Romanesque and Gothic. Note the façade with its portico consisting of three arches supported by fine capitals: the principal doorway is embellished by an exceptional sculptural decoration and a bronze door, dated 1191, whose borders depict the castles belonging to the abbey. The **interior** has the atmosphere of mystic sobriety so beloved by St Bernard and the Cistercians. Note the monumental **paschal candelabrum★** and the splendid **pulpit★★★** (12C); these are two of the finest examples of the Romanesque style in Abruzzi. The high altar consists of an early Christian sarcophagus dating from the 5C surmounted by a finely sculpted Romanesque **ciborium★★★**. The 9C crypt, with its cross vaulting supported by ancient columns, is one of the few remains of the original abbey.

Chiesa di San Clemente al Vomano

15km/9mi northwest of Atri. Currently closed for restoration. ☎ 085 89 81 28.

This church was founded in the 9C although it has undergone reconstruction several times since then. The fine classically inspired door (12C) gives access to the strikingly simple interior whose **ciborium★** (12C) stands out above all else. This ritual object is richly decorated with elegant fretwork and animal and vegetable motifs. The altarpiece underneath is embellished with Oriental patterns and inlaid terracotta. Parts of the original edifice can be seen through glass panes on the floor.

Abbazia di San Giovanni in Venere

35km/21mi southeast of Pescara on S 16. Open Mon-Fri 7.30am-1pm and 2-5pm, Sat 7.30-11am and 1.30-4pm, Sun and public holidays 9.15-11am and 1.30-4pm. No charge. ☎ 0872 60 132.

This abbey, founded in the 8C on the site of a temple dedicated to Venus and remodelled in the 13C, is situated in a panoramic **setting★** on the Adriatic Sea. On the façade note the 13C **Portale della Luna★** (Moon Doorway) adorned with low reliefs depicting sacred and profane subject matter. The austere Cistercian interior has a nave and two aisles with a raised chancel; the crypt rests on bare Roman columns and has 12C-15C frescoes.

Anagni★

Anagni is a small medieval town and the birthplace of several popes, including the infamous Boniface VIII (1235-1303). In 1303, after years of conflict, the French king, Philip the Fair, who had been excommunicated by the pope, sent a delegation to Anagni to assess its administration and to evaluate accusations of heresy and corruption. Boniface VIII was ignobly humiliated and this is what gave birth to the legend of the insult to the pope which became known as the "Slap (or Outrage) of Anagni".

Location

Population 20 144 – Michelin map 430 Q 21 – Lazio. Situated on a rocky spur which overlooks the Sacco Valley. Anagni is not far from the A 1, 30km/19mi from Frosinone. 🚻 *Piazza Innocenzo III Papa,* ☎ *0775 72 78 52.*

Worth a Visit

Cathedral★★

Open 9am-1pm and 4-7pm (winter 6pm). Crypt and the Museo del Tesoro (guided tours only), Museo Lapidario: €2.58 (for each museum); €6.71 inclusive ticket for all three museums. ☎ *0775 72 83 74.*

The town's most important building stands on the site of the former acropolis. This Romanesque cathedral was built in the 11C and 12C and remodelled in the 13C with Gothic additions. Walk round the outside to admire the three Romanesque apses with Lombard mouldings and arcades, the 14C statue of Boniface VIII over the loggia on the north side and the detached massive Romanesque campanile. The interior comprises a nave and two aisles; the 13C **paving★** was the work of the Cosmati. The high altar is surmounted by a Romanesque ciborium or canopy. The **paschal candelabrum** with a spiral column is adorned with multicoloured encrustations; it rests on two sphinxes and is crowned by an infant holding a cup. The work, like the nearby **episcopal throne**, is by Pietro Vassaleto and bears strong similarities with the style of the Cosmati. The **crypt★★★** with its beautiful pavement by the Cosmati also has magnificent 13C **frescoes** depicting the story of the Old Testament, scenes from the lives of the saints and men of science such as Galen and Hippocrates. The **treasury** contains some fine liturgical items, notably Boniface VIII's cope of embroidered red silk.

Medieval Quarter★

This quarter consists almost entirely of 13C buildings and is particularly evocative. The façade of **Boniface VIII's Palace** has two pierced galleries one above the other. One has wide round-headed arches while the other consists of attractive twinned windows with small columns. In Piazza Cavour is the 12C-13C **Palazzo Comunale** with a great **vault★** at ground level. The rear façade is in the Gothic style.

Excursions

Abbazia di Casamari★★

35km/22mi southeast of Anagni on S 6 and S 214. Guided tours only (except Sun morning). Open 9am-noon and 3-6pm. Donations welcome. ☎ *0775 28 23 71, 0775 28 28 00.*

The abbey occupies a lonely site which was originally a Benedictine foundation. It was consecrated in 1217 by Pope Honorius III, and later taken over by the Cistercians who rebuilt the abbey, modelling it on the abbey at Fossanova *(see TERRACINA)*, and in accordance with the rules of austerity and self-sufficiency laid down by St Bernard, the founder of the Cistercian Order.

This is a lovely example of early Italian Gothic architecture. Above the entrance porch of the abbey church is a gallery of twinned openings, which served as the abbots' lodging during the Renaissance. The simplicity of the façade is typically Burgundian with a round-headed doorway, the rose window, and rising above all the typically Cistercian transept tower.

The interior is spacious, austere and solemn. Built to a Latin cruciform plan, it has a nave and two aisles separated by massive cruciform piers with engaged columns supporting the lofty pointed vaulting. The later canopy seems out of place in the shallow chancel. The apse and arms of the transept are lit by windows with a wheel window above.

On the south side of the church are the cloisters with their twin columns, a well and a lovely flower garden. On the east side, in its traditional position, is the remarkable chapter house with delicate ribbed, pointed vaulting supported by clustered columns.

Alatri★

25km/15.5mi northwest of Casamari on S 214 and S 155. This important city, which was built in the 6C BC, retains several of its cyclopean walls (4C BC). The **acropolis★** which can be reached on foot from the grandiose Porta di Città is laid out on a trapezoidal plan and is one of the best preserved examples in Italy. It affords a very fine **view★★** of Alatri and the Frosinone Valley.

A maze of steep stairways and alleyways is lined with Gothic houses. The **Palazzo Gottifredi** *(Largo Luigi di Persiis)* is 13C and the church of **Santa Maria Maggiore★** in the transitional Romanesque-Gothic style has a façade with three porches. Inside there is interesting 12C-15C **carved woodwork★**. On the by-pass is the 13C church of San Silvestro which is built using the dry-stone technique and contains frescoes dating from the 13C to the 16C.

Subiaco

37km/23mi northwest of Alatri on S 155 and S 411 (scenic route). St Benedict, founder of the Benedictine Order, and his twin sister Scolastica retired to this spot at the end of the 5C and built 12 little monasteries before moving to Monte Cassino.

Access to the monasteries of Santa Scolastica and San Benedetto is 3km/2mi before Subiaco, shortly after the Aniene Bridge.

Monastero di Santa Scolastica – *Open 9.30am-12.30pm and 3.30-6.30pm, Sun and public holidays, 9-10am, 11.15am-12.30pm and 3.30-6.30pm. Guided tours only. Donations welcome.* ☎ 0774 85 525; www.benedettini-subiaco.org
Standing on a fine site overlooking the Aniene Gorges, the monastery has preserved a majestic 11C campanile, its church which was remodelled in the 18C, and three cloisters. The third, the work of the Cosmati, is admirable in its simplicity.

Monastero di San Benedetto★ – *Open 8.30am-12.30pm and 3-6.30pm. Book in advance. Donations welcome.* ☎ 0774 85 039.
This monastery, dedicated to St Benedict, stands above the previous one, clinging to the rock face in a wild site, overhanging the gorge. The buildings date from the 13C and 14C.

The church has two storeys. The **upper church** has walls painted with frescoes of the 14C Sienese school and the 15C Umbrian school. The **lower church**, itself with two storeys, is covered with frescoes by Magister Consolus, an artist of the 13C Roman school.

Visitors are admitted to the Sacred Cave (Sacro Speco) where St Benedict lived a hermit's existence for three years. A spiral staircase then leads up to a chapel which contains the earliest portrait of St Francis (without Stigmata or halo), painted to commemorate the saint's visit to the sanctuary. The Holy Staircase (Scala Santa) leads down to the Chapel of the Virgin (frescoes by the Sienese school) and the Shepherd's Cave. From there the visitor can enter the rose garden where St Benedict threw himself into brambles to resist temptation.

Ancona★

Ancona is a busy port and the main embarkation point for Croatia (Zara, Split and Dubrovnik) and Greece (Corfu, Igoumenitsa, Patras and Cephallonia). The town takes its name from the shape of the rocky promontory on which it is situated, forming as it does an acute angle (Greek *ankon* – elbow). Often ignored by tourists in a hurry to get to the port, Ancona offers a wealth of attractions, its historic centre packed with churches and museums.

Location

Population 98 329 – Michelin map 430 L 22 Town plan in the Michelin Atlas Italy Marches Ancona lies on A 14. South of the city is the splendid Riviera del Conero, one of the most beautiful and spectacular stretches of coastline on the Adriatic. 🏢 *(Jul-Aug) Stazione Marittima, ☎ 071 20 11 83.*
Surrounding area: see LORETO.

Worth a Visit

Duomo★

During the summer open daily 8am-noon and 3-7pm, rest of the year 8am-noon and 3-6pm. For information, contact the Curia Arcivescovile – Piazza Duomo 9. ☎ 071 20 03 91
The cathedral was dedicated to St Cyriacus, 4C martyr and patron saint of Ancona. The Romanesque building combines Byzantine (the Greek cross plan) and Lombard (mouldings and arcades on the outside walls) architectural features. The façade is preceded by a majestic Gothic **porch** in pink stone supported by two

Directory

WHERE TO EAT

• Moderate

La Moretta – *Piazza Plebiscito 52 –*
☎ 071 20 23 17 – Closed Sun, 1-10 Jan,
13-18 Aug – €23/39 + 10% service charge.
Run by the same family since 1897. Serves
traditional, local cooking – both meat and
fish dishes. Pleasant rustic-style interior, but
for atmosphere (lunchtime and evening) try
and get a table outside – the terrace looks
out on to the square and the church of San
Domenico.

WHERE TO STAY

• Moderate

Hotel City – *Via Matteotti 112/114 –*
☎ 071 20 70 949 – Fax 071 20 70 372 –
Closed 24-26 Dec – 🅿 ⏷ – 39 rm
€54.23/87.80. ⏷ A good solution for those
travelling by car and looking for accommodation in the centre of town. Rooms are
on the small side, but pleasant enough.
Furnishings are modern and functional. In
summer breakfast is served on the terrace.

lions. The interior is articulated by monolithic marble columns with Romanesque-
Byzantine **capitals**. Under the dome, note the clever transition from the square
base to the 12-sided drum supporting the dome. The tomb (1509) of Cardinal
Giannelli in the chancel is the work of the Dalmatian sculptor Giovanni da Traù.

Museo Archeologico Nazionale delle Marche

At the southern end of Piazza del Senato. (♿) *Open daily 8.30am-7.30pm. Closed Mon,*
1 Jan, 1 May, 25 Dec. €4. ☎ 071 20 26 02; www.regione.marche.it
The museum, installed in the Palazzo Ferretti, has interesting prehistoric and
archaeological collections on view. Particularly fine group of large **Roman bronzes
from Cartoceto**.

Chiesa di San Francesco delle Scale

This 15C church has a splendid Venetian Gothic doorway by the Dalmatian Giorgio
Orsini.

Galleria Comunale Podesti

Via Pizzecolli. Open daily 9am-7pm, Mon 9am-1pm, Sat 8.30am-6.30pm, Sun 3-7pm.
Closed public holidays and 4 May. €4. ☎ 071 22 25 045; www.comune.ancona.it
The public gallery displays works by Crivelli, Titian, Lorenzo Lotto, C Maratta and
Guercino. The gallery of modern art has canvases by Luigi Bartolini, Massimo
Campigli, Bruno Cassinari and Tamburini.
At the far end of the street, turn right towards the port.

Chiesa di Santa Maria della Piazza★

Open summer and public holidays, daily 7.30am-7.30pm, otherwise Mon-Sat 7.30am-
5.30pm, Sun 7.30am-7.30pm. For information, contact the Curia Arcivescovile – Piazza
Duomo 9. ☎ 071 20 03 91.
This small 10C Romanesque church has a charming façade (1210) adorned with
amusing popular figures. It was built over the site of two earlier (5C and 6C)
churches which retain fragments of mosaic pavements.

Loggia dei Mercanti★

This 15C hall for merchants' meetings has a Venetian Gothic façade which was the
work of Giorgio Orsini.

Arco di Traiano

The arch was erected in honour of the Emperor Trajan who built the port in AD 115.

Excursions

Jesi

30km/18mi southwest of Ancona. The ancient Roman settlement of *Aesis* became a
prosperous free commune in the 12C favoured by Frederick II of Hohenstaufen
who was born in Jesi in 1194. The city subsequently became part of the Papal states
and remained so until the unification of Italy. From its past Jesi retains an urban
nucleus, mainly medieval and Renaissance, surrounded by splendid **city walls★★**
(13C-16C) interspaced with gates and towers. The municipal theatre (18C) is dedicated to the celebrated composer of Jesi, Giovan Battista Pergolese. **Corso
Matteotti**, the main artery of the city, is bordered by fine palaces and churches.
Pinacoteca comunale★ – ♿ *Open mid-Jun to mid-Sep, 10am-1pm and 5-11pm, rest of*
the year 10am-1pm and 4-7pm, Sun and public holidays 10am-1pm and 5-8pm. Closed
Mon €2.07. ☎ 0731 53 83 42.
The municipal picture gallery is housed in Palazzo Pianetti. On the first floor there
is an admirable Rococo **gallery★** with an abundance of symbols and allegories. The
collection includes a considerable body of work by the Venetian artist **Lorenzo
Lotto** (*see LORETO*). The ***Pala di Santa Lucia*** is one of this artist's masterpieces.

Palazzo della Signoria★ – This palazzo was built to designs by the Sienese architect Francesco di Giorgio Martini, a pupil of Brunelleschi. Its imposing square structure has an elegant façade adorned by a stone tabernacle.

LA RIVIERA DEL CONERO★

Portonovo★

12km/8mi southeast of Ancona. Guided tours only (for information and to make a booking contact Portonovo Srl, c/o Hotel La Fonte, Loc. Portonovo, Ancona). ☎ *071 56 307.*
Portonovo lies in a picturesque setting formed by the rocky coastline of the **Conero Massif**. A private path leads through woodland to the charming 11C **church of Santa Maria★**, built on a square plan inspired by Norman churches.
Offering **panoramic views** the road winds south for about 20 kilometres passing through some of the prettiest villages in the area including **Sirolo** and **Numana**, from where there are boat trips to some of the delightful little coves dotted along the coast.

Arezzo★★

Arezzo is surrounded by a fertile basin planted with cereal crops, fruit trees and vines. The town is renowned for being the birthplace of many an artistic genius including Guido d'Arezzo (997-c1050) the Benedictine monk and inventor of the musical scale, Petrarch the poet (1304-74), Pietro Aretino the author, also known as The Aretine (1492-1556) and **Giorgio Vasari** the painter and art historian (1511-74). But it is to Piero della Francesca that Arezzo owes its greatest artistic heritage although the artist was not born here but in Sansepolcro, 40km/24mi down the road.

Location

Population 91 729 – Michelin map 430 L 17 – See also The Green Guide Tuscany. Arezzo is 11km/7mi from the Florence-Rome motorway, 81km/49mi from Florence.
🖪 *Piazza della Repubblica 28,* ☎ *0575 37 76 78.*
Surrounding area: see SANSEPOLCRO, SIENA.

Directory

WHERE TO EAT
• *Budget*
Trattoria il Saraceno – *Via Mazzini 6/A –* ☎ *0575 27 644 – Closed Wed, 7-25 Jan, 7-28 Jul – €20/25.* A delightfully old-fashioned family-run establishment. A chance to taste some authentic specialities of the region washed down with a decent bottle of wine. Also serves a wide choice of pizzas cooked in a traditional wood-burning oven.

WHERE TO STAY
• *Moderate*
Albergo Casa Volpi – *Localita Le Pietre 2 1.5km/0.9mi southeast of Arezzo in the direction of Sansepolcro –* ☎ *0575 35 43 64 – Fax 0575 35 59 71 –*
Closed 1-15 Aug – 🅿 🖽 *– 12 rm €61.97/82.63 –* 🖾 *€7.75 – Restaurant – €18/31.* A stone's throw from the city, this charming hotel lies tucked away amid splendid parkland. It is housed in a 19C villa which has been attractively refurbished. Rustic-style finish, complete with wrought-iron beds, frescoed ceilings and exposed beams. Fine views over Arezzo from the terrace.

EVENTS AND FESTIVALS
In summer, the Piazza Grande is the setting for the **Giostra del Saracino** (Saracen's Tournament), when costumed horsemen attack an armoured dummy, the Saracen, with lances.

Special Features

Chiesa di San Francesco

Open daily, in summer Mon-Fri 9am-6.30pm, Sat 9am-5.30pm, Sun and public holidays 1-5.30pm, rest of the year Mon-Fri 9am-5.30pm, Sat 9am-5pm, Sun and public holidays 1-5pm. By appointment only, ☎ *0575 90 04 04 or 06 32 810 (Internet bookings: www.pierodellafrancesca.it). Double-check your booking (you will be given a code number to be checked against your ticket). Closed 13 Jun, 4 Oct. €4.13 + €1.03 booking fee. For further details, contact the information office.*
This is a vast church, designed for the preaching of sermons and built in the Gothic style in the 14C for the Franciscan Order. It was altered in the 17C and 18C but restoration work has now returned it to its original austerity. The Franciscan friars,

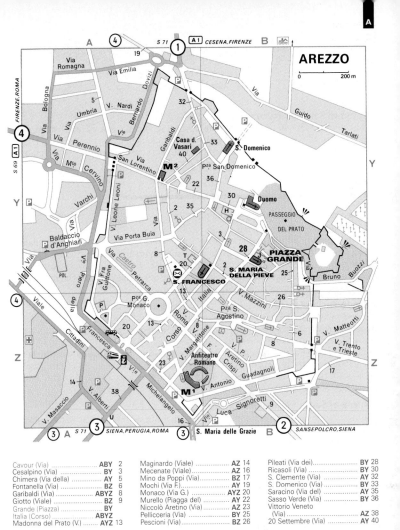

as custodians of the Holy Places, showed particular devotion to the True Cross and they commissioned Piero della Francesca to decorate the chancel of the church around this theme.

Affreschi di Piero della Francesca★★★ – The fresco cycle was executed between 1452 and 1466 and is considered to be one of the masterpieces of the Renaissance. The frescoes depict the Legend of the True Cross, a theme much revered by the Franciscans during the Middle Ages. The cycle is based on the *Legenda Aurea* (13C) a text by Jacopo da Varagine.

Walking about

Piazza Grande★

The **main square** is surrounded by medieval houses, some with crenellated towers. Also overlooking is the Romanesque galleried apse of the church of Santa Maria della Pieve.

Chiesa di Santa Maria della Pieve★ – This superb Romanesque parish church is crowned by a lofty campanile, which, owing to its numerous double bays (there are 40 of them in all), is referred to as the "Hundred Holes". Construction of the church began in the mid-12C and was completed in the 14C. In the 16C alterations were made, notably under the direction of **Giorgio Vasari**. The **façade**★★, which was inspired by the Romanesque style used in Pisa, is very ornate with three tiers of arcades supported by colonnettes.

Duomo

The cathedral was built from 1278 to 1511 but the façade is neo-Gothic. On the south side is an attractive Romanesque-Gothic portal dating from the first half of the 14C. The cathedral contains some **fine works of art★** including the fresco by Piero della Francesca depicting *Mary Magdalen*.

From Via Ricasoli turn into Via Sasso Verde.

Chiesa di San Domenico

This church, built in the Gothic style in the 13C but since restored, has an asymmetrical façade. It contains frescoes by the Duccio School, and by Spinello Aretino and his school. On the High Altar, there is an admirable *Crucifix★★* by Cimabue.

Worth a Visit

Museo d'Arte Medievale e Moderna★

Open 8.30-7.30pm. Closed 1 Jan, 1 May, 25 Dec. €4. ☎ 0575 40 90 50.
The museum of medieval and modern art is housed in the fully furnished Palazzo Bruni-Ciocchi. It contains sculptures, gold and silverware and numerous paintings dating from the Middle Ages to the 19C. The 19C is represented by some of the main *Macchiaioli* artists such as Fattori and Signorini. Look out for the outstanding collection of Renaisssance **maiolica★★** from Umbria.

Museo Archeologico

   Open 8.30am-7.30pm (last admission 7pm). Closed 1 Jan, 1 May, 25 Dec. €4, no charge during the town's National Heritage Week (Settimana dei Beni Culturali). ☎ 0575 20 882.
The archaeological museum stands adjacent to the oval **Roman amphitheatre** which dates from the 1C and 2C. It contains interesting collections of Etruscan and Roman bronze statuettes (from 6C BC to 3C AD), Greek vases (Euphronios' krater), Aretine vases, and ceramics.

Chiesa di Santa Maria delle Grazie

1km/0.6mi to the south via Viale Mecenate. In front of the church rises a graceful **portico★** by the Florentine, Benedetto da Maiano (15C). Inside is a marble **altarpiece★** by Andrea della Robbia.

Promontorio dell'**Argentario**★

This ancient promontory, now linked to the mainland by three ancient causeways formed by a build-up of sand *(tomboli)*, consists of the small limestone hill called **Monte Argentario** which rises to a height of 635m/2,083ft and is skirted by a road which affords fine views.

Location

Michelin map 430 O 15 – See also The Green Guide Tuscany. To get to the promontory, take the Via Aurelia and exit at either Albinia or Orbetello.
🅱 *Piazza della Repubblica, 1, Orbetello. ☎ 0564 86 04 47.*

Tour

TOUR OF THE PROMONTORY

Leaving from Orbetello. 43km/26mi – around 2hr.

Orbetello

Built on the central dike in the lagoon, it is situated at the end of the main access road to the peninsula (SS 440). The town was originally called *Urbs Tellus* literally the territory of the city (ie Rome), probably because it was given in AD 805 to the Abbazia delle Tre Fontane in Rome by Charlemagne. The **fortifications** are a reminder of the influence of the Sienese and, later, the Spaniards (16C-17C) who made the town the capital of a small State. The **cathedral** was built on the site of an ancient Etruscan-Roman temple.

Porto Santo Stefano ★★

This is the main town in the peninsula, and the embarkation point for trips to the island of Giglio. Its houses are built up the hillside on each side of a 17C Aragon-style fort from which there is a superb **view★** over the harbour and the Talamone Gulf.

Directory

WHERE TO EAT

• Budget

Il Moresco – *Via Panoramica 156, Cala Moresca – 58019 Porto Santo Stefano – 5.5km/3.4mi southwest of Porto Santo Stefano –* ☎ *0564 82 41 58 – Closed Tue, Jun-Sep and Wed lunchtime, Feb – €21/26.* Pleasantly situated in a quiet spot looking out to sea and the island of Giglio. A magical combination of good home cooking (fish and meat dishes) and fine views.

• Moderate

Il Cavaliere – *Strada Statale 440 39/41 – 58016 Orbetello Scalo – At the exit from the station underpass* ☎ *0564 86 43 42 – Closed Wed, 10-25 Nov –* 🖿 *– Booking recommended – €25/35.* Situated off the beaten track, away from the hordes of tourists, this restaurant is popular with the locals for its antipasti, as well as its fish-based starters and main courses. A simple, family-run restaurant (albeit a little noisy when the trains pass by).

WHERE TO STAY

• Moderate

Azienda Agraria Grazia – *Località Provincaccia 110 – 58016 Orbetello Scalo – 7km/4mi east of Orbetello, 140km/84mi along Via Aurelia in the direction of Rome –* ☎ *0564 88 11 82 – Fax 0564 88 11 82 – m.grazia.cantore@tin.it – ☎ – 3 studios €82.63/129.11* 🖿. Light, airy studios. Well equipped and comfortable, with modern-rustic style furnishings. Tucked away in an oasis of flora and fauna where deer, mouflon (wild sheep) and wild boar roam free. Suitable for horse riding and outdoor enthusiasts.

• Expensive

Antica Fattoria La Parrina – *Località Parrina – 58010 Albinia – 5km/3mi north of Orbetello Scalo, 146km/88mi from the Via Aurelia in the direction of Firenze –* ☎ *0564 86 55 86 – Fax 0564 86 26 26 – parrina@dada.it – ☎ – 16 rooms from €140 –* 🖿 *€5 – Restaurant €23/35.* Housed in a 19C villa that is now a working farm and guesthouse. Elegantly decorated with antique furniture. Breakfast and dinner served on the terrace in summer. A very stylish, rural retreat. Produces its own cheeses, wines and olive oil.

TAKING A BREAK

Bar Bagianni – *Piazza Garibaldi 8 – 58015 Orbetello –* ☎ *0564 86 81 34 – Mon-Sat 7am-1am, Sun 7am-1pm and 3pm-1am.* Ice cream bar, cocktail bar, internet café and tea room – all rolled into one establishment. Housed in an attractive building overlooking the main square. Popular with the locals from early in the morning until late into the night.

Baretto – *Lungomare Andrea Doria 41 – 58018 Porto Ercole –* ☎ *0564 83 26 54 – Open daily Jul-Aug 8am-3am; rest of the year, closed Wed; closed for a month in winter.* Of all the bars overlooking the harbour, the Baretto boasts the best location – right in the centre. Very popular with the locals (mainly young clientele) on account of its warm welcome and delicious cocktails made with fresh fruit.

Head north out of Porto Santo Stefano, taking the scenic route.

As the road ascends there is a succession of fine **views**★★ over the rocky creeks along the southwest coast, the island of Rossa (consisting of reddish rocks) and *(to the left)* you can see the hillside terraces and the Argentario promontory.

Porto Ercole⚬⚬

This seaside resort has a tiny old urban district beyond a medieval gateway with hoardings and machicolations that is linked to the fortress above the town by two parallel crenelated walls. From Piazza Santa Barbara lined by the arcading of the former Governor's Palace (Palazzo del Governatore, 16C), there are fine views.

Excursion

Rovine di Cosa★

11km/7mi south of Orbetello, at the far end of the southernmost bar, Tombolo di Feniglia. Open May-Sep 9am-7pm, rest of the year 9am-5pm. There is no charge for the archaeological site. Museum: €2. ☎ *0564 88 14 21.*

The ruins of Cosa, a Roman colony which flourished from the 3C BC to the 4C AD, have been found near the Via Aurelia.

The excavations have unearthed two separate parts of the settlement. On the brow of the promontory can be found the acropolis and further north is the main body of the colony.

Ascoli Piceno★★

A city of travertine and a hundred towers which is known as *piccola Siena* (little Siena) for the harmony and elegance of its medieval and Renaissance buildings, Ascoli is situated in a valley where the Tronto and Castellano rivers meet.

Location
Population 51 827– Michelin map 430 N 22 – Marches. Ascoli Piceno is on the Via Salaria, about 30km/18mi from the Adriatic. ❒ *Piazza del Popolo 17,* ☎ *0736 25 30 45.*

Walking about

Piazza del Popolo★★
The main square, elongated and well proportioned, is the public drawing room of the city. Paved with large flagstones, it is surrounded by imposing Gothic and Renaissance buildings and sheltered by elegant arcades.
The **Palazzo dei Capitani del Popolo★**, (People's Captains' Palace) erected in the 13C, owes its current appearance to additions made in the 16C by Cola dell'Amatrice, among others, who also designed the austere rear façade. Inside there is an attractive arcaded courtyard (16C).
The 13C-16C **church of San Francesco★** has several Lombard features. On the south side there is a fine 16C portal above which stands a monument to Julius II and the **Loggia dei Mercanti★** (Merchants' Loggia), a graceful early-16C building showing Tuscan influence, particularly in the capitals. On the left-hand side there are cloisters: the principal **Chiostro Maggiore**, 16C-17C, which shelters a colourful fruit and vegetable market, and the more intimate 14C **Chiostro minore** *(access from Via Ceci).* There is an elegant structure of double belltowers in the apse.

> ### HISTORICAL NOTES
> Several traces of the thriving Roman town of *Asculum* remain, although these are often incorporated into structures of a later date. In the Middle Ages and the Renaissance the city was the setting for bitter conflicts between opposing factions; in spite of this the town flourished and there was a proliferation in the construction of civic and religious buildings. The economic and artistic vigour of the town also attracted important figures from other parts of Italy. Among these it is worth noting the Venetian painter **Carlo Crivelli** (1430-94) who elected to settle in Ascoli permanently. Initially influenced by Mantegna and Bellini, Crivelli developed a highly original style which fused the solidity of Renaissance geometry with late Gothic decorative opulence and had a profound effect on local painters as well as initiating a flourishing of the arts in the entire region.

Corso Mazzini★
This is the grand street of the city and is lined with old palaces of varying epochs embellished by Latin and Italian inscriptions. At n° 224 the 16C **Malaspina Palace** has an original loggia with columns shaped like tree trunks. At the beginning of Via delle Torri is the Renaissance **church of Sant'Agostino** which has a fresco of Christ by Cola dell'Amatrice and a *Madonna dell'Umiltà* of the Fabriano school (14C). *For information and to make a booking contact Sig. Pulcini Renato:* ☎ *0736 25 92 88. Closed for restoration at time of publication.*

Directory

Via delle Torri

This street owes its name to the many towers that once stood here; of these two 12C **twin towers** remain. At the end of the street stands the 14C **church of San Pietro Martire**.

S.S. Vincenzo e Anastasio★

To arrange a visit contact Sig. Pulcini Renato: ☎ *0736 25 22 05.* This church of early Christian origin is a fine example of Romanesque architecture. Its 14C **façade★** is divided into 64 sections which were originally covered in frescoes. The strikingly simple interior houses a crypt of the 6C with remains of 14C frescoes.

Ponte romano di Solestà★

For information and bookings contact Sig. Pulcini Renato: ☎ *0736 29 82 04.* Heralded by a 14C gateway, this bridge is a bold construction of the Augustan Age supported by only one arch of 25m/82ft in height. From the far end there is an attractive view of the 16C public wash-tub (*lavatoio pubblico*).

Via dei Soderini

This street was once the main artery of the medieval city; this can be seen in its numerous mansions, feudal towers and picturesque side streets. The most interesting building is the **Palazzetto Longobardo** (11C-12C), a Lombard mansion which is flanked by the elegant Ercolani Tower (Torre Ercolani), more than 40m/130ft high. A typical Ascoli architrave stands above its doorway.

Worth a Visit

Duomo

Open 8am-12.30pm and 4-7.30pm. Donations welcome. ☎ *0736 25 97 74.*
The grandiose Renaissance façade of this 12C cathedral was the work of Cola dell'Amatrice. On the north side stands the **Porta della Musa**, a fine late Renaissance construction. Inside, in the Cappella del Sacramento (Eucharist Chapel – *south aisle*) there is a superb **polyptych★** by **Carlo Crivelli** in which the late Gothic grace of the *Madonna and Child* contrasts with the dramatic *Pietà* which derives from Mantegna.
To the left of the Duomo stands the 11C **Baptistery★**, a fine square structure crowned by an octagonal lantern with graceful trefoil openings. The entrance is surmounted by a triangular pediment. The draining channels carved into the stonework above the portal are typical of the local architecture.

Pinacoteca★

& *Open daily 9am-1pm and 3-7pm. Closed Mon afternoons winter and 1 Jan, 25 Dec* €3.10. ☎ *0736 29 82 13.*
The picture gallery is housed on the main floor of the town hall (Palazzo Comunale) and has a notable collection of figurative arts from the 16C-19C (Guido Reni, Titian, Luca Giordano, Carlo Maratta). Most notable among the paintings of the Marches region are works by **Carlo Crivelli**, **Cola dell'Amatrice** and, of Crivelli's circle, **Pietro Alamanno**. A precious, delicately worked 13C English relic **(piviale★)**, the cope donated in 1288 by Nicholas IV to the cathedral chapter, is a prized exhibit.
Opposite the town hall, in Palazzo Panichi, the **Museo Archeologico** displays ancient works of the Piceno age (9-6C BC) and Roman mosaics from the 1C AD. & *Open 8.30am-7.30pm. Closed 1 Jan, 1 May, 25 Dec.* €2.06. ☎ *0736 25 35 62.*
On the nearby Via Bonaparte, at n° 24, **Palazzo Bonaparte** is one of the best examples of domestic Renaissance architecture.

Excursion

Civitella del Tronto★

24km/15mi southeast. This charming village perched on a travertine mountain 645m/2 116ft above sea level enjoys a splendid **setting★★**. Its picturesque winding streets are lined with fine religious and civic architecture of the 16C-17C. The imposing structure of the 16C **Fortress★**, which dominates the entire village, was the last Bourbon stronghold to surrender to the Sardinian-Piedmontese armies in 1861. (&) *Open daily Mar-Sep 10am-7.30pm, Sat Sun and public holidays and Aug 10-24 10am-8pm, rest of year 10am-1pm and 2.30-5.30pm. Last entry 30min before closing.* €3.10. *You are advised to take some warm clothing because of the altitude.* ☎ *0861 91 588; www.fortezzacivitella.it*

Assisi★★★

The walled city of Assisi is closely associated with **St Francis**, as related in the numerous accounts of his life and work. Under the influence of the Franciscan Order of Minors founded by St Francis, a new, essentially religious, artistic movement developed which marked a turning-point in Italian art. The son of a rich Assisi draper, Francis preached poverty, humility and mysticism, and his teachings gave rise to a new artistic vision which found its expression in the purity and elegance of Gothic art.

During the 13C the stark, austere churches which were designed for preaching were embellished with a new splendour to reflect the tender and profound love of St Francis for nature and its creatures, as described in the tales of St Bonaventure. From the end of the 14C famous masters came from Rome and Venice to Assisi to work on the Basilica of St Francis. These artists abandoned the rigid traditions of Byzantine art in favour of a more dramatic art imbued with a spiritual atmosphere. Cimabue and later Giotto were its most powerful exponents.

Location

Population 25 464 – Michelin map 430 M 19 – Umbria. Assisi, prettily spread across the slopes of Monte Subasio, lies between Perugia and Foligno, on S 75.

🛈 *Piazza del Comune 12,* ☎ *075 81 25 34.*
Surrounding area: see PERUGIA.

Directory

WHERE TO EAT

• *Budget*

Da Erminio – *Via Montecavallo 19* – ☎ *075 81 25 06 – Closed Thu, 15 Jan-3 Mar, 1-15 Jul* – €15/31. Situated in a quiet, residential area beyond San Rufino, this small restaurant is well worth the climb! Serves traditional Umbrian dishes including strangozzi al tartufo (pasta dish with truffles). The open fire is an added attraction.

Da Cecco – *Piazza San Pietro 8* – ☎ *075 81 24 37 – Closed Wed, 10 Dec-15 Mar* – €20/28. A smart restaurant with a pleasant, friendly ambience. The cuisine is traditional but it has a distinctive personal touch. Simple decor with rustic and medieval elements.

WHERE TO STAY

• *Budget*

Casa di Santa Brigida – *Via Moiano 1* – ☎ *075 81 26 93 – Fax 075 81 32 16* – ⌷ 🅿 – *18 rm* €30.99/56.81 ⌷. With its flower-filled garden and shady trees this is a haven of peace and quiet. The interior is equally relaxing with rooms redolent of monastic calm. The half-board and full-board rates represent value for money. Light meals served, traditional cooking.

Hotel Berti – *Piazza San Pietro 24* – ☎ *075 81 34 66 – Fax 075 81 68 70* – *Closed 11 Jan-Feb – 10 rm* €38.73/61.97 – ⌷. €4.65. Former stable block used as a hostel by pilgrims heading for the Eremo delle Carceri. Small, family-run hotel with clean, pleasant rooms. Warm welcome. A stone's throw from the Da Cecco restaurant which is run by the same family.

Special Features

Basilica di San Francesco★★★

⚅ *Open daily 9.30am-noon and 2.30-6pm. Closed Sun.* ☎ *075 81 90 01.*
From the green esplanade or from the road that winds up to Assisi from the flat countryside, the basilica is an imposing and striking vision at all hours of the day. The simple façade has a Cosmati work *(see p 88)* rose window.

The group of buildings consists of two superimposed churches, resting on a series of immense arches. The whole building, erected after the death of St Francis to the plans of Brother Elias, was consecrated in 1253. It was this monk who influenced the Franciscans to use more splendour and decoration.

Basilica inferiore – Beyond the long narthex, the walls of the dark, sombre four-bay nave of the lower church are covered with 13C and 14C **frescoes★★★**. From the nave, enter the first chapel on the left with **frescoes★★** by Simone Martini (c 1284-1344) illustrating the life of St Martin. These are remarkable for their delicate drawing, graceful composition and bright colours. Further along, above the pulpit is a fresco of the *Coronation of the Virgin* attributed to Maso, a pupil of Giotto (14C). The choir **vaulting★★** is painted with scenes symbolising the Triumph of St Francis and the virtues practised by him. They are the work of one of Giotto's pupils.

ST FRANCIS

The son of a draper, St Francis of Assisi (1182-1226) had a privileged upbringing informed by courtly ideals, a period which he describes in his spiritual *Testamento* as "when I was in sin". His conversion took place in 1206 when the Crucifix of St Damian said to him: "Francis, go and repair my house which is falling into ruins". Having literally stripped himself of his family clothes and riches, Francis founded the Order of Minors, inspired by a spirit of **brotherhood** between all God's creatures, **minority**, in the sense of service to all, and of **absolute poverty**. He went on to dedicate himself to contemplation and to serving his neighbour, whom he would greet with the words *Signore ti dia pace* ("May God give you peace"), which was erroneously diffused as *pace e bene* ("peace and good").

The simplicity of his life was transmitted to even the most humble through both the use of the Umbrian dialect in which he wrote *Cantico delle Creature* (Canticle of the Creatures), one of the first and finest works of Italian literature, and through the joy he derived in coming up with new and effective ways of finding salvation for people. The Franciscans made popular several devotional practices in the Roman Catholic church, including the representation of the Christmas Manger – *presepio* – which is still strongly associated with the spiritual life of Assisi, where Francis is venerated as the patron saint.

The north transept is decorated with **frescoes**★★ of the Passion. Those on the ceiling, attributed to pupils of Pietro Lorenzetti, are valued for their narrative design and charm of detail; those on the walls, probably by Lorenzetti himself, are striking for their dramatic expression *(Descent from the Cross)*. In the south transept is the majestic work by Cimabue, a *Madonna with Four Angels and St Francis*★★.

From the Sixtus IV cloisters make for the **treasury**★★ with its many valuable items and the **Perkins collection** of 14C to 16C paintings.

At the bottom of the steps, beneath the centre of the transept crossing, is **St Francis' Tomb** which is both spare and evocative.

Basilica superiore – This accomplished Gothic work with its tall and graceful nave, bathed in light, contrasts with the lower church. The apse and transept were decorated with frescoes (many have since been damaged) by Cimabue and his school. In the north transept Cimabue painted an intensely dramatic *Crucifixion*★★★.

Between 1296 and 1304 **Giotto** and his assistants depicted the life of St Francis in a famous cycle of **frescoes**★★★. There are 28 clearly defined scenes, each showing a greater search for realism. They mark a new dawning in the figurative traditions of Italian art, which was to reach its apogee during the Renaissance.

Walking About

Via S. Francesco★

This picturesque street is lined by medieval and Renaissance houses. At n° 13a the Pilgrims' Chapel (Oratorio dei Pellegrini) is decorated inside with 15C frescoes, notably by Matteo da Gualdo. *Open daily, 9am-noon and 3-6pm. Closed Sun* ☏ *075 81 22 67.*

Piazza del Comune★

This square occupies the site of the forum: note the **Tempio di Minerva**★ (1C BC), a temple converted into a church, and, to the left, the People's Captains' Palace (13C).

Spectacular view of Assisi from the valley

ASSISI

Duomo di San Rufino★

The cathedral was built in the 12C and its Romanesque **façade★★** is one of the finest in Umbria, with a harmonious arrangement of its openings and ornamentation.

The interior, on a basilical plan, was rebuilt in 1571. To the right at the entrance is the baptismal font used for the baptism of St Francis, St Clare and Frederick II.

Chiesa di Santa Chiara★★

From the terrace in front of the church of St Clare there is a pretty view of the Umbrian countryside.

The church was built from 1257 to 1265 and closely resembles the Gothic upper basilica of St Francis. Inside there are numerous works of art including 14C frescoes depicting the life of St Clare; these were influenced by Giotto.

The Byzantine crucifix brought here from St Damian's Monastery *(below)*, which is said to have spoken to St Francis and caused his conversion to the Christian faith, can be seen in the small church of St George, which adjoins the south aisle. The crypt enshrines the remains of St Clare.

▶▶Rocca Maggiore★★ (view★★★); S. Pietro★

Excursions

Eremo delle Carceri★★

4km/2.5mi east. Open daily, Easter-Nov 6.30am-7.15pm, rest of the year 6.30am-5.30pm. ☎ 075 81 23 01.

The hermitage stands in a beautiful site at the heart of a forest of age-old green oaks. It is said that, having been blessed by St Francis, a huge flock of birds flew out of one of the trees, symbolising the spread of the Franciscan Order throughout the world. The hermitage was founded here by St Bernardino of Siena (1380-1444). The spot derives its name from the fact that Francis and his followers liked to retire from the world here as if they had been put into prison *(carcere in Italian)* in order, according to one of his biographers, to chase out "from the soul the tiniest speck of dust left in it by contact with mankind". Narrow passageways clearly indicating the structure of the monastery (built around the outline of the rock) lead to St Francis' Cave and the old refectory with its 15C tables.

Convento di San Damiano★

2km/1mi south of the gateway, Porta Nuova. Open daily, summer 10am-12.30pm and 2-6pm; winter 10am-12.30pm and 2-4.30pm. ☎ 075 81 22 73.

St Damian's Monastery and a small adjoining church stand alone amid olive and cypress trees and are closely associated with St Francis, who received his calling here and composed his *Canticle of the Creatures*, and also with St Clare who died here in 1253. The humble and austere interior is a moving example of a 13C Franciscan monastery.

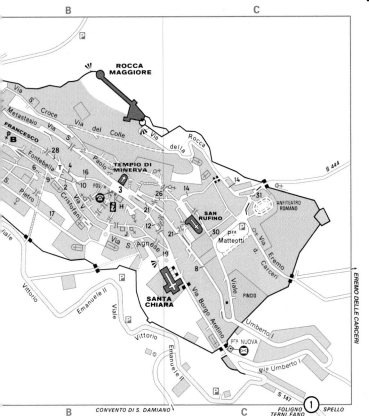

Basilica di Santa Maria degli Angeli★

5km/3mi southwest. Open daily, 6.30am-8pm, Aug also 9-11pm. ☎ *075 80 511.*
The basilica of St Mary of the Angels was built in the 16C around the **Porziuncola**, a small chapel named after the small plot (*piccola porzione* in Italian) of land on which it was built before the year AD 1000. It was in the Porziuncola that St Francis named Clare the "Bride of Christ". It contains a **fresco★** (1393) representing episodes from the history of the Franciscan Order *(above the altar)*. It was in the adjacent chapel, Cappella del Transito, that Francis died on 3 October 1226. The St Mary Major Crypt contains an enamelled terracotta **polyptych★** by Andrea della Robbia (c 1490). Near the church is the rose bush said to have lost its thorns when the saint threw himself onto it to escape temptation, and the cave in which he used to pray. In the corridor leading to the rose bush is a statue of the saint holding a nest where doves roost.

Spello★

12km/8mi southeast. A quiet, picturesque little town in which the bastions and gateways bear witness to its past as a Roman settlement. The **church of Santa Maria Maggiore** contains **frescoes★★** *(chapel on the left)* by **Pinturicchio** depicting the Annunciation, the Nativity, the Preaching in the Temple *(on the walls)* and the Sibyls *(on the vaulting)*. To each side of the high altar are frescoes by Perugino. Nearby, in the **church of Sant'Andrea**, which was built in 1025, is a painting by Pinturicchio and a crucifix attributed to Giotto. The village is also famous for its Flower Festival *(Le infiorate del Corpus Domini)* held on the Feast of Corpus Christi.

Foligno

18km/11mi to the southeast. Piazza della Repubblica is overlooked by the 14C Palazzo Trinci, built by the local overlords, and the cathedral (Duomo) with its magnificent doorway decorated with Lombard-style geometric decoration.

Palazzo Trinci – ♿ *Open daily, 10am-7pm. Closed Mon, 1 Jan, 25 Dec €2.58.* ☎ *0742 35 76 97.*
The focal point in this palazzo are the **frescoes★**, executed with an almost perfect technical grasp of perspective. The frescoes in the Loggia depict the legend of Romulus and Remus and seem almost three-dimensional. In the Studio (referred to as the "Rose room" as roses were presented to apostolic vicars such as the Trinci) there are depictions of the Trivium arts (Grammar, Rhetoric, Dialect) and the

Quadrivium arts (Arithmetic, Geometry, Music, Astronomy). Hours of the day are portrayed in relation to the ages of man and the planets. The Gothic thrones would suggest a northern attribution to these frescoes.

The frescoes and decorations along the corridor that leads to the cathedral represent great figures of Antiquity on one wall, and the seven ages of man on the other. Only the frescoes in the chapel, relating the life of Mary, are signed. They were completed by OttaViano Nelli in 1424.

Bevagna★

24km/14mi south of Assisi. Bevagna is a typical medieval town, divided up into four *guaite*, or quarters. Remains of various buildings bear witness to its Roman past, particularly from the 2C AD: ambulatory of the Roman theatre, temple and the **terme di Mevania** (thermal baths) with some fine mosaics depicting images of marine life. These are tucked away inside a doorway which is immediately on your right as you leave Piazza Garibaldi.

Piazza Silvestri – The square is typically medieval, overlooked by two churches – the late-11C church of San Michele and the late-12C church of San Silvestro (note the epigraph on the façade) – as well as the 13C **Palazzo dei Consoli**, which houses the charming **Teatro Torti**.

Bari

An agricultural and industrial centre, Bari is first and foremost a port. The Levantine Fair **(Fiera del Levante)**, held in September, is an important trade fair which was inaugurated in 1930 to encourage trade with other Mediterranean countries. Bari comprises the old town, clustered on its promontory, and the modern town with wide avenues, laid out on a grid plan in the 19C.

Location

Population 331 848 – Michelin map 431 D 32 – Puglia. The capital of Puglia, Bari overlooks the Adriatic. To get there, take either A 14 or S 16 motorway. 🄳 *Piazza Aldo Moro 32/A,* ☎ *080 52 42 244.*

Surrounding area: see Promontorio del GARGANO, PUGLIA.

Worth a Visit

Basilica di San Nicola★★

The basilica in the heart of the old town *(città vecchia)*, also known as the Nicholas "stronghold *(citadella)*", was begun in 1087 and consecrated in 1197

> **HISTORICAL NOTES**
>
> Legend has it that Bari was founded by the Illiri and then colonised by the Greeks. Between the 9C and 11C Bari was the capital of Byzantium's domain in Italy. In its role as a pilgrimage centre to St Nicholas' shrine and as a port of embarkation for the Crusades, Bari was a very prosperous city in the Middle Ages. It declined under the Sforza of Milan and Spanish rule in the 16C.

to St Nicholas, Bishop of Myra in Asia Minor, who achieved fame by resurrecting three children, whom a butcher had cut up and put in brine. St Nicholas' relics were brought home by sailors from Bari and it was decided to build a church to him. The building is one of the most remarkable examples of Romanesque architecture and it was the model for many churches built locally. The plain but powerful façade, flanked by two towers, is relieved by several twinned openings and a sculptured doorway with bulls supporting the flanking columns. On the north side there is the richly decorated 12C Lions' Doorway. Inside, the nave and two aisles with a triforium were reroofed in the 16C with a fine coffered ceiling. A large 12C ciborium (canopy) surmounts the high altar behind which is an unusual 11C **episcopal throne★** in white marble. In the north apse hangs a painting of the *Virgin and Saints* by the Venetian, Bartolomeo Vivarini, and opposite *St Jerome* by Costantino da Monopoli. The tomb of St Nicholas lies in the crypt. The marble columns are crowned by richly decorated capitals.

Cattedrale★

This 11C-12C Romanesque cathedral was added to and then altered at a later date. Inside, the nave and two aisles have oven-vaulted apses and there is a false triforium above the arches. The works of art include a pulpit made up of 11C and 12C fragments, and a baldachin rebuilt from 13C fragments.

> **WHERE TO EAT**
>
> Al Sorso Preferito *Via Vito Nicola De Nicolo 46* – ☎ *080 52 35 747* – Closed Wed, Sun evening – 🖱 – Booking recommended – €18/31. A popular restaurant and surprisingly good value. The management prides itself on the quality of its cooking and raw ingredients. Hearty, traditional cooking. Menu includes meat and fish dishes, and includes regional specialities.

In the north aisle is displayed a copy of the **Exultet** (the original is kept in the sacristy just outside the church), a precious 11C Byzantine parchment scroll in Beneventan script, typical of medieval southern Italy. The illustrations are on the reverse side so that the congregation could see them as the parchment was unrolled for the choristers.

Castello★

(&) *Open daily, 8.30am-7.30pm. Closed Mon, 1 Jan, 1 May, 25 Dec* €2.07. ☎ *080 52 86 210; www.castelli-puglia.org*
The Emperor Frederick II of Hohenstaufen built the castle in 1233 over the foundations of earlier Byzantine and Norman buildings. The irregular but four-sided courtyard and two of the original towers date from the Swabian period. The castle's defences were strengthened in the 16C.

Pinacoteca

On Lungomare Nazario Sauro beyond Piazza A. Diaz. & *Open daily, 9.30am-1pm and 4-7pm, Sun 9am-1pm. Closed Mon, public holidays.* €2.58. ☎ *080 54 12 423.*
The gallery, on the fourth floor (lift) of the Palazzo della Provincia, comprises Byzantine works of art (sculpture and paintings), a 12C-13C painted wood statue of **Christ★**, *The Martyrdom of St Peter* by Giovanni Bellini and canvases by the 17C-18C Neapolitan school.

Museo Archeologico

First floor of the university. Closed for restoration at time of going to press. ☎ *080 52 12 423.*
The archaeological museum displays Greco-Roman collections from excavations made throughout Puglia. The collections of vases and bronzes from the area are of special interest.

Excursion

Coast

The road from Bari to Barletta passes through many small but attractive coastal towns which were fortified against invasion by the Saracens during the Middle Ages and the Turks at the end of the 15C. These include **Giovinazzo** with its small 12C cathedral dominating the fishing harbour; **Molfetta** pinpointed by the square towers of its Apulian Romanesque cathedral in white limestone; and **Bisceglie**, a picturesque fishing village, with its cathedral finished in the 13C. The main doorway is flanked by two lions.

Bassano del Grappa★

Bassano del Grappa, a pottery town which also produces brandy **(grappa)**, is built on the banks of the Brenta River. The town is attractive, its narrow streets lined by painted houses and the squares bordered by arcades. At the centre is Piazza Garibaldi. The covered bridge (Ponte Coperto) is well known in Italy. Originally built in the 13C, it has been rebuilt many times since.

Location

Population 39 973 – Michelin map 429 E 17 – Veneto. The town with its famous bridge lies on S 47 which links Bassano del Grappa with Padua.
🖪 *Largo Corona d'Italia, 35,* ☎ *0424 52 43 51.*
Surrounding area: see PADOVA, TREVISO and VICENZA.

Worth a Visit

Museo Civico★

Open Tue-Sat 9am-6.30pm, Sun 3.30-6.30pm. Closed Mon, public holidays. €4.50, no charge on the first Sun of the month. ☎ *0424 52 22 35; www.x-land.it/museobassano*
The municipal museum is housed in the monastery next to the church of St Francis. The **picture gallery**, on the first floor, has several works by the local Da Ponte family. Jacopo da Ponte, otherwise called **Jacopo Bassano** (1510-92), was the best-known member. His works were marked by a picturesque realism and contrasts of light and shade. *St Valentine baptising St Lucilla* is his masterpiece.

Other Venetian painters include Guariento, Vivarini, Giambono (14C and 15C), Pietro Longhi, Giamattista Tiepolo and Marco Ricci (18C). There are also two lovely canvases by the Genoese painter Magnasco (18C) and a gallery devoted to the sculptor Canova.

Piazza Garibaldi

The square is dominated by the 13C square tower, **Torre di Ezzelino**, and over-looked by the church of San Francesco. The church, which dates from the 12C-14C, has an elegant porch (1306). Inside, the 14C Christ is by Guariento.

Excursions

Monte Grappa★★★

32km/20mi north – alt 1 775m/5 823ft. The road up passes through fine forests and bare mountain pastures, before reaching the summit, from where there is a magnificent **panorama** reaching as far as Venice and Trieste.

Asolo★

14km/9mi east. The streets of this attractive little town, dominated by its castle, are lined with palaces painted with frescoes. The town is closely associated with Robert Browning and Eleonora Duse, the famous Italian tragic actress who interpreted the works of Gabriele D'Annunzio. Duse is buried in the peaceful cemetery of Sant'Anna.

Marostica

7km/4mi west. **Piazza Castello★**, the main square of this charming small medieval city serves as a giant chessboard for a highly original game of chess – **Partita a Scacchi** – with costumed people as the chessmen.

Cittadella

13km/8mi south. This stronghold was built by the Paduans in 1220 to counter the Trevisans' construction of Castelfranco. Cittadella is encircled by fine brick **walls★**.

Possagno

18km/11mi northwest. This was the birthplace of the sculptor **Antonio Canova** (1757-1822), known for his neo-Classical works. The **house** where he was born and a **sculpture gallery** (Gipsoteca) nearby are open to the public. *Open May-Sep, daily 9am-noon and 3-6pm, rest of the year 9am-noon and 2-5pm. Closed Mon, 1 Jan, 1 May, Easter, 25 Dec. €3.10.* ☎ *0423 54 43 23.*

The **Tempio di Canova**, a temple designed by the master himself, crowns an eminence. Inside are the sculptor's tomb and his last sculpture, a **Descent from the Cross★**. *Open summer 9am-noon and 3-6pm, rest of the year 9am-noon and 2-5pm. For admission to the dome, contact the custodian. Closed Mon. No charge.* ☎ *0423 54 43 23.*

Castelfranco Veneto★

26km/16mi southeast. Castelfranco is a pleasant citadel surrounded by moats. It has a few pretty arcaded houses and is the birthplace of the artist **Giorgione** (1478-1510) . The cathedral contains his masterpiece, the *Madonna and Child with Saints★★*.

The artist's birthplace, (Casa natale di Giorgione) in *Piazza del Duomo* is now arranged as a museum. *Closed for restoration at time of publication.* ☎ *0423 49 12 40; www.bibliotecacastelfrancoveneto.tv.it*

Belluno★

This pleasant town stands on a spur at the confluence of the River Piave and River Ardo rivers and is surrounded by high mountains. To the north are the Dolomites with the Belluno Pre-Alps in the south. An independent commune in the Middle Ages, Belluno came under the aegis of the Venetian Republic from 1404.

Location
Population 35 077 – Michelin map 429 D 18 – Veneto. Belluno is on A 27 to Venice.
🛈 *Piazza dei Martiri 8,* ☎ *0437 94 00 83.*
Surrounding area: see DOLOMITI.

Walking About

Walk along via Rialto through the 13C gateway, Porta Dojona (remodelled in the 16C), across **Piazza del Mercato★**, bordered with arcaded Renaissance houses and adorned with a 1409 fountain, along via Mezzaterra and Via Santa Croce to the gateway, Porta Rugo. Via del Piave offers an extensive **view★** of the Piave Valley and the surrounding mountains. **Piazza del Duomo★** is surrounded by the late-15C Venetian-style **Rectors' Palace★** (palazzo dei Rettori), the Episcopal Palace (palazzo dei Vescovi) and the **cathedral** (Duomo), dating from the 16C with its Baroque campanile by Juvara. Inside, there are several good pictures by the Venetian school, notably by Jacopo Bassano and, in the crypt, a 15C **polyptych★** by the Rimini school. The Jurists' Palace (Palazzo dei Giuristi) houses the municipal museum (Museo civico) with an art gallery (local and Venetian works), a rich coin collection and documents on the *Risorgimento. Open Apr-Sep, daily 10am-noon and 4-7pm, Sun and public holidays, 10.30am-12.30pm; rest of the year, Mon-Sat 10am-noon, Tue-Fri also 3-6pm. €2.13.* ☎ *0437 94 48 36; www.comune.belluno.it*

Excursion

Feltre
31km/19mi southwest. Feltre, grouped around its castle, has kept part of its ramparts and in **Via Mezzaterra★**, old houses, adorned with frescoes in the Venetian manner. **Piazza Maggiore★** is a beautiful square with its noble buildings, arcades, stairways and balustrades. The **municipal museum** (museo civico) *(23 Via Lorenzo Luzzo, near the Porta Oria)* displays works by Lorenzo Luzzo, a local artist, Marescalchi, Bellini, Cima da Conegliano, Ricci and Jan Massys. The museum also includes a historical section on Feltre and an archaeological collection. (&) *Open summer, Tue-Fri 10.30am-12.30pm and 4-7pm, Sat-Sun and public holidays 9.30am-12.30pm and 4-7pm, rest of year Tue-Fri 10.30am-12.30pm and 3-6pm, Sat-Sun and public holidays 9.30am-12.30pm and 3-6pm. Closed Mon. €4.* ☎ *0439 88 52 42.*

Benevento

This was the ancient capital of the Samnites, who hindered the Roman expansion for some considerable time. In 321 BC they trapped the Roman army in a defile known as the Caudine Forks (Forche Caudine) between Capua and ancient Beneventum. The Romans occupied the town following the defeat in 275 BC of Pyrrhus (it was on this occasion that the victors transformed the old name **Maleventum** into **Beneventum**) and his Samnite allies. During the reign of Trajan, the town knew a period of glory and it was designated as the starting point for the Appian Trajan Way (Via Appia Traiana) leading to Brindisi. Under Lombard rule it became the seat of a duchy in 571 and later a powerful principality. Following the Battle of Benevento in 1266, Charles of Anjou who had defeated Manfred, the then king of Naples and Sicily, supported by Pope Urban IV, claimed the kingship.

Location
Population 63 284 – Michelin map 431 D 26 – Campania. To get to Benevento take S 88, which links the town with Isernia and A 16, or the Via Appia, which goes to Caserta. 🛈 *Via Nicola Sala 31,* ☎ *0824 31 99 11.*
Surrounding area: see Reggia di CASERTA.

Worth a Visit

Teatro Romano

Access from Via Port'Arsa, to the left of S. Maria della Verità church. & *Open daily 9am-1hr before sunset. Closed 1 May, 1 Dec. €2.* ☎ *0824 29 970.*

This is one of the largest Roman theatres still in existence; it was built in the 2C by the Emperor Hadrian and enlarged by the Emperor Caracalla. In the summer it is the arena for theatre, dance and opera performances.

From Piazza Duomo, dominated by the imposing cathedral which suffered heavy damages from bombardments in 1943 (of the original structure, only the façade and the substantial campanile remain, both 13C), turn into **Corso Garibaldi** which is lined with the most significant buildings from the city's history. Note the **Egyptian obelisk** from Isis' Temple (AD 88).

Arco di Traiano★★

From Corso Garibaldi turn left onto Via Traiano. The "Porta Aurea", erected in AD 114 to commemorate the emperor who had turned Benevento into an obligatory stopover on the journey to Apulia, is Italy's best-preserved triumphal arch. The low reliefs dedicated to the glory of the Emperor Trajan depicting scenes of peace on the side facing the city and scenes of war and life in the provinces facing the countryside, are of an exceptionally high standard.

Chiesa di Santa Sofia

Piazza Matteotti. Open daily, 8-11am (Sun 1pm) and 5-8pm, (winter 7pm). ☎ *0824 21 206.*

An 8C building which was rebuilt in the 17C. The interior has a bold and unusual layout consisting of a central hexagon enclosed by a decagonal structure. In the apses there are remains of 8C frescoes. Adjacent to the 12C **cloisters★** whose splendid columns support Moorish style arches, the **Museo del Sannio★** houses an important archaeological collection and some fine Neapolitan paintings of the 17C and 18C. (&) *Open daily, except Mon, 9am-1pm. Closed 1 Jan. €2.58.* ☎ *0824 21 818.*

►► Rocca dei Rettori.

Bergamo★★

Bergamo, one of the principal towns of Lombardy, is situated on the northern edge of the Lombardy plain at the confluence of the Brembana and Seriana valleys. It has a strong artistic heritage and is also a thriving business and industrial centre. The modern lower town is pleasant while the old upper town is quiet, picturesque and evocative of the past. It also has many delightful, old cake shops whose windows are filled with the small yellow cakes that are a local speciality, the "polenta e osei"

Directory

WHERE TO EAT

• *Budget*

Osteria D'Ambrosio – *Via Broseta 58/A, città bassa* – ☎ *035 40 29 26 – Closed Sat lunchtime, Sun and public holidays, 5-25 Aug, 25 Dec, Easter –* ⁊ – *Booking recommended – €15. An authentic, rustic-style osteria (tavern). Warm welcome assured by the rather eccentric but friendly proprietor. Communal-style eating, at basic tables, but with truly old-fashioned prices. Regional cuisine.*

• *Moderate*

Baretto di San Vigilio – *Via Castello 1, San Vigilio – 5min from the funicular in the città alta –* ☎ *035 25 31 91 – Closed Mon – €35/45. Situated just where the funicular arrives is this cosy café-restaurant. The food is both traditional and imaginative. The menu includes some regional and local specialities as well as delicious pastries. Seating outside in summer, with the added attraction of wonderful views over the town.*

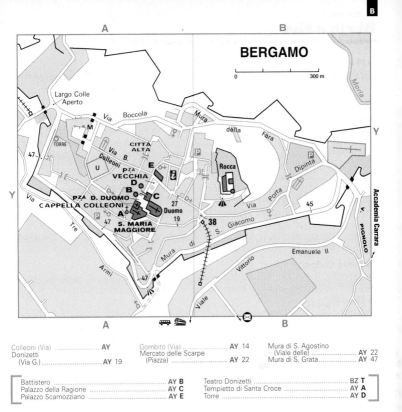

Location

Population 117 837 – Michelin map 428 E 10-11 – Lombardy. Crowned by the old town of Bergamo Alta, Bergamo dominates the local landscape and can be clearly seen from the A 4 motorway. The town is around 50km/30mi from Milan. It is ideally situated for excursions into the mountain valleys nearby and for visits to Lakes Como, d'Iseo and Garda. **🛈** *Viale Vittorio Emanuele II, 20, ☎ 035 21 02 04; Città Alta: vicolo Aquila Nera, 2, ☎ 035 24 22 26.*

Surrounding area: see BRESCIA, MILANO, Regione dei LAGHI.

Background

History – The Gauls seized the settlement in c 550 BC and called it Berghem. It was renamed Bergomum by the Romans when they took over in 196 BC. The city was destroyed by the barbarians before enjoying a period of peace under the Lombards and in particular in the reign of Queen Theodolinda. An independent commune from the 11C to the 13C, it then joined the Lombard League in its struggle against the Emperor Frederick Barbarossa. The town suffered during the struggles between the Guelphs (followers of the pope) and the Ghibellines (followers of the emperor). Under the rule of **Bartolomeo Colleoni** (1400-75), the town fell first to the Visconti family from Milan and then to the Republic of Venice which the famous mercenary leader served successively. Bergamo came under Austrian rule in 1814 and was liberated by Garibaldi in 1859.

Masques and Bergamasques – In addition to a large group of local artists, namely Previtali, Moroni, Cariani, Baschenis and Fra Galgario, numerous others worked in the town, including **Lorenzo Lotto**, Giovanni da Campione and Amadeo. Bergamo is also the home of the composer Donizetti (1797-1848). The vivacity of the people is displayed in the local musical folklore: the Bergamasque, a lively dance, is accompanied by pipers playing their *pifferi.*

The **Commedia dell'Arte** originated at Bergamo in the 16C. The comedy consists of an improvisation *(imbroglio)* based on a pre-arranged theme *(scenario)*, with gags *(lazzi)* uttered by masked actors representing stock characters: the valet (Harlequin), a stubborn but wily peasant from the Brembana Valley, the braggart (Pulcinella) the lady's maid (Columbine), the lover (Pierrot), the knave (Scapino), the old fox (Scaramouch), the clown (Pantaloon) and the musician (Mezzetino). This form of theatre was popular in France in the 17C and 18C.

Worth a Visit

CITTÀ ALTA★★★

You can either go by car *(park outside the walls)* or take the funicular *(station in Viale Vittorio Emanuele II)* which ends in **Piazza del Mercato delle Scarpe** (Square of the Shoe Market).

Piazza Vecchia★

This is the historic centre of the town. The **Palazzo della Ragione**, the oldest town hall in Italy, dates from 1199 but was rebuilt in the 16C. It has graceful arcades and trefoil openings and a central balcony surmounted by the Lion of St Mark symbolising Venetian rule. A 14C covered stairway leads to the majestic 12C tower with its 15C clock. *Open daily, except Mon, May-Sep 10am-8pm, Mar-April and Oct 10am-12.30pm and 2-6pm, Sat-Sun and public holidays 10am-6pm. Rest of year only Sat-Sun and public holidays 10.30am-4pm. €1.* ☎ *035 24 22 26; www.apt.bergamo.it*

The **Palazzo Scamozziano** opposite is in the Palladian style. The fountain in the centre was offered to Genoa in 1780 by the Doge of Venice, Alvise Contarini.

Through the arcades of Palazzo della Ragione make for **Piazza del Duomo★★** which is bordered by the chief monuments of the upper town.

Cappella Colleoni★★

&. *Open daily, Mar-Oct 9am-12.30pm and 2-6.30pm (last admission 6pm); rest of the year 9.30am-12.30pm and 2-4.30pm (last admission 4pm). Closed Mon (winter), 1 Jan, 25 Dec. No charge.*

The architect of the Carthusian monastery at Pavia, **Amadeo**, designed the chapel (1470-76), a jewel of Lombard-Renaissance architecture, as a mausoleum for Bartolomeo Colleoni, who directed that it should be built on the site of the sacristy of the basilica of St Mary Major. The funerary chapel opens into and is embedded in the north side of the basilica. The domed main structure is adjacent to the north porch which is skilfully used to counterbalance the recess.

The elegant **façade** is faced with precious multicoloured marble and lavishly decorated with delicate sculptures: figures of children *(putti)*, fluted and wreathed columns, sculptured pilasters, vases and candelabra, medallions and low reliefs combining sacred and secular elements after the contemporary fashion (allegories, scenes from the Old Testament, mythological figures including scenes from the life of Hercules with whom Colleoni identified himself).

The **interior** is sumptuously decorated with low reliefs of extraordinary delicacy, frescoes by Tiepolo and Renaissance stalls with intarsia work. The **Colleoni monument**, also by Amadeo, is surmounted by an equestrian statue of the leader in gilded wood and is delicately carved. The low reliefs of the sarcophagi represent scenes from the New Testament separated by niches housing statues of the Virtues. Between the two sarcophagi are portraits of the leader's children. His favourite daughter, Medea, who died at the age of 15, lies near him *(to the left)*, in a tomb by Amadeo which is a marvel of delicacy and purity.

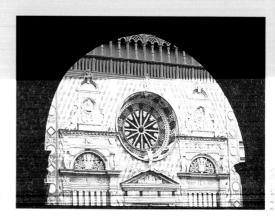

Cappella Colleoni, delicate Renaissance trefoil work.

Basilica di Santa Maria Maggiore★

Open daily, summer 9am-12.30pm and 2.30-6pm (winter 5pm), Sun and public holidays 9am-12.45pm and 3-6pm. Donations welcome. ☎ *035 22 33 27.*

This church, dedicated to St Mary Major, is 12C but the two lovely north and south **porches** with loggias and supported by lions in the Lombard Romanesque style were added in the 14C by Giovanni da Campione.

The interior, remodelled in the Baroque style (late 16C-early 17C), is richly decorated with stucco and gilding. The walls of the aisles and the chancel are hung
with nine splendid Florentine **tapestries**★★ (1580-86), beautifully designed after
cartoons by Alessandro Allori which relate the Life of the Virgin. On the west wall
of the nave hangs the sumptuous Flemish tapestry depicting the **Crucifixion**★★. It
was woven in Antwerp between 1696 and 1698 after cartoons by L Van Schoor.
This part of the church also contains Donizetti's tomb (1797-1848). Note also the
curious 18C Baroque confessional in the north aisle and the interesting 14C frescoes in the transept. Incorporated in the chancel screen are four superb **panels of
intarsia work**★★ depicting scenes from the Old Testament. They were made in the
16C after the designs of Lorenzo Lotto.

Leave by the door giving onto Piazza di Santa Maria Maggiore to admire the 14C
south porch, as well as the charming **Tempietto Santa Croce** which was built
c 1000 on the quatrefoil plan in the early-Romanesque style. To return to Piazza
del Duomo walk round the basilica's **east end**★ with its radiating chapels decorated
with graceful arcading

Battistero★

This charming octagonal baptistery is encircled by a red Verona marble gallery
with graceful, slender columns and 14C statues representing the Virtues. It is a
reconstruction of Giovanni da Campione's original work dating from 1340. It
originally graced the east end of the nave of St Mary Major but was deemed too
cumbersome and was demolished in 1660 and rebuilt on its present site in 1898.

▶▶Duomo; Via Bartolomeo Colleoni (Luogo Pio Colleoni); Rocca (views★).

CITTÀ BASSA★

The Carrara Academy is in the heart of a district of attractive alleyways, while
Piazza Matteotti is at the centre of the present-day business and shopping district
in the lower town.

Accademia Carrara★★

 ♿ *Open Apr-Sep 10am-1pm and 3-6.45pm, rest of the year 9.30am-1pm and 2.30-
5.45pm. Closed Mon, 1 Jan, Easter, 1 May, 25 Dec €2.58, no charge Sun.* ☎ *035 39 96 77;
www.accademiacarrara.bergamo.it*

This collection of 15C-18C Italian and foreign paintings is housed in a neo-Classical
palace.

Beyond the early-15C works, which still recall the International Gothic style, hang
two important portraits of *Giuliano de'Medici* by Botticelli and the elegant and
refined one of *Lionello d'Este* by Pisanello. These are followed by works of the
Venetian school: by the Vivarini family, Carlo Crivelli, Giovanni Bellini (gentle
Madonnas with dreamy expressions which are similar to those of his brother-in-
law, Mantegna), Gentile Bellini (delicate but penetrating portraits), Carpaccio
(Portrait of the Doge Leonardo Loredan) and by Lorenzo Lotto. Next come the late-
15C and early-16C works represented by Cosmè Tura, master of the Ferrarese
school (a very realistic *Virgin and Child* showing the influence of Flemish art), by
the Lombard Bergognone (soft light), and by the local artist, Previtali.

The 16C covers works by the Venetian Lorenzo Lotto (including a splendid *Holy
Family with St Catherine*), the fine local portraitist Cariani, and the Venetian masters, Titian and Tintoretto. The colours and delicate draughtsmanship of Raphael
greatly influenced Garofalo (Benvenuto Tisi) who was nicknamed the Ferrara
Raphael, while the Piedmontese Gaudenzio Ferrari and Bernardino Luini, the main
exponents of the Renaissance in Lombardy, were inspired by Leonardo da Vinci.
The 16C **portraits** are a particularly rich group, with the Ferrarese school which
specialised in this art and the local painter, Moroni (1523-78). Foreign artists
include Clouet *(Portrait of Louis de Clèves)* and Dürer.

The 17C-18C Bergamo school is represented by Baschenis (1617-77) and excellent
portraits by Fra Galgario (1655-1743). The 17C Flemish and Dutch section (Rubens,
Van Dyck, Brueghel etc) is dominated by a delightful Van Goyen seascape.

The museum also exhibits 18C Venetian painting: scenes of domestic interiors by
Pietro Longhi, topographical views by Carlevarijs, Bernardo Bellotto, Canaletto and
Francesco Guardi.

Old quarter★

The main street of this quarter is **Via Pignolo**★ which winds among old palaces,
mostly 16C and 18C and churches containing numerous works of art. Among these
are: the **church of San Bernardino** which has in the chancel a *Virgin Enthroned
and Saints*★ (1521) by Lorenzo Lotto (note the expressive use of colour with the
deep red of the Virgin's robe contrasting with the intense green of the drape held
up by the angels) and **Santo Spirito** which contains a *St John the Baptist surrounded
by saints* and a polyptych by Previtali, a polyptych portraying the Virgin by
Bergognone and a *Virgin and Child* by Lorenzo Lotto.

Piazza Matteotti★

This immense square is in the centre of the modern town. It is flanked by the **Sentierone**, the favourite promenade of the citizens of Bergamo. In the square stand the **Donizetti Theatre** and the **church of San Bartolomeo** which houses the superb *Martinengo Altarpiece* by Lorenzo Lotto depicting the enthroned Virgin surrounded by saints.

Excursions

▶▶Val Brembana★ *(25km/15mi north)*; San Pellegrino Terme♯♯; Museo del Presepio★ *(8km/5mi southwest. 4km/2.5mi from the Dalmine exit on the motorway. Follow directions for the museum.* 🅱 ☎ *035 56 33 83).*

Bologna★★

In traditional iconography Bologna is portrayed as being *dotta, grassa e rossa* (learned, self-indulgent and "red"). Bologna is without question learned (or better still, wise) thanks to its university which, along with that of Paris, is the oldest university in Europe. The self-indulgence associated with Bologna (in Italian it is known as Bologna the Fat) refers to the agricultural abundance of the city and its gastronomic opulence which has enshrined it as the food capital of Italy.

Its "redness", which over time has acquired political connotations, refers to the colour of its buildings, towers and 37km/23mi of arcades which buzz with activity and which helped to make the city the Cultural Capital of Europe in the year 2000.

Location

Population 381 161 – Michelin map 429 and 430 I 15-16 (together with town plan) – Emilia-Romagna. Bologna is well placed for access to the Adriatic and Tuscan coasts as well as the Dolomites. Indeed, the city is situated at an important motorway interchange, with access to A 1, A 14 to the Adriatic and A 13. It is also near the beginning of A 22, the Brenner transalpine route. 🅱 *Piazza Maggiore 6,* ☎ *051 24 65 41.*

Surrounding area. See MODENA.

Background

The Etruscan settlement of *Felsina* was conquered in the 4C BC by the Boïan Gauls, who were driven out in their turn by the Romans in 190 BC. Roman *Bononia* fell under the sway of the barbarians and did not recover until the 12C. In the subsequent century the city enjoyed the status of an independent commune and developed rapidly. A fortified city wall, towers, palaces and churches were built and the university flourished and acquired an excellent reputation for its teaching of Roman law.

In the struggle which confronted the Ghibellines, supporting the emperor, and the Guelphs, partisans of communal independence, it was the latter who prevailed when in 1249 they defeated the Imperial Army of Frederick II at Fossalta. The emperor's son, Enzo, was taken prisoner and remained at Bologna until his death 23 years later.

In the 15C, following a period of violent struggles between rival families, the city fell into the hands of the **Bentivoglio** family whose rule continued until 1506. The city then remained under papal control until the arrival of Napoleon Bonaparte. In the early 19C several insurrections were severely repressed by the Austrians and in 1860 Bologna was united with Piedmont.

Famous citizens include the Popes Gregory XIII, who established our present Gregorian calendar (1582), Gregory XV (17C) and Benedict XIV (18C). In 1530, following the defeat of François I at Pavia and the sack of Rome, the Emperor Charles V forced Pope Clement VII to crown him in the Basilica of St Petronius in Bologna.

Bologna School of Painting – This term covers the artistic movement founded by the brothers Agostino (1557-1602) and Annibale (1560-1609) and their cousin Ludovico (1555-1619) **Carracci**, who reacted against Mannerism with more "classical" composition and a more naturalistic art which aimed at expressing a simple and intimate spirituality. Numerous artists, in particular the Bolognese painters

Directory

GETTING ABOUT

By car – Situated 100km/62mi from Florence, 200km/125mi from Milan and 150km/93mi from Venice, Bologna is at a key intersection of a busy motorway network. For those intending to stay in the city for a while, it is advisable to leave your car in a car park and use public transport to get around.

By train – The railway station is in Piazza Medaglie d'Oro, at the end of Via dell'Indipendenza, for information ring ☎ 147 88 80 88 (from 7am to 9pm). Buses n⁰ˢ 17 and 25 go to Piazza Maggiore.

By plane – Guglielmo Marconi aiport is situated 6km/4mi northwest of the city in Borgo Panigale, ☎ 051 64 79 615. It is served by major national and international airline companies which connect it to major Italian and European cities.

The Aerobus – The Airbus offers a fast connection between the airport and the city centre, the railway station and the exhibition hall (fiera) district. Journey time between the railway station and airport is 20min. It runs from 5.20am to midnight (departures every 30min). €4.13 (including luggage transport) for a full journey, €2.07 for intermediate stops. Tickets can be purchased at ATC ticket offices, automated ticket machines or on board. For information contact ☎ 051 29 02 90.

Public transport – Bologna has a wide network of public transport. For information call ☎ 051 29 02 90. Tickets can be bought at ATC ticket offices, authorised vendors and automated ticket machines. There are various types of tickets: the City pass (€6.20) provides 7 journeys, no more than 60min long in the daytime, no more than 70min from 8.30pm to 6.30am, and can be used by one or more people at the same time; one-day tickets (€3.10) are valid for 24hr from the moment they are validated; one-hour tickets (€0.93) are valid for 60min in the daytime and for 70min between 8.30pm and 6.30am.

Taxis – CO.TA.BO. (Cooperativa Taxisti Bolognesi) radiotaxi ☎ 051 37 27 27 and C.A.T. (Consorzio Autonomo Taxisti) radiotaxi ☎ 051 53 41 41.

VISITING

Visitors can obtain a pass to all the municipal museums in the city. These can be purchased at the ticket office in the museums (marked with a diamond symbol) and the ATC ticket offices. *Tariff: €5.20 (valid for one day) or €8.26 (valid for 3 days).*

WHERE TO EAT
• Budget
Da Bertino – *Via delle Lame 55 – ☎ 051 52 22 30 – Closed Sun, Mon, 10 Aug-8 Sep, 1 Jan, 25 Dec –* 📷 *– €21/26.* An old-fashioned, traditional trattoria with a loyal following. Typical Bolognese dishes. Mouthwatering starters and home-made pasta dishes.

Gigina – *Via Henri Beyle Stendhal 1 – 4km/2.4mi northeast of the centre – ☎ 051 32 23 00 – Closed two weeks in Aug. – Booking recommended – €21/31.* Located just outside the city, this family-run trattoria has a good reputation for traditional food including regional specialities. The cooking is homely and the atmosphere cosy. Warm welcome.

• Moderate
Teresina – *Via Oberdan 4 – ☎ 051 22 89 85 – Closed Sun, 5-23 Aug – ⊄ – Booking recommended – €31/37.* Busy trattoria, with a menu which allows you to taste a little of everything. Simple surroundings inside, if a little cramped. Alfresco dining in the summer.

L'Anatra e l'Arancia – *Via Rolandino 1/2 – ☎ 051 22 55 05 – Closed Sun, 10-20 Aug. – €49/65.* Located within the precincts of the church of San Domenico, this fashionable bistro-restaurant is popular with the locals. Eclectic menu which recommends fish and seafood dishes to start with, followed by foie gras.

WHERE TO STAY

Note that most hotels have higher tariffs when exhibitions are being held at the fiera (exhibition hall). It is advisable to check prices by telephone beforehand and to book well in advance.

• Moderate
Albergo Accademia – *Via delle Belle Arti 6 – ☎ 051 23 23 18 – Fax 051 56 35 90 – www.hotelaccademia.it – ⊄ ▣ – 28 rm €41.32/108.46 ⌷.* An unpretentious but comfortable hotel in the historic centre. Modern and functional rooms, some without bath (these are cheaper). The hotel also has a garage (at a charge) which is a rare luxury in the historic centre of Bologna

Albergo San Vitale – *Via San Vitale 94 – ☎ 051 22 59 66 – Fax 051 23 93 96 – ⊄ – 17 rm €46.48/77.47.* This pleasant, well-kept hotel was originally an old convent (of which the garden remains). The rooms are simple but comfortable. Excellent value for money.

Albergo Villa Azzurra – *Viale Felsina 49 – 5km/3mi east of the historic centre, take Strada Maggiore – ☎ 051 53 54 60 – Fax 051 53 13 46 – Closed for around two weeks in Aug – ⊄ – 15 rm €54.23/77.47.* This is a peaceful hotel located in an attractive old villa with a pretty garden. Rooms are large and tastefully decorated. No credit cards. Very convenient for those arriving in Bologna by car who don't require accommodation in the city centre and are looking for a little peace and quiet.

Albergo Centrale – *Via della Zecca 2 – ☎ 051 22 51 14 – Fax 051 23 51 62 – Closed for around two weeks in Aug – 25 rm €61.97/82.63.* Housed in a fine old building, the hotel is light and airy. Rooms are spacious and pleasantly simple. Room 9 has preserved its original Art Deco furnishings. Rooms with a shared bathroom are cheaper.

• **Expensive**

Hotel Roma – *Via Massimo d'Azeglio 9 –*
☎ *051 22 63 22 – Fax 051 23 99 09 –* 🅿
📶 *– 82 rm from €86.76* 🍴 *– Restaurant*
€31.50/39.25. Situated in a quiet
pedestrianised street, a stone's throw from
the Basilica di S. Petronio. The hotel is of a
high standard, although the public areas and
rooms are a little cramped. Look out for the
kitsch touches including the floral upholstery
and bright red armchairs in the dining room.

Hotel Corona d'Oro 1890 – *Via Oberdan
12 –* ☎ *051 23 64 56 – Fax 051 26 26 79 –*
Closed 22 Jul-29 Aug – 📶 *– 35 rm. From
€201* 🍴*.* With many of the original features
tastefully preserved, this elegant hotel
exudes style. The wooden columns on the
first floor are a testament to its 14C
structure, there are 15C-16C caisson ceilings
along with a stunning Art Nouveau reception
hall.

TAKING A BREAK

Osteria dell'Orsa – *Via Mentana 1/F –*
☎ *051 23 15 76 – orsa@alinet.it – Open
noon-3pm, 7pm-1am.* Something of an
institution and popular with staff and
students from the University, this is a large
bar where some of the best jazz musicians
come and play live.

Paolo Atti & Figli – *Via Caprarie 7 –*
☎ *051 22 04 25 – info@paoloatti.com –
Open Mon-Wed, Fri 8.30am-1pm and 4.30-
7.15pm, Sat and Thu 8.30am-1pm.* Famous
Art Nouveau style patisserie founded in 1880
that has numbered Giosuè Carducci and the
painter Morandi among its frequenters. Also
an excellent delicatessen. Specialities include
the tortellini.

Tamburini – *Via Caprarie 1 –*
☎ *051 23 47 26 – Mon-Sat 8am-7pm.* This
is the smartest eatery in the area. It also
serves as a delicatessen, producing and
selling all the local culinary specialities. There
are hams, a variety of home-made pastas
and cheeses which can all be sampled there
and then or, if you can bear to wait, ordered
for later.

**Enoteca Regionale Emilia-
Romagna** – *Chiesa Santa Maria
dell'Assunta, Rocca Sforzesca – 45050
Dozza – 29km/17mi southeast of Bologna. –*
☎ *0542 67 37 82 – enoteca@tin.it – Tue-Sat
9.30am-1pm and 3-9pm, Sun 10am-1pm
and 3-9pm.* Located within the fort, this
large cantina has a wide selection of wines
from the Emilia Romagna region.

GOING OUT

Bottega del Vino Olindo Faccioli – *Via
Altabella 15/B –* ☎ *051 22 31 71 – Summer,
Mon-Fri; rest of the year, Mon-Sat 6pm-1am.
Closed Aug.* Handed down from father to
son in 1924, this wine shop stocks more
than 500 different wines from all over Italy.
A great place for discovering some of the
many wines that this country produces.
Tastings at the bar or in the main reception
area.

Cantina Bentivoglio – *Via Mascarella 4/B –*
☎ *051 26 54 16 –
jazz@bentivoglio.dsnet.it – Tue-Sun 8pm-
2am.* The elegant antique furnishings make
an excellent backdrop for wine tastings. The
wine cellar has more than 400 wines in
stock, including some very rare vintages. Live
jazz in the evenings.

Enoteca des Arts – *Via San Felice 9/A –*
☎ *051 23 64 22 – Mon-Thu 4.30pm-2am,
Fri-Sat 16.30pm-3am. Closed Aug.* A wine
bar-cantina, tucked away in a long
"corridor" with vaulted ceilings, the walls
feature displays of old bottles. Popular with
students at the University in Bologna who
have made friends with the proprietor who is
passionate about his choice of wines, Italian
or otherwise.

Il Circolo Pickwick – *Via San Felice 77/A –*
☎ *051 55 51 04 – Summer, Mon-Sat noon-
3pm and 6-11pm; rest of the year, noon-
3pm and 6pm-1am.* The pub's unusual
location, in an old pharmacy with its original
fittings, seem to make this a particularly
good venue for meeting up with friends or
making new ones. Serves a heady mix of
Italian wines, English beer and Cuban
cocktails.

Francesco Albani, **Guercino**, **Domenichino** and **Guido Reni**, followed this
movement known as the **Accademia degli Incamminati** (Academy of the
Eclectic), whose main teaching precept was the study of nature. In 1595 Annibale
Carracci moved to Rome to execute a commission for the Farnese family. His frescoes at Palazzo Farnese veer towards a sense of dynamism and illusionism which
herald Baroque art.

Worth a Visit

CITY CENTRE★★★

The two adjoining squares, **Piazza Maggiore** and **Piazza del Nettuno★★★**, together
with **Piazza di Porta Ravegnana★★**, the heart of Bologna, form a harmonious
ensemble.

Fontana del Nettuno★★

The fountain is the work of the Flemish sculptor known as Giambologna or
Giovanni Bologna (1529-1608). The gigantic muscular bronze Neptune (Nettuno),
is surrounded by four sirens spouting water from their breasts. The group has a
rather rough vigour in tune with the town's character.

BOLOGNA

Palazzo Comunale★

&. *Sala Rossa and Sala del Consiglio only if not in use. Cappella and Sala Farnese 8am-6.30pm, Cappella Palatina 8am-6pm. No charge. ☎ 051 20 31 11; www.comune.bologna.it/bolognaturismo*

The façade of the town hall is composed of buildings of different periods: 13C to the left, 15C on the right; in the centre the main doorway is 16C (the lower section is by Alessi) and is surmounted by a statue of Pope Gregory XIII. Above and to the left of the doorway is a statue of the *Virgin and Child* (1478) in terracotta by Niccolò dell'Arca. At the far end of the courtyard, under a gallery on the left, rises a great ramp, the so-called *Scala dei cavalli* (at one time climbed by horse-drawn carriages) leading to the richly decorated first-floor rooms, then up again to the second floor. Opening off the vast Farnese Gallery with 17C frescoes are the splendid rooms, at one time Cardinal Legato's rooms, which now display the **Collezioni comunali d'arte**, the town's art collections, with sections on furniture, the decorative arts and a selection of Emilian **paintings★** (14C-19C). They also house the **Museo Morandi★**, which boasts the largest collection of works by the painter and engraver from Bologna, including paintings, drawings, watercolours and etchings as well as a re-construction of the artist's studio with its collection of antiquities. *Exhibitions:* (&.) *Open 9am-6.30, Sun and public holidays 10am-6.30pm (last admission 6pm). Closed Mon, 1 Jan, 25 Dec €4.13. ☎ 051 20 36 29; www.comune.bologna.it/iperbole/ MuseiCivici*

Museum: Open 10am-6pm. Closed Mon, 1 Jan, 1 May, 25 Dec €4.13. ☎ 051 20 33 32; www.museomorandi.it

To the left of the Palazzo Comunale stands the austere 14C-15C Notaries' Palace (Palazzo dei Notari).

AN EXCEPTIONAL TALENT

The still-life painter **Giorgio Morandi** (1890-1964) lived most of his life in his native Bologna. Morandi used a limited palette of ochre, blue, white, ivory, brown and grey to portray a rigorous world, characterised by the absence of the human figure and by a restrained intensity. Bottles, vases, carafes, fruit bowls, all skilfully composed and re-composed in a myriad of variations, make up pictograms, while his geometric, subtle landscapes show the influence of Cézanne.

Palazzo del Podestà★

The Palazzo del Podestà and the Palazzo di re Enzo are only open during exhibitions and special events. For information, ☎ 051 22 45 00.

The Renaissance façade of the Governor's Palace facing Piazza Maggiore has arcades separated by Corinthian columns on the ground floor and is surmounted by a balustrade. The upper storey is punctuated by flat columns and is crowned by an attic pierced by oculi or round windows. The 13C **King Enzo's Palace** (Palazzo di Re Enzo) stands next to the Governor's Palace. It has a fine inner courtyard and a magnificent staircase leading up to a gallery, to the left of which is a courtyard overlooked by the Arengo Tower and the magnificent Podestà Chamber, to the left.

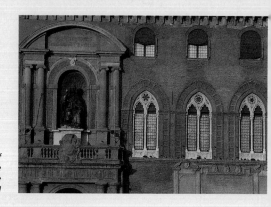

The composite façade of the Palazzo Comunale with the statue of Pope Gregorio XIII

Basilica di San Petronio★★

Building on the basilica, dedicated to St Petronius, began in 1390 to the plans of Antonio di Vincenzo (1340-1402) and was fully completed only in the 17C when the vaulting was finished. The façade, the upper part of which lacks its marble facing, is remarkable chiefly for the main **doorway★★** on which the Sienese Jacopo della Quercia worked from 1425 to 1438. The lintel, uprights and embrasures are adorned with highly expressive low reliefs.

The immense **interior** has many **works of art★** including frescoes by Giovanni da Modena (15C) in the first and the fourth chapels off the north aisle. Particularly striking is the fourth chapel, the right wall of which depicts *the Journey of the Kings* and the left wall an impressive *Inferno* and *Paradise*. Additional works include a *Martyrdom of St Sebastian* by the late-15C Ferrara school in the fifth chapel; a *Madonna* (1492) by Lorenzo Costa and the tomb of Elisa Baciocchi, Napoleon's sister, in the seventh chapel; and at the high altar a canopy (baldachin) by Vignola (16C). The 15C organ on the right is one of the oldest in Italy.

Near the basilica is the Museo Civico Archeologico *(see below)* and the 16C Bishop's Palace (Palazzo dell'Archiginnasio), the home of an extensive library (10 000 manuscripts) and the 17C-18C Anatomy Theatre (Teatro Anatomico). (&) *9am-1pm and 2-6.30pm. Closed Sun, 1 Jan, 1 May, 25 Dec and public holidays. No charge. ☎ 051 27 68 11 or 051 23 64 88; www.comune.bologna.it/archiginnasio*

In the nearby church of **Santa Maria della Vita**, note the dramatic **Mourning of Christ★**, a terracotta sculpture by Nicolò dell'Arca (15C).

Torri pendenti★★

There are two tall leaning towers which belonged to noble families in the attractive Piazza di Porta Ravegnana. They are symbols of the continual conflict between the rival Guelphs and Ghibellines in the Middle Ages. The taller, **Torre degli Asinelli**, nearly 100m-330ft high, dates from 1109. It is worth climbing the 486 steps that lead to the top in order to admire a **panorama★★** of the city. The second, known as **Torre Garisenda**, is 50m-165ft high and has a tilt of over 3m-10ft. N° 1 in the square is the Renaissance Linen Drapers' Hall (Casa dei Drappieri). *Torre degli Asinelli: Open daily, summer 9am-6pm, rest of the year 9am-5pm. €3. ☎ 051 24 65 44; www.comune.bologna.it.bolognaturismo*

The 14C Mercanzia or Merchants' House, in the next square, bears the coats of arms of the various guilds and several small statues.

JUST OUTSIDE THE HISTORIC CENTRE

Chiesa di San Giacomo Maggiore★

Open daily, Apr-Oct 10am-1pm and 3-7pm, rest of the year 10am-1pm and 2-6pm. Donations welcome. ☎ 051 22 59 70; http://web.tiscalinet.it/agostiniani

The church, dedicated to St James Major, was founded in 1267. On the north side is a fine Renaissance portico. Inside is the magnificent **Cappella Bentivoglio★** whose frescoes depicting *The Triumph of Fame and Death* and the beautiful

Madonna Enthroned with the Bentivoglio Family were executed by the Ferrarese painter Lorenzo Costa. The chapel also houses a masterpiece of Francesco Francia, the *Madonna Enthroned and Saints* (c 1494) which is imbued with an elegiac melancholy. Opposite the chapel, in the ambulatory, stands the **tomb★** (c 1433) of the jurist, Antonio Bentivoglio, by Jacopo della Quercia.

St Cecilia's Chapel *(entrance on Via Zamboni 15)* is a small church, founded in the 13C with additions made in the 15C. Inside there are remarkable **frescoes★** depicting St Cecilia (1506) by F Francia, L Costa and A Aspertini.

Further along via Zamboni is the Pinacoteca Nazionale (see below).

Strada Maggiore★

Along this elegant street, lined with some fine palaces (note Casa Isolani at no 19, a rare example of 13C architecture with a wooden portico) is the **Museo d'Arte industriale e Galleria Davia Bargellini**, housed in an attractive palace dating from 1658 (at no 44), which has collections of "industrial art" (applied and decorative arts) and paintings from the 14C-18C. (&) *Open daily, 9am-2pm, Sun 9am-1pm. Closed Mon, 1 Jan, 1May, 25 Dec, weekday holidays. No charge.* ☏ *051 23 39 41; www.comune.bologna.it/iperbole/MuseiCivici*

A little further down, on the right, is the church of **Santa Maria dei Servi** (founded in the 14C) which is heralded by a Renaissance quadrisection **portico★** and ends in a beautifully constructed apse. Inside, in the third chapel on the right, there is a splendid **Maestà★★** (Virgin in Majesty) by Cimabue.

Basilica di Santo Stefano★

Open daily, 9am-noon and 3.30-6pm, Sun and public holidays 9am-1pm and 3.30-6.30pm. ☏ *051 22 32 56.*

The basilica comprises a group of buildings (originally seven) overlooking the square with its Renaissance mansions. Entrance is through the **church of the Crucifix** (Crocifisso), an old Lombard cathedral initially restored in the 11C and heavily remodelled in the 19C. Turning left make for the atmospheric 12C **church of the Holy Sepulchre** (Santo Sepolcro) with its polygonal plan and the shrine of Bologna's patron saint, St Petronius. The black cipolin marble columns were originally part of the ancient Temple of Isis (AD 100) which was turned into a baptistery and later into a church. The font, originally consecrated with water from the Nile, was re-consecrated with water from the Jordan River. To the left make for the **church of San Vitale e Sant'Agricola** (8C-11C) with its plain, robust structure. Go through the Church of the Holy Sepulchre to reach the charming **Court of Pilate** (11C-12C) and, from there, through to the **church of the Trinity** (Trinità), 13C, the old *Martyrium* (4C-5C) where the bodies of martyrs were brought and which houses a fine *Adoration of the Magi* (14C) in wood. To the right of the Court of Pilate are the Romanesque cloisters where there is access to the small museum (paintings, statues and liturgical objects).

Chiesa di San Domenico★

The church, dedicated to St Dominic, was built at the beginning of the 13C and remodelled in the 18C. It houses the famous and beautiful **tomb★★★** *(arca)*: the fine sarcophagus is by Nicola Pisano (1267) while the arch with statues (1468-73) crowning it was executed by Niccolò da Bari, who was afterwards known as Niccolò dell'Arca, and completed by Michelangelo in 1494 with the two missing saints (Saint Procolo and Saint Petronius) and the angel on the right. The low reliefs by Nicola Pisano depict the life and miracles of St Dominic while the finial by Niccolò represents the celebration of creation symbolised by *putti* (the sky), garlands (the earth) and dolphins (the sea).

The chapel to the right of the presbytery has a fine painting by Filippino Lippi, the *Mystic Marriage of St Catherine* (1501). The choir has preserved its choir stalls executed by the monk Domenico da Bergamo in 1541.

Nearby, in Via D'Azeglio, is **Palazzo Bevilacqua★**, an admirable Renaissance, Florentine-style palace.

Chiesa di San Francesco★

This church was erected in the middle of the 13C and constitutes one of the first examples of Gothic architecture in Italy. From Piazza Malpighi note the three tombs of the glossarists (legal annotators) executed in the 13C. In the background rises the **apse structure★**, characterised by imposing flying

> ### THE LORD'S DOGS
> St Dominic was born in Spain in 1170. His mother was Blessed Joan de Aza de Guzmán who, when pregnant, had a vision that her unborn child was a dog bearing a torch, symbolising truth and the flame of faith. In 1216, St Dominic founded the Order of Preachers, more commonly known as the Dominicans. This name came from the Latin name for the legend (*Domini canes*, the Lord's dogs), and the dog and torch sometimes appear in representations of St Dominic. He established a friary in Bologna and died there in 1221.

buttresses of French influence. Inside, at the high altar, is a magnificent marble **altarpiece★** (1392), by the Venetian sculptor Paolo dalle Masegne.

A door on the right opens on to the Renaissance Chiostro dei Morti (cloisters) which afford a good view of the side of the church and the two bell towers.

Not far from the church of San Francesco is the Museo Civico Medievale (*see below*).

MUSEUMS

Pinacoteca Nazionale★★

Via Belle Arti 56, entrance on via Zamboni (off the map). ♿ *Open daily 9am-7pm. Closed 1 Jan, 1 May, 25 Dec. €4.13.* ☎ *051 24 32 22.*

An important collection of painting, predominantly of the Bolognese school from the 13C to the 18C. Among the Bolognese works are the energetic *St George and the Dragon*★ by Vitale da Bologna and Giotto's *Madonna Enthroned and Child*. The section on Renaissance painting boasts a dramatic fragment depicting Mary Magdalene by Ercole de' Roberti, Francesco del Cossa's *Mercanti Altarpiece*, Perugino's *Virgin and Child*★, which had a profound influence on the Bolognese school and *St Cecilia*★★ by Raphael, who portrays the theme of renunciation with symbolic instruments abandoned on the ground. The **Carracci Room★★** contains numerous masterpieces by Ludovico, one of the great interpreters of the new spirituality of the Counter-Reformation with his blend of quiet intimacy and high emotion: the graceful *Annunciation*, the *Bargellini Madonna* (note the view of Bologna), the *Madonna degli Scalzi* and the dramatic *Conversion of St Paul* which heralds Baroque painting. Of Agostino Carracci note the *Communion of St Jerome* and of Annibale Carracci's work, the *Assumption of the Virgin*, a masterpiece that can already be considered an example of Baroque painting. The **Guido Reni Room★★** houses some stunning work by this painter who, after an initial adherence to the work of the Carracci, leant towards a classicism that had its roots in Raphael and Classical art. In the famous *Massacre of the Innocents* the eternal moment is captured in a skilful composition and in the careful balance of architecture and figures forming a reversed triangle. The intense *Portrait of a Widow*, generally thought to be a portrait of the artist's mother, with its blend of keen psychological insight and balanced use of colour, is considered one of the finest portraits in Italian 17C painting. In the **Baroque corridor** is *St William*★, an early masterpiece of Baroque art by Guercino who added an expressive use of colour reminiscent of Titian to the lessons he had learnt from the Carracci. Of 18C painting note the works by Giuseppe Maria Crespi, one of the major painters of 18C Italy including the *Courtyard Scene*★ and the charming *Girl with a Rose and Cat*.

Museo Civico Archeologico★★

(♿) *Open daily, 9am-6.30pm, Sun and public holidays 10am-6.30pm (last admission 6pm). Closed 1 Jan, 1 May, 25 Dec. Guided tours available (allow 1-2hr). €4.* ☎ *051 23 38 49; www.comune.bologna.it/bologna/Musei/Archeologico/*

The atrium and inner courtyard of the municipal museum house an archaeological collection and the adjacent wing houses the plaster casts gallery. On the first floor is an extensive collection of funerary artefacts (7C BC) from the tombs in the graveyard in Verucchio (near Rimini), one of the major centres of Villanovian culture in Emilia. Also representative of this civilisation is the **askos Benacci**, thought to be an unguent and perfume jar. The museum also has prehistoric, Egyptian, Greek and Roman (fine Roman copy of the **head of Athena Lemnia**, the bronze statue by Phidias) and Etruscan-Italian sections.

Museo Civico Medievale

(♿) *Open Tue-Sat 9am-6.30pm, Sun and public holidays 10am-6.30pm (last admission 6pm). Closed Mon, 1 Jan, 1 May, 25 Dec. €4.13. ☎ 051 20 39 30, www.comune.bologna.it/iperbole/museiciv*

The Medieval Civic Museum is housed in the fine **Palazzo Fava-Ghisilardi★** (late 15C) which stands on the site of the Imperial Roman palace. The collections relate the development of art in Bologna from the Middle Ages to the Renaissance. Among the exhibited works note the University glossarists' tombs, the statue of Boniface VIII by Manno Bandini (1301), a beautiful English cope of the 13C and the fine memorial stone of Domenico Garganelli, made by Francesco del Cossa in about 1478.

Excursion

Madonna di San Luca

5km/3mi southwest. Leave the city centre by Via Saragozza. The 18C church is linked to the city by a **portico★** (4km/2.5mi long) of 666 arches. In the chancel is the *Madonna of St Luke*, a painting in the 12C Byzantine style. There is a lovely **view★** of Bologna and the Apennines.

Bolzano★

BOZEN

Nestling comfortably in the valley, the surrounding slopes covered with orchards and vineyards, the industrial and commercial town of Bolzano is now also a busy tourist centre. The architecture of the town shows a marked Tyrolean or Austrian influence which was exercised between the 16C and 1918. At the centre of the town are **Piazza Walther** and the delightful **Via dei Portici★**, overlooked by some lovely houses.

Location

Population 97 232 – Michelin map 429 C 15-16, town plan in the Michelin Atlas Italy – Trentino-Alto Adige. Capital of the Alto Adige, Bolzano lies on A 22, the Brenner transalpine route, at the confluence of the Adige and the Isarco.
🚪 *Piazza Walther 8,* ☎ *0471 30 70 00.*
Surrounding area. See DOLOMITI, TRENTO.

Directory

WHERE TO EAT
• *Moderate*
Vögele – *Via Goethe 3 –*
☎ *0471 97 39 38 – Closed Sat evening, Sun and public holidays, 15-30 Jul –* ✖ *–*
€26/43.50. A rustic-style eatery, situated near Piazza delle Erbe. Warm and friendly atmosphere, if a little on the noisy side. Regional cooking, wooden tables, no tablecloths. On the first floor, the dining facilities are more stylish and reserved for non-smokers.

WHERE TO STAY
• *Budget*
Albergo Belvedere-Schönblick – *39050 San Genesio –* ☎ *0471 35 41 27 –*
Fax 0471 35 42 77 –
schoenblick.bz@dnet.it – Closed 1 Jan – 🅿
🖳 *– 20 rm €38.73/72.30* 🖵. A short drive from Bolzano, this hotel has fine views over the city itself. An oasis of calm, popular with hikers as well as horse-riding and mountain bike enthusiasts. Cheerful, Tyrolean-style interior decor. High standard of cooking, local fare. The half-board rate represents very good value for money.

Worth a Visit

Duomo★
The cathedral is built of pink sandstone and roofed with multicoloured glazed tiles. Construction work was carried out during various periods including the early Christian Era (5C-6C), the Carolingian Era (8C-9C), the Romanesque (late 12C) and the Gothic periods (13C). The campanile (1501-19) rises to a height of 62m/203ft and includes late Gothic bays. On the north side is the "Small Wine Portal" *(porticina del vino)* on which all the decorative features have a connection with vines and grape harvesting. It indicates the privilege enjoyed by this particular church – an exclusive right to sell wine at this doorway. Inside, there are traces of 14C and 15C frescoes and a fine Late Gothic, carved sandstone **pulpit★** (1514).

Museo Archeologico dell'Alto Adige, "il museo di Ötzi"★
Via Museo 43, at the far end of Via dei Portici. Open daily 10am-6pm (last admission 5pm). Closed 1 Jan, 1 May, 25 Dec €6.70. In order to avoid a long wait, book your tickets in advance: ☎ *0471 98 20 98; www.iceman.it*
This archaeological museum, spread out over three floors, chronologically illustrates the history of the Alto-Adige region from the end of the last Ice Age (15000 BC) to the Carolingian age (AD 800).
The first floor houses the "Iceman", more commonly known as "Ötzi", whose remains were found by a couple of German mountain climbers near the Similaun glacier, in the Ötzi Alps, in 1991. Ötzi lived in the Copper Age and is 5 300 years old. In a study carried out in 2001 it was concluded that his death at about 45 years of age was the result of an arrow wound. His body was trapped in the ice which assured his preservation. He is now kept in refrigerated cells which maintain the mummy's temperature at –6°C/21°F with a level of humidity of about 100%. It is both touching and fascinating to see Ötzi on the other side of the glass with his various belongings such as a cape and an axe. Films and audioguides make the visit come alive for both adults and children.

Chiesa dei Domenicani

Piazza Domenicani. Open Mon-Sat 9.30am-6pm, Sun and public holidays 12-6pm. Donation appreciated. ☎ 0471 97 91 33; www.bolzano-bozen.it

The Dominican church was built in the early 14C in the Gothic style with a deep presbytery that is separated from the nave by a rood screen. The church was later altered and was subsequently damaged after the secularisation of 1785. To the right beyond the rood screen is the chapel of San Giovanni which is covered in frescoes from the Giotto School and is reminiscent of the Scrovegni Chapel in Padua. The frescoes depict scenes from the lives of the Blessed Virgin Mary, St John the Baptist, St Nicholas and St John the Evangelist. Another set of frescoes, by Friedrich Pacher (15C), can be seen in the cloisters to the right of the church.

Chiesa dei Francescani

Via Francescani 1. Open Mon-Sat 10am-noon and 2.30-6pm. Closed Sun and public holidays. Donation appreciated. ☎ 0471 97 72 93; www.bolzano-bozen.it

Burnt down in 1291, the Franciscan church was rebuilt in the 14C and the Gothic vaulting added in the 15C. The **Nativity altar★** is a remarkable wooden altarpiece carved by Hans Klocker (16C). The delightful little cloisters have elegant fan-vaulting decorated with frescoes by the Giotto School.

Antica parrocchiale di Gries

Access via Corso Libertà. Beyond Sant'Agostino. The original Romanesque building was replaced by a 15C Gothic parish church containing a Romanesque wooden Crucifix (opposite the door) and, to the right of the high altar, a side altar with an **altarpiece★** carved by Michael Pacher (1430-98), an Austrian painter and sculptor from the Tyrol. It depicts the Crowning of the Virgin between Archangel Gabriel who is about to strike the devil and St Erasmus who is holding out the winch that kills him by tearing out his guts. The back features the work of a Bavarian artist (1488). A particularly curious detail is the pair of glasses worn by the person at the bottom of the painting to the right.

Excursions

The Renon Plateau★ (Ritten)

The Renon (Ritten in German) is the plateau which dominates the Isarco Valley (Eisacktal) between Bolzano and Ponte Gardena.

It can be easily reached (by car from Bolzano north or with the funicular at Soprabolzano in Bolzano) and it can even be romantically explored on the electric train which goes from Maria Assunta (Maria Himmelfahrt) to Collalbo (Klobenstein).

The intense green of the plateau is interrupted only by wooden fences and little churches which appear as if from nowhere in their isolated setting, such as the church of Santa Verena, between Longostagno and Sant'Ingenuino.

The Renon overlooks the Dolomites which are best seen from the funicular that goes to Corno del Renon. The plateau is full of tiny charming villages, one of which, Barbiano, has a pretty leaning tower.

Some of the underlying earth is prone to erosion caused by a strange natural phenomenon called "earth pillars".

Water erodes the moraine earth circumventing the rocks thus protecting the underlying terrain. This forms columns surmounted by rocks which last for as long as they can stand the weight of the large stones. When the water makes them too thin, the rocks fall and the unprotected pinnacles crumble.

There are three groups of "pillars" on the Renon: at Soprabolzano, visible from the funicular, at Monte di Mezzo which can be reached by path n .24 from Longomoso, and at Auna di Sotto.

Riviera del **Brenta**★★

The Riviera del Brenta is a bucolic strip of land favoured by the Venetian nobility for their summer residences. For visitors to the area, whether they arrive by water, bicycle or car, these grandiose villas★, their reflections sparkling in the river which meanders slowly from Padua to the lagoon, still exude an aristocratic quality.

Location

Michelin map 429 F 18 – 35km/22mi east of Padua – Veneto. Standing alongside the Brenta canal between Strà and Fusina are numerous lovely Classical villas by Palladio *(see Index).* The tour can be done by boat – the **Burchiello** (boat) leaves from both Venice and Padua. By car take the road which follows the Brenta passing through Strà, Dolo, Mira and Malcontenta. *Surrounding area: see PADOVA, VENEZIA.*

> **A RIVER TRIP WITH A DIFFERENCE...**
> Experience life on the "Burchiello" in the 18C – if only for a day. Even if, these days, the boat is a modern one, it follows the old 18C transport route along the river. ♿ *(guided tour).* The "Burchiello" excursion runs from late Mar to late Oct. Departure from Padua (Piazzale Boschetti) on Wed, Fri and Sun at 8.15am and arrival in Venice (Piazza San Marco) in late pm including visits to Villa Pisani, Villa Widmann (also known as Barchessa Valmerana) and Villa Foscari (known as La Malcontenta). Departure from Venice (Pontile della Pietà) on Tue, Thu and Sat at 9am; same programme but visits in reverse order. Arrival in Padua in late pm. Closed Mon. €56.81. For further information contact: Il Burchiello di Sita Spa ☎ 049 87 74 712; www.ilburchiello.it

Worth a Visit

Strà

The **Villa Pisani**★ has a majestic garden with a delightful vista and basin. The spacious **apartments**★ of this 18C palace were decorated by various artists including Giovanni Battista Tiepolo who painted his masterpiece, *The Apotheosis of the Pisani Family*★★. *Open daily, Apr-Sep 9am-7pm, rest of the year 9am-5pm. Closed 1 Jan, 1 May, 25 Dec. Park €2.50, park and villa €5.* ☎ *049 50 20 74.*

Mira

The **Palazzo Foscarini** and **Villa Widmann-Foscari** are both 18C. The **ballroom**★ of the latter is entirely decorated with frescoes. *Villa Widmann:* ♿ *For information and bookings* ☎ *041 56 09 350.*

Malcontenta

Palladio built the Villa Foscari in 1574. Giovanni Battista Zelotti and Battista Franco were responsible for the frescoes. The villa was named after the wife of a Foscari who was ill-pleased *(malcontenta)* at being consigned to the villa. ♿ *€6.20. Information and bookings* ☎ *041 52 03 966.*

Villa Pisani, the residence of the doge Alvise Pisani

Brescia ★

The important industrial town of Brescia lies at the foot of the Lombard Pre-Alps. It has retained the regular street plan of the Roman camp *(castrum)* of Brixia. The town is dominated to the north by a medieval castle (Castello) and its bustling centre has many fine buildings from all periods: Roman, Romanesque, Renaissance and Baroque.

Location

Population 191 317 – Michelin map 428 2 429 F 12 – Lombardy. Brescia lies on A 4, not far from Lake Garda.
🛈 *Piazza Loggia 6,* ☎ *030 24 00 357; www.comune.brescia.it; www.gardanet.it/aptbs Surrounding area: see BERGAMO, Regione dei LAGHI, VERONA.*

Worth a Visit

Piazza della Loggia★

The **Loggia**, now the town hall, was built from the end of the 15C to the beginning of the 16C. Sansovino and Palladio were among those involved in the building of the upper storey. The **Clock Tower** opposite the Loggia is topped by two clockwork figures (Jacks) that strike the hours. On the south side of the square stand the graceful palaces, **Monte di pietà vecchio** (1484) and **Monte di pietà nuovo** (1497). To the north of the square is a picturesque popular quarter with arcades and old houses.

Piazza Paolo VI

The 17C **Duomo Nuovo** (New Cathedral) in white marble seems to crush the **Duomo Vecchio★** (Old Cathedral), a late 11C Romanesque building which succeeded an earlier sanctuary known as the rotunda after its shape. Inside, there is a magnificent sarcophagus in rose-coloured marble surmounted by the recumbent figure of a bishop, and in the chancel paintings by local artists, Moretto and Romanino. The organ was built in 1536 by Antegnati. To the left of the Duomo Nuovo, the **Broletto** is an austere Romanesque building dominated by a massive square tower. Proclamations were made from the balcony on the façade.

Pinacoteca Tosio Martinengo★

(&) *Open daily, Jun-Sep, 10am-5pm; rest of the year 9.30am-1pm and 2.30-5pm. Closed Mon, (open Easter Mon) Tue after Easter, 1 Jan and 25 Dec.* €2.50. ☎ *030 29 77 834; www.comune.brescia.it/musei*
The art gallery displays works of the **Brescia school**, characterised by richness of colour and well-balanced composition: religious scenes and portraits by Moretto, more sumptuous religious scenes in the Venetian manner by Romanino and other works, as well as canvases by Vincenzo Foppa and Savoldo. The works of Clouet, Raphael, the Master of Utrecht, Lorenzo Lotto and Tintoretto are also on view.

Via dei Musei★

This picturesque street has some interesting sites: the ruins of the **Capitoline Temple★** (AD 73), with the remains of the cells, the tribunal and the adjacent Roman theatre (**Teatro Romano**). Beyond the remains of the forum is the monastery founded in AD 753 by Ansa, the wife of the last king of the Lombards, Desiderio. Tradition has it that Desiderio's daughter, Ermengarda, wife of Charlemagne, who later repudiated her, died here. Included in the monastery complex were the basilica of **San Salvatore, the Romanesque church of** Santa Maria in Solario

BRESCIA

and the church of Santa Giulia which dates back to the Renaissance. The complex is now the **Museo della città★**. The City Museum's displays relate the history of the city from the Bronze Age to the present day. The Church of Santa Giulia has a dome decorated with a fresco of God the Father giving His blessing against a star-studded sky and **Desiderio's Cross★★** (8C-9C), richly decorated with precious stones cameos and coloured glass as well as a portrait thought to be that of Galla Placidia and her sons (3C-4C) *Museo della Città:* & *Open daily, Jun-Sep 10am-6pm; rest of the year 9.30am-5.30pm. Closed Mon (open Easter Mon) Tue after Easter, 1 Jan and 25 Dec. €5.16. ☎ 030 29 77 834; www.comune.brescia.it/musei*

HISTORICAL NOTES

Brixia flourished under the Roman Empire and the remains of monuments from this period include the Capitoline Temple and the forum. In the 8C Brescia became a Lombard duchy and then in the 12C and 13C a free commune and member of the Lombard League. The town was one of the most prosperous in Italy, owing to the manufacture of arms and armour. Brescia supplied all Europe until the 18C. From 1426 to 1797 Brescia was under Venetian rule and acquired numerous secular and religious buildings. A group of artists formed the Brescia school and the most important members were, in the 15C, Vincenzo Foppa and in the 16C, Romanino, Moretto, Savoldo and Civerchio.

Castello

Built in 1343 for the Visconti over the remains of a Roman temple, the castle was given additional bastions in the 16C and its entrance is decorated with the lion representing St Mark. It now houses the **Museo delle armi Luigi Marzoli**, an interesting collection of arms and armour from the 14C to 18C. Roman remains can be seen inside the museum. (&) *Jun-Sep 10am-5pm; rest of the year 9.30am-1pm and 2.30-5pm. Closed Mon (open Easter Mon), Tue after Easter, 1 Jan and 25 Dec. €2.50.* ☎ *030 29 77 834; www.comune.brescia.it/musei*

▶▶S. Francesco★ (8C); S. Maria dei Miracoli (façade★); S.S. Nazaro e Celso (*Coronation of the Virgin*★ by Moretto); S. Alessandro (*Annunciation*★ by Jacopo Bellini, *Descent from the Cross*★ by Civerchio); S. Agata (*Virgin of Pity*★ by the 16C Brescian School and the *Virgin with Coral*★); S. Giovanni Evangelista; Madonna delle Grazie; Madonna del Carmine.

Brindisi

Its name probably derives from the Greek *Brenteséion* (stag head), which evokes the shape of the old city which was enclosed by two "seni" (breasts) of water surrounding it from east and west. It was Trajan who replaced the old Appian Way beyond Benevento with the new Via Traiana which increased the importance of Brindisi from AD 109 onwards. After the Norman conquest the town became a port of embarkation for the Crusades to the Holy Land, and in particular saw the departure of the Sixth Crusade (1228).

Location
Population 93 454 – Michelin map 431 F 35 – Puglia. This important naval and trading port, on the Adriatic side of the 'boot's heel', has a daily shipping connection with Greece. Brindisi is on S 379. ❷ *Lungomare Regina Margherita,* ☎ *0831 52 30 72. Surrounding area: see LECCE, PUGLIA, TARANTO.*

Worth a Visit

The city centre contains the most interesting monuments. Principal access to the old city was through **Porta Mesagne** which was opened in the 13C. Guarding the Seno di Ponente stands the **Swabian Castle** (Castello Svevo) which was built on the initiative of Frederick II in 1227 and today houses the Navy. On the cape, near the port, stand two marble **Roman columns** which probably denoted the end of the Appian Way.

Piazza Duomo
The square is overlooked by the Balsamo Loggia (at the corner of Tarantini) which dates from the 14C, the Portico of the Knights Templar (14C) and the Romanesque cathedral (Duomo) which was rebuilt in the 18C. Inside, at the end of the north aisle and around the high altar are remains of the old mosaic flooring. The piazza also houses the **Museo Archeologico F. Ribezzo** which contains many artefacts from excavations. Note in particular the collection of Apulian, Messapici and Attic vases. *Tour: Open Mon-Fri, 9.30am-7.30pm. Also open Sat and Sun in Jul and Aug 9am-1.30pm. No charge.* ☎ *080 48 27 895; www.egnazia.3000.it*

Chiese
The historic centre contains numerous churches. The church of **San Giovanni al Sepolcro** is a Templar church erected in the 11C whose doorway is heralded by a porch held up by columns with stylised lion bases. The church of **San Benedetto** (11C) has a very simple interior consisting of a nave and two aisles divided by columns with Corinthian capitals and one column adorned with animal decorations (ox, lion, ram). The ceiling has ribbed vaulting. The adjacent cloisters are enclosed by a portico with polygonal columns with stylised capitals.

The small Romanesque church of **Santa Lucia** has 13C fresco remains in its interior (unfortunately these are very patchy). Underneath the church stands the old Basilian structure with its vaulted ceiling held up by columns with Corinthian capitals. The walls are covered with fine **frescoes** (12C), some of which are well preserved such as the *Virgin and Child* and, on the right, the *Maddalena Mirrofora* (Magdalene bearing Myrrh) holding a casket with two phials.

Excursion

Chiesa di Santa Maria del Casale★
5km/3mi to the north, near the airport. This is a splendid Romanesque-Gothic building built on the initiative of Philip d'Anjou and his wife Catherine of Flanders in the 14C. The façade, enlivened by bi-coloured geometric patterns, is characterised by a porch crowned by an embellishment consisting of Lombard arches which mirror the motif of the eaves on the façade. The interior has an interesting cycle of frescoes from the same period in the Byzantine style of which the *Day of Judgement* and the *Tree of the Cross* stand out.

Calabria

The colour of the sea, which is sometimes purple as suggested by the name of the coast between Gioia Tauro and Villa San Giovanni, can sometimes distract attention from the land itself which is half covered by mountains. From north to south the backbone of Calabria is formed by the Pollino Massif (Pollino Mountain has an altitude of 2 248m/7 375ft), which is a national park, and by the Sila and Aspromonte massifs. The olive groves produce excellent oil – Rossano oil has a very low level of acidity – and the citrus groves boast a wide variety of fruits including clementines and blond and bergamot oranges.

Location

Michelin map 431 G-N 28-33. Calabria is in the extreme south of the Italian peninsula, covering the narrow stretch of land between the Gulf of Policastro and the Gulf of Taranto. The main access road is A 3, the Salerno-Reggio Calabria motorway.

🛈 *for the* **Parco Nazionale del Pollino**: *Ente Parco Nazionale del Pollino, via Mordini 20, 85048 Rotonda (Potenza),* ☎ *0973 66 78 43, www.parcopollino.it*

HISTORICAL NOTES

The first colonies on the Ionian coast were founded by the Greeks in the 8C BC and they, together with the Byzantines and Basilian monks (**St Basil,** father of the Greek Church, lived from c AD 330-379) shaped the early art and history of this region. In the 3C BC, Rome undertook the conquest of southern Italy, but did not establish a complete and peaceful domination until Sulla reorganised the administration of these provinces in the 1C BC. After the fall of the Roman Empire, Calabria and the neighbouring regions fell under the sway of the Lombards, Saracens and Byzantines before being reunited with the Norman kingdom of the Two Sicilies and finally becoming part of a unified Italy in 1860. Natural disasters, such as the powerful earthquakes which struck in 1783 and 1908, famine, poverty, banditry, social and emigration problems have plagued Calabria which, thanks to agrarian reform and commitment to tourism and cultural activities, finally has occasion for real hope of a rebirth.

Special Features

Massiccio della Sila★★

Sila has an ancient name which signifies "primordial forest": the Greek version of the word is *hyla*, the Latin *silva*. It is a plateau measuring 1 700km²/656sq mi whose forests of larch pine and beech trees alternate with prairies. Average altitude is 1 200m/4 000ft.

On the Sila Grande are the two towns of Camigliatello and Lorica. About ten kilometres away from Camigliatello, the visitors' centre of the **Parco Nazionale della Calabria** offers the chance of taking walks along the fauna enclosures where deer and wolves can be seen in their natural habitat, viewed from wooden constructions with windows. The centre also offers botanical and geological walks.

The wooden houses which dot the landscape contribute to the illusory sensation of being in a northern country; this is the case particularly along the banks of lakes Cecita, **Arvo★** and Ampolino.

A tour of the lakes can come to an end at **San Giovanni in Fiore** where Joachim of Fiore (c 1130-1202) founded a hermitage and a new religious order *(ordine florense)* whose rule is similar to that of the Cistercians but stricter.

Aspromonte★

The Aspromonte Massif forms the southern tip of Calabria and culminates in a peak of 1 955m/6 414ft. The face overlooking the Tyrrhenian coast drops in terraces to the shore while the slope on the Ionian coast descends more gently down to the sea. The forest cover includes chestnut trees, oaks and beeches. The massif serves as a catchment area from which radiate deep valleys eroded by fast-flowing torrents *(fiumare)*. The wide riverbeds are dry in summer but may fill up rapidly and the waters become destructive. S 183 between S 112 and Melito di Porto Salvo runs through attractive scenery and affords numerous and often quite spectacular **panoramas★★★**.

Excursions

THE TYRRHENIAN COAST *Around 200km/120mi. Allow half a day.*

Paola

St Francis of Paola was born here around 1416. A **monastery** (santuario) visited by numerous pilgrims stands 2km/1mi away up the hillside. This large group of buildings includes the basilica with a lovely Baroque façade which enshrines the relics

Directory

WHERE TO EAT

• Budget

Hostaria de Mendoza – *Piazza degli Eroi 3 – 87036 Rende – 10km/6mi northwest of Cosenza –* ☎ *0984 44 40 22 – Closed Wed, Sun (Jul and Aug), 10-18 Aug –* 🚳 *– Booking advisable –* €13/18. An unpretentious restaurant with rustic ambience, heavy wooden furnishings and a multitude of objects hanging from the walls. Genuine home cooking. During the summer, meals are served under a large wooden gazebo on the piazza.

Il Normanno – *Via Duomo 12 – 89852 Mileto – 30km/18mi southeast of Tropea on S18 –* ☎ *0963 33 63 98 – Closed Mon (except Aug), 1-15 Sep –* 🚳 *–* €13/21. Attractive trattoria in the centre. Rustic-style interior with wood panelled walls. Small terraced area for dining in summer. Good, traditional home cooking. Very good value for money.

Trattoria del Sole – *Via Piave 14 bis – 87075 Trebisacce – 15km/9mi north of Sibari on S 106 –* ☎ *0981 51 797 – Closed Sun (except 15 Jun-15 Sep) –* €14/23. This simple eatery is tucked away in the maze of little streets in the historic centre. Warm and friendly atmosphere. Mouthwatering selection of fish (and a few meat) dishes prepared with the freshest ingredients. Ask the proprietor for his recommendations. In summer meals are served on the terrace.

• Moderate

Gambero Rosso – *Via Montezemolo 65 – 89046 Marina di Gioiosa Ionica – 10km/6mi north of Locri on S 106 –* ☎ *0964 41 58 06 – Closed Mon –* 🖥 *–* €34/46. A traditional restaurant located on the main thoroughfare. Good selection of antipasti, laid out on a large table in the entrance of the main dining room. Variety of delicious fish dishes, prepared with super fresh ingredients.

WHERE TO STAY

• Budget

Hotel Punta Faro – *Località Grotticelle, Capo Vaticano – 89685 San Nicolò di Ricardi – 10km/6mi southwest of Tropea –* ☎ *0963 66 31 39 – Fax 0963 66 39 68 – Closed 23 Sep-May –* 🅿 ⚓ *– 25 rm* €33.56/67.13 ⊆ *– Restaurant* €13.42/17.55. This hotel is well situated, a stone's throw from the seafront. Good parking facilities. Rooms are modern and functional in style. Lovely balcony with view out to the Aeolian Islands and Sicily. Free umbrella.

• Moderate

Stillhotel – *Via Melito di Porto Salvo 102/A – 88063 Catanzaro Lido – 14km/8mi south of Catanzaro –* ☎ *0961 32 851 – Fax 0961 33 818 –* 🅿 🖥 ⚿ *– 32 rm* €51.64/61.97 ⊆ *– Restaurant* €24/35. One of the main attractions of this rather unassuming hotel is its quiet, hillside location. Efficient staff. Rooms are spacious and well furnished. The restaurant serves both fish and meat dishes with a regional slant.

Hotel Aquila-Edelweiss – *Via Stazione 11 – 87052 Camigliatello Silano – 31km/19mi northeast of Cosenza on S 107 –* ☎ *0984 57 80 44 – Fax 0984 57 87 53 – Closed Nov and Dec – 48 rm* €51.65/82.63 *–* ⊆ €5.16 *– Restaurant* €25/50. A comfortable hotel, with a warm and friendly atmosphere, tucked away in the conifer woods in the Sita. Attractive 1950s furnishings and fabrics add to the ambience. Worth a detour for the restaurant alone, with its reputation for traditional cuisine and regional specialities.

Hotel Annibale – *Località Le Castella – 88841 Isola di Caporizzuto – 10km/6mi west of Caporizzuto –* ☎ *0962 79 50 04 – Fax 0962 79 53 84 –* 🅿 *– 20 rm* €72.30/82.63 ⊆ *– Restaurant* €28/39. This rather rustic-style hotel is situated in the heart of an old fishing village. Rooms furnished in heavy-duty pine. The dining room boasts a large fireplace and a profusion of pans and meats hanging from the wooden ceiling. Meals served in the garden in summer, under the pergola.

of the saint, cloisters and a hermitage hewn out of the rock which contains striking votive offerings. *Open daily, summer 6.30am-1pm and 2-8pm, winter 6.30am-1pm and 3-6pm* ☎ 0963 81 25 18.

Tropea★★

Tropea is built on a sandy clifftop. Opposite stands the solitary church of Santa Maria dell'Isola which clings to a rock. The most evocative reference to the past is to be found in the Romanesque-Norman **cathedral** which has its original façade. The Swabian **portico** which is grafted onto the façade links the church to the bishop's residence.

Palmi

This small town perched high above the sea has a small fishing harbour and a lovely sandy beach. The **Museo comunale** *(Casa della Cultura, Via San Giorgio)* has an **ethnographic section★** evoking the life and traditions of Calabria: local costumes, handicrafts, ceramics etc. *Open daily, 8am-2pm, Mon and Thu also 3-6pm. Closed Sat, Sun and public holidays.* €1.55. ☎ 0966 26 22 50.

Scilla★

The waters around Scilla, like the waters of Bagnara Calabra, contain swordfish. The name is mythological: Scilla was a woman who was forced to live the life of a sea monster. She was surrounded by dogs who devoured any passing creature. This was what happened to six of Ulysses' companions.

Opposite Scilla, near Messina, lurks Charybdis whom Zeus turned into a sea monster in punishment for her voracity. But even in the guise of a sea monster Charybdis did not lose her fame: three times a day she engulfs the surrounding waves thereby swallowing everything in the sea around her. Subsequently she spurts the water out thus creating a strong current. Ulysses narrowly escaped her clutches by grabbing a fig tree situated at the entrance of the monster's grotto.

The fisherman's district, the Chinalèa, is comprised of an intricate maze of houses and alleys going down to the water's edge. Higher up, Ruffo Castle (1255) extends its noble and reassuring gaze over the town.

AROUND THE "TOE" AND ALONG THE IONIAN COAST

Around 500km/300mi. Allow 2 days.

Pentedattilo★

Pentedattilo is a striking ghost town, totally abandoned by its inhabitants. Legend has it that the menacing rock resembling a hand that stands above it (in Greek *pentedàktylos* signifies "five fingers") put an end to men's violence. There is some truth to this: no voices have echoed in the narrow alleyways of the town since the mid-1960s as it was deemed unsafe due to the danger of collapse.

Locri

Locri was founded by the Greeks in the 7C BC. The town was ruled by the severe laws decreed by Zeleucos, the first legislator of *Magna Graecia,* and was one of the rival cities to Crotone which she defeated during the battle of Sagra. After having sided with Hannibal, along with the other towns on the Ionian coast during the Second Punic War, it declined in importance and was destroyed by the Saracens in the 9C AD. Most of the town's antiquities can be seen in the museum in Reggio di Calabria. There is an interesting excavation site *(Locri Epizefiri)* to the south of the town.

Gerace

Gerace rises up on a hill with an altitude of 480m/1 575ft. The town's symbol is a hawk which is reflected in its Greek name, *hierax.* For a long time Gerace preserved Greek culture and liturgy; for a time Byzantines and Normans lived there together, and it was subjected to invasions by the Swabians, French and Aragonese. It was also an illustrious episcopal seat. At one time Gerace possessed so many churches that it was known as "the city of a hundred bells". Its 11C **cathedral** has vast dimensions: 73m/240ft x 26m/85ft. The three aisles are divided by 20 Greek and Roman columns.

In the Largo delle Tre Chiese (square of three churches) stands the **Church of San Francesco**, which has an Arab-Gothic doorway and a **high altar★** in polychrome marble.

The Cattolica church in Stilo, a delicate expression of 10C Greek-Byzantine art

T. Zane/MICHELIN

Stilo

The native town of the philosopher **Tommaso Campanella** (1568-1639), filled with hermitages and Basilian monasteries, clings to the slopes of a mountain at an altitude of 400m/1 312ft. Further up, almost camouflaged, is the Byzantine jewel of a church, **La Cattolica★**. This 10C structure has a square plan and is roofed with five cylindrical domes. The elegant external decoration consists of brickwork, a traced central dome and roof tiles. Inside the Greek cross is composed of nine domed and barrel-vaulted sections each held up by four marble columns. Unfortunately one cannot admire the mosaics which are very damaged. (&) *Open daily, 21 Mar-21 Oct, 8am-8pm, rest of the year 8am-6pm. No charge.* ☎ *0964 77 60 06, www.recil.net/racil/stilo*

Capo Colonna

This cape was once called Capo Lacinio. From the last decades of the 8C BC one of the most famous temples of Magna Graecia stood here, the temple of Hera Lacinia. It had a golden age in the 5C BC but began to decline in 173 BC when the Consul Fulvio Flacco removed part of the marble roof which he was subsequently unable to repair due to the complexity of the original design. It was then plundered by pirates and became a quarry from which the Aragonese extracted material used for construction of the foundations of Crotone in the 16C. The temple was finally destroyed by an earthquake in 1683. Now only 48 columns remain of this Doric temple which was dedicated to the most important goddess of Olympus. In 1964 Pier Paolo Pasolini (1922-75) shot some scenes of his film *The Gospel According to St Matthew* here.

Crotone

The ancient town of Croton was an Achaean colony of Magna Graecia, founded in 710 BC and celebrated in Antiquity for its riches, the beauty of its women and the prowess of its athletes, such as Milo of Croton, so admired by Virgil. Around 532 BC Pythagoras founded several religious communities which devoted themselves to the study of mathematics and which, once they had become too powerful, were expelled northwards towards Metapontum (present-day Metaponto). The rival city of Locari defeated Croton in the mid-6C BC, which in turn defeated its other rival Sybaris. The city welcomed Hannibal during the Second Punic War before being conquered by Rome. Crotone is today a prosperous seaport and industrial centre as well as a popular holiday resort. The town also houses a **Museo Archeologico**. *Museum: & Open daily, 9am-8pm (last admission 7.30pm). Closed 1st and 3rd Mon of the month and when exhibitions are being set up. €2.07. ☎ 0962 23 082.*

Cattedrale di Santa Severina★

The 13C cathedral has a remarkable 8C circular **baptistery★** which shows a strong Byzantine influence. The Norman Castle is also of interest.

Rossano

The town spreads over a hillside clad with olive groves. In the Middle Ages it was the capital of Greek monasticism in the west, where expelled or persecuted Basilian monks came for refuge, living in the cells which can still be seen today. The perfect little Byzantine **church of San Marco** dates from this period. The flat east end has three projecting semicircular apses with graceful openings. To the right of the cathedral, the **Museo Diocesano** in the former archbishop's residence has a valuable **Purpureus Codex★**, a 6C evangelistary with brightly coloured illuminations. *(&) Open Tue-Sat 9.30am-12.30pm and 4-7pm, Sun and public holidays, 10am-noon and 4.30-6.30pm. Closed Mon €3.10. ☎ 0983 52 52 63.*

Situated 20km/12mi to the west of the town is a small church, **Santa Maria del Patire,** the only remaining building of a large Basilian monastery. The church has a nave and two apses ornamented with blind arcading and inside, mosaics portraying various animals.

Sibari

The town was founded in the 8C BC in a very fertile plain which was the source of the exceptional prosperity of the ancient city of **Sybaris**. It was razed in 510 BC by the neighbouring city of Crotone. There is a small archaeological museum (Museo Archeologico) and an excavation site (Parco Archeologico della Sibaritide**)** to the south of the town. *Museum: & Open daily, 9am-8pm. Closed 1st and 3rd Mon, 1 Jan, 1 May, 25 Dec €2 ☎ 0981 79 392; www.museodellacalabria.com Park: Open daily, 9am-1hr before sunset. Closed 1st and 3rd Mon, 1 Jan, 1 May, 25 Dec. No charge. ☎ 0981 79 166; www.museodellacalabria.com*

Rocca Imperiale★

This picturesque village has grown up around an imposing castle built by the Emperor Frederick II.

Touring Calabria

Cosenza

Town plan in the Michelin Atlas Italy. The modern town is overlooked by the old town where streets and palaces recall the prosperity of the Angevin and Aragonese periods. Cosenza was then considered the artistic and religious capital of Calabria. The 12C-13C **cathedral** (Duomo) has recently been restored to its original aspect. Inside is the **mausoleum★** containing the heart of Isabella of Aragon, the wife of Philip III, King of France and son of Louis IX (St Louis who died in Tunis). She died in 1271 outside Cosenza on the way back from Tunis with the sainted king's body and was buried in St-Denis Basilica in France.

Altomonte

30km/19mi south of Castrovillari. The large market town is dominated by an imposing 14C Angevin cathedral dedicated to **Santa Maria della Consolazione**. The façade is embellished with a doorway and an elegant rose window. Inside there are no aisles and the east end is flat. The fine **tomb★** is that of Filippo Sangineto. The small **museo civico** beside the church has several precious works of art in addition to a statue of *St Ladislas★* attributed to Simone Martini. *Tour: Open daily, Apr-Sep 9am-7pm, rest of the year 9am-1pm and 2-7pm, Sun and public hols 10am-1pm and 4-7pm.* €3. ☎ *0981 94 82 16; www.altomonte.comune.cs.it*

Serra San Bruno

Between the Sila and Aspromonte Massifs, amid the Calabrian mountains covered with oak and pine **forests★**, this small market town grew up around a **hermitage** founded by St Bruno. The 12C charterhouse *(1km/0.6mi from the town)* and the cave which served as hermitage *(4km/2.4mi southwest of the latter)* recall the memory of St Bruno who died in 1101.

Isola di **Capri**★★★

Capri has always been an enchanting place, with its ideal position off the Sorrento Peninsula, its beautiful rugged landscape, mild climate and luxuriant vegetation. Capri has long been a tourist hotspot. It captivated the Roman emperors Augustus and Tiberius and since the late 19C the island has been a magnet for numerous celebrities: artists and writers, as well as musicians and actors who mingle with the tourists in the fashionable lanes of Capri town. Marina Grande★ is the main port where boats arrive on the northern side of the isle. Here the houses, some white, some in varied hues, nestle around the bay framed by spectacular cliffs. A funicular railway connects Marina Grande to Capri, where there is a bus service to Anacapri.

Location

Population 7 235 – Michelin map 431 F 24 – Campania. Capri can be reached by ferry from Naples and Sorrento. 🄱 *for crossings: Caremar-Agenzia Angelina, Via C. Colombo 10, 80073 Capri,* ☎ *081 83 70 700; Alilauri, Marina Grande 2/4, 80073 Capri,* ☎ *081 83 76 995; Navigazione Libera del Golfo, piazza Vittoria, 80073 Capri,* ☎ *081 83 70 819. Funicular: €2.06 one-way ticket on funicular railway plus several bus routes, €6.71 cumulative ticket valid 1 day for two trips in funicular railway and unlimited bus rides for several routes. touristoffice@capri.it*
Surrounding area: see COSTIERA AMALFITANA, ISCHIA, NAPOLI, Golfo di NAPOLI.

Worth a Visit

CAPRI★★★

Capri is like a stage setting for an operetta with its small squares, little white houses and its quite Moorish-looking alleyways. Another of its charms is that wild and lonely spots can still be found near crowded and lively scenes.

Piazza Umberto I★

This famous piazzetta is the centre of town and the spot where fashionable crowds gather. The busy narrow side streets, such as **Via Le Botteghe★**, are lined with souvenir shops and smart boutiques selling luxury goods.

Belvedere Cannone★★

To reach the belvedere take **Via Madre Serafina★**, which is almost entirely vaulted. The belvedere presents the peaceful and mysterious aspect of Capri with its covered and winding stepped alleys.

Directory

WHERE TO EAT

• Budget

Le Arcate – *Viale T. De Tommaso 24 –*
80071 Anacapri – ☎ 081 83 73 325 –
www.caprionline.it – Closed Mon, 15 Jan-1
Mar. A simple eatery, just a stone's throw
from the centre. This place is popular with
tourists looking for a quick bite at
lunchtime. During the evening it is quieter
and more relaxing. Good for both pizzas
and pasta.

Pulalli Wine Bar – *Piazza Umberto I –*
80073 Capri – ☎ 081 83 74 108 –
pulalli@libero.it – Closed Tue, 1 Dec-15 Mar
(except 27 Dec-3 Jan) – 🖬 – €13. A pleasant
wine bar, situated up the steps by the tourist
office. Head for the much sought-after tables
on the little terrace where there is a good
view over the piazza. Inside dining area is
modern and elegant. Some excellent wines
and a good choice of first and second
courses. Also good for snacks.

Verginiello – *Via Lo Palazzo 25/A – 80073*
Capri – ☎ 081 83 70 944 – Closed 10-
25 Nov – 🖬 – €18/39. This unpretentious,
family-run restaurant is situated just as you
enter Capri. From the large terrace and
dining room there are fine views out to sea
and over the Marina Grande. Cooking is of a
high quality. Specialises in fish and seafood
dishes. Value for money.

La Savardina – Da Eduardo – *Via lo Capo*
8 – 80073 Capri – About 40min on foot
from Capri on the road to Villa Jovis –
☎ 081 83 76 300 – Closed Tue in Apr,
4 Nov-1 Mar (except 27 Dec-3 Jan) –
€21/26 + 10% service charge. If you decide
to visit Villa Jovis or are in the mood for a
walk, make sure you leave enough time for
lunch en route. The mouth-watering
flavours, shady citrus grove and unforgettable view will linger on in your memory.

• Moderate

Da Giorgio – *Via Roma 34 – 80073 Capri –*
☎ 081 83 75 777 – www.caprihotels.com –
Closed Tue, 8 Jan-Easter – €22/39 + 12%
service charge. A pleasant, unpretentious
restaurant with a wonderful veranda and
huge windows with splendid views over the
gulf of Capri. Traditional cuisine. Also serves
pizzas. Near the centre of Capri

Da Paolino – *Via Palazzo a Mare 11, Marina*
Grande – 80073 Capri – ☎ 081 83 76 102 –
Closed at lunchtime (late Sep), Nov-Easter –
€31/89 + 10% service charge. This

restaurant is best described as the
Mediterranean equivalent of the
Garden of Eden, deliciously scented
with the aroma of lemons. Warm and
friendly ambience. The wrought-iron tables
are a nice touch. Serves both meat and fish
dishes.

Aurora – *Via Fuorlovado 18 – 80073 Capri –*
☎ 081 83 70 181 – Closed Jan-Mar –
€28/57 +15% service charge. Pleasant
eatery, well-established and family run.
Popular with celebrities. Informal atmosphere
but elegant ambience. Good selection of
wines to accompany both fish and meat
dishes. Small dining area outside – very
sought after.

WHERE TO STAY

• Moderate

Hotel Florida – *Via Fuorlovado 34 – 80073*
Capri – ☎ 081 83 70 710 – Fax
081 83 70 042 – Closed 6 Nov-Feb – 19 rm
€51.65/87.80 – 🖵 €9.81. A small hotel,
centrally located and just two minutes from
the funicular down to the beach, but for all
that an oasis of calm. 1950s-style, simple
interior with a lacquer finish. Breakfast is
served on the terrace in the garden. Very
reasonably priced.

Hotel Villa Eva – *Via La Fabbrica 8 – 80071*
Anacapri – 100m from the bus-stop for the
Grotta Azzurra – ☎ 081 83 71 549 –
Fax 081 83 72 040 – Closed Nov-1 Mar – ✉
🛏 – Booking advisable – 10 rm. Double
€87.80/92.96 🖵. An oasis of peace and
quiet situated near the legendary Grotta
Azzurra. Surrounded by luxuriant greenery
are a number of small-scale buildings –
predominantly Mediterranean in style. You
can doze off in a hammock or head to the
swimming pool.

• Expensive

Capri Palace Hotel – *Via Capodimonte –*
80071 Anacapri – ☎ 081 83 73 800 –
Fax 081 83 73 191 – Closed Nov-Mar – 🛏
🖬 – 80 rm from €185.92 🖵 – Restaurant
€52. For sheer elegance, exquisite taste
and attention to detail, look no further
than this hotel. Facilities include suites and
rooms with private pool. And if this isn't
enough, indulge yourself with a treatment
at the spa.

Belvedere di Tragara★★

Access by Via Camerelle and Via Tragara. There is a magnificent view of the
Faraglioni.

Certosa di San Giacomo e Giardini d'Augusto

Open daily, 9am-2pm, Sun 9am-1pm. Closed Mon and public holidays. No charge.
☎ 081 83 76 218.
This 14C Carthusian Monastery of St James has two cloisters. In the smallest are
displayed Roman statues taken from the nymphaeum of the Blue Grotto.
From Augustus' Gardens there is a beautiful **view★★** of Punta di Tragara and the
Faraglioni. Lower down, **Via Krupp★**, clinging to the rock face, leads to Marina
Piccola.

One of many delightful viewpoints on Capri

Marina Piccola★

At the foot of the steep slopes of Monte Solaro is a harbour for fishing boats and there are beautiful small beaches.

Villa Jovis★★

Open 9am-1hr before sunset. Closed public holidays. €2.07. ☎ 081 83 70 381.

Jupiter's Villa was the residence of the Emperor Tiberius. Excavations have uncovered servants' quarters, the cisterns that supplied the baths, and the Imperial apartments with a loggia overlooking the sea.

From the esplanade overlooked by the church, there is a lovely **panorama★★** of the whole island.

Take the stairway behind the church to enjoy a view of **Tiberius' Leap★** (Salto di Tiberio), the impressive cliff from which the emperor is said to have had his victims thrown.

Arco naturale★

The sea has created this gigantic natural rock arch which rises well above sea level. Lower down is the **Grotta di Matromania**, a cave where the Romans venerated the goddess Cybele.

ANACAPRI★★★

Take Via Roma and a beautiful corniche road to reach Anacapri, a delightful village with shady streets, which is much less crowded than Capri.

Villa San Michele★

Access from Piazza della Vittoria. Open May-Sep, 9am-6pm. Rest of the year 9.30am-1hr before sunset. €5. ☎ 081 83 71 401; www.caprionline.com/axelmunthe

The villa was built at the end of the 19C for the Swedish doctor-writer, Axel Munthe (d 1949), who lived here up to 1910 and described the atmosphere of the island in his *Story of San Michele*. The house contains 17C and 18C furniture, copies of

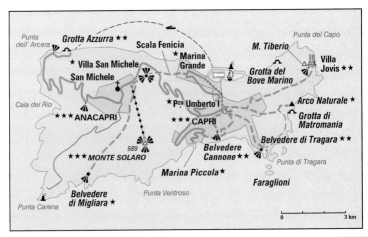

Classical works and some original Roman sculptures. The pergola at the end of the beautiful **garden** giddily overhangs the sea and provides a splendid **panorama**★★★ of Capri, Marina Grande, Mount Tiberius and the Faraglioni.

Just below the villa is a stairway, **Scala Fenicia**, which numbers nearly 800 steps and leads down to the harbour. It was for a long time the only link between the town and its port. This is where Axel Munthe met the old Maria "Porta-Lettere" who delivered the mail although she could not read, and who is depicted in his book.

Chiesa di San Michele

Open Jun-Sep, 9.30am-7pm, rest of the year 10am-1hr before sunset. €1.03. ☎ *081 83 72 396.*

From the organ gallery note the fine majolica **floor**★ (1761) after a cartoon by Solimena which represents the Garden of Eden.

Monte Solaro★★★

The chairlift operates from Apr to Oct, 9.30am-5pm, rest of the year 9.30am.3pm. Closed Tue (winter only) €5.50 return. ☎ *081 83 71 428.*

The chairlift swings pleasantly above gardens and terraces brimming over with luxuriant vegetation. From the summit there is an unforgettable **panorama**★★★ of the whole island and the Bay of Naples as far as the island of Ponza, the Apennines and the mountains of Calabria to the south.

Belvedere di Migliara★

1hr on foot there and back. Pass under the chairlift to take Via Caposcuro. There is a remarkable **view**★ of the lighthouse on the headland, Punta Carena, and of the sheer cliffs.

Excursions

Grotta Azzurra★★

Boats leave from Marina Grande. It is also possible to go by road (8km/5mi from Capri). Boat trip and visit to the cave all year, daily (except at high tide and when the sea is rough), 9am-1hr before sunset. Duration: 1hr. €8.10. Excursion from Marina Grande €12.65 with the following companies: Laser Capri (☎ 081 83 75 208), Gruppo Motoscafisti (☎ 081 83 75 646); the price includes trip by fast boat, small boat and grotto. Sun and public holidays, a supplement is payable: €0.36 for the small boat and €0.52 for the fast boat (Gruppo Motoscafisti).

The Blue Grotto is the most famous among the many marine caves on the island. The light enters, not directly, but by refraction through the water, giving it a beautiful blue colour.

Trip around the island★★★

Leave from Marina Grande. Boat trip all year (except when the sea is rough), departing from Marina Grande at regular intervals 9.30am-3pm (summer); 10am-noon (winter), with the following companies: Gruppo Motoscafisti (☎ 081 83 75 646), Laser Capri (☎ 081 83 75 208). Duration: about 2hr. €7.75-10.33 (depending on which company), + €8.01 for a trip to the Grotta Azzurra; prices higher on Sun and public holidays.

Visitors will discover a rugged coastline, pierced with caves and small peaceful creeks, fringed with fantastically shaped reefs and lined with sheer cliffs dipping vertically into the sea.

The island is quite small: barely 6km/4mi long and 3km/2mi wide. The particularly mild climate favours the growth of a varied flora: pine, lentisk, juniper, arbutus, asphodel, myrtle and acanthus.

The boats go in a clockwise direction and the first sight is the **Grotta del Bove Marino** (Sea Ox Cave), which derives its name from the roar of the sea rushing into the cave in stormy weather. Beyond is the headland (Punta del Capo) dominated by Mount Tiberius (Monte Tiberio). Once past the impressive cliff known as Tiberius' Leap (see above), the headland to the south, Punta di Tragara, is fringed by the famous **Faraglioni**, rocky islets eroded into fantastic shapes by the waves. The **Grotta dell'Arsenale** (Arsenal Cave) was used as a nymphaeum during the reign of Tiberius.

Continue past the small port of Marina Piccola to reach the more gentle west coast. The last part of the trip covers the north coast and includes the visit to the Blue Grotto.

Reggia di **Caserta**★★

As a sensible precaution, Charles III of Bourbon chose Caserta, which was far from the vulnerable Neapolitan coast, as the site for the construction of a magnificent royal palace that could compete with other courts of Europe. The Royal Palace of Caserta, together with Vanvitelli's Aqueduct and the San Leucio buildings (which housed the silk factory founded in 1789 by Ferdinand IV of Bourbon), have been included in UNESCO's World Heritage List.

Location

Michelin map 431 D 25 – Campania. Reggia di Caserta is situated just off A 1, about 20km/12mi from Naples.

Surrounding area. See BENEVENTO, COSTIERA AMALFITANA, NAPOLI, Golfo di NAPOLI.

Mysterious mythological figures adorn the park of the royal palace at Caserta

Worth a Visit

Palazzo

(&) *Open daily, 8.30am-7pm. Closed 1 Jan, 1 May, 25 Dec. €4.20.* ☎ *0823 44 71 47.*
In 1752 Charles III of Bourbon commissioned the architect **Luigi Vanvitelli** to erect a royal palace *(reggia)*. Compared to the grand royal residences of the period, Caserta is characterised by a more geometric, severe layout which reflects the personality of the architect. If its purity of line seems almost to anticipate the neo-Classical style, the theatrical design of its interior is still typically Rococo.
The building consists of a vast rectangle (249m/273yd long and 190m/208yd wide) containing four internal courtyards which are interconnected by a magnificent **entrance hall★**. The façade first seen by the visitor is adorned by a projecting colonnade and a double row of windows supported by a rusticated base: the principal façade, facing the garden, reproduces this motif but embellishes it with the use of pilaster strips bordering each window. The sumptuous **grand staircase★★** (scalone d'onore) a masterpiece of Vanvitelli, leads to the Palatine Chapel *(not open to visitors)* and to the luxurious royal apartments decorated in the neo-Classical style. The **Eighteenth Century Apartment** (Appartamento Settecentesco) is particularly interesting with its vaulted frescoed ceilings depicting the seasons and some wonderful views of ports by JP Hackert. The pretty **Queen's Apartment** (Apartamento della Regina) is decorated in a rather frivolous *rocaille* style: some curious pieces include a chandelier adorned with little tomatoes and a cage containing a clock and a stuffed bird. In the Elliptical Room (Sala Ellittica) there is an attractive 18C Neapolitan **crib★** *(presepe)*.

Park

(&) *Open daily, 8.30am-1hr before sunset. Closed Mon, 1 Jan, 25 Dec. €2.* ☎ *0823 44 71 47.*
This park epitomises the ideal grand Baroque garden. Its seemingly infinite expanse is arranged around a central axis consisting of a canal. The fountains and fish-ponds are powered by the Aqueduct, a monumentally ambitious work by Vanvitelli which spans five mountains and three valleys with a total length of 40km/25mi. Of the mythological sculptures adorning the park the most notable is the group of *Diana and Actaeon* which stands at the foot of the great **cascade★★** (78m/256ft high) and depicts the striking scene of a pack of hounds attacking a stag.
To the right of the cascade there is a picturesque English garden **(giardino inglese★★)** created for Maria-Carolina of Austria.

Excursions

Caserta Vecchia★

10km/6mi north. This small town is dominated by the ruins of its 9C castle. The town has a certain charm with its almost deserted narrow alleyways lined by old buildings with their brown tufa walls. The fine 12C **Cathedral** combines Sicilian-Arab, Apulian and Lombard motifs. Inside there is an attractive 13C pulpit. *Tour: Open daily, 9am-1pm and 3.30-7.30pm. No charge.* ☎ 0823 37 13 18.

Basilica di Sant'Angelo in Formis★★

15km/9mi northwest of Caserta Vecchia (take SS 87 to S. Iorio). Open daily, 10am-1pm and 3-6pm. If it is closed, contact Don Franco Duonnolo ☎ 0823 96 04 92.

One of the most beautiful medieval buildings in Campania. Erected in the 11C on the initiative of Desiderio, Abbot of Monte Cassino, the basilica combines a somewhat rudimentary architectural structure with one of the richest Romanesque cycle of frescoes. The interior, divided into a nave and two aisles, is covered in **frescoes**: the Last Judgement (east wall), the Life of Christ (nave), the Old Testament (north and south aisle) and Maestà (apse). Although of local production, these frescoes have a strong Byzantine influence (owing to the intervention of Greek painters who had worked at Monte Cassino), tempered by local culture as can be seen in the slightly crude use of colour and the liveliness of some images. In the apse there is a representation of the Abbot Desiderio offering the church to God (the unusual square halo indicates that the Abbot was still alive when the fresco was painted).

Capua

6km/4mi southwest of S. Angelo in Formis.

This walled city, founded by the Lombards, is the native town of Pier della Vigna, chancellor to Frederick II, and Ettore Fieramosca, Captain of the 13 Italian knights who vanquished the French in the Defeat of Barletta (1503).

On Piazza dei Giudici are the Baroque church of Sant'Eligio, a Gothic arch surmounted by a Loggia and the 16C town hall. The nearby church of the Annunciation (16C) has a lovely drum dome and, inside, a finely crafted wooden chancel and ceiling.

Duomo – *Open daily, 8.30-11.30am and 5-7pm, Sun and public holidays 8-11am.* ☎ 0823 96 10 81.

The cathedral, which dates from the 9C, has been destroyed and rebuilt several times since. The Lombard-style campanile incorporates some ancient fragments at its base. The columns of the atrium have lovely 3C **Corinthian capitals**, while the interior houses a 13C paschal candelabrum, an *Assumption* by F Solimena and, in the crypt, a *Dead Christ,* a fine sculpture of the 18C.

Museo Campano★ – *At the corner of Via Duomo and Via Roma. Open daily, 9am-1.30pm, Sun 9am-1pm. Closed Mon, public holidays.* €4.13. ☎ 0823 96 14 02.

This museum is housed in a 15C building with a fine lava stone Catalan **doorway**. The archaeological section has an astonishing collection of 6C to 1C BC *Matres Matutae,* Italic earth goddesses holding their newborn children and a charming **mosaic**. The medieval section groups some lovely sculptures from remains of the imposing gateway built by the Emperor Frederick II of Hohenstaufen around 1239. Note the head of a woman known as *Capua Fidelis.*

Southeast of the museum there is an area with an interesting series of Lombard churches (San Giovanni a Corte, San Salvatore Maggiore a Corte, San Michele a Corte, San Marcello).

Santa Maria Capua Vetere

3km/2mi southeast of Capua. This is the famous Roman Capua where the downfall of Hannibal was brought about by the temptations that were cast his way. Famous for the production of bronze and black ceramic vases, Capua was considered one of the most opulent cities of the Roman Empire. After Saracen attacks in the 9C, the inhabitants of the city moved to the banks of the River Volturno where they founded the present Capua. The **Anfiteatro Campano★** restored in the 2C AD, is the largest Roman amphitheatre after the Coliseum. It was the seat of the famous gladiator school in which the revolt headed by Spartacus erupted in 73 BC. *Tour: Open daily, 9am-1hr before sunset. Closed Mon, 1 Jan, 1 May, 25 Dec. €2.58 including the Mitreo and the Museo dell'Antica Capua.* ☎ 0823 79 88 64.

The **Mitreo** (2C AD) is an underground rectangular chamber adorned with a rare **fresco★** of the Persian god Mithras sacrificing a bull. *Open daily, 9am-8pm. Closed Mon, 1 Jan, 1 May, 25 Dec. €2.58 including the Anfiteatro and the Museo dell'Antica Capua.* ☎ 0823 84 42 06.

The pleasant **Museo Archeologico dell'Antica Capua** (*Via R. d'Angiò*) has interesting artefacts relating local history from the Bronze Age to the Imperial Age. These include some fine painted architectural terracotta pieces and three *Matres Matutae. Open daily, 9am-8pm. Closed Mon, 1 Jan, 1 May, 25 Dec. €2.58 including the Anfiteatro and the Mitreo.* ☎ 0823 84 42 06.

Parco Nazionale del **Cilento**★

The Cilento nature reserve was founded in 1991 and in 1997 was included in UNESCO's World Nature Reserve List. This Mediterranean park par excellence constitutes a perfect blend of nature and civilisation: it is situated at the cross-roads of the most diverse cultural influences, from the basin of the Mediter-ranean to the Apennines. The variety of the landscape lends itself to a variety of holiday experiences from excursions into the past to trips to the seaside: the coastline has some lovely beaches and is dotted with caves and rocky outcrops.

Location
Michelin map 431 F-G 26-28 – Campania. The territory of the Parco Nazionale del Cilento extends from the Tyrrhenian coast to the Diano Valley (a Pleistocene lake which was engulfed by the River Tanagro) and is bordered to the north by the Alburni Massif and to the south by the Gulf of Policastro. It lies off A 3 between Salerno and Reggio Calabria.
₿ *Via O. De Marsilio, 84078 Vallo della Lucania* ☎ *0974 71 99 11.*
Surrounding area: see CALABRIA.

Background

The vast variety of landscapes is the result of the twofold nature of the rocks. The *flysch* variety of the Cilento is to be found in the western part of the park and along the coast (Stella and Gelbison mountains) with its gentle landscape and Mediterranean vegetation. The calcareous rock of the interior (Alburni mountains and Mount Cerviati) and the southern coast (from Cape Palinuro to Scario) pro-duces a more barren landscape with beech forests and spectacular rock forma-tions, such as the numerous marine and earth caves. The most interesting floral species is the Palinuro primrose, symbol of the park, while typical fauna includes otters, wolves, foxes, hares and royal eagles.

Directory

Tours

Sights are listed based on an ideal itinerary which from Velia descends towards the coast and then makes its way up to the northwest. 170km/102mi. Allow at least 1 day.

Velia★
40km/25mi southeast of Paestum on S 18 and S 267. This colony was founded in 535 BC by Phoenician Greek refugees who had been expelled by the Persians. An active and prosperous port, Velia (known as Elea to the Greeks) became a Roman territory in 88 BC without, however, losing its cultural and linguistic Greek roots. The city was famous for its Eleatic school of philosophy which flourished in the 6C-5C BC and counted Parmenides and his pupil Zeno among its followers.
Ruins – *Pass under the railway line to reach this area. Open daily, 9am-1hr before sun-set. Closed 1 Jan, 1 May and 25 Dec. €2.* ☎ *0974 97 23 96.*
From the entrance there is an interesting view of the archaeological site of the **città bassa** (lower town) with its lighthouse, 4C BC city wall, the south sea-gateway and Roman baths from the Imperial era (mosaic and marble floor remains). From the baths, Via di Porta Rosa borders the marketplace and climbs up to the ancient gate-way (6C BC) and the **Porta Rosa★** (4C BC), a fine example of a cuneiform arch and the most important Greek civic monument in *Magna Graecia.*

The **acropolis** on the promontory above the lower town has remains of the medieval castle erected on the foundations of a Greek temple, and the Palatine Chapel which houses epigraphic material. Slightly lower down are the remains of the Greek theatre which was remodelled in the Roman era. Halfway down, towards the lower town, a Hellenistic villa with fresco remains has been discovered.

Capo Palinuro★★

30km/18mi southeast of Velia on S 447. The name Palinuro refers to Aeneas' mythical steersman who was killed and buried at sea here. From the port of Palinuro there are **boat trips** to the **Grotta Azzurra**★ and other caves that are scattered over the imposing promontory where in springtime the Palinuro primroses are in bloom. ♿ *Open daily, Apr-Nov 9am-6pm, (tour takes about 1hr30min including the caves as well as a short break on one of the beaches). €13. ☎ 0974 93 82 94 or 0974 93 16 04.*

From S 562 make for the natural arch at the mouth of the Mingardo River and the beautiful beaches on the coast *(see Gulf of POLICASTRO).*

66km/40mi northeast on SS 562, SS 447 (passing through Poderia and following signs for Policastro Busentino), SS 517 and SS 19.

Certosa di Padula★

♿ *Open daily, 9am-8pm (on Sat in mid-Jun to mid-Sep until 11pm). €4.13. ☎ 0975 77 745*

The charterhouse of San Lorenzo, founded in 1306, is one of the largest architectural complexes in southern Italy. Because of the vast dimensions, work on the buildings went on for centuries and for the most part its present-day appearance is Baroque. From the cloisters known as Chiostro della Foresteria a splendid 14C cedarwood doorway leads to the sumptuous Baroque **church** which houses the fine 16C Conversi and **Padri**★ chancels and the notable ceramic high altar. The vast **Great Cloisters** (104x149m/341x488ft) are surrounded by monks' cells. The left arcade leads to the dramatic 18C **staircase**★ inspired by the architecture of Vanvitelli.

35km/21mi northwest on SS 19.

Grotte di Pertosa

(♿) Guided tours only (1hr), Apr-Sep, daily, 9am-7pm, rest of the year 9am-4pm. €5.16 (short tour), €7.75 (long tour, recommended). ☎ 0975 39 70 37; www.vipnet.it/pert/grotte.html

These caves, which extend over an area of about 2.5km/1.5mi, are to be found in the evocative setting of the natural amphitheatre of the Alburni mountains and are reached via a small lake formed by an underground river. Inhabited since Neolithic times, the caves have fine concretions, mainly of sodium carbonate; the most interesting area is the so-called **Room of the Sponges** (Sala delle Spugne)

The S 166 leads up to the Sentinella Pass (932m/3 057ft) crossing some enchanting **landscapes**★ dotted with yellow broom.

42km/25mi northeast on SS 19.

Oasi WWF di Persano

(♿) Guided tours only (2hr); Jun-Sep 9am and 5pm; rest of the year 10am, 11am and 3pm (book at least one week in advance). Closed Mon, Tue, Thu, Fri. €5. No charge on the day of the Festa delle Oasi. ☎ 0828 97 46 84.

The "oasis" extends over 110ha/271 acres of alluvial plains formed by the River Sele between the Alburni and Picentini mountains. The most interesting flora can be found in the marshland, one of the last refuges of the otter, symbol of the oasis. Other fauna in the area include numerous aquatic birds, foxes, boars, badgers and weasels.

Cortona★★

Cortona occupies a remarkable site★★ planted with olive trees on the steep slope of a hill overlooking the Chiana Valley not far from Lake Trasimeno. It was part of the League of Twelve Etruscan Towns before coming under the control of Rome. It has retained its medieval town walls, commanded by a huge citadel (fortezza) which replaced the Etruscan precinct. The town, which was annexed to Florence in 1411, has barely changed since the Renaissance period.

Location

Population 22 436 – Michelin map 430 M 17 – See also The Green Guide Tuscany.

Cortona is situated just off S 71, which links Arezzo with Lake Trasimeno. Given its location at the top of a hill which overlooks the Val di Chiana some of the roads are very steep.

ℹ *Via Nazionale 42, ☎ 0575 63 03 52.*

Surrounding area: see AREZZO.

TOWN OF ARTISTS AND SAINTS

Cortona began to attract artists in the 14C and it was the Sienese School which predominated, until the arrival of Fra Angelico (c 1400-55). The town's main claim to fame, however, is that it was the birthplace of a number of famous old masters including **Luca Signorelli** (c 1450-1523) and **Pietro da Cortona** (1596-1669). **Gino Severini** (1883-1966) who was linked to the Futurist movement was also born here.

Directory

Worth a Visit

Piazza del Duomo, close up against the ramparts, affords a lovely view over the valley. The Romanesque cathedral (Duomo), remodelled at the Renaissance, contains some works of art.

Museo Diocesano★★

Opposite the Duomo. Open daily, Apr-Sep 9.30am-1pm and 3.30-7pm, Oct 10am-1pm and 3.30-6pm, rest of the year 10am-1pm and 3-5pm. Closed Mon €5. ☎ *0575 62 830.*
This former church houses a remarkable collection of paintings: a beautiful **Annunciation** and *Madonna and Saints* by Fra Angelico; works from the Sienese school by Duccio, Pietro Lorenzetti and Sassetta; an excellent group of works by **Signorelli**; and a remarkable ***Ecstasy of St Margaret*** by the Bolognese artist Guiseppe Maria Crespi (1665-1747). Note also the fine 2C Roman sarcophagus *(Battle of Lapiths and Centaurs).*

Palazzo Pretorio★

The Praetorian Palace was built in the 13C but altered during a later period. Its façade is original and is decorated with coats of arms while the façade overlooking Piazza Signorelli, which is preceded by a grand staircase, dates from the 17C. Inside, the **Museo dell'Accademia Etrusca★** displays Etruscan exhibits as well as Roman, Egyptian, medieval and Renaissance items. Among the Etruscan objects is a strange 5C BC bronze **oil lamp★★** with 16 burners shaped like human figures. The museum also displays works and memorabilia relating to Severini, bequeathed by the artist to his native town. *Open daily, Apr-Oct 10am-7pm, rest of the year 10am-5pm. Closed Mon, 1 Jan, 25 Dec. €4.20.* ☎ *0575 63 72 35; www.accademia-etrusca.net*

Santuario di Santa Margherita

This enshrines the fine Gothic **tomb★** (1362) of St Margaret. Via Santa Margherita leads off to the south of the church. Severini decorated the street with mosaics representing the *Stations of the Cross.*

Chiesa di San Domenico

Largo Beato Angelico. The church is dedicated to St Dominic. In the south apse is a *Madonna with angels and saints* by Luca Signorelli, a polyptych by Lorenzo di Niccolò at the high altar and a fresco by Fra Angelico.

Chiesa di Santa Maria del Calcinaio★

3km/2mi west. Santa Maria, built from 1485 to 1513 by **Francesco di Giorgio Martini**, strongly resembles the work of Brunelleschi. The church is remarkable for the grace and harmony of its design and its well-balanced proportions. The domed church is built on the Latin cross plan and the lofty interior is well lit.
In the oculus of the façade is a remarkable stained-glass window designed by a French artist, Guillaume de Marcillat (1467-1529).

Costiera amalfitana★★★

AMALFI COAST

With its charming fishing villages and luxuriant vegetation – a mixture of orange, lemon, olive and almond trees, as well as vines and bougainvillea – the region has long been popular with travellers and artists from all over the world. The wild and rugged landscape of the Amalfi coast contrasts with its reputation as a glamorous destination for the international jet set of the 1950s and 1960s who came aboard fabulous yachts in search of La Dolce Vita – as well as shoes, sandals and other brightly coloured fashions. These days the "Costiera" attracts tourists from all walks of life, while maintaining its reputation as a hot spot for the rich and famous.

Location
Michelin map 431 F 25 – Campania. Following the indentations of the rocky coast between Sorrento and Salerno, the corniche road hugs the Amalfi coast, arguably the most stunning coastline in Italy. The artistic and natural beauty of this area earned it a place in UNESCO's 1997 World Heritage List. **🚹** *Corso delle Repubbliche Marinare 27/29, 84011 Amalfi (Salerno), ☎ 089 87 11 07.*
Surrounding area: see CASERTA, NAPOLI, POMPEI, SALERNO. The first 4 itineraries are included in Golfo di NAPOLI which is the ideal point of departure or end to this journey.

Tour

ALONG THE COAST ⑤
79km/47mi – allow 1 day. The route below constitutes the continuation of itinerary ④, as described in Golfo di NAPOLI. For anyone wanting to explore the "Costiera" on its own, the best point of departure is Positano.

Positano♢♢♢
The white cubic houses of this old fishing village reveal a strong Moorish influence; lush gardens dotted on terraced slopes go down to the sea. Positano is "the only place in the world designed on a vertical axis" (Paul Klee). Much loved and frequented in the past by artists and intellectuals (Picasso, Cocteau, Steinbeck, Moravia and Nureyev who bought Li Galli island) and by the trend-setters of *La Dolce Vita* who used to meet up at the *Buca di Bacco* nightclub, today Positano is one of the most popular resorts of the Amalfi coast. "Positano fashion" was born here in the 1950s, with its brightly coloured materials and equally famous sandals that were desperately sought after by women of the jet set during their trips here.

Vettica Maggiore
Its houses are scattered over the slopes. From the esplanade there is a fine **view★★** of the coast and sea.

Positano

G. Targat/MICHELIN

Directory

WHERE TO EAT

• *Moderate*

Giardiniello – *Corso Vittorio Emanuele 17 – 84010 Minori – 5km/3mi northeast of Amalfi on S 163 – ☎ 089 87 70 50 – www.amalfinet.it/giardiniello – Closed Wed (except Jun-Sep), 6 Nov-6 Dec – €26/40.* Restaurant situated in the heart of the village with large airy dining room. Meals served under the pergola in summer. Delicious regional cooking. Specialises in fish. Pizzas also served in the evening. Very good value for money.

Chez Black – *Via del Brigantino 19/21 – 84017 Positano – ☎ 089 87 50 36 – Closed 7 Jan-7 Feb – €31/47 + 12% service charge.* Ideally located right on the seafront. The large dining room opens out on to the veranda and diners are assured of a sea view wherever they are seated. There is no pressure to have a three-course meal – the staff are equally happy for diners to order one dish, even a pizza.

Buca di Bacco – *Via Rampa Teglia 4 – 84017 Positano – ☎ 089 87 56 99 – Closed Nov-Mar – €35/63.* This restaurant is part of the hotel of the same name, situated in the centre of town. Specialises in fish dishes. Lovely terrace area with views out to sea. Popular with the artistic and intellectual jet set in the early 20C.

• *Expensive*

Palazzo della Marra – *Via della Marra 7/9 – 84010 Ravello – ☎ 089 85 83 02 – Closed Tue (except Apr-Oct), 5 Nov-3 Dec – Book – €43/57 + 15% service charge.* A charming restaurant housed in a splendid townhouse with noble pretensions which dates back to the 12C. Rather sombre interior with high vaulted ceilings. Medieval-style cuisine.

La Caravella – *Via Matteo Camera 12 – 84011 Amalfi – ☎ 089 87 10 29 – Closed Tue, 10 Nov-25 Dec – 🍽 – Book – €47/65.* Comprises three small elegant dining rooms – white walls and simple furnishings, much of it 1940s in style. Mouth-watering fish dishes, good wines and excellent service.

WHERE TO STAY

• *Moderate*

Albergo Hostaria di Bacco – *Via Lama 9 – 84110 Furore – ☎ 089 83 03 60 – Fax 089 83 03 52 – Closed 25 Dec (restaurant closed out of season) – 🅿 – 17 rm €57/73 – ☕ €5.16 – Restaurant. €21/36.* A comfortable, family-run hotel and restaurant with fine views out to sea. Good location, at the top end of the charming village of Furore, not far from the Amalfi coast. Represents value for money

Hotel Le Fioriere – *Via Nazionale 138 – 84010 Praiano – 11km/7mi southwest of Amalfi – ☎ 089 87 42 03 – Fax 089 87 43 43 – 🅿 🍽 – 14 rm €56.81/82.63 ☕.* A chance to live it up without breaking the bank. Simple, spacious rooms, modern in style. Some benefit from a pretty little terrace area overlooking the sea where breakfast (generous servings) can be taken in summer. A little on the noisy side.

Hotel Santa Lucia – *Via Nazionale 44 – 84010 Minori – 5km/3mi northeast of Amalfi on S 163 – ☎ 089 85 36 36 – Fax 089 87 71 42 – 🅿 🍽 (charge) – 30 rm €61.97/82.63 ☕ – Restaurant. €21/30.* A well-established, family-run hotel. Although it dates back to the 1960s there is a modern feel to the furnishings and general ambience. The beach (part of which has been reserved for hotel guests) is only 100m away. Both regional and national dishes on the menu.

• *Expensive*

Albergo Marincanto – *Via Colombo 36 – 84017 Positano – ☎ 089 87 51 30 – Fax 089 87 55 95 – Closed Nov-Mar – 🅿 🍽 – 25 rm from €108.46 ☕.* Rather retro and simple in style. Large parking area (charge) which makes the hotel very popular with visitors arriving by car. Lovely terrace-garden, with sea views.

Hotel Villa San Michele – *Via Carusiello 2 – 84010 Castiglione di Ravello – 5km/3mi south of Ravello – ☎ 089 87 22 37 – Fax 089 87 22 37 – Closed 7 Jan-10 Feb – 🅿 🍽 – 12 rm from €134.28 ☕ – Restaurant. €23.* Situated at the top of the cliff face, the hotel boasts magnificent views over the Gulf and the Capo d'Orso. Delightful setting with its luscious garden and the steps down to the beach. Decorated in blue and white with tiled floors, the rooms are beautifully sunny.

Hotel Aurora – *Piazza dei Protontini 7 – 84011 Amalfi – ☎ 089 87 12 09 – Fax 089 87 29 80 – Closed Nov-Mar (open 25 Dec) – 29 rm from €161 ☕.* A charming hotel, situated right on the seafront and a stone's throw from the hustle and bustle of the quayside. Light, airy rooms with modern furnishings. The majolica ware is a nice touch. Lovely terrace-garden, pleasantly shaded by the bougainvillea.

Hotel Palazzo Murat – *Via dei Mulini 23 – 84017 Positano – ☎ 089 87 51 77 – Fax 089 81 14 19 – Closed 4 Nov-20 Mar – 🍽 – 31 rm from €181 ☕ – Restaurant. €51.64/77.* A throwback to 18C Neapolitan Baroque architecture and the Vanvitelli school which so enthralled Joachim Murat (King of Naples) that he took it on as his summer residence. With their original features some of the rooms are particularly atmospheric. Surrounded by a botanical garden with a variety of exotic plants and brightly coloured flowers.

Vallone di Furore★★

The Furore Valley, between two road tunnels, is the most impressive section of the coast owing to the dark depths of its steep, rocky walls and, in stormy weather, the thunder of wild, rough seas. A fishermen's village has, nevertheless, been built where a small torrent gushes into the sea. The houses clinging to the slopes and vividly coloured boats drawn up on the shore are an unexpected feature in this bleak landscape. Anna Magnani, who came to Furore in 1948 with Roberto

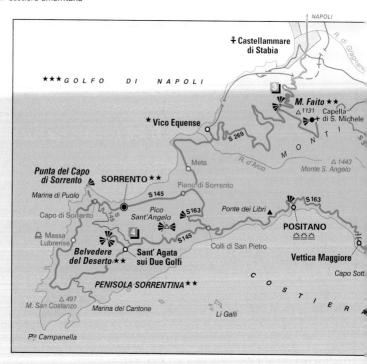

Rossellini to shoot *L'Amore*, fell under its spell and wanted to buy a fisherman's house. Those who wish to explore the spot on foot should take the path that goes along one side of the gorge. Note the **"Art walls"** ("Muri d'autore"), outdoor contemporary paintings and sculptures which relate local history.

Grotta dello Smeraldo★★

Access to cave by lift from street above 9am-4pm. €5.16 (lift and tour included). Visit also possible by boat from Amalfi harbour, €5.16 round trip (admission not included).
The exceptionally clear water of this marine cave is illuminated indirectly by rays of light which give it a beautiful emerald (*smeraldo*) colour. The bottom looks quite near, though the water is 10m/33ft deep, but it was not always covered by the sea. Fine stalactites add to the interest of the trip. The cave became submerged as a result of variations in ground level caused by the volcanic activity which affects the whole region.

Amalfi★★

Amalfi is a rather Spanish-looking little town with its tall white houses built on slopes facing the sea in a wonderful **setting★★★**. Amalfi enjoys a very mild climate, making it a popular holiday resort.

HISTORICAL NOTES

Amalfi is Italy's oldest republic founded in 840; by the end of the 9C it came under the rule of a doge. It enjoyed its greatest prosperity in the 11C, when shipping in the Mediterranean was regulated by the Tavole Amalfitane (Amalfi codex), the oldest maritime code in the world. Amalfi traded regularly with the Orient, in particular Constantinople, and the Republic had an arsenal to the left of Porta della Marina where many large galleys were built. This fleet of galleys played a large part in carrying Crusaders to the Levant.

Starting at Piazza Duomo, Via Genova, Via Capuano (its continuation) and **Via dei Mercanti** (parallel on the right) make up the **historic centre★** and business heart of the city with its picturesque variety of façades, flowering balconies and niches. The Islamic-looking layout of the town is characterised by winding alleyways, staircases and vaulted passages which open out onto delightful little squares with a fountain.

Duomo di Sant'Andrea★ – *Chiostro del Paradiso and Museo Diocesano: Open Jun-Sep 9am-9pm, Mar to mid-Jun and mid Sep to Oct 9am-7pm, rest of the year 10am-12.45pm and 2.30pm-5.15pm. €2.50. ☎ 089 87 10 59.*
Founded in the 9C, enlarged in the 10C and 13C and subsequently altered numerous times, the cathedral is a good example of the Oriental splendour favoured by maritime cities. The façade, rebuilt in the 19C on the original model, has a great deal of character: it is the focal point at the top of a stairway and its varied geometrical designs in multicoloured stone are striking. The campanile, on the left, is all that remains of the original church. A beautiful 11C bronze **door★**, cast in Constantinople, opens onto the vast atrium which precedes the church.

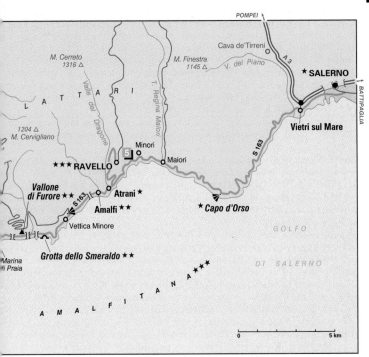

The atrium leads into the **Cloisters of Paradise★★** (Chiostro del Paradiso) which date from 1268. The architecture combines Romanesque austerity and Arab fantasy. The arcades shelter some sarcophagi. The Museo Diocesano is housed in the **Basilica del Crocefisso**, which used to be the site of the old 9C cathedral. Previously incorporated into the main building and transformed into the Baroque style, it has now reassumed its original Romanesque form (note the decorative mullioned triforium and the chapels with fresco remains). From the basilica make for the crypt which holds the relics of St Andrew the Apostle, brought over to Amalfi from Constantinople in 1206.

Atrani★

This pleasant fishermen's village at the mouth of the Dragon Valley (Valle del Dragone) has two old churches: Santa Maria Maddalena and San Salvatore. The latter was founded in the 10C and has a fine bronze door which is very similar to the one in Amalfi Cathedral. The road winds its way up the narrow Dragon Valley, planted with vines and olive groves, all the way to Ravello.

Ravello★★★

Ravello with its alleys, stairways and roofed passages clings to the steep slopes of the Dragon Hill. The **site★★★**, suspended between sea and sky, is unforgettable. The road from Amalfi climbs in hairpin bends up the narrow Dragon Valley, planted with vines and olive groves. The aristocratic restraint of Ravello has, over the centuries, beguiled artists, musicians and writers such as members of the Bloomsbury Group led by Virginia and Leonard Woolf *(see Villa Cimbrone below)*, DH Lawrence, Graham Greene, Gore Vidal, Hans Escher and Joan Miró.

Villa Rufolo★★★ – *Piazza Vescovado, next to the Duomo. (&) Open daily, Apr-Aug 9am-8pm, rest of the year 9am-6pm. Closed 1 Jan, 25 Dec. €4. ☎ 089 85 76 57.*
The villa was built in the 13C by the rich Rufolo family of Ravello (cited in Boccaccio's *Decameron*) and was the residence of several popes, Charles of Anjou and more recently, in 1880, of **Richard Wagner**. When the German composer, in search of inspiration for *Parsifal,* laid eyes on the villa's splendid garden he exclaimed, "the garden of Klingsor is found". A well-shaded avenue leads to a Gothic entrance tower. Beyond is a Moorish-style courtyard with typical sharply-pointed arches in the Sicilian-Norman style and interlacing above. This was originally cloisters in the 11C. A massive 11C tower overlooks the well-tended gardens and the elegant villa.
From the terraces there is a splendid **panorama★★★** of the jagged peaks as far as Cape Orso, the Bay of Maiori and the Gulf of Salerno. In the summer there are **concerts** in the gardens with an unequalled backdrop of trees, flowers and the sea.
For information contact the Società dei Concerti di Ravello, ☎ 089 85 81 49; Fax 089 85 82 49, or the Tourist Office (☎ 089 85 70 96); www.ravelloarts.org

Duomo – The cathedral, founded in 1086, was remodelled in the 18C. The campanile is 13C. The splendid **bronze door★** with its panels of reliefs was cast in 1179 by Barisanus da Trani. There is a magnificent mosaic-covered **pulpit★★** with a remarkable variety of motifs and fantastic animals (1272). On the left is an elegant 12C **ambo** adorned with green mosaics representing Jonah and the Whale. The small **museum** in the crypt has sculptural fragments, mosaics, a silver headreliquary with the relics of St Barbara. *Open daily, Mar-Oct 9.30am-1pm and 3-7pm; rest of the year only Sun and public holidays (Mon-Sat by appointment only).* €1.03. ☎ 089 85 83 11; www.diocesi.amalficava.it/ravello

To the left of the Duomo, the Cameo Factory houses a tiny **Coral museum** which displays some highly prized pieces. Of particular note is the snuffbox encrusted with cameos.

Chiesa di San Giovanni del Toro – *Open daily, Jul-Sep 9am-1pm and 3-6.30pm, rest of the year by appointment only. Donations welcome.* ☎ 089 85 83 11.

Via S. Giovanni del Toro, with its stunning **belvedere★★**, leads to this beautiful 11C church with three apses. Inside, antique columns support the arches. There is a richly-decorated 11C **pulpit★**, a Roman sarcophagus (south aisle) and 14C frescoes in the apses and the crypt.

Villa Cimbrone★★ – *Open daily, 9.30am-8pm.* €4.13. ☎ 089 85 74 59.

A charming **alley★** leads from Piazza Vescovado to the villa, passing on the way through the Gothic porch of the convent of St Francis. The villa was built at the beginning of the 19C by Lord William Bechett in an eclectic style with references to Villa Rufolo and the convent of St Francis. Villa Cimbrone is a homage to the history of Ravello and a point of reference for the **Bloomsbury Group** for whom the garden embodied the ideal aesthetic of clarity, order and harmony. On entering the grounds note the charming cloisters on the left and the lovely hall with ogival vaulting. A wide alley leads through the splendid garden to the belvedere, adorned with marble busts. There is an immense **panorama★★★** over the cultivated, terraced hillsides, Maiori, Cape Orso and the Gulf of Salerno.

Capo d'Orso★

The cape with its jagged rocks affords an interesting view of Maiori Bay.

Vietri sul Mare

At the eastern end of this stretch of coastline, the houses of Vietri sul Mare are terraced up the slope. The town is known for its ceramic ware. It affords magnificent **views★★** of the Amalfi coast.

Salerno★ *See SALERNO*

Cremona★

The original Gallic settlement became a Latin city before emerging as an independent commune in the Middle Ages. It suffered from the Guelph and Ghibelline troubles of the period. In 1334 the town came under Visconti rule and was united with the Duchy of Milan in the 15C. During the Renaissance the town was the centre of a brilliant artistic movement. In the 18C and 19C the French and Austrians fought for supremacy over Cremona until the Risorgimento. Cremona is the birthplace of the composer Claudio Monteverdi (1567-1643) who created modern opera with his *Orfeo* and *The Coronation of Poppea*.

Location

Population 71 611 – Michelin map 428 or 429 G 11-12 – Lombardy Cremona is an important agricultural market town in the heart of a fertile agricultural region, the Pianura Padana, on the banks of the River Po. It is easily reached from A 21 which links Brescia with Piacenza. 🏛 *Piazza del Comune 5,* ☎ 0372 23 233.

Surrounding area: see BRESCIA, PIACENZA.

> **TRATTORIA**
> Alba – *Via Persico 40* –
> ☎ 0372 43 37 00 – Closed Sun, Mon,
> 24 Dec-7 Jan, Aug – 🔲 – Book – €15/23.
> Typical trattoria with a family atmosphere.
> Simple interior with panelled walls. Hearty
> home cooking, traditional dishes with a
> regional flavour – at its best during the
> winter months. The cotechino (pork
> sausage) baked in a bread crust is
> particularly good.

THE VIOLINS OF CREMONA

From the late 16C the stringed-instrument makers of Cremona gained a reputation as violin and cello makers. The town was the birthplace of the greatest violin makers of all time and their instruments are still highly sought after by famous violinists today. The sound they produce is quite extraordinary, almost supernatural in tone and incredibly close to the human voice. The International School of Violin Making carries on this tradition.

The first of the famous violin makers of Cremona was **Andrea Amati**, from whom King Charles IX of France commissioned instruments in the 16C. His work was continued by his sons and his nephew, Nicolò, master of Andrea Guarneri and the most famous of all of them, **Antonio Stradivarius** (c 1644-1737), who made more than 1 000 instruments including the "Cremonese" which was made in 1715. **Andrea Guarneri** was the first of another renowned dynasty in which the most skilled violin maker of them all was Giuseppe Guarneri (1698-1744), better known as **Guarneri del Gesù** because of the three letters IHS (Jesus, Saviour of Mankind) inscribed on all his violins. Knowledgeable music lovers will find it easy to distinguish between the crystal-clear tones of a Stradivarius and the deeper, powerful tones of a Guarneri del Gesù.

A discourse on violin making must include reference to **Niccoló Paganini** (1782-1840), the violinist whose genius of interpretation, virtuosity and pyrotechnics were legendary. Paganini played a number of violins made in Cremona and these include the Guarneri (1743), known as "Il Cannone", which is now owned by the Comune of Genoa.

G. Biudzin/MICHELIN

Worth a Visit

Torrazzo★★★

Closed for restoration at time of publication.
The remarkable late-13C campanile is linked to the cathedral by a Renaissance gallery. Its massive form is elegantly crowned by an octagonal 14C storey. From the top (112m/367ft), there is a lovely **view**★ over the town. The astronomical clock, which dates from 1471, has undergone a number of alterations in its history, the last being in the 1970s. It is notable for its illustrations of the stars and the constellations of the zodiac.

Duomo★★

This magnificent Lombard cathedral was begun in the Romanesque and completed in the Gothic style (1107-1332). The richly decorated white marble façade is preceded by a porch. Numerous decorative features were later additions, namely the frieze by the followers of Antelami, the large 13C rose window and the four statue-columns of the central doorway.

The spacious **interior** is decorated with **frescoes**★ by the Cremona School (B Boccaccino, the Campi, the Bembo, Romanino da Brescia, Pordenone and Gatti). Also of interest, at the entrance to the chancel, are the **high reliefs**★★ by Amadeo, the architect-sculptor of the Carthusian Monastery at Pavia.

Battistero★

This harmonious octagonal baptistery, preceded by a Lombard porch and decorated with a gallery, was remodelled during the Renaissance.

Palazzo Comunale

    Open Tue-Sat 8.30am-6pm, Sun and public holidays 10am-6pm. Closed Mon (except summer), 1 Jan, 1 May, 25 Dec. €3.10. No charge during National Heritage Week. ☎ *0372 22 138 (to hear an old violin being played, book at least two weeks in advance); www.rccr.cremona.it*
This 13C palace was remodelled at a later date. Inside are displayed the most famous violins in the world: the *Charles IX of France* (Amati), the *Hammerle* (Amati), the *Quarestani* (Guarneri), the *Cremonese* 1715 (Antonio Stradivarius) and the *Stauffer* (Guarneri del Gesù).
To the left of the palace is the lovely 13C **Loggia dei Militi.**

Museo Civico Ala Ponzone

    Open Mon-Sat 8.30am-6pm, Sun and public holidays 10am-6pm. Closed 1 Jan, 1 May, 25 Dec. €5.16. ☎ 0372 46 18 85; www.rccr.cremona.it
Installed in a 16C palace, this municipal museum has a **picture gallery** with works of the Cremona School. Note the dramatic *St Frances in Meditation* by **Caravaggio**, the *Vegetable Gardener* by **Arcimboldo.**

Museo Stradivariano

    Mon-Sat 9am-6pm, Sun and public holidays 10am-6pm. Closed 1 Jan, 1 May, 25 Dec. €3.10. ☎ 0372 46 18 86; www.rccr.cremona.it
This museum has displays of wooden models and tools belonging to Stradivarius, as well as stringed instruments from the 17C-20C.

▶▶ Palazzo Fodri★, Palazzo Stanga, Palazzo Raimondi, S. Agostino, S. Sigismondo.

Delta del Po★

PO DELTA

This area around the Po Delta was once a malaria-infested marshy district. Land reclamation and drainage have since turned it into a fertile agricultural area and a designated nature reserve.

The Chioggia to Ravenna road (90km/56mi) traverses these flat expanses stretching away to the horizon and interrupted only by large solitary farms. Clumps of poplars and umbrella pines add touches of colour, especially in spring, to the monotony of this countryside where eel fishing is still common on the numerous canals which criss-cross the area.

In the southern part of the area the Valli di Comacchio, Italy's most important zone of lagoons, has its own special melancholy beauty.

The Polesine is the strip of the Pianura Veneta which stretches from Rovigo to the delta, and which takes in the ancient cities of Adria and Porto Tolle, the last town on the map before the River Po flows out to sea. What you see today is the result of the combined action of the Po, the Adige and man. In 1951 the Polesine was devastated by terrible flooding.

Location

Michelin map 429 H 18 – Emilia-Romagna, Veneto. The Po Delta is the region between Venice and Ravenna which takes in the provinces of Rovigo and Ferrara.

🛈 *for the Emilia-Romagna region: Castello Estense, Ferrara, ☎ 0532 29 93 03; Abbazia di Pomposa, ☎ 0533 71 91 10; Consorzio Parco del Delta, Via Cavour 11, 44022 Comacchio (Ferrara), ☎ 0533 31 40 03.*

🛈 *for the Veneto region: Via Dunant 10, 45100 Rovigo, ☎ 0425 36 14 81; Via dei Pini 4, 45010 Rosolina Mare, ☎ 0426 68 012.*

Surrounding area: see FERRARA, LAGUNA VENETA, RAVENNA, VENEZIA.

The melancholy charm of
the Po Delta near Ferrara

Worth a Visit

Comacchio

Comacchio is built on sand and water and in many ways it resembles Chioggia. The main activity of the townspeople is eel fishing. Its brightly coloured fishermen's houses, its canals spanned by some curious bridges, including an unusual triple bridge, and the fishing boats all lend it a special charm.

Castello di Mesola

28km/17mi north of Comacchio. A massive brick castle dating from 1583 which once belonged to the Este family.

Abbazia di Pomposa★★

(&) *Open daily, 8.30am-7pm. Closed 1 Jan, 1 May, 25 Dec. €4.13. ☎ 0533 71 91 30.*
This Benedictine abbey was founded in the 6C and enjoyed great fame in the Middle Ages, especially from the 10C to 12C when it was distinguished by its abbot, St Guy (Guido) of Ravenna, and by another monk, **Guido d'Arezzo**, the inventor of the musical scale and note system. In July and August the abbey hosts classical music concerts.

Directory

The fine pre-Romanesque **church** in the style typical of Ravenna is preceded by a narthex whose decoration exemplifies the Byzantine style. To the left, an admirable Romanesque campanile (1063) is remarkable for the progression in the number and size of its windows and the elegant simplicity of the Lombard bands and arches adorning its nine storeys; and finally, the variety of geometric decoration obtained with the use of bricks.

The nave has some magnificent **mosaic flooring** and two holy water stoups, one in the Romanesque style and the other in the Byzantine style. The walls bear an exceptional cycle of 14C **frescoes** based on the illuminator's art. From right to left the upper band is devoted to the Old Testament while the lower band has scenes from the Life of Christ; the corner pieces of the arches depict the *Apocalypse*. On the west wall are a *Last Judgement* and in the apsidal chapel *Christ in Majesty*.

Opposite the church stands the Palazzo della Ragione, where the abbot dispensed justice.

Dolomiti★★★

The DOLOMITES

Situated between the Veneto and Trentino-Alto Adige, the fan of so-called "Pale Mountains" (Monti Pallidi) take on red tints at sunset that suddenly vanish when the sun disappears. Their harsh, rocky contours embrace crystalline lakes and mysteries which have become the very stuff of numerous poetic legends.

Location

Michelin map 429 C 16-19 – Veneto – Trentino-Alto Adige.

For those travelling in the Trentino-Alto Adige region, the Dolomites are reached by taking A 22 off the Brennero transalpine route. Visitors to the Veneto region should take A 27 which goes to Belluno.

🅱 *Azienda di Promozione Turistica Dolomiti, Piazzetta S. Francesco 8, 32043 Cortina d'Ampezzo (Belluno),* ☎ *0436 32 31, www.apt-dolomiti-cortina.it*

🅱 *Consorzio Turistico Alta Badia, Strada Col Alt 36, 39033 Corvara,* ☎ *0471 83 61 76; Consorzio Turistico Val Gardena, Via Dursan 78/bis, 39047 S. Cristina,* ☎ *0471 79 22 77; Consorzio Turistico Rosengarten-Latemar, 39050 Ponte Nova,* ☎ *0471 61 03 10; Comitato Turistico Sciliar-Alpe di Siusi, Via Sciliar 16, 39040 Siusi,* ☎ *0471 70 70 24. Website for the whole of the Alto-Adige: www.hallo.com*

Surrounding area: see BELLUNO, BOLZANO, TRENTO.

Background

The rocky peaks of the Dolomites – a journey back in time

The Dolomites are made of a white calcareous rock, dolomite, which takes its name from the French geologist Déodat de Dolomieu who studied its composition in the 18C. Some 150 million years ago this land was submerged by the Tethys sea. On its sandy depths coral reefs and limestone began to shape the "Pale Mountains".

Tre Cime di Lavaredo

About 70 million years ago, during the Alpine orogenis (the corrugation of the earth's crust) the layers were violently compressed and forced to the surface. Thus the Dolomites were born out of the sea. Today visitors can still see fossils of marine life. The Dolomites were nearly completed in the Quaternary Era (about 2 million years ago) when glaciers softened and hollowed out the valleys. Only flora and fauna were missing at this stage; these began to inhabit the Dolomites when the glaciers retreated.

The massifs – To the southeast rise the Pelmo (3 168m/10 393ft) and the Civetta (3 220m/10 564ft) massifs. To the south, near the peak of the Vezzana, the Pale di San Martino, streaked by fissures, divide into three chains separated by a plateau. The Latemar (2 842m/9 324ft) and the Catinaccio (2 981m/9 780ft) massifs, together with the Torri del Vaiolet (Towers of Vaiolet), frame the Costalunga Pass. To the north of the pass rise the Sasso Lungo and the vast Sella Massif (Gruppo di Sella), skirted by a road.

To the east, the chief summits in the Cortina Dolomites are the Tofane, the Sorapis and the Cristallo. Finally, in the heart of the range, stands the **Marmolada Massif** (Gruppo della Marmolada, 3 342m/10 964ft), which dominates the Monti Pallidi.

Between Cortina and the Piave Valley the wooded region of **Cadore** boasts the Antelao (3 263m/10 705ft) and the triple peak, Tre Cime di Lavaredo (Drei Zinnen), which it shares with the Parco delle Dolomiti di Sesto in Alto Adige.

Flora and fauna – The Dolomite landscape is coloured by coniferous forests, crocuses, alpine gentians, edelweiss, rhododendron, lilies and alpine bluebells.

Tourist activity tends to drive away wild animals, but the Dolomites are still a refuge for chamois, marmots, royal eagles and woodcock.

THE LEGEND OF THE PALE MOUNTAINS

Legend has it that a prince who lived at the foot of the Alps married the daughter of the King of the Moon. The young girl loved flowers and meadows but was disturbed by the dark colour of the rocks. She so desperately missed the pale mountains of her home that she felt compelled to return to the Moon. Some dwarfs came to the disconsolate prince's aid and made some skeins of thread from the moon's rays, weaving them into nets which they placed on the mountains. The princess was thus able to return and the dwarfs were allowed to live in the kingdom.

At sunset, however, the Monti Pallidi assumed fiery hues, probably caused by the beautiful rose garden situated on one of the mountains where the King of the Dwarfs lived. One day, attracted by the rose garden, some foreign warriors arrived in the kingdom and imprisoned the king, who cursed the plant and ordered that roses would never be seen again, by day or night. The curse did not, however, mention sunset, a moment suspended between day and night. Thus, for those few minutes the Catinaccio mountain, which the Germans refer to as *Rosengarten* (rose garden), is still inflamed and throws light onto every rock of the Dolomites.

Tours

STRADA DELLE DOLOMITI*** [1]

From Bolzano to Cortina – 210km/131mi –allow two days.

The main touring route in the Dolomites is the great Dolomite Road, which is a wonderful and world-famous example of road engineering. The road was already used during the Renaissance by merchants travelling between Venice and Germany and it was also used during the First World War.

Bolzano★ *see BOLZANO*

Gola della Val d'Ega★

This narrow gorge, the Ega Valley, with pink sandstone walls, is guarded by the **Castel Cornedo.**

Nova Levante★

The Catinaccio Massif rises up behind this attractive village with its bulbous belfry and pretty houses.

Lago di Carezza★

This tiny lake is set in a dark expanse of fir trees with the jagged peaks of the Latemar and the Catinaccio Massifs in the background.

Passo di Costalunga★

From this pass on the Dolomite Road there is a **view★** over the Catinaccio on one side and the Latemar on the other.

Vigo di Fassa✳✳

This resort, in a picturesque **site★** in the famous Val di Farsa, is a mountaineering and excursion centre in the Catinaccio Massif (cable car).

Canazei✳✳✳

Canazei lies deep in the heart of the massif, framed between the Catinaccio, the Towers of Vaiolet (Torri del Vaiolet), the Sella Massif and the Marmolada. This is the usual base for most excursions and climbs in the Marmolada range. The church has a bulbous belfry and a façade with a painted image of St Christopher.

At Canazei turn right onto S 641.

This road affords very fine **views★★** of the Marmolada range and its glacier. As one comes out of a long tunnel a lake, **Lago di Fedaia★**, suddenly appears.

Marmolada★★★

This is the highest massif in the Dolomites, famous for its glacier and very fast ski-runs. The **cable car** from Malga Ciapela goes up to 3 265m/10 712ft offering admirable **panoramas★★★** of the Cortina peaks (Tofana and Cristallo), the Sasso Lungo, the enormous tabular mass of the Sella Massif and in the background the summits of the Austrian Alps including the Grossglockner.

Return to Canazei then after 5.5km/3mi turn left.

Passo di Sella★★★

Linking the Val di Fassa and Val Gardena this pass offers one of the most extensive **panoramas★★★** in the Dolomites, including the Sella, Sasso Lungo and Marmolada massifs.

Val Gardena★★★

One of the most famous valleys in the Dolomites both for its beauty and crowds of tourists. The inhabitants still speak a language which was born during the Roman occupation: the Ladin dialect which nowadays can only be heard in some valleys of the Dolomites, the Grigioni mountains and the Carniche Alps.

There are some skilful wood-workers as can be seen in some fine shops that are to be found in Selva (Wolkenstein), Santa Cristina and Ortisei (St Ulrich).

Selva di Val Gardena✳✳✳ – This resort is situated at the foot of the Sella Massif. It is an active craft centre: wooden objects, pewterware and ceramics.

Ortisei✳✳✳ – From Ortisei a cable car climbs up to **Alpe di Siusi✳** (Seiser Alm), a 60km²/23sq mi plateau in a delightful **setting★★** overlooking the Sasso Lungo and the Sciliar. This is a base for excursions to suit all tastes and abilities.

Return to the Dolomite Road.

Passo Pordoi★★★

The highest pass (2 239m/7 346ft) on the Dolomite Road lies between huge blocks of rock with sheer sides and shorn-off tops.

Passo del Falzarego

Nearing Cortina the scenery becomes more beautiful. The pass goes through the Tofane and skirts the barren landscape of the Cinque Torri which was a source of inspiration for Tolkien when he wrote *The Lord of the Rings.*

Cortina d'Ampezzo✳✳✳

Cortina, the capital of the Dolomites, is a winter sports and summer resort with a worldwide reputation. Set in the heart of the Dolomites at an altitude of 1 210m/4 000ft Cortina makes a good excursion centre for discovering the magnificent **mountain scenery★★★**.

Tondi di Faloria★★★ – *Cable car service to Faloria from Via Ria di Zeto. From Faloria to Tondi di Faloria: in winter, "Tondi" ski lift and "Girilada" chairlift; in summer, a jeep service operates.*

From the summit a grand panorama may be enjoyed. There are excellent ski slopes.

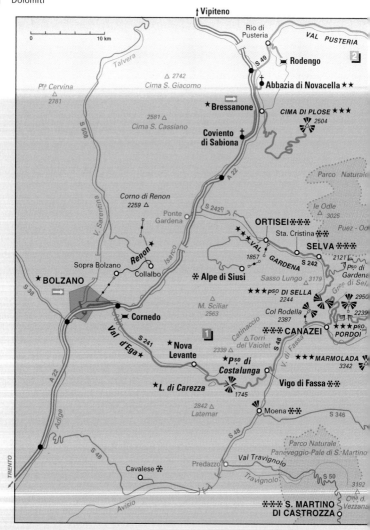

Italian and German

Adige/Etsch	Cervina (Punta)/Hirzerspitze
Alpe di Siusi/Seiseralm	Chuisa/Klausen
Badia/Abtei	Cornedo/Karneid
Badia (Val)/Gadertal	Corvara in Badia/Kurfar
Bolzano/Bozen	Costalunga (Passo di)/Karerpass
Braies (Lago di)/Pragser Wildsee	Croda Rossa/Hohe Geisel
Bressanone/Brixen	Dobbiaco/Toblach
Brunico/Bruneck	Ega (Val d')/Eggental
Campo Fiscalino/Fischleinboden	Gadera/Gaderbach
Carezza (Lago di)/Karersee	Gardena (Passo di)/Grödnerjoch
Catinaccio/Rosengarten	Gardena (Val)/Grödnertal

Tofana di Mezzo★★★ – *'Freccia del Cielo' cable car. For information telephone the tourist office (see above)*
A cable car climbs to 3 244m/10 643ft, from where there is a superb panorama over the surrounding mountains.

Belvedere Pocol★★ – *Open 1 Dec–Easter and 15 Jul–15 Sep. Hourly bus service from Piazza Roma.*
Lying to the southwest, this viewpoint affords a lovely view of Cortina which is best at sunset.

VAL PUSTERIA AND SURROUNDING AREA ②

Val Pusteria, or Pustertal, is bordered to the south by the Dolomites and by the central Alps to the north. From the end of the 13C until the 16C it belonged to the County of Gorizia and formed part of the Strada d'Alemagna, a road which linked

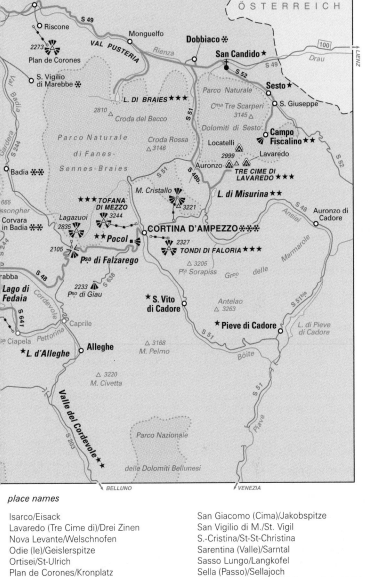

ÖSTERREICH

Brunico ✶✶
Riscone
S 49
Monguelfo
2273
Plan de Corones
VAL PUSTERIA
Rienza
Dobbiaco ✶
San Candido ★
S 52
S 49
Drau
LIENZ
100
S. Vigilio di Marebbe ✷
Parco Naturale
Cma Tre Scarperi
3145 △
Sesto ★
S. Giuseppe
L. DI BRAIES ★★★
2810 △
Croda del Becco
S 51
Dolomiti di Sesto
Locatelli △
Campo Fiscalino ★★
Lavaredo
S 52
Parco Naturale di Fanes-Sennes-Braies
Croda Rossa
△3146
2999 △
Auronzo △△ △
TRE CIME DI LAVAREDO ★★★
Badia ✶✶
S 244
665 ssongher
Corvara in Badia ✶✶
S 51
S 48b
M. Cristallo
★★★ TOFANA DI MEZZO
Lagazuoi
2835
3244
△ 3221
CORTINA D'AMPEZZO✶✶✶
L. di Misurina ★★
S 48
Ansiei
Auronzo di Cadore
★★Pocol
Pso di Falzarego
2105
2327
TONDI DI FALORIA ★★★
Marmarole
delle
△ 3205
Pta Sorapiss
Grpo
rabba
S 48
Cordevole
2233
Pso di Giau
S 638
★ S. Vito di Cadore
Antelao
△ 3263
S 51bis
Lago di Fedaia
S 641
Caprile
Pettorina
★ Pieve di Cadore
L. di Pieve di Cadore
a Ciapela
S 203
★ L. d'Alleghe
Alleghe
△ 3168
M. Pelmo
Bóite
S 51
Piave
△ 3220
M. Civetta
Parco Nazionale
delle Dolomiti Bellunesi
Valle del Cordevole ★★
BELLUNO
VENEZIA

place names

Isarco/Eisack
Lavaredo (Tre Cime di)/Drei Zinen
Nova Levante/Welschnofen
Odie (le)/Geislerspitze
Ortisei/St-Ulrich
Plan de Corones/Kronplatz
Plose (Cima d.)/Plose Bühel
Rienza/Rienz
Riscon/Reischach
San Candido/Innichen
San Cassiano (Cima)/Kassianspitze

San Giacomo (Cima)/Jakobspitze
San Vigilio di M./St. Vigil
S.-Cristina/St-St-Christina
Sarentina (Valle)/Sarntal
Sasso Lungo/Langkofel
Sella (Passo)/Sellajoch
Selva in Val Gardena/Wolkenstein in Gröden
Sesto (Val di)/Sextental
Talvera/Talfer
Tre Scarperi (Cima)/Dreischusterspitze
Vipiteno/Sterzing

Venice and Germany. This itinerary begins in Bressanone and continues into the Pusteria Valley.

Bressanone★

Set at the confluence of the River Rienza and River Isarco, Bressanone is an elegant, typically Tyrolean little town that enjoys a dry, invigorating climate with an exceptionally high number of hours of sunshine. There are many reminders of its eventful past. It was conquered by the Romans in 15 BC, was the seat of a Prince-Bishop from 1027 to 1803, became Bavarian for seven years from 1806 to 1813, and then belonged to Austria until 1919 when it became an Italian town.

Duomo – This Baroque cathedral which was orginally a Romanesque construction, has a neo-Classical west front designed by Jakob Pirchstaller (1783) flanked by two belltowers. The luminous interior is decorated with marble, stuccowork and frescoes by Paul Troger which are more striking for the gold leaf. The fine

Directory

WHERE TO EAT

• Budget

Concordia – *Via Roma 41 – 39046 Ortisei –
☏ 0471 79 62 76 – Closed Nov, mid-Apr to
May – €18/36.* One of the few restaurants in
the region to merit the definition. Tasty,
carefully-prepared dishes with a regional
flavour. Attractive surroundings and informal,
friendly atmosphere.

Gérard – *Via Plan de Gralba 37 – 39048
Selva di Val Gardena – ☏ 0471 79 52 74 –
Closed 15 Apr-10 Jun, 15 Oct-8 Dec – ⚲ –
€19.60/37.80.* If the cooking is typical of
the region, with the ubiquitous polenta
served alongside a variety of local products,
the wonderful views that this kind of refuge
affords (altitude 2 000m/6 560ft!) is unique:
the Sella and Sasso Lungo mountain ranges
are stunning. Overnight stays possible.

Rifugio Larin – *Località Senes – 32046 San
Vito di Cadore – 9km/5mi south of Cortina
d'Ampezzo on S 51 – ☏ 0436 91 12 –
Closed Oct-May – €22/31.* A classic
mountain hut-restaurant with lots of
atmosphere. Hearty but carefully prepared
food. Also accessible by car – although it
would be a shame to miss out on a pleasant
stroll. Wonderful views.

• Moderate

Unterwirt – *Località Gudon – 39043 Chiusa
d'Isarco – 34km/20mi northeast of Bolzano
on S 12 – ☏ 0472 84 40 00 – Closed Tue
and Wed, Jan-Mar – ⚲ – €28/51.* Although
the cooking has a traditional slant, it is
imaginative and the dishes are beautifully
presented. Lovely surroundings – take a stroll
in the garden or lounge by the swimming
pool after your meal. There are some
"ecologically friendly" rooms for overnight
stays. Charming village location.

WHERE TO STAY

• Budget

Hotel Gran Ancëi – *39030 San Cassiano –
26.5km/16mi west of Cortina d'Ampezzo –
☏ 0471 84 95 40 – Fax 0471 84 92 10 –
Closed 21 Apr-9 Jun, 11 Oct-3 Dec – 🅿 –
29 rm €27.50/61 ⌑ – Restaurant. €26/42.*
Surrounded by woodland and located near
the ski slopes, this is very much a mountain-
style hotel. Furniture and decor in the rooms
and public areas are mostly in wood.
Relaxing, peaceful ambience. Spacious and
airy with wonderful views over the Dolomites.

Hotel Erika – *39010 Braies – 5km/3mi
north of Lago di Braies
☏ 0474 74 86 84 – Fax 0474 74 82 55 –
Closed 20 Apr-15 Jun, 3 Nov-20 Dec – 🅿
⚴ 🝙 – 28 rm €31/62 ⌑ – €7.75
Restaurant. €19/24.* Friendly and enthusiastic staff on hand to ensure you get the best
out of your stay in the Dolomites – whatever
the season. Comfortable rooms with chunky
wooden furniture – the rooms on the third
floor are particularly attractive. Rates for
half-board and full-board accommodation.

• Moderate

Hotel Cavallino d'Oro – *Piazza Krausen –
39040 Castelrotto – 26km/16mi northeast of
Bolzano – ☏ 0471 70 63 37 –*

*Fax 0471 70 71 72 – Closed 10 Nov-5
Dec – 25 rm €43/116 ⌑ – Restaurant.
€22/32.* Would suit those looking for a
romantic ambience – complete with four-
poster beds and elegant antique Tyrolean-
style furniture. The dining area has an
equally intimate atmosphere, housed in the
17C "stuben" which are characteristic of the
local architecture.

Monika Hotel – *Via del Parco 2 – 39030
Sesto – ☏ 0474 71 03 84 –
Fax 0474 71 01 77 – Closed 3 Apr-19 May, 15
Oct-15 Dec – ⚲ 🅿 – 27 rm €43.38/141.50
⌑ – Restaurant. €24.26/40.77.* This hotel has
a "chocolate-box" appeal – Tyrolean in style,
stylish wooden interior, set in verdant, peaceful
surroundings. The rooms are simple but
comfortable. In contrast, the dining room is
more elegant.

Hotel Lavaredo – *Via M. Piana 11 – 32040
Misurina – ☏ 0435 39 227 – Fax
0435 39 127 – Closed Nov – 🅿 – 31 rm
€85/108.45 – ⌑ €10.35 – Restaurant.
€18.10/42.35.* Lakeside setting overlooked by
the magnificent mountain peaks of the Cime
di Lavaredo. Family-run hotel with comfortable
rooms and spacious public areas (lots of
wood!). Cooking has a national rather than
regional flavour: some international dishes.

• Expensive

Hotel Colfosco-Kolfuschgerhof – *Via Ronn
7 – 39030 Corvara in Badia – 2km/1.2mi east
of Passo Gardena on S 244 –
☏ 0471 83 61 88 – Fax 0471 83 63 51 –
Closed Oct-2 Dec, Apr to mid-Jun – 🅿 🝙
🕭 – 44 rm from €154.93 ⌑ – Restaurant.
€30/33.* Situated near the lifts, this hotel
would appeal to both summer and winter
mountain sports enthusiasts. The hotel also
has squash courts and table tennis tables;
other facilities include the sauna, Turkish baths
and massage rooms. The ambience is typically
Tyrolean. Friendly atmosphere. Good for
anyone in search of some peace and quiet.

GOING OUT

Enoteca – *Via Mercato 5 – 32043 Cortina
d'Ampezzo – ☏ 0436 86 20 40 – Mon-Sat
10.30am-1pm and 4.30-9pm, open throughout
the day in high season. Closed mid-May to mid-
Jun.* A beautiful old door opens onto this lovely
little wine bar with its wooden ceiling. A great
place for tasting the local wines.

SPORT AND LEISURE

Mountain footpaths

The Dolomites have a dense network of
footpaths. Whether you are an expert
climber or simply want to take a peaceful
walk, there is a vast choice of routes for
those wishing to get a better look at the
Monti Pallidi. Maps and guides listing paths,
mountain huts and bivouacs are on sale just
about everywhere.

Some mountain pathways include:

N° 2 (Bressanone-Feltre): This path crosses
the Plose, the Puez Group, the Gardenaccia,
the Sella and the Marmolada massif;

N° 3 (Villabassa-Longarone): This path winds
its way through Val Pusteria, the Croda

Rossa, Misurina, the Cristallo, the Sorapis and the Antelao;

N° 4 (San Candido-Pieve di Cadore): This track goes through the Sesto Dolomites, the Cadini di Misurina and the Marmarole.

To be fully prepared for a mountain excursion it is advisable to contact the tourist offices listed above.

Scuola di Volo Fly Ten – *Via Dolomiti 75 – 38031 Campitello di Fassa –* ☎ *335 67 57 667 (mobile phone) – Open 8.45am-noon.* No physical training is re-

quired before undertaking paragliding. For those brave enough to go through with it the sensation is absolutely exhilarating and the views are spectacular.

Gruppo Guide Alpine Scuola di Alpinismo – *Corso Italia 69/A – 32043 Cortina d'Ampezzo –* ☎ *0436 86 85 05 – guidecortina@mnet-climb.com – Mon-Sat 8am-noon and 4-8pm, Sun 4-8pm. Closed mid-Sep to last week in Jun.* Waterfalls, lakes, caves, routes with ropes (open to everybody) – a wide variety of organised excursions on offer for all the family

---

Romanesque **cloisters**★ feature 14C ribbed vaulting and interesting 14C and 15C frescoes. Access to the 11C church of San Giovanni Battista *(closed to visitors)* is via the cloisters. The church has 13C Romanesque and 14C Gothic frescoes.

Palazzo vescovile – Commissioned by Prince-Bishop Bruno de Kirchberg after 1250, the palace underwent numerous alterations in later years but retained its superb **courtyard**★ surrounded by three storeys of arcades. This was the Prince-Bishop's residence and the seat of the bishopric. It now houses the vast **Museo diocesano**★ containing a wonderful set of polychrome **wood carvings**★★ (Romanesque and Gothic Tyrolean art), a number of **altarpieces**★ carved in the round dating from the Renaissance, the cathedral **treasure**★ and **Nativity scenes**★ dating from the 18C to 20C. *Open mid-Mar to Oct 10am-5pm, Dec and Jan 2-5pm (also Jul). Closed Mon, Feb to mid-Mar and Nov. €4.13, €8.26 family ticket.* ☎ *0472 83 05 05; www.dioezesanmuseum.bz.it*

Head south towards Chiusa.

Convento di Sabiona

Leave the car in the car park north of Chiusa. To get to the convent from the village, go on foot (30min). This convent of Benedictine nuns in its attractive setting dates back to the 17C. It was built on the rock where the bishop's palace had stood, the palace having burnt down after being struck by lightning in 1535.

Turn round and head in the direction of Bressanone, turning right onto the road for Plose.

Plose★★

To the southeast. Alt 2 446 m/8 031ft. Cable car: from the village of S. Andrea, southeast of Bressanone, cable car to Valcroce (winter and Jul-Sep), then chairlift to Plose (operates in winter only). For further information contact Associazione Turistica di Bressanone. ☎ *0472 83 64 01, or Società Funivia Plose* ☎ *0472 20 04 33.*

The cable car from Valcroce and then another from Plose enable visitors to enjoy a wonderful **panorama**★★★ of the Dolomites to the south and the Austrian mountains to the north.

Retrace your steps and continue along SS 49. The Abbazia di Novacella is 3km/2mi north of Bressanone.

Abbazia di Novacella★★

3km/2mi north. Guided tours only, €3.90. For information on opening times ☎ *0472 83 61 89; www.kloster-neustift.it*

The abbey was founded in 1142 by Bishop Artmanno of Bressanone and run by monks of the Augustinian Order. The courtyard contains the **Well of Wonders** decorated with "eight" wonders of the world, one of which is the abbey itself. The **church** built in the Bavarian Baroque style is surprising for the ornateness and brilliance of the interior. Some of the detail in the painting, such as the leg of one of the characters which literally extends out of the fresco, is also striking. The **cloisters**, which were originally Romanesque, are covered with frescoes from a later period which were whitewashed over after the plague in the 17C. The memorial stones date back to the 18C. Only in this century were attempts made to recover the original frescoes. The magnificent Rococo **library** contains 76 000 rare books, and illuminated manuscripts.

The first village encountered when arriving on the State road which forks off the motorway is Rio di Pusteria. A few minutes away stands the **Castello di**

THE LADIN CULTURE

Ladin is a curious ancient language which has its roots in the Latin language and is spoken by around 30 000 people in and around the Dolomites. It had emerged by the 5C as a direct result of the earlier Roman expansion into the mountainous regions. At Ciastel de Tor, in San Martino in Badia, there is the **Museumladin**★, which has an impressive exhibition on the Ladin culture. The artistic displays and the creative use of the latest technology (projectors, computers, interactive exhibitions) make for an interesting visit. *Open Palm Sunday-Oct, Tue-Sat 10am-6pm, Sun 2-6pm, rest of the year Wed-Fri 2-6pm only. Closed Mon, Nov €5.16.* ☎ *0474 52 40 20; www.museumladin.it*

Rodengo, decorated with the oldest cycle of Romanesque frescoes (13C) with a pro-fane theme: the epic poem *Iwein* by Hartmann von Aue. *Open 15 May-Oct. Guided tours only (1hr) at 11am and 3pm. Closed Mon. €4. For information contact:* ☎ *0472 45 40 56.*

Brunico✳✳

This is the main town in the Pusteria Valley. There is an interesting **Ethnography Museum★** in **Teodone** covering an area of 3ha/7 acres) and including various types of rural building: country manor, hayloft, farm, grain store, oven, mill. They provide an effective illustration of the lifestyles and activities of peasants and noblemen in bygone days.

(&) *Open Tue-Sat 9.30am-5.30pm; Sun and public holidays 2-6pm (last admission 5.30pm). Closed Mon, Nov-Easter. €3.60.* ☎ *0474 55 20 87; www.provinz.bz.it/volkskundemuseen*

From Brunico go in the direction of Dobbiaco. After Monguelfo turn right where Lago di Braies is signposted.

Lago di Braies★★★

Alt 1 495m/4 905ft. This shimmering lake (called Pragser Wildsee in German) is encircled by the Croda del Becco mountains and can be circumnavigated in one hour. Boat trips can be made and it is also the starting point of some rather ardu-ous mountain footpaths.

Proceed through the Pusteria Valley. Turn right before Dubbiaco in the direction of Cortina which is signposted. Follow directions for Misurina and then for Tre Cime di Lavaredo. The last stretch of the route is a **toll-road.** *€18.08 per vehicle.*

Tre Cime di Lavaredo★★★

From the refuge at Auronza the Lavaredo shelter is reached in half an hour. From there the Locatelli shelter is reached in an hour. This last stretch of the path offers spectacular views of the Tre Cime range which forms part of the Parco Naturale delle Dolomiti di Sesto. The Tre Cime can also be reached from Sesto, along path n° 102 which leads to Locatelli in two and a half hours.

On the way back from Tre Cime a stop at Lago di Misurina is recommended.

Lago di Misurina★★

Alt 1 759m/5 770ft. This lake is set among a plantation of fir trees and is an excel-lent starting point for excursions to the surrounding mountains, from the Tre Cime di Lavaredo to the Cristallo.

Dobbiaco✳

Dobbiaco (Toblach in German) was an important town in the Middle Ages as it was at a crossroads with the Strada dell'Alemagna. In the centre of this village there is a late Baroque church dating from the second half of the 18C.

San Candido★

This pretty village, known as Innichen in German, has the most important Romanesque church in the Alto Adige. The **collegiata★** dates from the 13C, the campanile from the 14C. Above the south doorway there are frescoes by the painter and sculptor Michael Pacher (c 1430-98). The most striking piece however is the *Crucifixion,* an evocative wood sculptural group of the 13C with Christ's feet resting on Adam's head.

At San Candido turn right for Sesto leaving the Pusteria which eventually leads to Austria.

Sesto★

Sesto overlooks the Dolomites and offers a huge variety of walks, footpaths and alpine excursions which allow one to become better acquainted with this stunning landscape. The Monte Elmo funicular makes distances shorter. Those in search of a peaceful walk should consider path 4D which crosses the forest and high pastures and affords views of the Meridiana del Sesto (from Cima Nove to Cima Uno).

At San Giuseppe (Moos) the Val Fiscalino leads to **Campo Fiscalino★★** which affords truly stunning views of the Meridiana di Sesto and the Cima dei Tre Scarperi.

Worth a Visit

The Dolomites south of Cortina offer other views of the Dolomites.

Valle del Cordevole★★

The road from Caprile to Belluno is an extremely picturesque one with its hilltop vil-lages and impressive gorges. **Alleghe** on the bank of a **lake★** is a good excursion centre.

San Martino di Castrozza✳✳

An excellent starting point for numerous excursions.

Pieve di Cadore★

This town is pleasantly set at the head of a reservoir. It was the birthplace of the great artist, **Titian**. One of his works is to be found in the church, and the house where he was born is now a **museum.** *Open 20 Jun to mid-Sep 9.30am-12.30pm and 3-6pm, rest of the year 8.30am-12.30pm. Closed Mon (summer), Sun and holidays (winter). €1.50.* ☎ *0435 32 262.*

San Vito di Cadore★

This attractive village nestles at the foot of the Antelao.

Isola d'**Elba**★★

This is the largest island in the Tuscan Archipelago★★ which comprises the islands of Pianosa, Capraia, Giglio, Giannutri and Montecristo. The island's capital is Portoferraio. Elba is more of a holiday resort than a place for a day excursion but it is possible to tour the island in two days, either in one's own car or in a hire car available in Portoferraio.

Location
Michelin map 430 N 12/13 – See also The Green Guide Tuscany. The Isle of Elba is easily reached from Piombino, from where there are crossings to Portoferraio and Rio Marina.

🛈 *Calata Italia, 26, 57037 Portoferraio,* ☎ *0565 91 46 71, www.arcipelago.turismo.toscana.it*
🛈 *Crossing: Navarma-Moby Lines: Via Giuseppe Ninci 1, 57037 Portoferraio (Livorno),* ☎ *0565 91 81 01, www.mobylines.it; Toremar: Calata Italia 22, 57037 Portoferraio (Livorno),* ☎ *0565 91 80 80, www.toremar.it*

Excursions

Start from Portoferraio and follow one of the two itineraries indicated on the map below: **western Elba** *(about 70km/44mi, about 5hr)* and **eastern Elba** *(68km/42mi, about 3hr).*

Directory

WHERE TO EAT
• Budget
Da Pilade – *Località Marina di Mola – 57031 Capoliveri – On the road to Capoliveri –* ☎ *0565 96 86 35 – www.elbalink.it/hotel/dapilade – Closed mid-Oct to Easter – Book – €21/26.* This restaurant is not too far from the coast. Specialities include mouth-watering Aberdeen Angus steak *alla griglia* (grilled) and a wide range of unusual antipasti. Also has rooms and self-catering apartments, with a little garden or a terrace with sea view.

• Moderate
Affrichella – *Via S. Chiara 10 – 57033 Marciana Marina –* ☎ *0565 99 68 44 – Closed Wed – Book – €26/31.* This little restaurant, which is renowned for its seafood dishes, is situated just behind the Duomo. Boasts a variety of both hot and cold antipasti, and an interesting wine list. In summer meals are served at candlelit tables on the adjacent piazzetta.

La Lanterna Magica – *Via Vitaliani 5 – 57036 Porto Azzurro –* ☎ *0565 95 83 94 – Closed Mon (except Jun-Sep), Dec and Jan –* 🖻 *– €26/34.* With its huge windows looking out over the sea in the direction of Porto Azzurro, it is almost as if this restaurant has been erected on stilts sunk into the seabed. The menu has a regional flavour and features some local specialities. The wine and oil are produced on the family farm and are of an excellent quality.

WHERE TO STAY
• Moderate
Hotel Residence Villa Giulia – *Località Lido di Capoliveri – 57036 Porto Azzurro – 7.5km/4.5mi northwest of Capoliveri, heading towards Portoferraio –* ☎ *0565 94 01 67 – Fax 0565 94 01 10 – villagiulia@infoelba.it – Closed mid-Oct to Easter –* 🅿 *– 35 rm €51.65/82.63* 😋. The hotel is divided into four small buildings. The rooms are comfortable and well appointed, with rattan furniture, all with a balcony or a small terrace garden. During the summer months meals (only for guests) are served on the terrace which has lovely views out to sea.

Da Giacomino – *57030 Sant'Andrea – 6km/4mi northwest of Marciana –* ☎ *0565 90 80 10 – Fax 0565 90 82 94 – Closed Nov-Easter –* 🅿 ⬟ *– 33 rm €46.48/72.30 –* 😋 *€12.91 – Restaurant €19/40.* An ideal location for a holiday. The hotel rises up behind the cliffs and there is a wonderful garden which runs to the edge of the sheer cliff-face with stunning views down to the sea. The rooms are light and airy... and the staff are friendly.

GOING OUT
Calata Mazzini – *Calata Mazzini – 57037 Portoferraio.* There are various cafés and tea rooms along this (somewhat noisy) street. A good place to watch the boats coming and going in the busy little harbour.

SPORT AND LEISURE
Centro Velico Naregno – *Spiaggia di Naregno, northwest of Capoliveri – 57031 Capoliveri –* ☎ *0565 96 87 64 – cvn@centroveliconaregno.it – Open 8am-8pm, closed 15 Oct-Mar.* The Naregno sailing club runs various courses and hires out equipment including sailboards, catamarans, dinghies, scooters etc.

Nautilus Bagni Lacona – *Spiaggia Grande – 57031 Capoliveri –* ☎ *0565 96 43 64 – By appointment only, closed Nov-25 Apr.* For anyone who is not keen on scuba diving, this underwater vehicle is a very pleasant way of finding out about the multicoloured marine fauna and flora in the area. Sports enthusiasts can also hire motorboats, canoes, sailing boats and hang-gliders.

Isola d'Elba

Portoferraio

This island capital, guarded by ruined walls and two forts, lies at the head of a beautiful bay. In the upper part of the town is the **Musco Napoleonico** housed in the **Villa dei Mulini**, a simple house, with a terraced garden, which Napoleon sometimes occupied. His personal library and various mementoes are kept here. *Tour: Open daily 9am-8pm (last admission 7pm), Sun and public holidays 9am-2pm (last admission 1pm); in summer Sat 9am-11pm. Closed Tue, 1 Jan, 1 May, 25 Dec. €3. ☎ 0565 91 46 88; www.ambientepi.arti.beniculturali.it – www.elbaisola.com*

Beyond the great sandy beach at **Biodola**, the road goes towards **Marciana Marina**, a small port protected by two piers, one of which is dominated by a round tower, and climbs the wooded slopes of Monte Capanne.

Monte Capanne★★

Cable cars leave from Marciana. Alt 1 018m/3 339ft. Open daily, 10am-12.15pm and 2.30-5.30pm, Easter-Jun 10am-12.15pm and 2.30-5.30pm. Closed Nov-Easter €11.36 (round trip), €6.71 single. ☎ 0565 90 10 20.

From the summit not far from the terminus there is a splendid **panorama★★** of Elba, the Tuscan coast to the east and the coast of Corsica to the west.

Marciana

From this attractive village there is a lovely **view★** of Poggio, perched on its rocky spur, Marciana Marina and the Bay of Procchio. The small **Museo Archeologico** houses displays of prehistoric artefacts and Greek vases. *Closed for restoration at the time of writing.*

Madonna del Monte

Take the road up to the castle which dominates Marciana and from there a rocky path leads up to this sanctuary, built on the northern slope of Monte Giove. Beside the 16C chapel there is a curious semicircular fountain dated 1698 and a "hermitage" where Napoleon and his lover Maria Walewska spent a few days in the summer of 1814.

Marina di Campo

This small fishing port with its popular beach lies at the head of a lovely bay backed by a hinterland plain of olive groves and vineyards.

Museo Nazionale di Villa Napoleone di San Martino★

Open 9am-8pm (last admission 7pm), Sun and public holidays 9am-2pm (last admission 1pm); in summer, Sat 9am-11pm. Closed Mon, 1 Jan, 25 Dec. €3.☎ 0565 91 46 88; www.ambientepi.arti.beniculturali.it – www.elbaisola.com

In a setting of silent hills, planted with groves of evergreen oaks and vineyards, this modest house was the ex-emperor's summer residence. There is a lovely view of the Bay of Portoferraio.

Golfo Stella

Lower down there is a neo-Classical style villa, constructed by Prince Demidoff, son-in-law of King Jerome.

Capoliveri
Not far from this village there is a **panorama★★** of three bays: Portoferraio, Porto Azzurro and Golfo Stella.

Porto Azzurro ♒♒
This pretty port is overlooked by a fort which now serves as a prison.

Rio Marina
A pleasant port and mining village protected by a crenellated tower. Beyond **Cavo**, a small port sheltered by the Castello headland, the return journey to Portoferraio is by a high altitude **road★★** affording remarkable views of the ruins of Volterraio, the Bay of Portoferraio and the sea.

Ercolano★★

HERCULANEUM

Herculaneum was founded, according to tradition, by Hercules. Like Pompeii the Roman town was buried during the AD 79 eruption of Vesuvius. Numerous craftsmen and many rich and cultured patricians were drawn to the resort of Herculaneum because of its beautiful setting, overlooking the Bay of Naples. In 1997 Herculaneum was included in UNESCO's World Heritage List.

Location
Population 57 638 – Michelin map 431 E 25 – See also the local map in Golfo di NAPOLI.
Herculaneum is situated at the foot of Vesuvius, off A 3, the Naples-Pompeii-Salerno road.
Surrounding area: see COSTIERA AMALFITANA, NAPOLI, Golfo di NAPOLI.

Worth a Visit

2hr. NB: Some of the houses listed below may be temporarily closed for maintenance and restoration. (&) Apr-Oct 8.30am-7.30pm (last admission 6pm); Nov-Mar 8.30am-5pm (last admission 3.30pm). Closed 1 Jan, 25 Dec. €8.50 inclusive ticket (valid 1 day) for Pompeii, Oplontis, Stabia and Boscoreale; €13.50 (valid 3 days) for Pompeii, Herculaneum, Oplontis, Stabia and Boscoreale. ☎ 081 85 75 347; www.pompeiisites.org
Herculaneum is broadly divided into four sections which are delineated by the two main streets (*decumani*) and three other thoroughfares (*cardi*). The town has various examples of different types of dwellings, all of which were overwhelmed by the sea of mud which seeped into every nook. The particular interest of a visit to

Herculaneum is that all timber structures (frameworks, beams, doors, stairs and partitions) were preserved by a hard shell of solidified mud, whereas at Pompeii they were consumed by fire. The houses were empty, but death caught up with the inhabitants as they tried to flee the city or make for the sea.

The following itinerary starts at the bottom of Cardo III.

The **Casa dell'Albergo** was about to be converted into apartments for letting, hence its name. This vast patrician villa was one of the most badly damaged by the eruption.

The **Casa dell'Atrio a mosaico★★** takes its name from the chequered mosaic on the floor in the atrium. The garden on the right is surrounded by a peristyle. On the left are the bedrooms and at the far end, a pleasant *triclinium* (dining room). The terrace, flanked by two small rest rooms, offers an attractive view of the sea.

In the **Casa a graticcio★★** the framework (*graticcio*) of the walls was formed by a wooden trellis. It is a unique example of this type of house from Antiquity.

With its façade remarkably well preserved, the **Casa del Tramezzo carbonizzato★** is a good example of a patrician dwelling which housed several families. The atrium is separated from the *tablinium* (living room) by a wooden partition (*tramezzo*). Only the sides of the partition remain standing.

Next door is the **Bottega del tintore (A)**, the dyer's shop, which contains an interesting wooden clothes press.

The **Casa Sannitica★★**, was built on the very simple plan typical of the Samnites (an Italic people of the Sabine race). The splendid **atrium** is surrounded by a gallery with Ionic columns. The rooms are decorated with frescoes.

The **baths★★★** of Herculaneum which are in excellent condition were built at the time of Augustus. They are not sumptuous but they show a remarkable degree of practical planning. In the **men's baths** visit the *palestra*, the cloakroom, the *frigidarium* with frescoes on the ceiling, the *tepidarium* and the *caldarium*. The **women's baths** include the waiting-room, the cloakroom (*apodyterium*), adorned with a mosaic pavement depicting the sea god Triton, the *tepidarium* with a fine floor mosaic representing a labyrinth, and the *caldarium*.

The **Casa del Mobilio carbonizzato★ (B)** is a small but rather elegant house. It has the remains of a charred (*carbonizzato*) bed in one room.

The **Casa del Mosaico di Nettuno e Anfitrite★★** is equipped with a shop★, its counter opened onto the street. Mosaics depicting Neptune and Amphitrite adorn the nymphaeum.

Nearby is one of the most original houses in Herculaneum, the **Casa del Bel Cortile★ (C)**, with its courtyard (*cortile*), stone staircase and balcony.

The **Casa del Bicentenario★** was unearthed in 1938, 200 years after digging officially started. The house has fresco decorations and a small cross incorporated in a stucco panel. This is one of the oldest Christian relics which has been brought to light in the Roman Empire.

An inscription states that the **Pistrinum★★** (bakery) belonged to Sextus Patulus Felix. In the shop and back room may be seen flour mills, storage jars and a large oven.

The **Casa dei Cervi★★** was probably the most beautiful and most grandiose patrician villa overlooking the bay. It is adorned with numerous frescoes and works of art, including an admirable sculptured group of stags (*cervi*) being attacked by dogs.

The tour concludes with a visit to the **Terme Suburbane★**, elegantly decorated baths, and the **teatro★** (*entrance at Via Mare 123*), which could accommodate around 2 000 spectators.

Fabriano

Famous since the 13C for its manufacture of paper which is exported all over the world, Fabriano is a pleasant, tranquil town.

Location

Population 29 523 – Michelin map 430 L 20 – Marches. Fabriano is off S 76 which links Ancona with Umbria. **B** *Corso della Repubblica 70,* ☎ *0732 53 87.*
Surrounding area: see ANCONA, ASSISI, GUBBIO.

Worth a Visit

Piazza del Comune★

Characterised by its odd trapezoidal shape, the square is overlooked by the grim 13C **Governor's Residence** (Palazzo del Podestà), one of the finest examples of medieval civic architecture in the Marches, the Bishop's Palace (Palazzo Vescovile) and by the town hall (Palazzo Comunale) with its adjacent Loggia of St Francis. At the centre of the square stands the *Sturinalto*, a fine Gothic fountain somewhat similar to the Fontana Maggiore in Perugia.

> ### On paper... and canvas
> Fabriano was the birthplace of two delightful artists, **Allegretto Nuzi** (1320-73), the main exponent of the Fabriano School who was very much influenced by the Tuscans, and **Gentile da Fabriano,** (c 1370-1427), one of the principal exponents of the International Gothic style and a point of reference for artists such as Pisanello and Jacopo Bellini. Unfortunately the town does not house any of his work.

Piazza del Duomo

This peaceful and enchanting square is overlooked by the **Cathedral** dedicated to St Venanzo and decorated with frescoes by Allegretto Nuzi inside. Opposite stands the 15C ex-hospital Madonna del Buon Gesù which now houses an art gallery, the **Pinacoteca Civica**. The gallery illustrates the evolution of painting in Fabriano from the 13C to 15C. There are two fine **wood sculptures★** from the second half of the 14C, the *Adoration of the Magi* and the *Holy Representation* as well as a collection of tapestries. ♿ *The art gallery is temporarily housed in the Museo della Carta e della Filigrana – Largo Fratelli Spacca 2. Open Tue-Sat 10am-6pm, Sun and public holidays 10am-noon and 4-7pm. Closed Mon. €3.36.* ☎ *0732 70 92 30.*

Museo della Carta e della Filigrana★★

Largo Fratelli Spacca. (♿) Open Apr-Sep, 10am-6pm, Sun and public holidays 10am-noon and 4-7pm; rest of the year 10am-6pm, Sun and public holidays 10am-noon and 2-5pm. Closed Mon, 1 Jan, Easter, 1 May, 25 Dec. €3.36. ☎ *0732 70 92 97; www.museodella carta.com*
Housed in the ex-Convent of St Damian (15C) this is a lively museum which illustrates the manufacture of paper through the reconstruction of a fully operative medieval workshop. The museum also has displays of antique Fabriano paper and an international collection of watermarked paper.

Excursion

Grotte di Frasassi★★

15km/9mi northeast. (♿) Guided tours only (70min). Opening times vary. Closed 1 Jan, 10-30 Jan, 4 Dec and 25 Dec. €10.50. ☎ *0732 97 211; www.frasassi.com*
A tributary of the River Sentino has formed a vast network of underground caves (*grotte*). The largest, the **Grotta del Vento**, is composed of seven chambers where the visitor may admire stalagmites, stalactites and other diverse forms in a variety of colours.

Faenza

Having given its name to the ceramics known as faience, Faenza is synonymous throughout the world with its glazed and painted ceramics which have been produced locally since the 15C.

Location

Population 53 452 – Michelin map 429, 430 J 17 – Emilia-Romagna. Faenza is off S 9, the Via Emilia, which links Bologna with Rimini. 🔲 *Piazza del Popolo 1,* ☎ *0546 25 231.*
Surrounding area: see BOLOGNA, DELTA DEL PO, RAVENNA.

Special Features

CERAMICS

In Italy faience is also known as majolica, because during the Renaissance Faenza potters were inspired by ceramics which were imported from Majorca in the Balearic Isles. Faenza ceramics feature fine clay, remarkable glaze, brilliant colours and a great variety of decoration. An international competition and an international biennial of art ceramics bear witness to a vocation that is still strongly felt by artists and artisans.

Museo Internazionale delle Ceramiche★★

(&) *Open Apr-Oct 9am-7pm, Sun and public holidays 9.30am-1pm and 3-7pm; rest of the year 9am-1.30pm, Sat 9am-1pm and 3-6pm; Sun 9.30am-1pm and 3-6pm. Closed Mon, public holidays. €5.16.* ☎ *0546 21 240; www.micfaenza.org*
These vast collections present the development of ceramicwork throughout the world. On the first floor is a very fine collection of Italian Renaissance majolica, examples of the local ware, popular Italian pieces and an Oriental section. On the ground floor, as well as the contemporary Italian collection, there are fine pieces by Matisse, Picasso, Chagall, Léger, Lurçat and the Vallauris School.

Museo Internazionale delle Ceramiche

Late-15C plate

Worth a Visit

Pinacoteca Comunale★

Closed for restoration at the time of writing (although the old part is open to visitors). For information and bookings ☎ *0546 25 231.*
This important art collection includes works by Giovanni da Rimini, Palmezzano, Dosso Dossi, Rossellino, as well as canvases from foreign schools (portraits by Pombus).

Cattedrale

The 15C cathedral was built by Florentine architect Giuliano da Maiano but the façade is unfinished. It contains the tomb (1471) of Bishop St Savinus by Benedetto da Maiano. In Piazza della Libertà stands a charming 17C Baroque fountain.

Piazza del Popolo

The unusual elongated square has arcades surmounted by galleries. Around it are the 12C Palazzo del Podestà (governor's house) and the 13C-15C Palazzo del Municipio (town hall).

Excursions

Forlì

17km/10mi southeast. Situated on the Via Emilia, Forlì was an independent commune ruled by an overlord in the 13C and 14C. The citadel was heroically defended in 1500 by Caterina Sforza against Cesare Borgia.

The **basilica of San Mercuriale** (*Piazza Aurelio Saffi*) is dominated by an imposing Romanesque campanile. The lunette of the doorway to the basilica is adorned with a 13C low relief. The numerous works of art inside include several paintings by Marco Palmezzano and the tomb of Barbara Manfredi by Francesco di Simone Ferrucci.

At 72 Corso della Repubblica is the **pinacoteca**. The art gallery includes works by local 13C-15C artists. There is a delicate *Portrait of a Young Girl* by Lorenzo di Credi. (&) *Open 9am-1.30pm, Tue and Thu also 3-5.30pm, Sun 9am-1pm. Closed Mon, public holidays and 4 Feb. No charge.* ☎ *0543 71 26 06.*

Cesena

20km/12mi southeast of Forlì. The town lies at the foot of a hill on which stands the great 15C castle of the Malatestas. It contains the Renaissance library, **Biblioteca Malatestiana★** *(Piazza Bufalini)*. The interior of the library comprises three long aisles with vaulting supported on fluted columns capped with fine capitals. On display are valuable manuscripts, including some from the famous school of miniaturists at Ferrara, as well as the Missorium, a great silver-gilt plate probably dating from the 4C. (&) *Open daily, mid-Jun to Sep 8.30am-12.30pm and 4-7pm, (rest of the year 6pm); Sun and public holidays 10am-12.30pm. Guided tours only (45min). Closed 1 Jan.* €2.60. ☎ *0547 61 08 92; www.comune.cesena.fc.it*

Bertinoro

12km/7mi west of Cesena. This small town is famous for its panorama and its yellow wine (Albana). In the middle of the town is a "hospitality column" fitted with rings, each corresponding to a local home. The ring to which the traveller tethered his horse would determine which family should be his hosts. From the nearby terrace there is a wide **view★** of Romagna.

Fermo★

Fermo is a lovely town, enhanced by its beautiful hillside setting★, overlooking the surrounding countryside and sea. At the heart of the historic centre is the elegant Piazza del Popolo.

Location

Populaton 35 617 – Michelin map 430 M 23 – Marches. Fermo is not far from the Adriatic coast. Take A 14, exiting at Porto San Giorgio. ⊠ *Piazza del Popolo 6,* ☎ *0734 22 87 38.*

Worth a Visit

Piazza del Popolo★

This square in the centre of town is surrounded by arcades and elegant 16C porticoes. It is bordered by numerous palaces including the 15C-16C **Palazzo dei Priori** (Prior's Palace) with a statue of Sixtus V (once the Bishop of Fermo) on its façade, the Palazzo degli Studi, at one time the university and now the municipal library, and opposite, Palazzo Apostolico.

Pinacoteca Civica – *Open mid-Jun to Sep 10am-1pm and 3.30pm-7.30pm, Aug also 3.30-11.30pm; rest of the year 9.30am-1pm and 3.30-7pm. Closed Mon, 1 Nov.* €1.55. ☎ *0734 28 43 27.*

The municipal art gallery is housed on the first floor of the Palazzo dei Priori and boasts a fine collection, mainly of art from the Veneto and Marches. The most notable works include *Lu Margutta* (16C), a Saracen wood sculpture used as a target in knights' tournaments, the elegant Late Gothic *Scenes from the Life of Saint Lucy★* by Jacobello del Fiore (fl 1394-1439) and the *Adoration of the Shepherds★★* by Rubens (1577-1640), probably one of the finest works produced by the artist during his sojourn in Italy. In the Map Room there is a fine **terraqueous globe** from the 18C.

Near the Piazza, in Via degli Aceti, are the **Roman cisterns**, an imposing construction dating from the 1C AD comprised of 30 interconnecting chambers making up a total surface area of more than 2 000m²/21 528sq ft. These cisterns were used as a reservoir of water both for the city and the port. *Open mid-Jun to Sep 10am-1pm and 3.30-7.30pm, Aug also 3.30-11.30pm; rest of the year 9.30am-1pm and 3.30-7pm. Closed Mon, 1 Nov.* €2.58. ☎ *0734 21 71 40; www.sistemamuseo.it*

Off Piazza del Popolo is **Corso Cefalonia**, the main street of the historic centre, which is lined with fine Renaissance buildings (Palazzo Azzolino, Palazzi Vitali Rosati) and by the 13C Matteucci Tower.

Fermo

Piazza del Duomo

From this esplanade in front of the cathedral there are splendid **views★★** of the Ascoli area, the Apennines, the Adriatic and Conero Peninsula.

Duomo★ – *Open daily, 10am-12.30pm and 4-7.30pm (telephone to confirm opening times). Guided tours can be arranged. €2.07.* ☎ *0734 22 87 29.*

The Romanesque-Gothic cathedral (1227), built by the Maestri Comacini has a majestic **façade★** in white Istrian stone. A delicately carved doorway shows Christ with the Apostles on the lintel, and symbolic scenes or figures on the uprights. In the atrium, part of the old church, note the sarcophagus of Giovanni Visconti, lord of the city in the 14C. The 18C **interior** has a fine Byzantine **icon** and a 5C AD **mosaic★** in which a peacock drinking from a vase symbolises the resurrection of Christ.

Excursions

Montefiore dell'Aso

20km/12mi south. The collegiate church in this pretty town possesses a masterpiece of **Carlo Crivelli**, a **polyptych★★**, which although incomplete, is finely chiselled and highlighted with gold representing six saints. The depiction of Mary Magdalene represents a high point in the career of this artist. The saint, richly apparelled in gold and silk brocade with a scarlet mantle symbolising the passion of Christ, moves gracefully holding the vessel of ointment. *Open daily, 9am-noon and 3-8pm. No charge. For further information on opening times and guided tours contact* ☎ *0734 93 90 19; www.montefiore.net*

Chiesa di Santa Maria a piè di Chienti★

24km/14mi northwest. Open 8am-6pm, Sun and public holidays 9.30-10.30am and 11.30am-6pm. Donations welcome. ☎ *0733 86 52 41.*

This important Romanesque monument was founded in the 12C and subsequently remodelled on more than one occasion. The atmospheric **interior**, illuminated by the golden light of the alabaster windows, is divided into three aisles which open into an **ambulatory** with surrounding chapels of Cluniac influence. At the end of the 15C the raising of the presbytery created a second church whose apse is decorated with frescoes of the same period.

Ferrara★★

Ferrara is a tranquil town which is best explored in a leisurely manner. The streets lined with red-brick houses and austere palaces, and its charming squares – which were a source of inspiration to the 20C metaphysical painters De Chirico and Carrà – are easily accessible on foot or by bicycle. A splendid cultural centre during the Renaissance, these days Ferrara is a young and vibrant town and remains one of the major artistic and cultural centres in Italy.

Location

Population 132 127 – Michelin map 429 H 16 – Emilia Romagna. Ferrara rises up near the Po Delta, off A 13 which links Bologna with Padua. ◘ *Castello Estense, ☎ 0532 20 93 70.*
Surrounding area: see BOLOGNA, DELTA DEL PO.

Background

PATRONS OF THE ARTS

Initially an independent commune, Ferrara belonged to the **Este** family from 1208 to 1598, and despite numerous family dramas, often bloody, the Estes embellished their native city with fine buildings and patronised both men of letters and artists. **Niccolò III** (1393-1441) murdered his wife Parisina and her lover but he begat **Lionello** and **Borso**, moulding them into efficient administrators and enlightened patrons. **Ercole I** (1431-1505), who was responsible for his nephew's murder encouraged artists, as did his two famous daughters, Beatrice and Isabella d'Este. **Alfonso I** (1475-1534), the son of Ercole, became the third husband of Lucrezia Borgia, and **Ercole II** (1508-59) married Renée of France, the protector of the Calvinists. After the demise of **Alfonso II** (1533-97) who left no heirs, Ferrara came

Directory

under the rule of the Papacy and the Estes retired to the Duchy of Modena. Owing to the secular university (founded in 1391) and the patronage of the Este dynasty, the town witnessed a prodigious literary and artistic flowering. Three poets benefitted from the Este's largesse: **Matteo Maria Boiardo** (1441-94), **Ludovico Ariosto** and **Torquato Tasso** (1544-95).

The Ferrarese school

The leader of the Ferrarese school of painting *(known as the officina ferrarese)* was **Cosmè (Cosimo) Tura** (c 1430-95), a man of strong personality; the school's main characteristic was a meticulous realism, borrowed from the

PALADINS OF LOVE AND FAITH

Ludovico Ariosto, who spent his lifetime in the service of the Estes, in particular with Alfonso I, produced one of the greatest masterpieces of Italian literature, *Orlando Furioso (Roland the Mad)*. In relating the dramatic adventures of the knight Orlando and his lover Angelica, the poet gives free reign to his imagination, regaling his readers with theatrical descriptions of fantastic monsters and glorious battles. Tasso, a native of Sorrento, made several visits to Ferrara. During the first he wrote his epic poem *Gerusalemme Liberata (Jerusalem Delivered)* recounting the capture of Jerusalem by the Christians, enlivened by the love-story of Rinaldo and Armida.

Northern schools. This was combined with a rather grim expressionism which derived from Mantegna, and powerful modelling reminiscent of Donatello. The main members were **Francesco del Cossa** (1435-77), who tempered the severity and the metallic sense of form of Tura and whose free and luminous style is evocative of Piero della Francesca; **Ercole de' Roberti** (1450-96), who conversely adopted Tura's strong modelling tradition; and **Lorenzo Costa** (1460-1535) who moved his studio to Bologna where the dark tones of the Umbrian and Tuscan schools prevailed. In the 16C the colourist **Dosso Dossi** (c 1490-1542) and **Benvenuto Garofalo** (1481-1559) favoured a greater harmony of colour in line with the Venetian style and allied themselves to the classical tradition of Raphael and the Roman school.

Worth a Visit

OLD TOWN

Castello Estense★

(&) *Open all year 9.30am-5pm. Closed Mon, 1 Jan, 25 Dec. €4.10.* ☎ *0532 29 92 33; www.provincia.fe.it*

This massive castle, guarded by moats and four fortified gateways with drawbridges, was the seat of the Este family. The ground floor houses the spartan prison where Parisina and her lover were locked away. On the *piano nobile*, where the orangery

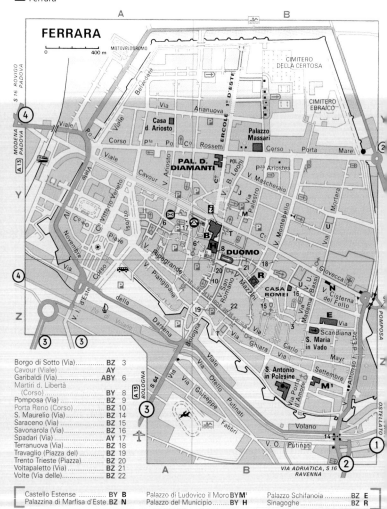

FERRARA

is, visitors may view the Ducal Chapel collection and the apartments decorated with frescoes by the Filippi, active in Ferrara in the second half of the 16C.

Duomo★★

The cathedral was built in the 12C in the Romanesque-Gothic Lombard style and presents a triple **façade★★** with a splendid **porch**. On the tympanum is depicted the *Last Judgement* recalling the decoration of French Gothic cathedrals. In the lunette above the central door, the sculpture of St George is by Nicholaus, an artist of the school led by the Romanesque master, Wiligelmo, who was responsible for the carved decoration of Modena cathedral. On the south side there are two tiers of galleries on the upper section; below is the Loggia dei Merciai, a portico occupied by shops in the 15C. Here stood the Portal of the Months; the panels are kept in the cathedral museum. The bell tower which was never completed was designed by Leon Battista Alberti. The semicircular apse with its decorative brickwork is by Biagio Rossetti.

The interior which was rebuilt in the 18C contains a number of works of art. In the south arm of the transept note *The Martyrdom of St Lawrence* by Guercino and two 15C bronze statues (St Maurelius and St George) and *The Last Judgement* by Bastianino on the vaulting in the apse.

Museo della Cattedrale – *Open all year 9.30am 2pm (telephone for confirmation of admission times). Closed Mon, public holidays. Donations welcome. ☎ 0532 76 12 99; www.comune.fe.it/musei-aa/schifanoia/htm* The museum contains two statues by Jacopo della Quercia, the **panels★★** of an organ painted by **Cosmè Tura** representing *St George slaying the Dragon* and *The Annunciation* and the admirable 12C **sculptures★** from the Portal of the Months, admirable in their immediacy and close observation of reality (the finest example is the month of September).

The 13C town hall, **Palazzo del Municipio**, facing the cathedral, was once the ducal palace.

Medieval streets

Via San Romano, which is still a commercial artery, linked the market square (Piazza Trento e Trieste) and the port (now Via Ripagrande). It is lined with several houses with porticoes, an unusual feature in Ferrara. **Via delle Volte**, which has a distinctive character, has become one of the symbols of the town. Covered alleyways *(volte)* linked the houses of the merchants and their warehouses, thus making more habitable space available. Along Via Mazzini are the **Sinagoghe** (synagogue complex) which comprise

three temples for different rites: the Italian and German traditions and that from Fano in the Marches. The synagogue complex was a gift of the Roman banker, Ser Samuel Mele, in 1481 to the Jewish community. *Open 10am-1pm (last admission noon). Closed Fri, Sat, Jewish feasts, Aug. €4. ☎ 0532 21 02 28; www.comune.fe.it/museoebraico*

Casa Romei*

Open all year 8.30am-7pm. Closed Mon, 1 Jan, 1 May, 25 Dec. €2. ☎ 0532 24 00 05.
This is a rare example of a 15C bourgeois residence combining late-Gothic features such as the decoration of the rooms on the ground floor (Room of the Sibyls, Room of the Prophets) and Renaissance elements like the portico of the main courtyard.

Palazzina di Marfisa d'Este*

Open 9.30am-1.30pm and 3-6pm. Closed Mon, public holidays. €2.07, €5.16 including admission to Palazzo Schifanoia. ☎ 0532 20 74 50; www.comune.fe.it/musei-aa/schifanoia/htm
This elegant single-storey residence (1559), formerly surrounded by loggias, pavilions and gardens, is where Marfisa d'Este entertained her friends, among them the poet Tasso. The interior is remarkable for the ornate ceiling decoration including grotesques, and elegant 16C-17C furniture. Pass into the garden to visit the Orangery (Loggia degli Aranci); the vault features a mock pergola complete with vine shoots and animals.

Palazzo Schifanoia*

Open all year 9.30am-7pm (last admission 6.30pm). Closed Mon, public holidays. €4.13, €5.16 including admission to Palazzina di Marfisa d'Este. ☎ 0532 64 178; www.comune.fe.it/musei-aa/schifanoia/htm
This 14C palace is where the Estes used to come to relax (*schifanoia* means carefree). There are splendid frescoes in the Room of the Months **(Salone dei Mesi★★)**. This complex cycle to the glory of Borso d'Este unfortunately retains only some of the 12 months. The three levels illustrate three different themes, notably everyday life at court, astrology and mythology. Several artists, including Francesco del Cossa (March, April, May) and Ercole de' Roberti (September), worked under Cosmè Tura. The frescoes, which demonstrate an extraordinary delicacy when portraying detail and a marvellous vivacity in both the use of colour and draughtsmanship, attest to Ferrara's great cultural achievements during the Renaissance.
The palace houses a museum, the **Museo Civico di Arte Antica**, which displays archaeological collections, medals, bronzes, marquetry and ivories. The museum is part of the **Lapidario** situated near a former church Santa Libera.
The 15C-16C church, **Santa Maria in Vado**, near the palace, is decorated inside with frescoes and paintings.

Palazzo di Ludovico il Moro*

♿ Open all year 9am-2pm (last admission 1.30pm). Closed Mon, 1 Jan, 1 May and 25 Dec. €4. ☎ 0532 66 299.
This palace was designed at the end of the 15C by Biagio Rossetti but building was not completed. There is a fine arcaded courtyard and a **grand staircase** with interesting marble decorations. The first floor houses an **archaeological museum** with an important collection of 5C-4C BC **Attic vases★** and burial accoutrements found at Spina, at one time one of the most important commercial ports in the Mediterranean. Spina was only brought to light in the 20C after an archaeological "mystery" that lasted over 2 000 years and fascinated Boccaccio among others.

Monastero di San Antonio in Polesine

Open all year 9.15-11.30am and 3.30-5pm. Closed Sat pm, Sun and public holidays, 1st day of the month. Donations welcome. For information ☎ 0532 64 068.
The convent founded in 1257 by Beatrice II d'Este, who joined the Benedictine order, stands in an isolated and peaceful setting.

The **church** has three chapels decorated with fine 14C-16C **frescoes★** by the Giotto and Emilian schools.

THE RENAISSANCE TOWN

In 1490 Ercole I d'Este commissioned **Biagio Rossetti** to extend the town to the north. The extension (**Addizione Erculea**) built around two main axes – Corso Ercole I d'Este and Corso Porta Pia, Bragio Rossetti and Porta Mare – is a great Renaissance town featuring parks and gardens. With this grandiose town-planning scheme Ferrara became the first modern city in Europe, according to the art historian Jacob Burckhardt, and in 1995 was included in UNESCO's World Heritage List.

Corso Ercole I d'Este★

The street lined with splendid Renaissance palaces but lacking any shops retains its original residential aspect. The focal point is the **Quadrivio degli Angeli** at the intersection with the other main axis, emphasised by three palaces with a rich angular decoration, including the Palazzo dei Diamanti.

Palazzo dei Diamanti★★

The most distinctive of all the works by **Biagio Rossetti**, the palace takes its name from the marble façade of 8 500 diamond bosses; the different angles at which they have been placed creates a curious optical effect. The palace was designed for a diagonal view: the central feature is therefore the corner embellished with pilasters and a balcony. On the first floor is the art gallery.

Pinacoteca Nazionale★ – & *Open all year 9am-2pm, Thu 9am-7pm, Sun and public holidays 9am-1pm. Closed Mon, 1 Jan, 1 May, 25 Dec, National Heritage Week (Apr). €4.13. ☎ 0532 20 58 44.*

The gallery displays paintings showing the development of the Ferrarese, Emilian and Venetian Schools from the 13C to 18C. Among the masterpieces are two **tondi** dedicated to San Maurelio by Cosmè Tura, a *Death of the Virgin* by the Venetian Carpaccio, a *Descent from the Cross* by Ortolano, an **altarpiece** by Garofalo and **frescoes** from churches in Ferrara. The Sacrati Strozzi Collection includes paintings of the *Muses* **Erato** and **Urania** from Leonello d'Este's Studiolo in Palazzo di Belfiore which was situated near the present Corso Ercole I d'Este and was later dismantled when the town was under Papal rule.

At nᵒ 17 in Corso Ercole I d'Este the **Museo Michelangelo Antonioni** presents the pictorial and photographic work of the great Ferrarese film director

Some of the "diamonds" on the Palazzo dei Diamanti ... a sort of optical illusion

Palazzo Massari

& *Open all year 9am-1pm and 3-6pm. Closed 1 and 6 Jan, Easter, 1 Nov, 25-26 Dec. €4.13, €6.70 with Museo Arte Moderna included. ☎ 0532 20 99 88; www.comune.fe.it*

This superb late-16C palace now houses the **Museo Boldini** containing oils, pastels and drawings that are representative of the artist's development (1842-1931) during the time he spent in Ferrara, Florence and Paris. There are a few works by other artists from Ferrara, including Previati.

Casa dell'Ariosto

Via Ariosto 67. Open all year 10am-1pm and 3-6pm, Sun and hols 10am-1pm. Closed Mon, 1 and 6 Jan, Easter, 1 Nov, 25-26 Dec. No charge. ☎ 0532 20 85 64; www.provincia.fe.it/musei-aci/schifanoia/htm

Ariosto's house is now a library but it still has the garden where the poet tended his roses and jasmine.

Fiesole★

The road from Florence winds uphill to Fiesole through olive-clad slopes, past luxuriant gardens and long lines of cypress trees, and affords views of this incomparable countryside★★★, so often depicted by the masters of the Italian Renaissance. The Etruscans founded this city in the 7C or 6C BC, strategically built high in the hills with a healthy climate. Fiesole was the most important city in northern Etruria and it dominated its neighbour and rival Florence until the 12C.

Location

Population 14 876 – Michelin map 430 K 15 – See also the Michelin Atlas Italy, The Red Guide Italia and The Green Guide Tuscany. Fiesole is 8km/5mi northeast of Florence.
🖪 *Via Portigiani 3,* ☎ *055 59 87 20.*
Surrounding area: see FIRENZE.

Worth a Visit

Convento di San Francesco★

Open 10am-12pm and 3-5pm and Sun pm. Closed Mon, Sat and Sun am. ☎ *055 59 175.*
The climb up to the convent which starts in front of the Duomo offers a splendid **view★★** over Florence (from a small terrace about halfway up). This humble Franciscan convent, with its charming small cloisters, is admirably set on the hilltop.

Duomo★

Founded in the 11C and enlarged in the 13C and 14C, the cathedral was extensively restored in the late 19C. The austere **interior★**, on a basilical plan with raised chancel, has columns supporting Antique capitals. There are two handsome **works★** by the sculptor Mino da Fiesole.

Zona archeologica

& – *Museum;* (&) – *Area Archeologica, Summer 9.30am-7pm, Apr and Oct 9.30am-6pm; rest of the year 9.30am-5pm. Closed Tue (winter), 1 Jan and 25 Dec. €6.20 including admission to Museo Bandini; €14.46 family ticket.* ☎ *055 59 477; www.ups.itpropart/museo-archeo-fiesole/*
This archaeological site, in its enchanting **setting★**, comprises a **Roman theatre★** (c 80 BC), which is still used for performances, a small **Etruscan temple** and the remains of **baths** built in the 1C BC by the Romans. The **museo archeologico★** exhibits finds dating from the Etruscan to the medieval period.

Antiquarium Costantini

Entrance near the archaeological site. Fine collection of Greek and Etruscan vases. In the basement are the results of the archaeological digs carried out on the museum site (Roman murals).

Museo Bandini

Opposite the entrance to the archaeological site. Summer 9.30am-7pm, Mar 9.30am-6pm, winter 9.30am-5pm. €6.20, including admission to the Museo Archeologico and the Cappella di San Giacomo. ☎ *055 59 477.*
The museum houses a collection of 14C and 15C Tuscan paintings. Note, on the first floor, Petrarch's masterpiece **Triumphs** illustrated by Jacopo del Sellaio.

Chiesa di San Domenico di Fiesole

2.5km/1.5m southwest (see also the plan of the built-up area of Florence on Michelin map 430). It was in this 15C church, remodelled in the 17C, that Fra Angelico took his vows. In the first chapel on the north side is a **Madonna and Saints★** by the artist. In the second chapel on the south is a **Baptism of Christ** by Lorenzo di Credi.

Badia Fiesolana

3km/2mi southwest (see also the plan of the built-up area of Florence on Michelin map 430). This former Benedictine convent was partially rebuilt in the 15C thanks to the generosity of Cosimo the Elder who often stayed here. The Romanesque **façade★** of the original church, with its decorative green and white marble geometrical motifs, was incorporated in the new building, left unfinished on the death of Cosimo the Elder. The interior and cloisters are typical of Brunelleschi's style.

Firenze★★★

FLORENCE

Acknowledged as one of Italy's most beautiful cities and one of the world's greatest artistic capitals, Florence is a testament to the Italian capacity for genius. The birthplace of Dante and the model for the Italian language, the city was the cradle of civilisation which nurtured the humanist movement and the Renaissance in the first half of the 15C.

Location

Population 376 662 – Michelin map 430 K 15 – See also The Green Guide Tuscany. Florence lies at the foot of the Apennines in the Arno valley. The city is situated at an important motorway interchange, at the point where A 1 and A 11 (Florence-coast route) meet. 🛈 *Via Cavour 1,* ☎ *055 29 08 32.*
Surrounding area: see FIESOLE, PRATO.

Background

Florence is without doubt the city where the Italian genius has flourished with the greatest display of brilliance and purity. For three centuries, from the 13C to the 16C, the city was the cradle of an exceptional artistic and intellectual activity from which evolved the precepts which were to dictate the appearance of Italy at that time and also the aspect of modern civilisation throughout Europe. The main characteristics of this movement, which was later to be known as the Renaissance, were partly a receptivity to the outside world, a dynamic open-minded attitude which encouraged inventors and men of science to base their research on the reinterpretation of the achievements of ancient Rome, and on the expanding of the known horizons. The desire to achieve universality resulted in a multiplication of the fields of interest.

Dante was not only a great poet but also a grammarian and historian who did much research on the origins and versatility of his own language. He was

one of Florence's most active polemicists. **Giotto** was not only a painter but also an architect. **Lorenzo the Magnificent** was the prince who best incarnated the spirit of the Renaissance. An able diplomat, a realistic politician, a patron of the arts as well as a poet himself, he regularly attended the Platonic Academy in the Medici villa at Careggi, where philosophers such as Marsilio Ficino and Pico della Mirandola and men of letters like Politian and others established the principles of a new humanism. This quest to achieve a balance between nature and order had its most brilliant exponent in **Michelangelo**, painter, architect, sculptor and scholar whose work typifies a purely Florentine preoccupation.

Florence is set in the heart of a serenely beautiful **countryside★★★** which is bathed by a soft, amber light. The low surrounding hills are clad with olive groves, vineyards and cypresses which appear to have been harmoniously landscaped to please the human eye. Florentine architects and artists have variously striven to recreate this natural harmony in their works, whether it be the campanile of La Badia by Arnolfo di Cambio, or that of the cathedral by Giotto, the façade of Santa Maria Novella by Alberti or the dome of Santa Maria del Fiore by Brunelleschi. The pure and elegant lines of all these works of art would seem to be a response to the beauty of the landscape and the intensity of the light. The Florentine preoccupation with perspective throughout the Quattrocento (15C) is in part the result of this fascination for the countryside and that other great concern of the period, the desire faithfully to recreate what the eye could see.

This communion of great minds, with their varied facets and fields of interest, expressed a common desire to push their knowledge to the limits, and found in the flourishing city of Florence an ideal centre for their artistic and intellectual development. The city's artists, merchants, able administrators and princely patrons of the arts all contributed to the creation of just the right conditions for nurturing such an intellectual and artistic community, which for centuries was to influence human creativity.

In the beginning ...

The colony of Florentia was founded in the 1C BC by Julius Caesar on the north bank of the Arno at a spot level with the Ponte Vecchio. The veteran soldiers who garrisoned the colony controlled the Via Flaminia linking Rome to northern Italy and Gaul.

The Middle Ages

It was only in the early 11C that the city became an important Tuscan centre when Count Ugo, Marquis of Tuscany, took up residence here, and again towards the end of the same century when the Countess Matilda affirmed its independence. During the 12C Florence prospered under the influence of the new class of merchants who built such fine buildings as the baptistery and San Miniato. This period saw the rise of trades organised in powerful guilds (*arti*), which soon became the ruling class when Florence became an independent commune. In the 13C one third of Florence's population was engaged in either the wool or the silk trades, both of which exported their products to the four corners of Europe and were responsible for a period of extraordinary prosperity. These tradesmen were ably supported by the Florentine money houses which succeeded the Lombard and Jewish institutions, and themselves acquired a great reputation by issuing the first-ever bills of exchange and the famous florin, struck with the Florentine coat of arms. The latter was replaced in the late 15C by the Venetian ducat. The main banking families were the Bardi-Peruzzi who advanced huge sums to England at the beginning of the Hundred Years War; they were soon to be joined in the forefront by the Pitti, Strozzi, Pazzi and of course the Medici.

The Guelph cause

Despite its prosperity, Florence did not escape the internal strife between the Ghibellines who were partisans of the Holy Roman Emperor and the Guelphs who supported the Pope. The Guelphs at first had the advantage; but the Ghibellines on being driven out of Florence, having allied themselves with other enemies of Florence, notably Siena, regained power after the Battle of Montaperti in 1260. The Guelphs counter-attacked and retook Florence in 1266. Under their rule the physical aspect of the city changed considerably, notably with the destruction of the fortified tower houses built by the Ghibelline nobility. They created the system of government known as the *signoria* which was made up of the *priori* (masters of the city's Guilds). There then occurred a split between the Black Guelphs and the White Guelphs who opposed the Papacy. During the split, Dante, who supported the White Guelphs, was exiled for life in 1302. In 1348 the Black Death killed more than half the population and put an end to the period of internal strife.

A glorious era (15C)

Among the numerous wealthy families in Florence, it was the **Medici** who gave the city several leaders who exercised their patronage both in the sphere of fine arts and finance. The founder of this illustrious dynasty was Giovanni di Bicci, a prosperous banker who left his fortune in 1429 to his son **Cosimo the Elder**, who in turn transformed his heritage into the city's most flourishing business. He discreetly exercised his personal power through intermediaries, and astutely juggled his own personal interests with those of the city, which assured Florence a kind of peaceful hegemony. His chief quality was his ability to gather around him both scholars and artists, whom he commissioned for numerous projects. Cosimo the Elder was a passionate builder and Florence owes many of her great monuments to this "Father of the Land". His son, Piero II Gottoso (the gouty) survived him by five years only and he in turn bequeathed all to his son **Lorenzo the Magnificent** (1449-92). Having escaped the Pazzi Conspiracy, Lorenzo reigned like a true Renaissance prince, although it was always unofficially. He distinguished himself by his skilful politics and managed to retain the prestige of Florence among its contemporaries while ruining the Medici financial empire. This humanist and man of great sensitivity was a great patron of the arts, and he gathered around him poets and philosophers, who all contributed to make Florence the capital of the early Renaissance.

A turbulent period

On Lorenzo's death, which had repercussions throughout Europe, the Dominican monk **Girolamo Savonarola**, taking advantage of a period of confusion, provoked the fall of the Medici. This fanatical and ascetic monk, who became the Prior of the Monastery of St Mark, preached against the pleasures of the senses and of the arts,

*Brunelleschi's dome –
a familiar landmark
in Florence*

and drove the citizens of Florence to make a "bonfire of vanities" in 1497 in Piazza della Signoria, on which musical instruments, paintings and books of poetry were burnt. A year later Savonarola himself was burnt at the stake on the same spot.

The Medici family returned to power with the help of the Emperor Charles V and they reigned until the mid-18C. **Cosimo I** (1519-74) brought some lost splendour back to Florence, conquered Siena and he himself became Grand Duke of Tuscany. He continued the tradition of patron of the arts protecting numerous artists.

Francesco I (1541-87), whose daughter Maria was to marry Henri IV King of France, took as his second wife the beautiful Venetian Bianca Cappello. The last prominent Medici was Ferdinand I (1549-1609) who married a French princess, Christine de Lorraine.

After the Medici, the Grand Duchy passed to the House of Lorraine, then to Napoleon Bonaparte until 1814, before returning to the House of Lorraine until 1859. When it became part of the Italian Kingdom, Florence was capital from 1865 to 1870.

FLORENCE, CAPITAL OF THE ARTS

The relatively late emergence of Florence in the 11C as a cultural centre and its insignificant Roman heritage no doubt contributed to the growth of an independent art movement, which developed vigorously for several centuries. One of its principal characteristics was its preoccupation with clarity and harmony which influenced writers as well as architects, painters and sculptors.

Dante Alighieri (1265-1321) established the use of the Italian vernacular in several of his works, thus superseding Latin as the literary language. He made an admirable demonstration with his *New Life (Vita Nuova)*, recounting his meeting with a young girl, Beatrice Portinari, who was to be the inspiration for his *Divine Comedy (Divina Commedia)*, in which Dante, led by Virgil and then by Beatrice, visits the Inferno, Purgatory and Paradise. Dante's description of those infernal circles where the damned are chastised, of the mountain of Purgatory where great crowds await redemption, and finally the dazzling vision of the divine splendour of Paradise, have inspired for generations not only Italian writers but men of letters everywhere. In the 14C Dante was responsible for creating an exceptionally versatile literary language to which Petrarch *(see Index)* added his sense of lyricism and Boccaccio *(see Index)* the art of irony.

Niccolò Machiavelli (1469-1527), born in Florence, was the statesman on whose account Machiavellism became a synonym for cunning; he recounted his experiences as a statesman in a noble and vigorous prose. He was the author of *The Prince (Il Principe* – 1513), an essay on political science and government dedicated to Lorenzo II in which he counselled that in politics the end justifies the means.

Francesco Guicciardini (1483-1540) wrote an important history of Florence and Italy, while **Giorgio Vasari** (1511-74), much later, with his work *The Lives of the Most Eminent Italian Architects, Painters and Sculptors,* was the first real art historian. He studied and classified local schools of painting, tracing their development from the 13C with the work of Cimabue, whom even Dante had praised in his *Divine Comedy.*

The Florentine school had its origins in the work of **Cimabue** (1240-1302) and slowly it freed itself from the Byzantine tradition with its decorative convolutions, while **Giotto** (1266-1337) in his search for truth gave priority to movement and expression. Later **Masaccio** (1401-28) studied spatial dimension and modelling. From then on perspective became the principal preoccupation of Florentine painters, sculptors, architects and theorists who continually tried to perfect this technique.

The Quattrocento (15C) saw the emergence of a group of artists like **Paolo Uccello** (1397-1475), **Andrea del Castagno** (1423-57), **Piero della Francesca** *(see Index)* a native of the Marches, who were all ardent exponents in the matters of foreshortening and the strictly geometrical construction of space; while others such as **Fra Angelico** (1387-1455), and later **Filippo Lippi** (1406-69) and **Benozzo Gozzoli** (1420-97) were imbued with the traditions of International Gothic *(see p 90)* and were more concerned with the visual effects of arabesques and the appeal of luminous colours. These opposing tendencies were reconciled in the harmonious balance of the work of **Sandro Botticelli** (1444-1510), whom Florence is proud to claim as a son. He took his subjects from Antiquity as the humanists in the court of Lorenzo de' Medici recommended, and he invented fables peopled by enigmatic figures with subtle linear forms, which created an impression of tension. At times a certain melancholy seems to arrest the movement and dim the luminosity of the colours. Alongside Botticelli, the **Pollaiuolo** brothers, **Domenico Ghirlandaio** (1449-94) and **Filippino Lippi** (1457-1504) ensure the continuity and diversity of Florentine art.

The High Renaissance with its main centres in Rome and other northern towns reached Florence in the 16C. **Leonardo da Vinci** *(see Index)*, **Michelangelo** *(see Index)* and **Raphael** *(see Index)*, all made their debut at Florence, and inspired younger Mannerist artists such as **Jacopo Pontormo**, **Rosso Fiorentino**, **Andrea del Sarto** (1486-1530) and the curious portraitist of the Medici, **Agnolo Bronzino**(1503-72).

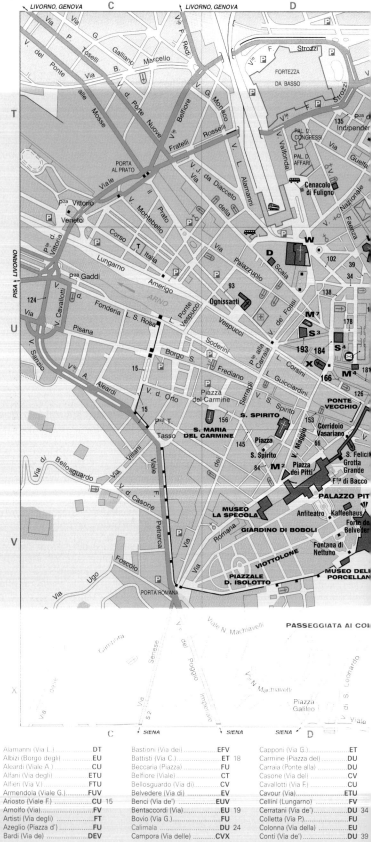

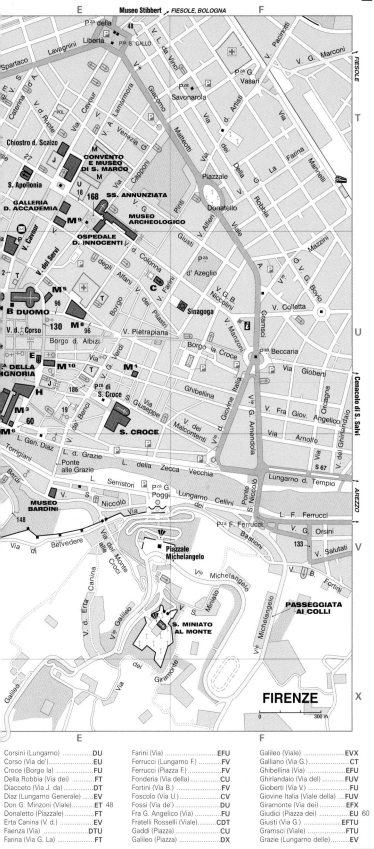

FIRENZE

Firenze

The emergence of a Florentine school of painting is, however, indissociable from the contemporary movement of the architects who were creating a style, also inspired by Antiquity, which united the classical traditions of rhythm, a respect for proportion and geometric decoration. The constant preoccupation was with perspective in the arrangement of interiors and the design of facades. **Leon Battista Alberti** (1404-72) was the theorist and grand master of such a movement. However it was **Filippo Brunelleschi** (1377-1446) who best represented the Florentine spirit, and he gave the city buildings which combined both rigour and grace, as in the magnificent dome of the cathedral of Santa Maria del Fiore which has become the symbol of Florence.

Throughout the Quattrocento (15C), buildings were embellished with admirable sculptures which became a harmonious part of the architectural whole. The doors of the baptistery were the object of a competition in which the very best took part. If **Lorenzo Ghiberti** (1378-1455) was finally victorious, **Donatello** (1386-1466) was later to provide ample demonstration of the genius of his art, so full of realism and style, as did **Luca della Robbia** (1400-82) and his dynasty who specialised in glazed terracotta decoration, **Andrea del Verrocchio** (1435-88) and numerous other artists who adorned the ecclesiastical and secular buildings of Florence. In the 16C **Michelangelo**, who was part of this tradition, confirmed his origins with his New Sacristy (1520-55) of San Lorenzo, which he both designed and decorated with sculpture. Later **Benvenuto Cellini** (1500-71), Giambolognga or **Giovanni Bologna** (1529-1608) and **Bartolomeo Ammannati** (1511-92) maintained this unity of style which was responsible for the exceptional beauty of the city of Florence.

The Procession of the Magi by Benozzo Gozzoli (detail showing Lorenzo the Magnificent), Palazzo Medici Riccardi

SCALA

Worth a Visit

Florence is such an important art centre that it takes at least four days to see the main sights. These are, however, situated fairly closely together in the city centre which is not adapted to heavy traffic. It is therefore advisable to do the sightseeing on foot and establish a visiting programme which takes into account the opening times.

PIAZZA DEL DUOMO★★★

In the city centre, the cathedral along with the campanile and baptistery, form an admirable group of white, green and pink marble monuments, which demonstrate the traditions of Florentine art from the Middle Ages to the Renaissance.

Duomo (Santa Maria del Fiore) ★★

Open daily 10am-5pm, Sat 10am-4.45pm, Sun and public holidays 1.30-4.45pm. Guided tours available in the morning and afternoon. Crypt, 10am-5pm. ☎ 055 23 02 885; www.operaduomo.firenze.it

One of the largest cathedrals in the Christian world, the Duomo is a symbol of the city's power and wealth in the 13C and 14C. It was begun in 1296 by Arnolfo di Cambio and was consecrated in 1436.

This essentially Gothic cathedral is an outstanding example of the Florentine variant of this style, with its sheer size, the predominance of horizontal lines and its polychrome decoration.

Exterior – Walk round the cathedral starting from the south side to admire the marble mosaic decoration and the sheer size of the **east end★★★**. The harmonious **dome★★★** by Brunelleschi took 14 years to build. To counteract the excessive thrust he built two concentric domes which were linked by props. The façade dates from the late 19C.

Top of the dome: Mon-Fri 8.30am-7pm, Sat 8.30am-5.40pm, (last admission 40min before closing). Closed Sun, from Maundy Thu to Easter Sun, 24 Jun, public holidays. €5.16. ☎ 055 23 02 885; www.operaduomo.firenze.it

Interior – The bareness of the interior contrasts sharply with the sumptuous decoration of the exterior. Enormous piers support sturdy arches which themselves uphold the lofty Gothic vaulting. The great octagonal **chancel** under the dome is surrounded by a delicate 16C marble balustrade. The dome is painted with a huge fresco of the Last Judgement. It is possible to go up to the inner gallery which offers an impressive view of the nave, and then climb to the top of the dome (464 steps) for a magnificent **panorama★★** of Florence.

The sacristy doors on either side of the high altar have tympana adorned with pale blue terracottas by Luca della Robbia representing the Resurrection and the Ascension. In the new sacristy (*left*), there are inlaid armorial bearings by the Maiano brothers (15C).

A dramatic episode of the **Pazzi Conspiracy** took place in the chancel. The Pazzi, who were rivals of the Medici, tried to assassinate Lorenzo the Magnificent on 26 April 1478, during the Elevation of the Host. Lorenzo, though wounded by two monks, managed to take refuge in a sacristy, but his brother Giuliano fell to their daggers.

Directory

GETTING ABOUT

Walking is by far the best solution. Florence has an ancient urban structure with narrow streets full of innumerable scooters and cars driven by Florentines who tend to be rather fast drivers. The one-way systems can be daunting if one doesn't know the city, traffic is often restricted to residents only and some car parks are also open to residents only. It's therefore a good idea to leave your car at the car parks at Fortezza da Basso or S. Maria Novella station and then walk or take a bus.

R. Mattes/MICHELIN

TALKING OF BUSES ...

A guideline of the main routes:
Lines 12 and 13 go to the Colli and Piazzale Michelangiolo,
Line 7 goes from the station to Fiesole.
Line 10 goes from the station to Settignano.
Line 17 goes from the station to the youth hostel.
Tickets with one hour validity cost €1, tickets valid for 3hr cost €1.80 and a booklet of four tickets valid for one hour costs €3.90.
Tourist tickets: valid for 24hr (€4),
2 days (€5.70), 3 days (€7.20)
and 7 days (€12).
For further information look at the ATAF website: www.ataf.net

to call a taxi ...

Dial either ☎ 055 4242, 055 4390, or ☎ 055 4798.

car rental

Cars can be rented at the airport or at offices in the city.

AVIS, Borgo Ognissanti 128r,
☎ 055 21 36 29, 055 23 98 826.

ITALY BY CAR, Borgo Ognissanti 134r,
☎ 055 28 71 61, fax 055 29 30 21, ☎
(airport) 055 30 04 13.

EUROPCAR, Borgo Ognissanti 53r,
☎ 055 29 04 37.

HERTZ, Via Maso Finiguerra 33r,
☎ 055 23 98 205.

GETTING AROUND BY BICYCLE

This is by far the best way of getting around Florence which is always beleaguered by traffic. Some hotels rent out bicycles but to meet the needs of all cyclists there is an association in Via S. Zanobi 120r/122r, called

Florence by bike

(www.florencebybike.it). Various types of bicycles can be rented and organised tours of the city by bike, with commentary on the sights by a tour leader, are also available.

SIGHTSEEING

To avoid the queues (of anything up to an hour) visitors are advised to book their tour of the Uffizi in advance. Booking office:
☎ 055 29 48 83.

WHERE TO EAT

It is not easy to eat well in Florence and it is even more difficult to get value for money. There is no shortage of bars selling sandwiches and ready cooked food as well as restaurants catering for tourists – but few of them are good. The best places to head for are the little trattorie which serve traditional Florentine dishes including tripe (*trippa* and *lampredotto*), vegetable soup (*ribollita*), bread cooked with tomatoes (*pappa al pomodoro*), various pasta dishes including *rigatoni strascicati*, steak (*bistecca*), stewed meatloaf (*polpettone in umido*), sausages with beans (*salsiccia con i fagioli all'uccelletto*) and the sweetened loaf *schiacciata dolce fiorentina*.

• Budget

Cantinetta dei Verrazzano – *Via dei Tavolini 18/20r, zona Piazza dalla Repubblica* – ☎ *055 26 85 90* – *cantinetta@verrazzano.com* – *Closed Sun* – €8/21. A charming little establishment with a winning formula which combines wonderful breads and pastries with good wines – and it's open 24 hours a day! The wine (which can be served by the glass) comes from the Fattoria di Verrazzano and is an excellent accompaniment to the wide variety of snacks on sale which include sliced ham and salami (affettati), rolls and sandwiches (panini), toasted bread (bruschette), cheeses (formaggi) and various desserts (dolci).

Enoteca Fuori Porta – *Via Monte alle Croci 10r, zona S. Niccolò* – ☎ *055 23 42 483* – *enos@ats.it* – *Closed Sun, 15 Aug, Easter, 25 Dec – Book* – €10/15. This very well-stocked enoteca was one of the first wine shops in Florence to offer quality wines. The young and enthusiastic proprietors of this

J. Malburet/MICHELIN

establishment also offer a "menù del giorno" which includes a number of first courses and some cold dishes. Highly recommended are the delicious and imaginative "crostoni".

Palle d'Oro – *Via Sant'Antonino 43/45r, zona S. Lorenzo* – ☎ *055 28 83 83 – Closed Sun, Aug –* 🍴 *– €10/23.* Situated a few minutes' walk from the market in San Lorenzo, this establishment dates back to the early 20C when the great-grandfather of the present owners set up a wine shop here. The menu features a number of Tuscan specialities and first courses. If you are short of time, there is a selection of sandwiches and rolls which can be consumed at the bar.

Vini e Vecchi Sapori – *Via dei Magazzini 3r, zona Piazza della Signoria* (☎ *055 29 30 45 – Closed Mon, Sun evening, 2 weeks in Aug –* 🚭 🍴 *– €13/15.* A small, but very pleasant establishment tucked away behind the Palazzo Vecchio. Local specialities include vegetable soup *(ribollita)* and tripe (including the *lampredotto* version) as well as *crostini*, sliced ham and salami *(affettati)* and cheeses *(formaggi)*. It can get very busy so be patient.

Osteria de' Benci – *Via de' Benci 11/13r, zona Santa Croce* – ☎ *055 23 44 923 – Closed Sun –* 🍴 *– Book – €20/39 + 10% service charge.* A traditional Tuscan trattoria with plenty of atmosphere and rustic ambience, wooden tables included. Traditional dishes with a regional flavour, based around seasonal produce. Good wine list – Tuscan wines only.

Trattoria 13 Gobbi – *Via del Porcellana 9r, zona S. Maria Novella* – ☎ *055 28 40 15 – Closed Mon lunchtime –* 🍴 *– Book – €20/40.* A well-known trattoria in Florence, popular for its authentic cooking and cheerful atmosphere. Rustic-style decor and furnishings in the two rooms which make up the dining area. During the summer meals are served in the lovely little courtyard.

• *Moderate*

Vineria Cibreino – *Via dei Macci 122r, zona Piazza Beccaria* – ☎ *055 23 41 100 – Closed Sun, Mon, 26 Jul-6 Sep, 31 Dec-6 Jan* (🚭 🍴 *– Book – €22/27.* This wine bar is located in the vicinity of the market in Sant'Ambrogio, adjacent to its sister restaurant. With its informal, friendly and trendy ambience it is one of the most popular establishments in the city. Delicious food and quality wines.

Del Fagioli – *Corso Tintori 47r, zona Santa Croce* – ☎ *055 24 42 85 – Closed Sat and Sun, Aug –* 🚭 *– €22/30.* A typical Tuscan trattoria with a relaxed, family atmosphere. Authentic home cooking and traditional Florentine dishes. A good place for a leisurely lunch.

Il Latini – *Via dei Palchetti 6r, zona S. Maria Novella* – ☎ *055 21 09 16 – Closed Mon, 24 Dec-5 Jan – €25/30.* Popular with Florentines and tourists alike this is a very lively establishment, the wooden tables always heaving with diners. Lots of witty banter and traditional Tuscan cooking.

Enoteca Pane e Vino – *Via S. Niccolò 70a/r, zona S. Niccolò* – ☎ *055 24 76 956 – Closed Sun and lunchtime, 7-21 Aug –* 🍴 *– €28/38.*

A delightful wine bar which successfully combines a rustic-style ambience with a more sophisticated dining experience. Imaginative menu based around traditional Tuscan produce. The wine list would satisfy even the most demanding connoisseur. Located on the far side of the Arno.

• *Expensive*

Cibreo – *Via dei Macci 118r, zona Piazza Beccaria* – ☎ *055 23 41 100 – Closed Mon, Sun, 31 Dec-6 Jan and 26 Jul-6 Sep –* 🍴 *– €56/65.* An informal but stylish establishment in the vicinity of the market in Sant'Ambrogio. The menu is based on traditional Tuscan cooking and the dishes are beautifully presented. The service is attentive and there is a good choice of wines. The wine bar next door also serves light snacks.

WHERE TO STAY

Florence is one of the most popular destinations in the world and between May and September this beautiful city is at the mercy of a massive tourist invasion. Our advice is to book your accommodation well in advance whether it is a small guesthouse *(pensione)* or a luxury hotel with all mod cons. Like Venice, prices are generally on the high side, but unlike other large cities, no one area is given over to accommodation for travellers on a tight budget – the historic centre of Florence has all sorts of hotels. Perhaps the only exception is the area around the station where there are a lot of small guesthouses which are popular with students but not particularly attractive. The heavy traffic in the centre of the city and the resulting noise and pollution remain a problem. Despite efforts to keep traffic out of the city centre during the day many areas are chock-a-block with cars and the parking is extremely difficult. Obviously the pedestrianised areas are the quietest. Many of the hotels have sought to reduce the noise levels by installing special glazing but if there is no air-conditioning in the summer you will have to decide which of the two evils you can best tolerate – and what a choice that is!

We have selected various types of accommodation ranging from the little pensione with a handful of rooms and shared bathrooms to smart hotels with all mod cons. Whatever your budget, if you want a room with a view expect to pay a supplement which will depend on how good the view is. Note that the hotels tend to put their prices up during trade fairs: do enquire about this when you make your booking.

N.B.: Yes, finding a hotel in some of Italy's busiest tourist destinations can be an arduous task and, alas, in Florence the relationship between quality and price often proves unfavourable for the visitor. However, it may be of interest to know that a number of religious orders offer accommodation; the prices are reasonable but there is one drawback: usually you have to be back in your room by 10.30pm.

Convents and monasteries

Casa della Madonna del Rosario – *Via Capo di Mondo 44* – ☎ *055 67 96 21 – Fax 055 67 71 33 –* 🚭 *– 32 rm*

Casa del Santo Nome di Gesù – *Piazza del Carmine 21 –* ☎ *055 21 38 56 – Fax 055 28 18 35 –* ⌿ *– 26 rm*

Istituto Gould – *Via dei Serragli 49 –* ☎ *055 21 53 63 – Fax 055 28 02 74 –* ⌿ *– 41 rm*

Casa del SS. Rosario – *Via Guido Monaco 24 –* ☎ *055 32 11 71 –* ⌿ *– 12 rm*

Convitto Ecclesiastico della Calza – *Piazza della Calza 6 –* ☎ *055 22 22 87 – Fax 055 22 39 12 – calza@calza.it –* ⌿ *– 50 rm*

Istituto Alfa Nuova – *Via E. Poggi 6 –* ☎ *055 47 62 80 – Fax 055 47 62 80 –* ⌿ *– 63 rm*

Istituto Salesiano dell'Immacolata – *Via del Ghirlandaio 40 –* ☎ *055 62 300 – Fax 055 62 30 282 – salesianifi@italwey.it –* ⌿ *– 55 rm*

Sette Santi Fondatori – *Via dei Mille 11 –* ☎ *055 50 48 452 – Fax 055 50 57 085 – 7santi@eidinet.com –* ⌿ *– 65 rm*

Istituto San Giovanni Battista – *Via di Ripoli 82 –* ☎ *055 68 02 394 – Fax 055 68 02 394 –* ⌿ *– 11 rm*

Istituto Santa Elisabetta – *Viale Michelangelo 46 –* ☎ *055 68 11 884 – Fax 055 68 11 884 – mabigus@tin.it –* ⌿ *– 29 rm*

Istituto Sant'Angela – *Via Fra Bartolomeo 56 –* ☎ *055 57 22 32 – Fax 055 57 22 32 –* ⌿ *– 11 rm*

Oasi del Sacro Cuore – *Via della Piazzola 4 –* ☎ *055 57 75 88 – Fax 055 57 48 87 – oasifirenze@.it –* ⌿ *– 58 rm*

Oblate dell'Assunzione – *Borgo Pinti 15 –* ☎ *055 24 80 582 – Fax 055 23 46 291 –* ⌿ *– 30 rm*

Pio X Artigianelli – *Via Serragli 106 –* ☎ *055 22 50 44 – Fax 055 22 50 44 –* ⌿ *– 18 rm*

Villa Agape – *Via della Torre del Gallo 8 –* ☎ *055 22 00 44 – Fax 055 23 37 012 –* ⌿ *– 28 rm*

Villa I Cancelli – *Via Incontri 21 –* ☎ *055 42 26 001 – Fax 055 42 26 001 –* ⌿ *– 31 rm*

Padri Filippini – *Via dell'Anguillara 25 –* ☎ *055 21 25 93 –* ⌿ *– 18 rm*

• *Budget*

Ostello Villa Camerata – *Viale Augusto Righi 2/4, zona Salviatino – 5km/3mi east of the centre towards Fiesole, bus line 17* ☎ *055 60 14 51 – Fax 055 60 13 00 –* ⌿ ✕ & *– 322 beds. €14.46 housed in a 15c villa which has been transformed with bunk beds, communal bathrooms and a restaurant, this cut-rate attractive hostel. Tucked away in the Tuscan hills with views over Fiesole, it's hard to believe that you are in one of the busiest cities in Italy.*

Albergo Scoti – *Via Tornabuoni 7, (2nd floor, no lift), zona S. Maria Novella –* ☎ *055 29 21 28 – Fax 055 29 21 28 – hotelscoti@hotmail.com –* ⌿ *– 7 rm €38.73/56.81 –* ⌧ *€4.13. An eclectic residence on Via Tornabuoni. The Renaissance palazzo with its richly frescoed salon creates a charming atmosphere of genteel aristocratic decline. Tiny, shared bathrooms.*

Youth Firenze 2000 – *Viale Raffaello Sanzio 16, zona S. Frediano –* ☎ *055 23 35 558 – Fax 055 23 06 392 – scatizzi@dada.it – Closed 15 Nov-15 Dec. –* ⌿ 🅿 🛏 ✕ & *– 76 beds – double rm €62* ⌧*. More of a hotel than a hostel with large private bathrooms and electronic keys which afford guests the luxury of privacy. Only 15min on foot from the Ponte Vecchio.*

Hotel Orchidea – *Borgo degli Albizi 111, (1st floor, no lift), zona Duomo –* ☎ *055 24 80 346 – Fax 055 24 80 346 – hotelorchidea@yahoo.it –* ⌿ *– 7 rm €40/65* ⌧*. This little pensione is housed on the first floor of a palazzo in the historic centre. The English lady who owns it has created a pleasantly relaxing, family atmosphere. The rooms are reasonably spacious, have high ceilings and are simply decorated. Shared bathrooms.*

Residenza Johanna I – *Via Bonifacio Lupi 14, zona Piazza della Libertà –* ☎ *055 48 18 96 – Fax 055 48 27 21 –* ⌿ *– 11 rm €41.32/67.14* ⌧*. A pleasant hotel where great attention has been paid to detail, to the extent that in some rooms there are niches full of books and magazines. Breakfast is served in a do-it-yourself formula: everything you need is set out on a tray in your room. This is an excellent address for its location (near Piazza S. Marco), atmosphere and reasonable prices.*

Residenza Johanna II – *Via Cinque Giornate 12, zona Fortezza da Basso –* ☎ *055 47 33 77 – Fax 055 47 33 77 –* ⌿ 🅿 *– 6 double rm €78* ⌧*. This small hotel, appropriately for Florence, is both restrained and welcoming. It is clean and in a pleasantly secluded position, if a little far from the city centre (half an hour on foot). There is also the advantage of a gravel courtyard where you can park your car (a real privilege in Florence!). Breakfast is served in a do-it-yourself formula: everything you need is set out on a tray in your room.*

• *Moderate*

Bed & Breakfast Dei Mori – *Via Dante Alighieri 12, zona Piazza della Signoria – deimori@b&b.it –* 🖭 *– 12 rm €46.48/87.80* ⌧*. This B&B is situated in a 15C palazzo, not far from Dante Alighieri's house and a stone's throw from the Duomo. Tastefully and imaginatively decorated – the painted headboards for the beds are a charming touch. Smokers tolerated but confined to the balcony.*

Albergo Firenze – *Piazza Donati 4, zona Piazza Repubblica –* ☎ *055 21 42 03 – Fax 055 21 23 70 –* & *– 60 rm €62/83. This hotel is housed in one of the 13C residences of the powerful Donati family. Welcoming public area. Rooms are modern and functional. Considering its location – not far from the Piazza della Repubblica – the prices are very reasonable.*

Residenze Johlea I e II – *Via San Gallo 76/80, zona Piazza della Libertà –* ☎ *055 46 33 292 – Fax 055 46 34 552 – www.johanna.it –* ⌿ *– 12 rm €67.14/92.96* ⌧*. The latest addition to a rather charming* chain of B&Bs housed in two small buildings. Stylish interior, comfortable rooms. Very relaxed and cosy family atmosphere. Highly recommended.

Locanda di Firenze – *Via Faenza 12, (3rd floor, no lift), zona S. Lorenzo –* ☎ *055 28 43 40 – Fax 055 28 43 52 –* ⬚ *6 double rm €108.46* ⬚. This guesthouse is situated on the third floor of a historic palazzo, a stone's throw from the market in San Lorenzo. It is run by an ex-University professor who has opened his home to tourists and is a very hospitable host. Very comfortable with great attention to detail.

• **Expensive**

Hotel Cimabue – *Via B. Lupi 7, zona Piazza S. Marco –* ☎ *055 47 56 01 – Fax 055 46 30 906 – info@hotelcimabue.it – 16 rm from €88* ⬚. Even if you do not have the good fortune to stay in one of the rooms with a frescoed ceiling or one of the suites, you will not be disappointed – the rooms are spacious and tastefully furnished. Welcoming and relaxing atmosphere.

Hotel La Scaletta – *Via Guicciardini 13, (1st floor, lift), zona Palazzo Pitti –* ☎ *055 28 30 28 – Fax 055 28 95 62 – info@lascaletta.com –* ⬚ *– 13 rm from €93* ⬚. This hotel has a pleasant, homely feel – lovely antique furniture in the breakfast and reading rooms. Wonderful roof terrace which overlooks the whole of the historic centre. Rooms are bright and airy.

Residenza Apostoli – *Borgo Santi Apostoli 8, (1st floor), zona Ponte Vecchio –* ☎ *055 28 84 32 – Fax 055 26 87 90 – residenza.apostoli@infinito.it – 11 rm from €118.79* ⬚. Housed in the 13C Palazzo del Siniscalco, not far from the Ponte Vecchio. Welcoming rooms designed with great attention to detail, tastefully furnished and with the occasional elegant retro-style concession. Breakfast served in your room. Excellent level of service.

Relais Uffizi – *Chiasso de' Baroncelli-chiasso del Buco 16, zona Piazza della Signoria –* ☎ *055 26 76 239 – Fax 055 26 57 909 –* ⬚ *– 10 rm from €140* ⬚. An elegant, convivial hotel housed in a fine medieval Florentine palazzo. Splendid lounge and breakfast area which overlook Piazza della Signoria – a very stylish start to the day.

TAKING A BREAK

Cafés

Rivoire – *Via Vaccherreccia 4r, Piazza della Signoria. –* ☎ *055 21 44 12 /0 55 21 13 02 – Tue-Sun 8am-midnight, closed 2 weeks in Jan.* Founded in 1862, the Rivoire is a well-established feature of Florentine café life and always very busy. One of its greatest attractions is its splendid location in Piazza della Signoria, overlooked by the Palazzo Vecchio and Cellini's statue of Perseus. Not so attractive are the prices (the coffee is the most expensive in Florence!).

Gran Caffè Giubbe Rosse – *Piazza della Repubblica 13/14r –* ☎ *055 21 22 80 – giubbe.rosse@tin.it – 8am-10pm.* The waiters here wear their red gilets with great pride – this café has long been popular with writers and artists. It is celebrated for its connections with the early Italian Futurist movement and hanging on the walls are a number of "pictorial" homages to this café where many of the artists of the time would gather.

Gilli – *Piazza della Repubblica 39r, on the corner of Via Roma –* ☎ *055 21 38 96 /055 23 96 10 – Summer Wed-Mon 7.30-1am; rest of the year Mon, Wed-Thu 7.30am-9pm and Fri-Sun 7.30am-1pm.* In its various incarnations – first as a bread shop, then a pasticceria and finally a café – the Gilli establishments have been in existence for 250 years and have changed address several times before eventually settling, in 1910, in their current premises in this lovely square.

Il Rifrullo – *Via San Niccolo 55r –* ☎ *055 23 42 621 – Open 8am-1am.* Situated off the beaten tourist track, one of the attractions of this bar is the large covered open-air area. It is popular with Florence's late-night revellers who can be found chatting into the early hours while sipping one of a wide selection of house cocktails.

Vip Bar – *Viale Giuseppe Poggi 5r, Piazzale Michelangelo. –* ☎ *0335 54 17 544 (mobile) – Winter: 8am-8pm, summer: 8am-3pm. Closed when it rains.* Like Michelangelo's David, this bar has one of the finest views in Florence! Ice creams and cocktails served on the vast terrace garden which boasts a spectacular panorama over the city.

Gelaterie (ice cream bars)

Caffè Ricchi – *Piazza Santo Spirito 8/9r –* ☎ *055 21 58 64 – www.caffericchi.it – Mon-Sat 7.30am-11pm.* This is one of most celebrated gelaterie in Florence and its ice creams are all home-made. Situated away from the touristy centre overlooking a lovely pedetrianised piazza and Brunellischi's elegant Santo Spirito church. Very busy on market days.

Il gelato di Vivoli – *Via Isola delle Stinche 7r –* ☎ *055 29 23 34 – vivoli@mail.cosmos.it – Tue-Sat 7.30am-1am, Sun 9.30am-1am.* There is no shortage of gelatarie in Florence but ice cream connoisseurs attest to this historic establishment (it dates back to 1930) being one of the very best. Eat in or take away.

Speciality shops

Dolci e Dolcezze – *Piazza Beccaria 8r –* ☎ *055 23 45 458 – Tue-Sun 8.30am-9.30pm.* With its coloured-marble decorations, glass chandeliers and green colour scheme, this tiny shop has a retro, slightly kitsch feel about it. But its reputation as one of the best pasticcerie is unquestionable. The celebrated lemon tart (torta al limone) and chocolate tart (torta al cioccolato) are among the best.

Procacci – *Via Tornabuoni 64r –* ☎ *055 21 16 56 – Tue-Sat 10.30am-8pm, closed Aug.* Founded in 1885 and now under the ownership of the Marchese Antinori, this exclusive delicatessen is something of an institution in Florence, celebrated for its fresh white truffles (on sale from Nov to Mar) and its delicious sandwiches.

Wine specialists

Enoteca Bonatti – *Via Gioberti 66/68r* – ☎ 055 66 00 50 – *Mon 4-8pm, Tue-Sat 9am-1pm and 4-8pm*. The Bonatti family's reputation as premium wine specialists goes back to 1934. The collection comprises more than 1 000 wines from all over Italy and a particularly good selection of Chianti and Brunello di Montalcino.

Enoteca Gola e Cantina – *Piazza Pitti 16* – ☎ 055 21 27 04 – *Summer, Tue-Sun 10am-1pm and 3-7pm; rest of the year closed Sun and Mon*. Situated under one of the porticoes in the Accademia Italiana, opposite the Palazzo Pitti, this wine specialist – there are also books on wine-making – boasts some of the finest vintages in Tuscany. Tastings conducted around an ancient marble counter or on the terrace.

Cantinetta Antinori – *Piazza degli Antinori 3, Palazzo Antinori*. – ☎ 055 29 22 34 – *Mon-Fri 12.30-2.30pm, 7-10.30pm*. Tastings of the world-famous Antinori wines – including the prestigious "Solaria" vintage – are held in the Marchese's splendid 15C palazzo. Some of the grand crus are on display in the very elegant wine bar.

GOING OUT

Antico Caffè del Moro "Café des artistes" – *Via del Moro 4r* – ☎ 055 28 76 61 – *Mon-Thu 7pm-1am, Fri-Sat 7pm-2am. Closed for 3 weeks in Aug*. In the 1950s the artists who frequented this establishment would often pay for their drinks with paintings which now decorate the walls of this cheerful cocktail bar. These days it is a favourite haunt of the student community and therefore very lively. The cocktails are made with fresh fruit.

Jazz Club – *Via Nuova dei Caccini 3, Angolo Via Borgo Pinti*. – ☎ 055 24 79 700 / 33 95 63 07 95 (mobile) – *Tue-Sun 9pm-2am. Closed Jun-Aug*. This is the jazz club of all jazz clubs in Florence! It is incredibly popular and you can see why – there are live concerts every evening with a different group (usually Italian) performing. Membership €5.16.

Meccano' – *Viale degli Olmi 1* – ☎ 055 33 13 71 – *Tue-Sat 11pm-4am*. The biggest and the most famous discotheque in Florence. There are several dance floors and a large garden area which is ideal for those long summer evenings. Techno, underground and progressive pop music.

Tenax – *Via Pratese 46* – ☎ 055 30 81 60 – *Open Tue-Sun, Closed Jun-Sep*. More than a discotheque – the Tenax also has live concerts during the week with the latest Italian and European rock bands coming to perform here. House music on Thursdays.

CONCERTS AND THEATRE

Florence is an art and music lover's city even at night, when plays and concerts animate its theatres. To find out what's on look in *La Nazione* and the pages on Florence in national daily newspapers or contact the theatres directly:

Box Office – *Via Alamanni 39r* – ☎ 055 21 08 04 – *Mon 3.30-7.30pm, Tue-Sat 10am-7.30pm*. Tickets on sale for a number of different theatres including Teatro della Pergola (from the Tue before the concert in question), Teatro Verdi, Teatro Comunale, Teatro Goldoni and Musicus Concentus. To find out what's on, buy a copy of Firenze Spettacolo.

Teatro Comunale – *Corso Italia 12* – ☎ 055 27 791 – *Tue-Fri 10am-4.30pm, Sat 10am-1pm*. Classical music is very much a feature of the cultural life of the city. Throughout the year concerts, operas and recitals are held at various different venues including Teatro Verdi, Teatro Comunale and Teatro della Pergola.

Teatro Verdi – *Via Ghibellina 99* – ☎ 055 21 23 20 – *info@teatroverdifirenze.it – Mon-Fri 10am-2pm, 7am-7pm, Sat 10am-1pm. Last admission 1hr before the performance begins. See Teatro Comunale*.

ETI – Teatro della Pergola – *Via della Pergola 18* – ☎ 055 22 641 – *Last admission to the theatre 1hr before the concert begins. See Teatro Comunale*.

The axial chapel contains a masterpiece by Ghiberti, the sarcophagus of St Zanobi, the first Bishop of Florence. One of the low reliefs shows the saint resurrecting a child. The frescoes in the north aisle include: in the first bay near the choir, one showing Dante explaining the *Divine Comedy* to the city of Florence (1465); further along to the right, two equestrian portraits of leaders of mercenary armies (*condottieri*) by Paolo Uccello (1436) and Andrea del Castagno (1456).

A stairway on the other side of the nave, between the first and second pillars, leads to the **Crypt of Santa Reparata**, the only remaining part of a Romanesque basilica which was demolished when the present cathedral was built. The basilica itself was formerly an early Christian church (5C-6C). Excavations have revealed traces of mosaic paving belonging to the original building and Brunelleschi's tomb (behind the railing-enclosed chamber, at the bottom of the stairs, on the left).

Campanile★★★

Open 8.30am-7.30pm (last admission 6.50pm). Closed 1 Jan, Easter, 8 Sep, 25 Dec. €5.16. Bookshop. ☎ *055 23 02 885; www.operaduomo.firenze.it*

The belltower is tall (82m/269ft) and slender and is the perfect complement to Brunelleschi's dome, the straight lines of the former balancing the curves of the latter. Giotto drew the plans for it and began building in 1334, but died in 1337.

The Gothic campanile was completed at the end of the 14C; its geometric decoration with its emphasis on horizontal lines is unusual. The admirable low reliefs at the base of the campanile have been replaced by copies. Those on the lower band were executed by Andrea Pisano and Luca della Robbia and those on the upper band by pupils of Andrea Pisano, but the overall design was by Giotto. The original low reliefs are in the Cathedral Museum.

From the top of the campanile (414 steps) there is a fine **panorama**** of the cathedral and town.

Battistero***

  ♿ *Open Mon-Sat noon-6.30pm, Sun and public holidays 8.30am-1.30pm. Closed 1 Jan, Easter, 24 Jun, 25 Dec. €2.58 ☎ 055 23 02 885; www.operaduomo.firenze.it*

The baptistery is faced in white and green marble in a sober and well-balanced Romanesque style. The **bronze doors***** are world-famous.

The south door *(entrance)* by Andrea Pisano (1330) is Gothic and portrays scenes from the life of St John the Baptist *(above)*, as well as the Theological Virtues (Faith, Hope, Charity) and the Cardinal Virtues *(below)*. The door frames, which show great skill, are by Vittorio Ghiberti, son of the designer of the other doors.

The north door (1403-24) was the first done by Lorenzo Ghiberti. He was the winner of a competition in which Brunelleschi, Donatello and Jacopo della Quercia also took part. Scenes from the Life of Christ are evoked with extraordinary nobility and harmony of composition.

The east door (1425-52), facing the cathedral, is the one that Michelangelo declared worthy to be the **Gate of Paradise**, the name by which it is known. In it Ghiberti recalled the Old Testament; prophets and sibyls adorn the niches. The artist portrayed himself, bald and cunning-looking, in one of the medallions.

Interior – With its 25m/82ft diameter, its green and white marble and its paving decorated with oriental motifs, the interior is grand and majestic. The dome is covered with magnificent **mosaics***** of the 13C. The Last Judgement is depicted on either side of a large picture of Christ the King; on the five concentric bands that cover the other five panels of the dome, starting from the top towards the base, are the Heavenly Hierarchies, Genesis, the Life of Joseph, scenes from the Life of the Virgin and of Christ, and the Life of St John the Baptist.

On the right of the apse is the tomb of the antipope John XXIII, friend of Cosimo the Elder, a remarkable work executed in 1427 by Donatello assisted by Michelozzo.

Under the 14C Gothic **Loggia del Bigallo** to the south of the baptistery, lost or abandoned children were exhibited.

Museo dell'Opera del Duomo**

  ♿ *Open Mon-Sat 9am-7.30pm (last admission 6.50pm), Sun and public hols 9am-2pm (last admission 1.20pm). Closed 1 Jan, Easter, 8 Sep, 25 Dec. €5.16 ☎ 055 23 02 885; www.operaduomo.firenze.it*

The museum contains items from the cathedral, campanile and baptistery; note models of Brunelleschi's dome on the ground floor. On the mezzanine is the famous **Pietà**** which Michelangelo left unfinished. In the large room on the first floor are two famous statues by **Donatello** – an impressive repentant **Magdalene*** carved in wood, and the prophets Jeremiah and Habakkuk, the latter being nicknamed *Zuccone* (vegetable marrow) because of the shape of his head.

In the same room are the famous **Cantorie****, choristers' tribunes from the cathedral, by Luca della Robbia and Donatello. The museum also houses the famous silver **altarpiece**** depicting the life of St John the Baptist, a 14C-15C masterpiece, and the admirable **low reliefs**** from the campanile: those by Andrea Pisano and Luca della Robbia depict scenes from the Book of Genesis and various human activities.

PIAZZA DELLA SIGNORIA**

Piazza***

Allow 1 day. This was, and still is, the political stage of Florence, with a wonderful backcloth formed by the Palazzo Vecchio, the Loggia della Signoria and, in the wings, the Uffizi Museum. The many statues make it virtually an open-air museum of sculpture: near the centre of the square, the equestrian statue of Cosimo I, after Giovanni Bologna, and at the corner of the Palazzo Vecchio, the Fountain of Neptune (1576) by Ammannati. In front of the Palazzo Vecchio are copies of the proud *Marzocco* or *Lion of Florence* by Donatello and Michelangelo's *David*.

Loggia della Signoria**

The Loggia, built at the end of the 14C, was the assembly hall and later the guardroom of the Lanzi (foot soldiers) of Cosimo I. It contains ancient (Classical) and Renaissance statues: the *Rape of a Sabine* (1583), *Hercules and the centaur Nessus* by Giovanni Bologna and the wonderful **Perseus***** holding up the severed head of Medusa, a masterpiece executed by Benvenuto Cellini from 1545 to 1553.

Palazzo Vecchio★★★

(&) *Open 9am-7pm; Thu and midweek holidays 9am-2pm. Closed 1 Jan, Easter, 1 May, 15 Aug, 25 Dec. Guided tours available. €5.68.* ☎ *055 27 68 465; www.comune.firenze.it*
The Old Palace's powerful mass is dominated by a lofty belltower, 94m/308ft high. Built from 1299 to 1314 probably to plans by Arnolfo di Cambio, it is in a severe Gothic style without any openings at ground level, a series of twinned windows above and battlements, parapet walk and crenellations on top with the tower.
The refinement and splendour of the Renaissance interior is a complete contrast. The **courtyard★** was restored by Michelozzo in the 15C and decorated in the following century by Vasari. The 16C fountain is surmounted by a delightful winged goblin, a copy of a work by Verrocchio (the original is housed in the palace).
Initially the seat of government (Palazzo della Signoria), the palace was then taken over in the 16C by Cosimo I as his private residence, as it was better suited to accommodating his large court. Most of the redecoration work done by Giorgio Vasari dates from this period. When Cosimo I abandoned the palace in favour of the Pitti Palace it was renamed Palazzo Vecchio. The apartments were lavishly decorated with sculptures by Benedetto and Giuliano da Maiano (15C) and with paintings by Vasari and Bronzino (16C) to the glory of Florence and the Medici.
On the first floor the great Sala dei Cinquecento, painted with frescoes by several artists including Vasari, contains a group carved by Michelangelo, *The Genius of Victory*. The walls of the magnificent **studiolo★★** or study of Francesco de' Medici, which was designed by Vasari, were painted by Bronzino, who was responsible for the medallion portraits of *Cosimo I* and *Eleanora of Toledo*. Leo X's apartment was decorated by Vasari and his assistants with scenes illustrating episodes from the history of the Medici family.
On the second floor, Cosimo I's apartments are open to the public. They are known as the Apartment of the Elements because of the allegories decorating the first chamber. The decoration was designed by Vasari around the theme of ancient mythology. Beyond these chambers are Eleonora of Toledo's apartments, again designed by Vasari with the exception of the chapel which is decorated with frescoes by Bronzino. Finally, in the apartments of the *Priori*, the best-known chamber is the **Sala degli Gigli★** (Chamber of Lilies) which has a magnificent coffered ceiling by Guiliano da Maiano and the **Sala del Guardaroba★** (dressing-room) lined with 16C maps.

GALLERIA DEGLI UFFIZI★★★

(&) *Open 8.30am-6.50pm, Sat during summer 8.30am-10pm. Closed Mon, 1 Jan, 1 May, 25 Dec. €6.20 (€8 during exhibitions). Book in advance to avoid the long queues.* ☎ *055 29 48 83 (booking office),* ☎ *055 23 88 651 (information); www.uffizi.firenze.it*
This is one of the finest art museums in the world. These collections were assembled by several generations of Medici and the visitor can follow the evolution of Italian art from its beginnings to the 17C.
The early nucleus was gathered together by Francesco I (1541-87) to which were added the collections of the Grand Dukes Ferdinand I and II, and Cosimo III. In 1737 the last member of the Medici dynasty, Anna Maria Luisa, Electress Palatine, bequeathed the Medici collection to her native city of Florence.
The Uffizi Museum was then housed in the Renaissance palace, designed by Vasari in 1560, which contained the offices *(uffizi)* of the Medici administration.

Galleries

The first gallery *(east)* is essentially dedicated to Florentine and Tuscan artists: there are works by Cimabue, Giotto, Duccio, Simone Martini (the **Annunciation**, a masterpiece of Gothic art), Paolo Uccello *(Battle of San Romano)* and Filippo Lippi. The Botticelli Room★★★ houses the artist's major works: the allegories of the *Birth of Venus* and *Spring* and the *Madonna with Pomegranate*. Other exhibits

Linking the Uffizi with the Palazzo Pitti: the Ponte Vecchio with its little shops

B. Perousse/MICHELIN

in the gallery include the **Adoration of the Magi** and the *Annunciation* by Leonardo da Vinci and a series of Italian and foreign paintings from the 15C and 16C (Perugino, Cranach, Dürer, Bellini, Giorgione, Correggio).

The first 11 rooms of the second gallery *(west)* contain works from the Italian Cinquecento (16C): *Tondo Doni* by Michelangelo, *Madonna and the Goldfinch* and *Leo X* by Raphael, *Madonna and the Harpies* by Andrea del Sarto, *Urbino Venus* by Titian and *Leda and the Swan* by Tintoretto. The other rooms are dedicated to both Italian and foreign paintings from the 17C and 18C: included in the collection are *Isabella Brandt* by Rubens, **Caravaggio**'s *Adolescent Bacchus* and works by **Claude Lorrain** and **Rembrandt**.

PONTE VECCHIO★★

As its name suggests, this is the oldest bridge in Florence. It has been rebuilt several times and spans the narrowest point of the Arno. Its original design includes a line of jewellers' shops and the **Corridoio Vasariano**, a passageway which was built by Vasari to link the Palazzo Vecchio to the Pitti Palace and which passes overhead.

PALAZZO PITTI★★

This 15C Renaissance building, of rugged but imposing appearance, with pronounced rustication and many windows, was built to the plans of Brunelleschi for the Pitti family, the rivals of the Medici. It was Cosimo I's wife, Eleanora di Toledo, who enlarged the palace by the addition of two wings. The court moved to the palace in 1560.

Galleria Palatina★★★ – & *Open daily 8.30am-6.50pm. Closed 1 Jan, 1 May, 25 Dec. €6.50. ☎ 055 29 48 83.* This gallery houses a marvellous collection of paintings: **groups**★★★ of works by Raphael (*Portrait of a Lady* or *La Velata*, *Madonna del Granduca* and *Madonna della Seggiola*) and Titian (portraits of *La Bella*, *The Aretino*, *The Concert* and the *Grey-eyed Nobleman*).

On the first floor are the **Appartamenti reali**★ (State Apartments). & *Open May-Oct, daily, 8.30am-6.50pm; Nov-Apr by appointment only. Closed Mon. €6.50. ☎ 055 23 88 611.*

The building also houses the **Galleria d'Arte Moderna**★ which mainly displays Tuscan works from the 19C and 20C. The section devoted to the **Macchiaioli** movement is represented by an exceptional **series**★★ by Fattori, Lega, Signorini, Cecioni. & *Open daily, 8.15am-1.50pm. Closed 1st, 3rd and 5th Mon of the month, 2nd and 4th Sun of the month, 1 Jan, 1 May, 25 Dec. Guided tours can be booked through Firenze Musei, ☎ 055 29 01 12. €4.13. No charge during National Heritage Week. ☎ 055 23 88 601; www.sbas.firenze.it*

In the other wing is the Silver Museum **(Museo degli Argenti**★★) presenting items largely from the Medici collections. *Open 8.15am-1.50pm. Closed 1st, 3rd and 5th Mon of the month, 2nd and 4th Sun of the month, 1 Jan, 1 May 25 Dec. €2. ☎ 055 23 88 709; www.sbas.firenze.it/argenti/*

GIARDINO DI BOBOLI★

Open daily, Jun-Aug 8am-7.30pm, Nov-Feb 8.15am-4.30pm, Mar 8am-5.30pm, rest of year 8am-6.30pm. Closed 1st and last Mon of the month, 1 Jan, 1 May, 25 Dec. €2.07. ☎ 055 23 48 63; www.ambientefi.arti.beniculturali.it/sbaafi/boboli.htm

This Italian-style terraced garden, behind the Pitti Palace, was designed in 1549 by Tribolo and is ornamented with antique and Renaissance statues. At one end of an avenue to the left of the palace is the **grotta grande**, a grotto created in the main by Buontalenti (1587-97). Cross the amphitheatre to reach the highest point of the garden from which, on the right, the **Viottolone**★, an avenue of pines and cypresses, runs down to **Piazzale dell'Isolotto**★, a circular pool with a small island, planted with citrus trees and adorned with a fountain by Giovanni Bologna. A pavilion houses a porcelain museum, the **Museo delle Porcelane**★. *Open daily, Jun to Aug 8.30am-7.30pm, Nov to Feb 8.15am-4.30pm, Mar 8.30am-5.30pm, rest of year 8.30am-6.30pm. Closed 1st and last Mon of month, 1 Jan, 1 May, 25 Dec. €2. ☎ 055 23 88 710.*

The **Forte del Belvedere**, at the top of the hill, affords a splendid **panorama**★ of Florence and the celebrated Florentine countryside. The elegant villa which dominates the bastion was designed by Buontalenti.

PALAZZO E MUSEO NAZIONALE DEL BARGELLO★★★

& *Open daily 8.15am-1.50pm (last admission 1.20pm). Guided tours (1hr) available in various languages. Closed Sun, 1st, 3rd and 5th of month, 2nd and 4th Mon of the month, 1 Jan, 1 May 25 Dec. €4, no charge during National Heritage Week. ☎ 055 23 88 606; www.sbas.firenze.it*

This austere palace was formerly the residence of the governing magistrate *(podestà)* and then became police headquarters *(bargello)*. It is a fine example of 13C-14C medieval architecture planned round a majestic **courtyard**★★ with a portico and loggia. The Volognona tower (57m/188ft) soars above the building. The palace is now a museum of sculpture and decorative arts with particularly good sections on Italian and Florentine Renaissance sculpture.

The rooms on the ground floor are devoted to the works of 16C Florentine sculptors: *Brutus* and the *Pitti Tondo* (a marble medallion depicting the Virgin and Child with St John) by Michelangelo; **low reliefs** from the pedestal of the Perseus bronze by Benvenuto Cellini.

There is an exceptional collection *(first floor)* of **sculpture★★★** by **Donatello** which includes his *Marzocco* (the Florentine heraldic lion), the bronze *David*, as well as the low relief of *St George* from Orsanmichele.

The rooms on the second floor display terracottas by Giovanni and Andrea della Robbia and works by **Verrocchio**, including the famous bronze statue of *David*.

CHIESA DI SAN LORENZO★★★

This was the Medici family parish church near the Medici Palace, and it was here that most of the family was buried. The **church★★** was begun by Brunelleschi c 1420. The interior is a perfect example of the sobriety of style introduced by **Brunelleschi** and typical of his thoughtful, measured, rigorous architectural style and its human dimension.

His great achievement is the **Old Sacristy★★** *(at the far end of the north transept)*. Donatello was responsible for part of the decoration of this and also the two **pulpits★★** in the nave with bronze panels, which are works of admirable virtuosity and full of a great sense of drama.

Biblioteca MeDecea Laurenziana★★

(&) *Open daily 8.30am-1.30pm. Closed 2 Jun and public holidays. No charge.* ☏ *055 21 07 60; www.bml.firenze.sbn.it*

Cosimo the Elder's library was added to by Lorenzo the Magnificent. Access is from the north aisle of the church or through the charming 15C **cloisters★** *(entrance to the left of the church)*. The vestibule was designed as an exterior and is occupied by a magnificent **staircase★★**, supremely elegant as the curved steps of the central flight lead up to the library proper. The staircase was built by Ammannati to Michelangelo's designs. The **library**, also by Michelangelo, displays in rotation some of its 10 000 manuscripts.

Cappelle Medicee★★

Entrance on Piazza Madonna degli Aldobrandini. Open daily 8am-5pm, Sun and public holidays 8am-1.50pm. Closed 1st, 3rd and 5th Mon of the month, 2nd and 4th Sun of the month, 1 Jan, 1 May, 25 Dec. €6. ☏ *055 23 88 602.*

The Medici Chapels include the Princes' Chapel and New Sacristy.

The **Princes' Chapel** (17C-18C), grandiose but gloomy, is faced with semi-precious stones and marbles and is the funerary chapel for Cosimo I and his descendants.

The **New Sacristy** was Michelangelo's first architectural work and despite its name was always intended as a funerary chapel. Begun in 1520, it was left unfinished when the artist left Florence in 1534. Michelangelo achieved a great sense of rhythm and solemnity by using contrasting materials, dark grey sandstone *(pietra serena)* and the white of the walls and marbles.

The famous **Medici tombs★★★** were also the work of Michelangelo. Giuliano, Duke of Nemours (d 1516), is portrayed as Action, surrounded by allegorical figures of Day and Night; and Lorenzo II, Duke of Urbino (d 1519), as a Thinker with Dawn and Dusk at his feet. Of the plans for Lorenzo the Magnificent's tomb only the admirable group of the Madonna and Child flanked by saints was completed. In the plain tomb underneath lie Lorenzo the Magnificent and his brother Giuliano.

PALAZZO MEDICI-RICCARDI★★

(&) *Open daily, 9am-7pm. Closed Wed. €4.* ☏ *055 27 60 340; www.palazzo-medici.it/medici-palace it/medici-building it*

This noble but austere building is typical of the Florentine Renaissance with its mathematical plan and rustication, massive at ground level and lighter on the upper level. The palace which has a square arcaded courtyard was begun in 1444 by Michelozzo on the orders of his friend Cosimo the Elder. From 1459 to 1540 it was a Medici residence and Lorenzo the Magnificent held court here, attended by poets, philosophers and artists alike. In the second half of the 17C the palace passed to the Riccardi who made extensive alterations to the building.

Cappella★★★

First floor. Entrance by the first stairway on the right in the courtyard. This tiny chapel was decorated with admirable **frescoes** (1459) by **Benozzo Gozzoli**. *The Procession of the Magi* is a vivid picture of Florentine life with portraits of the Medici and of famous dignitaries from the east who had assembled for the Council of Florence in 1439.

Sala di Luca Giordano★★

First floor: entrance by the second stairway on the right in the courtyard. The entire roof of this gallery built by the Riccardi at the end of the 17C and splendidly decorated with gold stucco, carved panels and great painted mirrors, is covered by a brightly-coloured Baroque fresco of the Apotheosis of the second Medici dynasty, masterfully painted by Luca Giordano in 1683.

SAN MARCO★★

(&) *Open Mon-Fri 8.15am-1.50pm, Sat 8.30am-6.50pm, Sun and public holidays 8.30am-7pm (last admission 30min before closing). Closed 1st, 3rd and 5th Sun of the month, 2nd and 4th Mon of the month, 1 Jan, 1 May, 25 Dec. €4. ☎ 055 23 88 608; www.sbas.firenze.it/sanmarco/*

The museum in a former Dominican monastery, rebuilt c 1436 in a very plain style by Michelozzo, is virtually the **Fra Angelico Museum★★★**. Fra Angelico took orders in Fiesole before coming to St Mark's, where he decorated the walls of the monks' cells with edifying scenes. Humility, gentleness and mysticism were the qualities expressed by this artistic monk in a technique influenced by the Gothic tradition. His refined use of colour, delicate draughtsmanship and gentle handling of the subject matter imbued these frescoes with a pacifying power, particularly appropriate for this oasis of calm and place of meditation.

The former guest hall, opening off the cloisters on the right, contain many of the artist's works on wood, especially the triptych depicting the **Descent from the Cross**, the famous **Last Judgement** and other religious scenes. The chapter house has a severe *Crucifixion* while the refectory contains an admirable **Last Supper★** by Ghirlandaio.

The staircase leading to the first floor is dominated by Fra Angelico's well-balanced and sober masterpiece, the **Annunciation**. The monks' cells open off three corridors, with lovely timber ceilings. Along the corridor to the left of the stairs are the *Apparition of Christ to the Penitent Magdalene (1st cell on the left)*, the *Transfiguration (6th cell on the left)* and the *Coronation of the Virgin (9th cell on the left)*.

At the far end of the next corridor are the cells of Savonarola, who was prior of St Mark's. Off the corridor on the right is the **library★**, one of Michelozzo's finest achievements.

GALLERIA DELL'ACCADEMIA★★

& *Open daily 8.30am-6.50pm (last admission 6.20pm). Closed 1 Jan, 1 May, 25 Dec. €6.20. ☎ 055 23 88 612; www.sbas.firenze.it/accademia/*

The museum gives the visitor some idea of the extraordinary personality of **Michelangelo** and the conflict between the nature of his raw materials and his idealistic vision. The **main gallery★★★** contains the powerful figures of **Four Slaves** (1513-20) and **St Matthew** (all unfinished) who would seem to be trying to struggle free from the marble. At the far end of the gallery, in a specially designed apse (1873), is the monumental figure of **David** (1501-04), the symbol of youthful but well-mastered force and a perfect example of the sculptor's humanism. The **picture gallery★** has works by 13C-15C Tuscan masters, including a painted chest by Adimari and two Botticellis.

CHIESA DI SANTA MARIA NOVELLA★★

Open Mon-Thu, Sat 9.30am-5pm; Fri and Sun and public hols 1-5pm. €2.50.

The Church of Santa Maria Novella and the adjoining monastery were founded in the 13C by the Dominicans. The church overlooks an elongated square which was originally the setting for chariot races.

The **church★★**, begun in 1279, was completed only in 1360, except for the **façade**, with harmonious lines and geometric patterns in white and green marble, which was designed by Alberti (upper section) in the 15C.

It is a large church (100m/328ft) designed for preaching. On the wall of the third bay in the north aisle is a famous **fresco★★** of the Trinity with the Virgin, St John and the donors in which Masaccio, adopting the new Renaissance theories, shows great mastery of perspective. At the far end of the north transept, the Strozzi di Mantora Chapel (raised) is decorated with **frescoes★** (1357) by the Florentine Nardo di Cione depicting the Last Judgement on a grand scale. The **polyptych★** on the altar is by Nardo's brother, Orcagna di Cione. The sacristy contains a fine **Crucifix★** *(above the entrance)* by Giotto and a delicate glazed terracotta **niche★** by Giovanni della Robbia.

In the Gondi Chapel *(first on the left of the high altar)* is displayed the famous **Crucifix★★** by Brunelleschi, which so struck Donatello that he is said, on first seeing it, to have dropped the basket of eggs he was carrying.

The chancel is ornamented with admirable **frescoes★★★** by **Domenico Ghirlandaio** who, on the theme of the Lives of the Virgin and of St John the Baptist, painted a dazzling picture of Florentine life in the Renaissance era.

The church is flanked by two cloisters. The finest are the **Chiostro Verde★** (Green Cloisters), so-called after the dominant colour of the frescoes painted by Paolo Uccello and his school (scenes from the Old Testament). Opening off these to the north is the **Cappellone degli Spagnoli** (Spaniards' Chapel) with late-14C **frescoes★★** by **Andrea di Bonaiuto** (also known as Andrea da Firenze). With an intricate symbolism the frescoes depict the Church Triumphant and the glorification of the deeds of the Dominicans. To the east is the refectory which houses the church's treasure.

Museum and cloisters: ♿ *Open 9am-2pm. Closed Fri and public holidays. Guided tours available. €2.58, €5.16 "carnet musei fiorentini" (50% reduction on the price of a stand-ard ticket for all the museums, valid for one year).* ☎ *055 28 21 87; www.comune.firenze.it*

CHIESA DI SANTA CROCE★★

Tour: Open Apr-Oct 9am-5.30pm, Sun and public holidays 3-5.30pm; rest of the year 9am-12.30pm and 3-5.30pm, Sun and public hols 3-5.30pm. ☎ *055 24 46 19.*

The church and cloisters of Santa Croce give onto one of the town's oldest squares. This is the church of the Franciscans. It was started in 1294 and completed in the second half of the 14C. The façade and the campanile date from the 19C.

The **interior** is vast (140m x 40m/460ft x 130ft) as the church was designed for preaching and consists of a single spacious nave and slender apse with fine 15C stained-glass windows. The church is paved with 276 tombstones and along the walls are ornate tombs.

South aisle: By the first pillar, a *Virgin and Child* by Antonio Rossellino (15C); opposite, the tomb of Michelangelo (d 1564) by Vasari; opposite the second pillar, the funerary monument (19C) to Dante (d 1321, buried at Ravenna); by the third pillar, a fine **pulpit★** (1476) by Benedetto da Maiano and facing it the monument to V Alfieri (d 1803) by Canova; opposite the fourth pillar, the 18C monument to Machiavelli (d 1527); facing the fifth pillar, an elegant low relief of the *Annunciation*★★ carved in stone and embellished with gold by Donatello; opposite the sixth pillar, the **tomb of Leonardo Bruni★★** (humanist and chancellor of the Republic, d 1444) by Bernardo Rossellino, and next to it the tomb of the composer Rossini (d 1868).

South transept: At the far end, the Baroncelli Chapel with **frescoes★** (1338) depict-ing the Life of the Virgin by Taddeo Gaddi and at the altar, the **polyptych★** of the Coronation of the Virgin from Giotto's studio.

Sacristy★ *(access by the corridor on the right of the chancel):* This dates from the 14C and is adorned with **frescoes★** including a Crucifixion by Taddeo Gaddi and, in the fine Rinuccini Chapel, with scenes from the Life of the Virgin and of Mary Magdalene by Giovanni da Milano (14C). At the far end of the corridor is the har-monious Medici Chapel (1434) built by Michelozzo, with a fine **altarpiece★** in glazed terracotta by Andrea della Robbia.

Chancel: The first chapel to the right of the altar contains evocative **frescoes★★** (c 1320) by Giotto depicting the life of St Francis; in the third chapel is the tomb of Julie Clary, the wife of Joseph Bonaparte. The chancel proper is covered with **frescoes★** (1380) by Agnolo Gaddi relating the legend of the Holy Cross.

North transept: At the far end is a famous *Crucifixion*★★ by Donatello, which Brunelleschi tried to surpass at Santa Maria Novella.

North aisle *(coming back):* Beyond the second pillar, a fine **monument to Carlo Marsuppini★** by Desiderio da Settignano (15C); facing the fourth pillar the tomb-stone of L. Ghiberti (d 1455); the last tomb (18C) is that of Galileo (d 1642).

Cappella dei Pazzi★★

At the far end of the first cloisters; entrance to the right of the church. (♿) Open Mar-Sep 10am-7pm; Oct-Feb 10am-6pm. Closed Wed, 1 Jan, 25 Dec. €4.13. ☎ *055 24 66 01.*

This chapel by Brunelleschi is entered through a domed portico, and is a master-piece of the Florentine Renaissance remarkable for its original conception, its pure, rigid lines, its skilful proportions and the harmony of its decoration (glazed terra-cotta from the Della Robbia workshop).

Chiostro Grande

Entrance at the far end of the first cloisters, on the right. These very elegant cloisters were designed by Brunelleschi shortly before his death (1446) and were completed only in 1453.

Museo dell'Opera di Santa Croce

(♿) Open daily 10am-6pm. Closed Wed. €4. ☎ *055 24 66 01.*

The museum is installed in the buildings around the first cloister and in particular in the former refectory. The museum contains a famous Crucifixion★ *by Cimabue which was seriously damaged by the 1966 floods that particularly affected Santa Croce.*

PASSEGGIATA AI COLLI★★

2h on foot or 1hr by car

For a drive to the hills take the road to the east along the south bank of the Arno to the medieval tower in Piazza Giuseppe Poggi. Poggi laid this fine road to the hills from 1865 to 1870. Take the winding pedestrian street to Piazzale Michelangiolo for a splendid **view★★★** of the whole city.

Not far from here, in a splendid **setting★★** overlooking the town, the church of **San Miniato al Monte★★**, built from the 11C to 13C, is one of the most remarkable examples of Florentine Romanesque architecture. Its very elegant façade is decorated with geometric designs in green and white marble, not unlike those of the baptistery. The harmonious interior also ornamented with multicoloured marble contains a 13C pavement. The **Chapel of Cardinal James of Portugal★** opening out of the north aisle is a fine Renaissance structure. In the centre of the nave is a Chapel of the Crucifix by Michelozzo. The pulpit and chancel screen *(transenna)* form a remarkable **ensemble★★** beautifully inlaid with marble (early 13C). In the apse is a mosaic depicting Christ giving His Blessing. The **frescoes★** (1387) in the **sacristy** are by Spinello Aretino. The 11C **crypt** has delicate columns with Classical capitals.

OTHER MUSEUMS AND MONUMENTS

Chiesa di Santa Maria del Carmine★★★
Cappella Brancacci: fresco cycle (1427) by **Masaccio** depicting Original Sin and the Life of St Peter. It was finished by Filippino Lippi. *Open 10am-5pm, Sun and hols 1-5pm. Closed Tue, 1 and 7 Jan, Easter, 1 May, 16 Jul, 15 Aug, 25 dec. Guided tours available. €3.10, €5.16 "carnet musei fiorentini" (50% reduction on the price of a standard ticket for all the museums, valid for one year). ☎ 055 23 82 195; www.comune.firenze.it*

La Badia
10C church of a former abbey *(badia)* with an elegant **campanile★**. The interior has a sumptuous coffered **ceiling★★** and houses several works of art including Filippino Lippi's **Virgin appearing to St Bernard★**, a delicate **relief★★** sculpture in marble by Mino da Fiesole and the **tombs★** carved by the same artist.

Museo Archeologico★★
Open Wed, Fri, Sat and Sun 8.30am-2pm, Mon 2-7pm, Tue and Thu 8.30am-7pm (last admission 30min before closing). Closed Mon, 1 Jan, 1 May, 25 Dec. €4.13. ☎ 055 23 575; www.comune.firenze.it/soggetti/sat
The museum has an important collection of Egyptian, Greek (**François vase★★**, found in an Etruscan tomb but of ancient origin), Etruscan (**Arezzo Chimera★★**, a 5C BC masterpiece) and Roman art.

Opificio delle Pietre Dure★
♿ *Open daily, 8.15am-2pm (Tue 8.15am-7pm). Closed Sun and public holidays, 24 Jun. €2. ☎ 055 26 51 357; www.dada.it/propart/opd.htm*
Lorenzo the Magnificent was responsible for reviving the ancient tradition of decorating with semi-precious stones in the form of mosaics *(pietre dure)*. This workshop now specialises in restoration work and there is a small **museum**.

Orsanmichele★
Originally a grain storehouse, Orsanmichele was rebuilt in the 14C. There are works by Donatello, Ghiberti and Verrocchio. Inside, there is a splendid Gothic **tabernacle★★** by Orcagna.

Palazzo Rucellai★★
The palace was designed by Leon Battista Alberti and built in the 15C. The façade is the first cohesive example of the three ancient orders placed one on top of the other.

Palazzo Strozzi★★
The building dates from the end of the 15C and is one of the finest palaces in Florence with its rusticated stonework, cornice and arcaded courtyard.

Piazza della SS. Annunziata★
This fine piazza is enhanced by Giambologna's equestrian statue of Ferdinando I de' Medici and two Baroque fountains.
Chiesa della Santissima Annunziata – The church dates from the 15C. In the chancel are some fine **frescoes★** by Rosso Fiorentino and Pontormo which were completed by Franciabigio. The interior is in the Baroque style; the north arm of the transept gives access to the Renaissance Cloisters of the Dead (Chiostro dei Morti)**.** The vault by the door is adorned with the **Madonna with the Sack★** by Andrea del Sarto (16C).
Ospedale degli Innocenti★ – *Open daily 8.30am-2pm. Closed Wed, 1 Jan, Easter, 1 May, 15 Aug, 25 Dec. €2.60. ☎ 055 20 37 323; www.minori.it/innocenti/index.htm*
Brunelleschi's **portico★★** is decorated by terracotta **medallions★★** by Andrea della Robbia. The Foundlings' Hospital houses a **gallery** displaying Florentine works.
►►Casa Buonarroti★, Cenacolo di S. Apollonia (*Last Supper★* by Andrea del Castagno), Cenacolo di S. Salvi★ (fresco★★ by Andrea del Sarto of the Last Supper), Ognissanti (*Last Supper★* in the church refectory), S. Spirito★ (works of art★), S. Trinità (Cappella dell'Annunciazione★ decorated with frescoes by Lorenzo Monaco and the frescoes in the Cappella Sassetti★★ by Ghirlandaio), Loggia del Mercato Nuovo★, Museo della Casa Fiorentina Antica★ (housed in the Palazzo Davanzati★), Museo Marino Marini, Museo di Storia della Scienza★.

Excursions

See the plan of the conurbation on Michelin map 430.

Ville Medicee★

In the 15C and 16C, the Medici built several elegant villas throughout the Florentine countryside.

Villa La Petraia★ – *3km/2mi north. Open daily, Jun-Aug 8.30am-7.30pm, Sep and Oct 8.30am-6.30pm, rest of year 8.15am-4.30pm (ticket office always closes 1hr early). Closed 2nd and 3rd Mon of month, 1 Jan, 1 May, 25 Dec. €2. Compulsory booking for groups. ☎ 055 45 26 91; www.ambientefi.arti.beniculturali.it*

In 1576 Cardinal Ferdinand de' Medici commissioned the architect Buontalenti to convert this former castle into a villa. In the 16C **garden**, there is a remarkable fountain by Niccolo Tribolo with a bronze statue of Venus by Giovanni Bologna.

Villa di Castello★ – *5km/3mi north of Castello. & Open (park only) Jun-Aug, 8.15am-7.30pm; Mar-May and Sep-Oct 8.15am-6.30pm; rest of the year 8.15am-4.30pm. Closed 2nd and 3rd Mon of the month, 1 Jan, 1 May, 25 Dec. €2.07. ☎ 055 45 47 91.*

This villa was embellished by Lorenzo the Magnificent and restored in the 18C. It has a very fine garden adorned with statues and fountains.

Villa di Poggio a Caiano★★ – *17km/11mi north by the Pistoia road, S 66. & Open 8.15am-1hr before dusk. Closed 2nd and 3rd Mon of the month, 1 Jan, 1 May, 25 Dec. €2. ☎ 055 87 70 12.*

Sangallo designed this villa for Lorenzo the Magnificent. The loggia is decorated by the Della Robbia. The magnificent drawing room has a coffered ceiling and **frescoes** by Pontormo representing Vertumnus and Pomona, gods of orchards and fruit.

Villa La Ferdinanda★★ – *26km/16mi west of Artimino.* This villa was commissioned from Buontalenti by Grand Duke Ferdinand I at the end of the 16C. Its many chimneys, its double spiral stairway and its magnificent setting overlooking the Arno valley give it a striking appearance. It houses a **museum of Etruscan archaeology**. *& Apr-Sep 9.30am-1pm, Sun and public hols 9.30am-12.30pm; Oct-Mar 9.30am-12.30pm. Closed Wed. €4. ☎ 055 87 18 124; www.po-NET.prato.it/MUSEI*

Certosa del Galluzzo★★

6km/4mi south by the Siena road. Guided tours only, Apr-Sep 9am-noon and 3-6pm; Oct-Mar 9am-noon and 3-5pm. Closed Mon. Donations welcome. ☎ 055 20 49 226.

The grandiose Carthusian monastery was founded in the 14C and underwent successive alterations until the 17C. The adjoining palace contains frescoes by Pontormo. The monks' cells are grouped around the Renaissance **cloisters**.

Gaeta★

Gaeta is a former fortress, still partly walled. South of Gaeta is a pleasant beach of fine sand, Serapo Beach.

Location

Population 22 687 – Michelin map 430 S 22 – Lazio. Gaeta is a small town in the south of Lazio, admirably sited on the point of a promontory bounding a beautiful **bay★**. The coastal road round the bay affords magnificent views. **🄱** *Corso Cavour 16, ☎ 0771 46 11 65.*

Surrounding area: see Abbazia di MONTECASSINO, TERRACINA.

Worth a Visit

Duomo

The cathedral is interesting, especially for its 10C and 15C Romanesque Moorish campanile adorned with glazed earthenware and resembling the Sicilian or Amalfi belltowers. Inside, the late-13C **paschal candelabrum★** is remarkable for its size and for its 48 low reliefs depicting scenes from the Lives of Christ and St Erasmus, the protector of sailors.

A picturesque medieval quarter lies near the cathedral.

Castello

The castle, dating from the 8C, has been altered many times. The lower castle was built by the Angevins, while the upper one was the work of the Aragonese.

Monte Orlando

Open summer 9am-9pm, rest of the year 9am-6pm. Access to the park by foot only. A shuttle bus operates to the summit from Jun to mid-Sep. €1.03 (round trip). For guided excursions apply to Cooperativa Elios, ☎ 0771 45 00 93; www.parks.it/parco.monte.orlando

Standing on the summit is the tomb of the Roman Consul Munatius Plancus (Mausoleo di Lucio Muniazio Planco), a friend of Caesar who founded the colonies of Lugdunum (Lyon) and Augusta Raurica (Augst near Basle).

Excursions

Sperlonga⌂

16km/10mi northwest. The village stands on a rocky spur, pitted with many caves, up in the Aurunci mountains.

Grotta di Tiberio e Museo Archeologico – ♿ *Open daily, 8.30am-7.30pm (summer until 11pm). €2.07. ☎ 0771 54 80 28.* The cave *(grotta)* lies below the Gaeta-Terracina road *(left after the last tunnel)*. It was in this cave that the Emperor Tiberius narrowly escaped death when part of the roof fell in. In the **museum**, by the roadside, there are 4C-2C BC statues, outstanding heads and busts and some realistic theatrical masks. There is also a reconstruction of a colossal group depicting the punishment meted out to the Cyclops Polyphemus by Ulysses.

At the Gaeta end of the tunnel are the charred ruins of Tiberius' Villa.

Promontorio del **Gargano**★★★

GARGANO PROMONTORY

The Gargano Promontory is one of the most attractive natural regions of Italy with its wide horizons, its deep and mysterious forests and its lonely, rugged coastline. This paradise for lovers of sun and sea is marred by one drawback: most of the beaches and bays are private as they belong to camping sites and hotels and are not easily accessible.

Location

Michelin map 431 B-C 28-30 – Puglia. The Gargano Promontory projects like a spur from the "boot" of Italy. The nearest main road is A 14.
Surrounding area: see PUGLIA, Isole TREMITI.

Tour

146km/91mi – allow one day.

Monte Sant'Angelo★

Monte Sant'Angelo stands in a **wonderful site★★**. The town is built on a spur (803m/2 634ft) dominated by the massive form of its castle and overlooks both the Gargano Promontory and the sea. It was in a nearby cave between 490 and 493 that the Archangel Michael, chief of the Heavenly Host, appeared three times to the bishop of Siponto. After a further apparition in the 8C it was decided to found an abbey. During the Middle Ages all the Crusaders came to pray to the Archangel Michael, the saintly warrior, before embarking at Manfredonia.

On 29 September the annual feast day includes the procession of the Archangel's Sword.

Santuario di San Michele★ – The church dedicated to St Michael, designed in the transitional Romanesque-Gothic style, is flanked by a detached octagonal campanile dating from the late 13C. Opposite the entrance a long covered stairway leads down to the very beautiful and richly worked **bronze door★** which is of Byzantine origin and dates from 1076. It gives access to both the nave with pointed vaulting which opens onto the cave (to the right) in which St Michael is said to have made his appearance. The marble statue of the saint is by Andrea Sansovino (16C) and the 11C episcopal throne is decorated in a style characteristic of Apulia.

Tomba di Rotari★ – *Go down the stairs opposite the campanile. Open 8.30am-1pm and 2.30-7.30pm; rest of the year, by appointment only. Donations welcome.* ☏ 0884 56 18 09. The tomb is to the left of the apse of the ruined church of San Pietro. Above the entrance are scenes from the Life of Christ. Inside, the tower rises in stages through a square, an octagon and finally a triangle to the dome. The tomb was supposed to contain the remains of Rotharis, a 7C king of the Lombards, but is really a 12C baptistery.

Chiesa di Santa Maria Maggiore – *Left of Tomba di Rotari.* The church, built in the Apulian Romanesque style boasts a fine doorway. Inside there are traces of the Byzantine frescoes which covered the walls. Note the figure of St Michael in the south aisle.

HISTORICAL NOTES
Geologically, Gargano is quite independent from the Apennine Mountains; it is a limestone plateau fissured with crevices into which runs water. Originally an island, Gargano was connected to the mainland by an accumulation of deposits brought down by the rivers from the Apennines. Today the massif is riven by high-altitude valleys, with fertile valley floors, and is heavily forested in the east. The scanty pastures and moors on the plateaux support flocks of sheep and goats as well as herds of black pigs. The picturesque Tremiti Islands belong to the same geological formation.

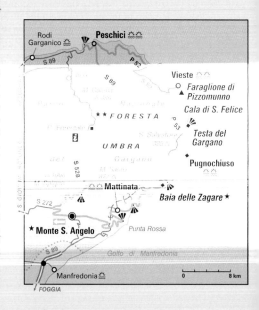

Directory

WHERE TO EAT
• Budget
Medioevo – *Via Castello 21 – 71037 Monte Sant'Angelo – ☎ 0884 56 53 56 – Closed Mon (except Jul-Sep) – €15/34.* Diners are given a warm welcome in this little trattoria which is tucked away up in the heart of the historic centre. Simple, modern-style dining room with a vaulted ceiling. Regional cuisine with some personal touches, dishes are lovingly prepared using the freshest ingredients – wonderful aromas.

Taverna al Cantinone – *Via Mafrolla 26 – 71019 Vieste – ☎ 0884 70 77 53 – Closed Fri (until May) and Nov-Easter – ⓕ – €16/26.* Simple, cheerful trattoria in the heart of the historic centre. Traditional home cooking. Recommended for its use of fresh, local produce and value for money.

• Moderate
La Collinetta – *Località Madonna di Loreto – 71010 Peschici – 2km/1mi southeast of Peschici – ☎ 0884 96 41 51 – Closed lunchtime, Oct-15 Mar – Book – €26/38.* Wonderful views over the coast from the terrace and excellent seafood dishes (prepared with super fresh ingredients) – a great combination. Friendly, enthusiastic staff. Overnight stays possible – pleasant rooms.

WHERE TO STAY
• Budget
Hotel Peschici – *Via San Martino 31 – 71010 Peschici – ☎ 0884 96 41 95 – Fax 0884 96 41 95 – Closed Nov-mid Mar – ▣ – 42 rm €31/49.10 – ⌂ €7.75.* One of the main attractions of this pension is its location – it is situated right in the heart of

the village and yet overlooks the sea. Rustic-style ambience enhanced by the vaulted ceiling. Rooms are simple but well maintained. Family-style guesthouse with a warm, friendly welcome.

• Moderate
Hotel Solemar – *Località San Nicola – 71010 Peschici – 3km/2mi east of Peschici – ☎ 0884 96 41 86 – Fax 0884 96 41 88 – Closed 21 Sep-19 May – ▣ ⌕ – 66 rm €51.65/92.96 – ⌂ €4.13 – Restaurant. €15/18.* An ideal location for a relaxing seaside vacation, this lovely hotel overlooks the bay (private) and is surrounded by greenery. The rooms are light and airy and all of them have a sea view. Guests can make their way down to the sea along the pleasantly shaded paths.

Park Hotel Paglianza e Paradiso – *Località Manacore – 71010 Peschici – 7km/4mi east of Peschici – ☎ 0884 91 10 18 – Fax 0884 91 10 32 – Closed 15 Oct-Mar – ▣ ⌕ ⓕ – 110 rm €54.23/72.30 ⌂ – Restaurant. €13/18.* Situated a few minutes walk from the sea, deep in a dense forest of pine trees, this establishment is the ideal solution for anyone looking for a comfortable, relaxing hotel with sporting facilities.

• Expensive
Hotel Svevo – *Via Fratelli Bandiera 10 – 71019 Vieste – ☎ 0884 70 88 30 – Fax 0884 70 88 30 – Closed 16 Oct-29 May – ▣ ⌕ ⓕ – 30 rm from €144.61 ⌂.* A charming hotel not far from the castle of the same name. Family run – the owners are very enthusiastic. Rooms are simple but well maintained. Wonderful terrace-solarium with swimming pool looking down over the sea and a fantastic panorama.

Foresta Umbra★★
Forests are rare in Puglia and this vast expanse of venerable beeches, elders, pines, oaks, chestnuts and linden trees as well as ancient yews, covers over 11 000ha/27 000 acres of undulating countryside. Visitors are welcome and the forest is well equipped with recreational facilities. Shortly after the turning to Vieste there is a forestry lodge (Casa Forestale) which now serves as a **visitor centre**.

Peschici⌂⌂
Well situated on a rocky spur jutting out into the sea, this fishing town is now a seaside resort.

Vieste⌂⌂
In a similar setting to Peschici, this small but ancient town, crowded on the clifftop, is dominated by its 13C cathedral. In the town centre there is an interesting shell museum, **Museo Malacologico**, displaying a large collection of shells from all over the world. ♿ *Open Jun-Aug 9.30am-1pm and 5pm-midnight; Sep-Nov and Mar-May 9.30am-1pm and 4-9pm. Closed Dec-Feb. No charge.* ☎ 0884 70 76 88.

To the south is a vast sandy beach with a limestone sea-stack, **Faraglione di Pizzomunno**, standing offshore.

Between Vieste and Mattinata there is a very fine **scenic stretch★★** of corniche road, overlooking the indented coastline. After 8km/5mi the square tower in **Testa del Gargano** marks the easternmost extremity of the massif: fine **view★** of the inlet, **Cala di San Felice**, which is spanned by a natural arch at the seaward end. Beyond the popular holiday resort of **Pugnochiuso⌂⌂**, there is another beauty spot, the **Baia delle Zagare★** (Bay of Zagare).

Mattinata⌂⌂
From the road running down towards Mattinata there is a fine **view★★** of this agricultural market town, a white mass amid a sea of olive groves encircled by a rim of mountains.

Genova★★

GENOA

The capital of Liguria, Italy's greatest seaport and the birthplace of Christopher Colombus, Genoa "la Superba" boasts a spectacular location★★. Sprawled across the slopes of a sort of mountainous amphitheatre, the port is overlooked by the colourful façades of a host of buildings. With its picturesque squares, it is a city of surprises and contrasts, where the most splendid palaces stand side by side with the humblest alleyways, known as carruggi. As a centre for the arts, the city has a vibrant cultural life which has earned it the title of European Capital of Culture (Capitale Europea della Cultura) in 2004.

Location

Population 636 104 – Michelin map 428 I 8 (with plans of the conurbation) – See the maps on pp 360 and 364 – Liguria.

The city is effectively enclosed by a long mountain range which curves around 30km/18mi of coastline. The historic centre, which huddles around the port, is a maze of little alleyways *(carruggi)* whereas in marked contrast the nearby modern part of the city is crossed by wide avenues and arterial roads. If you are travelling by car we recommend parking (payment) in Piazza della Vittoria or at the Porto Antico.
🚩 *Stazione Principe, ☎ 010 24 62 633; Via al Porto Antico (Palazzina S. Maria) ☎ 010 24 87 11.*

Surrounding area: see RIVIERA LIGURE.

Background

Genoese expansion was based on a strong fleet, which already in the 11C ruled supreme over the Tyrrhenian Sea, having vanquished the Saracens. By 1104 the fleet already comprised 70 ships, all built in the famous dockyards, making it a formidable power much coveted by foreign rulers such as the French kings, Philip the Fair and Philip of Valois.

The Crusaders offered the Genoese an opportunity of establishing trading posts on the shores of the Eastern Mediterranean. Following the creation of the Republic of St George in 1100, seamen, merchants, bankers and moneylenders united their efforts to establish the maritime supremacy of Genoa.

Initially Genoa allied itself with Pisa in the struggle against the Saracens (11C) and then became her enemy in a conflict concerning Corsica (13C). Finally it became the most persistent rival of that other great maritime republic, Venice (14C), disputing with her the trading rights for the Mediterranean. Genoa had colonies as far afield as the Black Sea.

In the 14C the Genoese merchant seamen controlled the trade in precious cargoes from the Orient; in particular they had the monopoly in the trading of alum used in the dyeing trade to fix colours.

Limited partnership companies flourished. Founded in 1408, the famous Bank of St George, grouping the maritime state's lending houses, administered the finances of the trading posts. The merchants became ingenious moneylenders and instituted such modern methods as bills of credit, cheques and insurance to increase their profits.

Porticciolo di Sturla

Directory

GETTING ABOUT

Information – ☎ 010 55 82 414,
www.amt.genova.it

Circonvallazione a monte – For a "tour of the avenues" take bus n° 33 (from Piazza Corvetto or the railway station) which takes in this panoramic route. The road is flanked by some fine 19C buildings.

A "passeggiata" by train – This is one of the locals' favourite Sunday outings. A trip into the country on a small, painted train (that runs on a narrow gauge line) up into the hills and little villages between Genoa and Casella. Frequent departures on a daily basis from the Genova-Casella station. For information contact ☎ 010 83 73 21.

Giro Giro Tour – Daily departure, leaving Piazza Caricamento (in front of the Acquario) at 3pm. A guided tour (multilingual) of the historic and cultural hotspots of the city (about 2hr). The ticket costs around €12.91. For information, contact: Macramè Viaggi ☎ 010 59 59 779.

Volabus Linea 100 – This bus links the airport with the city centre, departing every 30min. €2.07. For information contact: ☎ 010 55 82 414.

SIGHTSEEING

Card Musei – Includes entry to 20 museums in Genoa as well as discounts on certain attractions including the Acquario and exhibitions at the Palazzo Ducale. It costs €10.33 for 3 days and €15.49 for 7 days.

Libreria Ducale – In the Palazzo Ducale. ☎ 010 59 41 12. A specialist bookshop with a wide range of art books. Also stocks books on and maps of Genoa.

WHERE TO EAT

• Budget

Antica Osteria della Foce – *Via Ruspoli 72/74r* – ☎ *010 55 33 155 – Closed Sun, lunchtime on Sat and public holidays, 24 Dec-2 Jan, Aug, Easter – Book – €13/18.* A pleasant, friendly establishment, the atmosphere enhanced by the two large wood-burning ovens and the old bar. Cooking is based on traditional Ligurian specialities but the focaccia and savoury tarts (torte salate) are also good. Very speedy service and reasonable prices.

Cantine Squarciafico – *Piazza Invrea 3r* – ☎ *010 24 70 823 – ✍ – €18/26.* Located near the church of S. Lorenzo, this charming eatery is housed in the old cisterns of the 15C palazzo of the same name. Authentic Genovese cuisine.

• Moderate

Sul Fronte del Porto – Bar & Restaurants – *Calata Cattaneo, 3rd floor, Palazzo Millo – Porto Antico* – ☎ *010 25 18 384 – Closed Mon, Sat lunchtime, 15-30 Jan – ▣.* An innovative and highly original establishment which provides three restaurants, a cocktail bar and a snack bar all in one premises. There is the "Irifune" (€11-26), an authentic Japanese sushi bar, the rather eccentric "Compagnia delle

Aragoste" (€43-65) and lastly the "Portocarlo" brasserie (€22-55), which is a typical French bistro complete with oyster sellers outside. Located near the Acquario with all its hustle and bustle.

I Tre Merli – *Calata Cattaneo, Porto Antico – Palazzo Millo – ☎ 010 24 64 416 – info@itremerli.it – Closed Mon – ▣ – Book – €23/36.* An unusual wine bar which is housed in an old coffee warehouse in the Porto Antico near the Acquario. Elegant but curious interior decor which contrasts rough stone walls with coloured marble columns. Serves delicious fish dishes (the cuisine has a national rather than local feel to it) as well as the more traditional *focacce* and *farinate*.

Pintori – *Via San Bernardo 68/r* – ☎ *010 27 57 507 – Closed Sun, Mon 24, Dec-7 Jan, 10-31 Aug – Book – €27/44.* Even if it is difficult to find, located in a narrow "carruggio" in the old town, this trattoria is definitely worth hunting down. Meals are served at rustic-style tables in a lovely vaulted dining room. Authentic Ligurian cuisine with the odd Sardinian dish thrown in for good measure. Excellent wine cellar with more than 700 different wines. Very reasonably priced.

Antica Osteria del Bai – *Via Quarto 12, Quarto dei Mille – ☎ 010 38 74 78 – Closed Mon, 10-20 Jan, 1-20 Aug – ▣ ✗ – Book – €41.31/61.77.* A restaurant with a history. It is housed in an old fort which overlooks the beach from where Garibaldi set off with his "Thousand" men. The elegant, cheerful interior has a maritime feel to it as does the cooking. Dishes are cooked with super fresh ingredients.

WHERE TO STAY

It is worth noting that during the trade fairs, and in particular the international boat show **(Salone Nautico Internazionale)** which lasts for 10 days in October, the hotels tend to put their prices up. Do enquire about this when you make your booking.

• Moderate

Albergo Soana – *Via XX Settembre 23-8, (4th floor) – ☎ 010 56 28 14 – Fax 010 56 14 86 – soana@hotelsoana.it – Closed 23-28 Dec – 19 rm €46.48/77.47 – ☲ €3.62.* A small hotel with simple, modern rooms housed in an early 20C palazzo. Located in front of the Ponte Monumentale. A good hotel if you want to stay in the centre of town.

Albergo Cairoli – *Via Cairoli 14/4* – ☎ *010 24 61 454 – Fax 010 24 67 512 – 12 rm €51.65/77.47 – ☲ €5.16.* This small hotel is situated right in the heart of the city centre but has a cosy, homely ambience. The rooms are rather cramped but the terrace, with its mass of flowering plants, is particularly attractive.

Hotel Galles – *Via Bersaglieri d'Italia 13* – ☎ *010 24 62 820 – Fax 010 24 62 822 – ▣ – 20 rm €62/93 ☲.* A comfortable hotel strategically situated between the Porta Principe railway station and the Ponte dei

Mille seaport. Large, airy reception area – the vases of flowers are a nice touch. The rooms are spacious and welcoming with modern furnishings. Competitive prices.

• **Expensive**

Hotel Bristol – *Via 20 Settembre 35* – ☎ 010 59 25 41 – *Fax 010 56 17 56* – ▢ – 128 rm from €191 ☲. A luxurious, if rather austere hotel housed in a late 19C palazzo. The splendid entrance hall with its wonderful staircase sets the scene. The public areas and the rooms are all elegantly furnished with antiques. Very attentive service.

TAKING A BREAK

Mangini – *Piazza Corvetto 3r* – ☎ 010 56 40 13 – *Open daily, 7.30am-8.30pm*. Founded in 1876, this famous café-pasticceria, with its olde worlde charm, has long been popular with journalists and writers.

Romanengo – *Via Soziglia 74/76r* – ☎ 010 24 74 574 – *Open Tue-Sat 9am-1pm, 3.15-7.15pm*. Founded in 1780, this is one of the most famous confectionery shops in Italy. A cornucopia of sweet delights including candied fruit, pralines, chocolates, caramels and other sweets.

Caffè degli Specchi – *Salita Pollaiuoli 43r* – ☎ 010 24 68 193 – *Open Mon-Sat 7am-8.30pm*. This rather elegant but cosy café with its Art Nouveau interior has a reputation for being popular with the locals. Situated near the Palazzo Ducale.

Caffè del Barbarossa – Piano di S. Andrea, 21/23r – ☎ 010 24 74 574 – *Open Mon 7.30am-2.30pm, Tue-Fri 7.30am-2.30am, Sat-Sun 4.30pm-2.30am*. A small, friendly café/bar on two levels. Very popular with the locals and always heaving with people, particularly in the early evening.

Following continual struggles between the rival families of Genoa, the decision was taken in 1339 to elect a doge for life and to seek, essentially in the 15C, foreign protection.

In 1528 the great admiral **Andrea Doria** (1466-1560) gave Genoa its aristocratic constitution which gave it the status of a mercantile republic. The enterprising and independent Andrea was one of Genoa's most famous sons: he was an admiral, a legislator and an intrepid and wise leader who distinguished himself against the Turks in 1519 and, while serving François I, by covering the French retreat after their defeat at Pavia (1525). In 1528, indignant at François I's unjust treatment of him, he entered the service of Charles V, who plied him with honours and favours. Following his death and the development of ports on the Atlantic coast, Genoa declined as a port and it was Louis XIV who destroyed the harbour in 1684. In 1768, by the Treaty of Versailles, Genoa surrendered Corsica to France. Later, under the leadership of Giuseppe Mazzini, it became in 1848 one of the cradles of the Risorgimento.

Fine Arts in Genoa – As in many countries, the decline of commercial prosperity in the 16C and 17C coincided with intense artistic activity, evidenced in the building of innumerable palaces and the arrival at Genoa of foreign artists, especially the Flemish. In 1607 Rubens published a work on the *Palazzi di Genova (Palaces of Genoa)* and from 1621 to 1627 Van Dyck painted the Genoese nobility. Puget lived at Genoa from 1661 to 1667, working for patrician families such as the Doria and the Spinola.

The art of the Genoese school, characterised by dramatic intensity and the use of muted colours, is represented by Luca Cambiaso (16C), Bernardo Strozzi (1581-1644), the fine engraver Castiglione, and especially **Alessandro Magnasco** (1667-1749) whose sharp and colourful brushwork marks him out as a precursor of modern art.

In the field of architecture, Galeazzo Alessi (1512-72), when at his best, was the equal of Sansovino and Palladio in the nobility and ingenuity of his designs when integrating isolated buildings in the existing urban landscape.

Special Features

PORT★★

Boat tour departures daily from Aquarium and Ponte dei Mille (near Principe station). Hours vary depending on number of passengers. Duration: 45min. €6. Reserve in advance. May to Sep mini cruises for San Fruttuoso, Portofino, Cinque Terre, Porto Venere, and nature excursions for cetacean sightings in collaboration with WWF. Departures: 9am 12.30pm, return to Genoa by 7.30pm. €12-€33. Reserve well in advance. ☎ 010 26 57 12.

From the raised road *(Strada Sopraelevata)* which skirts the port, there are good views of Italy's principal port. To the east the **Porto Vecchio** (old port) includes a pleasure boat harbour, shipyards, and quays for ferries leaving for the islands or Africa. It is dominated by the **Bigo**, a metallic structure resembling a crane, designed by **Renzo Piano** (b 1937), and has a lift which affords an excellent bird's-eye **view★** of the *campanile* of the cathedral, the massive structure of Santa Maria di Carignano and Genoa's lighthouse, *la Lanterna*, symbol of the city. To the west the modern Porto Nuovo (port) is fringed by an industrial zone with steel and chemical plants as well as oil refineries. This busy port handles imported raw materials (oil and petrol, coal, minerals, cereals, metal and wood) and exports manufactured goods such as machines, vehicles and textiles.

Acquario★★

& *Open Mon-Fri 9.30am-7.30pm (in winter, Mon 10am-6pm), Sat, Sun and public hols 9.30am-8.30pm, Thu (in Jul and Aug) to 10pm (ticket office always closes 2hr early). Closed Mon in Nov. €11.60. Guided tours available and audioguides in various languages. €14.90 includes entry to Padiglione del Mare and Padiglione della Navigazione. ☎ 010 24 81 205; www.acquario.ge.it*

The aquarium has a modern, instructive layout. Illuminated panels describe (in Italian and English) the species and explain the varied habitats recreated in the tanks.

The visit begins with a film that provides an introduction to the underwater world. Then, a computerised system offers an opportunity for a "hands-on" experience and various observation points give visitors the impression that they are in amid the fish and marine mammals. There are also reconstructions of the underwater environments of the Mediterranean, the Red Sea, Madagascar, a tropical forest and a coral reef. Of particular interest are the seals, reptiles with striking camouflage, dolphins, sharks, penguins, and the tank filled with species that can be touched.

Antichi Magazzini del Cotone

Built in the 19C, the former cotton warehouse was restored by Renzo Piano to mark the celebrations honouring Christopher Columbus. On the first floor is the **Città dei Bambini★**, a space devoted to children between the ages of 3 and 14. Through a series of interactive games, young visitors are encouraged to explore their senses, the natural world, basic technological and scientific principles and to develop their social skills and the concepts of respect, tolerance and diversity. *Children only admitted if accompanied by one or two adults. Visit in sessions Tue-Sun, 10am-6pm. Closed Mon.€4.65 per person. ☎ 010 24 75 702; www.cittadeibambini.net/cdb/*

The third floor is occupied by the **Padiglione del Mare e della Navigazione★**, an interesting museum which gives an overview of the maritime tradition of the city through the display of instruments, the reconstruction of an arsenal, a 19C *carruggio* complete with shops (a sailmaker, a seascape painter, a figurehead carver), a shipyard and a steamship. & *Open Mar to Sep, Mon-Fri 10.30am-7pm, Sat-Sun and hols 11.30am-7.30pm; rest of year 10.30am-5.30pm, Sat-Sun and hols 10.30am-6pm (ticket office always closes 30min early). Closed Mon (Nov). €5.40; €14.90 including Aquarium. Guided tours available. ☎ 010 24 63 678; www.acquario.ge.it*

Sailors' quarter★

At the centre of this district is the 13C **Palazzo San Giorgio** which was the headquarters of the famous Bank of St George. The building was remodelled in the 16C. Behind the palace on **Piazza Banchi** (of the banks) is the Loggia dei Mercanti, which houses a fruit and vegetable market and sometimes a flee market.

Walking about

THE TOWN OF THE RENAISSANCE AND BAROQUE★★ *Allow 2hr*

Set off from Piazza Fontane Marose which is overlooked by a number of splendid palaces. Note the frescoes on the façade of the Palazzo Interiano Pallavicini (1565).

Via Garibaldi★★

Back in the middle of the 16C a number of patrician families decided to erect their residences on a street away from the historic centre. Once known as Via Aurea, this street of palaces was built to designs by Alessi in the 16C and is one of the loveliest streets in Italy. Alessi was also responsible for the designs of many of the actual palaces among which are N° 1 **Palazzo Cambiaso** (1565) and n° 4 the **Palazzo Carrega-Cataldi** (1588-61) which has preserved a delightful entrance hall decorated with grotesques. This leads into a large reception room that used to open onto the garden which was sacrificed to create more space for the building itself. In this new wing, on an upper floor, is a dazzling gilded **gallery★** in the Rococo style. (&) *Tours by reservation only, Mon-Fri, 9am-6pm. Closed Sat, Sun and hols. No charge. ☎ 010 27 04 358; www.lig.camcom.it/cciaa_ge*

Both n° 6, **Palazzo Doria**, and n° 7, **Palazzo Podestà** (1565-67), with its fine **nymphaeum** are by the same architect, GB Castello. The **Palazzo Municipale** (Town Hall), the former Palazzo Doria Tursi, at n° 9, has a lovely arcaded courtyard. The collections include manuscripts by Christopher Columbus (normally not on view) and the violin of Paganini *(to view ask at the mayor's office on the first floor).* & *For information ☎ 010 55 72 274; www.comunegenova.it*

Palazzo Bianco (n° 11) and **Palazzo Rosso** (n° 18) house a very fine **art gallery**★ and **picture gallery**★ (*see "Worth a Visit" below*)

Take Via Cairoli and Via della Zecca to get to Piazza del Carmine and the **church of the Santissima Annunziata** (17C). The sumptuous decoration inside this 17C church is a happy mixture of gilding, stucco and frescoes and is a good example of the Genoese Baroque style.

Via Balbi

This street is lined with palaces. The **Palazzo Reale** (Royal Palace), formerly the Balbi Durazzo, at n° 10, dates from 1650 and the principal floor has period furnishings of the 18C and 19C. There are frescoes on the ceiling by Domenico Parodi (1668-1740) who also designed the stunning **Mirrored Gallery**★ styled on the Gallery in the Doria Pamphili palace in Rome and the more famous one at Versailles. Beyond the sumptuous throne room, in the audience room is the *Portrait of Caterina Balbi Durazzo* by Van Dyck. The imposing 17C University building, **Palazzo dell'Universita**★, at n° 5 has a court and a majestic staircase. The 17C Palazzo Durazzo Pallavicini is at n° 1. *Palazzo Reale: Open Wed-Sun, 8.30am-7.15pm, Mon-Tue, 8.15am-1.45pm. Closed 1 Jan, 1 May, 25 Dec. €4; €6.50 including Palazzo Spinola. ☎ 010 27 101.*

From Via Balbi head back to Via Lomellini in the direction of the **church of San Siro**, its **interior**★ decorated with 17C frescoes by GB Carlone. The high altar, in marble and bronze, is the work of P Puget (1670).

Beyond Palazzo Spinola *(for a description, see under "Worth a Visit")*, is the church of **Santa Maria Maddalena**, the **interior**★ of which is one of the most characteristic examples of the local Baroque style.

Proceed along Vico Casana as far as the Piazza de Ferrari with its prestigious **Teatro Carlo Felice** and various other buildings, including the Accademia Ligustica di Belle Arti. Piazza G. Matteotti is dominated by the monumental façade of the **Palazzo Ducale** (1778). Of note inside is the lovely **chapel**★ with frescoes by GB Carlone which illustrate scenes from the history of the city.

The **church of Gesù**, erected by Tibaldi in 1597, houses in its sumptuous interior the *Assumption* by Guido Reni and two paintings by Rubens: *The Circumcision* and *The Healing by St Ignatius*.

OLD TOWN★★ *allow 2hr*

Heading east out of Porto Vecchio you wind your way up the charming, narrow alleyways which are flanked by some tall buildings.

The stroll that we are proposing is the continuation of the one described above. Skirt along the left side of the Palazzo Ducale as far as Piazza S. Matteo.

Piazza S. Matteo★

In the city centre, this small but harmonious square is lined with 13C-15C palaces that belonged to the Doria family. N° 17 is a Renaissance building presented to Andrea Doria by a grateful republic. The **church of San Matteo** has a Genoese-style façade with alternating courses of black and white stone. The tomb of Andrea Doria is in the crypt. To the left of the façade is the charming 14C cloister which you can see through the railings.

Cattedrale di San Lorenzo★★

Treasury: Open daily except Sun, 9am-noon and 3-6pm. Closed 1 Jan, Easter, 25 Dec. €5.50, €8 including Chiostro di San Lorenzo and Museo Diocesano. ☎ 010 24 71 831.

The cathedral, originally built in the 12C, with additions made through to the 16C, has a splendid Gothic **façade**★★ typical of the Genoese style. French influence appears in the placing of the 13C doorways and the large rose window. The carving on the central doorway represents a Tree of Jesse and scenes from the Life of Christ *(on the piers)* and the Martyrdom of St Lawrence and Christ between the Symbols of the Evangelists *(on the tympanum)*. The early-13C knifegrinder, at the right corner of the façade, resembles the angel of the sundial at Chartres and performs the same function. The transept crossing is crowned with a dome designed by Alessi.

The severe and majestic **interior**★ has marble columns in the nave and a false gallery above. The **Chapel of St John the Baptist**★ (at the end of the north aisle) once held the remains of St John. The **treasury**★ includes the famous **Sacro Catino**, a hexagonal cup in emerald green blown glass, which, according to legend, is said to be the Holy Grail. It also houses the reliquary for St John the Baptist (14C) in the International Gothic style, and a precious chalcedony plate (whose colour changes according to the light) of the 1C AD with the head of St John the Baptist in the centre (added in the 15C).

The Canons' cloisters house the **Museo Diocesano di Arte Sacra**. *Open Tue-Fri 10am-1pm, Sat-Sun and hols 10am-1pm and 3-7.30pm. Closed Mon. €5.16 (Guided tours available Sat pm and Sun). ☎ 010 25 41 250.*

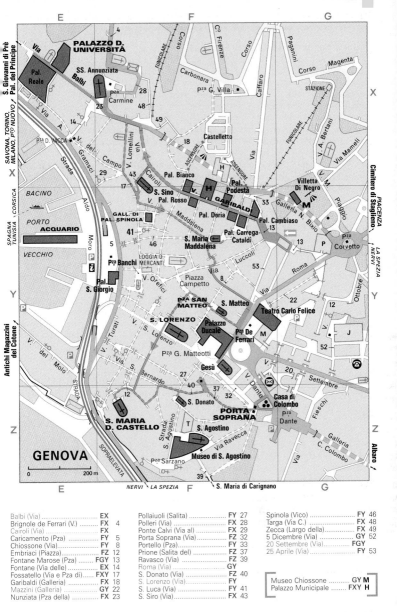

Head along Via Chiabrera as far as Piazza Embriaci.

Chiesa di Santa Maria di Castello★

Open daily, 9am-noon and 3.30-6pm. For reservations and information ☎ 010 25 49 511.
Three cloisters surround this Romanesque church, the nave of which is flanked by chapels added in the 15C and 17C. In the Grimaldi chapel, note the *Polyptych of the Annunciation* by Mazzone (1469). The second cloister (15C), the loggia of which overlooks the port, houses the fresco of the *Annunciation* by Giusto di Ravensburg.

Chiesa di San Donato

Built in the 12C and 13C, this church has its original doorway and a delightful Romanesque octagonal **campanile★**. The Romanesque interior is also alluring: it is worth noting the Madonna and Child (1401) in the south apse and the sumptuous *Adoration of the Magi★★* polyptych by Joos Van Cleve.
Via S. Donato leads into Piazza delle Erbe where the youth of Genoa gather in the evening. The Salita del Priore leads to **Porta Soprana**, one of the oldest entrances to the city (12C), characterised by two elegant twin towers. Just beyond Porta Soprana are the ruins of the so-called **Casa di Colombo**, with the elegant cloister of the church of Sant' Andrea (12C) adjacent to it.

Worth a Visit

Galleria Nazionale di Palazzo Spinola★

(&) Open Mon-Sat, 8.30am-7.30pm (ticket office closes 6.30pm), Sun and hols 1-8pm. Closed 1 Jan, 1 May, 25 Dec. €4. €6.50 includes Palazzo Reale. ☎ 010 27 05 300.

This palace, built at the end of the 16C by the Grimaldi family and then acquired by the Spinola family, has preserved its original interior decoration. The paintings and period furniture make for an atmospheric setting. The two principal floors are fine examples of 17C (first floor) and 18C (second floor) interior styles. It is thus possible to identify the evolution of fashions not just in furnishings but also in fresco painting of **ceilings★**. Tavarone's ceiling (17C) is richly Baroque, while those by L Ferrari and S Galeotti (18C) are more light and airy. The kitchen between the first and second floors can also be viewed. The **art collection★** comprises works by painters of the Italian and Flemish Renaissance among which an enchanting *Portrait of Ansaldo Pallavicino* by Van Dyck, a *Portrait of a Nun* by the Genoese painter Strozzi, *Sacred and Profane Love* by Guido Reni and, on the third floor (which houses the gallery proper), a moving *Ecce Homo★* by Antonello da Messina.

Pinacoteca di Palazzo Bianco★

Open Tue-Fri 9am-7pm, Sat-Sun 10am-7pm. Closed Mon and bank hols. €3.10. No charge Sun. ☎ 010 55 72 013.

The exquisite *Altarpiece with Scenes from the Lives of Saints Lawrence, Sixtus and Hippolitus* (13C), a gift from the Byzantine Emperor to the Genoese Republic to commemorate a treaty made in 1261, opens the collection. Numerous Flemish and Dutch paintings from the 15C to the 17C bear witness to the close commercial ties that linked Genoa to the Low Countries. Among these are a *Crucifixion* by Gerard David, highly dramatic in its use of dark colours and the restraint of its composition, the intense *Christ Blessing★* by Hans Memling, works by Jan Matsys, Van Dyck *(Christ of the Coin)* and Rubens *(Venus and Mars)*. Genoa also welcomed and appreciated Italian artists such as Veronese *(Crucifixion)* and Palma il Giovane *(Christ and the Samaritan Woman)*. Finally, there are works by Spanish (Murillo, 17C) and Genoese painters, among whom are Bernardo Strozzi (1581-1644), Domenico Piola (1627-1703) with *Charity* and Gregorio de Ferrari (1647-1726).

Galleria d'Arte di Palazzo Rosso★

Open Tue-Sat 9am-7pm, Sun and hols 10am-7pm. Closed Mon, 24 Jun, bank hols. €3.10. No charge Sun. ☎ 010 24 76 351.

On display are works by Palma il Vecchio, Guido Reni, Guercino *(The Eternal Father with an Angel)*, 1620, Mattia Preti and paintings of the Genoese school such as Guidobono. On the second floor (note the frescoed ceilings by the Genoese painters De Ferrari, Piola and Viviano) are some remarkable **portraits★** by Van Dyck. In addition there are collections of wooden sculpture of the Baroque era.

Palazzo del Principe★

Piazza Principe 4 (not on the map). Take either Via Balbi or Via Gramsci. (&) Open Tue-Sun, 10am-5pm. Closed Mon, Aug and public hols. €6.20. ☎ 010 25 55 09; www.doriapamphilj.it

This is the 16C residence of Andrea Doria who was granted the title of prince in 1531. **Perin del Vaga** (1501-47), a pupil of Raphael in Rome, was responsible for the **frescoes★** in the entrance hall, the Loggia degli Eroi and the symmetrical apartments of the prince and his wife, accessible from the loggia. The fresco in the Salone della Caduta dei Giganti (which takes its name from the subject) is particularly well preserved and contains a *Portrait of Andrea Doria★* by **Sebastiano del Piombo** (1526) and another portrait of Doria at the age of 92.

Chiesa di San Giovanni di Prè★

Via A. Gramsci, not far from the Palazzo del Principe. This Romanesque church has a portico on three levels which overlooks the port. Note the fine stone spire.

Museo di Sant' Agostino

(&) Open Tue-Sat, 9am-7pm, Sun 9am-12.30pm. Closed Mon and hols. €3.10. No charge Sun. ☎ 010 25 11 263.

This convent building complex, with its adjacent 13C church (today an auditorium), houses a collection of fragments and sculptures salvaged from destroyed churches and private houses. Of particular interest are the 13C tombstone of Simonetta Percivalle Lercari which almost has the appearance of a stone illuminated manuscript, the *Monument to Margaret of Brabant* by Giovanni Pisano (14C) and, on the second floor, sculptures by Pierre Puget *(Rape of Helen)* and Antonio Canova *(Penitent Magdalen)*.

Chiesa di Santo Stefano

From its elevated position on the Via XX Settembre, the church overlooks the town's main arterial road which is flanked by a number of elegant, Art Nouveau-style buildings. The Romanesque church has a fine Lombardy-style apse. Inside note the splendid painting by Giulio Romano, the *Martyrdom of St Stephen★* (c 1524).

Chiesa di Santa Maria di Carignano

Take Via Ravasco. This vast church was built in the 16C to plans by Alessi. Inside, there is a fine statue of *St Sebastian*★ by Puget.

Villetta Di Negro

On higher ground to the northwest of Piazza Corvetto, this is a sort of belvedere-labyrinth with palm trees, cascades and artificial grottoes. From the terrace there is a lovely **view**★ over the town and the sea. Standing on the summit is the **Museo Chiossone**★, which houses the collection of the Genoese engraver Chiossone, who was passionate about Oriental art after living in Japan for 23 years. The collection includes sculptures, buddhas, objets d'art, armoury and a remarkable assortment of prints, ivories and lacquerwork. *Open Tue-Fri 9am-1pm, Sat-Sun and hols 10am-7pm. Closed Mon and bank hols, 24 Jun. €3.10; €5.16 including 2 civic museums. Sun no charge. ☎ 010 54 22 85.*

Castelletto

From the terrace *(reached by lift)* there is a fine **view**★★ of the town.

Cimitero di Staglieno★

1.5km/1mi north. From Piazza Corvetto take Via Assarotti (off the map) and then turn left into Via Montaldo. In this curious cemetery there are ornate tombs and simple clay tumuli.

Albaro⌂

This is the location of the lido which has been built around wide avenues shaded with trees and flanked by elegant buildings. Albara has been a holiday resort since the end of the 14C and it retains some of the fine villas that were erected in the 16C, including the **villa Cambiaso Giustiniani**★, designed by Alessi. **Corso Itali**, where the locals head for their early evening "passeggiata", is flanked by some splendid Art Nouveau-style villas.

The little **porto di Boccadasse**★, overlooked by the multicoloured fishermen's houses, has retained its charm. From the top of Santa Chiara is a wonderful **view**★★ over the Riviera which stretches as far as the promontory at Portofino. The little streets, which are shaded by the foliage of the trees in the adjacent gardens, lead to the **porticciolo di Sturla**.

Villa Durazzo Pallavicini

Via Pallavicini 13 & Open daily except Mon, Apr to Sep 9am-7pm (ticket office closes 6pm), rest of year 9am-5pm (ticket office closes 4pm). Closed 1 Jan, 25 Dec, 31 Dec. €3.62. www.comune.genova.it

This is the most beautiful **park**★ in Genoa. It was designed around the middle of the 19C by Michele Canzio, the set designer at the Carlo Felice theatre. He arranged the garden in a series of theatrical scenes marked by little buildings, lakes, grottoes and waterfalls.

Gubbio★★

The small town of Gubbio, spread out over the steep slopes of Monte Ingino, has preserved almost intact its rich cultural and artistic heritage. Encircling ramparts, buildings of warm yellow stone roofed with Roman tiles, and distinctive towers and palaces outlined against a burnt and austere landscape make it one of the Italian towns in which the harsh atmosphere of the Middle Ages is most easily imagined.

Location

Population 31 483 – Michelin map 430 L 19 – Umbria. Gubbio lies off S 298, about 40km/24mi from Perugia. 🄱 *Piazza Oderisi, 6, ☎ 075 92 20 693.*

Surrounding area: see ASSISI, PERUGIA.

GUBBIO

Special Features

OLD TOWN★★

Piazza Grande stands at the heart of this charming but austere area of the old town with its steep, narrow streets, sometimes stepped, spanned by arches converted into living quarters. The houses, flanked by palaces and towers of nobility, are often used as ceramic artists' workshops. The façade, often built of a mixture of brick, rubblework and dressed stone, sometimes has two doors; one, narrower than the main door, is known as the Door of Death through which coffins were brought out.

The most picturesque streets are Via Piccardi, Baldassini, dei Consoli, 20 Settembre, Galeotti and the embankments along the River Camignano leading to Piazza 40 Martiri.

Directory

WHERE TO EAT

• *Moderate*

Fabiani – *Piazza 40 Martiri 26/AB – ☎ 075 92 74 639 – Closed Tue, Jan – €23/34 An elegant restaurant that has retained the style and ambience of the 15C palazzo in which it is housed. Umbrian specialities on the menu. Meals served outside in the courtyard in the summer. Car park nearby.*

EVENTS AND FESTIVALS

Gubbio has its traditional festivals; the most spectacular is the Candle Race. Three "candles", or *ceri*, strange wooden poles 4m/13ft tall, each topped with the statue of a saint (including St Ubald, patron saint of the town), are carried through the crowded streets in a frenzied race covering a distance of 5km/3mi, from the historical town centre to the basilica of Sant'Ubaldo situated at an altitude of 820m/2 665ft. During the race the "candle"-carriers, dressed in medieval costumes, demonstrate their skill by attempting not to drop their "candles" and carrying St Ubald into the church first, before the doors are slammed shut after the other two statues have arrived. These three strange *ceri*, whose origins date back to the pre-Christian era, grace Umbria's coat of arms.

The splendid Palazzo dei Consoli

Palazzo dei Consoli★★

 ♿ *Open daily, Apr to Sep, 10am-1pm and 3-6pm, rest of year 10am-1pm and 2-5pm. Closed 1 Jan, 14-15 May, 25 Dec. €3.62.* ☏ *075 92 74 298.*

Overlooking Piazza Grande, this imposing Gothic building, supported by great arches rising above Via Baldassini, has a majestic façade which reflects the palace's internal plan. The stairway leads up to the vast hall *(Salone)* where popular assemblies were held and which contains collections of statues and stonework.

Next is a museum, Museo Civico, where the **Tavole eugubine** have pride of place. The bronze tablets (2C-1C BC) are inscribed in the ancient language of Umbria. This document is unique in the fields of linguistics and epigraphy. The tablets record the political organisation and religious practices of the region in Antiquity.

Palazzo Ducale★

(♿) *Open daily except Wed, 8.30am-7.30pm. Closed 1 Jan, 25 Dec. €2.* ☏ *075 92 75 872.*

The Ducal Palace, which dominates the town, was built from 1470 onwards for Federico de Montefeltro. The design is attributed to Laurana, although it was probably finished by Francesco di Giorgio Martini, who was inspired by the ducal palace at Urbino. The elegant courtyard is delicately decorated. The rooms are adorned with frescoes and lovely chimney pieces; the Salone is particularly interesting.

Churches

Duomo – The plain façade of the cathedral is adorned with low reliefs showing the Symbols of the Evangelists. The interior consists of a single nave. The **Episcopal Chapel** opens to the right. It is a luxurious sitting room decorated in the 17C, from which the bishop could follow the services.

Chiesa di San Francesco – The inside walls of the north apse are covered with remarkable early-15C **frescoes★** by the local painter, Ottaviano Nelli. The church is dedicated to St Francis.

Chiesa di Santa Maria Nuova – Houses a fine **fresco★** by Ottaviano Nelli.

Teatro romano

This reasonably well preserved Roman theatre dates from the reign of Augustus.

Isola d'**Ischia**★★★

Ischia, known as the Emerald Island because of its luxuriant vegetation, is the largest island in the Bay of Naples and one of its major attractions. A clear, sparkling light plays over a varied landscape: a coast covered with pinewoods, indented with bays and creeks sheltering villages with their colourful cubic houses; the slopes covered with olive trees and vineyards (producing the white or red Epomeo wine); and an occasional village with its quaint white houses. The cottages, sometimes roofed with a dome and with an outside staircase, often have walls covered with vines.

The island rose out of the sea during the Tertiary Era at the time of a volcanic eruption. The soil is volcanic and there are many hot springs with various medicinal properties.

Location

Ischia: Population 18 105 – Michelin map 431 E 23 – Campania.

A tour of the island, which is fairly small, can be done in a matter of hours.

Surrounding area: see Isola di CAPRI, COSTIERA AMALFITANA, NAPOLI, Golfo di NAPOLI.

Directory

GETTING THERE

Ischia and Procida can be reached from Naples, Capri and Pozzuoli. For **Ischia**: from Naples there are daily ferry crossings (1hr 25min); from Capri there are daily hovercraft crossings (40min) from April to October; from Pozzuoli there are daily ferry crossings; from Procida there are daily ferry crossings (30min) and hovercraft crossings (15min). For **Procida**: from Naples there are daily ferry crossings (1hr) and hovercraft crossings (35min); from Ischia there are daily ferry crossings (25min); from Pozzuoli there are daily ferry crossings (30min) and hovercraft crossings (15min).

◪ for crossings from/to Naples, Pozzuoli, Procida: Travels and Holidays Office, Via Iasolino, Pontile 93, ☎ 081 98 48 18; Traghetti Pozzuoli, Via Iasolino, ☎ 081 99 28 03; Alilauro, Via Porto, ☎ 081 99 18 88; ☎ 081 89 67 280; Alilauro, Traghetti Pozzuoli, Via Roma, 80078 Pozzuoli, ☎ 081 52 67 736.

WHERE TO EAT

• *Moderate*

Da "Peppina" di Renato – *Via Montecorvo 42 – 80075 Forio – ☎ 081 99 83 12 – Closed lunchtime, Tue (except Jun-Sep), Dec-Feb – Book – €23/34.* The climb up the narrow, winding path is worth it for the spectacular view over the sea and the coastline. If you're looking for good home cooking, packed with flavour, this is the place to come. Meals are served under the shady pergola with unusual wrought-iron benches that have been constructed from the headboards of antique beds.

Il Melograno – *Via Giovanni Mazzella 110 – 80075 Citara – 2.5km/1mi south of Forio – ☎ 081 99 84 50 – Closed Mon, Tue from Nov-7 Jan, 7 Jan-15 Mar – Book – €33/50 + 10% service charge.* This restaurant specialises in fish dishes which are cooked with great skill and attention to detail. The

menu varies on a daily basis depending on the availability of the "raw materials". Meals are served in two very cheerful dining rooms complete with a splendid fireplace, or, weather permitting, in the garden under the shade of the olive trees.

WHERE TO STAY

• *Moderate*

Hotel Providence Terme – *Via Giovanni Mazzella 1 – 80075 Citara – ☎ 081 99 74 77 – Fax 081 99 80 07 – Closed Nov-Mar – ☷ ▣ ▨ (payment) ⌧ – 69 rm €53/85 – ⌧ €8 – Restaurant. €16/24.* This hotel boasts a splendid setting, near the famous "Poseidon" gardens and the beach at Citara, as well as some excellent spa facilities. Modern-style rooms and a pleasant terrace area with a swimming pool. Everything you need for a relaxing, restorative holiday.

Villa Angelica – *Via 4 Novembre 28 – 80076 Lacco Ameno – ☎ 081 99 45 24 – Fax 081 98 01 84 – Closed Nov-15 Mar – ⌧ – 20 rm €62/104 ⌧ – Restaurant. €15/21.* A charming hotel with enthusiastic, friendly staff. At the centre of the light and airy public areas is a lovely, little garden. The rooms are spacious and modern in style. The spa facilities including a swimming pool (half indoors/half outdoors). Half- and full-board rates on request. One of our favourites.

Hotel San Giorgio Terme – *Spiaggia dei Maronti – 80070 Barano d'Ischia – Southeast of Serrara Fontana – ☎ 081 99 00 98 – Fax 081 99 08 76 – Closed 29 Oct- 6 Apr – ▣ ⌧ – 81 rm €56.81/113.62 ⌧.* From the large terrace – where drinks are served – or the swimming pool (thermal water) guests can enjoy fine views over one of the most beautiful beaches on the island. The public areas are light and spacious, the rooms are all very individual in style. An ideal base for a relaxing holiday.

Tour

40km/25mi: follow the itinerary on the map. The narrow road, as it winds between rows of vines, offers numerous fine viewpoints of the coast and the sea.

Ischia★

The capital is divided into two settlements, **Ischia Porto** and **Ischia Ponte.** The Corso Vittoria Colonna, an avenue lined with cafes and smart shops, links the port in a former crater, and Ischia Ponte. The latter owes its name to the dike built by the Aragonese to link the coast with the rocky islet on the summit of which stands the **Castello Aragonese★★**, a beautiful group of buildings comprising a castle and several churches. *Open daily, Jun to Aug 9.30am-7pm, rest of year 9am-6pm. €8 ☎ 081 99 19 59, www.castelloaragonese.it*

There is an enchanting **view★★** from the terrace of the bar of the same name. On the outskirts are a large pinewood and a fine sandy beach.

Monte Epomeo★★★

Access is by a path which branches off in a bend of the road once level with the public gardens. 1hr 30min on foot there and back. From the summit of this tufa peak there is a vast **panorama** of the entire island and the Bay of Naples.

Serrara Fontana

Not far from this settlement a belvedere offers a plunging **view★★** of the site of Sant'Angelo with its beach and peninsula.

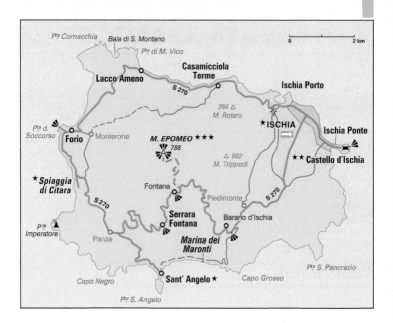

Sant'Angelo★

The houses of this peaceful fishing village cluster round the small harbour. Nearby is the vast Maronti Beach **(Marina dei Maronti)** which has been transformed by the opening of many thermal establishments *(access by a footpath)*.

Spiaggia di Citara★

This fine beach is sheltered by the majestic headland, Punta Imperatore. Another thermal establishment, Giardini di Poseidone, is laid out with numerous warm-water swimming pools amid flowers and statues.

Forio

The town centre is Piazza Municipio, a tropical garden overlooked by old buildings.

Lacco Ameno

This was the first Greek colony on the island and was called Pithecusa (meaning lots of monkeys) by the Greeks. It is now a holiday resort. The church of Santa Restituta *(Piazza Santa Restituta)* was built on the remains of an early-Christian basilica and a necropolis. There is a small archaeological museum. The tour of the island ends with the important thermal spa of **Casamicciola Terme.**

Excursion

Procida★

Procida was formed by craters levelled by erosion and remains the wildest island in the Bay of Naples. The fishermen, gardeners and winegrowers live in a picturesque setting of colourful houses with domes, arcades and terraces.

Procida: Mediterranean colours and light

Regione dei **Laghi**★★★

LAKE DISTRICT

Narrow and long, these lakes are all of glacial origin and their banks are covered with a varied and luxuriant vegetation which flourishes in the particularly mild climate. This fairyland of blue waters at the foot of shapely mountains has always been a favourite haunt of artists and travellers. The charm and originality of these Pre-Alpine lakes are due to the juxtaposition of Alpine and southern scenery, the numerous villas with attractive gardens on the lakesides, the great variety of flowers throughout the year, the small sailing villages with their flotillas of boats where fresh fish is the speciality. Each lake has its own specific character, making it quite different from its neighbour.

Location
Michelin map 428 D-F 7-14 – Piedmont – Lombardy – Trentino-Alto Adige – Veneto. The Lake District extends from Piedmont to Veneto and from Switzerland to Trentino in the north.

Worth a Visit

LAGO MAGGIORE★★★
Lake Maggiore is the most famous of the Italian lakes, in part for its legendary beauty at times both majestic and wild, and also for the Borromean Islands. It is fed by the River Ticino, which rises in Switzerland, and its waters change from a jade

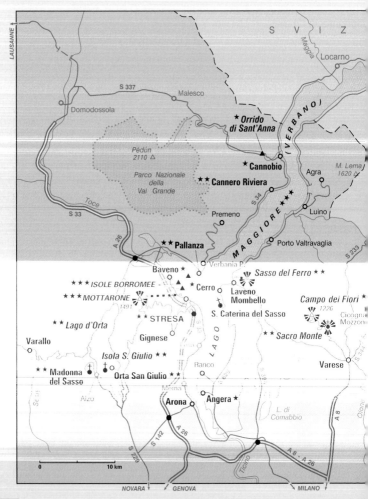

green in the north to a deep blue in the south. The mountains of the Alps and Pre-Alps shelter the lake which enjoys a constantly mild climate in which a luxuriant and exotic vegetation flourishes.

Angera★

This wonderful holiday resort stands in the shadow of the **Rocca Borromeo**. There is a vast panoramic view from a tower, the **Torre Castellana.** Known since the days of the Lombards (8C), the Rocca still has Law Courts decorated with admirable 14C **frescoes★★** depicting the life of Archbishop Ottone Visconti. The fortress also houses the **Museo della bambola★** (Doll Museum) with an extensive collection of exhibits showing the development of the doll *(bambola)* since the early 19C. *Museum: Open daily, 9.30am-12.30pm and 2-6pm, except Oct 9.30am-12.30pm and 2-5pm. Closed Nov to 26 Mar. €5.68.* ☎ *0331 93 13 00.*

Arona

The chief town on Lago Maggiore is overlooked by the gigantic statue, **Colosso di San Carlone★**, of **St Charles Borromeo**, the Cardinal Archbishop of Milan who distinguished himself by the authority he showed in re-establishing discipline and morals in the Church and by his heroic conduct during the plague of 1576. The statue is 24m/78ft high with a 12m/39ft base. *Open daily, mid-Mar to Sep 8.30am-12.30pm and 2-6.30pm, Oct 8.30am-12.30pm and 2-5pm; rest of year, Sat-Sun and hols 9am-12.30pm and 2-5pm. €3. No charge 4 Nov.* ☎ *0322 24 96 69.*

At the summit of the old town the church of **Santa Maria** contains a lovely **polyptych★** (1511) by Gaudenzio Ferrari. From the **Rocca,** the ruined castle, there is a **view★** of Lake Maggiore, Angera and its mountain setting.

Baveno★

This quiet holiday resort, once visited by Queen Victoria, has a Romanesque church and an octagonal Renaissance baptistery.

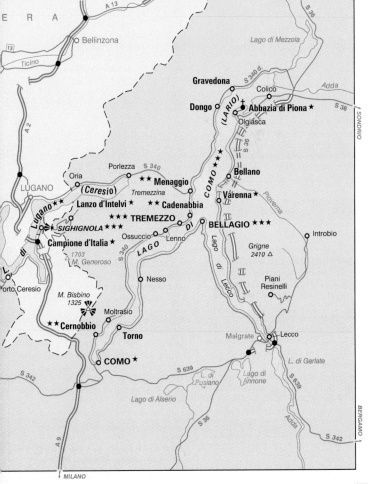

Directory

GETTING THERE

One of the most pleasant ways to get around the lakes is to take a boat trip. See below for details.

Lago Maggiore

Boat from Arona and/or Angera to Locarno, lunch available on board. From Stresa and/or Laveno for the Borromee Islands and Villa Taranto. Car ferry between Laveno and Intra. All-day tickets also available. Discounts for groups and senior citizens. Night cruise in summer. For information ☎ 800 55 18 01. The delightful **Borromee Islands** are situated in the middle of the lake. All-day ticket valid for the islands: €6 (2 islands round trip); €8 (3 islands round trip); €10 (3 islands and Villa Taranto round trip). For information, contact Ufficio Navigazione Lago Maggiore ☎ 0323 31 261.

Lago d'Orta

Departures from Orta San Giulio: Easter-Oct, daily, every 30min, rest of year, only Sun and hols, every 45min. (Oct, Nov and Mar also Sat). Duration 5min. Price varies during the season. ☎ 0322 84 48 62. There is also a motor boat service (€2.07 round trip). For information, contact Sig. Urani ☎ 338 30 34 904 (mobile) or Sig. Fabris ☎ 330 87 98 39 (mobile).

Lago di Lugano

"Grande Giro del lago" cruise daily from Apr to mid-Oct, dep Lugano 2.40pm, return 5.15pm. Restaurant on board. Explanations in four languages. Other boat excursions possible year-round in Italian and Swiss waters. For information contact Società Navigazione del Lago di Lugano. ☎ 0041 91 97 15 223.

Lago di Como

Boat from Como to Colico, Tremezzo, Bellagio or Menaggio. From Tremezzo to Dongo, Domaso and Colico. Hydrofoil from Como to Tremezzo, Bellagio and Menaggio. Car ferries: between Bellagio, Varenna, Menaggio and Cadenabbia. All-day ticket valid for Lago Crociere, Sat night, in the summer. Discounts for groups and senior citizens. For information: ☎ 800 55 18 01.

Lago d'Iseo

Departures in high season, from Sarnico, two or twelve around the lake, return in late pm, lunch available on board, stop at Monte Isola. Duration approx 7hr. From Iseo afternoon excursion to the three islands, duration 3hr. From Sarnico, Iseo, Lovere or Montisola, tour of lake, afternoon departure and return in evening. For information contact LA.T. in Iseo, Lungolago Marcone 2C ☎ 030 98 03 209.

Lago di Garda

Boat tour from Desenzano and/or Peschiera to Riva del Garda, lunch available on board. Boat excursion across the lake taking in Sirmione, Gardone, Salò, Limone. Car ferry between Maderno and Torri. All-day tickets also available. Discounts for groups and senior citizens. Night cruise in summer. For information ☎ 800 55 18 01.

SIGHTSEEING

The towns and sights for each lake are listed in alphabetical order. For places in Switzerland see The Green Guide Switzerland.

WHERE TO EAT

• Budget

Café delle Rose – Via Ruga 36 – 28922 Verbania Pallanza (L. Maggiore) – ☎ 0323 55 81 01 – Closed Sun from May to Sep – ⌷ – €7. Fin de siècle ambience, enhanced by the furniture and furnishings which are mostly antique. At lunchtime, the café serves a variety of dishes and offers a very reasonably priced menu. In the evening the place transforms itself into a wine bar offering panini and other snacks late into the night. Excellent choice of music.

Al Porto – Via Zanitello 3 – 28922 Verbania Pallanza (L. Maggiore) – ☎ 0323 55 71 24 – Closed Nov, Mon and lunchtime – €15. An unusual rustic-style establishment, which resembles the galley of an old sailing ship. Open late into the night for drinks as well as food, from simple home-made snacks to meals. Different menu every day. There is a wonderful view of the lake from the terrace on the first floor.

Papa – Via Bell'Italia 40 – 37010 San Benedetto di Lugana (L. di Garda) – 2.5km/1mi west of Peschiera del Garda – ☎ 045 75 50 476 – €18/28. A traditional establishment with a loyal clientele who come back year after year to spend their holidays here. Regional cuisine, reasonable prices. Meals served under a lovely wisteria-covered pergola. Pleasantly decorated rooms.

Ristoro Antico – Via Bottelli 46 – 28041 Arona (L. Maggiore) – ☎ 0322 46 482 – Closed Sun evening, Mon, Jul – ▢ – Book – €18/29. This family-style restaurant serves very authentic, homely food. Great attention to detail and a menu that changes on a daily basis. Rustic-style interior with roof tiles exposed. Offers excellent value for money.

Il Gabbiano – Via I Maggio 19 – 28831 Baveno (L. Maggiore) – ☎ 0323 92 44 96 – Closed Wed, Thu (except 15 Jul-15 Sep), 15 Jan-15 Feb – Book – €18/34. Housed in an old farmhouse just outside Baveno, this is a trattoria-restaurant with a difference. The menu is a wonderful mixture of simplicity and creativity and the dishes are imaginatively presented. Rustic-style ambience.

Italia – Via Ugo Ara 58, Isola dei Pescatori – 28838 Stresa (L. Maggiore) – ☎ 0323 30 456 – Closed Jan – €21/26. The establishment comprises a bar area complete with an old coloured cement floor – you might just be able to spot a snack here – and a large terrace area overlooking the lake which is closed off and heated in winter. Fish from the lake is its staple fare, simply and traditionally prepared. Private moorings at night.

Aurora – Via Ciucani 1/7 – 25080 Soiano del Lago (L. di Garda) – 10km/6mi north of

Desenzano on S 572 – ☎ 0365 67 41 01 – Closed Wed – €22/28.50. A rare combination of quality and value for money. The cuisine is traditional and regional in style but has a very distinctive touch, and the dishes are stylishly presented. The dining room is light and airy, with elegant rustic-style furnishings.

• *Moderate*

Le Oche di Bracchio – *Via Bracchio 46 – 28802 Mergozzo (L. Maggiore) – 10km/6mi northwest of Pallanza* – ☎ 0323 80 122 – Closed 10 Jan-15 Feb – Book – €25/34. A simple, rather alternative establishment which caters for vegetarians and those following a macrobiotic diet. The building is rather basic but is well maintained. The setting is enhanced by the fruit trees. Also offers facilities for various Eastern disciplines. A great place if you're looking to "find yourself" or simply looking for a bit of peace and quiet.

Agriturismo Il Bagnolo – *Località Bagnolo – 25087 Serniga (L. di Garda) – 1km/0.6mi northwest of Gardone Riviera* – ☎ 0365 20 290 – Closed Tue, Oct-Apr open only Fri evening-Sun – Book – €27/35. This farm guesthouse is an excellent example of its kind, and boasts a wonderfully verdant setting. In keeping with the agriturismo concept, the cooking is based on the farm's own produce and is delicious. Elegant rooms with a romantic feel about them and all very individual in style.

Gatto Nero – *Via Monte Santo 69 – 22012 Rovenna (L. di Como) – North of Cernobbio* – ☎ 031 51 20 42 – Closed Mon, Tue lunchtime – Book – €35/47. A very popular establishment where people come to enjoy the panoramic setting complete with views of the lake and the mountains. Traditional cooking with a number of fish dishes on the menu. Warm and cosy inside, with rustic-style decor. The view from the summer terrace is breathtaking. Would appeal to couples looking for romance!

WHERE TO STAY

• *Budget*

Agriturismo Il Monterosso – *Località Cima Monterosso – 28922 Verbania (L. Maggiore) – 6km/3.6mi from Pallanza on the road which winds its way up to the top of Colle Monterosso* – ☎ 0323 55 65 10 – Fax 0323 51 97 06 – ilmonterosso@iol.it – Closed Jan, Feb; restaurant closed Mon and Tue – 8 double rm €50 ☕ – Rest €40. What a setting to this little turreted farmhouse situated at the top of Colle Monterosso! It is surrounded by chestnut, pine and beech woods and boasts breathtaking views over the four surrounding lakes below as well as the Monte Rosa massif. This agriturismo combines good taste with simplicity and authentic home cooking. A good spot for walking and horse riding.

Hotel Il Chiostro – *Via F.lli Cervi 14 – 28921 Verbania Intra (L. Maggiore)* – ☎ 0323 40 40 77 – Fax 0323 40 12 31 – chiostrovb@libero.it – 🅿 ♿ – 108 rm €36.15/77.47 ☕. This lovely hotel is housed in what was a 17C convent and an old cotton factory which have been sympathetically converted. The hotel has also managed to retain some of the monastic calm while offering all mod cons – a rare achievement. The frescoed reading room and the charming cloisters are particularly lovely. The rooms, some of which look out onto the cloister, are simple in style. Highly recommended.

• *Moderate*

Hotel Miravalle – *Via Monte Oro 9 – 38066 Riva del Garda (L. di Garda)* – ☎ 0464 55 23 35 – Fax 0464 52 17 07 – Closed Nov-Mar – 🅿 🏊 – 29 rm €49.06/82.62 ☕. The main attractions here are the location (not far from the centre), the lovely garden and the swimming pool. The rooms are pleasantly old-fashioned and the buffet-style breakfast is particularly good.

Albergo Silvio – *Via Carcano 10 / 12 – 22021 Bellagio (L. di Como) – 2km/1.2mi southwest of Bellagio* – ☎ 031 95 03 22 – Fax 031 95 09 12 – Closed 10 Jan-20 Feb. – ⛔ 🅿 – 17 rm €51.65/77.47 ☕ – Restaurant. €23/36. Quiet, simply decorated rooms (particularly those in the roof which are very attractive). However, the main attraction is the cooking. Fish from the lake – caught by the owner himself – feature large on the menu. Meals served in a lovely dining room with fine views or under the large pergola. Situated very near the centre of town.

Hotel Palazzina – *Via Libertà 10 – 25084 Gargnano (L. di Garda)* – ☎ 0365 71 118 – Fax 0365 71 528 – Closed 10 Oct-Mar – 🅿 🏊 – 25 rm €49.06/69.72 – ☕ €8.01 – Restaurant €18/23. This popular, family-run hotel has a very easy-going, 1960s feel about it and its loyal clientele return year after year. The two large panoramic terraces, one of which has a swimming pool, are particularly lovely.

Hotel Cangrande – *Corso Cangrande 16 – 37017 Lazise (L. di Garda) – 5km/3mi south of Bardolino on N 249* – ☎ 045 64 70 410 – Fax 045 64 70 390 – Closed 20 Dec-10 Feb – 🅿 – 17 rm €57/99 ☕. This hotel is housed in a 1930s building, close to the medieval walls, which also serves as the offices for the Girasole winery. The elegant rooms are modern in style. The huge barrels in the public areas add to the atmosphere. Wine enthusiasts might like to visit the extensive cellar.

Hotel La Fontana – *Strada statale del Sempione 1 – 28838 Stresa (L. Maggiore)* – ☎ 0323 32 707 – Fax 0323 32 708 – Closed Dec and Jan – 🅿 – 20 rm €60/70 – ☕ €7. The 1940s villa which houses this hotel is surrounded by lovely gardens. All the rooms have a little terrace with a view of lake. Decor is slightly retro in style. Centrally located and reasonably priced.

Hotel Rigoli – *Via Piave 48 – 28831 Baveno (L. Maggiore)* – ☎ 0323 92 47 56 – Fax 0323 92 51 56 – Closed Nov-Easter – 🅿 – 31 rm €67.14/87.80 – ☕ €9.30 – Restaurant €22/35. The rooms are spacious, with modern pale-coloured furnishings, and the public areas are sunny and pleasant. This hotel exudes a real holiday atmosphere, nowhere more than the lakeside terrace-garden area which has lovely views out to the Borromee Islands. Half-board rates available.

Hotel Desirée – *Via San Pietro 2 – 25019 Sirmione (L. di Garda) –* ☎ *030 99 05 244 – Fax 030 91 62 41 – Closed mid Nov-mid Mar –* 🅿 🅾 *(payment) – 34 rm €69/94* 🍽 *– Rest €21/26.* A simple, unpretentious hotel in a quiet location, not far from the beach and the thermal baths. The furnishings in the public areas are a little old-fashioned but the rooms have their own balcony. The dining room is lovely and light, with windows on three sides.

Hotel Garni La Contrada dei Monti – *Via Contrada dei Monti 10 – 28016 Orta S. Giulio (L. d'Orta) –* ☎ *0322 90 51 14 – Fax 0322 90 58 63 – www.orta.net/lacontradadeimonti/ – Closed 3-31 Jan –* ♿ *– 17 €69.72/77.47 –* 🍽 *€7.75.* A jewel of light and harmony, this charming little hotel is housed in an 18C palazzo which has been lovingly restored. Great attention to detail in the rooms: mirrors with hand-painted frames in the bathrooms, a frescoed vaulted ceiling in the hall. Would appeal to couples looking for romance!

TAKING A BREAK

Bar di Lago – *Via Mazzini 13 – 28832 Feriolo (L. Maggiore) –* ☎ *0323 28 101 – Open daily in summer, 7am-midnight; rest of the year, Thu-Tue.* Located off the beaten track in a quiet, little marina between Stresa and Baveno. The bar has wonderful views over the lake and is a great spot for savouring an ice cream or a granita ... while dangling your feet in the water!

Caffè Broletto – *Piazza del Popolo 24 – 28041 Arona (L. Maggiore) –* ☎ *0322 46 640 – Tue-Sun 10am-2am, closed 10 days in winter.* From one of the loveliest outdoor terraces in Arona you get a view of this traffic-free piazza, a small church and the blue water of the lake. Try one of the fruit cocktails (with or without alcohol).

Gardesana – *Piazza Calderini 20 – 37010 Torri del Benaco (L. di Garda) –* ☎ *045 72 25 411 – gardesana@easynet.it – Summer, 9am-midnight; rest of the year, Wed-Mon, closed 10 Nov-Jan.* Nestling between the splendid tower which overlooks the port and the old houses with their wrought-iron balconies, is an elegant hotel and tea room. Try and get a seat under the little portico which is covered in flowers. In summer, musicians come to play classical music every evening.

Gelateria Cremeria Fantasy – *Via Principessa Margherita 38 – 28838 Stresa (L. Maggiore) –* ☎ *0349 35 64 327 – 9-24, Closed Nov-Jan except public holidays.* While it is not easy to find a gelateria which stands out from the rest, try this little parlour. The 32 flavours of ice cream and semifreddi – all home-made – are exceptionally good.

Gelateria Oasi – *Via Ruga 15 – 28922 Verbania Pallanza (L. Maggiore) –* ☎ *0323 50 19 02 – Mon-Sat 10am-9.30pm, Sun 9.30am-24.30am.* Pistacchio, walnut, vanilla, carrot, basil ... just some of the numerous and unusual flavours produced by this artisanal ice cream parlour which was established four years ago. Very popular.

LEISURE

Garda Yachting Charter – *Lungolago Zanardelli – 25088 Maderno (L. di Garda) – In the port, beyond the landing stage –* ☎ *0365 54 83 47 – gyc@mail.gyc.it – Book ahead.* Motorboats (with or without a licence) and sailing boats (3.65m/12ft to 8.50m/26ft) for hire.

Isole Borromee★★★

Town plan in the Michelin Atlas Italy, under Stresa. A large area of the lake was given to the princely Borromeo family in the 15C but only gradually did they purchase all the islands in the tiny archipelago. In the 17C, Charles III established a residence on **Isola Bella**, named after his wife, Isabella. The palace, built in the Lombard Baroque style, has several state rooms – medals room, state hall, music room, Napoleon's room, ballroom and Hall of Mirrors. The most unusual feature is the caves where those living in the palace could find cooler air on very hot days. The decoration of light and dark coloured stones and shells is designed to represent an underwater world. The gardens filled with a variety of exotic plants, form an amazing Baroque composition, a truncated pyramid of ten terraces ornamented with statues, basins, fountains and architectural perspectives simulating stage sets. At the top of the garden is the shell-shaped "amphitheatre" providing an extraordinary scenic effect. Boat trips are available to the **Isola dei Pescatori**, which has retained its original charm, and the **Isola Madre**, an island totally covered with a splendid garden of flowers and rare or exotic plants. In the palazzo, note the Puppet Theatre that once belonged to the House of Borromeo.

Cannero Riviera★★

The houses of this resort rise in tiers above the lake amid olive trees, vineyards, and orange and lemon groves.

Cannobio★

Cannobio is a small resort near the Swiss border. In addition to the Renaissance church of the Madonna della Pietà there are several other fine old houses. About 3km/2mi out of town *(on the Malesco road)* is the **Orrido di S. Anna★**, a precipice formed by the torrent.

Cerro★

This peaceful village on a well-shaded part of the lakeside has a tiny fishing port and an interesting **ceramics museum**.

Laveno Mombello

From here a cablecar climbs up to the summit of **Sasso del Ferro★★** from where there is a vast **panorama** over the entire Lake District. *Daily 10am-5.30pm. For information* ☎ *0332 66 80 12.*

Pallanza★★

Everywhere flowers deck and scent this wonderful resort. Its **quays★★**, sheltered by magnolias and oleanders, offer lovely views of the lake. On the outskirts of the town on the Intra road is the **Villa Taranto★★** with its famous **gardens** featuring azaleas, heather, rhododendrons, camellias, dahlias and maples. (&) *Open daily, 8.30am-6.30pm. Closed Nov-Mar. €7.* ☎ *0323 40 45 55 or 0323 55 66 67, www.villataranto.it*

Eremo di Santa Caterina del Sasso

About 500m/550yd from Leggiuno. Open daily, Apr to Oct 8.30am-12pm and 2.30-6pm, rest of year 9am-noon and 2-5pm (Nov to Feb, Sat-Sun and hols only). Donation appreciated. ☎ *0332 64 71 72, www.provincia.va.it/santacaterina*

This hermitage was founded in the 13C by an anchorite, Alberto Besozzo. In a picturesque setting, the building clings to a rock overlooking the lake.

Stresa★★

Town plan in the Michelin Atlas Italy. This pleasant resort, which attracts many artists and writers, enjoys a magnificent situation on the west bank of Lago Maggiore facing the Borromean Islands, and is a delightful place with all the amenities of both a holiday resort in spring, summer and autumn and a winter sports resort. The ski slopes are on **Mottarone★★★** *(take the Armeno road: 29km/18mi; the scenic toll-road from Alpino: 18km/11mi; or the cablecar)* which from its summit provides a magnificent **panorama** of the lake, the Alps and the Monte Rosa massif. *Charge for access via Strada Borromea: €4 (car); €2.50 (motorcycle) round trip with cableway from Stresa. For information on Strada Borromea* ☎ *0323 30 399.*

Standing on the outskirts of the town, off the Arona road, is the **Villa Pallavicino★** with its wildlife park. *Open daily, 9am-6pm. Closed Nov-Feb. €6.40.* ☎ *0323 31 533; www.parcozoopallavicino.it*

From Stresa, follow the Vezzo Gignese direction.

At **Gignese** *(8km/5mi southwest)* there is the **Museo dell'Ombrello e del Parasole**, a small, interesting museum which illustrates the history, from 1850 to the present day, of the umbrella and sunshade, particularly in the context of Lago Maggiore which has a celebrated umbrella-making tradition. (&) *Open Tue-Sun, 10am-noon and 3-6pm. Closed Mon (except Jul and Aug). €2.* ☎ *0323 20 80 64.*

LAGO D'ORTA★★

Lake Orta, one of the smallest Italian lakes, is separated from Lake Maggiore by the peak known as Il Mottarone, rising to the northeast. It is perhaps the most delightful and the most gracious of all the lakes with its setting of wooded hills and the tiny islet, Isola San Giulio.

Orta San Giulio

The lakesides have been inhabited since earliest times and in the 4C the people were converted to Christianity by St Julius.

Chiesa della Madonna dal Sasso★★

5km/3mi from Alzo. From the church terrace there is a magnificent view of the lake in its verdant mountain setting.

Orta San Giulio★★

This small resort has a delightful site on the tip of a peninsula. The alleyways are lined with old houses adorned with elegant wrought-iron balconies. The **Palazzotto★** or 16C town hall is decorated with frescoes.

Sacro Monte d'Orta★

1.5km/1mi from Orta. This sanctuary dedicated to St Francis of Assisi and set on a hilltop comprises 20 chapels. These are decorated in the Baroque style and the frescoes serve as background to groups of lifelike terracotta statues.

Isola di San Giulio★★

Boats leave from Orta. On this jewel of an island, 300m/330yds long and 160m/175yds wide, stands the **basilica di San Giulio** which is said to date from the 4C, when St Julius came to the island. Inside there is a lovely 12C **ambo★** decorated with frescoes by the school of Gaudenzio Ferrari (16C). Note also, in the crypt, the shrine containing the relics of St Julius. *Open 9.30am-12.05pm and 2-6.35pm (winter 5.35pm), Sun and hols 9.30-10.45am, 2-4.45pm and 5.45-6.35pm (winter 5.35pm). No visits during Mass. No charge. Closed till 11am Mon.* ☎ 0322 91 19 37.

Varallo

About 20km/12mi west. This industrial and commercial town in the Val Sesia is famous for its pilgrimage to the **Sacro Monte★★** with its 43 chapels. Again these are decorated with frescoes and groups of life-size terracotta figures (16C-18C) which illustrate the Fall of Man and scenes from the Life of Christ. They were the work of several artists including Gaudenzio Ferrari (1480-1546), a local painter who was a pupil of Leonardo da Vinci. Ferrari showed definite originality and picturesque realism in his work.

LAGO DI LUGANO★★

Most of **Lake Lugano**, also known as Lake Ceresio by the Italians, is in Swiss territory. Lugano is wilder than Lakes Maggiore and Como and with its irregular outline has none of the grandeur or majesty of the others. Its mild climate and its steep mountain countryside make it an ideal place for a holiday.

Campione d'Italia★

An Italian enclave in Switzerland, Campione is a colourful, smiling village which is highly popular on account of its casino. A chapel, the oratory of San Pietro, is a graceful building dating from 1326. It was the work of the famous **Maestri Campionesi** who vied with the Maestri Comacini in spreading the Lombard style throughout Italy *(see Italian Art, p 86).*

Lanzo d'Intelvi★

Set in the heart of a pine and larch forest, this resort (alt 907m/2 976ft) is also a ski centre in winter. Some 6km/4mi away is the **belvedere di Sighignola★★★**, also known as the "balcony of Italy" because of its extensive view of Lugano, the Alps as far as Monte Rosa and on a clear day Mont Blanc.

Varese

13km/8mi southwest of Porto Ceresio. Town plan in the Michelin Atlas Italy. This busy but pleasant modern town stands not far from the lake of the same name. One of its advantages is a mild and sunny climate due to its proximity to the Italian lakes. At 3km/ 5mi to the west rises the hilltop known as **Sacro Monte★★**, with its important pilgrimage church dedicated to the Virgin. The road up to the basilica is lined with 14 chapels decorated with frescoes in *trompe l'œil* and groups of life-size terracotta figures. From the summit there is a magnificent **view★★** of the lakes and surrounding mountains.

At a distance of 10km/ 6mi to the northwest is the long mountainous ridge, **Campo dei Fiori★★**, which raises its forest-clad slopes above the plain. There is a vast **panorama★★** of the Lake District.

About 10km/ 6mi to the south, on the road to Tradate, is **Castiglione Olona**, which has some fine **frescoes★** by **Masolino da Panicale** (c 1383-1440) in the Collegiata *(Story of the Virgin Mary)* and in the Baptistery *(Story of St John the Baptist).*

Villa Cicogna Mozzoni a Bisuschio

8km/5mi northeast of Varese on the road to Porto Ceresio. (ở) *Guided tours only, by reservation. Closed Easter, mid-Oct to mid-Mar €6. For information on opening times* ☎ *0347 47 11 34.* The villa, set in fine Italian terraced gardens, was originally a hunting lodge in the 15C which was extended in the 16C with the addition of a residence. In the first floor rooms, complete with furnishings, the upper part of the walls and the ceilings are adorned with fine frescoes in the Renaissance style.

LAGO DI COMO★★★

Set entirely within Lombardy, **Lake Como**, of all the Italian lakes, has the most variety. Pretty villages, tiny ports, villas in shady exotic gardens succeed one another along the banks of this Pre-Alpine lake. Bellagio stands on a promontory at the confluence of its three arms.

Bellagio★★★

Bellagio occupies a magnificent site on a promontory dividing Lake Lecco from the southern arm of Lake Como. It has a worldwide reputation for the friendliness of its people and its excellent amenities. The splendid lakeside **gardens★★** of **Villa Serbelloni** and **Villa Melzi**, with their fragrant and luxuriant vegetation, are the main sights in Bellagio. It is pleasant to stroll up and down the pretty, steep little streets on the hillside. *Villa Serbelloni: Open daily except Mon, 11am-12.30pm and 4-5.30pm. Closed Nov to Mar. €5.50. For information and reservations* ☎ *031 95 02 04; www.bellagiolakecomo.com*
Villa Melzi: Open daily, 9am-6pm. Closed Oct-Feb. €5.☎ *031 95 02 04.*

Bellano

This small industrial town stands on the River Pioverna at the mouth of the valley (Valsassina), with the great mass of the Grigne towering behind. The attractive 14C **church** with a façade by Giovanni da Campione is in the Lombard Gothic style.

Cadenabbia★★

This delightful resort occupies an admirable site opposite Bellagio. A splendid avenue of plane trees, Via del Paradiso, links the resort with the Villa Carlotta and Tremezzo.
From a chapel, **Capella di San Martino** *(1hr30min on foot there and back)* there is a good **view★★** of Bellagio on its promontory, Lakes Como and Lecco and of the Grigne.

Cernobbio★★

This splendid location is famous for the **Villa d'Este**, the opulent 16C residence now transformed into a hotel and surrounded by fine parkland *(access to both the villa and the park is limited to hotel guests)*. The best view of the villa (from the ground) is from Piazza del Risorgimento, near the landing stage with the Liberty-style roof.

Chiavenna

Ancient Chiavenna owes its name to its key (*clavis* in Latin) position in the Splügen and Maloja transalpine passes between Italy and Switzerland. Chiavenna is also famous for its **crotti**, restaurants housed in natural caves and serving local specialities (found only in Valtellina) such as *pizzoccheri* (buckwheat pasta served with melted cheese) and *bresaola* (dried meat). Nearby, above the Palazzo Balbini (15C) is **Il Paradiso**, a rock that was once a fortified site and is now set out as a pleasant garden, the **Giardino botanico e archeologico**. *Open daily except Mon, 10am-noon and 2-6pm in summer, rest of year 2-5pm, Sun and hols 10am-noon and 2-5pm. €1.55.* ☎ *0343 33 795.*

See also the strange frescoes decorating the exterior of the Palazzo Pretorio and the doorways in the Via Dolzino on which the inscriptions date back to the days of the Reformation.

Collegiata di San Lorenzo – ♿ *Open Mar to Oct, daily except Mon, 3-6pm, Sat also 10am-noon, rest of year, daily 2-4pm, Sat also 10am-noon, Sun to 5pm. €3.10. Call in advance for Baptistery* ☎ *0343 37 152.*
The Collegiate Church of St Lawrence, built during the Romanesque period and reconstructed in the 16C after a fire, contains two paintings, one by Pietro Ligari (1738) (2nd chapel on the right) and one by Giuseppe Nuvoloni (1657) (1st chapel on the left).
The **Baptistery** has a Romanesque **font★** (1156) in *ollare* stone: the name of the stone being a reference to its being used to make *olle* (urns and vases). The low reliefs illustrate a baptismal scene depicting various social classes (nobleman hunting with his falcon, soldier and craftsman), a child with his godfather, a priest and acolyte, and members of the clergy. The inscription reveals the identity of the sponsors of the work. The **treasury** houses a wonderful 12C binding for an evangelistary.

Strada del passo dello Spluga★★

30km/19mi from Chiavenna to the pass. The Splügen Pass Road is one of the boldest and most spectacular in the Alps. The **Campodolcino-Pianazzo section★★★** is grandiose as it climbs the sheer mountainside in tight hairpin bends.

Como★

The city was already prosperous under the Romans but reached its zenith in the 11C. It was destroyed by the Milanese in 1127, rebuilt by the Emperor Frederick Barbarossa and from 1355 onwards shared the fortunes of Milan. The **Maestri Comacini** known as early as the 7C, were masons, builders and sculptors who spread the Lombard style *(see Italian Art, p 86)* throughout Italy and Europe.

Duomo★★ – Begun in the late 14C the cathedral was completed during the Renaissance and crowned in the 18C with an elegant dome by the architect, Juvarra. It has a remarkable **façade★★** which was richly decorated from 1484 onwards by the **Rodari brothers**, who also worked on the **north door**, known as the Porta della Rana because of the frog *(rana)* carved on one of the pillars. They were also responsible for the exquisitely delicate **south door**.

The **interior★**, full of solemn splendour, combines Gothic architecture and Renaissance decoration. In addition to the curious banners, hung between the pillars, and the magnificent 16C-17C **tapestries★**, there are canvases by B Luini *(Adoration of the Magi, Virgin and Child with Saints★)*, and G Ferrari *(Flight into Egypt)*, in the south aisle as well as a *Descent from the Cross★* (1489) carved by Tommaso Rodari in the north aisle. Note also the organ in five parts, comprising 96 registers and 6 000 pipes. Various 17C artists were involved in its construction although its current form is the work of the organ-makers Balbiani and Vegezzi-Bossi.

Adjoining the façade is the **Broletto★★**, or 13C town hall, with an arcade at street level and a lovely storey of triple-arched windows above.

Chiesa di San Fedele★ – In the heart of the picturesque old quarter, this church is in the Romanesque Lombard style. The nave and two aisles are terminated by a splendid polygonal Romanesque **chancel★** with radiating chapels. The whole east end is graced by two storeys of arcading.

Basilica di Sant'Abbondio★ – This masterpiece of Romanesque Lombard architecture was consecrated in 1093. The noble but severe **façade★** has a lovely doorway. The nave and four aisles are separated by columns. The remarkable 14C **frescoes★** evoke the Life of Christ.

Villa Olmo – *3km/2mi north by S 35 and then S 340 to the right. Open Mon-Sat, 9.30am-noon and 3-6pm. Closed Sun and hols. No charge. ☎ 031 24 25 43.*
This is a large neo-Classical building dating from the late 18C, with a small theatre and gardens, from which there is a lovely **view★** of Como in its lakeside setting.

Dongo

It was in this village that Mussolini and his mistress, Clara Petacci, were captured on 27 April 1945.

Gravedona

This fishing village has an attractive Romanesque church, **Santa Maria del Tiglio★**. The 5C baptistery was remodelled in the Lombard style in the 12C.

Menaggio★★

Favoured by a cool summer breeze, this is one of the lake's smart resorts.

Abbazia di Piona★

2km/1mi from Olgiasca. This graceful monastery, which was founded in the 11C by Cluniac monks, and which adopted Cistercian rule a century later under St Bernard of Clairvaux (1090-1153), has pretty Lombard Romanesque **cloisters★** (1252).

Torno

On the outskirts of this attractive port, the 14C church of **San Giovanni** has a fine Lombard Renaissance **doorway★**.

Tremezzo★★★

A mild climate and a beautiful site combine to make Tremezzo a favourite place for a stay. The terraced gardens, **Parco comunale★**, are a haven of peace.
The 18C **Villa Carlotta★★★** *(entrance beside the Grand Hotel Tremezzo)* occupies an admirable site facing the Grigne Massif.

The enchanting Villa Carlotta, Tremezzo

In the 20C the problem was exacerbated by the growth of industrial sites around Mestre and Porto Maghera accommodating petrol-tankers with obvious implications on the environment of the lagoon. The reduction in oxygenated water flowing through the canals of Venice is gradually eroding the ability of plant and marine life to survive.

Tidal flooding

The tide along these coasts can fluctuate wildly; for it to be classified as tidal flooding its level has to reach or exceed 1.10m/3ft 6in. The last such occurrence happened on 4 November 1966 when consequences were felt way beyond the shores of Venice – the Arno overflowed in Florence with tragic results. That year an alarming prediction was rumoured that Venice might possibly disappear – fortunately, radical action against further subsidence, including the closure of artesian wells on the mainland, have proved the prophecy false.

Similar crises of this kind are documented as far back as 589. Contemporary personal accounts are terrifying. **Paolo Diacono** (c 720-99) wrote of the first flood tide: "non in terra neque in aqua sumus viventes" (neither on earth nor in water were we alive). Records from 1410 state that "almost one thousand people coming from the fair at Mestre and other places drowned".

Since the 17C the water level of the Venetian lagoon has dropped by 60cm/24in. In past centuries, once every five years, the tide would rise above the damp-proof foundations made of Istrian stone that were built to protect the houses against salt deposits. Nowadays, in the lower areas, these foundations are immersed in water more than 40 times in a single year and the buildings can do very little to stall the degradation process.

Flora and fauna

At the lower end of the food chain are different types of molluscs. But the principal category of fauna is undoubtedly that of the **fish** kingdom, which has defined both the very character of the lagoon with its distinctive collection in shoals around sandbanks, and the interaction of man within this environment as he seeks to exploit such rich resources.

Crab and **shrimp** are central to the fishing industry and to Venetian cuisine. From a boat it soon becomes obvious where the fishing banks are situated as these attract various species of aquatic birds: **wild duck** (mallard and teal), tens of thousands of

Directory

WHERE TO EAT

• *Budget*

Al Bragosso del Bepi el Ciosoto – *Via Romea 120 – 30010 Sant'Anna di Chioggia – 8km/5mi south of Chioggia on S 309 Romea – ☎ 041 49 50 395 – Closed Wed, Jan – 🖻 – €19/34*. The counter and bar made out of an old boat set the scene in this lovely trattoria which specialises in fish. The dishes are prepared with the freshest of ingredients, all of an excellent quality. The prices are very reasonable. Also has accommodation.

Da Luigi – *Via Dante 25 – 30020 Torre di Fine – 40km/24mi northeast of Venice – ☎ 0421 23 74 07 – Closed Wed (except Jun-Aug), Oct – 🖻 – €20/30*. This trattoria is renowned for its traditional, homely cooking. Great care is taken to use produce of a high quality. The seafood dishes alla griglia are excellent. Also has rooms which are simply furnished but comfortable.

La Colombara – *Via Zilli 42 – 33051 Aquileia – 2km/1mi northwest of Aquileia – ☎ 0431 91 513 – Closed Mon – €21/31*. Although it is a little off the beaten track, this fish restaurant is well worth the detour. Cooked with great attention to detail and a lightness of touch, the dishes are always prepared with the freshest ingredients. Rustic-style decor and a welcoming family atmosphere. Pleasant outside dining area.

WHERE TO STAY

• *Budget*

Hotel Cristina – *Viale Martiri della Libertà 11 – 34073 Grado – ☎ 0431 80 989 – Fax 0431 85 946 – Closed Oct-May – 🅿 – 26 rm €36/77.50 ⚏ – Restaurant €22/32*. More of a guesthouse than a hotel, in a panoramic setting. The 1970s feel extends to the public areas as well as the rooms. Lots of outdoor areas for lounging around. Meals served outside in summer. Authentic, homely cooking.

• *Moderate*

Hotel Park – *Lungomare Adriatico 74 – 30019 Lido di Sottomarina – 10km/6mi east of Chioggia – ☎ 041 49 65 032 – Fax 041 49 01 11 – 🅿 🖻 – 41 rm €56.81/67.14 ⚏ – Restaurant €16/27*. A simple, family-run establishment situated right on the beach. It has a restaurant and a private bathing area. The rooms are spacious, the decor functional.

Eurotel – *Calle Mendelssohn 13, at Lignano Riviera – 33054 Lignano Sabbiadoro – 7km/4mi southwest of Lignano Sabbiadoro – ☎ 0431 42 89 92 – Fax 0431 42 87 31 – eulignano@orgeurotels.it – 🏊 🖻 – 70 rm €67.14/72.30 ⚏*. One of the main attractions of this 1970s-style hotel is its peaceful, verdant setting. The rooms are spacious and most of them have a small cooking area. Private beach and swimming pool. Free umbrella and lounger for guests staying on a weekly basis.

coots, **herons** and **marsh harriers**. The very rich bird life of the lagoon also includes the little **egret**, recognisable by its elegant carriage and startlingly white feathers with which ladies adorned themselves at the beginning of the 20C.

Among the mammals **rodents** provides a somewhat harmful presence. The ra the so-called *pantagena*, is at home anywhere, on the city squares as well as in rul bish dumps and attics.

The sandbanks are abundantly cloaked in vegetation: **glasswort**, **sea lavender** an **asters** turn the mounds first green, then red, then blue, then grey. Rooted in th water are various **reeds** and **rushes** with long stalks and spiky flowers.

Tour

Following the coastline, departing from Grado and finishing in Chioggia. 220km/132mi

Grado⌂⌂

At the time of the barbarian invasions the inhabitants of Aquileia founded Gradc which was from the 5C to the 9C the residence of the Patriarchs of Aquileia. Today Grado is a busy little fishing port and seaside resort with a growing reputation. The town situated in the middle of the lagoon is an imposing sight.

Quartiere vecchio★ – This is a picturesque district with a network of narrow alleys *(calli)* running between the canal port and the cathedral. The Duomo di Santa Eufemia, is on the basilical plan and dates from the 6C. It has marble columns with Byzantine capitals, a 6C mosaic pavement, a 10C ambo and a valuable silver-gilt **altarpiece★**, a Venetian work of the 14C. Beside the cathedral a row of sarcophagi and tombs leads up to the 6C basilica of Santa Maria delle Grazie which has some original mosaics and fine capitals.

Aquileia

While the plan of the town was being outlined (181 BC) with a plough, according to Roman custom, an eagle (aquila) hovered overhead: hence its name. Aquileia was a flourishing market under the Roman Empire and was used as general head-quarters by Augustus during his conquest of the Germanic tribes. The town then became one of Italy's most important patriarchates (554-1751) ruled by bishops.

Basilica★★ – The Romanesque church was built in the 11C on the foundations of a 4C building and restored in the 14C. It is preceded by a porch and flanked by a campanile. The interior with its nave and two aisles is in the form of a Latin cross. The splen-did 4C mosaic **paving★★**, which is one of the largest and richest in western Christendom, depicts religious scenes. The timber ceiling and the arcades are both 14C, the capitals are Romanesque and the decoration of the transept Renaissance. The 9C Carolingian crypt known as **Cripta degli affreschi** is decorated with fine Romanesque **frescoes★★**.

The **Cripta degli Scavi** is reached from the north aisle. Finds from the excavations are assembled here, notably admirable 4C mosaic **paving★★**. *Open Apr to Oct, Mon-Sat, 8.30am-7pm, rest of year Mon-Sat, 8.30am-12.30pm and 2.30-5.30pm, Sun and hols 8.30am-1pm and 2.30-6pm. Basilica: no charge. Crypts: €2. ☎ 0431 91 067 (Basilica), 0431 91 97 19 (office); www.aquileia.it*

Aree archeologiche★ – (&) *Open daily, 8.30am to 1hr before sunset. Closed 1 Jan, 25 Dec. No charge. ☎ 0431 91 016; www.museoarcheo-aquileia.it*

Excavations have uncovered the remains of Roman Aquileia: behind the basilica, the Via Sacra leading to the river port, houses and the forum. The **Musei Archeologico e Paleocristiano** (Archaeological and Early-Christian Museums) contain an import-ant collection of finds from local excavations. The remarkable series of portraits, including those of Tiberius and of Augustus as a youth, in the archaeological museum is noteworthy. *Museo Archeologico & Open Tue-Sat 8.30am-7.30pm, Mon 8.30am-2pm. Closed 1 Jan, 1 May €4. ☎ 0431 91 016; www.museoarcheo-aquileia.it Museo Paleocristiano: Open Tue-Sun, 8.30am-7.30pm, Mon 8.30am-1.15pm. Closed 1 Jan, 1 May. No charge. ☎ 0431 91 131; www.museoarcheo-aquileia.it*

Lignano

Lignano, the largest seaside resort on the coastline of Friuli, lies on a long, sandy peninsula covered with pine woods. Stretching east from the mouth of the Tagliamento, it closes off part of the Marano Lagoon, an angling reserve. Its **beach★★**, facing Grado, the Trieste Gulf and the coastline of Istria (which is often visible), is popular for its 8km/5mi of fine, golden sand that slopes very gently into the sea; it is a safe holiday resort for families with children. The resort comprises three areas. At the tip of the peninsula is **Lignano Sabbiadoro**, the oldest part of the town and a convivial place with old houses, shopping streets and a large yacht-ing marina (the *darsena*). Separated from Sabbiadoro by a large expanse of pine wood that belongs to the Vatican and is reserved for children's holiday camps is **Lignano Pineta**, an elegant, modern part of the town laid out like a spiral and divided off by streets radiating out from the central square. **Lignano Riviera** gets its name from the nearby Tagliamento. The water offshore from its beach is slightly colder but the vegetation is thicker here. ... ... holidaymakers can enjoy the 18-hole golf course and visit the zoo, the **Parco zoo Punt...** ... which presents animals from all over the world. ♿ *Open Mar to Oct, 9am to sunset, re... ... ...d hols, 9am-4pm. Closed Nov to Jan. €8.* ☎ *0431 42 87 75, www.parcozoopuntaverde.it* ...

Venezia★★★ *see VENEZIA*

Chioggia
Strictly speaking, Chioggia is not one of the lagoon islands, resting as it does on two parallel islands, linked to terra firma by a long bridge.

La città – The main street, the **Corso del Popolo**, runs parallel to the Canale della Vena – the Fossa Clodia of ancient times – rendered more colourful and lively by its fish market, to terminate in Piazzetta Vigo. The column bearing a winged lion marks the end of the Fossa Clodia. To cross the canal, walk over the stone bridge, the Ponte Vigo built in 1685.

The corso is dotted with the Duomo and several of the Chioggia churches: among these are the **Church of San Andrea** with its 11C Romanesque campanile rising from a square base; **San Giacomo** which was rebuilt in the 18C and **San Francesco delle Muneghette** founded in the 15C but rebuilt in the 18C.

The island's principal church is the **Duomo★**, dedicated to Santa Maria Assunta, which was founded in the 11C. It was razed to the ground by fire, and so was rebuilt in 1633 by Baldassare Longhena (1598-1682). It is still shadowed by its 14C square bell tower, although originally, the church would have been orientated on a different axis.

The Isola di San Domenico extends at the far end of Chioggia. This promontory – reached by following Calle di San Croce, beyond Ponte Vigo – accommodates in the church, a painting of Saint Paul by Carpaccio (c 1465-c 1526). The campanile is 13C.

L'Aquila★

Overlooked by Gran Sasso, the highest massif in the Abruzzi region, this rather austere town boasts both a long history and a wealth of artistic treasures. Equally enticing are its charming buildings and the intriguing legends surrounding its mysterious past.

Location
Population 69 839 – Michelin map 430 O 22 – Local map in the Michelin Atlas Italy – Abruzzi. L'Aquila lies at the heart of the Abruzzi, off A 24. ▯ *Piazza Santa Maria di Paganica 5,* ☎ *0862 41 08 08; Via XX Settembre 8,* ☎ *0862 22 306. Surrounding area: see ABRUZZO.*

Background

According to legend L'Aquila was founded in the 13C when the inhabitants of 99 castles in the valley at the foot of the Gran Sasso joined forces to form a city in which each castle had a corresponding church, square and fountain. Caught up in the vicissitudes of the Kingdom of Naples, L'Aquila was besieged, destroyed and rebuilt several times until it became the second most important city of the Kingdom in the 15C. Rich in splendid monuments, it also had a resurgence thanks to the commerce all over Europe of saffron, "red gold", which grows on the plateaux of Navelli. This was the period in which St Bernardino of Siena (who died in L'Aquila in 1444) resided in the city; the initials IHS (Iesus Hominum Salvator – Jesus Saviour of Mankind) marked on several doorways, bear witness to his presence.

Worth a Visit

Basilica di Santa Maria di Collemaggio★★
Open daily, 8am-noon and 5pm to sunset. No charge. ☎ *0862 23 165.*
For both its historical and architectural value this is the most celebrated basilica in the Abruzzi region. It was begun in 1287 in the Romanesque style on the initiative of Pietro da Morrone, the future Pope **Celestine V**, who was crowned there in 1294. The ample, horizontally crenellated **façade★★**, beautifully adorned with geometrical patterns in white and pink stone, is pierced with rose windows and doorways added in the 15C. On the left side of the basilica stands the **Porta Santa**, a beautiful richly decorated Romanesque doorway. The interior contains the 16C Lombard Renaissance-style tomb of Pope Saint Celestine V.

Chiesa di San Bernardino★★

Open daily 8a̶̶ ̶ ̶ ̶and 4pm to sunset.
☎ 0862 22 255.

This superb church, a masterpiece of **Cola dell'Amatrice** (1527), has a majestic and rich **façade★★** which is articulated by entablatures that give definition to the three orders of double columns (Ionic, Doric and Corinthian). The spacious and well-lit interior, in the form of a Latin cross, is roofed with a lovely Baroque wooden ceiling and contains the **mausoleum of St Bernardino★** which is adorned with figures by the local sculptor, Silvestro dell'Aquila, as is the elegant **tomb★** of Maria Pereira.

> ### COLUI CHE FECE PER VILTADE
> ### IL GRAN RIFIUTO...
> *He who made the Great Refusal, impelled by cowardice*
> Dante, *Inferno*, Canto III, 59-60.
> Pietro da Morrone (1215-96), hermit and founder of the Celestine order of the Morronese Abbey near Sulmona, was unexpectedly elected pope in September of 1294. Overwhelmed by the intrigues and plots of the pontifical court, Pope Celestine V abdicated after only a few months and was banished to the castle of Fumone by his successor, Boniface VIII. He died there shortly afterwards and in 1313 was canonised by Pope Clement V.

Castello★

Museum: (&) *Open daily except Mon 9am-8pm (ticket office closes 7.30pm). Closed 1 Jan, 1 May, 25 Dec. €4.* ☎ *0862 63 32 39; www.muvi.org/museonazionaledabruzzo*
Built in the 16C to by Pirro Luigi Escribà who also designed Castel Sant'Elmo in Naples, this square castle, reinforced with powerful bastions, is a good example of 16C military architecture. The great rooms now house a museum, the **Museo Nazionale d'Abruzzo★★**. On display on the ground floor are the *Archidiskodon Meridionalis Vestinus*, the fossil remains of an ancestor of the elephant that lived about one million years ago, and some interesting exhibits from Abruzzi in Roman times, including the *Calendario Amiterno*. On the first floor the section on **Sacred Art** (12C-17C) constitutes the core of the museum and displays some significant examples of painting, sculpture and decorative arts of the Abruzzi region. Among these it is worth noting the polychrome wooden sculptures, the *Croce processionale★* by Nicola di Guardiagrele, a masterpiece of workmanship in gold, and the wooden statue depicting *St Sebastian* by Silvestro d'Aquila.

Fontana delle 99 cannelle★

This imposing fountain which was begun in 1272 commemorates the legendary founding of L'Aquila with its 99 castles. It is made of pink and white stone in a trapezoidal form and is adorned with 99 gargoyles, each different from the others.

Lecce★★

Nicknamed "the Baroque Florence", the town boasts a profusion of incredibly decorative buildings. At night, decked in lights, it resembles a sumptuous theatrical set. Lecce was in Roman times the prosperous town of Lupiae. The Normans greatly favoured the town and made it the capital of the region known as Terra d'Otranto. From the 16C to the 18C, Lecce knew a period of great splendour during which it was embellished with Renaissance, Rococo and Baroque monuments. The local finely grained limestone was particularly easy to work, and the town's numerous Baroque buildings are remarkable for the abundance of decorative work. The most inventive artists came from the Zimbalo family: their work is to be found in both churches and palaces and is widespread throughout the Salentina Peninsula.

Location

Population 93 705 – Michelin map 431 F 36 – Puglia. Lecce is set in the very heart of the Salento region, off S 613. ☐ *Corso Vittorio Emanuele 24,* ☎ *0832 24 80 92. Surrounding area: see PUGLIA.*

Special Features

BAROQUE LECCE★★

The historic centre, once surrounded by ramparts (16C), of which only traces remain, and a **castle** (built by Charles V on an existing Angevin fort), is now delineated by a ring of avenues. The heart of the city is the lively **Piazza S. Oronzo** which is dominated by a statue of the patron saint on top of one of the two columns that mark the end of the Appian Way, the other being in Brindisi (*see BRINDISI*).

Directory

To the south side of the square, parts of a **Roman amphitheatre** (2C), originally double tiered, have been unearthed. Also in the piazza are the small church of **San Marco**, attributed to Gabriele Riccardi and built by the Venetian colony, and the very old **palazzo del Seggio** which temporarily houses a papier mâché statue of San Giuseppe Patriarca (19C).

Basilica di Santa Croce★★

Several architects worked on this basilica in the 16C and 17C and it constitutes the best example of the Baroque style of Lecce. The façade is sumptuously decorated without being overbearing (the lower part is Renaissance in structure). The upper storey is almost without doubt the work of Zimbalo and is richly ornamented. The two storeys are linked by a long balcony held up by animal atlantes and caryatids while the parapet is adorned with cherubs holding mitres and books. The central rose window above seems as if it were fashioned by an expert lace-maker. The **interior** is light and airy and the plainer architectural style is reminiscent of the Florentine Renaissance idiom. There is also abundant Baroque decoration of great delicacy. The side chapel at the end of the north aisle contains a fine **high altar** with sculptured low reliefs by Francesco Antonio Zimbalo and depicts scenes from the life of San Francesco da Paola.

Palazzo del Governo

Adjoining the basilica the Governor's residence, a former Celestine monastery, has a rusticated façade with a frieze above and intricately decorated window surrounds, especially at first-floor level, designed by Zimbalo (ground floor) and Cino.

Chiesa del Gesù (or del Buon Consiglio)

The austere style of this church, built by the Jesuits (1575-79), makes a stark contrast to the other churches in Lecce. Inside there is an ornate **Baroque altar★**.

The delicate Baroque modelling on the façade of Santa Croce

Chiesa di Sant'Irene

Built by Francesco Grimaldi for the monks of the Theatine order, this church has lavish **Baroque altars** attributed to Francesco A Zimbalo.

Piazza del Duomo★★

Completely enclosed in a homogeneous body of Baroque buildings and heralded by an arch facing Corso Vittorio Emanuele, this is one of the most remarkable squares in southern Italy. To the left, the **campanile** (1661-82) and the adjacent **Duomo** (1659-82) are by Giuseppe Zimbalo, the 17C **Palazzo Vescovile** and the **Seminario,** dating from 1709, by Giuseppe Cino. In the courtyard of the latter there is an ornately decorated **well★** by the same sculptor.

LECCE

Aragona (Via F. d')	YZ 3	Imperatore Augusto (V)	Y 15	Realino (Via Bernardino)	Z 29
Caracciolo (Via Roberto)	Z 7	Jacobis (V. Agostino de)	Z 17	Rubichi (Via Francesco)	Y 32
Cavallotti (Viale F.)	Y 8	Ludovico (Via)	Y 21	S. Oronzo (Piazza)	Y
Fazzi (Via Vito)	Y 12	Marche (Viale)	Y 22	Taranto (Via)	Y 38
Imperatore Adriano (V.)	Y 14	Orsini del Balzo (Via)	Z 25	Trinchese (Via Salvatore)	Y
		Palazzo dei Conti		Vitt. Emanuele (Cso)	Y 42
		di Lecce (Via del)	Z 26	Vittorio Emanuele (Pza)	Y 43
		Pietro (Via M. de)	Y 28	25 Luglio (Via)	Y 44

Duomo – The first sighting of the Duomo is in fact of the north side. It is the most ornate façade of the church with its imposing entrance and arcade with a statue of St Oronzo. The main façade *(visible from the square)* is more restrained. Inside, the **crypt**, rebuilt in the 16C on an existing medieval structure, is held up by 92 columns with capitals adorned by figures of animals.

Chiesa del Rosario (or di San Giovanni Battista)★

This church was Giuseppe Zimbalo's last work and the façade features an abundance of decoration which is both intricately detailed and yet graceful.
The **interior**★ is adorned with Baroque altars and some fine 17C altarpieces.

Via Palmieri

Several elegant buildings border this street, particularly noteworthy are the ones at Piazza Falconieri, Palazzo Marrese and Palazzo Palmieri (18C). At the end of the street, **Porta Napoli** (or Arco di Trionfo) was built in the 16C in honour of Charles V.

Chiesa di Sant'Angelo

Although unfinished, this façade is typical of Zimbalo's style (1663) and is decorated with garlands, cherubs and angels.

Chiesa di San Matteo★

This church with its harmonious façade by Achille Carducci (1667-1700) shows the distinct influence of Borromini and his Roman work, the church of San Carlo alle Quattro Fontane.

Worth a Visit

Museo Provinciale San Castromediano★

Open daily except Mon, 9am-1.30pm (ticket office closes 1.15pm) and 2.30-7.30pm (ticket office closes 7.15pm). ☎ 0832 30 74 15.
Housed in a modern building, the museum has a rich archaeological section *(ground floor)* and a very important **ceramics collection**★★ *(first floor)*. Of particular inter-

est are the Attic vases decorated with red figures. There is also a collection of epigraphs of various origins and two beautiful bronze statues (a figure of a woman and a priest). There is an art gallery on the third floor.

▶▶S.S. Nicolò e Cataldo.

Excursion

Abbazia di Santa Maria di Cerrate★

14km/9mi north on the road to Brindisi, then turn right (follow directions). This enchanting Benedictine abbey, in its isolated country setting, dates back to the 12C. The **church★**, closed on the north side by a fine portico with capitals embellished with figurative scenes (13C), has an elegant doorway whose vault is decorated with scenes from the New Testament. The interior retains part of the frescoes that probably once covered its entire surface. Some fresco fragments are conserved in the **Museo delle Tradizioni Popolari** which is housed in monastery rooms. The museum also has displays of traditional wares such as oil-presses (the abbey has an underground olive-press). *Open daily except Mon, 9am-1.30pm and 2.30-7.30pm. Closed 1 and 6 Jan, 25-26 Dec. No charge.* ♿ ☎ *0832 30 74 15.*

Loreto ★

The small city of Loreto is grouped around its well-known church which is the scene of a famous pilgrimage to the "House of Mary". The old quarter is partially encircled by massive brick ramparts dating from the 16C.

Location

Population 11 298 – Michelin map 430 L 22 – Marches. Loreto is situated 5km/3mi from Porto Recanati. Rising up over the surrounding plain, it is easily spotted from the motorway. **🛈** *Via Solari 3,* ☎ *071 97 02 76.*
Surrounding area: see ANCONA.

Worth a Visit

Il Santuario della Santa Casa★★

Open daily, Apr to Sep 6.45am-8pm, rest of year 6.45am-7pm (Santa Casa closed 12.30-2.30pm). ☎ *071 97 01 04; www.santuarioloreto.it*

Many famous architects, painters and sculptors contributed to the building and decoration of this church, the Sanctuary of the Holy House. Construction started in 1468 and was only completely finished in the 18C. The architects included firstly Giuliano da Sangallo, then Bramante who built the side chapels, and finally Vanvitelli who designed the bulbous campanile. Go round the outside of the church to admire the lovely triple **apse★★** and Sangallo's elegant dome. The sober and harmonious façade with its double buttresses surmounted by clocks at the corners is typical of the late Renaissance.

> **ANGELS IN FLIGHT FROM NAZARETH TO LORETO**
>
> It is said that the Santa Casa (Holy House) or House of Mary was miraculously carried from Nazareth in several stages by angels and set down in a wood of laurels (*lauretum* in Latin), which gave its name to Loreto. In fact three walls of the House of Mary were transported in 1294 by the Angeli (angels in Italian), a noble family which ruled over Epiros where Nazareth is located.

The three **bronze doors★★** are adorned with fine late-16C and early-17C statues. The interior has a nave and two aisles. At the end of the south aisle the **Sacristy of St Mark★** (San Marco) is crowned by a dome painted with frescoes (1477) by Melozzo da Forlì with an exceptional sense of foreshortening, showing angels carrying the Instruments of the Passion. In the **Sacristy of St John★** (San Giovanni) is a lavabo designed by Benedetto da Maiano under a vault painted with frescoes by Luca Signorelli. Standing at the transept crossing is the **Santa Casa★★** which was sumptuously faced with marble carved in the 16C by Antonio Sansovino and other sculptors. The north transept leads to a room decorated by Pomarancio (1605-10).

Piazza della Madonna★, in front of the basilica, is lined by the unfinished portico of the Palazzo Apostolico, which now houses a picture gallery, the **Pinacoteca★**. This contains a remarkable collection of **works★** by **Lorenzo Lotto**, and paintings by

Simon Vouet and Pomarancio. The Flemish tapestries were woven to designs by Raphael and there is a superb collection of Urbino faience vessels. & *Open Apr to Oct, daily except Mon, 10am-1pm and 4-7pm, rest of year 10am-1pm and 3-6pm (ticket office always closes 30min early). Closed 1 Jan, Easter, 1 May, 15 Aug, 25 Dec. Donation recommended.* ☎ *071 97 77 59; www.santuarioloreto.it*

Outskirts

Recanati

7km/4mi southwest. This little town, perched on a hill, was the birthplace of the poet **Giacomo Leopardi** (1798-1837), the most perceptive but melancholy of Italian poets whose work was very melodious. The **Palazzo Leopardi** contains mementoes of the writer. & *Open daily, 9am-12.30pm and 2.30pm to 1hr before sunset. Closed 1 Jan, 25 Dec. €4.* ☎ *071 75 73 380; www.giacomoleopardi.it*

The **Museo Civico**, housed in the Villa Colloredo Mels complex *(via Gregorio XII)*, has several important works by Lorenzo Lotto, including an *Annunciation*. Other exhibits include various historical and archaeological finds, as well as some pieces of modern and contemporary art. & *Open daily except Mon, 9am-noon and 3pm to 1hr before sunset. Closed 25 Dec. €3.10.* ☎ *071 75 70 410.*

Lucca★★★

Situated in the centre of a fertile plain, Lucca has preserved within its girdle of ramparts, in many parts tree-topped, a rich heritage of churches, palaces, squares and streets which gives the town a charming air, unscathed by contemporary developments. The ramparts (4km/2.5mi long) extend all the way round the old town. They were built in the 16C and 17C and include 11 bastions, linked by curtain walls, and four gateways.

Location

Population 85 484 – Michelin map 430 K 13 – See also The Green Guide Tuscany. Lucca is situated 74km/44mi from Florence and 20km/12mi from Viareggio.
🅑 *Piazza S. Maria 35,* ☎ *0583 91 99 31.*
Surrounding area: see COLLODI, GARFAGNANA, MONTECATINI TERME, PESCIA, PISA, VERSILIA.

Background

Lucca was colonised by the Romans in the 2C BC and it has retained the plan of a Roman military camp, with the two principal streets perpendicular to one another. During the Middle Ages a complicated system of narrow alleys and oddly shaped squares was added to the original network. The town became an independent commune at the beginning of the 12C and flourished until the mid-14C with the silk

Piazza dell'Anfiteatro

Directory

WHERE TO EAT

• Budget

Osteria Baralla – *Via Anfiteatro 5/7/9 – ☎ 0583 44 02 40 – Closed Sun, mid-Jan to mid-Feb – Book – €15/21*. A charming restaurant housed in what was the entrance to the servants' quarters in a medieval palazzo. There are two dining areas, one of which has a vaulted ceiling. The other room is smaller and more intimate. The menu changes daily and features typical Tuscan dishes.

Da Giulio-in Pelleria – *Via delle Conce 45, Piazza S. Donato – ☎ 0583 55 948 – Closed Mon, Sun (except May, Sep, Dec), 20-31 Dec – Book – €18/22*. Historic trattoria where the large number of covers does not impact on the quality of the food. Regional cooking, and reasonable prices. Despite all the comings and goings, the atmosphere is pleasant and the service attentive.

WHERE TO STAY

• Budget

Ostello San Frediano – *Via della Cavallerizza 12 – ☎ 0583 46 99 57 – Fax 0583 61 007 – ⊠ ⚹ – 148 rm €16 – ⚌ €1.55 – Meals €8*. This hotel is part of the former Real Collegio and is adjacent to the church of San Frediano. With all the comforts of a hotel but at guesthouse prices. The public areas are comfortable and spacious, and there is also a lovely garden area. Perfect for relaxing and winding down after a tiring day tramping round the historic centre.

• Moderate

Piccolo Hotel Puccini – *Via di Poggio 9 – ☎ 0583 55 421 – Fax 0583 53 487 – 14 rm €55/80 – ⚌ €3.62*. Not far from the church of San Michele in Foro, is this little hotel which prides itself on its Puccini memorabilia.

A great place for soaking up the magical atmosphere of this historic town. The management and the staff are friendly and enthusiastic, and also extremely knowledgeable! Very clean.

Albergo San Martino – *Via Della Dogana 9 – ☎ 0583 46 91 81 – Fax 0583 99 19 40 – ⊡ ⚹ – 10 rm €74/104 – ⚌ €8*. A stone's throw from the Duomo, this hotel is ideally situated. The other main attraction are the spacious, airy rooms. The hotel has all mod cons, with pleasant, modern furnishings. The staff are young and dynamic, just what you need to put a spring in your step. Guided tours of the town can be arranged.

TAKING A BREAK

Antico Caffè Di Simo – *Via Fillungo 58 – ☎ 0583 49 62 34 – Apr-Oct 8-24; Nov-Mar, Tue-Sun 8am-8.30pm*. With origins dating back to 1846, this café has seen a number of great Italian artists pass through its doors, among them Puccini, Verdi and Leopardi. The perfect place for immersing yourself in the history and cultural life of Lucca, while sipping one of the house cocktails.

Gelateria Sergio Santini – *Piazza Cittadella 1 – ☎ 0583 55 295 – Summer 9am-midnight; rest of the year, Tue-Sun 9am-8pm*. This is the place to head for if you fancy sitting out in the sun enjoying one of the best chocolate ice creams in town, listening to Puccini. The ice cream is all home-made. Other specialities include paciugo and panettone gelato.

EVENTS AND FESTIVALS

Every year, a most unusual commemorative procession, **Luminara di Santa Croce**, passes through the illuminated town after dark *(see under Events and Festivals in the Practical Points section)*.

trade as its main activity. In the early 14C the town enjoyed a great period of prosperity and prestige under the control of the mercenary soldier and leader Castruccio Castracani (d 1328). Lucca's finest religious and secular buildings date from this period. Luccan architects adopted the Pisan style to which they added their own characteristic refinement and fantasy.

From 1550 onwards the town became an important agricultural centre and with this new prosperity came a renewed interest in building. The countryside was dotted with villas, the town encircled by ramparts and most of the houses were either rebuilt or remodelled.

In the early 19C, Elisa Bonaparte ruled the city for a brief period from 1805 to 1813. Following Napoleon's Italian campaigns he bestowed the titles of Princess of Lucca and Piombino on his sister. She showed a remarkable aptitude for public affairs and ruled her fief with wisdom and intelligence, encouraging the development of the town and the arts.

The Legend of the Holy Cross – The **Volto Santo** (Holy Visage) is a miraculous Crucifix kept in the cathedral. It is said that after Christ had been taken down from the Cross, Nicodemus saw the image of his face on it. The Italian Bishop Gualfredo, when on pilgrimage in the Holy Land, succeeded in tracing the Volto Santo and embarked in a boat without a crew or sails which drifted ashore on the beach at Luni, near La Spezia. As the worshippers at Luni and Lucca disputed possession of the Holy Image, the Bishop of Lucca had it placed on a cart drawn by two oxen; they immediately set off towards Lucca.

The fame of the Volto Santo, spread by merchants from Lucca, gained ground throughout Europe.

Walking About

Città vecchia

The streets and squares of old Lucca are full of atmosphere with their Gothic and Renaissance palaces, their towers of the nobility, old shops, sculptured doorways and coats of arms, elegant wrought-iron railings and balconies. Starting from **Piazza San Michele**, follow Via Roma and Villa Fillungo to **Piazza del Anfiteatro** situated inside the Roman amphitheatre. From here go towards Piazza San Pietro (12C-13C church) and then take Via Guinigi where at N° 29 stands **Casa dei Guinigi** with its **tower** (**panorama★** of town from the top) crowned with trees which rises above the great façade with its Gothic windows. The houses opposite at N⁰ˢ 20 and 22 also belonged to the Guinigi family. *Tower: Open daily, Mar to Sep 9am-7.30pm, Oct 10am-6pm, rest of year 9am-5.30pm. €3.10.* ☎ *0583 48 524.*

Continue to the Romanesque church of **Santa Maria Forisportam**, so-called because it stood outside the Roman walls. Via Santa Croce, Piazza dei Servi and Piazza dei Bernardini, where the 16C palace of the same name stands, lead back to Piazza San Michele.

Worth a Visit

Duomo★★

The cathedral, dedicated to St Martin, was rebuilt in the 11C. The exterior was re-modelled almost entirely in the 13C, as was the interior in the 14C and 15C. The strength and balance of the green and white marble **façade★★**, designed by the architect Guidetto da Como, are striking despite its asymmetry. The upper section with its three superimposed galleries is the first example of the Pisan Romanesque style *(see PISA)* as it developed in Lucca; the idiom is characterised by lighter, less rigid lines and by inventive ornamentation. The ornate sculpture and marble-inlaid designs are of great interest.

LUCCA

The slim and powerful campanile harmoniously combines the use of brick and marble, and the number of openings increases with the height.

The sculptural decoration of the porch is extremely rich: pillars with naïvely carved columns, arcading, friezes and a variety of scenes.

The Gothic **interior** has elevations where the round-headed main arches with their robust piers contrast with the delicacy of the elegant triforium. On the west wall is an unusual Romanesque sculpture of St Martin dividing his cloak. The classical and sober lines of this sculpture herald the style of Nicola Pisano. In the north aisle is the lovely shrine *(tempietto)* built by the local artisan Matteo Civitali (1436-1501) to house the Volto Santo. The great 12C figure of **Christ★** in wood blackened through time shows a distinctly Oriental influence because of its hieratic aspect. It is said to be a copy of the legendary holy image.

In the sacristy is one of the masterpieces of Italian funerary sculpture by the Sienese artist, Jacopo della Quercia (1406): the **tomb of Ilaria del Carretto★★**, wife of Paolo Guinigi, lord of Lucca in the early 15C. The recumbent figure wears a long, delicately draped robe and at her feet lies a small dog, a symbol of fidelity. Other works of art include a *Presentation of the Virgin in the Temple* by Bronzino *(north aisle)* and the large-scale *Last Supper★* with its subtle lighting by Tintoretto *(south aisle)*.

Chiesa di San Michele in Foro★★

The white mass of the 12C-14C church on the site of the Roman forum dominates the adjoining square which is lined by old mansions and the Palazzo Pretorio.

The exceptionally tall **façade★★** (the nave itself was to have been taller) is a good example of the Lucca-Pisan style, despite the fact that the lower part was remodelled last century. The four superimposed galleries surmount blind arcading and are decorated with varied motifs. At the top, two instrument-playing angels flank a statue of the Archangel Michael slaying the dragon.

The simplicity of the Romanesque **interior** is a direct contrast to the ornate exterior. On the first altar of the south aisle is a *Madonna★* by Andrea della Robbia. The south transept is adorned with a lovely **painting★** with brilliant colours by Filippino Lippi.

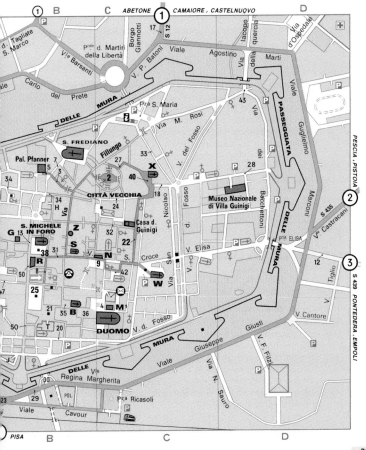

Chiesa di San Frediano★

This great church, dedicated to St Frigidian, was rebuilt in the original Lucca-Romanesque style in the 12C before the influence of the Pisan school was felt. The sober façade is faced with white marble from the Roman amphitheatre. The upper middle section, remodelled in the 13C, is dominated by a Byzantine-style mosaic depicting the Ascension by local artists.

The interior comprises a nave and two aisles with wooden ceilings (flanked by Renaissance and Baroque side chapels) on the plan of the Early-Christian basilicas: the nave which ends in a semicircular apse is articulated by antique columns crowned with fine capitals.

To the right on entering is a curious Romanesque **font★** (12C) with low reliefs depicting the story of Moses. The Chapel of Sant'Agostino is decorated with frescoes by the Ferraran painter Amico Aspertini: one of these depicts the translation of the Volto Santo from Luni to Lucca.

Pinacoteca

The **apartments** of this 17C palace have remarkable interior **decoration★** (17C-18C). The **Pinacoteca** includes works by 17C Italian artists (Salimbeni and Barocci) and foreign paintings. ♿ *Open Mon-Sat 9am-7pm, Sun and hols 9am-2pm. Closed 1 Jan, 1 May, 25 Dec. €4; €6.50 combined ticket with with Museo Nazionale Villa Guinigi. ☎ 0583 55 570; www.ambientepi.arti.beniculturali.it*

Museo Nazionale di Villa Guinigi

Via della Quarquonia. ♿ Open Mon-Sat 8.30am-7.30pm (ticket office closes 7pm), Sun and hols 8.30am-1.30pm (ticket office closes 1pm). Closed 1 Jan, 1 May, 25 Dec. €4. ☎ 0583 49 60 33; www.ambientepi.arti.beniculturali.it

The villa which once belonged to Paolo Guinigi now contains archaeological, sculpture (Romanesque, Gothic and Renaissance) and painting (Lucca and Tuscany) sections. There are some remarkable panels of intarsia work.

Excursions

Villa Reale di Marlia

8km/5mi to the north. (♿) Garden only. Closed Mon.€6. For information ☎ 0583 30 108.

The Villa Reale is surrounded by magnificent 17C **gardens★★** modified by Elisa Bonaparte. Unusual features include a lemon grove, a 17C nymphaeum and an open-air theatre.

Villa Grabau

Near the Villa di Marlia. ♿ Mar-Nov: Open Wed-Sun 10am-1pm and 3-7pm, rest of the year Sun 11am-1pm, 3-5.30pm. Closed over the Christmas period. Park and villa €5.16, park only €4.13. ☎ 0583 40 60 98, www.island.pisa.it/grabau

The villa stands in the centre of a particularly magnificent perspective which draws the eye from the entrance avenue to the Italian garden, and beyond.

Fountains with bronze mascarons and white marble statues add to the elegant appearance of the **park★★**, which covers an area of 9ha/22 acres and is, in reality, a botanical garden. The layout of the park includes an outdoor theatre, an informal English garden with large trees and exotic plants, and an Italian garden, decorated with old 18C and 19C lemon trees in their original containers.

Other features include a winter greenhouse and an unusual 17C-18C **Lemon House.**

Villa Mansi

At Segromigno, 11km 7mi to the northeast ♿ Open Apr to Oct, daily except Mon, 10am-6pm, rest of year 10am-5pm. Closed 1 Jan, 21 Dec. to 6 Jan. €6.50 ☎ 0583 92 00 96 www villamansi.it

This 16C villa, transformed in the 18C, has a façade covered with statues and a vast shady **park★** where statue-lined alleys lead to a lovely pool.

Villa Torrigiani (or di Camigliano)★

13km 8mi to the northeast ♿ Open daily, 10am-12.30pm and 3pm to 1hr before sunset. No charge for gardens, Palazzo guided tours only. Closed Nov to Mar €8. ☎ 0583 92 80 41, www.uchha.org/it/Toscana/camigliano.htm

This 16C villa was converted in the 17C into an elegant summer residence by Marques Nicolao Santini, ambassador of the Lucca republic to the Papal Court and to the Court of Louis XIV. The gardens designed by Le Nôtre, are adorned with fountains, grottoes and nymphaea. The villa, which has a delightful Rococo façade, contains rooms adorned with frescoes.

Mantova★★

MANTUA

Mantua is set in the heart of a flat fertile plain which was formerly marshland on the southeastern border of Lombardy. It is encircled to the north by three lakes formed by the slow-flowing River Mincio. This active and prosperous town has important mechanical and petrochemical industries. The region is also the number one producer of hosiery worldwide.

Location
Population 48 288 – Michelin map 428 or 429 G 14. Mantua lies at the southeast corner of Lombardy. The main access roads are the A 22 Brennero pass and S 236 from Brescia. 🛈 *Piazza Andrea Mantegna 6,* ☎ *0376 32 82 53.*
Surrounding area: see VERONA.

Background

Although, according to a legend quoted by Virgil, Mantua was founded by Monto, daughter of the divine Tiresias, its origins would seem to be Etruscan dating back to the 6C or 5C BC. It passed to the Gauls before becoming Roman in the 3C BC. In 70 BC **Virgil** (Publius Virgilius Maro), the great poet, was born in the Mantua area. Author of the *Aeneid* in which he recounts the wanderings of Aeneas, the exiled Trojan prince, and the foundation of the earliest settlement from which Rome was to spring, Virgil describes his beloved Mantuan countryside, with its soft misty light, and the pleasures of rural life in his own harmonious but melancholy style in the *Eclogues* or *Bucolica* and in the *Georgics.*

In the Middle Ages Mantua was the theatre for numerous struggles between rival factions which successively sacked the town, before it became an independent commune in the 13C and finally the domain of Luigi Gonzaga, nominated Captain General of the People. Under the **Gonzaga** family, who were enlightened rulers and patrons of the arts and letters, Mantua became an important intellectual and artistic centre in northern Italy of the 15C and 16C. Thus Gian Francesco Gonzaga (ruled 1407-44) placed his children in the charge of the famous humanist Vittorio da Feltre (1379-1446) and commissioned the Veronese artist **Pisanello** (1395-1455) to decorate his ducal palace.

His son Ludovico III (1444-78), a mercenary army leader by profession, was a typical Renaissance patron: he gave land to the poor, built bridges and favoured artists. The Sienese humanist Politian (1454-94), the Florentine architect Leon Battista Alberti (1404-72) and the Paduan painter **Andrea Mantegna** (1431-1506) all belonged to his court. Francesco II (1484-1519) married Isabella d'Este, a beautiful and wise woman who contributed to the fame of Mantua. Their son Federico II was made duke by the Emperor Charles V in 1530 and he commissioned the architect and artist **Giulio Romano** (1499-1546), Raphael's pupil, to embellish his native town; the artist worked on the ducal palace and cathedral and the Palazzo Te.

In 1627 Vicenzo II died without heirs and the succession passed to the Gonzaga-Nevers family, the cadet line. The Habsburg Emperor Ferdinand II opposed the French succession, and in 1630 sent an army which sacked the town and then

Directory

deserted it following a plague which decimated Milan and Lombardy (the background to these dramatic events is described in the novel *I Promessi Sposi* by Manzoni). The Gonzaga-Nevers, however, restored the fortunes of the town until 1707 when they were deposed. Mantua became part of the Austrian Empire which ruled until 1866, except for a period under Napoleonic rule (1787-1814), when it joined the Kingdom of Italy.

Worth a Visit

Palazzo Ducale★★★

(&) *Open daily, 8.45am-7.15pm (ticket office closes 6.30pm). Closed 1 Jan, 1 May, 25 Dec. €6.50.* ☏ *0376 38 21 50.*

The imposing Ducal Palace comprises buildings from various periods: the Magna Domus and the Palazzo del Capitano erected in the late 13C by the Bonacolsi, Lords of Mantua from 1272 to 1328; the Castello di San Giorgio, a 14C fortress, and other inner sections built by the Gonzaga in the 15C-16C, including the 15C Palatine chapel of Santa Barbara.

Apartments★★★ – Start from the 17C Ducal Stairway which gives access to the first floor. One of the first rooms displays *The Expulsion of the Bonacolsi and the Triumph of the Gonzaga on 16 August 1328* by Domenico Morone (1442-1517). The painting shows the medieval aspect of Piazza Sordello with the old façade of the cathedral. The **Pisanello rooms** on the first floor have fragments of frescoes and remarkable **sinopie★★** (preparatory sketches using a red earth pigment), which were discovered in 1969 and are a good example of the refined and penetrating work of Pisanello. These lyrical scenes draw inspiration from the feats of the Knights of the

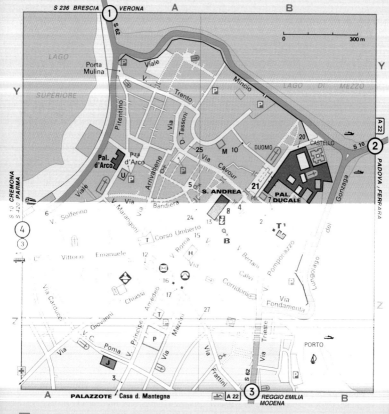

In the Palazzo Ducale plump cherubs gaze from the ceiling of the Camera degli Sposi

Round Table and the fantastic and timeless world of medieval chivalry. The **Tapestry Room** (Appartamento degli Arazzi), formerly known as the **Green Apartment** (Appartamento Verde), in the neo-Classical style, is hung with nine splendid Brussels tapestries after Raphael. The **Room of the Zodiac** (Camera dello Zodiaco) leads to the **Room of the Moors** (Stanzino dei Mori), in the Venetian style, and to the **Hall of the Rivers** (Sala dei Fiumi) which overlooks the **Hanging Garden** (Giardino Pensile). The giants depicted on the walls represents the rivers of Mantua. The **Corridor of the Moors** (Corridoio dei Mori) leads into the famous **Hall of Mirrors** (Sala degli Specchi) used for dancing and music. In the elegant **Room of the Archers** (Sala degli Arcieri), the antechamber to the ducal apartments, hang paintings by Rubens and Domenico Fetti. The **Ducal Apartments** (Appartamento Ducale) comprise a suite of rooms remodelled for Vincenzi I in the early 17C by Antonio Maria Viani, and including the Paradise Room (Appartamento del Paradiso) and the tiny Room of the Dwarfs (Appartamento dei Nani). The building known as the **Rustica** and the **Equestrian Court** (Cortile della Cavallerizza) are by Giulio Romano; the courtyard is lined by a **gallery**, Galleria della Mostra, built in the late 16C by Antonio Maria Viani to house Vicenzo I's art collection, and by the **Hall of the Months** (Galleria dei Mesi) erected by Giulio Romano.

In the **Castello di San Giorgio** may be viewed the celebrated **Room of the Spouses★★★** (Camera degli Sposi) – so-called because this is where marriages were recorded – executed from 1465 to 1474 by **Andrea Mantegna**. The walls are covered with a cycle of frescoes which glorify the superb and refined world of the Gonzaga court. Mantegna creates an illusion of space with his knowledge of fore-shortening and perspective and his skilful use of volume and materials. The painted *trompe l'oeil* and carved stucco decorations and garlands of foliage and fruits are also admirable. On the north wall look for Ludovico II turned towards his secretary, and his wife Barbara seated full-face. The children cluster round their parents, as do other members of the court including an enigmatic dwarf.

On the west wall the fresco presents Ludovico with his son, Cardinal Francesco, against the background of a town with splendid monuments, which could well be Rome as imagined by Mantegna who had not yet visited the city. Mantegna has por-trayed himself as the figure in purple which can be glimpsed on the right of the dedication. His great mastery of *trompe l'oeil* culminates in the ceiling oculus from which gaze cupids and servants. This invention was highly successful and intro-duces a note of wry humour and even oddness to this otherwise rather solemn ensemble.

Piazza Sordello★

This square, which was the centre of old Mantua, has retained its medieval aspect. To the west is the 13C Palazzo Bonacolsi – the tall Tower of the Cage (Torre della Gabbia) still bears on its façade the cage *(gabbia)* in which wrongdoers were ex-hibited – and the 18C Palazzo Vescovile where telamones adorn the 18C façade. To the east are the oldest buildings of the Palazzo Ducale: the Magna Domus and the crenellated Palazzo del Capitano.

On the north side stands the **Cathedral** (Duomo) which features varied elements and styles: the neo-Classical façade, the late-Gothic right wing and a Romanesque campanile. The 16C interior was designed by Giulio Romano.

Piazza Broletto

This was the centre of public life at the time of the commune (13C) when was built the Palazzo Broletto, a 13C communal palace, partly remodelled in the 15C. On its façade it has a seated statue of Virgil (1225). At the right corner rises the Torre Comunale, a tower later converted into a prison.

Piazza delle Erbe★

The Square of Herbs derives its name from a fruit and vegetable market. It is lined to the north by the rear façade of the Palazzo Broletto and to the east by the 13C Palazzo della Ragione, flanked by the 15C Clock Tower and the Romanesque church known as the **Rotonda di San Lorenzo★**. Sober and elegant, this circular building has a colonnaded ambulatory with a loggia above, and a dome crowning all. & *Open daily 10am-noon and 2.30-4.30pm. Donation recommended.*

Basilica di Sant'Andrea★

The basilica dedicated to St Andrew, built in the 15C to the plans of Alberti, is a masterpiece of the Italian Renaissance. The façade retains Classical architectural features: the tympanum, the triumphal arch, the niches between the pilasters. The **interior** has a single nave. The barrel vaulting and walls are painted in *trompe l'oeil*. The first chapel on the left contains the tomb of Mantegna. The transept crossing is crowned by a dome built from 1732 to 1765 by Filippo Juvarra. In the crypt two urns housed in a reliquary contain a relic of the Blood of Christ brought to Mantua by the Roman soldier Longinus.

Teatro Accademico

& *Open daily except Mon, 9.30am-12.30pm and 3-6pm. Closed 1 Jan, 1 May, 15 Aug, 25 Dec. €2.07. ☎ 0376 32 76 53.*
This small, pretty 18C theatre by Bibiena has a stage set in imitation marble with four architectural orders in pasteboard and a monochrome decor. The theatre which welcomed the 13-year old Mozart on 13 December 1769, is still used for concerts.

Palazzo d'Arco

Piazza d'Arco. Open Mar to Oct, Tue-Sun 10am-12.30pm and 2.30-6pm, rest of year only Sat-Sun and hols 10am-12.30pm and 2-5pm (ticket office closes 30min early). Closed Mon and bank hols. €3. ☎ 0376 32 22 42.
This neo-Classical palace in the Palladian tradition *(see VICENZA)* contains interesting collections of 18C and 19C furniture, paintings and ceramics.

Palazzo di Giustizia

The monumental façade of the Law Courts with caryatids is early 17C. At n° 18 in the same street is Giulio Romano's house built in 1544 to his own designs.

Casa del Mantegna

47 Via Acerbi. This rather severe-looking brick building was in all probability built to designs by Mantegna himself in 1476. It has a delightful courtyard.

Palazzo Te★★

(&) *Open daily, 9am-6pm, except Mon am. Closed 1 Jan, 1 May, 25 Dec. €8. ☎ 0376 36 38 83.*
This large country mansion was built on the plan of a Roman house by Giulio Romano for Federico II from 1525 to 1535. It combines Classical features and melodramatic invention, such as the amazing "broken" entablature in the main courtyard, and is a major achievement of the Mannerist style. The **interior** was ornately decorated by Giulio Romano and his pupils. In the **Room of the Horses** (Salone dei Cavalli), used for receptions, some of the finest horses from the Gonzaga stables are depicted. In the **Room of Psyche** (Sala di Psiche), used for banquets, the sensual and lively style of Giulio Romano is the best illustration of the hedonistic character of the palace. The frescoes in the **Room of the Giants** (Sala dei Giganti), the most celebrated room of the palace, depict the wrath of Jupiter against the Titans. The overall decoration which covers the walls and vaulted ceiling creates an indefinite spatial illusion and the dome above gives a sense of artificiality, in sharp contrast to the effect sought by Mantegna in the Camera degli Sposi in the Palazzo Ducale.

Excursions

Sabbioneta★

34km/20mi southwest of Mantua. The town was built from 1558 by Vespasiano Gonzaga (1531-91), a mercenary leader in the service of Philip II of Spain who conferred on his loyal servants the glorious order of the Golden Fleece. The order was created in 1429 by Philip the Good, Duke of Burgundy. Vespasiano was a cultured man and he wanted to take personal charge of the construction of his ideal town.

Town★ – *Tours organised by Ufficio del Turismo Comunale, Piazza d'Armi 1.* Its hexagonal walls, star plan and monuments make Sabbioneta a jewel of Italian Mannerism.

The **Garden Palace (**Palazzo del Giardino) was designed for festivities and its walls and ceilings were richly painted with frescoes by Bernardino Campi (1522-1591) and his school. The great **Galleria** (96m/315ft long) is one of the longest Renaissance galleries.

The **Olympic Theatre** (Teatro Olimpico), a masterpiece by Vicentino Scamozzi (1552-1616), was built from 1588 to 1590 and is one of the oldest covered theatres in Europe. The interior is decorated with frescoes by the school of Veronese and there is a ducal box adorned with colonnades and statues of the gods.

The **Ducal Palace** (Palazzo Ducale), has finely carved wooden and coffered ceilings. There are interesting equestrian statues of the Gonzaga family. The Galleria degli Antenati is also noteworthy.

Vespasiano Gonzaga is buried in the **church of the Incoronata** with its octagonal plan and dome. Vespasiano's mausoleum is adorned with a bronze statue by Leone Leoni (1509-90); he is depicted as Marcus Aurelius.

The **Museo d'Arte Sacra** displays the order of the **Golden Fleece** discovered in 1988 in Vespasiano's tomb *(see above)* in the church.

The 19C **Synagogue** (Sinagoga) traces the story of the town's Jewish community whose great legacy was the elegant printworks also used by Vespasiano.

Massa Marittima★★

The name Massa Marittima is believed by some to indicate that the territory formerly extended as far as the sea; others think it refers to the nearby Maremma region. This old medieval town stands in rolling countryside and blends harmoniously with the various activities – mining, farming and craftwork – on which its prosperity has been based since its very beginnings.

Location

Population 8 823 – Michelin map 430 M 14 – See also The Green Guide Tuscany. Massa Marittima is on the road that links Follonica with Siena, nestling in the foothills and surrounded by picture-postcard Tuscan countryside. 🏛 *Via Parenti 22, ☎ 0566 90 27 56.Surrounding area: see SIENA.*

DIRECTORY
Osteria da Tronca – *Vicolo Porte 5 – ☎ 0566 90 19 91 – Closed Wed, 29 Dec-Feb – 🏠 – €19/26.* The motto *Amo talmente il vino che maledico chi mangia l'uva* ("I love wine so much that damned be those who eat the grapes") leaves guests in no doubt as to what kind of establishment this is. Regional cooking, rustic-style interior and plenty to drink!

Worth a Visit

Piazza Garibaldi★★
This lovely square is lined by some fine medieval buildings, three of which are of Romanesque origin – Palazzo del Podestà with its many double-windowed bays, the crenellated Palazzo Comunale and the cathedral.

Duomo★★
The cathedral was probably built in the early 11C. In addition to the Romanesque style, Gothic-style features were added in 1287 by **Giovanni Pisano**. The majestic building is adorned with blind arcades in the lower part and dominated by a fine campanile, at one time crenellated but now surmounted by a spire with four bellcotes, pierced with windows which increase in number with the height.

The interior, in the form of a Latin cross, comprises three aisles which are divided by two rows of columns crowned with capitals of different styles. The inside wall of the façade is decorated with striking pre-Romanesque low reliefs revealing the Byzantine influence (10C). There is an unusual baptismal font (1267). In the chapel to the left of the choir stalls is the panel of the *Virgin of the Graces* which has been attributed to **Duccio di Buoninsegna** and the remains of the *Presentation of Christ at the Temple* by Sano di Pietro (1406-81). In the chapel to the right of the choir stalls is a *Crucifixion* by Segna di Bonaventura (recorded from 1298 to 1327).

Palazzo del Podestà
The palace, which dates back to 1225-30, was the residence of the town's most eminent magistrate (*podestà*). The façade is decorated with the coat of arms of the *podestà*. The building now houses the **Museo archeologico**: exhibits include an

Massa Marittima, a medieval jewel in the country

interesting stele by Vado dell'Arancio *Open daily except Mon, Apr to Oct 10am-12.30pm and 3.30-7pm, rest of year 10am-12.30pm and 3-5pm. €2.58. ☎ 0566 90 22 89; www.coopcollinemetallifere.it*
The palace also houses the splendid *Virgin in Majesty* by Ambrogio Lorenzetti (1285-c 1348).

Museo della miniera
& *For information on opening times ☎ 0566 90 22 89; www.coopcollinemetallifere.it*
The museum, which is situated near Piazza Garibaldi, evokes the mining activities in the 700m/770yds of tunnels in the surrounding area; note the supporting timberwork and extraction techniques.
►►Fortezza dei Senesi e Torre del Candeliere★, S. Agostino.

Excursions

Abbazia and eremo di San Galgano★★
32km/20mi northeast. This ruined, but still impressive, Gothic Cistercian Abbey, the first Gothic church in Tuscany, was built by monks from 1224 to 1288, and dedicated to **St Galgan** (1148-81). The remains of the old monastery include the cloisters, the chapter house and the scriptorium.

Grosseto
52km/31mi southeast. This modern-looking provincial capital is situated in the fertile Ombrone Plain. The old town is encircled with late-16C ramparts and their powerful bastions built by the Medici. There is an interesting **Museo Archeologico**. & *Open May-Oct, daily, 10am-1pm and 5-8pm; Mar and Apr, daily, 9am-1pm and 4-6pm; rest of year, Tue-Fri 9am-1pm, Sat-Sun and hols 9am-1pm and 4-6pm. Closed 1 Jan, 1 May, 25 Dec. €5. ☎ 0564 48 87 50; www.gol.grosseto.it*
The 13C abbey church of **San Francesco** contains small frescoes by the 14C Sienese school and a lovely painted 13C crucifix.

Matera★★

Matera overlooks a ravine separating it from the Murge Hills in Puglia. This provincial capital stands in the heart of a region dissected by deeply eroded gorges – a desolate landscape with wide horizons. Modern Matera, the town's centre of activity, is laid out on a plateau overlooking the lower town with its many rock dwellings *(sassi)*, now mostly abandoned. In the town and surrounding area there are some 130 churches hewn out of the rock. These date back to the 8C BC and the arrival of Oriental (non-Latin) monastic communities who settled locally and in Puglia. They were adept in this form of underground architecture which shows a Byzantine influence.

Location
Population 56 924 – Michelin map 431 E 31 – Basilicata. Matera lies at the heart of Basilicata, on S 7, Via Appia.
🖪 *Via De Viti de Marco 9, ☎ 0835 33 19 83. Surrounding area: see CALABRIA, PUGLIA.*

Worth a Visit

The Sassi★★
The two main troglodyte quarters are on either side of the rock crowned by the cathedral. The roofs on some houses serve as walkways while the lower storeys are hewn out of the rock. Little limewashed houses and stairways overlap and over-hang one another in a labyrinth which is difficult to unravel.

Strada dei Sassi★★
This panoramic street skirts the wild gorge and runs round the cathedral rock. The natural rock walls are riddled with both natural and man-made caves.

Duomo★
The cathedral was built in the 13C Apulian-Romanesque style; the façade has a lovely rose window and a projecting gallery above the single doorway. The walls are embellished with blind arcades. On the south side are two richly sculpted door-ways. The interior was remodelled in the 17C and 18C. The Byzantine fresco por-traying the Madonna dates from the 12C-13C, the Neapolitan crib is 16C and the lovely carved stalls of the choir are 15C. The **Chapel of the Annunciation**★ has a beautiful Renaissance decoration.

Chiesa di San Pietro Caveoso
Open daily, 10am-noon and 3.30-5.30pm. No charge. ☎ *0835 31 15 10.*
This Baroque church stands at the foot of Monte Errone, which has several churches hewn out of the rock and decorated with frescoes, namely Santa Lucia alle Malve, Santa Maria de Idris and San Giovanni in Monterrone.

Museo Nazionale Ridola
& *Open daily except Mon am, 9am-8pm. Closed 1 Jan, 25 Dec.* €2.50☎ *0835 31 00 58.*
This museum in a former monastery has an interesting collection of archaeologic-al finds, which were discovered locally.

▶▶Views of Matera★★ from the two belvederes *(4km/2.4mi by the Altamura road, then take the Taranto road and finally turn right and follow the "chiese rupestri" – rock churches – signpost).*

Merano★★

MERAN

Merano is an important tourist centre and spa. With its mild climate and thermal waters, it attracts people seeking relief from blood disorders, meta-bolic disorders and respiratory problems, rheumatism and other chronic conditions. Other attractions include the Gran Premio Ippico, the most famous steeplechase race in Italy, which Merano hosts. There are numerous cable cars and chairlifts up to Merano 2000, a good winter sports centre also popular in summer for excursions into the mountains.

Location
Population 34 120 – Michelin map 429 B-C 15 – Trentino-Alto Adige. Merano lies at the start of the wider upper valley of the Adige, known as the Val Venosta. There is a motorway link with Bolzano. 🛈 *Corso della Libertà 35,* ☎ *0473 23 52 23.*
Surrounding area: see BOLZANO.

Worth a Visit

Passeggiate d'Inverno and d'Estate★★
These winter and summer promenades run along the Passirio River. The win-ter one, facing south, is shady and flower-decked and attractively lined with shops, cafés and terraces and is by far the busier. It is prolonged by the Passeggiata Gilf which ends near a powerful waterfall. The summer prom-enade, on the opposite bank, meanders through a lovely park planted with pines and palm trees.

DIRECTORY
Sissi – *Via Galilei 44 –*
☎ *0473 23 10 62 – Closed Mon, 8-22 Jan, 1-15 Jul –* 🚫 🅿 *– Book – €38/49.* A quiet, elegant establishment. Lovely public lounge with picture windows and Art Nouveau lamps – very atmospheric in the evening. More intimate "snugs" on the first floor. Innovative cuisine using seasonal produce.

Passeggiata Tappeiner★★

This magnificent promenade (4km/2.4mi long) winds high above Merano affording remarkable viewpoints as far as the Tyrol.

Duomo di San Nicolò

This Gothic cathedral has a huge belfry and a west front with a crenellated gable. The right-hand side is decorated with a 14C statue of St Nicholas and a gigantic statue of St Christopher that was repainted in the 19C. The interior, roofed with beautiful ribbed **Gothic vaulting★**, includes two 15C stained-glass windows and two painted wooden **Gothic polyptychs★** (16C) by Knoller, a native of the Tyrol. In the neighbouring **Cappella di Santa Barbara** standing at the start of the old footpath leading to Tirolo is a 16C high relief of the *Last Supper.*

Via Portici (Laubengasse)★

This arcade-lined street is overlooked by houses with painted façades and oriel windows. The shops have curiously sculpted façades.

Castello Principesco★

Open daily except Mon, 10am-5pm, Sun and hols 10am-1pm. Closed 1 Jan, 25 Dec, Jan and Feb. €2. ☎ 0473 25 03 29; www.comune.merano.bz.it/tuttocittà/cultura
Built in the 14C and extended in the 15C, this castle has crenellated gables and a tower with a pepper-pot roof. It was used by the Princes of Tyrol as their residence when they stayed in the town. It has some fine apartments that are stylishly if austerely furnished.

Excursions

Avelengo★

10km/6mi to the southeast. A scenic road leads to the plateau of Avelengo which dominates the Merano valley.

Merano 2000∗

Access by cable car from Val di Nova, 3km/1.9mi east. Open Jun to 7 Nov and 18 Dec-10 Apr, daily, 9am-5pm. ☎ 0473 23 48 21.
This conifer-clad plateau is a winter sports centre. It also makes a good base for excursions into the mountains in summer.

Tirolo★

4km/2mi north. It can also be reached by ski lift from Merano. This charming Tyrolean village in the middle of vineyards and orchards is dominated by its castle, **Castel Tirolo**, built in the 12C by the Counts of Val Venosta. *Open mid-Mar to Oct, daily except Mon, 10am-5pm. Closed in winter. €2.60 – €5.20. ☎ 0473 22 02 21.*
Castel Fontana (also known as the **Brunnenburg**) is a strange set of 13C fortifications rebuilt at a later date. The American poet Ezra Pound worked on his *Cantos* here from 1958, when the accusation of collaboration with the Nazi regime based on his radio programmes was lifted.

Tours

VAL PASSIRIA★

50km/31mi to the Rombo Pass; 40km/25mi to the Monte Giovo Pass. The road follows the Passiria Valley as far as the attractive Tyrolean village of **San Leonardo**, which clusters round its church. The **Rombo Pass Road★** (Timmelsjoch), steep and often cut out of the living rock, offers impressive views of the mountain peaks on the frontier. The **Monte Giovo Pass Road★** (Jaufenpass) climbs amid conifers. On the way down, there are splendid **views★★** of the snow-capped summits of Austria.

VAL VENOSTA★

From Merano, take S 38 in the direction of Resia. Val Venosta is a long, sunny valley covered in apple orchards which gradually becomes wider and wider to the west as it climbs towards the Resia pass. It can be reached from Merano, just after the attractive Birreria Forst. It is bordered by the Valtellina at the **Stelvio Pass**, by Switzerland at the Tubre mountain pass and by Austria at the Resia pass.
Val Venosta's history reaches far back into time and is best recounted through its most famous inhabitant, Ötzi, who lived 5 300 years ago and whose body was preserved by the ice in the spot where he died, in Val Senales, a bifurcation of Val Venosta. (*Ötzi is now an important exhibit in the Archaeological Museum of Bolzano. See BOLZANO*).

Naturno – From Merano take the road in the direction of the Resia pass for 15km/9mi. After passing the massive Birreria Forst, the road leads to Naturno which stands at a crossroads of the Val Venosta and the Val Senales. This "junction" is dominated by the 13C **Juval Castle**, now owned by the mountain climber Reinhold Messner who has decorated the castle with priceless souvenirs from his explorations in Tibet. *Open daily except Wed, 10am-4pm. Closed Jul and Aug, Nov to Palm Sun. €7. ☎ 348 44 33 871.*

Before entering the town, the slightly hidden church of **San Procolo★**, surrounded by fruit orchards, can be seen. The tiny structure houses the oldest frescoes in the German-speaking part of the Alto Adige (8C). The most notable fresco is the **Saint on a Swing**, a jolly and expressive figure who is thought to portray Procolo, the Bishop of Verona who fled the city. The scene portrays his flight; the saint undulates on the swing watched by the curious gazes of the men watching from the upper "windows" and the six people on the right. ♿ *Open daily except Mon, 9.30am-12pm and 2.30-5.30pm. Closed Mon (except hols), 5 Nov to mid-Apr €1.70. ☎ 0473 66 73 12.*

Sluderno – This town is dominated by **Coira Castle** which dates from 1253. Its current appearance is Renaissance; the internal loggia (1570) is particularly beautiful and adorned with the family tree of the owners, the Trapp family. The castle is also renowned for its very large and old armoury. *Open daily except Mon, 20 Mar to Oct 10am-12pm and 2-4.30pm. Guided tours only. Closed Mon (except hols). €5.1, €12.91 family ticket. ☎ 0473 61 52 41.*

Glorenza – This old city counts less than 1 000 inhabitants. Glorenza was already documented in 1178 and is well worth a visit as it is the only fortified town in the Alto Adige where time has stood still. It is entirely surrounded by ramparts and has the only arcading in the whole valley. The parish church, situated outside the city walls, has a frescoed exterior (1496) depicting *The Last Judgement*.

Malles – Malles is home to a jewel of Romanesque architecture, the Church of **San Benedetto★**, dating from the 9C. Note the frescoes depicting a Frankish nobleman holding a sword and an ecclesiastic holding a model of the church. Their faces are framed by two square haloes. *Guided tours only. For information, Ufficio Turistico Malles ☎ 0473 83 11 90.*

Burgusio – Those en route to the Resia pass cannot fail to see the huge white abbey of **Montemaria**. Even when it is snowing the sloping roof and the bulbous towers and campanile are still visible.

A visit to the **crypt** will reveal extraordinary Romanesque frescoes dating from the 12C when the abbey was founded. The paintings are based on the *Apocalypse* and show a clear Byzantine influence. The Pantocrator (Christ the Almighty) is depicted in a lozenge bordered by a rainbow, a symbol of peace. On the sides are cherubim and seraphim with their wings fanning out above their heads, lower down the Evangelists are portrayed. The painting on the opposite walls depicts the walls of celestial Jerusalem. *Open Jul to Sep, Mon-Fri 10am, 11am, 3pm and 4pm, Sat 10am and 11am; Apr-Jun Mon-Fri 10.45am and 3pm, Sat 10.45am; rest of year by reservation only. Closed Sun and hols €3. ☎ 0473 83 13 06.*

Lago di Resia – A campanile mysteriously appears out of the waters of the lake: originally part of the church of Curono Vecchia, it was submerged by the waters of this artificial basin in 1950.

An enchanting sight: the old campanile rising up from the Lago di Resia

Milano★★★

MILAN

Milan is Italy's second city in terms of population, politics and cultural affairs. But the real spirit of Lombardy's capital lies in its commercial, industrial and banking activities which have made Milan, set in the heart of northern Italy at the foot of the Alps, the country's financial heartland. The enterprising spirit of its people has built upon the city's history to make Milan one of the country's most dynamic towns.

Location

Population 1 300 977 – Michelin map 428 F 9 (with plans of the conurbation) and the Michelin City Map 46 of Milan. Milan lies at the heart of a network of motorways that includes A 4 (Turin-Venice), A 7 (Milan-Genoa), A 1 (Milan-Florence) and A 8 (the Lake District). The town is bounded by two concentric boulevards: the shorter, enclosing the medieval centre, has replaced the 14C ramparts, of which traces remain, among them the Porta Ticinese and the Porto Nuovo. The outer wall marks the town's expansion during the Renaissance. After 1870 Milan expanded rapidly beyond its fortifications, particularly along the main communication axes.
🗐 *Via Marconi 1,* ☎ *02 72 52 41.*
Surrounding area: see BERGAMO, Regione dei LAGHI, PAVIA.

Background

HISTORY

Milan is probably Gallic (Celtic) in origin, but it was the Romans who subdued the city of Mediolanum in 222 BC and ensured its expansion. At the end of the 3C Diocletian made Milan the seat of the rulers of the Western

Empire, and in 313 Constantine published the **Edict of Milan** which gave freedom of worship to the Christians. In 375 **St Ambrose** (340-96), a Doctor of the Church known for his eloquence, became bishop of the town, thus adding to its prestige.

The barbarian invasions of the 5C and 6C were followed by the creation of a Lombard kingdom with Pavia as capital. In 756 Pepin, King of the Franks, conquered the area, and his son Charlemagne was to wear the Iron Crown of the Kings of Lombardy from 774. In 962 Milan once again became capital of Italy.

In the 12C Milan allied itself to other cities to form the Lombard League (1167) to thwart the attempts of the Emperor Frederick Barbarossa to conquer the region. With the decisive victory at **Legnano** the cities of the league achieved their independence. In the 13C the **Visconti**, Ghibellines and leaders of the local aristocracy, seized power. The most famous member was **Gian Galeazzo** (1347-1402), an able war leader, man of letters, assassin and pious builder of Milan's Cathedral and the Carthusian Monastery of Pavia. His daughter, Valentina, married Louis, Duke of Orleans, the grandfather of Louis XII of France. This family connection was the reason for the later French expeditions into Italy.

After the death of the last Visconti, Filippo-Maria (d 1447), and three years of the Ambrosian Republic, the Sforza took over the rule of Milan, thanks to Francesco, the son of a simple peasant and son-in-law of Filippo-Maria Visconti. The most famous figure in the **Sforza** family, **Ludovico il Moro** (1452-1508) made Milan a new Athens by attracting to his court the geniuses of the time, Leonardo da Vinci and Bramante. However, Louis XII of France proclaimed himself the legitimate heir to the Duchy of Milan and set out to conquer the territory in 1500. His successor François I renewed the offensive but was thwarted at Pavia by the troops of the Emperor Charles V. From 1535 to 1713 Milan was under Spanish rule. During the plague, which ravaged the town from 1576 to 1630, members of the Borromeo family, St Charles (1538-84) and Cardinal Federico (1564-1631) distinguished themselves by their religious and humanitarian work.

Directory

GETTING THERE

By car and train – A good network of motorways serves the city (A 4 Turin-Venice, A 8/A 9 Milan-Lakes, A 7 Milan-Genoa, A 1 Autostrada del Sole which heads south).

By air – A train connects Malpensa airport with Cadorna station (every half-hour; journey time 40min) which in turn connects to the underground system. Tickets cost €9.30 (single), €12.39 (return). Information: www.malpensaexpress.com, ☎ 02 27 763 (recorded message), ☎ 02 20 222.

There are also buses from the airport which leave approximately every 20 minutes (journey time 45min/1hr depending on traffic). They stop at both the Stazione Centrale and the Stazione Cadorna (in this case the bus serves as a substitute when the train doesn't run: before 6.50am and after 8.20pm). Tickets cost €7.75.

Note that taxis are rather expensive as the airport is about 40km/25mi away from the city.

For flights landing at Linate airport there are buses which go to San Babila (line 73). Tickets cost €0.77.

GETTING ABOUT

By public transport – It is highly advisable to use public transport: in general it is punctual and quick (especially the three underground lines). It also avoids problems like getting stuck in heavy traffic, losing one's way (particularly in the city centre with its obligatory traffic systems that frequently result in leading you far away from your required destination) and wandering around looking for parking spaces which often seem like mirages.

By car – If you do use a car bear in mind that parking in the city centre and the Fiera (exhibition centre) district is by payment only and subject to regulations. Yellow lines indicate parking for residents only, blue lines allow parking for up to 2 hours as long as pre-paid cards, purchased from parking attendants or at tobacconists, are displayed (1hr €1.29, 2hr €2.58). It is advisable to park in designated car parks (look out for blue signposts) or just outside the central zone of the city, but only where blue lines are displayed. Prices here are slightly lower than in the city centre and sometimes flat rates are charged before you leave your car (find out from the parking attendant what the charges are).

WHERE TO EAT

Milanese cooking is best known for its *costoletta di vitello fritta* (fillet of veal fried in breadcrumbs with cheese), *l'ossobuco* (a knuckle of veal with the marrowbone), *risotto allo zafferano* (rice cooked with saffron) and *minestrone* (a soup of green vegetables, rice and bacon). In terms of wine, look out for the Valtellina and Oltrepò Pavese labels, which are local to the region.

• **Budget**

Premiata Pizzeria – *Alzaia Naviglio Grande, zona Navigli* – ☎ 02 89 40 06 48 – ✍. Tasty pizza in a setting where everything from the signboard to the covered courtyard is pleasant. Very crowded (on arrival leave your name and you will be told how long you will have to wait, then go and have a walk in the neighbouring vicolo dei Lavandai until your table is ready).

Rino Vecchia Napoli – *Via G. Chavez 4, zona Piazzale Loreto* – ☎ 02 26 19 056 – ✍. Excellent pizzas that deserve manifold awards. Go there armed with patience (it's always very crowded) and be prepared to make way for the next customers. Needless to say service is speedy. Don't forget to book!

Pizzeria Geppo – *Via G. B. Morgagni 37, zona Piazzale Loreto* – ☎ 02 29 51 48 62 – ✍ – *Book*. Practically a broom cupboard that serves delicious, large but thin pizza. Booking is recommended, as everyone knows about this place!

Dulcis in Fundo – *Via Zuretti 55, zona Stazione Centrale* – ☎ 02 66 71 25 03 – *dulcis@iol.it* – *Closed Mon, evenings (except Thu)* – ✍ 🍽 – €15/23. Post-Modern meets 1970s... A rather extraordinary establishment housed in an old industrial building which has been painted in pastel colours and decked out with an eclectic jumble of tables and chairs. On the menu is a vast selection of tarts, puddings and savouries as well as a limited number of unusual main courses. Thursday evening is a complete riot. Children very welcome.

Mykonos – *Via Tofane 5, zona Naviglio Martesana* – ☎ 02 26 10 209 – *Closed Tue, lunchtime, 9am-midnight Aug* – ✍ – *Book* – €20/24. A simple, rustic-style Greek restaurant housed in a pretty building. The cuisine draws on tradition but the proprietor, who hails from Greece, also brings a personal touch to a number of typically Greek dishes.

• **Moderate**

Trattoria all'Antica – *Via Montevideo 4, zona Navigli* – ☎ 02 58 10 48 60 – *Closed Sat lunchtime, Sun, Aug, 26 Dec-7 Jan* – 🍽 – €24/32. A great combination – authentic regional cooking, a cheerful ambience and an eccentric proprietor. Not for the fainthearted or those on a diet – the portions are very

Panettone

generous! *The risotto allo zafferano* (rice cooked with saffron) and *cotechini fumanti* (Italian pork sausage) are excellent as are the *affettati* (sliced cold meats and salami). More varied menu in the evening.

Al Mercante – *Piazza Mercanti 17, zona Centro Storico* – ☎ *02 80 52 198 – Closed Sun, 1-7 Jan, 3-28 Aug –* 🗑 *– €34/46.* A busy restaurant focusing on traditional, regional cooking. Smart interior with lovely *outside* dining area overlooking the little square. Specialities include risotto and ossobuco. Despite all the comings and goings, the staff are polite, friendly and efficient.

Masuelli San Marco – *Viale Umbria 80, zona Porta Romana-Porta Vittoria –* ☎ *02 55 18 41 38 – Closed Sun and Mon lunchtime, 25 Dec-6 Jan, 16 Aug-10 Sep –* 🗑 *– Book – €35/47.* A popular restaurant which has been in the same family for eight generations. Classic, regional cooking which is closely linked to the seasons and the tradition of serving certain dishes on certain days, for example, "Cassoela" on Thursdays.

• *Expensive*

Savini – *Galleria Vittorio Emanuele II, zona Centro Storico* – ☎ *02 72 00 34 33 – Closed Sun, 1-6 Jan, 6-27 Aug –* 🗑 *– Book – €62/89 + 12% service charge.* One of the city's most historic establishments situated in one of the most atmospheric arcades in Italy. Would appeal to those looking for a gastronomic (but unpretentious) experience and a decadent *fin de siècle* atmosphere. The excellent cuisine draws on tradition but is also innovative.

WHERE TO STAY

It is worth noting that during trade fairs and exhibitions the hotels tend to put their prices up. Do enquire about this when you make your booking. The better hotels tend to be very expensive and in view of this, travellers on a tight budget might want to try and find accommodation outside the city (see PAVIA).

• *Moderate*

Hotel Garden – *Via Rutilia 6, zona urbana Sud-Est –* ☎ *02 55 21 28 38 – Fax 02 57 30 06 78 – Closed Aug –* 🅿 *– 23 rm €56.81/82.65.* For value for money, this is a real find. An unpretentious hotel, with functional, comfortable rooms. Quiet situation, with good links to the city centre. There is also a lovely garden shaded by a large plane tree. Breakfast not included.

Albergo Città Studi – *Via Saldini 24, zona Città Studi –* ☎ *02 74 46 66 – Fax 02 71 31 22 –* 🗑 *– 45 rm €64.55/108.45 –* ☕ *€7.74.* Located in one of the busiest University areas in town. Quiet, simple hotel, with adequate facilities. Most importantly it represents excellent value for money.

Hotel des Etrangers – *Via Sirte 9, zona Navigli –* ☎ *02 48 95 53 25 – Fax 02 48 95 53 25 –* 🗑 *– 69 rm €69.72/134.28* ☕. This hotel is situated near the trade fair district and is well served by public transport. It is reasonably quiet with functional, modern rooms. Represents extremely good value for money.

• *Expensive*

Hotel Gala – *Viale Zara 89, zona urbana Nord-Est –* ☎ *02 66 80 08 91 – Fax 02 66 80 04 63 – Closed Aug –* 🅿 🗑 *– 23 rm from €90 –* ☕ *€10.* This family-run hotel is particularly well situated for anyone arriving by car. Other attractions include easy access to the centre, quiet location and lovely garden. Definitely one for the address book.

Hotel Regina – *Via Cesare Correnti 13, zona Centro Storico –* ☎ *02 58 10 69 13 – Fax 02 58 10 70 33 – Closed 24 Dec-7 Jan, Aug. –* 🗑 ♿ *– 43 rm from €129* ☕. A rather grand and elegant hotel with 18C overtones. The internal courtyard, the vaulting supported by columns, has been covered over with glass creating a very atmospheric entrance hall. Highly recommended.

Hotel Cavour – *Via Fatebenefratelli 21, zona Centro Direzionale –* ☎ *02 65 72 051 – Fax 02 65 92 263 – Closed 24 Dec-6 Jan, Aug –* 🗑 *– 113 rm from €174* ☕. There is an understated elegance about this hotel which extends to both the public areas and the rooms which are functional but comfortable. Efficiently and professionally managed by one of Milan's oldest family of hoteliers.

Hotel Spadari al Duomo – *Via Spadari 11, zona Centro Storico –* ☎ *02 72 00 23 71 – Fax 02 86 11 84 –* 🗑 *– 39 rm from €208* ☕. A stylish, comfortable hotel with a very contemporary feel overlooking the spires of the Duomo. On display are various pieces of modern art and sculpture, the work of some of the city's more avant-garde artists, along with a collection of original designer furniture.

TAKING A BREAK

Bar Basso – *Via Plinio 39, zona Stazione Centrale –* ☎ *02 29 40 05 80 – Tue-Sun 7.30am-8.30pm.* This is where the "wrong" Negroni cocktail was invented, using champagne instead of gin.

Bar Bianco – *Giardini di Palestro, zona Porta Venezia.* Establishment specialising in milk-based drinks and other such products.

Bar Magenta – *Via Carducci 13, zona S. Ambrogio –* ☎ *02 80 53 808 – 8-2.30am.* This is one of the most famous bars in Milan, frequented by people of different generations and ideological extractions, according to the fashion of the moment. It is worth tasting the very rich *aperitivo* while taking a look around: the counter is typical of the decor of this Art Nouveau style bar.

Bar della Crocetta – *Corso di Porta Romana 67 –* ☎ *02 54 50 228 – 8-1.30am.* The perfect place for sandwich enthusiasts. They come in an impressive array of shapes and sizes and with a wide variety of fillings. Well located for anyone heading for the Teatro Carcano.

Crota piemunteisa – *Piazza Cesare Beccaria 10, zona Centro Storico –* ☎ *02 80 52 707 – Tue-Sun 7am-2am, Mon 5pm-2am.* This tiny space behind the Duomo is just big enough to hold tables and wooden stools, a jukebox, two counters (one for beer, one for sandwiches – be sure to try the excellent frankfurters and sauerkraut). Over the decades this establishment has attracted a mixed bag of people who seem to have no common denominator.

Gattullo – *Piazzale Porta Lodovica 2.* One of the best places for a freshly baked brioche and a good cappuccino.

Gelateria Marghera – *Via Marghera 33, zona Fiera* – ☎ 02 46 86 41 – *8am-midnight.* Not far from the Teatro Nazionale and the Fiera district. Excellent selection of creamy ice creams.

Moscatelli – *Corso Garibaldi 93, zona Brera* – *10-1am.* The perfect place to taste Italian wines accompanied by something to nibble on.

Taveggia – *Via Visconti di Modrone 2, zona S. Babila* – ☎ 02 76 02 12 57. This establishment serves one of the best hot chocolates – dark and syrupy – in Milan.

Viel – *Corso Buenos Aires 15* – ☎ 02 29 51 61 23 – *9-1am* – *Viale Abruzzi 23* – ☎ 02 20 40 43 9. Famous for its milkshakes, this bar has been a student hang-out for decades.

LIFE IN MILAN

The most frequented parts of Milan are around Piazza del Duomo, Via Dante and Via Manzoni. At the *Galleria Vittorio Emanuele* II, the Milanese come to talk, read their *Corriere della Sera* or drink coffee side by side with the tourists. For visitors looking for luxury items or just wanting to stroll through the most fashionable districts in the city, the Corso Vittorio Emanuele II, the Piazza San Babila, the Corso Venezia, and the Via Monte Napoleone and Via della Spiga – where the couture houses are – are pleasant areas to explore. The Corso Magenta and the streets around Sant'Ambrogio have retained all the charm of the Milan of another age with old houses and winding, narrow streets lined with old cafés and antique shops.

GOING OUT

Head for the picturesque Brera District, which is popular with artists and full of art galleries, and buzzing with life in the evening.

Le Scimmie – *Via A. Sforza 49, zona Navigli* – ☎ 02 89 40 28 74 – *9-1am.* A large trattoria with four rooms in total and live music (mostly jazz).

ENTERTAINMENT

Milan has a very lively cultural and artistic scene. The city hosts a number of musical events – classical, jazz, klezmer – where some of the world's most famous stars come to perform. There are also a number of theatres.

Music

La Scala – *Piazza Scala, zona Centro Storico* – ☎ 02 72 00 37 44. Stages opera and ballet. The season traditionally starts on St Ambrose's day.

Auditorium di Milano – *Corso S. Gottardo, zona Navigli* – ☎ 02 83 38 92 01. Performances of classical, jazz, klezmer and other types of music. Also hosts literary evenings, events for children as well as audiences with well-known artistes.

Conservatorio – *Via Conservatorio 12, zona S. Babila* – ☎ 02 76 21 101. Varied programme of chamber and orchestral music.

drama

Teatro Dal Verme – *Via San Giovanni sul Muro 5, zona Centro Storico. Box office: via Rovello* – ☎ 02 72 33 32 22.

Piccolo Teatro – The Piccolo Teatro di Strehler comprises three theatres, all of which are centrally located: *Teatro Strehler, Largo Greppi; Teatro Grassi, via Rovello 2; Teatro Studio, via Rivoli 6* – ☎ 02 72 33 32 22; *info@piccoloteatro.org; www.piccoloteatro.org*

Teatro Carcano – *Corso di Porta Romana 63* – ☎ 02 55 18 13 77.

Teatro Manzoni – *Via Manzoni 40, zona Centro Storico* – ☎ 02 76 36 901.

Under Napoleon, Milan became the capital of the Cisalpine Republic (1797) and later of the Kingdom of Italy (1805). In 1815 Milan assumed the role of capital of the Venetian-Lombard Kingdom.

FINE ARTS

The Cathedral (Duomo) marks the climax of architecture of the Gothic period. Prominent architects during the Renaissance were the Florentine Michelozzo (1396-1472) and especially **Donato Bramante** (1444-1514), favourite master mason of Ludovico il Moro before he left for Rome. An admirer of Classical art, he was both a classicist and a man of great imagination who invented the **rhythmic articulation** (a façade with alternating bays, pilasters and niches) which imparted much of their harmony to many Renaissance façades.

The Lombard school of painting sought beauty and grace above all else. Its principal exponents were Vincenzo Foppa (1427-1515), Bergognone (1450-1523) and Bramantino (between 1450 and 1465-1536). The works of Andrea Solario (1473-c 1520), Boltraffio (1467-1516) and especially the delicate canvases of **Bernardino Luini** (c 1480-1532) attest to the influence of **Leonardo da Vinci** who stayed in Milan for some time.

Today Milan is the capital of Italy's publishing business and is an important centre, with its numerous art galleries, for contemporary art.

Special Features

PIAZZA DUOMO AND SURROUNDING AREA

Duomo★★★

Exterior – This Gothic marvel of white marble, both colossal and ethereal, bristling with belfries, gables, pinnacles and statues, stands at one end of a great paved esplanade teeming with people and pigeons. While they are part of the setting, the pigeons are largely responsible for the building's deterioration. Its recent restoration was a lengthy and highly technical process. It should be seen late in the afternoon in the light of the setting sun. Building began with the chevet in 1386 on the orders of Gian Galeazzo Visconti, and continued in the 15C and 16C under the direction of Italian, French and German master masons. The façade was finished only between 1805 and 1809, on the orders of Napoleon.

Walk round the cathedral to view the **east end** with three vast bays of curved and counter-curved tracery and wonderful rose windows. The overall design is the work of a French architect, Nicolas de Bonaventure, and of a Modenese architect, Filippino degli Organi.

From the 7th floor of the Rinascente store in Corso Vittorio Emanuele there is an interesting close-up view of the architectural and sculptural features of the roofs.

Interior – In contrast with the exterior this is bare, severe and imposing, an impression further strengthened by the dim light. The nave and four aisles are separated by 52 pillars of tremendous height (148m/486ft). The width across the transepts is 91m/299ft. The windows of the nave, aisles and transept have fine stained glass, which dates in part back to the 15C and 16C.

The mausoleum of Gian Giacomo Medici in the south arm of the transept is a fine work by Leoni (16C). In the north arm is the curious statue of St Bartholomew (who was flayed alive), by the sculptor Marco d'Agrate. Pass under the dome and in front of the monumental chancel (1570-90) with the high altar by Pellegrino Tibaldi. The magnificent bronze candelabrum in the north transept is a French work of the 13C. In the crypt (cripta) and treasury (tesoro), visitors can see the silver urn containing the remains of St Charles Borromeo, Bishop of Milan, who died in 1584, as well as ivories and gold and silver church plate.

On the way out, you can see the entrance to the Early-Christian baptistery (battistero) and the 4C basilica of Santa Tecla whose outline has been marked out on the parvis. Crypt and treasury, open daily, 9am-12pm and 2.30-6pm. Baptistery, open daily, 9.45am-5pm.45. €1. No charge for crypt of S. Carlo. ☎ 02 72 02 26 56; www.interlandia.com/duomo

Visit to the roof★★★ – ♿ Open daily, Feb to Nov 9am-5.45pm, rest of year 9am-3.15pm. Closed 1 Jan, 1 May, 25 Dec. Life €5, on foot €3.50; €7 including museum. ☎ 02 72 02 26 56; www.interlandia.com/duomo

Take a walk on the roof to view the 135 pinnacles, numerous white marble statues (2 245 in all!), full of grace and elegance, and the Tiburio or central tower (108m/354ft), surmounted by a small gilt statue, the Madonnina (1774).

Museo del Duomo★★ – ♿ Open daily, 10am-1.15pm and 3-6pm. Closed Easter, 25 Apr, 1 May, 25 Dec. €6. €7 including life to roof, €12 with Pinacoteca included. ☎ 02 72 02 26 56; www.interlandia.com/duomo

Housed in the royal palace built in the 18C by Piermarini, the cathedral museum shows the various stages in the building and restoration of the cathedral, and houses sculptures, tapestries and old stained-glass windows. Also of note are the splendid **Aribert Crucifix★** (1040), the original support for the Madonnina (1772-73), and the large wooden **model★** (modellone) of the cathedral made to a scale of 1:20 in the 16C-19C.

Cross over to the **Galleria Vittorio Emanuele II★**, which was laid out in 1877 to the plans of Giuseppe Mengoni, and a focus of the city's political and social life. The far end opens out on to Piazza della Scala.

Teatro alla Scala★★

Traditionally recognised as being the most famous opera house in the world, La Scala surprises people seeing it for the first time because of the simplicity of its exterior, which gives no hint of the magnificence of its auditorium. Built from 1776 to 1778 with six levels of boxes, it can seat an audience of 2 000 people.

The **Museo teatrale alla Scala★** presents memorabilia relating to Toscanini and Verdi, including busts, portraits and stage costumes. From the museum, you can go into one of the boxes and see the auditorium. Museum: Open daily except Sun, 9am-12pm and 2-5pm. Closed Nov-Apr, hols. €3.10. ☎ 02 88 79 473; www.museoteatrale.com Turn into via S. Margherita.

Via and Piazza dei Mercanti★

In Via Mercanti stands the Palace of Jurisconsults (Palazzo dei Giureconsulti), built in 1564 with a statue of St Ambrose teaching on the façade. The Piazza dei Mercanti is quiet and picturesque. The charming Loggia degli Osii (1316) is decorated with heraldic shields, statues of saints and the balcony from which penal sentences were

Galleria Vittorio Emanuele

proclaimed. To the right of the loggia is the Baroque palace of the Palatine schools, with statues of the poet Ausonius and St Augustine in the niches. Opposite is the town hall, the **Palazzo della Ragione** or Broletto Nuovo **(D)**, which was built in the 13C and extended in the 18C. The **equestrian statue** on the façade, of the governing magistrate *(podestà)* Oldrado da Tresseno, is a Romanesque work by Antelami.

Worth a Visit

MUSEUMS

Pinacoteca di Brera★★★

Open daily, 8.30am-7.30pm (ticket office closes 45min early). Closed 1 Jan, 1 May, 25 Dec. €5. ☎ 02 89 42 11 46.

The Brera Art Gallery forms part of a series of institutes – the Accademia di Belle Arti (Fine Arts Academy), the Biblioteca (library), the Osservatorio Astronomico (observatory) and the Istituto Lombardo di Scienze, Lettere ed Arti (The Lombardy Institute of Science, Arts and Letters) – all of which are housed in a fine 17C building. In the courtyard looms a statue of Napoleon (1809) depicted as a victorious Roman emperor by Canova.

The tour of the gallery starts with the Jesi collection which introduces the main artistic movements of the first half of the 20C: note the sense of movement and dynamism of the Futurist painters (Boccioni's *La Rissa in galleria*, see p 97) and the clean geometry of the metaphysical works by Carrà *(The metaphysical muse)* and Morandi *(Still Life)*. The sculpture collection is dominated by three artists: Medardo Rosso, Arturo Martini and Marino Marini. Along the passage to the left, it is possible to admire the Maria Theresa Room and the library, Biblioteca Braidense. The Cappella Mocchirolo gives a brief review of Italian painting from the 13C to 14C *(Polyptych of Valle Romita)* by Gentile da Fabriano.

The Brera holding of **Venetian paintings** is the largest and most important one outside Venice. Masterpieces include the *Pietà*★★ by Giovanni Bellini, in which the tragic event is echoed by the deserted landscape and metallic sky, and the famous *Dead Christ*★★★ by Mantegna, an admirable meditation on death with a realism given added pathos by the artist's skill in foreshortening. In the Napoleon Rooms hang major works by Tintoretto *(Miracle of St Mark★)*, Veronese *(Dinner at the house of Simon)* and Giovanni and Gentile Bellini *(St Mark preaching at Alexandria in Egypt)*.

The **Lombard school** is well represented and pride of place is given to a *polyptych with Madonna and saints★* by Vicenzo Foppa, whose work shows the influence of the Paduan school and Mantegna in particular, and the lovely, Leonardesque *Madonna of the rose garden★★* by Bernardino Luini.

One room contains two Renaissance masterpieces from **Central Italy**: the *Montefeltro altarpiece★★★* by Piero della Francesca, in which the ostrich egg symbolises both the Immaculate Conception and the abstract and geometrical perfection of form sought by the artist, and the *Marriage of the Virgin★★★* by

Raphael, in which the graceful, delicate figures merge in the background with the circular Bramante-style building. Further along, Caravaggio's magnificent *Meal at Emmaus*★★★ is a fine example of the artist's use of strong contrast between light and shade and of his realism.

In the Room of 18C Venetian painting *Rebecca at the Well*★★ by Piazzetta is an exquisite portrayal of the girl's gaze, with expressions of both astonishment and innocence, even though the portrait is in profile.

The last rooms are dedicated to 19C-20C painting. Paintings on display include the *Carro rosso* by Fattori and *The Kiss* by Hayez. Among the foreign artists are Ribera, Van Dyck, Rubens and Reynolds.

Castello Sforzesco★★★

Open daily except Mon, 9.30am-5.30pm. Closed 1 Jan, 1 May, 15 Aug, 25 Dec. No charge. ☎ 02 86 46 36 51.

This huge brick quadrilateral building was the seat of the Sforza, Dukes of Milan. The **municipal art collections** are now on display in the castle.

Museo di Scultura★★ – *Ground floor.* The minimalist approach of the museum's layout is particularly effective. Romanesque, Gothic and Renaissance works are mainly by Lombard sculptors. Interesting works include the **tomb of Bernabò Visconti**★★ (14C) surmounted by his equestrian statue from the Romanesque period; and the **reclining figure of Gaston de Foix** with accompanying **statues**★★ (1523) by Bambaia in his usual classical and harmonious style, as well as the unfinished *Rondanini Pietà*★★★ by Michelangelo, both from the Renaissance.

Pinacoteca★ – *1st floor.* The gallery displays works by Mantegna, Giovanni Bellini, Crivelli, Bergognone, Luini, Moretto, Moroni, Magnasco, Tiepolo, Guardi, Lotto etc.

Museo degli strumenti musicali★ – An extensive collection of stringed instruments, some of which are made to resonate by the use of a bow and others which are plucked, wind instruments and keyboards.

Museo Archeologico – *In the vault under the Rochetta courtyard.* The museum includes a prehistory collection, Egyptian art and a lapidary exhibition. Another section of the museum is housed in the monastery of San Maurizio *(see below).*

Pinacoteca Ambrosiana★★

Open daily except Mon 10am-5.30pm. Closed 1 Jan, Easter, 1 May, 25 Dec. €6.20. ☎ 02 80 692; www.ambrosiana.it

This palace, erected in 1609 for Cardinal Federico Borromeo, was originally one of the first libraries open to the public. A few years later the gallery was added and housed the collection donated by the cardinal.

This is one of the richest libraries in the world and boasts a fine collection of drawings including Leonardo's **Codice Atlantico** series.

The gallery is housed on the first floor and opens with the original body of work donated by the cardinal, as well as subsequent acquisitions of the same period (15C and 16C). Note the *Portrait of a Lady* by De Predis and the delightful *Infant Jesus and the Lamb*★★ by Bernardino Luini, imbued with the warm intimacy that the artist expresses to bring alive a tender moment. One of the most notable paintings of the Lombard School is the *Sacra Conversazione* by Bergognone (1453-1523), with its Madonna dominating the composition whose use of perspective is still very much anchored in the Middle Ages. The *Musician*★★ by Leonardo da Vinci has an unusually dark background for the artist who tended to create a strong relationship between the dominant figures and their surrounding space. In Room 3 the *Madonna Enthroned with Saints*★ by Bramantino is striking for the huge toad at the feet of St Michael (symbolising the dragon slain by the saint) contrasting with the grotesque swollen figure of Arius (a reference to the defeat of the Arian heresy led by St Ambrose, see p 274). Note also the slightly masculine appearance of the Madonna's face which seems to be veiled by the hint of a beard. The delicate *Nativity*, a copy from Barocci, is pervaded by a glowing light which irradiates from the child, illuminating the Virgin's tender face. The splendid preparatory **cartoons**★★★ for Raphael'a School of Athens (the fresco was painted in the Vatican *Stanze* in Rome) are the only surviving example of large Renaissance cartoons. Caravaggio's *Basket of Fruit*★★★ made the still-life a key subject matter in painting. On a monochrome background shrivelled leaves and almost rotten fruit render the idea of death and the transitory nature of life. The cardinal's collection also includes a series of fine Flemish paintings by Paul Bril and Jan Brueghel's remarkable *Mouse with a Rose*★, painted on copper. Other rooms are mainly devoted to Italian art from the 16C-19C and focus on painting from Lombardy. Of particular note are four stunning **portraits**★ by Francesco Hayez.

Museo Poldi Pezzoli★★

Open daily except Mon, 10am-6pm. Closed hols. €6.20. ☎ 02 79 48 89.

Attractively set out in an old mansion, the museum displays collections of weapons, fabrics, paintings, **clocks**★, and small bronzes. Among the paintings on the 1st floor (at the top of an old staircase built into an irregular, octagonal-shaped stairwell) are works by the Lombard School (Bergognone, Luini, Foppa, Solario, Boltraffio), **portraits**★★ of Luther and his wife by Lucas Cranach and, in the Golden

MILANO

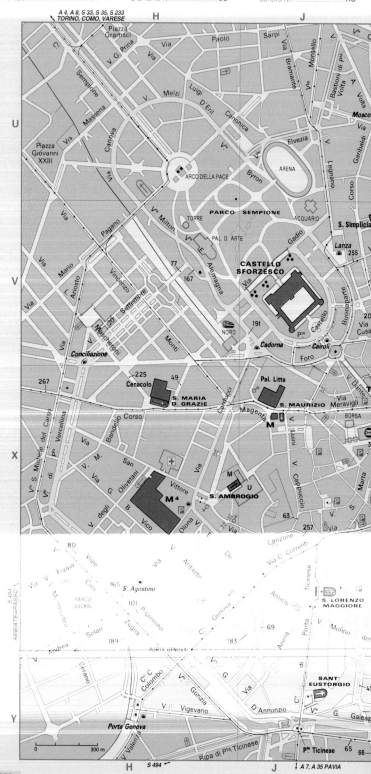

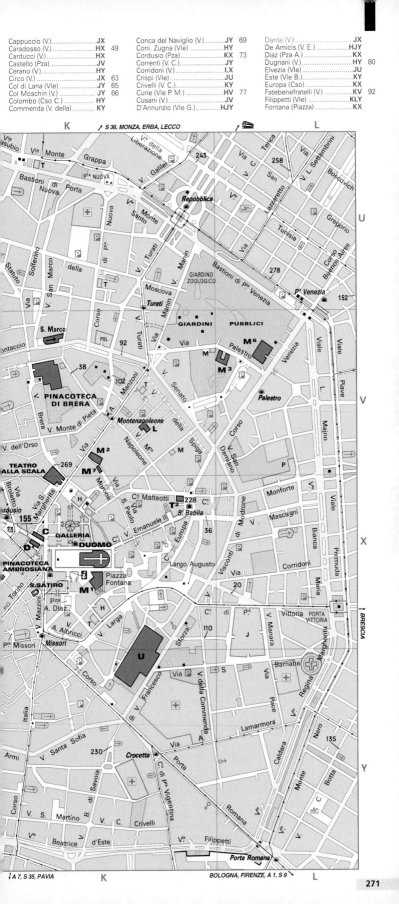

Milano

Hall decorated with a **Persian carpet**, the famous *Portrait of a Woman*★★★ by Piero del Pollaiolo, a **Descent from the Cross** and a *Madonna and Child*★★ by Botticelli, and a **Dead Christ**★ full of pathos by Giovanni Bellini. The other rooms are hung with works by Pinturicchio, Palma il Vecchio (*Portrait of a Courtesan*), Francesco Guardi, Canaletto, Tiepolo, Perugino and Lotto.

Palazzo Bagatti Valsecchi★★

Open Tue-Sun, 1-5.45pm. Closed Mon and bank hols. €6, €2 Wed. ☎ 02 76 00 61 32, www.museobagattivalsecchi.org

The façade of the palace is divided into two parts: they are connected by a loggia (*1st floor*) surmounted by a balcony. All that can be seen of the present residence (*opposite*) of the Bagatti Valsecchi family is the beautiful internal courtyard.

Museum – At the top of the flight of steps embellished with a wrought-iron railing is the *piano nobile* of the residence of Fausto and Giuseppe Bagatti Valsecchi, who, at the end of the 19C, decided to furnish their house in the Renaissance style, as was customary at the time. They used authentic pieces and faithful reproductions, adding their own personal touch. The two private apartments, belonging to Fausto and Giuseppe, are open to the public as well as the reception rooms.

Fausto's rooms comprise the **Fresco Room** (depicting the *Madonna of Mercy*, 1496), the **library** decorated with two splendid 16C leather globes (the blue one is a particularly fine example) and various objects including a 17C German roulette set and the **bedroom** which is dominated by a magnificent bed carved with *Christ's Ascent to Calvary* and various battle scenes. The bathroom is particularly charming: the bath is set in a Renaissance-style niche. The **Labyrinth Passage**, which is aptly named after the ceiling decoration, leads to the **Domed Gallery**, an area that serves to link the various rooms on the floor. The **room** containing a stove from Valtellina (Sala della stufa valtellinese) gives access to Giuseppe's apartment: the warm atmosphere is due to the fine wood panelling embellished with a sculpted frieze with human figures, animals and floral patterns. The **Red Room**, used by Giuseppe and Carolina Borromeo, his wife, contains children's furniture including a baby walker, commode and two cradles as well as a 17C Sicilian bed; Giuseppe's room, all in green, has a fine sculpted ceiling. Access to the formal rooms is via the domed gallery: the huge **reception hall,** heated by an impressive chimney, the **Arms Room** with its fine collection of bayonets and the **Dining Room** decorated with 14C Flemish tapestries, paintings and 17C ceramics.

Casa di Manzoni★

Via G. Morone 1. Open Mon-Fri, 9am-noon and 2-4pm. Closed weekends, hols, Aug, mid-Dec to mid-Jan. No charge. ☎ 02 86 46 04 03.

It was in this luxurious mansion that Alessandro Manzoni lived for 60 years. On the ground floor, visitors can see the library with the writer's books and desk. On the first floor are memorabilia, photographs, portraits, letters and illustrations of his most famous novel, **The Betrothed**. The bedroom where he died still has its original furniture.

Museo Civico di Storia Naturale★

Corso Venezia 55. Open daily Mon-Fri, 9am-6pm, Sat-Sun and hols, 9am-6.30pm. Closed 1 Jan, 1 May, 25 Dec. No charge. ☎ 02 88 46 32 80; www.reteculturale.regione.lombardia.it/adm

The Natural History Museum has been completely restructured. It contains interesting geological, palaeontological and zoological collections. The instructive layout with numerous dioramas is particularly suitable for children.

Museo della Scienza e della Tecnica Leonardo da Vinci★

♿ Open Tue-Fri, 9.30am-5pm (ticket office closes 4pm), Sat-Sun and hols 9.30am-6pm (ticket office closes 5pm). Closed 1 Jan, 25 Dec. €6.20. ☎ 02 48 55 51, www.museoscienza.org

This vast museum exhibits interesting scientific documents. In the **Leonardo da Vinci Gallery**, visitors can see models of the Tuscan artist's inventions. The other sections of the museum deal with acoustics, chemistry, telecommunications and astronomy. Large pavilions are given over to displays relating to the railways, aircraft and shipping.

Museo Civico di Archeologia★

Open daily except Mon, 9am-5.30pm. Closed 1 Jan, Easter, 1 May, 25 Dec. No charge. ☎ 02 80 53 972.

The museum housed in the extant buildings of the great Benedictine monastery is divided into five sections: Roman and barbarian art on the ground floor and Greek, Etruscan and Indian (Gandhara) art in the basement. The most outstanding Roman exhibits are the 4C **Trivulzio cup★** with fine openwork cut from a single piece of glass, and the large **silver platter from Parabiago★** (4C) featuring the festival of the goddess Cybele.

There are interesting remains of the 3C Roman wall in the garden.

Opposite the museum stands **Palazzo Litta** with its 18C façade

Galleria d'Arte Moderna

Via Palestro 16. Open daily except Mon, 9.30am-5.30pm. Closed 1 Jan, Easter, 1 May, 15 Aug, 25 Dec. No charge. ☎ 02 76 00 28 19.

The Modern Art Gallery has been set out in the Villa Reale built in 1790 which also houses the Marino Marini Museum and the Grassi Collection. It includes **The Fourth Estate** by Pelliza da Volpedo, works by Giovanni Segantini **(The Two Mothers, The Angel of Life)**, a famous **Portrait of Alexander Manzoni** by Francesco Hayez, and sculptures by the Milanese sculptor, Medardo Rosso (1858-1928). The **Carlo Grassi Collection** comprises works by Gaspare Van Wittel, Pietro Longhi, Cézanne, Van Gogh, Manet, Gauguin, Sisley, Corot, Toulouse-Lautrec, Boccioni and Balla. The **Marino Marini Museum** displays sculptures and paintings by the artist. The **Contemporary Art Pavilion (PAC)** *(Via Palestro 14)* has been designed for temporary exhibitions *(additional charge)*.

CHURCHES AND BASILICAS

Chiesa di San Maurizio Monastero Maggiore★★

This is a monastery church built in the Lombard-Renaissance style (early 16C). The bare façade, which often goes unnoticed on Corso Magenta despite the narrowness of the pavement, conceals an interior divided into two, well-lit sections and entirely decorated with **frescoes★** by Bernardino Luini. To reach the chancel (where concerts are held), take the passageway situated to the left at the back of the church.

Basilica di Sant'Ambrogio★★

The basilica was founded at the end of the 4C by St Ambrose and it is a magnificent example of the 11C-12C Lombard-Romanesque style with its pure lines and fine **atrium★** adorned with capitals. The façade pierced by arcading is flanked by a 9C campanile to the right and a 12C one to the left. The doorway was renewed in the 18C and has 9C bronze panels. In the crypt, behind the chancel, lie the remains of St Ambrose, St Gervase and St Protase.

Inside the basilica there is a magnificent Byzantine-Romanesque **ambo★** (12C) to the left of the nave, and at the high altar a precious gold-plated **altar front★★** which is a masterpiece of the Carolingian period (9C). In the chapel of San Vittore in Ciel d'Oro *(at the end of the south transept)* there are remarkable 5C **mosaics★**. From the far end of the north transept one can gain access to Bramante's portico.

Chiesa di Santa Maria delle Grazie★

This Renaissance church erected by the Dominicans from 1465 to 1490 was finished by Bramante. The interior (restored), is adorned with frescoes by Gaudenzio Ferrari in the fourth chapel on the right, and with the impressive **dome★**, gallery and cloisters all by Bramante. The best view of the **east end★** is to be had from Via Caradosso.

Cenacolo – *Open daily except Mon, 8.30am-6.45pm, by reservation only. €6.50 + €1 reservation. ☎ 02 89 42 11 46; www.cenacolo.brera.it*

In the former refectory *(cenacolo)* of the monastery is the famous portrayal of *The Last Supper*★★★ by **Leonardo da Vinci**, painted between 1495 and 1497 at the request of Ludovico il Moro. It is a dramatic and skilful composition that creates the illusion that the painted space is a continuation of the room itself.

Christ is depicted at the moment of the institution of the Eucharist: His half-open mouth suggests that he has just finished speaking. Around Him there is a tangible sense of shock and premonition of imminent disaster with its intimation of Judas' betrayal.

The technique used (Leonardo chose egg tempera, possibly mixed with oil and placed the image on the coldest wall in the room), dust, the ravages caused by a bomb falling on the refectory in 1943 and, more recently, smog have all contributed to the necessity for considerable restoration work (it has been documented that the painting has undergone restoration 10 times). In fact the condition of the painting was already compromised in 1517, and in 1901 Gabriele D'Annunzio wrote an ode with an explicit title: *On the Death of a Masterpiece.*

In May 1999, after 21 years of restoration work, the Cenacolo was finally unveiled and its original colours and use of *chiaroscuro* admired.

Opposite the fresco is a superb *Crucifixion★* (1495) by Montorfano, unfortunately somewhat overshadowed by *The Last Supper.*

Chiesa di Sant'Eustorgio★

This church was used by the inquisition prior to moving to Santa Maria delle Grazie. The earliest basilica dates back to the 5C-6C, from which period date the remains of the apse and the early-Christian cemetery. What remains visible today combines elements from various periods. The exterior of the church merits a closer look, particularly the south side and apse, which probably date from the 10C, and the Cappella Portinari. The church is dedicated to St Peter Martyr, the inquisitor, murdered by a blow to the head in 1252.

> **SAINT OF MILAN**
>
> Ambrose (c 337/339-397), an Imperial civil servant born in Treviri, was one of the key figures in the later Roman Empire. He brought peace to the Christians of Milan who were disunited following the death of the Arian bishop Aussenzio (Arianism was a heresy which denied the divine nature of Christ) and by public acclaim was declared Bishop of Milan before having even been baptised.
>
> He was authoritative with emperors and even imposed a public penitence on Emperor Theodosius who had been responsible for the massacre of Thessalonicans.
>
> The power of his sermons proved crucial in the conversion of St Augustine whom he baptised in 387.
>
> Ambrose also renewed the liturgy and calendar of the Milanese Church which even today follows the "Ambrosian" rite.

Cappella Portinari★★ – *(& only if assisted). Open daily except Mon, 9.30am-noon and 3.30-6pm (4-8pm in Aug). €5.16. ☎ 02 89 40 26 71.*

This chapel, a jewel of the Lombard-Renaissance style, houses the finest cycle of paintings by the Milanese artist **Vincenzo Foppa** (c 1427-1515).

Facing the entrance, the *Annunciation* provides a background to the balcony connecting two Renaissance palaces. Above the entrance is the *Assumption.*

On the right hand wall St Peter is depicted preaching from the pulpit, at that time made in wood. This recalls the moment when a heaven-sent cloud appeared, protecting the throng from the strong rays of the sun. The rather amusing character peeking through the beams is an example of Foppa's ability to subtly introduce elements of everyday life into his paintings.

The adjacent scene represents the unmasking of the devil in one of his ruses. Assuming the guise of the Madonna and Child his true identity is revealed at the sight of the Host (you can see his horns).

On the wall in front, the saint is reattaching the foot to a boy's leg – his foot having been cut off as a punishment for striking his mother.

The final scene takes place in the Barlassina woods, between Como and Milan, where Peter's earthly story reaches its conclusion. The landscape not only serves as a backdrop but has a reality entirely independent of the dramatic scenes.

Basilica di San Satiro★

With the exception of the 9C square campanile and the west front, which dates from 1871, the basilica, like the baptistery, was designed by Bramante. The architect adopted a totally Classical idiom to solve the problem posed by lack of space, skilfully integrating gilded stucco and *trompe l'oeil* work to create the impression of a chancel. The **dome★** is also remarkable. The basilica also includes a small Oriental-style chapel on the plan of a Greek cross, decorated with a 15C painted terracotta statue of the *Descent from the Cross* and fragments of 9C-12C frescoes.

Basilica di San Lorenzo Maggiore★

The basilica was founded in the 4C and rebuilt in the 12C and 16C. It has kept its original octagonal plan. In front of the façade is a majestic **portico★** of 16 Roman columns, all that remains of the Roman town of Mediolanum. The majestic interior is in the Byzantine-Romanesque style and has galleries exclusively reserved for women, a vast dome and a spacious ambulatory. From the south side of the chancel pass through the atrium and then a 1C Roman doorway to a chapel, the **Cappella di Sant'Aquilino★** dating from the 4C. It has retained its original plan and the palaeo-Christian mosaics. *Cappella: Open daily, 8am-6.45pm.* €2. ☎ *02 89 40 41 29.*

Further on, the **Porta Ticinese**, a vestige of the 14C ramparts, leads to the attractive quarter where the artists gather, the Naviglio Grande.

Chiesa di San Marco

In the Brera district is the **church of San Marco** which is open to the public. It was rebuilt in 1286 over much older foundations. It houses an interesting black and white fresco painted by the Leonardo da Vinci School *(north aisle)* representing a *Madonna and Child with St John the Baptist*. It was discovered in 1975.

Basilica di San Simpliciano

This was built in AD 385 on the orders of St Ambrose, Bishop of Milan. A few extensions were made to the early-Christian basilica during the early Middle Ages and the Romanesque period. On the vaulting in the apse is a *Coronation of the Virgin* by Bergognone (1481-1522).

Both these churches host excellent concerts.

▶▶ Ca' Granda-Ex Ospedale Maggiore★ (University)

Excursions

Abbazia di Chiaravalle★

7km/4mi southeast. Leave by Porta Romana then consult the plan of the built-up area on Michelin map 428. Open daily except Mon, 9-11.45am and 3.30-6pm. Donation recommended. ☎ *02 57 40 34 04.*

The abbey, founded by St Bernard of Clairvaux (hence Chiaravalle) in 1135, is dominated by an elegant polygonal **bell tower★**. It is an early example of Gothic architecture in Italy. Brick and white stone are combined in the typical Cistercian style. The porch was a 17C addition. Inside, there are a nave and two aisles and 14C frescoes on the dome. Another fresco in the south transept represents the Tree of the Benedictine Saints. The small cloisters are delightful.

Monza

21km/13mi north. Monza is quite an attractive industrial town specialising mainly in textiles. It stands on the edge of the Brianza, a lovely green hilly area dotted with lakes, attractive towns and villas set in lovely gardens.

Duomo★ – This cathedral was built in the 13C-14C and has an attractive Lombard **façade★★** (1390-96) in alternating white, green and black marble, which is remarkable for its harmonious proportions and variety of openings. It was the work of Matteo da Campione, one of the famous *Maestri Campionesi (see Index)*, who spread the Lombard style throughout Italy. The **interior★** was remodelled in the 17C. The splendid silver gilt **altar front★** dates from the 14C. To the left of the chancel is the Chapel of the Queen of the Longobards, Theodolinda (6C-7C), with its fascinating 15C **frescoes★** depicting scenes in the life of this pious sovereign.

The **treasury★** *(tesoro)* has the famous 5C-9C **Iron Crown★★** of the Kings of Lombardy, which was offered by Pope Gregory I the Great to the queen. In addition there are fine pieces of 6C to 9C plate, 17C reliquaries and 16C tapestries. *Treasury: Open daily except Mon, 9-11.30am and 3-5.30pm, Sun and hols 10.30am-noon and 3-5.45pm (no visits during religious ceremonies). Closed Mon (museum)* €3.50. ☎ *0397 32 34 04.*

Parco di Villa Reale★★ – The majestic neo-Classical royal villa was the residence of Eugène de Beauharnais (Napoleon's stepson) and Umberto I of Italy, who was assassinated at Monza in 1900 by an anarchist. This vast park is landscaped in the English manner. In the northern part of the park there are several sporting facilities and the Monza racing circuit which is the venue for the annual Grand Prix Formula One race.

Modena*

Modena, situated between the River Secchia and River Panaro, at the junction of the Via Emilia and the Brenner Autostrada, is an active commercial and industrial centre (manufacture of shoes and cars and railway engineering) and one of the most important towns in Emilia-Romagna. However, Modena with its archbishopric and university, remains a quiet town whose old quarter in the vicinity of the cathedral is adorned by several spacious squares lined with arcades. It is in this part of the town that one finds such gastronomic specialities as *zamponi* (stuffed pigs' trotters) and Lambrusco, a sparkling red wine which is produced locally.

Location

Population 176 022 – Michelin map 428, 429 or 430 I 14 – Town plan in the Michelin Atlas Italy – Emilia-Romagna. Modena is about 40km/24mi from Bologna. The main access road isA 1. **🛈** *Piazza Grande 17, ☎ 059 20 66 60.*
Surrounding area: see BOLOGNA, PARMA.

Worth a Visit

Duomo★★★

The cathedral is dedicated to St Geminian and is one of the best examples of Romanesque architecture in Italy. Here the Lombard architect, **Lanfranco**, gave vent to his sense of rhythm and proportion. The *Maestri Campionesi (see Index)* put the finishing touches to his work. Most of the sculptural decoration is due to **Wiligelmo**, a 12C Lombard sculptor.

The façade is divided into three parts and is crowned by the Angel of Death carrying a fleur-de-lis, a work carried out by the *"Campionesi"* masters. The central portal is enhanced by a porch supported by two lions by Wiligelmo whose name can be seen on one of the stones to the left of the portal. The doorway also includes the date 1099, the year in which the church was founded. The low reliefs above the side doors and to each side of the central portal depict episodes from the Book of Genesis.

The south side overlooking the square is remarkable for its architectural rhythm. From left to right, are the Prince's Doorway carved by Wiligelmo, the Royal Entrance, a gem carved by the *"Campionesi"* masters in the 13C and a 16C pulpit decorated with the symbols of the four Evangelists.

G. Biudzin/MICHELIN

To reach the other side of the church, walk under the Gothic arches linking the cathedral to the huge Romanesque campanile built of white marble (88m 286ft) known as *Ghirlandina* because of the bronze garland on its weather-vane. On the north side is the Fishmarket Door, so called because it used to lie near the fish market at the bishop's palace; it was carved by the Wiligelmo School. The recessed orders of the arches are decorated with episodes from the Breton cycle, one of the first examples of this subject matter in Italy.

The **interior** of the cathedral reveals the ebullience of Gothic churches and the simplicity of Romanesque architecture. In the north aisle beyond the 15C Altare delle Statuine (with small statues), rises a 14C pulpit and, opposite this, a rough wooden seat traditionally said to have been used by the public executioner. The choir stalls in the presbytery, the work of Lendinara, date from the 15C. The **rood screen★★★**, a Romanesque masterpiece, is supported by Lombardy lions and telamones and is the work of *"Campionesi"* masters dating from the 12C-13C. The parapet is decorated with scenes from Christ's Passion. The atmospheric crypt has a large number of slender columns. It contains a terracotta sculpture group of the *Holy Family*★ (15C) by Guido Mazzoni, and St Geminiano's tomb. In the south aisle of the church is an exquisite 16C terracotta Nativity scene.

The **Museo del Duomo** contains the famous 12C **metopes**★★, low reliefs which used to surmount the flying buttresses. They represent wandering players or symbols incomprehensible today, but whose modelling, balance and style have an almost Classical air.

&. Open mid-Apr to Oct, daily except Mon, 9am-12.30pm and 4-7pm, rest of year 9.30am-12.30pm and 3.30-6.30pm. Closed 2 Sep, Aug, 1 Jan, Easter, 25 Dec (am). €3.10. ☎ 059 21 60 78.

Palazzo dei Musei

This 18C palace contains the two most important art collections gathered by the Este family.

Biblioteca Estense★ – *1st floor, staircase on the right. &. Open daily except Sun, 8.30am-1.45pm Closed 31 Jan, 1st and 2nd week of Sep €2.60. ☎ 059 22 22 48.*

This is one of the richest libraries in Italy, containing 600 000 books and 15 000 manuscripts, the most interesting of which are on display. The prize exhibit is the **Bible of Borso d'Este**★★. It has 1 020 pages illuminated by a team of 15C Ferrara artists, including Taddeo Crivelli.

Galleria Estense★ – *&. Open daily except Mon, 8.30am-7.30pm (ticket office closes 7pm). Closed 1 Jan, 1 May and 25 Dec. €4. ☎ 059 43 75 911; www.galleriaestense.it*

This gallery opens with the **Marble bust of Francesco I d'Este**, a masterpiece of Gian Lorenzo Bernini. The 15C Modena School is well represented (Bonascia, Francesco Bianchi Ferrari); it owes much to the Ferrarese School which is represented by the powerfully modelled *St Anthony*★ by Cosmè Tura. There is also a fine collection of Venetian masters (Cima da Conegliano, Veronese, Tintoretto, Bassano), 16C Ferrarese painting (Dosso Dossi, Garofalo) and works linked to the Accademia degli Incamminati in Bologna (the Carracci, Guido Reni, Guercino). The foreign schools are also well represented; note the **Portrait of Francesco I d'Este** by Velasquez.

As well as paintings, the gallery also has some fine terracotta figures, typical works by Modenese sculptors from the 15C-16C. (Nicolò dell'Arca, Guido Mazzoni, Antonio Begarelli). There are also collections of ceramics and musical intruments; note the splendid **Este harp** (1581).

Palazzo Ducale★

This noble and majestic building, the ducal palace, was begun in 1634 for Francesco I d'Este and has an elaborately elegant design. Today it is occupied by the Infantry and Cavalry schools.

Excursions

Abbazia di Nonantola

11km/7mi north. Open daily, 7am-10.30pm. ☎ 059 54 90 25; www.abbazia.nonantola.net

The abbey was founded in the 8C and flourished during the Middle Ages. The 12C abbey church has some remarkable **Romanesque sculpture**★ carved by Wiligelmo's assistants in 1121.

Carpi

18km/11mi north. This attractive small town has a 16C Renaissance cathedral by Peruzzi, overlooking **Piazza dei Martiri**★. The **Castello dei Pio**★, an imposing building bristling with towers, includes a courtyard by Bramante and contains a small museum. *Open Thu, Sat, Sun and hols, 10am-12.30pm and 3.30-7pm (ticket office closes 15min early). Closed 10-20 Aug, 1 Jan, 25 Dec. €2.10. ☎ 059 64 92 98; www.carpidiem.it/musei*

The 12C-16C Church of Sagra has a tall Romanesque campanile, **Torre della Sagra**.

Molise

Molise is an ancient land of passage for seasonal movement of cattle, for armies and for travellers. Mountains dominate the territory and inhabitants of the region have always looked to them as a natural defence and refuge: strongholds, fortified castles and villages nestling on hillsides characterise its landscape.

Location

Michelin map 431 A-C 24-27. Molise is shaped like a wedge inserted between the Apennines and the sea , and between the Abruzzi and Puglia. The main access road is A 14.
Surrounding area: see ABRUZZO, PUGLIA.

Worth a Visit

Sights are listed in alphabetical order.

Agnone

42km/26mi northeast of Isernia. This old village owes its fame to the **Fonderia pontificia Marinelli**, the oldest bell factory in the world, founded in the 10C. It now houses the **Museo Internazionale della Campana**. (&) *By reservation only, noon and 4pm. Closed Easter, 15 Aug, 25 Dec. €4.50.* ☎ 0865 78 235.
The central street, Via Vittorio Emanuele, is bordered by the **church of Sant'Emidio** (15C) and the Italo-Argentinian theatre which was founded in the last century with funds raised from emigrants in South America. **Via Garibaldi**, lined with houses embellished by lions which bear witness to the community of Venetian merchants, leads to the **Ripa★**, a garden with a fine view over the Verrino Valley.

Altilia Saepinum★

25km/15mi south of Campobasso on S 87. Open daily, May to Sep 8.30am-7.30pm, rest of year 8.30am to 1hr before sunset. Closed 1 Jan, 25 Dec. €2. ☎ 0874 79 02 07.
The ruins of *Saepinum* rise in the middle of an attractive town on which construction began in the 17C using plundered stone. The Samnites founded the city which was subsequently occupied by the Romans who made it a municipality and in the Augustan Age built a city wall measuring 1 250m/4 101ft with four fortified doors and articulated by 25 towers.
Access is through the Porta di Terravecchia gateway at the extreme south of the *cardo*, the city's principal street. At the crossroads of the *cardo* and the *decumanus* streets *(see p 62)* are the remains of the **basilica** (with Ionic columns on its peristyle) to the left and, to the right, the **forum**, a huge paved rectangular area. Turning right on the *decumanus* note the remains of the senate house *(curia)*, the temple dedicated to Jupiter, Juno and Minerva, some remains of mosaic flooring, a semicircular recess belonging to the "house of oil-presses" with four brick oil containers, and the impluvium of a Samnite house. To the extreme east of the *decumanus*, beyond the **Porta di Benevento** gateway, lies the **Mausoleum of Ennius Marsus**, a fine semicircular crenellated building standing on a square plinth.
Returning to the main crossroads and continuing up the *decumano* cross the old residential and commercial quarters with remains of workshops and the *macellum* (market). At the eastern end of the street rises the **Porta di Boiano★**. From the top there is a good view of the western part of the fortifications and the ruins of the well-preserved central part of the city. Outside the fortifications turn right and make for the **Mausoleum of Numisius Ligus**. This square tomb is crowned by four acroteria and has a simple elegance.
Against the inner face of the wall, the intimate **theatre★** has preserved its monumental entrance of white stone. The pretty adjacent buildings house a **museum** which has displays of material pertaining to *Saepinum*.

Pietrabbondante

5km/3mi northeast of Isernia. In an evocative natural setting stands the **Italic Sanctuary of Pietrabbondante★**. This was a sacred site for the Samnites who turned it into a political as well as religious centre and thus a symbol of anti-Roman resistance. All that remains of the sanctuary are the foundations of the **high temple**, remains of the minor temple and the fine **theatre** which stands on the slopes of the hill. *Open daily, 8.30am to 1hr before sunset. Closed 1 Jan, 1 May, 25 Dec. €2.* ☎ 0865 76 129.

Monastero di Santa Maria di Canneto

36km/22mi southeast of Vasto. This monastery, erected in the 8C, is a fine expression of Lombard-Cassinese culture. The **church** has two admirable sculptural works: the **pulpit★** (8C) and the **altarpiece★** portraying the refectory (10C). Adjacent to the church, remains of a Roman villa have been discovered, with traces of mosaic flooring (3C-4C AD).

Monastero di San Vincenzo al Volturno

28km/17mi northwest of Isernia. Guided tours (approx 2hr) of excavation area and church, conducted by Associazione Culturale Atena. Reserve 3-4 days in advance. €2.58. ☎ 0865 95 13 66.

In an enchanting natural setting with the backdrop of the Mainarde mountains and striking hilltop towns, stands this Benedictine monastery which was founded in the 8C and repeatedly destroyed by Saracen attacks. The **church**, rebuilt in around 1950 using remains from previous constructions, is heralded by a **sequence of arches** of the 13C. The **excavations** currently being carried out beyond Volturno have brought to light some priceless remains of the original abbey.

Termoli

Termoli is the only port in Molise and the departure point for the Tremiti islands *(see p 424)*. It has a fine **castle** (13C) which forms part of the fortifications ordered by Emperor Frederick II to defend the port. The narrow alleyways wind their way up to the **Cathedral★★** (12C), one of the most significant examples of Romanesque architecture in Molise. The façade is enlivened by lesenes and blind twin arches. The motif of the arches continues on the left side and on the apse which dates from the 13C. Inside, the crypt has mosaic flooring from the 10C-11C.

Abbazia di **Montecassino**★★

MONTE CASSINO ABBEY

The massive hulk of the mighty and majestic abbey rising up over the summit of Monte Cassino is an awesome sight. The access road up to one of the holiest places of Roman Catholicism climbs in hairpin bends, affording wonderful views over the valley.

Location

Michelin map 430 R 23. Monte Cassino lies off A 1 which links Rome with Naples. *Surrounding area: see GAETA.*

Worth a Visit

The monastery of Monte Cassino, the mother house of the Benedictines, was founded in 529 by **St Benedict** (d 547). It was here that the saint drew up a complete and precise set of rules combining intellectual study and manual labour with the virtues of chastity, obedience and poverty. In the 11C under Abbot Didier the abbey's influence was at its height. The monks were skilled in the arts of miniatures, frescoes and mosaics and their work greatly influenced Cluniac art. The abbey has been destroyed several

A TRAGIC EVENT

Monte Cassino was the setting for one of the most terrible battles of the Second World War which resulted in the deaths of thousands of men and the destruction of one of the greatest centres of Christianity. After the Allies had taken Naples in 1944, the Germans made Cassino the key stronghold in the system of defences guarding the approaches to Rome. On 17 May the Allies launched their final assault, with the Polish corps as the spearhead. After a raging battle, the Germans abandoned Cassino on the following day, allowing the Allies to join forces and leaving open the road to Rome.

times since its foundation and was most severely damaged at the Battle of Cassino. It has since been rebuilt to the original plans.

Abbey★★

Open mid-Mar to Oct, daily, 8.45am-12.30pm and 3.30-6.30pm, rest of year 8.45am-noon and 3-5pm. No charge. ☎ 0776 31 15 29; www.officine.it/montecassino

It is preceded by a suitably solemn suite of four communicating cloisters. The bare façade of the basilica quite belies the sumptuousness of the **interior★★** where marble, stucco, mosaics and gilding create a dazzling if somewhat austere ensemble in the 17C-18C style. The chancel has lovely 17C walnut stalls and the marble tomb enshrining the remains of St Benedict.

Museo abbaziale★★

Open Feb-Oct, daily, 9am-noon and 3-6.30pm, rest of year Sun and hols only, 9am-12pm and 3-5pm. €2. ☎ 0776 31 15 29. www.apt.frosinone.it

The museum presents documents on the abbey's history and works of art which survived the 1944 bombing.

On the way down to Cassino are a museum, the **Museo archeologico nazionale**, and the neighbouring excavation site (amphitheatre, theatre and tomb of Umidia Quadratilla). ♿ *Open daily, 9am-8pm. Closed 1 Jan, 1 May, 25 Dec. €2. ☎ 0776 30 11*

Montecatini Terme‡‡‡

The spring water at Montecatini has been famous for its medicinal properties for centuries. With its parks, wide variety of entertainment and racecourse the town provides the ideal setting for an enjoyable break.

Location

Population 20 360 – Michelin map 430 K 14. Map in The Red Guide Italia. See also The Green Guide Tuscany. Montecatini Terme is situated between Florence and Lucca, off the motorway that links Florence to the coast.

🖪 *Viale Verdi 66/A, ☎ 0572 77 22 44. Surrounding area: see LUCCA, PISTOIA.*

*A typical little square
in Italy:
Montecatini Alto*

G. Bludzin/MICHELIN

Facilities

Montecatini is one of the most elegant and popular spa resorts in Italy. The spring water here is used to treat metabolic disorders, liver, stomach and intestinal complaints and rheumatism. Numerous different therapies are used, including mud baths and balneotherapy, but the commonest form of treatment is drinking the water straight from the spring.

►► Museo dell'Accademia d'Arte (works by the Italian artists Guttuso, Primo Conti, Messina and some of the personal belongings of Verdi and Puccini).

Excursions

Collodi★★

15km/9mi west. Collodi was the pen-name adopted by Carlo Lorenzini, the author of *Pinocchio*, whose mother was born in the village. A park, **Parco di Pinocchio**, in the form of a maze is laid out on the banks of the River Pescia. (&) *Open daily, 8.30am to sunset. €7. ☎ 0572 42 93 42; www.pinocchio.it*

Directory

Castello e Giardino Garzoni – *Open daily, 9am to 1hr before sunset (castle closed for restoration at time of publication, only garden open to visitors). For information* ☏ *0572 42 95 90.*
The villa is an amazing building dating from the Baroque period and the 17C. In the **gardens** are vistas, pools, clipped trees, grottoes, sculpture and mazes creating a charming and imaginative spectacle.

Montefalco★

Ramparts from the 14C still girdle this charming little town, which lies among vineyards and olive groves. It is perched – as its name suggests – like a falcon on its nest and has been called the Balcony of Umbria. Montefalco, won over to Christianity in 390 by St Fortunatus, has its own saint, Clara, not to be confused with the companion of St Francis of Assisi.

Location
Population 5 601 – Michelin map 430 N 19 – Umbria. Montefalco is not far from S 3, which links Foligno with Spoleto.
Surrounding area: see ASSISI, PERUGIA.

Worth a Visit

Torre Comunale
Closed for restoration at time of publication. From the top (110 steps) of the communal Tower there is a beautiful **panorama★★★** of nearly the whole of Umbria.

L'antica chiesa di San Francesco
Open Jun to Aug, daily, 10.30am-1pm and 2-6pm. For information ☏ *0742 37 95 98.*
This historic Franciscan church, now deconsecrated, provides an enchanting setting for the **museum** which contains mid-15C **frescoes★★** depicting scenes from the life of St Francis and St Jerome by Benozzo Gozzoli, a *Nativity* by Perugino and an awe-inspiring *Crucifix* by the Expressionist Master of Santa Chiara (active in Umbria from the end of the 13C to the beginning of the 14C), who possibly collaborated with Giotto in the basilica in Assisi. The museum also houses a gallery displaying works by Francesco Melanzio (c 1487-1526), a native of Montefalco.

Chiesa di Sant'Illuminata
The church is Renaissance in style. The tympanum of the main doorway and several niches in the nave were painted by Francesco Melanzio.
▶▶ S. Agostino (Gothic, with frescoes by Umbrian painters of the 14C, 15C and 16C), S. Fortunato *(1km/0.6mi south)* (fresco★ by Benozzo Gozzoli).

Montepulciano★★

Montepulciano is an attractive little town typical of the Renaissance period. It occupies a remarkably picturesque setting★★ on the top of a tufa hill separating two valleys.
The town was founded in the 6C by people from Chiusi fleeing the barbarian invasions. They named it Mons Politianus, which explains why people from the town are known as Poliziani. Poets have long sung the praises of its ruby-red wine ("vino nobile").

FAMOUS INHABITANTS

This was the birthplace of **Angelo Poliziano** (1454-94), one of the most exquisite Renaissance poets. The poet was a great friend of Lorenzo de' Medici, whom he called Lauro (Laurel) and whom he saved from assassination during the Pazzi Conspiracy (see Duomo in FIRENZE). The *Stanzas*, Poliziano's masterpiece, describe a sort of Garden of Delight haunted by attractive women. Parallels can be drawn between Poliziano's verse and the paintings of his friend Botticelli.

Antonio da Sangallo il Vecchio, one of the two senior members of the famous family of Renaissance sculptors and architects, bequeathed some of his most famous works to Montepulciano.

Directory

WHERE TO EAT

• Moderate

Borgo Buio – *Via Borgo Buio* – ☎ *0578 71 74 97* – *borgobuio@bccmp.com* – *Closed Thu* – *€23/28.* With its wide selection of snacks and pasta dishes (all home-made) this is definitely one for the address book; the establishment also has some good wines. Interior decoration is somewhere between elegant and rustic: the brick-vaulted ceiling adds to the atmosphere.

La Grotta – *Località San Biagio – 1km/0.6mi southwest of Montepulciano on S 146* – ☎ *0578 75 74 79 – Closed Wed, Jan and Feb – €37/48.* Housed in a fine 16C palazzo – complete with vaulted ceiling – this restaurant has built its reputation on its authentic Tuscan cooking. Alfresco dining in the lovely garden in summer!

WHERE TO STAY

• Budget

Agriturismo Relais Ai Battenti – *Via dell'Antica Chiusina 23 – 1.5km/1mi south of Montepulciano* – ☎ *0578 71 70 09 – Fax 0578 71 70 09 – www.agriturismodella toscana.it – Closed 10 Jan-20 Mar. – ⊠ – 4 rm €41.32/92.96 ⌷.* This establishment has a great family atmosphere. Breakfast here is a particularly homely affair with guests seated at a long wooden table in the lovely dining room which has a wonderful fireplace. Comfortable, country-style rooms, all with a private bathroom (although not always en suite).

• Moderate

Albergo Meublé Il Riccio – *Via Talosa 21* – ☎ *0578 75 77 13 – Fax 0578 75 77 13 – www.ilriccio.net – Closed the first 2 weeks in Jun and Sep – 6 rm €51.65/77.47 – ⌷ €7.75.* A quiet, pleasant hotel housed in a medieval palazzo. One of the main attractions of this establishment is the wonderful view from the two terrace areas: from here you look down on Montepulciano, and out over the surrounding valley and nearby lakes. Rooms are simple and on the functional side.

TAKING A BREAK

Caffè Poliziano – *Via Voltaia nel Corso 27/29* – ☎ *0578 75 86 15* – *caffepoliziano@libero.it* – *Open 6.30am-1am.* First opened in 1868, this lovely café has long been popular with artists and writers – previous visitors have included the writer Luigi Pirandello and the film-maker Federico Fellini! The large, elegant room with its picture windows is an ideal spot for relaxing with a hot chocolate (there are more than 30 different varieties on the menu) or a glass of red wine. The Nobile and Rosso di Montepulciano are excellent.

Location

Population 13 890 – Michelin map 430 M 17 – See also The Green Guide Tuscany. Montepulciano lies off S 146, which goes from San Quirico d'Orcia to Chiusi. 🖪 *Via di Gracciano nel Corso 59/A,* ☎ *0578 75 73 41.* *Surrounding area: see PIENZA.*

Walking About

Città antica★

Beyond the gateway, Porta al Prato, the high street, the first part of which bears the name Via Roma, loops through the monumental area in the old town. At n° 91 Via Roma stands the 16C **Palazzo Avignonesi** attributed to Vignola; n° 73, the palace of the antiquarian Bucelli, is decorated with stone from Etruscan and Roman buildings; further along, the **Renaissance façade★** of the church of **Sant'Agostino** was designed by Michelozzo (15C); a tower opposite has a Pulcinello as Jack o'the clock. At the Logge del Mercato (Grain Exchange) bear left into Via di Voltaia nel Corso: Palazzo Cervini (n° 21) is a fine example of Florentine Renaissance architecture with its rusticated stonework and curvilinear and triangular pediments designed by Antonio da Sangallo, a member of an illustrious family of architect-sculptors, who designed some of the most famous buildings in Montepulciano. Continue along Via dell'Opio nel Corso and Via Poliziano (n° 1 is the poet's birthplace).

Piazza Grande★★ – Forming the centre of the city, this square with its irregular plan and varying styles avoids architectural monotony while blending into a harmonious whole. The **Palazzo Comunale★** (Town Hall) is a Gothic building which was remodelled in the 15C by Michelozzo. From the top of the square **torre** (tower) there is an immense **panorama★★★** of the town and its environs. *Tower: For information* ☎ *0578 71 21.*

The majestic Renaissance **Palazzo Nobili-Tarugi★** facing the cathedral is attributed to Antonio da Sangallo the Elder. The palace has a portico and great doorway with semicircular arches; six Ionic columns, standing on a lofty base, support the pilasters of the upper storey. The square also has an attractive **well★** adorned with an admirable sculpture of lion supporters holding aloft the Medici coat of arms. Inside the 16C-17C **Duomo**, to the left of the west door, lies the recumbent figure of Bartolomeo Aragazzi, secretary to Pope Martin V; the statue was part of a monument by Michelozzo (15C), as were the low reliefs on the two first pillars and the statues flanking the high altar. The monumental **altarpiece★** (1401) above the high altar is by the Sienese artist, Taddeo di Bartolo.

Continue along the high street to Piazza San Francesco for a fine **view** of the surrounding countryside and of the church of San Biagio. Walk down Via del Poggiolo and turn right into Via dell'Erbe to return to the Logge del Mercato.

►► Museo Civico – Pinacoteca Crociani (glazed terracotta by Andrea della Robbia; Etruscan remains and paintings dating from the 13C to 18C)

Excursions

Chiesa della Madonna di San Biagio★★

1km/0.6mi. Leave by the Porta al Prato and then take the Chianciano road before turning right. This splendid church built in pale-coloured stone and consecrated in 1529 is an architectural masterpiece by **Antonio da Sangallo**. The building, which was greatly influenced by Bramante's design for St Peter's in Rome, is a useful example of Bramante's concepts. San Biagio's design is simpler although it is planned in the shape of a Greek cross and is crowned by a dome. Two campaniles flank the main façade; one is unfinished and the other includes the three architectural orders (Doric, Ionic and Corinthian). The south transept is prolonged by a semicircular sacristy. The interior gives the same impression of majesty and nobility. To the left of the west door is a 14C Annunciation. The 16C marble high altar is imposing.

Opposite the church stands the Canonica (canonry), an elegant porticoed building.

Chianciano Terme‡‡

10km/6mi southeast. This fashionable thermal spa is pleasantly situated. The healing properties of its waters (which can help relieve kidney and liver disorders) were known to the Etruscans and the Romans. There are some fine parks and plenty of sophisticated hotels and spas.

Chiusi

27km/16mi southwest. Standing on a hill covered with olive groves, Chiusi is today a quiet and hospitable little town. It was once one of the 12 sovereign cities of Etruria.

Museo Archeologico★ – *Via Porsenna.* (&) *Open daily, 9am-8pm. Closed 1 Jan, 1 May, 25 Dec. €4.* ☎ *0578 20 177.*

The museum presents the various finds from the burial grounds in the neighbourhood: sarcophagi, rounded tombstones *(cippi)*, alabaster and stone funerary urns, burial urns *(canopae)* in the shape of heads, clay ex-votos as well as a variety of utensils, vases, lamps and jewellery. The objects all display the Etruscan taste for fantasy and realism.

Napoli★★★

NAPLES

Naples is a universe in its own right, imbued with fantasy and fatalism, superstition and splendour. It is a city of a thousand faces: it may be chaotic and heaving with traffic but it is rich with history, art and culture, ready to surrender its mysteries to anyone who scratches the surface. Then there is the lovely bay: with its horizon bounded by Posillipo, the islands, the Sorrento Peninsula and lofty Vesuvius, it is one of the most beautiful in the world. In essence Naples is a city of many facets where the present weaves its way through its long history, and its alluring charms and architectural splendours have been praised by innumerable poets and writers. Even UNESCO's committee fell under her spell, to the extent that in 1995 they included the historic centre of the city in their World Heritage List.

Location

Population 1 002 619 – Michelin map 431 E 24 (with plans of the conurbation) – Campania.

The main access roads to Naples include A 1, Autostrada del Sole, A 3 for those arriving from the south and A 16 which links Naples to the Adriatic. ⌂ *Piazza dei Martiri 58,* ☎ *081 40 53 11, Piazza del Plebiscito (Palazzo Reale),* ☎ *081 41 87 44.*

Surrounding area. See CAPRI, CASERTA, COSTIERA AMALFITANA, ISCHIA, Golfo di NAPOLI, POMPEI, SALERNO.

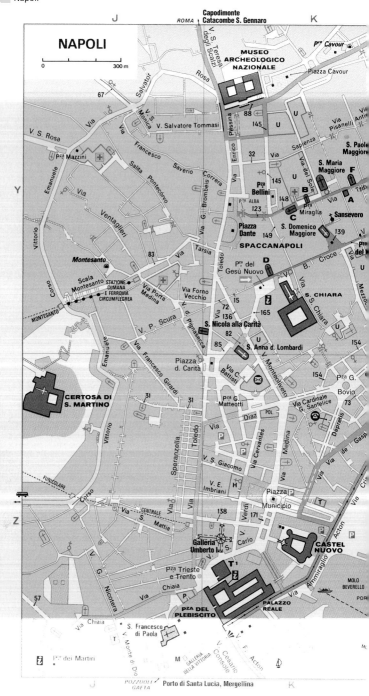

Background

HISTORICAL NOTES

According to legend, the siren Parthenope gave her name to a town which had sprung up round her tomb, which is why Naples is called the Parthenopaean City. In fact, Naples originated as a Greek colony named Neapolis, conquered by the Romans in the 4C BC. Rich inhabitants of Rome like Virgil, Augustus, Tiberius and Nero used to spend the winter there, but the Neapolitans themselves retained the Greek language and customs until the decline of the Empire.

Since the 12C seven princely dynasties have reigned over Naples. The Normans, Hohenstaufens, Angevins, Aragonese, Spanish and Bourbons ruled successively until the end of the 18C. The French Revolution of 1789 brought in French troops, and in 1799 a **Parthenopaean Republic** was set up, followed by a French kingdom (1806-15) under Joseph Bonaparte (Napoleon's brother) and afterwards Joachim Murat (Napoleon's brother-in-law), both of whom promoted excellent reforms. From 1815 to 1860 the restored Bourbons remained in power in spite of the 1820 and 1848 revolts.

Directory

GETTING ABOUT

It is preferable to get to Naples by train or plane as traffic in the city is chaotic and few hotels have garages. Capodichino Airport, ☏ 081 78 96 111 or 848 86 56 41/2 (for international ALITALIA flights), 848 86 56 43 (for general information), is 6km/4mi away from the city. Buses to Naples include n° 14 (the terminus is in Piazza Garibaldi where the railway station is) and n° 3 S which stops at the station and at Molo Beverello.

Naples has a generally good network of public transport although overground transport does fall prey to traffic which can be chock-a-block.

Information listed is intended for guidance only; for details check transport maps available from Tourist Offices.

Trains – The **Cumana** and **Circumflegrea** trains (terminus in Piazza Montesanto) connect Naples to Bagnoli and the Campi Flegrei district. The **Circumvesuviana** train (terminus in Corso Garibaldi) has swift connections to Herculaneum, Pompeii, Castellammare, Vico Equense and Sorrento.

Underground – The **Metropolitana FS** crosses the city vertically from Piazza Garibaldi down to Pozzuoli, while the **metropolitana collinare** from Piazza Vanvitelli goes back up to Piscinola/Secondigliano. The new link goes from Piazza Vanvitelli to the Museo Archeologico.

Funicular railway – Three routes offer swift connections to the Vomero: the **Funicolare centrale** (Via Toledo-Piazza Fuga), the **Funicolare di Chiaia** (Via del Parco Margherita-Via Cimarosa) and the **Funicolare di Montesanto** (Piazza Montesanto-Via Morghen). The **Funicolare di Mergellina** links Via Mergellina to Via Manzoni.

Tickets – "GiraNapoli" tickets allow travel on buses, trams, the funicular railway and the underground (both the Metropolitana FS and the Metropolitana collinare). There are two types of ticket: 90min tickets and 1-day tickets. Monthly passes are also available.

Radiotaxi – There are 5 radiotaxi companies in operation: **Cotana** ☏ 081 57 07 070, **Free** ☏ 081 55 15 151, **Napoli** ☏ 081 55 64 444, **Partenope**

☏ 081 55 60 202 and **Consor Taxi** ☏ 081 55 25 252.

Sea connections – Ferry and hovercraft crossings to Capri, Ischia, Procida and Sorrento leave from Molo Beverello and Mergellina port.

Bring your broken dolls to the Dolls' Hospital to be "cured".

WHERE TO EAT

• Budget

Pizzeria Di Matteo – *Via Tribunali 93/94, zona Spaccanapoli* – ☏ *081 45 52 62* – *Closed Sun, 2nd and 3rd week of Aug* – Long a haunt of the rich and famous: previous visitors include the Italian film-star Marcello Mastroianni and more recently Bill Clinton. Simple surroundings, tasty pizzas. Excellent prices and quick service. Mind you don't bang your head going up the stairs to the first floor!

Trianon da Ciro – *Via Pietro Colletta 42/46, zona Castel Capuano* – ☏ *081 55 39 426* – *Closed 25 Dec, 1 Jan* – . 1920s-style establishment with stucco ceilings and walls painted a splendid yellow ochre colour. Very traditional and with plenty of atmosphere. Don't be surprised if your delicious pizza is accompanied by a few lines of poetry from the proprietor who is passionate about both pizzas and poetry.

Antica pizzeria Da Michele – *Via Cesare Sersale 1/3/5/7, zona Via Duomo* – ☏ *081 55 39 204 Closed Sun, 3 weeks in Aug* – . A very popular pizzeria: the decor is unpretentious and the main attraction is the excellent pizzas. Come armed with bags of patience – queuing is part of the experience and almost obligatory.

Antica pizzeria Gino Sorbillo – *Via Tribunali 32, zona Spaccanapoli* – ☏ *081 44 66 43* – *ginosorbillo@libero.it* – *Closed Sun, 6-25 Aug* – + 10% service charge. One of the best pizzerias in town! As explained in the menu, the young and enthusiastic proprietor Gino comes from a long line of pizzaioli – 21 in all. Great ambience... and fantastic pizzas.

Galleria Umberto I

Luigi Lombardi a S. Chiara – *Via Benedetto Croce 59, zona Piazza S. Domenico Maggiore* – ☎ *081 52 20 780* – *www.paginegialle.it/lombardilu* – *Closed Mon, Aug* – 🖻 *+ 13% service charge*. This pizzeria has been in the same family since the mid-19C – a veritable dynasty of pizzaioli. Over the years it has satisfied the hunger pangs of generations of students and Neapolitan intellectuals. Splendid dining room divided into smaller, more intimate alcoves behind brick-built arches. Excellent pizzas and various other traditional dishes.

Brandi – *Salita di S. Anna di Palazzo 2, zona Piazza di Plebiscito* – ✒. Tradition has it that the mythical Margherita pizza was born here on 11 June 1889, so called in honour of Queen Margherita. One for the address book of all pizza connoisseurs. A good place to head for after a little light afternoon shopping.

Osteria della Mattonella – *Via Nicotera 13, zona Piazza S. M. degli Angeli* – ☎ *081 41 65 41 – Closed Sun evening* – ✒ 🖻 *– Book* – *€15/18*. If you're looking for traditional Neapolitan cooking and an authentic setting, you couldn't do better than this. Paper napkins and informal, friendly service. Limited menu but genuine home cooking and generous portions.

Beverino – *Via S. Sebastiano 62, zona Piazza Bellini* – ☎ *081 29 03 13 – Closed Mon, Sun evening, 15-22 Aug* – *€13*. Situated near the atmospheric Piazza Bellini. Good for both lunch and informal dinners. Good wine list to accompany various pasta dishes and cold appetisers. Rustic ambience. Like any self-respecting wine bar it is housed in a vaulted cellar underground – perfect for getting away from the summer heat.

Trattoria Castel dell'Ovo – *Via Luculliana 28, zona S. Lucia* – ☎ *081 76 46 352 – Closed Thu* – ✒ *– €15/21 + 13% service charge*. A very simple, unpretentious trattoria with tables at the side of the small harbour in the charming Borgo Marinaro. Equally suitable for romantic suppers and lunches with wonderful view over the grandiose Castel dell'Ovo, the bay and the fishing boats.

'A Tiella – *Riviera di Chiaia 98/100, zona Piazza della Repubblica* – ☎ *081 76 18 688 – Closed Sun evening* – *€15/23*. What better way to end a gentle stroll along the seafront than a meal at this lovely, little restaurant? The main focus of the menu is fish but other dishes are included. Another attraction is the Neapolitan-style home-made pasta. Charming surroundings complete with vaulted ceiling and small courtyard. Other nice touches include the lemon- and ivy-themed decor and lovely photographs of old Naples.

Taverna dell'Arte – *Rampe S. Giovanni Maggiore 1/A, (across Via Mezzocannone), zona Spaccanapoli* – ☎ *081 55 27 558 – Closed Sun, 4-25 Aug* – 🖻 *– Book* – *€18/30*. For a truly authentic gastronomic experience complete with wines from the Campania region, this is the place to come. Understated but elegant in its rusticity. It is a very popular restaurant and you are advised to book well in advance.

Marino – *Via Santa Lucia 118/120, zona Santa Lucia* – ☎ *081 76 40 280 – Closed Mon, Aug* – 🖻 *– €18/31 + 15% service charge*. A typical Neapolitan trattoria, always crowded and noisy. Run by the same family for many years, with generation after generation faithfully adhering to the same gourmet recipes for both meat and fish dishes. A particularly mouth-watering and abundant display of antipasti.

• **Moderate**

L'Europeo di Mattozzi – *Via Campodisola 4/6/8, zona Corso Umberto I* – ☎ *081 55 21 323 – Closed Sun, evenings (except Thu-Sat and before public holidays), 15-31 Aug* – 🖻 *– €23.24/33.50*. Authentic, home cooking inspired by regional traditions and seasonal ingredients which are always super-fresh. Friendly staff combine great courtesy with infectious enthusiasm for food. Simple surroundings and pleasantly noisy.

La Chiacchierata – *Piazzetta Matilde Serao 37, zona Piazza del Plebiscito* – ☎ *081 41 14 65 – Closed evenings (except Fri), Aug; from Jun-Sep also Sat and Sun – Book* – *€25/37*. Bijou, family-run restaurant with a loyal clientele. Simple, homely cooking with a choice of meat and fish dishes. You can even watch the chef at work: the kitchen is on view. Informal atmosphere. Very centrally located and very reasonably priced.

WHERE TO STAY

• **Budget**

I Vicoletti – *Via S. Domenico Soriano 46, (4th floor, no lift) zona Piazza Dante* – ☎ *081 56 41 156 – Fax 081 54 48 006* – ✒ 🖻 *– 5 rm €30.99/56.81* ☷. The main attraction of this establishment is the vast terrace with views over the Castel Capuano. Other strong points include the rooms which are spacious, simply furnished but very colourful, and the friendly, enthusiastic staff. Situated in the heart of the historic centre, this hotel exudes a very Mediterranean atmosphere. Shared bathrooms and lots of stairs!

• **Moderate**

La Locanda dell'Arte – *Via Enrico Pessina 66, (2nd floor, with lift) zona Museo Archeologico* – ☎ *081 56 44 640 – Fax 081 56 45 427* – 🖻 *– 6 rm €51.65/92.96* ☷. This historic hotel is housed in an early 19C building located in a pedestrian area opposite the Accademia di Belle Arti. It has been tastefully decorated, with great attention to detail. The rooms are quiet and elegant, with dark wooden furniture, tiled floors and large windows looking out over the pedestrian area.

Bed & Breakfast Napoli t'amo – *Via Toledo 148, (1st floor, no lift)* – ☎ *081 55 23 626 – Fax 081 55 23 626 – info@napolitamo.it* – *12 rm €56.81/72.30* ☷. A stylish setting for this B&B: it is housed on the first floor of a fine 16C palazzo (complete with coat of arms above the rather grandiose portal) in one of the smartest shopping streets in the city. The rooms and public areas are very spacious, with simple, functional furnishings. Pity about the cramped bathrooms.

Hotel Le Orchidee – *Corso Umberto I 7, (5th floor, with lift) zona Corso Umberto I* – ☎ *081 55 10 721 – Fax 081 25 14 088* – ✒

⊡ – 7 rm €67.14/82.63 ⊡ €3.10. This small hotel is very well situated, a stone's throw from the historic centre and not far from the embarkation point for the islands. Housed in an old palazzo, it offers comfortable accommodation. The rooms are spacious and well maintained with simple, modern furnishings.

Hotel Ausonia – *Via Francesco Caracciolo 11, zona Mergellina* – ☎ *081 68 22 78 – Fax 081 66 45 36* – ⊡ – *19 rm €72.30/98.13* ⊡. Very close to the Porto di Mergellina. The marine theme is carried through the hotel: from the bedsteads featuring rudders and portholes to a 17C barometer in the small entrance area. For a nautical experience without leaving terra firma.

Soggiorno Sansevero – *Vicolo S. Domenico Maggiore 9, (1st floor, with lift) zona Piazza S. Domenico Maggiore* – ☎ *081 55 15 742* – ⊠ ⊡ – *6 rm €72.30/92.96* ⊡. The Sansevero group of hotels offers stylish accommodation in three 18C palazzi in the heart of Naples. Good-sized rooms have been attractively decorated, with wickerwork furniture and wrought-iron beds. Cheerful, sunny atmosphere makes for a very pleasant stay. The prices are reasonable and it is worth noting that the rooms with shared bathrooms are even cheaper.

Albergo Sansevero – *Via S. Maria di Costantinopoli 101, (1st floor, with lift) zona Spaccanapoli* – ☎ *081 21 09 07 – Fax 081 21 16 98* – ⊡ – *8 rm €72.30/92.96* ⊡.

Albergo Sansevero (Degas) – *Calata Trinità Maggiore 53, (3rd floor, with lift) zona piazza del Gesù Nuovo* – ☎ *081 55 11 276* – ⅙ – *9 rm €82.63/92.96* ⊡.

• *Expensive*

Hotel Suite Esedra – *Via Cantani 12, zona Corso Umberto I* – ☎ *081 28 74 51 – Fax 081 28 74 51* – ⊡ – *16 rm from* €92.96 ⊡. A historic hotel in what was a rather fine patrician residence. Elegant interior with damask upholstery and a 19C table for breakfast. All the rooms have their own individual style and there is even a suite with a hydromassage bath for two. Facilities also include a small gym. Service is of a very high standard.

Bed & Breakfast Parteno – *Lungomare Partenope 1, (1st floor, with lift)* – ☎ *081 24 52 095 – Fax 081 24 71 303 bnb@parteno.it* – ⊡ *6 rm from* €107 An elegant and rather stylish B&B with the décor and furnishings chosen by a well known local artist. Warm, welcoming atmosphere enhanced by the setting: it is housed in a splendid nobleman's residence that has been carefully restored. Facilities include a sauna and gym.

Hotel Villa Capodimonte – *Via Moiariello 66, zona Capodimonte* – ☎ *081 45 90 00 Fax 081 29 93 44* – ⊡ ⅞ – *57 rm from* €145 ⊡ – *Rest* €27/41. A little off the beaten track but easy to get to. Splendid setting with lovely parkland surrounding this villa-style hotel and wonderful views over the Bay of Naples. Spacious rooms with Art Nouveau-style décor and deluxe facilities. Most have a balcony.

TAKING A BREAK

Gran Caffè Gambrinus – *Via Chiaia 1/2* – ☎ *081 41 75 82 – Daily 8am-1am.* The most famous of all the Neapolitan cafés, it exudes an air of historical importance. Its sumptuously decorated rooms have witnessed 150 years of the most important events of Neapolitan history.

Intra Moenia – *Piazza Bellini Vincenzo 70* – ☎ *081 29 07 20 – Daily 10am-3am.* Situated in the old heart of the Naples, this establishment has long been popular with the city's intellectual élite. A café, bookshop and gelateria all rolled into one, the building also houses a publishing house, one of the few that is still in operation.

La Caffettiera – *Piazza dei Martiri 25/26* – ☎ *081 76 44 243 – Daily 7.30am-11pm.* Good coffee and delicious brioches.

Scaturchio – *Piazza S. Domenico Maggiore 19* – ☎ *081 55 16 944 – Daily 7.30am-8.40pm.* The place to try the *sfogliatella riccia* (a flaky pastry stuffed with ricotta and candied fruit, flavoured with orange oil) straight out of the oven or a baba, a cake of foreign origin but very much appreciated in the Kingdom of Naples.

GOING OUT

Dizzy Club – *Corso Vittorio Emanuele 19/20* – *Thu-Tue 8pm-2am.* Over 150 cocktails to choose from here! Also the place to go if you fancy a game of cards or chess.

ENTERTAINMENT

Teatro San Carlo – *Via San Carlo 98* – ☎ *081 79 72 111* – *biglietteria@teatrosancarlo.it* – *Opera season: Dec-May – Box office: Tue-Sun 10am-1pm and 4.30-6.30pm.* With its opera company permanently in residence, the San Carlo is one of the best opera houses in the world.

SHOPPING

The figurines from the Nativity scenes (head for Via San Gregorio Armeno) make lovely souvenirs and presents. The best place for cameos and coral pieces is the Napoletano (especially Torre del Greco).

EVENTS AND FESTIVALS

With all their pomp and circumstance and magnificent ceremonial trimmings, there are a number of well-known religious festivals. These include Madonna di Piedigrotta (8 Sep), Santa Maria del Carmine (16 Jul) and especially the Feast of the Miracle of St Januarius (1st Sun in May and 9 Sep). During the Christmas period (until 6 Jan), the churches are decorated with wonderful Nativity scenes.

USEFUL TELEPHONE NUMBERS

Carabinieri Police ☎ 081 54 81 111
State Police ☎ 081 79 41 111
Road Police ☎ 081 59 54 111
City Police ☎ 081 75 13 177
Emergency Ambulance ☎ 081 75 28 282 or 081 75 20 696
Railway Information ☎ 147 88 80 88

Ferdinand of Aragon's fleet in Naples harbour (15C)

GIRAUDON

ART IN NAPLES

A royal patron of the arts

Under the princes of the House of Anjou, Naples was endowed with many ecclesiastical buildings, which were greatly influenced by the French Gothic style. **"Robert the Wise" of Anjou** (1309-43) attracted poets, scholars and artists from various regions of Italy to his court in Naples. Boccaccio spent part of his youth in Naples where he fell in love with Fiammetta, whom some believe to have been the king's own daughter. His friend Petrarch also spent some time in this city. In 1324 Robert the Wise brought the Sienese sculptor **Tino di Camaino** to adorn many of the churches with his monumental tombs. Other churches were embellished with frescoes by the Roman artist Pietro Cavallini, slightly later by Giotto whose works have unfortunately disappeared, and by Simone Martini.

The Neapolitan School of Painting (17C-early 18C)

The busiest period in Neapolitan painting was the 17C which began with the arrival in Naples in 1607 of the great innovator in painting, **Caravaggio**. The master's style was bold and realistic: he often used real people as models for his crowd scenes. He used chiaroscuro with dramatic effect with light playing a fundamental part. So a new school of painting flourished, its members greatly inspired by the master. The principal followers were Artemisia Gentileschi, the Spaniard **José de Ribera** alias Spagnoletto, **Giovanni Battista Caracciolo** and the Calabrian Mattia Preti. One pupil who differed greatly from the others was **Luca Giordano** whose spirited compositions were full of light. His decorative work heralds the painting of the 18C. **Francesco Solimena** perpetuated Giordano's style but he was also influenced by the more sombre style of Mattia Preti and by Classicism. His paintings are characterised by chiaroscuro effects which lend solidity to shapes and a strong balance to the use of space.

The Baroque period

Numerous architects built fine Baroque buildings in Naples and the surrounding area. **Ferdinando Sanfelice** (1675-1748) had a highly inventive and theatrical approach to staircases, which he placed at the far end of the courtyard where they became the palace's most important decorative feature. It was, however, **Luigi Vanvitelli** (1700-73) who was the great Neapolitan architect of the 18C. The Bourbon King Charles III entrusted Vanvitelli with the project to build another Versailles at Caserta *(see CASERTA)*. It was in the 17C that Naples began to specialise in the marvellous **Christmas Mangers** *(presepi)* which were to become famous.

Special Features

SPACCANAPOLI AND THE DECUMANUS MAXIMUS★★

Visit: 4hr on foot. To get the most out of this itinerary, including gaining access to all the churches and buildings, you are advised to set out in the morning.

The main axis of old Naples, formed by the Via S. Benedetto Croce, Via S. Biagio dei Librai and Via Vicaria Vecchia is nicknamed Spaccanapoli, meaning the street which bisects Naples. It follows the course of one of the main roads through ancient Naples, the **Decumanus Maximus** which now more or less forms the Via Tribunali. Strolling through these streets is to witness Naples' evolution through the centuries, beginning with the Greeks and the Romans.

In Piazza del Gesù Nuovo, which is dominated by the impressive Baroque monument of the Virgin, is the church of **Gesù Nuovo** with its fine façade and diamond pointed facing, a unique testimony to the 15C Palazzo Sanseverino nearby. The inside of the façade is decorated with Solimena's *Expulsion of Heliodorus from the Temple. Open daily, 9am-1pm and 4-7pm.* ☎ 081 55 18 613.

Enter Via Benedetto Croce.

Chiesa di Santa Chiara★

Open Mon-Sat, 7.30am-12.30pm and 4.30-8pm, Sun and hols, 8am-1pm and 4.30-8pm. ☎ 081 55 26 209, www.santachiara.org

Sancia of Majorca, the wife of Robert the Wise of Anjou, had this Church of the Poor Clares built in the Provençal-Gothic style. The simple façade is preceded by a porch in peperino, the grey colour of which is in pleasant contrast to the yellow tufa. The interior, having been restored with Baroque features, was destroyed in the 1943 bombing and then rebuilt in its original form. A bare, lofty nave, lit by tall, narrow twin windows, opens onto nine chapels. At the end, in place of an apse, a long wall is lined with memorials to the Anjou dynasty: including the **tomb★★** of Robert the Wise, the work of Florentine sculptors, and on the right the tomb of Charles of Anjou, attributed to **Tino di Camaino** who is also responsible for the **tomb★** of Marie de Valois *(near the south wall)*. To the right of the presbytery a vestibule leads to the 14C **chancel★** which is accessed via a fine marble doorway: on the walls there are remains of frescoes by Giotto's followers.

Cloisters★★ – The current layout is the work of Domenico Antonio Vaccaro who, in the 18C, transformed the interior of the cloisters into a garden. It was divided into four parts with two covered avenues that intersect at the centre to form a cross. He was also responsible for embellishing the wall of the portico, the seats and the columns lining the avenues with fine **majolica decoration★** which features floral motifs, landscapes, pastoral scenes and mythological subjects.

Chiesa di San Domenico Maggiore

Open daily, 8am-1pm and 4-7pm. ☎ 081 55 73 111.

The church apse gives onto a square ornamented with a small Baroque votive monument *(guglia)* to St Dominic. The interior of the church has both Gothic (**caryatids** by Tino di Camaino support a huge paschal candelabrum) and Baroque features. In the side aisle to the right, the second chapel is decorated with frescoes by Pietro Cavallini (1309). The 18C sacristy lined with panelling contains numerous coffins of members of the court of Aragon *(in the balustrade)*.

Cappella Sansevero

Open daily except Tue, 10am-8pm, Sun and hols 10am-1.30pm. €4.13. ☎ 081 55 18 470; www.ic-napoli.com/sansevero

This 16C chapel was completely restored in the 18C by Raimondo de Sangro, an eccentric whose passion for alchemy and scientific study gave rise to a certain notoriety. There are even two skeletons complete with "petrified" circulatory system *(in an underground chamber, access from the south aisle)*.

In the chapel there are fine marble **sculptures★**: on either side of the choir are *Chastity* (the veiled woman) and *Despair* (the latter being symbolised by a man struggling with a net); the central one depicts the splendid ***Christ covered by a shroud★***, a masterpiece by **Giuseppe Sammartino**. The folds of a thin shroud are draped on the peaceful recumbent figure.

Just before Via S. Biagio dei Librai, is the charming **Piazzetta del Nilo** which derives its name from a statue of the Nile found in the square. A little further along, to the left, is the attractive Via S. Gregorio Armeno. It is lined with small shops and workshops where the small figurines for the Nativity scenes *(presepio)* are produced. The skills required have been handed down from father to son since the 19C. These days the statuettes include modern figures. The area is particularly charming around Christmas time. At the end of the street, at the bend, rises the campanile of the church of San Gregorio Armeno.

Chiesa di San Gregorio Armeno

Open daily, 9.30am-noon. Donation recommended. ☎ 081 55 20 186.

This church is dedicated to St Gregory. A spacious atrium leads onto the **interior★** of the church which is opulently Baroque in style. The frescoes along the nave and in the cupola are the work of Luca Giordano. At the end of the nave are two huge Baroque **organs**. Of particular interest in the presbytery is the high altar with intarsia work in polychrome marble and, to the right, the *comunichino*, a brass screen from behind which the nuns followed Mass. The beautiful ceiling, in gilded wood, features medallions decorated by Teodoro di Enrico.

The **cloisters** *(access via the steps in the monastery)* have a splendid fountain *(centre)* decorated with statues of Christ and the Samaritan woman (late 18C).

At the end of Via S. Gregorio Armeno is Via dei Tribunali which runs into the Decumamus Maximus that dates back to ancient Rome.

Chiesa di San Lorenzo Maggiore

Open 8am-noon and 5-7pm. For excavations: Mon-Fri 9am-1pm and 3-5.30pm, Sat 9am-5.30pm, Sun 9.30am-1.30pm. €2.58.

The church of St Lawrence was built in the 14C over an early Christian church, the remains of which include the perimeter walls and the columns from the nave. Restored in the Baroque style, it was eventually returned to its original appearance after recent restoration work.

It is built on the plan of a Latin cross with an elegant **arch★** that spans the transept crossing. The nave, a simple, austere rectangular space (except for a chapel on the west wall which has kept its splendid Baroque additions) is a testament to the Franciscan influence. The **polygonal apse★** is an interesting specimen of French Gothic architecture in southern Italy. It is surmounted by elegant arches crowned by twin bays and terminates in an ambulatory onto which open chapels with frescoes by disciples of Giotto. The north transept houses a large chapel dedicated to St Anthony and, on the altar, a painting of the saint surrounded by angels (1438), on a gold background. To the right of the high altar is the remarkable **tomb★** of Catherine of Austria, attributed to Tino di Camaino.

From the cloisters of the church make for the **chapter house**, with its frescoed walls and vault, which houses a unique "illustrated Bible" – terracotta figurines placed inside nutshells which date from the 1950s. Access to the **ruins** is also from the cloisters. The ruins reveal a crucial part of Naples' Greco-Roman history: along with the forum there are traces of the treasury, bakery and *macellum* (large covered market). *Ruins: (&. – entrance from Vico dei Maiorani). Open Mon-Sat, 9am-1pm and 3.30-5.30pm, Sun and hols 9am-1.30pm. Guided tours available (1hr). €2.58. ☎ 081 45 49 48.*

Duomo★

Treasury of San Gennaro open to visitors Mon-Fri, 8am-12.30pm and 4.30-7pm, Sat 8am-12.30pm and 4.30-7.30pm, Sun and hols 8am-1.30pm and 5-7.30pm. ☎ 081 44 90 97.

Built in the 14C, the cathedral was considerably altered at a later date. Held in great veneration by the people, the **Tesoro di San Gennaro★** (Chapel of St Januarius), in a rich Baroque style, is preceded by a remarkable 17C bronze grille: behind the high altar are two glass phials containing the saint's blood which is supposed to liquefy, failing which disaster will befall the town. The Feast of the **Miracle of St Januarius** is held twice annually on the first Sunday in May and on 19 September. The dome is decorated with a Lanfranco fresco showing an admirable sense of movement.

The south transept houses an *Assumption* by Perugino and the Gothic **Minutolo Chapel** which has a beautiful 13C mosaic floor and frescoed walls. The **succorpo** (crypt) is an elegant Renaissance structure.

A door in the middle of the north aisle gives access to the 4C **Basilica di Santa Restituta**, which was transformed in the Gothic period and again in the 17C. At the far end of the nave, the 5C **Baptistery of San Giovanni** is a fine structure containing **mosaics★★** of the same period. From the north apse make for the **archaeological displays** which afford some evocative time travel through Greek, Roman and medieval Naples.

Decumanus Maximus★★

Broadly takes the course of the Via dei Tribunali. Tour of decumanus monuments, daily 9am-1.30pm. Pio Monte della Misericordia. ☎ 081 44 69 44

Turn right to get to the 17C **Pio Monte della Misericordia** which houses six panels; the themes are linked to the charitable works carried out by the institute. Of particular interest are *St Peter freed from Prison* by Caracciolo and the fine *The Seven Works of Mercy★★★* by **Caravaggio**.

Turn back and at the junction of Via Duomo turn right.

Quadreria dei Girolamini – *Entrance from Via Duomo 142.* Housed on the first floor of a convent, this collection has a considerable body of work from the Neapolitan, Roman and Florentine schools of the 16C-18C. These include paintings by Luca Giordano, GB Caracciolo, José de Ribera *(Apostles)*, Guido Reni and Francesco Solimena *(Prophets)*. The convent also houses a Library with a splendid **18C room★**.

The **chiesa dei Girolamini** has works of art by Pietro Bernini (father of Lorenzo), Pietro da Cortona, Luca Giordano and Francesco Solimena.

A little further on is the church of **San Paolo Maggiore**. In front is a splendid flight of steps; the interior is Baroque and very ornate: note the polychrome altar. The sacristy houses fine **frescoes★** by **Solimena**: *The Fall of Simon Magus* and the *Conversion of St Paul (side walls)* are among this artist's masterpieces.

Further along, to the right, is the church of **Purgatorio ad Arco** with its tiny underground cemetery *(cimitero sotterraneo)* where, until recently, the unique practice of cleaning the bones was carried out for the purposes of receiving grace, a widespread practice in Naples.

At no 362 is **Palazzo Spinelli di Laurino** with a curious elliptical courtyard embellished by one of Sanfelice's staircases.

On the parvis of the church of **Santa Maria Maggiore**, also known as Pietrasanta, with its beautiful flooring in brick and majolica (1764) rise, to the left, the Renaissance chapel, Cappella Pontano, and, to the right, a fine campanile which dates back to the original church (11C).

Beyond **Croce di Lucca**, a 17C church with coffered ceiling of gilded wood, is the church of **San Pietro a Majella**. It has Gothic overtones but was restored in the 17C. Features include the fine carved choir stalls and the frescoes in the apse.

The tour ends in Piazza Bellini which is a pleasant place to spend the evening. In the centre are the ruined Greek walls. A little further on is **Piazza Dante**, overlooked by a semicircular range of buildings, the work of Vanvitelli.

Worth a Visit

MUSEO ARCHEOLOGICO NAZIONALE*** *Visit: 2hr*

& *Open daily except Tue, 8.30am-2pm or 8.30am-7.30pm (ticket office closes 1hr early). Closed 1 Jan, 1 May, 25 Dec. €6.20. For information on opening times ☎ 84 88 00 288; www.athena.cib.na.cnr.it/vhf-it/sanc/welcome.html*

The National Archaeological Museum occupies a group of 16C buildings which were originally intended to house the royal cavalry, and then became the seat of the university from 1610 to 1777. The collections comprise mainly works of art belonging to the Farnese family and treasures discovered at Pompeii and Herculaneum. It is one of the richest museums in the world for Greco-Roman antiquities.

Ground floor

Greco-Roman sculpture***

The large atrium displays sculptures from Pompeii and Herculaneum. At the front of the room a staircase on the right leads to the section in the basement dedicated to the **epigraphy section** (ancient inscriptions) and the **Egyptian collection**.

Galleria dei Tirannicidi – *Turn right on entering the Atrium.* The Tyrant-Slayers Gallery is devoted to Archaic art. The **Aphrodite Sosandra** with a fine, proud face and elegantly-draped robe is a splendid copy of a Greek bronze (5C BC), while the powerful marble group of the **Tyrant-Slayers**, a copy of a Greek bronze, represents Harmodios and Aristogiton who delivered Athens from the tyrant, Hipparchus, in the 6C BC.

Galleria dei Grandi Maestri – *Access from the Galleria dei Tirannicidi.* The Great Masters' Gallery contains the majestic statue of the Farnese Pallas (Athena), Orpheus and Eurydice bidding each other farewell, a low relief of touching simplicity copied from an original by Phidias (5C BC), and the **Doryphorus**, the spear-bearer, a copy of the famous bronze by Polyclitus.

At the end of the Galleria dei Tirannicidi, to the left, is a gallery displaying the famous **Callipygian Aphrodite** (Callipige signifies "with lovely buttocks", 1C) and the lovely statue of **Artemis of Ephesus** (2C) in alabaster and bronze, representing the deity venerated at the famous temple by the Aegean Sea. She is sometimes considered as a nature goddess in the Oriental tradition and is represented with numerous breasts symbolising her maternal nature.

Galleria del Toro Farnese – *Access from the preceding gallery.* This gallery houses the monumental sculptural groups found at the Baths of Caracalla in Rome in the 16C.

In the centre is the colossal *Flora farnese*. In the last room is the impressive sculptured group called the **Farnese Bull** depicting the death of Dirce, a legendary queen of Thebes. It was carved from a single block of marble. It is a 2C Roman copy, which like many works in the Farnese collection has undergone much restoration, thereby altering its original characteristics. In the right wing is the **Farnese Hercules**, resting after his famous labours.

From this gallery make for the section dedicated to **engraved gemstones** which includes one of the greatest masterpieces of the museum, the celebrated **Tazza Farnese***, an enormous cameo in the shape of a cup made in Alexandria in the 2C BC.

Mosaics**

To the left on the mezzanine. Although most of these come from Pompeii, Herculaneum and Stabia, they offer a wide variety of styles and subject matter. There are two small works (*Visit to a Fortune-Teller* and *Roving Musicians*) by Dioscurides of Samos along with the *Actors on stage* found in the Room of the Tragic Poet *(Room LIX)*. Mosaics including a *Frieze with festoons and masks* and the splendid mosaic of the **Battle of Alexander and Darius** *(Room LXI)* which paved the floor of the House of the Faun at Pompeii, are housed in Rooms LX and LXI.

The latter reveals a remarkable sense of depth (rear view of a horse in the foreground) and movement (the horses champing at the bit, the lances crossed and the Persian king prostrate in front of Alexander). The collection also includes some fine examples of *opus sectile.*

First floor

Works from Villa di Pisone and dei Papiri★★★

At the beginning of the Salone della Meridiana, on the right. The villa, which was discovered at Herculaneum in the 18C but was later reburied, is thought to have belonged to L Calpurnius Pison who was Julius Caesar's father-in-law. The owner had turned the house into a museum. The documents and splendid works of art from his collections are priceless. The Sala dei Papiri (Room CXIV) contains photographs of some of the 800 papyri from the library. In Room CXVI are exhibited **bronze statues** that adorned the peristyle of the villa: the **Drunken Faun** lost in euphoria, a **Sleeping Satyr** with a beautiful face in repose; the two lifelike **Wrestlers** are inspired from Lysippus (4C BC); the famous **Dancers from Herculaneum** are probably in fact water-carriers; the famous **Hermes at Rest,** with a tall strong figure, reflects Lysippus' ideal.

In Room CXVII, is the **portrait** mistakenly identified as that of **Seneca**, one of the most remarkably expressive works handed down from Antiquity.

Silver, ivory, terracotta and glass gallery★

At the beginning of the Salone della Meridiana, on the left. These rooms are mostly devoted to finds brought back from Pompeii and Herculaneum. Exhibits include silver found in the House of Menander in Pompeii, ivory ornaments, Greek and Italic weapons, glass objects, among which note the stunning **Blue vase★★** decorated with *putti* and harvest scenes.

From this section make for the room displaying the cork **model of Pompeii** made in the 19C.

Sale del Tempio di Iside★★★

After the room above. The room features objects and pictures from the Temple of Isis discovered behind the Great Theatre at Pompeii. Three areas have been partially reconstructed to evoke the original structure: the portico, the *ekklesiasterion* (the assembly room where the worshippers of Isis met) and the *sacrarium* (sanctuary). The frescoes on the walls illustrate a still life (figs, grapes, geese and doves are all elements linked to the worship of this Egyptian goddess and were part of the Isis cult). Of particular interest are the beautiful large panels which are well preserved and depict sacred rites and scenes illustrating the myths surrounding Io (Isis).

Sale degli affreschi★★★

At the far end of the Salone della Meridiana, on the left, or after the Sale del Tempio di Iside. The collection includes some splendid frescoes from Pompeii, Herculaneum and Stabia in particular. The diversity of style and colour is a testament to the richness of this form of decorative art practised by the Romans *(see POMPEI).* Exhibits include beautiful paintings with mythological subjects such as Heracles, Ariadne, and the tragic Medea and Iphigenia, and epic poems including episodes from the Trojan war which are often inserted in architectural perspectives, friezes of cupids, satyrs and maenads. The female figures found at Stabia which represent *Leda, Medea, Flora* and *Artemis* are notable for their grace and gentleness. The medallions depicting Campanian landscapes were originally in a villa at Boscotrecase.

At the far end of the Salone della Meridiana, to the right, a **Topographical section** is in the process of being set up. It will display artefacts from Campania dating from prehistory to the Roman age.

PALAZZO AND GALLERIA NAZIONALE DI CAPODIMONTE★★

Visit: 2hr. North of the city. & Open daily, 8.30am-2pm or 8.30am-7.30pm (ticket office closes 1hr early). Closed 1 Jan, 1 May, 25 Dec. €7.23. For information on opening times ☎ 84 88 00 288 (Freephone); www.beniculturali.it

This former **royal estate★** extends over high ground to the north of the city. The whole includes a massive and austere palace which was built from 1738 to 1838, an extensive park, and the remains of the famous 18C porcelain factory. The palace itself has an art gallery in addition to the royal apartments.

Pinacoteca

The nucleus of the holding is the Farnese collection, inherited by the Bourbons and enriched over the years. The works are presented mostly in chronological order and trace the main trends in the evolution of Italian painting; there are also important works by foreign artists.

The collections open with the Farnese Gallery which displays famous portraits of the most important members of the Farnese family. Note the portrait of *Paolo III with his nephews★★*, a masterpiece by Titian showing all his penetrating psychological insight.

In the intense **Crucifixion★★★** by Masaccio, the figure of Mary Magdalene in a bright red dress with arms dramatically stretched towards the cross is a fine example of perspective that made Masaccio such a key figure in the revolution that was the Renaissance. The hunched figure of Christ is not an error but results from the fact that originally the painting was placed above another polyptych and therefore had to be looked at from below. Renaissance painting is represented by the works of Botticelli (*Madonna and Child with Saints*), Filippino Lippi and Raphael. A fine example of the Venetian school is the **Transfiguration★★** by Giovanni Bellini; the soft colours and light convey a sense of serenity which suffuses the landscape. In the Venetian section note the celebrated **Portrait of Fra Luca Pacioli**, possibly by a Spanish artist. Among the main exponents of Mannerism are Sebastiano del Piombo **(Portrait of Clement VII★)**, Pontormo and Rosso Fiorentino. Titian's study of light is exemplified in the sensual **Danae** and in the works of his pupil El Greco; light is an important feature in the *Boy lighting a candle with a firebrand*. Serenity and tenderness are evoked in a small canvas, **The Mystic Marriage of St Catherine** by Correggio and in the *Holy Family* by Parmigianino, which stresses the essential role of the mother: the child is only partly shown. By the same artist note the *Lucrezia* and the elegant **Antea★**. The section devoted to Flemish artists includes two fine works by the Flemish master, Peter Bruegel the Elder (*The Misanthrope* and **The Parable of the Blind★★**).

The second floor houses the "Neapolitan Gallery", a collection formed by Gioacchino Marat of works acquired from suppressed monastic orders. Masterpieces on display include **St Ludovic of Toulouse** by Simone Martini, the celebrated **St Jerome in his studio** by Colantonio and the **Flagellation★★** by Caravaggio. There are also works by Caracciolo, Ribera, Mattia Preti, Luca Giordano and Francesco Solimena.

The third floor is devoted to collections of contemporary art.

Royal apartments

1st floor. The rooms have fine furnishings. Of particular note is the **room★** with walls faced in porcelain and decorated with chinoiserie flowers and scenes. Also on view are a fine porcelain collection including the elegant *Procession of Aurora* in biscuit porcelain dating from the 19C, and an especially rich collection of royal armoury.

CERTOSA DI SAN MARTINO★★

Visit: 1hr Open daily except Mon, 8.30am-7.30pm (ticket office closes 6.30pm). Closed bank hols. ☎ 84 88 00 288 (Freephone).

This immense Carthusian monastery dedicated to St Martin is beautifully situated on a spur of the Vomero hill. The **Castel Sant'Elmo**, a massive structure with bastions, overlooks the monastery to the west; it was rebuilt by the Spaniards in the 16C and was for a long time used as a prison. From the drill square *(access on foot or by lift)* there is a wonderful view over the city and the bay. The monastery was founded by the Anjou dynasty in the 14C and was almost completely remodelled in the 16C and 17C. The monastic buildings can be visited, as well as the museum which is arranged in the buildings overlooking the Procurators' Cloisters.

Church

The **interior★★** is lavishly Baroque and is adorned with paintings by Caracciolo Guido Reni and Simon Vouet. To the left of the choir, beyond the sacristy with its superb furnishings embellished with inlay, is the treasury decorated with frescoes by Luca Giordano and a painting by Ribera, *La Pietà*.

The **great cloisters** is a harmonious ensemble, the work of the architect-sculptor Cosimo Fanzago.

Museum★

The section devoted to festivals and costumes contains an exceptional collection of figurines and Neapolitan **cribs★★** *(presepi)* in polychrome terracotta from the 18C and 19C. The collection is a wealth of objects (from baskets of fruit and vegetables in wax to animals and utensils) widely used in Neapolitan cribs; the four cribs on display are fine examples. The tour concludes with a large, impressive crib from the late 19C (some of the figures date back to the 18C).

To the left of the cloisters there is also an interesting **sculpture** section including works by Tino di Camaino.

CITY CENTRE★★ *Visit: 2hr 30min*

Castel Nuovo (or Maschio Angioino)★★

(♿) *Open Mon-Sat 9am-7pm (ticket office closes 6pm), Sun 9am-2pm courtyard only €5.16. ☎ 081 79 52 003.*

This imposing castle, surrounded by deep moats, was built in 1282 by Pierre de Chaulnes and Pierre d'Agincourt, the architects of Charles I of Anjou. It was modelled on the castle at Angers. A remarkable **triumphal arch★★** embellishes the entrance on the town side. This masterpiece bearing sculptures to the glory of the House of Aragon, was built to designs by Francesco Laurana in 1467. Access to the

Sala dei Baroni is via the staircase in the inner courtyard *(at the far end on the left)*. The fine vaulting is star shaped, formed by the tufa groins intersecting with other architectural features. The **Cappella Palatina** (14C) features an elegant Renaissance doorway which was previously surmounted by Laurana's splendid **Virgin** now kept, along with other works by the same artist in the sacristy.

Teatro San Carlo★

  Guided tours only, Sat-Sun 2-3.30pm. €2.58. ☎ 081 79 72 331; www.teatrosancarlo.it
The theatre was built under Charles of Bourbon in 1737 and rebuilt in 1816 in the neo-Classical style. The opera house is an important institution in the Italian world of music.
The splendid auditorium, with boxes on six levels and a large stage, is built entirely of wood and stucco to achieve perfect acoustics.

Piazza del Plebiscito★

This noble semicircular "square" (19C) is enclosed on one side by the royal palace, on the other by the neo-Classical façade of the church of **San Francesco di Paola**, built on the model of the Pantheon in Rome and prolonged by a curving colonnade. The equestrian statues of Ferdinand I and Charles III of Bourbon are by Canova.

Palazzo Reale★

  Open daily except Wed, 9am-8pm, May to Oct, Sat 9am-11pm. Closed 3-17 Mar, 1 Jan, 1 May, 25 Dec. €4.13. ☎ 081 79 44 021.
The royal palace was built at the beginning of the 17C by the architect Domenico Fontana and has been remodelled several times. The façade retains more or less its original appearance. Since the late 19C the niches on the façade have contained eight statues of the most famous Kings of Naples. A huge **staircase** with twin ramps and crowned by a coffered dome leads to the **apartments★** and the sumptuously decorated **royal chapel**. It was only after 1734 that royalty lived in the apartments. The richly ornamented rooms have retained their numerous works of art, tapestries, paintings, period furniture and fine porcelain. Of particular interest are the splendid **door knockers★** made of wood: putti, nymphs and animals are set off against a gilded background in a floral pattern.

Porto di Santa Lucia★★

See plan of the built-up area on Michelin map 431. Santa Lucia is the name of the small suburb that juts out towards the sea. It is best known as the name of a tiny port, immortalised by a famous Neapolitan song, nestling between a rocky islet and the jetty linking it to the shore. **Castel dell'Ovo** is a severe edifice built by the Normans and remodelled by the Angevins in 1274. Legend has it that Virgil hid a magic egg (*uovo*) within its walls and that the destruction of the egg would result in a similar fate for the castle.
From the jetty there is a splendid **view★★** of Vesuvius on the one hand and of the western side of the bay on the other. In the evening, go further along to Piazza Vittoria which offers a **view★★★** of the residential suburbs on the Vomero and Posillipo hillsides, brightly lit up by a myriad of twinkling lights.

ELSEWHERE IN THE HISTORIC CENTRE

Chiesa di Sant'Anna dei Lombardi

Open Tue-Sat, 9am-12.30pm. Closed Mon, Sun and hols. ☎ 081 55 13 333.
This Renaissance church, dedicated to St Anne of the Lombards, is rich in contemporary Florentine **sculpture★**. Inside is the tomb of Mary of Aragon *(1st chapel on the left)* by Antonio Rossellino and an *Annunciation (1st chapel on the right)* by Benedetto da Maiano. In the oratory to the right of the choir is a **Descent from the**

Legend and mystery around Castel dell'Ovo

Cross, a late-15C terracotta by Guido Mazzoni who introduced this style of rather theatrical realism to Naples which was to become very popular in southern Italy. The former sacristy has lovely stalls which are attributed to Fra Giovanni da Verona (1457-1525).

Palazzo Como★

This majestic late-15C palace, with its rusticated stonework, is a reminder of the Florentine Renaissance. It contains the **Museo Civico Filangieri** which displays collections of arms and armour, ceramics and porcelain, furniture and paintings by Ribera, Carracciolo, Mattia Preti etc. *Closed for restoration at time of publication.*

Porta Capuana★

This is one of the fortified gateways in the walls built in 1484 to the plans of Giuliano da Maiano. The **Castel Capuano** nearby was the former residence of the Norman princes and the Hohenstaufens.

Chiesa di San Giovanni a Carbonara★

An 18C stairway leads to the elegant Gothic doorway of this 14C church. Inside are the tomb of Ladislas of Anjou (15C) and many works of art in two chapels, the Carracciolo del Sole *(behind the choir)* and the Carracciolo del Vico *(to the left)*.

Chiesa di Santa Maria Donnaregina★

Go through the cloisters adorned with 18C faience. A Baroque church of the same name precedes the small 14C Gothic church which shows a French influence. Inside is the **tomb★** of the founder, Mary of Hungary, widow of Charles II of Anjou, by **Tino di Camaino**. The walls of the nuns' chancel are decorated with 14C **frescoes★**.

OUTSIDE THE HISTORIC CENTRE

The following places of interest are not on the town plan. See the map of the built-up area on Michelin map 431.

Villa Floridiana★

To the west of Naples. This graceful small white palace *(palazzina)* in the neo-Classical style stands high up on the Vomero hillside and is surrounded by a fine park. The façade overlooks the gardens which afford a splendid **panorama★**. The villa houses the **Museo Nazionale di Ceramica Duca di Martina★**, which displays a collection of enamels, ivories, faience and especially porcelain. ♿ *Open daily, 8.30am-2pm or 8.30am-7.30pm (ticket office closes 1hr early). Closed 1 Jan, 1 May, 25 Dec. €2.58. For information on hours,* ☎ *84 88 00 288 (Freephone).*

Catacombe di San Gennaro★★

North of the city. Guided tours only (40min), daily, 9.30am, 10.15am, 11am and 11.45am. Closed 1 Jan €2.58. ☎ *081 74 11 071.*
The catacombs dug in the volcanic rock extend over two floors and consists of vast galleries illuminated by a gentle light. The galleries open out to form a "baptistery" in the lower section and a spacious basilica with three aisles (4C-6C) in the upper section. The tomb of St Januarius, whose remains were transferred here in the 6C, is decorated with frescoes of the saint. There are beautiful paintings in the niches (3C-10C). In the upper section, the vault of the atrium is adorned with early Christian work and portraits of the dead adorning the family tombs. The Bishops' Crypt above the tomb of St Januarius contains fine mosaics depicting the bishops.

Villa Comunale

In the direction of Mergellina, along the seafront. Vanvitelli laid out these public gardens along the waterfront in 1780 and they are very popular with Neapolitans for their evening stroll. At the centre of the gardens is the **Aquarium** which presents a large variety of sea creatures to be found in the Bay of Naples. ♿ *Open daily except Mon, Mar to Oct 9am-6pm, Sun and hols 10am-7.30pm, rest of year 10am-7.30pm, Sun and hols 10-14. €1.55.* ☎ *081 58 33 263.*

Museo Principe di Aragona Pignatelli Cortes

Riviera di Chiaia, opposite the Villa Comunale. ♿ *Open daily, 8.30am-2pm (ticket office closes 1pm). Closed 1 Jan, 1 May, 25 Dec.* ☎ *84 88 00 288 (Freephone).*
The ground floor of the summer residence of the Princess Pignatelli (she lived here until the 1950s) is open to visitors. Furnishings date back to the 19C. In the garden, the old stables house an interesting collection of carriages from the same period. The vehicles which have been very well preserved are of English, French and Italian origin.

Mergellina★

Mergellina, at the foot of the Posillipo hillside with the small port of Sannazzaro, is one of the few places in Naples ideal for a stroll. It affords a splendid **view★★** of the bay: the Vomero hillside, crowned by Castel Sant'Elmo, slopes down gently towards the Santa Lucia headland and Castel dell'Ovo beyond, with Vesuvius in the distance.

Golfo di **Napoli**★★★

Bay of NAPLES

The Bay of Naples, extending from Cumae to Sorrento, has a rich history and is one of the most beautiful Italian bays. It is an area of striking contrasts where one may find in close proximity isolated areas conducive to meditation, such as the archaeological sites, the bare slopes of Vesuvius, the Sibyl's Cave or Lake Averno, and others bustling with activity, noisy, crowded with traffic, all of which are enlivened by the exuberance of the local people. Its legendary beauty is somewhat marred by the uncontrolled sprawl of industrial development which has reached the outskirts of Naples. However, its islands, capes and mountains are as lovely as they were two thousand years ago.

Location

Michelin map 431 E-F 24-26 – Campania. The main access roads to the Bay of Naples are A 1, the so-called Autostrada del Sole, A 3 if you are arriving from the south and A 16, which links Naples to the Adriatic. ◙ *in Naples: Piazza dei Martiri 58,* ☎ *081 40 53 11, Piazza del Plebiscito (Palazzo Reale),* ☎ *081 41 87 44.*
Surrounding area. See CAPRI, CASERTA, COSTIERA AMALFITANA, ISCHIA, NAPOLI, POMPEI, SALERNO.

Directory

WHERE TO EAT
• Budget
Taverna Azzurra-da Salvatore – *Via Marina Grande 166 – 80067 Sorrento –* ☎ *081 87 72 510 – Closed Mon (Jan-May) –* ◙ *– Book – €15/39.* This taverna is mainly frequented by the locals – they know where to head for some of the best seafood in town! The fish is always of the best quality and super-fresh, and what the chef purchases depends on what is on sale at the daily fish market. Simple surroundings, with a marine theme to the decor. If you are lucky you might get a table right by the beach.

Zi'ntonio – *Via De Maio 11 – 80067 Sorrento –* ☎ *081 87 81 623 – Closed Tue (except Mar-Oct) –* ◙ *– €22/40.* This establishment is popular with the locals and tourists alike. Charming majolica-tiled dining area. There is also an intermediate floor with a rustic-style wooden finish. Combines authentic regional cooking with some national dishes. Also serves delicious pizzas. One for the address book.

• Moderate
Taverna del Capitano – *Piazza delle Sirene 10/11, Località Nerano – 80068 Marina del Cantone – 5km/3mi southwest of Sant'Agata sui Due Golfi –* ☎ *081 80 81 028 – Closed Mon (except Jun-Sep), 8 Jan-Feb –* ◙ *– Book – €47/65.* A quiet, elegant restaurant with vast picture windows overlooking the sea. Typical Mediterranean cooking, with an emphasis on fish. Dishes prepared with excellent, super-fresh ingredients. Stylish decor and well-maintained surroundings. Also has rooms (very pleasant).

WHERE TO STAY
• Moderate
Hotel Sant'Agata – *Via dei Campi 8/A – 80064 Sant'Agata sui due Golfi –* ☎ *081 80 80 800 – Fax 081 53 30 749 – Closed Nov-15 Mar –* ◙ ◙ *(payment) – 30 rm €58/80* ☺ *– Restaurant €18/23.* This hotel is ideally situated for a holiday touring the beautiful Amalfi coast and the sites of Pompeii and Herculaneum. The public areas are roomy and light; the rooms have been tastefully decorated. The attention to detail also extends to the cuisine. Very reasonably priced.

Hotel Désirée – *Via Capo 31/bis – 80067 Sorrento –* ☎ *081 87 81 563 – Fax 081 87 81 563 – Closed Feb –* ☇ ◙ *– 22 rm €51.65/82.63* ☺. A small, rather old-fashioned hotel with a charming family atmosphere and simple surroundings. Perched high above the sea, there are wonderful views taking in the Bay of Naples and Vesuvius. Facilities include a terrace-solarium and private beach (you take a lift to get down there!). Extremely reasonably priced.

Hotel Regina – *Via Marina Grande 10 – 80067 Sorrento –* ☎ *081 87 82 722 – Fax 081 87 82 721 – Closed Nov-Feb –* ◙ *– 36 rm €72.40/149.80* ☺ *– Restaurant €36.20.* A stone's throw from the centre, yet lovely and quiet. Facilities at the hotel include a lovely citrus-grove garden and a terrace-solarium with wonderful views. Panoramic restaurant on the top floor.

TAKING A BREAK
Bar Ercolano – *Piazza Tasso 28 – 80067 Sorrento –* ☎ *08 18 07 29 51 – Wed-Mon 6am-1am.* Situated right on the main square, this is the perfect spot for whiling away a warm summer's evening.

Circolo dei Forestieri – *Via L. De Maio 35 – 80067 Sorrento –* ☎ *081 87 73 263 – Daily, 9.30am-1am.* Amazing views from the superb terrace area at the top. Live music almost every night.

Excursions

We have suggested 4 itineraries (the first two departing from Naples), each of them a natural progression from the previous one. For itinerary 5, see COSTIERA AMALFITANA.

CAMPI FLEGREI★★ ⬑

From Naples to Cuma. 45km/28mi – about 6hr. This volcanic area, the Phlegrean Fields, which received its name from the ancients ("phlegrean" is derived from a Greek word meaning "to blaze"), extends in an arc along the Gulf of Pozzuoli. Hot springs, steam-jets and sulphurous gases rise from the ground and from the sea, and are proof of an intense underground activity. Lakes have formed in the craters of extinct volcanoes. This stretch of coastline is subject to variations in ground level due to volcanic activity.

Naples★★★ *See NAPOLI*

Posillipo★

This famous hill forms a promontory and separates the Bay of Naples from the *Gulf of Pozzuoli*. Posillipo, dotted with villas and their lovely gardens and modern buildings, is Naples' main residential area. It affords splendid views of the bay.

Marechiaro★

This small fishermen's village built high above the sea was made famous by a Neapolitan song *Marechiare*.

Parco Virgiliano

Also called the **Garden of Remembrance**, the park has splendid **views★★** over the Bay of Naples, from Cape Miseno to the Sorrento Peninsula, as well as the islands of Procida, Ischia and Capri.

Museo Vivo di Città della Scienza a Bagnoli★

Open Tue-Sat 9am-5pm, Sun and hols 10am-7pm (call ahead to confirm opening times). Closed 1 Jan, 15 Aug, 25 Dec. €7; Planetarium €1.50, on reservation. ☎ 081 37 23 728; www.cittadellascienza.it/

A fine industrial building from the mid-19C now houses the innovative Science Center, helpfully divided up into various sections – each with a different theme (physics, classical world, nature, evolution, communications). Worth a visit is the **Officina dei Piccoli**, where children from 0 to 10 can learn through play, and the Planetarium.

Pozzuoli*

Pozzuoli, which is of Greek origin, became an active trading port under the Romans. As the town is at the centre of the volcanic area known as the Phlegrean Fields and is constantly affected by changes in the ground level which occur in this region, the town centre has been evacuated. The town has given its name to pozzolana, a volcanic ash with a high silica content which is used in the production of certain kinds of cement.

Anfiteatro Flavio★★ – *Corso Terracciano. Open daily, 9am to 1hr before sunset. Closed 1 Jan, 1 May, 25 Dec. €2.07. ☎ 081 52 66 007.*
This amphitheatre is one of the largest in Italy and dates from the reign of Vespasian, the founder of the Flavian dynasty. It could accommodate 40 000 spectators. Built of brick and stone, it is relatively well preserved: note the outer walls, the entrances and the particularly well-preserved **basements**★★.

Tempio di Serapide★ – *Set back from Via Roma.* The temple, dedicated to Serapis, which is situated near the sea, was really the ancient market place and was lined with shops. There is a sort of apse in the end wall which contained the statue of Serapis, the protecting god of traders. The central edifice shows the effects of variations in ground level: the columns reveal signs of marine erosion.

Tempio di Augusto★ – The temple, dedicated to Augustus, dated from the early days of the Empire and was converted into a Christian church in the 11C. A recent fire has revealed a grandiose marble colonnade with its entablature.

Solfatara★★

♿ *Open daily, Apr to Oct 8.30am-7pm, Mar 8.30am-6pm, rest of year 8.30am-4.30pm. €4.60. ☎ 081 52 62 341; www.solfatara.it*
Although extinct, this crater still has some of the features of an active volcano such as jets of steam charged with sulphurous fumes, strong smelling and with traces of yellow, miniature volcanoes spitting hot mud, and bubbling jets of sand. The ground gives a hollow sound and the surface is hot. The sulphurous vapours have been used for medicinal purposes since Roman times.

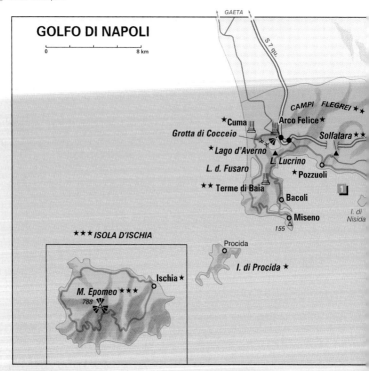

Lago Lucrino

In Antiquity, oyster farming was practised here on the lake and the banks were lined with elegant villas. One of these belonged to Cicero and another was the scene of Agrippina's murder, on the orders of her son Nero.

Terme di Baia★★

Open daily except Mon, 9am to 1hr before sunset. €2.07. ☎ 081 86 87 592; www.ulixes.it
This Greek colony was in Roman times a fashionable beach resort, as well as a thermal spa *(terme)* with the most complete equipment in the world for hydrotherapy. The Roman emperors and patricians had immense villas, all of which disappeared under the sea after a change in ground level. However, ruins of the famous baths remain on the hilltop overlooking the sea. Facing the hill, these include from left to right the baths of Venus, Sosandra and Mercury.

Bacoli

On the high ground in the old town rises the **Cento Camerelle★** *(Via Cento Camerelle, to the right of the church)*. This huge reservoir, which belonged to a private villa, is built on two levels: the grandiose upper level built in the 1C AD has four sections and immense arches; the lower part, built much earlier, has a network of narrow galleries forming a cross, that emerge high above sea level. The famous **Piscina Mirabile★** *(at the church take the road to the left, Via Ambrogio Greco, and then Via Piscina Mirabile to the right)* was an immense cistern designed to supply water to the Roman fleet in the port of Miseno. It is 70m long, 25m wide and nearly 15m high (230ft × 82ft × 49ft) and is divided into five sections with 48 pillars supporting the roof. There are remarkable light effects. *Cento Camerelle: Open daily, 9am to 1hr before sunset. Contact custodian on Via Cento Camerelle. Donation recommended. For additional information ☎ 081 56 35 541 (Ufficio Beni Culturali del Comune di Bacoli).*

Piscina Mirabile: Open daily, 9am to 1hr before sunset. No charge. Donation recommended. For additional information ☎ 081 56 35 541 (Ufficio Beni Culturali del Comune di Bacoli).

Miseno

This name is given to a lake, a port, a promontory, a cape and a village. Lake Miseno, a former volcanic crater, was believed by the ancients to be the Styx, across which Charon ferried the souls of the dead. Under the Emperor Augustus it was linked by a canal to the port of Miseno, which was the base of the Roman fleet. The village of Miseno is dominated by Monte Miseno, on which Misenus, the companion of Aeneas, is said to have been buried. The slopes of the promontory were studded with luxurious villas, including the one where in AD 37 the Emperor Tiberius choked to death.

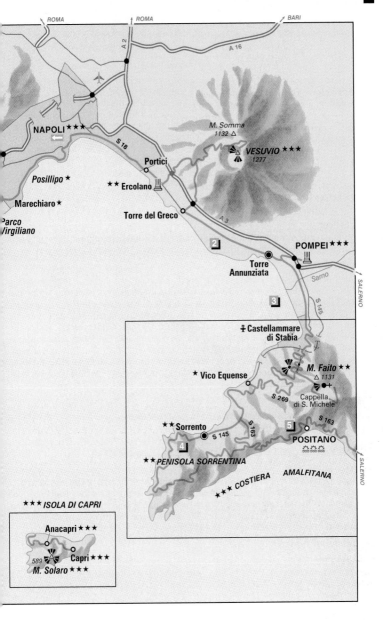
The map shows the following labelled locations:

- ROMA — A 2
- ROMA
- BARI
- A 16
- NAPOLI ★★★
- S 18
- M. Somma 1132 △
- VESUVIO ★★★ 1277
- Portici
- Posillipo ★
- ★★ Ercolano
- Marechiaro ★
- Parco Virgiliano
- Torre del Greco
- A 3
- POMPEI ★★★
- Torre Annunziata
- Sarno
- SALERNO
- ‡ Castellammare di Stabia
- M. Faito ★★ △ 1131
- ★ Vico Equense
- S 269
- Cappella di S. Michele
- ★★ Sorrento
- S 145
- S 163
- S 163
- POSITANO
- ★★ PENISOLA SORRENTINA
- ★★★ COSTIERA AMALFITANA
- SALERNO
- ★★★ ISOLA DI CAPRI
- Anacapri ★★★
- 589
- M. Solaro ★★★
- Capri ★★★

Lago del Fusaro

A lagoon with a small island on which Vanvitelli built a hunting lodge for King Ferdinand IV of Bourbon in 1782.

Cuma★

Cumae, one of the oldest Greek colonies, was founded in the 8C BC. The city soon dominated the whole Phlegrean area including Naples, leaving an important Hellenic heritage. Its splendour was at its height under the tyrant Aristodemus. After its capture by the Romans in 334 BC, decline set in and continued until AD 915 when it was pillaged by the Saracens. The ancient city of Cumae stands in a serene and solemn setting near the sea. Visitors have access to the ruins of the acropolis, the upper town where most of the temples stood. In the lower town, excavations have revealed the remains of an amphitheatre, a temple dedicated to the Capitoline Triad (Jupiter, Juno and Minerva) and baths.

Parco Archeologico★★ – (&) *Open daily, 9am to 1hr before sunset. Closed 1 Jan, 1 May, 25 Dec. €4.* ☎ *081 85 43 060.*
The acropolis is built on a hill of volcanic material (lava and tufa) in a lonely site and is reached by an alley lined with laurels. After the vaulted passageway, the path to the left leads to the Sibyl's Cave, **Antro della Sibilla★**, one of the most vener-

ated places of Antiquity. Here the Sibyl delivered her oracles. The cave was hollowed out of the rock by the Greeks in the 6C or 5C BC and it is rectangular in shape with three small niches.

Take the stairway up to the sacred way (Via Sacra). From the belvedere there is a good **view★** of the sea. Some finds from the excavations are on display. On the right are the remains of the **Tempio di Apollo** (Temple of Apollo) which was later transformed into a Christian church. Further on is the **Tempio di Giove** (Temple of Jupiter)which was also converted by the early Christians. In the centre stands a large font and there are several Christian tombs near the sanctuary.

THE CUMAEAN SIBYL

In Antiquity the Sibyls were virgin priestesses dedicated to the cult of Apollo and deemed to be semi-divine creatures with powers of divination. The Sibyl from Cumae (one of the main centres of Greek civilisation in Italy) was a famous prophetess. She is reputed to have sold the Sibylline Books, collections of the Sibyls' prophecies, to the Etruscan King of Rome, Tarquin the Elder or Tarquin the Superb (6C BC). The oracles were later used by the rulers to answer their subjects' petitions and expectations. One of the best-known depictions of the Cumaean Sibyl by Michelangelo adorns the ceiling of the Sistine Chapel in the Vatican.

Arco Felice★

The minor road in the direction of Naples leads to this triumphal arch which was erected on the Via Domitiana; there are still traces of the paved Roman way.

Lago d'Averno★

The lake lies below the Cumae-Naples road: belvedere on the right approximately 1km/0.6mi beyond Arco Felice. This lake within a crater is dark, still and silent and wrapped in an atmosphere of mystery, which was all the more intense in Antiquity as birds flying overhead were overcome by fumes and dropped into the lake to be swallowed up. Virgil regarded it as the entrance to the Underworld. Under the Roman Empire, Agrippa, a captain in the service of the Emperor Augustus, developed it as a naval base and linked it by canal with Lake Lucrino (*see above*), which in turn was linked to the open sea. An underground gallery 1km/0.6mi long, known as **Grotta di Cocceio** (Cocceio's Cave), connected Avernus with Cumae, and was used by chariots.

VESUVIO★★★ ②

From Naples to Torre Anunziata 45km/28mi – allow one day

The coast road relieves the Salerno motorway across a densely-populated industrial zone, once a favoured resort of the Neapolitan aristocracy (18C-19C). There are two important sites located a short distance from the road.

Portici

The road crosses the courtyard of the **royal palace** built in 1738 for the Bourbon King Charles III. Today the palace buildings are the home of the Naples Faculty of Agronomy. In his opera *The Mute Girl of Portici (Muette de Portici)*, the French composer, Auber, features the 17C revolt against the Spaniards, instigated by **Masaniello**, a young fisherman from Portici.

Herculaneum★★ *See ERCOLANO*

Il Vesuvio★★★

The outline of Vesuvius, one of the few still active volcanoes in Europe, is an intrinsic feature of the Neapolitan landscape. It has two summits: to the north **Monte Somma** (alt 1 132m/3 714ft) and to the south Vesuvius proper (alt 1 277m/4 190ft). Over time the volcanic materials on the lower slopes have become fertile soil with orchards and vines producing the famous *Lacryma Christi* wine.

The eruptions of Vesuvius – Until the earthquake of AD 62 and the eruption of AD 79 which buried Herculaneum and Pompeii, Vesuvius seemed extinct; its slopes were clothed with famous vines and woods. By 1139, seven eruptions had been recorded. Then came a period of calm during which the slopes of the mountains were cultivated. On 16 December 1631 Vesuvius had a terrible awakening, destroying all the settlements at its foot; 3 000 people perished. The eruption of 1794 devastated Torre del Greco. The volcano had minor eruptions in 1858, 1871, 1872, from 1895 to 1899, 1900, 1903, 1904, a major eruption in 1906, 1929, and one in 1944 altering the shape of the crater. Since then, apart from brief activity linked with the 1980 earthquake, Vesuvius has emitted only a plume of smoke.

Climbing the volcano – *From Herculaneum and via Torre del Greco, 27km/17mi plus 45min on foot there and back. Wear good walking shoes. Paid parking, on street or in Herculaneum, bus service from railway station, Circumvesuviana line. Guide required to go to edge of crater €5.16. Head guide: Sig. Pompilio ☎ 0335 24 71 54, Sig. Maddaloni ☎ 0337 94 22 49. Collegio Regionale Guide Alpine, via Panoramica 172, Ercolano, ☎ 081 77 75 720.*

A good road leads to a junction in the midst of lava flows. Take the left fork (*car park a few kilometres further on*). The path is an easy but most impressive climb up the volcano, scattered with cinders and lapilli.

From the summit there is an immense **panorama★★★** over the Bay of Naples with the Sorrento Peninsula in the south and Cape Miseno in the north. Beyond is the Gulf of Gaeta.

The crater affords an unforgettable sight for its sheer size and the sense of desolation on the slopes of the jagged walls, for the great yawning crater, which takes on a pink colour in the sun, and for the spouting steam-jets.

Torre del Greco

This town which has been repeatedly destroyed by the eruptions of Vesuvius, is well known for its ornaments made of coral and volcanic stone, and its cameos.

Torre Annunziata

This town is the centre of the famous Neapolitan pasta industry. It has been buried under the lava of Vesuvius seven times. It is the site of the sumptuous Villa di Oplontis which is open to the public and in 1997 was included in UNESCO's World Heritage List.

Villa di Oplontis★★ – *Open daily, Apr to Oct 8.30am-7.30pm (ticket office closes 6pm), Nov to Mar 8.30am-5pm (ticket office closes 3.30pm). Closed 1 Jan, 25 Dec. €8.26 inclusive (valid 1 day) for Pompeii, Oplonti, Stabia and Boscoreale. €13.42 (valid 3 days) for Pompeii, Herculaneum, Oplonti, Stabia and Boscoreale. Access from Porta Marina (Via Villa dei Misteri or Piazza Esedra) or from Piazza Anfiteatro. Information desk open at Porta Marina (9am-5pm). ☎ 081 85 75 347; www.pompeiisites.org*

This fine example of a Roman suburban villa is thought to have belonged to Poppea, wife of Nero. The vast building, in which can be identified the slaves' quarters (to the east) and the area given over to the imperial apartments (to the west), has many well-preserved examples of beautiful original **wall paintings**. In particular, there are landscape scenes featuring architectural elements, portrait medallions and still-life paintings, including a basket of figs and details of fruit (in the two recesses or *triclinia* to the east and west of the atrium respectively). Of the various animals depicted, the peacock appears so frequently as to have supported the theory that the name of the villa was derived from it. Within the villa, the kitchens are easily identified (with ovens and sink), as are the latrines which represent an advanced drainage system. The area to the west of the piscina, perhaps used as a conservatory, has fine wall paintings with foreshortened flowers and fountains.

BETWEEN VESUVIUS AND THE PENISOLA SORRENTINA★★★ ③

70km/42mi – allow 1 day
The departure point for this itinerary is Torre Annunziata.

Pompeii★★★ *See POMPEI*

Castellammare di Stabia‡

This was an ancient Roman spa town. Occupied successively by the Oscans, the Etruscans, the Samnites and finally the Romans in the 4C BC, Stabiae rebelled against Rome but was destroyed by Sulla in the 1C BC. The town was rebuilt in the form of small clusters of houses, while luxury villas for rich patricians spread over the high ground. In the AD 79 eruption of Vesuvius the new town was wiped out along with Herculaneum and Pompeii. The naturalist Pliny the Elder, who came by boat to observe the phenomenon at close range, perished by asphyxiation. In the 18C the Bourbons undertook excavations, repaired the port, and built shipyards which are still in use.

Antiquarium★ – *Via Marco n° 2. Closed for restoration at time of publication.*
The finds from the excavations are displayed here and include a magnificent series of **mural paintings** from the villas and some very fine stucco **low reliefs**.

Roman villas – *2km/1mi to the east. Arriving from the north take S 145, follow directions for Agerola-Amalfi, take the flyover and after the tunnel turn left to reach the excavation site. Open daily, Apr to Oct 8.30am-7.30pm (ticket office closes 6pm), Nov to Mar 8.30am-5pm (ticket office closes 3.30pm). Closed 1 Jan, 25 Dec. €8.50 inclusive (valid 1 day) for Pompeii, Oplonti, Stabia and Boscoreale. €13.50 (valid 3 days) for Pompeii, Herculaneum, Oplonti, Stabia and Boscoreale. Access from Porta Marina (Via Villa dei Misteri or Piazza Esedra) or from Piazza Anfiteatro. Information desk at Porta Marina (9am-5pm). ☎ 081 85 75 347; www.pompeiisites.org*
Villa di Arianna (Ariadne's Villa) was one of the luxurious villas facing the sea with an incomparable view of the bay and of Vesuvius. The architectural refinement of **Villa San Marco** with its two storeys was enhanced by gardens and swimming pools. It was probably a sumptuous country residence.

Monte Faito★★

Access is from Vico Equense via a scenic route; alternatively there is a cable car which departs from Piazza Circumvesuviana in Castellammare di Stabia. The cableway (10min) operates from Apr to Oct, departures every 20-30min, 9.25am-4.25pm; mid-Jun to Aug, 7.25am-7.15pm. €6.20. For information ☎ 081 87 11 334.
Monte Faito is part of the **Lattari range**, a headland which separates the Bay of Naples from the Gulf of Salerno and forms the Sorrento Peninsula. Its name is derived from the beech trees (*fagus* in Latin) which offer shade in summer. From

Belvedere dei Capi there is a splendid **panorama★★★** of the Bay of Naples. From there the road continues up to a chapel, **Cappella San Michele,** which affords another enchanting **panorama★★★** – the wild landscape of the Lattari mountains contrasts strongly with the smiling scenery of the Bay of Naples and the Sarno plain.

Vico Equense★

This is a small health and seaside resort on a picturesque rocky site.

SORRENTO AND THE PENISOLA SORRENTINA★★ 4

30km/18mi – allow half a day

The innumerable bends on this road afford constantly changing views of enchanting landscapes, wild, fantastically shaped rocks plunging vertically into a crystal-clear sea, deep gorges spanned by dizzy bridges and Saracen towers perched on jagged rock stacks. The Amalfi coast, with its wild and rugged landscape, is formed by the jagged fringe of the Lattari Mountains, a deeply eroded limestone range. Contrasting with these awe-inspiring scenes are the more charming views of fishing villages and the luxuriant vegetation, a mixture of orange, lemon, olive and almond trees, vines and all the Mediterranean flora. The region is very popular with foreigners and artists. A significant part of the attraction is the local cuisine with abundant seafood (fish, crustaceans and shellfish), and the local *mozzarella* cheese washed down with the red Gragnano or white Ravello and Positano wines.

Sorrento★★

This important resort, known for its many beautiful gardens, overlooks the bay of the same name. Orange and lemon groves are to be found in the surrounding countryside and even encroaching on the town. Local craftsmen produce various marquetry objects. The poet **Torquato Tasso** *(see FERRARA)* was born in Sorrento in 1544.

Museo Correale di Terranova★ – *Open daily except Tue, 9am-2pm. Closed Jan, bank hols. €6.* ☎ *081 87 81 846.*

Housed in an 18C palace, the museum has some splendid examples of local intarsia work (*secretaire*, 1910), a small archaeological section and, on the first floor, a collection of 17C and 18C furniture as well as an interesting collection of 17C-18C Neapolitan paintings. Two rooms are devoted to the landscape painters of the **Posillipo School** which flourished in the 1830s, including the main exponent of this school, **Giacinto Gigante** (1806-76). On the second floor there is a fine collection of porcelain and ceramics. From the terrace, beyond the orange grove, there is a very fine **view★★** over the Gulf of Sorrento.

The historic centre – Via S. Cesareo, the *decumanus* of the Roman city, leads to the **Sedile Dominova**, seat of city administration in the Angevin period. It consists of a loggia decorated with frescoes surmounted by a 17C ceramic dome. The steeply sloping street, Via San Giuliani, leads to the church di S. Francesco. This Baroque church has a bulbous campanile and is flanked by delightful 13C **cloisters★** whose vegetable-motif capitals sustain interlaced arcades in the Sicilian-Arab style.

The nearby public gardens, **Villa Comunale**, offer a good **view★★** of the Bay of Naples.

Penisola Sorrentina★★

Leave Sorrento to the west by S 145 and at the junction take the road to the right to Massa Lubrense.

This winding road skirts the Sorrento Peninsula and affords fine views of the hillsides covered with olive groves, orange and lemon trees and vines. The vines cling to the trelliswork which supports rush matting in winter to protect the citrus trees from the cold.

From the headland (**Punta del Capo di Sorrento**) *(footpath: from the church in the village of Capo di Sorrento take the road to the right and after the college the paved path, 1hr there and back)* there is a superb **view★★** of Sorrento.

At Sant'Agata sui Due Golfi, perched on a crest which dominates both the Gulf of Salerno and the Bay of Naples, the **Belvedere del Deserto** (a Benedictine monastery situated 1.5km/1mi west of the town) affords a splendid **panorama★★**. *Since this is a closed monastery, visits must be reserved in advance by calling the monastic community.* ☎ *081 87 80 199.*

Beyond Sant'Agata, the road which descends steeply to Colli di San Pietro is spectacular. From here you could return to Sorrento by S 163 which offers some superb **views★★** over the Bay of Naples, or you could head for Positano (see itinerary 5 described in COSTIERA AMALFITANA).

THE ISLANDS★★★

Capri★★★ *see CAPRI*

Ischia★★★ *see ISCHIA*

Procida★ *see ISCHIA*

Orvieto★★

This important Etruscan centre later became a papal stronghold and it was here that Clement VII took refuge in 1527 when Rome was sacked by the troops of the French King Charles V. Orvieto is a pleasant city with a wealth of historic buildings and it enjoys a particularly remarkable site★★★ on the top of a plug of volcanic rock. The area produces an excellent white wine, Orvieto, which has a fresh and fragrant aroma.

Location

Population 20 703 – Michelin map 430 N 18 – Umbria. Orvieto is situated in southern Umbria, not far from Lake Bolsena. The main access road is A 1. ◻ *Piazza del Duomo 24,* ✆ *0763 34 17 72.*
Surrounding area: see TODI, VITERBO.

Directory

WHERE TO EAT
• Moderate
I Sette Consoli – *Piazza Sant'Angelo 1/A –* ✆ *0763 34 39 11 – Closed 24-26 Dec, 15-25 Feb, Wed, and Sun evenings (Nov to mid-Mar) – Book – €35/44.* Rarefied, imaginative cooking and even a few fish dishes on the menu. Although the rustic-style interior, enhanced with a few rather more refined stylistic features, is perfectly nice, nothing can compare with the pleasure of eating outside in the garden with its wonderful view of the Duomo.

WHERE TO STAY
• Moderate
Albergo Filippeschi – *Via Filippeschi 19 –* ✆ *0763 34 32 75 – Fax 0763 34 32 75 – Closed 25 Dec –* ▣ *– 15 rm €54.23/82.64 –* ☲ *€5.16.* A simple, family establishment housed in an old palazzo. Excellent location – ideal for those exploring the town on foot.

EVENTS AND FESTIVALS
Towards the end of the year, Orvieto hosts the winter session of the **Umbria Jazz** festival *(see PERUGIA).*

Worth a Visit

DUOMO★★★

Visit: 1hr. Cappella di S. Brizio: Open Apr to Sep, Mon-Sat 10am-12.45pm and 2.30-7.15pm (6.15pm Mar and Oct, 5.15pm rest of year), Sun and hols, 2.30-6.45pm (5.45pm winter). No visits during religious services. €1.55. ✆ *0763 34 24 77.*
In the heart of the town, the quiet Piazza del Duomo, of majestic proportions, is lined with several interesting buildings. The cathedral, a perfect example of the transitional Romanesque-Gothic style, was begun in 1290 to enshrine the relics of the Miracle of Bolsena. Over 100 architects, sculptors, painters and mosaicists took part in the building of the cathedral which was completed only in 1600. The austere Palace of the Popes, **Palazzo dei Papi★** now houses the Cathedral Museum, **Museo dell'Opera.** *Museum: Closed for restoration at time of publication.*

Marble, mosaics and intricate stone patterns enliven the façade of the Duomo

R. Mattes/MICHELIN

Façade★★★

This is the boldest structure and the richest in colour among Italian Gothic buildings. The vertical lines are accentuated by the slender gables and especially by the soaring buttresses, which are clad with small panels of coloured marble, elongated in shape and further prolonged by pinnacles. The sumptuous decorative effect is obtained by the use of sculptures lower down with multicoloured marbles and mosaics above.

The original design, elaborated (c 1310-30) by the Sienese Lorenzo Maitani, was further developed by Andrea Pisano, Andrea Orcagna and Sanmicheli. Maitani was also responsible for the astonishing **low reliefs★★** adorning the pillars which, reading from left to right, portray: *Genesis, Jesse's Tree, Scenes from the New Testament,* and the *Last Judgement.*

Orcagna was the designer of the rose window, fitted into a square frame and surrounded by statues of the Apostles and the Prophets. The mosaics on the spire depict the *Coronation of the Virgin* and date from the end of the 18C.

Interior

A nave and two aisles built in alternating courses of black and white stone rest on semicircular arches supported by lovely bracketed capitals. A moulding projects above the arches. The nave and aisles are roofed with a timber ceiling, while Gothic vaulting covers the transepts and the chancel. The paving slopes up towards the chancel, reducing the perspective. Alabaster window-panes let in plenty of light. At the entrance stand the 15C stoup and the Gothic font. A fresco of the *Virgin and Child* (1425) in the north aisle is by Gentile da Fabriano.

In the north transept under the 16C monumental organ is the entrance to a chapel, the **Cappella del Corporale**, which enshrines the relics of the Miracle of Bolsena and notably the linen cloth (corporal) in which the bleeding Host was wrapped. A tabernacle encloses the **Reliquary★★** of the corporal, a masterpiece of medieval goldsmiths' work (1338) encrusted with enamels and precious stones. In the chapel on the right is a *Madonna of Pity* (1320) by the Sienese painter Lippo Memmi. A fine Gothic stained-glass **window★** in the chancel illustrates the Gospel with recognisable figures of theologians and prophets.

The south transept gives access, beyond a wrought-iron grille (1516), to the famous **Cappella della Madonna di San Brizio**, painted with admirable **frescoes★★**. These were begun in 1447 by Fra Angelico who began by decorating the vaulting. He left them unfinished and the work was taken up in 1490 by **Luca Signorelli** (c 1445-1523). As the human figure was his main interest, while landscape and colour remained secondary considerations, the theme of the frescoes, the Last Judgement, enabled him to perfect his talent. Although he lacked the spiritual depth of Michelangelo, he can be considered the latter's predecessor in terms of an almost sculptural approach to painting, the careful portrayal of human anatomy, dramatic compositions and the sense of pathos he confers on his figures.

A FEW MINUTES IN FRONT OF LUCA SIGNORELLI'S FRESCOES

The atmosphere which permeates the Chapel of San Brizio is even more disturbing if one considers the images as the anticipation of an apocalyptic day which could strike at any time. Monsters, the torture of the damned and the corpse-like colour of the demons all contribute to a sense of anguish. Every detail is imbued with a monstrous quality, even the grotesques.

The frescoes should be read starting from the north wall. The first is a portrayal of the *Preaching of the Antichrist*; the Antichrist, who has the devil as his adviser, has taken on the appearance of Christ. Signorelli has portrayed himself in the noble dark figure on the extreme left. This image is followed by the *Calling of the Elect to Heaven*.

On the wall of the altar, on the left: the *Angels leading the Elect to Paradise*; on the right: *Angels chasing out the Reprobates*, with scenes of hell.

On the right wall: *The Damned in Hell* and the *Resurrection of the Dead*.

On the west wall, in the *End of the World*, the sun and moon have lost all traces of familiarity, the earth is in the throes of an earthquake. A sibyl, a prophet and demons are all represented in this scene.

Underground Orvieto

(&) *Guided tours only. €5.50. For information on opening times and reservations* ☎ *0339 73 32 764.*

Orvieto lies on a bed of volcanic earth. To understand the history and structure of the city it is worth visiting its "cellars". The majority of the underground chambers (already present in Etruscan times) which have been dug out of the hill are in fact cellars. A visit to these caves (of which more than 1 000 are officially listed) will reveal medieval niches for funerary urns, the foundations of a 14C oil mill and the 6C BC base of a well with steps to enable ascent and descent.

Pozzo di San Patrizio★★

Open daily, Apr to Sep 10am-7pm, rest of year 10am-6pm. €3.10; €4.13 including Museo Emilio Greco. ☎ *0763 34 37 68.*

St Patrick's Well was dug in the volcanic rock by order of Pope Clement VII de' Medici to supply the town with water in case of siege. Sangallo the Younger was entrusted with the work. Two spiral staircases, lit by 72 windows, wind up and down without meeting. The well is over 62m/203ft deep and its water cold and pure.

Palazzo del Popolo★

The town hall is built of volcanic rock in the Romanesque-Gothic style. The façade has a majestic balcony, elegant windows and curious fluted merlons.

Quartiere Vecchio★

This quiet, unfrequented quarter has retained its old houses, medieval towers and churches. At the western extremity stands the church of **San Giovenale;** the Gothic apse is decorated with 13C-15C frescoes.

Museo Archeologico Faina

(&) *Open daily, 31 Mar to 28 Sep 9.30am-6pm, rest of year 10am-5pm. Closed Mon (winter), 1 Jan, 25-26 Dec. €4.13.* ☎ *0763 34 15 11; www.systemnet.it/museo-faina*

This important **Etruscan Collection★** includes splendid painted vases, carved terracotta funerary urns and a rare 4C sarcophagus.

Chiesa di San Bernardino

This charming Baroque church is dedicated to St Bernardino. The oval interior is delightfully decorated and has an organ carved with figures.

Piazza della Repubblica

It stands on the site of the ancient forum, dominated by the church of Sant'Andrea, dedicated to St Andrew, with its lovely 12-sided Romanesque tower.

▶▶ Etruscan Necropolis of Crocifisso.

Excursions

Bolsena

22km/13mi southwest of Orvieto.
Bolsena, the ancient Etruscan city of Volsinii, stands on the banks of Italy's largest lake of volcanic origin; its level is continually changing owing to earth tremors. Its shady shores welcome many visitors attracted by a gentle and limpid light. In the old part of the town, its sombre-coloured houses are clustered together, clinging to the hillside. There is a good view from S 2, the Viterbo-Siena road.

> **THE MIRACLE OF BOLSENA**
> The famous miracle at the Bolsena Mass took place in 1263. A Bohemian priest had doubts about the doctrine of transubstantiation, that is, the incarnation of Christ in the Host at consecration. According to legend, as he was celebrating Mass in St Christina's church, the Host began to bleed profusely at the moment of consecration. The priest no longer doubted the mystery and the Feast of Corpus Christi was instituted.

Chiesa di Santa Cristina★ – *For information on opening times at the church and cata-combs* ☎ *0761 79 90 67.*

The 3C Saint Christina is said to have belonged to the Bolsena region. She was a victim of the persecutions of Diocletian. Although the church is 11C the façade, articulated by gracefully carved pilasters, is Renaissance. The columns inside are Roman. The north aisle leads to the **Chapel of the Miracle**, where the pavement stained by the blood of the Host is revered, and then to the Grotto of St Christina. In the latter is the Altar of the Miracle and a reclining statue of the saint attributed to the Della Robbia.

Padova★★

PADUA

An art and pilgrimage centre, Padua is a busy town. At the heart of the historic centre is **Piazza Cavour**, while the neo-Classical **Caffè Pedrocchi**, which was a meeting-place of the liberal elite in the Romantic period, is nearby.

Location

Population 211 391 – Michelin map 429 F 17 – Veneto. Padua is off A 4, around 40km/24mi from Venice. It is linked to Bologna by A 13. **🚆** *Stazione Ferrovie dello Stato,* ☎ *049 87 52 077.*

Surrounding area: see Riviera del BRENTA, LAGUNA VENETA, TREVISO, VENEZIA, VICENZA.

Background

History – There are few traces of ancient *Patavium* which was one of the most prosperous Roman cities in the Veneto during the 1C BC owing to its river trade, its agriculture and the sale of horses. In the 7C Padua was destroyed by the Lombards, and from the 11C to 13C it became an independent city-state. This was the period when numerous churches and palaces were built. The city underwent its greatest period of economic and cultural prosperity under the enlightened rule of the lords of Carrara (1337-1405). In 1405 Padua came under the sway of the Venetian Republic and remained a loyal subject until 1797 when the Venetian Constitution was abolished by Napoleon.

The city of St Anthony the Hermit – The saint is venerated in Padua. He was born in Lisbon in 1195 and died at the age of 36 in the environs of Padua. This Franciscan monk was a forceful preacher. His help was invoked by the shipwrecked and those in prison and he is generally represented holding a book and a lily.

A famous university – The University of Padua founded in 1222 is the second oldest in Italy after Bologna. It expanded rapidly and attracted students from the whole of Europe. Galileo was a professor and among its students were the Renaissance scholar Pico della Mirandola, the astronomer Copernicus and the poet Tasso.

Directory

PADOVA

Art in Padua – In 1304, **Giotto** came to Padua from Florence to decorate the Scrovegni Chapel. He painted a cycle of frescoes which is one of the masterpieces of Italian art.

In the 15C the Renaissance in Padua was marked by **Donatello**, another Florentine, who stayed in the city from 1444 to 1453. Also in the 15C Paduan art flourished under the guiding influence of the Paduan artist, **Andrea Mantegna** (1431-1506). A painter of powerful originality, he was fascinated by anatomy and archaeology and was also a technical innovator in the field of perspective.

Worth a Visit

Frescoes by Giotto in the Scrovegni Chapel★★★

Closed for restoration at time of publication. ☎ *049 82 04 550, www.padovanet.it/museicivici*

The cycle of 39 frescoes was painted c 1305-10 by Giotto on the walls of the **Cappella degli Scrovegni**. The chapel, built in 1303, illustrates the lives of Joachim and Anna (the parents of the Virgin), Mary and Jesus: the *Flight into Egypt, Judas' Kiss* and the *Entombment* are among the most famous. On the lower register, the powerful monochrome figures depict the Vices *(left)* and Virtues *(right)*. The *Last Judgement* on the west wall completes the cycle.

This work shows an exceptional unity and is Giotto's masterpiece, displaying great dramatic power, harmonious composition and intense spirituality. On the altar stands a **Virgin★** by the Tuscan sculptor Giovanni Pisano.

Frescoes in the Chiesa degli Eremitani★★

The 13C church of the Hermits was badly damaged by bombing in 1944 but has been rebuilt in the original Romanesque style. In the Cappella Ovetari *(the second on the right of the Cappella Maggiore)* are fragments of frescoes by **Mantegna.** The various scenes *(Martyrdom of St James* on the north wall, *Assumption* in the apse and *Martyrdom of St Christoper* on the south wall) display his powerful visionary talent and his careful attention to perspective and architectural detail. The Lady Chapel (Cappella Maggiore) has splendid frescoes by **Guariento**, Giotto's Venetian pupil.

Museo Civico agli Eremitani★

    Open daily, 9am to 1hr before sunset. Closed Mon (except hols), 1 Jan, 1 May, 15 Aug, 25-26 Dec. €5.16 including Cappella degli Scrovegni. ☎ *049 82 04 550, www.padovanet.it/museicivici/informazioni.html*

The municipal museum in the Hermitage of St Augustine (Sant'Agostino) comprises several collections: archaeology (Egyptian, Etruscan, Roman and pre-Roman), coins (Bottacin Bequest) and 15C-18C Venetian and Flemish paintings (Emo Capodilista collection).

The museum also contains the extensive collection from the former Art Gallery including furniture, ceramics and sculptures as well as **paintings★★**, most of them from the Venetian School (14C-18C). In particular, note works by Giotto.

Basilica del Santo★★

Open daily, May-Oct 6.20am-8pm, rest of year 6.20am-7pm. ☎ *049 87 55 23 25; www.mess-s-antonio.it/basilica*

This important pilgrimage church dedicated to St Anthony overlooks the square in which Donatello erected an **equestrian statue★★** of the Venetian mercenary leader **Gattamelata** (nickname of Erasmo di Nardi who died in Padua in 1443). This bronze was the first of its size to be cast in Italy.

The basilica with its eight-tiered bulbous domes was built from 1232 to 1300 in the transitional Romanesque-Gothic style and brings to mind St Mark's in Venice. The imposing **interior★★** contains numerous works of art: off the north aisle is the **Cappella del Santo★★**, a Renaissance masterpiece, which contains the tomb-cum-altar of St Anthony (Arca di Sant'Antonio) by Tiziano Aspetti (1594); on the walls are magnificent 16C **high reliefs★★** by several artists. In the chancel the **high altar★★** is adorned with bronze panels (1450) by Donatello. The third chapel, off the south aisle, has **frescoes★** by Altichiero (14C), an artist from Verona.

There is a fine **overall view★** of the building from the cloisters to the south of the basilica.

Oratorio di San Giorgio and Scuola di Sant'Antonio★

    Open daily, Apr to Sep 9am 12.30pm and 2.30-7pm, rest of year 9am-12.30pm and 2-5pm. €2. ☎ *049 82 25 52; www.mess-s-antonio.basilica/index.htm*

St George's oratory was built as a funerary chapel and is decorated with 21 **frescoes★** (1377) by Altichiero and his pupils, depicting various religious scenes.

In the adjacent Scuola di Sant'Antonio (a religious charitable institution), a room on the first floor contains 15-16C **frescoes★** relating the life of St Anthony. Four of these are by Titian.

Palazzo della Ragione★

    Open daily except Mon, Feb to Oct 9am-7pm, rest of year 9am-6pm. Closed Mon (except hols), bank hols. €3.62. ☎ *049 82 05 006; www.padovanet.it/museicivici/monumenti/regione.html*

The Law Courts, standing between two attractive **squares★**, the Piazza della Frutta and the Piazza delle Erbe, are remarkable for their loggias and roof in the form of an upturned ship's keel. The first-floor **salone★★** is adorned with a 15C cycle of frescoes depicting the *Labours of the Months*, the *Liberal Arts*, the *Trades* and the *Signs of the Zodiac*.

Piazza dei Signori

This square is lined by the 14C-15C Palazzo del Capitano, one-time residence of the Venetian Governors, the clock tower, **Torre dell'Orologio★**, with its arcade, and the graceful Renaissance gallery, Loggia del Consiglio.

Università

The University is housed in a palace known as the "Bo" from the name of an inn with an ox as its sign which once stood on the site. It has retained a lovely 16C courtyard and an anatomy theatre, **Teatro Anatomico** (1594). *Guided tours only: Mon, Wed and Fri 3pm, 4pm and 5pm, Tue, Thu and Sat 9am, 10am and 11am. Closed Sun and bank hols. €2.59. ☎ 049 82 09 711.*

University life is very animated here. One of the most attractive spectacles is graduation day when the students are celebrating, dressed up in their pointed hats.

Caffè Pedrocchi

This neo-Classical building, erected in 1831, is a café with white, red and green rooms. It was here that the student rebellion against the Austrians was played out in 1848. On the upper storey are rooms for meetings and concerts **(sale)** built in a range of different styles. *Open daily except Mon, 9.30am-12.30pm and 3.30-6pm. Closed bank hols. €2.58. ☎ 049 82 05 007; www.padovanet.it/musei civici/monumenti/pedrocchi.html*

Battistero

The baptistery adjoining the Duomo has interesting frescoes and a polyptych by Menabuoi (14C).

Chiesa Santa Giustina

This 16C domed classical-style church, dedicated to St Justina, is reminiscent of the basilica del Santo. At the far end of the chancel is an **altarpiece★** by Veronese.

Orto Botanico

(&) *Open daily Apr to Oct 9am-1pm and 3-6pm, rest of year 9am-1pm. Closed Sun (winter). €2.58. ☎ 049 82 72 119.*

The botanical gardens are among the oldest of their kind in Europe. They were laid out in 1545 and contain many exotic species including the palm tree which inspired Goethe in his reflections on the development of plants.

Prato della Valle

This 17C oval garden is planted with plane trees and encircled by the still waters of a canal, lined with statues of famous men.

Excursions

Montagnana★

47km/29mi southwest. This small town is girt with impressive 14C **ramparts★★** reinforced with 24 polygonal towers and four gateways. The **Duomo**, attributed to Sansovino, contains a *Transfiguration* by Veronese at the high altar and 16C frescoes and stalls. The church of **San Francesco**, with its lovely Gothic belfry, abuts the town wall.

Colli Euganei★

The Euganean hills to the south of Padua are of volcanic origin. This pleasant hilly area is planted with orchards and vineyards and was already appreciated in Roman times for its numerous hot springs and its wines.

Abano Terme‡‡‡ – This modern and elegant thermal spa well shaded by pines is one of Italy's most famous spa towns.

Montegrotto Terme‡‡ – Although less important than Abano it is rapidly growing in importance. This was the ancient *Mons Aegrotorum* (mountain of the sick).

Monselice★ – This town, whose Latin name *Mons Silicis* (mountain of granite) bears witness to its importance as a mining community during Roman times, has retained a large section of its walls and is dominated by the ruins of a castle. From Piazza Mazzini, go up the picturesque Via del Santuario to reach the 13C-14C castle, the Romanesque cathedral, the early-17C Sanctuary of the Seven Churches and the Villa Balbi with its Italian garden. The upper terrace affords a lovely **view★** of the region.

Arquà Petrarca★ – *6.5km/4mi northwest of Monselice.* It was here, in these tranquil, medieval surroundings, that **Petrarch** (1304-74) died. He was born in Arezzo but his stormy life took him to various places in Italy and abroad. In a church in Avignon, he met Laura, the woman with whom he fell in love for all time and whom he immortalised in his collection of sonnets entitled the *Canzoniere*. His works became a reference throughout Europe for lyric poetry and, during the Renaissance, they gave rise to attempts at imitation after the poet had become virtually a cult figure.

Petrarch's house★) where he lived and died is open to the public. It has 16C frescoes and the original coffered ceiling. Exhibits include memorabilia of the poet and autographs of famous visitors such as Carducci or Byron. His pink marble funerary monument was erected on the church square in 1380. *Open Feb to Sep, daily except Mon, 9am-12pm and 3-7pm, rest of year daily except Mon, 9am-noon and 2.30-5pm. Closed Mon (except Bank Hol Mon), 1 May, 15 Aug, 25-26 Dec. €3.10. ☎ 0429 71 82 94; www.padovanet.it/museicivici/monumenti/petrarca.html*

Este – Cradle of the Este family, rulers of Ferrara, the town still has an attractive section of **town wall★** to the north. The **Museo Nazionale Atestino★** (*Ateste* was the name of the town during Roman times) is housed in the 16C Mocenigo Palace. It has an extensive archaeological collection relating to local farming from the Paleolithic to the Roman eras, displayed chronologically. The Duomo, on an elliptical plan, contains a large canvas (1759) by Tiepolo. *Museum:* ♿ *Open daily, 9am-8pm. Closed 1 Jan, 1 May, 25 Dec. €2. ☎ 0429 20 85.*

Riviera del Brenta★★ *see Riviera del BRENTA*

Paestum★★★

One of Italy's most important archaeological sites, Paestum was discovered by chance around 1750, when the Bourbons started to build the road which crosses the area today. The initial settlement was an ancient Greek colony founded around 600 BC under the name of Poseidonia by colonists from Sybaris. Around the year 400 BC the city fell to a local tribe, the Lucanians. It became Roman in the year 273 BC but began to decline towards the end of the Empire because of the malaria which finally drove out its inhabitants. The temples, built of a fine yellow limestone, stand amid the ruins of dwellings sheltered by cypresses and oleanders.

Location

Michelin map 431 F 26-27 – Campania. Paestum is on the coast, not far from S 18, 48km/29mi south of Salerno. **🔒** *Via Magna Grecia 165, ☎ 0828 81 10 16. Surrounding area: see COSTIERA AMALFITANA, SALERNO.*

Worth a Visit

The suggested itinerary (2hr) proceeds from south to north. Those wishing to visit the museum first should start from the north. ♿ *Open daily, 9am to 2hr before sunset. Closed 1 Jan, 1 May, 25 Dec. €4; €6.50 including museum. ☎ 0828 81 10 16; www.paestum.org* Take the Porta della Giustizia through the 5km/3mi-long city wall, **Cinta muraria★**, and follow the **Via Sacra,** the principal street of the Greek and Roman city.

Basilica★★

The rear of the "Basilica", so-called by 18C archaeologists, stands to the right of the Via Sacra. This mid-6C BC temple, the oldest in the city, was dedicated to Hera, sister and bride of Zeus. The great age of the monument is attested to by the pronounced swelling at the centre of the columns (*entasis*) and the squashed echini (moulding above the capital) of the columns. These deformations convey the way in which architectural structures were considered living entities which swell and squash when submitted to undue pressure. The porch (*pronaos*) leads into the central chamber divided into two aisles, probably indicating that two cults were practised here.

Tempio di Nettuno★★★

When Paestum was first discovered this well-preserved temple was thought to have been dedicated to Neptune (or Poseidon in Greek, hence the town's name Poseidonia). It has since been proved that it was dedicated to Hera and more recent hypotheses suggest that it may have been dedicated to Zeus or Apollo. Dating from the mid-5C BC, it is in an admirably harmonious Doric style. One of the most impressive structural devices is the slight convexity (2cm) of the horizontal lines which makes the numerous columns look straight. For this same reason the fluting on the corner columns veers slightly inwards.

In the centre of the city stands the **forum**, surrounded by a portico and shops, and overlooked by the **curia**, the adjacent *macellum* (covered market) and the *comitium* (3C BC), the most important public building where magistrates were elected. To the left of the *comitium* stands the **Temple of Peace** (2C-1C BC) constructed on a north-south plan according to Italic custom.

To the east of the forum stands the **amphitheatre**, constructed between the Republican and Imperial ages and divided by the main road. Unusually it is not located outside the city centre, a measure that was adopted to enable an easy flow of people to and from the amphitheatre.

The *gimnasium* (c 3C BC) was probably a sanctuary with a pool. During ritualistic celebrations the statue of the divinity was immersed in the pool and then placed on a platform on the west side. The pool was buried in the 1C AD and the structure subsequently housed the gymnasium.

The **Tempietto Sotterraneo** (small underground temple, 6C BC) has been interpreted as being a *heroon*, a kind of cenotaph devoted to the cult of the city's founder who was made a hero after his death. Some bronze vases with traces of honey were also found here; these are housed at the museum.

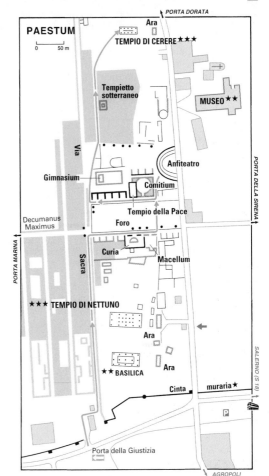

Tempio di Cerere★★

Originally erected in the late 6C BC in honour of Athena, the Temple of Ceres combines an interesting mix of styles: the Doric colonnade is solid and massive whereas the internal Ionic columns are more graceful and decorative. Near the entrance of the temple, on the east side, is the sacrificial altar, the **ara**.

Museo★★

The masterpieces in this museum include the famous **metopes★★**, 6C BC low reliefs in the Doric style which adorned both the *Thesauròs*, or temple of Hera (scenes from the life of Heracles and the Trojan Wars), and the High Temple (Dancing Girls) of the Sanctuary of Hera at Sele *(10km/6mi north near the mouth of the River Sele)* as well as the Tomb of the Diver. The **Tomba del Tuffatore★★** constitutes a rare example of Greek funerary painting with lively banquet scenes and the famous dive, symbol of the passage from life to death, which is directed beyond the columns of Hercules, the frontier of the known world. The museum also houses the stunning **vases★** (6C BC) from the underground temple, a true masterpiece of bronze sculpture, the painted Lucanian tombs (4C BC) and the representations, executed in a style which is typical of Paestum art, of Hera Argiva with a pomegranate (symbol of fertility) and the flower-woman in terracotta, used as an incense burner.

Parma★★

Parma is an important market town with a rich musical heritage (the famous
20C conductor Arturo Toscanini was born here). The town has a certain refined charm and a gastronomic reputation which centres on two of the country's most prized culinary possessions, Parmesan cheese and dry-cured ham.
**At the heart of the town is Piazza Garibaldi, a popular meeting-place for the
townspeople.**

Location
Population 168 717 – Michelin map 428, 429 H 12-13 – Emilia-Romagna. Parma is situated near A 1, between the Po and the Apennines. ☐ *Via Melloni 1/B,*
☎ *0521 21 88 89.*
Surrounding area: see MODENA, REGGIO EMILIA.

Background

A settlement was founded on this site by the Etruscans in 525 BC and it became a
Roman station on the Via Emilia in 183 BC. It declined but revived in the 6C under
the Ostrogoth king, Theodoric. After having been an independent commune from
the 11C-13C, it became a member of the Lombard League *(see Index)*. After the fall
of the commune's government in 1335, Parma was governed in turn by the
Visconti, the Sforza and, later, the French before being annexed by the Papacy in
1513. In 1545 Pope Paul III, Alessandro Farnese gave two papal territories, Parma
and Piacenza, having made them a duchy, to his son Pier Luigi Farnese, who was
assassinated in 1547. However, the **Farnese** dynasty continued to reign until 1731
and several members of the house were patrons of the arts and letters, collectors
and great builders.

When it passed to the Bourbons, its first sovereign was Charles, successively King
of Naples then King of Spain. When Don Philip, the son of Philip V of Spain and
Elizabeth Farnese, married Louise Elizabeth, the favourite daughter of Louis XV,
the town underwent a period (1748-1801) of great French influence in several
domains (customs, administration and the arts).

Numerous Frenchmen came to work in Parma while others like Stendhal chose
to live here; he made Parma the setting of his well-known novel, *The
Charterhouse of Parma.* The Bourbons of Parma had their Versailles at Colorno,
north of the town.

Directory

WHERE TO EAT
• *Moderate*
Osteria del Gesso – *Via Ferdinando Maestri
11 –* ☎ *0521 23 05 05 – Closed 25 Jul-18
Aug, Sun and Mon lunchtime (from 19 Jun-
Aug); rest of the year, Wed and Thu
lunchtime –* ⊡ *– Book – €27/36.* Given its
location near the law court, this restaurant is
popular with lawyers and magistrates' clerk.
Upmarket ambience. One criticism – the
tables are a little too close together. Offers
flavoursome regional cooking with a light row
of touch and dishes are beautifully presented.

WHERE TO STAY
Note that most hotels have higher tariffs
when exhibitions and trade fairs are being
held. It is advisable to check prices by
telephone beforehand
• *Moderate*
Hotel Button – *Via della Salina 7 –*
☎ *0521 20 80 39 – Fax 0521 23 87 83 –
Closed 23 Dec-2 Jan, 5-31 Jul – 40 rm
€62/88 –* ⊡ *€8.* Situated in the heart of
the historic centre, between the Teatro Regio
and Piazza del Duomo, and very convenient

for anybody arriving by train. Housed in
an old convent, this rather smart hotel
combines several styles including
various Art Nouveau features.

SHOPPING
Tasting the dry-cured ham for which Parma is
so famous is an absolute must.

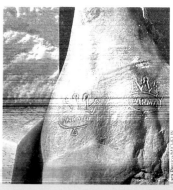

A label and a guarantee

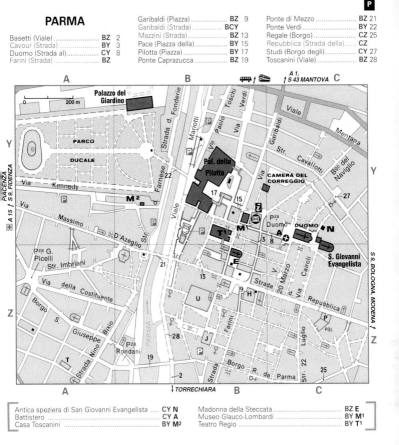

THE PARMA SCHOOL

The school is represented by two main artists, Correggio and Il Parmigianino, whose works formed the transition between the Renaissance and Baroque art. Antonio Allegri (1489-1534), known as **Correggio**, was a master of light and chiaroscuro; his work shows a gracefully sensual and optimistic vision which seem to herald 18C French art. Francesco Mazzola (1503-40), or **Il Parmigianino** (The Parmesan) as he was commonly known, was a more troubling and melancholy personality. His elongated forms and cold colours were characteristic of Mannerism. His canon of feminine beauty influenced the Fontainebleau school and all the other European Mannerists of the 16C, through the intermediary of Niccolò dell'Abbate and Il Primaticcio.

Worth a Visit

This historic core of the city comprises the Romanesque **Episcopal Centre★★★** including the cathedral and baptistery, the Baroque church of San Giovanni and the surrounding palaces as well as the Palazzo della Pilotta (16C-17C) and Correggio's Room.

Duomo★★

The cathedral is in the Romanesque style and is flanked by an elegant Gothic campanile. The façade includes a Lombard porch supported by lions and surmounted by a loggia and three tiers of galleries with little columns. Inside, the dome is decorated with the famous **frescoes** painted by Correggio from 1522 to 1530. The ascending rhythm of the *Assumption of the Virgin* with the central figure amid a swirling group of cherubim is remarkable. The artist's mastery of perspective and movement is expressed in an original and exuberant style virtually Baroque in spirit. In the south transept the *Descent from the Cross* (1178) by the sculptor Antelami clearly shows the influence of the Provençal School, although the solemnity of the figures distinguishes it. In the nave, the frescoes are by Gambara (1530-74); on the vaulting they were painted by Bedoli (16C). The gilded copper *Angel* (1284) which crowned the spire of the bell tower is now on the third pillar to the left of the nave.

Battistero★★★

This is Italy's most harmonious medieval monument. The octagonal baptistery in Verona rose-coloured marble was started in 1196 and the architecture and carved decoration, which show great unity of style, date from the 13C. The baptistery is attributed to Antelami who was also responsible for the sculptures; his signature appears on the lintel of the north door, dedicated to the Virgin. Inside (the interior is a 16-sided polygon), the admirable 13C **frescoes** of Byzantine inspiration depict scenes from the *Life of Christ* and the *Golden Legend*.

Chiesa di San Giovanni Evangelista

This Renaissance church, dedicated to St John the Evangelist, has a Baroque façade. Inside, the **frescoes on the dome★★**, painted by Correggio (1520-24), depict the *Vision of St John at Patmos* and the *Translation of St John the Evangelist*. Those on the arches of the chapels to the north (1st, 2nd and 4th) were executed by Parmigianino.

In the convent next door are the **Renaissance cloisters**. *Monastery: open Mon-Sat 9am-noon and 3-6pm, Sun and hols 10am-1pm and 3.30-6pm. Church: open daily, 8am-noon and 3.30-8pm. Donation recommended.* ☎ *0521 23 55 92; www.offigm.com/sangiovanni*

Antica spezieria di San Giovanni Evangelista

&. *Open daily, 8.30am-2pm (ticket office closes 1.30pm). Closed 1 Jan, 1 May, 25 Dec. €2.* ☎ *0521 23 36 17 o 0521 23 33 09.*

This 13C pharmacy was started by the Benedictine monks. The furnishings date from the 16C.

Palazzo della Pilotta

The palace was so-called because the game of fives *(pilotta)* was played in its courtyards. This rather austere building, erected by order of the Farnese from 1583 to 1622, now houses two museums, the Palatine Library and the Farnese Theatre *(see below)*.

Camera del Correggio or di San Paolo★

&. *Open daily, 8.30am-2pm (ticket office closes 1.45pm). Closed 1 Jan, 1 May, 25 Dec. €2.* ☎ *0521 23 33 09.*

Correggio's Room was the dining room of the Abbess of St Paul's Convent. The ceiling frescoes depicting mythological scenes with a luminous quality are Correggio's first major work (1519-20). The garlands of flowers and trelliswork and the reliefs and architectural detail at the base of the vault reveal the influence of Mantegna, whom he met in his youth in Mantua *(see MANTOVA)*. The next room was decorated by Araldi (1504).

Chiesa di Santa Maria della Steccata

Open daily, 10.30am-noon, 3-4pm and 5.30-6.30pm. Donation recommended. ☎ *0521 23 49 37; www.santuari.it/steccata*

This 16C church, designed by the architects Bernardino and Zaccagni, contains fine **frescoes★** by Parmigianino representing *The Foolish and the Wise Virgins*, placed between the figures of Adam and Moses, and Eve and Aaron. The mausoleum of Neipperg, husband of the former French Empress Marie-Louise who became Duchess of Parma, is on the left, and the tombs of the Farnese family and the Parma Bourbons are in the crypt.

Teatro Regio

The Royal Theatre, built between 1821 and 1829 at the request of Marie-Louise of Habsburg, has a Classical frontage. The inaugural performance was of Bellini's opera *Zaira*. The acoustics are excellent.

Palazzo del Giardino

The Parco Ducale★ (ducal garden) was landscaped by the French architect Petitot and adorned with statues by another Frenchman, Boudard.

Palazzo della Pilotta

Museo Archeologico Nazionale★ – &. *Open Tue-Fri, 8.30am-2pm, Sat-Sun and hols 8.30am-7.30pm. Closed Mon, 1 May, 25 Dec. €2.* ☎ *0521 23 37 18.*

The National Museum of Antiquities displays pre-Roman and Roman artefacts including the finds made in the excavation of Velleia to the west of Parma.

Galleria Nazionale★★ – &. *Open daily, 8.30am-2pm (ticket office closes 1.30pm). Closed 1 Jan, 1 May, 25 Dec. €6.* ☎ *0521 23 33 09.*

The well laid out gallery exhibits Emilian, Tuscan and Venetian paintings of the 14C, 15C and 16C by: Fra Angelico, Dosso Dossi, El Greco, Canaletto, Bellotto, Piazzetta and Tiepolo. Parmigianino is represented by his astonishing portrait *Turkish Slave*, which is of considerable elegance, and Correggio by one of his masterpieces, *The Virgin with St Jerome* (1528), as well as other works. The gallery also houses a sketch by Leonardo da Vinci, *(La Scapigliata)*.

Teatro Farnese★★ – &. *Open daily, 8.30am-2pm (ticket office closes 1.45pm). Closed 1 Jan, 1 May, 25 Dec. €2. ☎ 0521 23 33 09.*
This imposing theatre was built in wood in 1619 by G B Aleotti, following the model of Palladio's Olympic Theatre in Vicenza *(see VICENZA)*. Inaugurated for the marriage of Margaret de' Medici and Odoardo Farnese, the theatre was almost totally destroyed in 1944 and was rebuilt exactly as before in the 1950s.

Fondazione-Museo Glauco Lombardi★

(&) *Open Tue-Sat 10am-3pm, Sun and hols 9am-1pm (ticket office closes 30min early). Closed Mon, bank hols €4.☎ 0521 23 37 27; www.museolombardi.it*
The Glauco-Lombardi museum is chiefly devoted to life in the Duchy of Parma and Piacenza in the 18C and 19C. It contains paintings and mementoes of the former Empress Marie-Louise who governed the duchy. There are numerous works by French artists: Nattier, Mignard, Chardin, Watteau, Fragonard, Greuze, La Tour, Hubert Robert, Vigée-Lebrun, David and Millet.

Casa Toscanini

Closed Mon and Sun pm. €1.55. For further information on opening times ☎ 0521 28 54 99; www.archivio.biblcom.unipr.it/museotoscanini
The birthplace of the famous conductor **Arturo Toscanini** (1867-1957) houses interesting documents for anybody with a love of music. On show are distinctions and decorations granted to the musician, sculptures and objects connected with the Toscanini family, Verdi and Wagner, letters from Mazzini, Garibaldi, D'Annunzio and Einstein, and numerous reminders of the master's work in America. There is also an audio-visual presentation of the conductor's career.

Excursions

Castello di Torrechiara★

17km/11mi south by the Langhirano road. Open daily except Mon, May to Oct 8.30am-7.30pm, rest of year 8am-4pm. Closed 1 Jan, 1 May ☎ 0521 35 52 55.
This 15C fortress, built on a hilltop, is powerfully fortified by double ramparts, massive corner towers, a keep and machicolated curtain walls. The upper rooms (the Gaming and Gold Rooms) have remarkable **frescoes**★. From the terrace there is a superb **view**★ which reaches as far as the Apennines.

Fidenza

23km/14mi west. Leave Parma by Via Massimo D'Azeglio. This attractive agricultural town has a remarkable 11C **Duomo**★ which was completed in the Gothic style in the 13C. The lovely sculptured decoration of the **central porch**★★ is most likely the work of the Parmesan sculptor, Antelami. The three fine **Romanesque doors** are adorned with lions, a typically Emilian feature.

Fontanellato

19km/12mi to the northwest by the Fidenza road and then the road to Soragna, to the right. The vast moat-encircled castle, **Rocca Sanvitale**, stands in the centre of town. The ceiling of one of the rooms is decorated with a **fresco**★ depicting Diana and Actaeon by Parmigianino. The fine furnishings date from the 17C. (&) *Open daily, Apr to Oct, 9.30-11.30am and 3-6pm, rest of year 9.30-11.30am and 3-5pm. Closed Mon (Nov to Mar), 1 Jan am, 25 Dec. €6.40. ☎ 0521 82 90 55; www.fontanellato.org*

Pavia★

This proud city is rich in buildings from the Romanesque and Renaissance periods. An important military camp under the Romans, it became, successively, the capital of the Lombard kings, rival of Milan in the 11C, famous intellectual and artistic centre during the 14C under the Visconti, a fortified town in the 16C and one of the most active centres of the 19C independence movements. The university, one of the oldest and most famous in Europe, was founded in the 11C and its students included Petrarch, Leonardo da Vinci and the poet Ugo Foscolo.

Location

Population 73 752 – Michelin map 428 G 9 – Lombardy. On the banks of the River Ticino, Pavia is 38km/23mi from Milan, to which it is linked by A 7 and S 35.
🚏 *Via Fabio Filzi 2, ☎ 0382 22 156.*
Surrounding area: see MILANO, PIACENZA.

Directory

WHERE TO EAT

• **Budget**

Enoteca Enotria – *Via dei Mille 160/162* – ☎ *0382 56 67 55* – *Closed Sun, Mon and lunchtimes* – *Book* – €*18/26*. This wine bar is situated on the far side of the river, in the charming Borgo Ticino. The enthusiastic proprietor has a flair for matching classical dishes with interesting wines. Informal, family atmosphere. Pleasant dining room with tiled floor and rose-tinted walls.

WHERE TO STAY

• **Budget**

Agriturismo Tenuta Camillo – *27010 Pavia* – ☎ *0382 66 509* – *Fax 0382 66 509* – *agrimillo@libero.it* – *Closed Sep-Oct* – ✍ **P** ⌿ – *2 rm, 2 studios* €*30.99/61.97* – *Restaurant* €*23*. Nestling in a flower-filled "basin", between the rice fields and the lines of poplar trees, this is a lovely spot which is also well located for getting to Milan. The rooms and studios have been tastefully decorated with plain, country-style furnishings: the beds have painted headboards. Authentic, home-cooked food.

Worth a Visit

Castello Visconteo★

Open Tue-Fri, Mar to Jun, Sep and Nov 9am-1.30pm, Sat-Sun 10am-7pm, rest of year 9am-1.30pm, Sun 9am-1pm. Closed Mon and hols. €*4.10;* €*1 for castle courtyard only.* ☎ *0382 33 853.*

This impressive brick building was built by the Visconti. It now houses the **Musei Civici★**, the municipal collections, which are rich in archaeological finds, medieval and Renaissance sculpture and, particularly, paintings. The **pinacoteca★**, the picture gallery, on the first floor, has numerous masterpieces including a lovely altarpiece by the Brescian artist Vincenzo Foppa, a *Virgin and Child* by Giovanni Bellini and a very expressive *Christ bearing the Cross* by the Lombard artist, Bergognone. The last room contains a 16C model of the cathedral by Fugazza after plans by Bramante.

Duomo★

This vast cathedral, surmounted by one of Italy's largest domes, was begun in 1488: both Bramante and Leonardo da Vinci are said to have worked on the plan. The façade is 19C. To the left of the façade stood an 11C municipal tower, which fell down in March 1989, while opposite is the 16C Bishop's Palace. The adjoining Piazza Vittoria is overlooked by the 12C **Broletto** or town hall. The square affords an interesting view of the cathedral's chevet.

Chiesa di San Michele★★

This lovely Romanesque church, dedicated to St Michael, has a pale-coloured sandstone **façade★** which is quite remarkable for the balance and variety of its sculptural ornamentation. An impressive Romanesque doorway on the south side has a lintel on which Christ is seen giving a papyrus volume to St Paul and the Keys of the Church to St Peter. Inside, there are interesting architectural features (dome on squinches, the friezes and modillions beneath the galleries, the elevated chancel, mosaics, capitals etc). The apse is decorated with a lovely 15C **fresco★** portraying the *Coronation of the Virgin*.

Chiesa di San Pietro in Ciel d'Oro★

This Lombard-Romanesque church, dedicated to St Peter, which was consecrated in 1132, has a richly decorated west **door★**. In the chancel is the **Arca di Sant'Agostino★** (the tomb of St Augustine – 354-430), the work of the *Maestri Campionesi (see Index)*.

Chiesa di San Lanfranco

2km 1mi west. In the chancel of this church, a **cenotaph★** (late 15C) by Amadeo commemorates Lanfranc, who was born in Pavia and became Archbishop of Canterbury, where he is buried (d 1089).

Excursions

CERTOSA DI PAVIA★★★

10km/6mi to the north. Open daily, May to Sep, 9-11.30am and 2.30-6pm, rest of year until sunset. Guided tours available (1hr). Donation recommended. The "*Gratiarum Cartusia*" (Charterhouse of the Graces), is one of the most remarkable and characteristic examples of Lombard art as well as being home to a small community of **Cistercian monks**. It was founded as a family mausoleum in 1396 by Gian Galeazzo Visconti of Milan. Most of the monastery was built in the 15C and 16C to the plans of successive architects. The former palace of the Dukes of Milan (1625) is on the right of the courtyard, and on the left are the studios of the sculptors in charge of the decoration.

The Certosa is a harmonious blend of late-Lombard Renaissance, Gothic and monastic spirituality

B. Juge/MICHELIN

Façade – The façade is an elaborate, richly detailed work whose underlying structure is, however, characterised by a restrained elegance. The more ornate lower part (1473-99) was the work of the Mantegazza brothers, the famous architect and sculptor Amadeo, who worked also in Bergamo, and his pupil, Briosco. The upper part was completed in 1560 by another architect and sculptor, Cristoforo Lombardo.

The façade is adorned with multicoloured sculptures in marble, with medallions at the base, statues of saints in the niches and an endless variety of foliage, garlands and ornaments. Round Amadeo's famous windows are scenes from the Bible, the Life of Christ and the life of Gian Galeazzo Visconti. The low reliefs round the central doorway by Briosco depict events in the history of the Carthusians. Before entering the church, walk round to the left for a general view of the late Lombard-Gothic style, with its galleries of superimposed arcades.

Interiore and cloisters – The interior has a certain solemn grandeur and, although it is essentially Gothic, the beginnings of the Renaissance can be detected in the transept and the chancel.

Upon entering, look up: above the south chapels a painted Carthusian monk peeks out at visitors from a window with twin openings. From higher up, visitors are observed by stars which emblazon the intense blue of the vaulting.

The south arm of the transept is decorated with a *Virgin and Child* (1481-1522) by **Bergognone** who was also responsible for the *Madonna del tappeto* above the entrance of the **small cloisters**, with their Lombard terracottas.

Adjacent to the small cloisters, the ceiling of the **refectory** is decorated with the *Madonna del Latte*, also by Bergognone.

The atmospheric **large cloisters** occupy a vast space; above the arcades, note the roofs and chimneys of the 24 monks' cells which until 1968 were inhabited by Carthusian brothers.

Enter one of the cells and observe the surprising interior: although spartan in the extreme, each cell is a veritable apartment which looks out on the garden.

Back in the church, on the vaulting of the right altar of the transept, note the *Virgin Enthroned* receiving the charterhouse from Gian Galeazzo Visconti. The latter's tomb dates from the late 15C.

In the **lavatorium** note the *Madonna del Garofano* (Virgin with Carnation) by Bernardino Luini (c 1480-1532).

The transept is separated from the chancel by a marble partition wall. The inlay work of the choir stalls was executed to plans by Bergognone.

The **old sacristy** houses a *Triptych* by Baldassare degli Embriachi (late 14C), made from ivory and hippopotamus teeth, with scenes from the lives of the Virgin and Christ. In the middle of the sacristy note the *Virgin and Child*, a recurring theme in the monastery which attests to the profound gratitude felt by Gian Galeazzo's wife Catherine to the Virgin.

The north arm of the transept contains another work by Bergognone, the *Ecce Homo*, as well as the cenotaph of Ludovico il Moro and Beatrice d'Este, by Cristoforo Solari (1497).

Proceeding towards the exit, in the second chapel on the north side note the *Eternal Father* by Perugino (c 1445-1523).

LA LOMELLINA

This region lying between the Ticino and the Po is the great rice-growing area of Italy and a landscape of vast stretches of flooded land divided by long rows of willows and poplars. The chief towns of architectural interest are: **Lomello** *(32km/20mi southwest of Pavia),* whose 11C church of Santa Maria and 8C baptistery form a particularly harmonious ensemble; **Mortara** *(15km/9mi north of Lomello on S 211)* with its 14C church of San Lorenzo (paintings by Gaudenzio Ferrari) and finally **Vigevano** *(12km/7mi northeast of Mortara on S 494)* with its outstanding elliptical **Piazza Ducale★★**. The square (possibly designed by Leonardo da Vinci) lies at the foot of the Sforza castle and is dominated by Bramante's imposing tower.

Also of interest in the area, even if it is in Piedmont, is **Novara**, an industrial and commercial centre. Worth a visit is the **basilica di San Gaudenzio★**. It was

built from 1577 to 1659 to the designs of the Lombard architect Pellegrino Tibaldi, it was crowned with a tall slender **dome★★** (1844-78), an audacious addition by a local architect, A Antonelli. Inside are several interesting works of art, including paintings by Morazzone (17C) and Gaudenzio Ferrari (16C) and the silver **sarcophagus★** of the city's patron saint (St Gaudentius).

Also of interest is the **Cortile del Broletto**. This lovely courtyard has several interesting buildings including the 15C Palazzo Podestà, the 13C Broletto (Town Hall) and the Palazzo degli Paratici, now the **Museo Civico** (art gallery and archaeological section). Finally, there is the **Duomo**. This neo-Classical cathedral by Antonelli has a 6C-7C palaeo-Christian baptistery. The chancel is adorned with a black and white Byzantine-style mosaic **floor★**.

Perugia★★

Perugia was one of the 12 Etruscan city-states known as *lucumonies* which comprised the federation of Etruria in the 7C and 6C BC. The massive Etruscan wall with its gateways gives some idea of the splendour of that age. The town also has numerous ecclesiastical and secular buildings from the Middle Ages. Today the capital of Umbria is an industrial and commercial centre and a university town.

Location

Population 156 673 – Michelin map 430 M 19 – Umbria. Perugia is perched atop a hill, in the heart of Umbria. The main access road is E 45 which links the town with Emilia-Romagna.

🅱 *Piazza IV Novembre 3,* ☎ *075 57 23 327.*
Surrounding area: see ASSISI, GUBBIO.

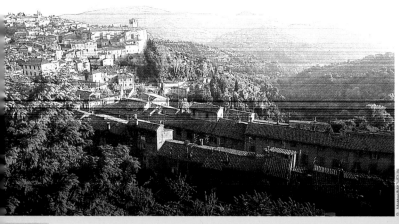

Directory

WHERE TO EAT

• Budget

Dal Mi' Cocco – *Corso Garibaldi 12 –* ☎ *075 57 32 511 – Closed Mon, 25 Jul-15 Aug –*🖅 *–Book – €12.91.* "Like going to stay with friends" is the motto and the reality of this rather alternative establishment housed in some old stables. Diners are welcomed with a glass of red wine and treated to some Vin Santo later on in the meal. The fixed-price menu features a number of Umbrian specialities. Bread and pasta are cooked on the premises.

Locanda degli Artisti – *Via Campo Battaglia 10 –* ☎ *075 57 35 851 – Closed Tue, 10-20 Jan –*🖾 *– €19/34.* This restaurant is housed in a brick-walled vault, in a medieval palazzo in the historic centre. Tasty regional cooking as well as some specialities from Lucania. The menu also includes some national dishes as well as various pizzas. Pictures by aspiring artists hang on the walls. Musical entertainment in the evenings.

• Moderate

Caffè di Perugia – *Via Mazzini 10 –* ☎ *075 57 31 863 – www.caffediperugia.it –* Housed in what was a medieval palazzo which has been tastefully restored to its former glory, much to the joy of the locals.

Choose from the grill-pizzeria in the old vault, or the elegant dining room with its frescoed ceiling, or the well-stocked wine bar. Imaginative menus.

WHERE TO STAY

• Moderate

Hotel Priori – *Via dei Priori –* ☎ *075 57 23 378 – Fax 075 57 23 213 – 60 rm €60/85* 🖵. The main attraction of this pleasant, no-frills hotel is the splendid terrace which looks down over the little old alleyways and the roofs of the historic centre. Simple rooms, some with a view, with dark wooden furniture.

Hotel La Rosetta – *Piazza Italia 19 –* ☎ *075 57 20 841 – Fax 075 57 20 841 – 94 rm €76/115* 🖵 *– Restaurant €23/37 + 15% service charge.* Whereas some of the rooms have frescoed ceilings and gorgeous antique furnishings, others, although pleasant and spacious, have a more cluttered feel and are not quite so elegant. Located in the vibrant heart of the city.

EVENTS AND FESTIVALS

Perugia has been the atmospheric backdrop for the **Umbria Jazz** festival for around 30 years. For information, contact ☎ 075 57 32 432.

Special Features

PIAZZA IV NOVEMBRE★★

Visit: 2hr. This square in the heart of Perugia is one of the grandest in Italy. Here are grouped the chief buildings of the city's glorious period as an independent commune: the Priors' Palace, the Great Fountain and the Cathedral. Leading off from the far end of the square is the picturesque **Via Maestà delle Volte★** with its medieval houses and vaulted passageways.

Fontana Maggiore★★

The Great Fountain was built to the designs of Fra Bevignate (1278) and is admirably proportioned. The sculpted panels are the work of Nicola Pisano (lower basin) and his son Giovanni (upper basin). Copies replace some of the originals, which are on display in the National Gallery of Umbria.

Palazzo dei Priori★★

The Priors' Palace was begun in the 13C and enlarged in the following centuries. It forms an ensemble of impressive grandeur. The façade overlooking the square has a majestic outside staircase leading up to a marble pulpit from which the priors harangued the people. The Corso Vannucci façade boasts a fine 14C doorway. Inside, the palace rooms are decorated with either 14C frescoes or beautifully carved 15C panelling in the Notaries' Chamber and College of the Mercanzia.

Galleria Nazionale dell'Umbria★★

♿ *Open daily, 8.30am-7.30pm (ticket office closes 7pm). Closed 1st Mon of the month, 1 Jan, 25 Dec. €6.50.* ☎ *075 57 41 257.*

The National Gallery of Umbria, housed on the top floor of the Priors' Palace, presents a large selection of Umbrian art showing its development from the 13C to the late 18C.

ARTISTIC HERITAGE

In harmony with their peaceful countryside, the Umbrian painters had gentle, mystic souls. They loved landscapes with pure lines, punctuated with trees; and in their stylised compositions, the women are depicted with a tender gracefulness, sometimes too mannered. Their technique is characterised by extremely delicate draughtsmanship and soft colours. The masters were **Giovanni Boccati** (1410-c1485), **Fiorenzo di Lorenzo** (d 1520) and especially Pietro Vannucci alias **Perugino** (1445-1523), the teacher of Raphael. His favourite subjects were religious; in them he showed his sense of space, atmosphere and landscape, marred only by a touch of mannerism. The historical artist Pinturicchio (1454-1518) was influenced by Perugino but his charmingly realistic scenes were painted more naïvely than those of his predecessor.

PERUGIA

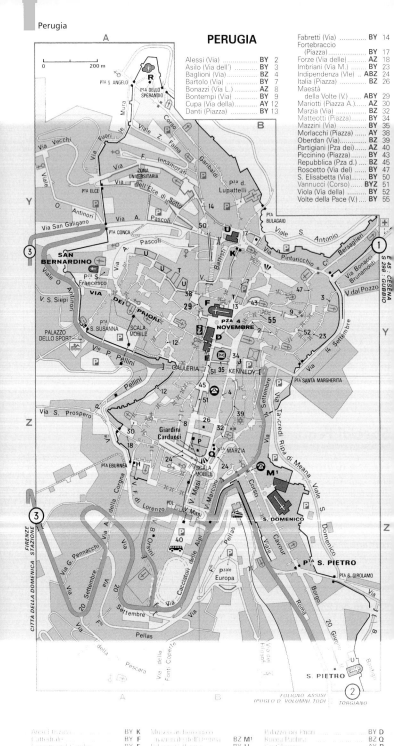

On display are: a *Madonna* by Duccio, a *Crucifix* by the unknown master, Maestro di San Francesco, a *polyptych of St Anthony* by Piero della Francesca and works by Fra Angelico, Boccati and Fiorenzo di Lorenzo.

Masterpieces by Pinturicchio and Perugino include a *Dead Christ* with its black background and an admirable *Madonna of Consolation*. Note also the marble statuettes by Nicola and Giovanni Pisano from the Great Fountain, and other works by Arnolfo di Cambio. The 17C is represented by Federico Barocci, Pietro da Cortona and Orazio Gentileschi.

The 15C Priors' Chapel is dedicated to the city's patron saints: St Herculanus and St Louis of Toulouse, whose story is told by Benedetto Bonfigli (d 1496) in a remarkable cycle of **frescoes**. The museum also has some lovely 13C and 14C French enamels and ivories.

Cattedrale★

The cathedral is Gothic, but the Piazza Dante façade was completed with a Baroque doorway.

The south chapel contains an interesting *Descent from the Cross* by Barocci, which inspired Rubens in his *Antwerp Descent.* In the north chapel is a ring said to be the Virgin's wedding ring. In both these chapels, note the superb **stalls** with 16C marquetry work.

Worth a Visit

Chiesa di San Pietro★★

To reach the church, dedicated to St Peter, go through the **Porta San Pietro★**, a majestic but unfinished work of the Florentine Agostino di Duccio. The church was built at the end of the 10C and remodelled during the Renaissance. Inside are 11 excellent canvases by Vassilacchi, alias Aliense, a Greek contemporary of El Greco. Also of note are the **carved tabernacle** by Mino da Fiesole and the marvellous 16C **stalls★★**.

Chiesa di San Domenico★

The interior of this imposing Gothic church, dedicated to St Dominic, was altered in the 17C. To the right of the chancel is the 14C **funerary monument** of Pope Benedict XI.

Museo Archeologico Nazionale dell'Umbria★★

   Open daily except Mon am, 8.30am-7.30pm. Closed 1 Jan, 1 May, 25 Dec. €2. ☏ *075 57 59 61; www.archeopg.arti.beniculturali.it*

The National Archaeological Museum comprises prehistoric, Etruscan and Umbrian sections. The remarkable collections include funerary urns, sarcophagi and Etruscan bronzes.

Collegio del Cambio★

Open Mar to Oct and 20 Dec to 6 Jan, Tue-Sat 9am-12.30pm and 2-5.30pm, Sun and hols 9am-12.30pm, rest of year 8am-2pm. Closed Mon, 1 Jan, 25 Dec. €2.58. ☏ *075 57 28 599; www.perusia.it/cambio/*

The Exchange was built in the 15C for the money-changers. In the Audience Room are the famous **frescoes★★** of Perugino and his pupils. These frescoes display the humanist spirit of the age, which sought to combine Classical civilisation and Christian doctrine. The statue of Justice is by Benedetto da Maiano (15C).

Oratorio di San Bernardino★★

To reach the oratory of St Bernardino, walk along the picturesque **Via dei Priori★**. This Renaissance jewel (1461) by Agostino di Duccio is exquisite in its harmonious lines, the delicacy of its multicoloured marbles and its sculptures. The low reliefs on the façade depict St Bernardine in glory on the tympanum, the life of the saint on the lintel and delightful angel musicians on the shafts. Inside the church, the altar consists of a 4C early-Christian sarcophagus.

Via delle Volte della Pace★

The picturesque medieval street is formed by a long 14C Gothic portico as it follows the Etruscan town wall.

Sant'Angelo★

This small church is circular in plan and dates from the 5C-6C. The interior includes 16 ancient columns.

Rocca Paolina★

Access via Porta Marzia. These are the remains of a fortress built in 1540 on the orders of Pope Paul III – hence the name "Pauline". The impressive interior still has huge walls, streets and wells dating from the 11C to 16C. Escalators have been built to facilitate access within the fortress.

Arco Etrusco★

This imposing Etruscan Arch is built of huge blocks of stone. A 16C loggia surmounts the tower on the left.

Alongside, the majestic 18C **Palazzo Gallenga** serves as a summer school for foreign students.

Giardini Carducci

There is a superb **view★★** from the Carducci Gardens, which dominates the San Pietro quarter, over the Tiber Valley.

Excursions

Ipogeo dei Volumni★

6km/4mi southeast. Open Jul to Aug, daily, 9am-12.30pm and 4.30-7pm, rest of year 9am-1pm and 3.30-6.30pm. Closed 1 Jan, 1 May, 25 Dec. €2.07. ☏ 075 39 33 29.
This vast Etruscan hypogeum hewn out of the rock, comprises an atrium and nine burial chambers. The Volumnian tomb is the largest; it contains six rounded tombstones *(cippi)*, the biggest being that of the head of the family (2C BC).

Torgiano

16km/10mi southeast. This village dominating the Tiber Valley has the interesting **Museo del Vino★** (Lungarotti Foundation) describing wine-growing traditions in Umbria and Italy since the days of the Etruscans: excellent historical and photographic documents. *Open daily, summer 9am-1pm and 3-7pm (6pm winter). Closed 25 Dec. €4. ☏ 075 98 80 200, www.lungarotti.it*

Panicale

32km/20mi southwest. Take S 220, turn right after Tavernelle and follow directions. Panicale is a medieval town perched on a hillside overlooking Lake Trasimeno. The church of San Sebastiano houses a *Martyrdom of St Sebastian* by Perugino.

Città della Pieve

42km/26mi southwest on S 220. This warm ochre-coloured town, founded in about AD 7-8 and originally called *Castrum Plebis*, was the birthplace of Pietro Vannucci, better known as **Perugino**. Some of his works are housed in the cathedral *(Baptism of Christ. Virgin with St Peter, St Paul, St Gervase and St Protasius)*, in the oratory of Santa Maria dei Bianchi (*Adoration of the Magi*, an elegant composition balanced by the portrayal of the gentle Umbrian countryside) and in Santa Maria dei Servi *(Descent from the Cross)*.
In the oratory of San Bartolomeo there are mid-14C frescoes by the Sienese artist, Jacopo di Mino del Pellicciaio *(Weeping of the Angels)*.
Among the numerous monuments in the city, which date from the Middle Ages to the 18C, note the Palazzo della Corgna, built in the middle of the 16C by the Perugian architect Galeazzo Alessi and frescoed by Niccolò Pomarancio and Salvio Savini.

Pesaro★★

At the mouth of the smiling Foglia Valley, the town was the birthplace of the composer Gioacchino Rossini.

Location

Population 88 987 – Michelin map 430 K 20 – Town plan in the Michelin Atlas Italy –Marches. Pesaro is situated on the Adriatic coast, off A 14.
ℹ *Viale Trieste 164, ☏ 0721 69 341.*
Surrounding area: seeRIMINI, Repubblica di SAN MARINO, URBINO.

Worth a Visit

Museums★

The **picture gallery** in the Municipal Museum contains several works by the Venetian, **Giovanni Bellini**. The famous **Pala di Pesaro** (1475) is an immense altarpiece representing the Virgin being crowned on the central panel, and numerous other scenes on the predella.
In the **ceramics section★★**, the Umbrian potteries are well represented but there are also examples of work from the Marches region. *Open Jul and Aug, daily, 9.30am-12.30pm and 5-8pm (11pm Tue and Thu); rest of year Tue and Wed 9.30am-12.30pm, Thu-Sun also 4-7pm. Closed Mon, 1 Jan, 25 Dec. €2.58, €4.13, including Casa Rossini. ☏ 0721 38 75 41.*

Palazzo Ducale

The great mass of the Ducal Palace, built for a member of the Sforza family in the 15C, overlooks the Piazza del Popolo with its fountain adorned with tritons and sea horses. The crenellated façade has an arcaded portico with, above, windows adorned with festoons and cherubs.

►►Museo Oliveriano (archaeological items), remains of the old church of S. Domenico.

GIOACCHINO ROSSINI (Pesaro 1792-Passy 1868)

Rossini's career was characterised by a "crescendo" which catapulted him from Pesaro into a realm of the most prestigious recognition, first from the important Italian cities and later from the principal European courts. He is often hastily labelled as a "light" composer but in reality his work contains a kind of aloof sense of irony about the worries of the world, in the context of a typically theatrical humour, and ultimately attains a pessimistic view similar to that of Leopardi, who was also from the Marches. Aged 37, at the peak of his career, Rossini stopped composing and retired from public life.

Among his most celebrated works are *The Italian Girl in Algiers*, *The Barber of Seville*, *Cinderella* and *William Tell*.

The composer's **house** *(at n° 34 Via Rossini)* is now a museum. *Open Jul and Aug, daily, 9.30am-12.30pm and 5-8pm (11pm Tue and Thu); rest of year Tue and Wed 9.30am-12.30pm, Thu-Sun also 4-7pm. Closed Mon, 1 Jan, 25 Dec. €2.58, €4.13, including Musei Civici.* ☎ *0721 38 75 41.*

Excursions

Gradara

15km/9mi northwest. Gradara is a medieval town, almost intact, surrounded by walls and battlemented gateways. The **Rocca★**, built on a square plan with corner towers, is a well-preserved example of military architecture in the 13C and 14C. It is here that **Gianni Malatesta** is said to have come upon and then murdered his wife, Francesca da Rimini, and her lover, his brother Paolo Malatesta, who were in the throes of passion while reading a courtly romance. Dante portrayed the inseparable couple in his *Divine Comedy*. ᴧ *Open Mon-Sat 8.30am-7.15pm (ticket office closes 6.45pm), Sun and hols 8.30am-2pm (ticket office closes 1.15pm). Closed 1 Jan, 1 May, 25 Dec. €4.* ☎ *0541 96 41 15.*

Fano⌂

11km/7mi southeast. This town, now a favourite seaside resort, was ruled by the Malatesta family from Rimini in the 13C-15C.

Corte Malatestiana★ – This 15C Renaissance ensemble includes a courtyard-garden and palace, and it would make an ideal theatrical set. The palace houses a museum, the **Museo Civico**. *Open Tue-Sun, 9.30am-12.30pm and 4-7pm, in summer also 9-11pm. Closed Mon and bank hols. €3.* ☎ *0721 82 83 62.*

Chiesa di Santa Maria Nuova – 16C-18C. This contains **works★** by Perugino, which are admired for their fine draughtsmanship and their delicate colours.

Fontana della Fortuna – *Piazza XX Settembre.* This 16C fountain presents the protecting goddess Fortune, perched on a pivoting globe, with her billowing cloak acting as a weather-vane.

Arco d'Augusto – *At the far end of the street of the same name.* This 1C arch has a main opening and two side ones for pedestrians. A low relief on the façade of the church of San Michele nearby portrays the arch in its original form. To the left of the arch are the remains of the Roman wall.

Piacenza★

Piacenza was originally built by the Romans at the end of the Via Emilia on the south bank of the Po. It flourished in the Middle Ages and was a member of the Lombard League. In 1545 Pope Paul III, Alessandro Farnese, gave the papal lands of Piacenza and its neighbour Parma to his natural son Pier Luigi along with a dukedom. After this the Farnese ruled Piacenza until 1731 when the dukedom passed to the Bourbons.

Location

Population 98 384 – Michelin map 428 G 11 – Town plan in the Michelin Atlas Italy –Emilia-Romagna. Piacenza is situated on the banks of the River Po. It is the first city you reach as you enter Emilia from Lombardy on A 1. The main road connecting it to Turin and Brescia is A 21. **⎀** *Piazzetta Mercanti 7,* ☎ *0523 32 93 24. Surrounding area: see CREMONA.*

Worth a Visit

Piazza Cavalli

The old political and economic centre of the city, this square derives its name from the **equestrian statues★★** of Dukes Alessandro and Ranuccio I Farnese, a Baroque masterpiece by Francesco Mochi (1580-1654).

The square is very much dominated by the imposing **"Gotico"★★**, the old town hall, a masterpiece of 13C Lombard-Gothic architecture. The building is both severe and harmonious and displays a notable contrast between the marble lower part and the brick upper storeys, the great openings and the elegantly decorated windows.

To the left of the square is the façade of the 13C **church of San Francesco**, an interesting example of Franciscan Gothic architecture, embellished by a fine splayed doorway.

Duomo★

Open daily, 7.30am-noon and 4-7pm. No charge. ☎ 0523 32 93 24.

This remarkable Lombard-Romanesque cathedral dates from the 12C-13C. The façade is adorned with a rose window and a porch with three notable doorways. The two lateral doorways are influenced by the sculptural styles at Modena and Nonantola. The **interior** on the plan of a Latin cross is simple but enriched by the sweeping frescoes (Guercino, Morazzone, 17C) which adorn the dome, and by the canvases in the chancel (Camillo Procaccini and Ludovico Carracci).

Basilica di Sant'Antonino

Piazza S. Antonino. Open Mon-Sat, 8am-noon and 4-6.45pm, Sun and hols 8.15am-12.30pm and 8-9.30pm. No charge. ☎ 0523 32 93 24.

This former palaeo-Christian basilica dedicated to St Anthony was remodelled in the 11C and has interesting features: an octagonal tower (40m/131ft high) and the north "Paradise" vestibule (1350) in the Gothic style.

Galleria d'Arte Moderna Ricci-Oddi

Via S. Siro 13. ♿ Open daily except Mon, 10am-noon and 3-6pm. Closed bank hols. €4; no charge last Thu of the month. ☎ 0523 32 07 42.

The modern art collections include Italian paintings from various regions ranging from the Romantic period to the 20C: works by the landscape painter Antonio Fontanesi, the Macchiaioli (Fattori), artists influenced by the Impressionist school (Boldini, Zandomeneghi), works in an Oriental and figurative idiom (De Pisis), Futurist (Boccioni) and metaphysical (De Chirico, Carrà) paintings. There are also sculptures (Medardo Rosso) and works by foreign artists such as Klimt who influenced Italian art. **Chiesa di San Savino**

Near the junction of Via G. Alberoni with Via Roma. Open daily, 9am-noon and 4-5pm. No charge. ☎ 0523 32 26 61.

This 12C church, with its very pure architectural lines, contains priceless traces of the original construction, such as the fine capitals and the **mosaic flooring★** in the chancel and in the crypt.

Palazzo Farnese

This imposing late-Renaissance palace, built to designs by Vignola but never completed, now houses the **Museo Civico★**. ♿ *Open Tue-Sun, 9am-1pm, also 3-6pm Fri-Sun and hols. Closed Mon, bank hols. €5.25. ☎ 0523 32 69 81; www.farnese.net*

On the ground floor the sumptuous *Fasti farnesiani★* cycle of frescoes by Draghi and Ricci is richly framed in stuccowork. The images portray stories of Alessandro Farnese who became Pope Paul III. There are also collections of ceramics and glass, frescoes from local churches (14C-15C) and a series of Romanesque sculptures of the "Piacenza School" which combine influences both from the contemporary French school and Wiligelmo (*The Prophets David and Ezekiel*, 12C). Note also the bronze **Etruscan divining liver★★**, a soothsayer's device dating from the 2C-1C BC. The first floor, with its richly decorated ceiling, houses collections of paintings from the 16C-19C Emilian, Lombard and Ligurian schools, a *Virgin and Child with St John* by Botticelli and the *Fasti Farnesiani* dedicated to Elisabetta Farnese. There is also a Carriage Museum and a Risorgimento Museum.

Chiesa di San Sisto

At the northern end of Via S. Sisto. Open Mon-Fri, 7.10am and 4.30-6.30pm, Sat 7.10am and 3-6pm, Sun and hols 7.10am and 3-5.30pm. No charge. ☎ 0523 32 93 24.

This rather curious 16C building was designed by Alessio Tramello, an architect from Piacenza. The façade is preceded by a doorway, dated 1622, which opens onto a 16C atrium. The **interior** has an interesting Renaissance decoration and a splendid 16C **wood chancel**. Raphael painted the famous *Sistine Madonna* for this church, now replaced by a copy.

Chiesa della Madonna di Campagna★

Via Campagna. Open daily, 7am-noon and 3-7pm. ☎ 0523 32 93 24.

This beautiful church, in the form of a Greek cross and built in the idiom of Bramante, constitutes one of the most important Renaissance buildings in Italy. The interior contains splendid **frescoes★** by Pordenone (1484-1539), an exponent of the Mannerist style whose painting was characterised by a vivid use of colour and sculptural forms.

Galleria Alberoni

Via Emilia Parmense 77, 2.5km/1.5mi southeast. By reservation only. ☎ *0523 32 20 74 or 0523 32 93 24.*

The gallery is situated within the precincts of a college founded in the 18C by Cardinal Alberoni, and comprises a fine collection of 16C-17C Flemish and Italian **tapestries** as well as a rich collection of 15C-19C Italian (Guido Reni, Baciccia, Luca Giordano) and Flemish (Jan Provost) paintings. The jewel of the collection is the moving *Ecce Homo*★★ by Antonello da Messina.

Pienza★★

Pienza displays a remarkable unity of style, especially in its main square, and is a perfect example of Renaissance town planning. It was commissioned by Pope Pius II, the diplomat and humanist poet, who wanted to build the ideal town. The architectural unity was intended to reflect the utopian concepts of the "ideal city", as conceived by the 15C humanist movement.

Location

Population 2 258 – Michelin map 430 M 1 – See also The Green Guide Tuscany. Pienza is off S 146, between San Quirico d'Orcia and Montepulciano.
🖪 *Via Casenuove 22,* ☎ *057 87 48 072.Surrounding area: see MONTEPULCIANO.*

Worth a Visit

The centre of Pienza is the work of the Florentine architect, **Bernardo Rossellino** (1409-82), a pupil of Alberti, whose design centred on having the principal monuments line the town's main axis. The town hall, with its ground-floor loggia, is opposite the cathedral. The other sides of the square are framed by the Bishop's Palace (simply restored in the 15C) and the Palazzo Piccolomini; a pretty well in front of the latter enhances the overall plan. There is a fine **view**★ over the Orcia Valley from behind the cathedral.

Cattedrale★

The cathedral, which was completed in 1462, has a Renaissance façade. The interior (restored) shows Gothic influences and contains several paintings by the Sienese school, including an *Assumption*★★, a masterpiece by Vecchietta.

Museo Diocesano

♿ *Open mid-Mar to Oct, daily except Tue, 10am-1pm and 3-6pm, rest of year only Sat, Sun and hols, 10am-1pm and 3-6pm. Closed Tue €4.13.* ☎ *0578 74 90 71; www.infinito.it/utenti/ufficio.turistico*
The Cathedral Museum contains pictures of the 14C and 15C Sienese school and a remarkable 14C historiated cope made in England.

Palazzo Piccolomini★

Open daily except Mon, 10am-12.30pm and 3-6pm (ticket office closes 30min early). Closed Mon (except hols). €3. ☎ *0578 74 85 03.*
Rossellino's masterpiece was greatly influenced by the Palazzo Rucellai in Florence (*see FIRENZE*). The three sides facing the town are similar; the fourth, overlooking the Orcia Valley, has three tiers of loggias and gives onto hanging gardens which are among the earliest to have been created. The elegant inner courtyard features slim Corinthian columns. The palace still has its armoury, and the incunabula and a Baroque bed from the papal bedchamber.

Excursions

Montalcino★

24km/15mi west. In addition to part of its 13C walls, this small hillside town still has its magnificent **fortezza**★★ built in 1361, a consummate example of defensive forts at that time. It is shaped like a pentagon and its tall walls, with machicolations and parapet walk, are punctuated by five towers. One of them was used as officers' quarters and, in case of siege, could be used by the nobility. The ordinary people would seek shelter within the outer walls. It was here that the government of Siena took refuge when the town was captured by Holy Roman Emperor Charles V in 1555. *Open daily except Mon, Apr to Oct 9am-8pm, rest of year 9am-6pm. €2.07; €5.16 including the Museo Civico and Museo Diocesano.* ☎ *0577 84 93 31; www.prolocomontalcino.it*

In the Monastery of Sant'Antimo silence is transformed into music as the small community sings Gregorian chants

Montalcino is also famous for its **Brunello,** a red wine of excellent quality produced in a small vineyard. The town is a picturesque labyrinth of medieval streets leading to a Romanesque and Gothic church, to the 13C town hall, the **Palazzo Comunale★** flanked by a loggia and topped by a tall tower, or to the small **Museo Civico e Diocesano**. & Open daily except Mon, 10am-1pm and 2-6pm. €4.13, €5.16 cumulative with fortress. ☎ *05777 84 60 14; www.prolocomontalcino.it*

Abbazia di Sant'Antimo★★

35km/22mi southwest. Open Mon-Sat, 10.30am-12.30pm and 3-6.30pm, Sun and hols 9.15-10.45am and 3-6pm. Masses sung in Gregorian chant. Gratuity recommended. *www.antimo.it* ☎ *0577 83 56 59; www.antimo.it*

The abbey, which was founded in the 9C, stands in an isolated hill **site★** amid cypress and olive groves. Its prosperity was at its peak in the 12C when the **church** was built. It is a fine example of Cistercian Romanesque architecture with Burgundian (ambulatory and apsidal chapels) and Lombard (porch, bell tower with Lombard bands and façades) influences. The interior is spacious and austere. Columns topped by fine alabaster capitals divide the nave with its wooden roof from the aisles which have groined vaulting. Only some of the monastic buildings remain standing.

Pisa★★★

Pisa has the atmosphere of a minor capital city which has lost some of its hustle and bustle. Its superb buildings reflect past splendours.

The city is more spacious than Florence and less austere thanks to its yellow, pink or yellow-ochre house fronts but, like Florence, it is bisected by the River Arno, which forms one of its most majestic meanders at this point. Pisa also owes its charm to its somewhat aristocratic air, the genteel lifestyle that this seems to encourage, and the special quality of the light, probably due to the proximity of the sea.

The city is almost totally encircled by walls and is traversed from north to south by a main street lined with shops; on the south bank this is the Corso Italia and on the north bank a narrow street flanked by arcades, Borgo Stretto. The winding, Via Santa Maria, linking Piazza del Duomo to the Arno, is one of the most characteristic streets in Pisa with its noble yet cheerful appearance. These two streets on the north bank flank the busiest district in the city, full of shops and restaurants.

Location

Population 92 379 – Michelin map 430 K 13 – See also The Green Guide Tuscany. Pisa is situated near the mouth of the River Arno, with the Parco Naturale di Migliarino-S. Rossore-Massaciùccoli between the town and the sea. ᛁ *Via Carlo Cammeo 2, 050 56 04 64.Surrounding area: see LUCCA, VERSILIA.*

Directory

WHERE TO EAT

• **Budget**

Osteria Dei Mille – *Via dei Mille 32* – ☎ *050 55 62 63* – *osteriadeimille@csinfo.it* – 📶 ✖ – *€12/25 + 15% service charge*. This charming establishment is just five minutes from the hustle and bustle of the Piazza dei Miracoli. Authentic Tuscan cooking with a wide selection of vegetarian dishes. The copper saucepans hanging on the walls are a nice touch.

La Clessidra – *Via Santa Cecilia 34* – ☎ *050 54 01 60* – *Closed Sat lunchtime, Sun, 27 Dec-8 Jan, 5-25 Aug* – 📶 – *Book* – *€17/23*. A simple, pleasant restaurant with a very able and hard-working chef. The cuisine is typically Tuscan but with an innovative touch and a few variations on the traditional themes. Located in one of the smartest and best-preserved parts of town.

WHERE TO STAY

• **Budget**

Hotel Galileo – *Via S. Maria 12, (1st floor, no lift)* – ☎ *050 40 621* – *www.csinfo.it/hotelgalileo* – *9 rm €36.15/49.06*. A good solution for anyone wanting to stay in the centre of town, within easy reach of the famous piazza, and at a reasonable price! The rooms are simple, with modern furnishings and have large windows. They all have private bathrooms but not always en suite.

• **Expensive**

Hotel Francesco – *Via S. Maria 129* – ☎ *050 55 41 09* – *Fax 050 55 61 45* – *info@hotelfrancesco.it* – 📶 ♿ – *13 rm from €87.79* 🚗. This comfortable hotel is situated in a quiet part of town, a stone's throw from the Leaning Tower. Modern-style, wooden furniture throughout. Spacious rooms and bathrooms. Breakfast al fresco in summer – there is a lovely terrace area outside.

TAKING A BREAK

Caffè dell'Ussero – *Lungarno Pacinotti 27* – ☎ *050 58 11 00* – *Open Sun-Fri 7.30am-9pm, closed Aug*. Situated on the ground floor of the Palazzo Rosso is this rather grand café, which dates back to the 18C. It has had an interesting past: initially the meeting-place for Pisa's intellectual elite, it has also been a cinema! These days it is a pleasant tea room which hosts some quite smart social gatherings. Overlooks the River Arno.

Background

Sheltered from raiding pirates, Pisa was a Roman naval base and commercial port until the end of the Empire (5C). It became an independent maritime republic at the end of the 9C and continued to benefit from its geographical location. Pisa became the rival of Genoa and Venice, and the Pisans waged war against the Saracens in the Mediterranean basin. It was in the 12C and the beginning of the 13C that Pisa reached the peak of its power and prosperity. This period was marked by the construction of some fine buildings and the foundation of the university.

During the 13C struggles between the Emperor and the Pope, Pisa supported the Ghibellines (*see Index*) and thus opposed Genoa on the seas and Lucca and Florence on land. In 1284 the Pisan fleet was defeated at the naval **Battle of Meloria**. Ruined and racked by internal strife, Pisa's maritime empire foundered; Corsica and Sardinia which she had ruled since the 11C were ceded to Genoa. Pisa herself passed under Florentine rule and the Medici took a special interest in the city, especially in the study of science there. Its most famous son was the astronomer and physicist **Galileo** (1564-1642). His patron was Cosimo II, Grand Duke of Tuscany. Nevertheless Galileo, aged 70, had to defend his theory of the rotation of the earth before the Inquisition and in fact renounced it.

The economic prosperity of the powerful maritime Pisan Republic from the 11C to the 13C fostered the development of a new art style which is particularly evident in the fields of architecture and sculpture. The **Pisan-Romanesque style**, with the cathedral as the most rigorous example, is characterised by external decoration: the alternate use of different coloured marbles to create geometric patterns, a play of light and shade due to the tiers of loggias with small columns on the upper parts of the façade, and intarsia decoration showing the strong influence of the Islamic world and of Christian countries of the Near East which had relations with the maritime republic. Alongside architects such as Buscheto, Rainaldo and Diotisalvi there were numerous sculptors to embellish the exteriors. Pisa became an important centre for Gothic sculpture in Italy, thanks to the work of **Nicola Pisano** (1220-c 1280), originally from Puglia, and his son **Giovanni Pisano** (1250-c 1315).

Special Features

PIAZZA DEL DUOMO (CAMPO DEI MIRACOLI)★★★

Visit: 3 hr. In and around this famous square, also known as **Campo dei Miracoli** (Field of Miracles), are four buildings which form one of the finest architectural complexes in the world. It is advisable to approach on foot from the west through the **Porta Santa Maria** to enjoy the best view of the Leaning Tower.

Duomo★★

Open Mon-Sat, Apr to Sep 10am-7.40pm, Sun and hols 1-7.40pm, rest of year 10am-12.45pm and 3-4.45pm, Sun and hols 3-4.45pm. €2. ☎ 050 56 05 47; www.duomopisa.it
This splendid cathedral was built with the fantastic spoils captured during the expeditions against the Muslims. Building started in 1063 under Buscheto and was continued by Rainaldo, who designed the façade.

The **west front★★★** is light and graceful with four tiers of small marble columns and a decorative facing of alternating light- and dark-coloured marble. The church itself is built on the plan of a Latin cross. The original doors were replaced by **bronze doors★** cast in 1602 to designs by Giovanni Bologna. The south transept door has very fine Romanesque bronze **panels★★** (late 12C) by Bonanno Pisano, depicting the Life of Christ in a naïve but free creative style.

The **interior**, with its nave and four aisles, is impressive for its length (100m/330ft), its deep apse, its three-aisled transept and the forest of piers which offer an astonishing variety of perspectives. Note in particular the beautiful **pulpit★★★** of **Giovanni Pisano** on which he worked from 1302 to 1311. It is supported by six porphyry columns and five pillars decorated with religious and allegorical statues.

The eight panels of the pulpit evoke the Life of Christ and group a multitude of personages with dramatic expressions. Near the pulpit is Galileo's lamp, which gave the scholar his original idea for his theory concerning the movement of the pendulum.

Torre Pendente★★★

Open daily, Apr to Sep 8am-8pm, Mar and Oct 9am-6pm, rest of year 9am-5pm (ticket office closes 4.20pm). By reservation only. €15. ☎ 050 56 05 47; www.duomo.pisa.it
The **Leaning Tower of Pisa** is both a bell tower and belfry. This white marble tower (58m/189ft high) was begun in 1173 in a pure Romanesque style by Bonanno Pisano and completed in 1350. Built, like the towers of Byzantium, as a cylinder, the tower has six storeys of galleries with

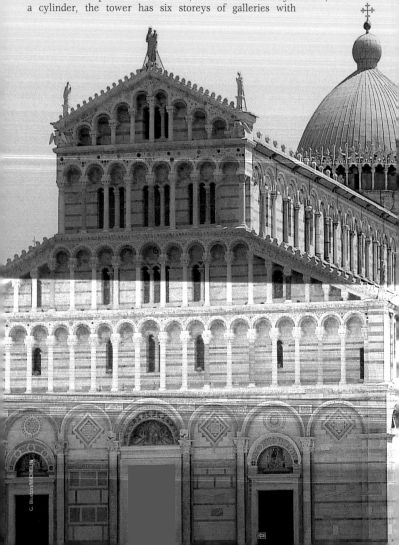

G. Biudzar/MICHELIN

columns which seem to wind round in a spiral because of the slope of the building. On the lower level is the blind arcading decorated with lozenges that is specific to the architecture of Pisa. The tower slowly began leaning in 1178 and has continued to do so at a rate of between 1 and 2 millimetres a year. The movement is caused by the alluvial soil on which the tower is built, soil that is insufficiently resistant to bear the weight of the building. Over the years, architects tried in vain to correct the unfortunate "lean". The tower was closed to the public in 1990 and a committee was formed to debate how best to find a long-term solution to the problem. In 1992 the tower was surrounded by two stainless steel cables at first-floor level and, in 1993, the base was strengthened by a reinforced concrete "corset", which included 670 tonnes of lead to counterbalance the lean; progression of the lean was effectively stopped for several years. Another restoration attempt in September 1995 ended in disaster when the tower shifted 2.5 millimetres in one night, double the annual rate. Engineers dumped lead on the base of the North side, and the tower was prevented from falling. No further restoration work took place until 1998, when steel-cable "braces" were attached to the tower. They were removed in 2001 when the tower had moved a further 40 centimetres towards the vertical, returning the tower to the angle it was at in 1838. The tower was reopened to the public later that year.

Battistero★★★

(&) *Open daily, Apr to Sep 8am-8pm (ticket office closes 7.40pm), Mar and Oct 9am-6pm (ticket office closes 5.40pm), rest of year 9am-5pm (ticket office closes 4.40pm). Closed 1 Jan, 25 Dec. €5. ☎ 050 56 05 47; www.duomo.pisa.it*

Work on the Baptistery began in 1153 and the two lower storeys are in the Pisan-Romanesque style, while the frontons and pinnacles above the first-floor arcades are Gothic. The building is roofed with an unusual dome and has four doorways with fine carving. The majestic interior is full of light and has a diameter of 35m/115ft. The sober decoration consists of light- and dark-coloured marble; in the centre is a lovely octagonal **font**★ (1246) by an artist from Como, Guido Bigarelli. The masterpiece of the baptistery is the admirable **pulpit**★★ (1260) by Nicola Pisano. It is less ornate than the one done by his son for the cathedral and stands on simple columns. The five panels of the pulpit depict the Life of Christ: its noble, classical-style sculptures are no doubt inspired by Roman art and the sarcophagi to be found in the neighbouring Camposanto.

Pisa

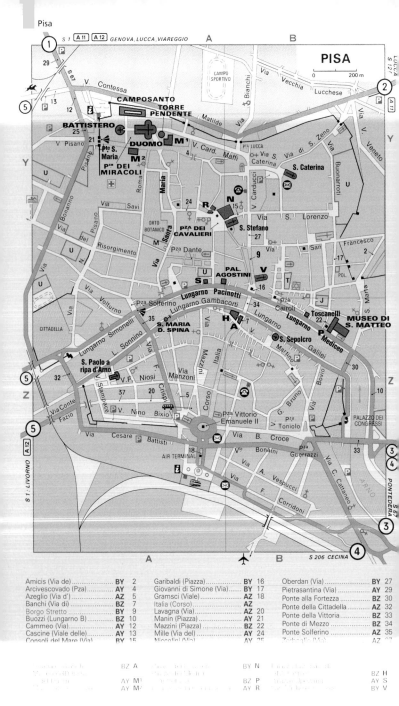

Camposanto★★

&. Open daily, Apr to Sep 8am-8pm (ticket office closes 7.40pm), Mar and Oct 9am-6pm (ticket office closes 5.40pm), rest of year 9am-5pm (ticket office closes 4.40pm) Closed 1 Jan, 25 Dec. €5. ☎ 050 56 05 47. www.duomo.pisa.it

This burial ground was begun in 1277 by Giovanni di Simone, one of the architects of the Leaning Tower. Work was interrupted by the naval Battle of Meloria (*see above*) and completed only in the 15C.

The large rectangular area is bounded on the outside by a blind portico. Inside, the majestic semicircular arcading includes four delicate lancet windows with Gothic tracery.

One of the most famous cycles comprising *The Triumph of Death*★★★ and the *Last Judgement*★★ and *Hell*★ by a 14C artist was saved and is displayed in the north gallery. The transience and vanity of wordly pleasures are illustrated with great realism.

Museo dell'Opera del Duomo★★

 ♿ *Open daily, Apr to Sep 8am-8pm (ticket office closes 7.20pm), Mar and Oct 9am-6pm (ticket office closes 5.20pm), rest of year 9am-5pm (ticket office closes 4.20pm). Closed 1 Jan, 25 Dec. €5.* ☎ *050 56 05 47; www.duomo.pisa.it*

The Cathedral Museum contains works of art from the monuments in Piazza del Duomo: 12C-16C sculptures (Romanesque period influenced by Islamic and Burgundian art, Gothic and Renaissance); cathedral treasure (ivory **Madonna and Child** by Giovanni Pisano) and silver ware. On the first floor are displayed 15C-18C paintings and sculpture; fragments of Renaissance stalls and 12C-13C illuminated manuscripts; episcopal vestments and ornaments; archaeological artefacts found in the early 19C in the cemetery by Carlo Lasinio, who made a series of engravings of the Camposanto frescoes.

Museo delle Sinopie★

(♿) *Open daily, Apr to Sep 8am-8pm (ticket office closes 7.40pm), Mar and Oct 9am-6pm (ticket office closes 5.40pm), rest of year 9am-5pm (ticket office closes 4.40pm). Closed 1 Jan, 25 Dec. €5.* ☎ *050 56 05 47; www.duomo.pisa.it*

This museum contains the sketches or *sinopie* (sketches in a reddish-brown pigment which came from Sinope on the Black Sea) which were under the frescoes and were brought to light by a fire following the bombing in 1944. They have been well restored and give a good idea of the vitality and free draughtsmanship of these 13C-15C painters.

Worth a Visit

Piazza dei Cavalieri★

This, the historic centre of Pisa, gets its name from the Cavalieri di Santo Stefano (Knights of St Stephen), a military order which specialised in the struggle against the infidel. Around the square are: the **Palazzo dei Cavalieri** with a **façade★** decorated by Vasari; the **church of Santo Stefano** built in 1569 with its white, green and pink marble façade and dedicated to St Stephen; and the **Palazzo Gherardesca** designed in 1607 by Vasari to stand on the site of a former prison, Torre della Fame, where Count Ugolino della Gherardesca and his children were condemned to die by starvation, having been accused of treason after the naval defeat at Meloria.

Museo Nazionale di San Matteo★★

(♿) *Open Mon-Sat, 8.30am-7.30pm (ticket office closes 7pm), Sun and hols 8.30am-1.30pm (ticket office closes 1pm). Closed 1 Jan, 1 May, 25 Dec. €4.* ☎ *050 54 18 65; www.ambientepi.arti.beniculturali.it*

The National Museum houses works created in Pisa between the 13C and 15C. Of note are the **Virgin Mary Nursing** by Nino Pisano and Masaccio's **St Paul**.

Chiesa di Santa Maria della Spina★★

This early-14C church, dedicated to St Mary of the Thorn, resembles a finely worked reliquary shrine with all its gables, pinnacles, statues and statuettes by the Pisano, their assistants and followers. Some of the originals have been replaced by replicas.

►►S. Caterina (façade★), S. Michele in Borgo (façade★), Lungarni (Palazzo Agostini★), S. Sepolcro (chancel★), S. Paolo a Ripa d'Arno (façade★).`

Excursions

Basilica di San Piero a Grado★

6km/4mi southwest. Leave by ⑤ on the map, the Via Conte Fazio. This Romanesque church stands on the spot on which St Peter is said to have landed when he came from Antioch. The apse with its three apsidal chapels is remarkable.

Livorno

24km/14mi southwest of Pisa. The important seaport of Leghorn deals mainly in timber, marble, alabaster, cars and craftwork from Florence. Cosimo I de' Medici started rebuilding the harbour to replace the silted-up Porto Pisano, and it was finished in 1620 under Cosimo II. The main streets are Via Grande lined with arcaded buildings, Via Cairoli and Via Ricasoli. In the Piazza Micheli, from which the Fortezza Vecchia (Old Fortress) can be seen, stands the **monument★** to the last prominent Medici, the Grand Duke Ferdinand. The four bronze Moors (1624) were the work of Pietro Tacca.

Montenero

9km/6mi south of Livorno. The 18C pilgrimage church dedicated to Our Lady of Grace consists of a richly decorated Baroque church, a monastery and behind railings the *famedio*, a series of chapels reserved for the burial of distinguished citizens of Livorno.

Pistoia ★★

This industrial town has a rich historic centre which is evidence of its importance in the 12C-14C. Both Lucca and Florence coveted Pistoia, but it was Florence and the Medici who annexed it for good in 1530.

Location

Population – Michelin map 430 K 14 – See The Green Guide Tuscany. Pistoia is located between Florence and the coast, about 36km/22mi from Florence.
🖪 *Piazza del Duomo (Palazzo dei Vescovi),* ☎ *0573 21 622.*
Surrounding area: see FIRENZE, MONTECATINI TERME, PRATO.

Worth a Visit

Piazza del Duomo★★

This is a most attractive and well-proportioned square lined with elegant secular and religious buildings.

Duomo★ – *Cappella di S. Jacopo: For information on opening times* ☎ *0573 29 095; www.diocesi.pistoia.it*
Rebuilt in the 12C and 13C, the cathedral has a **façade★** that is a harmonious blend of the Pisan-Romanesque style (tiers of colonnaded galleries) and the Florentine-Renaissance style (porch with slender columns added in the 14C). The lower part of the campanile is quite massive but it becomes more graceful towards the top with three tiers of colonnaded galleries. The interior was remodelled in the 17C. Inside is the famous **altar of St James★★★**, a masterpiece of silversmith work dating from the 13C, which was modified and extended in the following centuries. The saints surround the Apostle seated in a niche, with Christ in Glory above. Scenes from the Old and New Testaments complete the composition. In the chapel to the left of the chancel is a lovely **Madonna in Majesty★** (c 1480) by Lorenzo di Credi.

Battistero★ – *Open daily Tue-Sat, Apr to Sep 9.30am-12.30pm and 4-7pm, rest of year 9.30am-12.30pm and 3.30-6.30pm, Sun and hols 9.30am-12.30pm. Closed Mon. No charge.* This Gothic octagonal baptistery with polychrome marble facing dates from the 14C. The tympanum of the central doorway bears a statue of the **Virgin and Child** between St Peter and St John the Baptist, attributed to Nino and Tommaso Pisano.

Palazzo Pretorio – This palace was built in the 14C as the residence of the governing magistrate *(podestà)* and remodelled in the 19C.

Palazzo del Comune – The Town Hall was built from 1294 to 1385 and has a graceful arcaded **façade★** with elegant paired windows or triple bays. The palace houses the **Museo Civico** with a collection of paintings and sculptures from the 13C-20C Tuscan school. ⑤ *Open Mon-Sat, 10am-7pm, Sun and hols 9am-12.30pm. Closed 1 Jan, 1 May, 25 Dec. €3.10.* ☎ *0573 37 12 96; www.comune.pistoia.it*

Chiesa di Sant'Andrea★

This church dedicated to St Andrew is in the pure Pisan-Romanesque style and has a famous **pulpit★★** executed (1298-1308) by Giovanni Pisano in his dramatic but intensely lively manner: the panels represent five scenes from the Life of Christ. The lovely **crucifix★** in gilded wood is by Giovanni Pisano *(in a niche beyond the first altar on the right).*

▶▶ Palazzo del Tau (Information Centre on the works of Marino Marini), Ospedale del Ceppo (frieze★★ by Giovanni della Robbia), S. Giovanni Fuorcivitas (north façade★, pulpit★, *Visitazion*★★ by Luca della Robbia).

Excursions

Vinci★

11km/7mi south. The great Leonardo da Vinci was born not far from this town. The **Museo Leonardiano★** is housed in the castle in honour of its famous son. (⑤) *Open daily, Mar to Oct 9.30am-7pm, rest of year 9.30am-6pm (25 Dec, 3-6pm only). €3.62; €4.13 including the Museo Collegiata in Empoli and Museo Ceramica in Montelupo.* ☎ *0571 56 055.*
The birthplace, or **casa natale** of the artist lies 2km/1.2mi to the north amid olive trees. ⑤ *Open daily, Mar to Oct 9.30am-7pm, rest of year 9.30am-6pm (25 Dec, 3-6pm only). No charge.* ☎ *0571 56 055.*

Golfo di **Policastro**★★

Gulf of POLICASTRO

This magnificent gulf extending from the tip of Infreschi to Praia a Mare is backed by high mountains whose sharp, needle-like peaks soar skywards. The lower slopes are planted with cereals and olive groves with clumps of chestnut trees above.

Location

Michelin map 431 G 28 – Campania – Basilicata – Calabria. The main access roads to the Gulf of Policastro are A 3 and S 18.
Surrounding area: see CALABRIA.

Directory

WHERE TO EAT
• *Budget*
Taverna Antica – *Piazza Dei Martiri 3 – 87028 Praia a Mare – 12km/7mi southeast of Maratea on S 18 – ☎ 0985 72 182 – Closed Tue (except Jun-Oct) – 🍴 – Book – €18/26.* Here you can enjoy excellent fish cuisine, the type of fish dependent on availability. Whether it's on the little terrace or in the cosy rustic-style dining room, why not sit back and let the friendly and knowledgeable proprietor make your choices for you.
La Tana – *Località Castrocucco – 85040 Maratea Porto – South of Maratea – ☎ 0973 87 72 88 – Closed Thu (except 15 Jun-15 Sep) – €18/31.* The large tank used for breeding and cleaning shellfish, is an indication of what this restaurant specialises in: seafood. Imaginative cooking and dishes are attractively presented. Accommodation also available: attractive rooms with either terrace or garden and private access.

WHERE TO STAY
• *Moderate*
Hotel Germania – *Via Roma 44 – 87028 Praia a Mare – 12km/7mi southeast of Maratea on S 18 – ☎ 0985 72 016 – Fax 0985 72 755 – Closed Oct-Mar – 🅿 ♿ – 60 rm €43.90/67.14 – ☕ €7.75 – Rest €15.50/17.05.* An unpretentious establishment, with bright and spacious public lounges overlooking the limpid blue sea. Shame about the furnishings and decor which are a little dated. Lovely location right on the beach. Another attraction is the huge sun terrace on the top floor.
Hotel Martino – *Via Citrosello 16, Località Marina di Maratea – 85046 Maratea - –7km/4mi southeast of Maratea – ☎ 0973 87 91 26 – Fax 0973 87 93 12 – 🅿 🏊 – 33 rm €51.65/82.63 – ☕ €4.13 – Restaurant €15/26.* This hotel has a lovely setting: it overlooks the sea with the mountains in the background. Beautiful, good-sized rooms that have been tastefully furnished. Try and get one of the rooms with a private terrace (and a view!). Indoor swimming pool and private beach. Half- and full-board rates available.

Worth a Visit

Between **Sapri** and **Praia a Mare** the corniche road overlooks the green waters which lap the charming creeks. A series of small villages succeed one another along this enchanting coast.

Maratea⌂⌂
This seaside resort has many beaches and creeks and its hotels and villas are hidden behind a screen of luxuriant vegetation. The village itself is spread over the slopes of Monte Biagio, on the summit of which stands the basilica of San Biagio and the great white figure of the Statue of the Redeemer (22m/72ft tall), the work of Innocenti (1965). Nearby there is a superb **panorama**★★ of the Gulf of Policastro and the Calabrian coast.

Pompei★★★

POMPEII

Pompeii, the opulent town which was buried in AD 79 in one of the most disastrous volcanic eruptions in history, provides important evidence of the ancient way of life. The extensive and varied ruins of the dead city, in its attractive setting, movingly evoke on a grand scale a Roman city at the time of the Empire. In 1997 Pompeii was included in UNESCO's World Heritage List.

A girl – who may represent Dionysus herself – reading the rites under the watchful gaze of two women priests, Villa dei Misteri.

Location

Population 26 018 – Michelin map 431 E 25 – Campania. Pompeii is situated at the foot of Vesuvius, to which it owes its fame. The main access road is A 3. ❶ *Via Sacra 1, ☎ 081 85 07 255*

Surrounding area: see COSTIERA AMALFITANA, CAPRI, ISCHIA, NAPOLI, Golfo di NAPOLI, SALERNO.

Background

Pompeii was founded in the 8C BC by the Oscans, but by the 6C BC a Greek influence was already prevalent in the city from its neighbour Cumae, which was then a powerful Greek colony. From the end of the 5C BC, when it came under Samnite rule, to the beginning of the 1C AD, the city knew great prosperity; town planning and art flourished. In the year 80 BC, the town fell under Roman domination and then it became a favourite resort of rich Romans. Roman families settled there. Pompeii adopted Roman organisation, language, lifestyle, building methods and decoration. When the eruption of Vesuvius struck, Pompeii was a booming town with a population of about 25 000. The town was situated in a fertile region, made flourished and there was even some industrial activity; it also had a port. The numerous shops and workshops which have been uncovered, its wide streets and the deep ruts made in the cobblestones by chariot wheels are evidence of the intense activity that went on in the town.

The people had a lively interest in spectacles, games and active politics, as can be seen in a fresco housed at the Archaeological Museum in Naples. In AD 59, after a bloodthirsty fight between rival supporters, the amphitheatre was closed for 10 years and only re-opened after Nero's wife Poppea interceded. In the year AD 62, an earthquake extensively damaged the town but before all could be put to rights, Vesuvius erupted (August AD 79) and also destroyed Herculaneum and Stabiae. In the space of two days Pompeii was buried under a layer of cinders 6m to 7m/20ft to 23ft deep. Bulwer-Lytton describes these events in his novel *The Last Days of Pompeii*.

It was only in the 18C, under the reign of Charles of Bourbon, that systematic excavations began. The finds had a tremendous effect in Europe, creating a revival of Antique art and the development of a so-called Pompeiian style.

ARCHITECTURE AND DECORATION

Building methods – Pompeii was destroyed before a degree of uniformity in building methods had been achieved and it presents examples of the diverse methods and materials used: *opus quadratum* (large blocks of freestone piled on top of one another, without mortar of any kind); *opus incertum* (irregularly shaped blocks of tufa or lava bonded with mortar); *opus reticulatum* (small square blocks of limestone or tufa arranged diagonally to form a decorative pattern); *opus testaceum* (walls are faced with triangular bricks laid flat with the pointed end turned inwards). Sometimes the walls were faced with plaster or marble. There are several types of dwelling in Pompeii: the sober and austere house of the Samnites, which became larger and more richly decorated through Greek influence. With the arrival of the Romans and the problems arising from a growing population, a new kind of house evolved in which limited space is compensated for by richness of decoration.

Pompeiian painting – A large number of paintings which adorned the walls of the dwellings have been transferred to the Archaeological Museum in Naples. However, a visit to the dead city gives a good idea of the pictorial decoration of the period. There are **four different styles**. The 1st style by means of relief and light touches of colour imitates marble. The 2nd style is by far the most attractive: walls are divided into large panels by false pillars surmounted by pediments or crowned by a small shrine, with false doors all designed to create an illusion of perspective. The artists show a partiality for the famous Pompeiian red, cinnabar obtained from mercury sulphide, and a dazzling black, both of which make for a very striking style. The 3rd style abandoned *trompe l'oeil* in favour of scenes and landscapes altogether more ethereal and painted in pastel colours. Most of the frescoes uncovered at Pompeii belong to the 4th style. It combines elements from the 2nd style with others from the 3rd style to produce ornate compositions.

Worth a Visit

Allow 1 day. NB: some of the houses listed may occasionally be closed for cleaning and maintenance. Open daily, Apr to Oct 8.30am-7.30pm (ticket office closes 6pm), Nov to Mar 8.30am-5pm (ticket office closes 3.30pm). Closed 1 Jan, 1 May, 25 Dec. €8.50 inclusive (valid 1 day) for Pompeii, Oplonti, Stabia and Boscoreale. €13.50 (valid 3 days) for Pompeii, Herculaneum, Oplonti, Stabia and Boscoreale. Access from Porta Marina (Via Villa dei Misteri or Piazza Esedra) or from Piazza Anfiteatro. Information desk at Porta Marina (9am-5pm). ☎ 081 53 65 154; www.pompeiisites.org

Porta Marina

This was the gateway through which the road passed to go down to the sea. There were separate gates for animals and for pedestrians.

Streets

The streets are straight and intersect at right angles. They are sunk between raised pavements and are interrupted at intervals by blocks of stone to enable pedestrians to cross without getting down from the pavement. This was particularly useful on rainy days when the roadway was awash; these stepping-stones were positioned so as to leave enough space for chariots. Fountains, of simple design, were set in square basins.

Foro★★★

The forum was the centre of the town and the setting for most of the large buildings. In this area, religious ceremonies were held, trade was carried out and justice was dispensed. The immense square, closed to traffic, was paved with broad marble flagstones and adorned with statues of past emperors. A portico surmounted by a terrace enclosed it on three sides.

The **Basilica**★★ is the largest building (67m by 25m/220ft by 82ft) in Pompeii where judicial affairs and business were conducted.

The **Tempio di Apollo**★★ is a temple dedicated to Apollo which was built before the Roman occupation and stood against the majestic background of Vesuvius. The altar was placed in front of the steps leading to the shrine *(cella)*. Facing each other are copies of the statues of Apollo and Diana found on the spot (the originals are in the Naples Museum).

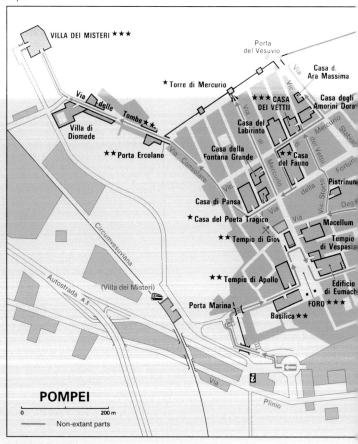

The **Tempio di Giove★★**, in keeping with tradition, has pride of place. The temple dedicated to the Capitoline Triad (Jupiter, Juno and Minerva) is flanked by two triumphal arches, formerly faced with marble.

The **Macellum** was a large covered market lined with shops. In the centre, a kiosk surrounded by pillars and crowned by a dome contained a basin used for cleaning fish.

The **Tempio di Vespasiano**, dedicated to the Emperor Vespasian, contained a marble altar adorned with a sacrificial scene.

A fine **doorway★** with a marble frame decorated with carvings of plants gives access to the **Edificio di Eumachia** (Building of Eumachia), built by the priestess Eumachia for the powerful guild of the *fullones (see below)* of which she was the patron.

Foro Triangolare★

There are several Ionic columns of a majestic propylaeum which preceded the Triangular Forum. A few vestiges of its small **Doric temple** provide rare evidence of the town's existence in the 6C BC.

Teatro Grande★

The Great Theatre was built in the 5C BC, remodelled in the Hellenistic period (200-150 BC) and again by the Romans in the 1C AD. It was an open-air theatre which could be covered by a canopy on sunny days and could hold 5 000 spectators.

Caserma dei Gladiatori

The barracks for the gladiators has a large esplanade bounded by a gateway, originally used as a foyer for the theatres.

Odeion★★

Odeums, or covered theatres, were used for concerts, oratorical displays and ballets. This held only 800 spectators. It had a wooden roof and it dates from the early days of the Roman colonisation.

Tempio d'Iside★

The cult of the Egyptian goddess Isis spread in the Hellenistic period thanks to contact with the Orient and Egypt. The small building stands on a podium in the middle of an arcaded courtyard. To the left of the temple is the *purgatorium*, a site set aside for purification ceremonies which contained water from the Nile. The pictorial decorations of the temple are housed in the Archaeological Museum in Naples.

STABIAN BATHS	
Palestra	A
Swimming pool	B
Changing room	C
Central heating	D
WOMEN'S BATHS	
Changing-rooms	e
Tepidarium	f
Caldarium	g
MEN'S BATHS	
Changing-rooms	h
Frigidarium	k
Tepidarium	l
Caldarium	m

Casa di Lucius Ceius Secundus

This is an interesting house *(casa)* with its façade faced with stucco in imitation of stone as in the 1st style *(see above)*, and with its pretty little *atrium*.

Casa del Menandro★★

This large patrician villa named after Menander, was richly decorated with paintings (4th style) and mosaics and had its own baths. Part of the building was reserved for the servants' quarters. In the *atrium* is a *lararium* (shrine to the household gods) arranged as a miniature temple in one corner. It has a remarkable peristyle with Doric columns faced with stucco, between which stands a low wall adorned with plants and animals.

The house opens onto **Via dell'Abbondanza★★**, a commercial street which is now most evocative with its shops and houses.

Casa del Criptoportico

After passing through the peristyle (note the painting in the *lararium*: Mercury with a peacock, snakes and foliage), go down to the Cryptoporticus, a wide underground passage surmounted by a fine barrel vault and lit by small windows. This type of corridor, which was very popular in Roman villas during the Empire, was used as a passage and for exercise as it was sheltered from the sun as well as from bad weather.

Fullonica Stephani★★

N° 7. This is an example of a dwelling-house converted into workshops. The clothing industry flourished in Roman times as the full, draped costume required a lot of material. In the *fullonicae,* new fabrics were finished and clothes were laundered. Several of these workshops have been uncovered in Pompeii. The *fullones* (fullers) cleaned the cloths by trampling them underfoot in vats filled with a mixture of water and soda or urine.

Termopolio di Asellina

This was a bar which also sold pre-cooked dishes *(thermopolium)*. A stone counter giving directly onto the street formed the shop front; jars embedded in the counter contained the food for sale.

Termopolio Grande★

This bar, which is similar to the previous one, has a painted *lararium*.

Casa di Trebius Valens
The inscriptions on the wall are electoral slogans. At the far end of the peristyle the polychrome fresco is in imitation of a stone wall.

Casa di Loreius Tiburtinus★
This was a rich dwelling, judging from the fine marble *impluvium*, the *triclinium* adorned with frescoes and the **decoration**★ against a white background of one of the rooms, which is among the best examples of the 4th Pompeiian style. But its most luxurious feature was the splendid **garden**★ which was laid out for water displays.

Villa di Giulia Felice★
Built just within the town boundary, it has three main parts: the dwelling, the baths which the owner opened to the public, and a section for letting, including an inn and shops. The large garden is bounded by a fine **portico**★ and embellished by a fine series of basins.

Anfiteatro★
This is the oldest Roman amphitheatre known (80 BC). It was built away from the city centre to enable easy access. On particularly hot days spectators were pro-tected from the heat by a linen drape held up by wooden poles. Alongside is the great **palestra** used as a training ground by athletes.

Necropoli fuori porta Nocera★
According to custom, tombs line one of the roads leading out of town, via the Nocera Gate.
Take the Via di Porta Nocera to return to the Via dell' Abbondanza, then turn left.

Terme Stabiane★★★
These baths, the oldest in Pompeii (2C BC), are divided into sections for men and women. The entrance is through the gymnasium (*palestra*) for athletic games, to the left of which are changing-rooms (*spogliatoio*), and a swimming pool (*piscina*).
The **women's baths** begin at the far end on the right, with changing-rooms fitted with lockers, a *tepidarium* (lukewarm bath) and a *caldarium* (hot bath). The central heating apparatus is between the men's and women's baths. The **men's baths** have large, well-preserved changing-rooms, a *frigidarium* (cold bath), a *tepidarium* and a *caldarium*. There is a fine stucco decoration on the coffered ceiling.

Lupanare
The official brothel of Pompeii is decorated with licentious subject matter, aimed at illustrating the "specialities" of the prostitutes. Graffiti on the walls describes the customers' opinions on services received.

Pistrinum
The baker's oven and flourmills.

Casa dei Vettii★★★
The Vettii brothers were rich merchants. Their dwelling, the most lavishly decor-ated in the town, is the finest example of a faithfully restored house and garden. The reroofed *atrium* opens directly onto the peristyle surrounding a delightful gar-den with statues, basins and fountains.
The **frescoes** in the *triclinium*, on the right of the peristyle, depict mythological scenes and friezes of cupids, and are among the finest from Antiquity.

Casa degli Amorini Dorati★
This house shows the refinement of the owner, who probably lived during the reign of Nero, and his taste for the theatre. The glass and gilt medallions depicting cupids (*amorini*) have deteriorated. But the building as a whole, with its remarkable peristyle with one wing raised like a stage, is well preserved. There is an obsidian mirror set in the wall near the passage between the peristyle and *atrium*.

Casa dell'Ara Massima
There are well preserved **paintings**★ (one in *trompe l'œil*).

Casa del Labirinto
One of the rooms opening onto the peristyle has a mosaic of the Labyrinth with Theseus killing the Minotaur.

Casa del Fauno★★
This vast, luxurious house had two atriums, two peristyles and dining rooms for all seasons. The bronze original of the famous statuette of the faun that adorned one of the impluviums is in the Naples Museum. The rooms contained admirable mosaics including the famous *Battle of Alexander and Darius* (Naples Museum) which covered the area between the two peristyles.

Casa della Fontana Grande
Its main feature is the large **fountain**★ (*fontana*) shaped as a niche decorated with mosaics and fragments of coloured glass in the Egyptian style.

Torre di Mercurio★
A tower on the town wall, dedicated to the god Mercury, now affords an interesting **view**★★ of the excavations.

Casa del Poeta Tragico★
This house takes its name from a mosaic now in the Naples Museum. A mosaic of a watchdog at the threshold bears the inscription *Cave Canem* (Beware of the dog).

Casa di Pansa
A very spacious house partly converted for letting.

Porta Ercolano★★
The Herculaneum Gate was the main gateway of Pompeii, with two gates for pedestrians and one for vehicles.

Via delle Tombe★★
A great melancholy feeling pervades this street lined with monumental tombs and cypresses. There are examples of all forms of Greco-Roman funerary architecture: tombs with niches, small round or square temples, altars resting on a plinth, drum-shaped mausoleums, simple semicircular seats or exedrae.

Villa di Diomede
This important dwelling dedicated to Diomedes has a loggia overlooking the garden and the swimming pool.

Villa dei Misteri★★★
Located outside the city centre this ancient patrician villa is comprised of two areas: a luxurious residential part (west) and the eastern half reserved for domestic and agricultural work and the servants' quarters. In the area inhabited by the owners, the dining room *(from the apsed room in the west of the villa, enter the tablinium, turn right into the cubiculum and right again into a room which leads into the triclimium)* contains the splendid **fresco** from which the villa derives its renown as well as its name. This vast composition, which fills the whole room, depicts against a Pompeiian red background the initiation of a young bride to the mysteries *(misteri)* of the cult of Dionysus (from the left: Child reading the rites; scenes of offerings, sacrifices and Dionysian rites; flagellation of a girl; dancing Bacchante; dressing of the bride). The mistress of this house was probably a priestess of the cult of Dionysus, which was then very popular in southern Italy. There is a fine peristyle and an underground passage *(criptoportico).*

Promontorio di **Portofino**★★★

PORTOFINO PROMONTORY

This rocky, rugged promontory offers one of the most attractive landscapes on the Italian Riviera. The coastline is dotted with small villages in sheltered bays. Part of the peninsula has been designated as a nature reserve (Parco Naturale) to protect the fauna and flora. By taking the corniche roads and the numerous footpaths the visitor can discover the secret charms of this region.

Location
Michelin map 428 J 9 – Liguria. The Portofino promontory is about 40km/24mi from Genoa, just off S 1. ▐ *Via Roma 35,* ☎ *0185 26 90 24.*
Surrounding area: see GENOVA, RIVIERA LIGURE.

Special Features

Portofino★★★
Private road with free entrance. For information on route, contact Hotel Portofino Kulm ☎ *0185 73 61. Crossing: From Rapallo, Santa Margherita, Portofino and S. Fruttuoso from* €2.58 *to* €12.39 *(round trip), Servizio Marittimo del Tigullio* ☎ *0185 28 46 70.* To reach the port which gave the peninsula its name, take the road that passes via **Santa Margherita Ligure**▵▵ *(5km/3mi)*, a fashionable seaside resort, and then the **corniche road**★★ (Strada Panoramica) which affords lovely views of the rocky coast. This small fishing village with its gaily coloured houses lies at the head of a sheltered creek. The **walk to the lighthouse**★★★ *(1hr on foot there and back)* is beautiful, especially in the evening, when the setting sun shines on the Gulf of Rapallo. Wonderful views unfold between the olive trees, yews and sea pines. From the

castle – formerly Castello San Giorgio *(take the stairway which starts near the harbour and the church of San Giorgio)* – there are splendid **views**★★★ of Portofino and the Gulf of Rapallo. Continue along the pathway to the lighthouse, from where the view extends right round the coast as far as La Spezia. *Open daily except Tue, summer 10am-6pm, winter 10am-5pm. Closed 1 Jan, Easter. €1.55. ☎ 0185 26 90 46.*

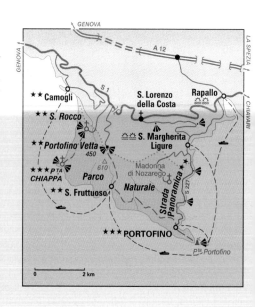

Chiesa di San Lorenzo della Costa

10km/6mi north. At Santa Margherita Ligure take the **scenic road**★★ which offers a succession of lovely views over the Gulf of Rapallo. The church of **San Lorenzo** contains a **triptych**★ (1499) by an artist from Bruges. It may have been the work of Gerard David (Gheeraert Davit) who spent some time in Genoa.

Portofino Vetta★★

14km/9mi. From this elevated site (450m/1 476ft) there is a lovely view of the peninsula and the Ligurian coast.

San Fruttuoso★★

On foot: *take the signposted footpath starting in Portofino (4hr30min there and back) or another from Portofino Vetta, but the final stages are difficult (3hr there and back).* **By boat:** *services operate from Rapallo, Santa Margherita Ligure, Portofino and Camogli.* This small village stands at the head of a narrow cove in the shadow of Monte Portofino. There is a beautiful abbey, **Abbazia di San Fruttuoso**, built from the 13C to 14C.

Belvedere di San Rocco★★

13km/8mi northwest. From the terrace beside the church there is a view of Camogli and the western coast from the headland, Punta della Chiappa, right round to Genoa. A path leads to **Punta della Chiappa**★★★ *(2hr30min there and back by a stepped footpath which starts to the right of the church).* There are unforgettable views of the peninsula and, from the chapel, of the Genoa Coast.

Camogli★★

15km/9mi northwest. Tall houses crowd round a small harbour.

Directory

Prato★★

For a long time Prato was in conflict with Florence, but in 1351 she fell under the sway of her illustrious neighbour and remained thus until the 18C. In the 14C a fortified wall in the form of a hexagon was erected around the old town.

Location

Population 172 473 – Michelin map 430 K 15 – See also The Green Guide Tuscany. Prato is only 17km/10mi from Florence. The main access roads are A 1 (Bologna-Florence), and the road that links Florence with the coast. ▯ *Piazza delle Carceri 15,* ☎ *0574 24 112.*
Surrounding area: see FIRENZE, PISTOIA.

Worth a Visit

Duomo★

The cathedral, built in the 12C and 13C and extended in later centuries, presents a harmonious blend of the Romanesque and Gothic styles. The façade owes its elegance to its lofty central part, its finely carved decoration and the graceful circular pulpit with a canopy (15C) by Michelozzo and Donatello.
The interior of the church, sober in style, has massive columns of green marble and numerous works of art: the **Capella del Sacro Cingolo** (Chapel of the Holy Girdle) is enclosed by two delicately worked bronze **screens★** and decorated with frescoes (1392-95) by Agnolo Gaddi and his pupils. The *Virgin and Child★* (1317) is by the sculptor Giovanni Pisano.
In the axial chapel are **frescoes★★** by **Filippo Lippi**. Note the *Banquet of Herod★★★* and *Salome's Dance*. Note also the marble **pulpit★** with the unusual shape of a chalice, and in a niche the moving *Virgin of the olive tree★*, a terracotta statue (1480) by Benedetto da Maiano.

Palazzo Pretorio★

This austere and massive building, a curious mixture of the Romanesque and Gothic styles, overlooks a charming small square, **Piazza del Comune**, with an elegant bronze fountain (1659) by Tacca. Three floors of the building are occupied by the **Galleria Comunale** which presents works by the 14C and 15C Tuscan school, notably an important collection of **polyptychs★**.
►►Castello dell'Imperatore, S. Maria delle Carceri, S. Francesco (frescoes★), Museo dell'Opera del Duomo (panels★ carved by Donatello).

Puglia

With the exception of the Gargano Promontory and the limestone Murge Hills which rise behind Bari, Puglia is a flat plain planted with cereals, olive trees and vines or in pasture. Away from the main tourist haunts, Puglia offers the visitor beautiful yet austere scenery, quiet beaches and some marvellous architectural gems, both religious and military.

Location

Michelin map 988 D-H 29-37. This region takes its name from the ancient Roman province of Apulia. It extends from the spur of the Italian "boot" right down to the heel, all along the Adriatic coast in the south of the country. The main access roads are A 14 from the north and A 16 from Naples.
See also BRINDISI, Promontorio del GARGANO, LECCE, TARANTO, Isole TREMITI.

Background

As early as the late 8C BC, Greeks from Laconia and Sparta founded the towns of Gallipoli, Otranto and, most significantly, Taranto on the Apulian coast. In the 5C and 4C BC Taranto was the most prosperous town in Magna Graecia. The local tribe, the Lapyges, tenaciously resisted Greek colonisation; in the 3C BC the Greek cities and the Italiots both came under Roman domination.
Taranto declined as Brindisi, a trading post facing the eastern part of the Mediterranean, flourished. The latter was linked to Rome when Trajan prolonged the Appian Way. The Roman colonisation greatly benefited this area by introduc-

Off the coast of Puglia

ing improved communications and political organisation. Christianity was firs
introduced to the area in the 3C and was strengthened in the 5C with the appear
ances of the Archangel Michael at Monte Sant'Angelo *(see p 213)*.

The area was occupied successively by the Byzantines, Lombards and Arabs befor
Puglia sought help in the 11C from the Normans who then dominated the entir
area. Puglia greatly increased its trade and its architectural heritage thanks to th
early Crusades, most of which embarked from the Apulian ports, and to the reig
of Roger II of Sicily (1095-1154).

It was under the Emperor Frederick II of Hohenstaufen, an unusual, authoritaria
and cruel character, an atheist but a cultured and highly intelligent person, that th
region knew a period of splendour in the first-half of the 13C. The sovereign wa
captivated by the country and chose to reside here. This favoured trade, unifica
tion and the establishment of an efficient administration. His son Manfred con
tinued his work but had to submit to Charles of Anjou in 1266. The French lost inter
est in the region and it began to lose its vitality and prestige. Puglia then passed t
the Aragon dynasty who, by isolating the region, greatly contributed to its decline.

After a period of Austrian domination, the Bourbons of Naples improved to som
small extent the misery and stagnation to which the country had been reduced by
the Spanish rulers. The brief Napoleonic period followed a similar policy. In 186
Puglia was united with the rest of unified Italy. During the 20C Puglia progressively
emerged from the difficult position of inferiority which was prevalent throughou
the rest of the Italian south or Mezzogiorno. The region has achieved a certai
independence and vigour and now claims two thriving industrial towns, Tarant
and Lecce, a Trade Fair in Bari and several newly founded universities.

TOURING PUGLIA

Sights given in alphabetical order.

Altamura

This large market town in the Murge Hills has an old quarter on a hilltop. The 13C
Duomo in the transitional Romanesque-Gothic style forms the focal point at th
upper end of the main street. The façade is crowned with two bulbous bell towers
has 16C additions, and is pierced by a delicately decorated 13C **rose window★** an
a richly sculptured 14C-15C **doorway★**.

Bari *see BARI*

Barletta

In the 12C and 13C the town of Barletta was an embarkation port for the Cru
sades and many military or hospitaller
Orders chose this as the site for an institution.

Now a commercial and agricultural
centre, the town has a fine historic nucleus comprising several medieval religious and secular buildings. The symbol of the town is a statue dating back
to the Roman era. The **Colosso★★** or
Statua di Eraclio is a gigantic statue
over 4.5m/15ft tall of a Byzantine emperor whose identity is uncertain
(Valentinian I?). Probably 4C, this
work is of interest as it marks the transition from decadent Roman to early
Christian art. The stiffness of the figure
is offset by the intense expression.

THE BARLETTA CHALLENGE

In 1503 the town, which was held by the Spanish,
was besieged by French troops. The Italians,
accused of cowardice by a French prisoner, issued
a challenge, following which 13 Italian knights led
by Ettore Fieramosca met and defeated 13 French
knights in single combat.

In the 19C this deed was deemed a fine example
of patriotism and Ettore Fieramosca became a
heroic figure. In 1833 the author Massimo
d'Azeglio based a novel on this event, *Ettore
Fieramosca or the Tournament of Barletta*
(Ettore Fieramosca o la disfida di Barletta).

Directory

WHERE TO EAT

• Budget

Trattoria Iolanda – *Via Montanara 2 – 73014 Lucugnano – 12km/7mi north of Santa Maria di Leuca on S 275, then turn left* – ☎ *0833 78 41 64 – Closed Wed (except 16 Jun-Sep)* – ✂ – *Book* – *€13/18*. You have been warned: there's no sign-board, the striped awning is made out of plastic, the bread is served in baskets made of the same material and you have no say in what you choose to eat. It's a sort of initiation ritual but worth the effort required. There are very few establishments like this left...

Trattoria delle Ruote – *Via Monticello 1 – 74015 Martina Franca – 4.5km/3mi east of Martina Franca* – ☎ *080 48 37 473 – Closed Mon* – ✂ ✸ – *Book* – *€18.08/25.82*. This trattoria is housed in a 19C trullo which has been modernised. The proprietor and his family are most welcoming and offer good, homely food which is steeped in tradition. Agricultural implements and wheels hang on the walls.

U.P.E.P.I.D.D.E. – *Corso Cavour, ang. Trapp. Carmine – 70037 Ruvo di Puglia* – ☎ *080 36 13 879 – Closed Mon, 10 Jul-10 Aug* – *€18/28*. The cuisine is traditional but has a very distinctive personal touch. Flame-grilled dishes are the house speciality. With their uneven ceilings and stone walls, the dining rooms have a cosy feel to them and are very atmospheric. Good selection of regional and other Italian wines.

Osteria del Tempo Perso – *Via Tanzarella Vitale 47 – 72017 Ostuni* – ☎ *0831 30 33 20 – Closed Mon, lunchtime (except Sun and public holidays), 10-31 Jan* – *Book* – *€20/37*. Have you ever eaten in a cave? Well, this is as good a time as any. The authentic, traditional food complements the rustic setting beautifully. There is also a second dining room which, while less "troglodytic", has a certain rusticity. Farm workers' tools (and religious items!) decorate the walls.

Baccosteria – *Via San Giorgio 5 – 70051 Barletta* – ☎ *0883 53 40 00 – Closed Mon, Sun evenings, 1-20 Aug* – ◎ – *Book* – *€22/34*. Fortunately for us, nostalgia got the better of this dynamic American couple and they returned to their homeland to set up a rather smart bistro. Specialities include spaghetti with sea urchins (ricci di mare) and squid (calamari) stuffed with ricotta cheese. The glass floor that allows diners to see into the wine cellar below is a nice touch.

• Moderate

Da Mimì – *Via del Mare – 73053 Patù – 5km/3mi north of Santa Maria di Leuca* – ☎ *0833 76 78 61 – Closed Nov – Book* – *€22.47/36.93*. Panoramic clifftop setting, with lovely shady terrace overlooking the sea. Fish dishes are served here, prepared with fresh, good quality ingredients. Very reasonable prices.

WHERE TO STAY

• Budget

Agriturismo Curatori – *Via Conchia 227, Contrada Cristo delle Zolle – 70043 Monopoli – 15km/9mi northeast of Castellana Grotte on S 377* – ☎ *080 77 74 72 – Fax 080 77 74 72 – 2 dbl rm €51.65* ☕. An 18C farm, surrounded by old olive trees. Accommodation extends to studios with kitchens and simple rooms (lovely wrought-iron beds). Cosy, family atmosphere. Meals on request, prepared with produce made on the farm.

• Moderate

Hotel Rosa Antico – *Strada statale 16 – 73028 Otranto* – ☎ *0836 80 15 63 – Fax 0836 80 15 63* – 🅿 ◎ – *12 rm €46.48/82.63* ☕. More like staying at a friend's house than going to a hotel, such is the warmth of the welcome you are likely to receive. The rooms are simple but attractive, with great attention paid to detail. Delicious breakfasts, generous portions.

Hotel Lo Scoglio – *On a small islet which you can get to by car – 73010 Porto Cesareo – 30km/18mi north of Gallipoli* – ☎ *0833 56 90 79 – Fax 0833 56 90 78* – 🅿 ♿ – *47 rm €51.65/82.63* ☕ – *Restaurant €18/34*. Situated on two islets which are linked to the coast by a wharf. The hotel is tucked away among luscious vegetation in a flower-filled garden, almost entirely surrounded by the sea. Rather like being on a tropical island! If it is a relaxing holiday you are after, this is the place to come.

Hotel Novecento – *Contrada Ramunno – 72017 Ostuni – 1.5km/1mi south of Ostuni* – ☎ *0831 30 56 66 – Fax 0831 30 56 68* – 🅿 🛳 ◎ – *16 rm €61.97/103.29* ☕ – *Rest €15.49/25.82*. A real oasis of peace and quiet. Although it has been modernised, this splendid villa has retained its former charms and ambience. Half- and full-board rates available.

Hotel Orsa Maggiore – *Coastal road towards Santa Cesarea Terme 303 – 73030 Castro Marina – 18km/11mi south of Otranto on S 173* – ☎ *0836 94 70 28 – Fax 0836 94 77 66* – 🅿 ◎ – *30 rm €70/93* ☕ – *Restaurant €18/30*. This hotel is situated near the famous Grotta di Zinzulusa, overlooking the sea from its clifftop position. Wonderful views which lift the spirit. Very reasonably priced meals: the cooking is at its best in the fish dishes. Simple rooms, with panoramic views.

Grand Hotel D'Aragona – *Strada provinciale, towards Cozze – 70014 Conversano – 10km/6mi northwest of Castellana Grotte on S 634* – ☎ *080 49 52 344 – Fax 080 49 54 265* – 🅿 🛳 ◎ – *68 rm from €80.05* – ☕ *€6.20* – *Restaurant €23/36*. A little off the beaten track but you are unlikely to be disappointed. There are bathing facilities to suit everybody: experienced swimmers, beginners and children are all catered for. Rooms are spacious with modern furnishings. Large, well-tended garden, ideal for relaxing.

SHOPPING

The little terracotta whistles *(figuli)* with their colourful designs make lovely gifts. They are produced in Rutigliano, near Bari.

The statue stands in front of the basilica of **San Sepolcro** which dates from the 12C-14C and possesses a fine **reliquary★**, with Limoges enamels on the base.

The **Castello★** is an imposing fortress built by the Emperor Frederick II of Hohenstaufen and later remodelled, especially by Charles V in the 16C. The latter is responsible for its curious plan with four pointed corner bastions; inside are two large superimposed semicircular blockhouses. The castle houses a **pinacoteca** exhibiting a fine **collection★** of paintings by the local artist, Giuseppe de Nittis (1846-84), who worked mainly in Paris. *Open May to Sep daily, 9am-1pm and 4-8pm, rest of year daily, 9am-1pm and 3-7pm. Closed 1 Jan, 1 May, 25 Dec. €2.58. ☎ 0883 57 86 20.*

In Via Cialdini, on the ground floor of the 14C Palazzo di Don Diego de Mendoza is the **cellar** where the famous Barletta challenge, **la disfida di Barletta**, was issued. Further along is the 17C **Palazzo della Marra**; its façade is richly decorated in the Baroque style.

Bitonto

17km/11mi southwest of Bari. Set amid a sea of olive groves, this small town has a fine **Duomo★** which strongly resembles those in Trani and Bari. The three-part façade is enlivened by large, richly sculptured openings. On the south side an elegant gallery with small columns surmounts the ground-floor arcade. Inside, columns with fine capitals support a gallery with triple openings. The fine pulpit dates from 1229.

Brindisi *see BRINDISI*

Canosa di Puglia

23km/14mi southwest of Barletta. The inhabitants of this Greek, then Roman, city were known for their ceramic vases *(askoi)*. The 11C Romanesque **Duomo** which shows a certain Byzantine influence, was remodelled in the 17C following an earthquake. The façade is 19C. Inside note the 11C episcopal throne and the **tomb★** of Bohemond, Prince of Antioch (d 1111), the son of Robert Guiscard (1015-85), a Norman adventurer who campaigned in southern Italy. This curious mausoleum is in the form of a domed cube. In the Via Cadorna there are three 4C BC hypogea, the **Ipogei Lagrasta,** and to the right of the Andria road stand the remains of the palaeo-Christian basilica of **San Leucio** which was itself built on the site of a Roman temple. *Ipogei: For information on opening times ☎ 0883 66 21 83.*

Canne della Battaglia

12km/8mi southwest of Barletta. The strategic importance of the site in late Antiquity is evidenced by a famous battle in AD 216 when the Carthaginians led by Hannibal won a decisive victory over the Roman army under the leadership of Scipio. There are ruins of a medieval necropolis and of an Apulian village; and on the opposite slope, a stronghold where the main Roman axis, the *decumanus*, intersected by streets *(cardi)* is still visible, as well as the remains of a medieval basilica and of a Norman castle.

Castel del Monte★★

29km/18mi southeast of Barletta. (♿) *Open daily, Mar-Sep 10am-1.30pm and 2.30-7.30pm, rest of year 9am-1.30pm and 2.30-6.30pm (ticket office closes 30min early). Closed 1 Jan, 1 May, 25 Dec. €3.10.☎ 080 52 86 238.*

The Emperor Frederick II of Hohenstaufen built this powerful castle c 1240. It stands, proud and solitary, on the summit of one of the Murge Hills. With its octagonal plan the Castel del Monte is the sole exception in a series of 200 quadrilateral fortresses built by this sovereign on his return from the Crusades. The octagonal plan of the fortress, built in a pale-coloured stone, is strengthened at each of its angles by an octagonal tower (24m/79ft tall). The overall plan combines balance, logic and strict planning with delicate decoration.

The superb Gothic gateway takes the form of an ancient triumphal arch and opens into the inner courtyard. Arranged around this at ground-floor level are eight vast trapezoidal chambers with pointed vaulting. Above, the eight identical rooms are lit by delicately ornamented windows. The arrangement of the water conduits is quite ingenious: water runs from the rooftops into the cisterns of the towers and is then piped into the different rooms.

Grotte di Castellana★★★

40km/25mi southeast of Bari, at Castellana-Grotte. Guided tours only, also in English, French and German at scheduled times. Short tour (1km, approx 1hr): Apr to Nov, 8.30am-1pm and 2.30-7pm (departs hourly). €7.75. Long tour to Grotta Bianca (3km, 2hr): same period 9am-12pm and 3-6pm (departs hourly). €12.91. Tour not recommended for heart patients. For information ☎ 800 21 39 76 or 080 49 98 211.

This network of caves was created by the underground rivers which filter down through the limestone soil of the Murge Hills. The vast chambers were discovered in 1938 and have an infinite variety of magnificent concretions: curtain as well as richly coloured stalactites and stalagmites. This grand spectacle reaches a climax at the White Cave, **Grotta Bianca★★★**, which glistens with calcite crystals.

Foggia

Town plan in the Michelin Atlas Italy. Foggia is set in the heart of a vast cereal-growing plain, the Tavoliere. This trading and industrial centre was founded in 1050 by the Norman conqueror, Robert Guiscard. In 1223 the Emperor Frederick II of Hohenstaufen built a castle which has now disappeared.

The present **Duomo** incorporates parts of an earlier building (13C), notably the lower walls with some blind arcading and a sculptured cornice above, and the crypt. This earlier structure, which was destroyed by the 1731 earthquake, has been rebuilt.

Galatina

This craft and wine-making centre stands on the flat and stony Salento Peninsula. The cathedral with its Baroque façade recalls the gracious style of Lecce. The 14C church of **Santa Caterina di Alessandria★**, commissioned by Raimondello del Balzo Orsini, is decorated with a marvellous cycle of **frescoes★** by several 15C artists. Many of the women depicted in the frescoes bear the features of Maria d'Enghien, Raimondello's wife. In the nave: scenes of the Apocalypse (first segment); Genesis (second); scenes from the life of Christ (third). In the south aisle: the Life of the Virgin. In the chancel: Scenes from the life of St Catherine. The octagonal apse with its ribbed vaulting dates from 1455-60.

Galatone

24km/15mi southwest of Lecce. The **church of the Crocifisso della Pietà** has a lovely **façade★** embellished in the Baroque style typical of the Lecce area. The sumptuous interior decoration includes gilding and stucco ornamentation.

Gallipoli☖

The old town with its attractive small port is set on an island and linked to the modern town by a bridge. Note the imposing **castle**, rebuilt in the 16C on the site of an Angevin fortress, and the **cathedral** with a Baroque façade which recalls Lecce (the interior contains many paintings of the 17C and 18C). Along the Riviera, which follows the outline of the old city wall, stands the church **della Purità**; the **interior★** is sumptuously decorated with ornate stuccowork, some fine 18C paintings and a remarkable ceramic floor.

Promontorio del Gargano★★★ *see Promontorio del GARGANO*

Gioia del Colle

In the centre of the town stands the massive **Norman castle** built on the site of a Byzantine fortress and very much foreshadowing the lines of the castles erected by Frederick II of Hohenstaufen in Puglia. From the square courtyard there is access to the ground floor rooms which house the Archaeological Museum (note the fine 4C BC Apulian red-figure bowl depicting a burial temple at the centre), as well as the old bakery and prison. On the upper storey the **Throne room**, illuminated by a mullioned opening, is notable for its large round arch. (&) *Open daily except Mon, 8.30am-7.30pm. Closed 1 Jan, 1 May, 25 Dec. ☎ 080 34 81 305.*

Lecce★★ *see LECCE*

Lucera

Already important in Roman times, Lucera was ceded by the Emperor Frederick II of Hohenstaufen to the Saracens of Sicily, who in turn were expelled by Charles II of Anjou. Lucera has an imposing 13C **fortress★** built by the Angevins, which affords a fine **panorama★** of the Tavoliere Plain. The historic centre is dominated by the 14C **Duomo** which overlooks a fine square, the focal point of the town. Nearby stands another imposing Romanesque church with sober architectural lines which is dedicated to St Francis of Assisi but is linked with San Francesco Fasani who lived in the area in the 18C and restored the building. Further along, a fine palace, unfortunately in poor condition, houses the **Museo Civico G. Fiorelli** which displays a marble **Venus★**, a Roman replica of a model by the school of Praxiteles. *Open Tue-Sat, 9am-1pm and 4-7pm, Sun and hols, 9am-1pm. No charge. ☎ 0881 54 70 41.*

Santa Maria di Leuca

A short distance from the centre stands a well-preserved **Roman amphitheatre★** built during Augustus' reign.

Manfredonia⌂

Manfred, the son of the Emperor Frederick II of Hohenstaufen, founded the port in the 13C. It is guarded by a fine 13C **castle** and a bastion pierced with pointed openings. The church of **Santa Maria di Siponto★** *(3km/2mi south by S 89)* is an elegant 11C building in the Romanesque style which shows influences both Oriental (square plan and terraced roof hiding the dome), and Pisan (blind arcades with columns enclosing lozenges).

The late-11C church of **San Leonardo** *(beyond the church of Santa Maria, take the Foggia road to the right)* has a fine delicately sculptured **doorway★** dating from the early 13C.

Ostuni★

35km/22mi west of Brindisi. This large market town now spreads over several hill-sides. At the centre of the old town with its white alleyways and Aragonese ramparts stands the late-15C **Cattedrale** which has both Romanesque and Gothic elements. The **façade★** is crowned by an unusual pattern of concave (central section) and convex (side sections) lines enhanced by an arched decoration. In the centre there is a beautiful **rose window★** with complex symbolism relating to the passage of time: 24 external arcades, standing for the hours in a day, 12 internal ones standing for the months of the year, while Christ, in the centre, is surrounded by seven angels' heads which stand for the days of the week. Nearby the church of San Vito (or Santa Maria Maddalena dei Pazzi) houses a small **archaeological museum** which displays the plaster cast of **Delia**, a young woman who lived about 25 000 years ago and died shortly before childbirth (her skeleton shows the foetus' tiny bones). (⌂) *Open Tue-Sat 9am-1pm, Tue and Thu also 3.30-7pm, Sun and hols 10am-12.30pm and 3.30-7pm. Closed Mon. €1.55.* ☎ *0831 33 63 83.*

Otranto

Otranto lies on the Adriatic coast of the "heel" of the peninsula. This fishing port was once capital of "Terra d'Otranto", the last remaining Byzantine stronghold, and resisted the Lombards and then the Normans for some considerable time. In the 15C when the town was besieged by the troops of the Turkish ruler Mohammed II the townspeople took refuge in the cathedral where they were massacred. Survivors were taken prisoner and killed on the summit of a hill, Colle della Minerva, where a sanctuary was built to the memory of the martyrs. Greek influence has been so strong in the "Terra d'Otranto" that even today inhabitants speak a dialect which is very similar to Greek.

Citta Vecchia – There is a good view of the old town from the northeast pier; to the left is the 15C **Castello Aragonese,** trapezoidal in form and flanked by massive cylindrical towers. To reach this stronghold perched on the clifftop pass through the gateways Porta di Terra and the 15C Porta Alfonsina.

Cattedrale★ – This 12C cathedral was altered in the late 15C. The interior, with Classical columns separating the nave from the two aisles, is remarkable for its aston-ishing mosaic **floor** which was executed between 1163 and 1165 by Pantaleone, a priest. The decoration has simple, almost primitive patterns but the vivacity of the figures' poses and attitudes, the freshness of the colours and variety of symbols make this a fascinating illustrated story. The central nave portrays the Tree of Life which is held up by two Indian elephants. The tree's outstretched branches embrace bibli-cal scenes, creatures from a medieval bestiary, heroes of courtly poems, mythological images and the cycle of months and astrological signs. This pattern is taken up at the end of the two aisles with two other trees and representations of Paradise and Hell on the left and biblical and mythological figures on the right. Equally interesting is the vast **crypt** which is divided into five aisles and sustained by a veritable forest of Ancient capitals (Classical, Byzantine and Romanesque).

Chiesetta di San Pietro – Erected between the 9C and 10C this Byzantine-style church (built in the form of a Greek cross within a square and with a central dome on pendentives) has fine frescoes of the same period; unfortunately these are in very poor condition.

The coast to the south★ – Between Otranto and **Santa Maria di Leuca** *(51km/32mi)* the road offers fine views of this wild and indented coastline. At the head of an inlet is a cave, **Grotta Zinzulusa**, with concretions and two lakes, one salt water and the other fresh, which are inhabited by rare marine species. *Open daily, mid-Jul to mid-Sep 9.30am-7pm, rest of year 10am-4pm. Guided tours only (20min), no tours when sea is rough. €2.60. ☎ 0836 94 38 12; www.castro.it*

Ruvo di Puglia

34km/21mi west of Bari. On the edge of the Murge Hills, Ruvo has an Apulian-style Romanesque **cathedral★** with a sober façade embellished by a rose window, a twin opening, a sculptured doorway and at the very top a frieze of arches. Inside the lofty nave, tall arches carry a deep cornice supported by sculptured corbels. The **Museo Archeologico Jatta** has a fine collection of Attic, Italic and Apulian **vases★**. Of these the superb **Crater of Talos★★**, a red-figured vase with a black background, is particularly notable. *Open daily, 8.30am-1.30pm, Sat also 2.30-7.30pm. Closed 1 Jan, 1 May, 25 Dec. No charge. ☎ 080 36 12 848.*

Take Via De Gaspari, with its 16C clock tower, the Torre dell'Orologio – opposite is the Renaissance Palazzo Caputi – to reach Piazza Matteotti which is flanked by fine palaces and the ruins of a medieval castle.

San Giovanni Rotondo

43km/27mi northeast of Foggia on S 89 and S 272. This is a site of pilgrimage dear to myriad devotees of **Padre Pio** (1887-1968). The Capuchin monk from **Pietrelcina**, near Benevento, was ordained and lived here. In 1918 Stigmata appeared on his body which disappeared on his death. He was canonised in 2002.

Trani

This wine-growing town has an ancient port surrounded by old houses. The 11C-13C Romanesque **cathedral★★** is one of the finest in Puglia and is dedicated to St Nicholas the Pilgrim, a humble Greek shepherd who arrived in Trani on the back of a dolphin.

Blind arcades encircle the building and there is a fine **bronze door★** which was cast in 1180. Beyond the lofty transept the chancel has a delicately decorated window. To the south rises the bell tower. Inside, one detects a strong Norman influence. The nave and aisles are slightly raised as they are built over two immense crypts, the lower of which is a forest of ancient columns. The upper church is well lit but severe with slender twin columns carrying the main arches and an elegant gallery with triple openings.

From the **public gardens★** to the east of the port there is an attractive view of the old town and its tall cathedral. The **castle** (restored) on the seashore was built by Frederick II.

Troia

17km/11mi southwest of Foggia. This agricultural market town is well situated on a hilltop overlooking the Tavoliere plain. The Romanesque **cathedral** in the Apulian style was begun in the 11C and completed two centuries later. The façade is embellished with blind arcading and a lovely **rose window★**. A fine 12C **bronze door★** in the Byzantine tradition opens into the nave and two aisles separated by columns with finely worked capitals. The north doorway has a sculptured **tympanum** depicting Christ flanked by two angels.

Taranto★ *see TARANTO*

Isole Tremiti★ *see Isole TREMITI*

Terra dei Trulli★★★

This region extending between Fassano, Ostuni, Martina Franca and Alberobello takes its name from the very curious buildings, the *trulli*, which are to be found almost everywhere. These square structures have conical roofs covered with *chiancarelle*, local grey limestone roof slabs. Originally built without using mortar, the walls and the edges of the roof are whitewashed. They are crowned with differently shaped pinnacles, each with a magical significance. Each dome corresponds to a room and each abode usually comprises three or four *trulli*. A tall chimney crowns the side of the building. The external staircase leads to the attic. The doorway stands in a recessed arch surmounted by a triangular gable. Inside, the rooms are domed.

The conical roofs of the trulli: Alberobello

Alberobello★★★ – This small town has an entire district of *trulli* (about 1 400) which often abut one another. They spread over the hillside to the south of the town (Zona Monumentale, Rioni Monti and Aia Piccola). On the hilltop stands the church of **Sant'Antonio** also in the form of a *trullo (take Via Monte Sant'Angelo)*. Inside, the transept crossing is covered with a dome, similar to those in the *trulli*.

It is possible to visit some of these strange dwellings: from the rooftops there is often a good view of the site. A good example can be visited at the **Museo del Territorio** (in the new quarter, Piazza XXVII Maggio), a large 18C *trullo* which is now used for exhibitions. The **Trullo Sovrano★**, a two-storeyed *trullo*, the largest in Alberobello, stands near the principal church on Piazza Sacramento. Built in the mid-18C it has a total of 12 cones and has preserved enough of its furnishings for it to be possible to make out what the various rooms were used for. (&) *Open daily, 10am-7.15pm. €1.50. Closed 25 Dec.* ☎ *0335 80 32 082*

Locorotondo – This town takes its name from the layout of its alleyways which wind in concentric circles (*loco rotondo:* round place) around the hill on which it is set. Buildings of note in the **historic centre★** include the neo-Classical church of San Giorgio and the church of Santa Maria la Greca whose façade is adorned with a fine Gothic rose window.

The road from Locorotondo to Martina Franca follows the **Valle d'Itria★★**, a vast and fertile plain planted with vines and olive trees and dotted with *trulli*.

Martina Franca★ – This white city rises on a hilltop in the Murge Hills. The architecture of the old town, girdled by its ramparts, is an attractive combination of the Baroque and Rococo styles.

The pleasant **Piazza Roma** is bordered by the former **Palazzo Ducale** (1668) whose principal floor is enriched by beautiful 18C frescoes. *Open Mon-Sat, 9am-1pm and 3-7pm, Sun and hols 9am-12pm. No charge.* ☎ *080 48 36 252.*

Make for Corso Vittorio Emanuele which leads to Piazza del Plebiscito, dominated by the white façade of the collegiate church of **San Martino**. The saint's image is depicted in the high reliefs above the doorway. Inside, the high altar (1773) is flanked by two fine marble statues portraying Hope and Charity. The adjacent square, Piazza Maria Immacolata, has attractive arcades and leads into **Via Cavour★** which is lined by numerous Baroque palaces. Nearby, in Via Principe Umberto, the church of San Domenico has a lovely Baroque façade.

Ravenna ★★★

In the peaceful provincial-looking town of Ravenna, the sober exteriors of its buildings belie the wealth of riches accumulated initially when Ravenna was the capital of the Western Empire and later when it was an Exarchate of Byzantium. The mosaics which adorn the city's ecclesiastical buildings are breathtakingly beautiful in the brightness of their colours, richness of decoration and powerful symbolism which evokes a sense of great spirituality.

Location

Population 138 418 – Michelin map 429, 430 I 18. Ravenna lies south of the Po Delta which is crossed by S 309. Other access roads include A 14: exit just after the junction for Imola. 🚹 *Via Salara 8/12,* ☎ *0544 35 404.*
Surrounding area: see DELTA DEL PO, RIMINI.

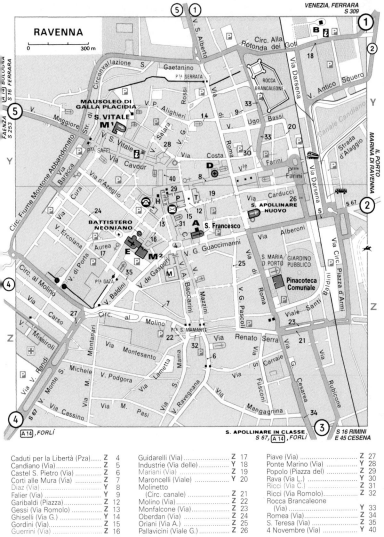

Directory

WHERE TO EAT

• *Budget*

Ca' de' Vén – *Via C. Ricci 24 –*
☎ *0544 30 163 – Closed Mon – ⚞ – Book –*
€13/18. Once the smartest grocer's shop in
Ravenna – with origins dating back to 1876 –
now a trattoria-wine bar where diners are
seated at long wooden tables. The menu
offers mainly cold dishes (although there are a
handful of cooked dishes). Renowned for its
sandwiches and particularly its wonderful
piadine (toasted sandwiches), a regional
speciality. Good selection of Italian wines.

WHERE TO STAY

• *Budget*

Casa di accoglienza Galletti Abbiosi –
Via di Roma 140 – ☎ *0544 21 51 27 –*

Fax 0544 21 11 96 –
info@ostellora.org – ♿ *– 70 beds*
€25.82 ☐. This 19C palazzo has been
restored to its former glory. One of the best
features is the wonderful staircase up to the
rooms which tend to be rather plain and
functional (although some have a frescoed
ceiling!). Popular with university students in
winter, but you should not have a problem
the rest of the year.

Hotel Ravenna – *Via Maroncelli 12 –*
☎ *0544 21 22 04 – Fax 0544 21 20 77 –*
🅿 *– 26 rm €30.99/56.81.* This well-
maintained, home-from-home hotel would
appeal to those not wanting to spend a
fortune but looking for value for money.
Simple, uncluttered rooms. Does not serve
breakfast.

Background

After the division of the Empire in AD 395 by Theodosius, Rome, already in decline, was abandoned in AD 404 by the Emperor Honorius who made Ravenna the capital of the Roman Empire. Honorius' sister, **Galla Placidia**, governed the Western Empire with pomp and splendour before the barbarian invasions brought the Ostrogoth kings Odoacer (476-93) and **Theodoric** (493-526) to Ravenna; they embellished Ravenna in their turn. The strategic location of Ravenna's port, Classis, on the Adriatic sea facing the Greek world, inevitably led to trading with Byzantium which had become the Imperial capital in 476. Ravenna came under Byzantine rule in 540 in the reign of the **Emperor Justinian** (482-565), and was administered by Exarchs. From then on Ravenna exercised considerable influence over a large part of the Italian peninsula.

Special Features

THE MOSAICS

The oldest mosaics are in the Neonian Baptistery and the Tomb of Galla Placidia (5C). Next in chronological order are those adorning the Baptistery of the Arians, St Apollinaris the New, St Vitalis, and finally St Apollinaris in Classe (6C). The mosaic heritage of the city combines the two great schools of the Ancient world: The Hellenic-Roman School, characterised by a realistic rendition of figure and landscape, and the Byzantine School whose rarefied and stylised figures seem to be fixed on their gold background. In 1996 these early Christian monuments of Ravenna were included in UNESCO's World Heritage List.

The mosaics in St Andrew's Chapel: the Museo Arcivescovile

Visit – *Below are the opening times for the buildings with mosaics. Basilica di S. Vitale, Mausoleo di Galla Placidia, Battistero Neoniano, Museo Arcivescovile and Basilica di S. Apollinare Nuovo: Open daily, Apr to Sep 9am-7pm, Mar and Oct 9am-5.30pm, rest of year 9am-4.30pm. Closed 1 Jan, 25 Dec. €6 including all diocesan monuments in Ravenna.* ☎ *0544 21 81 58.*
Battistero degli Ariani: ♿ *Open daily, 8.30am-7.30pm. No charge.* ☎ *0544 34 424.*
Museo Nazionale: ♿ *Open daily, 8.30am-7.30pm (ticket office closes 7pm). Closed 1 Jan, 1 May, 25 Dec. €4; €5 including Mausoleo di Teodorico; €6.50 including Mausoleo di Teodorico and S. Apollinare in Classe.* ☎ *0544 34 057.*
S. Apollinare in Classe: Open daily, 8.30am-7.30pm (ticket office closes 7pm) €2. €5 including Museo Nazionale; €6.50 including Museo Nazionale and Mausoleo di Teodorico ☎ *0544 47 36 12.*

Basilica di San Vitale★★★

Access to the basilica affords a view of the fine recomposed **fresco** by Pietro da Rimini (c 1330), originally in the Church of Santa Chiara. Consecrated in 547 by Archbishop Maximian, the basilica is an architectural masterpiece; the splendour, originality and light effects are typical features of the later period of Ancient art. The church, dedicated to St Vitalis, has an octagonal plan, two storeys of concave exedrae encircled by an ambulatory and a deep apse. The richly decorated interior is dazzling: precious marbles, splendidly carved Byzantine capitals, frescoes and especially the **mosaics** of the apse with their brilliant colours. The chancel is adorned with sacrificial scenes from the Old Testament; on the side walls of the apse are wonderful groups representing the **Empress Theodora** with her retinue and the **Emperor Justinian** attended by his court. These works display the splendour, hieratic power and strong outlines which are typical of Byzantine art. On the ceiling *Christ in Majesty* is enthroned between St Vitalis and Bishop Ecclesio (on the right), the founder of the church.

Mausoleo di Galla Placidia★★★

This mid-5C mausoleum in the form of a Latin cross has a great architectural harmony and is embellished by wonderful mosaics. The vaulting, shining with stellar and floral motifs, and the dome are painted a deep blue whose magic is enhanced by the shadowy light created by the alabaster windows. On the tympanum and pendentives the symbolic scenes are full of serenity, in particular the idyllic Good Shepherd, on the west wall. The sarcophagi in the projecting arms of the mausoleum were made to house Galla Placidia and her family.

The Benedictine monastery adjacent to the basilica houses the **Museo Nazionale** with displays of late-Roman and palaeo-Christian artefacts, textiles, ivories, Cretan-Venetian icons and mosaics.

Battistero Neoniano (or degli Ortodossi)★

The baptistery, erected in the 5C by Bishop Neoni, is also known as the Orthodox Baptistery in contrast to the Arian baptistery erected by the Goth Theodoric. It has an octagonal plan and comprises two orders of arcades supporting the vault which is covered in splendid mosaics: in the dome there is a portrayal of the *Baptism of Christ* accompanied by the Apostles; the lower section portrays eight small temples with altars and thrones surmounted by the cross, an Eastern iconography which refers to the preparation of the Almighty's throne for the Last Judgement. Around the side windows there are Byzantine low relief sculptures depicting the prophets.

> ### What is Arianism?
> The spread of Arianism began in the 4C following the preaching of the Alexandrian priest Arius (280-336). The Arian heresy maintained that Christ was not fully divine. Condemned by the Council of Nicaea in 325, Arianism flourished in the East in the 4C and among Goths, Vandals and Lombards until the 6C.

Museo Arcivescovile

The Episcopal Palace museum displays a small lapidary collection and Archbishop Maximian's **throne★★** (6C), a masterpiece in carved ivory. The **Capella di Sant'Andrea★** contains remarkable mosaics.

Battistero degli Ariani

The **Arians' Baptistery** was built by the Goth Theodoric in the 6C. The dome is decorated with fine **mosaics** which make use of the same iconography, if a little less elegantly, as the Neoniano Baptistery.

Basilica di Sant'Apollinare Nuovo★★

Erected between 493 and 526 by Theodoric, probably as a Palatine church, St Apollinaris is divided into a nave and two aisles articulated by beautifully crafted columns in Greek marble with Corinthian capitals. The north and south walls are decorated with a series of **mosaics** on a gold background distributed over three sections: the upper sections date from Theodoric's reign while the lower section was remodelled under Justinian who eliminated any reference to Arianism. On both sides the upper registry portrays Scenes from the Life of Christ, inserted into a "naturalistic" background which still shows a Greco-Roman influence. In the middle section between the large windows are representations of saints and prophets. The lower registry on the south side shows a **Procession of martyrs** leaving Theodoric's palace led by St Martin making their way towards Christ the King. The drapes of the sumptuous palace replace the previous portrayals of Theodoric's dignitaries; of these only the spectral hands on the columns remain. The opposite side shows a **Procession of virgins** led by the Magi leaving the city of Ravenna and the port of Classis with its three anchored ships. Their colourful, dynamic appearance makes a notable contrast with the measured, hieratic procession of martyrs. Around the figure of Christ observe the tender portrayal of the Virgin and Child surrounded by angels.

Basilica di Sant'Apollinare in Classe★★

5km/3mi south. Leave Ravenna by S 67.

The basilica stands in open country not far from the sea. The basilica was begun in 534 and consecrated in 549; a cylindrical campanile was added in the 11C.

The majestic interior is composed of a nave and two aisles separated by arches on marble columns with splendid Corinthian capitals. In the aisles lie superb Christian sarcophagi (5C-8C). The triumphal arch and apse feature magnificent 6C-7C **mosaics** with a marked freedom and simplicity of composition and a lovely harmony of colour. The triumphal arch shows Christ the Saviour surrounded by symbols representing the Evangelists; underneath there are two groups of six lambs (the Apostles) leaving two towered cities (Bethlehem and Jerusalem). The vaulting of the apse shows the Transfiguration: dominated by the hand of God, the cross bearing an image of Christ stands out, with its surrounding starry sky. At the ends of the arms the Greek letters alpha and omega indicate that Christ is the beginning and the end. There are depictions of the prophets Moses and Elijah; the three sheep represent St Peter, St James and St John, witnesses of the Transfiguration. Below there is a charming portrayal of a meadow with the figure of Apollinaris surrounded by his sheep (the flock of the faithful).

Worth a Visit

Mausoleo di Teodorico★

Open daily, summer 8.30am-7pm (ticket office closes 6.30pm), winter 8.30am-4.30pm (ticket office closes 4pm). Closed 1 Jan, 1 May, 25 Dec. €2; €5; including Museo Nazionale; €6.50 including Museo Nazionale and S. Apollinare in Classe. ☎ 0544 45 16 83.

This curious mausoleum, erected by Theodoric around 520, is built of huge blocks of freestone assembled without mortar. The two-storey building is covered by a remarkable monolithic dome 11m/36ft in diameter in Istrian stone. Inside, the decoration is sober and austere. A Romanesque porphyry basin has been transformed into a sarcophagus.

Sepolcro di Dante

Dante was exiled from Florence and took refuge first at Verona and then at Ravenna, where he died in 1321. The Classical building in which the tomb now stands was erected in 1780.

Chiesa di San Francesco

This 10C Romanesque church, dedicated to St Francis, is flanked by a campanile of the same period. Remodelled after the Second World War, it still retains some fine Greek marble columns, a 5C high altar and a 10C crypt.

Pinacoteca comunale

Open Mon-Sat 9am-1.30pm, Sun and hols 3-6pm. Guided tours by reservation (Signora Nadia Ceroni). ☎ 0544 48 20 54 or 0544 48 23 56; www.comune.ravenna.it or www.racine.ra.it/ravenna/pinacoteca

The ex-monastery of the Lateran Canons, whose façade facing the Public Gardens has a **Lombard loggia** (16C), houses the municipal picture gallery. Collections include works from most of the Italian schools (in particular the Emilian and Romagna schools) from the 14C to the 20C. The **recumbent effigy★** (1525) of a young knight, Guidarello Guidarelli, by Tullio Lombardo, is the jewel of the museum.

TO ALL YOUNG WOMEN SEARCHING FOR A HUSBAND...
It might be cheering to know that according to legend, women who kiss Guido Guidarelli will marry within the year. It is advisable not to wait until the last days of December.

Reggio di Calabria

Reggio, which backs against the Aspromonte Massif, is a pleasant town of modern appearance, rebuilt after the earthquake of 1908 along the Straits of Messina. Reggio is surrounded by rich groves of olives, vines, orange and lemon trees, and fields of flowers used for making perfume. Half the world production of bergamot (a citrus fruit) comes from Reggio.

Location

Population 179 617 – Michelin map 431 M 28 – Town plan in the Michelin Atlas Italy. Calabria. Reggio is right at the bottom of A 3. ▯ Corso Garibaldi 329, ☎ 0965 89 20 12. Surrounding area: See CALABRIA, MESSINA.

Worth a visit

Lungomare★

This long and elegant seafront promenade lined with palm trees and magnolias affords views of the Sicilian coastline and Etna.

Museo Nazionale Archeologico★★

&. *Open daily, 9am-8pm. Closed 1st and 3rd Mon of month, 1 Jan, 1 May, 25 Dec. ☎ 0965 81 22 55.*

Although most visitors come to this museum wanting to look at the mysterious bronze warriors, it would be a pity not to have a look at other, smaller historic mementoes housed here. Stop and look at the *pinakes★*, terracotta low reliefs that were used in Locri as ex-votos in the 5C BC. They were dedicated to Persephone, bride of Hades who carried her off to the Underworld while she was picking flowers. There is also an intimate and familiar scene portrayed in the *Woman putting a peplum into a decorated chest.*

The lower floor is "home" to the two **Riace Warriors★★★**, found in the sea of Riace in 1972.

Reggio Emilia

This rich industrial and commercial centre, set on the Via Emilia, was the birthplace of the poet Ariosto (1474-1533) and the landscape painter Antonio Fontanesi (1818-82). Like Modena and Ferrara, it belonged to the Este family from 1409 to 1776.

Location

Population 143 664 – Michelin maps 428, 429 H 13 – Town plan in the Michelin Atlas Italy – Emilia-Romagna. Reggio Emilia is just off A 1, between Parma and Modena.
🛈 *Piazza Prampolini 5/C,* ☎ *0522 45 11 52.*
Surrounding area: see MODENA, PARMA.

Worth a Visit

The historic centre

Piazza Prampolini, the political, religious and economic centre of the town, is overlooked by the cathedral, which was remodelled in the 15C but dates back further, the Romanesque baptistery and the Town Hall with its 16C Bordello tower.

To the right of the cathedral is the picturesque and lively **Via Broletto** which leads into Piazza San Prospero. This square is dominated by the 18C façade and unfinished campanile of the **church of San Prospero** which has a fine cycle of frescoes in the apse by C. Procaccini and B. Campi as well as a fine wooden chancel. ☎ *0522 43 46 67.*

Musei Civici

Via Spallanzani 1. Open Tue-Sat, mid-Apr to mid-Sep 9am-noon and 9pm-12am, rest of year 9am-noon, Sun and hols 10am-1pm. Closed Mon. No charge. ☎ *0522 45 64 77; www.musei.comune.re.it/servizi/*

The municipal museums include the Spallanzani Museum of Natural History, an anthropological section with artefacts from the area around Reggio, Roman and medieval mosaics, marbles, paintings of the local school (15C-20C) among which is **Solitude★** by Antonio Fontanesi, and a section dedicated to the film director M Mazzacurati (1908-69).

Chiesa della Madonna della Ghiara★

Corso Garibaldi. Open Mon-Sat, 10am-noon and 4-5.30pm, Sun and hols 10.25-10.50am and 3.30-5pm. ☎ *0522 43 97 07.*

This is a beautiful church, erected at the beginning of the 17C following a miracle. The **interior** contains splendid frescoes, altarpieces and paintings which constitute a fine anthology of 17C Emilian painting. One of the most significant paintings is the dramatic *Crucifixion* by Guercino.

▶▶Galleria Parmeggiani.

Excursions

Brescello

28km/17mi northwest. The town owes
its name (*Brixellum*) to the Celts who
settled in the Po Plain and who, as they
had moved along the plain, had already
founded the settlements of Bressanone
(Brixen) and Brescia (Brixia).

In spite of its ancient origins, Brescello
nowadays is famous for being the setting of the films about **Don Camillo**
and **Peppone**. The **museum** contains
memorabilia and posters relating to the films and as well as objects used during the
filming such as bicycles, a motorcycle and sidecar and even a tank. (&) *Open Mon-
Sat 10am-noon and 3-6pm, Sun and hols 9.30am-12.30pm and 2.30-7pm (reserve visit
several days in advance: Sig. Carpi, 8am-1.30pm). Donation recommended.
☎ 0522 68 75 26; www.pragmanet.it/pro-loco/museo-it.htm.*

> **A SMALL WORLD FULL OF POETRY**
> Giovanni Guareschi (1908-68), a journalist and
> novelist who liberally dipped his pen in humour,
> together with Giovanni Mosca (1908-83) founded
> a newspaper (the *Candido*) and wrote *The Small
> world of Don Camillo* which was made into a
> famous film starring Fernandel and Gino Cervi.

Castello di Canossa

32km/20mi southwest. Only the romantic ruins, perched on a rock, remain of the
imposing stronghold which belonged to the great Countess of Tuscany, Matilda
(1046-1115), who supported the Pope against the Emperor for 30 years during the
quarrel over the investiture of bishops and abbots. The Emperor Heinrich IV of
Germany came barefoot and in his shirtsleeves through the snow, to make amends
to Pope Gregory VII in 1077. He had to wait three days for his absolution. This is the
origin of the expression "to go to Canossa"; that is, to humble oneself after a quarrel.

Rieti

Rieti lies at the junction of several valleys in the heart of a fertile plain and
is the geographical centre of Italy. It is also a good excursion centre from
which to follow in the footsteps of St Francis of Assisi, who preached locally.

Location

Population 46 100 – Michelin map 430 O 20 – Lazio. Rieti lies at the foot of Mount
Terminillo. The main access roads are S 4, the Via Salaria, which links the town to
L'Aquila and A 1, and S 79 which goes to Terni. ᛒ *Piazza Vittorio Emanuele 17 –
Portici del Comune, ☎ 0746 20 32 20.
Surrounding area: see ABRUZZO.*

Walking about

Piazza Cesare Battisti

This is the centre of the town, where the most important buildings are to be found.
Take the gateway to the right of the 16C-17C Palazzo del Governo with its elegant
loggia to reach the pleasant **public garden★**, from where there is a lovely view of
the town and its surroundings.

Duomo

This cathedral has a 15C porch and a lovely Romanesque campanile dating from
1252. Inside, the fresco of the Madonna dates from 1494 while the **crypt** is 12C.

Palazzo Vescovile

Behind the cathedral. This 13C episcopal building has heavily ribbed **vaulting★** over
the two vast naves.

Excursions

Convento di Fonte Colombo

*5km/3mi southwest. Take the Contigliano road and after 3km/2mi turn left. Open daily,
9am-12.30pm and 3.30-6.30pm. Guided tours available on request. Donation recommended. ☎ 0746 21 01 25; www.fratilazio.it*

It was in the old monastery that **St Francis** underwent an eye operation. He dic-
tated the Franciscan Rule in the grotto after having fasted for 40 days. Visitors will
see the 12C Chapel of St Mary Magdalene adorned with frescoes depicting the "T",

the emblem of the Cross designed by St Francis; the St Michael Chapel and the grotto where the saint fasted; the tree-trunk in which Jesus appeared to him; the old monastery; and the 15C church.

Convento di Greccio★

15km/9mi northwest. Take the road via Contigliano to Greccio and continue for 2km/1.2mi. Leave the car on the esplanade at the foot of the monastery. Open Mon-Sat, 9am-12.45pm and 3-6.45pm, Sun and hols 9am-6.30pm. ☎ 0746 75 01 27.

This 13C monastery clings to a rocky overhang at an altitude of 638m/2 093ft. It was here that St Francis celebrated Christmas in 1223 and said Mass at a manger *(presepio)* between an ox and an ass, thus starting the custom of Christmas Nativity scenes. Visitors have access to the Chapel of the Crib (Cappella del Presepio – frescoes by the school of Giotto) and the areas where St Francis and his companions lived. On the upper floor is the church of 1228 with its original furnishings.

Convento di Poggio Bustone

10km/6mi north by the Terni road. Open daily, 9am-noon and 3-6pm. Tours by reservation only. No charge. ☎ 0746 68 89 16.

Perched at an altitude of 818m/2 684ft in a lovely green setting, the monastery consists of a 14C church, much altered, with its 15C to 17C frescoes, charming 15C-16C cloisters, a 14C refectory, and two caves in which St Francis is said to have lived.

Convento La Foresta

5km/3mi north. Open daily, summer 8.30am-noon and 3-7pm, winter 8.30am-noon and 2.30-6pm. Guided tours only. ☎ 0746 20 00 85.

It was in this mountain retreat that St Francis wrote his *Canticle of the Creatures* and performed the miracle of the vine. In the wine cellar is the vat which was filled by the miraculous grape. The cave where St Francis stayed is also open to visitors.

Rimini☼☼☼

Once the destination for the rich and famous (even King Umberto I came here), today Rimini is an internationally known seaside resort with modern hotels, a marina, an airport and a great beach of fine sand. But Rimini is not just a summer hotspot: it has an illustrious past, well documented in its historic centre.

Location

Population 131 062 –Michelin maps 429, 430 J 19 – Town plan in the Michelin Atlas Italy. The main access roads to Rimini are A 14, S 9 (the Via Emilia), and S 16.
i *Piazzale Cesare Battisti 1 (at the station), ☎ 0541 51 331.*
Surrounding area: see PESARO, RAVENNA, SAN MARINO.

Background

This Umbrian and Gallic colony, with its strategic situation at the junction of the Via Emilia and the Via Flaminia, flourished during the Roman Empire. In the 13C the town grew to fame with the notoriety of its ruling house, the **Malatesta**. In *The Divine Comedy* Dante immortalised the fate of the tragic lovers, Paolo Malatesta and Francesca da Rimini, who were murdered by Gianni Malatesta (the brother of Paolo and the husband of Francesca). Later Sigismondo I Malatesta (1417-68) combined open-minded political action with a patronage of the arts that summoned Piero della Francesca and Leon Battista Alberti to his court. In the 16C Rimini became a papal town.

In the arts Giotto's work in the church of St Francis (now the Tempio Malatestiano) engendered the development of a **Riminese school** in the 14C which is similar to Giotto's style but sharper and more dramatic.

More recently, the city has achieved international fame as the birthplace of the film director **Federico Fellini** (1920-93), who paid homage to his roots in cinematic masterpieces such as *I vitelloni* and *Amarcord*.

Worth a Visit

Tempio Malatestiano★★

The church was built in the 13C by the Franciscans and became the Malatesta mausoleum in the 14C. It was remodelled from 1447 by **Leon Battista Alberti** on Sigismondo I's orders. Based on the principal that the church was to glorify Sigismondo and his beloved wife Isotta by housing their tombs, Alberti decided to

Directory

WHERE TO EAT

• Budget

La Baracca – *Via Marecchiese 373 – 47037 Vergiano – 4.5km/3mi southwest of Rimini –* ☎ *0541 72 74 83 – Closed Wed –* €18/26. A simple, little restaurant with a friendly, family atmosphere. Offers a traditional meat-based menu. Represents value for money. A trip to La Baracca would also give you an opportunity to explore the hinterland behind Rimini.

Dei Cantoni – *Via Santa Maria 19 – 47020 Longiano – 22km/13mi northwest of Rimini off the Via Emilia –* ☎ *0547 66 58 99 – Closed Wed, Jan –* 🏠 *–* €19/22. This lovely restaurant is situated in the historic centre, under the walls of the Castello Malatestiano. Delicious, regional cuisine which is closely linked to the seasons. Al fresco dining in summer. Warm welcome assured.

• Moderate

Osteria la Sangiovesa – *Via Saffi 27 – 47822 Santarcangelo di Romagna – 13km/8mi west of Rimini on the Via Emilia –* ☎ *0541 62 07 10 – Closed lunchtime, 1 Jan, 25 Dec –* 🏠 *–* €26/33. A gastronomic experience, as recommended by many hotels on the Riviera. The excellent cuisine draws on tradition but is also innovative and beautifully presented. Good selection of wines. Pleasant surroundings in a mixture of styles.

Acero Rosso – *Viale Tiberio 11 –* ☎ *0541 53 577 – Closed lunchtime (except Sun and public holidays); Jun-Sep, Mon; rest of the year, Sun evening and Mon; 12 Aug-16 Aug and 23 Dec-26 Dec –* €36.92/49.92. If you're celebrating a special occasion or simply looking to treat yourself to a gourmet meal, how about a lobster *risotto* with a red wine and seafood sauce or a *carpaccio* of scampi with a basil sauce? Elegant ambience with tables outside in summer.

WHERE TO STAY

• Budget

Hotel Diana – *Via Porto Palos 15 – 47811 Viserbella – 8km/5mi north of Rimini –* ☎ *0541 73 81 58 – Fax 0541 73 80 96 – Closed Oct-Mar –* 🅿 🛇 🏠 *(payment) –* 38 rm €33.5/60 – 🍴 €5.50 – Restaurant €15.70/18.10. The rooms which are modern and well kept overlook the swimming pools catering for adults and children which back onto the vast beach. Extremely courteous, friendly staff. Definitely one for the address book.

Hotel Rondinella e Dependance Viola – *Via Neri 3 –* ☎ *0541 38 05 67 – Fax 0541 38 05 67 –* 🅿 🛇 🏠 *(payment) –* 55 rm €36.15/51.64 – 🍴 €4.13 – Restaurant €12.91/15.49. One of the many establishments along the coast sporting a 1970s-style exterior. Having said that, nothing is too much trouble for the staff who are warm and friendly. The hotel is also spotlessly clean...and very reasonably priced. What more could you ask for?

• Moderate

Hotel Giglio – *Viale Principe di Piemonte 18 – 47831 Miramare di Rimini – 7km/4mi south of Rimini –* ☎ *0541 37 20 73 – Fax 0541 37 74 90 – Closed Oct-Easter –* 🅿 🛇 🏠 *(payment) –* 42 rm €46.50/72.30 – 🍴 €5.17 – Restaurant €16.53/19.11. If you're keen on taking it easy and basking in the sun, this is the hotel for you. It is directly on the beach, has a lovely sunbathing terrace and you can get from the rooms (modern) to the sea in a nanosecond. Friendly, family atmosphere and good food.

Hotel Villa Lalla – *Via Vittorio Veneto 22 –* ☎ *0541 55 155 – Fax 0541 23 570 –* 🏠 *–* 40 rm €50/83 🍴 – Restaurant €15.50/26. Situated in a residential district, just a few minutes' walk from the sea and the centre, this hotel would be a good solution for anyone wanting to add on a few days to a business trip. Ecologically-friendly rooms with breakfast served on the veranda.

Hotel Avila In – *Via San Salvador 192 – 47812 Torre Pedrera – 9km/5mi north of Rimini –* ☎ *0541 72 01 73 – Fax 0541 72 11 82 – Closed Nov –* 🅿 🛇 🏠 *–* 65 rm €47/103.30 🍴 – Restaurant €16/26. A very comfortable hotel right on the seafront. An added bonus is the lovely gardens where you can escape from the heat of the day. For sports enthusiasts there are swimming pools and a tennis court. Also facilities for children and a health club.

• Expensive

Grand Hotel – *Parco Fellini 1 –* ☎ *0541 56 000 – Fax 0541 56 866 –* 🅿 🛇 🏠 🚻 *–* 105 rm from €201.42 🍴 – Restaurant €44/62. Inextricably linked to the great film-maker Federico Fellini, this establishment is in the finest tradition of a grand palace hotel. Elegant interior with furnishings dating back to the 15C, the Grand Hotel exudes an aura of a bygone age. For a taste of how the other half live, this is the place to come.

TAKING A BREAK

Bounty – *Via Weber 6 –* ☎ *0541 39 19 00 – Jun-Sep 7.30am-3am; Oct-May, Tue and Wed, Fri-Sun.* The largest pub in Rimini and the town's main nightspot, this vast bar has been decked out like a sailing vessel. Organises events such as cabaret evenings, and orchestral and theatre performances.

GOING OUT

Antica Drogheria Spazi – *Piazza Cavour 5 –* ☎ *0541 23 439 – 11am-3pm and 6pm-midnight.* An elegant winery/wine bar in the upper part of the town. Away from the madding crowds and the beach, there is plenty of space and it has a lovely outdoor area. Wines from all over Italy as well as international vintages.

Club Paradiso – *Via Covignano 260 –* ☎ *0541 75 11 32 – info@paradisoclub.it – 5-20 Aug, daily 9pm-5am; rest of the year, Fri and Sat.* With its luxuriant gardens and Baroque furnishings, the Paradise club is without doubt the most attractive discotheque in Rimini. Established 45 years ago as a venue for parties it is still going strong and embraces all types of music!

Mon Amour – *Viale Principe di Piemonte 30* – ☎ *0541 37 34 34* – *Tue, Fri-Sun from 10.30pm.* This discotheque-piano bar would appeal to the over-30s who will appreciate the understated decor and Latin American ambience. Popular with Italian businessmen on holiday in Rimini.

Shopping

Stamperia Ruggine – *Via Bertani 36* – ☎ *0541 50 811* – *Tue-Sat 9am-1pm and 3.30-7.30pm.* This is the place to come to watch the local craftsmen at work applying large floral designs to fabric and ceramics, a traditional art form in Rimini.

Sport and Leisure

Blue Beach Center – *Zona Pascoli – Opposite beaches 62, 63, 63 A, 63 B, 64, 65.* – ☎ *0541 38 24 56* – *www.spiaggia63a.it* – Open 8am-7.30pm, Closed 20 Sep-May. Of all the private swimming pools, this is the best. As well as activities for children, a treatment (massage) room, fitness centre, television room and various other sports facilities you can also learn to water ski and jet ski here! Pleasant, airy public area on the lower floor and there are tables outside on the piazza.

Delfinario – *Lungomare Tintori 2* – ☎ *0541 50 298* – *dolphins@iper.net* – Apr-Sep, daily; Oct, Sat and Sun, Closed Nov-Mar. This little dolphinarium will delight and entertain the children. After a tour of the aquatic museum there is a live show (40min) with five dolphins performing. These dolphins are also used in therapy for autistic children.

---

adopt the Classical model of a triumphal arch (inspired by the nearby Arch of Augustus) and a whole series of Classical elements. Although unfinished, Rimini's "temple" was the first of a new kind of religious building and a point of reference a few decades later for the church of Sant'Andrea in Mantua.

The **interior** includes an allegorical decoration exquisitely and subtly crafted by Agostino di Duccio who composed a kind of medieval encyclopaedia updated with pagan and Classical elements (note the enchanting *Childhood games* in the second chapel on the right). The south aisle houses Sigismondo's tomb and the reliquary chapel *(if closed contact the sacristy)* with the famous portrait *Sigismondo Malatesta and St Sigismondo* ★★ by Piero della Francesca. In the adjacent chapel, Isotta's tomb rests on elephants (her husband's favourite animal) who hold up Sigismondo's crest (SI). In the third chapel on the right, the signs of the zodiac and the planets (note the view of Rimini in Cancer, the city's sign) celebrate the divine creation, contrasting with human activity which is represented by the liberal arts in the opposite chapel in the north aisle. Behind the altar is Giotto's **painted 14C crucifix★★**.

Arco d'Augusto
Piazzale Giulio Cesare. The arch of Augustus was built in 27 BC and has a majestic appearance, with fine fluted columns and Corinthian capitals.

The historic centre
Piazza Cavour is bordered by the Town Hall (Palazzo Comunale), Palazzo dell'Arengo and the Palazzo del Podestà, all dating from the 13C-14C but considerably remodelled since then. Going through the arcades of the fish market and turning right onto Via Cairoli make for the **church of Sant'Agostino** which has interesting examples of 14C Riminese painting. In the nearby Piazza Malatesta stands the imposing **Castel Sigismondo**, an austere building erected by Sigismondo 1 who consulted Brunelleschi with regard to its design.

Museo della Città
Via Tonini 1. &. Open Mon-Sat, mid-Jun to mid-Sep 10am-12.30pm and 4.30-7.30pm, Sun and hols 4.30-7.30pm (Jul and Aug 10am-12.30pm, 4.30-7.30pm and 9-11pm), rest of year 8.30am-12.30pm and 5-7pm, Sun and hols 4-7pm. Closed Mon. €4. No charge Sun. ☎ 0541 21 482; www.comune.rimini.it/cultura/musei/musei_pagina.htm
The museum has collections of archaeological artefacts pertaining to Roman Rimini *(Ariminum)* as well as works dating from the 14C-19C. Of particular note are the Riminese paintings and crucifixes, the delicate *Pietà*★ by Giovanni Bellini, the **San Vincenzo Ferrer Altarpiece** by Domenico Ghirlandaio and, in the 17C section, paintings by Guercino and Guido Cagnacci.

Ponte di Tiberio
The bridge was begun under Augustus and completed under Tiberius in AD 21. The building material is massive blocks of Istrian limestone.

Riviera Ligure★★

The enchanting Italian or Ligurian Riviera is like the French Riviera, a tourist paradise. The mild climate makes it particularly popular in winter. The coast is dotted with popular resorts with good amenities and a wide range of hotels. The hinterland provides a large choice of walks for those who prefer solitude.

Location
Michelin map 428 I-K 4-12 – Liguria. From Ventimiglia to the Gulf of La Spezia, the coast describes a curve backed by the slopes of the Alps and the Ligurian Apennines, with Genoa in the middle. The coastal roads include A 10 (Riviera di Ponente), A 12 (Riviera di Levante) and S 1 (Via Aurelia).
See: GENOVA, Promontorio di PORTOFINO.

Excursions

RIVIERA DI PONENTE★ ①
The map below locates the towns and sites described in the guide, and also indicates other beauty spots in small black type.

From Ventimiglia to Genoa *175km/109mi – Allow one day.*
The main road of the Riviera, the Via Aurelia, is of Roman origin. It is difficult, as it is winding and narrow, and carries heavy traffic. Nevertheless, there are remarkable viewpoints from the stretches of corniche road or when the road runs close to the blue waters of the Ligurian Sea. Slightly inland the A 10 motorway with its many tunnels and viaducts runs parallel. The road passes through a succession of resorts with villas often screened by luxuriant and varied vegetation, or crosses a stretch of coastal plain traversed by mountain torrents. With its exceptionally good exposure to the sun the Riviera specialises in the growing of flowers, often under glass, throughout the year.
The hinterland provides a sharp contrast, with the tranquillity of its wild, forested landscapes.

Ventimiglia
Not far from the French border, Ventimiglia has an old quarter (Città Vecchia) criss-crossed by narrow alleyways, the 11C-12C Duomo, an 11C octagonal baptistery, the 11C-12C church of San Michele and the 17C Neri Oratory. The **Giardini Hanbury★★** (Hanbury Gardens) in Mortola Inferiore *(6km/4mi west, towards the French border)*, with their varied and exotic vegetation, are laid out in terraces, overlooking the sea. (&) *Open daily except Wed (winter only), mid-Jun to Sep 9am-7pm, Apr to mid-Jun and Oct 10am-5pm, rest of year 10am-4pm (ticket office always closes 1hr early). Closed Wed (winter only). €6.*
☎ *0184 22 95 07; www.cooperativa-omnia.com*

Bordighera
The villas and hotels of this famous resort are scattered among flower gar-

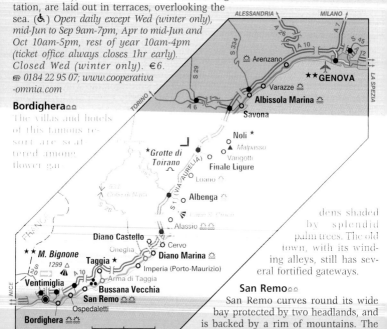

dens shaded by splendid palm trees. The old town, with its winding alleys, still has several fortified gateways.

San Remo
San Remo curves round its wide bay protected by two headlands, and is backed by a rim of mountains. The luxurious capital of the Riviera di Ponente

Directory

Where to Eat

• Budget

Osteria Mezzaluna-Wine Bar – *Vico Berna 6 – 17021 Alassio – ☎ 0182 64 03 87 – osteria.mezzaluna@iol.it – Closed Mon in winter –* ⊭ – A charming little establishment with majolica-tiled tables and walls, vaulted ceilings hung with marine paraphernalia (oars, rudders and old lifejackets). Wide selection of cold meats, cheese, *bruschette* (toasted bread snacks) and other warm and cold dishes. Even the live music is good.

Luchin – *Via Bighetti 51 – 16043 Chiavari – ☎ 0185 30 10 63 – Closed Sun –* ⊭ *– €13/18.* With origins dating back to 1907, this establishment has a reputation for authentic Ligurian cooking: specialities include *farinata di ceci* (chickpea polenta). Unpretentious, but welcoming ambience with large refectory-style tables.

La Favorita – *Località Richelmo – 18030 Apricale – 16km/10mi north of Ventimiglia – ☎ 0184 20 81 86 – Closed Tue (except Aug), 24 Jun-8 Jul, 12 Nov-6 Dec – Book – €20/25.* What was once an old farmhouse is now a great restaurant run with tremendous enthusiasm by the family owners. The fresh flowers on the tables and the walls decorated with climbing plants give a sense of continuity with the countryside which you can see through the lovely picture windows. Authentic, homely cooking.

Sotto la Scala – *Via Cerisola 7 – 16035 Rapallo – ☎ 0185 53 630 – Closed Sun evening, Mon, (except Jul-Aug), lunchtime (except public holidays) – Book – €22/33.* Not far from the railway station is this charming little villa furnished with rustic-style antique furniture and period light fittings. On the walls, pictures and various utensils from the 19C. Traditional cuisine with flair. Some meat dishes on the menu.

• Moderate

U Giancu – *Via San Massimo 78 – 16035 Rapallo – ☎ 0185 26 12 12 – Closed 23 Dec-2 Jan, 3 Jan-Easter (open only Fri-Sun), 5-25 Nov – Book – €23/33.* With its splendid collection of old cartoons on the walls and a country-style ambience outside, it is easy to forget that the sea is only minutes away. There is a children's area and the train where they can take their meals is a nice touch.

Da Casetta – *Piazza San Pietro 12 – 17022 Borgio Verezzi – 4km/2.4mi southwest of Finale Ligure sulla Via Aurelia – ☎ 019 61 01 66 – Closed Tue and lunchtime (except Sat, Sun and public holidays Sep-Jun). – Book – €27/38.* Somewhere between rustic and elegant with its brick vaulted ceilings and limewashed walls with traces of natural rock picked out here and there. The cuisine here is mainly regional and the vegetables are all supplied by the family market garden business.

Quintilio – *Via Gramsci 23 – 17041 Altare – 12km/7mi northwest of Savona on S 29 – ☎ 019 58 000 – Closed Sun evening, Mon, lunchtime (except Sun), Jul – €32/43.* A mixture of elegant and rustic, simply decorated and furnished. Homely cooking focuses on regional (Ligurian and Piedmontese) specialities prepared with flair and imagination. Accommodation also available: rooms are clean and comfortable.

Where to Stay

• Budget

Albergo Rosita – *Via Mànie 67 – 17024 Finale Ligure – 3km/2mi northeast – ☎ 019 60 24 37 – Fax 019 60 17 62 – Closed 5-20 Jan, Nov –* ⊭ 🅿 *– 9 rm €41.40/58 – ☕ €6.20 – Restaurant €21.60/28.20.* Splendid clifftop location in a verdant setting. Light, airy public areas furnished in wood. Rooms are comfortable and have a balcony with sea view. Breakfast served on the veranda off the terrace-solarium.

Pensione Miramare – *V. Fiascherino 22 – 19030 Tellaro – 4km/2.4mi southeast of Lerici – ☎ 0187 96 75 89 – Fax 0187 96 65 34 – Closed Nov-22 Dec, 9 Jan-Easter –* 🅿 *– 14 rm €50/62 – ☕ €6 – Restaurant €20/33.* An unpretentious but welcoming pensione which is extremely well run. Overlooking Tellaro and the Golfo dei Poeti, there is a lovely garden terrace. Offers very good value for money.

• Moderate

Hotel Delle Rose – *Via de Medici 17 – 18014 Ospedaletti – 6km/4mi northeast of Bordighera on the Via Aurelia – ☎ 0184 68 90 16 – Fax 0184 68 97 78 – 14 rm €54.23/72.30 ☕ – Restaurant €23/34.* The main attractions here are the lovely garden full of exotic plants and the warmth and hospitality of the family owners. Classic, if slightly old-fashioned rooms and public lounges. Slightly off the beaten track.

Hotel Ca' d'Andrean – *Via Discovolo 101 – 19010 Manarola – ☎ 0187 92 00 40 – Fax 0187 92 04 52 – Closed 10-25 Nov –* ⊭ *– 10 rm €55/73 – ☕ €6.* This small, rather charming hotel is situated in the pedestrianised area in the upper part of the village. The rustic finish is a reminder that this was once, in the not too distant past, an agricultural building. Modern-style rooms are spacious and light. Pleasant lounge area with its lovely fireplace. Beautiful garden with lemon trees.

Hotel Due Gemelli – *Via Litoranea 9, Località Campi – 19017 Riomaggiore – 4.5km/3mi east of Riomaggiore – ☎ 0187 92 06 78 – Fax 0187 92 01 11 –* 🅿 *– 13 rm €67.14/77.47 – ☕ €6.20 – Restaurant €21/36.* You may not have direct access down to the sea, but there are splendid panoramic views from the balconies in the rooms and the terrace restaurant. A simple, family establishment which would make an ideal base for exploring the Cinque Terre.

Taking a Break

Caffè Gino – *Piazza Milite Ignoto 1 – 17026 Noli – ☎ 019 74 84 57 – 8am-1am, Closed mid-Jan to mid-Feb.* From the tables set out in the piazza (pedestrians only) you have a great view of the red clock tower and the flower-filled balconies of the old houses. An oasis of peace and quiet in this charming little village.

Cafè S.M.S. – *Via Chiesa 1 – 17011 Albissola Capo – On the promenade –* ☎ *019 48 32 83 – 7.30am-1am, winter Tue-Sun* A small café with tables right on the promenade overlooking the sea. Cheerful, welcoming atmosphere.

Enoteca Marone – *Via San Francesco 61 – 18038 San Remo – ☎ 0184 50 69 16 – Mon 4-7.30pm, Tue-Sat 8.45am-12.30pm and 4-7.30pm.* For 18 years the dynamic and enthusiastic owners of this wine bar have been choosing the wines direct from the producers, and very knowledgeable they are too. The cellar extends to around 1 200 different wines which are elegantly displayed.

Enoteca Olioteca San Giorgio – *Via Volta 19 – 18010 Cervo – ☎ 0183 40 01 75 – Tue-Mon 9am-3pm and 5.30pm-3am.* This wine bar also specialises in olive oil products (including extra virgin olive oil and the regional delicacy, pesto). Good choice of traditional wines from Liguria including Vermentino, Pigato, Vignamare, Ormeasco and Rosolio.

Gelatomania – *Via Cavour 56/D – 18039 Ventimiglia – ☎ 0184 35 26 16 – Summer, Mon 3-11.30pm, Tue-Thu, Sat 9am-noon and 2.30-11.30pm, Fri 9am-11.30pm, Sun 9am-1pm and 4-11.30pm; rest of the year, Tue-Sun 9am-12.30pm and 3-11.30pm.* This is the oldest gelateria in town, as well as one of the best. Give yourself plenty of time to choose from the 44 flavours which include seasonal fruits and meringue.

Gelateria Haiti – *Via Roma 28 – 18039 Ventimiglia – ☎ 0184 35 16 18 – Summer, 10am-1pm and 2.30pm-midnight, rest of the year, Thu-Tue.* The almond nougat and Nutella flavours are a must. This is also the place to try ice cream made with soya.

Living Garden – *Giardino Vittorio Veneto 1 – 18038 San Remo – ☎ 0184 50 34 64 – Mon 2pm-1am, Wed-Sun 10am-1am.* Located in front of the casino on the seafront. During the day it is a pleasant tea room and in the evening it is transformed into a throbbing discotheque which is very popular with local young people. Also hosts theme nights.

Mondino – *Via Roma 38/B – 18039 Ventimiglia – ☎ 0184 35 13 61 – Mon-Sat 7am-1pm and 3.30-7.30pm; closed mid-Sep to mid-Oct.* Excellent pasticceria (confectioner's and pastry shop) which sells delicious *panettoni* (cakes) and other regional specialities.

Pasticceria-Focacceria Scalvini – *Via Colombo 3 – 17026 Noli –* ☎ *019 74 82 01 – Summer, 7.15am-1pm and 3.30-8pm; rest of the year, Wed-Mon 8am-1pm and 3.30-7.30pm.* Founded in 1820, this *pasticceria* has a long tradition of pastry making. Specialities include *torta di mandorla* (almond tart), different Genoese-style breads, *amaretti*, and other pastries made with fresh fruit.

U Gumbu – *Via Matteotti 31 – 18010 Cervo – Tue-Mon 10am-noon and 3-6pm.* This lovely little house, built in stone and wood, houses the Museo dell'Oliva. On sale are various artisanal products including extra virgin olive oil, pesto and jams.

Vino e Farinata – *Via Pia 15/r – 17100 Savona – Tue-Sat noon-2pm and 6-9.30pm; Closed 10 days in Aug-Sep* As you walk through the little tiled doorway to the oldest bakery in town nothing has changed here for 130 years. Pastries like those made with *farina di ceci* (chickpea flour) are prepared according to age-old recipes, baked in a large oven which towers over the counter.

GOING OUT

Bagni Miramare – *Corso Bigliati – 17012 Albissola Marina – Opposite Piazza del Popolo. – ☎ 019 48 02 85 – Closed Oct-Feb.* While the children play water games and throw themselves off the diving-board, their parents can sip cocktails at the attractive, Bali-style bar. In the evening the Miramare transforms itself into a discotheque and hosts theme nights.

Casinò Municipale di San Remo – *Corso Inglesi 18 – 18038 San Remo – ☎ 0184 53 40 01 – 10am-2.30am.* This is the town's main nightspot. The casino is housed in a rather grand building with plenty of atmosphere and original early-19C furnishings. The level of service and the professionalism of the croupiers recalls the casinos of a bygone age.

LEISURE

La Superba – *Pontile Marinetta – 17100 Savona – Beneath the Torre Pancaldo –* ☎ *010 26 57 12 – Bookings only.* Day trips to Genoa (visiting the Acquario and the Lanterna), Portofino (and San Fruttuoso), or the Cinque Terre (including a tour of Isola Palmaria). Of particular interest are the whale watching trips accompanied by experts from the WWF, which enable you to see whales in their natural habitat.

enjoys a pleasantly warm temperature all the year round and the highest number of sunshine hours on the Ligurian coast. In addition to these advantages San Remo boasts a wide choice of hotels, thermal establishments, a pleasure boat harbour, casino, racecourse, lively festivals and other cultural and sporting events.

San Remo is the main Italian flower market and millions of roses, carnations and mimosa flowers are exported worldwide. The flower market takes place from October to June from 6am to 8am.

Corso Imperatrice – This is Liguria's most elegant seafront promenade and it is particularly known for its Canary palms.

La Pigna★ – This is the name given to the old town, because of its pointed shape (*pigna* meaning beak). It has a medieval aspect with its winding alleys lined with

tall and narrow houses. From Piazza Castello climb up to the Baroque church of the Madonna della Costa, from where there is an attractive **view**★ of the town and bay.
▶▶Monte Bignone★★ (panorama★★).

Bussana Vecchia
The medieval fortified village was destroyed by an earthquake in 1887 and was deserted until the 1960s, when some artists, mostly foreigners, set about restoring the houses and moved in. At first somewhat reserved and solitary, they eventually opened up shops selling their work and crafts.

Taggia
Taggia, set amid vineyards, orchards and olive groves, commands the Argentina Valley. In the 15C and 16C Taggia was an important art centre frequented by Louis (Ludovico) Bréa from Nice, the Piedmontese artist Canavese, and Perino del Vaga and Luca Cambiaso from Genoa.
The church of **San Domenico**, dedicated to St Dominic, has a fine collection of **works**★ by Louis Bréa (*Virgin of Pity* and the *Baptism of Christ*).

Diano Marina⌂
From here it is possible to visit the fortified village of **Diano Castello** and its 12C Chapel of the Knights of Malta (Cappella dei Cavalieri di Malta) with its multi-coloured wooden roof.

Albenga⌂
Albenga lies a short distance inland, in an alluvial plain with rich market gardens. The medieval **old town**★ is clustered round the **Cattedrale** with its imposing late-14C campanile. The vaulting of the nave is covered with *trompe l'oeil* frescoes. The octagonal 5C baptistery has a baptismal font and a charming palaeo-Christian mosaic in the style typical of Ravenna.

Grotte di Toirano★
Open daily, Jul and Aug 9.30am-12.30pm and 2-5.30pm, rest of year 9.30am-12.30pm and 2-5pm. Guided tours only. Closed 1 Jan, 10-25 Dec. €9. ☎ 0182 98 062.
The caves were inhabited in the late-Neolithic period. There are traces of human footprints, torch marks, the remains and prints of bears, and mud balls used as missiles. The caves open into a series of chambers bristling with stalagmites and stalactites. The last section is the most interesting: a cave once filled with water, which has hollowed it out and given it its round shape.

Finale Ligure
Finale Marina has a basilica with a fanciful Baroque façade. In **Finale Pia** the abbey church is graced with an elegant late-13C campanile. The old town of **Finale Borgo**★, 2km/1.2mi inland, still has its town walls and its collegiate church of San Biagio with an elegant 13C polygonal campanile. Inside are a polyptych of St Catherine (1533) and a 16C painting of St Blaise surrounded by saints.
From **Castel San Giovanni** (*1hr on foot there and back; start from Via del Municipio*) there is a **view**★ of Finale Ligure, the sea and the hinterland. Higher up, **Castel Gavone** retains a 15C round tower with diamond-shaped rustication.

Noli★
This fishing village still has ancient houses, 13C towers and a Romanesque church with a huge wooden statue of Christ, also of the Romanesque period.

Savona
Italy's seventh port, Savona handles crude oil, coal, cellulose and Italian cars for export to Britain and the United States. The old town has several Renaissance palaces, its 16C Duomo and on the seafront a 16C fortress, **Fortezza Priamar**, where the Italian patriot Mazzini was imprisoned in 1830.

Albissola Marina⌂
This town is known for its production of ceramics, which carries on a 13C tradition. At the end of the 16C a Duke of Nevers, a member of the Italian Gonzaga family, summoned the Conrade brothers from Albisola to Nevers to found a faïence factory. The 18C **Villa Faraggiana** with its exotic **park**★, now houses the Ligurian Ceramics Centre. The exhibits include: the rich Empire furnishings, ceramic pavements and flooring, and the superb **ballroom**★ with its stucco and fresco decoration. (&) *Open daily except Mon, 3-7pm. Closed Easter, Oct to Feb. €4.20. ☎ 019 48 06 22.*

Genoa★★ *see GENOVA*

RIVIERA DI LEVANTE★★★ ②

From Genoa to La Spezia *173km/108mi – Allow one day.*
This stretch of coast has more character and is wilder than the Riviera di Ponente. Sharp promontories, little sheltered coves, tiny fishing villages, wide sandy bays, cliffs, the pinewoods and olive groves of the hinterland, all lend it charm. The road is often winding and hilly but there are fewer stretches of corniche road and the road often runs much further from the coast.

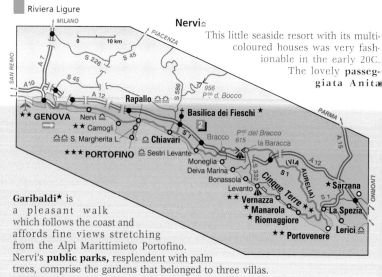

Nervi☆

This little seaside resort with its multi-coloured houses was very fashionable in the early 20C. The lovely **passeggiata Anita Garibaldi★** is a pleasant walk which follows the coast and affords fine views stretching from the Alpi Marittimieto Portofino. Nervi's **public parks,** resplendent with palm trees, comprise the gardens that belonged to three villas.

Portofino★★★ see *Promontorio di PORTOFINO*

Rapallo☆☆

This sophisticated seaside resort is admirably situated at the head of a bay to the east of the Portofino peninsula. The Lungomare Vittorio Veneto is a lovely palm-shaded **promenade★** along the seafront.

Chiavari☆

This seaside resort has a vast beach and a pleasure-boat harbour. In San Salvatore 2km/1.2mi to the northeast is the small 13C **Basilica dei Fieschi★** with its alternating courses of black and white marble. The vaulting is pointed. Opposite stands the Palazzo Fieschi, a graceful 13C Genoese Gothic building.

Cinque Terre★★

Lying northwest of the Gulf of La Spezia, the Cinque Terre (Five Lands) is, even today, an isolated region best reached by train or boat (parking difficult). This rugged coast is wild but hospitable, with its vineyards and fishing villages where the people remain strongly attached to their old customs and traditions. In 1997 Cinque Terre, together with Portovenere and the Palmaria, Tino and Tinetto islands, were included in UNESCO's World Heritage List.

A coastal path linking all five villages: Riomaggiore, Manarola, **Corniglia**, Vernazza and **Monterosso** affords fine views.

Vernazza★★ – This is the most attractive village with its tall colourful houses and its church clustered together at the head of a well-sheltered cove.

Manarola★ – This fishing village with its small 14C church is set in a landscape of terraced vineyards. Starting from the station there is a splendid **walk★★** *(15min on foot)* which offers lovely views of the coast and the other villages.

Riomaggiore

Riomaggiore★ – *Take the branch road off the La Spezia-Manarola road.* The old houses of this medieval village lie in a narrow valley. The tiny fishing harbour backs against the strange black rock strata, typical of the region.

La Spezia

Town plan in the Michelin Atlas Italy. 🚹 *viale Mazzini 47,* ☎ *0187 77 09 00.* This naval base and important port comprises Italy's largest naval dockyard and specialises in the manufacture of arms.

Museo Lia★★ – (&) *Open Tue-Sun, 10am-6pm. Closed Mon (except Easter Mon), 1 Jan, 1 May, 25 Dec, hols. €6. For information and reservations* ☎ *0187 73 11 00; www.castagna.it/mal*

Housed in a completely restored 17C monastery, this collection was accumulated by Amedeo Lia who amassed (and then donated to the city) 1 110 works of art in his lifetime, dating from Roman times to the 18C. The museum has important sections on ivory, enamels, crosses and devotional objects, a beautiful series of illuminated manuscripts, paintings, glass and rock crystal. Listed here are some of the most significant pieces (numbers used are those used in the museum). Room 1: the collection opens with an Umbrian *Virgin and Child* in polychrome wood (13C). To the right of the entrance, in a glass case devoted to Roman art, is an **amethyst head**, probably a portrait of one of Caligula's sisters. To the left are some ivories (note the sumptuous German Baroque Cup with Alboin and Rosamund – A20), enamels (St George and the Dragon in enamel and gold) and a gold and enamel medallion portraying the Adoration of the Magi (565). At the end of the room note the crosses, in particular the 13C Limoges cross (516). Room II: This room displays illuminated manuscripts with three complete antiphonaries and numerous illuminated pages, mostly Italian (14C-16C). The paintings (13C-18C) begin in Room IV and are displayed in chronological order. Among the numerous artists it is worth noting the followers of Giotto, Bernardo Daddi and Pietro Lorenzetti *(St John the Evangelist)* and Alvise Vivarini *(St Jerome).* Painters from the 16C include Giampietrino *(Madonna and Child with St John),* Bellini and **Pontormo** (self-portrait). The 17C and 18C are represented respectively by followers of Caravaggio and Venetian landscapes and portraits (Longhi, Guardi). Rooms XI and XII have displays of bronze figures, rock crystal and Roman glass – note the bottle with gilded bands dating from the 1C BC. The last room has a collection of mainly 17C still-life paintings.

►► Museo Navale.

Sarzana★

16km/10mi north. The busy town of Sarzana was once an advance base of the Republic of Genoa, a rival of Pisa, and its numerous historic buildings bear witness to its past importance. The **Cattedrale** has a marble **altarpiece★** (1432) delicately carved by Riccomani. In a chapel to the right of the chancel is a phial which is said to have contained the Blood of Christ. In the chapel to the left is a *Crucifixion★* (1138), a Romanesque masterpiece of the artist, Guglielmo, probably from Lucca. The **Fortezza di Sarzanello★** (1322) is a fortress built on a height to the northeast of the town, by the *condottiere* (leader of a mercenary army) from Lucca, Castruccio Castracani. It is a curious example of military architecture with deep moats and massive curtain walls guarded at intervals by round towers. *For information contact the Cultural Office* ☎ *0187 61 42 48, 0187 61 42 90, 0187 61 42 27 (8am-1.30pm).* From the top of the keep there is a magnificent **panorama★★** of the town and the Apennine foothills.

Portovenere★★

This small, severe-looking town is dominated by a 12C-16C citadel. Some of the houses date as far back as the 12C and were in fact once fortified by the Genoese. The church of San Lorenzo dates from the 12C, while the church of San Pietro incorporates parts dating from the 6C. From the terrace there is a very fine view of the Gulf of La Spezia and the Cinque Terre region.

Lerici⌂

At the head of a well-sheltered cove Lerici has an important 13C castle (*castello*) which was rebuilt in the 16C by the Genoese.

Roma ★★★

ROME

The capital of the Roman Empire to which it owes its name, and the centre of Christendom since the fall of the Empire, Rome is rich in monuments of its ancient history which justify its renown as the Eternal City. Today Rome is no longer the marble city left behind by Augustus and the Emperors, nor is it the opulent court of the Papal era: since 1870, the year in which it was proclaimed capital of Italy, Rome has seen a widespread and, especially after the Second World War, uncontrolled urban expansion.

The best views of this urban complex sprawling over the seven hills are from the belvederes on the Janiculum (Gianicolo), the Aventine (Aventino) and the Pincio hills. At dusk the visitor will discover a city bathed in a golden light, the green masses of the gardens, the silhouettes of umbrella pines shading the areas of ruins, as well as the numerous domes and bell towers rising above the pink-tiled roofscape.

The surrounding countryside has been more fortunate, so that even today those landscapes dotted with pine trees and cypresses, under a pure blue sky and bathed in a golden light, form an unforgettable panorama.

Location

Population 2 643 581 – Michelin map 430 Q 19, with plans of the conurbation. Michelin map 38 Rome – See also The Green Guide Rome. "All roads lead to Rome", so they say. In fact, Rome lies at the hub of a complicated motorway network with the traffic from A 1, A 12, A 24 all converging on the very busy Raccordo Anulare (ringroad). ☑ *via Parigi 5,* ☎ *06 48 89 92, Aeroporto di Fiumicino,* ☎ *06 65 95 60 74.*

Surrounding area: see TERRACINA, TIVOLI.

B. Morandi/MICHELIN

Background

No other city in the world has managed to combine so successfully such a diverse heritage of Classical antiquities, medieval buildings, Renaissance palaces and Baroque churches. Far from being discordant they constitute a logical continuity where revivals, influences and contrasts are evidence of the ingenuity of Roman architects and builders. Of course, the ruins no longer present the splendour they displayed under the Empire, when they were faced with marble, and only a few of the palaces have retained the painted decoration of their façades. And even the city more recently acclaimed by Goethe and Stendhal has changed, owing to the damage caused by heavy traffic and the developments resulting from the modernisation of a busy capital city.

However, today's visitor cannot fail to be impressed by the immensity of the great centre of ancient civilisation and lively modern activity that is Rome. The best overall views of this urban complex sprawling over the seven hills are from the belvederes with the numerous domes and bell towers in the distance. Rome with some 300 churches is the city of churches, where it is not uncommon to find two side by side. It is often impossible to stand back and admire their façades but the richness of the decoration and the ingenious use of *trompe l'oeil* tend to compensate for this drawback. Often the interiors are astonishing for their silence and light and the inventiveness and audacity of the ultimate design. In the older districts of Rome (Vecchia Roma) around the Pantheon, the Piazza Navona and the Campo dei Fiori, there is a wealth of fine palaces. Those who wander through these districts will often catch a glimpse between ochre-coloured façades of a small square with all the bustle of a market, or several flights of stairways descending to a fountain. In the evening these areas are lit by tall street lights and are bathed in a soft glow which gives them a certain charm, a pleasant change from the bustling main arteries.

Luxury shops are to be found around the Piazza del Popolo, Via del Corso, Piazza di Spagna and the streets which open off them. Via Veneto lined with cafés and luxurious hotels is a fashionable tourist centre. Piazza Navona is another fashionable meeting-place while the **Trastevere**, which has never lost its popular character, has a variety of restaurants. Antique and second-hand shops line Via dei Coronari.

LOST IN THE MISTS OF TIME ...

The legendary origins of Rome were perpetuated by both Roman historians and poets, such as Livy in the more than 100 volumes of his monumental opus, *Roman History,* and Virgil in the *Aeneid.* Both claimed that Aeneas, son of the goddess Aphrodite, fled from Troy when it was captured, and landed at the mouth of the Tiber. Having defeated the local tribes he founded Lavinium. His son Ascanius (or Iulus) founded Alba Longa. It was here that Rhea Silvia the Vestal, following her union with the god Mars, gave birth to the twins Romulus and Remus, who were abandoned on the Tiber. The twins, transported by the current of the river, came to rest at the foot of the Palatine where they were nursed by a wolf. Later Romulus marked a furrow round the sacred area on which the new city was to be built. Jesting, Remus stepped over the line; Romulus killed him for violating the sacred precinct. Romulus populated his village with outlaws who settled on the Capitol and married women who had been seized from the Sabines. An alliance grew up between the two peoples who were ruled by a succession of kings, alternately Sabine and Latin, until the Etruscans arrived.

But beyond legend modern historians emphasise the strategic location of Rome's seven hills especially that of the Palatine, which was a staging-post on the salt road (Via Salaria). This no doubt led to the development of settlements around the Palatine in the 8C BC.

Two centuries later the Etruscans had transformed these villages of shacks into a well-organised town, with a citadel on the Capitol. The last Etruscan king, Tarquin the Superb, was thrown out in 509 BC and the Consulate was instituted.

The Republican era was an ambitious one of territorial expansion. During the 2C and 1C BC the Republican regime tore itself to pieces in a civil war. To restore order disrupted by the rival political factions and rule the newly conquered territories, it required a clever man of very determined character. **Julius Caesar** (101-44 BC) emerged from amid the contenders by reason of his audacious strategies (he conquered the whole of Gaul in 51 BC), his grasp of political affairs, his talents as an orator and his unbounded ambition. Appointed consul and dictator for life, he was assassinated on the Ides of March, 15 March 44 BC. He was succeeded by his great-nephew, **Octavian**, a young man who was of delicate health and had won no military glory. Octavian was to demonstrate tenacity of purpose and political genius and ably rid his path of possible rivals. In 27 BC the Senate granted Octavian the title **Augustus**, which invested him with an aura of holiness. He soon became the first Roman emperor. His achievements were considerable: he extended Roman government and restored peace to the whole of the Mediterranean basin.

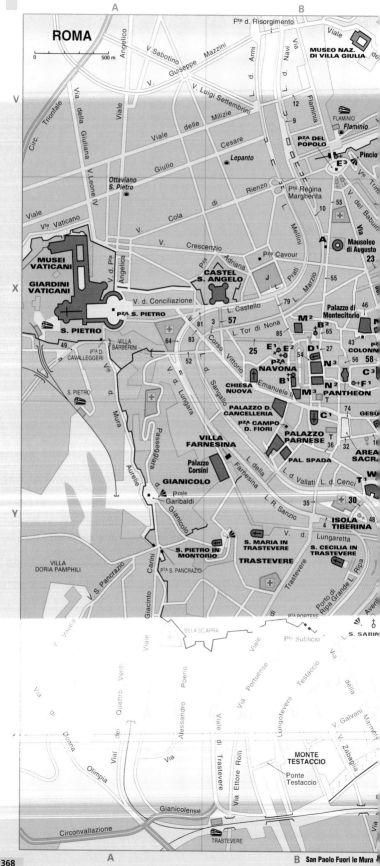

ROMA

0   500 m

MUSEO NAZ. DI VILLA GIULIA

Pte d. Risorgimento

Viale

Via Giuseppe Mazzini

V. Sabotino

Angelico

V. d. Armi

L. d. Navi

V. Luigi Settembrini

Viale delle Milizie

Flaminia

FLAMINIO

Flaminio

PZA DEL POPOLO

E³

Pincio

Cesare

Lepanto

Giulio

Ottaviano S. Pietro

V.

Cola di

Rienzo

Pte Regina Margherita

10

55

V. del Babuino

Crescenzio

Adriana

Pza Cavour

Mausoleo di Augusto 23

A

MUSEI VATICANI

GIARDINI VATICANI

V. d. Pta Angelica

Pza

CASTEL S. ANGELO

J

55

L. Mazzio

Palazzo di Montecitorio 46

V. d. Conciliazione

L. Castello

79

M² B²

65

27

43

PZA COLONN

S. PIETRO

VILLA BARBERINI

81   3 — 57

L. Tor di Nona

25

E¹ E²

54

D¹

N³

56 58

C³

49

PTA D. CAVALLEGGERI

64 — 83

Corso Vittorio

PZA NAVONA

B¹

M³

N²

PANTHEON

F¹

S. PIETRO

52

Emanuele II

74

GESÙ

CHIESA NUOVA

T

C¹

PALAZZO D. CANCELLERIA

16

VILLA FARNESINA

V. d. Lungara

PZA CAMPO D. FIORI

PALAZZO FARNESE

36

32

AREA SACRA

Passeggiata

Palazzo Corsini

L. della Farnesina

PAL. SPADA

W

GIANICOLO

Aurelia

Pzale Garibaldi

L. d. Vallati

L. d. Cenci

T¹

Gianicolo

L. R. Sanzio

35

30

ISOLA TIBERINA

48

4

VILLA DORIA PAMPHILI

Carini

S. PIETRO IN MONTORIO

PTA S. PANCRAZIO

S. MARIA IN TRASTEVERE

V. d. Lungaretta

S. CECILIA IN TRASTEVERE

TRASTEVERE

Trastevere

Porto di Ripa Grande

L. Ripa

V. S. Pancrazio

Giacinto

PTA PORTESE

Aventi

S. SABIN

Viale

VILLA SC. ARRA

Viale

Pte Sublicio

Testaccio

V. Galvani

della

V. Vitellia

V. di Donna Olimpia

Viale dei Quattro Venti

Alessandro Poerio

Viale di Trastevere

Via Portuense

Lungotevere Testaccio

V. Zabaglia

Marmo

Via

Via Ettore Rolli

MONTE TESTACCIO

Via

Gianicolense

Ponte Testaccio

Circonvallazione

TRASTEVERE

A   B

V

X

Y

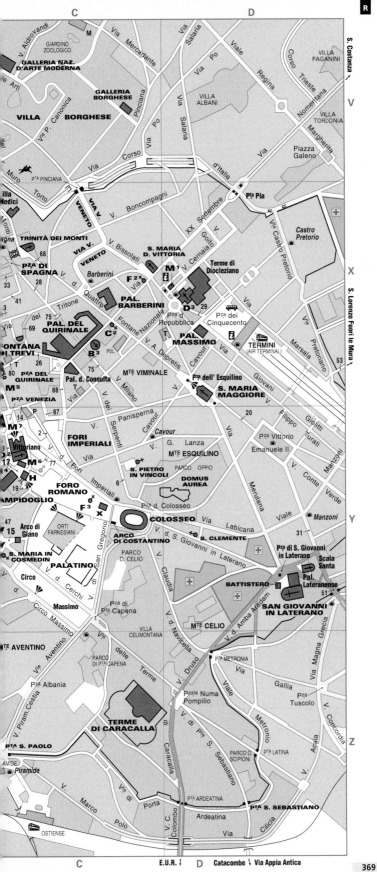

INDEX OF STREET NAMES AND SIGHTS IN ROME

Directory

R

GETTING THERE

By car – Driving in Rome is not advisable as parking in the city can be a major problem (visitors should note that most of the hotels in the city centre do not have private garages or parking). The few private car parks that do exist are extremely expensive and access to the city centre by car is severely restricted (a special permit is required).

By train – The mainline national and international trains arrive at Stazione Termini or Tiburtina, which are linked to the city centre on both Metro lines A and B. For information contact: ☎ 8488 88 088, or consult the website www.trenitalia.com

By air – The main airport is Leonardo da Vinci, at Fiumicino (26km/16mi southwest of Rome). It is linked to the centre by train. Services from Stazione Termini depart every 30min (no stop, €9.30), and from the stations at Tiburtina, Tuscolana, Ostiense every 15min (€4.65). There is also a night bus service to the airport from Stazione Tiburtina (45min).

Useful numbers – **Aeroporto "Leonardo da Vinci" – Fiumicino,** ☎ 06 65 951; **Ciampino,** ☎ 06 79 49 41. **Domestic flight reservations**: ☎ 06 65 641 (Alitalia), 06 65 95 52 19 (other flights). **Passenger information**: ☎ 06 65 95 36 40 and 06 65 95 44 55.

By car – Most city traffic makes use of two ring roads: the outer ring road (Grande Raccordo Anulare), lies on the outskirts of the city at a junction of main national roads as well as A 1, A 2, A 24, A 18 motorways; the second ring-road is the Tangenziale Est which forms part of the traffic network within the city. It connects the Olympic stadium to Piazza San Giovanni in Laterano, passing through the eastern quarters of the city (Nomentano, Tiburtino, Prenestino).

GETTING ABOUT

By taxi – Radiotaxi telephone numbers are: ☎ 06 88 22, 06 49 94, 06 55 51, 06 41 57.

By bus, tram or underground – City route plans are on sale in bookshops and kiosks; the plan Rete dei Trasporti Urbani di Roma, published by ATAC (Azienda Tramvie e Autobus del Comune di Roma, ☎ 06 46 951), is sold at the information kiosk in Piazza dei Cinquecento. Tickets should be purchased before the beginning of the journey and punched in the machine in the bus and on the underground to be validated.

By car – Driving in Rome is not advised as access to the city centre is very difficult and parking severely restricted; many streets are reserved for pedestrians, taxis, buses and local residents. The historic centre is delineated as blue zone (fascia blu) from which private cars are excluded almost all day. There are two large underground car parks in central Rome: Villa Borghese, near the Porta Pinciana and Parking Ludovisi, Via Ludovisi 60. The pedestrianised areas are: Colosseo, Fori imperiali and Appia Antica. For information contact: www.comune.roma.it

SIGHTSEEING

The city of Rome has information booths located at strategic points of the city centre (Largo Goldoni, Piazza Sonnino, Piazza Cinque Lune, corner of Via Minghetti (zona Fontana di Trevi). These offer information on all cultural and tourist events in the capital. Open Tuesday to Saturday from 10am to 6pm and on Sundays from 10am to 1pm, up-to-the-minute information is provided to tourists in Italian and English.

Internet users can visit the website: www.comune.roma.it

Facilities for the disabled – For information in Italy on which monuments are accessible to disabled travellers, contact **CO.IN** (Consorzio Cooperative Integrate), Via Enrico Giglioli 54/a; ☎ and Fax 06 71 29 011, 800 27 10 27 (toll-free number for the Servizio Vacanze Serene). Offices are open Mon-Fri, 9am-5pm and Sat 9am-1pm. Information also available on the website: www.coinsociale.it

B. Pérousse/MICHELIN

WHERE TO EAT

Visitors are spoilt for choice in Rome, with a wide selection of places to eat, ranging from pizzerias and simple trattorias to elegant restaurants serving fine cuisine.

DIFFERENT TYPES OF RESTAURANTS
Restaurants, trattorias and osterie

Although the distinction between these different types of restaurants is not as obvious as it once was, in general, a **ristorante** offers elegant cuisine and service, while a **trattoria or osteria** is more likely to be a family-run establishment serving home-made dishes in a more relaxed, informal atmosphere. Prices are usually lower in the latter and house wine (of varying quality) is served by the carafe. In typical trattorias, the waiter will often tell you what dishes of the day are on offer – if ordering these, make sure that you know how much you are paying ahead of time to avoid any unpleasant shocks when the bills arrives! (a list is usually available; if in doubt ask to see it). Be wary of choosing the tourist menu, which usually has very limited choice.

In Rome, lunch is usually served from 12.30-3pm and dinner from 8-11pm; restaurants generally close around midnight. Most places will close for one day a week, which varies from restaurant to restaurant, but is not usually at weekends. Many restaurants, especially trattorias, close for two to three weeks in August.

Wine bars

Wine bars (enoteche) have become increasingly popular in Italy in recent years, offering customers the chance to sample a selection of fine wines accompanied by various hors d'oeuvres and delicate snacks, without having to order a full meal.

Pizzerias

Pizzerias are usually only open in the evening and are good meeting-places for those who want to eat out at reasonable prices. As a result, they tend to be very popular and visitors are advised to book in advance where possible to avoid the inevitable queue outside. The addresses below include a number of pizzerias which specialise in the Neapolitan-style pizza, which is becoming more and more popular. Neapolitan-style pizzas have a rim and are thicker than the Roman variety. The Romans tend to prefer their pizza thin, crispy and drenched in olive oil. They are also unlikely to forego the traditional entrée of **bruschetta** (toasted bread rubbed with raw garlic, sprinkled with salt, drizzled with olive oil and in some cases topped with freshly chopped tomatoes, basil or capers) or **fritto misto alla romana**. Fritto misto comprises a number of different seasonal delicacies, such as courgette flowers stuffed with mozzarella and anchovies, fillets of salted cod, stuffed giant green Ascoli olives, and potato croquettes dipped in batter and deep-fried. Those not wishing to order pizza may like to try a **crostino** instead – this toasted bread is similar to bruschetta, but is covered with melted cheese and parma ham, or perhaps with porcini (cep) mushrooms.

For those not wishing to sit down for a large meal at lunchtime, or who are on a limited budget, there are a number of self-service restaurants and places offering slices of pizza (pizzeria al taglio) in the city. These small stalls, which are usually only open during the day, often have a bar area with stools for customers to sit and enjoy their pizza. In addition to the numerous pizzerie al taglio in the city, slices of pizza can also occasionally be bought at bakeries, some of which are particularly well known for their plain or tomato topped pizza. Visitors should be aware that these bakeries keep shop opening hours and will not therefore be open at lunchtime.

Pizzeria Da Baffetto – Via del Governo Vecchio 114, Piazza Navona district – ☎ 06 68 61 617 – ✂. Excellent crispy pizza served in a traditional pizzeria which has been popular with students since the 1960s. Expect to queue, but once you're seated the service is remarkably swift.

Pizzeria Dar Poeta – Vicolo del Bologna 45, Trastevere district – ☎ 06 58 80 516 –

www.darpoeta.it – ✂. This warm and lively pizzeria serves pizzas made from a special dough. Also on offer is a wide selection of bruschette and even a ricotta and Nutella calzone for those with a sweet tooth.

Restaurants and trattorias

• Budget

Eau Vive – Via Monterone 85, Pantheon district – ☎ 06 68 80 10 95 – Closed Sun and Aug – 🖻 ✂ – Booking recommended – €8/26. This restaurant is run by missionary nuns of different nationalities and is located inside the 16C Palazzo Lante, near the Pantheon. French specialities can be sampled in the large, frescoed dining room on the first floor.

Enoteca La Bottega del Vino da Anacleto Bleve – Via S. Maria del Pianto 9/A, Largo Argentina district – ☎ 06 68 65 970 – Closed evenings and public holidays – Booking recommended – €10/26. This wine bar is situated in the heart of the Jewish quarter. Before sitting down, choose from the delicate soufflés, roulades, salads and cheeses displayed at the bar. Delicious lemon or coffee ice cream. Family run with attentive service.

Augusto – Piazza de' Renzi 15, Trastevere district – ☎ 06 58 03 798 – Closed Sat evening and Sun – ✂ – €13/17. During the summer this family-run restaurant has large wooden tables outside, overlooking one of the most typical squares in this district. The food here is simple and the atmosphere warm and informal. Expect to wait for a table.

Da Francesco – Piazza del Fico 29, Piazza Navona district – ☎ 06 68 64 009 – Closed Tue lunchtime – ✂ – Booking recommended – €15/31. The attractive Piazza del Fico is home to this lively trattoria which serves typical Roman dishes, including pizzas, an excellent focaccia with dry-cured ham and various types of pasta. A cheerful atmosphere, with a mixed clientele of tourists and well-known faces.

Trattoria dal Cavalier Gino – Vicolo Rosini 4, Montecitorio district – ☎ 06 68 73 434 – Closed Sun and Aug – ✂ – €18/23. A friendly atmosphere and good food at affordable prices make this trattoria a popular choice with office workers of the surrounding neighbourhood. For this reason, and because of the restaurant's limited capacity, it can be difficult to get a table here at lunchtime.

• Moderate

Ditirambo – Piazza della Cancelleria 74, Piazza Navona district – ☎ 06 68 71 626 – Closed Mon lunchtime and Aug – ✂ – Booking recommended – €23/39. Situated directly behind Campo dei Fiori, this friendly restaurant has two small, well-furnished rooms where a range of sophisticated dishes are served. The different types of bread, the pasta and the desserts are home-made. A popular choice.

Pommidoro – Piazza dei Sanniti 44, San Lorenzo Fuori le Mura district – ☎ 06 44 52 692 – Closed Sun – €26/31. A genuine Roman *trattoria* specialising in game dishes and grilled meat and fish. Frequented by politicians, artists and journalists.

La Penna d' Oca – *Via della Penna 53, Piazza del Popolo district* – ☎ *06 32 02 898 – Closed Sun, Sat lunchtime, for 10 days in Jan and 20 days in Aug – Booking recommended* – €26/62. Not far from Piazza del Popolo, this charming restaurant serves traditional cuisine, innovative fish and seafood dishes (try the conch pie served with red onion) and home-made bread. Meals are served on a pleasant veranda in summer.

Paris – *Piazza San Callisto 7/A, Trastevere district* – ☎ *06 58 15 378 – Closed Sun evening, Mon and Aug* – 🖻 – €28/52. This restaurant is situated in the heart of Trastevere and offers mainly Roman-Jewish cuisine, served in an attractive Baroque-style room. Dishes include *tagliolini al sugo di pesce* (thin noodles in a fish sauce), *carciofi alla giudia (artichoke hearts fried in olive oil with garlic and parsley)*, fried vegetables, and to end your meal, delicious ricotta cheese.

Checchino dal 1887 – *Via Monte Testaccio 30, Testaccio district* – ☎ *06 57 46 318 – Closed 24 Dec-2 Jan, Aug, Sun and Mon – Booking recommended* – €34/62. A good address for quality Roman cuisine, accompanied by the best Italian wines. Specialities include *rigatoni all pajata*, sweetbreads in a white wine sauce and oxtail. Cheaper meals based on cheese and vegetables available at lunchtime.

Sora Lella – *Via di Ponte Quattro Capi 16, Isola Tiberina district* – ☎ *06 68 61 601 – Closed Sun, 1 Jan, Easter, Aug and 24-26 Dec.* – 🖻 – €34/67. This famous restaurant was once run by Lella Fabrizi, the sister of the actor Aldo. It is now managed by her son, who has extended the traditional range of family recipes to include new specialities. Don't miss the *formaggi alle marmellate* (cheese with sweet fruit jelly) and the home-made desserts.

• *Expensive*

La Rosetta – *Via della Rosetta 9, Pantheon district* – ☎ *06 68 61 002 – Closed Sat lunchtime, Sun and 8-22 Aug* – 🖻 – *Booking recommended* – €70/108. This restaurant is well-known throughout Rome because of the high quality of its fish and seafood specialities. Don't miss the delicious Mediterranean sashimi (raw fish).

La Terrazza – *Via Ludovisi 49, Piazza di Spagna district* – ☎ *06 47 81 21* – 🖻 – *Booking recommended* – €80/120. The roof-garden of the Hotel Eden is home to this elegant restaurant, which offers stunning views of the city and is popular with famous personalities. The creative cuisine served here is mainly based on fish and seafood recipes. Prices for Sunday brunch are more affordable.

CAFÉS

Caffè Greco – *Via dei Condotti 86, Piazza di Spagna district* – ☎ *06 67 91 700 – 8am-8.30pm*. The café was founded by a Greek in 1760 and was frequented by writers and artists such as Goethe, Berlioz, Leopardi,

D'Annunzio, Andersen (who lived in the same building) and Stendhal, whose last Roman residence was at n° 48. On 24 March 1824, Pope Leo XII forbade his citizens to enter the café, subject to a term of three months' imprisonment. This decision proved so unpopular that the café owner continued to serve customers through an opening in the window. The long, narrow, inner room known as the "omnibus" contains portraits of famous people.

S. Eustachio – *Piazza S. Eustachio 82, Pantheon district* – ☎ *06 68 61 309 – 8.30am-1am*. This café is famous for its delicious, creamy coffee known as a *gran caffè speciale*, the secret recipe of which is jealously guarded by its creator. Let the waiter know if you like your coffee unsweetened, as coffee is usually served with the sugar already added.

Tazza d'Oro – *Via degli Orfani 84, Pantheon district* – ☎ *06 67 89 792 – Mon-Sat, 7am-8pm*. This specialist coffee bar serves strong and aromatic coffee and has a wide selection of coffee to take away. In the summer, don't miss the coffee *granita* with double helpings of cream.

Rosati – *Piazza del Popolo 4, Piazza del Popolo district* – ☎ *06 32 25 859 – 7.30am-midnight*. This traditional, elegant café/restaurant and terrace is situated right on the piazza and is a pleasant meeting-place.

Bar del Fico – *Piazza del Fico 26/27, Piazza Navona district* – ☎ *06 68 65 205 – 8am-2am*. The Bar del Fico, one of the busiest in the district, has tables set out in the shade of the fig tree which gives both the bar and the piazza their name. Temporary exhibitions of paintings and photography can be admired inside the bar. The bar serves delicious canapés and snacks at aperitif time and plays a good selection of music

Antico Caffè della Pace – *Piazza della Pace 4, Piazza Navona district* – ☎ *06 68 61 216 – 10am-2am*. Situated in a lovely little square near the main piazza, this café attracts a number of personalities from the theatre, especially in the evening when they can be seen sitting at the outdoor tables. The two rooms inside the café have a Central European feel, with padded sofas, soft lights and tinted mirrors.

Caffè Capitolino – *Piazzale Caffarelli 4, Campidoglio, Capitolino district* – ☎ *06 67 10 20 71 – Mon-Sat, 9.30am-9pm*. Situated on the terrace of Palazzo Caffarelli, the Capitoline Museum bar provides a stunning panorama of the surrounding area. Sandwiches and hot and cold drinks, including a range of cocktails, are served here. The view is particularly impressive at sunset.

ICE CREAM PARLOURS

If you ask a Roman where you can buy the best ice cream in the city, he will nearly always give you the address of a *gelateria* in his own neighbourhood. Good ice cream is not difficult to find in Rome and many producers have their own specialities. What better way to cool down on a hot summer's day or evening in the capital than with an ice cream cone or a *granita* or *grattachecca* in your favourite flavour.

The *grattachecca* is the Roman version of the crushed ice drink known as *granita* elsewhere in Italy and sold in kiosks on street corners in the summer months. The pieces of ice, which are scraped off large blocks with a spatula, are placed in paper cups and covered with sweet, colourful syrups. Pieces of fresh fruit are then added on top.

Il Gelato di S. Crispino – *Via della Panetteria 42, Fontana di Trevi district –* ☎ 06 67 93 924 – *Wed-Mon, 11am-midnight.* The owners of this *gelateria*, considered to be one of the best in Rome, only make flavours which they like themselves. Try the ice cream with honey, ginger and cinnamon, cream with Armagnac, liquorice, meringue with hazelnut or chocolate and cream with Pantelleria raisin wine.

Giolitti – *Via Uffici del Vicario 40 –* ☎ 06 67 98 147 – *Open 7am-2am.* Despite having no outdoor tables, this pleasant gelateria is an excellent meeting-point in the heart of the city and serves a wide range of ice creams and milk shakes.

WHERE TO STAY

From modest *pensioni* to luxury hotels, Rome has a wide range of accommodation options to suit all budgets and tastes, although finding value for money can sometimes prove difficult. As the capital is very popular with tourists and pilgrims throughout the year, visitors are advised to book well in advance in order to be sure of securing accommodation and avoiding any unpleasant surprises. Generally speaking, the low season includes January, the first half of February, the last two weeks of July, the months of August and November and the first two weeks of December. During these periods many hotels offer reasonable rates and special weekend deals or short breaks. Visitors are advised to choose a hotel with air-conditioning during the summer, as it is particularly hot during this period (hotels with air-conditioning are indicated in the list given below).

It is worth noting that during trade fairs and exhibitions the hotels tend to put their prices up. Do enquire about this when you make your booking.

SELECTING A DISTRICT

A good selection of pensioni and hotels can be found in the **historic centre**, where the atmosphere and high concentrations of tourist sights and shops make it particularly popular with visitors; however, many of these establishments have limited capacity and as a result are often full. The attractive village-like quarter of **Trastevere**, with its lively nightlife, would also be a pleasant area in which to stay, although accommodation options here are somewhat limited.

The **Vatican and Prati** districts are close to the centre and are quieter and more reasonably priced than the historic centre and Trastevere (especially the Prati district, which has a good choice of hotels). The choice of accommodation around **Via Cavour** (near the

Rione Monti district), between Termini Station and the Fori Imperiali, is also good, especially for mid-range hotels.

Many of the cheaper *pensioni* and smaller hotels are concentrated in the area around **Termini Station**, slightly away from the city centre and somewhat lacking in character, but well served by public buses and the metro system.

The majority of the city's luxury hotels can be found on the **Via Veneto** and in the area around **Villa Borghese**.

CONVENTS AND MONASTERIES

As well as providing accommodation for pilgrims, convents and monasteries are also a good option for those on a limited budget. Rooms are reasonably priced, although visitors are usually expected to be in by a specified hour (usually 10.30pm). Occasionally men and women are required to sleep in separate rooms.

For further information, contact the **Peregrinatio ad Petri Sedem**, *Piazza Pio XII 4 (Vaticano – San Pietro district),* ☎ 06 69 88 48 96; Fax 06 69 88 56 17.

HOTEL RESERVATIONS

Visitors can book hotel rooms through the **Hotel Reservation Service**, ☎ 06 69 91 000, open 7am-10pm. This service is free of charge and offers a choice of 350 hotels in the capital. Visitors booking any of these hotels may also take advantage of a shuttle service from Fiumicino airport, at a cost of €9.55 per person. Reservations can be made by phone or from the airport desk (in the International, European and National Arrival halls), from Termini Railway Station (opposite platform 20), at Ciampino airport and at the Tevere-Ovest service station on the A1 Milan-Rome motorway. The same service is also available on the internet at www.hotelreservation.it

• Budget

Ostello Foro Italico A. F. Pessina – *Viale delle Olimpiadi 61, Monte Mario district – From Termini station, metro A to Ottaviano, then bus 32 (7 stops) –* ☎ 06 32 36 267 – Fax 06 32 42 613 – 🖵 – 400 beds €14.46 🖵 – Meal €8. This modern building surrounded by gardens is the only official hostel in Rome and has a self-service restaurant and a bar. The hostel offers dormitory accommodation only, with 6-bedded rooms for men and 10-bedded rooms for women. Rooms are cleaned between 10am and 2pm, when they must be vacated by guests. Closed between midnight and 7am.

Pensione Ottaviano – *Via Ottaviano 6, (2nd floor, lift), Vatican district –* ☎ 06 39 73 81 38 – gt.costantini@agora.stm.it – 🖵 – 25 rooms €15.49/46.48. Particularly popular with young foreign visitors, this cheerful *pensione* is decorated with paintings and posters left by previous guests. After 8.30pm guests can check their e-mail free of charge. Breakfast not available.

Hotel Pensione Tizi – *Via Collina 48, (1st floor, lift), Porta Pia district –*

☎ 06 48 20 128 – Fax 06 47 43 266 – ✉ – 25 rooms. €36.15/56.81 – ⬚ €5.16. The lobby of this small *pensione* is similar to the entrance hall in houses belonging to a typical Roman family. The hotel is named after the owner's daughter, Tiziana, who is usually at reception to welcome guests. Quiet, attractive rooms, both with and without bathrooms. Good value for money.

Pensione Panda – *Via della Croce 35, Piazza di Spagna district* – ☎ 06 67 80 179 – Fax 06 69 94 21 51 – *www.hotelpandaparadise.com* – 20 rooms. €36.15/61.97. This well-kept *pensione* in a 17C palazzo not far from the Spanish Steps has quiet, simply furnished rooms, some with shared bathroom. Although lacking in overall charm, the hotel is recommended for its excellent location and reasonable rates.

Bed & Breakfast Maximum – *Via Fabio Massimo 72, (1st floor), Vatican district* – ☎ 06 32 42 037 – Fax 06 32 42 156 – *bbmaximum@tiscalinet.it* – ✉ – 4 rooms. €36.15/72.30 ⬚. This B&B situated close to St Peter's offers colourful rooms fitted with ceiling fans. The rooms and bathrooms, one of which has a hydromassage tub, are arranged allong an elegant, arched corridor. Breakfast is served in the rooms. Special offers available in low season.

• *Moderate*

Hotel Perugia – *Via del Colosseo 7, Colosseo district* – ☎ 06 67 97 200 – Fax 06 67 84 635 – htlperugia@isl.it – 13 rooms. €56.81/90.38 ⬚. Given its excellent location close to the Colosseum, this small hotel is very reasonably priced. One of the rooms on the fourth floor has a small balcony with views of the amphitheatre, but no private bathroom.

Hotel Navona – *Via dei Sediari 8, (1st floor, no lift), Piazza Navona district* – ☎ 06 68 21 13 92 – Fax 06 68 80 38 02 – *info@hotelnavona.com* – ✉ ⋈ – 30 rooms. €72.30/103.29 ⬚. This delightful hotel has cool, attractive rooms decorated in English style, as a result of the owner's long period of residence in Australia. The hotel is located in a 16C palazzo which was built on top of much older foundations. Breakfast is served at a long table.

Hotel Trastevere Manara – *Via Luciano Manara 24/A-25, Trastevere district* – ☎ 06 58 14 713 – Fax 06 58 81 016 – *hoteltrastevere@tiscalinet.it* – 9 rooms. €77.47/98.13 ⬚. An excellent location, just a stone's throw from the attractive Piazza Santa Maria in Trastevere. The hotel rooms, all furnished in modern style, include individual safety deposit boxes.

Pensione Barrett – *Largo Torre Argentina 47, Torre Argentina district* – ☎ 06 68 68 481 – Fax 06 68 92 971 – ✉ ⬚ – 20 rooms. €77.47/92.96 – ⬚ €5.16. Simple, but well looked after and in an excellent location. The rooms have thoughtful and unusual touches, such as a small footbath and tea- and coffee-making facilities. Visitors in search of peace and quiet should avoid the rooms overlooking the busy square.

Hotel Coronet – *Piazza Grazioli 5, Pantheon district* – ☎ 06 67 92 341 – Fax 06 69 92 27 05 – *hotelcoronet@tiscalinet.it* – 13 rooms. €77.47/144.61 ⬚. Located in the Palazzo Doria Pamphili, this small hotel is well maintained and offers spacious, comfortable rooms. A romantic atmosphere and good service.

Hotel Pensione Suisse – *Via Gregoriana 54, (3rd floor, lift), Piazza di Spagna district* – ☎ 06 67 83 649 – Fax 06 67 81 258 – *suisse.hotel@tiscalinet.it* – 12 rooms. €85.22/129.11 ⬚. In an elegant mansion near the Casa dei Mostri, this hotel is run by a friendly multilingual family and has well-appointed rooms arranged around an internal courtyard. Guests are requested to return to the hotel no later than 2am. Breakfast is served in the rooms.

• *Expensive*

Hotel Due Torri – *Vicolo del Leonetto 23, Piazza Navona district* – ☎ 06 68 76 983 – Fax 06 68 65 442 – ⬚ – 26 rooms. €98.13/165.27 ⬚. Once the residence of high prelates, this delightful centrally located hotel is situated in a quiet, attractive street. Each room has its own unique decor and is furnished with a parquet floor and high quality furniture, including some genuine antiques. One of our favourite addresses in Rome.

Hotel Cisterna in Trastevere – *Via della Cisterna 7/8/9, Trastevere district* – ☎ 06 58 17 212 – Fax 06 58 10 091 – ⬚ – 19 rooms. €98.13/118.79 ⬚. This hotel, housed within a small 18C palazzo, is located in a narrow street named after an unusual fountain, known as the "cisterna" ("well" in English). Some of the rooms have dormer windows and wooden beams, and one on the top floor even has a small balcony.

Hotel Venezia – *Via Varese 18, Stazione Termini district* – ☎ 06 44 57 101 – Fax 06 49 57 687 – ⬚ – 61 rooms. €103.29/139.44 ⬚. A comfortable, well-kept hotel, with good facilities. The public rooms of the hotel are particularly attractive, with wrought-iron candelabra, beautifully made rustic furniture and delicate fabrics. Recommended.

Hotel Teatro di Pompeo – *Largo del Pallaro 8, Campo dei Fiori district* – ☎ 06 68 30 01 70 – Fax 06 68 80 55 31 – ⬚ – 13 rooms. From €139.44 ⬚. The unusual dining room of this delightful hotel still retains the original vaults of Pompey's Theatre. The hotel rooms are spacious and simply furnished, with coffered ceilings and tiled floors.

Sant'Anselmo – *Piazza Sant'Anselmo 2, Aventino district* – ☎ 06 57 48 119 – Fax 06 57 83 604 – 44 rooms. €118.79/180.76 ⬚. This hotel, situated away from the traffic of the city amid the greenery of the Aventine hill, offers rooms with antique furniture in three residential villas. The hotel is surrounded by delightful gardens and graced with a beautiful veranda on which breakfast is served. A wonderful way to experience Rome.

Hotel Fontana – *Piazza di Trevi 96, Fontana di Trevi district* – ☏ *06 67 86 113 – Fax 06 67 90 024 – 25 rooms. From €180.76* ⚏. One way of admiring the Trevi fountain without having to fight through the crowds is to stay at this delightful hotel situated in Piazza di Trevi, where the charming rooms will satisfy the most romantic of travellers.

Hotel Lord Byron – *Via De Notaris 5, Villa Giulia district* – ☏ *06 32 20 404 – Fax 06 32 20 405 –* 🖵 *– 32 rooms. From €229.82* ⚏. This small, elegant hotel overlooks the Villa Borghese gardens and has an attractive 1920s atmosphere. The hotel restaurant, the **Relais Le Jardin**, serves fine cuisine.

GOING OUT

For those who enjoy music and dancing, Rome has a wide selection of venues ranging from the best-known nightclubs to disco bars and bars with live bands. Nightlife is mainly concentrated in three areas, each offering different kinds of entertainment and attracting a different crowd. The district between **Piazza Campo dei Fiori** and **Piazza Navona** has a wide choice of pubs and bars, drawing a mix of young students, foreign tourists and the theatre crowd (especially in the elegant bars around Piazza Navona). On the streets of **Trastevere**, the bars and restaurants are generally typically Roman in character and host shows with live music. The majority of the city's most popular nightclubs are concentrated in the Testaccio district, particularly in Via di Monte Testaccio, and more recently, in the nearby Via di Libetta.

SHOPPING

Unlike other capital cities in Europe, Rome does not have many large department stores, preferring a wide range of small shops and boutiques to suit all tastes and budgets. Visitors will have no difficult in buying antiques, craft products and high quality food produce throughout the city, especially in the historic centre, as well as an excellent selection of the latest fashions.

In general, clothes stores are closed on Monday morning, while food shops close on Thursday afternoon. With the exception of the historic centre, where shops tend to stay open all day, shops are open 10am-1pm and 4-7.30pm (winter) or 5-8pm (summer). Credit cards are accepted in most stores, with the exception of small food shops.

FASHION

Many luxury stores are located in **Via Veneto**, while some of the best-known names in the Italian fashion world can be found in the area between **Via del Corso** and **Piazza di Spagna**, especially in Via Frattina, Via Borgognona (Laura Biagiotti, Versace, Fendi etc) and Via Bocca di Leone (Versace). Particularly worthy of mention in this district is **Bulgari**, one of the original goldsmiths in Rome, which is situated at the beginning of **Via dei Condotti**. In the same street, **Raggi** is very popular with young people for its reasonably priced and striking jewellery. Other famous names in this district include Armani, Gucci, Prada and Valentino.

Via del Corso, which is packed with young people on a Saturday afternoon, is home to a variety of shops selling all kinds of goods at reasonable prices, as are Via Nazionale, Via del Tritone and Via Cola di Rienzo.

MARKETS

Borgo Parioli – *Via Tirso 14, Catacombe di Priscilla district – Open Sat-Sun, 9am-8pm.* This antiques market is held in a large garage and has a selection of paintings, prints, frames, clocks, embroidery, lace, books and magazines. Unusual culinary specialities may also be sampled here.

Mercato di Via Sannio – *Via Sannio, San Giovanni in Laterano district – Mon-Sat, 10am-1pm.* A wide choice of reasonably priced new and second-hand clothes, as well as shoes sold at factory prices.

Porta Portese – *Trastevere district – Sun, from dawn to 2pm.* This market sells a bit of everything and is often referred to as the flea market. It opened officially during the Second World War, formed by stalls from other local markets, and is held along Via Portuense. Articles on sale include general bric-a-brac, new and second-hand clothes, photographic equipment, books and records.

Among Augustus' successors there were those who were driven by madness and cruelty (Caligula, Nero and Domitian); and others who continued the good work of Roman civilisation: the good administrator, Vespasian; Titus who was known as the love and delight of the human race; Trajan, the "best of Emperors" and great builder, and Hadrian, an indefatigable traveller and passionate Hellenist.

CHRISTIANITY

As the old order passed away, undermined from within by economic misery and the concentration of authority in the hands of one man, and from without by barbarian attacks, a new force – Christianity – began to emerge. It had first reached Rome in the reign of Augustus. The religion of Jesus of Nazareth originated in Palestine and Syria, and was spread throughout the pagan world by his disciples, eventually reaching Rome. During the last years of the 1C and the early years of the 2C the Christian

Church became organised, but transgressed the law from the beginning because the Emperor embodied religious power. It was not until the **Edict of Milan** (313), which allowed Christians to practise their religion openly, and the conversion of **Constantine** (314), that the Church could come out into the open.

From the first days of Christianity, the bishop was Christ's representative on earth. The bishop of Rome, capital of the Empire, claimed primacy. Gradually the name **"Pope"**, which had been used for all bishops, was reserved for the Bishop of Rome alone. For 19 centuries the popes at the head of the Roman church have influenced the history of Christianity and given the Eternal City its particular character. In the 11C **Gregory VII** restored order to the Christian Church, which had by then an appalling reputation. He dealt with two scourges: the buying and selling of church property, and the marriage of the clergy. In so doing he started the **Investiture Controversy**, which set in opposition the Sovereign Pontiff and the Holy Roman Emperor.

During the Renaissance numerous popes distinguished themselves as ambitious patrons of the arts, bringing to their court such artists as Raphael and Michelangelo whose genius contributed to the embellishment of the capital. They included Pius II, Sixtus IV (who built the Sistine Chapel, Santa Maria della Pace and Santa Maria del Popolo), Julius II (who commissioned Michelangelo to decorate the ceiling of the Sistine Chapel), Leo X (who had a great personal fortune and nominated Raphael as intendant of the arts), Clement VII, Sixtus V (a great builder) and Paul III who built the Farnese Palace.

Worth a Visit

No other city in the world has such a wealth of Classical antiquities, medieval buildings, Renaissance palaces and Baroque churches. With this in mind, a minimum stay of two or three days is recommended. The following paragraphs give general information on some 20 of the best-known sights. The section entitled "Additional Sights" lists by type other interesting buildings, beauty spots or museums highlighting the city's outstanding wealth of places to visit.

EVERY STONE TELLS A STORY...

Campidoglio★★★
On the hill which symbolised the power of ancient Rome, there now stand the city's administrative offices, the church of Santa Maria d'Aracoeli, Piazza del Campidoglio and its palaces, and pleasant gardens.

Chiesa di Santa Maria d'Aracoeli★★
The church has a lovely staircase built as a votive offering after the plague of 1346, and a beautiful, austere façade. It was built in 1250 on the spot where the Sibyl of Tibur (Tivoli) announced the coming of Christ to Augustus. In the first chapel on the right are **frescoes★** painted by Pinturicchio in about 1485.

Piazza del Campidoglio★★★
Capitol Square was designed and partly laid out by Michelangelo from 1536 onwards. It is framed by three palaces and a balustrade with statues of the Heavenly Twins or Dioscuri. In the centre stood the equestrian statue of Marcus Aurelius installed by Michelangelo and now housed in the Capitoline Museums.

Musei Capitolini★★★ – *Open daily except Mon, 9.30am-8pm (ticket office closes 7pm). Closed 1 Jan, 1 May, 25 Dec. €6.20. ☎ 06 39 96 78 00.*

The Dioscuri and the Palazzo Senatorio

The museums are housed in the **Palazzo Nuovo** (New Palace), built in 1655 by Girolamo Rainaldi, the 12C **Palazzo Senatorio**, remodelled between 1582 and 1602 by Giacomo della Porta and Girolamo Rainaldi, and the **Palazzo dei Conservatori**. Some sections of the collection, particularly the Roman remains, are housed in the **Centrale Montemartini★★**, at Viale Ostiense 106. ᵹ *Open daily 9.30am-7pm. Closed Mon, 1 Jan, 1 May, 25 Dec. €4.13. ☎ 06 57 48 030.*

Of note in the Palazzo Nuovo are the **equestrian statue of *Marcus Aurelius*★★** (late 2C); the ***Dying Gaul*★★★**, a Roman sculpture based on a bronze of the Pergamum school (3C-2C BC); the **Sala degli Imperatori★★** (Emperors' Room) with portraits of all the emperors; the ***Capitoline Venus*★★**, a Roman work inspired by the Venus of Cnidus by Praxiteles; and the **Mosaic of the Doves★★** from Hadrian's Villa at Tivoli.

The Palazzo dei Conservatori, built in the 15C and remodelled in 1568 by Giacomo della Porta, houses the ***She-Wolf*★★★** (6C-5C BC), the ***Boy Extracting a Thorn*★★**, a Greek original or a very good copy dating back to the 1C BC, and a **Bust of *Junius Brutus*★★**, a remarkable head dating from the 3C BC placed on a bust in the Renaissance period. The picture gallery or **pinacoteca★** (*2nd floor*) contains mainly 14C to 17C paintings (Titian, Caravaggio, Rubens, Guercino, Reni).

From Via del Campidoglio there is a beautiful **view★★★** of the ruins.

Terme di Caracalla★★★ (Baths of Caracalla)

ᵹ *Open daily in summer 9am to 1hr before sunset, other months 9am-5.30pm (ticket office always closes 1hr early). Closed Mon pm, 1 Jan, 25 Dec. €5, €20 "roma archeologica" card valid for 9 sites. ☎ 06 39 96 77 00; www.pierreci.it*

These baths built by Caracalla in AD 212 extend over more than 11ha/27 acres and could take 1 600 bathers at a time. The main rooms (*caldarium, tepidarium* and *frigidarium*) occupy the middle part of the central section; the secondary rooms (vestibule, palaestra and *laconicum*) are symetrically positioned at the sides. The ruined caldarium for the very hot bath, a circular room (34m/112ft in diameter), is the setting for operatic performances in summer.

Catacombe★★★

There are numerous underground Christian cemeteries alongside the Via **Appia Antica ★★**. In use from the 2C they were rediscovered in the 16C and 19C. They consist of long galleries radiating from an underground burial chamber (*hypogeum*) which belonged to a noble Roman family of the Christian faith. They permitted fellow Christians to use the galleries. The decorations of the catacombs (carvings or paintings of symbolic motifs) are precious examples of early Christian art.

The visitor with little time to spare should visit the following catacombs:

Catacombe di San Callisto★★★ along the Appian Way, **Catacombe di San Sebastiano★★★**, along the Appian Way **Catacombe di Domitilla★★★** *(entrance at Via delle Sette Chiese 282). Guided tours only (45-60min), available in several languages, 8.30am-12.30pm, 2.30-5.30pm (to 5pm in winter). €4.13, no charge on the last Sun in Sep. S. Callisto: Open every day except Wed. Closed 1 Jan, Feb, Easter, 25 Dec. ☎ 06 51 30 15 80. S. Sebastiano Open every day except Sun. Closed Jan, Easter, from mid Nov to mid Dec, 25 Dec. ☎ 06 78 50 350. Domitilla Open every day except Tue. Closed 1 Jan, Easter and 25 Dec. ☎ 06 51 10 342. www.catacombe.domitilla.it*

Castel Sant'Angelo★★★

Open daily except Mon 9am-8pm (ticket office closes 7pm). Closed 1 Jan, 25 Dec. €5, €20 "roma archeologica" card valid for 9 sites. ☎ 06 39 96 76 00; www.pierreci.it

The imposing fortress was built in AD 135 as a mausoleum for the Emperor Hadrian and his

The angel standing watch over Castel Sant'Angelo

amily. In the 6C, Gregory the Great erected a chapel on top of the mausoleum to commemorate the apparition of an angel who, by putting his sword back into its sheath, announced the end of a plague. In the 15C Nicholas V added a brick storey to the ancient building and corner towers to the surrounding wall. Alexander VI 1492-1503) added octagonal bastions.

n 1527, during the sack of Rome, Clement VII took refuge in the castle and installed an apartment which was later embellished by Paul III; the **Popes' Apartment★** stands isolated at the summit of the fortress and testifies to the gra-ciousness of the popes' life style.

A long passageway (Il Passetto) links the fortress to the Vatican palaces. A fine spiral ramp dating from antiquity leads to the castle. From a terrace at the summit there is a splendid **panorama★★★** of the whole town. The Castel Sant'Angelo is linked to the left bank of the Tiber by the graceful **Ponte Sant'Angelo★**, which is adorned with Baroque angels carved by Bernini and with statues of St Peter and St Paul (16C).

Domus Aurea★★

In the Parco Oppio. ঐ *Open daily, 9am-7.45pm (ticket office closes 6.45pm). Closed 1 Jan, 25 Dec. €5 + €1 for reservation (required).* ☎ *06 39 96 77 00; www.pierreci.it*
This was the luxurious residence erected by Nero after the fire of AD 64. The grotto-like underground rooms are decorated with geometric designs, grapes, faces and ani-mals. These "grotesques" were a great source of inspiration to Renaissance artists.

Colosseo★★★ (Colosseum)

ঐ *Open daily in summer 9am to 1hr before sunset, other months 9am-5.30pm (ticket office always closes 1hr early). Closed 1 Jan, 25 Dec. €8 including Palatino, €20 "roma archeologica" card valid for 9 sites.* ☎ *06 39 96 77 00; www.pierreci.it*
This amphitheatre, inaugurated in AD 80, is also known as the Flavian Amphitheatre after its initiator, Vespasian, first of the Flavian emperors. It took the name of the Colosseum either because it stood near the huge bronze statue of Nero, the Colossus, which was 36m/120ft high (its position is marked by a few slabs of stone on the ground near the beginning of Via dei Fori Imperiali), or because of its own colossal dimensions (527m/576yds in circumference and 57m/187ft high). With its three superimposed Classical orders (Doric, Ionic and Corinthian), it is a masterpiece of classical architecture. The projections supported wooden poles inserted through holes in the upper cornice: the poles carried a linen awning which could be extended over the amphitheatre to protect the spectators from sun or rain. In all there was probably space for about 50 000 spectators. Fights between men and beasts, gladiatorial contests, races and mock naval battles took place in the arena. The excavations revealed an underground warren where the wild animals waited before being brought to the surface by a system of ramps and lifts.
Now an integral part of the Coliseum, the **arco di Costantino★★★** is an arch erected to commemorate Constantine's victory over Maxentius in AD 315. Some of the low reliefs were removed from other 2C monuments erected in honour of Trajan, Hadrian and Marcus Aurelius.

Fori Imperiali★★★ *Entrance in Via IV Novembre.* These were built by Caesar, Augustus, Trajan, Nerva and Vespasian. There are hardly any remains of the latter two. The Via dei Fori Imperiali, laid out in 1932 by Mussolini, divides the imperial forums.
The **Mercati Traianei★★**, which have kept their semicircular façade, were a distri-bution and supply centre as well as a retail market. They comprised about 150 shops. (ঐ) *Open daily except Mon, Apr to Sep 9am-6pm, rest of year 9am-4.30pm. Closed 1 Jan, 1 May, 25 Dec, hols pm. €6.20.*☎ *06 67 90 048; www.comune.roma.it/cultura*
The **Torre delle Milizie★** (Tower of the Militia) is part of a 13C fortress. All that remains of the largest and finest of the imperial forums, **Foro di Traiano★★★** (Trajan's Forum), is the **Colonna Traiana★★★** (Trajan's column) which depicts, in over 100 scenes, episodes of the war waged by Trajan against the Dacians. It is an unrivalled masterpiece.
Of the Augustan Forum, **Foro di Augusto★★** (*view from Via Alessandrina*), there remain a few columns of the Temple of Mars the Avenger, and vestiges of the stair-way and of the wall enclosing the forum (behind the temple). The forum is domin-ated by the House of the Knights of Rhodes (Casa dei Cavalieri di Rodi), built in the Middle Ages and rebuilt in the 15C amid the ancient ruins. Of Caesar's Forum, the **Foro di Cesare★★** (*view from Via del Tulliano*), there remain three lovely columns from the Temple of Venus Genitrix.

Foro Romano★★★

ঐ *Open daily in summer 9am to 1hr before sunset, other months 9am-5.30pm (ticket office always closes 1hr early). Closed 1 Jan, 25 Dec. No charge.*☎ *06 39 96 77 00.*
The remains of the Roman Forum, the religious, political and commercial centre of ancient Rome, reflect the 12 centuries of history which created Roman civilisa-tion. The forum was excavated in the 19C and 20C.

The **Basilica Emilia** was the second basilica to be built in Rome (170 BC).

Take the Sacred Way, **Via Sacra★**, along which victorious generals marched in triumph to the **Curia★★**, rebuilt in the 3C by Diocletian. Senate meetings were held here; nowadays it houses the **Plutei di Traiano★★**), low reliefs sculpted low-relief panels depicting scenes from the life of the Emperor Trajan, and sacrificial animals.

After the Romans attacked Antium (modern Anzio) in 338 BC and captured the prows *(rostra)* of the enemy ships which they fixed to the **orators' platform★**; this then became known as the Rostra.

Nearby rises an imposing Triumphal Arch, **Arco di Settimio Severo★★**, built in AD 203 to commemorate the Emperor's victories over the Parthians. At the foot of the Capitol stood some remarkable monuments: the late 1C **Tempio di Vespasiano★★** (Temple of Vespasian) of which only three elegant Corinthian columns remain; the **Tempio du Saturno★★★** (Temple of Saturn) which retain eight 4C columns; and the **Portico degli Dei Consentis★**, a colonnade of pillar with Corinthian columns dating back to restoration work of AD 367 – the portico was dedicated to the 12 principal Roman deities.

The **Colonna di Foca★** (Column of Phocas) was erected in AD 608 in honour of the Byzantine Emperor Phocas who presented the Pantheon to Pope Boniface IV. The **Basilica Giulia★★**, which has five aisles, was built by Julius Caesar and completed by Augustus. It served as a law court and exchange.

Almost nothing is left of the **Tempio di Cesare** which started the cult of Emperor worship. It was consecrated by Octavian in 29 BC to the "god" Julius Caesar.

Three beautiful columns with Corinthian capitals remain of the **Tempio di Castore e Polluce★★★** (Temple of Castor and Pollux). The circular **Tempio di Vesta★★★** stands (Temple of Vesta) near the **Casa delle Vestali★★★** (House of the Vestal Virgins).

The **Regia** was held to have been the residence of King Numa Pompilius, who succeeded Romulus and organised the State religion.

The **Tempio di Antonino e Faustina★★** (Temple of Antoninus and Faustina) was dedicated to the Emperor Antoninus Pius and his wife (note the fresco of grotesques and candelabra). The temple now houses the church of San Lorenzo in Miranda rebuilt in the 17C.

The remains of the **Tempio di Romolo** (the Romulus to whom the temple is thought to be dedicated was not the founder of Rome but the son of the Emperor Maxentius who died in 307) include the concave façade and the bronze doors between two porphyry columns

The grandiose **Basilica di Massenzio★★★** (Basilica of Maxentius) was completed by the Emperor Constantine. The **Arco di Tito★★** (Triumphal Arch of Titus), erected in 81, commemorates the capture of Jerusalem by this emperor, who reigned for only two years.

Palatino★★★

Open daily, 9am-1hr before sunset (the ticket office closes 1hr before this time). Closed 1 Jan, 25 Dec. €6.20. Guided visit (75min) and audioguide available. ☎ 06 39 96 77 00. www.prc.it

The Palatine Hill, where Romulus and Remus were discovered by the wolf, was chosen by Domitian as the site for the Imperial Palace. The **Domus Flavia★** (or official state apartments) was made up of three main areas: the basilica, where the Emperor dispensed justice, the throne room and the *lararium*, the Emperor's private chapel. Also of note were the peristyle courtyard and the dining room or *triclinium* which opened onto two small leisure rooms, *nymphaea*. The rooms in the **Domus Augustana★★** (private imperial apartments) are arranged around two peristyles on two floors. Then there was the **Stadium★** designed to stage private games and spectacles for the Emperor.

The **Casa di Livia★★** (House of Livia) *(closed for restoration at the time of writing)* probably belonged to Augustus (fine vestiges of paintings). The **Orti Farnesiani** (Farnese Gardens), laid out in the 16C on the site of Tiberius' palace, afford **views★★** of the Forum and town.

Leave the Palatine and head along Clivus Palatinus then turn into Via Sacra near the Arco di Tito

Tempio di Venere e di Roma★

The Temple of Venus and Rome, built between 121 and 136 by Hadrian, was the largest in the city (110m/361ft by 53m/174ft). It was unique in that it comprised two *cellae* with apses back to back. One was dedicated to the goddess of Rome and faced the Forum; the other was dedicated to Venus and faced the Colosseum.

Chiesa del Gesù★★★

The mother-church of the Jesuits in Rome, built by Vignola in 1568, is a typical building of the Counter-Reformation. On the outside, the engaged pillars replace the flat pilasters of the Renaissance, with light and shade effects and recesses. The interior, spacious and ideal for preaching, was lavishly decorated in the Baroque style: on the dome, the **Baciccia frescoes★★** illustrate the *Triumph of the Name of Jesus* (1679); the **Cappella di Sant'Ignazio★★★** *(north transept)*, a chapel where the remains of St Ignatius Loyola rest, is the work (1696-1700) of the Jesuit Brother Andrea Pozzo and is sumptuously decorated.

Pantheon★★★

& *Open Mon-Sat, 8.30am-7.30pm, Sun 9am-6pm (midweek holidays, 9am-1pm). Closed 1 Jan, 1 May, 25 Dec. No charge.* ☎ *06 68 30 02 30.*

The Pantheon, an ancient building perfectly preserved, founded by Agrippa in 27 BC and rebuilt by Hadrian (117-125), was a temple which was converted into a church in the 7C.

Access is through a porch supported by 16 single granite columns, all ancient except for three on the left. The doors are the original ones. The **interior★★★**, a masterpiece of harmony and majesty, is dominated by the **ancient dome★★★**, the diameter of which is equal to its height. The side chapels, adorned with alternately curved and triangular pediments, contain the tombs of the kings of Italy and that of Raphael *(on the left)*.

Piazza del Popolo★★

The **Piazza del Popolo** was designed by Giuseppe Valadier (1762-1839). The **Porta del Popolo★** was pierced in the Aurelian wall in the 3C, and adorned with an external façade in the 16C and with an inner façade designed by Bernini in the 17C.

The Renaissance church of **Santa Maria del Popolo★★** was remodelled in the Baroque period. It contains 15C **frescoes★** by Pinturicchio *(first chapel on the right)*; two **tombs★** by Andrea Sansovino *(in the chancel)*; two **paintings★★★** by **Caravaggio**: the *Crucifixion of St Peter* and the *Conversion of St Paul (first chapel to the left of the chancel)*; and the **Cappella Chigi★** *(2nd on the left)*, a chapel designed by Raphael. Leading off the Piazza del Popolo is the main street of central Rome, **Via del Corso**, lined with handsome Renaissance palaces and fashionable shops.

Pincio

This fine public park was laid out in the 19C by Giuseppe Valadier. It is bordered by the gardens of the Villa Borghese and affords a magnificent **view★★★** particularly at dusk when the golden glow so typical of Rome is at its mellow best.

Piazza di Spagna★★★

This square, a popular tourist attraction, was so named in the 17C after the Spanish Embassy occupied the Palazzo di Spagna. It is dominated by the majestic Spanish Steps, the **Scalinata della Trinità dei Monti★★★**, built in the 18C by the architects De Sanctis and Specchi, who adopted the baroque style of perspective and *trompe l'oeil*. At the foot of the stairway are the **Fontana della Barcaccia★** (Boat Fountain) by Bernini's father, Pietro (17C), and Keats' House where the poet died in 1821.

At the top of the stairs, the church of the **Trinità dei Monti★** is the French church, built in the 16C and restored in the 19C. It contains a ***Deposition from the Cross★*** *(2nd chapel on the left)* dating from 1541 by Daniele da Volterra, a great admirer of Michelangelo.

Piazza di Spagna, one of the most atmospheric "stage sets" in Italy

Leading off from this square is **Via dei Condotti** lined with elegant shops. It is also renowned for the Caffè Greco *(see p 373)*, a famous establishment which was opened in 1760 and frequented by celebrities (Goethe, Berlioz, Wagner, Stendhal etc).

Piazza Navona★★★

The square built on the site of Domitian's stadium retains its shape. A pleasant and lively pedestrian precinct, it is adorned at the centre with Bernini's Baroque masterpiece, the **Fontana dei Fiumi★★★** (Fountain of the Four Rivers), completed in 1651. The statues represent the four rivers – Danube, Ganges, Rio de la Plata and Nile – symbolising the four corners of the earth.
Among the churches and palaces lining the square are **Sant'Agnese in Agone★★** with a Baroque façade by Borromini and attractive **interior★** on the plan of a Greek cross, and the adjoining 17C **Palazzo Pamphili**.

Piazza Venezia★

This Piazza in the centre of Rome is lined with palaces: Palazzo Venezia, Palazzo Bonaparte, where Napoleon's mother died in 1836, and the early-20C Palazzo delle Assicurazioni Generali di Venezia.

Palazzo Venezia★

This palace, built by Pope Paul II (1464-71), is one of the first Renaissance buildings. A **museum**, on the first floor, presents collections of medieval art (ivories, Byzantine and Limousin enamels, Italian Primitive paintings on wood, gold and silver work, ceramics and small bronzes of the 15C-17C. (&) *Open daily except Mon, 8.30am-7.30pm. Closed 1 Jan, 1 May, 25 Dec. €4. ☎ 06 67 98 865.*
The **basilica di San Marco**, which was incorporated within the palace in the 15C, has a fine Renaissance **façade★** overlooking Piazza di San Marco.

Monumento a Vittorio Emanuele II (Vittoriano)

This huge memorial by Giuseppe Sacconi, begun in 1885 in honour of the first king of a united Italy, Victor Emanuel II, overshadows the other monuments of Rome by its sheer size and dazzling white colour. It affords a **view★★** of the Eternal City.

Basilica di San Giovanni in Laterano★★★

Open daily, 7am-6.30pm. ☎ 06 69 88 64 93.
St John Lateran, the cathedral of Rome, is among the four major basilicas in Rome. The first basilica was founded by Constantine prior to St Peter's in the Vatican. It was rebuilt in the Baroque era by Borromini and again in the 18C.
The main façade by Alessandro Galilei dates from the 18C and the central door has bronze panels that originally belonged to the Curia of the Roman Forum (modified in the 17C). The vast and grandiose interior has a 16C **ceiling★★** which was restored in the 18C. In the nave the **Statues of the *Apostles*★** by pupils of Bernini stand in niches built by Borromini. The elegant **Cappella Corsini★** *(first in the north aisle)* was designed by Alessandro Galilei. The transept **ceiling★★** dates from the end of the 16C.
The **Cappella del Santissimo Sacramento** (Chapel of the Blessed Sacrament – *north transept*) has fine ancient **columns★** in gilded bronze. The pretty **cloisters★** are the work of the Vassalletto (13C), marble-masons who were associates of the Cosmati. The **baptistery★**, built in the 4C, is decorated with beautiful 5C and 7C mosaics.
In **Piazza di San Giovanni in Laterano** rises a 15C BC Egyptian obelisk, the tallest in Rome.
The **Palazzo Lateranense** (Lateran Palace), rebuilt in 1586, was the papal palace until the papal court returned from Avignon. The staircase, **Scala Sancta**, is a precious vestige from the medieval papal palace and is traditionally identified as the one Christ used in the palace of Pontius Pilate. Worshippers climb the stairs on their knees. At the top is the papal chapel, called the Sancta Sanctorum, with its many precious relics.

Basilica di Santa Maria Maggiore★★★

For information and reservations for the Basilica and Loggia ☎ 347 33 31 943.
This is one of the four major basilicas in Rome. It was built by Pope Sixtus III (AD 432-440) and is dedicated to St Mary Major. It has since undergone extensive restoration. The campanile, erected in 1377, is the highest in Rome. The façade is the work of Ferdinando Fuga (1743-1750). The adjoining **loggia** is decorated with **mosaics★** by Filippo Rusuti (end 13C), much restored in the 19C.
The impressive **interior★★★** contains remarkable **mosaics★★★**: in the nave, those above the entablature are among the most ancient Christian mosaics in Rome (5C) and depict scenes from the Old Testament; on the 5C triumphal arch are scenes from the New Testament; in the apse, the mosaics are composed of 5C elements but were completely redone in the 13C.
The coffered **ceiling★** is said to have been gilded with the first gold brought from Peru. The floor, the work of the **Maestri Cosmati** (12C) was subject to much restoration in the 18C. The **Cappella di Sisto V** *(south aisle)* and the **Cappella**

Paolina (north aisle) were both built in the form of a Greek cross and surmounted by a cupola. Another chapel was added at the end of the 16C and one in the 17C: they were richly decorated in the Baroque style. Popes Sixtus V, Pius V, Clement VIII and Paul V are buried here.

Leave the church by the door at the far end of the south aisle.

From **Piazza dell'Esquilino**, with its Egyptian obelisk, there is a **view★★** of the church's imposing 17C chevet.

Basilicia di San Paolo Fuori Le Mura★★

Open daily, 7am-6.30pm (6pm winter). ☎ *06 54 08 383.*

One of the four major basilicas, St Paul's "Outside the Walls", was built by Constantine in the 4C on the site of St Paul's tomb. It was rebuilt in the 19C, after it had been wholly destroyed by fire in 1823, on the original basilical plan of early Christian churches.

The impressive **interior★★★** contains: an 11C bronze door cast in Constantinople *(at the entrance of the first south aisle);* and a Gothic **ciborium★★★** (1285) by Arnolfo di Cambio, placed on the high altar which stands above a marble plaque inscribed with the name Paul and dated 4C. In the **Cappella del Santissimo Sacramento★** (Chapel of the Blessed Sacrament) *(left of the chancel)* are: a 14C wooden figure of Christ attributed to Pietro Cavallini; a statue of St Brigitta kneeling, by Stefano Maderno (17C); a 14C or 15C statue of St Paul; and the **paschal candelabrum★★**, a 12C Romanesque work of art by the Vassalletto. The **cloisters★** are also attributed, at least in part, to this same family of artists.

Fontana di Trevi★★★

A late-Baroque creation, the Trevi Fountain was commissioned from Nicola Salvi in 1762 by Pope Clement XIII. The central figure, the Ocean, rides in a chariot drawn by two seahorses and two tritons.

Tourists continue the tradition of throwing two coins over their shoulders into the fountain – one coin to ensure their return to Rome and the other for the fulfilment of a wish.

ART AND FAITH IN THE ETERNAL CITY: THE VATICAN

The Vatican City is bounded by a wall, overlooking Viale Vaticano, and to the east by the colonnade of St Peter's Square. This makes up the greater part of the Vatican state as laid down in 1929 in the Lateran Treaty. The Vatican City, now reduced to only 44ha/109 acres and with less than a thousand inhabitants, stems from the Papal States, a donation made in the 8C by Pepin the Short to Pope Stephen II, and lost in 1870 when Italy was united into one kingdom with Rome as its capital. The Vatican State, with the Pope as ruler, has its own flag and anthem and prints its own stamps. The Vatican, like Italy, started using euro notes and coins at the beginning of 2002. In 1970, Pope Paul VI dissolved the armed forces, retaining only the Swiss Guard who wear a colourful uniform said to have been designed by Michelangelo.

The Pope, who is the Head of State, is also the Supreme Head of the Universal Church, and from this very small State, the spiritual influence of the Church radiates throughout the world through the person of the Sovereign Pontiff. When the Pope is in residence, he grants **public audiences** on Wednesdays.

Giardini Vaticani★★★

€9. *Reservations required at Vatican Museums.* ☎ *06 69 88 44 66 or 06 69 88 45 87, Fax 06 69 88 51 00.*

The vast, magnificent gardens are adorned with fountains and statues, gifts from various countries. Of particular interest is the Casina of Pius IV, a fine 16C building decorated with stuccowork and paintings. From the gardens are glorious views of the cupola.

Piazza San Pietro★★★

This architectural masterpiece was begun in 1656 by Bernini, master of the Baroque. The two semicircles of the colonnade which adorn the square and frame the façade of the basilica form an ensemble of remarkable sobriety and majesty. At the centre of the square stands a 1C BC obelisk brought from Heliopolis in Egypt to Rome in AD 37 by order of Caligula. It was erected here in 1585 on the initiative of Sixtus V by Domenico Fontana. At the top is a relic of the Holy Cross.

Basilica di San Pietro★★★

Open daily in summer 7am-7pm, in winter 7am-6pm (depending on scheduled pontifical ceremonies). For information ☎ *06 69 88 44 66.*

Constantine, the first Christian Emperor, decided in AD 324 to build a basilica on the site where St Peter was buried after he had been martyred in Nero's circus. In the 15C it proved necessary to rebuild.

For two centuries, the plan of the new basilica was constantly revised. The plan, of a Greek cross surmounted by a dome designed by Bramante and adopted by Michelangelo, was altered to a Latin cross at the behest of Paul V in 1606, when he

instructed Carlo Maderna to add two bays and a façade to Michelangelo's square
plan. From 1629 onwards, the basilica was decorated in a sumptuous Baroque style
by Bernini.

The **façade** (115m/377ft long and 45m/151ft high) was completed in 1614 by Carlo
Maderna; it is surmounted by colossal figures, and masks the dome. In the centre
is the balcony from which the Sovereign Pontiff gives his benediction *Urbi et Orbi*
(to the City and the World).

Under the **porch**, the first door on the left has bronze panels carved by Giacomo
Manzù (1964); the bronze central door dates from the Renaissance (1455); the door
on the right, or Holy Door, is opened and closed by the Pope to mark the beginning
and end of a Jubilee Year.

Inside, it is customary to first approach the stoups in the nave which at first glance
appear of normal size but are in fact huge. Such size emphasises the gigantic
dimensions of the basilica, otherwise not apparent because of the harmony of its
proportions. The length of St Peter's can be compared to that of other great basilicas throughout the world by means of markers inlaid in the pavement of the nave.
The first chapel on the right contains the *Pietà*★★★, the moving and powerful masterpiece carved by Michelangelo in 1499-1500, which shows his creative genius.
In the right aisle, adjoining the Cappella del SS Sacramento, **Gregory XIII's
Monument**★ is adorned with low reliefs illustrating the institution of the Gregorian
calendar devised by that pope. Immediately beyond the right transept, **Clement
XIII's Monument**★★★ is a fine neo-Classical design by Canova dating from 1792.
The apse is dominated by the **Cattedra di San Pietro**★★★ (St Peter's Throne) by
Bernini (1666), a great carved throne in bronze encasing a 4C episcopal chair but
symbolically attributed to St Peter, and surmounted by a "glory" in gilded stucco.
In the chancel on the right is **Urban VIII's Monument**★★★, again by Bernini
(1647), a masterpiece of funerary art. On the left stands **Paul III's Monument**★★★
by Guglielmo della Porta (16C), a disciple of Michelangelo.
St Leo the Great's Altar *(chapel to the left of the chancel)* has a fine Baroque **altarpiece**★ carved in high relief by Algardi. Nearby, **Alexander VII's Monument**★★
characterised by extreme exuberance, is a late work by Bernini (1678) assisted by
his pupils. The **baldaquin**★★★ which crowns the pontifical altar and is 29m/95ft tall
(the height of the Farnese Palace) was strongly criticised: partly because the bronze
had been taken from the Pantheon and partly because it was thought to be too theatrical and in bad taste. It does, however, fit in well with the overall architectural
plan.
The **dome**★★★ designed by Michelangelo, which he himself built as far as the
lantern, was completed in 1593 by Giacomo della Porta and Domenico Fontana.
From the **summit** *(leave the basilica by the right aisle for access)* there is a **view**★★★
of St Peter's Square, the Vatican City and Rome from the Janiculum to Monte
Mario. *Open daily, Apr to Sep 8am-6pm, rest of year 8am-5pm. €4.13 in lift, €3.62 on
foot. For information ☎ 06 69 88 44 66.*
The 13C bronze **Statue of St Peter**★★ overlooking the nave is attributed to Arnolfo di
Cambio and is greatly venerated by pilgrims, who come to kiss its feet. **Innocent VIII's
Monument**★★★ *(between the second and third bays in the left aisle)* is a Renaissance work
(1498) by Antonio del Pollaiuolo. The **Stuart Monument** *(between the first and second
bays in the left aisle)* carved by Canova is adorned with beautiful **angels**★ in low relief.
The **Museo Storico**★ (Historical Museum) *(entrance in the left aisle, opposite the Stuart
Monument)* has many treasured items from St Peter's. ♿ *Open daily, Apr to Sep 9am-7pm
(ticket office closes 6.30pm), rest of year 9am-6pm (ticket office closes 5.30pm). Closed Easter,
25 Dec. €4.13. ☎ 06 69 88 18 40.*

Musei Vaticani★★★

*Entrance in Viale Vaticano ♿ Two equipped itineraries available for disabled visitors:
Itinerary A: Classical and Etruscan antiquities. Itinerary B: Palazzi Vaticani,
Pinacoteca (a map of the itineraries is available at the information desk). Open Mar to
Oct, Mon-Fri, 8.45am-5.45pm (ticket office closes at 3.20pm). Sat, last Sun of the month
and the rest of the year 8.45am-1.45pm (ticket office closes 12.20pm). Closed Sun (except
last Sun of month), 1 and 6 Jan, 11 Feb, 19 Mar, Easter and Easter Mon, 1 May,
Ascension, Corpus Christi, 29 Jun, hols. Audioguide tours in Italian, French, Japanese,
English, Spanish, German €10, no charge 27 Sep and last Sun of the month. Bar, coffee
shop and self service facilities. ☎ 06 69 88 49 47.*

The museums of the Vatican occupy part of the palaces built by the popes from the
13C onwards, which have been extended and embellished to the present day.
These include on the first floor the **Museo Pio-Clementino**★★★ (Greek and Roman
antiquities) with its masterpieces: the **Belvedere Torso**★★★ (1C BC), greatly admired
by Michelangelo; the **Venus of Cnidus**★★, a Roman copy of Praxiteles' Venus; the
Laocoon Group★★★, a 1C BC Hellenistic work; the **Apollo Belvedere**★★★, a 2C
Roman copy; **Perseus**★★, a neo-Classical work by Canova, which was purchased by
Pius VII; **Hermes**★★★, a 2C Roman work inspired by the work of Praxiteles; and the
Apoxyomenos★★★, the athlete scraping his skin with a strigil after taking exercise,
a 1C Roman copy of the Greek original by Lysippus.

Stanze di Raffaello:
Coronation of Carlo
Magno *(detail)*

The **Museo Etrusco★**, on the second floor, has a remarkable 7C BC gold **fibula★★** adorned with lions and ducklings in high relief *(Room II)* and the *Mars*★★ found at Todi, a rare example of a large bronze statue from the 5C BC *(Room III)*.

The **Sala della Biga** derives its name from the **two-horse chariot★★** *(biga)*, a 1C Roman work reassembled in the 18C.

The four **Stanze di Rafaello★★★** (Raphael Rooms), the private apartments of Julius II, were decorated by Raphael and his pupils from 1508 to 1517. The result is a pure Renaissance masterpiece. The frescoes are remarkable: the *Borgo Fire*, the *School of Athens*, *Parnassus*, the *Expulsion of Heliodorus from the Temple*, the *Miracle of the Bolsena Mass* and *St Peter delivered from prison*. The **Collezione d'Arte Moderna Religiosa★★**, assembled by Pope Paul VI, is displayed in the apartment of Pope Alexander VI.

On the first floor the **Cappella Sistina★★★** (Sistine Chapel) is open to the public; its splendid vault, painted by Michelangelo from 1508 to 1512, illustrates episodes from the Bible, with the Creation, the Flood and, above the altar, the Last Judgement, which was added by the artist in 1534. The lowest sections of the side walls were decorated by Perugino, Pinturicchio and Botticelli. The **Pinacoteca★★★** (Picture Gallery) also contains some first-class works: three **compositions★★★** by **Raphael** (*The Coronation of the Virgin*, *The Madonna of Foligno* and *The Transfiguration* – Room VIII); *St Jerome*★★ by Leonardo da Vinci *(Room IX)* and a *Descent from the Cross*★★ by Caravaggio *(Room XII)*.

AND IF YOU STILL HAVE TIME ...

▶▶ **Churches:** Chiesa Nuova★, S. Andrea al Quirinale★★, S. Andrea della Valle★ (façade★★, dome by Maderno★★), S. Agnese Fuori le Mura★, S. Agostino★ (*Madonna of the Pilgrims*★★ by Caravaggio), S. Carlo alle Quattro Fontane★★, S. Cecilia in Trastevere★ (*Last Judgement*★★★ by Cavallini), S. Clemente★★ (mosaics★★★ in the apse), S. Ignazio★★, S. Lorenzo Fuori le Mura★★, S. Luigi dei Francesi★★ (works★★★ by Caravaggio), S. Maria degli Angeli★★, S. Maria in Cosmedin★★ ("Bocca della Verità"), S. Maria sopra Minerva★★, S. Maria della Pace★, S. Maria in Trastevere★★ (Mosaics★★★ in the chancel), S. Maria della Vittoria★★ (*Ecstasy of St Teresa*★★★ by Bernini), S. Pietro in Montorio★ (Bramante's tempietto★★), S. Pietro in Vincoli★ (*Moses*★★★ by Michelangelo), S. Sabina★★, S. Susanna★★.

▶▶ **Museums and palaces:** Galleria Borghese★★★, Museo Nazionale Romano★★★ (Palazzo Massimo alle Terme★★★, Palazzo Altemps★★★, Aula Ottagona★★★), Museo Nazionale di Villa Giulia★★★, Palazzo Barberini★★ (Galleria Nazionale di Arte Antica★★), Palazzo della Cancelleria★★, Palazzo Farnese★★, Palazzo del Quirinale★★, Villa Farnesina★★, Palazzo Braschi★ (Museo di Roma★), Palazzo Doria Pamphili★ (art gallery★★), Palazzo della Sapienza (S. Ivo★★), Palazzo Spada★, Galleria Nazionale d'Arte Moderna★

Who will dare place a hand in the notorious Bocca della Verità?

▶▶ **Monuments from Antiquity:** Ara Pacis Augustae★★, Area Sacra del Largo Argentina★★, Tempio di Apollo Sosiano★★, Piramide di Caio Cestio★, Tempio della Fortuna Virile★, Tempio di Vesta★, Tomba di Cecilia Metella★.

▶▶ **Squares, streets, parks and gardens:** Piazza del Quirinale★★, Villa Borghese★★, Piazza Bocca della Verità★, Piazza Campo dei Fiori★, Piazza Colonna★ (Colonna di Marco Aurelio★), Piazza S. Ignazio★, Porta S. Paolo★, Porta di S. Sebastiano★, Via dei Coronari★, E.U.R.★ (Museo della Civiltà Romana★★), Isola Tiberina★ (Ponte Fabricio★), Gianicolo★ (views★★★).

Excursions

Castelli Romani★★

Castelli Romani, or Roman Castles, is the name given to the region of the Alban Hills (Colli Albani), which are of volcanic origin and lie to the southeast of Rome. In the Middle Ages, while anarchy reigned in Rome, the noble families sought refuge in the outlying villages which they fortified. Each of these villages was strategically set on the outer rim of an immense crater, itself pitted with small secondary craters, some of which now contain lakes (Albano and Nemi). Pastures and chestnut groves cover the upper slopes while lower down there are olive groves and vineyards, which produce an excellent wine.

Nowadays the Romans readily leave the capital in summer for the "Castelli" where they find peace, fresh air, good walking country and pleasant country inns.

Tour of the Castles – *122km/76mi, allow half a day.* Leave Rome by the Via Appia in the direction of **Castel Gandolfo★★**, now the Pope's summer residence. It is thought that Castel Gandolfo was built on the site of ancient Alba Longa, the traditional and powerful rival of Rome. Their rivalry led to the famous combat of the Horatios for Rome and the Curiaces for Alba, as recounted by the Roman historian Livy. **Albano Laziale** was built on the site of Domitian's villa. Today the town boasts an attractive church, **Santa Maria della Rotonda★**, built in the villa's nymphaeum, which has a massive Romanesque campanile, and public gardens, the **Villa Comunale★**, which house a villa that belonged to Pompey (106-48 BC). Not far from Borgo Garibaldi is the so-called **tomb of the Horatios and the Curiaces★**.

Ariccia has a lovely square designed by Bernini, a palace which belonged to the Chigi banking family, and the church of Santa Maria dell'Assunzione.

Velletri is a prosperous town lying south of the Alban Hills in the heart of a wine-producing region.

Take Via dei Laghi out of Velletri.

This scenic road winds through groves of chestnut and oak trees to reach **Nemi**, a small village in a charming **setting★★** on the slopes of the lake of the same name. The road then climbs to **Monte Cavo** (alt 949m/3 124ft) which was crowned by the Temple of Jupiter. First a monastery and now a hotel have occupied the buildings. From the esplanade there is a fine **view★** of the Castelli region with Rome on the horizon. Beyond the attractively set **Rocca di Papa**, facing the Alban lakes, the road passes through **Grottaferrata** with its **abbey★** which was founded in the 11C by Greek monks. **Tusculo** was the fief of the powerful Counts of Tusculum who governed the Castelli region. Next comes **Frascati★** pleasantly situated on the slopes facing Rome. It is known for its wines and its 16C and 17C villas, particularly the **Villa Aldobrandini★** set above its terraced gardens.

The road back to Rome passes **Cinecittà**, the Italian Hollywood. *Gardens: open Mon-Fri, 9am-1pm and 3-6pm (5pm winter). Closed Sat, Sun and hols. Permit required for visit, to be picked up at IAT, Piazza Marconi 1, ☎ 06 94 20 331.*

Ostia Antica★★

Ostia, at the mouth of the Tiber, takes its name from the Latin word *ostium* meaning mouth. According to Virgil, Aeneas landed here but its foundation dates in reality back to the 4C BC when Rome embarked on her conquest of the Mediterranean. From that time on, Ostia's development has reflected that of Rome: a military port during the period of expansion, a commercial port once Rome had established an organised system of trade. At first there was simply a castle to protect the port from pirates but by the 1C BC, Ostia had become a real town around which Sulla built ramparts in 79BC. Like Rome, Ostia began to decline in the 4C.

Slowly the harbour silted up and malaria decimated the population. Ostia was soon covered by alluvium deposited by the Tiber. It was 1909 before Ostia was discovered and regular excavations began.

On this extensive site the visitor can discover a variety of interesting remains: warehouses (*horrea*); baths; sanctuaries; examples of the substantial dwelling-house, the *domus* built around its atrium or courtyard; and the more usual blocks of flats, several storeys high (*insula*). They were nearly all built of brick and unrendered. Some had elegant entrances framed by a triangular pediment resting on two pillars. Here and there a porch or a balcony added interest to the street front.

Nowadays it is hard to imagine the feverish activity that surrounded the forum and Capitol

B. Kaufmann/MICHELIN

In addition there are the numerous meeting-places for both business and pleasure, and the forum which was the hub of both political and social life. During the empire Ostia was a town with a population of 100 000 which included a large number of foreigners.

Excavations – (& *only for museum and with guide*) *Museum and excavations: Apr to Oct 8.30am-7.30pm (ticket office closes 6pm); rest of year 8.30am-5.30pm (ticket office closes 4pm). Closed 1 Jan, 1 May, 25 Dec. €4.☎ 06 56 35 809.*

Once past the **Via delle Tombe**, just outside the **Porta Romana** (the main entrance to the town coming from Rome) is the **Decumanus Maximus,** the east-west axis of all Roman towns; in Ostia it was paved with large slabs and lined with porticoed houses and shops.

On the right are the **Terme di Nettuno.** This 2C baths building has a terrace with a view of the fine **mosaics★★** which depict the marriage of Neptune and Amphitrite. A little further on, on the opposite side is the **Horrea di Hortensius★**, grand 1C warehouses built round a pillared courtyard which is lined with shops. The theatre has been much restored but is nevertheless very evocative of life in a Roman city.

The **Piazzale delle Corporazioni★★★** was surrounded by a portico housing the offices of the 70 trading corporations which represented the trading links with the Roman world. The mosaic pavement portrays their emblems, which in turn indicate the commodity they traded in and the country of origin. The temple in the centre of the square is sometimes attributed to Ceres, goddess of corn and the harvest.

On the right is the Casa di Apuleio and then the **Mitreo**, a temple to Mithras and one of the best preserved in Ostia.

The **Thermopolium★★** was a bar with a marble counter where hot drinks were served (hence its name).

The **Casa di Diana★** is a striking example of an *insula* (block of flats) with rooms and passages arranged around an inner courtyard.

The **Museo★** displays objects found in Ostia: crafts, oriental religious cults (numerous in Ostia), sculptures and **portraits★**, and examples of the rich interior decoration found in Ostia.

Dedicated to the Capitoline triad (Jupiter, Juno and Minerva) the **Capitolium★★** was the largest temple in Ostia, built in the 2C. Some of the pillars of the surrounding portico in the **forum** (extended in the 2C) are still standing. At the far end stands the 1C Temple of Rome and Augustus (Tempio di Roma e Augusto), faced with marble.

Beyond the **Casa del Larario★**, so-called because of the red and ochre brick decoration, is the **Horrea Epagathiana★**, a warehouse with a fine doorway featuring columns and fronton.

Built in the 4C facing the seashore, the **Casa di Amore e Psiche★★** has interesting remains of mosaic and marble floors and a lovely nymphaeum.

There is a series of baths *(terme)* starting with the **Terme di Mitra** with traces of the steps and *frigidarium*. Further along are the **Insula del Serapide★** and the **Terme dei Sette Sapienti★** – there is a handsome mosaic floor in the large circular room. Beyond the walls are the **Terme della Marciana** with a beautiful **mosaic★** in the *frigidarium*.

The **Schola del Traiano★★** is an impressive 2C to 3C building which was the headquarters of a guild of merchants. Inside can be seen several porticoed courtyards and a rectangular basin.

Make for the **Basilica cristiana**, a 4C Christian basilica; a row of columns separates the aisles which end in apses. An inscription on the architrave of a colonnade marks the entrance to what has been identified as the baptistery.

A little further on are the **Terme del Foro★** which are the largest baths in Ostia. Along one side is a good example of a public lavatory. In the rectangular enclosure of the **Campo della Magna Mater** are the remains of a temple dedicated to Cybele (or the Magna Mater, the Great Mother).

Cerveteri

The ancient Caere was a powerful Etruscan centre, which stood on an eminence to the east of the present town of Cerveteri. Caere attained great prosperity in the 7C and 6C BC and was renowned as an important cultural and religious centre. In the 4C BC Caere began to decline. It was only at the beginning of the 20C that excavation work began on this site. Most of the finds are now displayed in the Villa Giulia in Rome. *(See The Green Guide Rome.)*

Necropoli della Banditaccia★★ – *Open daily except Mon, 8.30am to 1hr before sunset. Closed 1 Jan, 25 Dec. €4.* ☎ *06 99 40 001.*
The splendid necropolis which is to be found 2km/1mi to the north of Cerveteri is an important testimonial to Etruscan burial cults. It is laid out like a city with numerous tumuli lining a main street. The site is pervaded by a great sense of peace. The tombs generally dating from the 7C BC add a strange note to the scene. These conical earth mounds, often grass covered, rest on a stone base, which is sometimes decorated with mouldings, with the burial chambers underneath. Other tombs consist of underground burial chambers reached through simply decorated doors. A vestibule leads into the burial chambers which often contain two funeral beds placed side by side: one is adorned with a small column if the deceased was a man (the breadwinner) and the other with a small canopy in the case of a woman (guardian of the home). One of the tombs without a tumulus is the **Tomba delle Rilievi**★★ with its painted low-relief stuccoes giving a realistic picture of everyday Etruscan life.

Tour around Lake Bracciano★★
From Cerveteri go 18km/11mi north to Bracciano (see The Green Guide Rome). At 164m/538ft above sea level, Lake Bracciano extends over an area of 57.5km²/22sq mi (making it the eighth largest Italian lake) with a maximum depth of 160m/525ft. *Lacus Sabatini* has played an important role in supplying water to Rome: Trajan, for example, erected a 30km/18mi long aqueduct which brought water to Trastevere and survived until the 17C.

Bracciano★ is dominated by the splendid **Castello Orsini-Odescalchi**★★★ (14C-15C) outlined by six imposing cylindrical towers and two castle walls. **The interior** has lovely frescoed rooms, 15C ceilings and furnishings from subsequent periods. There are stunning views of the lake and town from the castle but the real jewel of this place is the enchanting **Central Courtyard**★, a real time machine that magically transports one to the period of the legendary feats of knights and heroes. *Call ahead for information on opening times. Closed Mon, 1 Jan, 25 Dec. €5.*☎ *06 99 80 43 48; www.odescalchi.it*
Clinging to the promontory the charming medieval village of **Anguillara Sabazia**★ offers magnificent views of the lake which is reached by enchanting little streets.
Trevignano Romano is a typical medieval village with its fishermen's houses near the lake arranged in a herringbone pattern.

Salerno★

Salerno, lying along the graceful curve of its gulf, has retained a medieval quarter on the slopes of a hill crowned by a castle. From the Lungomare Trieste★ promenade, planted with palm trees and tamarinds, there is a wide view of the Gulf of Salerno.

Location
Population – Michelin map 431 E-F 26 – Campania Salerno lies at the tip of the Amalfi coast. The main access roads are A 3 and S 18, as well as the panoramic coastal road, the 163 ▢ *Piazza Ferrovia or Vittorio Veneto, ☎ 089 23 14 32. Surrounding area: see COSTIERA AMALFITANA, NAPOLI, Golfo di NAPOLI, PAESTUM.*

Worth a Visit

Duomo★★
Open daily, 8am-noon and 4-8pm. Donation recommended. ☎ *089 23 13 87.*
The cathedral is dedicated to St Matthew the Evangelist, who is buried in the crypt. It was built on the orders of Robert Guiscard and consecrated by Pope Gregory VII in 1085. The Norman-style building was remodelled in the 18C and suffered considerable damage in the 1980 earthquake. The church is preceded by a delightful arcaded **atrium** built of multicoloured stone with ancient columns. The square tower to the right is 12C. The central doorway has 11C **bronze doors**★ cast in Constantinople.

The interior is of impressive dimensions. The two **ambos★★** encrusted with decorative mosaics and resting on slender columns with marvellously carved capitals, along with the **paschal candelabrum** and the elegant iconostasis which encloses the chancel, form an outstanding 12C-13C group. The Crusaders' Chapel at the far end of the south aisle is where the Crusaders had their arms blessed. Under the altar is the tomb of Pope Gregory VII who died in exile at Salerno (1085). In the north aisle stands the tomb of Margaret of Durazzo, the wife of Charles III of Anjou.

Museo Archeologico

(&) *Open Mon-Sat, 9am-8pm, Sun and hols 9am-2pm. No charge.* ☎ *089 23 11 35.*
Housed in the attractive St Benedict monastery complex, the museum has artefacts dating from prehistory to the late Imperial era. Of particular note is the bronze **Head of Apollo★** (1C BC) and a fine collection of pre-Roman amber.

Via Mercanti★

This street is one of the most picturesque with its shops, old houses and oratories. At its west end stands an arch, **Arco di Arechi,** built by the Lombards in the 8C.

Saluzzo★

This pretty town, situated on the slopes of a hill, has an imposing castle at the heart of its medieval buildings. From the 12C-16C Saluzzo was the seat of a powerful marquisate making it a prosperous centre of art and culture. Take a pleasant stroll around the narrow streets with their stone stairways or have a glance at the shops selling antiques, woodwork and wrought iron.
Saluzzo was the birthplace of the patriot and writer Silvio Pellico (1789-1854), author of *My Prisons*.

Location I

Population 15 746 – Michelin map 428 I 4 – Piedmont. Saluzzo is situated between Cuneo and Turin, the main link roads to these towns being S 20 and S 662.
🖪 *Via Griselda 6,* ☎ *0175 46 710.*
Surrounding area: see TORINO.

Worth a Visit

Casa Cavassa★

Open Apr to Sep, Wed-Sat 9am-12.15pm and 3-6.15pm, Sun and hols 9am-12.15pm and 2-6.45pm, rest of year Wed-Sat 9am-12.15pm and 2-5.45pm, Sun and hols 9am-12.15pm and 2-5.45pm. Closed Mon, Tue. €2.60; €3.10 including Torre Civica. ☎ *0175 46 710.*
The fine Renaissance portal of this elegant 15C house is surmounted by the motto *"droit quoy qu'il soit"* (forward at all costs) and by the emblem of the Cavassa family, a fish swimming upstream (in the dialect of Lyon, fish is *chavasse*). The gallery of the beautiful panoramic loggia is adorned with a *grisaille* decoration depicting the *Labours of Hercules* by the Flemish-Burgundian artist Hans Clemer. In the various rooms which open on to the loggia are original Renaissance furnishings and a splendid altarpiece, **Madonna della Misericordia★**, also by Hans Clemer, which is surrounded by fine 15C choir stalls.

Chiesa di San Giovanni

Open daily, 8am-noon and 3-7pm. No charge. ☎ *0175 24 03 52; www.comune.saluzzo.cn.it*
The austere façade of this 14C church conceals a rich interior. In the north aisle there is a fine cycle of 15C **frescoes★** with scenes from the life of Christ framed by views of the city and lively groups of figures. The masterpiece of the church is the extraordinary **apse★★**, a jewel of Burgundian Gothic art, "embroidered" in green Sampeyre stone. The niche on the left houses the **Tomb of Ludovic II**, by Benedetto Briosco (master builder of the Charterhouse of Pavia after Amedeo). The niche on the right was to have housed the tomb of Ludovic's wife, Marguerite de

Foix, who was ultimately buried in Spain (note the corbel in the left hand corner with the strange figure of a prophet wearing glasses). From the north aisle make for the cloisters and the chapter house with the **Mausoleum of Galeazzo Cavassa**. Near the church, on the other side of the square, stands the **Torre Civica**, erected by Marquess Ludovic I in the 15C. The effort required to reach the top of the tower is rewarded by the fine **view★** at the top. *Open Apr to Sep, Wed-Sat 9am-12.15pm and 3-6.15pm, Sun and hols 9am-12.15pm and 3-6.45pm, rest of year Wed-Sat 9am-12.15pm and 2-5.15pm, Sun and hols 9am-12.15pm and 2-5.45pm. Closed Mon; Tue by reservation only. €1.30; €3.10 including Casa Cavassa. ☎ 0175 46 710.*

Excursions

Abbazia di Staffarda★

10km/6mi north on S 589. Open daily, Apr to Sep 9am-12.30pm and 2-6pm, rest of year 9am-12.30pm and 2-5pm. €5.17. ☎ 0175 27 32 15; www.mauriziano.it
This imposing monastery was erected by Cistercian monks in the 12C-13C in the Romanesque-Gothic style and constituted an important economic centre that hosted fairs and markets. The guest rooms on the right after the entrance have a fine Gothic refectory and a little beyond, to the left, is the 13C Loggia del Mercato. Opposite, from the long building which housed the lay brothers, make for the **cloisters**. At the end of the monastery buildings, on the right, stands the **church**, preceded by a portico. The solemn austerity of the interior, whose only decorative motif consists of the contrast formed between the red bricks and the white stone, is given movement by an asymmetry which seems to allude to the imperfection of Man. In the apse you may feel you are being watched by the slightly perplexed gaze of the sun's face on the vaulting (15C).
On the street leading up to the abbey note the fine **apse complex**.

Castello della Manta

4km/2.5mi south on S 589. Open daily except Mon, Feb-Sep 10am-1pm and 2-6pm, rest of year 10am-1pm and 2-5pm. Closed Jan, last 2 weeks Dec. €5. ☎ 0175 87 822.
This 12C stronghold was turned into an aristocratic residence in the 15C by Valerano, son of Tommaso III, Marquess of Saluzzo. The splendid **frescoes★★★** in the Baronial Room (first half of the 15C), with all the taste and decorative elegance of the International Gothic Style, depict the *Procession of Heroes and Heroines*. The characters portrayed derive from the courtly poem *The Wandering Knight*, written by Tommaso III. There is also a lively representation of the allegory of the Fountain of Youth.
On the return journey, a short detour to **Savigliano** (*13km/8mi east of Saluzzo on S 662*) is recommended. Note the atmospheric **Piazza Santarosa★**, bordered by Renaissance and medieval buildings.

Le Langhe

From Bra to Alba, a 90km/56-mile itinerary. The River Tanaro and River Bormida di Spigno mark the borders of this region of limestone hills, notable for its pointed peaks and deep valleys which have been carved out by torrents. The hill peaks are covered in vineyards which produce prized wines such as Barolo and Nebbiolo. Other typical products include the famous white truffles from Alba and hazelnuts. Specialities of this region can be tasted in the numerous wine bars *(enoteche)*. This route starts from Bra and, passing through La Morra, Monforte, Dogliani, Belvedere Langhe, Bossolasco, Serralunga d'Alba and Grinzane Cavour, finally reaches Alba. The landscape is dominated by castles and vineyards and affords splendid panoramic **views★**. The castle at Grinzane Cavour has hosted the literary prize of the same name since 1982.

Alba – Alba was the ancient Roman city of Alba Pompeia, the birthplace of the Roman Emperor Pertinax (AD 126-193). It is a gourmet centre famous for its delicious **tartufi bianchi** or white truffles (annual truffle fair in autumn) and its wines.

The town boasts several **feudal towers**, churches and medieval houses. Inside the Gothic **Duomo** dedicated to St Lawrence are Renaissance choir stalls inlaid with intarsia work of very delicate craftsmanship.

PRICELESS MUSHROOMS

White truffles are an underground mushroom tuber which grow in symbiosis with the roots of oaks, willows or poplars in damp, clay soil which has little exposure to the sun. They are mainly composed of water and mineral salts which are absorbed through the roots of the trees. They are hunted out by "*trifolai*" (from "trifola", a dialect word for truffle), accompanied by highly trained dogs who must find the truffles without damaging them.

San Gimignano★★★

Rising up from the Val d'Elsa, San Gimignano is surrounded by gently-rolling countryside dotted with vines and olive trees. Its 14 grey stone towers set on a hilltop are enclosed within an outer wall including five gates. It has all the charm of a small medieval town, built mainly of brick, and has been amazingly well preserved.

Location

Population 7 027 – Michelin map 430 L 15 – See also The Green Guide Tuscany. San Gimignano is easily accessible from Florence. Take the Florence-Siena dual carriageway as far as Poggibonsi. Follow the signs for San Gimignano (13km/8mi from Poggibonsi). **B** *Piazza Duomo, 1, ☎ 0577 94 00 08. Surrounding area: see SIENA, VOLTERRA.*

Directory

WHERE TO EAT
• *Budget*
Osteria del Carcere – *Via del Castello 13 –* ☎ *0577 94 19 05 – Closed Wed, Thu (winter only), Jan and Feb – 🗗 – €15/21.* This simple, rustic-style eatery is situated in the vicinity of the Piazza della Cisterna. Check the blackboard for the day's specials. Excellent meat dishes prepared with stuffed joints of meat from the famous butcher in Panzano in Chianti. Good selection of wines and cheeses.

WHERE TO STAY
• *Budget*
A La Casa de' Potenti – *Piazza delle Erbe 10 –* ☎ *0577 94 31 90 – Fax 0574 94 31 90 – 🖥 – 6 rm €38.35/56.80 – 🍽 €5.* This 14C palazzo is as central as it gets in San Gimignano. Some of the rooms overlook the piazza and have a view of the Duomo. You cannot fail to be impressed by the position, the decor (very atmospheric) and the prices!
• *Moderate*
Agriturismo Il Casale del Cotone – *Via Cellone 59 – 2.5km/1mi north of San Gimignano in the direction of Certaldo –*

☎ *0577 94 32 36 – info@casaledelcotone – Closed 2 Nov, 23 Dec – 🗓 – 11 rm €72.30/92.96* 🛏An elegant farmhouse which dates back to the 18C. Tasteful mixture of antiques and country furnishings. Nearby is also an annexe with apartments to rent. An ideal base for a relaxing holiday in a rural setting.

TAKING A BREAK
Caffè delle Erbe – *Via Diacceto 1 –* ☎ *0577 90 70 83 – Jun-Oct, Wed-Mon 8am-midnight, rest of the year 8am-8pm.* The smartest café in town: its warm and friendly ambience make it a very popular place. Musicians come and play in the small bar area with wrought-iron furniture and paintings on the walls. Lovely intimate but airy dining room upstairs (you get a glimpse of it through the skylight in the bar downstairs). There are also tables outside in the piazza.

SHOPPING
Via San Giovanni – This is the main shopping street with plenty of souvenir and wine shops, as well as a number of delicatessens selling the local speciality, wild boar meat.

Worth a Visit

Piazza della Cisterna★★
The square is paved with bricks laid on their edges in a herring-bone pattern and it derives its name from a 13C cistern or well *(cisterna)*. It is one of the most evocative squares in Italy with its tall towers and austere 13C-14C mansions all around.

Piazza del Duomo★★
The collegiate church, palaces and seven towers of nobility line this majestic square.
Collegiata★ – *Open daily, Apr to Oct 9.30am-7.30pm, rest of year 9.30am-5pm. Closed 21 Jan-Feb €3.50, €5.50 including Basilica Santa Maria Assunta.* ☎ *0577 94 22 26.*
This 12C Romanesque church was extended in the 15C by Giuliano da Maiano. The façade was restored in the 19C. Inside are a **Martyrdom of St Sebastian** (1465) by Benozzo Gozzoli and an **Annunciation** in wood by Jacopo della Quercia *(west wall).* The walls of the left aisle are adorned with **frescoes** evoking scenes from the Old Testament by Bartolo di Fredi (14C), while the **frescoes★★** (c 1350) of the right aisle are by Barna da Siena and depict scenes from the Life of Christ *(start at the top).* They display an elegant draughtsmanship and delicate colours. In the **Cappella di Santa Fina** (railings) designed by Giuliano da Maiano, the harmonious **altar★** is by his nephew Benedetto da Maiano and the **frescoes★** (1475) by Domenico Ghirlandaio.

Palazzo del Popolo★
The 13C-14C Town Hall is dominated by a tall **tower,** from the top of which unfolds an unusual **view★★** over the brown roofs and towers of the town. The Council Chamber has a remarkable **Maestà★** (Madonna and Child enthroned in Majesty, 1317) by Lippo Memmi, which was restored c 1467 by Benozzo Gozzoli.

▶▶Palazzo del Podestà, S. Agostino (frescoes★★, tomb★ of St Bartolo, the work of Benedetto da Maiano).

Excursions

San Vivaldo★

17km/10mi northwest. Leave by ①. In 1500 Franciscan monks settled here to honour the body of St Vivaldo who died here in 1320. During the next 15 years they built a monastery and a series of chapels (17 are still extant) recreating the holy places of Jerusalem in miniature. The chapels of the **sacro monte** contain painted terracottas which depict nearly-to-scale scenes ranging from the Passion to Whitsuntide. *By appointment only ☎ 0571 68 01 14.*

Certaldo

13km/8mi north. It was in this village, in the wooded Elsa Valley, that **Giovanni Boccaccio** (1312-75) spent the last years of his life. Along with Dante and Petrarch, he was one of the three great Italian writers. In the upper town are the **Casa del Boccaccio**, now converted into a museum, the church of San Jacopo where the writer is buried and the **Palazzo Pretorio**. *House museum: Open May to Sep, daily 10am-7pm, except Tue 10.30am-1.30pm; Oct and Apr, Mon-Fri 10.30am-4.30pm, Sat-Sun 9am-7pm, rest of year daily except Tue 10.30am-4.30pm. Closed Tue (winter), 25-26 Dec. €3.10. ☎ 0571 66 42 08. Palazzo Pretorio: Open Apr to Oct, daily 9.30am-1pm and 2-7.30pm, rest of year daily except Mon, 10.30am-12.30pm and 2-5pm. Closed Mon. (winter). €2.60. ☎ 0571 66 12 19; www.comune.certaldo.fi.it*

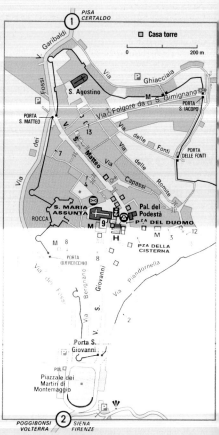

Repubblica di **San Marino**★

SAN MARINO REPUBLIC

One of the smallest states in the world (61km²/23sqmi), San Marino stands in an admirable site★★★ on the slopes of the jagged sandstone ridge of Monte Titano. This ancient republic strikes its own coinage, issues its own postage stamps and has its own army and police force.

San Marino is believed to have been founded in the 4C by a pious mason, Marinus, who was fleeing from the persecutions of the Emperor Diocletian. The system of government has changed little in nine centuries, and the leading figures are still the two Captains Regent, who are chosen from among the 60 members of the Grand Council and installed every six months during a colourful ceremony *(see under Events and Festivals in the Practical Points section)*. The economy is based on tourism, trade, the sale of postage stamps, craft industries and agriculture. San Marino produces a very pleasant wine, Moscato.

Location

San Leo: population 2 675 – Michelin maps 429, 430 K 19 – Town plan in the Michelin Atlas Italy. San Marino is 22km/13mi from Rimini, on S 72.
🛈 *Palazzo del Turismo, contrada Omagnano 20, ☎ 0549 88 29 98.*
Surrounding area: see RIMINI.

Worth a Visit

Palazzo Pubblico

Piazza della Libertà. Open daily, Apr to Sep 8am-8pm, rest of year 8.50am-5pm. Closed 1 Jan, 25 Dec, 2 Nov pm. €2.07 includes Museo di S. Francesco. ☎ 0549 88 27 08.
Government House was rebuilt in the Gothic style in the late 19C. The Great Council Chamber is open to visitors.

Basilica di San Marino

The basilica contains the relics of St Marinus. In the nearby church of San Pietro there are two niches hewn in the rock, in which St Marinus and his companion St Leo are said to have slept.

"Rocche" (Guaita, Cesta and della Fratta, Montale)

These three peaks are crowned with three towers *(torri)* which are linked by a watchpath. From the towers there are splendid **views**★★★ of the Apennines, the plain, Rimini and the sea as far as the Dalmatian coast. In the Torre Cesta there is a museum, **Museo delle Armi Antiche**, with a collection of firearms. *Open daily, Mar to mid-Sep 8am-8pm, rest of year 8.50am-5pm. Closed 1 Jan, 2 Nov pm, 25 Dec. €2.07. ☎ 0549 88 26 70.*

Museo-Pinacoteca di San Francesco

Open daily, 8.50am-5pm. Closed 1 Jan, 2 Nov pm, 25 Dec. €2.07. ☎ 0549 88 26 70.
Paintings from the 12C to 17C and 20C as well as Etruscan pottery and funerary objects.

Excursions

San Leo★★

16km/10mi southwest. Leave to the north then take the road to the left leading down to the Marecchia Valley. Just before Pietracuta and S 258 bear left.
A steep winding road climbs to the summit of the huge limestone rock (alt 639m/2 096ft) in an impressive **setting**★★, made famous by Dante in his *Divine Comedy*, with the historic village of San Leo and its 15C **fortress**★, designed by Francesco di Giorgio Martini, where the charlatan Count Cagliostro (18C) was imprisoned and died. From the fortress, which houses a **museum**, there is an immense **panorama**★★★ of the Marecchia Valley, Montefeltro and San Marino.

The cathedral, which is in the Lombard-Romanesque style (1173), and the pre-Romanesque parish church (restored) are noteworthy. The 16C Palazzo Mediceo (*Piazza Dante Alighieri 14*) houses the **Museo d'Arte Sacra**, with works from the 14C-18C. *Museums: Open Mon-Sat, Apr to Sep 9am-7pm (10.30pm Jul and Aug), rest of year 9am-6pm, Sat-Sun and hols 9am-6.30pm. Closed 25 Dec am. Museo d'Arte Sacra: €3; Museo Civico della Fortezza: €7.* ☎ *0541 91 63 06 or 800 55 38 00; www.comune.san-leo.ps.it*

Sansepolcro★

This small industrial town (famous for its pasta) still has its old town walls and numerous old houses★ dating from the Middle Ages up to the 18C, a reminder of its early, but long-lasting, prosperity. The finest streets are the Via XX Settembre and the Via Matteotti where there is also an austere Romanesque-Gothic cathedral. However, Sansepolcro's main claim to fame is the birth here in c 1415 of the most important artist of the Italian Quattrocento (15C), Piero della Francesca.

Location
Population 15 760 – Michelin map 430 L 18 – See also The Green Guide Tuscany. Sansepolcro is off the dual carriageway that links Cesena with Perugia. The town is only just inside Tuscany, on the border with Umbria. 🚩 *Piazza Garibaldi 2,* ☎ *0575 74 05 36.*
Surrounding area: see AREZZO.

Worth a Visit

Museo civico★★
Via Aggiunti 65. (🚻) *Open daily, Jun-Sep 9am-1.30pm and 2.30-7.30pm, rest of year 9.30am-1pm and 2.30-6pm. €6.20.* ☎ *0575 73 22 18; www.sansepolcro.net*
The most interesting exhibits in the municipal museum are the admirable **paintings★★★** by **Piero della Francesca:** his *Resurrection* (an impressive example of a mature style of art), the beautiful polyptych of the *Virgin of Mercy* and two fragments of frescoes, one of *St Julian* and the other of *St Ludovic*. The museum also has works by Bassano, Signorelli, and the Della Robbia School, as well as etchings and a few pieces of church plate. From the upper floor, there is a beautiful view of Via Matteotti and fragments of frescoes and sinopies (red chalk drawings) from the 14C. The basement contains sculptures and architectural ornamentation dating from the 13C to the 18C.
▶▶ S. Lorenzo (*Descent from the Cross★* by Rosso Fiorentino).

Excursions

Camaldoli★★
76km/47mi northwest. Camaldoli, situated in a great forest in the heart of the mountains, was the cradle of the Camaldulian Order, founded in the 11C by St Romuald. The monastery, standing at the head of an austere valley, was rebuilt in the 13C. Higher up in a grim, isolated site is the **Hermitage★** (*Eremo*) a cluster of buildings encircled by ramparts. These include St Romuald's cell and a fine 18C church.

Convento della Verna★
36km/22mi northwest. The monastery, pleasantly situated, was founded in 1213 and it was here that St Francis of Assisi received the Stigmata. The basilica and the small church of Santa Maria degli Angeli are adorned with terracottas by Andrea della Robbia.

Poppi★
61km/38mi northwest. This proud and attractive town, formerly the capital of the Casentino, overlooks the Arno Valley. The town itself is crowned by its proud-looking **castello★**, former seat of the Counts of Guidi. This 13C Gothic palace has a curious **courtyard★** decorated with coats of arms. *Open daily, mid-Mar to Oct 10am-6pm (ticket office closes 5.30pm), rest of year 10am-5pm (ticket office closes 4.30pm). Closed 1 Jan am. €3.* ☎ *0575 52 05 16; www.casentino.net/poppi*

Monterchi
17km/11mi south. The cemetery chapel has a strange but compelling work by Piero della Francesca, the **Madonna del Parto★**, which has been detached and placed above the altar. This is a rare depiction of the pregnant Virgin in Italian art.

Siena★★★

More than anywhere else Siena embodies the aspect of a medieval city. With its yellowish-brown buildings (from which the colour "sienna" is named) and encircled by massive ramparts the city extends over three converging clay hills at the very heart of the high Tuscan plateau. As a centre for the arts, Siena is an enticing maze of narrow streets, lined with tall palaces and patrician mansions, which come together on the famous Piazza del Campo.

Location
Population 54 256 – Michelin map 430 M 15/16 – See also The Green Guide Tuscany.
Siena is 68km/41mi from Florence. There is a dual carriageway linking Siena with the region's capital.
🛈 *Piazza del Campo 56,* ☎ *0577 28 05 51. Surrounding area: see VOLTERRA.*

Background

Siena's greatest period of prosperity was the 13C-14C, when it was an independent republic with a well-organised administration of its own. It flourished essentially on trade and banking. During the Guelphs versus **Ghibellines** conflict, Siena was opposed to its powerful neighbour Florence. One of the most memorable episodes of this long struggle was the Battle of Montaperti (1260), when the Sienese Ghibellines resoundingly defeated the Florentine Guelphs. During this troubled time Siena acquired her most prestigious buildings, and a local school of painting evolved which played a notable part in the development of Italian art.

In 1348 the plague decimated Siena's population and the city began to decline as dissension continued to reign among the rival factions. By the early 15C Siena's golden era was over.

The mystical city of Siena was the birthplace in 1347 of **St Catherine**. By the age of seven, it seems, she had decided on her spiritual marriage with Christ. She entered the Dominican Order aged 16 and had many visions and trances throughout her life. She is said to have received the Stigmata at Pisa. In 1377 she helped to bring the popes back from Avignon to Rome, which they had left in 1309. **St Bernardine** (1380-1444) is also greatly venerated in Siena. He gave up his studies to help the victims of the plague in the city. At the age of 22, he entered the Franciscan order and was a leader of the Observants, who favoured a stricter observance of the rule of St Francis. A great preacher, he spent much of his time travelling throughout Italy.

SIENESE ART

It was not only in political matters that Siena opposed Florence. In Dante's city, Cimabue and Giotto were innovators, but were greatly influenced by the Roman traditions of balance and realism which led to the development of Renaissance art in all its glory. Siena, on the other hand, remained attached to the Greek or Byzantine traditions, in which the graceful line and the refinement of colour gave a certain dazzling elegance to the composition, which was one of the chief attractions of Gothic painting. **Duccio di Buoninsegna** (c 1255-1318/19) was the first to experiment with this new combination of inner spirituality and increased attention to space and composition as well as the splendour of the colours.

Simone Martini (c 1284-d 1344 in Avignon) followed in Duccio's footsteps but imitated nature more closely with his exquisite harmonies of colour and taste for detail. He had a considerable reputation in Europe and worked at the Papal Court in Avignon.

His contemporaries **Pietro** and **Ambrogio Lorenzetti** introduced an even greater realism with minute delicate details, while at the same time remaining true to the sense of line of their predecessors. One of the favourite themes of the Sienese school was the Virgin and Child.

The Sienese artists of the Quattrocento (15C) continued in the spirit of the Gothic masters. While Florence concentrated on rediscovering antiquity and its myths, minor masters such as **Lorenzo Monaco, Giovanni di Paolo** and **Sassetta** continued to emphasise preciocity in figure design, flexibility of line and subtlety of colour which made Siena an ideal refuge for Gothic sensibilities.

In the field of secular architecture, the Gothic style gave Siena its own special character with the use of elements which made for a more graceful aspect. Brick and stone were often associated on the lower storeys, while windows became more numerous, especially in the Sienese style with a depressed triple arch supporting a pointed one.

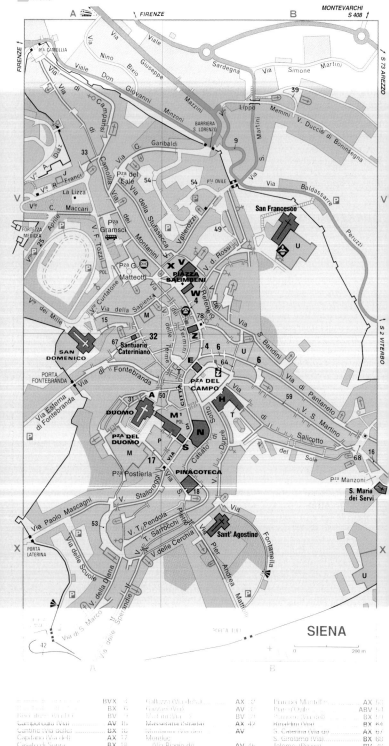

SIENA

0   200 m

Directory

WHERE TO EAT

• Budget

Osteria la Chiacchiera – *Costa di Sant'Antonio 4* – ☎ *0577 28 06 31* – *€12/25.* Be patient – there's not much room inside and you may have to wait a long time for a table but it's worth it. During the summer when there are tables out in the little street that runs between Santa Caterina and the Piazza del Campo, service is much quicker. Traditional Tuscan cooking.

Hosteria Il Carroccio – *Via Casato di sotto 32* – ☎ *0577 41 165* – *Closed Wed, 3 weeks in Jan, Feb* – *€18/23.* This establishment is renowned for its authentic Sienese cooking and delicious salads. A small but welcoming rustic-style trattoria which is popular with the locals. Located a few minutes' walk from the Piazza del Campo.

Antica Trattoria Papei – *Piazza del Mercato 6* – ☎ *0577 28 08 94* – *Closed Mon, except public holidays, and 20-30 Jul.* – *€20.14/26.34.* Classic Sienese trattoria, with a lively and friendly atmosphere. Simple, unpretentious decor. In the summer meals are served outside in the busy Piazza del Mercato, with the Torre del Mangia in the background. Represents good value for money.

• Expensive

Antica Trattoria Botteganova – *Strada statale 408, per Montevarchi* – ☎ *0577 28 42 30* – *Closed Mon* – 🖥 *– Book* — *€43/55 + 10% service charge.* This is deemed to be one of the best restaurants in town and worth the detour even if it is a little out of the way. Stylistically it is somewhere between rustic and elegant. Delicious if elaborate cooking: meat and fish dishes on the menu.

WHERE TO STAY

• Budget

Bed & Breakfast Casa per Ferie Convento San Francesco – *Piazza San Francesco 5/6* – ☎ *0577 22 69 68* – *Fax 0577 22 69 68* – *Closed 3 weeks in Jan* – 🚻 *– 16 rm €20.66/41.32* – 🍽 *€5.16.* Located within the Basilica complex, this small but welcoming establishment is in keeping with the simple tenets of the Franciscan order. Modern, functional rooms: one bathroom for every two rooms. No specific restrictions.

Santuario Casa di S. Caterina Alma Domus – *Via Camporegio 37* – ☎ *0577 44 177* – 🚽 *– 30 rm €41.32/54.23* – 🍽 *€5.16.* If luck is on your side you may get one of the rooms with a little balcony overlooking the Duomo. Whatever happens you can always repair to the lovely reading room or the little chapel (access on the second floor). Ask for a "room with a view"!

• Moderate

Albergo Cannon d'Oro – *Via Montanini 28* – ☎ *0577 44 321* – *Fax 0577 28 08 68* – *cannondoro@libero.it* – *30 rm €67.14/80.05* – 🍽 *€6.71.* This was once the home of Sapia, who appears in Dante's Divine Comedy (Purgatory, Canto XIII). Guests must still negotiate the three flights of old stairs, although rooms are available on the ground floor for those who experience difficulty walking.

TAKING A BREAK

Piazza del Campo – It is difficult to choose from the large number of cafés that surround this wonderful square. Look for the most comfortable chairs and get a table in the sun!

Nannini – *Via Banchi di Sopra 22/24* – ☎ *0577 23 60 09* – *7.30am-midnight.* Probably the most famous café in town and its association with various Sienese specialities extends throughout Italy as well as internationally. Push the boat out and treat yourself to a pastry or an ice cream. It's an experience you won't forget.

Pasticceria Bini – *Via dei Fusari 9/13* – ☎ *0577 28 02 07* – *Tue-Sun 7am-1.30pm and 3.30-8pm.* Founded in 1943, this pasticceria remains one of the best in Siena. Specialities include *panforte margherita* (cake with honey, almonds and candied citrus fruit), *panforte oro* (with candied melon), *copate* (small white wafer biscuits) and *cannoli* (pastries filled with ricotta and candied fruit). All the various Sienese specialities under one roof!

WINE BARS

Enoteca Italiana – *Fortezza Medicea* – ☎ *0577 28 84 97* – *info@enoteca-italiana.it* – *Mon noon-8pm, Tue-Sat noon-1am, Closed 10 days in Jan.* Set up with the aid of State funding in the castle ramparts, this wine cellar/bar promotes Italian and especially Tuscan wines. Organises tastings of more than 1 000 wines. Also hosts lectures for the larger wine-growers.

Antica Drogheria Manganelli – *Via di Città 71/73* – ☎ *0577 28 00 02* – *admanganelli@tin.it* – *9am-8pm, closed Jan.* With origins dating back to 1879, this splendid delicatessen sells a marvellous selection of quality products supplied by some of the best producers in the area. As well as wine you can buy *cantucci* (little biscuits made with almonds), pasta and even a wonderful 80 year-old balsamic vinegar made with hazelnuts!

EVENTS AND FESTIVALS

Twice a year, on 2 July and 16 August, Siena becomes a hotbed of feverish anticipation, excitement and vociferous rivalry when the famous bareback horse race, the **Palio delle Contrade** takes place.

The Palio

B. Morandi/MICHELIN

Building activity was concentrated on the cathedral where construction work and transformations lasted over two centuries. There again the façade is in a unique Gothic style where one can detect the transition from the Romanesque to the Flamboyant Gothic in a sumptous and detailed interpretation.

Sculpture, also influenced by the building of the cathedral, was enriched by the output of two Pisan artists, Nicola and Giovanni Pisano. The latter decorated the cathedral façade with a series of highly expressive figures and his work influenced **Tino di Camaino**, born in Siena in 1280 but who spent the last years of his life at the Angevin Court in Naples. However, the important figure in Sienese sculpture is **Jacopo della Quercia** (1371-1438), who successfully combined Gothic traditions with the Florentine Renaissance style.

Special Features

Piazza del campo★★★

Visit: 1hr15min. This piazza forms a monumental ensemble of almost matchless harmony. It is shaped like a scallop or a fan and is paved with brick and encircled by a ring of stone slabs. The piazza slopes down to the long brick and stone façade of the Palazzo Pubblico. Eight white lines radiate outwards dividing the area into nine segments, each symbolising one of the forms of government which ruled Siena. This consisted of nine members representing trade and banking who ruled the city during its greatest period of prosperity from the late-13C to the mid-14C.

At the upper end is the **Fonte Gaia** (Fountain of Joy) so-called because of the festivities which followed its inauguration in 1348. Fountains were at that time a symbol of the city's power. It was embellished with panels sculpted by Jacopo della Quercia but these, now badly deteriorated, have been replaced by replicas.

The Piazza del Campo is the venue twice annually for the popular festival **Palio delle Contrade**. The whole town participates in the preparation of this event for weeks beforehand and it recalls the medieval administrative organisation of Siena with its three main quarters, themselves subdivided into parishes *(contrade)*. Stands are put up for spectators around the piazza, and the surrounding houses are decked with pennants. The festivities begin with a procession of the *contrade* in costume, who then compete in a dangerous horse race round the square. There is much betting on the outcome. The *palio*, a standard bearing the effigy of the Virgin, the city's protectress, is awarded to the winner.

Palazzo Pubblico★★★

Open daily, mid-Mar to Oct 10am-7pm, rest of year 10am-6.30pm. €6.50 (without reservation), €6 (with reservation); including Torre and Museo €9.50 (without reservation), €9 (with reservation). ☎ 0577 29 22 26; www.comune.siena.it

The Town Hall, built between the late-13C and mid-14C in the Gothic style, is of a rare elegance with its numerous triple bays under supporting arches, which adorn the gently-curved façade. High up on the central part is a circular bronze panel inscribed with the monogram IHS (*Iesus Hominum Salvator* Jesus Men's Saviour) used as a badge by St Bernardine. From one end of the façade rises the slim form

The fan-shaped Piazza del Campo which echoes with the cries of the crowd and the whinnying of the horses as the Palio gets underway.

of the **Torre del Mangia**, a tower (88m/289ft high) designed by Lippo Memmi. At the foot of the tower, **Cappella di Piazza** is a chapel in the form of a loggia dating from 1352, built to mark the end of the plague. It was remodelled in the Renaissance style a century later. *Tower: Open daily, mid-Mar to Oct 10am-7pm, rest of year 10am-4pm. €5.50 (without reservation), €5 (with reservation); including Torre and Museo €9.50 (without reservation), €9 (with reservation).*

This palace was the seat of Siena's successive governments and most of the great artists of the Sienese school contributed to its decoration.

Sala dei Priori: in the Priors' Room, frescoes (1407) by Spinello Aretino recount the struggles between Pope Alexander III and the Emperor Frederick Barbarossa.

Cappella★: the chapel contains frescoes by Taddeo di Bartolo portraying the Life of the Virgin, a very lovely **railing★** and its magnificent early-15C **stalls★★** with intarsia work illustrating the Creed, and on the high altar a Holy Family by Sodoma.

Sala del Mappamondo★★: in the Globe Room the admirable *Maestà★★* (1315) is Simone Martini's earliest known work, and opposite is the famous *equestrian portrait★★* of the Sienese general, Guidoriccio da Fogliano, by the same artist. Note the curious contrast between the realism with which the figure is portrayed and the unreality of the background landscape.

Sala della Pace★★: in the Peace Room are the famous frescoes, although badly damaged (1335-40), of Ambrogio Lorenzetti, entitled *Effects of Good and Bad Government★★*, where the artist has achieved a happy combination of a scholarly and noble allegorical approach with that of meticulous narrative detail.

Torre★★: from the top of the tower there is a superb **panorama★★** of Siena's chaotic rooftops and of the gently-rolling Sienese countryside beyond.

Worth a Visit

Duomo★★★

Open Mon-Sat, mid-Mar to Oct 7.30am-7.30pm, Sun and hols 1.30-7.30pm, rest of year 7.30am-5pm. No charge. ☎ 0577 28 30 48; www.operaduomo.it

The richly decorated façade of the cathedral was begun in the 13C by Giovanni Pisano who added some remarkably expressive statues. The upper part was modelled on Orvieto Cathedral. The sober Romanesque campanile dates from 1313.

The walls of the **interior** are faced with alternating bands of black and white marble. The profusion of pillars provides a multitude of perspectives as one moves about. The 15C-16C **paving★★★** is unique. About 40 artists including **Beccafumi** worked on the 56 marble panels which portray, either in graffiti or intarsia work, mythological figures such as Sibyls, Virtues and Allegories and scenes from the Old Testament in a lively and delicate manner.

In the chancel is a 15C bronze tabernacle by Vecchietta and richly decorated 14C-16C **stalls★★**. At the entrance to the north transept stands the famous **pulpit★★★** carved from 1266 to 1268 by **Nicola Pisano**, who relates the Life of Christ in seven panels in a grandiose and exceptionally dramatic style.

From the north aisle a charming doorway leads to the famous library, **Libreria Piccolomini**, built in 1495 by Cardinal Francesco Piccolomini, the future Pope Pius III, to house his uncle's books. The Umbrian painter **Pinturicchio** adorned it with **frescoes★★** (1502-09) depicting episodes in the life of Aeneas Silvius Piccolomini (Pius II). The delicate draughtsmanship is typical of miniatures, while the brilliant colours are more typical of illuminations. In the centre stands the famous marble statue of the *Three Graces*, a 3C Roman sculpture (damaged) showing Hellenistic influence.

Museo dell'Opera Metropolitana★★

Open daily, mid-Mar to Sep 9am-7.30pm, Oct 9am-6pm, rest of year 9am-1.30pm. Closed 1 Jan, 25 Dec. €5.50; €7.50 including Libreria, Battistero, Oratorio S. Bernardino, Museo Diocesano d'Arte Sacra. ☎ 0577 28 30 48; www.operaduomo.it

The museum is in the extant part of the vast building started in 1339. The present cathedral was to have been its transept. The project was abandoned owing to technical problems and especially the terrible plague of 1348. The museum contains Giovanni Pisano's statues which originally adorned the cathedral façade, a low relief by Jacopo della Quercia and the famous *Maestà* (Virgin in Majesty) by **Duccio.** This altarpiece was originally painted on both sides (now separated). The panels of the reverse side depict scenes from the Passion of Christ, with a wealth of intimate details.

Battistero di San Giovanni★

Open daily, mid-Mar to Sep 9am-7.30pm, Oct 9am-6pm, rest of year 10am-1pm and 2-5pm. Closed 1 Jan, 25 Dec. €2.50; €7.50 including Museo dell'Opera, Libreria, Oratorio S. Bernardino, Museo Diocesano d'Arte Sacra. ☎0577 28 30 48; www.operaduomo.it

The baptistery, dedicated to St John, lies below the cathedral, under an extension of the chancel, and dates from the 14C. The façade started in the Gothic style was never completed.

The interior is decorated with 15C frescoes. The **font★★** is adorned with panels designed by Jacopo della Quercia. The bronze panels were by several Tuscan masters such as Lorenzo Ghiberti and Donatello. Of note is the latter's *Feast of Herod*.

Pinacoteca Nazionale★★

& *Open Mon-Sat 8.30am-7.15pm (except Mon pm), Sun and hols 8.15am-1.15pm. Closed Mon pm, 1 Jan, 1 May, 25 Dec. €4. ☎ 0577 28 61 43.*

The extensive collection of 13C-16C Sienese paintings is displayed in the 15C **Palazzo Buonsignori★**.

On the second floor is the rich section of the **Primitives.** Beyond the late-12C to early-13C painted Crucifixes and the works of a local artist, Guido da Siena, are the masterpieces of the Sienese school such as Duccio, with the **Madonna of the Franciscans**. The **Virgin and Child** is by Simone Martini. There are also numerous works by the Lorenzetti brothers including the **Pala del Carmine.** Note the *Virgin of Humility* by Giovanni di Paolo.

On the first floor note Pinturicchio's works, a **Birth of the Virgin Mary** by Beccafumi and **Christ on the Pillar** by Sodoma.

Via di Città★, Via Banchi di Sopra

These narrow, flagstoned streets bordered by remarkable **palaces★** bustle with life. Coming from Via San Pietro the visitor will see in the Via di Città, on the left the 15C **Palazzo Piccolomini** or Palazzo delle Papesse with the lower part of its façade rusticated in the Florentine manner. Practically opposite stands the long curving Gothic façade of the **Palazzo Chigi-Saracini**, now the home of the Academy of Music. Farther along, on the right, the **Loggia dei Mercanti** or Merchants' Loggia, in the transitional Gothic-Renaissance style with a 17C top storey, is the seat of the Commercial Courts.

Beyond on the left is the 13C **Palazzo Tolomei**, an austere but elegant building. Robert of Anjou, King of Naples, stayed here in 1310. The **Piazza Salimbeni★** is enclosed on three sides by buildings with different architectural styles: at the far end the 14C **Palazzo Salimbeni** is Gothic; on the left the 15C **Palazzo Spannocchi** is Renaissance; while the 16C **Palazzo Tantucci** on the left is Baroque.

Basilica di San Domenico★

St Catherine experienced her trances in this 13C-15C Gothic conventual church. Inside, there is an authentic portrait of the saint by her contemporary Andrea Vanni.

In the Cappella di Santa Caterina *(halfway down the south aisle)* is a lovely Renaissance **tabernacle★** carved in marble by Giovanni di Stefano which contains the head of the saint. The **frescoes★** by Sodoma on the walls depict scenes from the life of the saint.

Casa di Santa Caterina

St Catherine's house has been transformed into a series of superimposed oratories. In the basement is the cell where St Catherine lived. Above is the 13C painted crucifix in front of which the saint is said to have received the Stigmata.

Chiesa di Sant'Agostino

This 13C church, dedicated to St Augustine, has a Baroque interior. There is a remarkable **Adoration of the Crucifix★** by Perugino, and the Cappella del Santo Sacramento contains **works★** by Ambrogio Lorenzetti, Matteo di Giovanni and Sodoma.

Excursions

Abbazia di Monte Oliveto Maggiore★★

36km/22mi southeast of Siena. (&) Open daily, 9.15am-noon and 3.30-6pm (5pm winter). ☎ 0577 70 76 11; www.tbee.it/montoliveto.

The extensive rose-coloured brick buildings of this famous **abbey** lie hidden among cypresses, in a countryside of eroded hillsides. Monte Oliveto is the Mother House of the Olivetans, a congregation of the Benedictine Order which was founded in 1313 by Blessed Bernard Tolomei of Siena.

Chiostro Grande – The great cloisters are decorated with a superb cycle of 36 **frescoes★★** depicting the life of St Benedict by **Luca Signorelli** from 1498 and by **Il Sodoma** from 1505 to 1508. The frescoes begin on the right by the west door at the great arch, with two of Sodoma's masterpieces: *Christ of the Column* and *Christ bearing His Cross*. The majority of the frescoes are by Il Sodoma, a refined artist, who was influenced by Leonardo da Vinci and Perugino *(see Index)* and shows great interest in the flattering representation of different human types, landscapes and picturesque details, as illustrated in the following frescoes: no 4 depicting St Benedict receiving his hermit's robe; no 12 the saint greeting two young men in a crowd – the people are shown in different poses; no 19 where voluptuous courtesans have been sent to seduce the monks (splendid architectural elements open onto a long perspective). Signorelli *(see Index)*, who completed only eight frescoes, is more concerned with the powerful, sculptural nature of the figures and the dramatic effect of the compositions where landscape is only secondary: in no 24 St Benedict resuscitates a monk who has fallen off a wall.

The cloisters lead to the refectory (15C), the library and the pharmacy.

Chiesa abbaziale – The interior of the abbey church was remodelled in the Baroque style in the 18C. The nave is encircled by inlaid **stalls★★** (1505) by Fra Giovanni da Verona. Access to the crib is to the right of the chancel.

Spoleto★

This former Roman municipium became the capital of an important Lombard duchy from the 6C to the 8C. The town covers the slopes of a hill crowned by the Rocca dei Papi. The city was dear to St Francis, who loved its austere character, tempered by the grace of the narrow winding alleys, the palaces and numerous medieval buildings.

Location
Population 37 647 – Michelin map 430 N 20 – Umbria. Spoleto lies off S 3, the Via Flaminia, which links Foligno with Terni. 🚇 *Piazza Libertà 7,* ☎ *0743 22 03 11. For Norcia and the Parco dei Monti Sibillini:* 🚇 *Casa del Parco, Via Solferino 22, Norcia,* ☎ *0743 81 70 90.*
Surrounding area: see ASSISI.

Directory

WHERE TO EAT
• *Moderate*
Apollinare – *Via Sant'Agata 14 –* ☎ *0743 22 32 56 –* €*31/36.* An elegant, very reputable restaurant which is popular with the locals. The subtle yellow and the blue decor provides a harmonious contrast to the old stone walls and beamed ceilings. Evening meals served by candlelight. The excellent cuisine draws on tradition but is also innovative.

WHERE TO STAY
It is worth noting that during the trade fairs and exhibitions, the hotels tend to put their prices up. Do enquire about this when you make your booking.

• *Moderate*
Hotel Aurora – *Via Apollinare 3 –* ☎ *0743 22 03 15 – Fax 0743 22 18 85 –* ⚿ *– 23 rm* €*59.39/75.40* ⚏. Tucked away in a quiet corner of town is this lovely little family-run hotel which represents very good value for money. Modern, functional rooms. Full- or half-board rates with meals at the adjacent Apollinare restaurant *(see above).*

EVENTS AND FESTIVALS
Each summer the town hosts an international arts festival, the Spoleto Festival, which was originally set up by the Italian-American impresario and composer Giancarlo Menotti.

Worth a Visit

Duomo★★
Flanked by a baptistery, the cathedral provides the focal point of **Piazza del Duomo★**. The façade is fronted by a fine Renaissance porch and adorned above by a rose window and 13C mosaic. Inside note the altar cross painted on parchment applied to wood by Alberto Sozio (1187), frescoes *(first chapel on the south side)* by Pinturicchio, Fra Filippo Lippi's burial monument *(south transept)* and in the apse **frescoes** depicting the life of the Virgin by Fra Filippo Lippi and his assistants. In the episode depicting the Dormition of the Virgin, note the self-portrait of Lippi dressed in Dominican vestments.

Ponte delle Torri★★
A pleasant walk leads to the Bridge of Towers (80m/262ft high with a length of 230m/755ft), built in the 13C over a Roman aqueduct which was used as a foundation. The bridge with its ten Gothic arches is guarded by a small fortified gatehouse at one end.

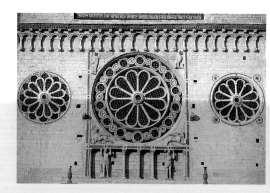

Rose windows of the Duomo

Basilica di San Salvatore★

St Saviour's Basilica, one of the first Christian churches in Italy, was built by Oriental monks in the 4C and modified in the 9C. Roman materials were re-used in the building of the later edifice.

Chiesa di San Gregorio Maggiore★

This 12C Romanesque church, dedicated to St Gregory Major, was modified in the 14C. The 14C baptistery to the left of the entrance porch has walls covered with frescoes *(Massacre of the Innocents)*. The campanile is built of stone from ancient buildings.

The dark, bare nave and aisles rest on massive columns with roughly hewn capitals. In the chancel note the 15C fresco and a carved stone cupboard of the same period.

Arco di Druso

This arch was built in AD 23 in honour of Tiberius' son, Drusus.

Chiesa di San Domenico

This lovely 13C church, dedicated to St Dominic, is built of alternating courses of white and pink stone. The nave is decorated with 14C and 15C frescoes and the south transept contains a canvas by Lanfranco.

Excursions

Fonti del Clitunno★

13km/8mi north. Open in spring; for information on hours ☎ 0743 52 11 41. €0.77.
These crystal-clear waters which surge amid aquatic plants were sacred to the Romans. They plunged animals into the water for purification prior to sacrifice. About 1km/0.6mi below stands the **tempietto★** of Clitumnus, a minuscule early Christian building dating from the 5C. It boasts columns and a carved pediment.

Monteluco road★

8km/5mi east. An attractively-winding road leads up to **Monteluco**. On the way up, the church of **San Pietro** has a lovely 13C Romanesque **façade★** with relief sculptures. On the summit, **Monteluco★** was once the seat of an ancient cult, but is now a health resort. The monastery founded by St Francis still exists.

Tours

SOUTHERN UMBRIA

This long *(150km/93mi)* but scenic route in southern Umbria ends in the heart of the Monti Sibillini. From Spoleto head for Carsulae along S 418 and continue in the direction of San Gemini and San Gemini Fonte.

Roman ruins: Carsulae

16km/10mi northwest. Go via S. Gemini and S. Gemini Fonte. These are the remains of a Roman town destroyed in the 9C.
Head in the direction of Terni along S 3 bis.

Terni

Terni, an important industrial centre, has an old town with several fine palaces, the church of San Francesco with its 15C bell tower, and the church of San Salvatore, which has early Christian (5C) origins. The bustling town centre comprises Piazza della Repubblica and Via Roma.
Follow S 79 as far as Cascate delle Marmore.

Cascata delle Marmore★★

For information on hours and prices, contact Infopoint ☎ 0744 43 18 42. This artificial waterfall created by the Romans falls in three successive drops down sheer walls of marble *(marmore)* to disappear at the bottom of a wooded ravine. *Take the Macerata road, S 209 (7km/4mi east of Terni), or the Rieti road, S 79 (9km/6mi to the east plus 30min there and back on foot).*

Take S 209 as far as Ferentillo.

Ferentillo*18km/11mi northeast.* This picturesque village is dominated by two ruined castles. From here *(5km/3mi north, then 2km/1.2mi further by a poor road)* it is possible to reach the solitary abbey of **San Pietro in Valle**, which was founded in the 7C and rebuilt in the 12C. The cloisters are decorated with 12C frescoes and there are Roman sarcophagi. *Open daily, 10am-noon and 2-5pm. Donation recommended. ☎ 0744 78 03 16; www.umbria2000.it*

Proceed along S 209 as far as the junction with S 320. Head in the direction of Norcia.

Norcia★

The quiet, walled town of Norcia is located within the **Parco dei Monti Sibillini**, whose highest peak is Monte Vettore (2 476m/8 170ft). St Benedict, patriarch of Western monasticism and patron saint of Europe, was born here in 480.

The walk along the Corso Sertorio towards Piazza S. Benedetto is a visual and olfactory delight. The shop windows are piled high with tempting displays of truffles, cheeses, hams, salamis and different types of pasta as well as vegetables and pulses. Overlooking Piazza S. Benedetto is the **Castellina** fortress, erected in the 16C by Vignola, which now houses the **Museo Civico-Diocesano**, and the 13C church of **San Benedetto**, with its Gothic façade. The frescoes inside date back to the 14C.

La montagna a ridosso di Norcia – Around 20km/12mi from Norcia, in the direction of Ascoli Piceno, the hilltop village of **Castelluccio** looms up (1 453m/4 790ft) against a backdrop of tundra-like scenery, heralding the beginnings of the immense upland plain of the **Piano grande★★**, which is carpeted with flowers in spring. Look out for the inscriptions on the limewashed walls of the stables and their ironic comments on village life.

Castelluccio: little hilltop village which is renowned for its lentil production

Sulmona★

Sulmona was the birthplace of the Roman poet Ovid, who immortalised his origins in the verse "Sulmo mihi patria est" (hence the acronym SMPE of the town's emblem). Sulmona was and still is a lively commercial and crafts centre, renowned for its goldsmiths' workshops.

Location
Population 25 407 – Michelin map 430 P 23 – Abruzzi. 🚩 *Corso Ovidio 208,* ☎ *0864 53 276. Sulmona lies at the head of a fertile basin framed by majestic mountains. The main access roads are A 25 from Pescara, or S 5, the Via Tiburtina Valeria.*
Surrounding area: see ABRUZZO.

SHOPPING
Confetti Pelino – *Via Stazione Introdacqua 55 –* ☎ *0864 21 00 47 – www.pelino.it* If you are looking for a present for a wedding, baptism or an anniversary this is the place to go.

Worth a Visit

Porta Napoli★
Southern town gateway. This Gothic gate has historiated capitals (14C). The exterior has an unusual decoration of gilded bosses, Angevin coats of arms and Roman low reliefs. The elegant **Corso Ovidio**, which cuts through the medieval heart of the city, commences here.

Piazza Garibaldi
This square is the scene on Wednesdays and Saturdays of a large and highly colourful market. The square is bordered by the pointed arches of the 13C **aqueduct★**, the Baroque corner of Santa Chiara and the Gothic doorway of San Filippo. At the corner of the aqueduct by Corso Ovidio stands the Renaissance fountain, **Fontana del Vecchio** which derives its name from the inscription under the bearded head above the curved gable.

Sugared almonds from Confetti Pelino

On Easter Sunday, the **feast of the "Madonna che scappa in piazza"** is celebrated in Piazza Garibaldi: the statue of the Virgin is borne to a meeting with the Risen Christ; as she comes within sight of Him, she sheds her mourning clothes and appears in a resplendent green robe.

Chiesa di San Francesco della Scarpa
This church was erected in the 13C by Franciscan monks who had shoes and so did not limp (hence its name, *scarpa* being the Italian for "shoe"). It has a fine Romanesque **doorway★** on Corso Ovidio flanked by a campanile and the remains of the apse.

Palazzo dell'Annunziata★★
This monumental construction documents four centuries of Sulmonese art. Built by a Brotherhood of Penitents from 1415, the palace constitutes a synthesis of Gothic (the rich Gothic doorway with statues of the Virgin and St Michael, the ornate **trefoil openings**, and statues of four Doctors of the Church), Renaissance (the elegant middle doorway, the right portal and the two twin openings) and Baroque art (the theatrical façade of the adjacent church). There is an astonishingly carved **frieze★** halfway up the façade depicting hunts and love scenes. Inside, the palace houses the **Museo Civico**. *Open daily except Mon, 10am-1pm and 4-7pm. €0.52.* ☎ *0864 21 02 16.*

COLOURFUL LITTLE DELICACIES
From the windows of Corso Ovidio colourful and unusual bunches of flowers peep out: these are the famous Sulmona sweets which were created at the end of the 15C. A taste of these little sweets will hold some pleasant surprises in store: a glacé of pure sugar hides Sicilian almonds, hazelnuts, chocolate, candied fruit and rosolio. To find out more, go to the small museum, **Museo dell'Arte e della Tecnologia confettiera**, at the Pelino factory in Via Introdacqua 55. ♿ *Guided tours only, Mon-Sat 9am-12pm and 3.30-6.30pm. Closed Sun and hols. No charge.* ☎ *0864 21 00 47; www.pelino.it*

Excursions

Basilica di San Pelino★

13km/8mi northwest, near the village of Corfinio. Open daily, summer 8.30am-noon and 3-6.30pm, rest of year by appointment only. Donation recommended. ☎ 0864 72 81 20.

This bishop's seat was erected in the 11C and 12C. The rear of the basilica offers a good view of the **apse complex★** and the adjacent oratory of Sant'Alessandro. The **interior** houses a fine 12C **ambo**.

Popoli

17km/10mi northwest. This pretty town is clustered around Piazza Matteotti. The square is bordered to the left by the church of San Francesco, with its Gothic façade and Baroque crenellations, and to the right by the theatrical staircase which leads up to the 18C church of the Santissima Trinità. Next to the square stands the **Taverna Ducale★**, an elegant 14C Gothic building adorned with coats of arms and low reliefs which in the past was used a storeroom for tithes.

Taranto★

Taranto is a well-protected naval base at the end of a great roadstead, closed at the seaward end by two fortified islands. Taranto was founded in the 7C BC and became one of the most important colonies of Magna Graecia.

During Holy Week many impressive ceremonies take place in the town, including several processions between Thursday and Saturday, one lasting 12 hours and another 14 hours, which go from church to church at a very slow pace *(see Events and Festivals, p 45).*

Location

Population 208 214 – Michelin map 431 F 33 – Town plan in the Michelin Atlas Italy – Puglia. Tucked away behind the "heel", Taranto lies off S 106 (if you are travelling from Calabria), S 7, Via Appia and S 172. **𝐁** *Corso Umberto 113,* ☎ *099 45 32 392. Surrounding area: see BRINDISI.*

Worth a Visit

Museo Nazionale★★

Central office closed for restoration at time of publication. To visit, contact Palazzo Pantallo: daily 8.30am-7.30pm. Closed 1 Jan, 1 May, 25 Dec. No charge. The National Museum has a good collection of local archeological finds which illustrate the history of Magna Graecia. Among the statues it is worth mentioning the figure of **Poseidon★★** which was discovered at Ugento (near the tip of the "heel"). This bronze statue, probably of local manufacture and dating from the 6C BC, most likely depicts the god of the sea or possibly **Zeus** holding a thunderbolt and a bird (both lost). The museum also houses a notable **collection of ceramics★★** with elegantly decorated vases in the Corinthian, Attic, proto-Italiot and Apulian styles and an astonishing collection of Hellenic **gold jewellery★★★** (4C and 3C BC) which was found in local tombs. These pieces are composed of filigree and lamina which are sometimes enriched by stones and enamels.

Giardini comunali Villa Peripato★

From the municipal gardens, a haven of exotic and luxuriant vegetation, there is a magnificent view over the harbour's inner basin, the Mare Piccolo.

Lungomare Vittorio Emanuele★

This is a long promenade planted with palm trees and oleanders.

La città vecchia

The old city is an island connected to the mainland by two bridges, one of which is a revolving bridge. At the eastern extremity of the island stands the **Aragonese Castle** which today is the seat of the Navy.

Duomo – The 11C-12C cathedral with a Baroque façade has been greatly remodelled. The nave and two aisles are separated by ancient columns with Romanesque or Byzantine capitals and the ceiling is 17C. The chapel of **San Cataldo★** was faced with polychrome marble and embellished with statues in the 18C.

Chiesa di San Domenico Maggiore – This 14C church was considerably remodelled in the Baroque era. There is a fine, if rather damaged, façade with an ogival portal surmounted by a rose-window.

Tarquinia*

The town of Tarquinia crowns a rocky platform, facing the sea, in a barley- and corn-growing region interspersed with olive groves. Tarquinia is famous for the Etruscan burial ground which lies quite near.

Location

Population 15 079 – Michelin map 430 P 17 – Lazio. Tarquinia is located off S 1 (the Via Aurelia) in northern Lazio. *Piazza Cavour 1, ☎ 0766 85 63 84.*
Surrounding area: see Promontorio dell'ARGENTARIO.

HISTORICAL NOTES

According to legend, the town was founded in the 12C or 13C BC. Archaeologists have found 9C BC vestiges of the Villanovian civilisation which derived its name from the village of Villanova near Bologna, and developed around the year 1000 BC in the Po Plain, in Tuscany and in the northern part of Latium, where the Etruscans later settled. Standing on the banks of the River Marta, Tarquinia was a busy port and in the 6C BC ruled the coast of Etruria. Under Roman rule, Tarquinia was decimated by malaria in the 4C BC and was sacked by the Lombards in the 7C AD. The inhabitants then moved to the present site about two kilometres to the northeast of the original position.

Worth a Visit

Necropoli etrusca**

4km/2.5mi southeast. Open daily except Mon, 8.30am to 1hr before sunset. Closed 1 Jan, 25 Dec. €4; €6.50 including museum. The burial ground is on a bare, windswept ridge parallel with that on which the former Etruscan city stood. The necropolis extends over an area 5km/3mi long and 1km/0.6 mile wide and contains around 600 tombs dating from the 6C-1C BC. As at Cerveteri *(see p 388)* there are no visible remains at ground level but there are remarkable **paintings***** on the walls of the underground burial chambers. These colourful and lively paintings are of the utmost importance for the light they shed on the Etruscan civilisation.

The most important tombs include: the **Tomba del Barone** (tomb of the Baron), dating from the 6C BC; the 5C BC **Tomba del Leopardi** (tomb of the Leopards), one of the finest, in which are depicted leopards as well as scenes of a banquet and dancing; the 6C BC **Tomba dei Tori** (tomb of the Bulls) with its erotic paintings; the **Tomba delle Leonesse** (tomb of the Lionesses) dating from around 530-520 BC; the 4C BC **Tomba Gigliogi** (Giglioli tomb) decorated with *trompe l'oeil* paintings of costumes and arms; and the late-6C BC **Tomba delle Caccia e della Pesca** (tomb with Hunting and Fishing Scenes) which consists of two chambers displaying the return from the hunt, a banquet and the art of fishing.

Museo Nazionale Tarquiniese*

(&) *Open daily except Mon, 8.30am-7.30pm. Closed 1 Jan, 25 Dec. €4; €6.50 including Monterozzi museum and necropolis. ☎ 0766 85 60 36.*

The National Museum is housed in the **Palazzo Vitelleschi*** built in 1439 and has a most remarkable collection of Etruscan antiquities originating from the excavations in the necropolis. Artefacts include sarcophagi, pottery, ivories, votive offerings and 6C BC Attic kraters and amphorae.

The following exhibits are of great interest: two admirable **winged horses***** in terracotta and on the second floor several reconstructed tombs, notably the **Tomba del Letto Funebre** (tomb with the Funeral Bed) (460 BC) and the **Tomba del Triclinio** (tomb of the Triclinium) (450-470 BC), one of the finest in the necropolis.

Chiesa di Santa Maria in Castello*

To visit, contact Signora Colomba Bassi, who lives behind the tower. Donation recommended.

This Romanesque church (1121-1208), dedicated to St Mary, stands near a tall tower built in the Middle Ages and was part of the fortified citadel guarding the town. It has an elegant doorway decorated with Cosmati work *(see Index)* and an imposing interior.

The Winged Horses, Museo Nazionale

Excursions

Civitavecchia

20km/12mi south. Civitavecchia, the Roman *Centumcellae*, has been the port of Rome since the reign of Trajan and now handles maritime traffic with Sardinia. The port is guarded by the Fort of Michelangelo, a massive Renaissance construction which was begun by Bramante, continued by Sangallo the Younger and Bernini, and completed by Michelangelo in 1557. Henri Beyle, known under the pen-name Stendhal (1783-1842), was appointed French Consul at Civitavecchia in 1831. In his leisure time Stendhal wrote numerous works, including *The Charterhouse of Parma* (1839).

Museo Nazionale Archeologico – *Largo Plebiscito nº 2 A.* ♿ *Open daily except Mon, 9am-7.30pm. No charge.* ☎ *0766 23 604.*
The museum has Etruscan and Roman collections composed of finds from local sites.

Terme di Traiano (or Terme Taurine) – *3km/2mi northeast.* (♿) *Open daily except Mon, 9am to 1hr before sunset. €5.* ☎ *0368 77 06 631; www.comune.civitavecchia.rm.it /terme.html*
There are two groups of baths *(terme)*: the first (to the west) dates from the Republican period and the second, the better preserved, was built by Trajan's successor, the Emperor Hadrian.

Tuscania★

25km/16mi north. Tuscania was a powerful Etruscan town, a Roman municipium and an important medieval centre. The town retains fragments of its walls and two superb churches, a little way out of town. Tuscania's artistic heritage was considerably damaged by the earthquake of February 1971.

Chiesa di San Pietro★ – The golden-hued façade of St Peter's stands at the far end of an empty square on the site of the Etruscan acropolis. To the left are two medieval towers and to the right the former bishop's palace. The harmonious façade dates from the early 13C. The symbols of the Evangelists surround a rose window, probably of the Umbrian school. Lower down an atlante (or a dancer?) and a man (Laocöon?) being crushed by a snake probably came from Etruscan buildings.
The interior was built by Lombard masons in the 11C. Massive columns with beautiful capitals support curious denticulated arches. The nave retains its original and highly decorative paving. The frescoes in the apse are 12C. The **crypt★★** is a forest of small columns, all different and of various periods – Roman, pre-Romanesque and Romanesque – supporting groined vaulting. *Crypt: General visiting hours, 9am-1pm and 2.30-7pm (5pm in winter).* ☎ *0761 43 63 71.*

Chiesa di Santa Maria Maggiore★ – This late-12C church, dedicated to St Mary Major, is modelled on St Peter's. The 13C Romanesque **doorways★★** are decorated with masterly sculptures.
Inside is an ambo rebuilt with 8C, 9C and 12C fragments. Above the triumphal arch there is a realistic 14C fresco of the *Last Judgement.*

Terracina ☋

In the Roman era it was already a fashionable country resort. Terracina has retained part of its medieval wall and some Roman remains.

Location

Population 38 662 – Michelin map 430 S 21 – Lazio. Terracina stands in an attractive setting at the head of a bay and is backed by a limestone cliff. . The main access roads are S 148 and S 213. ▣ *Via Leopardi,* ☎ *0773 72 77 59.*
Surrounding area: see GAETA.

Worth a Visit

Duomo

The cathedral overlooks the attractive **Piazza del Municipio** which still has the paving of the Roman forum. It was consecrated in 1075 and is fronted by a portico on ancient columns which support a 12C mosaic frieze. The campanile with its small columns is in the transitional Romanesque-Gothic style. Inside, the **pulpit** and **paschal candelabrum★**, a lovely 13C work by the Cosmati *(see Index)*, are of special interest.

Tempio di Giove Anxur★

4km/2.5mi plus 15min on foot there and back by Via San Francesco Nuovo. Although there are few remains other than the foundations, a vaulted gallery and an underground passage *(cryptoporticus)*, it is worth visiting the site of the Temple of Jupiter for its beauty alone and for the extensive **panorama★★** of the town, the canals and port, Monte Circeo and the Pontine marshes, the plain of Fondi with its lakes, and the coast as far as Gaeta.

Excursions

Parco Nazionale del Circeo★

Designated in 1934, this park covers a narrow coastal strip between Anzio and Terracina and includes part of the former Pontine marshes. Some of the most attractive beauty spots are: **Monte Circeo**, the refuge of the witch Circe who transformed Ulysses' companions into a herd of pigs; **Lago di Sabaudia**, a lake which can be reached by a bridge leading to the town of **Sabaudia**⌂, a pleasant country resort; the **scenic route** *(5km/3mi from the San Felice – Torre Cervia road)* is lined with luxury villas and brightened by typically Mediterranean plants and flowers. The park is one of UNESCO's protected nature reserves.

Abbazia di Fossanova★★*Open daily 7am-noon, 4-6pm and 6.30-7.30pm, Sun and hols 9-10.30am and 4-5.30pm. Guided tours by appointment. ☎ 0773 93 90 61.*

Standing, as the rule prescribes, in a lonely site, the **Cistercian abbey of Fossanova** is the oldest of the Order in Italy. Monks from Citeaux in France settled here in 1133. In 1163 they began to build their abbey church, which was to serve as a model for many Italian churches (Casamari for instance). Although rather heavily restored, Fossanova has kept its original architecture and plan intact. It was designed in accordance with the rules of austerity laid down by St Bernard. The buildings are laid out to suit the activities of the monks and lay-brothers

Chiesa – The church (consecrated in 1208) is in the Burgundian style but such decoration as there is recalls the Lombard tradition with traces of the Moorish style. As regards the exterior, the Latin cross plan with flat east end, the octagonal transept crossing tower, the rose windows and the triple-bayed window of the east end are typically Cistercian. The well-lit and lofty interior has a central nave balanced by aisles with groined vaulting.

Chiostro – The cloisters are picturesque with three Romanesque sides and the fourth or south side in the late-13C pre-Gothic style (transitional Romanesque Gothic style). The small columns are Lombard in form and decoration. The fine Gothic chapter house opens into the cloisters through wide twin bays. It was in the guest house, which stands apart, that the teacher and scholar St Thomas Aquinas died on 7 March 1274.

Anzio⌂

66km/40mi north of Terracina. Anzio backs against a promontory facing out to sea and forms with **Nettuno**⌂ a pleasant modern seaside resort. It has a popular yachting harbour.

Anzio is the Antium of antiquity, a Volscian city where Coriolanus took refuge, having abandoned his original intention of engaging in a fratricidal struggle with Rome. Antium was also the birthplace of Nero, in whose villa were found the statues of the Apollo Belvedere, the Fanciulla (young girl) of Anzio and the Borghese Gladiator, now respectively in the Vatican, the Museo Nazionale Romano in Rome and the Louvre in Paris. The name of Anzio is also remembered for the

Directory

Anglo-American landing of 22 January 1944, which, after a long struggle, ended in the taking of Rome on 4 June 1944. Several military cemeteries, monuments, memorials and museums recall those who gave their lives during this operation.

Isola di Ponza★*Access from Anzio or Formia (ferry 2hr30min, motorboat 1hr) and from Terracina (ferry 2hr).* This volcanic island, lying beyond the Gulf of Gaeta, has a verdant ridge and white or blue-grey cliffs, which are either bordered by narrow beaches or drop abruptly into the sea. At the southeast end of the island is the village of **Ponza**⚐⚐ with its serried ranks of cubic and gaily painted houses in a semicircle around a small harbour. The latter is busy with fishing boats, coasting vessels, pleasure craft and the ferries which ply back and forth to the mainland. The island is popular with underwater fishermen.

Tivoli★★★

The villas testify to Tivoli's importance as a holiday resort from the Roman period through to the Renaissance. Tivoli or Tibur in antiquity came under Roman control in the 4C BC and it was there that a Sibyl prophesied the coming of Jesus Christ to the Emperor Augustus.

Location

Population 52 809 – Michelin map 430 Q 20 – Lazio. Tivoli, a small town on the lower slopes of the Apennines where the River Aniene plunges in cascades into the Roman plain , lies off S 5, the Via Tiburtina, 36km/22mi from Rome.
🛈 *Piazza Garibaldi,* ☎ *0774 31 12 49.*
Surrounding area: see ROMA.

Special Features

Villa d'Este★★★

Allow 2hr. Open daily, 8.30am to 1hr before sunset. Closed 1 Jan, 1 May, 25 Dec. €6.50. For information on hours ☎ *0774 31 20 70.*
In 1550 Cardinal Ippolito II d'Este, who had been raised to great honours by François I of France but had fallen into disgrace when the king's son Henri II succeeded to the throne, decided to retire to Tivoli, where he immediately began to convert the former Benedictine convent into a pleasant country seat. The Neapolitan architect Pirro Ligorio was invited to prepare plans. The simple architecture of the villa contrasts with the elaborate terraced gardens. The statues, pools and fountains enhance the natural beauty with all the grace of the Mannerist style. To the left of the main entrance stands the old abbey church of **Santa Maria Maggiore** with its attractive Gothic façade and a 17C bell tower. Inside, in the chancel, are two 15C triptychs: above the one on the left is a painting of the Virgin by Jacopo Torriti, who also worked in mosaic at the end of the 13C.

Palace and gardens★★★ – From the former convent cloisters go down through the elaborately-decorated Old Apartments. From the ground-floor level there is a pleasant **view★** of the gardens and Tivoli itself. A double flight of stairs leads to the

The Canopo: Villa Adriana

upper garden walk. A fountain with a shell-shaped basin, **Fontana del Bicchierone**, is attributed to Bernini. To the left the **Fontana Rometta**, or "Mini Rome", reproduces some of the well-known monuments of Classical Rome. From here a splendid avenue lined with fountains, **Viale delle Cento Fontane★★★**, leads to the Oval Fountain, **Fontana dell'Ovato★★★**, dominated by a statue of the Sibyl. At a lower level the Fishpond Esplanade, **le Peschiere,** is overlooked at one end by the Organ Fountain, **Fontana dell' Organo★★★**, in which a concealed water-powered organ once played music. Right at the very bottom of the garden is the Nature Fountain, **Fontana della Natura,** with a statue of Diana of Ephesus. Return by the central avenue to admire the Dragon Fountain, **Fontana dei Draghi**, built in 1572 in honour of Pope Gregory XIII, then turn right to pass the Bird Fountain, **Fontana della Civetta**, which used to produce birdsong, and finally the modernised Fountain of Proserpina, **Fontana di Proserpina.**

Villa Adriana★★★

6km/4mi southwest by the Rome road, S 5, and then a local road to the left, 4.5km/3mi from Tivoli. Allow 2hr30min. Open May to Sep, daily 9am-8pm, Oct-Apr, daily 9am-5pm (ticket office closes 90min early). Closed 1 Jan, 1 May, 25 Dec. €6.20. ☎ 06 39 96 79 00.

This was probably the richest building project in antiquity and was designed entirely by the Emperor **Hadrian** (AD 76-138), who had visited every part of the Roman Empire. He had a passion for both art and architecture and he wished to recreate the monuments and sites he had visited during his travels. In AD 134 the villa was almost finished, but the 58 year-old Hadrian, ill and grief-stricken by the death of his young favourite Antinoüs, was to die four years later. Although later emperors probably continued to visit Tivoli, the villa was soon forgotten and fell into ruin. The site was explored from the 15C to the 19C and the recovered works were dispersed to various museums and private collections. It was only in 1870 that the Italian government organised the excavation of Tivoli, thus revealing this magnificent complex.

Before exploring the site it is advisable to study a model of the villa displayed in a room next to the bar. *Follow the itinerary shown on the accompanying plan.*

Pecile★★ – The water-filled Pecile takes its name from a portico in Athens. It was built in the shape of a large rectangle with slightly curved ends and is lined with a portico; it was oriented so that one side was always in the shade. The apsidal chamber called the **Sala dei Filosofi** (philosophers' room) was perhaps a reading room.

Teatro Marittimo★★★ – The circular construction consists of a portico and a central building surrounded by a canal. It provided an ideal retreat for the misanthropic Hadrian. Bear south to pass the remains of a **nymphaeum** (*ninfeo*) and the great columns which belonged to a building comprising three semicircular rooms round a courtyard (*cortile*).

Terme★★ – The layout of the baths shows the high architectural standards attained in the villa. First come the Small Baths and then the Great Baths with an apse and splendid vaulting.

The tall building, called the **Pretorio** (Praetorium), was probably a storehouse.

Canopo★★★ – Beyond the **museum** which contains the finds from the most recent excavations is a complex which evokes the Egyptian town of Canope with its famous Temple of Serapis. The route to Canope from Alexandria consisted of a canal lined with temples and gardens. At the southern end of this site is a copy of the Temple of Serapis.

Having reached the ruins overlooking the nymphaeum, turn right before skirting the large fishpond surrounded by a portico.

Palazzo imperiale – The palace complex extended from Piazza d'Oro to the Libraries. The rectangular **Piazza d'Oro★★** was surrounded by a double portico and was an aesthetic indulgence serving no useful purpose. On the far side are traces of an octagonal chamber and a domed chamber opposite.

Sala dei Pilastri Dorici★★ – The hall takes its name from the surrounding portico which was composed of pilasters with Doric bases and capitals.

Also visible are the **Caserma dei Vigili** (firemen's barracks), remains of a summer dining room and a nymphaeum. These buildings overlook a courtyard which is separated from the **library court** by a cryptoporticus, part of a network of underground passages which ran from one villa to another without emerging above ground. The suite of ten rooms along one side of the library court was an infirmary. Note the fine mosaic **paving★**. According to custom the **library** was divided in two for a Greek section and a Latin section. The route to the **Terrazza di Tempe** goes past rooms paved with mosaic which belonged to a dining room. The path runs through the trees on the slope above the valley past a **round temple** attributed to the goddess Venus, and skirts the site of a **theatre**, on the left, before ending at the entrance.

Villa Gregoriana★

Closed for restoration at time of publication. ☎ *0774 31 12 49.*

This wooded park has a tangle of paths which wind down the steeply wooded slopes to the River Aniene where it cascades through the ravine. The waters of the Aniene plunge down at the Great Cascade, the **Grande Cascata★★**, disappear out of sight at the Siren's Cave or **Grotta della Sirena** and burst from the rock-face in Neptune's Cave, **Grotta di Nettuno**. Climb the slope overlooking the ravine to leave the Villa Gregoriana and visit the **Tempio della Sibilla** (Sibyl's Temple), also known as the Temple of Vesta. This elegant Corinthian-style structure dates from the end of the Republic. An Ionic temple stands alongside.

Excursion

Palestrina★

23km/14mi southeast. With its panoramic position overlooking the Prenestini mountains, an old historic centre and the remains of the celebrated Temple of Fortuna Primigenia, Palestrina makes for an extremely pleasant excursion. This splendid town flourished from the 8C to 7C BC; after various vicissitudes it submitted to Roman domination. The Romans turned it into a holiday resort for emperors and nobles. The cult of the goddess Fortuna prospered until the 4C AD when the sanctuary was abandoned and the medieval city born on its remains.

Tempio della Fortuna Primigenia★ – This magnificent sanctuary, one of the finest examples of Hellenic architecture in Italy, dates from the 2C-1C BC and originally comprised a series of descending esplanades. In the Lower Sanctuary the Basilical Room remains as well as two side buildings, a natural grotto and the Apse Room from where the celebrated Nile fresco was taken *(see below)*. The Upper Sanctuary was built on the fourth esplanade of the temple (now Piazza della Cortina). In the 11C Palazzo Colonna, later Barberini, now the archaeological museum, was built here. From the terrace there is a fine **view of the town★** and the valley.

Museo Archeologico Prenestino – (♿) *Open daily, 9am-7.30pm. €3.* ☎ *06 95 38 100.* The museum has artefacts from several necropoleis as well as objects from the Barberini collection. The museum's masterpiece is the magnificent **Nile mosaic★★** which portrays Egypt with the Nile flooding.

Todi★★

Todi, a charming old town perched on an attractive site, has retained three sets of walls dating from the Etruscan (Marzia Gateway), Roman and medieval periods.

Location

Population 16 905 – Michelin map 430 N 19 – Umbria. Todi is roughly the same distance from Perugia, Terni, Orvieto and Spoleto. The main road to Perugia is S 3 bis.
🄱 *Piazza Umberto I 6,* ☎ *075 89 43 395.*
Surrounding area: see PERUGIA, ORVIETO, SPOLETO.

Directory

WHERE TO EAT
• *Budget*
Antica Osteria De La Valle – *Via Ciuffelli 19 –* ☎ *075 89 44 848 – Closed Mon –* *€21/28.* A one-room rustic-style establishment complete with bar and bottles on display. The owner, who is also in charge of the cooking, offers a variety of dishes drawing inspiration from seasonal, local produce.

WHERE TO STAY
• *Moderate*
Bed & Breakfast San Lorenzo Tre – *Via San Lorenzo 3 (2nd floor) –* ☎ *075 89 44 555 – Fax 075 89 44 555 – Closed Jan, Feb –* 🖃 *– 6 rm €51.65/98.13* ⛵. If you're looking for a quiet, elegant establishment, with historic overtones but a homely feel, this is the place for you. The rooms, which are all very individual in style, are tastefully furnished with period pieces. Ask for a rooms with a view out over the countryside.

Worth a Visit

Piazza del Popolo★★

This square in the centre of Todi is surrounded by buildings which are evidence of the town's flourishing commercial life in the Middle Ages. The 13C Gothic **Palazzo dei Priori★** was formerly the seat of the governor (*podestà*). Its windows were remodelled at the Renaissance and it is dominated by a curious 14C tower on a trapezoidal plan.

The 13C **Palazzo del Capitano★** has attractive windows in groups of three flanked by small columns. Both this and the neighbouring building have arcades with round-headed arches and massive pillars at ground level. The adjoining **Palazzo del Popolo★**, one of the oldest communal palaces in Italy (1213), houses a lapidary museum, a picture gallery and a museum of Etruscan and Roman antiquities. ♿ *Open daily except Mon, 10.30am-1pm and 2.30pm-sunset. Closed Mon (except Apr), 1 Jan, 25 Dec. €3.10.* ☎ *075 89 56 216; www.umbrars.com/sistemamuseo*

Chiesa di San Fortunato★★

Piazza della Repubblica. Building on the church, dedicated to St Fortunatus, lasted from 1292 to 1460; the structure combines Gothic and Renaissance features. The **central doorway★★** catches the eye with the richness and delicacy of its decoration. The well-lit and lofty interior has **frescoes** (1432) by Masolino (fourth chapel to the south) and the tomb of **Jacopone da Todi** (1230-1307), a Franciscan monk, a poet and author of the *Stabat Mater*.

Duomo★

This great early-12C Romanesque building is preceded by a majestic staircase leading up to its harmonious façade, all in pink and white marble, with a great rose window pierced and fretted in the Umbrian manner. Walk round the building to admire the Romanesque apse. Inside note the Gothic capitals, the Renaissance font and the lovely stalls with intarsia work dating from 1530.

Piazza Garibaldi

This square adjoining the Piazza del Popolo is graced with a monument to Garibaldi. From the terrace, there is a pretty **view★★** of the valley and distant rounded hills.

Rocca

Pass to the right of St Fortunatus and walk up to the ruins of the 14C castle. There is a well-shaded and pleasant public garden.

Chiesa di Santa Maria della Consolazione★

1km/0.6mi west on the Orvieto road. This Renaissance church was built of pale stone from 1508 to 1609 by several architects who drew inspiration from the designs of Bramante. The plan is that of a Greek cross; four polygonal apses are reinforced by pilasters with composite capitals. The dome, whose drum is designed in accordance with Bramante's rhythmic principle, rises roundly from the flat terrace roof. The interior is austere and well lit. The dome was decorated in the 16C and the 12 statues of the Apostles are by Scalza (16C).

Tolentino

This small town in the Marches region was where Napoleon Bonaparte and Pope Pius VI signed the Treaty of Tolentino (1797) ratifying the surrendering of Avignon to France.

Location

Population 15 934 - Michelin map 430 M 21 - Marches. Linked by S 77 and the dual carriageway, Tolentino is 18km/11mi from Macerata.
🛈 *Piazza Libertà 18, ☎ 0733 97 29 37.*

Worth a Visit

Basilica di San Nicola★★

Basilica: Open 7am-noon and 3-7.30pm. Museums: Open 9.30am-noon and 4-7pm. ☎ *0733 97 63 11; www.sannicoladatolentino.it*

The basilica is dedicated to the Augustine monk who was venerated for his magic powers. St Nicholas died in Tolentino in 1305 and was buried in the basilica's crypt. Building lasted from 1305 to the 18C and the exterior reflects the different construction periods. The façade, remodelled in the 17C in the Baroque style, has an elegant late-Gothic doorway by the Florentine sculptor Nino di Bartolo (15C), a pupil of Donatello.

The **interior** is striking for the opulence of its marble, gold and stucco decoration and the magnificent coffered ceiling (1628). In the first chapel on the south side is the *Vision of St Anne* by Guercino (1591-1666).

Cappellone di San Nicola – The chapel serves as south transept and is the most famous part of this pilgrimage church, owing to its cycle of 14C **frescoes★★** by an unknown master of the Rimini school. The images on the vaulting portray the Evangelists and the Doctors of the Church while the walls recount episodes from the Lives of the Virgin and Christ (upper and central frescoes) and scenes from the life of St Nicholas of Tolentino (lower frescoes).

Museums – These include the **Museo delle Ceramiche** (Ceramics Museum), the **Museo dell'Opera**, which has a fine 14C wood **nativity** and the **Galleria degli ex voto** (Gallery of ex-votos), which is striking for the ingenuous and spontaneous devotion reflected in the votive offerings.

Museo dell'Umorismo nell'arte

Piazza della Libertà. ☕ *Open Tue to Sun 10am-1pm and 3-6.30pm. Closed 1 Jan, 1 May, 25 Dec. €2.59.* ☎ *0733 96 97 97; www.biennaleumorismo.org*

In 1961 a group of artists from Tolentino founded the Biennale Internazionale dell'Umorismo nell'arte (The International Biennial of humour in art). The growing success of this exhibition led to the creation of the rather unusual Museo della Caricatura (Caricature Museum).

Excursion

San Severino Marche

11km/7mi northwest. The medieval and Renaissance heart of this town clusters around the elliptical-shaped **Piazza del Popolo**. There is a delightful **view★** of the town and surrounding mountains from the hill where the cathedral stands *(go up Via della Pitturetta).*

Pinacoteca Civica – *Palazzo Tacchi-Venturi, via Salimbeni 39. Open daily except Mon, summer 9.30am-1pm and 4.30-7pm, rest of year 9am-1pm and 4.30-6.30pm. Closed 2nd and 4th Sun of month in winter. €2.07.* ☎ *0733 63 80 95; www.comunesanseverino marche.it*

This picture gallery has a fine collection of interesting local paintings: **Lorenzo Salimbeni** and his brother **Jacopo** revolutionised the idiom of 15C painting by adding a vivid realism to the International Gothic Style. The collection also includes an opulent **polyptych** by Vittore Crivelli and the delicate *Madonna della Pace* by Pinturicchio (1454-1513).

Nearby *(turn left at the end of Via Salimbeni)* is the church of **San Lorenzo in Doliolo** (11C) which is architecturally very interesting and has a beautiful **crypt★** covered in frescoes attributed to the Salimbeni brothers and their school. *Open daily, 8am-7pm.* ☎ *0733 63 83 51.*

Torino★★

TURIN

Turin is unwilling to reveal its true character to the rushed visitor who will almost certainly fail to capture the profound contrasts which comprise the soul and charm of this city. On two occasions Turin has had to reinvent itself as a capital: first of the newly created Kingdom of Italy and more recently of the automobile industry. Now the city is attempting to shake off the role of "factory-city" and become an important cultural centre for the new millennium. Technology has always been its economic and cultural motor although Turin has never lost a rather conservative spirit which has always had trouble in adjusting to those historic and social changes in which it has played an active role.

The military tradition of the ruling Savoy dynasty has given Turin a rather severe imprint which is reflected in its splendid but restrained, balanced Baroque architecture, a far cry from the opulence of Rome. For centuries the city has jealously guarded the Turin Shroud at the same time cherishing a vocation for the esoteric which has attracted personalities such as Paracelsus, Nostradamus and Cagliostro. Nietzsche lived his last lucid years in Turin where he wrote his major works. He claimed that "Turin is the first place where I am possible".

Location

Population 903 705 – Michelin map 428 G 4-5 – Plans of the conurbation in the Michelin Atlas Italy – Piedmont. Situated at the foot of the Alps, against a backdrop of wonderful alpine scenery, Turin lies at the hub of a motorway network which takes in A 4, as well as A 5 (to the Valle d'Aosta), A 32 (to the Val di Susa) and A 32 (to Moncenisio), A 21 (to Piacenza) and A 6 (to Cuneo).

🛈 *Piazza Castello, 161,* ☎ *011 53 51 81; Stazione Porta Nuova,* ☎ *011 53 13 27.*
Surrounding area: see VALLE D'AOSTA.

Background

HISTORICAL NOTES

During the 1C the capital of the Celtic tribe, the Taurini, was transformed by the Romans into a military colony and given the name of Augusta Taurinorum. Converted to Christianity, it became the seat of a bishopric in the early 5C and then a century later a Lombard duchy before passing under Frankish rule. From the 11C onwards and for nearly nine centuries the destiny of Turin was linked to that of the **House of Savoy**. This dynasty descended from Umberto the Whitehanded (d 1056), reigned over Savoy, Piedmont, Sardinia and finally all of Italy. It was Italy's reigning royal family from 1861 to 1946. They were skilful rulers, often siding with the pope rather than the emperor, and playing France off against the Dukes of Milan. They slowly extended their rule over the area. It was in the early 18C that Charles Emmanuel II and Victor Amadeus II embellished their adopted city with splendid buildings by Guarini and Juvarra.

Charles Emmanuel III increased the importance of Turin during his long reign (1732-73) by reorganising the kingdom's administration and by establishing in his capital a court with very formal etiquette, similar to the one at Versailles. In 1798 Charles Emmanuel IV was expelled from Turin by French troops who wanted to impose a regime based on the revolutionary principles of 1789. On the fall of Napoleon Bonaparte, Victor Emmanuel I was restored without difficulty to his kingdom and promoted a policy against any foreign interference in Piedmontese affairs. Turin then became the centre of the struggle against the Austrians and for the unification of Italy.

Following the reorganisation of Piedmont by the statesman Camillo Cavour, the Franco-Piedmontese alliance against Austria, the victories at Solferino and Magenta (1859), Victor Emmanuel II was proclaimed the first King of Italy and Turin became the seat of the Italian government, to be replaced by Florence in 1865. The House of Savoy reigned over Italy until the proclamation of an Italian Republic in 1946.

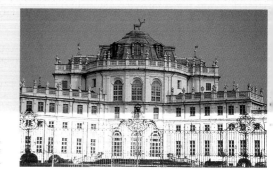

The elegance and clean lines of Juvarra's Stupinigi Hunting Lodge

ECONOMY

The intense activity of its suburban industries has made Turin the capital of Italian engineering. It was in the Piedmontese capital that the **Italian motor industry** was born with FIAT, founded in 1899 by Giovanni Agnelli, and Lancia, created in 1906 by Vincenzo Lancia and eventually taken over by the FIAT group in 1969. The **Lingotto**, the famous FIAT factory which was built in 1920 with such avant-garde technical features as the spectacular test ramp on the roof, was defined by Le Corbusier as "one of the most striking spectacles provided by industry". When production ceased, the building was transformed by **Renzo Piano** into a highly modern conference and exhibition centre with an auditorium and a commercial area. Important tyre manufacturers and well-known coachbuilders (one of the most famous was the great Pinin Farina) have contributed to the prosperity of the motor industry in Turin itself.

Directory

GETTING ABOUT

By car – In spite of its decentralised position (the city is only about 100km/62mi from the French border) there is a good network of motorways linking Turin to various cities. Furthermore, thanks to its famous octagonal plan and wide 19C avenues, traffic, although heavy at times, is manageable and it is easier to travel in and around Turin by car than it is in many other Italian cities.

Bus – The terminus is in Corso Inghilterra at the corner of Corso Castel Fidardo, ☎ 011 53 52 47.

By train – The main railway stations in the city are:

Porta Nuova, Corso Vittorio Emanuele II 53, ☎ 8488 88088 (toll-free number);

Porta Susa, piazza XVIII Dicembre 8, ☎ 8488 88088 (toll-free number).

By air – Turin's international airport is situated 11km/7mi north of the city in Caselle, ☎ 011 56 76 361/2, Fax 011 56 76 420, www.turin-airport.com It is served by major national and international airline companies and has flights to principal Italian and European cities.

Taxi journeys to the city centre (about 30min) vary from €23.24 (daytime) to €38.73 (evenings). Airport taxi service ☎ 011 99 14 419.

Buses operated by Sadem ensure connections to the city every 45min, from 5.15am to 10.30pm (departs from Porta Nuova – Corso Vittorio Emanuele II at the corner of Via Sacchi – and Porta Susa – Corso San Martino at the corner of Piazza XVIII Dicembre) and from 6.30am to 11.30pm (departs from the airport, arrivals floor, opposite the national flights exit). Tickets cost €4.13 and can be purchased from ticket counters adjacent to the terminals or on the vehicle when leaving from Turin and from the newspaper stand in the departure lounge, the automated ticket machine or the ticket office (€0.52) in the National Arrivals lounge when departing from the airport.

TORINO CARD (AND MUSEUMS)

The card includes free transport for 48hrs (from the date on the back of the card) on all public transport in the city as well as free entrance to all the museums, discounts for concerts and various other events. The card costs €13 (one adult and child under 12). For information contact Turismo Torino.

ENJOYING TURIN BY DAY ...

The best way of discovering the city is on foot. Although Turin is a large city the historic centre is rather compact and can be pleasantly covered on foot; pedestrians are protected from inclement weather by the elegant arcades lining the main streets.

Public transport – ATM (City transport company) has its head office in Corso Turati 19/6, ☎ 800 019 152 (toll-free number), www.comune.torino.it/atm Tickets can be purchased at tobacconists, newspaper stands

and authorised bars. There are various types of tickets: the biglietto ordinario urbano (€0.77) is valid for 70min, a biglietto giornaliero (one-day ticket – €2.58) allows unlimited travel all day, the Shopping ticket (€1.55) is valid for four hours from when it is stamped, from 9am to 8pm, the Shopping insieme ticket (€2.58) is valid only on Saturdays and allows unlimited travel for three people from 2.30pm to 8pm.

Taxi – Central Taxi Radio ☎ 011 57 44 o 011 57 48, Centrale Radio ☎ 011 57 37, Radio Taxi ☎ 011 57 30.

SOME SUGGESTIONS FOR DISCOVERING THE CITY

Boat trips on the Po – Boat trips of varying lengths are operated along the Po (departure from the river bank at Lungopo Diaz). For information ☎ 011 58 11 900.

Touristbus – This service operates tours of the city, the hills and the Savoy residences. For booking and information contact Turismo Torino ☎ 011 58 11 900.

Get on your bike ... – through the magnificent Mandria a Venaria Reale Park (1340 ha/3311 acres of parkland 15km/9mi northwest of the city centre), where bicycles can be rented. The park also offers excursions on horseback and nature walks. For information call ☎ 800 48 66 64 (toll-free number).

WHERE TO EAT

• Budget

Pizzeria La Stua – *Via Mazzini 46 –* ☎ *011 81 78 339 – Closed Mon, Sun lunchtime – 🗺 – Book.* During the winter the regular customers in the know head for the little dining room on the ground floor where there is a lovely fire crackling and spitting in the fireplace. If there's no room left, head up the narrow winding staircase to the first floor.

Pizzeria Gennaro Esposito – *Via Passalacqua 1/G – ☎ 011 53 59 05 – Closed Sat lunchtime, Sun – Book.* Small, rather eccentric establishment. Look out for the good-luck charms and pictures of celebrities hanging on the walls. If you want to avoid the queues, get there by 7pm.

Porto di Savona – *Piazza Vittorio Veneto 2 – ☎ 011 81 73 500 – Closed Mon, Tue lunchtime – 🗺 🖾 – €21/26.* A typical old-fashioned trattoria of a kind few and far between these days. Walls decorated with old photographs of the city and famous regulars. A good selection of traditional, regional dishes on the menu.

• Expensive

Del Cambio – *Piazza Carignano 2 –* ☎ *011 54 37 60 – Closed Sun, 3-31 Aug –* 🖾 *– Book – €46/60 + 15% service charge.* Valuable works of art, Baroque mirrors and gilded stuccowork all make for a very refined ambience where time seems to have stood still. Count Cavour could still be dining at his table, pondering the façade of the magnificent Palazzo Carignano.

WHERE TO STAY

It is worth noting that during the trade fairs and commercial exhibitions, the hotels tend to put their prices up. Do enquire about this when you make your booking

• Budget

Hotel Centrale – *Via Mazzini 13 –* ☎ *011 81 24 182 – Fax 011 88 33 59 – ⊠ – 12 rm €41.32/72.30.* The rooms are modern and functional but comfortable. Very reasonably priced. If you are travelling alone you could ask for one of the single rooms (without ensuite bathroom) and save some money.

• Moderate

Hotel Magenta – *Corso Vittorio Emanuele II 67 –* ☎ *011 54 26 49 – Fax 011 54 26 49 – 18 rm €46.48/61.97.* A stone's throw from the Porta Nuova station and very convenient for anyone arriving by train. Fine period palazzo with basic but attractive rooms. Some have shared bathrooms.

Hotel Artuà – *Via Brofferio 1 (4th floor, with lift) –* ☎ *011 51 75 301 – Fax 011 51 75 141 – info@artua.it –* ▣ ▣ ✕ – *20 rm €65/100* ⌂. Housed in a lovely old building located away from the hustle and bustle, near Piazza Solferino. Simple but comfortable rooms: prices vary. The cheapest rates do not include breakfast.

Hotel Dogana Vecchia – *Via Corte d'Appello 4 –* ☎ *011 43 66 752 – Fax 011 43 67 194 –* ▣ *– 50 rm €82.63/134.28* ⌂. The inn of the old customs-house, built at the end of the 18C and situated in the heart of the historic centre, was a stopping place for travellers, some of the most illustrious of which include Mozart, Napoleon and Verdi. The prettiest rooms are those decorated with antique furnishings, but there are a few modern, functional rooms for the more practical minded.

• Expensive

Hotel Roma e Rocca Cavour – *Piazza Carlo Felice 60 –* ☎ *011 56 12 772 – Fax 011 56 28 137 – hotel.roma@tin.it – 90 rm from €85.22* ⌂. Elegant, old-fashioned hotel: antique furniture, magnificent wood or marble floors, precious rugs, Murano glass chandeliers. The hotel offers excellent discounts on weekends, in the month of August and during the Easter and Christmas holidays. In August 1950 Cesare Pavese put an end to his tormented life in room 346.

Villa Sassi – *Strada al Traforo del Pino 47 –* ☎ *011 89 80 556 – Fax 011 89 80 095 – Closed Aug –* ▣ ^ *– 17 rm from €170.43 – Restaurant €43.89/56.81.* An exclusive retreat with overtones of faded grandeur. Situated just 4km/2.5mi from the historic centre this 17C villa is surrounded by beautiful parkland (over 2ha/5 acres). Spacious, comfortable rooms with period furnishings. Reasonable prices.

TAKING A BREAK

Al Bicerin – *Piazza della Consolata 5 –* ☎ *011 43 69 325 – Tue-Sat 11am-7.30pm.* This café was founded in 1763. Cavour came here to take refuge from the troubles of politics.

Baratti & Milano – *Piazza Castello 29 –* ☎ *011 56 12 666 – Mon and Tue, Thu-Sat 8.30am-7.30pm, Sun 8.30am-1pm and 3.30-7.30pm.* Founded in 1875, this was originally a confectionery shop. With its elegant Art Nouveau rooms the café was a favourite with the ladies of Turin's high society. Also serves light lunches.

Caffè San Carlo – *Piazza San Carlo 156 –* ☎ *011 53 25 86 – Tue-Sun 7am-midnight.* This opulent café, founded in 1822, was a patriotic stronghold during the Risorgimento and later became a salon frequented by artists, literary personalities and statesmen.

Caffè Torino – *Piazza San Carlo 204 –* ☎ *011 54 51 18 – 8am-1am.* Founded in 1903, this Art Nouveau café is adorned with gilded friezes, huge chandeliers and marble and wood fireplaces. It was frequented by members of the royal family, intellectuals and actors such as James Stewart, Ava Gardner and Brigitte Bardot.

Lara Pessina/MICHELIN

Caffè Torino

Fiorio – *Via Po 8 –* ☎ *011 81 73 225 – Tue-Sun 8am-1am.* Founded in 1780, this was the traditional meeting-place for aristocrats and conservative intellectuals. Its ice cream is one of the glories of Turin.

Hafa Cafè – *Via S. Agostino 23/C – 11.30am-1am.* Connected to the shop of the same name which sells ethnic furniture and objects (closing time 9pm), this Moroccan cafe is decorated with exquisite taste. North African specialities are served with music in the background.

Mulassano – *Piazza Castello 15 –* ☎ *011 54 79 90 – 7.30am-9pm.* Founded in 1907, this charming and intimate café, decorated in marble, bronze, wood and leather, was frequented by members of the Savoia family and performers from the nearby Teatro Regio. It counted the comedian Macario and the poet Guido Gozzano among its *habitués*.

Platti – *Corso Vittorio Emanuele II 72 –* ☎ *011 50 69 056 – Tue-Sat 7.30am-midnight, Mon and Sun 7.30am-9pm.* Founded in 1870, this was originally a shop selling liqueurs and later became an Art Nouveau café. It was frequented predominantly by intellectuals and writers such as Cesare Pavese. It has since been completely refurbished and also has a restaurant.

Stratta – *Piazza San Carlo 191 – ☎ 011 54 79 20 – Tue-Sat 9.30am-1pm and 3-7.30pm, Mon 3-7.30pm.* Confectioner's founded in 1836, famous for its multicoloured sweets.

GOING OUT

Tre Galli – *Via Sant'Agostino 25 – ☎ 011 52 16 027 – 7pm-2am.* A pleasant wine bar-restaurant with a rustic-minimalist atmosphere. Tables outside in the summer. A good after-theatre place.

ENTERTAINMENT

Music lovers ... – There are several prestigious concert halls in Turin including the **Auditorium Giovanni Agnelli** del Lingotto, Via Nizza 262/43, ☎ 011 66 44 551 (classical music) and the **Conservatorio Giuseppe Verdi**, Via Mazzini 11, ☎ 011 88 84 70. Without forgetting the **Teatro Regio**, in Piazza Castello 215, ☎ 011 88 15 241, where with a bit of luck you will be able to enjoy an opera or ballet.

SHOPPING

There are 18km/11mi of arcades in the historic centre. On Via Roma, which the architect Piacentini modernised in the 1930s, particularly in the first stretch *(coming from Porta Nuova station),* there are luxurious shops and the elegant San Federico gallery.

Art and antique lovers should head for the nearby Via Cavour, Via Maria Vittoria and Via San Tommaso in search of furniture, ceramics and Art Nouveau objets d'art. Most antiquarian bookshops are concentrated around Via Po, Via Accademia Albertina and Piazza San Carlo, while Via Lagrange is a gourmet's paradise. Turin specialities include agnolotti pasta, *bagna cauda*, the famous grissini breadsticks and naturally chocolate (chocolates with fillings, hazelnut-chocolate *gianduiotti, bonet*). All of which can be accompanied by prestigious local wines or vermouth which was created in Turin at the end of the 18C.

Two streets lead off Piazza Castello: the famous Via Po *(see below)* and the lively shopping street Via Garibaldi, one of the longest pedestrian streets in Europe, characterised by a young informal style. On the second Sunday of the month an unmissable appointment is the **Balôn** in Porta Palazzo, Turin's traditional flea market which has been in existence since 1856.

But Turin boasts other very solid traditions. There are numerous publishing companies such as Bollati Boringhieri, Einaudi, Lattes, Loescher, Paravia, SEI and UTET as well as one of the major national newspapers, *La Stampa*, founded in 1895. Music also thrives in Turin thanks to the presence of the RAI National Symphony Orchestra and the prestigious *Teatro Regio*.

These diverse traditions are all displayed in the numerous fairs and exhibitions hosted by the city: the *Salone dell'Automobile* (every two years), the *Salone del Libro* (Book Fair), the *Salone della Musica* and the *Settembre Musica* festival which also encompasses the prestigious *Cinema Giovani* (Young cinema) festival, a homage to the "tenth art" in a city which until the First World War was the Italian capital of cinema.

NOT JUST FIAT...

For many Turin is synonymous with FIAT but numerous companies known all over the world were born here or have their central offices in or around the city. Among these are: Lavazza, Cinzano, Martini & Rossi, Gancia, Caffarel and Peyrano in the food and drink sector; the textile group GFT, producers of the Armani, Valentino, Cerruti and Ungaro brands; the Istituto Bancario San Paolo and the Cassa di Risparmio di Torino (the second largest bank in Italy) in the banking sector; SAI, Toro and Reale Mutua Assicurazioni in the insurance sector; STET-Telecom Italia in the telecommunications sector; Robe di Kappa, Superga and Invicta in the sports clothing sector and De Fonseca in the shoe manufacturing industry. Without forgetting Michelin naturally, who opened their first factory outside France in 1906 in the famous building on Via Livorno.

Worth a Visit

HISTORIC CENTRE

Piazza San Carlo★★

This is a graceful example of town planning. The churches of **San Carlo** and **Santa Cristina**, symmetrically placed on the south side, frame the Via Roma. The curious façade of Santa Cristina *(on the left)*, surmounted by candelabra, was designed by the famous Sicilian-Turinese architect Juvarra, who was responsible for many of Turin's lovely buildings. On the east side is the 17C palace which was the French Ambassador's residence from 1771 to 1789. In the centre of the square stands the famous "bronze horse" by C Marocchetti (1838), an equestrian monument to Emanuele Filiberto of Savoy who, after defeating the French at the battle of San Quintino in 1557, salvaged his states after 25 years of French occupation (Treaty of Cateau-Cambrésis).

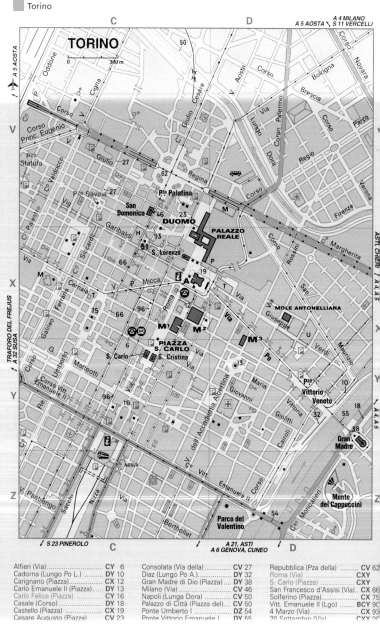

Palazzo dell'Accademia delle Scienze

This 17C palace by Guarini now houses two major Italian museums.

Museo Egizio★★★ – *Ground and first floors* (&) *Open daily, 8.30am-7.30pm (ticket office closes 6.30pm) Closed 1 Jan, 1 May, 25 Dec. €6.50. ☎ 011 56 18 393. www.museoegizio.it*

The Egyptian Museum is one of the richest collections of Egyptian antiquities in the world. The basement houses the finds from the excavations carried out in 1911 by two Italian archaeologists, Schiaparelli and Farina. On the ground floor is the section on **statuary art** with 20 seated or standing figures of the lion-headed goddess Sekhmet from Karnak, and an important series of **statues of Pharaohs** of the New Kingdom (1580-1100 BC), Egypt's Golden Age. The **Rock Temple of Thutmose III** (c 1450 BC), a gift from the United Arab Republic, originated from Ellessya 200km/124mi to the south of Aswan.

The collections on the first floor evoke all aspects of Egyptian civilisation, in particular: the **sarcophagi** – simple examples dating from the Middle Kingdom (2100-1580 BC) and sculpted ones during the New Kingdom; a collection of **canopic urns;** and an important number of mummies and copies of funerary papyri rolls known as the **Book of the Dead.** In addition to the recreated **funeral chambers** (*mastabas*, Giza 2500 BC), there is an exceptional collection of **funerary steles** dating from the Middle and New Kingdoms. Jewellery and pottery from the pre-dynastic civilisations, known as Nagadian, date from 4000-3000 BC. The influence of the Greek world made itself felt from the 4C BC following the conquest by Alexander the Great (masks and statuettes), followed by the Romans from 30 BC (bronze vases). Another room is devoted to **inscriptions**; the hieroglyphs (deciphered by Champollion in 1824), and texts in hieratic script using cursive on papyrus, limestone flakes and fragments of pottery.

Galleria Sabauda★★ – *2nd and 3rd floors.* (&) *Open daily except Mon, 8.30am-7.30pm. Closed 1 Jan, 1 May, 25 Dec.* €4; €8 including Museo Egizio. ☎ 011 54 74 40.
The gallery houses the collections of the House of Savoy and is divided into various thematic and chronological sections.
On the second floor the section on **14C to 16C Piedmontese painting★** has works by Martino Spanzotti (1455-1528), the principal exponent of the Late Gothic Piedmontese school, his pupil Defendente Ferrari (1510-31), Macrino d'Alba (1495-1528) and Gaudenzio Ferrari (1475-1546), an artist closely linked to the Milanese school. One of his masterpieces is the *Crucifixion★*. The section on **14C to 16C Italian painting** includes works by Fra Angelico, Antonio and Piero Pollaiolo (Tuscan school), Bergognone (Lombard school), Bartolomeo Vivarini and Giovanni Bellini (Venetian school). The **Prince Eugene Collection** has both Italian and European painting including a collection of **Dutch and Flemish painting★★**. One of the richest in Italy, it includes the *Stigmata of St Francis* by Van Eyck (1390-1441), *Scenes from the Passion of Christ* by Hans Memling (c 1435-94), the *Old Man Sleeping* by Rembrandt (1606-69) and enchanting **landscapes** by Jan Brueghel (1568-1625).
On the third floor the **Dynastic Collections**, divided into three sections presented in chronological order, include fine examples of Italian and European painting from the 15C to 18C. Some of the most notable works include the *Visitation★* by the Flemish artist Van der Weyden (1400-64), *The Meal at the House of Simon★*, an early work of Veronese (1528-1588), the *Trinity* by Tintoretto (1519-94), the great canvases by the **Bassano** family (16C) whose dynamic use of light heralds the work of Caravaggio, the *Assumption★★* by Orazio Gentileschi (1563-1639), one of the artist's masterpieces characterised by a violent realism, the *Sons of Charles I of England★*, a fine portrait by Van Dyck (1599-1641), *The Four Elements* by the Bolognese painter F. Albani (1578-1660) whose classicism derives from the work of the Carracci and Guido Reni, the portrait of *Philip IV of Spain* by Velasquez (1599-1660), *The Triumph of Aurelius* by Tiepolo (1696-1770) and the beautiful **views★** by the Venetian painter Bellotto (1720-80), a nephew of Canaletto. The fine **Gualino Collection** includes works from the fine and decorative arts of various periods and nationalities, among which some very fine Chinese sculpture.

Palazzo Carignano★★
Victor Emmanuel II (1820-78), responsible for the Unification of Italy and the country's first king (1861), was born in this beautiful Baroque palace by **Guarini**. It houses the **Museo del Risorgimento Italiano★★**, a rich collection of documentation pertaining to the history of Italy from the end of the 18C to the Second World War with particular reference to the Risorgimento. The museum includes a visit to the **Sala del Parlamento Subalpino★**, where from 1848-1860 speakers included Cavour, Garibaldi, Verdi and Manzoni. It is also possible to visit the **Aula del Parlamento Italiano**, built to accommodate the growing number of members of parliament but never actually used as, during its construction, Florence was made the capital of Italy. *Open daily except Mon, 9am-7pm.* €4.13. ☎ 011 56 21 147; *www.regione.piemonte.it/cultura/risorgimento/index.htm*

Piazza Castello
The political and religious heart of the city, this square was designed by the architect Ascanio Vitozzi (1539-1615). The main city streets lead off this square and it is bordered by the Royal Palace and the arcades of the **Teatro Regio**, inaugurated in 1740. Severely damaged by bombardments in the Second World War, it was rebuilt and opened to the public in 1973. In the theatre's atrium there is a gateway designed by the artist Umberto Matroianni entitled *Musical Odyssey*. In the centre of the square stands the imposing castle from which it derives its name. The castle was later named Palazzo Madama.

Palazzo Madama★
(&) *Open Tue-Sun 10am-8pm (11pm Sat). Closed 1 Jan, Easter, 1 May, 25 Dec. No charge.* ☎ 011 44 29 911.

The palace derives its name from the two "Madame Reali" who stayed here in the 17C-18C: Maria Cristina of France, widow of Victor Amadeus I and Giovanna of Savoia-Nemours, widow of Charles Emmanuel II. The castle was erected in the 14C and 15C on the remains of the Roman gateway, Porta Pretoria, which formed part of the Augustan ramparts, while the west façade was designed in the 18C by Juvarra. Part of a more ambitious project which was brought to a halt by the death of Giovanna of Nemours, the classically elegant façade and the grand staircase are based on French and Roman models although tempered by the restraint of Turin Baroque.

There is a museum of ancient art, the **Museo d'Arte Antica★**, on the ground floor. The exhibits include Gothic carvings, 15C choir stalls, canvases of the 15C-16C Piedmontese school (Gian Martino Spanzotti, Macrino d'Alba, Defendente and Gaudenzio Ferrari), a *Portrait of a Man* (1475) by Antonello da Messina and a 14C *Madonna* by Barnaba da Modena. The decorative arts section comprises Greek, Roman and barbarian gold work, enamels, ivories, wooden caskets, ceramic ware, a large collection of engraved glass, and 15C furniture.

Palazzo Reale★

The princes of the House of Savoy lived in this plain building until 1865. The façade was designed by Amedeo di Castellamonte in the 17C. The sumptuous **apartments (*appartamenti*)** are accessed by the fine staircase, **Scala delle Forbici** designed by Filippo Juvarra and are decorated in the Baroque, Rococo and neo-Classical styles. ⚓ *Open daily, summer 8.30am-7.30pm, rest of year 9am-7pm. Closed 1 Jan, 1 May, 25 Dec. €4.13.* ☎ *011 43 61 455.*

The Royal Armoury, **Armeria Reale★**, contains a splendid collection of arms and armour and interesting military memorabilia dating from the 13C to 20C. *Open daily, 8.30am-7.30pm (ticket office closes 7pm). Closed 1 Jan, 1 May, 25 Dec. €2.* ☎ *011 51 84 358.*

To the left of the palace stands the **church of San Lorenzo** to which the architect Guarini added a dome and rather daring crenellations.

Duomo★

Open daily, 7am-noon and 3-7pm☎ 011 43 61 540.

This Renaissance cathedral, dedicated to St John, Turin's patron saint, was built at the end of the 15C for Cardinal Della Rovere. The façade has three finely carved doorways; the crown of the brick campanile was designed by Juvarra.

Inside, behind the high altar surmounted by a dome, a Baroque masterpiece by Guarini, is the **Cappella della Santa Sindone** (Chapel of the Holy Shroud) which enshrined the precious but much-contested **Holy Shroud★★★** in which Christ is said to have been wrapped after the Descent from the Cross. In 1997 a raging fire caused grave damage to Guarini's dome (temporarily replaced by a *trompe l'oeil*) but fortunately the urn containing the precious relic was saved.

There are some interesting Roman remains near the cathedral: remains of a 2C AD theatre and the **Porta Palatina** (1C AD), a fine example of a Roman city gateway. Via IV Marzo crosses the oldest part of the city and leads to the harmonious, elegant **Piazza del Palazzo di Città**, dominated by the Town Hall which was erected in the 17C by Francesco Lanfranchi.

Nearby *(turn right onto Via Milano)* stands **San Domenico** (14C), the only Gothic church in the city which inside has works by Ferrari and Spanzotti and a beautiful cycle of 14C frescoes. *Open daily, 7am-noon and 4-6.30pm.* ☎ *011 52 29 711.*

FROM PIAZZA CASTELLO TO THE PO

Via Po★

Created between the 17C and 18C to connect the historic centre to the River Po and bordered by harmoniously arranged palaces and arcades, this is one of the most beautiful streets in Turin.

Nearby stands the **Pinacoteca Albertina**, a picture gallery which has collection of Piedmontese, Lombard and Venetian painting, a section on Flemish and Dutch painting as well as a fine group of **cartoons★** by Gaudenzio Ferrari and his school. *Open daily except Mon, 9am-1pm and 3-7pm. Closed hols.* €4.13. ☎ 011 81 77 862. *www.accademialbertina.torino*

Mole Antonelliana★

This unusual structure, towering 167m 548ft up into the air, is the symbol of Turin. Its daring design was the work of the architect Alessandro Antonelli (1798-1888). Originally destined to be a temple for the Jewish community (1863), it was ceded to the city in 1877. The summit affords a vast **panorama★★** of Turin. Inside is the **Museum of Cinema**. (⚓) *Open Tue-Fri 9am-8pm, Sat 9am-11pm. Closed Mon.* €5.16; €6.71 *including museum and panoramic elevator.* ☎ 011 81 25 658, *www.museonazionaledelcinema.org*

Piazza Vittorio Veneto

This large 19C square affords a wonderful **view★★** of the hills and dips down towards the river which can be reached by going down to the **Murazzi** (Lungopo Diaz), ramparts erected in the 19C. Beyond the Victor Emmanuel I bridge, erected by Napoleon, stands the imposing neo-Classical church of the **Gran Madre**.

To the right of the church, **Monte dei Cappuccini** (alt. 284m/932ft) affords an exceptional **panorama★★★** of the city.

Parco del Valentino

This wooded park extends along the Po for about 1.5km/1mi and affords a pleasant walk along the river. To the north stands the **Castello del Valentino**, erected in the first half of the 17C for Duchess Marie Christine of France. There is also the Palazzo delle Esposizioni (Exhibition Hall), the Teatro Nuovo and the **Borgo Medievale★**, an interesting reconstruction of a medieval town and Fénis Castle. & – *all sights accessible except the Fortress. Borgo, open daily except Mon, summer 9am-8pm, rest of year 9am-7pm, fortress 9am-7pm. Closed 1 Jan, Easter, 1 May 25 Dec. No charge for Borgo; €2.58 for fortress. No charge 1st Fri of the month. ☎ 011 44 31 701; www.medieval-revival.org*

ADDITIONAL SIGHTS

Galleria Civica di Arte Moderna e Contemporanea★★

Via Magenta 31. & Open daily except Mon, 9am-7pm. €5.16. No charge 1st Fri in month. ☎ 011 44 29 518; www.gamtorino.it

This ample collection of fine art gives a good overview of Italian art and its main exponents, focusing on the 19C and 20C Piedmontese schools. The second floor, devoted to 19C art, has the largest body of work by the Reggio artist **Antonio Fontanesi** (1818-82), whose landscapes are notable for their solemn compositions, veiled light and dense, rich colours. The first floor, devoted to the 20C, shows the development of Italian and European art through the work of the more significant artists and movements: Balla, Casorati, Martini, the Milanese Novecento group, the Ferrara metaphysical paintings (Carlo Carrà, Giorgio de Chirico), the Roman school (Scipione, Mafai), Turin's "Gruppo dei Sei" (Jessie Boswell, Gigi Chessa, Nicola Galante, Carlo Levi, Francesco Menzio and Enrico Paolucci), examples of Informal Art and "Arte Povera" from the 1960s. The ground floor has collections of international art of the last 30 years.

Museo dell'Automobile Carlo Biscaretti di Ruffia★★

South of the town. Take Corso Massimo d'Azeglio and then follow the plan of the built-up area in the Michelin Atlas Italy. The address is Corso Unità d'Italia 40. & Open daily except Mon, 10am-6.30pm. Closed 1 Jan, 25 Dec. €5. ☎ 011 67 76 66; www.museoauto.org

A vast modern building houses an extensive collection of cars, chassis and engines as well as graphic documents outlining the history of the automobile from its beginnings to the last 20 years.

Another **room devoted to the history of tyre manufacture** traces the tremendous development of materials, structure, technology and research, famous car races, types of vehicle (cycles to planes etc). The museum also includes a library and archives *(open by appointment only).*

A much-deserved homage to Turin's motor industry: the Museo dell'Automobile Carlo Biscaretti di Ruffia

Museo dell'Automobile Carlo Biscaretti di Ruffia

Excursion

Plan of the built-up area in the Michelin Atlas Italy.

Palazzina di Caccia di Stupinigi★

11km/7mi southwest. (&) Open daily, summer 10am-6pm (ticket office closes 5.20pm), rest of year 10am-5pm (ticket office closes 4.20pm). Closed 1 Jan, 1 May, 25 Dec. €6.19. ☎ 011 35 81 220.

This huge building was a hunting lodge built by Juvarra for Victor Amadeus II of Savoy. Napoleon stayed here before assuming the crown of Italy. The palace now houses a **Museo d'Arte e del Mobilio** (Fine Arts and Furniture Museum). The apartments are richly decorated in the Rococo style of the 18C. A magnificent park surrounds the *palazzina.*

Tours

HILLS AROUND TURIN★

32km/19mi. Leave Turin heading east.

Basilica di Superga★

Open daily, Apr to Oct 9am-noon and 3-6pm (5pm rest of year). ☎ *011 89 80 083.* This masterpiece was built by Juvarra from 1717 to 1731 on a hill (670m/2 198ft high). The basilica is circular in plan and roofed with a dome and its most remarkable feature is its monumental façade with its imposing columns and pilasters. The chapel dedicated to the Virgin, in the chancel, is a pilgrimage centre. The basilica is the Pantheon of the Kings of Sardinia.

Tombe dei Reali: The royal tombs in the crypt include that of Victor Amadeus II, who built the basilica to fulfil a vow made when his capital was being besieged by a French and Spanish army in 1706. Alongside are the tombs of Charles-Albert and other princes of the House of Savoy. From the esplanade there is a fine **view★★★** of Turin, the Po Plain and the Alps.

Colle della Maddalena★

From Superga take the scenic route via Pino Torinese which affords good **views★★** of Turin. From Pino Torinese continue to the hilltop, **Colle della Maddalena,** and the **Parco della Rimembranza,** a very popular large public park which commemorates those who died in the First World War. On the way down there are more lovely **views★** of Turin. The **Parco Europa** at Cavoretto overlooks the southern part of the town.

VAL DI SUSA★

150km/93mi, allow one day. From Turin take the west exit in the direction of Corso Francia

Castello di Rivoli

Victor Amadeus II commissioned Juvarra to build a grandiose residence (18C) in the Baroque style. Only the left wing (some rooms are decorated) and the lower part of the central range were built. The château now houses a museum of contemporary art, **Museo d'Arte Contemporanea★** (1960 to the present day as well as temporary exhibitions). ♿ *Open Tue-Fri 10am-5pm, Sat-Sun 10am-7pm (1st and 3rd Sat 10am-10pm). Closed 1 Jan, 1 May, 25 Dec.* €6.20. ☎ *011 95 65 222; www.castellodirivoli.torino.it* Take S 25. From S 25 follow the turn-off 6km/4mi after Rivoli.

> ### 4 MAY 1949
> Heavy rain and fog over Turin. An aeroplane flies over Superga with its illustrious passengers: 18 players from Grande Torino, the legendary football team who won five championships in a row and provided Italy's national team with ten players. They were on their way back from Lisbon where they had played a friendly and were accompanied by technicians, executives and journalists. With zero visibility, at 5.05pm the plane loses radio contact and plunges down, its left wing hitting the basilica, finally crashing to the ground. The city of Turin is paralysed with grief, the Grande Torino team dies and its memory is imbued with a sense of nostalgia and the desire to make the sport live forever.

Abbazia di Sant'Antonio di Ranverso★

Open daily except Mon, summer 9am-12.30pm and 2.30-6pm, rest of year 9am-12.30pm and 2-5pm. €2.58. ☎ *011 93 67 450.*

This abbey was a resting place for pilgrims as well as a centre for the curing of "St Anthony's Fire" (egotism). The church, founded in the 12C, has a fine façade and three 15C doorways adorned with gothic pediments and pinnacles. The interior has beautiful **frescoes★** by **Giacomo Jaquerio** (1401-53) who combined the realism of Burgundian art with the refinement of the International Gothic Style. The frescoes in the sacristy are better preserved; the scene portraying two peasants offering two pigs refers to the tradition of curing St Anthony's fire with pork fat. At the high altar there is a fine **polyptych** by Defendente Ferrari (1510-31).

Avigliana

Until the 15C this town was one of the Savoia family's favourite residences. The heart of the historic centre is the pretty square, **Piazza Conte Rosso**, dominated by the ruins of a **Castle** (15C). Nearby stands the Romanesque-Gothic parish church of **San Giovanni**. Southeast of the ruins stands the church of **San Pietro★** (10C-11C) which has a fine cycle of frescoes (mainly 14C-15C). *Open daily, Apr to Oct 9am-noon and 3-6pm (by appointment only).* ☎ *011 93 28 300.*

A scenic road skirts the two **lakes of Avigliana**, originally glaciers, eventually leading up to the abbey of San Michele. *(13.5km/8mi).*

Sacra di San Michele★★★

Open mid-Mar to mid-Oct, Tue-Sat 9.30am-12.30pm and 3-6pm, Sun and hols 9.30am-noon and 2.40-6pm, rest of year 9.30am-12.30pm and 3-5pm, Sun and hols 9.30am-noon and 2.40-5pm. Guided tours Sun pm only. Closed Mon (except hols). €2.50; €3.50 Sun. ☎ *011 93 91 30; www.sacradisanmichele.com*

Sacra di San Michele: a magnificent but haunting sight.

This Benedictine abbey, perched on a rocky site (alt 962m/3 156ft), was a powerful establishment in the 13C with over 100 monks and 140 sister houses. It was built at the end of the 10C by Hughes de Montboissier from Auvergne and its layout bears a strong resemblance to the abbey at Mont Saint Michel in France. After passing through the iron doors of the entrance gatehouse, climb the great staircase leading to the **Zodiac Door**; its pilasters and capitals were decorated by the famous Master Nicolò (1135). The Romanesque-Gothic **church** built on top of the rocky eminence has 16C frescoes. The early-16C triptych on the high altar is by Defendente Ferrari. The carved capitals are outstanding.

From the esplanade there is a lovely **view★★★** of the Alps, the Dora Valley, the Po and the Turin plains.

Head back along S 25 or A 32 through the Fréjus tunnel.

Susa★

Situated at the foot of an impressive mountain range dominated by the Rocciamelone (3 538m/11 608ft) stands Susa, at a junction of two roads which lead to France. This has resulted in its being referred to as "Italy's gateway". Because of its strategic position Susa, which was founded by the Celts and flourished in Roman times, was destroyed on several occasions (by Constantine in 312 and by Barbarossa in 1174).

The symbol of the city is the **Savoy Door★** which takes its name from the French region and dates from the late 3C to early 4C AD when the ramparts were built. Next to the door stands the **Cathedral**, founded in the years 1027-29 with Gothic additions made in the 14C. To the south side of the church is a small square, Piazza San Giusto which is dominated by the magnificent **Romanesque campanile★★**.

In a delightful corner stands the elegant **Arco di Augusto★**, the oldest monument in the city (8 BC). The arch is decorated with low reliefs which depict an alliance between Cozio, Lord of Susa, and Augustus. In front of the arch there are remains of the **Roman Aqueduct** (4C AD); beyond stand the Celtic **rocks** (6C-5C BC), used by Druid priests for sacrificial rites.

To the south, in a typically decentralised position stands the **amphitheatre**, erected in the 1C-2C AD.

Abbazia della Novalesa – *8km/5mi northeast. Open daily, Jul and Aug 10.30am-4.30pm, rest of year only Sat-Sun 9-11.30am. Due to the fragility of the frescoes, the Cappella di S. Eldrado is not open to visitors during snow or rain. Donation recommended.* ☎ *0122 65 32 10.*

This powerful Benedictine abbey was founded in the 8C and destroyed by Saracens in the 10C. It was later rebuilt but began to decline in the 13C. The real jewel of this abbey are the extraordinary **frescoes★★** in the **Cappella Sant'Eldrado** (12C) which depict scenes from the lives of Saints Eldrado and Nicola of Bari.

MONFERRATO★

150km/93mi, allow one day. From Turin head east on S 10.

The proposed itinerary takes the visitor through this attractive region of limestone hills, bordered to the north by the Po, to the east by the plains of Alessandria and to the southwest by the Langhe hills. The valley of Villafranca d'Asti and the lower part of the River Tanaro divide the area into Lower and Upper Monferrato (north and south respectively in spite of their names). Defended by numerous strongholds and covered in castles, towers and fortified towns, Monferrato is a generous region which has given Piedmont some of its finest wines: Barbera, Dolcetto and Grignolino among red wines, Cortese and Gavi among white wines and the dessert wines Asti Spumante, Moscato and Brachetto.

Chieri

This town is known for its cuisine. It has some fine Piedmontese Gothic monuments such as the 15C cathedral flanked by the Romanesque-Gothic baptistery and the 13C-15C church of San Domenico with its fine campanile.

Follow directions for Castelnuovo Don Bosco (4km/2.5mi south at **Colle Don Bosco** is the house where St John Bosco was born, as well as the sanctuary) and Albugnano.

Abbazia di Vezzolano★

17km/10mi northeast of Chieri. Open daily except Mon, summer 9.30am-12.30pm and 2-6pm, rest of year 9.30am-12.30pm and 2-5pm. Closed 1 Jan, 1 May, 26 Dec. No charge. ☎ *011 99 20 607.*

Immersed in a silent green valley, this abbey is one of the finest examples of Piedmontese Romanesque-Gothic architecture. Its beautiful terracotta and sandstone façade has a doorway adorned with low reliefs. Beyond stands the real jewel of Vezzolano, the splendid *jubé*★★ (rood screen) dated 1189, whose beautiful polychrome low reliefs depict episodes from the life of the Virgin. These structures served to separate the faithful from those areas reserved for the monks. The interior of the church, with two aisles, has pointed arches and cross vaulting supported by pilasters. At the end of the south aisle there is access to the evocative and elegant **cloisters★** (which have incorporated one of the church's aisles) with 13C-14C fresco remains.

Rejoin S 458.

Asti

38km/24mi southeast on S 458. The home town of the tragic poet, Vittorio Alfieri (1749-1803), is the scene of an annual horse race *(palio)* which is preceded by a procession with over 1 000 participants in 14C and 15C costume *(see Events and Festivals, p 45)*. The 12C **baptistery of San Pietro★**, the 15C church of San Pietro and the Gothic cloisters form an attractive group. In the heart of the old town the 14C Gothic **Cattedrale** is decorated with Baroque paintings.

Take E 74 dual-carriageway and then S 456 for Acqui Terme.

Strada dei castelli dell'Alto Monferrato★

From Acqui Terme to Gavi *(24km/15mi to Ovada on S 456 and another 24km/15mi to Gavi on minor roads)* this scenic route, also known as the wine route, follows the crest of the hillsides covered with vineyards. **Acqui Terme‡‡**, famous in Roman times for its healing mud and spa water, is a pleasant town with remains of Roman and medieval architecture. Along the road there is a series of hilltop villages, each one guarded by a castle. Among these are Visone, Morsasco, Cremolino, Molare, Tagliolo, Lerma, Casaleggio, Mornese and, making a short detour to the northeast, Montaldeo, Castelletto d'Orba and Silvano d'Orba.

Isole **Tremiti**★

TREMITI ISLANDS

This tiny archipelago, the only one on the Adriatic coast, comprises two main islands, San Nicola and San Domino as well as two uninhabited isles, Capraia and Pianosa; the latter is much further out in the Adriatic. The boat trip out from Manfredonia offers unforgettable views★★★ of the Gargano coastline with its dazzling white limestone cliffs. As the boat rounds the promontory there are also good views★★★ of the coastal towns of Vieste, Peschici and Rodi Garganico set on their precipitous sites. On the points of the rocky headlands there are typical platforms *(trabocco)* equipped with square fishing nets.

Directory

Location

Population 373 – Michelin map 431 A 28 – Puglia. The Tremiti islands lie offshore from the Gargano Promontory and belong to the same geological formation. *Surrounding area: see Promontorio del GARGANO, PUGLIA.*

Special Features

San Nicola★
High on the clifftop stands the **Abbazia di Santa Maria al Mare**, an abbey originally founded by the Benedictines in the 9C. A fortified ramp leads up to the abbey. Of particular interest are the remains of an 11C mosaic pavement, a 15C Gothic polyptych and a 13C Byzantine crucifix. From the cloisters there are good glimpses of the second island, San Domino. *Open Jun to Sep, daily, 9.30am-7.30pm, rest of year 8.30am-2pm.* ☎ *0882 46 30 63.*

San Domino★
Take a boat trip round this island and discover the wild beauty of its very indented and rugged coasts covered in pine forests. *Excursions: To tour the island of San Nicola or the entire archipelago, contact Società Cooperativa AMAR BLU,* ☎ *0360 37 35 27.*

Trento★

TRENT

Austrian and Italian influences meet here. This agricultural and industrial centre stands at an important crossroads with the converging of routes from the Brenner Pass, Brescia and Venice.

Location

Population 104 906 – Michelin map 429 D 15 – Town plan in the Michelin Atlas Italy –Trentino-Alto Adige. Trent, capital of Trentino, stands on the Adige not far from the Brenta Massif and is encircled by rocky peaks and valleys. The town lies off A 22, the Brenner transalpine pass.
🛈 *Via Manci 2,* ☎ *0461 98 38 80.*
Surrounding area: see BOLZANO, DOLOMITI, Regione dei LAGHI.

HISTORICAL NOTES
This Roman colony under the Empire became an episcopal see in the 4C, was occupied successively by the Ostrogoths under Theodoric, and by the Lombards in the 6C before being united to the Holy Roman Empire in the late 10C. From 1004 to 1801 the town was governed by a succession of prince-bishops.
The Council of Trent (1545-63), called by Pope Paul III to study methods of combating Protestantism, met in the town. These important deliberations marked the beginning of the Counter-Reformation and the findings were to change the character of the Church. The main decisions which aimed at the re-establishment of ecclesiastical credibility and authority, concerned compulsory residence for bishops and the abolition of the sale of indulgences.
After a period of Napoleonic rule in the 19C, Trent was ceded to the Austrians in 1814. In 1918, the town was liberated, after a long hard struggle, by Italian troops.

Worth a Visit

Piazza del Duomo★
This cobbled square is the town centre. All around stand the cathedral, the Palazzo Pretorio (13C, restored), the belfry and the Rella houses painted with 16C frescoes.

Duomo★
The majestic 12C-13C cathedral is in the Lombard-Romanesque style. The façade of the north transept is pierced with a window representing the Wheel of Fortune which determines man's destiny: Christ stands at the summit, the Symbols of the Evangelists rise towards him.
Inside, note the unusual sweep of the stairway leading to the towers. To the right, in the 17C Chapel of the Crucifix (Cappella del Crocifisso), is a large wooden Christ

Directory

WHERE TO EAT

• **Budget**

Antica Trattoria Due Mori – *Via San Marco 11 – ☎ 0461 98 42 51 – Closed Mon – ⌂ – €21/31*. Rustic setting – with 15C wooden barrel-vaulted ceilings – for a classical restaurant. The menu focuses largely, but not exclusively, on traditional dishes and draws inspiration from produce that is in season.

• **Moderate**

Osteria a Le Due Spade – *Via Don Rizzi – angolo Via Verdi 11 – ☎ 0461 23 43 43 – Closed Sun and Mon lunchtime – Book – €38/51*. A culinary experience not to be missed, if you can get a table that is. With origins dating back to the 16C, this small, charming establishment -housed in what was an old cellar – offers regional dishes with an innovative flair. Attentive service.

WHERE TO STAY

• **Moderate**

Hotel Aquila d'Oro – *Via Belenzani 76 – ☎ 0461 98 62 82 – Fax 0461 98 62 82 – Closed 23 Dec-7 Jan – ⌂ – 19 rm €51.65/71.47 ⌂*. This little hotel is situated in the heart of the historic centre, a stone's throw from the Duomo. If the public areas are rather cramped the rooms are spacious with modern furnishings. Pleasant bar (with the same name) next door open to the public.

Hotel America – *Via Torre Verde 50 – ☎ 0461 98 30 10 – Fax 0461 23 06 03 – ⌂ – 66 rm €70/103 ⌂ – Restaurant €20.50/33*. Wood and pale colours throughout – from the public lounges to the rooms – creating a very relaxing atmosphere. Lovely views over the town and the Castello del Buonconsiglio and out over the surrounding mountains. A very pleasant spot.

in front of which the decrees of the Council of Trent were proclaimed. In the south transept is the tomb of the Venetian mercenary leader Sanseverino, who was killed in 1486.

The remains of a 5C early-Christian basilica, **basilica paleocristiana★,** lie beneath the chancel.

Open Mon-Sat, 10am-noon and 2.30-6pm. Closed Sun and hols. Basilica: €1.50. ☎ 0461 23 44 19; www.asteria.it/museo.htm

Museo Diocesano★

& *Open mid-Jul to mid-Oct, Mon-Sat 9.30am-12.30pm and 2.30-6pm, Sun and hols 10am-6pm (rest of year closed Sun and hols). Closed 1 Jan, 15 Aug, 8 Dec, 25 Dec. €3. ☎ 0461 23 44 19; www.asteria.it/museo.htm*

The Diocesan Museum installed in the Palazzo Pretorio displays the most important items from the cathedral's treasury: paintings, carved **wooden panels★, altarpiece★** and eight early-16C **tapestries★** which were woven in Brussels by Pieter Van Aelst.

Via Belenzani

This street is lined with palaces in the Venetian style. Opposite the 16C town hall (Palazzo Comunale) stand houses with walls painted with frescoes.

Via Manci

The Venetian (loggias and frescoes) and mountain (overhanging roofs) styles are intermingled all along the street. Nº 63, the Palazzo Galazzo with its embossed stonework and huge pilasters is 17C.

Castello del Buon Consiglio★★

& *Open daily except Mon, Apr to Sep 9am-noon and 2-5.30pm (summer 10am-6pm), rest of year 9am-noon and 2-5pm. Closed Mon (except hols), 1 Jan, 2 Nov, 25 Dec. €5. ☎ 0461 23 37 70.*

From the 13C to the dawn of the 14C this castle was the residence of Trent's prince-bishops. Castelvecchio (Old Castle), as its name implies, is the oldest part of the castle and incorporates the **Torre Aquila** *(there are excellent guided tours of the tower: contact the guard at the Loggia del Romanino)*, which an artist of Bohemian origin decorated with frescoes depicting the **months★★** in a fine expression of the International Gothic Style. Everyone will have a favourite: the month of January portrays the inhabitants of the castle throwing snowballs; the month of May depicts the season of love; and the month of December shows the gathering of fire-burning wood for the winter months.

The prince-bishop who most influenced life in Trent in the 16C was Bernardo Cles who enlarged the castle adding the Magno Palazzo. Cles was a true Renaissance prince, calling renowned artists to decorate his residence. The Ferrarese painters Dosso and Battista Dossi adorned the most important rooms, such as the Sala Grande. The frescoes on the vaulting and lunettes of the **loggia** depict biblical and mythological scenes and are by the Brescian artist Gerolamo Romanino.

The castle also houses collections of paintings, coins and archaeological artefacts as well as a Risorgimento Museum.

Palazzo Tabarelli★

This remarkable building is in the Venetian-Renaissance style with pilasters, pink marble columns and medallions.

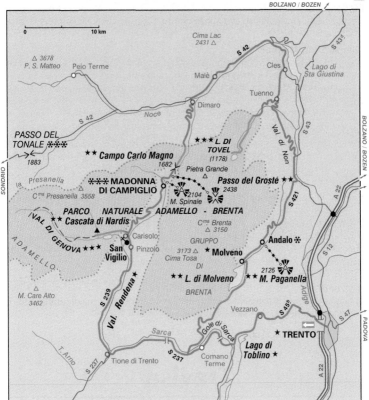

Chiesa di Santa Maria Maggiore

Numerous meetings of the Council of Trent were held in this Renaissance church, dedicated to St Mary Major, with its Romanesque campanile. The elegant marble organ loft (1534) in the chancel is by Vincenzo and Girolamo Grandi. At the second altar on the right, in the nave, is a 16C altarpiece of the *Madonna and saints* by Moroni.

Chiesa di Sant'Apollinare

This small Romanesque church on the west bank of the Adige has a curious pointed roof covering two Gothic domed vaults. It is dedicated to St Apollinaris.

Tour

GRUPPO DEL BRENTA★★★

Round trip starting from Trent: 233km/145mi – allow 2 days.

The wild limestone Brenta Massif prolongs the Dolomites beyond the Adige Valley. Its characteristic features are deep valleys, solitary lakes and erosion-worn rocks.

The map below locates the towns and sites described in the guide and also indicates other beauty spots in small black type. Take S 45b in the direction of Vezzano.

Lago di Toblino★

This charming lake fringed with tall rushes, stands against a background of rocky walls. An attractive little castle, once the summer residence of the bishops of Trent, stands on a small peninsula.

Val Rendena★

This wide valley clad with firs and larches has charming villages with fresco-covered churches, protected by overhanging roofs.

The church of **San Vigilio** near Pinzolo has a remarkable *Dance of Death* (1539) by Simone Baschenis.

Val di Genova★★★

The valley crosses the granite Adamello Massif and is known for its wild grandeur. The road follows a fast-flowing river as it tumbles and foams along the rock-strewn bed to reach a waterfall, **Cascata di Nardis★★,** where the waters drop over 100m/330ft.

Madonna di Campiglio★★★
This pleasant resort and winter sports centre has many hotels and numerous possibilities for excursions.

Campo Carlo Magno★★
A supposed visit by Charlemagne gave this place its name. It has become a winter sports centre. From the **Passo del Grosté** – *cable car and then on foot* – there is a fine **panorama★★** of the Brenta Massif. *Cable car: For information on cableway schedule* ☎ *0465 44 77 44.*
Continue to Dimaro and Malè and at Cles turn right towards Tuenno.

Lago di Tovel★★★
Pass through wild gorges to reach this lovely lake fringed by wooded slopes. In hot weather the waters of the lake take on a reddish tinge due to the presence of microscopic algae.

Andalo❋
This small holiday resort is set in majestic scenery amid a great pine forest and overlooked by the crests of the Brenta Massif. From the summit of **Monte Paganella** *(cable car)* at 2 125m/6 972ft there is a splendid **panorama★★** of the whole region, and in clear weather as far as Lake Garda. *Access for cableway or chairlift from end Jun to mid-Sep and from Dec to Apr. Access also possible from Fai della Paganella by chairlift, same schedules. For information* ☎ *0461 58 55 88; www.paganella.it*

Molveno★
This choice resort is situated amid gently sloping meadows at the north end of a **lake★★** which lies on the floor of a cirque.

Treviso★

Treviso, situated in the rich Venetian plain, is an important agricultural and industrial centre but has retained its old walled town. Ever since the 14C its fortunes have been linked with those of Venice.

Location
Population 81 771 – Michelin map 429 E-F 18 – Town plan in the Michelin Atlas Italy – Veneto. Treviso is close to Venice, linked by the S 13. 🛈 *Piazza Monte di Pietà 8,* ☎ *0422 54 76 32.*
Surrounding area: see LAGUNA VENETA, PADOVA, VENEZIA.

Worth a Visit

Piazza dei Signori★
This forms the historic centre of Treviso and is bordered by impressive monuments: the Palazzo del Podestà with its tall municipal belltower, the **Palazzo dei Trecento★** (1207) and the Renaissance Palazzo Pretorio. Lower down in Piazza del Monte di Pietà is the former municipal pawn shop, the **Monte di Pietà**, with the Chapel of the Rectors (Cappella dei Reggitori).
In Piazza San Vito there are two adjoining churches **San Vito** and **Santa Lucia**, the latter adorned with remarkable **frescoes★** by Tommaso da Modena, one of the finest 14C artists after Giotto.

Chiesa di San Nicolò★
This large Romanesque-Gothic church, dedicated to St Nicholas, contains interesting frescoes, especially those on the columns which are by Tommaso da Modena. In the Onigo Chapel there are portraits of people from Treviso by Lorenzo Lotto (16C). The *Virgin in Majesty* at the far end of the chancel is by Savoldo (16C). In the adjoining **monastery**, the chapter house has portraits of famous Dominicans by Tommaso da Modena.

Museo Civico Bailo★
Borgo Cavour 22. (♿) *Open Tue-Sat 9am-12.30pm and 2.30-5pm, Sun and hols 9am-noon. Closed Mon and hols. €1.55.* ☎ *0422 65 84 42.*
In the municipal museum are works by Tommaso da Modena, Girolamo da Treviso (15C) and others of the Venetian school such as Cima da Conegliano, Giovanni Bellini, Titian, Paris Bordone, Jacopo Bassano and Lorenzo Lotto.

Duomo

The 15C and 16C cathedral has seven domes, a neo-Classical façade and a Romanesque crypt. Left of the cathedral stands an 11C-12C baptistery. In the Chapel of the Annunciation (Cappella dell'Annunziata), to the right of the chancel, there are frescoes in the Mannerist style by Pordenone and on the altarpiece an *Annunciation* by Titian.

Chiesa di San Francesco

Viale Sant'Antonio da Padova. This church in the transitional Romanesque-Gothic style has a fine wooden ceiling, the tombstone of Petrarch's daughter and the tomb of one of Dante's sons, as well as frescoes by Tommaso da Modena in the first chapel to the left of the chancel. The church is dedicated to St Francis.

Excursions

Maser

29km/18mi northwest by S 348. This small agricultural town is known for its famous **villa★★★** built in 1560 by Palladio for the Barbaro brothers: Daniele, Patriarch of Aquileia, and Marcantonio, ambassador of the Venetian Republic. The interior was decorated from 1566 to 1568 with a splendid cycle of **frescoes★★★** by Veronese. It is one of his best decorative schemes and he used all his amazing knowledge of perspective, *trompe l'oeil*, foreshortening and his sense of movement and colour. *Open Mar to Oct, daily, 3-6pm, rest of year only Sat-Sun and hols 2.30-5pm. Closed Sun am, Easter, 24 Dec to 6 Jan. For information on winter hours and prices ☎ 0423 92 30 04.*

Not far from the villa is a **Tempietto**, a graceful circular chapel with a dome which was also the work of Palladio.

Conegliano

28km/17mi north. Conegliano is surrounded by pleasant hills clad with orchards and vineyards, which produce an excellent white wine. This was the birthplace of **Cima da Conegliano** (1459-1518), an admirer of Giovanni Bellini, and a superb colourist who introduced idealised landscapes bathed in a crystal-clear light. The **Duomo** has a fine **Sacra Conversazione★** by this artist. *By appointment only, Sat 10am-noon, Sun and hols 3-6pm. €1.55. ☎ 0438 22 606; www.conegliano2000.it*

The **castello** houses two small **museums** and affords a lovely **panorama★** of the town and its setting. *Museo Civico del Castello: Open daily except Mon, Apr to Sep 10am-12.30pm and 3.30-7pm, rest of year 10am-12.30pm and 3-6.30pm. Closed Nov. €1.55. ☎ 0438 22 871; www.conegliano2000.it*

Next to the cathedral the walls of the **Scuola dei Battuti** are decorated with 15C and 16C **frescoes★** in both the Venetian and Lombard styles.

Vittorio Veneto

41km/26mi north. The name of this town recalls the great victory of the Italians over the Austrians in 1918. In Ceneda to the south of the town, the **Museo della Battaglia**, which presents documents on this victory, is installed in a 16C loggia (Loggia Cenedese) with a frescoed portico by Sansovino. *Open daily except Mon, May to Sep 10am-12.30pm and 3.30-7pm, rest of year 9.30am-12.30pm and 2-5pm. Closed 1 Jan, Easter, 1 Nov, 25 Dec. €3. ☎ 0438 57 695.*

The suburb of Serravalle in the north has retained a certain charm. The church of **San Giovanni** *(take Via Roma and then Via Mazzini)* has interesting **frescoes★** attributed to Jacobello del Fiore and Gentile da Fabriano (15C).

Portogruaro★

56km/35mi east. The town grew up from the 11C onwards along the banks of the River Lemene, a trade route that brought the town its wealth. Two fine main streets lined with attractive porticoes flank the river banks and there are numerous palaces built in a style that is typically Venetian, dating from the late Middle Ages and the Renaissance (14C-16C). On the **Corso Martiri della Libertà★★** (the busiest of the shopping streets) not far from the 19C cathedral and its leaning Romanesque campanile is the strange **Palazzo Municipale★**, built in a late-Gothic style (14C), on which the façade is crowned with Ghibelline merlons. Behind the palace is the river: note, to the right, the two 15C watermills (now restored) and a small 17C fishermen's chapel (Oratorio del Pesce) with its own landing-stage. In the Via del Seminario (the main street on the opposite bank) stands the **Museo Nazionale Concordiese** *(at n° 22)*. This has Roman exhibits (small bronze of Diane the Huntress) and palaeo-Christian artefacts from Concordia Sagittaria *(3km/2mi south)*, a Roman colony founded in 40 BC. *Open daily, 9am-8pm (11pm Sat in summer). Closed 1 Jan, 1 May, 25 Dec. €2.07. ☎ 0421 72 674.*

Trieste★

With its lively cultural life, there is something of the Central European city about Trieste. It is also the largest seaport on the Adriatic. Its extensive port (12km/7.5mi of quays stretch as far as the Slovenian border) handles more goods from abroad than from Italy. An oil pipeline links Trieste to refineries in Austria and Bavaria. The vast shipyards, specialising in the building of large vessels, are important to the local economy.

Location
Population 216 459 – Michelin map 429 F 23 – Friuli-Venezia Giulia. Trieste is a modern town which stands at the head of a bay of the same name and at the foot of the Carso Plateau. The edge of the latter forms a steep coast with magnificent white cliffs as far as Duino in the north. The A 4, which begins in Turin and then crosses the Po Valley, ends here. ∄ *Via San Nicolò 20,* ☎ *040 67 96 11.*
Surrounding area: see LAGUNA VENETA.

Background

Trieste is of very ancient origin; the Celts and Illyrians fought over the town before the Romans made it their great trading centre of Tergeste, which had the important role of defending the eastern frontiers of the Empire. In the Middle Ages it came under the sway of the Patriarch of Aquileia and then, in 1202, under Venice. In 1382 Trieste rebelled and placed itself under the protection of Austria and it played the role of mediator between the two powers until the 15C. In 1719 Charles VI declared it a free port and established the headquarters of the French trading company Compagnie d'Orient et du Levant in the city. Trieste then enjoyed a second period of prosperity and was embellished by numerous fine buildings. Many political exiles sought refuge in the city. It was only in 1919 after fierce fighting that Trieste was united with the Kingdom of Italy.

At the beginning of the 20C Trieste boasted an active literary group under the leading influence of the novelist Italo Svevo and the poet Umberto Saba. James Joyce lived in the town for some years until 1914.

Directory

Worth a Visit

Colle di San Giusto★★
Visit: 1hr. This hilltop was the site of the ancient city and today the **Piazza della Cattedrale**★ is lined with the ruins of a Roman basilica, a 15C-16C castle, a 1560 Venetian column, the altar of the Third Army (1929) and the basilica of San Giusto.
Basilica di San Giusto★ – It was founded in the 5C on the site of a Roman building, but the present buildings date in large part from the 14C. The façade is pierced with a fine Gothic rose window and decorated with a low relief and bronze busts. The massive campanile has fragments of Roman columns built into its lowest storey and bears a 14C statue of St Justus. From the top there is an attractive **view**★ of Trieste.

The **interior★** comprises a nave and four aisles. The side aisles belonged to two separate basilicas which were joined together in the 14C by the building of the nave. In the south aisle are a lovely 13C mosaic and 11C frescoes depicting the life of St Justus. A magnificent 12C **mosaic★★** in the north apse shows the Virgin in Majesty between the Archangels Michael and Gabriel, and the Apostles.

Castello di San Giusto – *Open daily, Apr to Sep 9am-7pm, rest of year 9am-5pm. Closed 1 Jan, 1 May, 25-26 Dec. €1.55.☎ 040 31 36 36; www.triestecultura.it*
The castle houses a **museum** of furniture and a fine collection of **arms★**.

Museo di Storia e d'Arte – The Museum of History and Art contains a remarkable collection of red-figured **Greek vases★** and charming **small bronzes★** dating from the Roman Archaic period. *Open daily except Mon, 9am-1pm (7pm Wed). Closed hols. €1.55. ☎ 040 31 05 00; www.triestecultura.it*

Teatro romano – The remains of an early-2C Roman theatre lie at the foot of the Colle di San Giusto.

Lower town

Piazza dell'Unità d'Italia★ – Three early-20C palaces line this square, namely the Palazzo del Governo (Government Palace), Palazzo del Comune (Town Hall) and the offices of Lloyd Trieste.

Museo del Mare★ – *Via Campo Marzio. Access in Riva Nazario Sauro. Open daily except Mon, 8.30am-1.30pm. Closed bank hols. €2.58. ☎ 040 30 49 87; www.rete-civica.trieste.it/museicivici*
The history of seafaring is traced from its beginnings to the 18C. The **fishing section★★** is of special interest.

Excursions

Santuario del Monte Grisa

10km/6mi north. Leave by Piazza della Libertà in the direction of Prosecco and then Villa Opicina and follow the signposts to "Monte Grisa".
This modern sanctuary is dedicated to the Virgin. From the terrace there is a splendid **panorama★★** of Trieste and its bay.

Villa Opicina

9km/6mi north. Leave by Via Fabio Severo. After 4.5km/3mi turn left off S 14 to take S 58. It is also possible to take the funicular which leaves from Piazza Oberdan in Trieste. Open daily, 7am-8pm (departing from Opicina), 7.11am-8.11pm (departing from Piazza Oberdan). The Opicina cableway runs every 20min. €0.77. ☎ 800 01 66 75.
Villa Opicina stands on the edge of the Carso Plateau (alt 348m/1 142ft). From the belvedere with its obelisk there is a magnificent **view★★** over Trieste and its bay.

Grotta Gigante★

13km/8mi north. Follow the above directions to Villa Opicina and then turn left in the direction of Borgo Grotta Gigante. Open Tue-Sun, Apr to Sep, 10am-6pm guided tours every 30min, Mar and Oct, 10am-4pm hourly, rest of year 10am-noon and 2-4pm hourly. Closed Mon (except hols), 1 Jan, 25 Dec. (Jul and Aug open daily). €6.71. ☎ 040 32 73 12.
An impressive stairway leads down to this chamber of amazing size where one can walk among the splendid concretions. There is a **speleological museum** *(Museo di Speleologia)* at the entrance to the cave.

Castello di Miramare★★

8km/5mi northwest by the coast road. ♿ Open daily except Mon, 9am-7pm (ticket office closes 6.30pm). €4. ☎ 040 22 47 013; www.castello-miramare.it
Standing on the point of a headland, this castle with its lovely terraced **gardens** was built in 1860 for Archduke Maximilian of Austria, who was shot in Mexico in 1867, and his wife, Princess Charlotte, who died insane. *Garden: Open daily, Apr to Sep 8am-7pm, Mar and Oct 8am-6pm, rest of year 8am-5pm. No charge. ☎ 040 22 41 43; www.castello-miramare.it*

Muggia

14km/9mi south. Leave by Riva Nazario Sauro. Facing Trieste, this small Venetian-looking town boasts a 15C Gothic cathedral with an attractive pointed campanile and an elegant façade in Istrian limestone.

Udine★

This charming town was the seat of the Patriarchs of Aquilea from 1238 to 1420 when it passed under Venetian rule. Udine nestles round a hill encircled by a picturesque lane, Vicolo Sottomonte, and with a castle on its summit. The charm of Udine lies in its Gothic and Renaissance monuments, its secluded squares and narrow streets, often lined with arcades. The town was badly damaged, like most of Friuli, by the 1976 earthquake.

Location

Population 94 932 – Michelin map 429D 21 – Town plan in the Michelin Atlas Italy – Friuli-Venezia Giulia. Udine is connected to A 4 by A 23, the road that links up with the Tarvisio pass. ▯ *Piazza I Maggio 7,* ☎ *0432 29 59 72.*
Surrounding area: see LAGUNA VENETA.

Directory

WHERE TO EAT

• Budget

Al Vecchio Stallo – *Via Viola 7 –* ☎ *0432 21 296 – Closed Sun, 25 Dec-4 Jan –* ⊘ *– €13/21.* A real find indeed: a good old-fashioned eatery which has been in the same family for generations. Rustic-style ambience in this 17C palazzo (note the horses' harnesses on the walls). Authentic regional cooking at very reasonable prices.

• Moderate

Alla Vedova – *Via Tavagnacco 9 –* ☎ *0432 47 02 91 – Closed Sun evening, Mon, 10-25 Aug – €24/31.* The profusion of objects hanging on the walls (copper utensils, hunting trophies, old firearms and, in a more innocuous vein, an odd collection of little spoons) bear witness to the passing of time at this century-old establishment. Divided up into several small dining rooms (some with fireplace). Specialises in grilled meats and game.

WHERE TO STAY

• Moderate

Hotel Clocchiatti – *Via Cividale 29 –* ☎ *0432 50 50 47 – Fax 0432 50 50 47 – Closed 20 Dec-15 Jan –* ▯ ▯ *– 13 rm €61.97/92.96 –* ⊇ *€7.75.* A cosy and welcoming little hotel. Simply furnished

rooms with all the basics (the rooms in the attic on the second floor are particularly attractive). The small bar area where breakfast is served leads out to an outdoor terrace.

SHOPPING

When it comes to dry-cured ham two names spring to mind: *prosciutto di Parma* and the famous *San Daniele,* which originated in San Daniele del Friuli, near Udine.

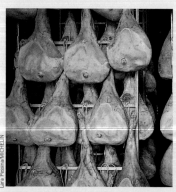

Prosciutto di San Daniele: the famous dry-cured ham

Worth a Visit

Piazza della Libertà★★

This very harmonious square has kept its Renaissance character and is bordered by several public buildings. The former town hall is also known as the **Loggia del Lionello** (1457), from the name of its architect. Its Venetian-Gothic style is characterised by the elegant arcades and its white and rose-coloured stonework. Opposite on a slightly higher level is the 16C **Loggia di San Giovanni,** a Renaissance portico surmounted by a 16C clock tower, with Moorish jacks (*Mori*) to strike the hour, similar to the ones in Venice. A 16C fountain plays in the centre of the square, not far from statues of Hercules and Cacus and the columns of Justice and St Mark.

Castello

& *Open Tue-Sat 9.30am-12.30pm and 3-6pm, Sun and hols 9.30am-12.30pm. Closed Mon, 12 Jul pm, hols. €2.58. No charge Sun and hols.* ☎ *0432 50 18 24; www.comune.udine.it*
This imposing early-16C castle is preceded by an esplanade from which there is a good view of Udine and the surrounding Friuli countryside. This was the seat of the representatives of the Most Serene Republic (Venice).
Alongside is the 13C church of **Santa Maria del Castello** with a 16C façade and campanile which bears a statue of the Archangel Gabriel at its summit. Inside, there is a 13C fresco of the *Descent from the Cross.*

Duomo

This 14C Gothic cathedral remodelled in the 18C has a lovely Flamboyant-Gothic doorway. The massive campanile has, on one of its faces, statues of the Angel of the Annunciation and of Archangel Gabriel (14C). Inside, there is attractive **Baroque decoration★**: organ loft, pulpit, tombs, altarpieces and historiated stalls. Tiepolo painted the remarkable *trompe l'oeil* frescoes in the Chapel of the Holy Sacrament (Cappella del Santo Sacramento).

The oratory **della Purità**, to the right of the cathedral, has a ceiling decorated with a remarkable *Assumption* (1757) by Tiepolo. *Open Tue-Sat 9am-noon and 4-6pm, Sun and hols 4-6pm. Closed Mon. Donation recommended.* ☎ *0432 50 68 30; www.spazio-cultura.it/duomoud*

Palazzo Arcivescovile

Open Wed-Sun, 10am-noon and 3.30-6.30pm. Closed Mon, Tue. €3.62.

The 16C-18C Archbishop's Palace boasts **frescoes★** by Tiepolo. The ceiling of its grand staircase depicts the *Fall of the Rebel Angels*, while the apartments are decorated with scenes from the Old Testament.

Piazza Matteotti

This lovely square bordered by arcaded houses is the site of a lively open-air market. Also of interest are: the elegant 16C Baroque church of San Giacomo, a 16C fountain and a 15C column of the Virgin. It is pleasant to stroll in Via Mercato Vecchio and Via Vittorio Veneto with their shops beneath the arcades.

Excursions

Villa Manin★★

30km/18mi southwest, in Passariano. ♿ *Open daily except Mon, 9am-12.30pm and 3-6pm. No charge.* ☎ *0432 90 66 57.*

Having lived in the Friuli area (territory under Venetian control) since the 13C, the Manin family occupied very high-ranking positions in the service of the Republic. The villa was a summer residence, the counterpart of their palace on the Grand Canal. The 16C villa was rebuilt in the 17C and rapidly completed with two wings set at right angles to the main part of the building, recalling the grandeur of Versailles. Finally, it was extended by semi-circular outbuildings based, in design, on St Peter's Square in Rome. It was here that Napoleon stayed prior to the Treaty of Campoformio *(8km/5mi southwest of Udine)* marking the end of the Venetian Republic: an irony given that this was the residence of the last Doge, Ludovico Manin.

In the right wing of the villa, visitors can see the magnificent chapel and its sacristy, the stables with their 18C and 19C coaches and carriages, and the weapons room (15C-18C arms). The superb grounds are decorated with statues.

Cividale del Friuli★

16km/10mi west. This is the ancient *Forum Julii*, which gave the town situated high above the River Natisone its modern name. The Lombards, who came from Scandinavia, settled here in the 6C and founded the first of their many duchies in northern Italy. The town later became the residence of the Patriarchs of Aquileia. From the 15C onward it belonged to Venice. Since the 1976 earthquake, Cividale has been rebuilt.

Duomo – It was extensively rebuilt in the 16C in the Renaissance style by Piero Lombardo (1435-1515) but retains some Gothic features on the façade and in the interior. The high altar has a 12C Veneto-Byzantine silver-gilt altarpiece. The small **Museo christiano**, a museum of Lombard art *(opening off the south aisle)*, contains numerous valuable items: the octagonal baptismal font of the Patriarch Callisto, reconstructed in the 8C using Byzantine fragments, and the 8C "altar" of Duke Ratchis in marble with carved sides depicting scenes from the Life of Christ. *Museum: Open Mon-Sat, 9.30am-12pm and 3-7pm (winter to 6pm). Closed Sun, hols am. No charge.* ☎ *0432 73 11 44.*

Museo Archeologico Nazionale★★ – *To the left of the cathedral.* ♿ *Open Tue-Sun, 8.30am-7.30pm (ticket office closes 7pm), Mon 9am-2pm (ticket office closes 1.30pm). €2.* ☎ *0432 70 07 00.*

Housed in a superb late-16C palace said to have been designed by Palladio, the museum displays on the second floor the numerous items discovered in Lombard graveyards in Cividale and the surrounding area. They include jewellery, weaponry and everyday objects that provide an excellent insight into Lombard culture and art from the 6C to the Carolingian era. Note the Roman sarcophagus which was re-used at a later date, and the objects taken from the grave of Duke Gisulfo (7C).

Tempietto★★ – *Near the Piazza San Biagio.* (♿) *Open Apr to Oct, daily 9am-12.30pm and 3-6.30pm, Sun and hols 9.30am-1pm and 3-7.30pm, rest of year 9.30am-12.30pm and 3-5pm, Sun and hols 9.30am-12.30pm and 2.30-6pm. €2.07.* ☎ *0432 70 08 67; www.comune.cividale-del-friuli.ud.it*

This elegant 8C Lombard building is a square chamber with quadripartite vaulting and an admirable Lombard **decoration** of friezes and stylised stuccos. It is a unique example of the architecture of this period.

Urbino★★

The walled town of Urbino, with its rose-coloured brick houses, is built on two hills overlooking the undulating countryside bathed in a glorious golden light. Urbino was ruled by the Montefeltro family from the 12C onwards and reached its peak in the reign (1444-82) of Duke Federico da Montefeltro, a wise leader, man of letters, collector and patron of the arts. Urbino was the birthplace of Raphael (Raffaello Sanzio) (1483-1520).

In 1998 Urbino's evocative historic centre was added to UNESCO's World Heritage List.

Location
Population 15 147 – Michelin map 429, 430 K 19 – Marches. Urbino is 36km/22mi from Pesaro, to which it is linked by S 423. **⯑** *Piazza Rinascimento 1, ☎ 0722 26 13. Surrounding area: see PESARO.*

Directory

WHERE TO EAT
• **Budget**

Nenè – *Via Crocicchia – 2km/1.2mi northwest of the town –* ☎ *0722 29 96 –* €15/27. Situated in open countryside, but only 2km/1.2mi from the Palazzo Ducale, is this lovely rural farmhouse which has been fully restored. Good food. Also offers accommodation with independent access: the rooms are somewhere between elegant and rustic.

Vanda – *Via Mari 4 – 61029 Castelcavallino – 8km/5mi northwest of Urbino (direction Montecalende) –* ☎ *0722 34 91 17 – Closed Wed and lunchtime (except public holidays), 22 Dec-22 Jan, 8-23 Jul –* €19/48. The restaurant's out-of-town location is also a good excuse to head out into the countryside – very scenic. The main dining room with its lovely wooden finish is a sort of windowed veranda which has fine views over the castle. Delicious, regional cuisine. Al fresco dining in summer.

Worth a Visit

Palazzo Ducale★★★
Visit: 90min. The palace (1444-72), started by order of Duke Federico by the Dalmatian architect **Luciano Laurana** and completed by the Sienese **Francesco di Giorgio Martini**, is a masterpiece of harmony and elegance. The design hinges on the panorama to the west of the old town, and the original façade overlooking the valley is pierced by superimposed loggias and flanked by two tall round towers. The severe east wing facing Piazza Rinascimento has irregularly spaced windows, while the austerely majestic north façade is punctuated by three great doors at ground level and four rectangular windows on the first floor.

The inner courtyard, inspired by earlier Florentine models, is a classic example of Renaissance harmony with its pure, delicate lines, serene architectural rhythm and subtle combination of rose-coloured brick and white marble.

On the ground floor are a museum, the **Museo Archeologico** (lapidary fragments: inscriptions, steles, architectural remains etc), a library, the **Biblioteca del Duca**, and cellars or **cantine**

Galleria Nazionale delle Marche★★ – (⯑) *Open Tue-Sun, 8.30am-7.15pm (ticket office closes 6.15pm). Mon 8.30am-2pm (ticket office closes 1pm). Closed 1 Jan, 1 May, 25 Dec. €4.13. ☎ 0722 27 60.*

The palace's first floor rooms with their original decoration are the setting for the National Gallery of the Marches which contains several great **masterpieces★★★**, a predella of the *Profanation of the Host* (1465-69) by Paolo Uccello, *Madonna di Senigallia* and a curious *Flagellation of Christ* by Piero della Francesca (see Index), the *Ideal City (see PIENZA)* by Laurana and the famous portrait of a woman, known as *The Mute*, by Raphael. Duke Federico's **studiolo★★★** is decorated with magnificent intarsia panelling.

A collection of 16C-17C Italian paintings and 17C-18C maiolica is displayed on the second floor.

To the north of the palace stands the early-19C cathedral built by Valadier.

Casa di Raffaello★
57 Via Raffaello. (⯑) Open Mar to Oct, Mon-Sat 9am-1pm and 3-7pm, Sun and hols 9am-1pm; rest of year Mon-Sat 9am-2pm, Sun and hols 9am-1pm. Closed 1 Jan, 25 Dec. €3. ☎ 0722 32 010; www.comune.urbino.ps.it

Raphael lived here up to the age of 14. This typical 15C house belonged to the boy's father, Giovanni Sanzio or Santi, and contains mementoes and period furniture.

The grandeur and magnificence of the Palazzo Ducale

Chiesa di San Giovanni Battista e San Giuseppe

Via Barocci. Open Mar to Oct, Mon-Sat 10am-12.30pm and 3-5.30pm, Sun 10am-12.30pm; rest of year Mon-Fri 10am-12.30pm and 3-5pm, Sat 10am-noon and 3-5pm, Sun 10am-12.30pm. €2, for each church. ☎ 347 67 11 181.

Of these two adjacent churches, the first is 14C and contains curious **frescoes★★** by the Salimbene brothers depicting the life of St John the Baptist. The second, dating from the 16C, has in the nave a colossal statue of St Joseph (18C) painted in grisaille, and a very lovely stucco **crib★**, a life-size work by Federico Brandani (1522-75).

Strada panoramica★★

Starting from Piazza Roma, this scenic road skirts a hillside and affords admirable **views★★** of the town walls, the lower town, Ducal Palace and cathedral: a wonderful scene in various hues of pink brick.

Valcamonica

The valley which stretches from Lovere to Edolo, and is linked to the Valtellina by the Passo di Gavia, may be given over to industry at the lower level, but the higher you climb the more picturesque it is, the upper slopes dotted with the ruins of numerous castles. Over a stretch of land of around 60km/36mi is a series of rock carvings (added to UNESCO's World Heritage List), which date back to between prehistoric and early Roman times.

Location

Michelin map 428 and 429 E-D 12-13 – Lombardy. The Valcamonica follows the course of the River Oglio as far as Lago d'Iseo. The main access road from Bergamo is S 42. *Surrounding area: see BERGAMO, BRESCIA, Regione dei LAGHI.*

Special Features

Rock carvings★★

Eroded by the alpine glaciers (which disappeared 10 000 years ago), the rocks of the Valcamonica became a highly polished, smooth surface which lent itself to figurative engravings. Created by tapping or scratching away at the stone, the carvings are a testament to the daily life of the people who inhabited the region. Having dedicated themselves to hunting during the Palaeolithic era (c 8000-5000 BC), they adopted agricultural farming methods during the Neolithic era and then metallurgy during the Bronze Age (from 1800 BC) and the Iron Age (from 900 BC). There are four basic types of representation: deer (hunting scenes); ploughs and other agricultural machinery; weaponry and warriors; religious representations: prayers, symbols, idols.

The carvings can be seen in the **Parco Nazionale delle Incisioni Rupestri di Naquane** *(visit: 2 hr – access from Capo di Ponte)* and in the **Riserva Naturale Regionale di Ceto, Cimbergo e Paspardo**: for admission to the Riserva contact the **Museo di Nadro di Ceto**. *Open daily except Mon, 9am-5pm. Closed Easter, 25 Dec. €4. Park:* ♿ *Open Mar to mid-Oct 8.30am-7.30pm, rest of the year 8.30am-5pm, closed Mon (except Bank holiday Mon). €4.13* ☎ *0369 92 190. Reserve:* (♿) *Open summer 9am-6pm, winter 9am-noon and 1.30pm-5pm. Closed 1 Jan, 25 Dec. €1.55 with entry to the Museo di Nadro.* ☎ *0364 43 34 465; www.kernunos.it Museo di Nadro:* (♿) *Open daily 9am-5pm. Closed 1 Jan, 25 Dec. €1.55.* ☎ *0364 43 34 65; www.g3informatica.it/museo; www.kernunos.it*

▶▶Breno: 10C castle, church of S. Antonio (14C-15C), church of S. Salvatore.

Valle d'Aosta

AOSTA VALLEY

With its secluded valleys, numerous castles, villages with balconied houses roofed with flat stone slabs *(lauzes)*, the Valle d'Aosta is one of the most attractive tourist areas in Italy offering various possibilities for excursions and scenic routes leading up to glaciers. This region comprising the Dora Baltea and adjacent valleys is surrounded by high peaks of both the French and Swiss Alps: Mont Blanc, the Matterhorn (Cervino), Monte Rosa, Grand Combin, Dent d'Hérens, Gran Paradiso and Grande Sassière.

Since 1948 the Valle d'Aosta has been, for administrative purposes, an autonomous region: inhabitants still speak a Franco-Provençal dialect and public documents are published both in Italian and French.

Location

Michelin map 428 E 3-4. Flanked by France and Switzerland, the Valle d'Aosta covers the northwest corner of the Italy. It is crossed by A 5.

🗉 *Piazza Chanoux 8,* ☎ *0165 23 66 27.*

Special Features

Parco Nazionale del Gran Paradiso★★

The Gran Paradiso National Park Department organises outings in each valley with park guides who will help visitors discover the unique features of the protected area. Contact the appropriate Park Office. ☎ *and Fax 0124 90 10 70, sturpngp@misper.it*

This national park covering an area of almost 70 000ha/270sqmi includes an area previously preserved as a royal hunting ground. It can be reached by the Rhêmes, Savarenche, Cogne and Locana valleys or the Nivolet Pass road. The park is rich in wildlife and is important as a reserve for endangered species, such as the ibex, and some of the rarest specimens of alpine flora.

Facilities

Owing to its marvellous situation the Valle d'Aosta offers some splendid viewpoints★★★. It is also a ski-lover's paradise (resorts at **Breuil-Cervinia**★★★, **Courmayeur**★★★, **La Thuile**★★, **Gressoney**, **Champoluc**★). The slopes wind

The unmistakable outline of the Matterhorn

Directory

Where to Eat

• *Budget*

Casale – *Frazione Condemine 1 – 11020 Saint Christophe – 4km/2.5mi northeast of Aosta – ☎ 0165 54 12 03 – Closed Sun evening, Mon (winter), 5-20 Jan, 5-20 Jun – €20.66/33.57.* Good food that is a mixture of the traditional and original. Welcoming, family atmosphere. Helpful proprietor. Comfortable rooms on the first floor. Lovely terrace with views over the valley.

• *Moderate*

Hostellerie de la Pomme Couronnée – *Frazione Resselin 3 – 11020 Gressan – 3km/1.8mi southwest of Aosta – ☎ 0165 25 11 91 – Closed Tue, Wed lunchtime – ⌂ – Book – €32/48.* Situated in a small, rural farmhouse which has been restored with as many original features as possible including the entrance and the stone walls in the dining room. Apples reign supreme and are a key feature of the cuisine here.

Where to Stay

• *Budget*

Hotel Miravalle – *Località Porossan – ☎ 0165 23 61 30 – Fax 0165 35 705 – 🚭 🅿 – 24 rm €41.32/77.47 ☕.* Of note are the fireplace (a fire is lit in the evenings) and the light and spacious breakfast room with lovely picture windows (fine views) as well as the sun terrace. The harmonious, if unusual, decor (complete with porcelain ornaments and some beautiful dolls) and the courteous service enhance the old-fashioned ambience.

A l'Hostellerie du Paradis – *Eau Rousse – 11010 Eau Rousse – 3km/1.8mi south of Valsavarenche – ☎ 0165 90 59 72 – Fax 0165 90 59 71 – 🏊 ♿ – 30 rm €41.32/51.65 – ☕ €7.75 – Restaurant €21/46.* Entirely in keeping with its surroundings this hotel is situated in a charming and quiet mountain hamlet. Facilities include a reading room and snooker room. Rooms are very welcoming and all individually decorated: some have a fireplace. Traditional fare.

• *Moderate*

Albergo La Barme – *Località Lillaz – 11012 Cogne – 4km/2.5mi southeast of Cogne – ☎ 0165 74 91 77 – Fax 0165 74 92 13 – Closed Oct and Nov – ♿ – 13 rm €40/80 ☕ – Restaurant €18/32.* A small, family-run hotel ideally situated for excursions into the Parco del Gran Paradiso in summer and for cross-country skiing in winter. Complementing the stone and wooden structure are the pale furnishings. Complete with restaurant, garden and a sauna.

Albergo Dei Camosci – *Località La Saxe – 11013 Courmayeur – ☎ 0165 84 23 38 – Fax 0165 84 21 24 – Closed May, mid-Jun, 23 Sep-3 Dec – 🅿 ♿ – 23 rm €46.48/69.72 ☕ – Restaurant €21/28.* Classic mountain-style hotel: stone and wood structure with functional but welcoming rooms. Comfortable public areas. Great views of Mont Blanc. The proprietors are also in charge of the cooking which focuses on regional dishes and specialities.

Albergo Granta Parey – *Località Chanavey – 11010 Rhêmes-Notre-Dame – 1.5km/1mi north of Rhêmes-Notre-Dame – ☎ 0165 93 61 04 – Fax 0165 93 61 44 – Closed Nov – 🅿 – 33 rm €41.32/81.63 – ☕ €7.75 – Restaurant €21/29.* Children are particularly welcome in this family-run hotel which is situated very near the ski-lifts. Comfortable rooms with parquet floor and pine furniture. Separate dining room for guests.

Hotel Tourist – *Via Roma 32 – 11028 Valtournenche – 8km/5mi south of Cervinia – ☎ 0166 92 070 – Fax 0166 93 129 – Closed Oct and Nov – 🅿 ♿ – 34 rm €61.97 – ☕ €7.75 – Restaurant €18/23.* A welcoming, airy establishment (pale walls and lots of wood and stone) – spacious rooms with furniture in cherrywood. Cuisine typical of the region is served in the restaurant and a free shuttle-bus to the nearby ski-pistes is available.

Taking a Break

La Bottega degli Antichi Sapori – *Via Porta Praetoria 63 – ☎ 0165 23 96 66 – Mon-Sat 8am-1pm and 3-7.30pm.* Cheeses, hams, wines ... there's no shortage of specialities in the Aosta region. This lovely grocer's (air-conditioned) has a fine selection of them, along with various types of pasta and delicious sauces.

Old Distillery Pub – *Via Près Fosses 7 – ☎ 0165 23 95 11 – Summer, Tue-Sun 6pm-2am; daily, rest of the year.* The coloured glass, flowery curtains and old tables combine to create a an authentic-seeming Scottish pub: a little piece of Scotland transported to Italy. Lots of atmosphere guaranteed!

Going Out

Caffè della Posta – *Via Roma 51 – 11013 Courmayeur – ☎ 0165 84 22 72 – Thu-Tue 8.30am-2.30am, closed 2 weeks in winter and summer.* Housed in a stone building, this lovely café is just the place to gather your strength for the long winter ahead. Cosy up to the wonderful fireplace that has been warming its visitors since 1911.

down through breathtaking landscapes comprised of woods, forests and glaciers, such as the stunning one at Monte Rosa. Ski-lovers can immerse themselves in the heart of the Parco Nazionale del Gran Paradiso (**Cogne****).

Economic activities in the region include cattle breeding and crafts such as wood-carving. Furniture (chests, benches), smaller pieces such as the typical *grolle* (wooden goblets), sculptures and toys (particularly animals such as stylised cows and donkeys) can all be found.

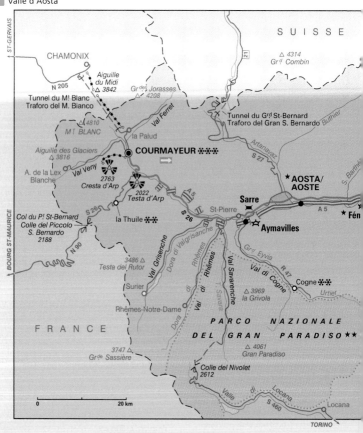

Tour

FROM COURMAYEUR TO IVREA

160km/100mi – allow one day

Courmayeur✱✱✱

Plans of the town and surrounding areas in the Michelin Atlas Italy. This well-known mountaineering and winter sports resort is a good excursion centre. Take a cable car to the Cresta d'Arp and to cross the Mont Blanc Massif and make a short detour into France *(for the area beyond La Palud see The Green Guide French Alps)*. By car you can explore the following valleys: Veny, Ferret or Testa d'Arpi and the road to the Little St Bernard Pass, one of the busiest transalpine routes which was used by the Romans in ancient times.

Once through St-Pierre and past the road south up the Cogne valley, on the left stands **Castello di Sarre**, the former summer residence of the Counts of Savoy. Further on, to the right, is the 14C **Fortezza d'Aymavilles**, impressively quartered with great round crenellated towers.

Aosta✱

Aosta stands in the valley of the same name and is the capital of the region. It has retained the geometric plan of a military camp *(castrum)* and some interesting monuments from the Roman period. Aosta, an active religious centre in the Middle Ages, was the birthplace of the theologian St Anselm, who became Archbishop of Canterbury where he died in 1109. Today it is an active industrial town and, since the opening of the Mont Blanc Tunnel in 1965, an important tourist centre, at the junction of the transalpine routes to France and Switzerland via the St Bernard Tunnel.

Roman Monuments✱ – These are grouped in the centre of Aosta and include a gateway, the **Porta Pretoria**, a majestic arch, **Arco di Augusto**, both dating from the 1C BC, a **Roman bridge**, a **theatre** and the ruins of an **amphitheatre**.

Complesso Ursino – The church, dedicated to St Orso, has some lovely carved 15C **stalls** and a Baroque rood screen. Beside the 11C **crypt** a doorway opens onto charming little Romanesque **cloisters✱** with historiated **capitals✱✱** illustrating biblical and secular scenes. The **Priorato di Sant'Orso** is a Renaissance-style priory

with elegant **windows★**. *Open Mon-Sat, Mar to Jun and Sep 9am-7pm, Jul and Aug 9am-8pm, rest of year 10am-12.30pm and 1.30-5pm, Sun and hols 10am-12.30pm and 1.30-6pm. To view frescoes of the Complesso, contact the custodian. ☎ 0165 23 66 27; www. regione.vda.it*

Cattedrale – The cathedral was built in the 12C and has been remodelled several times; it now boasts a neo-Classical façade (1848). The chancel has 12C mosaic paving, 15C Gothic stalls and the 14C tomb of Thomas II of Savoy. The sacristy contains a rich **treasury**. The cloisters are 15C. *Treasury: ♿ Open Apr to Sep, daily, 8-11.30am and 3-6.30pm, Sun and hols 8-10am and 3-5.30pm. Rest of year, Sun and hols only 8-10am and 3-5.30pm. Contact custodian on weekdays. ☎ 0165 40 413. €2.07. ☎ 0165 54 02 51; www.regione.vda.it/turismo*

Castello di Fénis★

Open daily, Mar to Jun and Sep 9am-7pm, Jul and Aug 9am-8pm; rest of year, daily except Tue, 10am-12.30pm and 1.30-5pm, Sun and hols 10am-12.30pm and 1.30-6pm. Ticket office always closes 30min early. Closed 1 Jan (am only), 25 Dec. €3.10. ☎ 0165 23 66 27; www.regione.vda.it

This imposing fortress contains fine carved furniture in the local style. The inner courtyard has remarkable frescoes portraying the Golden Legend.

Breuil-Cervinia✳✳✳

This winter sports resort is admirably situated at 2 050m/6 822ft. Cable cars climb up to the Rosa Plateau (Plan Rosa) and the Furggen Pass at 3 491m/11 453ft.

Saint-Vincent★

The Casino de la Vallée in its fine park is very popular.
The road passes two castles: Castello di Montjovet and the 14C **Castello di Verrès** which curiously enough has no keep or corner towers.

Castello d'Issogne★

Open Mon-Sat, Mar to Jun and Sep 9am-7pm, Jul and Aug 9am-8pm; rest of year 10am-12.30pm and 1.30-5pm, Sun and hols 10am-12.30pm and 1.30-6pm (closed Wed in this season). Ticket office always closes 30min early. Closed 1 Jan (am only), 25 Dec. €5.16. ☎ 0165 23 66 27; www.regione.vda.it

The castle was built at the end of the 15C by Georges de Challant. It has a fine courtyard with a fountain surmounted by a wrought-iron pomegranate tree. The arcaded gallery is painted with 15C frescoes and inside the furniture is typical of the Valle d'Aosta area.

Fortezza di Bard★

The colossal fortress, dismantled on the orders of Napoleon in 1800 and rebuilt during the 19C, commands the upper Dora Baltea Valley.

Pont-Saint-Martin

This village is named after the Roman bridge which was guarded by a chapel dedicated to St John Nepomuk.

Ivrea

This busy industrial town stands at the mouth of the Valle d'Aosta. To the east of Ivrea is the largest moraine in Europe, the Serra d'Ivrea.

Venezia★★★

VENICE

Venice is a legendary city. She chose the waters of the lagoon for her regal existence of more than a thousand years, the same water that has saved her from the clutches of time and yet threatens her very being.

She is a city of a multitude of moods and faces: lively and affectionate to the inhabitants that fill her streets with their chatter; on the verge of a painful farewell for those who prefer her in the tragic guise of *Death in Venice*. Each visitor to Venice takes away a highly personal impression of the city's essence.

Location

Population 277 305 – Michelin map 429 F 18-19 – See also The Green Guide Venice.

The main access road to Venice is A 4. It is linked to Mestre by the Ponte della Libertà.

🖪 *Calle Ascensione, San Marco 71/F, ☎ 041 52 98 711.*

Surrounding area: see Riviera del BRENTA, LAGUNA VENETA, PADOVA, TREVISO.

Background

Venice is built on 117 islands; it has 150 canals and 400 bridges. A canal is called a *rio*, a square a *campo*, a street a *calle* or *salizzada*, a quay a *riva* or *fondamenta*, a filled-in canal *rio Terrà*, a passageway under a house *sottoportego*, a courtyard a *corte* and a small square a *campiello*. The squares are charming, with their well curbs (*vera da pozzo*) often sculpted.

Gondolas – For centuries gondolas have been the traditional means of transport in Venice. The gondola is an austere and sober craft except for its typical iron hook, which acts as a counterweight to the gondolier. The curved fin is said to echo the doge's *corno* (horn-shaped hat) and the prongs to represent the *sestieri* or districts of the city. The prong on the back of the stern symbolises the Giudecca.

The Venetians – The Venetians are both proud and fiercely traditional, known for their commercial and practical skills. The **"bautta"** (black velvet mask) and **domino** (a wide hooded cape), once very popular with the locals and still worn in Venice at Carnival time, add to their elusiveness. Skilled courtesans, diplomats and spies have given Venice a reputation for intrigue and manoeuvring in love and politics. Venetian is a very lively dialect which is used in place of Italian, even in place names.

The Grand Canal winds through Venice

Historical notes

Venice was founded in AD 811 by the inhabitants of Malamocco, near the Lido, fleeing from the Franks. They settled on the Rivo Alto, known today as the Rialto. In that year the first doge – a name derived from the Latin *dux* (leader) – Agnello Partecipazio, was elected and thus started the adventures of the Venetian Republic, known as La Serenissima, which lasted 1 000 years. In 828 the relics of St Mark the Evangelist were brought from Alexandria; he became the protector of the town.

The Venetian Empire – From the 9C to the 13C Venice grew steadily richer as it exploited its position between East and West. With its maritime and commercial power it conquered important markets in Istria and Dalmatia. The guile of Doge Dandolo and the assistance of the Crusaders helped the Venetians capture Constantinople in 1204. The spoils from the sack of Constantinople flowed to Venice, while trade in spices, fabrics and precious stones from markets established in the East grew apace. **Marco Polo** (1254-1324) returned from China with fabulous riches. He related his amazing adventures in French in his *Book of the Wonders of the World* and won great fame throughout Europe. The 14C war with Venice's rival Genoa ended in victory for the Venetians in 1381.

The first half of the 15C saw Venetian power at its peak: the Turks were defeated at Gallipoli in 1416 and the Venetians held the kingdoms of Morea, Cyprus and Candia (Crete) in the Levant. In mainland Italy, from 1414 to 1428, they captured Verona, Vicenza, Padua, Udine, and then Brescia and Bergamo. The Adriatic became the Venetian Sea from Corfu to the Po.

The capture of Constantinople by the Turks in 1453 started the decay. The discovery of America caused a shift in the patterns of trade and Venice had to keep up an exhausting struggle with the Turks who were defeated in 1571 in the naval battle of **Lepanto**, in which the Venetians played an important part. Their decline, however, was confirmed in the 17C when the Turks captured Candia (Crete) after a 25-year siege.

The "Most Serene Republic" came to an end in 1797. Napoleon Bonaparte entered Venice and abolished a thousand year-old constitution. Then, by the **Treaty of Campoformio,** he ceded the city to Austria. Venice and the Veneto were united with Italy in 1866.

The government of the Republic was from its earliest days organised to avoid the rise to power of any one man. The role of doge was supervised by several councils: the Grand Council drew up the laws; the Senate was responsible for foreign affairs, and military and economic matters; the Council of Ten, responsible for security, kept a network of secret police and informers which created an atmosphere of mistrust but ensured control of all aspects of city life.

Venetian painting

The Venetian school of painting with its marked sensuality is characterised by the predominance of colour over draughtsmanship, and by an innate sense of light in hazy landscapes with blurred outlines. Art historians have often noted the contrast between the scholarly and idealistic art of the Florentines and the freer, more spontaneous work of the Venetians, which later influenced the Impressionists.

The real beginnings of Venetian painting are exemplified by the **Bellini** family: Jacopo, the father, and Gentile (1429-1507) and **Giovanni** (or **Giambellino**, 1432-1516), his sons. The latter, who was the younger son, was a profoundly spiritual artist and one of the first Renaissance artists to integrate landscape and figure compositions harmoniously. In parallel, their pupil **Carpaccio** (1455-1525) recorded Venetian life with his usual imagination and care for detail while **Giorgione** remained a major influence. His pupil, **Lorenzo Lotto**, was also influenced by the realism of Northern artists.

The Renaissance came to a glorious conclusion with three great artists: **Titian** (c 1490-1576) who painted dramatic scenes where dynamic movement is offset by light effects; Paolo **Veronese** (1528-88), whose sumptuous ornamentation and rich colours reflected the splendour of La Serenissima; and **Tintoretto** (1518-94), a visionary whose dramatic technique reflects an inner anxiety.

The artists of the 18C captured Venice and its peculiar light, grey-blue, iridescent and slightly misty: **Canaletto** (1697-1768) whose works won favour with English Grand Tourists, and his pupil Bellotto (1720-80), were both inspired by townscapes; Francesco **Guardi** (1712-93) who painted in luminous touches; **Pietro Longhi** (1702-58), the artist of intimate scenes; **Giovanni Battista (Giambattista) Tiepolo** (1696-1770), a master decorator who painted frescoes with sacred and secular scenes full of light and movement. His son, Giovanni Domenico (1727-1804), adopted a similar style.

Spontaneity and colour are also found in the musicians of Venice, of whom the best known is **Antonio Vivaldi** (1678-1741), who was master of violin and viola at a hospice, Ospedale della Pietà, for many years. (Hospices were charitable institutions and orphanages but were also academies of music and drama).

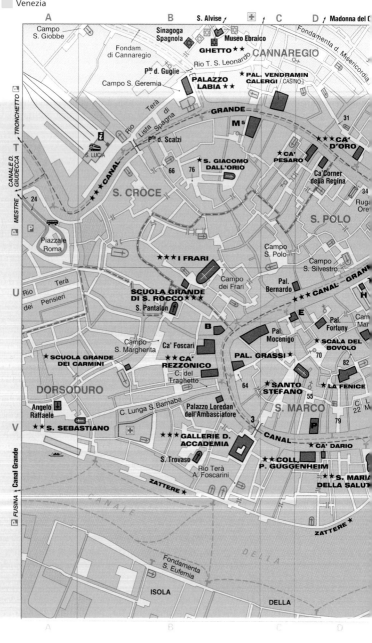

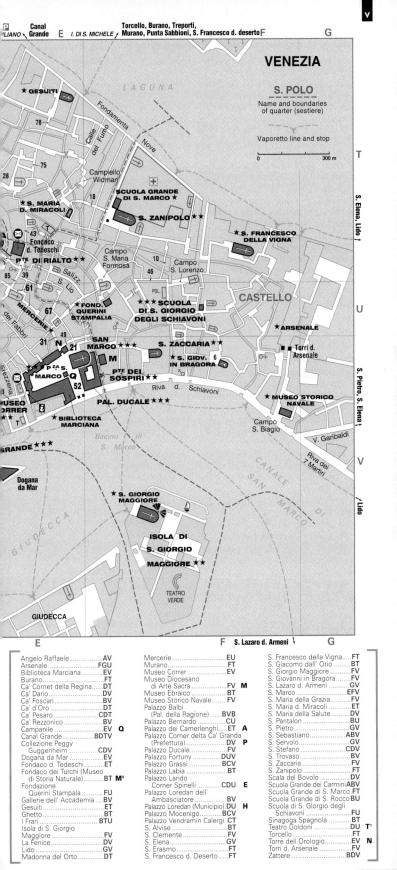

VENEZIA

S. POLO
Name and boundaries of quarter (sestiere)

Vaporetto line and stop

0 — 300 m

CASTELLO

Directory

Visitors spending one day in Venice should take in Piazza San Marco. You would need another day or two to get round the Accademia, the *Scuole* (Schools) and the churches which house many of the city's treasures. Anyone who has the luxury of a week in Venice will get a real feel for the place strolling along the narrow streets and exploring the islands in the lagoon.

The hub of public life is Piazza San Marco (see below) where tourists and citizens sit on the terraces of the famous Florian and Quadri cafés. The Florian is the most celebrated of all the cafés in Venice; founded in 1720 it has received Byron, Goethe, George Sand, Musset and Wagner within its mirrored and allegory-painted walls.

The shops in St Mark's have sumptuous window displays of lace, jewellery, mirrors and the famous glassware from Murano. The Mercerie – shopping streets – lead to the Rialto Bridge.

On the far side of this are the displays of greengrocers' *(erberie)* and fishmongers' shops *(pescherie)*.

GETTING ABOUT

It goes without saying that in Venice public transport uses only liquid roads. It is important to bear in mind that heavy traffic on the Grand Canal and the fact that stops do not always take one "door to door" mean that walking can sometimes be quicker. However, on arrival in the city, the very sight of the first bridge (Ponte degli Scalzi, opposite the station, is particularly steep) can be tiring for visitors carrying heavy luggage. Likewise, walking up and down bridges all day can put even the most energetic walker to the test.

Visitors will find that they will happily make use of the famous Venetian water-boats, the **vaporetti**.

Listed below are the two most convenient routes:

– **Line 1** stops at all stops along the Grand Canal. Terminates at the Lido after stopping at piazzale Roma, the station and San Marco.

– **Line 82** is faster than Line 1 as it makes fewer stops. Stops at Tronchetto, Piazzale Roma, the Giudecca, San Giorgio, San Marco and the Lido.

One-way tickets cost € 3.10; return journeys €5.16; 24hr €9.30; and 72hr €18.08) tickets can also be purchased; these need be stamped only on the initial journey. Weekly passes cost €30.99.

Anyone needing a taxi should make sure that the cab has a yellow strip which carries the black symbol (for the area code) and the number, and that the taximeter or tariff is clearly visible. The Italian Tourist Board recommends that in the event of a dispute over the price, take down the number of the taxi and the time, and, most important of all, get a receipt with details of the route and the price you paid for the trip.

Visitors are urged not to use the unauthorised mini cabs that hang around outside railway stations, airports and other waiting areas.

To call a taxi in Venice, dial:

Radio Taxi, ☎ 041 522 23 03, 72 31 12

Ferrovia, ☎ 041 71 62 86

Piazzale Roma (S. Chiara), ☎ 041 71 69 22

Rialto, ☎ 041 523 05 75, 72 31 12

S. Marco (Molo), ☎ 041 522 97 50

Lido, ☎ 041 526 00 59

Aeroporto (Marco Polo), ☎ 041 541 50 84

Visitors who opt to walk will be relieved to learn that as well as a choice of three bridges crossing the Grand Canal (Scalzi, Rialto, Accademia) they can be "ferried" across the canal in a gondola. This service is available at seven points along the Grand Canal (Station, S. Marcuola, S. Sofia, al Carbon, S. Tomà, S. Samuele, S. Maria del Giglio): it is a very rapid journey and costs only €0.36 (except when exhibitions are on at Palazzo Grassi, in which case the S. Samuele crossing costs €0.52. Be careful to keep your balance!

Visitors who want to enjoy the full experience of a **gondola** ride must be prepared to spend considerably more: a 50 minute journey through canals costs €61.97 (official starting price which does not include musical accompaniment). This price can be divided among six people who can be accommodated in a gondola. Each 25min after the initial 50min costs €30.99. A tour in a gondola by night is an unforgettable experience but incurs considerable costs: from 8pm to 8am a 50min journey costs €77.47, each 25min thereafter costs €38.73. For more information contact the Istituzione per la Conservazione della Gondola e la Tutela del Gondoliere, ☎ 041 528 50 75.

FOR YOUNG VISITORS

For those who are lucky enough to be aged between 14 and 29, the *Rolling Venice* card (cost €2.58) offers a range of discounts on youth hostels, hotels, campsites, public transport, university canteens, restaurants, museums, the Biennale and various shops taking part in this scheme. Cards can be purchased with proof of identity at the following places:

at the ACTV ticket offices;

at San Marco, corte Contarina 1529, at the offices of the Assessorato alle politiche giovanili, ☎ 041 27 47 645 (Mon-Fri morning from 9.30am to 1pm; Tue-Thu from 3pm to 5pm);

in Santa Croce, corte Canal 659, at the Agenzia Arte e Storia, ☎ 041 52 49 232 (Mon-Fri morning from 9am to 1pm and from 3.30pm to 6.15pm);

in San Polo, calle del Castelforte San Rocco 3101, at the Associazione Italiana Alberghi per la Gioventù, ☎ 041 52 04 414 (Mon-Sat from 8am to 2pm).

An additional fee of €5.16 provides a guided tour of Venice and a book of useful information. €7.75 will get you a pass, a guide, an information booklet and/or a *Rolling Venice* T-shirt.

WHERE TO EAT

Lunch or dinner in one of the trattorias is one of the pleasures of Venetian life. High up the list of things to try are the fish and seafood (in particular the squid, cuttlefish, eels and mussels), as well as *fegato alla veneziana* (calf's liver fried with onions). There are some excellent local wines to accompany these dishes including Valpolicella, Bardolino and Amarone (red) along with Soave and Prosecco (white).

• Budget

Da Sergio – *5870/A, Castello* – ☎ *041 52 85 153 – ⌗ – €13*. A typical Venetian trattoria serving simple, traditional food at reasonable prices. As you would expect in any self-respecting establishment of this nature there is a good selection of local specialities including *polpette* (croquette-style meatballs) on display at the bar.

Alla Patatina – *San Polo 2741/A, Calle Saoneri* – ☎ *041 52 37 238 – www.lapatatina.it – Closed Sun, 3 weeks in Aug, 1 week in Dec – Book – €13*. Pleasant 1950s-style establishment with a lively atmosphere. On offer at the bar are plenty of vegetable antipasti (including, of course, the delicious roast potatoes they do so well here) along with *polpette al sugo* (meatballs with sauce). Standard table service also available.

Gam-Gam – *Fondamenta Pescaria 1122* – ☎ *041 71 52 84 – www.jewishvenice.org – Closed Fri, Sat luncthime (Sat evening in summer) – ⌗ – Book – €15/34*. For anyone looking for something a little different or even a complete change of scene, you could try this rather pleasant Jewish restaurant. Modern, if austere decor. Strictly kosher food.

S. Trovaso – *1016, Dorsoduro* – ☎ *041 52 03 703 – giorgiocassan@tin.it – Closed Mon, 31 Dec – Book – €15/41*. This establishment is conveniently situated near the Accademia. It is always very crowded so remember to book! Good selection of dishes as well as pizzas.

La Zucca – *Sestiere S. Croce 1762* – ☎ *041 52 41 570 – Closed Sun, 1 week in Aug and Dec – Book – €21/31*. If you're in the mood for more varied and exotic dishes, prepared with a lightness of touch, this is the place to go. A simple trattoria, it offers a particularly good selection of vegetables dishes – the decor itself is a celebration of the pumpkin *(zucca)*!

• Moderate

Ai Frati – *Fondamenta Venier 4 – 30141 Murano* – ☎ *041 73 66 94 – Closed Thu, Feb – €26/42 + 12% service charge*. Founded as a wine shop in the mid-19C, it has since mutated into an eatery. For more than half a century now it has been serving good, authentic home cooking. The dining room is very pleasant but for a real treat try and get a table on the terrace overlooking the canal.

Al Mascaron – *Calle Longa Santa Maria Formosa 5225* – ☎ *041 52 25 995 – Closed Sun, 15 Dec-15 Jan – ⌗ – €32/53*. This is arguably the most successful restaurant in Venice...and that is saying something. It is a very lively, noisy place and always busy. Excellent home cooking. Definitely one for the address book.

Trattoria Favorita – *Via Francesco Duodo 33 – 30126 Venezia Lido* – ☎ *041 52 61 626 – Closed Mon, Tue lunchtime, 15 Jan-15 Feb – €37/50*. What could be better after a long walk or a sunny day by the sea, than some delicious seafood or a traditionally cooked fish dish? Rustic-style ambience and tables outside. Very popular with the locals.

Alle Testiere – *Calle del Mondo Novo 5801, Castello* – ☎ *041 52 27 220 – Closed Sun and Mon, 24 Dec-12 Jan, 25 Jul-25 Aug – ⌗ – Book – €40/55*. A small, informal establishment. The napkins might be made of paper but the cooking is a rather gastronomic affair. The menu, which focuses mostly on fish dishes, depends on what was on sale at the market that morning. A real treat for you (and your wallet!).

• Expensive

Harry's Dolci – *Fondamenta San Biagio 773, Giudecca* – ☎ *041 52 24 844 – Closed Tue, 8 Nov-26 Mar – €54/77 + 12% service charge*. Both restaurant and pasticceria, this is a little less expensive than its more famous sister establishment across the way. Stylistically it owes much to the Harry's tradition with diners seated close together in comfy chairs at low tables. Spectacular view from the large terrace overlooking the Canale della Giudecca.

WHERE TO STAY

• Budget

Istituto San Giuseppe – *Ponte della Guerra 5402, Castello* – ☎ *041 52 25 352 – ⌗ – 11 rm*

Casa Caburlotto – *Fondamenta Rizzi 316, S. Croce* – ☎ *041 71 08 77 – Fax 041 71 08 75 – 30 rm*

Casa Capitanio – *S. Croce 561* – ☎ *041 52 03 099 – Fax 041 52 23 975 – ⌗ – 12 rm*

Casa Cardinal Piazza – *Cannaregio 3539/A* – ☎ *041 72 13 88 – Fax 041 70 02 33 – 24 rm*

Casa Murialdo – Circolo ANSPI – *Cannaregio 3512* – ☎ *041 71 99 33 – Fax 041 72 00 02 – ⌗ – 12 rm*

Domus Civica – *S. Polo 3082* – ☎ *041 72 11 03 – Fax 041 52 27 139 – ⌗ – 100 beds*

Foresteria Valdese – *Castello 5170* – ☎ *041 52 86 797 – Fax 041 24 16 238 – ⌗ – 6 rm*

Opera Pia Istituto Ciliota – *Calle delle Muneghe 2976* – ☎ *041 52 04 888 – Fax 041 52 12 730 – ⌗ – 39 rm*

Patronato Salesiano Leone XIII – *Castello 1281* – ☎ *041 24 03 611 – Fax 041 24 03 610 – ⌗ – 15 rm*

Santa Fosca – *Cannaregio 2372* – ☎ *041 71 57 75 – Fax 041 71 57 75 – ⌗ – 121 beds*

Ostello della Giudecca – *Fondamenta Zitelle 86, Isola della Giudecca* – ☎ *041 52 38 211 –*

Fax 041 52 35 689 – vehostel@tin.it – ⌿ – 260 beds €15.49 ⌷ – Meal €8. An excellent base for exploring (by vaporetto!) one of the most fascinating cities in the world...and without burning a hole in your pocket. Marvellous situation – on the Giudecca, overlooking the lagoon and the city.

Hotel Bernardi – Semenzato – *Calle dell'Oca 4366 – Vaporetto Cà d'Oro – ☎ 041 71 04 01 – Fax 041 71 08 17 – Closed 1 week at the end of Nov, mid- Dec to 25 Dec, 15 Jan-31 Jan – 25 rm €33.57/98.13* ⌷. A no-frills hotel (stylewise the rooms leave a bit to be desired) but it is well situated (in a small street behind Campo S.S. Apostoli, near the Rialto bridge) in a less touristy part, although right at the heart, of the city.

R. Mattes/MICHELIN

• **Moderate**

Locanda Cà Foscari – *Calle della Frescade 3887/B – Vaporetto San Tomà – ☎ 041 71 04 01 – Fax 041 71 08 17 – valtersc@tin.it – Closed mid-Nov to mid-Jan – ⌿ – 11 rm €51.65/82.63* ⌷. A very simple but pleasant establishment with light, airy rooms and a family atmosphere. Offers extremely good value for money – a very rare thing in Venice.

Hotel Locanda Fiorita – *Campiello Novo 3457/A, San Marco – ☎ 041 52 34 754 – Fax 041 52 28 043 – ⌷ – 10 rm €77.47/108.46* ⌷. A good little hotel housed in a lovely old building. It is situated in one of the city's most attractive little squares, just a stone's throw from the very famous Piazza S. Marco. The rooms are rather functional and the public areas could be better but who wants to stay in their room when there is the whole of Venice to explore?

Hotel Serenissima – *Calle Goldoni 4486, San Marco – ☎ 041 52 00 011 – Fax 041 52 23 292 – Closed 15 Nov-2 Feb – 37 rm €77/170* ⌷. This unpretentious hotel is ideally located between the Rialto Bridge and St Mark's Square. The rooms are simply furnished but tastefully decorated (some in Venetian style) and well kept. One of the main attractions here is the staff who are very pleasant, creating a friendly, family atmosphere.

La Calcina – *Fondamenta Zattere ai Gesuati 780, Dorsoduro – Vaporetto Zattere – ☎ 041 52 06 466 – Fax 041 52 27 045 –* ⌷ *– 29 rm €77/176* ⌷. Only a photograph remains in the hallway of the "La Calcina" inn where Ruskin stayed in 1876, but this hotel, completely remodelled, stands on that very site. And it is as pleasant now as it was then; in the breakfast room as in the bedrooms, on the roof terrace as on the waterside terrace. The fine location on the Grand Canal adds to its charm as does the light which floods in, a rarity in Venice's narrow streets.

• **Expensive**

Hotel La Residenza – *Campo Bandiera e Moro 3608, Castello – ☎ 041 52 85 315 – Fax 041 52 38 859 – ⌷ – 13 rm from €93* ⌷. A stone's throw from Piazza San Marco is this lovely 16C palazzo which has been lovingly restored to its former glory – the perfect setting for a dream holiday. Features include 18C stuccowork, along with period light fittings and furnishings. The other main attraction is the wonderful view of the campo. Reasonably priced.

Pensione Seguso – *Zattere 779 – ☎ 041 52 86 858 – Fax 041 52 22 340 – Closed Dec-Feb – 35 rm from €100.71* ⌷. Whether it is the wooden panelling or the round windows, but there is something rather pleasantly old-fashioned and Anglo-Saxon about this hotel. Previous visitors include Italo Calvino and Ezra Pound.

Hotel Paganelli – *Riva degli Schiavoni 4687, Castello – ☎ 041 52 24 324 – Fax 041 52 39 267 – ⌷ – 22 rm from €113.62* ⌷. This family-run hotel overlooks the Bacino di San Marco. Some rooms (all decorated in the Venetian style) enjoy this view, others (in an adjoining building) look out onto Campo San Zaccaria.

Hotel Falier – *Salizzata San Pantalon 130, Santa Croce – ☎ 041 71 08 82 – Fax 041 52 06 554 – 19 rm from €129.11* ⌷. Close to I Frari but away from the bustling town centre, this hotel is a quiet haven of peace. Rustic-style decor with classic overtones. Charming little back garden where breakfast is served.

Hotel Abbazia – *Calle Priuli dei Cavalletti 68, Cannaregio – ☎ 041 71 73 33 – Fax 041 71 79 49 – Closed 7 Jan-7 Feb – ⌷ – 39 rm from €144.61* ⌷. An ideal location for visitors wishing to stay near the station. This hotel once housed a Carmelite monastery and retains many of its original features, including the pulpit in the entrance hall. Attentive, professional staff. The rooms are plain but spacious and there is a lovely garden.

Hotel Danieli – *Riva degli Schiavoni 4196, Castello – ☎ 041 52 26 480 – Fax 041 52 00 208 – ⌿x – 233 rm from €320.98 – ⌷ €48 - Rest €86/124.* Possibly the most famous hotel in the world! For many the image conjured up by Venice is that of palaces in the mist, decadent shapes and colours blurred in the mind's eye with cinematic and literary associations. Walking into Palazzo Dandolo, the Hotel Danieli since 1822, is like walking into that imaginary portrait. The columns, staircase, open gallery and architectural embroidery are reminiscent of the decorative richness of King Ludwig's castle at Neuschwanstein in Bavaria.

TAKING A BREAK

Caffè Florian – *Piazza San Marco 55. – ☎ 041 52 05 641 – www.paginegialle.it/caffeflorian – Open 10am-midnight.* You can't go to Venice without experiencing the city's most famous café, named after its first proprietor Floriano Francesconi. With its elegant 18C salons, smart waiters and magnificent exterior it is a throw-back to its past even with all the hustle and bustle. Past habitués of renown have included the playwright Goldoni (1707-93) and the neo-Classical sculptor Canova (1757-1822). Also hosts musical soirées.

Caffè Quadri – *Piazza San Marco 120 – ☎ 041 52 22 105 – quadri@quadrivenice.com – 9am-midnight.* You will need a break from all that sightseeing so why not treat yourself to a top-quality cup of coffee? In the arcaded portico of the Procuratie Vecchie is the elegant Caffè Quadri, which was founded by Giorgio Quadri in 1775 and was one of the first cafés in Venice to serve Turkish coffee.

Da Zorzi – *San Marco 4359 – Rialto – ☎ 041 52 08 816.* If you like your cream whipped...we recommend that you head straight for this place where the cream is still whipped by hand.

Devil's Forrest – *San Marco (Calle degli Stagneri) 5185 – S. Giorgio degli Schiavoni. – ☎ 041 52 00 623 – Tue-Sun 10am-1am.* Beer, beer and more beer. You can even play darts here!

Harry's Bar – *San Marco (Calle Vallaresso) 1322 – Piazza San Marco. – ☎ 041 52 85 777 – 10.30am-11pm.* Not far from the Piazza San Marco is the legendary Harry's Bar. Opened in 1931 by Giuseppe Cipriani, it boasts the writer Ernest Hemingway as one of its regulars. These days, it is popular with the locals and tourists alike who come and enjoy the elegant surroundings while sipping the house cocktail, a "Bellini", which is made with champagne and peach juice.

Marchini – *San Marco 2769 – La Fenice – near Campo Santo Stefano, in the busy thoroughfare, Calle del Piovan, heading for San Marco. – ☎ 041 52 29 109 – www.golosessi.com – Wed-Sun 8.30am-8.30pm.* Elegant pasticceria with a very inviting window display!

Paolin – *Sestiere San Marco 3464 – La Fenice. – ☎ 04 15 22 07 10 – Sun-Fri 6.30am-11pm.* Offers an imaginative selection of delicious ice creams (all made with milk of course). Flavours include Tiramisù, Torrone (nougat) and Yogurt. For an even more luxurious experience there are a number of extras on offer including candied fruit, whipped cream, custard and there is even a liquorice/aniseed topping for the more adventurous.

Piero e Mauro – *Calle dei Fabbri 881 – Piazza San Marco. – ☎ 04 15 23 77 56 – 6.30am-2am.* Good selection of sandwiches, crostini (toasted bread snacks) and beers.

The decor is fun too: the rather cramped room is decorated like the interior of a boat.

Rosa Salva – *San Marco (Marzaria San Salvator) 5020 – La Fenice. – ☎ 041 52 25 385 – Mon-Sat 7.45am-8.30pm, Sun 8am-9pm.* You might have to stand up but it's worth it. They say this place serves the best cappuccino in Venice. Why not have a delicious pastry with it?

The Fiddler's Elbow – *Cannaregio (Corte dei Pali) 3847 – Ca' D'Oro – ☎ 041 52 39 930 – 5pm-1am.* If you fancy an Irish coffee or a pint, how about a trip to this Irish pub?

GOING OUT

Al Volto – *San Marco 4081 – La Fenice – very near Campo Manin. – ☎ 041 52 28 945 – Mon-Sat 10am-2.30pm and 5-10pm.* With its collection of vintage wines, this wine bar is popular with serious wine buffs. Warm, welcoming atmosphere – can get very busy.

Il Paradiso perduto – *Cannaregio (Fondamenta della Misericordia) 2540 – Ca' D'Oro – ☎ 041 72 05 81 – Mon-Fri 7pm-1am, Sat 7pm-2am; Closed Wed.* An unusual establishment with live music, poetry readings and good food.

Linea d'Ombra – *Dorsoduro (Punta della Dogana) 19 – La Salute. – ☎ 041 52 85 259 – 8pm-2am; Closed Wed and Sun evening.* This rather elegant piano bar is situated round the corner from the Dogana del Mar, on the Zattere. Wonderful views of the Giudecca. Serves good cocktails.

ENTERTAINMENT

Music and theatre have always formed an intrinsic part of the spirit of Venice. As well as the three major theatres, concerts and plays are also held in numerous churches such as the Pietà, the Frari, S. Stefano, all ideal concert halls. See the *Gazzettino* for all information on concerts and shows in the city.

Gran Teatro La Fenice – It is not true that the Fenice no longer exists: to find out what's on (concerts are temporarily being held at the PalaFenice, on the island of Tronchetto) look at the relevant posters on view all over the city. For further information call ☎ 041 78 65 28 or ☎ 041 52 10 161.

Teatro Goldoni – Situated on the Calle del Teatro. Offers a rich season of plays and concerts. ☎ 041 520 54 22.

Teatro a l'Avogaria – Situated in Calle Avogaria, 1617 in the Dorsoduro quarter. ☎ 041 520 61 30.

Teatro Fondamenta Nuove – Situated on the Fondamenta Nuove, near the Sacca della Misericordia (Cannaregio 5013). Plays, concerts and dance. For information call ☎ 041 522 44 98.

Special Features

SAN MARCO, THE DRAWING ROOM OF VENICE

Piazza San Marco★★★

St Mark's Square is the heart of Venice. All around, the covered galleries of the **Procuratie** (procuratorships) shelter famous cafés (Florian, Quadri), and luxury shops. The square opens on the Grand Canal through the delightful **Piazzetta San Marco**. The two granite columns crowned by "Marco" and "Todaro" (St Mark and St Theodore) were brought from the East in 1172.

Basilica★★★ – St Mark's combines the Byzantine and Western styles. Building was carried out throughout the 11C and when the basilica was consecrated in 1094, the body of St Mark, stolen from Alexandria in 828, had been miraculously recovered. Visitors are overcome by a feeling of awe, perhaps owing to the rich decoration of marble and **mosaic**. Built on the plan of a Greek cross, the basilica is crowned by a bulbous dome flanked by four smaller domes of unequal height placed on the arms of the cross.

Façade – This is pierced by five large doorways adorned with variegated marbles and sculptures. The central doorway has three arches adorned with Romanesque-Byzantine low reliefs, and above are copies of the four famous **bronze horses** (the originals are in the gallery of the basilica).

On the first arch on the left is depicted the Translation of the Body of St Mark. On the south side near the Doges' Palace stands the porphyry group, known as the **Tetrarchs★** (4C). At the corner is the proclamation stone (pietra del bando), where laws were proclaimed. The pretty Piazzetta dei Leoncini lies to the north.

Atrium: As an introduction to the narrative told in mosaic inside the basilica, the mosaics in the atrium depict scenes from the Old Testament. The atrium gives access to the **Galleria e Museo marciano** which displays the **gilded bronze horses★★**. Open daily, Apr to Sep 9.45am-5pm, rest of year 9.45am-4pm. €1.50. ☎ 041 52 25 205; www.chorus-ve.org

Interior: The dazzling decoration of St Mark's combines the luminous mosaics (1071) by artists from Constantinople and a 12C pavement decorated with animal and geometric motifs – its uneven surface has been caused by subsidence. An iconostasis separates the raised presbytery (sanctuary) from the nave. Beyond, a ciborium raised on **alabaster columns★★** precedes the **Pala d'Oro★★★** (Golden Altarpiece), a masterpiece of Gothic art dating from the early 10C. The relics of St Mark rest under the high altar. Pala d'Oro: Open daily, Apr to Sep 9.45am-5pm, rest of year 9.45am-4pm. €2. ☎ 041 52 25 205; www.chorus-ve.org

The mosaic decoration depicts the New Testament, starting with the dome of the apse with Christ as Pantocrator (ruler of all) and ending with the Last Judgement in the area above the atrium. Near the entrance, the Arch of the Apocalypse illustrates the visions described in the gospel of St John. The dome nearest the doorway is dedicated to Pentecost. As one approaches the central dome, the west arch presents a synthesis of the Passion and Death of Christ. The south arch opening onto the south transept depicts the Temptation of Christ and His Entry into Jerusalem, the Last Supper and the Washing of the Feet. In the centre is the Dome of the Ascension depicting the Apostles, the Virgin, the Virtues and the Beatitudes. Christ in Benediction dominates the scene. The Presbytery Dome is dedicated to the Season of Advent. The mosaics on the north arch giving onto the north transept, are after cartoons by Tintoretto (St Michael, Last Supper and Marriage at Cana) and Veronese (Healing of the Leper). The Dome of St John the Evangelist in the left transept illustrates the Sermon on the Mount and scenes from the Life of St John the Evangelist.

The south transept gives access to the **treasury★** which contains a collection of religious objects and ornaments which came into Venice's possession after the conquest of Constantinople. Open daily, Apr to Sep 9.45am-5pm, rest of year 9.45am-4pm €2.50 041 52 22 205; www.chorus-ve.org

Campanile★★ – For information on hours ☎ 041 52 24 064; www.chorus-ve.org

The bell tower (99m 325ft high) which dominates the square is the symbol of Venice. It is a careful reconstruction of the 15C campanile which collapsed in 1902. The **panorama★★** from the top extends from the Giudecca Canal to the Grand Canal across a sea of roofs and beyond, to the islands in the lagoon.

At the base of the campanile is the **Loggetta Sansoviniana**: statues of Minerva, Apollo, Mercury and Peace adorn the niches. The terrace is enclosed by a balustrade punctuated by a 17C gate.

Palazzo Ducale★★★

(♿) Open daily, Apr to Oct 9am-7pm (ticket office closes 5.30pm), rest of year 9am-5pm (ticket office closes 3.30pm). Closed 1 Jan, 25 Dec. ☎ 041 52 24 951.

The palace was a symbol of Venetian power and glory, and was the residence of the doges and the seat of government and the law courts as well as being a prison. It was built in the 12C but was completely transformed between the end of the 13C and the 16C.

A pretty, geometric pattern in white and pink marble lends great charm to the two **façades**. The groups at the corners of the palace represent, from left to right, the *Judgement of Solomon* (probably by Bartolomeo Bon), *Adam and Eve*, and *Noah's Drunkenness* (14C-15C Gothic sculptures). The small loggia on the first floor is a delicate structure with quatrefoil motifs. The main entrance is the **Porta della Carta★★**, so called perhaps because of the scribes who worked there or the archives kept inside. It is in the Flamboyant-Gothic style (1442) and has on its tympanum a Lion of St Mark before which kneels Doge Foscari (19C copy). The gateway leads into the Porticato Foscari; directly opposite is the **Scala dei Giganti** (Giants' Staircase) dominated by statues of Mars and Neptune by Sansovino.

Interior – Start at the top of Sansovino's **Scala d'Oro** (Golden Staircase) and pass through a suite of rooms as follows: the **Sala delle Quattro Porte** (Room of the Four Doors) where the ambassadors waited for their audience with the doge; an antechamber, the **Sala dell'Antecollegio**, for diplomatic missions and delegations; the **Sala del Collegio** where the doge presided over meetings; the Senate Chamber, **Sala del Senato or "dei Pregadi"**, where the members of the Senate submitted their written request to participate in the meetings. The **Sala del Consiglio dei Dieci** (Chamber of the Council of Ten) is where met the powerful magistrates who used the secret police and spies to safeguard the institutions. Beyond the **Sala della Bussola**, the waiting-room for those awaiting interrogation and the armoury (Armeria) is the **Sala del Maggior Consiglio** (Grand Council Chamber). In this vast room (1 300m² – 14 000sq ft) sat the legislative body which appointed all public officials; here also was conducted the constitutional election of the new doge. In the chamber hang paintings and portraits of 76 doges as well as Tintoretto's *Paradise*. Proceed to the **Sala dello Scrutinio** (Ballot Chamber) where the counting of the votes took place; the **Prigione Nuove** (new prisons) and the Bridge of Sighs (Ponte dei Sospiri). Further along are the Censors' Chamber **(Sala dei Censori),** the seat of the judiciary, and the Sala dell'Avogaria – the *avogadori* were lawyers appointed by the state whose duty was to ensure that the law was obeyed.

Ponte dei Sospiri★★

The Bridge of Sighs connects the Doges' Palace with the prisons. It was built in the 16C-17C and owes its name to romantic literary notions which held that the prisoners would suffer their final torment at the enchanting view of Venice from the window.

Torre dell'Orologio

Closed for restoration at time of publication. For information call ☎041 52 24 951.
At the top of the Clock Tower, which dates from the late 15C, are the famous Moors *(Mori)*, a pair of giant bronze jacks, which strike the hours.

Museo Correr★★

(&) *Open daily, Apr to Oct 9am-7pm (ticket office closes 5.30pm), rest of year 9am-5pm (ticket office closes 3.30pm). Closed 1 Jan, 25 Dec. €9.50. ☎ 041 52 25 625.*
Next to the Ara Napoleonica which bounds the square to the west is a museum which traces the 1 000 year-old history of the city: paintings, sculpture and artefacts.

Libreria Sansoviniana★

This noble and harmonious building was designed by Sansovino in 1553. At N° 7 is a library, **Biblioteca Nazionale Marciana**, where it is possible to view manuscripts, maps and engravings.

CANAL GRANDE★★★ (GRAND CANAL)

The Grand Canal (3.8km/2.3miles long, between 30m and 70m/100-230ft wide and, on average, 5.5m/18ft deep) takes the form of an inverted S and affords the best view of the palazzi. On the left bank you will see:

*The delicate tracery work
of the windows of a
palace on the Grand Canal*

G. Targat/MICHELIN

Palazzo Labia★★

The elegant late-18C residence of the Labia family who were Spanish merchants.

Palazzo Vendramin Calergi★

An early-16C mansion, the residence of the Codussi, where Wagner lived and died.

Ca' d'Oro★★★

Although it has lost the gilded decoration which gave it its name, the mansion retains an elegant façade in the ornate Gothic style. It houses the **Galleria Franchetti** which displays a fine *St Sebastian★* by Mantegna. *Gallery: & Open Tue-Sun 8.30am-7.15pm, Mon 8.15am-2pm (ticket office closes 30min early). Closed 1 Jan, 1 May, 25 Dec. €3.* ☎ *041 52 22 349.*

Ponte di Rialto★★

The Rialto Bridge was built by Antonio da Ponte and was opened in 1591. The present structure is the sixth version but the first one to be built of stone. It is the main crossing between the two banks. The original 12C bridge was built of wood.

Palazzo Grassi★

It was built in the 18C by Giorgio Massari and was the last great Venetian palace to be constructed before the fall of the Republic. It is the venue for major exhibitions. On the right bank are:

Ca' Pesaro★

The palace built by Longhena has an unusual ground floor with diamond-pointed rustication. It is the home of the **Museo d'Arte Orientale** (Museum of Oriental Art) and the **Galleria Internazionale di Arte Moderna** (International Gallery of Modern Art). *Museo di Arte Orientale: Open daily, 8.15am-2pm (ticket office closes 1.30pm). Closed 1 Jan, 1 May, 25 Dec. €2.07; €9.30 including Galleria Accademia, Galleria Franchetti at Cà D'Oro; €4.13including Galleria Franchetti at Cà D'Oro.* ☎ *041 52 41 173.*

Gallery: Closed for restoration at time of publication.

Ca' Rezzonico★★

This was the last palace designed by Longhena which was completed by Massari. It houses the **Museo del Settecento Veneziano** (Museum of 18C Venice). *(&) Apr to Oct 10am-6pm, rest of year 10am-5pm. Closed Tue; 1 Jan, 1 May, 25 Dec. €6.50.* ☎ *041 24 10 100.*

Ca' Dario★

The small late-15C palazzo is embellished with polychrome marble decoration. It has gained a sinister reputation owing to the death in suspicious circumstances of several of its owners.

Worth a Visit

VENICE ON CANVAS

Gallerie dell'Accademia★★★

Open Tue-Sun 8.30am-7.15pm, Mon 8.15am-2pm. Closed 1 Jan, 1 May, 25 Dec. €6.50 ☎ *041 52 00 345.*

The Academy presents the most important collection of Venetian art from the 14C to the 18C. Masterpieces include a *Madonna enthroned* and the *Virgin and Child between St Catherine and Mary Magdalene* by Giovanni Bellini; the *Calling of the Sons of Zebedee* by Marco Basaiti; *St George* by Andrea Mantegna; *The Tempest* by Giorgione, the crystallisation of a state of mind rather than the representation of a specific moment; a *Portrait of a young gentleman in his study* by Lorenzo Lotto, which suggests that the sitter is distracted from his book by a thought or memory; an impressive but sinister *Pietà* by Titian; *Christ in the House of Levi* by Veronese; the cycle of luminous paintings of the *Miracles of the Relics of the True Cross* by Gentile Bellini and Carpaccio. The latter also painted the colourful and magical series of canvases relating the *Story of St Ursula*.

CHURCHES

Santa Maria della Salute★★

The church, dedicated to St Mary of Salvation, was built in the 17C to fulfil a vow by the Venetians and marking the end of a plague epidemic (1630). The white church designed by Longhena is a distinctive landmark with its modillions and concentric volutes (known as *orrechioni* – big ears). In the sacristy hangs a *Wedding at Cana* by Tintoretto in which the artist has included himself as the first Apostle on the left.

San Giorgio Maggiore★

The church on the island of San Giorgio, was designed by Palladio. The top of the tall **campanile** affords the finest **view★★★** of Venice. In the presbytery (sanctuary) hang two large paintings by Tintoretto, the *Last Supper* and the *Harvest of Manna*. *Campanile: (& – only if accompanied.) Ascent daily, 9.30am-12.30pm and 2.30pm to 30min before sunset; Sun and hols closed 11am-noon. €3 (with lift). Accommodation available. For information and reservations ☎ 041 52 27 827.*

San Zanipòlo★★

The square in which stands an **equestrian statue★★** of the mercenary leader Bartolomeo **Colleoni** by Verrocchio is flanked by the deceptive perspective of the **Scuola Grande di San Marco★** to one side, and is dominated by the Gothic church of Santi Giovanni e Paolo, dedicated to St John and St Paul (in the Venetian dialect Zanipòlo is a contraction of the two names). The grandiose and solemn church is a fitting setting as the burial place for the doges and is lit by the brightly coloured stained-glass windows in the right transept.

The view from Piazza San Marco: San Giorgio Maggiore

R. Mattes/MICHELIN

I Frari★★★

Open all year 9am (1pm Sun and public holidays)-6pm. €1.55. Chorus Associazione Chiese di Venezia ☎ 041 27 50 462, www.chorus-ve.org

This great Franciscan church – its name is derived from the abbreviation of Fra(ti Mino)ri – can be compared to San Zanipòlo on account of its imposing appearance and its funerary monuments. The focal point of the perspective is an **Assumption of the Virgin** by Titian in the main chapel, Cappella Maggiore.

San Zaccaria★★

The Renaissance-Gothic Church of St Zachary has a tall white façade with its three tiers of round-headed windows; it is visible from the windows of the Palazzo Ducale. The interior is covered with paintings; the most important is Giovanni Bellini's **Sacra Conversazione**, a work of great sensitivity.

San Sebastiano★★

This church has frescoes by Veronese depicting the saint to which it is dedicated.

THE VENETIAN SCUOLE

Instituted during the Middle Ages, the *scuole* (literally meaning schools) were lay guilds drawn from the middle classes which were active in all aspects of life, be it devotional, charitable or professional, until the fall of the Republic. Each school had its own patron saint and *mariegola*, a rule book and constitution of the guild. In the 15C the *scuole* were housed in magnificent palaces with their interiors decorated by famous artists.

To appreciate the rich artistic heritage of the guilds, visit the **Scuola di San Rocco★★★**, decorated with scenes from the Old and New Testaments by Tintoretto, and the **Scuola di San Giorgio degli Schiavoni★★★**, a perfect setting for the exquisite paintings in warm colours by Carpaccio relating the lives of St George, St Tryphon and St Jerome. *S. Rocco: (&) Open daily, 28 Mar to 2 Nov 9am-5.30pm (ticket office closes 5pm), rest of year 10am-4pm (ticket office closes 3.30pm). Closed 1 Jan, Easter, 25 Dec. €5.16. No charge 16 Aug (feast of St. Rocco). ☎ 041 52 34 864; www.sanrocco.it S. Giorgio degli Schiavoni: & Open Tue-Sun (except pm), Apr to Oct 9.30am-12.30pm and 3.30-6.30pm, rest of year 10am-12.30pm and 3-6pm. Closed Sun pm, Mon, hols. €3. ☎ 041 52 28 828.*

OTHER AREAS AND MUSEUMS OF VENICE

Arsenale★
There was a dockyard in Venice as early as 1104 when the crusades stimulated shipbuilding activity. The Arsenal is enclosed by a medieval wall punctuated by towers and has two entrances: the land gateway surmounted by lions from Ancient Greece, and the watergate marked by two towers through which passes the *vaporetto*.

Ghetto★★
The Jewish quarter (ghetto) is a hauntingly beautiful and secret corner of the Canneregio district close to the bustling Strada Nuova. It was the first Jewish quarter to be differentiated as such in Western Europe. In the Venetian dialect the term *geto* referred to a local mortar foundry. The g, normally pronounced soft (as in George) was hardened by the first Jews who came from Germany. The term ghetto now evokes the persecutions endured by the Jewish people. A museum, the Museo Ebraico and synagogues, **sinagoghe** are open to visitors.

Giudecca
Giudecca Island offers visitors a simple, quiet charm as well as a glorious view of Venice. The Palladian church of **Il Redentore★**, *(Fondamenta S. Giacomo)* was built like Santa Maria della Salute after the 1576 plague. On the third Sunday in July the church celebrates the Feast of the Redeemer which ends with a spectacular fireworks display.

Collezione Peggy Guggenheim★
Open daily except Tue, 10am-6pm (10pm Apr to Oct). Closed 25 Dec. €8. ☎ 041 24 05 411; www.guggenheim-venice.it
An 18C palazzo where the American Peggy Guggenheim lived from the end of the Second World War until her death, is the setting for an interesting collection of paintings and sculpture by some of the best 20C artists.

Fondazione Querini-Stampalia★
(&) *Open Tue-Thu, 10am-6pm, Fri-Sat 10am-10pm. Closed Mon, Sun and hols €6. ☎ 041 27 11 411; www.provincia.venezia.it/querini*
The museum is a must for those interested in the Venice of old. There is a charming series of **panels★★** by Pietro Longhi dedicated to the sacraments and to the hunt.

Excursions

Lido○○
Venice's seaside resort on the Adriatic has a slightly decadent air. It has a casino, which is one of the few in Italy, and hosts a prestigious annual film festival.

Murano★★
By the end of the 13C, the threat of devastating fire was constant in Venice with its wooden buildings and the Grand Council decided to move the glassworks away from the city to Murano. It became known as the glassmaking island and a museum, **Museo di Arte Vetraria★**, displays a unique collection of glassware. The furnaces, the shouts of the vendors coaxing visitors into the glassware shops, should not detract from the artistic atmosphere of the island. The apse of the fine basilica, **Santi Maria e Donato★★**, is a masterpiece of 12C Veneto-Byzantine art and the mosaic floor★★ recalls that of St Mark's. *Museo di Arte Vetraria (&) Open daily except Wed, Apr to Oct 10am-5pm, rest of year 10am-4pm. Closed 1 Jan, 1 May, 25 Dec. €4. ☎ 041 73 95 86.*

Burano★★
This is the most colourful of the islands in the lagoon. At the doors and windows of the brightly painted houses the women are engaged in lace-making.

Torcello★★
It is almost a ghost island where only the stones speak of its glorious past. In 639 the inhabitants of Altinum fleeing from the Lombards settled on the island and built a church. Torcello became a bishopric. The 10C witnessed the glorious ascent of Venice whose power extended over the lagoon, but an aura of gloom pervaded the island as malaria decimated the population. *Basilica: Open daily, summer 10.30am-5.30pm, rest of year 10am-5pm. €3. ☎ 041 27 02 464.*

Verona★★★

Verona stands on the banks of the Adige against a hilly backdrop. It is the second most important art centre in the Veneto region after Venice. The fashionable Piazza Bra is linked by Via Mazzini to the heart of the old town.

Location

Population 255 268 – Michelin maps 428, 429 F 14-15 – Town plan in the Michelin Atlas Italy. Verona is very well situated with easy access to Venice (take A 4) and the Brenner transalpine pass (take A 22). Also nearby are Lake Garda and the Euganean Hills (Colli Euganei). *🛈 Via degli Alpini 9, ☎ 045 80 68 580; Stazione Porta Nuova, ☎ 045 80 00 861; Villafranca airport, ☎ 045 86 19 163.*

Surrounding area: see BRESCIA, Regione dei LAGHI, MANTOVA, VICENZA.

Bird's-eye view of Verona

Background

This Roman colony under the Empire was coveted by the Ostrogoths, Lombards and Franks. The town reached the peak of its glory under the **Scaligers** who governed for Holy Roman Emperor from 1260 to 1387. Then it passed to the Visconti of Milan before submitting to Venetian rule from 1405. Verona was occupied by the Austrians in 1814 and united as part of the Veneto with Italy in 1866.

> **ROMEO AND JULIET**
> The setting for this apocryphal drama was Verona in 1302 when political conflict raged...The tragic young couple immortalised by Shakespeare belonged to rival families: Romeo to the Montecchi (Montagues), who were Guelphs and supported the Pope, and Juliet to the Capuleti (Capulets), who were Ghibellines and supported the Emperor.

Pisanello – Artists of the Veronese school were influenced by Northern art from the Rhine Valley and they developed a Gothic art which combined flowing lines with a meticulous attention to detail. **Antonio Pisanello** (c 1395-c 1450), a great traveller, active painter, prodigious medal-maker and enthusiastic draughtsman, was the greatest exponent of this school. His painting, with soft colours, meticulous details and flowing lines, was reminiscent of the rapidly disappearing medieval world and heralded the realism typical of the Renaissance.

Walking About

Our route takes you through the prettiest streets and squares in Verona, and into its churches and theatres. Set off from Piazza delle Erbe.

Piazza delle Erbe★★

The Square of Herbs was the former Roman forum and it is today attractive and lively, especially on market day. In line, down the middle of the square, stand the market column; the *capitello* (a rostrum from which decrees and sentences were

Directory

WHERE TO EAT

• Budget

La Stueta – *Via Redentore 4/B* – ☎ *045 80 32 462 – Closed Mon, Tue lunchtime, 7-14 Jan, 4-25 Jul – €21/25.* A reasonably priced trattoria not far from the Roman amphitheatre. Traditional decor and cooking. Polenta lovers will not be disappointed.

San Basilio alla Pergola – *Via Pisano 9* – ☎ *045 52 04 75 – Closed 1-15 Jan, 14-21 Sep – €21/31.* With its rustic-style dining rooms and splendid wooden floors, there is a pleasant, country feel to this restaurant. Complementing the ambience is the chef's traditional but imaginative cooking. Offers good value for money.

• Moderate

Ciccarelli – *Via Mantovana 171, Località Madonna di Dossobuono – 8km/5mi southwest of Verona on S 62 in the direction of Mantua* – ☎ *045 95 39 86 – Closed Fri evening and Sat, 3-16 Aug – 🖻 – €25/31.* It almost goes without saying that the dishes dones best by this very traditional trattoria are roast and boiled meats (accompanied by a wide selection of cooked or raw vegetables). The puddings are all home-made. If you are on your own you may have to share a table.

WHERE TO STAY

It is worth noting that during trade fairs and exhibitions the hotels tend to put their prices up. Do enquire about this when you make your booking.

• Moderate

Cavour – *Vicolo Chiodo 4* – ☎ *045 59 01 66 – Fax 045 59 05 08 – Closed 9 Jan-9 Feb – 🖻 🖻 – 22 rm €73/117 – ☟ €9.* The main benefit of this hotel is its quiet, central location. Simple rooms with modern furnishings (some have exposed beamed ceilings). In fact, you could quite happily stay in your room and listen to opera were it not such a magical experience going to the Arena.

Hotel Torcolo – *Vicolo Listone 3* – ☎ *045 80 07 512 – Fax 045 80 04 058 – Closed 7 Jan-8 Feb – 🖻 – 19 rm €70/99 – ☟ €10.30.* Having trouble finding a decent hotel in the centre without facing financial ruin? Look no further ... and the staff are keen to please. Pleasant rooms (some with a slightly retro feel). Breakfast served in your room or, when possible, outside.

EVENTS AND FESTIVALS

The opera and theatre summer seasons both draw large crowds.

---

proclaimed) of the 16C governors *(podestà)*; the fountain known as the Verona Madonna, with a Roman statue symbolising the town; and a Venetian column surmounted by the winged Lion of St Mark (1523).

Palaces and old houses, some with pink marble columns and frescoes, make an attractive framework round the square: on the north side is the Baroque **Palazzo Maffei**.

In Via Cappello (N° 23) is the **Casa di Giulietta** (Juliet's House); in fact it is a Gothic palace which is said to have belonged to the Capulet family; the famous balcony is in the inner courtyard. *Open Tue-Sun 8.30am-7.30pm, Mon 1.30-7.30pm (ticket office closes 6.45pm). €3.10.* ☎ *045 80 34 303.*

Piazza dei Signori★★

Take Via della Costa to reach this elegant square which resembles an open-air drawing-room. On the right is the 12C **Palazzo del Comune** (Town Hall), also known as the Palazzo della Ragione dominated by the **Torre dei Lamberti**, a tower built of brick and stone and with an octagonal upper storey. This building is connected by an arch with the **Palazzo dei Tribunali** (Law Courts), formerly the Palazzo del Capitano (Governor's Residence) which is also flanked by a massive brick tower, Torrione Scaligero. The **Loggia del Consiglio** on the opposite side is an elegant edifice in the Venetian-Renaissance style.

At the far end of the square, the late-13C **Palazzo del Governo** with its machicolations and fine Classical doorway (1533) by Sammicheli was initially a Scaliger residence before it became that of the Venetian Governors.

Arche Scaligere★★

The Scaliger built their tombs between their palace and their church. The sarcophagi bear the arms of the family, with the symbolic ladder *(scala)*.

The elegant Gothic mausolea are surrounded by marble balustrades and wrought-iron rails, and are decorated with carvings of religious scenes and statues of saints in niches. Over the door of the Romanesque church of **Santa Maria Antica** is the tomb of the popular Cangrande I (d 1329) with his equestrian statue above *(the original is in the Castelvecchio Museum).*

Duomo★

The cathedral has a 12C Romanesque chancel, a Gothic nave and a Classical-style tower. The remarkable main doorway in the Lombard-Romanesque style is adorned with sculptures and low reliefs by Maestro Nicolò. The interior has fine pink marble pillars. The altarpiece *(first altar on the left)* is decorated with an *Assumption* by Titian. The marble chancel screen is by Sammicheli (16C). The canons' quarters are pleasant to walk through.

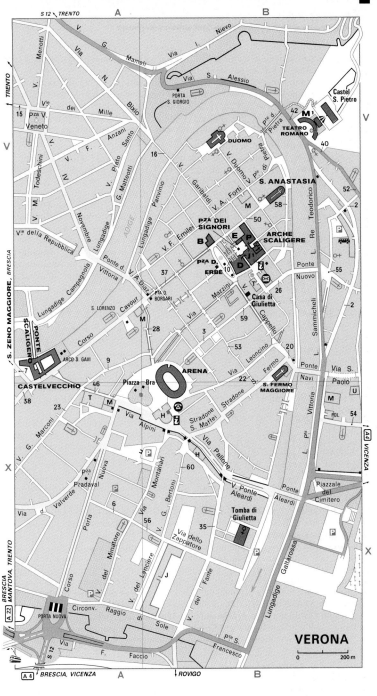

Worth a Visit

Arena★★
   Open Tue-Sun 9am-7pm, Mon 1.45-7.30pm (during opera season, 9am-3pm and open Mon). Closed Mon. €3.10. ☎ 045 8003 204.

This amphitheatre, among the largest in the Roman world, could accommodate 25 000 spectators with its 44 tiers of seats. It is built of blocks of pink marble, flint and brick; this indicates that it probably dates from the late 1C. In summer it is the venue for a prestigious opera season. From the topmost row there is a good **panorama★★** of the town in its hilly setting, which on a clear day reaches as far as the Alps.

Castelvecchio and Ponte Scaligero★★
This splendid fortified complex was built in 1354 by Cangrande II Scaliger. The castle itself is divided into two parts separated by a passageway guarded by a keep.

The castle contains the **Museo d'Arte★★** created by the architect Carlo Scarpa. The **collection** shows the development of Veronese art from the 12C to 16C and its links with Venice and the International Gothic *(see Index)*. There are frescoes by local artists and canvases by Stefano da Verona, Pisanello, Giambono, Carlo Crivelli (splendid *Madonna of the Passion*), Mantegna and Carpaccio as well as the Bellinis. The rooms on the upper floor contain works from the Renaissance period by Veronese artists: Morone, Liberale da Verona *(Virgin with a Goldfinch)*, Girolamo dai Libri and Veronese. There are also some Venetian works by Tintoretto, Guardi, Tiepolo and Longhi. Also on display are arms, jewellery and sculpture. *Museum: Open Tue-Sun 8.30am-7.30pm, Mon 1.45-7.30pm. Closed 1 Jan, 25-26 Dec. €3.10. No charge 1st Sun in month. ☎ 045 59 47 34.*

Chiesa di San Zeno Maggiore★★
Access via Largo D. Bosco. Plan of the built-up area in the Michelin Atlas Italy.

St Zeno is one of the finest Romanesque churches in northern Italy. It was built on the basilical plan in the Lombard style in the 12C. The façade is decorated with Lombard bands and arcading; the side walls and campanile have alternate brick and stone courses. In the entrance porch resting on two lions, there are admirable bronze **doors★★★** (11C-12C) with scenes from the Old and New Testaments. On either side are low reliefs by the master sculptors Nicolò and Guglielmo (12C). On the tympanum of the doorway is a statue of St Zeno, patron saint of Verona.

The imposing interior has a lofty, bare nave with a cradle roof flanked by aisles with shallow roofing. On the high altar is a splendid **triptych★★** (1459), a good example of Mantegna's style characterised by precise draughtsmanship and rich ornamentation. There are 14C statues on the chancel screen and a curious polychrome statue of St Zeno laughing in the north apse.

To the north of the church are small Romanesque cloisters.

Chiesa di Sant'Anastasia★
Open Mar to Oct, Mon-Sat 9am-6pm, Sun and hols 1-6pm; rest of year Sat 10am-5pm, Sun and hols 1-5pm. €2. For information contact Associazione Chiese Vive ☎ 045 59 28 13; www.veronatuttintorno.it

This church was begun at the end of the 13C and completed in the 15C. The campanile is remarkable and the façade is pierced with a 14C double doorway adorned with frescoes and sculpture. The lofty interior contains several masterpieces: four **figures of the Apostles** by Michele da Verona; Pisanello's famous fresco *(above the Pellegrini Chapel, to the right of the high altar)* of **St George delivering the Princess of Trebizond★★** (1436), which has an almost surreal combination of realistic precision and Gothic fantasy; 17 **terracottas★** by Michele da Firenze in the Cappella Pellegrini; and the fresco showing *Knights of the Cavalli family being presented to the Virgin★* (1380) by the Veronese artist, Altichiero (first chapel in the south transept).

Chiesa di San Fermo Maggiore★
The church, dedicated to St Firmanus Major, was built in the 11C-12C and remodelled at a later date. The façade is in the Romanesque and Gothic styles. The aisleless church is covered by a stepped, keel-shaped roof. On the left by the west door the Brenzoni mausoleum (1430) is framed by a fresco of the *Annunciation★* by Pisanello.

Teatro romano★
Open Tue-Sun 8.30am-7.30pm, Mon 1.30-7.45pm (ticket office closes 6.45pm) During Verona summer theatre season, 9am-3pm. Closed 1 Jan, 25 Dec. €2.60. No charge 1st Sun in month. ☎ 045 80 00 360.

The Roman theatre dates from the time of Augustus but has been heavily restored. Theatrical performances are still given here. A former monastery, **Convento di San Girolamo** *(access by lift)* has the small **Museo Archeologico** and there is a lovely **view** over the town. *Museum: Open Tue-Sun 8.30am-7.30pm, Mon 1.30-7.30pm (ticket office closes 6.45pm). During Verona summer theatre season, 9am-3pm. Closed 1 Jan, 25 Dec. €2.60. No charge 1st Sun in month.*

Castel San Pietro
Take the stairway which leads off Regaste Redentore. St Peter's Castle dates back to the Visconti and the period of Venetian rule. The terraces afford splendid **views**★★ of Verona.

Tomba di Giulietta
Via del Portiere. Open Tue-Sun 8.30am-7.30pm, Mon 1.45-7.30pm (ticket office closes 45min early). Closed 1 Jan, 25-26 Dec. €2.60. ☎ *045 80 00 361.*
Juliet's tomb is in the cloisters of the church of San Francesco al Corso, where, it is said, Romeo and Juliet were married.

Versilia★

Versilia is a district with a mild climate and contrasting landscapes lying between the sea coast and the mountains, which form a natural barrier against the north wind. The gently rolling hills give way to the lush coastal plain which was formed in the Quaternary Era by the alluvium deposited by the streams tumbling down from the mountain peaks.

Along the coast is a string of superb resorts boasting fine sandy beaches (up to 100m/110yd wide), which slope gently into the sea and are ideal for families with young children. In the distance one can see the Apuan Alps which give Upper Versilia the wonderful natural resources of white and red marble and slate. In the hinterland and on the mountains Nature has the upper hand and the traditional small villages, surrounded by olive and chestnut trees, provide a contrast to the crowded coast.

The Apuan Alps have been designated a Parco Naturale which includes Camaiore, Pietrasante, Seravezza and Stazzema. The park is an ideal place for outdoor activities – rambling, climbing, gliding, pony trekking, mountain biking and pot-holing.

Location
Michelin map 430 J 12 – K12/13 – See also The Green Guide Tuscany. Versilia is easily accessible from the motorways that link Genoa to Livorno and Florence to the coast. ⋿ *Azienda di Promozione Turistica Versilia, Ufficio Informazioni, Via G. Donizetti 14, 55045 Pietrasanta (Lucca),* ☎ *0584 20 331; Viale Carducci 10, 55049 Viareggio (Lucca),* ☎ *0584 96 22 33.Surrounding area: see LUCCA, PISA.*

Tour

FROM QUARRY TO QUAYSIDE
50km/30mi. Allow half a day.

Cave di Carrara
The wild countryside and the gigantic nature of the quarrying operations afford a spectacular sight. The impressive quarries, **Cave dei Fantiscritti**★★ *(5km/3mi northeast)* in a wild site, and the **Cave di Colonnata**★ *(8.5km/5mi east)* in a greener setting, are both actively worked and regularly despatch quantities of marble *(marmo).* **Marina di Carrara** *(7km/4mi southwest)* is the main port, where marble blocks are stacked high.

Marina di Massa and Marina di Carrara
A somewhat deserted stretch of coast precedes these two resorts, which have a number of fine turn-of-the-century buildings. Between them is the harbour from which marble is exported, with huge marble warehouses on the quayside.

Forte dei Marmi≙≙≙
This particularly elegant resort, which is set deep in a pine forest, is popular with artists and the Italian jet set. The beach has regular rows of delightful little cabins painted different colours. To the north the mountains of Liguria turn west towards the coast and plunge into the sea, marking the end of the gentle Versilian coastline.

Marina di Pietrasanta≙≙
Like Lido di Camaiore, this part of the shoreline, which includes the towns of Focette, Motrone, Tonfano and Fiumetto, is named after the village situated inland at the foot of the mountains.
The seaside resort has a long beach (over 5km/3mi), delightful paths through the pine woods, ideal for walking or cycling, and a wide range of sports amenities. There is also excellent nightlife.

Directory

WHERE TO EAT

• Budget

Rino – *Via della Chiesa 8 – 55040 Bargecchia – 4km/2.5mi south of Camaiore –* ☎ *0584 95 40 00 – Closed Tue (Oct-Jun) –* €*13/22.* Right in the heart of the village is a very traditional establishment (both in terms of decor and cuisine). Specialities include fresh pasta and grilled meats. There is a lovely garden where meals are served in summer. Accommodation also available: simple rooms next to the restaurant.

Mokambo – *Viale della Repubblica 4 – 55042 Forte dei Marmi –* ☎ *0584 89 446 – Closed Wed –* 🍴 ✗ – €*13/31 + 10% service charge.* After a day in the sun by the sea, this is the ideal spot for a quick pizza, a sandwich or even a proper meal (fish of course!). With its cheerful ambience and spacious surroundings, this place is popular with families and groups of youngsters.

Osteria alla Giudea – *Via Barsanti 4 – 55045 Pietrasanta –* ☎ *0584 71 514 – Closed Mon –* 🍴 *– Book –* €*17.50/22.50 + 10% service charge.* The proprietors are also the chefs here – you will see them hard at work in the kitchen which is on show. With its marble and wrought-iron tables there is a French bistro feel to the place, but the cooking is firmly rooted in the traditions of the region. The dishes of the day are written up on the blackboard near the entrance.

• Moderate

Il Centro Storico – *Via Cesare Battisti 66 – 55041 Camaiore –* ☎ *0584 98 97 86 – Closed Mon –* €*23/34.* A simple trattoria with a family atmosphere. Authentic regional cooking with truffles and mushrooms serving as the inspiration for many of the dishes. Accommodation also available: the rooms are well kept.

Il Puntodivino – *Via Mazzini 229 – 55049 Viareggio –* ☎ *0584 31 046 – Closed lunchtime from 15 Jul to 31 Aug, 7-28 Jan –* 🍴 *–* €*23.24/31.* A great place for a quick lunch – the dishes of the day are written up on a blackboard near the entrance. In the evening, there is more choice and you can sample several dishes if you choose the *menu degustazione.* Good selection of wines which you can also buy. Young, trendy ambience.

Trattoria al Porto – *Via Coppino 319 – 55049 Viareggio –* ☎ *0584 38 38 78 – Closed Sun and Mon lunchtime, 15 Dec-15 Jan –* 🍴 *– Book –* €*41/46.* You will have to book several days in advance if you want to dine here – this establishment is always busy! Jovial, lively atmosphere (the menu will be read out to you in a rather flamboyant manner). Specialises in seafood; the dishes prepared with the freshest of ingredients.

WHERE TO STAY

• Budget

Hotel Grande Italia – *Via Torino 5, Tonfano – 55044 Marina di Pietrasanta –* ☎ *0584 20 046 – Fax 0584 24 350 – Closed 20 Sep-May –* ✗ 🅿 *– 23 rm* €*41/73 –* ⌂ €*7 – Restaurant* €*16/21.* Dating back to the early 20C this hotel remains largely unchanged and would appeal to retro enthusiasts. Simple surroundings and a family atmosphere. The lovely pinewood which surrounds the hotel enhances the sense of peace and quiet.

• Moderate

Albergo Dei Cantieri – *Via Indipendenza 72 – 55049 Viareggio –* ☎ *0584 38 81 12 – Fax 0584 38 85 61 – Closed 20-30 Nov –* ✗ *– 7 rm* €*50/85* ⌂. At the edge of the pinewood, south of the town, are two pavilions (in the grounds of a patrician villa) which have been tastefully restored. Weather permitting, breakfast is served in the gazebo in the middle of the garden. The rooms and the public areas are well kept.

Hotel Sylvia – *Via Manfredi 15 – 55043 Lido di Camaiore –* ☎ *0584 61 79 94 – Fax 0584 61 79 94 – Closed Oct-Mar –* 🅿 *– 21 rm* €*51.64/63.13 –* ⌂ €*7.75.* A simple, very pleasant family pensione which is surrounded by a lovely garden. Quiet location, not far from the sea. Light, airy rooms. Facilities include a reading room (on the ground floor) for the use of guests. Good, home cooking.

Hotel Arcangelo – *Via Carrara 23 – 55049 Viareggio –* ☎ *0584 47 123 – Fax 0584 47 314 – Closed Oct-Easter – 19 rm* €*51.65/64.56 –* ⌂ €*6.20 – Restaurant* €*18/21.* This hotel, housed in what was once a private dwelling, benefits from a peaceful setting (despite the location in a street off the seafront). Lovely garden at the back. 1950s-style rooms (simple) and public areas (well kept). Friendly staff.

Hotel Pardini – *Viale Carducci 14 – 55049 Viareggio –* ☎ *0584 96 13 79 – Fax 0584 96 16 79 – hotelpardini@virgilio.it – Closed 3 weeks in Nov –* ♿ *– 14 rm* €*67.14/92.96 –* ⌂ €*7.75.* A family-run hotel on the main drag, within easy reach of restaurants, shops and bathing areas. Pleasant ambience and peaceful atmosphere. Spacious rooms, with simple, modern furnishings. Attentive, courteous service.

TAKING A BREAK

Pasticceria Bar Fappani – *Viale Marconi, Lungomare – 55049 Viareggio –* ☎ *0584 96 25 82 – Tue-Sun 8am-midnight.* With its large terrace area overlooking the sea, this is a good spot to indulge any yearnings for something sweet. A family-run establishment since 1921, it has a relaxing, cosy atmosphere.

GOING OUT

Discotheques in Versilia – *Seafront between Lido di Camaiore and Forte dei Marmi – 55042 Forte dei Marmi.* Every night the seafront is transformed into one long dance hall. From Viareggio to Forte dei Marmi, there is one discotheque after another – and they are all very different. It was actually La Bussola, which opened back in 1970, that established Versilia's reputation for its lively nightlife. Generally speaking the younger generation (aged between 25 and

30) head for the Seven Apples (which has a swimming pool) or the Capannina which organises theme nights. The local youth tend to hang out at the Faruck, the Agorà and the Midho' (where the Kupido annex is given over to tecno music). Last of all, as you head out of Forte dei Marmi, there is the Canniccia, which is popular with the over-30s: it has four dance floors and a large garden.

Agorà – *Viale Cristoforo Colombo 666 – 55043 Lido di Camaiore –* ☎ *0584 61 04 88 – Wed-Thu and Sat 9pm-4am.*

Faruk – *Viale Roma 53/55, Tonfano – 55044 Marina di Pietrasanta –* ☎ *0584 21 57 8/ 05 84 21 744 –Thu-Sat midnight-4am.*

La Bussola – *Viale Roma 44, Focette – 55044 Marina di Pietrasanta –* ☎ *0584 22 737 – Thu-Sun 10pm-4am.*

La Canniccia – *Via Unità d'Italia 1, exit on A 12 for Versilia – 55044 Marina di Pietrasanta –* ☎ *0584 23 225/ 0584 74 56 85 – Fri-Sun 11pm-4.30am.*

La Capannina – *Viale della Repubblica 18 – 55042 Forte dei Marmi –* ☎ *0584 80 169 – Fri-Sat 5.30pm-5am.*

Midho' and Kupido – *Viale Achille Franceschi 12 – 55042 Forte dei Marmi –* ☎ *0584 89 114 – Fri-Sat and Tue 11.30pm-4am.*

Seven Apples – *Viale Roma 109, Focette – 55044 Marina di Pietrasanta –* ☎ *0584 20 458/ 0584 22 433 – www.geniusnet.it/seven – Fri-Sun 8.30pm-4am.*

Shopping

Laboratorio di Cartapesta – *Via Morandi – 55049 Viareggio – Guided tours of the* papier-mâché *workshops. Information in Piazza Mazzini.*

The carnival in Viareggio is internationally famous for the procession of allegorical papier-mâché floats (some of them very large). Visitors are welcome to go and see how they are made.

On the outskirts of Marina di Pietrasanta, on the other bank of the Fiumetto, set slightly back from the beach, is **Versiliana Park** (about 80ha/200 acres of wood-land). The poet Gabriele D'Annunzio was a regular visitor to the early-20C house. The park is traversed by pleasant paths and in summer it plays host to various cultural events.

Lido di Camaiore⊛⊛

Lido di Camaiore is more modern and more of a family resort than Viareggio, its prestigious neighbour, but they are so close that they tend to run into one another. It has the same fine sandy beach, the same pine woods and a delightful esplanade along the front.

The coast road then becomes more open and the vegetation more lush. The hotels are spaced further apart and are set about with vegetation. There is a splendid view of the Apuan Alps inland.

Viareggio⊛⊛

This fashionable seaside resort, on the Tyrrhenian Coast, has some lovely beaches and plenty of amenities for holidaymakers. As the rebuilding of Viale Regina Margherita and its prolongation, Viale Guglielmo Marconi, was accomplished in a short time, the two streets provide fine examples of the architectural style of the late 1920s, somewhere between Art Nouveau and Art Deco, such as the splendid Gran Caffè Margherita with high coloured Baroque cupola. At **Torre del Lago Puccini** *(5km/3mi to the southeast)* the composer Puccini wrote the majority of his operas. The **Villa Puccini** contains the tomb and other mementoes of Puccini. *Villa:* (&) *Open daily except Mon, May to Sep 10am-12.30pm and 3-6.30pm, Mar and Apr 10am-12.30pm and 3-5.30pm, rest of year 10am-12.30pm and 2.30-5pm. Closed Nov, 25 Dec. €5; 29 Nov no charge.* ☎ *0584 34 14 45; www.giacomopuccini.it*

The stylish Viale Regina Margherita in Viareggio

Massaciuccoli★

Head for the Via Aurelia (SS 1) going north towards Viareggio; turn left to Torre del Lago.
This road crosses part of the **Migliarino-San Rossore-Massaciuccoli** Country Park
including the lake (average depth 1.60m/5ft), the Massaciuccoli Marshes and all
that remains of the ancient Pisan Forest which used to stretch uninterrupted from
La Spezia (north) to Castiglioncello (south of Livorno). The lake is well stocked
with fish and turtles. Over 250 species of birds live and nest there or visit the lake
during migration; some of the species are rare. The huge area of forest in the
remainder of the park is indicative of the large-scale planting of parasol pines from
the 16C onwards, despite the presence of other varieties.

Vicenza★★

Strategically located at the crossroads of the routes that link the Veneto with
the Trentino, the proud and noble city of Vicenza is now a busy commercial
and industrial centre. In addition to its traditional textile industry, and newer
mechanical and chemical industries, Vicenza has a reputation as a gold-
working centre.
The gastronomic speciality of Vicenza is *baccalà alla Vicentina,* salt cod with
a sauce served with slices of *polenta* (maize semolina), which is best with wine
from the Berici Mountains (Barbarano, Gambellara and Breganze).

Location

*Population 109 738 – Michelin map 429 F 16 – Town plan in the Michelin Atlas
Italy –Veneto.* Vicenza lies in a pretty setting at the foot of the Berici Mountains. The
main access road is A 4. ☐ *Piazza Matteotti 12,* ☎ *0444 32 08 54.*
Surrounding area: see LAGUNA VENETA, PADOVA, VERONA.

Background

The ancient Roman town of Vicetia became an independent city state in the 12C.
After several conflicts with the neighbouring cities of Padua and Verona, Vicenza
sought Venetian protection at the beginning of the 15C. This was a period of great
prosperity, when Vicenza counted many rich and generous art patrons among its
citizens and it was embellished with an amazing number of palaces.

Directory

WHERE TO EAT
• Budget
Al Pestello – *Contrà Santo Stefano 3 –*
☎ *0444 32 37 21 – Closed Sun, 24-30 May
and 10-30 Oct – €18/34.* Serves tasty food
in lovely surroundings – note the huge fresco
in the dining room. There is also a lovely
outdoor area. The menu, in dialect, includes
a number of traditional, local specialities.

• Moderate
Antica Osteria da Penacio – *Via Soghe 22,
località Soghe – 36023 Arcugnano
10km/6mi south of Vicenza on S 247 –
☎ 0444 27 30 81 – Closed Wed, Thu
lunchtime, 20-30 Jan, 20-30 Jul, 20-30 Oct
– ✦ €34/51.* From the outside it looks like a
rather old taverna but the interior is
surprisingly elegant. Both dining rooms are
modern in style and there is a small but well-
stocked wine cellar which adds to the
atmosphere. The cuisine is of a high
standard.

WHERE TO STAY
• Moderate
Hotel Victoria – *Strada Padana (in the
direction of Padua) 52 – 7km/4mi east of
Vicenza on SS 11 – ☎ 0444 91 22 99 – Fax
0444 91 25 70 – ☐ ◉ ♿ – 56 rm €55/62
✦. Combines reasonable prices with
comfortable surroundings – a rare thing in
Vicenza. Offers good-sized rooms and
apartments; stylewise they are somewhere
between classical and functional. Given its
situation – not far from the motorway and
yet a few minutes' from the centre – this
hotel would be a good solution for anyone
arriving by car.

• Expensive
Giardini – *Via Giuriolo 10 –
☎ 0444 32 64 58 – Fax 0444 32 64 58 –
Closed 23 Dec-3 Jan – ☐ ◉ ♿ – 17 rm
from €103.29 ☷.* Situated just a stone's
throw from the Teatro Olimpico, is this little
hotel that from the outside – Venetian villa in
style – pays homage to the great Palladio.
Inside it is comfortable with attractive,
modern rooms.

Andrea Palladio

Vicenza was given the nickname of "Venice on *terra firma*" due to an exceptionally gifted man, Andrea di Pietro, known as Palladio, who spent many years in Vicenza. The last great architect of the Renaissance, Palladio was born at Padua in 1508 and died at Vicenza in 1580. He succeeded in combining, in a supremely harmonious idiom, the precepts of ancient art with the contemporary preoccupations. Encouraged by the humanist Trissino, he made several visits to Rome to study her monuments and the work of Vitruvius, a Roman architect of the time of Augustus. He perfected the Palladian style and in 1570 published his **Treatise on Architecture**, in four volumes, which made his work famous throughout Europe.

The **Palladian style** is characterised by rigorous plans where simple and symmetrical forms predominate and by harmonious façades which combine pediments and porticoes, as at San Giorgio Maggiore in Venice *(see VENEZIA)*. Palladio was often commissioned by wealthy Venetians to build residences in the countryside around Venice. He combined architectural rhythm, noble design and, in the case of the country mansions, a great sense of situation, decoration and height, so that the villas seemed to rise like a series of new temples on the banks of the Brenta *(see Riviera del BRENTA)* or the slopes of the Berici Mountains. His pupil, Vicenzo Scamozzi (1552-1616), completed several of his master's works and carried on his style.

Worth a visit

Piazza dei Signori★★

Like St Mark's Square in Venice, it is an open-air meeting-place recalling the forum of Antiquity. As in the Piazzetta in Venice, there are two columns, here bearing effigies of the Lion of St Mark and the Redeemer.

With the lofty **Torre Bissara★**, a 12C belfry, the **Basilica★★** (1549-1617) occupies one whole side of the square. The elevation is one of Palladio's masterpieces, with two superimposed galleries in the Doric and Ionic orders, admirable for their power, proportion and purity of line. The great keel-shaped roof, destroyed by bombing, has been rebuilt. The building was not a church but a meeting-place for the Vicenzan notables. *Open Tue-Sun, Jul and Aug 9am-7pm, rest of year 9am-5pm. Closed Mon. No charge.* ☎ *0444 32 36 81; www.comune.vicenza.it*

The 15C **Monte di Pietà** (municipal pawn shop) opposite, its buildings framing the Baroque façade of the church of San Vincenzo, is adorned with frescoes. The **Loggia del Capitano★**, formerly the residence of the Venetian Governor, which stands to the left, at the corner of the Contrà del Monte, was begun to the plans of Palladio in 1571 and left unfinished. It is characterised by its colossal orders with composite capitals and its statues and stuccoes commemorating the naval victory of Lepanto *(see Index)*.

Teatro Olimpico★★

(&) *Open Tue-Sun, Jul and Aug 9am-7pm, rest of year 9am-5pm. Closed Mon.* €6.70 *including Museo Civico and Museo Archeologico;* €7.80 *including Museo Civico, Museo Archeologico and Museo del Risorgimento.* ☎ *0444 22 28 00; www.comune.vicenza.it*

This splendid building in wood and stucco was designed by Palladio in 1580 on the model of the theatres of Antiquity. The tiers of seats are laid out in a hemicycle and surmounted by a lovely **colonnade** with a balustrade crowned with statues. The **stage★★★** is one of the finest in existence with its superimposed niches, columns and statues and its amazing perspectives painted in *trompe l'œil* by Scamozzi who completed the work.

Corso Andrea Palladio★

This, the main street of Vicenza, and several neighbouring streets are embellished by many palaces designed by Palladio and his pupils. At the beginning is the **Palazzo Chiericati** *(see below)*, an imposing work by Palladio; at Nº 147 the 15C **Palazzo Da Schio** in the Venetian-Gothic style was formerly known as the Ca d'Oro (Golden House) because it was covered with frescoes with gilded backgrounds. The west front of **Palazzo Thiene** overlooking Contrà S. Gaetano Thiene was by Palladio, while the entrance front at Nº 12 Contrà Porti is Renaissance, dating from the late 15C.

The **Palazzo Porto-Barbaran** opposite is also by Palladio. At Nº 98 the **Palazzo Trissino** (1592) is one of Scamozzi's most successful works. Next is the Corso Fogazzaro, where the **Palazzo Valamarana** (1566) at Nº 16 is another work by Palladio.

Museo Civico★

On the first floor of Palazzo Chiericati. & *Open daily except Mon, July to 2 Sep 9am-7pm, rest of year 9am-5pm. Closed 1 Jan, 25 Dec.* €6.71 *including other Vicenza museums. For information* ☎ *0444 32 13 48.*

The collection of paintings includes Venetian Primitives (*The Dormition of the Virgin* by Paolo Veneziano); a *Crucifixion*★★ by Hans Memling; canvases by Bartolomeo Montagna (pupil of Giovanni Bellini), Mantegna and Carpaccio, one of the most active artists in Vicenza. There are Venetian works by Lorenzo Lotto, Veronese, Bassano, Piazzetta, Tiepolo and Tintoretto as well as Flemish works by Brueghel the Elder and Van Dyck.

Chiesa della Santa Corona

Contrà Santa Corona. The church was built in the 13C in honour of a Holy Thorn presented by St Louis, King Louis IX of France, to the Bishop of Vicenza. The nave and two aisles have pointed vaulting while the chancel is Renaissance. Works of art include: a *Baptism of Christ*★★ by Giovanni Bellini *(fifth altar on the left)* and an *Adoration of the Magi*★★ (1573) by Veronese *(third chapel on the right).* The fourth chapel on the right has a lovely coffered **ceiling**★, richly painted and adorned with gilded stucco, and a *Mary Magdalene and Saints* by Bartolomeo Montagna.

Duomo

The cathedral, built between the 14C and 16C, has an attractively colourful Gothic façade and a Renaissance east end. Inside, the lovely **polyptych**★ (1356) is by Lorenzo Veneziano.

Giardino Salvi

This garden is attractively adorned with statues and fountains. Canals run along two sides of the garden and two lovely Palladian 16C and 17C loggias are reflected in the waters.

Excursions

Villa Valmarana ai Nani★★

2km/1mi south by the Este road and then the first road to the right. Open Tue-Sun, May to Sep 10am-noon and 3-6pm; Mar and Apr, Oct and Nov, 10am-noon and 2.30-5.30pm. Closed Mon, 6 Nov to 14 Mar. €6. ☎ *0444 32 18 03.*
The villa dates from the 17C. Both the Palazzina and the Forestiera buildings were adorned with splendid **frescoes**★★★ by **Giovanni Battista (Giambattista) Tiepolo** and his son **Giovanni Domenico**.

La Rotonda★

2km/1mi southeast by the Este road and then the second road to the right. Open Tue-Sun, 10am-noon and 3-6pm (tour of interior Wed only). Closed Mon, 6 Nov to 14 Mar €6 for interior, €3 for garden ☎ *0444 32 17 93.*
The Rotonda is one of Palladio's most famous creations and the plan of Chiswick House in London was inspired by it. The gracefully proportioned square building is roofed with a dome and fronted on each side by a pedimented portico, making it look like an ancient temple.

Basilica di Monte Berico and Monti Berici★

2km/1mi south by Viale Venezia and then Viale X Giugno. As the Viale X Giugno climbs uphill, it is lined with an 18C portico and chapels. On the summit is the Baroque basilica roofed with a dome. From the esplanade there is a wide **panorama**★★ of Vicenza, the Venetian plain and the Alps. Inside, there is a *Pietà* (1500) by Bartolomeo Montagna.
From here the road runs southwards to Arcugnano and Barbarano, where one can catch occasional glimpses of former patrician villas now used as farmhouses in this attractive countryside of volcanic hills.

Montecchio Maggiore

13km/8mi southwest by S 11. The ruins of these two castles brings to mind one of Romeo and Juliet. There are good **views**★ of the Po Plain and Vicenza.
On the outskirts of Montecchio on the Tavernelle road the **Villa Cordellina-Lombardi** has one room entirely covered with **frescoes**★ by Tiepolo. *Open Apr to mid Oct. The Fri 9am-1pm, Sat Sun and hols 9am-noon and 3-6pm. Closed 16 Oct to 31 Mar €2.10* ☎ *0444 69 60 85.*

Vipiteno

STERZING

Only 15km/9mi from the Austrian border, Vipiteno is a pretty town grouped around one street lined with typical Tyrolean houses (Erker) and arcading. Vipiteno's long history began in the Bronze Age. In Roman times there was a road station named *Vipitenum* and in 1180 the town was documented as *Stercengum* (from which Sterzing derives). Vipiteno flourished between the 15C and 16C when silver and lead were mined in nearby valleys (a visit to the mines in the nearby Val Ridanna and Valle Aurina, in Predoi, will provide an insight into mining activity in the Alto Adige).

Location

Population 5 702 – Michelin map 429 B 16 – Trentino-Alto Adige. Vipiteno is the last exit off A 22, the Brennero transalpine pass. **⌂** *Piazza Città 3,* ☎ *0472 76 53 25. Surrounding area: see DOLOMITI, MERANO.*

Walking About

The 15C tower, Torre dei Dodici, cuts the street in half, the more picturesque **Città Nuova★** (New City) street lying to the south and the **Città Vecchia** (Old City) street to the north. On Via Città Nuova stands the 16C town hall.
In the square where the two streets converge stands the church of the Holy Spirit (Chiesa dello Spirito Santo), richly decorated with 15C frescoes.

Vipiteno: typical of the colourful villages in the Valle Isarco

T. Zane/MICHELIN

Excursions

Cascate di Stanghe

Take the road in the direction of Racines and then follow directions to Stanghe. Open daily, May to Jun 9.30am-5.30pm, Jul and Aug 9am-6pm, Sep and Oct 9.30am-5.30pm, rest of year by request only. €2.60. ☎ *0472 75 66 66; www.ratschings.org*
This waterfall descends a narrow gorge that, having been eroded by the water, is coloured white and green. Walking through the winding gorge is facilitated by the presence of long passageways and small wooden bridges attached to the rocks. A walk through the ravine and the wood near the town is pleasant and can be done uphill (obviously more tiring) or downhill. To vary the excursion it is possible to descend via the waterfall (leaving the car at the top where there is a cafeteria and a small chapel) and return up via footpath n° 13 which passes through meadows and affords fine views of the pastures. Whether one chooses the waterfall or footpath route, the journey time is roughly the same: about an hour to ascend and three quarters of an hour to descend.

Montecavallo

Along the Brennero road, just after Via Città Vecchia, there is a cable car to Montecavallo (alt 2 000m/6 500ft). On arrival there is a wide choice of footpaths and walks.

Viterbo*

Viterbo, still girdled by its walls, has kept its medieval aspect, notably in the San Pellegrino quarter★★, a working-class area which houses many craftsmen. Here there are typical vaulted passageways, towers and external staircases.

Location

Population 60 212 – Michelin map 430 O 18 – Lazio. Viterbo is situated 20km/12mi southeast of Lago di Bolsena. Access to A 1 is by dual carriageway. ∎ *Piazza San Carluccio,* ☎ *0761 30 47 95.*
Surrounding area: see ORVIETO.

Worth a Visit

Piazza San Lorenzo★★

This square, which occupies the site of the former Etruscan acropolis, takes one back to the Middle Ages with a 13C house on Etruscan foundations (now a chemist's), its cathedral dating from 1192 and adorned with a fine Gothic campanile, and its 13C papal palace, **Palazzo dei Papi★★** – one of the most interesting examples of medieval secular architecture in Lazio. From the Piazza Martiri d'Ungheria there is a lovely view of the piazza.

Museo Civico

Piazza F. Crispi. ♿ *Open daily except Mon, Apr to Oct 9am-7pm (6pm winter). Closed bank hols. €3.10.* ☎ *0761 34 82 76.*
The municipal museum is housed in the former monastery of Santa Maria della Verità and contains collections of Etruscan and Roman objects discovered in the area: sarcophagi and grave artefacts from the tombs. The picture gallery, on the first floor, has a terracotta by the Della Robbia as well as works by Salvator Rosa, Sebastiano del Piombo and a local painter, Pastura (15C-16C).

Excursions

Teatro Romano di Ferento★

9km/6mi north. ♿ *Open daily except Mon, 9am-1.30pm. €2.07.* ☎ *0761 32 59 29.*
The 1C Roman theatre is quite well preserved and is the most important vestige of the Ancient Ferentium, the ruins of which lie scattered over a melancholy plateau. The theatre ruins stand between the road and the Decumanus (main road) and consist of a brick back wall as well as a portico of well-dressed blocks without any mortar, and 13 tiers of seats.

Santuario della Madonna della Quercia

3km/2mi northeast. The church, dedicated to the Madonna of the Oak *(quercia),* is in the Renaissance style with a rusticated façade and tympana by Andrea della Robbia. The cloisters are part Gothic, part Renaissance.

Villa Lante di Bagnaia★★

5km/3mi northeast. (♿) Open daily, 8.30am to 1hr before sunset. Visit to Italian gardens and loggias beneath the two buildings (30min). Closed 1 Jan, 1 May, 25 Dec. €2.07 ☎ *0761 28 80 08*
This elegant 16C villa was built to the designs of Vignola and became the residence of several popes. A lovely Italian terraced garden with geometric motifs and numerous fountains makes an ideal setting for the villa.

One of the fountains at Villa Lante di Bagnaia

Bomarzo

21km/13mi northeast by S 204. Extending below the town is the **Parco dei Mostri**, a Mannerist creation of Vicino Orsini (16C) adorned with a series of fantastically shaped **sculptures★**. *Park Open daily, 8am to sunset. €7.75.* ☎ *0761 92 40 29.*

Lago di Vico★

18km/11mi southeast by the Via Santa Maria di Gradi. This solitary but charming lake occupies a crater with forested slopes (beech, chestnut, oak and, on the lake shores, hazel trees).

Civita Castellana

36km/22mi southeast. Civita Castellana occupies the site of the Etruscan city Falerii Veteres which was destroyed by the Romans in 241 BC, but rebuilt in the 8C or 9C. The **Duomo** is fronted by an elegant **portico★** built in 1210 by the Cosmati *(see Index)*. The late-15C castle or **Rocca** was built by Sangallo the Elder and became the residence of Cesare Borgia.

Palazzo Farnese di Caprarola

18km/11mi southwest. Open daily, 8.30am-6.45pm (guided tours every 30min). Closed 1 Jan, 1 May, 25 Dec. €2.07. ☎ *0761 64 60 52.*
The five-storey building is arranged around a delightful circular inner courtyard. To the left of the entrance hall is Vignola's **spiral staircase★★** which rises majestically through tiers of 30 paired Doric columns, and is decorated with grotesques and landscapes by Antonio Tempesta. The paintings which adorn several rooms are by the Zuccaro brothers, Taddeo (1529-66) and Federico (c 1540-1609) as well as Bertoja (1544-74). These are typical of the refined and sophisticated Mannerist style of the late Italian Renaissance period.

Montefiascone

17km/10.5mi northwest. Montefiascone stands in the vineyard country which produces the delicious white wine *Est, Est, Est.*
The imposing **Duomo** has a dome designed by Sammicheli, while the curious church of **San Flaviano★**, in the Lombard-Romanesque style, is in reality two churches superimposed. In the lower church, frescoes illustrate the *Story of the Three Dead and the Three Living Men* symbolising the brevity and vanity of human life; opposite stands the tombstone of Johann Fugger, a German prelate who died on his way to Rome. As he was fond of good food and wine, he sent one of his servants ahead of him with orders to mark the inns where the wine was the best, with the word *est* ("is", short for *Vinum est bonum* in Latin). When he arrived at Montefiascone the faithful servant found the wine so good that he wrote, in his enthusiasm, *"Est, Est, Est"*. And his master, becoming enthusiastic in his turn, drank so much, much, much of it that he died.

Volterra★★

A commanding position★★ overlooking beautiful countryside makes a harmonious setting for the Etruscan and medieval town of Volterra with its well-preserved walls. To the northwest of the town there is a view of the **Balze★**, impressive precipices, which are part of a highly eroded landscape furrowed by gully erosion.
Large salt pans to the west are used in the manufacture of fine salt and soda.

Location

Population 11 686 – Michelin map 430 L 14 – See also The Green Guide Tuscany. Volterra rises up on the summit of a hill that separates the Cecina and Era valleys. The main access road is S 68 which links Poggibonsi with Cecina. 🚹 *Piazza dei Priori 20, 0588 87 257.Surrounding area: see SAN GIMIGNANO, SIENA.*

Worth a Visit

Piazza dei Priori★★

The piazza is surrounded by austere palaces. The 13C Palazzo Pretorio has paired windows and is linked with the Torre del Podestà, also known as Torre del Porcellino because of the wild boar sculpted high up on a bracket. The early-13C Palazzo dei Priori, opposite, is decorated with terracotta, marble and stone shields of the Florentine governors.

Volterra

Duomo and battistero★

The cathedral in the Pisan-Romanesque style, although it has been remodelled several times, stands in the picturesque Piazza San Giovanni. The interior comprises a nave and two aisles with monolithic columns and 16C capitals. On the second altar in the nave, on the left is a lovely late-15C *Annunciation*. The transept contains, in the north arm, a *Virgin* of the 15C Sienese school, and in the south arm, a 13C painted wooden sculpture, **Descent from the Cross★★**. The nave has a superb 17C pulpit with 12C low reliefs. The octagonal baptistery dates from 1283.

Via dei Sarti

This street is lined with palaces: N° 1, Palazzo Minucci-Solaini attributed to Antonio da Sangallo which now houses the art gallery *(see below)*, and N° 37, the **Palazzo Viti** with its superb Renaissance façade designed by Ammanati. In 1964 Luchino

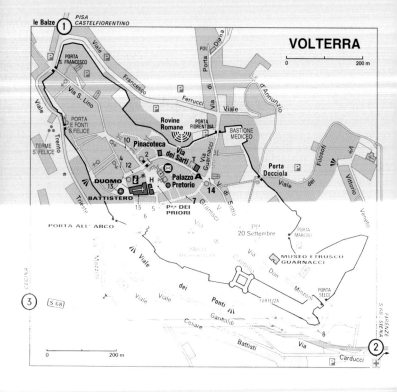

Visconti shot some scenes from his film *Vaghe stelle dall'orsa* here. Some beautiful Indian robes that belonged to Giuseppe Viti, a trader in alabaster who was also the Emir of Nepal, are conserved here. *Open daily, 10am-1pm and 2.30-6.30pm. Closed 5 Nov to 29 Mar €4. For information ☎ 0588 84 047; www.palazzoviti.it*

Pinacoteca

Via dei Sarti 1. Open daily, mid-Mar to Oct 9am-7pm, rest of year 9am-1.45pm Closed 1 Jan, 25 Dec. €7 including Museo Etrusco and Museo Arte Sacra. ☎ 0588 86 290; www.volterratur.it

The Art Gallery displays numerous works of art by 14C to 17C Tuscan artists, notably a lovely *Annunciation* by Luca Signorelli and a *Descent from the Cross*, a masterpiece of Florentine Mannerism by Rosso Fiorentino.

Museo Etrusco Guarnacci★

 ♿ *Open daily, mid-Mar to Oct, 9am-7pm, rest of year 9am-1.45pm. Closed 1 Jan, 25 Dec. €7.*

More than 600 Etruscan funerary urns, made of tufa, alabaster and terracotta, make up the exhibition.

▶▶ Porta all'Arco★ (Etruscan gateway), Teatro romano, Porta Docciola, Viale dei Ponti (views★★).

Excursion

Larderello

33km/21mi south. Larderello is situated in the heart of the **Colline Metalliferi★**, the "metal-bearing hills". In the past they were mined for iron ore, copper and pyrites. Larderello is one of Tuscany's more unusual places with its desolate landscapes, the hissing of its volcanic steam jets, belching smoke from the blast furnaces and the rumble of machinery.

The furrowed landscape of the Balze

The clear blue waters of Maddalena island, Sardinia

The Islands

SARDEGNA

SARDINIA

Sardinia offers an almost primeval landscape of rocks sculpted by the wind and sea, forests of holm and cork oaks, oleander, aromatic plants and shrubs, the clear blue waters of the Mediterranean and the silence of an earlier age broken only by the sounds of nature.

Location

Sardinia is the largest island in the Mediterranean after Sicily. It is surrounded by the Tyrrhenian sea to the east and south, the Mediterranean Sea to the west and the Straits of Bonifacio, which divide the island from Corsica, to the north. The island has a number of bays, among them Golfo dell'Asinara in the north, Golfo di Orosei in the east, Golfo di Cagliari in the south and Golfo di Oristano in the west. A number of smaller islands lie off the Sardinian coast, such as Asinara, Maddalena, Caprera, Tavolara, Sant'Antioco and San Pietro. The Punta la Marmora in the Gennargentu mountains is the highest peak of the island with an altitude of 1 834m/6 017ft.

Directory

TRAVELLING IN SARDINIA

Sardinia offers endless opportunities for visitors with its rugged scenery, views of the sea and megalithic remains. Visitors should allow at least a week in order to explore the island fully.

When exploring the east side of the island it is advisable to leave with a full tank of petrol, as petrol stations are few and far between.

Sights described in this section are marked on the map in bold, while additional itineraries for visitors with more time at their disposal are marked in small black type.

GETTING THERE

Ferries leave from Civitavecchia, Genoa, La Spezia, Livorno, Palermo and Trapani for the ports of Cagliari, Golfo Aranci, Olbia, Porto Torres and Arbatax *(see Practical Points section at the beginning of the guide)*. Visitors are advised to book their crossing in advance if travelling in the summer season.

Sardinia can also be reached by **air**, with airports in Alghero, Cagliari, Olbia and Sassari.

Consult *The Red Guide Italia* and Michelin map 433 for further information on companies and specific routes.

WHAT TO EAT

The traditional recipes of Sardinia are simple but tasty, flavoured with the many aromatic plants and herbs that grow in profusion on the island.

Bread is often the soft-doughed *carasau*, known as *carta da musica* in the rest of Italy. Gnocchetti sardi, a type of pasta shell which has nothing to do with the traditional Italian gnocchi, are also known as *malloreddus*, and are often served with a sausage and tomato sauce. Meat-lovers should try the suckling pig (*porchetto da latte*) roasted on a spit. The island has many different varieties of cheese, including goats' cheese, Sardinian *fiore* and Sardinian *pecorino*.

Local desserts include the rhomboid-shaped *papassinos*, which are often covered with icing and sprinkled with small coloured sugar balls, and *sebadas*, round doughnuts which are fried and covered with honey.

The best known local wines are the *Anghelu Ruju* and *Cannonau*; *Mirto* is an excellent local liqueur.

Our recommendations for restaurants in Sardinia are listed in the relevant sections.

ARTS AND CRAFTS

Sardinia is also well known for its cottage industries, which produce a range of products including goldwork, ceramics, leather, wood and cork, tapestries and basketware.

Colourful Sardinian costume

B. Morandi/MICHELIN

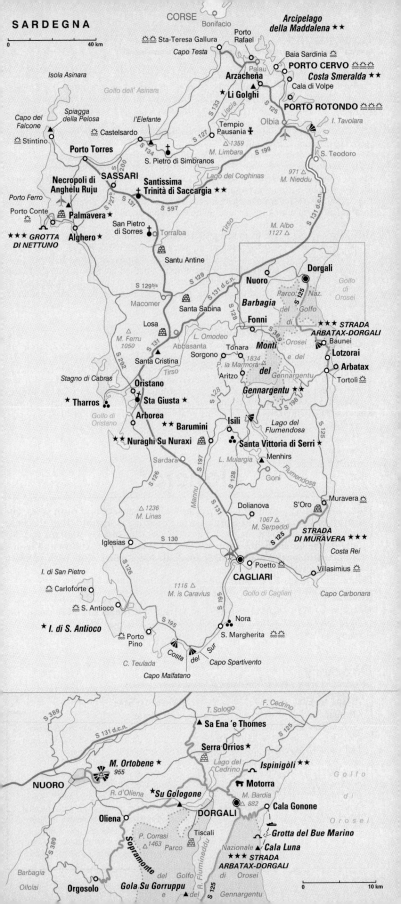

Background

A long and eventful history

Earliest inhabitants – Sardinia has traces of human settlement dating back to pre-historic times – *domus de janas* (fairies' houses) with their disturbing human-like features, dolmens standing alone in the middle of fields and ancient *nuraghi* unchanged by the passing centuries.

The Nuraghic civilisation lasted from 1800 to 500 BC; its golden age is considered have lasted from 1200 to 900 BC.

The island has over 7 000 **nuraghi** or fortified tower houses, structures in the form of a truncated covered cone. The name comes from the root *nur*, also found in *nurra*, which means both "mass" and "cavity". The nuraghi were built of huge blocks of stone without any mortar, possibly using an inclined plane along which they would have been pushed or rolled. They were used as dwellings, as watch-towers from which to keep an eye on both livestock and territory and, when built together as a group, as fortresses.

Other structures remain from this prehistoric period, including dolmens, "covered avenues" or *allées couvertes*, funeral monuments comprising a rectangular room covered by stone slabs and a tumulus, and Giants' Tombs *(see ARZACHENA)*.

As water was a rare commodity on the island, it played an important part in the nuraghic religion. The god who lived in the wells and rivers and who had the power to overcome periods of drought was represented by the bull, often pictured throughout the island.

Successive invasions

Sardinia has been subject to a number of invasions throughout history. The first to arrive were the Phoenicians in the 8C BC, followed by the Romans in 238 BC, the Vandals in AD 455 and the Byzantines in AD 534. The Saracens arrived in the 7C and after the year 1000 the island was fought over by the Pisans and Genoese. It then fell to the Spanish in 1295 and later, during the War of Succession, to the Austrian Empire in 1713. The Kingdom of Sardinia was created in 1718 by Vittorio Amedeo II of Savoy and the island was annexed to the new united Italy in 1861. Sardinia was granted the special status of an autonomous region in 1948.

Alghero★

The early history of this pleasant little walled port set amid olive trees, eu-calyptus and parasol pines is unknown. Coral divers operate from the port which is the main town on the Riviera del Corallo. In 1354 Alghero was oc-cupied by the Catalans; the town still has a Catalan-Gothic centre and its in-habitants still speak Catalan. Its Spanish air has earned it the nickname of the Barcelonetta of Sardinia.

The beach extends 5km/3mi to the north of the village.

Location

Population 40 574 – Michelin map 433 F 6. Alghero is located 35km/21mi southwest of Sassari. **i** *Piazza Portaterra 9 –* ☎ *079 97 90 54.*

Surrounding area: see SASSARI.

Directory

WHERE TO EAT	WHERE TO STAY
• *Budget*	• *Moderate*
La Muraglia – *Bastioni Marco Polo 7* *07041 Alghero – ☎ 079 97 55 77 – Closed Wed – €27/51. Marvellous situation, housed within the fortifications. The view from the top floor, which takes in the harbour and stretches as far as the Capo Caccia promontory, is breathtaking. Excellent cooking to boot. You will need to book in advance to get a table outside!*	**Hotel Al Gabbiano** – *Viale Mediterraneo 5 – 08013 Bosa Marina – 45km/27mi south of Alghero on the coastal road –* ☎ *0785 37 41 23 – Fax 0785 37 41 09 –* **P** |⚑| *30 rm €69.72/72.30 –* ⚏ *€5.16 – Restaurant €22.73/33.58.* Simplicity and courtesy sum up this establishment. Facilities include its own private beach and a pizzeria as well as a traditional restaurant. If this isn't enough to tempt you, how about complete privacy in one of the Art Nouveau-style apartments with its own entrance.

Walking About

Città vecchia★

The fortifications encircle a network of narrow streets in the old town. The **Duomo** *(Via Roma)* has a beautiful doorway and a campanile in the Catalan-Gothic style. The 14C-15C church of **San Francesco** has a Gothic interior and lovely **cloisters** in golden-coloured tufa.

The fishing harbour stands close against the fortifications in the northern part of the town. The harbour is the embarkation point for the boat trips to the **Grotta di Nettuno★★★** (Neptune's Cave). *Open daily, Apr to Sep 9am-7pm, Oct 10am-5pm, rest of year 9am-2pm. Closed 25 Dec. €8.* ☎ *079 94 65 40; www.infoalghero.it*

Alghero:
the splendid tiled dome
of San Michele

Excursions

Grotta di Nettuno★★★

27km/17mi west; access also possible by boat. The road out to the headland, **Capo Caccia**, offers splendid **views★★** of the rocky coast. Neptune's Cave is on the point. A stairway (654 steps) leads down the cliff face. There are small inner lakes, a forest of columns, and concretions in the form of organ pipes.

Nuraghe Palmavera★

10km/6mi on the Porto Conte road. Open daily, Apr to Oct 9am-7pm, rest of year 9.30am-4pm. €2.10. ☎ *079 95 32 00.*
This nuraghe is surrounded by the remains of a prehistoric village, formed by approximately 50 individual dwellings crowded closely together. The nuraghe is a particularly fine building in white limestone with two vaulted towers and two separate entrances.

Necropoli di Anghelu Ruju

10km/6mi from Alghero on the Porto Torres road. Open daily, Apr to Oct 9am-7pm, rest of year 9.30am-4pm. €2.10.
This necropolis comprises 38 hypogea (underground chambers) dating from the Neolithic era (c 3000 BC).

Arzachena

Arzachena, once an agricultural market town, owes its fame to its position in the heart of the Costa Smeralda hinterland at the foot of a curious mushroom-shaped rock (Fungo) and its proximity to important archaeological remains.

Location

Population 10 448 – Michelin map 433 D 10. Arzachena is on S 125, the road that traverses the hinterland behind the Costa Smeralda. 🛈 *Via Paolo Dettori,* ☎ *0789 82 624. Surrounding area: see COSTA SMERALDA.*

Directory

WHERE TO EAT

• Budget

Pinocchio – *Località Cascioni – 07021 Arzachena – Strada provinciale (in the direction of Porto Cervo) –* ☎ *0789 98 886 –* €*21/31*. A traditional establishment which specialises in fish, the dishes inspired by traditional recipes of the area. Also serves excellent pizzas cooked in a wood-fired oven. Reasonably priced accommodation available: simple, comfortable rooms with private access from the garden. Not far from the Costa Smeralda.

WHERE TO STAY

• Budget

Centro Vacanze Isuledda – *07020 Cannigione – 6.5km/4mi northeast of Arzachena –* ☎ *0789 86 003 – Fax 0789 86 089 – www.isuledda.it –* €*34.09.* Great position overlooking the Maddalena archipelago with accommodation to suit the most and least adventurous travellers: there are tents, bungalows, rooms, mobile homes and "tukul". Other facilities include supermarkets, shops and various essential services. Lively atmosphere.

Hotel Citti – *Viale Costa Smeralda 197 – 07021 Arzachena –* ☎ *0789 82 662 – Fax 0789 81 920 – hotelcitti@katamail.com – Closed 25 Dec-6 Jan –* 🅿 ⌶ *– 50 rm* €*41.32/72.30* ⌷. One of the main attractions of this establishment is that it offers excellent value for money, making it a

good base for exploring the entire Costa Smeralda. The street on which it is situated may be slightly busy but the rooms are spacious and comfortable and there is a lovely sun lounge with a pool at the back.

• Moderate

Hotel Selis – *Località Santa Teresina – 07021 Arzachena – Strada provinciale (in the direction of Porto Cervo) –* ☎ *0789 98 630 – Fax 0789 98 631 –* 🖬 *– 18 rm: half-board* €*92.96* ⌷ *– Restaurant* €*28.* The splendid stone building which houses this hotel is off the beaten track. The good-sized rooms are light and airy, with tiled floors and wrought-iron beds: some have a small garden-terrace which makes a lovely children's play area or a sunbathing place (and would also suit anyone travelling with their dog).

• Expensive

Residence Hotel Riva Azzurra – *Località Banchina – 07020 Cannigione – 6.5km/4mi northeast of Arzachena –* ☎ *0789 89 20 05 – Fax 0789 88 072 – rivazzurra@tiscalinet.it – Closed 15 Apr-15 Oct –* 🖬 ⌶ 🖬 ⛆ *– 21 apartments for 4 people: from* €*1301.47 a week.* Attractive pastel-coloured, Mediterranean-style hotel which blends in well with the setting. The comfortable, two-roomed apartments laid out in an arc around a lovely garden, a stone's throw from the beach. Friendly, welcoming atmosphere.

Special Features

MEGALITHIC STONES

The remains of a **Giants' Tomb** (Tomba dei Giganti di Li Muri) and a necropolis can be seen not far from Arzachena.

Tomba di Giganti di Li Golghi*

Follow signs for Luogosanto from Arzachena; take a right turn after about 7km/4mi. Signposted. This megalithic tomb dates from between 1800 and 1200 BC. It would once have been covered by an ellipsoidal tumulus 27m/88ft in length.

Necropoli di Li Muri

Return to the junction and follow signs to Necropoli di Li Muri. Park by the first or second house (the road after this becomes narrow and bumpy) and continue on foot for the last 500m/550yd. This circular necropolis dates from 3500-2700 BC. It consists of a central dolmen, the tomb, surrounded by five concentric stone circles which supported a tumulus.

GIANTS' TOMBS

Popular tradition gave the name Giants' tomb to these tombs dating from the nuraghic period. The funeral chambers lined and roofed with megalithic slabs (like a dolmen) were preceded by an arc of standing stones forming the exedra or area of ritual. The front of the structure is formed by a central stele with fascia in relief, which leads to the corridor of stones. This "false door" may have symbolised the connection with the afterlife.

Barbagia

Wild and evocative, this area is full of steep ravines, known only to local shepherds, and has a wide variety of flora (holm oak, chestnut, hazelnut, holly, dwarf juniper, thyme and yew) and fauna (golden and Bonelli eagle, peregrine falcon, golden kite, wild boar, fox and moufflon).
The Monti del Gennargentu★★ and Supramonte, a limestone plateau in the Orgosolo, Oliena and Dorgali areas, are also situated in this region.

Location
Michelin map 433 G-H 9-10. This region of Sardinia, with its pastoral farming traditions, lies behind the immense Gennargentu massif.*Surrounding area: see NUORO.*

Directory

WHERE TO EAT
• *Moderate*
Ristorante presso Hotel Monteviore – *On S 125 (at the 196km/118mi point), Località Monteviore – 08022 Dorgali – 9km/5mi south of Dorgali – ☎ 0784 96 293 – €24/30.* Surrounded by greenery and off the beaten tourist track is this old farmhouse which has been tastefully restored. Authentic, traditional cooking with a regional bias. There is accommodation: the rooms are spacious and attractive. Also has a campsite in the area ... for naturists.

WHERE TO STAY
• *Moderate*
Hotel L'Oasi – *Via Garcia Lorca 13 – 08020 Cala Gonone – ☎ 0784 93 111 – Fax 0784 93 444 – Closed 10 Oct-Easter – 🅿 🖵 (payment) – 30 rm €61.97/82.63 – ⌂ €10.85 – Restaurant €13.43/18.* Previously a private residence, it is now a small hotel which offers good-sized rooms and apartments which are attractively furnished. The main attraction is the building that houses the restaurant: it is perched up on the cliff overlooking the sea with a splendid view of the bay.

Tour

WILD LANDSCAPES, HISTORY AND THE SEA

Tortolì
Tortolì is the main town of **Ogliastra**, a wild region characterised by cone-like rocks known as "Tacchi". The land in the interior is used for sheep rearing, while arable farming is practised along the coast.
The sea is calm along this coastline, especially at Gairo, where the pebbles are called "*coccorocci*" (literally coconut rocks). Juniper plants grow at **Orri**.

Arbatax
This isolated port is situated in a beautiful mountain setting overlooking the Tortolì sea and is particularly well known for the outcrops of porphyry rock not far from the harbour. A more secluded bay can be found at Cala Moresca *(follow signs)*. The magnificent stretch of **road★★★** between Arbatax and Dorgali *(70km/43 miles)* skirts impressive gorges.

Between Lotzorai and Baunei
The SS 125 road **from Arbatax to Dorgali★★★** passes through an increasingly atmospheric landscape as it runs further into the Barbagia region.
At Lotzorai, a yellow sign indicates the turn-off for the **Domus de janas**. This archaeological area contains approximately ten of these unusual stone constructions, which are occasionally built so that the opening in the rock gives the impression of a human face.
It is worth stopping at the highest point of the road (1 000m/3 300ft) to admire the view. In summer the mountains are dotted here and there with patches of sweet-smelling yellow broom.

Dorgali
This town, the main resort in the Barbagia, lies in the bay of Cala Gonone and is the cultural, culinary and craft-work centre of the region. Its main street, via Lamarmora, offers a pleasant stroll past traditional shops selling local rugs made with a distinctive knot, while the archaeological remains in the region take the visitor back to prehistoric times. The local *cannonau* grape has been producing excellent wine for the past two thousand years.

> **DOMUS DE JANAS**
> These attractively named hypogea (*domus de janas* means "house of fairies") were built from the beginning of the fourth to the middle of the third millennium.
> They are constructed from sandstone, granite, limestone and basaltatic rock and some are decorated with drawings of oxen and goats.

The nuraghic village of **Serra Orrios★** lies not far from Dorgalio on the road leading to S 129, while the Giants' Tomb **Sa Ena'e Thomes** is situated on the Lula road. This tomb has the traditional layout of a Giants' Tomb. The funerary chamber, in the form of a passage roofed with large slabs like a dolmen, is preceded by a series of stones forming the arc of a circle. The larger central stone is carved with a moulding and pierced with a small passageway at ground level.

Cala Gonone

A winding **road★★** leads to this resort built in an attractive bay with a small harbour. Boat trips leave from the port.

Cala Luna – This attractive white sandy beach is lapped by calm, clear water and backed by oleanders. There are a number of caves around the bay.

Grotta del Bue Marino – *By appointment only. Closed Nov to Apr. For information on opening times and prices ☎ 0784 96 243, 0784 93 696 or 0784 93 305; www.dorgali.it*
The *bue marino* or sea ox refers to the monk seal which occupied this cave until the end of the 1970s. The galleried cave has some lovely concretions and a small spring at the back of the area which can be visited.

Dolmen Mottorra

Head north. After a bend in the road, at the km 207 point on S 125, a sign marks the path to the dolmen. The dolmen is situated in the middle of a field which is reached after following the path for approximately five minutes. It consists of an almost circular slab of schist supported by seven upright stones and dates from the beginning of the third millennium BC.

Grotta di Ispinigòli★★

The road to the cave is approximately 7km/4mi from Dorgali on S 125. By appointment only. For information on opening times, prices and reservations ☎ 0784 96 243; www.dorgali.it
On entering the cave, the visitor immediately comes to a large chasm and realises that the cave is formed by an immense cavity and not by a tunnel. The eye is caught by an impressive **stalagmite column** which appears to support the roof. This column (38m/125ft) is the second tallest in the world (the tallest is in New Mexico). The cave is now a fossil, as there is no more water to form new concretions, which are lamellar (in the shape of knives or drapes) or cauliflower (formed under water, like coral) in form.
The dominant colour is red, because the rock strata of the roof is thin. Had it been thicker, water would have filtered through depositing limestone, which would have given the concretions a white colour.
The abundant flow of water in the past quickly built up deposits on the floor of the cave; as a result the stalagmites are much larger than the stalactites.
Phoenician jewellery and human bones have been found in the cave, suggesting that it was perhaps used for sacrificial purposes or as a burial chamber for the nuraghic people.

Su Gologone★

20km/12.5mi to the southeast of Nuoro, on the Oliena-Dorgali road. The large town of **Oliena** stands at the foot of a particularly steep slope of the Sopramonte.
Just beyond Oliena take a local road to the right for about 6km/4mi. The lovely spring at Su Gologone gushes from a rocky face (300 litres per second) in a picturesque green setting.
Not far from Supramonte di Dorgali a cave open to the sky hides the **nuraghic village of Tiscali**.

Orgosolo

20km/12mi south. This market town with its calm appearance is notorious for being the stronghold of bandits and outlaws (popularised by the Italian film producer Vittorio de Seta in his film *Banditi a Orgosolo* made in 1961). Today it is a pleasant town with bright murals adding a touch of life and colour to its streets.

Fighting spirit: a mural in Orgosolo

Barumini★★

The town of Barumini is surrounded by numerous traces of the earliest period of Sardinian history.

Location

Population 1432 – Michelin map 433 H 9. Barumini is situated in the heartland of Sardinia, 10km/6mi north of Villanovaforru, off S 197.
Surrounding area: see ORISTANO.

Special Features

Nuraghe Su Nuraxi★★

2km/1.2mi west, on the left-hand side of the Tuili road. Open daily, 9am to 1hr before sunset. €4.20. ☏ 070 93 68 510.
The oldest part of Su Nuraxi dates from the 15C BC. The fortress was consolidated as a result of the threat posed by the Phoenician invaders between the 8C and 7C BC and was later taken by the Carthaginians between the 5C and 4C BC. The settlement was gradually enlarged over the centuries until it was abandoned in the 3C with the arrival of the Romans.

Nuraghic settlement: Su Nuraxi

B. Morandi/MICHELIN

Excursion

Santa Vittoria di Serri★

38km/24mi east by the Nuoro road and a road to the right in Nurallao. There are remains of a prehistoric religious centre. On the way out, the road passes through the village of **Isili** with two thriving craft industries (furniture-making and weaving).

Cagliari

Cagliari is the capital of the island. It is a modern-looking town with a busy harbour and an old nucleus surrounded by fortifications, built by the Pisans in the 13C. Before becoming Roman it was a flourishing Carthaginian city called Karalis.
The Terrazza Umberto 10 affords a fine view★★ of the town, harbour and bay. The Feast of St Efisio (an officer in Diocletian's army who converted to Christianity and became the patron saint of Sardinia) is undoubtedly one of the most splendid in the whole of Italy *(see under Events and Festivals in the Practical Points section).*

Location

Population 165 926 – Michelin map 433 J 9. Cagliari is located in the south of the island, overlooking the Golfo di Cagliari. The road network which converges on the town includes S 195, S 130, S 131, S 125 and the coastal road which goes to Villasimius. *🅱 Piazza Matteotti 9, ☏ 070 66 92 55.*
Surrounding area: Isola di SANT'ANTIOCO.

Worth a Visit

Cattedrale

Built in the 13C Pisan style, the cathedral was remodelled in the 17C. Inside are magnificent **pulpits★★** (1162) by Guglielmo of Pisa with carved panels illustrating the Life of Christ. A little door on the right of the choir leads down to the Sanctuary or **Santuario**, a crypt with 17C decoration, which contains the remains of 292 Christian martyrs in urns placed along the walls. A door opens on the right into a chapel containing the tomb of Marie-Louise of Savoy, the wife of the future King Louis XVIII of France and sister of the King of Sardinia.

ADDRESS BOOK

Lillicu – *Via Sardegna 78 – 09124 Cagliari – ☎ 070 65 29 70 – Closed Sun, 10 Aug-1 Sep – ⬚ – €18/28.* You could easily get round Cagliari in a day and this is the place to head for lunch or supper. Authentic, local cooking: dishes are well prepared and not too heavy. Diners are seated together at large marble tables – all very cosy.

Museo Archeologico Nazionale★

♿ *Open daily, 9am-8pm. Closed Mon, 1 Jan, 1 May, 25 Dec. €5, €8 including Pinacoteca Nazionale.* ☎ *070 65 59 11.*
The National Archaeological Museum has a large collection of arms, pottery and small **bronzes★★★**, grave artefacts from the earliest period of Sardinian history. Phoenician, Punic and Roman art are represented in the other rooms.

Torre dell'Elefante and Torre San Pancrazio★

The early-14C Elephant and St Pancras towers were part of the Pisan fortifications.

Anfiteatro Romano

This amphitheatre is the most important Roman monument in Sardinia.

▶▶ Orto Botanico

Excursion

Strada di Muravera★★

30km/19mi from Cagliari, the SS 125 road enters wild gorges with reddish-coloured walls of porphyritic granite, dotted with oleander bushes and prickly pear cacti.

Costa Smeralda★★

EMERALD COAST

This wild and undulating region has one of the most indented coastlines of the island. It is a succession of pink granite headlands, covered with maquis scrub and overlooking the sea which is a clear emerald green.

Not so long ago the region was one of farmers and shepherds, but in 1962 it was discovered by the international jet set. The development of the Emerald Coast was promoted by a consortium originally presided over by the Aga Khan. This eastern peninsula of the Gallura region now offers a range of tourist facilities and is the perfect spot for those keen on windsurfing, sailing, golf and tennis. The main resorts are Porto Cervo◌, Cala di Volpe and Baia Sardinia◌.

Location

Michelin map 433 D 10. The Costa Smeralda is the wonderful stretch of coastline towards the northeast of the island where the water really is emerald green.
Surrounding area: see ARZACHENA.

GALLURA

Gallura is the northeastern point of Sardinia. The interior is dominated by Monte Limbara (1 359m/4 461ft) and boasts a dramatic landscape of granite plateaus, cork oaks and caves, while the wild indented coastline offers visitors glimpses of the clear waters of the Mediterranean.

Directory

WHERE TO EAT
• Budget
Panino Giusto – *Piazzetta Clipper – 07020 Porto Cervo – ☎ 0789 91 259 – Closed Nov-May –* 🍽 Situated at the entrance to Porto Cervo Marina, overlooking the yachting harbour, this establishment would suit anyone looking for a snack or a light meal but who does not want to stray far from the beach. Open all day, it serves simple meals, salads and sandwiches. You can eat outside looking over the boats moored in the harbour, or inside where there is a pub-style dining area.

La Vecchia Costa – *Località La Punga – 07021 Arzachena – 5km/3mi southwest of Porto Cervo (in the direction of Arzachena) – ☎ 0789 98 688 –* 🍽 *– €21/26.* If you are in the mood for a good pizza, this is the place to head for. Made with the soft-doughed bread, called "carasau", that is peculiar to Sardinia, the pizzas are deliciously thin and crispy, as well as vast! Very reasonable prices, unusual in this area.

Tattoo – *Liscia di Vacca Alta – 07020 Porto Cervo – 2km/1.2mi from Porto Cervo – ☎ 0789 91 944 – Closed Oct-Mar –* 🍽 🖲 *– €21/26.* Surrounded by smart pastel-coloured, Mediterranean-style villas, this establishment is not far from the beach (very exclusive!) at Liscia di Vacca. The Tattoo is also fashionable enough to hold its own and is popular with the jet set.

La Terrazza – *Via Villa Glori 6 – 07024 La Maddalena – ☎ 0789 73 53 05 – Closed Sun (except May-Sep) –* 🖲 *– €21/36.* Having fallen in love with Sardinia, the dynamic owners (originally from Bologna) have adopted the island's delicious gastronomy as their own. The varied menu focuses on fish – always super-fresh and of the best quality – and includes a number of regional specialities. Meals are served out on the terrace which boasts a wonderful panoramic view.

OFF THE BEATEN TRACK ...
Terza Spiaggia – *Località Terza Spiaggia – 07020 Golfo Aranci – 44km/27mi southeast of Arzachena – ☎ 0789 46 485 – Closed Oct-Mar – €21/41.* What could be better than relaxing on the beach next to the crystal-clear sea and with a wonderful view of the Golfo degli Aranci, while tucking into a delicious sandwich? Or maybe you would prefer a simple fish dish (prepared with fish caught by the owners themselves earlier that day). Meals are served inside (simple beach-style café interior).

Il Portico – *Via Nazionale 107 – 08020 Budoni – 34km/20mi southeast of Olbia on S 125 – ☎ 0784 84 44 50 – Closed Mon (winter), 10 Oct-10 Dec –* 🖲 *– €21/41.* Creative home cooking with lots of seafood and Sardinian specialities prepared with the freshest of ingredients. The dining facilities extend to a large veranda, small outdoor terrace and dining room inside. In summer, they also serve pizzas cooked in a wood-burning oven.

WHERE TO STAY
• Moderate
Hotel Da Cecco – *Via Po 3 – 07028 Santa Teresa di Gallura – 17km/10mi west of Palau on S 133b – ☎ 0789 75 42 20 – Fax 0789 75 56 34 – Closed Nov-24 Mar –* 🅿 *– 32 rm €41.32/67.14 –* 🍴 *€7.75.* From the rooms and the sun lounge there is a magnificent view over the Straits of Bonifacio beyond the Saracen tower. This is a small, modern hotel which would suit visitors looking for a relaxing holiday and the best of Sardinian hospitality.

• Expensive
Hotel Villa Gemella – *Baia Sardinia – 07020 Baia Sardinia – ☎ 0789 99 303 – Fax 0789 99 560 – hotelvillagemella@tiscalinet.it –* 🅿 🛋 *– 26 rm from €147.19* 🍴 *– Restaurant €31.* One of the main attractions of this hotel is the lovely flower-filled garden which is a great spot for relaxation. There is also a swimming pool ... not to mention the sea (the Bay of Sardinia) nearby. The rooms, which are light and airy, have been tastefully furnished; some have a terrace and a view (ask when booking).

Special Features

ARCIPELAGO DELLA MADDALENA★★
The Maddalena Archipelago consists of the islands of Maddalena, Caprera, Santo Stefano, Spargi, Budelli, Razzoli, Santa Maria and other islets found in the **Straits of Bonifacio**.

These isolated islands, occasionally frequented by Corsican shepherds, were annexed to the Kingdom of Sardinia in 1767. Maddalena then became a military base and has recently been used as such by NATO. The archipelago was made a **national park** in 1996.

Maddalena★★
A lovely scenic route *(20km/12mi)* follows the magnificent coastline of this small island, providing views of small creeks and bays and the clear blue waters of the Mediterranean.

Caprera★
This island was once the home of Garibaldi and is connected to Maddalena by the Passo della Moneta causeway. It now houses a well-known sailing centre.

Crystal-clear water

Casa di Garibaldi★ – (&) *Open daily, Jun to Aug 9am-6.30pm, rest of year 9am-1.30pm. Closed 1 Jan, 1 May, 25 Dec. €2.* ☎ *0789 72 71 62.*
The tree planted by Garibaldi (1807-82) on the birth of his daughter Clelia (1867) can still be seen in the garden of his one-time home. Objects and clothes that belonged to the "generalissimo", his wife and family are exhibited in the museum. From one of the rooms there are fine views of Corsica, where Garibaldi died in 1882. He is buried in the garden with his sons and his last wife.

Nuoro

Nuoro lies at the foot of Monte Ortobene, on the borders of the Barbagia region to the north of the Gennargentu Mountains. In this large town of central Sardinia the customs, traditions and folklore have remained unchanged since ancient times.
The Sagra del Redentore (Feast of the Redeemer) includes a procession through the town in local costumes and a folk festival *(see under Events and Festivals in the Practical Points section).* The author Grazia Deledda, a native of Nuoro, won the Nobel Prize for Literature in 1926 for her descriptions of Sardinian life.

Location
Population 37 863 – Michelin map 433 G 9-10. Nuoro is situated off S 131. 🛈 *Piazza Italia 19,* ☎ *0784 30 083.*
Surrounding area: see BARBAGIA.

Worth a Visit

Museo della Vita e delle Tradizioni Popolari Sarde
Via A Mereu 56. (&) Open daily, mid Jun to Sep 9am-8pm, rest of year 9am-1pm and 3-7pm. €3.10. ☎ 0784 31 29 00.
The museum, evoking the popular traditions of the island, has a fine collection of Sardinian costumes.

Excursion

Monte Ortobene★
9km/6mi east. This is a popular excursion with local people. The summit affords several good viewpoints.

Oristano

Oristano is the main town on the west coast. Founded in 1070 by the inhabitants of nearby Tharros, Oristano put up a strong fight against the Aragonese in the 14C.

Location

Population 33 007 – Michelin map 433 H 7. The town of Oristano overlooks the gulf of the same name. The main access road is S 131. ▯ *Via Vittorio Emanuele 8,* ☎ *0783 70 621.*
Surrounding area: see BARUMINI.

Walking About

Piazza Roma

The crenellated tower, Torre di San Cristoforo, overlooking this vast esplanade, was originally part of the town wall built in 1291. Opening off Piazza Roma is **Corso Umberto**, the town's main shopping street.

Chiesa di San Francesco

The church, rebuilt in the 19C, has some interesting **works of art★** including a wooden statue of Christ by the 14C Rhenish school, a fragment of a polyptych *(St Francis receiving the Stigmata)* by Pietro Cavaro, a 16C Sardinian artist, and a statue of *St Basil* by Nino Pisano (14C).

Excursions

Basilica di Santa Giusta★

3km/2mi south. This church, built between 1135 and 1145, stands in the town of the same name, on the banks of a lake.

The sober elegance of Santa Giusta is characteristic of all Sardinian churches where Pisan and Lombard influences mingle. The façade, divided into three sections in the Lombard manner, has an attractively carved doorway typical of the Pisan style. Inside, the columns are either of marble or of granite and have bases and capitals often taken from Roman and early-medieval buildings. The central nave is slighty raised, the roof is trussed and the side aisles are covered by cross vaults. The chapels in the right aisle and the bell tower are modern constructions. There is a crypt under the slightly raised choir.

Tharrosa

On Capo San Marco, on the northern side of the gulf. The Phoenicians founded Tharros on the Sinis Peninsula north of the Gulf of Oristano in the 8C-7C BC. It was an important depot on the Marseilles-Carthage trading route, before it was conquered by the Romans in the 3C BC. The inhabitants left the site for Oristano around the year 1000 before it was buried under wind-blown sand.

Zona archeologica – *Open daily, 9am to 1hr before sunset. €4.* ☎ *0783 37 00 19.*
The excavation site lies near a hill crowned by a Spanish tower (Torre di San Giovanni). Here are remains of Punic fortifications, a sewerage system, tanks, baths, a Punic temple with Doric half-columns and, on the hilltop, a tophet *(see SANT'ANTIOCO).* The two white columns standing alone are reconstructions dating from the 1960s.

Arborea

18km/11mi south. This charming little town was planned and laid out in 1928 by the Fascist government, following the draining of the marshes and the extermination of the malaria mosquito.

Isola di **Sant'Antioco**★

This volcanic island is the largest of the Sulcis Archipelago. It has a hilly terrain with high cliffs on the west coast.

The chief town, also called Sant'Antioco, is linked to the mainland by a road. Catacombs, some of which have been transformed from Punic hypogea, can be seen under Sant'Antioco church. They date from the 6C and 7C AD.

Location
Population 11 827 – Michelin map 433 J-K 7. Sant'Antioco lies off the southwest coast of Sardinia. The main access road is S 126. ⓘ Piazza Repubblica 31/A, ☎ 078 18 20 31. Surrounding area: see CAGLIARI.

Special Features

Vestigia di Sulcis★
(&) *Open daily, 9am-1pm and 3.30-7pm, (6pm in winter). Closed hols. €5.16.* ☎ *0781 83 590.*
The ancient town of Sulci, founded by the Phoenicians in the 8C BC, gave its name to this group of islands.

The archaeological site is divided into a number of different areas. The tombs in the **necropolis**, carved out of volcanic tufa, were used by the Carthaginians until the Roman period. The **archaeological museum** displays finds from the excavations and includes a fine collection of **steles★**. The archaeological area comprises the Phoenician-Punic **tophet★**, once believed to be where the first-born male child was sacrificed, but now understood to be a cemetery for still-born babies or children who died in infancy.

Excursions

Tratalias
18km/11mi from Sant'Antioco. The 13C Pisan-Romanesque church of Santa Maria towers above this small village, which has a hint of the Wild West about it.

Monte Sirai
19km/12mi from Sant'Antioco. Traces of a Phoenician-Punic settlement remain on this hill. The Phoenicians arrived here in 750 BC. Their city was destroyed by the Cathaginians who settled here in 520 BC, building a new fortress. This fortress was in turn destroyed by the Romans in 238 BC, and they remained on Monte Sirai until 110 BC, when the site was abandoned.

Sassari

Sassari is the second largest town in Sardinia. Its spacious, airy modern quarters contrast with its medieval nucleus, nestling round the cathedral. The busiest thoroughfares are the Piazza d'Italia and the Corso Vittorio Emanuele II.

Location
Population 120 303 – Michelin map 433 E. Town plan in the Michelin Atlas of Italy. Sassari is situated about 20km/13mi from the Golfo dell'Asinara. The main access roads are S 131, S 291 and S 597. ⓘ Via Roma, 62, ☎ 079 23 17 77. Surrounding area: see ALGHERO.

Worth a Visit

Museo Nazionale Sanna★
& *Open daily, 9am-8pm. Closed 1 Jan, 1 May, 25 Dec. €2. ☎ 079 27 22 03.*
The museum contains rich archaeological collections, including an interesting section devoted to Sardinian ethnography and a small picture gallery.

THE SYMBOL OF SASSARI
This is the Fontana di Rosello, the huge fountain near the church of the Holy Trinity. It is a rather grand and elaborate Renaissance structure which was erected by the Genoese in 1605, although records show that there has been a fountain on this spot since the end of the 13C.

Duomo

The cathedral is built in many styles and has a 13C campanile with a 17C upper storey, a late-17C Spanish Baroque **façade**★ and a Gothic interior.

Excursions

Santissima Trinità di Saccargia★★

17km/11mi southeast by the Cagliari road, S 131, and then the road to Olbia, S 597.

This former Camaldulian abbey church, dedicated to the Holy Trinity, was built in the 12C in decorative courses of black and white stone, typical of the Pisan style. The elegant façade includes a porch added in the 13C and is flanked by a slender campanile. Inside, the apse is adorned with fine 13C frescoes showing a strong Byzantine influence and depicting scenes of the Passion, including the Virgin and the Apostles in the upper section and Christ surrounded by angels and archangels on the vault.

A Romanesque jewel: Santissima Trinità di Saccargia

B. Morandi/MICHELIN

Porto Torres

Situated at the head of a large bay, Porto Torres is the port for Sassari. Founded by Caesar it enjoyed considerable importance in the Roman period, as can be testified by the remains in the vicinity of the station.

Chiesa di San Gavino★ – The church was built at the end of the 11C by the Pisans (the long series of blind arcades on the north side are characteristic of the Pisan style) and enlarged shortly afterwards by Lombard master builders. It is a fine example of medieval Sardinian art. A 15C doorway in the Catalan-Gothic style interrupts the arcades. Inside, piers alternate with groups of four clustered columns giving a harmonious result. A large **crypt** enshrines the relics of St Gavin and a very fine Roman **sarcophagus**★, decorated with sculptures portraying the Muses.

SICILIA

SICILY

From sun-scorched earth in the summer, the land turns a brilliant green as soon as the spring rain arrives. With its mountainous terrain at the heart of the island, and glorious coastline, Sicily has much to offer. Visitors who come to relax by the sea or marvel at the island's rich artistic heritage and traditional way of life, are rewarded with a marvellous collage of colourful images and sensations.

Location

Sicily, the largest of the Mediterranean islands, has an area of 25 709km²/9 927sq miles. It is triangular in shape and was named Trinacria (Greek for "three points") under Greek rule.

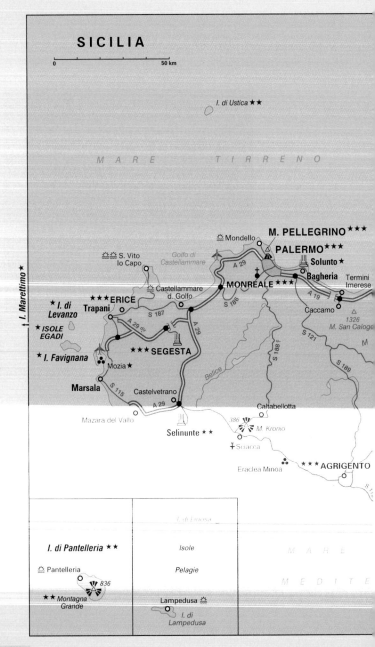

SICILIA

0 ——— 50 km

I. di Ustica ★★

MARE TIRRENO

M. PELLEGRINO ★★★
Mondello
PALERMO ★★★
Solunto ★
S. Vito lo Capo
Golfo di Castellammare
Bagheria
Termini Imerese
MONREALE ★★★
A 29
★★★ ERICE
Castellammare d. Golfo
★ I. di Levanzo
Trapani
S 186
S 187
A 29 dir
Caccamo
1326
M. San Caloge
★ ISOLE EGADI
A 29
S 121
★★★ SEGESTA
★ I. Favignana
S 188
S 169
Mozia ★
Belice
M
★ I. Marettimo
Marsala
S 115
Castelvetrano
Caltabellotta
A 29
386
M. Kronio
Mazara del Vallo
Selinunte ★★
Sciacca
★★★ AGRIGENTO
Eraclea Minoa

Linosa

I. di Pantelleria ★★   Isole   MARE

Pantelleria   Pelagie   MEDITE
836
★★ Montagna Grande   Lampedusa
                              I. di Lampedusa

484

Nearly 5 million people live on the island, which is generally mountainous and reaches at its highest point, Mount Etna (an active volcano), an altitude of 3 340m/10 958ft. Throughout its history Sicily has suffered numerous earthquakes: the earthquake in 1693 damaged most of the towns in the southwest of the island, in 1908 Messina was almost entirely destroyed, and the earthquake in 1968 badly affected the western part of the island.

Background

Historical and Artistic Notes

Sicily has been a constant pawn for marauding forces in the Mediterranean because of its strategic location, lying, as it does, near the Italian peninsula and controlling the Mediterranean. Firstly came the Greeks in the 8C BC who discovered an island divided between two ethnic groups: the **Sicani**, the oldest inhabitants, and the **Siculi** (Sicels) who came from the mainland.

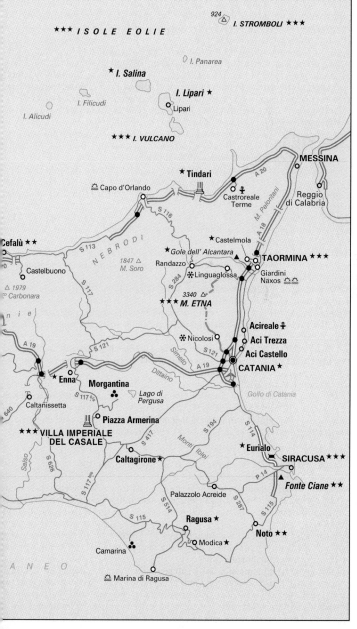

The Carthaginians were for several centuries the main rivals of the Greeks. Although they had colonised the coastal areas, they were finally pushed back to the western part of the island, where they remained until the siege of Motya by Dionysius I of Syracuse in 397 BC.

The 5C BC, excluding the rules of the tyrants of Gela and Syracuse (see SIRACUSA), was the apogee of Greek rule in Sicily (Magna Graecia). After erecting some magnificent buildings, they neutralised their enemies and Syracuse grew to become the rival of Athens.

This fragile peace was broken by the arrival of the Romans who coveted the island for the richness of its soil.

By 241 BC, at the end of the First Punic War, the whole of Sicily had been conquered and it became a Roman province, governed by a praetor. The Romans exploited the island's resources to the full with the help of more or less dishonest officials. The island was also a victim of the numerous barbarian invasions which ravaged southern Italy.

In 535 the island passed to the Byzantines before experiencing a period of great prosperity under the Muslims of the Aghlabid dynasty (Tunisia), in the 9C. The Saracens were in turn expelled by the Normans (11C).

The son of the Great Count Roger I of Sicily, **Roger II** (1095-1154), created the Norman Kingdom of Sicily. He established his court at Palermo and during his reign the island was to enjoy a prosperous period of considerable political power and cultural influence.

The name of the Hohenstaufen Emperor **Frederick II** dominated the reign of this Swabian dynasty. The house of Anjou followed in 1266; however, Charles of Anjou was expelled following the Palermo revolt of 1282 known as the **Sicilian Vespers**. Power passed to the Aragon dynasty and it was Alfonso V the Magnanimous who reunited Naples and Sicily and took the title of King of the Two Sicilies (1442).

The island passed to the Bourbons of Naples by marriage until they were overthrown by the Expedition of Garibaldi and the Thousand (1860).

The Second World War left its mark on Sicily; the Anglo-American landings between Licata and Syracuse in 1943 ended in the abandonment of the island by the Germans after more than a month of heavy fighting.

Each period has left its mark on the island's heritage, be it in the field of art or customs and daily life. The Greeks built admirable Doric temples with the mellow local limestone, and also splendid theatres. During the brief period when the Normans dominated the island, Sicily knew an era of economic prosperity and artistic development.

This style was unique for its blending of a variety of different influences. The architectural style was still essentially Norman but the decoration (horseshoe-shaped arches, bulbous bell towers and intricately decorated ceilings) showed a strong Moorish influence, while the decoration of the walls with dazzling mosaics on golden backgrounds was Byzantine.

Known variously as **Sicilian-Norman** or **Arab-Norman**, this style can be seen at Palermo, Monreale, Cefalù and Messina.

If the Renaissance has left few traces in the island – with some outstanding exceptions by **Antonello da Messina** (see Index) who usually worked on the mainland – the Sicilians adopted the Spanish-influenced Baroque style with great fervour in the late 18C. The main exponents were the architects **Rosario Gagliardi** in Noto and Ragusa, **Vaccarini** in Catania, and **Giacomo Serpotta** who embellished numerous oratories in Palermo with his sculpted fantasies.

Sicilian literature is particularly rich, especially in the 19C, with **Giovanni Verga** (see Index) who created a new form of Italian novel, and **Luigi Pirandello** (see Index). Noteworthy among the 20C writers to describe contemporary life are **Elio Vittorini** (1908-66) and **Leonardo Sciascia** (1921-89). Other writers include **Gesualdo Bufalino** (1920-96) and the poet **Salvatore Quasimodo** (1901-68).

Sicily Today

The long period of foreign domination in Sicily has left its imprint not only on the art, culture and literature of the island but also on its economy. Following the Arab invasions, the island's economy was neglected by its foreign rulers, with the exception of the Normans and Swabians. Vegetation and forests were cleared, the locals exploited, and the island was prevented from developing and making the most of its potential.

Today Sicily survives on an assisted economy in the hope that new development projects will stem the emigration of its young people, increase the wealth of the island and return it to its former glory.

Geographically and economically Sicily can be divided into three regions. The first region comprises the provinces of Catania, Syracuse and the southern part of Messina. Industries established in this area include chemical and petrochemical plants and oil refineries. The agriculture of the region tends to be intensive and of high quality. Palermo, Trapani and the north of Messina make up the second

Directory

GETTING ABOUT

The main connections to Sicily **by boat** leave from Cagliari, Genoa, Livorno, Naples, Reggio di Calabria, Villa San Giovanni.

If you are travellling by air you will arrive at either Palermo or Catania, the island's two main airports. There are also airports at Trapani, Pantelleria and Lampedusa and there are connecting flights to these airports at busy times of the year (Easter and in summer). Another possibility is the airport at Reggio di Calabria, which, although not in Sicily itself, is very near the Straits of Messina. *See the Practical Points section at the beginning of the guide for further details.*

SIGHTSEEING

You could just about get round the island in a week. In addition to the places and areas that are described in this guide, the map highlights other areas of interest and beauty (indicated in small, black type). *See The Green Guide Sicily for further information.*

SHOPPING

Ceramics are perhaps the island's most celebrated artisanal trade: the most important centres are Caltagirone, Santo Stefano di Camastra and Sciacca. If, on the other hand, you are in the Trapani area, you might be interested in the necklaces and other objects made out of coral, and in Erice there is a rug-making tradition. Natural sponges are the thing to buy on Pantelleria, and in Syracuse the papyrus may be of interest. The antique and junk shops are a good place to look for Sicilian puppets and carts.

region, in which the services sector and the building industry are highly developed. Finally, the poorest part of Sicily consists of the provinces of Agrigento, Caltanissetta and Enna. This region is underdeveloped economically and has poor agricultural land, which has resulted in a flow of emigration.

The fishing industry is still of prime importance to the Sicilian economy; island specialities include tuna from Trapani and swordfish from Messina.

Traditions

The folk traditions and customs which once animated the streets have almost completely disappeared. It is only on feast days and in the museums that the visitor can now see the famous **Sicilian carts** which were gaily decorated with bright colours and intricate wrought-iron work. These colourful carts were the main method of transport for over a century, until the end of the 1950s. In Palermo the popular **puppet** *(pupi)* **theatres** can still be seen showing their dramatised versions of the 12C *Song of Roland* and Ariosto's *Orlando Furioso (Roland the Mad)* can still be seen.

Agrigento★★★

Agrigento, the Greek city of Akragas, is attractively set on a hillside facing out to sea. The Greek poet Pindar referred to Agrigento as "man's finest town". It includes a medieval quarter on the upper slopes above the modern town, and impressive ancient ruins strung out along a ridge below, wrongly called the Valley of the Temples (declared a UNESCO World Heritage Site in 1997).

Directory

WHERE TO EAT
• *Budget*

Kokalo'S – *Via Cavaleri Magazzeni 3, Valle dei Templi* – ☎ *0922 60 64 27* – *Book* – €*10/34.* Having satisfied your thirst for learning in the Valley of the Temples, this rustic-style establishment, which is also a wine bar, could be just the place to quench your (less spiritual) thirst with a refreshing drink. Also serves pizzas and other simple dishes.

WHERE TO STAY
• *Moderate*

Hotel Villa Eos – *Contrada Cumbo, villaggio Pirandello* – *On S 115* – ☎ *0922 59 71 70* – *Fax 0922 59 71 88* – 🅿 🏊 📷 – *23 rm* €*77.47/98.13* 🍽 – *Restaurant* €*22/29.* After a tiring day's sightseeing what could be more restorative than a dip in the swimming pool, or a game of tennis if you still have the strength. Well situated just a stone's throw from the sea and not far from Pirandello's house. Attractive, well-kept rooms.

■ Agrigento

Location

*Population 55 521 – Michelin map 4432
P 22. Agrigento is linked to Palermo by
S 189 and the north coast of the island
by S 640 and A 19. ▣ Via Cesare Battisti
15, ☎ 0922 20 454.*

Special Features

VALLE DEI TEMPLI
(VALLEY OF THE TEMPLES)★★★

*Allow 3hr. Open daily, 8.30am-9pm.
€4.50; €6 including Museo Archeologico
Regionale. ☎ 0922 29 702.*

Of the many temples from the late 6C to the late 5C BC, parts of nine are still visible.
The destruction of the temples was for long thought to have been caused by earth-
quakes but is now also attributed to the anti-pagan activities of the early Christians.
Only the Temple of Concord was spared when it became a church in the late 6C AD.

Tempio di Zeus Olimpio★

Had this now-ruined temple been completed, its size (113m/371ft long by
56m/184ft wide) would have made it one of the largest in the ancient world. The
entablature of the Temple of Olympian Zeus (Roman Jupiter) was supported by
20m/66ft tall columns, between which stood **telamones**
(columns in the form of male figures). One of these
colossal statues, standing 7.5m/25ft high, has been
reconstructed and is now on view in the
Archaeological Museum *(see below)*. A reproduction of the giant, lying on the ground in the
centre of the ruins, gives some idea of the
immense size of the building.

Tempio dei Dioscuri★★

Of the hexastyle temple of Castor
and Pollux, only four of the
columns supporting part of the
entablature remain. The small
rose at the corner of the entablature is a typical decorative
feature.

Alongside is a **sacred area** dedicated to Demeter and Persephone the chthonic or un-
derground gods: there are
two sacrificial altars, one of
which is circular, with a holy
well in the middle, and the
other square.
*Return to the square and take
Via dei Templi.*

Tempio di Eracle★★

Dating from the late 6C, the
Temple of Hercules is probably the oldest of the Agrigento temples and is built in
the ancient Doric style.
Eight of its columns
have been raised.

Further on to the
left can be seen
the deeply
grooved ruts
thought to
have been
made by
ancient
wheeled ve-
hicles. The deep marking
is possibly due to the ruts
having been used at a later
date as water channels.

Temple of Castor and Pollux

TYRANTS, PHILOSOPHERS AND WRITERS

The town was founded in 580 BC by people from
Gela who originated from Rhodes. Of the governing "tyrants", the cruellest in the 6C was
Phalaris, while **Theron** (5C) was renowned as a
great builder. The 5C philosopher **Empedocles**
was a native of Agrigento, as was **Luigi
Pirandello** (1867-1936), winner of the Nobel
Prize for Literature in 1934 and innovator in modern Italian drama (Six Characters in Search of an
Author), whose plays were woven around the
themes of incomprehension and absurdity.

Tempio della Concordia★★★

The Temple of Concord is the most massive, majestic and best preserved of the Doric temples in Sicily. It has a peristyle of 34 tufa limestone columns, the original stucco facing having disappeared. It is not known to what deity it was dedicated and its present name (Concordia) is taken from a Roman inscription found nearby. The internal arrangement dates from the Christian period (mid-5C).

Tempio di Hera Lacinia★★

Set on the edge of the ridge, this temple, dedicated to Hera (Roman Juno), conserves part of its colonnade. On the east side there is a sacrificial altar and behind the temple an ancient cistern.

Worth a Visit

Museo Archeologico Regionale★

Enter via the cloisters of the church of St Nicholas (see below). Open Tue-Sun 9am-1.30pm and Tue-Sat 2-6pm. Closed Mon, Sun and hols pm. €4.50. ☎ 0922 40 15 65.
The museum contains a fine collection of **Greek vases★** including the *Dionysius Cup* and the *Perseus and Andromeda Cup* on a white background. One room is devoted to the **telamones★** from the Temple of Zeus. There are also the 5C BC marble statue of a youth, the *Ephebe of Agrigento★★ (Room 10)* and the beautiful *Gela Cup★★ (Room 15)* which illustrates a centaur in the upper part and the battle between the Greeks and the Amazons in the lower part.

Oratorio di Falaride

Open Mon-Sat, 8am-5pm. Closed Sun and hols. For ticket price, ask on site. Legend has it that the palace of Phalaris, the first tyrant of Agrigento, was in the vicinity. The building is in fact a small Roman-Hellenistic temple which was transformed during the Norman period.

Chiesa di San Nicola

Open daily, 9.30am-noon and 3.30-7.30pm.
This sober church, dedicated to St Nicholas, in the transitional Romanesque-Gothic style contains a magnificent **Roman sarcophagus★** on which the death of Phaedra is portrayed. From the terrace there is a fine **view★** of the temples.

Quartiere ellenistico-romano★

♿ Open Mon-Sat 8.30am-5pm, Sun and hols 8.30am-1.30pm. For prices, ask on site.
In the Greco-Roman quarter, the layout of the main streets lined with houses is a good example of 4C BC town planning.

Town centre

The centre of the town is concentrated around the shady **Piazzale Aldo Moro**, which leads into the attractive **Via Atenea**, a busy shopping street. Crowning the old town with its stepped streets is the **Cattedrale**, a Norman building which was greatly altered in the following centuries. On the way back down to Piazzale Aldo Moro visit a small abbey church, **Abbaziale di Santo Spirito★**, which has four charming **high reliefs★** in stucco attributed to Giacomo Serpotta.
To visit, contact adjoining monastery.

Excursions

Tomba di Terone

Visible from the Caltagirone road. The tomb (3m/10ft high), said to be that of Theron, Tyrant of Agrigento, in fact dates from the Roman era and is thought to have been erected in honour of soldiers who died during the Second Punic War.

Casa di Pirandello

6km/4mi west by the Porto Empedocle road, S 115. Turn left shortly after the Morandi viaduct. (♿) Open daily, Apr to Nov 9am-1pm and 2-7pm, Jan to Mar 9am-1pm and 2-6pm. €2. ☎ 0922 51 17 98; www.regione.sicilia.it
This small house surrounded by vineyards was the birthplace of the famous dramatist Luigi Pirandello (1867-1936), who is buried under a nearby pine tree.

Caltagirone★

Caltagirone is famous for its pottery which is not only displayed in profusion in the local shops (vases, plates, household goods) but also adorns bridges, balustrades, balconies (note the lovely balcony of the 18C Casa Ventimiglia), and the façades of palaces lining Via Roma in the town centre.

Location
Population 39 225 – Michelin map 432 25 P. Caltagirone lies just off S 417 which links Catania with Gela. 🛈 *Palazzo Libertini,* ☎ *0933 53 809.*
Surrounding area: see Villa Imperiale del CASALE.

Worth a Visit

Santa Scala di S. Maria del Monte★
The stairway built in the 17C to join the old and new town, has 142 steps in volcanic stone; the risers are decorated with polychrome ceramic tiles with geometric, floral and other decorative motifs. On 24 and 25 July the stairway is covered in lights which form different patterns: the most frequent is the symbol of the town, an eagle with a shield on its breast.

Villa Comunale★
This beautiful garden was designed in the mid-19C by Basile as an English garden. The side flanking Via Roma is bounded by a balustrade adorned with maiolica vases. On an esplanade stands the delightful Arab-style **palchetto della musica** (bandstand) decorated with ceramics.

Museo della ceramica
(♿) *Open daily, 9am-6.30pm. €2.58.* ☎ *0933 21 680.*
The **Teatrino**, a curious little 18C theatre decorated with ceramics, houses an interesting museum which traces the history of local ceramics from prehistory to the early 20C. The importance of this craft is illustrated by a fine **cup★** dating from the 5C BC depicting a potter and a youth working at the wheel.

Villa Imperiale del **Casale**★★★

This immense 3C or 4C Roman villa (3 500m²/37 670sq ft) probably belonged to some dignitary and is important for its mosaic pavements which cover almost the entire floor space. These picturesque mosaics, in a wide range of colours, were probably the work of African craftsmen and portray scenes from mythology, daily life, and events such as hunts or circus games.
The Villa Romana del Casale was declared a UNESCO World Heritage Site in 1997.

Location
Michelin map 432 0 25. The villa is situated near Piazza Armerina, off S 117b. 🛈 *Via Cavour 15,* ☎ *0935 68 02 01.*
Surrounding area: see CALTAGIRONE, ENNA.

Was the bikini really not "invented" until the 20C?

Worth a Visit

Mosaics★★★

Open daily, 8.30am-7.30pm (ticket office closes 6.30pm). €4.13. ☎ 0935 68 00 36.
The most noteworthy mosaics portray **cupids★★** fishing or playing with dolphins, a hunting scene in the **Sala della Piccola Caccia★★★**, the capturing and selling of **wild animals** for circus use in the **Ambulacro della Grande Caccia★★★** and sports practised by young girls who appear to be wearing modern swimwear in the **Sala delle Dieci Ragazze in Bikini★★**. Finally, the mosaics of the **triclinium★★★** portray the *Labours of Hercules.*

Excursion

Piazza Armerina

5km/3mi southwest. The interesting **medieval centre★** of Piazza Armerina huddles round its Baroque **cathedral** on the pleasantly green slopes of a valley. *Open daily, 7.30am-12.30pm and 3.30-6.30pm. ☎ 0935 68 02 14.*

Catania★

Catania is a busy seaport and industrial town which has developed considerably in recent years, despite being destroyed several times by the eruptions of Mount Etna. This fine city has wide, regular streets overlooked by numerous Baroque buildings by the architect Vaccharini, who rebuilt Catania after the 1693 earthquake.
Natives of the town include the musician Vicenzo Bellini (1801-35), composer of the opera *Norma*, and the novelist, Giovanni Verga.

Location

Population 337 862 – Michelin map 432 O 27 (including a plan of the built-up area).
Catania is situated on the east coast, overlooking the Ionian Sea. The main access roads are A 18 (from Messina), A 19 (from Enna), and S 114, which links the town with Syracuse. Catania holds the heat record for the whole of Italy: over 40°C (104°F). ❸ *Via Cimarosa 10, ☎ 095 73 06 211.*
Surrounding area: see ETNA, SIRACUSA, TAORMINA.

Directory

WHERE TO EAT	WHERE TO STAY
• *Moderate*	• *Moderate*
Cantine del Cugno Mezzano – *Via Museo Biscari 8* – ☎ *095 71 58 710* – *Closed Sun lunchtime, 10-28 Aug* – *€23/36.* This is a very trendy, fashionable establishment housed in an old 18C palazzo in the centre of town. Rustic-style ambience, with large wooden tables, but a modern approach to the cuisine. Also has a good wine list.	**Hotel La Vecchia Palma** – *Via Etnea 668* – ☎ *095 43 20 25 – Fax 095 43 20 25 –* ⓒ – *11 rm €46.48/72.30* ☕. An Art Nouveau-style building with many of the original features, this hotel offers good-sized, comfortable rooms with all mod cons. It is a family-run establishment and guests are made to feel very at home. Definitely one for the address book.

Worth a Visit

Piazza del Duomo★

This square is the centre of town and is surrounded by a Baroque ensemble designed by Vaccarini which includes the **Fontana dell'Elefante** (Elephant Fountain) dating from 1735, the **Palazzo Senatorio or degli Elefanti** (town hall) with its well-balanced façade, and the **Duomo★** dedicated to St Agatha, the town's patron saint. The cathedral, built at the end of the 11C by the Norman, Roger I, was remodelled after the 1693 earthquake and has an elegant **façade★** by Vaccarini. To the left of the cathedral, the beautiful abbey church **Badia di Sant'Agata★** contributes to the harmony of the square.

Catania

CATANIA

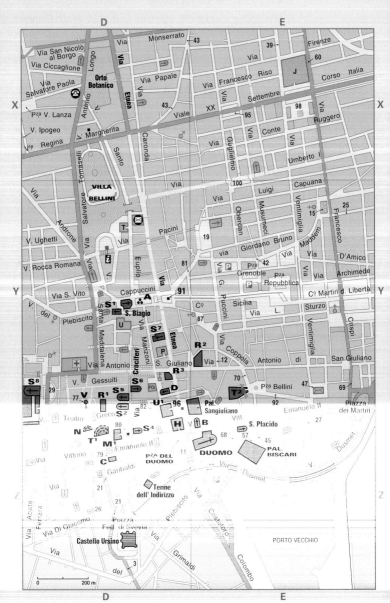

Not far from here, in via Museo Biscari, stands **Palazzo Biscari★**, one of the most beautiful examples of civil architecture in the city. The south side of the mansion has a highly decorated **façade★★** with figures, cherubs and scrolls. *Open daily, 9.30am-12.30pm and 4-7pm. Guided tours only (20min), Mon-Sat 9.30am-12.30pm and 4-7pm. By appointment only.* ☎ 095 32 18 18.

Via Etnea★
The town's main shopping artery is over 3km/2mi long. All the way along it affords a view of Etna. It is bordered by numerous palaces and churches and the **Villa Bellini★** gardens.

Quartiere Occidentale
This district to the west of the town runs through Via Vittorio Emanuele II, along which the old theatre, **Teatro Antico**, can be seen. It is is crossed by **Via Crociferi★**, considered to offer some of the best examples of Baroque architecture in Catania. *Theatre closed for restoration at time of publication.* ☎ 095 74 72 111.

Castello Ursino
Open Tue-Sat, 9am-1pm and 3-6pm, Sun and hols 9am-1pm. Closed Mon. ☎ 095 34 58 30.
This bare, grim castle, fortified by four towers, was built in the 13C by the Emperor Frederick II of Hohenstaufen and houses the **Museo Civico**.

Excursion

Acireale
17km/11mi north. The route passes through **Aci Castello**, with its **castle★** built from black volcanic rock, and **Aci Trezza**, a small fishing village. Offshore, the **Faraglioni dei Ciclopi★** (Cyclops' Reefs) emerge from the sea. These are supposed to be the rocks hurled by the Cyclops Polyphemus after Ulysses had blinded him by thrusting a blazing stake into his single eye. The road leads to **Acireale**, a modern town with numerous Baroque buildings which include those of the **Piazzo del Duomo★** with the Basilica of St Peter and St Paul and the Town Hall, as well as the church of **San Sebastiano** with its harmonious **façade★** embellished with columns, niches and friezes.

Cefalù★★

Cefalù is a small fishing town in a fine setting★★, hemmed in between the sea and a rocky promontory. It boasts a splendid Romanesque cathedral.

Location
Population 14 026 – Michelin map 432 M 24. Cefalù is situated on the north coast, overlooking the Tyrrhenian Sea. The main access roads are A 20 (from Palermo), and S 113 (from Messina). ᵈ *Corso Ruggero 77,* ☎ *0921 42 10 50.*
Surrounding area: see PALERMO.

Worth a Visit

Duomo★★
Open daily, summer 8am-noon and 3.30-7pm, rest of year 8am-noon and 3.30-5pm. ☎ *0921 92 20 21.*
Built of a golden-tinted stone which blends in with the cliff behind, this cathedral was erected to fulfil a vow made by the Norman King, Roger II (12C), when in danger of shipwreck. The church (1131-1240) has well-marked Norman features in its tall main apse flanked by two slightly projecting smaller ones and especially in its façade, abutted by the two square towers. The portico was rebuilt in the 15C by a Lombard master.
The timber ceiling of the two aisles and the transept galleries are also Norman. The columns are crowned with splendid **capitals★★** in the Sicilian-Norman style *(see Historical and Artistic Notes on Sicily, p 485).*
The presbytery is covered with beautiful **mosaics★★** on a gilded background, displaying a surprising variety of colour and forming an admirable expression of Byzantine art. Above is Christ Pantocrator (Ruler of All) with underneath, on three different levels, the Virgin with four archangels and the 12 Apostles. In the choir, the angels on the vaulting and the prophets on the side walls date from the 13C. Note the episcopal throne (south side) and the royal throne (north side), both in marble and mosaic.

▶▶ Museo Mandralisca (*Portrait of an Unknown Man★* by Antonello da Messina).

Isole **Egadi** ★

EGADI ISLANDS

The islands are popular for their wild aspect, clear blue sea and beautiful coastlines. It was here in 241 BC that the treaty ending the First Punic War was concluded, in which Carthage surrendered Sicily to Rome.

Location
Population 4410 – Michelin map 432 M-N 18-19. The three islands – Favignana, Levanzo and Marettimo – which make up this small archipelago lie offshore from Trapani.
🚩 *piazza Madrice 8,* ☎ *0923 92 16 47.*
Surrounding area: see ERICE, TRAPANI, SEGESTA.

Directory

GETTING ABOUT
There are daily departures from Trapani: ferries (1-2hr 45min) and hydrofoils (15min-1hr).
Shipping company: Catalano Viaggi, molo San Leonardo, 91023 Favignana (Trapani), ☎ *0923 92 13 68.*

WHERE TO STAY
• *Budget*
Hotel Egadi – *Via Colombo 17 – 91023 Favignana –* ☎ *0923 92 12 32 – Fax 0923 92 12 32 – Closed Oct-mid May – 12 rm €44/78* 🍽. This hotel has become something of an institution on the island, such is the level of hospitality and courtesy.

The rooms are simple but spotlessly clean and the cooking is good. In the evening there is a wide selection of imaginative dishes, carefully put together and prepared with good quality ingredients.
• *Moderate*
Hotel Aegusa – *Via Garibaldi 11/17 – 91023 Favignana –* ☎ *0923 92 24 30 – Fax 0923 92 24 40 –* 🖥 *– 28 rm €72.30/123.95* 🍽 *– Restaurant €23/31.* This hotel has a real holiday feel about it. Inviting (and reasonably priced) menu with a good selection of fish and other traditional dishes. Meals served in the lovely courtyard-garden. Rooms are light and airy with wicker furniture.

Worth a Visit

Favignana★
The island covers an area of 20km²/8 sq miles and is butterfly-shaped. The **Montagna Grossa** culminating at 302m/991ft runs right across the island and ends as an indented coastline. The islanders were masters in the art of tuna fishing which took place for about 50 days between May and June. Having captured the tuna in a series of nets, they would perform a dangerous manoeuvre and pull in the fish towards the shore where they were harpooned.

The main town of the group of islands, **Favignana**, is guarded by the fort of Santa Caterina, a former Saracen lookout tower, which was rebuilt by the Norman King, Roger II, and served as a prison under the Bourbons. To the east of the harbour are the former **tufa quarries★** now drowned by the sea. Boat trips take visitors to the various caves (contact the fishermen at the harbour), including the **Grotta Azzurra★** which is situated on the west coast.

The wild allure of Levanzo

Levanzo★
This tiny island is only 6km²/2sq miles in size. In 1950 traces of life in prehistoric times were found in the **Grotta del Genovese★**, which is reached on foot or by boat from Cala Dogana. *To visit, contact Sig. Castiglione, Via Calvario, Levanzo.* ☎ *0923 92 40 32, 0360 63 92 61 or mobile 339 74 18 800.*

Marettimo★
Off the beaten tourist track, Marettimo with its attractive **harbour** *(no landing stage, rowing boats take visitors to the quay)* has several restaurants but no hotels. Take a **trip★★** around the island in a boat (contact the fishermen at the harbour) to discover the numerous caves which riddle the cliff faces.

Enna★

Surrounded by a sun-scorched landscape, Enna's isolated but panoramic site★★ has earned it the nickname of the Belvedere of Sicily.
According to legend it was on the shores of a lake, Lago di Pergusa, *(10km/6mi to the south)*, that Pluto carried off the youthful Proserpine (or Persephone), future Queen of the Underworld.

Location
Population 28 424 – Michelin map 432 O 24. At the centre of the island, Enna rises to an altitude of 942m/3 091ft. The main access road is A 19.
₿ *Piazza N. Colajanni 6,* ☎ *0935 26 119.*
Surrounding area: see Villa Imperiale del CASALE.

Worth a Visit

Castello di Lombardia★
Open daily, mid-Apr to mid-Oct 8am-8pm, rest of year 9am-1pm and 3-5pm. No charge. ☎ *0935 40 347.*
This medieval castle has six of its original 20 towers. From the top of the tallest there is an exceptional **panorama★★★** of the hilltop village of Calascibetta, Mount Etna and most of the Sicilian mountain peaks. Beyond the castle, the **belvedere**, once the site of a temple to Demeter, offers a fine **view★** of Calascibetta and of Enna itself.

Duomo
Open daily, 8am-1pm and 4-7pm. ☎ *0935 50 31 65.*
The cathedral was rebuilt in the Baroque style in the 16C and 17C but still has its 14C Gothic apses. Inside the building the finely carved coffered **ceiling★** is worthy of note, with its strange winged creatures at the end of each beam.

Torre di Federico★
At the far end of Via Roma facing the castle. In the past Enna could have been described as the town of towers. The town's strategic, defensive function accounts for the large number of these. The octagonal tower built by Emperor Frederick II of Hohenstaufen Swabia is impressively located at the centre of a small public garden.

Isole **Eolie**★★★

AEOLIAN or LIPARI ISLANDS

The Aeolian Islands, also known as the Lipari Islands, are so called because the ancients thought Aeolus, the God of the Winds, lived there. The archipelago comprises seven main islands, Lipari, Vulcano, Stromboli, Salina, Filicudi, Alicudi and Panarea, all of exceptional interest for their volcanic nature, their beauty, their light and their climate.

A deep blue, warm, clear sea, ideal for underwater fishing, interesting marine creatures including flying fish, swordfish, turtles, sea horses and hammerhead sharks, make the islands a refuge for those who like to live close to nature. Boat trips provide good views of the beautiful indented coastlines and hidden coves and bays. The inhabitants of the islands fish, grow vines and quarry pumice stone.

Location
Population 11 026 – Michelin map 432 L 25-27 and K 27. The Aeolian Islands lie off the coast near Milazzo, in the Tyhrrenian sea.

Worth a Visit

Lipari★
This, the largest island in the archipelago, is formed of volcanic rock dipping vertically into the sea. In ancient times Lipari was a source of obsidian, a glassy black volcanic rock, from which pumice stone was quarried on the east coast (the industry is now in decline). Today the islanders fish and grow cereals and capers.

Two bays (Marina Lunga with its beach and Marina Corta) frame the town of **Lipari★**, dominated by its old quarter encircled by 13C-14C walls. Inside is the castle rebuilt by the Spaniards in the 16C on the site of a Norman building. The castle houses the **Museo Archeologico Eoliano★★** which exhibits a re-creation of Bronze Age necropoli, a lovely collection of **red-figure kraters★**, **amphorae★** and terracotta **theatrical masks★★**. (&) *Open daily, 9am-1.30pm and 3-7pm. €4.13.* ☎ 090 98 80 174; *www.museolipari.org*

There are **boat trips★★** leaving from Marina Corta which take the visitor round the very rugged southwest coast of the island. When making a **tour of the island by car**, stop at Canneto and Campo Bianco to visit the pumice stone **quarries★**. The splendid **view★★** from the **Puntazze** headland includes five of the islands: Alicudi, Filicudi, Salina, Panarea and Stromboli. However, it is the belvedere at **Quattrocchi** which affords one of the finest **panoramas★★★** of the whole archipelago.

Vulcano★★★
This 21km²/8sq mile island is in reality four volcanoes. According to mythology it is here that Vulcan, the god of fire, had his forges – whence the term volcanism. Although there has been no eruption on the island since 1890 there are still important signs of activity: fumaroles (smoke-holes), spouting steam-jets often underwater, hot sulphurous mud flows greatly appreciated for their therapeutic properties. The island has a wild but forbidding beauty, with its rugged rocky shores,

The sulphurous vapours of Vulcano

Directory

GETTING ABOUT

Ferries run regularly from Milazzo, Messina, Reggio di Calabria, Palermo and Naples.
🖪 Ferries: Eolian Tours, Via Amendola 10, 98055 Lipari (Messina), ☎ 090 98 11 312; Eoltravel, Via Vittorio Emanuele 83, 98055 Lipari (Messina), ☎ 090 98 11 122.

WHERE TO EAT

• Moderate

E Pulera – Via Diana – 98055 Lipari – ☎ 090 98 11 158 – Closed lunchtime; Nov-May – Book – €29/37 + 12% service charge. One of the main attractions is the beautiful flower-filled garden where guests have dinner (authentic local fare). In July and August diners are entertained with live music and folk dancing displays.

Filippino – Piazza Municipio – 98055 Lipari – ☎ 090 98 11 002 – Closed Mon (except Jun-Sep), 16 Nov-15 Dec – 🍽 – €30/38 + 12% service charge. With its large open-air area in Piazza della Rocca, this place has become something of an institution throughout the archipelago and, indeed, the whole of Sicily. The menu (mostly fish) is dicated by the morning's catch, the dishes cooked according to tradition. Informal ambience and excellent (quick and efficient) service.

Punta Lena – Via Marina, località Ficogrande – 98050 Stromboli – ☎ 090 98 62 04 – Closed Nov-Mar – €31/43. The fish is always ultra-fresh and of very good quality, and the dishes are tasty, but if the seafood specialities lack a little imagination, you will be consoled by the setting. Meals are served under a lovely pergola with a splendid view of the sea.

WHERE TO STAY

• Moderate

Hotel Ericusa – 98050 Alicudi – ☎ 090 98 89 902 – Fax 090 98 89 910 – Closed Oct-May – 🛏 – 12 dbl rm €77.47 🍽 – Restaurant €31. This simple, small hotel is the only accommodation on the island. It is right on the beach and the rooms have their own private entrance. On the menu are lots of vegetables and fish (caught that morning). Would appeal to those looking for a sunny, seaside vacation and, most of all, peace and solitude!

Hotel La Canna – Contrada Rosa – 98050 Filicudi – ☎ 090 98 89 956 – Fax 090 98 89 966 – Closed Nov – 🍽 – 7 rm €51.64/103 – 🍽 €7.74 – Restaurant €27/31. Housed in an Aeolian-style building which is in keeping with the landscape, this hotel enjoys a panoramic setting overlooking the port and the sea. There are two very romantic rooms with a little terrace reserved for "honeymoon couples" but the wonderful swimming pool and sun lounge are open to everybody.

Hotel Poseidon – Via Ausonia 7 – 98055 Lipari – ☎ 090 98 12 876 – Fax 090 98 80 252 – Closed Nov-Feb – 🍽 – 18 rm €56.81/108.46 – 🍽 €7.75. Very centrally located. A small, Mediterranean-style establishment – lots of white and blue. Light and airy rooms with modern, functional furnishings. Sun lounge. Helpful staff.

• Expensive

Locanda del Barbablù – Via Vittorio Emanuele 17/19 – 98050 Stromboli – ☎ 090 98 61 18 – Fax 090 98 63 23 – Closed lunchtime, Nov and Feb – 🛏 – 6 dbl rm from €123.95 – Restaurant €31. You will receive a warm welcome here. Attractive, stylish rooms which successfully combine antique pieces with artisanal works. Imaginative and varied menu with something for everyone.

---

desolate areas and strangely coloured soils due to the presence of sulphur, iron oxides and alum. The island's main centre, **Porto di Levante**⚓, stands below the great crater. The beach is known for its particularly warm water due to the underwater spouting steam-jets.

Excursions to the **Great Crater★★★** (about 2hr on foot there and back) are interesting for the impressive views they afford of the crater and of the archipelago. The headland **Capo Grillo** affords a view of several islands.

A tour of the island by boat (starting from Porto Ponente) offers the visitor many curious views, especially along the northwestern coast, which is fringed with impressive basalt reefs.

Stromboli★★★

The volcano of Stromboli, with its plume of smoke, has a sombre beauty, and is a wild island with steep slopes. There are very few roads and such soil as can be cultivated is covered with vines yielding a delicious golden-coloured Malvasia wine. The little square, white houses are markedly Moorish in style.

The **crater★★★**, in the form of a 924m/3 032ft cone, has frequent minor eruptions with noisy explosions and accompanying flows of lava. To see the **spectacle★★★** climb up to the crater (about 5hr on foot there and back, difficult climb, visitors are advised to make the ascent in the company of a guide) or watch from a boat the famous flow of lava along the crevasse named Sciara del Fuoco towards the sea. Excursions: Authorised CAI-AGAI guides, Porto di Scari and Piazza San Vincenzo, Stromboli. ☎/Fax 090 98 62 11, 090 98 62 63, 368 66 49 18 or mobile 330 96 53 67.
At night the scene becomes both beautiful and awesome.

Salina★

The island is formed by six extinct volcanoes of which two have retained their characteristic outline. The highest crater, **Monte Fossa delle Felci** (962m/3 156ft) dominates the archipelago. There is a pleasant panoramic road round the island. Caper bushes and vines grow on the lower terraced slopes. The latter yield the delicious golden Malvasia wine.

Erice★★★

Occupying a unique and beautiful setting★★★ this ancient Phoenician and Greek city presents two faces: during the hot summers it is bright and sunny and the sun-drenched streets of the village, strategically located, offer splendid views★★ over the valley, whilst in winter Erice is wreathed in mist and seems a place lost in time.

In Antiquity Erice was a religious centre famous for its temple consecrated to Astarte, then to Aphrodite and finally Venus, who was venerated by mariners of old.

Location

Population 31 026 – Michelin map 432 M 19. Erice, rising almost vertically (750m/2 461ft) above the sea, is about 14km/8mi from Trapani, on the western side of the island. *Viale Conte Pepoli 11,* ☎ *0923 86 93 88.*

Surrounding area: see Isole EGADI, SEGESTA, TRAPANI.

Directory

WHERE TO EAT

• *Moderate*

Monte San Giuliano – *Vicolo San Rocco 7 –* ☎ *0923 86 95 95 – Closed Mon, 7-25 Jan and 5-23 Nov – Book – €24.27/34.09.* Located at the heart of the village is this lovely little establishment which serves authentic, local fare. Fine, rustic-style dining room but perhaps even more appealing is the pergola in the internal courtyard – very light and airy.

WHERE TO STAY

• *Budget*

Azienda Agricola Pizzolungo – *Contrada S. Cusumano – 96016 Erice Casa Santa –* ☎ *0923 56 37 10 – Fax 0923 56 97 80 – fraadr@tin.it –* ✉ 🖬 *– 6 apartments: per* head €30.99. A stone's throw from the sea is this 19C farmhouse surrounded by a lovely garden. A romantic and rustic establishment – how about a refreshing dip in an old stone trough? Apartments for 2, 4 and 6 people, complete with kitchen and private access.

• *Moderate*

Hotel Baglio Santacroce – *91019 Valderice – 2km/1.2mi east of Valderice –* ☎ *0923 89 11 11 – Fax 0923 89 11 92 –* 🅿 🏊 *– 25 rm €67/108* 🍽 *– Restaurant €18/23.* What was once a 17C farmhouse is now a charming, small hotel. Glorious, verdant setting with wonderful views of the Golfo di Cornino. The rooms may not be spacious but have plenty of character with exposed beams and tiled floors.

Walking About

Castello di Venere

This castle, built by the Normans in the 12C, crowns an isolated rock on Monte Erice, on the site of the Temple of Venus (Venere). From here and the nearby gardens (Giardino del Balio) there are admirable **views**★★ in clear weather the Tunisian coast can be seen.

Chiesa Matrice★

This church was built in the 14C using stones quarried from the Temple of Venus. The porch was added in the 15C and flanked by the square battlemented bell tower (13C) with its elegant openings.

Etna★★★

Etna is the highest point in the island (3 340m/10 950ft), and is snow-capped for most of the year. It is still active and it is the largest and one of the most famous volcanoes in Europe.
Etna was born of undersea eruptions which also formed the Plain of Catania, formerly covered by the sea.

Location

Michelin map 432 N-O 26-27. Etna dominates the Ionic coastline between Catania and Taormina. In 1987 the **Parco dell'Etna** was created, covering an area of 59 000ha/145 790 acres; in the centre of the park, the mountain has the appearance of a huge, black, distorted cone which can be seen from a distance of 250km/155 miles. On its lower slopes, which are extremely fertile, orange, mandarin, lemon and olive trees flourish as well as vines which produce the delicious Etna wine. Chestnut trees grow above the 500m/1 500ft level and give way higher up to oak, beech, birch and pine. Above 2 100m/6 500ft is the barren zone, where only a few clumps of *Astralagus siculus* (a kind of vetch) will be seen scattered on the slopes of secondary craters, among the clinker and volcanic rock.
Surrounding area: see CATANIA, TAORMINA.

> ### THE GIANT AWAKES
> Etna's eruptions were frequent in ancient times: 135 are recorded. But the greatest disaster occurred in 1669, when the flow of lava reached the sea, largely devastating Catania as it passed. The worst eruptions in recent times occurred in 1910, when 23 new craters appeared, 1917, when a jet of lava squirted up to 800m/2 500ft above its base, and 1923, when the lava ejected remained hot 18 months after the eruption. Since then, stirrings of Etna have been numerous...the last, in 2001, which involved the crater on the southeast side, swept away the lifts and the funicular platform and threatened to destroy the Sapienza Refuge and the town of Nicolisi.

Special Features

Ascent of the volcano★★★

By the south face from Catania via Nicolosi, or by the northeast face from Taormina via Linguaglossa. As the volcano may erupt at any time, tourist facilities (roads, paths, cable cars and refuge huts) may be closed, moved or withdrawn. Excursions may be cancelled in the case of bad weather (fog) or volcanic activity. The best time for the ascent is early morning. Wear warm clothing even in summer (anorak, thick pullover) and strong shoes (no heels – the stony terrain of the paths through the lava can cause injuries, particularly to ankles). Wear sunglasses to avoid the glare.

South face – *Depending on snow conditions, excursions take place from the week before Easter to 31 Oct. Duration: approx 3hr round trip. €28.41 including insurance and guide. For further details and information on excursions leaving at sunset, contact Gruppo Guide Alpine Etna Sud, Via Etnea 49, Nicolosi, ☏ 095 79 14 755 or Funivia dell'Etna, Piazza V. Emanuele 45, Nicolosi, ☏ 095 91 11 58 or 095 91 41 41. Another*

Etna

M. Magni/MICHELIN

option is to book a private trip with one of the alpine guides who organise trekking, alpine skiing as well as expeditions into the caves created by the lava flow. Some sections of the upper slopes have been destroyed by the eruption in 2001 and some of the paths to the summit are no longer accessible. The cable-car has also been replaced by a minibus service.

The ascent depends on the conditions on the volcano and stops close to the grandiose valley, **Valle del Bove,** which is hemmed in by walls of lava (1 200m/3 900ft high) pierced with pot holes and crevasses belching smoke.

Northeast face – *May-Oct. Excursions leave from Piano Provenzana. Duration: approx 3hr round trip. €36.15, including alpine guide. For further details and information on excursions leaving at dawn and at sunset, contact STAR, Via Santangelo Fulci 40, ☎ 095 37 13 33 – or ask at the Hotel Le Betulle di Piano Provenzana, Linguaglossa, ☎ 095 64 34 30.*

The road goes through Linguaglossa, a lovely pinewood and the winter sports resort of Villaggio Mareneve.

The surfaced road ends at Piano Provenzana (1 800m/5 900ft). There is a magnificent **view★★** from the area around the new observatory. The climb ends amid an extraordinary landscape of lava, which still smokes at times.

Circumetnea

This road runs around Etna, offering varied views of the volcano and passing through a number of interesting villages.

Messina

Despite having been destroyed numerous times throughout the centuries, Messina – the ancient Zancle of the Greeks – is today an active market town. Messina may have suffered repeated earthquakes (especially the 1908 one which destroyed 90% of the town and killed 60 000 in the region), as well as epidemics and bombings, but the townspeople remain remarkably resilient, buoyed by the cultural and commercial ties they have forged with other areas of Sicily and Europe.

Location

Population 259 156 – Michelin map 432 M 28 (including town plan). Messina overlooks that stretch of sea which separates Sicily from the main land. ☑ *Via Calabria, isol 301b, ☎ 090 67 42 36.*
Surrounding area: see TAORMINA.

Worth a Visit

Museo Regionale★

North of the town at the end of the Viale della Libertà (&) Open Tue-Sat, 9am to Sep 9am-7pm, also 4-6.30pm Tue, Thu and Sat (3-5.30pm in winter); Sun and hols 9am-1pm (ticket office always closes 30min early). Closed Mon. €4.13. ☎ 090 36 12 92.

The museum comprises an art gallery and a sculpture and decorative arts section. In the sculpture section there is a fine wooden crucifix dating from the early 15C. The painting section displays a *polyptych of St Gregory* (1473)

> **ANTONELLO DA MESSINA**
>
> The artist was born in Messina in 1430 and he studied in Naples where he was influenced by the then popular Flemish art. Later he was to be attracted by the innovations of Tuscan painting which, with its increasing use of perspective, emphasised volume and architectural details. His works show a complete mastery of his art, forms and colours, skilfully balanced, enhance an inner vision which greatly influenced the Venetian painters of the Renaissance, notably Carpaccio and Giovanni Bellini. Antonello died on his native island around 1479.

by Antonello da Messina, a remarkable composition which combines the Tuscan idiom with the earliest Flemish influences, a remarkable **Descent from the Cross** by the Flemish artist Colin van Coter (15C); and two Caravaggios, **Adoration of the Shepherds** and **Resurrection of Lazarus**, both painted towards the end of his life from 1608 to 1610. The **Berlina del Senato★** painted in 1742 is particularly worthy of note.

Duomo
Open Mon-Sat, 9.30am-7pm, Sun 10.30-11am and 4-7pm. ☎ 090 77 48 95.
The cathedral, almost entirely rebuilt after the 1908 earthquake and the bombings of 1943, still displays the main features of its original Norman style (12C). The finely carved central **doorway★** dates from the 15C. To the left stands the campanile (60m/196ft tall) with its **astronomical clock★** which was made in Strasbourg in 1933 and is believed to be the world's largest.

Santissima Annunziata dei Catalani
Take the Via Cesare Battisti from the south side of the cathedral. The church which was built in 1100 during the Norman reign and altered in the 13C, takes its name from the Catalan merchants who owned it. The **apse★** is characteristic of the composite Norman style which blends Romanesque (small columns supporting blind arcades), Moorish (geometric motifs and polychrome stonework) and Byzantine (dome on a drum) influences.

Excursion

Tindari★*62km/37mi west.* The ancient Greek Tyndaris, founded in 396 BC, is perched on the summit of the cape of the same name. At the very point stands a **sanctuary** with a Black Virgin which is a place of pilgrimage. The **ruins** *(rovine)* are essentially those of the city **ramparts**, the **theatre** on a site facing the sea, and the so-called **Basilica**, a fine arcaded Roman building (access by the main street, the Decumanus) which preceded the forum. *Open daily, 9am to 2hr before sunset.* €2.07.☎ 0941 36 90 23.

Noto★★

Noto, which dates from the time of the Siculi, was completely destroyed by the terrible earthquake of 1693. It was rebuilt on a new site 10km/6mi distant from the original town. Lining the streets, laid out on a grid plan, are handsome palaces, churches and other Baroque monuments in the local white limestone, which has mellowed with time to a golden hue. Several Sicilian architects worked together on this project. The most inventive was probably Rosario Gagliardi.

Location
Population 21 663 – Michelin map 432 Q 27. Noto is situated deep in the south of the island. The main access road is S 115. 🄳 *Piazza XVI Maggio,* ☎ 0931 83 67 44. *Surrounding area: see RAGUSA, SIRACUSA.*

Special Features

The Baroque centre★★
The hub of the town is **Corso Vittorio Emanuele**, which widens into three squares overlooked by the monumental façades of churches designed in an imposing but flexible Baroque style: **San Francesco all'Immacolata** and the **cathedral★★** (the cupola and much of the central nave collapsed in 1996) in the attractive **Piazza Municipio★**, and **San Domenico★**. *S. Francesco: Open daily, Jun to Sep 7.30am-12.30pm and 4-8pm, rest of year 7.30am-noon and 3.30-7.30pm.* ☎ 0931 83 50 05. *S. Domenico: Currently closed for restoration.* ☎ 0931 83 50 05.
To the right of San Domenico is **Via Corrado Nicolaci★**, a gently sloping street which offers an enchanting vista with the church of Montevergine as focal point. It is lined with palaces sporting splendid balconies; the most notable is **Palazzo Nicolaci di Villadorata** with exuberantly fanciful **balconies★★★**.

Palermo★★★

Palermo, the capital and the chief seaport of Sicily, is built at the head of a wide bay enclosed to the north by Monte Pellegrino and to the south by Capo Zafferano. It lies on the edge of a wonderfully fertile plain bounded by hills and nicknamed the Conca d'Oro (Golden Basin), where lemon and orange groves flourish.

Location
Population 683 794 – Michelin map 432 M 21-22 (including plan of built-up area). Palermo is situated on the northern coast. The main access roads are A 19 and A 29. ▤ *Piazza Castelnuovo 34,* ☎ *091 58 38 47.*
Surrounding area: see CEFALÙ, USTICA.

Background

Palermo was founded by the Phoenicians, conquered by the Romans and later came under Byzantine rule. From 831 to 1072 it was under the sway of the Saracens, who gave the city its special atmosphere suggested today by the luxuriance of its gardens and the shape of the domes on some buildings. Conquered by the Normans in 1072, Palermo became the capital under **Roger II**, who took the title of King of Sicily. This great builder succeeded in blending Norman architectural styles with the decorative traditions of the Saracens and Byzantines: his reign was the golden age of art in Palermo. Later the Hohenstaufen and Angevin kings introduced the Gothic style (13C). After more than three centuries of Spanish rule, the Bourbons of Naples gave Palermo its splendid Baroque finery.

The Sicilian Vespers
Since 1266 the brother of Louis IX of France, Charles I of Anjou, supported by the pope, had held the town. But his rule was unpopular. The Sicilians had nicknamed the French, who spoke Italian badly, the *tartaglioni* or stammerers. On the Monday or Tuesday after Easter 1282, as the bells were ringing for vespers, some Frenchmen insulted a young woman of Palermo in the church of Santo Spirito. Insurrection broke out, and all Frenchmen who could not pronounce the world *cicero* (chick-pea) correctly were massacred.

Special Features

Palazzo dei Normanni★★
Of the immense royal palace built by the Normans on the site of an earlier Moorish fortress, only the central part and the massive Pisan Tower are of the Norman period.
Cappella Palatina★★★ – *1st floor of Palazzo dei Normanni.* Built in the reign of Roger II from 1130 to 1140, it is a wonderful example of Arab-Norman decoration. Ten Classical columns separate the nave and two aisles. The upper walls, the dome and the apses are covered with dazzling **mosaics★★★** which, along with those of Constantinople and Ravenna, are the finest in Europe. This splendid decoration is complemented by the carved stalactite ceiling, marble paving, and the ornate pulpit and paschal candelabrum.

Open Mon-Fri 9am-noon and 3-5pm, Sat 9am-noon, Sun 9.10am and noon-1pm (ticket office closes 30min earlier). Closed Sat and Sun pm, hols. No charge. ☎ 091 70 54 879.
On the second floor the old royal apartments, **Antichi appartamenti reali★★**, house the 12C King Roger's chamber, **Sala di re Ruggero**, which is adorned with mosaics of the chase. (&) *Guided tours only (30min), Mon, Fri and Sat 9am-noon, for groups with prior authorisation from police headquarters. Fax 091 70 54 737, www.ars.sicilia.it*

The attractive gardens, **Villa Bonanno★**, boast superb palm trees.

Walking About

FROM PALAZZO DEI NORMANNI TO THE CALA
Visit: 3hr. The route begins at Palazzo dei Normanni, the focus of Sicilian politics, both past and present, passes through two pretty squares which form the busy centre of Palermo and ends at the Cala, the old harbour of the city.

Chiesa di San Giovanni degli Eremiti★★

Open Mar to Oct, Mon-Sat 9am-7.30pm, Sun and hols 9am-2pm; rest of year 9am-7pm, Sun and hols 9am-1.30pm (ticket office always closes 30min early). €4.13. ☎ 091 65 15 019.

Only a stone's throw from the Palazzo dei Normanni, this church, with its surrounding gardens, is a green oasis where even the noise of the traffic is dulled. The church, dedicated to St John of the Hermits, was built with the aid of Arab architects in 1132 at the request of King Roger II and is picturesquely crowned with pink domes. Beside it is a garden of tropical plants with pleasant 13C **cloisters★** of small twin columns.

Turn into Via Vittorio Emanuele, the main thoroughfare in the centre of the city, which divides Palermo into two parts. The cathedral is on the left.

Flavour of the East: San Giovanni degli Eremiti

Cattedrale★

Open Mon-Sat, 7am-7pm, Sun and hols 8am-1pm and 4-7pm. ☎ 091 33 43 76.

Founded at the end of the 12C, the cathedral is built in the Sicilian-Norman style *(see Historical and Artistic Notes on Sicily, p 485)* but has often been modified and added to (the 15C south porch and the 18C dome). The **apses★** of the east end have retained their typically Sicilian-Norman decoration.

In the interior, which was modified in the 18C in the neo-Classical style, note the tombs of the Emperor Frederick II and other members of the Hohenstaufen dynasty as well as of Angevin and Aragonese rulers. The **Treasury** *(Tesoro)* displays the ornate **imperial crown★** which belonged to Constance of Aragon. *Treasury: Open Mon-Sat, 10am-12.30pm and 2-4pm. €1.03; €1.55 including Treasure and Crypt.*

Quattro Canti★

Two main streets, Via Vittorio Emanuele and Via Maqueda, intersect to form this busy crossroads with four canted corners *(Quattro Canti)* decorated with statues and fountains. The crossroads form a fine early-17C ensemble in the Spanish Baroque style. The church of **San Giuseppe ai Teatini** has an astonishingly decorative **interior★**.

La Martorana★★

Open daily Apr to Sep, 8am-1pm and 3.30-7pm, rest of year Mon-Sat, 8am-1pm and 3.30-5.30pm, Sun and hols 8.30am-1pm. Donation recommended. ☎ 091 61 61 692.

The real name of this church is Santa Maria dell'Ammiraglio (St Mary of the Admiral). It was founded in 1143 by the Admiral of the Fleet to King Roger II and altered in the 16C and 17C by the addition of a Baroque façade on the north side. Pass under the elegant 12C belfry-porch to enter the original church which is decorated with beautiful Byzantine **mosaics★★** depicting scenes from the New Testament *(Annunciation, Nativity, Death of the Virgin)* and in the cupola, the imposing figure of *Christ Pantocrator* (Christ as Ruler of All) surrounded by angels, the Prophets and the Evangelists. At the very end of the two side aisles note the two panels depicting *Roger II crowned by Christ (right),* and *Admiral George of Antioch kneeling before the Virgin (left).*

Chiesa di San Cataldo★★

Open Mon-Fri, 8.30am-3pm, Sat 8.30am-1pm, Sun 9am-1pm. Closed hols. ☎ 091 87 28 047.

This splendid church, founded in the 12C, recalls Moorish architecture with its severe square shape, its domes, its decorative crenellations and the traceried openings of the façade.

The two churches face each other on the small **Piazza Bellini★**. The Moorish and Norman features of the square are particularly evident in the three rose-coloured cupolas of San Cataldo.

Directory

GETTING THERE

The easiest and quickest way to get to Palermo is by **air**. The city airport, Falcone-Borsellino, named after two judges who were murdered in 1992 (and formerly known as Punta-Raisi), is situated 30km/18mi north of Palermo, off the A 29 dual carriageway, ☎ 091 70 20 111. It is served by various airlines including Alitalia, Alpi Eages, Air Sicilia, Med Airlines, Meridiana and Air Europe. A bus links the airport with the city centre every 30min, stopping in Via le Lazio, Piazza Ruggero Settimo in front of Hotel Politeama, and at the main railway station. The 1hr journey costs €4.65 (single). For information contact ☎ 091 58 04 57.

The island can also be reached by **ferry** from:

Genoa: Grandi Navi Veloci, Via Fieschi 17 ☎ 010 58 93 31, Fax 010 55 09 225 (20hr).

Livorno: Grandi Navi Veloci, Varco Galvani Darsena 1, ☎ 0586 40 98 04, Fax 0586 42 97 17, (only certain days, 17hr).

Naples: Tirrenia Navigazione, Stazione Marittima, Molo Angioino, ☎ 081 25 14 740, Fax 25 14 767 (11hr); Aliscafi SNAV, Via Caracciolo 10, ☎ 081 76 12 348, Fax 081 76 12 141 (from Apr to Oct, 4hr30min).

Cagliari: Tirrenia Navigazione (www.tirrenia.it), agenzia Agenave, Molo Sanità, Stazione Marittima, ☎ 070 66 60 65, Fax 070 65 23 37 (only one departure a week, 13hr30min).

Getting around – It is best to avoid driving in Palermo because of traffic congestion and the difficulty of finding somewhere to park. Large car parks can be found on the outskirts of the city (marked by a 🅿 on the map). There is also a free car park in Piazza Maggiore, 300m from the Botanical Gardens. Other parking facilities (for which there is a charge) include Piazza Giulio Cesare 43, Porto, Via Guardione 81, Porto and Via Stabile 10.

However, by far the best way to see the city is by public transport and taxi for longer distances and on foot once in the old town.

Bus – There are two types of ticket: tickets valid for 90min cost €0.77 and the daily tickets (which expire at midnight) cost €2.58 and are a good option if you intend to use public transport more than three times during the course of the day.

Taxis – Autoradio Taxi ☎ 091 51 27 27 and Radio Taxi Trinacria ☎ 091 22 54 55.

WHERE TO EAT

• *Budget*

Pizzeria Tonnara Florio – Discesa Tonnara 4, zona Arenella – ☎ 091 63 75 611 – Closed Mon – ⌀. This attractive Liberty-style building, unfortunately in need of restoration, has a beautiful garden and a number of rooms once used for processing tuna and repairing fishing boats. The old tuna room in the building now houses a pizzeria. There is also a nightclub.

Antica Focacceria San Francesco – Viale Sandro Paternostro 58 – ☎ 091 32 02 64 – ⌀. This establishment is situated in the heart of the medieval quarter, in front of the church of San Francesco. With its marble tables and an unusual counter carved out of an old cast-iron stove, it has a pleasantly old-fashioned feel about it. Specialities include *focaccie farcite* (flat-pizza dough baked with various fillings, *arancini* (deep-fried rice balls) and *torte salate* (savoury pastries).

Di Martino – *Via Mazzini 54* – ⌀. After a morning's sightseeing – taking in 19C Palermo and maybe the Museo d'Arte Moderna – you will probably have worked up an appetite. If you are not in the mood for a full-blown lunch, this is the place to head for a sandwich: they are both exquisitely presented and delicious. Tables outside.

Lara Pessina/MICHELIN

Puppets

• *Moderate*

Capricci di Sicilia – *Via Istituto Pignatelli 6, angolo piazza Sturzo* – ☎ 091 32 77 77 – ⌂ – €24/40. A rather unusual establishment – you will probably see the odd mime artist and even the street vendors poking their head round the door. Simple surroundings and informal service, but its main attraction is the excellent quality of the cooking which draws its inspiration from the cuisine and produce of the area.

Bye Bye Blues – *Via del Garofalo 23, zona Mondello* – ☎ 091 68 41 415 – Closed at lunchtime (except Sun and public holidays), Tue – Book – €23/46. This is a must as much for the ambience as the food. The menus, imaginative, the dishes (both fish and meat, in equal measure) are well put together and there is an excellent wine list. Not to be missed!

Santandrea – Piazza Sant'Andrea 4 – ☎ 091 33 49 99 – Closed Sun (Jul and Aug), Tue, Jan – Book – €31/41. This restaurant, in the heart of the Vucciria district, serves traditional Sicilian cuisine.

WHERE TO STAY

• *Budget*

Hotel Azzurro di Lampedusa – *Via Roma 111, (5th floor, with lift)* – www.hotelazzurrodilampedusa.it – 16 rm €36.15/54.23 ⌀. Housed in a palazzo right in the historic centre, this establishment would appeal to visitors looking for the real Palermo and a bit of local colour. No-frills rooms with basic facilities. Offers good value for money.

Hotel Moderno – *Via Roma 276 –* ☎ *091 58 86 83 – Fax 091 58 82 60 –* 🖵 *– 38 rm €46.48/61.97 –* 🖵 *€2.58.* The main attraction here is the warm, friendly welcome from the staff who will do their utmost to make guests feel at home. Simple, good-sized rooms although the modern furnishings are possibly just a little too spartan.

• **Moderate**

Hotel Gardenia – *Via Mariano Stabile 136 –* ☎ *091 32 27 61 – Fax 091 33 37 32 – gardeniahotel@gardeniahotel.com –* 🖵 *– 16 rm €61.97/87.80* 🖵. A small, family-run hotel housed on the upper floors of an old palazzo in the city centre. Simple rooms (some have a balcony overlooking the city). Reasonably priced.

• **Expensive**

Massimo Plaza Hotel – *Via Maqueda 437 –* ☎ *091 32 56 57 – Fax 091 32 57 11 –* 🖵 *– 15 rm from €98.13* 🖵. Small but elegant and stylish, this hotel is situated opposite the neo-Classical Teatro Massimo. Very attentive service. The rooms (spacious) and the public areas are all tastefully decorated with warm colours, attractive furnishings and wooden floors.

Centrale Palace Hotel – *Corso Vittorio Emanuele 327 –* ☎ *091 33 66 66 – Fax 091 33 48 81 –* 🅿 🖵 ♿ *– 63 rm from €144 –* 🖵 *€10.33 – Restaurant €33/51.* The elegant, tasteful Centrale Palace is located in a 17C mansion and offers

excellent hospitality. This hotel has attractive public areas, including a panoramic restaurant on the top floor.

TAKING A BREAK

Bar Costa – *Via G. d'Annunzio 15 – Wed-Mon 8am-9pm.* Specialises in all kinds of cakes and pastries (especially lemon and orange mousses).

Mazzara – *Via Generale Magliocco 15 –* ☎ *091 32 14 43 – Sun-Fri 8am-9pm, Sat 8am-11.30pm.* The long-established *pasticceria* (pastry shop), where Giuseppe Tomasi di Lampedusa, the author of *Il Gattopardo (The Leopard)* used to stop for breakfast.

Oscar – *Via Mariano Migliaccio 39 –* ☎ *091 68 22 381 – Wed-Mon 8am-9pm.* The best-known speciality here is a Devil's food cake.

SHOPPING

The food markets in Palermo are full of life and regional character, with a range of colourful lamp-lit stalls selling fresh fruit, vegetables and local fish. The most famous is without a doubt **Vucciria** market, a vibrant, colourful food market which is held every morning (except Sunday) until 2pm not far from the quayside in Via Cassari-Argenteria and the surrounding area (almost up to Piazza San Domenico). Other lively markets include the **Ballarò** food market in the area around Piazza del Carmine, and **Capo** market, the most interesting part of which sells food (Piazza Beati Paoli) and the second section of which sells a variety of clothing (Via San Agostino and Via Bandiera).

Piazza Pretoria at night

Piazza Pretoria★★

The square has a spectacular **fountain★★** surmounted by numerous marble statues, the work of a 16C Florentine artist. The **Palazzo Pretorio**, now the town hall, occupies one side of this square.

Immediately to the north of the last stretch of Corso Vittorio Emanuele, is a lively food market, the **Vucciria**, which is open every morning except Sunday. To the other side is a quieter area where visitors can enjoy exploring the churches and palaces.

Chiesa di San Francesco d'Assisi★

Open Mon-Fri, 10am-4pm, Sat 9am-noon. Closed Sun. Contact the pastor several days in advance. ☎ *091 58 23 70.*

The church, dedicated to St Francis of Assisi, was built in the 13C. After its destruction during the Second World War it was rebuilt in the original style. Particularly noteworthy are the **portal** (original) and the rose window on the façade. The spacious, simple interior contains statues of allegorical figures by Giovanni Serpotta.

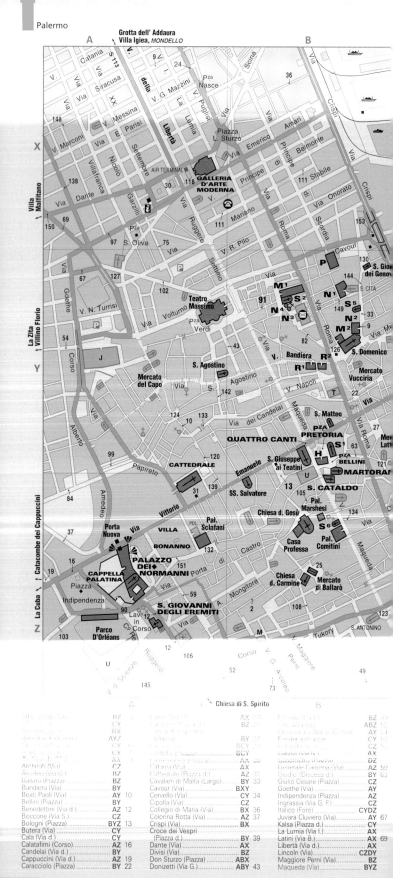

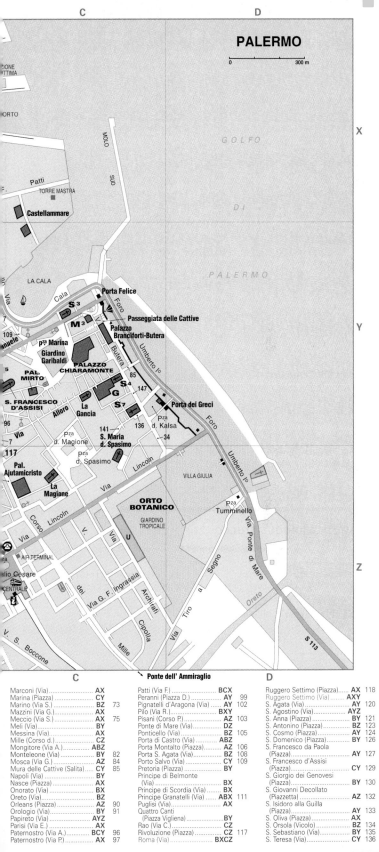

PALERMO

0   300 m

GOLFO

DI

PALERMO

LA CALA

Porta Felice

Passeggiata delle Cattive

Palazzo
Branciforti-Butera

p.za Marina
Giardino
Garibaldi

PALAZZO
CHIARAMONTE

PAL.
MIRTO

S. FRANCESCO
D'ASSISI

Alloro
La
Gancia

Porta dei Greci

P.za
d. Kalsa

S. Maria
d. Spasimo

P.za
d. Magione

P.za
d. Spasimo

Pal.
Ajutamicristo

La
Magione

Lincoln

VILLA GIULIA

ORTO
BOTANICO

GIARDINO
TROPICALE

P.za
Tumminello

AIR TERMINAL

llio Cesare

CENTRALE

V. S. Boccone

Ponte dell' Ammiraglio

Sammartino (Via)	AX	138
Scienze (Via d.)	AZ	
Scina (Via)	BX	
Scuole (Via d.)	AZ	139
Siracusa (Via)	AX	
Spasimo (Piazza d.)	CYZ	
Spasimo (Via d.)	CY	141
Spirito Santo (Via d.)	ABY	142
Squarcialupo (Via)	BY	144
Stabile (Via M.)	AYBX	
Stazzone (Piazza)	AZ	145
Tiro a segno Nazionale (Via)	DZ	
Torremuzza (Via)	CY	147
Tukory (Corso)	ABZ	
Turrisi (Via N.)	AY	
Turrisi Colonna (Via)	AX	148
Valver de (Via)	BY	149
Verdi (Piazza)	ABY	
Villafranca (Via)	AX	
Virgilio (Piazza)	AX	150
Vittoria (Piazza d.)	AZ	151
Vittorio Emanuele (Corso)	AZCY	
Volturno (Via)	AY	
XIII Vittime (Piazza d.)	BX	153
XX Settembre (Via)	AX	

Cappella Palatina	AZ	
Casa Professa	BZ	
Castello a Mare	CXY	
Catacombe dei Cappuccini	AZ	
Cattedrale	AZ	
Chiesa del Carmine	BZ	
Chiesa del Gesù	BZ	
Chiesa di S. Spirito	ABZ	
Galleria d'Arte Moderna (Teatro Politeama)	AX	
Galleria Regionale di Sicilia (Pal. Abatellis)	CY	G
Giardino Garibaldi	CY	
Grotta dell'Addaura	AX	
La Gancia	CY	
La Magione	CZ	
La Cuba	AZ	
La Ziza	AY	
Martorana	BY	
Mercata Vucciria	BY	
Mercato di Ballarò	BZ	
Mercato di Capo	AY	
Mercato Lattarini	BY	
Museo Archeologico Regionale	BY	M1
Museo Internazionale delle Marionette	CY	M3
Museo del Risorgimento	BY	M2
Oratorio del Rosario di S. Cita	BY	N1
Oratorio del Rosario di S. Domenico	BY	N2
Oratorio di S. Caterina d'Alessandria	BY	N3
Oratorio di S. Filippo Neri	BY	N5
Oratorio di S. Lorenzo	CY	N4
Orto Botanico	CDZ	
Palazzo Ajutamicristo	CZ	
Palazzo Branciforti-Butera	CY	
Palazzo Chiaramonte	CY	
Palazzo Comitini	BZ	
Palazzo dei Normanni	AZ	
Palazzo Marchesi	BZ	
Palazzo Mirto	CY	
Palazzo Oneto di Sperlinga	BY	R1
Palazzo Pretorio (Municipio)	BY	H
Palazzo Sclafani	AZ	
Palazzo Termine	BY	R2
Parco d'Orléans	AZ	
Passeggiata delle Cattive	CY	
Ponte dell'Ammiraglio	CDZ	
Porta dei Greci	CY	
Porta Felice	CY	
Porta Nuova	AZ	
Prefettura	BY	P
Quattro Canti	BYZ	
S. Agostino	AY	
S. Cataldo	BZ	
S. Caterina	BY	S1
S. Domenico	BY	
S. Francesco d'Assisi	CY	
S. Giorgio dei Genovesi	BY	
S. Giovanni degli Eremiti	AZ	
S. Giuseppe ai Teatini	BY	
S. Ignazio all'Olivella	BY	S2
S. Maria della Catena	CY	S3
S. Maria della Pietà	CY	S4
S. Maria dello Spasimo	CYZ	
S. Maria di Valverde	BY	S5
S. Matteo	BY	
S. Orsola	BZ	S6
S. Teresa alla Kalsa	CY	S7
SS. Salvatore	BZ	
Teatro Massimo	AY	
Villa Bonanno	AZ	
Villa Igiea	AX	
Villa Malfitano	AX	
Vucciria	BY	

Palazzo Chiaramonte★

This fine Gothic palace (1307) served as a model for many buildings in Sicily and southern Italy.

In the gardens, **Giardino Garibaldi**, opposite there are two spectacular **magnolia-fig trees★★** (*Ficus magnolioides*).

The Cala

The old harbour of the city is known as the *cala*, and was once enclosed by chains kept in the Gothic-Renaissance style church of **Santa Maria alla Catena★**.

Worth a Visit

A RIOT OF BAROQUE STUCCO

Oratorio del Rosario di San Domenico★★★

For information on tours ☎ 329 61 95 122.

The stucco decor of this church was the work of **Giacomo Serpotta**, an important artist of the Baroque period. The freedom of movement achieved in the figures of the putti is particularly striking.

Oratorio del Rosario di Santa Cita★★★

Open daily, 9am-1pm and 3-5pm. Sun contact the nuns at the nearby Istituto del Sacro Cuore. Donation recommended. ☎ 091 33 27 79.

This church is considered to be the masterpiece of **Giacomo Serpotta**, who worked on it between 1686 and 1718. Panels depicting the Mysteries are framed by a group of rejoicing angels and cherubim.

Oratorio di San Lorenzo★★★

Open 9am-1pm. A late work and masterpiece of **Giacomo Serpotta** decorated with stuccowork recalling scenes from the lives of St Francis *(on the right)* and St Lawrence *(on the left)*. It is a highly imaginative riot of rejoicing putti.

PALAZZI AND MUSEUMS

Galleria Regionale della Sicilia★★

Open Mon-Sat 9am-2pm, Tue and Thu also 3-8pm, Sun and hols 9am-1.30pm (ticket office closes 30min early). €4.13. ☎ 091 62 30 011.

This museum and gallery is housed in the attractive 15C **Palazzo Abatellis★**. It includes a medieval art section and a picture gallery featuring works from the 11C to the 18C. The design of the gallery, which was built by Carlo Scarpa in the 1950s, is particularly interesting. The famous architect and designer concentrated on finding the best backdrop for the most important paintings, focusing on the frame and background, the materials and colours in order to maximise the impact of the natural light. Outstanding works include the dramatic fresco of **Death Triumphant**★★★ from Palazzo Sclafani and a very fine **bust of Eleonora of Aragon**★★ by Francesco Laurana. Paintings of note include the **Annunciation**★★ by Antonello da Messina, with Mary's face exuding both a sense of peace and acceptance, and a triptych, the **Malvagna Altarolo**★★, by the Flemish artist Mabuse.

Museo Internazionale delle Marionette★★

Open Mon-Fri 9am-1pm and 4-7pm. Closed Sat-Sun and hols €3. ☎ *091 32 80 60, 091 32 80 60, www.museomarionettepalermo.it*

This museum is a testament to the lively tradition of puppet *(marionette)* shows in Sicily. These animated spectacles were an even bigger part of Sicilian life in the past. Shows generally concentrated on chivalric themes, in particular the adventures of two important heros, Rinaldo and Orlando, who personified very different characters and temperaments.

The museum houses a splendid collection of Sicilian puppets. The delicate features of Gaspare Canino's puppets are admirable: these puppets are among the oldest in the collection (19C). The second part of the museum is dedicated to both European and non-European craftsmanship and features puppets from all over Asia and Africa. The darkness of the room lends an air of mystery to the collection.

Museo Archeologico Regionale★

(&) *Open daily, 8.30am-7pm (ticket office closes 6.30pm). €4.13; €7.75 including Palazzo Abatellis and Palazzo Mirto.* ☎ *091 61 16 805.*

The archaeological museum, which is housed in a 16C convent, contains the finds from excavations of the numerous ancient sites in Sicily. On the ground floor are displayed two Phoenician sarcophagi, an Egyptian inscription known as the Palermo Stone and pieces from Selinus. These last include a fine series of twin stelae and the reconstruction of a temple pediment *(Sala Gabrici)* and especially the remarkable **metopes**★★ from the temples (6C and 5C BC). On the first floor are displayed bronzes including **Heracles with stag**★ and the famous **Ram**★★, a Hellenistic work from Syracuse, and marble statues, notably **Satyr**★, a copy of an original by Praxiteles. On the second floor are two fine mosaics (3C BC), *Orpheus with animals* and the *Mosaic of the seasons.*

Palazzo Mirto★

& *Open Mon-Sat 9am-6.30pm, Sun and hols 9am-1pm. €2.58; €5.16 or €7.75 to include two or three museums.* ☎ *091 61 64 751; www.manol.com/soprintendenza.pa*

The main residence of the Lanza-Filangieri princes contains its original 18C and 19C furnishings. Outside the palace, the **stables**★ which date back to the 19C, are of interest. The piano nobile *(1st floor)* with its drawing-rooms and formal rooms is open to visitors. The splendid **Salottino cinese** (Chinese Room) has leather flooring and silk wall coverings depicting scenes from everyday life, while the walls in the unusual **Smoking Room**★ are decorated with painted and engraved leather. The **Salottino Pompadour** (Pompadour Room) is impressive for the richness of the silk that covers the walls. Exhibits of note include a 19C Neapolitan dinner service depicting figures in traditional costume *(in the passageway facing the Chinese Room)* and the 18C Meissen porcelain decorated with flowers and animals *(in the dining room).*

ADDITIONAL SIGHTS

Villa Malfitano★★

Off the map. Follow Via Dante. Guided tours only (30min), daily except Sun 9am-1pm. Closed Sun, hols and 15 Jul. €2. ☎ *091 68 20 522.*

Surrounded by beautiful **gardens**★★, this Liberty-style villa has retained its elegant interior decor, including many Oriental furnishings. Particularly worthy of note is the **decoration** of the **Sala d'estate** (Summer Room) by Ettore de Maria Bergler; the *trompe l'oeil* effect transforms the room into a cool veranda surrounded by greenery.

Catacombe dei Cappuccini★★

Access by Via dei Cappuccini, at the bottom of Corso Vittorio Emanuele. Open daily, summer 9am-noon and 3-5.30pm, rest of year 9am-noon and 3-5pm. €1.29. These Capuchin catacombs are an impressive sight. About 8 000 mummies were placed here from the 17C to 19C and have been preserved by the very dry air. They are decked out in their finery and are placed in a line.

La Zisa★

Access by Corso Finocchiaro Aprile. (&) *Open Mar to Oct, Mon-Sat 9am-7.30pm, Sun and hols 9am-2pm, rest of year Mon-Sat 9am-7pm, Sun and hols 9am-1.30pm (ticket office always closes 30min early). €4.13.* ☎ *091 65 20 269.*

This magnificent pleasure palace in the Arab-Norman style was built in the 12C and remodelled in the 17C. The palace (restored) now houses a collection of Egyptian works from the Mameluke and Ottoman periods, which probably complemented the decoration of the palace. The austere exterior is in contrast to the very ornate decoration inside.

Orto Botanico★

Open Mon-Fri 9am-5pm, Sat-Sun and hols 9am-1pm. Closed 1 Jan, Easter, 15 Aug, 25 Dec. €3.10. ☎ 091 62 38 241.

A quiet and secluded garden with a fine collection of exotic plants and trees, including some magnificent **magnolia-fig trees★★** (*Ficus magnolioides*).

Parco della Favorita

3km/2mi north along Via Diana. This park was laid out for the Bourbons in the 18C. Beside the Chinese pavilion (Palazzina Cinese) is a museum, the **Museo Etnografico Pitrè**, which displays a number of traditional Sicilian objects. (&)
Open daily except Fri, 8.30am-8pm (ticket office closes 7.30pm). Closed mid-week hols and Easter. €3.10 ☎ 091 74 04 893.

Excursions

Monreale★★★

8km/5mi southwest. The town, dominating the green plain known as the Conca d'Oro (Golden Basin) of Palermo, grew up around the famous Benedictine **abbey** founded in the 12C by the Norman King, William II.

Duomo★★★ – *Open daily, 8am-6.30pm. Treasury in Cappella del SS. Crocifisso 9.30-11.45am and 3.30-5.45pm. €2.07. Lift to terraces: 9.30-11.45am and 3.30-5.45pm. €1.55.*
The finely carved central doorway of the cathedral has beautiful **bronze doors★★** (1185) embellished with stylised figures, which were carved by Bonanno Pisano. The more Byzantine north **doorway★** is the work of Barisano da Trani (12C). The decoration of the **chevet★★** is remarkable for the blending of Moorish and Norman styles. The cathedral has a basilical plan. The interior is dazzling with multicoloured marbles, paintings, and especially the 12C and 13C **mosaics★★★** adorning the oven vaults and the walls. They represent the complete cycle of the Old and New Testaments. A gigantic ***Christ Pantocrator*** (Ruler of All) is enthroned in the central apse. Above the episcopal throne, in the choir, a mosaic represents King William II offering the cathedral to the Virgin. Another mosaic opposite, over the royal throne, shows the same King William receiving his crown from the hands of Christ.

From the **terraces★★★** there are magnificent **views★★** of the cloisters and over the fertile plain of the Conca d'Oro.

Chiostro★★★ – (&) *Open Mon-Sat, summer 9am-7.30pm, Sun and hols 9am-2pm; rest of year 9am-7pm, Sun and hols 9am-1.30pm. €4.13. ☎ 091 64 04 403.*
The cloisters to the right of the church are as famous as the mosaics. They afford views of the abbey church. On the south side there is a fountain that was used as a lavabo by the monks. The galleries, with their sharply pointed arches, are supported by twin columns with remarkably carved capitals.

Monte Pellegrino

14km/9mi north. The road out of the city affords splendid **glimpses★★★** of Palermo and the Conca d'Oro. On the way up, the road passes a 17C sanctuary, **Santuario di Santa Rosalia**.

Bagheria

16km/10mi east. Bagheria is known for its Baroque villas and especially for the **Villa Palagonia★**, which is decorated with **sculptures★** of grotesques and monsters. Villa Cattolica houses the **Civica Galleria d'Arte Moderna e Contemporanea Renato Guttuso** as well as the tomb of the painter himself by Giacomo Manzù (1912-1987). *Villa Palagonia. Open daily, Apr-mid Oct 9am-1pm and 4-7pm, rest of year 9am-1pm and 3.30-5.30pm. €4.13. ☎ 091 93 20 88. www.villapalagonia.it. Galleria d'Arte Moderna e Contemporanea. & Open daily except Mon, May-Sep 10am-8pm, rest of the year 9am-7pm. Closed 1 Jan, Easter, 15 Aug, 25 Dec. €4.13. ☎ 091 90 34 38.*

Rovine di Solunto★

19km/12mi east. Open Mar to Oct, Mon-Sat, 9am-6.30pm, rest of year 9am-1.30pm, Sun and hols 9am-1pm. €2.50. ☎ 091 90 45 57.
Soluntum has a splendid site on a rocky ledge on the promontory which overlooks a headland, Capo Zafferano. It was a Phoenician city before it fell under the sway of Rome in the 3C BC.

The site (**zona archeologica**) includes ruins of the baths, forum, theatre, streets, houses, drainage system and numerous cisterns. Take Via Ippodamo da Mileto to reach the summit. There is a splendid **view★★** of the bay of Palermo and Monte Pellegrino.

Isola di **Pantelleria**★★

PANTELLERIA ISLAND

Known as the "Black Pearl of the Mediterranean", the island is full of character with its indented coastline, steep slopes covered with terraces under cultivation, and its Moorish-looking cubic houses *(dammusi)*. The highest point of this volcanic island is Montagna Grande (836m/2 743ft). The vineyards produce some pleasant wines such as the sparkling Solimano and the muscat Tanit. Capers are also grown on Pantelleria.

Pantelleria has remains of prehistoric settlements and, like Sicily, later suffered invasions by the Phoenicians, Carthaginians, Greeks, Romans, Vandals, Byzantines, Moors and Normans who in 1123 united the island with Sicily.

Location

Population 7 436 – Michelin map 432 Q 17-18. Situated in the Sicilian Channel, the Island of Pantelleria is only 84km/52miles away from Cape Bon in Tunisia. It is the westernmost island of the Sicilian group and lies on the same latitude as Tunis.

> **GETTING THERE**
> The quickest way to reach the island is by air with connecting flights from Trapani and Palermo. There are also direct flights from Rome and Milan during the summer months. **⌘** *Aeroporto:* ☎ *0923 91 13 98.* Ferries (5-6hr) and hydrofoils (2hr 30min) leave from Trapani. **⌘** *Agenzia Rizzo, Via Borgo Italia 22,* ☎ *0923 91 11 04.*

Excursions

Tour of the island by car★★

About 40km/24mi: 3hr. The very picturesque coastal road gives the visitor a good chance to discover the beauty of the indented coastline, cliffs, inlets, caves, thermal springs and lakes. Driving south from Pantelleria, road signs indicate a Neolithic village, where the **sese grande**★, a flat, elliptic funerary monument can be seen. Further along the road, the village of **Scauri**★ boasts a lovely site. On the south coast towards **Dietro Isola** the corniche road affords beautiful plunging **views**★★ of this coastal area. The cape, **Punta dell'Arco**★, is terminated by a splendid natural rock arch in grey volcanic stone known as the **Arco dell'Elefante**★ (Elephant Arch). On the northeast coast the inlet **Cala dei Cinque Denti**★, and the rest of the coastline further north make a lovely volcanic landscape. From here, you can go on to visit the **Specchio di Venere**★ (Venus' Mirror), a beautiful green lake.

Montagna Grande★★

13km/8mi southeast of Pantelleria. From the summit of this peak there is a splendid **panorama**★★ of the island. In clear weather the view extends as far as Sicily and Tunisia.

Ragusa★

Ragusa, partly rebuilt following the 1693 earthquake, boasts a splendid setting on a plateau between deep ravines. The modern town lies to the west while the old town, Ragusa Ibla, clusters on an outlier of the hills, Monti Iblei, to the east. The Syracuse road offers magnificent **views**★★ of the old town.

Asphalt and oil are produced or refined locally in large industrial complexes.

Location

Population 69 631 – Michelin map 432 Q 26. Ragusa is situated at the southernmost point of the island. The main access road is S 115.

⌘ *Via Capitano Bocchieri 33 (Ibla-Palazzo La Rocca),* ☎ *0932 62 14 21.*

Surrounding area: see NOTO.

Worth a Visit

Ragusa Ibla★★

The medieval area is a maze of streets, but much of the old town was rebuilt in the Baroque style. Here many of the beautiful buildings are adorned with richly decorated corbels depicting exaggerated figures and masks. The hub of the town is Piazza del Duomo, where the elegant Baroque church of **San Giorgio★★** stands. The church was designed by the architect Rosario Gagliardi who also worked in Noto. The pink stone façade has a convex central section which is flanked by three orders of columns and two wings crowned with scrolls. *Open daily, 9am-noon and 4-6pm.* ☎ *0932 22 00 85.*

The nearby church of **San Giuseppe★** shares certain similarities with San Giorgio, suggesting that it may be the work of the same architect. *Open daily, 9am-noon and 3.30-5pm (since this is a monastery run by the Benedictine nuns in perpetual adoration of Our Lord, utmost silence must be observed).*

Città nuova

The new town is laid out in a grid pattern around the 18C cathedral of **San Giovanni**, which is fronted by a wide terrace. *Open daily, 8am-noon and 4-7.30pm, Sun and hols 8am-12.30pm and 4.30-8pm. Donation recommended.* ☎ *0932 62 15 99.*

Not far away, the **Museo Archeologico Ibleo** *(Palazzo Mediterraneo, Via Natalelli)* contains the finds from excavations undertaken locally, notably from the ancient Greek city of Camarina. *Open daily, 9am-1.30pm and 4-7.30pm. €2.07.* ☎ *0932 62 29 63.*

Excursion

Modica★

15km/9mi south. This village, situated in a narrow valley, has retained many of its magnificent Baroque buildings, the most impressive of which is the majestic church of **San Giorgio**, preceded by a long flight of stairs. *Open daily, summer 7.30am-8pm, winter 7.30am-7.30pm. Donation recommended.* ☎ *0932 94 12 79.*

The **Museo delle Arti e Tradizioni Popolari★** offers interesting reconstructions of old workplaces, including workshops and a farm. (&) *Open daily, Jun to Oct 10am-1pm and 4.30-7.30pm, rest of year 10am-1pm and 3.30-6.30pm. Closed 1 Jan €2.50.* ☎ *0932 75 27 47; www.ragusaonline.com*

Segesta★★★

Splendidly situated against the hillside, its ochre colours in pleasant contrast to the vast expanse of green, the archaeological park is dominated by a fine Doric temple standing in an isolated site. Probably founded, like Erice, by the Elimi, Segesta soon became one of the main cities in the Mediterranean basin under Greek influence, rivalling Selinus in importance. It was probably destroyed by the Vandals.

Location

Michelin map 432 N 20. Segesta is situated 35km/21mi southeast of Trapani.

Surrounding area: see ERICE, SELINUNTE, TRAPANI.

The elegant Doric temple at Segesta

Worth a Visit

Tempio★★★

Open daily, summer 9am-7pm (ticket office closes 6pm), rest of year 9am-5pm (ticket office closes 4pm). €4.13. Shuttle to the theatre €1.03. Bar and restaurant service. ☎ *0924 95 23 56.*

The temple of Segesta stands alone, on an eminence encircled by a deep ravine, in a landscape of receding horizons. The Doric building (430 BC), pure and graceful, is girt by a peristyle of 36 columns in golden-coloured limestone. The road leading up to the theatre *(2km/1mi; shuttle bus available, see above)* affords a magnificent **view**★★ of the temple.

Teatro★

This Hellenistic theatre (63m/207ft in diameter) is built into the rocky hillside. The tiers of seats are orientated towards the hills, behind which, to the right, is the Gulf of Castellammare.

Antica città di **Selinunte**★★

SELINUS (Ancient City)

Selinus was founded in the mid-7C BC by people from the east coast city of Megara Hyblaea and was destroyed twice, in 409 and 250 BC, by the Carthaginians. The huge ruins of its temples with their enormous platforms, probably wrecked by earthquakes, are impressive.

Location

Michelin map 432 O 20. Selinus is situated on the south coast. The main access roads are S 115 and S 115d. 🖪 ☎ *092 44 62 51.*
Surrounding area: see SEGESTA.

Special Features

Zona archeologica

♿ *Open daily, 9am to 3hr before sunset. €4.13.* ☎ *0924 46 277.*

Visitors to the site first reach an esplanade around which are grouped the remains of three **temples**. The first to come into view is **Temple E** (5C BC) which was reconstructed in 1958. To the right stands **Temple F**, completely in ruins. The last of the three, **Temple G**, probably dedicated to Apollo, was one of the largest in the ancient world. It was over 100m/330ft long; its columns were built of blocks each weighing several tonnes. The rubble of the fallen stonework gives some indication of its great size.

Cross the depression, Gorgo Cottone, to reach the **acropolis** with its perimeter wall. The site is dominated by the partially reconstructed (1925) columns of **Temple C** (6C BC), the oldest. There are four more ruined temples in the immediate vicinity.

To the west, on the opposite bank of the River Modione stand the remains of a sanctuary to Demeter Malophoros (the dispenser of pomegranates).

Siracusa★★★

SYRACUSE

Syracuse, superbly situated at the head of a beautiful bay, enjoys a very mild climate. It was one of Sicily's, if not Magna Graecia's, most prestigious cities and at the height of its splendour rivalled Athens.

Location
Population 126 282 – Michelin map 432 P 27. Syracuse is situated on the east coast, overlooking the Ionian Sea. The main access roads are S 114 (from Catania) and S 115 (from the south). **⌷** *Via della Maestranza 33, ☎ 0931 65 201.*
Surrounding area: see CATANIA, NOTO.

Background

Greek colony
Syracuse was colonised in the mid-8C BC by Greeks from Corinth who settled on the island of Ortigia. It soon fell under the yoke of the tyrants, and it developed and prospered. In the 5C-4C BC the town had 300 000 inhabitants. Captured by the Romans during the Second Punic War (212 BC), it was occupied successively by the barbarians, Byzantines (6C), Arabs (9C) and Normans.

Tyrants and intellectuals
In the Greek world, dictators called tyrants (from the Greek word *turannos*) exercised unlimited power over certain cities, in particular Syracuse. Already in 485 BC **Gelon**, the tyrant of Gela, had become master of Syracuse. His brother **Hiero** an altogether more unpleasant person, nonetheless patronised poets and welcomed to his court both **Pindar** and **Æschylus**, who died in Gela in 456.

Dionysius the Elder (405-367 BC) was the most famous but even he lived in constant fear. He had a sword suspended by a horsehair above the head of Damocles, a jealous courtier, to demonstrate to him the many dangers which threatened a ruler. He rarely left the safety of his castle on Ortigia, wore a shirt of mail under his clothing and changed his room every night. He had Plato expelled from the city when the philosopher came to study the political habits of the people under his dictatorship.

Directory

WHERE TO EAT
• *Moderate*
Darsena-Da Jannuzzo – *Riva Garibaldi 6 –* As soon as you reach the island of Ortigia, turn right – ☎ 0931 61 522 – Closed Wed – ⌷ – €24/30. You only need to cast your eye over the display of fresh fish at the entrance to know that you are in for a treat. The cooking is simple and tasty, the dishes prepared with fish caught that morning. Meals are served either inside simple surroundings or out on the veranda with views over the waterfront.

WHERE TO STAY
• *Moderate*
Agriturismo La Perciata – *Via Spinagallo 77 – 10km/6mi southwest of Syracuse on the Maremonti road (in the direction of Canicattini Florida junction) –* ☎ 0931 71 73 66 – Fax 0931 62 301 – pergiata@pergiata.it – ⌷ – 9 rm €46.48/72.30 ⌷. There is a very Mediterranean feel to this villa which enhances the very relaxing ambience. The hotel's rural location also means that guests can go horse riding if they wish. Other attractions include a tennis court and hydromassage facilities. Elegant, rustic-style rooms and apartments which have all mod cons.

Bed & Breakfast Dolce Casa – *Via Lido Sacramento 4, Località Isola – S 115 (in the direction of Noto, heading off left for Isola –* ☎ 0931 72 11 35 – Fax 0931 72 11 35 – giuregol@qconsult.it – ⌷ ⌷ – 10 rm €51.60/72.50 – ⌷ €5.50. What was once a private dwelling has been transformed into a very pleasant and welcoming B&B halfway between Syracuse, with all its various attractions, and the sea. The good-sized rooms are light and airy, with rustic-style furnishings, and have a rather romantic feel to them. There is also a lovely garden with lots of palm trees and a pinewood.

• *Expensive*
Albergo Domus Mariae – *Via Vittorio Veneto 76 –* ☎ 0931 24 854 – Fax 0931 24 858 – ⌷ – 12 rm from €92.96 – Rest €18/23. This is a hotel with a difference...run by nuns! In every other respect it is a very traditional establishment. The rooms (spacious) and public areas (a little cramped) are elegant and have been tastefully furnished and there is a lovely sun lounge with sea views. Altogether very relaxing.

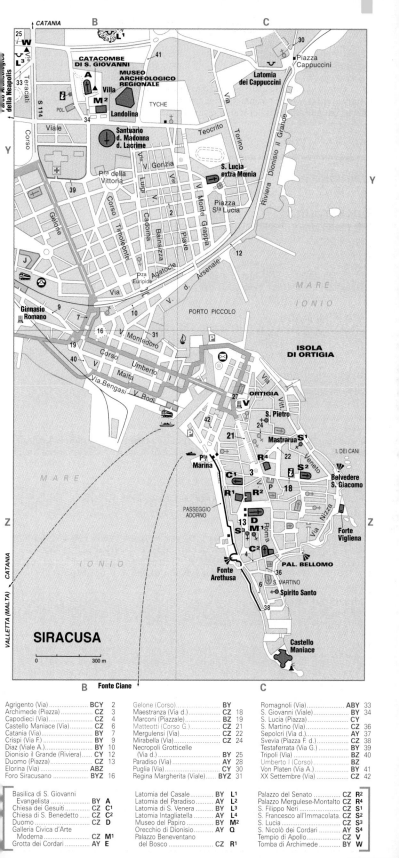

SIRACUSA

Archimedes, the famous geometrician born at Syracuse in 287 BC, was so absent-minded that he would forget to eat and drink. It was in his bath that he discovered his famous principle: any body immersed in water loses weight equivalent to that of the water it displaces. Delighted, he jumped out of the bath and ran naked through the streets shouting "Eureka" (I have found it!). When defending Syracuse against the Romans, Archimedes set fire to the enemy fleet by focusing the sun's rays with a system of mirrors and lenses. But when the Romans succeeded in entering the town by surprise, Archimedes, deep in his calculations, did not hear them, and a Roman soldier ran him through with his sword.

Worth a Visit

L'ORTIGIA★★★

Visit: 45min. The island of Ortigia boasts numerous medieval and Baroque palaces. The latter are found mainly in **Via della Maestranza★**. These narrow streets are shaded in summer and are ideal for a stroll.

The **Piazza Duomo★** is particularly attractive, lined by palaces adorned with wrought-iron balconies and the monumental façade of the **Duomo★**. It was built in the 7C on the foundations of a Doric temple dedicated to Athena, some columns of which were re-used in the Christian building (*north and interior*). Inside, there are several sculptures (including the *Madonna of the Snow*) which are attributed to the **Gagini**, a family of artists who settled in Sicily in the 16C. *Open Mon-Sat, summer 8am-12.40pm and 4-6.30pm; rest of year 8am-12.40pm; Sun and hols 9-10.15am and 4-5.30pm.*

Fonte Arethusa★

This is the legendary cradle of the city. The nymph Arethusa, pursued by the river-god Alpheus, took refuge on the island of Ortigia where she was changed into a spring (*fonte*) by Artemis. Though near the sea, the fountain, built into a wall, runs with fresh water.

The **Passaggio Adorno,** a favourite walk for the Syracusans, starts below.

Galleria Regionale di Palazzo Bellomo★

Open daily except Mon, 9am-2pm (ticket office closes 1.30pm), Wed also 3-7pm (ticket office closes 6/6.30pm). €2.58. ☎ 0931 69 511.

The museum is housed in a beautiful 13C palace which was remodelled in the Catalan style in the 15C. The art gallery has an admirable **Annunciation★** (damaged) by Antonello da Messina and **The Burial of St Lucy★** by Caravaggio. There is also a collection of goldsmiths' work, Sicilian cribs, liturgical objects and furniture.

PARCO ARCHEOLOGICO DELLA NEAPOLIS★★★

2hr on foot. Access by Via Rizzo or Via Paradiso. ♿ Open daily, Apr to Oct 9am-6pm, rest of year 9am-3pm. €4.50. ☎ 0931 48 11 11.

Teatro greco★★★

The Greek theatre dates from the 5C BC and is one of the largest of the Ancient world. The tiers of seats are hewn out of the rock. The first performance of *The Persians* by Æschylus was held here.

Behind the theatre stretches the road of the tombs, **Via dei Sepolcri**, which is hewn out of the rock.

Latomia del Paradiso★★

This former quarry, now an orange grove, dates from ancient times. Part of its roof fell in during the 1693 earthquake.

The **Orecchio di Dionisio★★★** (Ear of Dionysius) is an artificial grotto in the form of an earlobe. The grotto was so named in 1608 by the painter Caravaggio as a reminder of the legend recounting how the exceptional echo enabled the tyrant Dionysius to overhear the talk of the prisoners he confined in a room below.

The tour of the park concludes with the **Ara di Ierone II**. This huge altar (c 200m-656ft long), partly hewn out of the rock, was used for public sacrifices.

The **Roman amphitheatre★** dates from the Imperial period and is hewn out of the rock.

MUSEO ARCHEOLOGICO REGIONALE PAOLO ORSI★★

(♿) Open Tue-Sat 9am-2pm (ticket office closes 1pm), Mon and Wed 3.30-7.30pm (ticket office closes 6.30pm), Sun and hols call for information. Closed Mon am. €4.13. ☎ 0931 46 40 22; www.regione.sicilia.it

In the charming grounds of the **Villa Landolina** stands the museum built in memory of the archaeologist Paolo Orsi (1859-1935). It presents the history of Sicily from prehistoric times up to the Greek colonies of Syracuse (7C BC).

The first section explains the local geology and early fauna (skeletons of the two dwarf elephants) and prehistory, starting from the Upper Palaeolithic, when man made his first appearance in Sicily.

The second part features the Greek colonisation (from mid-8C BC onwards); many artefacts were salvaged in the Lentinoi excavations (marble kouros) but more importantly at Megara Hyblaea and at Syracuse: chalk statue of the **goddess-mother★**, ceramics, architectural fragments and small-scale replicas of the great sanctuaries of Ortigia, the oldest district in Syracuse. The **Venus Anadiomede★**, a Roman copy of a Greek statue by Praxiteles, is on temporary display just before the section dedicated to Syracuse.

The third part of the museum is devoted to the various Syracusan colonies. The town became very powerful and in 664 BC it founded Akrai (Palazzolo Acreide). Then followed Kasmenai (Monte Casale) in 644 BC and Camarina (598 BC): chalk statues, horsemen used in the ornamentation of temples etc. This part of the building also shows artefacts from the Greek colonies inland (large statue of Demeter or Koré enthroned) and the excavations at Gela and Agrigento, which were conducted by Paolo Orsi.

CATACOMBE DI SAN GIOVANNI★★

Open daily except Mon, 9am-1pm and 2.30-5.30pm. €3.50. ☎ 0931 67 955.

After the catacombs in Rome, these are the finest examples in Italy. In contrast to those in Rome which have been dug out of fragile tufa, the catacombs in Syracuse have been excavated from solid rock to create spacious chambers, big enough to hold up to seven tombs. They consist of a main gallery off which branch secondary galleries ending in circular chapels or rotundas; several of the tombs are in the form of arched niches.

Excursions

Fonte Ciane★★

8km/5mi southwest. It is best to visit by boat. By reservation only. For information contact Sig. Vella. ☎ 0931 39 889 or 368 72 96 040 (mobile).

The River **Ciane★★**, rising here, is lined with papyrus beds, which are unique in Italy. It was here that the nymph Ciane was changed into a spring when she opposed the abduction of Proserpine by Pluto.

Castello Eurialo★

9km/6mi northwest of the plan. Open daily, 9am to 1hr before sunset. No charge. ☎ 0931 71 17 73.

This was one of the greatest fortresses of the Greek period; it was built by Dionysius the Elder. Fine **panorama★**.

Taormina★★★

Taormina stands in a wonderful site★★★ at an altitude of 250m/820ft and forms a balcony overlooking the sea and facing Etna. It is renowned for its peaceful atmosphere and its beautiful monuments and gardens. The nearby seaside resort of Giardini Naxos also hosts a number of cultural and musical events.

Location

Population 10 669 – Michelin map 432 N 27 – Town plan in the current Michelin Italy Atlas. Taormina is situated on the east coast, overlooking the Ionion Sea. The main access road is A 18.

🖪 *Piazza Santa Caterina (Palazzo Corvaja), ☎ 0942 23 243.*

🖪 *for Giardini Naxos: Via Tysandros 54, 98030, Giardini Naxos (ME), ☎ 0942 51 010.*

Surrounding area: see CATANIA, ETNA, MESSINA.

Worth a Visit

Teatro greco★★★

(♿) Open daily, 9am to 2hr before sunset. €4.13. ☎ 0942 23 220; www.regione.sicilia.it

The Greek theatre dates from the 3C BC but was remodelled by the Romans who used it as an arena for their contests. Performances of Classical plays are given in summer. From the upper tiers there is an admirable **view★★★** between the stage columns of the coastline and Etna.

The theatre and Mount Etna, Taormina

Corso Umberto★

The main street of Taormina has three gateways along its course: Porta Catania; the middle one, Porta di Mezzo, with the Torre dell' Orologio (Clock Tower); and Porta Messina.

The Piazza del Duomo is overlooked by the Gothic façade of the **cathedral** and adorned by an attractive Baroque fountain. *Cathedral open daily, 8.30-11.30am and 4-6pm.* ☎ *0942 23 123.*

Almost halfway along, the **Piazza 9 Aprile★** forms a terrace which affords a splendid **panorama★★** of the gulf. The Piazza Vittorio Emanuele was laid out on the site of the forum and is overlooked by the 15C **Palazzo Corvaja**.

Giardino di Villa Comunale★★

From these terraced public gardens of flowers and exotic plants there are views of the coast and the sea.

Directory

WHERE TO EAT
• *Moderate*
Vicolo Stretto – *Via Vicolo Stretto 6* – ☎ *0942 23 849* – *Closed Mon (except 15 Jun-15 Sep), 9-20 Dec, 8 Jan-12 Feb* – 🖸 – *Book* – €26/44. Wherever you are seated, whether it is in the lovely little dining room (warm and welcoming) inside or the terrace (open and airy) overlooking the rooftops of Taormina, just sit back and relax. The cooking – mostly fish – draws inspiration from the cuisine in the Trapani area where the chef comes from and includes dishes such as tuna fish with couscous, delightful!

WHERE TO STAY
• *Budget*
Bed & Breakfast Villa Regina – *Punta San Giorgio – 98030 Castelmola – 53 m/3mi northwest of Taormina* – ☎ *09-12 28 228* – *Fax 0942 28 083 – www.tao.it/intelisano* – *10 rm €30.99/49.06* – ⚁ – €7.75. A very simple but charming establishment, with a lovely little shady garden, that boasts wonderful views of Taormina and the coast. Definitely one for the address book especially for couples looking for a bit of privacy and romance. And it is reasonably priced!

• *Moderate*
Andromaco Palace Hotel – *Via Fontana Vecchia* – ☎ *0942 23 436* – *Fax 0942 24 985* – 🛉 🖸 – *20 rm €82/114* ⚁. Notwithstanding the rather grandiloquent name, this is a small, rather gracious, family-run hotel. Panoramic position not far from the centre. Comfortable rooms. Warm welcome assured.

TAKING A BREAK
Caffè San Giorgio – *Piazza S. Antonio 1 98030 Castelmola* – ☎ This café was founded in the early 20C, and previous habitués include a number of famous personalities, among them Rolls and Royce as well as Rockefeller. One of the main attractions is the breathtaking view of Taormina and the coast from the splendid terrace area

Excursions

Castello

4km/2.5mi northwest by the Castelmola road, and then a road to the right. It is also possible to walk up (1hr there and back). The castle was built in the medieval period on the summit of Monte Tauro (390m/1 280ft), on the remains of the former acropolis. There are splendid **views★★** of Taormina.

Castelmola★

5km/3mi northwest. This tiny village is strategically located near Taormina and enjoys a splendid **site★** with panoramic views. The focus of the village is the attractive Piazzetta del Duomo with its fine, intricate paving. From various points there are fine **views★** of Etna, the north coast and the beaches below Taormina.

Gole dell'Alcantara★

17km/11mi west. Open daily, May-Oct 7am-8pm, rest of year 7am-5pm. €2.07. To rent boots and overalls €6.71. Prices may vary. ☎ 0942 98 50 10.
The volcanic walls of these narrow gorges are formed by irregular geometrical shapes, turning the waterfalls which occasionally cascade down the rock into prisms of light. Visitors can hire boots and overalls at the entrance to the gorge in order to explore the first section of the river bed.

Trapani

Situated within sight of the Egadi Islands, Trapani has a sheltered port which is important to the salt trade.

Location

Population 69 453 – Michelin map 432 M 19. Trapani is situated at the westernmost point of the island. The main access roads are A 29 and S 113. ▯ *Piazza Saturno, ☎ 0923 29 000.*
Surrounding area: see Isole EGADI, ERICE.

Worth a Visit

Santuario dell'Annunziata★

For information, contact the pastor several days in advance. ☎ 0923 53 91 84. Donation welcome.
Built in the 14C, the church was remodelled and enlarged in the 17C. The campanile is Baroque. On the north side the attractive **Cappella dei Marinai** (Renaissance Sailors' Chapel) is crowned with a dome. Inside, access to the **Cappella della Madonna★** is through a Renaissance arch carved in the 16C; the chapel contains the graceful statue of the Virgin (14C) known as the **Madonna di Trapani** and attributed to Nino Pisano.

Museo Pepoli★

Open Mon-Sat, 9am-1.30pm, Sun and hols 9am-12.30pm. €2.58 ☎ 0923 55 32 69.
The Pepoli Museum is located in the former Carmelite convent which adjoins the Annunziata. The works include sculpture (by the Gagini) and paintings, such as the 15C Trapani polyptych, a **Pietà★** by Roberto di Oderisio and *St Bartholomew* by Ribera. There is also a display of local crafts: coral work and a very delicate crib.

Centro storico★

The old town is built on the promontory that juts into the sea, with the Villa Margherita to the east. It contains a number of beautiful old mansions, especially along Rua Nova (now Via Garibaldi) and Rua Grande (now Corso Vittorio Emanuele).

Excursions

Salt pans

30km/18mi from Trapani to Marsala. Allow one day, including a trip to Mozia. The coastal road which leads from Trapani to Marsala is lined with salt pans *(saline)* and fine open **views★★**; the water is divided into a multicoloured grid by strips of land. In places there are windmills, a reminder of times gone by when they were the main way to pump water and grind the salt. The view is even more evocative in the summer, at harvest time, when the rose-coloured tint of the water in the basins is more intense (the colour changes as the saline content increases) and the shimmering pools of water inland are drying out in the sun. At Nubia there is the small, but interesting **Museo del Sale** housed in a 17C saltworks where an exhibition illustrates this ancient craft with tools and display panels. & *Open Mon-Sat, 9.30am-1pm and 3.30-6.30pm (5pm winter), Sun am only. Guided tours available (30min). Audiovisual program. €1.03. ☎ 0923 86 71 42.*

A restored **mill** can be visited not far from Mozia *(see below). Wind permitting, the windmill operates in summer, Wed and Sat 4-6pm, rest of year Sat-Sun and hols only on request. €2.58. For information contact Saline Ettore and Infersa, ☎ 0923 96 69 36*

Isola di Mozia★

14km/9mi south of Trapani. Leave the car at the jetty. Fishermen provide a ferry service to the island. This ancient Phoenician colony was founded in the 8C BC on one of the four islands of the **Laguna dello Stagnone**. Visitors can explore the ruins of the Phoenician city by following the path around the island *(about 1hr30min; anti-clockwise direction recommended)*. A small **museum** houses exhibits found on the island, including the magnificent **Ephebe of Mozia★★**, a noble figure of rather haughty bearing clothed in a long, pleated cloak which shows an obvious Greek influence. & *Access to island and visit to museum, daily 9am-1pm and 3pm to 1hr before sunset. Ferry €3, admission to museum €6. ☎ 0923 71 25 98.*

Marsala

Marsala, the ancient Lilybaeum on Capo Lilibeo, the westernmost point of the island, owes its present name to the Saracens, who first destroyed and then rebuilt the city, calling it Marsah el Ali (Port of Allah). It is known for its sweet Marsala wine which an English merchant, John Woodhouse, rediscovered in the 18C.

It was at Marsala in 1860 that Garibaldi landed at the start of the **Expedition of the Thousand,** which freed southern Italy from the sway of the Bourbons.

Piazza della Repubblica is the hub of city life, lined by the cathedral and Palazzo Senatorio.

A former wine cellar, near the sea, now houses a museum, the **Museo Archeologico di Baglio Anselmi** *(Via Boeo)*: the exhibits include the wreck of a **warship★** which fought in the Punic War and was found off the coast near Mozia. & *Open daily, 9am-2pm, also 4-7pm Wed, Sat, Sun and hols. €4.13. ☎ 0923 95 25 35.*

Ustica★★

This small volcanic island boasts an indented coastline which hides magnificent caves, inlets and small bays. It has been a marine reserve since 1987.

Location

Population 1 373 – Michelin map 432 K 21. Ustica is situated off the coast around Palermo.

Surrounding area: see PALERMO.

Special Features

Island

The small village of **Ustica★** is built overlooking the bay and harbour. An extensive **prehistoric village★** dating from the Bronze Age has been discovered near Faraglioni in the Colombaia district.

The other is always visible through the tono. The coastline is dotted with small beaches and rocky inlets, such as the **piscina naturale★**, the bay known as the natural swimming pool.

Riserva marina

Open daily, 8am-7pm. Are also 4-10pm No charge. For information ☎ 091 84 49 456.

This marine reserve was established in 1987 to preserve and protect the fauna and natural marine environment around Ustica, where the sea is particularly free of pollution (Ustica is located right in the middle of the Atlantic current). The reserve organises guided tours to some of the caves around the island as well as snorkelling trips. Experienced divers can enjoy a spectacular **underwater show★★** near **Scoglio del Medico**.

> **GETTING THERE**
> There are regular ferry departures from Palermo. During the summer months, there is also a hydrofoil service (route: Trapani-Favignana-Ustica-Napoli). ⓑ Agenzia Militello, Piazza Di Bartolo 7, ☎ 091 84 49 002.

Index

URBINO *Marches*...Town, sight or tourist area covered as a chapter in the guide, followed by the region
Trains ....Practical information
Sirmione *Lombardy* ....Place of interest, followed by the region
Vivaldi, Antonio...People, events and artistic styles mentioned in the guide